THE DARTNELL

SALES MANAGER'S

HANDBOOK

FIRST EDITION—1934
SECOND EDITION—1937
THIRD EDITION—1940
FOURTH EDITION—1945
FIFTH EDITION—1947
SIXTH EDITION—1949
SEVENTH EDITION—1956
EIGHTH EDITION—1959
NINTH EDITION—1962
TENTH EDITION—1965
(Second Printing)—1966
ELEVENTH EDITION—1968
(Second Printing)—1970

International Standard Book Number: 0-8513-003-4
Library of Congress Catalog Card Number: 56-59050

Printed in the U. S. A. by
DARTNELL PRESS, INC., 4660 Ravenswood Avenue, Chicago, Illinois 60640

THE DARTNELL
SALES
MANAGER'S
HANDBOOK

Edited by Ovid Riso

Created by John Cameron Aspley

Eleventh Edition - 1968

THE DARTNELL CORPORATION

CHICAGO and LONDON

FOREWORD

Eleventh Edition

MANAGEMENT'S recognition of the marketing function as the primary and most significant factor in the success of any business operation has created new vistas and responsibilities for sales executives, requiring broader viewpoints and greater alertness to the challenges of fast-changing markets.

"This is a selling era," states Robert A. Stringer, general manager, distribution, sales services division of General Foods Corporation, "a phase in the business cycle when marketing holds the key to future growth. *More than any other single factor,* marketing of goods and services will determine our business success or failure, because marketing is the all-important link between production and consumption."

This eleventh revision of the Sales Manager's Handbook, originally issued in 1934 and until now edited by J. C. Aspley, reflects this "selling era," already imprinted with the unpredictable power of the computer and with the far-reaching concern of government for the consumer.

Present-day sales practices and policies of countless American companies of every size and the practical experience of successful executives have been distilled within these pages.

Managers, salesmen and others in distributive fields will find this book of practical value. The tasks and situations confronted by the modern sales manager, and the contemporary policies of many leading companies in organizing their marketing activities, are examined and analyzed in eight sections. The entire marketing process is viewed through the critical eyepiece of experience.

In accomplishing this, we have received the generous cooperation of many companies, corporate officers, marketing executives, industry organizations, trade associations, business publications, and management consultants, to all of whom we are indebted. The government has contributed through various divisions of the Departments of Commerce and Labor, and the Small Business Administration especially.

The illuminating results of a number of comprehensive Dartnell surveys also have been helpful in the preparation of this edition. The companies studied, to determine current practices, represent a cross section of American business.

Some of the marketing activities discussed or illustrated carry portents of the future. From computerized marketing research to "The House of Tomorrow"; from shopping-at-home via television to startling technological advances in every field, they point unwaveringly to the new and greater marketing challenges in a space-age world.

A glimpse of the proportions of the markets immediately ahead was provided by former Secretary of Commerce Alexander B. Trowbridge. "Our domestic market," he said, "which now encompasses just under 200 million persons, will number 300 million by the turn of the century." Referring to this, former Agriculture Secretary Orville Freeman added: ". . . we shall need twice as much water, one-third more food, housing for another 100 million Americans and roads for three times the number of automobiles we now have."

These are some of the dazzling aspects of the great new targets ahead for marketing men. They are already coming into focus.

Another very interesting and useful part of this book is the gold mine of information in the Ready-Reference Section, with its appropriate, pertinent data and examples for sales and marketing executives.

Earlier editions included the subject of sales promotion; its importance grew to such dimensions that it is now treated in a companion volume, *The Dartnell Sales Promotion Handbook.*

Ending on a personal note: So many business executives are familiar with the name "Dartnell," and acquainted with its work, that it has been a pleasure to engage in the planning and research which have gone into this book.

Ovid Riso

ABOUT OVID RISO . . .

This edition of *The Dartnell Sales Manager's Handbook* was edited by Ovid Riso, former vice-president of Philco International Corporation. Previously, Mr.  Riso was advertising and sales-promotion manager of RCA International, manager of the international division of Young & Rubicam, and a staff editor of McGraw-Hill Publishing Company. He was president of the Philadelphia chapter of the International Advertising Association, former vice-president of the Philadelphia chapter of the Public Relations Society of America, and a member of the U.S. Regional Export Expansion Council. He is currently a consultant; also editor of *Poor Richard's Almanack,* monthly publication of the Poor Richard Club of Philadelphia, and editor of *The Philco World,* published by Philco-Ford Corporation for its distributors and dealers.

OVID RISO

CONTENTS

PART 5—COMPETITIVE TRADE PRACTICES

PART 6—MODERN SALES POLICIES

PART 7—ORGANIZING FOR SELLING

PART 8—OPERATING THE SALES FORCE

READY-REFERENCE SECTIONS

PART 1

THE
EVOLUTION
OF
SALES
MANAGEMENT

Chapter 1

SALES AND MARKETING MANAGEMENT TODAY

A T THE national convention of Sales and Marketing Executives International, speakers referred to some of the changes taking place in sales and marketing management.

One of the most significant changes noted was the trend among an increasingly large number of companies toward the organization of their activities to meet modern marketing requirements. This was summed up in the expression, "the marketing concept."

"The marketing concept is focused on the customer, not the company or the product, as the center of the business universe," declared Dr. Arnold Corbin in an address before the British Institute of Management. "It represents a change in philosophy from 'we sell what we make' to 'we make and sell what will sell.' "

The marketing concept requires that a company be customer oriented rather than product oriented. "It involves getting the right product, in the right form, at the right price, at the right time and to the right people," says consultant Robert J. Lavidge, president of Elrick & Lavidge, Inc., Chicago, and past president of the American Marketing Association.

Who are the right people for any product or service? The wants and needs of people resulting in the things they buy in both quantity and quality are subject to the circumstances and conditions around them. These are constantly changing.

What Is "Marketing"?

There have been, and will continue to be, myriad definitions of marketing. Here is one idea of what is meant by "marketing":

Marketing is ascertaining, creating, and satisfying the wants of the people, and doing it at a profit.

This definition is not perfect, but it states the ultimate objective of marketing, which is to make a profit, and it clearly defines the way in which the objective is realized: namely, by learning and satisfying the wants of people.

William F. May, chairman and chief executive officer of the American Can Company, was called upon to detail the marketing-oriented business philosophy of his company before the annual marketing conference of the National Industrial Conference Board in New York. He said:

"The whole concept of marketing is of crucial importance not only to the American Can Company, but to the entire U.S. economy. Indeed, when our system is working at its best, the marketplace is the economy, and, in the corporate sense at least, we thrive or dwindle on how successfully we keep pace with our markets.

"There are three key phrases to this matter of keeping pace: (1) Anticipating the needs and desires of the market and satisfying them as quickly as possible; (2) then being quick to recognize when the market has changed, or is about to change, and (3) being ready to meet that change with a corresponding shift in product or service.

"If a company can manage to do well in each phase, it should be strong and successful; if not, sooner or later it will find itself in trouble."

The Mustang Story

A good illustration of the marketing concept in action is the story behind the phenomenally successful Mustang car introduced by the Ford Motor Company.

The first step was basic consumer marketing research dealing with the composition of the automobile buyers' market. This revealed a real opportunity among younger, educated, married people. It was found that half the sales of new cars in the 1960's were in the 18-to-34 age group. The research also uncovered real interest in a sports-type car, with a wide selection of "options" in terms of engines, colors, and transmissions, without a sports-car price.

The conclusion was reached that here was a market looking for a product, rather than the reverse. It seemed a great opportunity, so Ford went ahead with designing a car to meet the requirements of the market. Thus was the Mustang born. It was a success from the start—orders for the car far outdistanced production facilities.

Then a strange thing happened. Mustang owners became so emotionally excited about the cars that their unanticipated reactions triggered a refreshingly new approach to motor-car marketing.

Normally, you sell a motor car by telling people that it has great performance, it has high horsepower, it will do 100 m.p.h., it won this race or that; i.e., you appeal to rational motivations. However, Ford was deluged by thousands of letters from people who had bought Mustangs and then just had to write to the company to say that the car through styling alone had dramatically influenced their lives and their whole personalities!

The Problem of Survival

Failure to meet the challenge of marketing in a fast-changing world can be highly disastrous.

Speaking at a meeting of the Louisville chapter of the American Marketing Association, Robert A. Strain, Chicago branch manager for the Maytag Company, illustrated the problems of survival with two examples:

1. In the automobile industry, more than 215 million cars have been produced in the United States alone, yet only four of 1,500 manufacturers survive.

2. Even though the home-laundry-appliance industry has manufactured and sold more than 50 million washing machines, there are some 200 manufacturers of washing machines who have gone broke, leaving the market to less than 20 remaining.

The Maytag executive outlined marketing basics as: (1) recognizing the need for a product, (2) building a product to fulfill that need, (3) exposing the product, (4) "hooking up" the product with a prospect, (5) writing the order, and (6) standing behind the product, making certain it performs exactly as represented.

"We must sell something other than price alone," emphasized Mr. Strain, adding that failure to do so means that profits will continue to dwindle, and "for a business without profits there's no tomorrow."

Since the objective of nearly all businesses is to "market" goods and services, and thereby to make a profit, the whole business may be said to be a marketing enterprise, and the *sole* activity of the business is therefore marketing. This, of course, would be the broadest possible interpretation of the term "marketing." But such an interpretation would not be helpful in an exploration of the problems of the marketing function, for obviously engineering, manufacturing, purchasing—and possibly product research and development—while contributing to the marketing objectives of a business, are not, of themselves, part of the responsibility of the marketing department.

Major Forces at Work

Many observers have noted the forces which govern marketing to be five in number: consumer habits, mass merchandising, technologic advances, federal control, and world trade. Each of these factors will be recognized in the pages which follow.

One of the most cogent summaries of the effect of these forces on modern sales and marketing management was presented at a marketing-strategy conference of the Sales Executives Club of New York by Walter E. Brunauer, an executive of the Sperry and Hutchinson Company. Mr. Brunauer said, in part:

In the successful marketing strategies of many diversified companies, a single thread winds through them and links them all together. That thread is *change;* it is the quickening pace of change— of the new demands and the great opportunities that change is creating for the marketing executive . . . also, it is the twin consequences that change offers: On the one hand, opportunity; on the other, obsolescence.

For there *are* new dimensions in marketing strategy. They are being drawn by the external forces that affect and encompass your marketing operation.

The Consumer

Americans are taking home a record number of dollars to spend. Their impact on your marketing plans will be felt increasingly in the future. In 1975 (according to a recent report from the Twentieth Century Fund), there will be 235 million people in the United States —44 million more than today. And half of them will be under 26 years of age.

There will be two million marriages a year. There will be five million births.

The average family's income will hit $9,525 a year. Two families out of every five will rank in the over-$10,000 class, compared with only about one out of five today.

Seventy-two out of every 100 people will live either in cities or their suburbs. And 60 percent of all consumers will be concentrated in the coastal states of the East, South, and West.

Add to all this the profound effects of government programs in the areas of antipoverty, civil rights, industrial training, the Peace Corps, etc., designed with the hope that they will cut down unemployment, reduce poverty, and increase family income, thus setting new and higher standards of living.

Social Security for the aged, rent subsidization, and unemployment compensation also tend to maintain or increase purchasing power among consumer groups with limited means.

Finally, of course, we have increased minimum-wage rates, ever-increasing union-contract wages, and more and better fringe benefits being enjoyed by wage earners.

These affluent consumers will be on the move, seeking leisure and recreation, gaining new levels of education, enjoying broader culture, indulging in new home conveniences—from ultrasonic washing machines to television and telephone in every room.

It will be the era of the electronic home and the age of the all-American family with two college degrees, three automobiles, a four-week vacation, and a five-figure income.

More than half of these new consumers by 1975 will have been born into the age of the electronic media. As never before, the average consumer will be able to see through an advertising claim or perhaps tune it out completely. The "noise level" of advertising is already a problem; it can only grow into a larger one.

Also, with greater insistence than ever before, the consumer will demand product quality and product service. She will neither be conned by a product claim, nor will she tolerate any guff from the retailer.

The "Education Explosion"

Of course, the seeds of many of these changes are taking hold right now. But it is their rate of growth that is increasing so rapidly. In another decade, for example, we in marketing will have witnessed what is now emerging as the "education explosion." The number of college-educated adults has more than doubled in the past two decades—from 7½ million to more than 16 million. The forecast is that by 1975 more than 24 million people will boast college degrees; by 1980, more than 28 million.

This social phenomenon is by no means unrelated to practical marketing. It already affects broad segments of our markets; its influence is spreading into others. Its more awesome effects are on consumer attitudes—toward business, toward products and their functions, toward advertising and promotion in general, and toward specific advertising claims and appeals.

Don't underrate the significance of this single force. Increasingly, college graduates will dominate the higher income brackets. They will exert leadership influences in the marketplace—setting new tastes, molding opinion, determining the buying behavior of the masses.

And, naturally, none of us plans to underestimate the impact of the civil-rights movement. Its implications are many, and they are shattering. They affect not only to whom we sell, but who sells it, who advertises it, and even who makes it . . . and, while this racial revolution is fermenting, we will see, the sociologists tell us, at first a sharper segmentation of ethnic markets, followed perhaps by a gradual assimilation of them.

These are just some of the forces that are being created by consumers—by their characteristics and by their proclivities. And, while consumers are changing, another great force—that of the marketplace—is changing almost as rapidly.

The Marketplace in Ferment

The mad rush of the mass merchandisers to grow bigger and to look alike—to sell the same products, at the same prices or discounts, with the same services, or lack of them—could spell real trouble for many manufacturers.

Note the swift changes. The discounters now threaten to dominate retailing; many offer traditional department-store services.

To compete, the department stores open suburban and exurban branches; they offer new services, sell by catalog, mail, and phone, even send representatives to the home.

Supermarkets edge more into nonfood and variety lines.

Variety chains begin more and more to resemble full-fledged general merchandisers.

Door-to-door selling spreads and tries to upgrade its image.

Automatic vending booms, and moves into nonfood and higher-than-a-dollar lines.

Mail-order chains become merchandising giants.

And, meanwhile, all the traditionalists—the food, drug, and variety chains—rush to open competitive discount subsidiaries.

The traditional retail images are blurring. And in this retail rat race, the weaker merchants are shaken out; the big chains get bigger, invade new fields, grow and merge, and emerge still bigger. The survivors wield vast economic power—they are tougher to sell; they are more choosy about new products; they demand more attractive deals and better profit opportunities.

Paradoxically, in the midst of this chaos, the small specialty convenience store is finding its own way to compete. It is winning new customers by offering the housewife quality products, in pleasant surroundings, ease of shopping, and flawless service.

To the marketing executive, all this furor in the marketplace means that he must think more boldly in terms of distribution strategy. For his best customers can become, almost overnight, his biggest headache. He must watch them closely; he must anticipate their changes in policy or mood. He cannot afford to get squeezed or lost in the hectic hurly-burly of today's marketplace.

Technology on the Move

The consumer and the marketplace have been the traditional and pervasive forces that have shaped our marketing plans. But the newest and most rapidly developing force of change is that of technology. It is embracing us completely . . .

The most immediate sign of the new technology is, of course, the computer. We employ it in marketing research, in inventory control, in improving our sales effectiveness—in short, in making more information available more quickly so that we can make more enlightened decisions and more swift actions. And our customers, it seems, are virtually living with the computer. Whether they be industrial companies or large retailers, their computer applications are putting new demands on our pricing, discounts, deals, deliveries, inventories, even on the billing forms we send.

Eventually, the strongest effects of the technological advance will be realized in the broad universe of market, materials, and products. The tempest that is stirred by technological change means shorter life-cycles for products; it implies greater costs and risks in attempting to launch new ones. It guarantees new competition from companies and industries and products that were in an earlier day incapable of presenting a worthy marketing challenge.

The overall impact of technological change on the consumer or competitor—be it a 30-year-old housewife who buys your product or a $300-million manufacturer that might run you out of business overnight—is something that we must study carefully. It will inevitably demand new innovations in our basic product concepts as well as in our marketing approaches to our ultimate consumers. As Arthur Fatt of Grey Advertising noted recently, "Prediction of the future is uncertain—but addiction to the past is deadly."

World Barriers Are Coming Down

Still another emerging force is that of world trade. And for the truly ambitious man or company, this force may hold the greatest challenge . . . There will be debate, argument, dissension; there could be anger and walkouts. Yet, inevitably, the age-old trade barriers will begin to crumble. It will be a result of sheer selfishness as well as of the recognition of the dire necessity of gaining new markets and sources of supply.

Whether your market area consists of a couple of counties or entire hemispheres, this will mean new markets and new competition. It will bring new customers, who have different needs and respond to different appeals. Of its very nature, it will mean a broader and very much more challenging world of opportunity.

One footnote must be added to this mention of the force of world trade: As today we see many of our companies sweep beyond our continent and around the world, we note the similarities in market development. We see, for example, European countries now accepting convenience foods and products; South America in need of hardware and durables; and Africa crying for the basic necessities. All that has been learned in marketing—U.S.A.-style (after all, we *are* the greatest test market of all)—can be applied with full vigor in these developing world markets.

The Influence of Government

There remains one major force that affects, and usually constricts, your marketing strategy. It is that of big government. Marketers today are being virtually engulfed by its influence.

Today the long arms of government stretch out and encompass almost every major business decision—mergers, taxes, capital investment, plant locations, overseas investment, price increases, price decreases, list prices, fair trade, advertising, packaging, financing, credit. In too many companies, scarcely can a plan be laid or a decision made without casting an eye toward Washington to see which way the wind is blowing.

This is a highly complex situation—a double-edged sword if there ever was one. The front edge, the one seen day to day, is that of federal enforcement: the Federal Trade Commission, the Justice Department, the Food & Drug Administration, Internal Revenue—many other government agencies. The other edge of that sword is federal legislation; in the long run, it can cut the deepest. The legislative wheels of our Government move slowly indeed. But they are moving.

There is a final aspect of big government, and to some it is the most disturbing of all. It is neither federal enforcement nor federal legislation. We might call it "federal frustration."

It derives from the actions—lawful ones, but at times debatable ones—of members of the Congress or the administration. The steel industry, the drug companies, virtually every basic industry, has seen it—even reeled under it . . .

This force seems to blow with the wind. But it is always with us, and as government gets bigger, as business grows bigger, it has to be reckoned with in a greater way in our marketing planning.

That brings us back to the lonely marketing executive who flies almost as though in the eye of the hurricane about which these winds of force swirl.

He must detect these forces of change. He must anticipate and measure their impact, before his competitors do. He must prepare his organization and his people to meet the change, whether it be a new wrinkle in supermarket buying or the latest government drive against some particular business practice.

This demands wisdom, courage, up-to-date information, and a unique array of marketing talents.

What of Tomorrow?

We find of interest and value a presentation by Arthur C. Fatt, chairman of the board of Grey Advertising, Inc., on the evolution of distribution. Mr. Fatt has outlined 10 areas in which sales management, marketing, distribution, and advertising merge. In answer to the question, "What must manufacturers do to prepare for the evolution in distribution in the next decade?" he suggests:

1. They must learn to read the signs which indicate the important distribution currents in the decade ahead. Manufacturers who looked ahead and correctly read the signs in the past were not caught off base by so many marketing developments which we blithely call the "distribution revolution."

2. Advertisers should work unceasingly to help reduce the cost of distribution for the retailer by more efficient methods of getting the goods from the factory, through the stores, to the consumer, in order to counteract the price advantage and other inducements of the private label.

3. Some manufacturers will have to ask themselves: "Will I be better off to work with the large retailers and produce their private brands, so as to get more cooperation from them in moving our advertised brands and at the same time keeping competitors out?"

4. The new breed of manufacturers' representatives (now called salesmen) will have to be better schooled in merchandising, promotion, advertising, and display, as well as in the arithmetic of retailing, because they will be confronted by buyers with exact information speedily gathered by computers.

5. Advertisers will have to recognize that marginal brands, having an insignificant share of the market, will be most vulnerable against the onslaught of strongly advertised private labels. It's understandable that only brands which enjoy a significant market share, and which have adequate sales velocity, will find space in the retail stores.

6. We must intensify the drive for new products, especially those which will create new markets. Examples: fabric softeners, dietary food-drinks, electric toothbrushes, and development of the recreation market. Nevertheless, "me-too" products will come out of the laboratories more often than breathtaking innovations. Positioning such products in the marketplace will be an even greater challenge to marketing and advertising ingenuity in the years ahead. It's safe to say a great many more brands will have to depend on nuances in copy and advertising strategy to insure their market positions.

7. We shall have to learn much more about test marketing than we know today. We must develop new research methods and better use of computers to take many risks out of marketing decisions.

8. We must change some of today's advertising concepts. Advertisers must spur the application of mathematical models to help figure out how advertising works in relation to the other marketing functions. It is conceivable that 10 years from now we should have a clearer and better understanding of the true selling effectiveness of advertising.

9. We must give thought to developing a variety of advertising campaigns to run concurrently, but keyed to specific buying motives of different segments, geographical, ethnic, economic, social and psychological.

10. Advertisers and their agencies will have to work more closely to make advertising in the seventies more exciting, more ingenious in content and in format. Contrary to some prevailing opinions, mathematics, science, and technology will sharpen rather than dull advertising's creative urge.

We are indebted to famed advertising executive Leo Burnett and *Journal of Marketing* for the following "Fallacies of Marketing."

Fallacy as to Marketing Foresight

The first fallacy is that the people already in the marketing field are the ones who understand it best and know what the potential customer wants.

Yet in actuality the only person who really knows what he wants is the customer himself. For example, if television producers *really* knew what the public wanted in entertainment, the mortality rate in programs would not be so wastefully high each new season.

Fallacy as to New Markets

The second fallacy is a limited definition of "competition," under which the chief marketing strategy is to attain the largest possible share of the existing market rather than to create new markets and add to total consumption.

A few years ago the Brookings Institution completed a comprehensive study of successful and unsuccessful industries. The difference between success and failure hinged on a really simple thing— product leadership. Industries that failed to innovate and that failed to keep ahead of the market also failed to grow with the economy, and perished or were absorbed.

Fallacy as to Competition

The third fallacy in the marketing world is that competition is a closed system, and that our competitors are those making substantially the same products or offering the same services that we are.

In studying Nielsen share-of-market reports, do we sometimes know *too much* about our competitors? By putting such high priority on "me-too" products and competitive countermoves, are there not serious dangers of standardization of products rather than market expansion?

Fallacy as to Income Brackets

A fourth fallacy is the marketing theory of appealing mainly to present income brackets.

In the past, it was commonly believed, and it was generally true, that people bought "according to income." But today people increasingly are buying according to *expectations of future income*. Individual purchases have come to be more and more like company purchases—based on a projection into the next few years, and not necessarily on current income alone.

Fallacy as to Decision-Making

> *The fifth fallacy is that because we are living*
> *in the age of the specialist, only qualified experts*
> *with specialized skills will be competent in the future*
> *to make basic decisions.*

Actually, quite the reverse is happening. Our greatest need today is for the synthesizer, much more than for the specialist. He is not necessarily a computer programmer, but he understands how computers work and what they can do and cannot do.

What does all this mean to us as marketing men? It means that change and the rate of change have been so rapid, and that the need for new marketing power is so great, that many a marketing man has been caught with his rusty calculus showing. He has not yet learned how to use the amazing new tools of cybernetics, electronic data processing, and game theory, and is in fact scared silly by them, as he is by taking any kind of calculated risk.

Chapter 2

EVALUATING PRESENT
SALES MANAGEMENT

IN DISCUSSING the marketing role of the chief executive of a company, Clarence E. Eldridge, formerly vice-president in charge of marketing for the General Foods Corporation, and currently executive vice-president-marketing for Campbell Soup Company, in a series of essays commissioned by the Association of National Advertisers (reprinted in *Printers' Ink*), comments:

"The chief executive must discharge his ultimate responsibility for the satisfactory execution of the marketing function not by performing that function himself or by interfering with its performance by his duly appointed delegate, but at an entirely different level and in an entirely different way.

"First, he can and should lay out a long-term plan for the company. The plan should indicate company policy with respect to diversification—whether to diversify at all, and if so, the direction the diversification should take. It should enunciate the policy of the company with respect to new products and the possible elimination or downgrading of existing products.

"Second, the chief executive should let the marketing director (or in the case of a decentralized company, the general managers of the divisions) know what the company's profit requirements are for the forthcoming year. This is important, for major marketing decisions frequently depend on the company's overall financial capability and need for profit.

"Third, the chief executive can retain effective control of the marketing operation by his review and his plan.

"In smaller companies, the chief executive should approve such a plan for each major product. For larger companies, which function through semiautonomous operating divisions, the chief executive should require submission to him of a single such plan for each division.

"The fourth control tool which the chief executive possesses consists of progress reports by either the marketing director or the division general manager.

"The fifth tool is regular meetings of the chief executive's staff. Since this staff consists of the heads of all principal departments of the business, it provides an opportunity to keep the entire management informed of developments throughout the company.

"Sixth, it is both a responsibility and a privilege of the chief executive to decide how the company should be organized for maximum marketing effectiveness."

The Marketing Director

Next, we come to the marketing director. Of this executive, Eldridge says:

"The role of the marketing director is rather easy to describe. That role is the assumption of almost complete responsibility for the marketing function, thereby relieving the chief executive or the general manager of the impossible task of planning and supervising the company's marketing activities while at the same time trying to coordinate all the functions of the business and to formulate and achieve the company's overall objectives.

"The second requisite is that he should be an executive—a manager. While his immediate responsibility is to the marketing function, that responsibility should be exercised in consonance with company objectives and policies.

"There are other respects in which he must be an executive. One of his most important jobs is the selection and supervision of his aides: the advertising director, the product manager, the sales manager, the promotion manager, the marketing-research director, and the advertising agency. In addition to supervising the activities of all these aides and giving final approval to their recommendations, an important part of his job is to weld them together into a smoothly functioning unit, each part of which has its own responsibilities while simultaneously sharing in the group responsibility: To advance the approved marketing objectives.

"Contrary to a quite prevalent view, he need not have had in-advance familiarity with the particular kind of products he is now called upon to market. Such familiarity is not undesirable, but it should not be assigned priority over an understanding of the principles of marketing.

"What he does need to have is a knowledge of what marketing is all about, and of the elements—such as product line, product quality, pricing, packaging, distribution, advertising, selling, promotion, and marketing research—which constitute the totality of marketing and of the complete interdependence of all those elements.

"Even in his specific role as marketing director, he needs to have a knowledge of at least the fundamentals of economics. He must know how to keep his marketing expenditures in correct relationship to gross profit and thereby insure that the end result of his activities—namely, the production of an operating profit—is compatible with the company's objectives.

"Perhaps most important of all, he must be an analyst, a planner. He must be able to plan not only for the upcoming year but for the years ahead. He must be able to diagnose the problems of the business and to prescribe a course of action designed to meet those problems. There is probably no single activity of the marketing director that is more important or that can influence more strongly the effectiveness of the marketing program than his analysis of and approval of the marketing plan. He must be able by virtue of his own knowledge of the situation to spot fallacies in the plan. He must be able to detect omissions in the proposed plan, such as alternative conclusions or courses of action."

Relation of the marketing manager to other corporate executives.

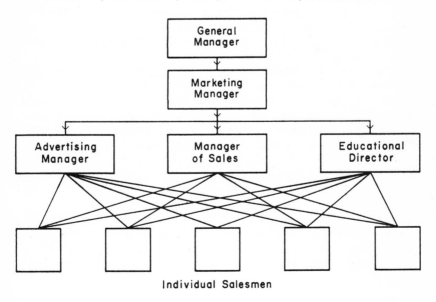

Individual Salesmen

Many companies have what are called "profit centers." In some companies the product manager is said to be "responsible for profits." This can be true only in the most limited sense. Not even the marketing director is responsible for profits. Just as there are many factors besides advertising that are responsible for sales results, there are many factors besides marketing that are responsible for profits.

Plan for Profit

The marketing department can influence but has no direct control over product quality or manufacturing costs. It must take the situation as it finds it. But the marketing director does have some responsibility for profits. It is his responsibility to formulate a plan which, on the basis of estimated product costs and his own estimate of sales, will produce an acceptable profit. It is likewise his responsibility if, during the currency of the plan, the budgeted profits are in jeopardy for whatever reason—higher costs, necessary price reductions or concessions, less than anticipated sales or whatnot— to modify the marketing plan or at least to acquaint the chief executive with the changed conditions. The marketing plan makes it possible for the chief executive to relieve himself of the necessity for "running" the marketing department of the business and at the same time leaves him in complete control of the entire operation.

What does the chief executive expect from his top marketing man? Robert B. Walker, president and chairman of the board of the American Tobacco Company, in an article in *Printers' Ink,* outlined his requirements as follows:

"My top marketing man must be smart enough to know his objectives and strong enough not to be distracted from them.

"He must be a bold innovator—not only sensitive to changes in the marketplace but also capable of anticipating the unstated needs of the consumer.

"He must have the courage to make decisions in the face of uncertainty, and defend his decisions against criticism and second guessing from others—including myself.

"How do you judge the marketing man in action? Looking hard at this question, one word comes to my mind—*results*. But certain questions can be asked about any marketing operation:

"How long does it take to move from the idea to the product to the marketplace? Are we doing this faster than competition?

"How well-positioned are we to make strategic adjustments within the marketing program to meet competitive actions?

"Do we beat competition to the punch a fair share of the time—that is, do we develop our share of product 'firsts'?

"Is the long-range marketing plan clearly defined—in other words, do we know just what we're trying to achieve and how we expect to do so?

"While I would expect marketing objectives to be in practical alignment with business trends, I would also expect marketing objectives to be sprinkled with imaginative thinking about the shape of things to come.

"It has been said that a marketing genius is a man who shoots at something no one else can see—and hits it. This portrays the successful marketing executive—he is possessed with the ability to imagine and do the unexpected. And I believe it is the duty of the chief executive officer to create an atmosphere for bold innovation."

The Sales Manager

This brings us to the sales manager's role and responsibilities.

Raymond O. Loen, management consultant, writing in the *Harvard Business Review*, points out that:

"Even though sales managers understand many aspects of managing, they have trouble distinguishing the elements of managing from those of nonmanaging activities in their day-to-day activities. Experience indicates that most sales managers have difficulty deciding which activities are managing, and which are nonmanaging or 'doing.'

"Managing can be defined as planning, directing, and controlling the activities of other people in the same organization in order to achieve or exceed desired objectives. It does have other meanings, but the managing we are concerned with here is the direction one is expected to give when he wants to get results through others.

"It is easy to confuse selling with managing because one who sells is expected to get sales results through customers and prospects. *Selling is not managing, however.* The essential difference is that a person in a managerial position has authority and responsibility to get a job done through others in the same organization—and these others are expected to recognize his authority and responsibility to help accomplish the overall objectives of the enterprise.

"Managing responsibility is generally greater or more important than 'doing' responsibility. Accordingly, it is important for the sales manager to have an awareness that he is not managing when he personally does selling, public relations, or the like. Only with this kind of awareness is he apt to strive to do as much managing

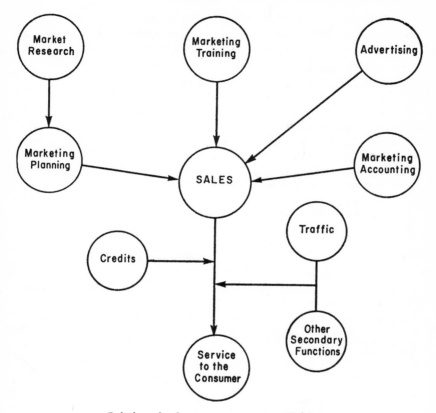

Relation of sales to other corporate divisions.

as he should in his current job; only with this awareness is he apt to be able to develop himself as much as he should for the broader responsibilities where managing activities assume even greater importance to his company."

The president, marketing director, and sales manager exert their decision-making responsibilities so as to produce the best profit-producing sales policies for their organization. Naturally, these policies will vary from company to company, so there is no one way of evaluating them specifically. In broad terms, however, they may be reviewed and tested from the following checklist, in which the questions have been classified according to organization, policies, activities, and programs concerned with the overall effectiveness of sales organizations.

EVALUATION CHECKLIST

A. STAFF—SALES-MANAGEMENT GROUP

1. Does background and ability of all department heads fit 90 percent or more of the requirements set by job specifications?

2. Are all department heads working together in reasonable harmony?

3. Is each department head training a possible successor?

4. Is turnover of trainees, assistants, or other employees excessive:
   a. In any one department?
   b. In the management staff as a whole?

5. Does one executive have full responsibility for forward planning from the sales and comprehensive policy position?

6. What is the degree of coordination between sales policies and advertising and production policies?

7. Are members of the sales-management group selected solely on merit and accomplishment?

8. Is each member of the group able to understand current competitive threats?

9. Does each member of the group recognize current and future potentials for enlarging markets and shares of markets?

10. Does executive compensation plan provide incentives to spur accomplishment of top-management objectives?

11. Is top sales executive (or company officer responsible for sales) aware of and able to use motivation devices appropriate to the men he directs and the conditions under which they work?

12. Are changes in, or additions to, the sales-management staff planned to strengthen or improve it during the next year or two?

    (If necessary insert additional factors considered vital to the effective and progressive operation of this phase of your business.)

B. STAFF—SALES-OPERATING GROUP

1. Is field manpower adequate in number?

2. Is field manpower adequate in quality?

3. What is being done to improve effectiveness of first-line salesmen?

4. Does each territory or division have a good salesman-recruiting program?

5. Does each territory or division have a good salesman-selection program?

6. Is our salesman-training program adequate for current needs in each territory or division?

7. Is morale of salesmen at a satisfactory level in each territory or division?

8. If morale of salesmen is not satisfactory do we know what to do to find and remedy factors which have negative effect on productivity?

9. Are our channels of communication between the sales-management staff and field sales force adequate for today's conditions?

10. If channels of communication are adequate, are we using them with maximum effectiveness?

11. Have we recently checked into the effectiveness of the sales methods and techniques used by our salesmen in their daily selling contacts?

12. If these methods are considered satisfactory for today's requirements, what is planned ahead for improvement and application to conditions and problems we will be facing in the next two years?

13. Are the sales tools, manuals, exhibits, and similar equipment used by our salesmen adequate for today's needs?

14. What is being planned for their improvement?

15. Do we explain to each salesman how quotas are calculated and why they are important?

16. If we are doubtful about the accuracy or utility of our present quota system, what is being done about improving or replacing it?

17. Do our sales records, at the regional or divisional level nearest point of contact with the buyer, provide adequate control to assure that good accounts can't be lost before the danger of such loss is brought to the attention of the management men responsible for results?

18. Do we have some method for periodic merit review of field salesmen by their immediate supervisors?

19. If not, do we have factors in our compensation plan which provide incentives for steady and continuing improvement of sales performance?

20. If the answers to questions 18 and 19 are both "No"—are our first-line sales supervisors able to constantly inspire salesmen to better efforts in the absence of these factors?

C. POLICIES

1. Are all major policies clearly stated, dated, and circulated to those concerned?

2. Does a standard procedure exist for policy review?

3. Is it clearly understood which executives are responsible for establishing policy in given areas?

4. Are sales personnel in the field and on the first line of supervision consulted when decisions about policies are under consideration?

5. Do we have a clear-cut, comprehensive marketing policy for the company as a whole?

6. Does each unit or division within the company have a basic policy established for guidance and control?

7. Has our master marketing policy been stated in terms of what it means to our buyers and those who use or consume our product or service?

8. Do we have a well-understood pricing policy?

9. Does our pricing policy contain elements that enable us to make healthy adjustments, when necessary, within a framework consistent with the best long-term interests of all concerned?

10. Have we taken steps to "sell" our pricing policy to our own executives, sales supervisors, and salesmen?

11. Is the authority for making pricing decisions assigned to the executive responsible for the profit contribution of the product, service, or division?

12. Have we recently compared our pricing policies with those of our competitors and with those used by other companies of similar size and nature in other industries?

13. Are we constantly studying the pricing policies successfully used by leaders in all fields to determine which elements in them might find profitable application to our problems?

14. Have we allowed financial, production, or other executives to assume influence or power in making price policy?

15. Is it possible that these influences from other departments are leading to price policies which will have a negative effect on sales or profits?

16. Have we established some channels for wholesalers, dealers, or other links in the chain of distribution, to express their ideas to us about price and other policies?

17. Are we interested in what the end user or consumer thinks about our price policy?

18. Have we discussed our marketing and price policies with our public-relations counsel?

19. If not, have we considered the public-relations aspects of the impact of these policies? Since they have been established have we reviewed possible changes in public opinion?

20. Has our marketing policy been "sold" internally to engineering, production, and all other personnel in terms of what it means to them?

21. Has our marketing policy been translated into quality and performance terms for use in stimulating production employees to improve quality and performance?

D. PROGRAMS—1. MARKETING

1. Do we know where our company as a whole stands today in relation to our competitors?

2. Do we have similar information for each product, service, or division?

3. Have we established what our next goals should be?

4. Do we know how we are going to get there?

5. Have we recently tabulated our sales by product for as many years as data is available?

6. Have we compared these figures with total sales in the industry and with similar figures of our strongest competitors?

7. Have we made similar comparisons on a price-per-unit basis?

8. Have we plotted these elements on a graph to show the relationships between costs, volume, and price per unit?

9. Are we using the significance of such comparisons and relationships in our advance marketing planning?

10. Did we recently review our marketing program with a fair amount of objectivity?

11. Do we occasionally review marketing programs with the aid of qualified individuals who were not personally involved in the development of original plans?

12. Before deciding on marketing programs, do we double check for possible information sources that may be influenced by a natural bias? (Such as market data furnished by media representatives who are more interested in selling space, programs, etc., than in supplying unvarnished facts which may not favor their special case.)

13. Have we checked our established and potential markets to find out if any shifts have occurred?

14. Have we analyzed any changes that seem likely to occur in the demand for our products by our principal customers or accounts?

15. Have we reappraised with care the adequacy of channels of distribution used in the past?

16. Do we know whether conditions have changed enough to warrant a revision of distribution channels?

17. Before making any changes, do we give careful consideration to factors which may show that unsatisfactory results may be due to poor utilization of a distribution channel rather than any fault or lack in the channel as such?

18. Have we checked our price structure to locate any special areas which price-conscious competitors could select as "soft-targets" to aim at?

19. Did we review our discount policies to see if they meet today's conditions with realism or are they merely a set of figures most people accept as a tradition?

20. Do we make it a regular practice to analyze accounts for the "Profit Contribution Factor"?

21. Have we been making progress toward the improvement of "Profit Contribution Factors"?

22. Did we set standards for controlling the costs of servicing accounts of various sizes?

23. Do we know if the use of such standards is bringing us a satisfactory increase in profits?

24. Are present facilities adequate to supply and service the preferred customers and prospects who are the targets of our marketing plan?

25. Have we made provision for adequate supervision of the sales force needed for the success of the marketing plan?

26. Are we planning to develop and improve these supervisors so that they will be well equipped to help their salesmen meet and beat the increasingly keen competition that is expected?

27. Are we planning to help our wholesalers, dealers, jobbers, etc., overcome the problems they expect to face in the next two years?

28. Did we check marketing-staff personnel to insure timely availability of specialists and others with the skills needed to implement the marketing plan?

29. Did we review and evaluate the present mailing list of customers and prospects?

30. Did we set up a plan to add new names to the mailing list?

31. Do we have an effective direct-mail program?

32. Did we set up a plan for periodic review, correction, and improvement of catalogs, displays, presentations, samples, etc., to be used in selling?

33. Is one person in charge of the above activity?

34. Is our advertising agency making a first-rate contribution to our marketing program?

35. Have we given them an adequate description and explanation of our marketing program?

36. Have we established a centralized liaison link between our advertising agency and our top marketing executive?

37. If our advertising agency is primarily "media-minded," is the marketing function adequately represented by one or more marketing specialists in our own top executive positions?

38. If this is not the case, do we encourage our executives to consult with or retain the services of first-rate marketing counsel?

39. If we have reason to suspect that competitors (both within and from outside our own industry) are likely to make faster progress than we expect to make, in the use of advanced marketing techniques, are we taking precautionary steps to insure quick availability and utility of plans to take necessary countermeasures?

40. Have we established a policy for evaluating whether or not we should undertake a vigorous program for the development of new products?

41. If we are looking for new products, have we established a "yardstick" of important factors the new product or service must offer?

42. In evaluating new products, do we consider the possible profit contribution as an important factor?

43. Have we established "break-even" points for our present products or services?

44. Do we know, from our "break-even" information, at what point it pays us to invest additional sales-promotion dollars to "buy" unit volume calculated to produce a high (or above-average) profit return per dollar of sales volume?

45. Do we have some method of determining how a new product will change our "break-even" points?

46. Have we considered the possible advantages of seeking new products sold through different channels, or to markets that stand a good chance of

improving or remaining stable, if our present markets should suffer a setback?

47. If our present method of distribution relies heavily on the ability of others to establish our product or brand recognition with the eventual buyer or user, should we consider the possible advantages of doing more and better advertising and promotion work aimed directly at the buyer or user?

48. If the above is desirable but subject to limiting factors, have we considered the advantages to be gained from more careful selection of distributors with renewed emphasis on their ability to meet our requirements for better recognition at the point of sale?

49. Have we recently reviewed the possible advantages to be gained by setting up more effective distributors by some program which would put them under more control in areas we know are vital?

50. Did we recently review our total distribution pattern to discover possible areas of duplication or neglect which were allowed to develop because of conditions which have since changed?

51. Have we given serious consideration to benefits to be derived from a continuing study of the actual results of our marketing program compared with the long-range intent of our marketing policies?

52. If the day-to-day operations of the sales force have developed resentments or antagonism toward the company on the part of some wholesalers, dealers, or users, are we aware of the nature and extent of these feelings?

53. Do we have a method for determining our cost of sales as a percent of sales?

54. Can we prepare a comparison schedule showing the trend in our cost of sales as a percent of sales compared to a similar trend of costs as experienced by our major competitors?

55. Is our cost-of-sales factor under control?

56. In the last two years, have we introduced new models, brought out new products, or given other evidence of ability to innovate or develop advanced ideas?

57. If we have been considered leaders in our line, is this leadership being threatened?

58. If we have been consistently gaining on the leaders in our line, have we maintained our rate of gain with some consistency?

59. If steady progress is our goal, have we taken steps to make all executives and employees aware of this?

D. PROGRAMS—2. CONTACT SELLING

1. Is our recruiting program delivering an adequate supply of qualified candidates for contact-selling jobs?

2. Do we have a recruiting policy and a consistent program geared to current needs?

3. Have we given serious consideration to encouraging the development of and seeking out of those company employees who might be good prospects for contact-selling jobs?

4. Do we have a carefully planned and well-supervised salesman-selection procedure?

5. Does this procedure bring the supervisor, under whom the salesman will work, into the interviewing and final selection steps?

6. Do we know our rate of turnover and reasons why those salesmen who leave us make the decision to do so?

7. Do we have a good idea of what this turnover rate is costing us?

8. Have we recently checked turnover rates to see if we are "in line" for our type of selling and to determine how those with better rates achieved them?

9. If some of our field supervisors have higher turnover rates than others, are we investigating causes?

10. Is our salesmen's compensation plan in step with the times?

11. Does our salesmen's compensation plan provide some form of incentive as a reward for better-than-average performance?

12. If not, are we able to make our salesmen feel that chances for advancement, prestige, or other nonfinancial rewards are worthy of serious study and work?

13. Are we avoiding the error of training salesmen and then losing them to our competitors?

14. Have we found a way to build for the future by developing men who eventually go into business for themselves either selling or using our products; or who are sought by our distributors as valuable employees?

15. Do we have some form of systematic merit review for our salesmen?

16. Do we have a system for finding out the vital statistics for territories and individual sales performance?

17. Does this system reveal for the individual salesman the average number of calls required per sale by customer?

18. Does this system show, promptly, sales performance against quota?

19. Does this system allow periodic review of selling costs by territory, by man; and if necessary by product, city, or type of customer?

20. Does our system show progress against plans for selling new products or setting up new accounts?

21. If we require salesmen to send in reports, do we have records of their receipt and provisions for acknowledgment?

22. Have we recently surveyed reports and other paperwork required from salesmen to see what can be eliminated or reduced to provide more time and attention for active selling?

23. Do we encourage our supervisors to work with their men in the field?

24. Do we provide inspirational and instructive opportunities to our salesmen so that those who want to improve skills and performance have guidance and encouragement?

25. Do we sometimes consult with our supervisors and ask them for ideas and suggestions; and by this means encourage them to do the same with their men?

26. Do we provide training and development opportunities for older or "advanced" salesmen as well as for beginners and newcomers?

27. Do we provide a sales manual that actually helps our men sell?

28. Is our sales training based mostly on the real needs of our salesmen?

29. Do we have some effective method of evaluating the effectiveness of our sales-training efforts?

30. Is each member of our sales force kept completely and promptly informed about every product improvement, price change, and other data?

31. Do we make all possible efforts to personally sell our salesman on our product, make it easy for him and his family to own or use it?

32. Do we take special pains to put our salesmen on all mailing lists to receive material being sent to customers, stockholders, and employees?

33. Do we make an honest and consistent effort to get salesmen to feel a part of the company as a whole and not just "outside men" with different interests?

34. Do we constantly encourage our salesmen by words and examples to make the best use of selling time?

35. Do we require our supervisors to be readily available to their men?

36. Do we encourage our supervisors to stay at least one step ahead of their men by being outstanding pace-setters and real leaders?

37. Do we set high yet obtainable standards for individual performance goals?

38. Are we sure our supervisors know how to assign men to the selling jobs for which they are best fitted?

39. Do our records, forms, systems, etc., lend themselves to the production of clearly understandable job assignments?

40. Have we provided our sales supervisors with systems and procedures that give them the means to hold good control over the activities of their men?

41. Is each supervisor held responsible for the results management has asked him to produce?

42. Does each supervisor hold his men responsible for the results they are assigned to produce?

43. Are supervisors trained to analyze and locate causes of trouble rather than to be content with constantly treating the symptoms?

44. Do we require a periodic check to see that each salesman has all the necessary sales tools and aids required for his job?

45. Do we require a periodic check to see that all salesmen are using these tools and aids properly?

46. If a sales tool or aid can be proved unnecessary or inefficient, do we have a procedure for withdrawing or replacing it?

47. Are we always careful to avoid even the appearance of playing favorites?

48. Do our supervisors thoroughly understand the meaning of turnover and do we supply them with adequate information to direct salesmen's efforts where and when needed to have the best influence on turnover? (If "turnover" is a factor in our operation.)

49. Have our salesmen been trained enough, or do they have ample experience, in the use of turnover pros and cons when speaking to customers and prospects?

50. Do we supply special visual aids, surveys, reports, testimonials, and similar items designed to emphasize the plus benefits of turnover qualities associated with our products?

51. Have we established a good system for developing a steady flow of prospects for our salesmen?

52. Have we been able to train and develop our salesmen to find their own prospects?

53. Do we have some method of dividing leads, or names of prospects, fairly among all members of the sales force?

54. In the development of new business, do we have definite standards to qualify it by and specific minimum order limits?

55. Are we constantly striving to train our salesmen to sell benefits rather than things?

56. Have we satisfied ourselves that those who train our salesmen have access to information they need to place heavy emphasis on benefits in ways that meet the needs of possible buyers?

57. Does our training program include attention to ways and means of handling the difficult buyer?

58. Do we also stress techniques of overcoming objections?

59. Do we have at least one tested and proved procedure recommended for closing the sale?

60. Do our men understand, fully, the details of how delivery promises are made?

61. If such promises must be changed, do we have a way of notifying both salesman and customer?

62. Have our salesmen been briefed on credit policies and practices?

63. Do our salesmen understand our guarantee and know how to explain it as a customer benefit?

64. Do our salesmen thoroughly understand service problems that may arise and are they in a position to help customer get assistance or action?

65. Do our salesmen know effective methods for handling customer complaints in accordance with company policies?

66. Whenever we establish a policy within our own department, do we make a habit of putting it in writing and circulating it to all concerned?

67. Do we make a steady effort to be impartial when setting up and assigning selling territories?

68. To keep this reputation for impartiality, do we do our best not to reduce a territory without an especially good reason?

69. If it should be necessary to take a good account out of a territory, do we make every possible effort to substitute an even better one in its place?

70. Do we have good reason to believe it would increase profits if we supply our customers with certain aids in using or reselling our product?

71. Do our salesmen thoroughly understand the uses and benefits of our customer-aid materials?

72. Do we have some way of checking on the results obtained when salesmen are supposed to be giving special attention to customer aids?

73. Do we have a good method for reading all sales reports and sending prompt replies or acknowledgments back to the field?

74. Do we make a special effort to run sales meetings that hold the interest, stimulate the individual, and deliver a desired result?

75. If we run contests, do we take special pains to base the awards on a fair relationship of "prize points" to dollars of sales revenue?

76. In running contests, are we careful to avoid the type where only a few top men win and all others get nothing?

77. When we participate in trade association or similar convention activities, do we look for opportunities to broaden the contacts and experience of the salesmen most likely to benefit from participation?

78. Have we found a way to make "exhibit duty" an honor and a challenge rather than a task to be ducked?

79. If packaging is important to our product, have we been doing a good job of improving the salesman's ability to talk and think in packaging terms that will help his customers?

E. ORGANIZATION

1. Is the sales and marketing function adequately represented in the top-management group?

2. Have we considered the advantages to be gained from inviting top executives from other departments to attend meetings and other activities which will increase their knowledge and understanding of sales and marketing?

3. Does an up-to-date organization chart exist for the sales department?

4. Does this chart clearly show line-and-staff relationships?

5. Does this chart show definite areas of responsibility and authority?

6. Have we recently given serious consideration as to whether or not our functional and geographic groupings of the organization are best designed to serve current and future requirements?

7. Where geographic groupings exist, are we sure they were determined on sound marketing principles?

8. Where functional groupings exist, are we sure they were determined on sound marketing principles?

9. If some of these groupings originated through the special abilities or influences of individuals, have we considered how new developments might make different groupings, based on sounder principles, safer and more advantageous?

10. Is each sales manager's sphere of operations set up so that the profitability factor for each division or product is accurately known at all times?

11. Have we recently studied what might be gained from organizing all activities related to one product or service under one executive who is then completely responsible for the profit contribution of his division?

12. If we are now operating under a division manager pattern, have we made a recent check to see if results are following according to plan?

13. In setting up our lines of organization, did we consider the effective "span of control" for each assignment?

14. In setting up our organization, did we give adequate consideration to principles of good communications:

    a. Between individuals?
    b. Between departments inside the sales group?
    c. Between headquarters and the field?
    d. Between departments outside the sales group?

15. Have we analyzed the flow of reports in theory and checked this against practice?

16. If our organization chart is just an "interesting antique curiosity," are we taking steps to remedy the situation?

17. Do we have good reasons to believe a company policy manual would be worth preparing?

18. If we already have such a manual, is it up to date?

19. Is our organization manual clear enough to be fairly well understood by a new executive during his first day on the job?

20. Do we make regular checks to find out whether our organization structure is so rigid it acts as a hindrance to progress?

21. Do we make a periodic check to see if our sales activity is properly focused on new or allied products recently added to our line?

22. Each time we do the above, do we consider the advantages to be gained by setting up a separate sales division for those products or services?

Chapter 3

THE TASKS OF SALES MANAGEMENT

MOST of the problems of business and the tasks which they create for sales management may be classified in three general areas. They are product, distribution, and pricing. Of course, there are secondary or associated responsibilities calling for judgment and decision on the part of sales managers.

The emphasis on marketing involves sales executives in product design, in which they must have a voice if they are to be held responsible for profitability. The responsibility of the sales manager for distribution is, of course, a primary one. And, since one of the chief objectives of marketing is profit, pricing policies, price levels, discounts, and other terms all exert a force toward this end.

Experts Pose the Problems

Sales Management queried six company officers and marketing executives concerning their biggest marketing problems. Their replies were as follows:

Our marketing problem is to bolster sales in the face of declining demand.

Stimulating sales through sharpening salesmanship, stronger merchandising, promotional efforts, offering better values, and general "belt tightening" are the order of the day in this business (and this industry) at this time.

> David J. Brunn, president
> Drexel Furniture Company
> Drexel, N. C.

Our major marketing problem is in mounting competitive pressure. To combat the problem we are (1) strengthening our sales force and distributor organization, (2) spending $3.2 million to expand brewery facilities for increased plant capacity to keep pace with consumer demand, (3) enlarging our distribution area to broaden our marketing base and (4) maintaining brand vitality through advertising despite continually rising media costs.

> Harvey J. Bolser
> Vice-president, marketing
> Pearl Brewing Company
> San Antonio, Texas

Some of our problems are (1) increasing difficulty in finding skilled workers, (2) rising costs of virtually everything, (3) many plants operating dangerously near capacity, (4) some shortages and extended deliveries of important materials and (5) some major customers are balancing their inventories, which will require rescheduling of our production and shipment in 1967.

> Ralph C. Charbeneau
> Director of advertising
> Ex-Cell-O Corporation
> Detroit, Michigan

My greatest marketing problem in 1967 is to capitalize the tremendous opportunities available to us for expansion and growth.

We have a strong organization, with a nucleus of experienced key people eager and capable of stepping up to greater responsibility and productivity. My main objective is to provide the leadership and climate, as well as the organizational followthrough that will allow these people to assume greater responsibility and to develop their individual potential to a larger degree.

> W. W. Clements
> Executive vice-president
> Dr. Pepper Company
> Dallas, Texas

Because we manufacture window shades, woven woods, and venetian blinds, we feel the immediate effects of consumer tastes. Our problem is to *accelerate* a changing market, and stay just the *right* distance ahead of a market we are anticipating, creating and *selling* all at the same time.

Now our marketing challenge falls into consistent focus: We must maintain a lead in fashion authority against competitive imitation, and at the same time force a filtering down of the new high-fashion image to capture the enthusiasm of middle-market consumers.

> Frank Lambert
> General sales manager
> Breneman, Inc.
> Cincinnati, Ohio

Our marketing challenge is clear. Most fresh meat has been marketed on a commodity basis rather than on a differentiated product approach. Within grade and quality groupings, all goods of a type have been assumed to be fully interchangeable. Brand preference was of little or no consequence. Price has tended to be the one competitive weapon, with profits generated by efficiencies in production.

At Swift, increasing efforts are being directed to establishing *product differentiation*. We are examining all the ways we can discover and satisfy *special* demands, either from retailers or consumers. Our program tries to bring manufacturing, distribution, and retailing together in places and through channels especially suited to a particular product.

> R. W. Reneker, president
> Swift and Company
> Chicago, Illinois

Elements of a Long-Range Plan

While a sound plan for expanding any business must include many factors, present-day conditions place particular emphasis on distribution. So the sales phases of the plan need painstaking consideration.

It may well be that our present policy is adequate. But at least we should check it to be sure it meets the larger test of public service, as well as company security. While selling may not undergo any sudden changes, it is clear there will be progressive changes.

During the past several years, Dartnell has carefully observed the trend of sales management. Members of the staff have enjoyed close relations with many sales leaders in all lines of business. The following conclusions have been reached as to what a sound customer-relations policy for the average business should encompass:

Principle No. 1

Your long-range sales policy should speed the movement of goods and services into the hands of those who can use or sell them at a profit.

This means you should predetermine those customers who are able to use your products, the quantities in which they can use them, and then eliminate, so far as possible, those functions which add to the cost of distributing to those customers. It means putting "profit" ahead of "coverage" as a main consideration in sales planning, administration, and concentration of sales effort.

Principle No. 2

Your long-range sales policy should provide for selling and moving goods and services in economic quantities, at economically sound prices, through the most economically sound channels of distribution.

One of the most important jobs of sales management is to determine how much is needed to sell any given customer to earn a profit on his purchases. Millions of distribution dollars have been wasted because too many customers had the turnover craze, and bought in such small quantities that there was no profit to the supplier, and the purchaser penalized himself by carrying inadequate stocks.

Another great loss results from too careless selection, or no selection at all, of distribution outlets. Too many companies undercut established markets by selling mass distributors at stripped cost prices. Such a policy is unsound.

Principle No. 3

Your long-range policy should include the training of every salesman, distributor, wholesaler, dealer, and consumer to sell and buy in economical quantities.

This is fundamental in any program aimed at the reduction of prices to the consumer. It makes no difference whether a buyer buys too much or too little; if the quantity is uneconomical, costs are needlessly increased and waste results.

The control of this waste calls for intensive buyer and seller education. It cannot be done overnight. But provision should be made in sales planning for more of this all-important work. We must lay aside any ideas we have about selling buyers all we can get them to order and pay for, and sell them economical quantities determined by dealer and consumer studies.

Principle No. 4

Your long-range sales policy should seek to determine, by trustworthy means, the customer structure of each customer's business. This determines his chances for survival.

It is reasonable to assume that the establishments which will survive highly competitive selling will be those which had the foresight to build a solid customer structure. The manufacturer's sales policy should be aimed in that direction. His customers and their customers in turn must be educated to build the same kind of foundation for lasting relationships.

Principle No. 5

Your long-range sales policy should determine the sales objective, measure the sales power needed to reach that objective, then seek to apply the needed sales power to attain the objective at an economical cost.

This means more than just establishing the potential sales expectancy from a territory. It means first of all determining a break-even point in sales production. It means the intelligent allocation of that volume among all sales-production factors, with a corresponding allocation of the sales effort.

And more than anything else it means focusing the sales effort, by the use of scientific controls and proper budgeting of expense, upon the main objectives, with the least possible dissipation of effort on side shows and frills. In short, it means doing a superlative job of planning; of doing the first things first, of planning the work and then working the plan.

In developing distribution for most products in the general classification of consumer goods, the distributor and dealer require the most important considerations of sales management.

"Dealer coverage" means sales-territory coverage, and sales volume falls or rises in proportion to the number of good dealers selling the product. They are on the firing line. They confront the consumer.

Importance of Product Exposure

The task of obtaining and maintaining product exposure at the retail level was selected as one of the most important problems facing American industry by William H. Derbius, vice-president, domestic marketing, The Parker Pen Company, who wrote Dartnell as follows:

Because of the way The Parker Pen Company products are sold, the greatest problem we face on a day-to-day basis is that facet of distribution related to the product's availability at the retail counter.

With the costs of getting products up to retail counters constantly increasing and the costs of moving them across counters constantly increasing, maintaining the delicate balance between supply and demand in these outlets is a problem that will become more and more complex.

Like other marketers of packaged durable consumer hard goods, we utilize some 50,000 to 60,000 retail outlets. It is in this complex assortment of retail outlets where the challenge lies for us because:

1. Retailers, large and small, are becoming more and more conscious of the costs involved in inventories. As a result, the larger-volume retailers are installing sophisticated inventory-control systems. Under these conditions a product is carefully monitored and it has to perform by giving the retailer what he considers an acceptable number of "turns" or it will be taken out of stock.

2. The concept of brand proliferation practiced by many of the major marketers today makes it a constant challenge for an older brand to hold its shelf position. With the number of new products on the increase and finding their way onto retail counters, the ability of an established product to claim satisfactory performance per square foot of counter space becomes increasingly difficult.

3. The willingness and capability of some manufacturers to launch a new product and continue to support it with a sustained saturation advertising campaign can result in one, two, or even three established brands losing shelf or counter position to the new entrant. If this counter space is to be regained, it has to be at great expense and effort in support of the older brand.

4. Retailers, in their quest to control inventories more efficiently, are demanding more and more services from manufacturers and their salesmen. Those manufacturers who cannot afford the manpower to perform up to the level required by the retailer will ultimately get less and less cooperation from the retailer and, consequently, less and less shelf or counter space. Therefore, the smaller manufacturer with the third or fourth brand in a market will probably have to face an ever-decreasing share of market.

Where there is an opportunity to apply tested principles, success comes not so much in techniques and methods as in the approach to sales planning.

Fringe Accounts and Small Orders

One fundamental of any sales management program should be to speed the movement of goods *only* into the hands of those who could use or sell them at a profit.

How are we to know who these people are? Perhaps we should set up standards for selecting customers, just as we define standards for selecting salesmen. But to do that we need to go back into our records and check fringe accounts—the customers we may have served at a loss, and who, in turn, made very little or no money on what we sold them.

How many of these fringe accounts developed into profitable accounts? Did the profit on the accounts which developed satisfactorily compensate you for the total loss the company sustained on the other fringe accounts which did *not* develop? You might find you can lop off about half your accounts and make more money yourself, and help your profitable customers make more, too.

Another problem is to move goods in economical quantities. We know quite well that many profitable accounts have been built out of fringe business. One company made a tidy profit selling accounts which hide-bound competitors turned down. Perhaps you might not want to adhere to this principle.

But before you decide, get the facts. Have you ever made an honest-to-goodness analysis of small orders? True, the accounting department can prove you lost money on them, and you probably do. But does the accounting department know? Does it know the break-even point on your sales? Does it know how much more you can spend to get "plus" business? How does it figure costs on small orders? On a prorata basis or on a "run-on" basis? If you did not have the extra volume on these small orders, how would the loss of volume affect overall profits?

The Product Mix

The product mix in many companies includes items with varying profit margins. While it would be highly desirable to have the sales force concentrate all its efforts on high-profit products, the volume and the contribution provided by less profitable items are often necessary in order to cover factory burden. Nonetheless, it is still the objective of most sales and marketing managers to upgrade the mix to include more profitable products. In an attempt to do this, companies offer better incentives for sales of the high-profit items. Other companies use focused product promotion as the catalyst to provide increased field efforts where desired. Here is where all the advertising tools available can be coordinated with one another and with the field sales effort. Strong space advertising and direct mail, plus special sales tools keyed to primary markets, can be combined to produce dramatic results.

You have to know the answers to those questions to do an intelligent job of sales planning. To get the correct answers you have to dig deeper than the costs which may be established by an ultraconservative controller.

Then there is the matter of how far to go in training personnel. Sales managers agree that it is desirable to train people. But do we know how much we can afford to appropriate for that sort of thing? Do we know what sales results were derived from money previously spent for training work of various kinds? That is not easily answered. But we have to know and not guess that our training program is effective. It can be evaluated by breaking down sales of individual salesmen and by adequate sales analysis.

What About Our Customers' Customers?

Another rather vital point disregarded in the past, or at least slighted in our desire to get sales coverage, is the customer structure of the accounts we are serving. If a customer was able to pay our bills, that was about all we cared. If he couldn't pay them, that was the credit department's worry.

Is that a wise policy to follow in the future? Maybe we have a competitive situation which justifies grabbing all business we can get, and let tomorrow look out for itself. Market coverage might be more important than stabilization of our distribution. What we do in the next few years to build a solid and enduring sales foundation will pay handsome dividends. At least, it is important enough for us to get the facts before deciding on policy.

Similarly we need to get more facts on the long-term profit resulting from intensive selling. We hear a lot of loose talk about pressure selling having outlived itself—that future selling will be low-pressure selling. How about that? Enough pressure should be applied to produce the sales power needed to attain the future objective we establish. It is dangerous to generalize on this point. What every sales manager will have to determine for himself, in the light of his objective and previous experience with pressure methods, is how much pressure he can profitably and safely use.

What we want to avoid is overselling brought about by too much pressure. But at the same time, we must get sufficient sales volume to keep our people employed at good wages. Somewhere there is a point of diminishing returns. Where is that point? Once we know, we have the answer to how much pressure to put behind sales— whether we want quotas or not, whether to use contests or not, whether to use a lot of salesmen or a few salesmen, etc.

The selling process is linked up with the whims and foibles of human nature. It would be rash to say what will work and what won't work. Every business has within its own experience, just as every salesman has within his own experience, tested principles which should be more fully utilized. Every business faces different problems which must be solved if it is to measure up to its future responsibility. There is no such thing as a made-to-order selling plan for every business. Each one must be tailored to fit.

The "Language Gap"

Frank Laseter, president of Gondas Corporation, Miami, claims that a "language gap" exists between sales managers and their salesmen. When managers and salesmen were asked to list the 10 most important factors for employees, the two lists differed greatly.

Heading the list of morale factors for salesmen was "full appreciation for work done." Yet the sales supervisors put that factor eighth on their list of the same 10 basic motivations.

Feeling "in" on things, which the sales supervisors surveyed thought was of least concern to sales employees, turned out to be *second* on the list of the salesmen's own consensus. "Teach your salesmen all of the ramifications of your business," Laseter emphasized, "or you cannot expect them to involve themselves wholly in your mutual drive for business success.

"The poorest asset you can have in your company is an ill-prepared and poorly trained salesman."

After proper training, Laseter thought *leadership* was a second necessary essential of good sales supervision.

Motivation is the third necessary ingredient to achieve good, effective sales supervision. This means that a salesman must have some good reason for being a salesman in the first place. One of these reasons is compensation.

But the salesman himself is somewhat adrift as regards proper compensation methods. "Like management," Laseter observed, "salesmen are caught in a conflict of values." Laseter concluded: "It is clear that new ways of motivating today's salesmen must be found."

Plugging "Profit Leaks"

Wasteful practices, too, creep into distribution and they must be constantly watched and corrected.

Summarizing all this, it will be useful to note the following list of "profit leaks" prepared for review by a West Coast manufacturer.

1. Unreasonably small shipments because of no planned buying procedure.

2. High transportation costs due to small shipments.

3. Allowing merchandise to be returned or exchanged means excessive and duplicated costs.

4. Burden of merchandise replacements made as matter of "policy" to avoid losing dealer's goodwill, and not because of defects in material or workmanship.

5. Cost of keeping up poor selling items showing unsatisfactory turnover.

6. Rush service because of dealers' starved stocks, which means peak load staff at all times.

7. Made-to-order size service for eastern or low-end buyers not regularly handling our lines.

8. Losses due to bad debts through not selecting best accounts for solicitation.

9. Long terms and high discounts increase cost of essential credit accommodation.

10. Chiseling deductions and improper claims allowed because "not worth fighting."

11. Annual dividends, rebates, etc., which are not reflected in retail prices.

12. Costly freight allowances which result in nearby customers carrying the overhead load of servicing far off customers.

13. Allowances for advertising, which are sometimes wasteful because some retailers don't spend the other fellow's money as carefully as their own.

14. Excessive solicitation, which must be paid for by someone.

15. Split shipments, which mean duplicated costs—usually unnecessary.

16. Excessive number of errors due to excessive number of transactions per $1,000 of business.

17. Manufacturing costs higher and quality lower because of:
    a. Too many varieties of merchandise.
    b. Too many sizes made.
    c. Excessive amount of made-to-order service.
    d. Lack of continuity of sales.
    e. Pressure of rush deliveries.

It will be noted that many of the items in the list are obviously competitive and are probably continued at the demand of customers. It is not easy for one seller to refuse to do something which his competitors are doing. It is in this area of distribution that trade associations can be of great service to society. By means of gentlemen's agreements and voluntary action, distribution wastes can at least be restricted, if not entirely eliminated. Trade associations can and do prepare lists of inefficient marketing practices which have fastened themselves upon the industry, and constantly educate members to eliminate them as far as possible.

Chapter 4

THE MODERN SALES ORGANIZATION

A S STATED by Herbert A. Simon in *Administrative Behavior* (Macmillan), the task of management is to attain its objectives by utilizing available resources in the best calculated ways through a systematic plan of action. A form of cooperation must be provided, by which persons associated in the enterprise are induced to submerge their personal interests and work toward a common end. This requires a plan for the division of work in which the participants share a common goal, and for the coordination of effort by giving each member of the group his status or role in relation to the other members.

To put these principles into actual practice requires the formation of an organization. Lyndall Urwick, in *Elements of Administration* (Harper & Row), defines the concept of organization as requiring that the coordinating authority operate throughout the entire structure of management always in two contrary senses; one in which the dividing lines are vertical, indicating different kinds of duties, and the other in which the dividing lines are horizontal, indicating different levels of authority. It is impossible to fix any function of management accurately in the organizational structure except in both these senses.

The vertical divisions encompass the functional areas of work. In a small manufacturing company these include, but are not limited to, sales, production, and financial matters. In a one-man operation, these functions are all handled by the one individual; he supplies the limited capital needed, makes the product, sells it, and keeps such records as are needed to evaluate his efforts. He is president, treasurer, production manager, sales manager and controller. Even though he be but one man, all of these functions, and more, must be handled.

As sales increase, he hires additional help in the production area. This requires him to authorize one of them to watch over and direct

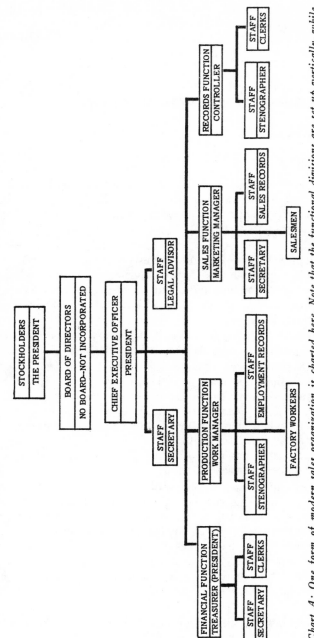

Chart A: One form of modern sales organization is charted here. Note that the functional divisions are set up vertically, while the various levels of authority line up horizontally. The sales manager (or marketing manager) is on the second level of authority, lining up with the three other major executives.

the efforts of the others; thus a horizontal structure begins to emerge. The president, as production manager, has a production supervisor who directs the factory workers, and who reports to the president.

The company grows, and the president is forced to delegate more of his functions. He hires salesmen, then a sales manager to supervise them; he hires bookkeepers, then a controller to supervise them. Probably he retains the function of treasurer, because he owns all the capital.

The company prospers and in time each functional manager needs assistance to help in the planning and record-keeping of his department. New personnel enters the organization as staff. They are assigned certain duties and maintain necessary records. The purpose of staff is to increase the effectiveness of the executive it serves, to investigate, and recommend action. The staff provides a liaison for preliminary exploration of interdepartmental and interdivisional problems as they arise.

The greatest contribution of the staff may be in the planning area, for action to be authorized by the functional executive; but the staff members have no authority other than that reflected by the chief executive's authority. The staff earns respect by the thoroughness of its work and astuteness of its recommendations. It gets things done, without formally delegated authority, through its ability to gain the consent of those it governs.

How Organizations Evolve

Thus, for the illustrative company, an organization has evolved as shown in Chart A. Note that all the functional divisions are divided vertically, with the various levels of authority lined up horizontally. The lines of authority flow from the president through his functional managers to the workers, primarily in the factory and sales territories; the other workers are shown as staff. This shows the usual differential between function, line, and staff.

Persons in both the functional and line positions have full authority over those below them, particularly in matters of hiring, firing, and compensation (within company policies), while staff men have no such authority.

Action comes through the work of line personnel. Planning is conducted by both line and staff personnel, but it is the duty of staff to furnish statistical and creative data, to recommend plans for action which the line personnel put into effect.

The chart also indicates that the president, as chief executive officer, is the focal point of all authority. He delegates authority to his individual functional managers, who in turn further divide it and pass certain portions of it to their subordinates. However, in this delegation, the president does not relinquish his centralized responsibility for results; in like manner each subordinate maintains his control over results expected of him. Authority may be delegated and responsibilities charged to individuals, but an executive can never properly divest himself of his responsibility.

Conflicts to Be Expected

Robert J. Lavidge, president of Elrick & Lavidge, Inc., and past president of the American Marketing Association, has said:

"It is inevitable that there will be conflicts in most any organization between the customer-oriented point of view and the point of view of those who are primarily concerned with production, product engineering, accounting, and other functions."

Philip Kotler of Northwestern University noted a number of these in an article in the *Harvard Business Review:*

SUMMARY OF ORGANIZATIONAL CONFLICTS

Other Departments	Their Emphasis	Emphasis of Marketing
Engineering	Long design lead time	Short design lead time
	Functional features	Sales features
	Few models with standard components	Many models with custom components
Purchasing	Standard parts	Nonstandard parts
	Price of material	Quality of material
	Economic lot sizes	Large lot sizes to avoid stock-outs
	Purchasing at infrequent intervals	Immediate purchasing for customer needs
Production	Long order lead times and inflexible production schedules	Short order lead times and flexible scheduling to meet emergency needs
	Long runs with few models	Short runs with many models
	No model changes	Frequent model changes
	Standard orders	Custom orders
	Ease of fabrication	Aesthetic appearance
	Average quality control	Tight quality control
Inventory Management	Fast-moving items, narrow product line	Broad product line
	Economic levels of stock	Large levels of stock

Finance	Strict rationales for spending	Intuitive arguments for spending
	Hard-and-fast budgets	Flexible budgets to meet changing needs
	Pricing to cover costs	Pricing to further market development
Accounting	Standard transactions	Special terms and discounts
	Few reports	Many reports
Credit	Full financial disclosures by customers	Minimum credit examination of customers
	Low credit risks	Medium credit risks
	Tough credit terms	Easy credit terms
	Tough collection procedures	Easy collection procedures

W. N. Mitchell, partner, A. T. Kearney Company, management consultants, has said:

"Authority represents the mandate setting forth limits within which the one to whom it is granted may perform the function of management. Responsibility is the obligation to supervisors to see that authority, to the measure possessed, is exercised.

"Accountability represents the personal liability as the object of sanctions or penalties imposed in the event, and to the extent, responsibility is not accepted and acted upon."

In the division of labor among the various levels of the organization, long-run and future considerations fall primarily on the shoulders of the top executive group, and the short-run or immediate ones on those in the lower levels. It has been aptly said, "The president thinks today in terms of what the workmen will be doing 5 to 10 years hence."

The Geographically Structured Company

There is no typical organization that will serve all companies. Each must be tailored to fit the demands of the enterprise. The marketing department may be structured on a geographical basis. If so, all products produced by the company would be sold by the same salesmen, as shown in Chart B.

Note that the product managers of products A, B, C, and D are staff to the chief marketing executive; their purpose is to investigate, plan, and record results of the marketing of their respective products. The salesmen sell all four lines of products, reporting to branch managers who are assigned specific branch territories and who, in turn, report to one of the two district managers.

The advantages of such an organization lie principally in its

MARKETING ORGANIZATION

GEOGRAPHICAL STRUCTURE

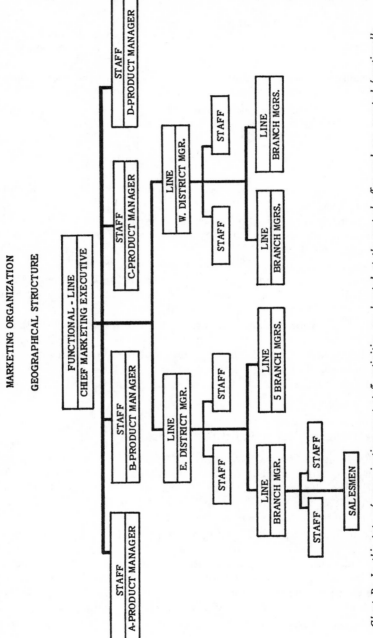

Chart B: In this type of organization, most staff activities are located at the central office and are grouped functionally.

simplicity and its economy of operation. Line authority and chain of command are direct; field services are not duplicated; and decisions can be made at the level nearest the need.

The principal disadvantages of this type of organization lie in the breadth of product knowledge which the salesmen must attain to operate effectively. They may become "Jacks-of-all-trades-but-masters-of-none." Communications may become quite snarled as the four product managers vie with each other in trying to get equal field sales representation. One product line, although important to the company, may become submerged and neglected due to the superior promotional effort by the manager of another product, or because the first product is a little harder to sell and the salesmen shun it.

Functional activities vary considerably within companies. Many take on line characteristics, such as the sales manager of a product; others tend toward staff. Even with staff classification, a short line of authority exists from department manager, to supervisors, to clerks. Typical staff activities might include, but be not limited to, the following:

Advertising	Customer correspondence
Promotions	Sales-personnel correspondence
Catalogs	Sales service and engineering
Pricing service	Quotations
Product research	Order entry
Market research	Order expediting
Personnel employment	Estimating costs
Personnel training	Expense checking and recording

In a geographically structured company, most of these activities are located at the central office and are grouped functionally. For instance, advertising, promotions, catalogs and pricing service may in themselves be under separate department heads who report to a director of advertising, who in turn reports to the chief marketing executive. These departments would serve all product groups, and each department might have a man assigned to only one or to two of the products.

The Product-Structured Company

In a product-structured company, each product manager would have some of these activities under his jurisdiction, even though

	Today	1 week ahead	1 month ahead	3 mo. to 6 mo. ahead	1 year ahead	2 years ahead	3 yrs. to 4 yrs. ahead	5 yrs. to 10 yrs. ahead
PRESIDENT	1%	2%	5%	17%	15%	25%	30%	5%
VICE PRESIDENT	2%	4%	10%	29%	20%	20%	13%	2%
WORKS MANAGER	4%	8%	15%	38%	20%	10%	5%	
SUPERINTENDENT	6%	10%	20%	43%	10%	9%	2%	
DEPARTMENT MANAGER	10%	10%	25%	39%	10%	5%	1%	
SECTION SUPERVISOR	15%	20%	25%	37%	3%			
GROUP SUPERVISOR	38%	40%	15%	5%	2%			

How far should sales executives plan in advance? A study made by a sales-consulting organization came up with this thought-provoking analysis of averages among a group of companies.

there might be central directors of each function who would keep watchful eyes over all functional work in each product division.

A typical product-structured organization is shown on Chart C. Note that the staff of the chief marketing executive is small, as each product sales manager has his own supporting staff to concentrate only on the products of his department. Since there are no branch managers (in this example), an additional district manager would be needed to hold to 10 the number of salesmen reporting to each district manager.

The advantages of this system include the possibility of more specialization; the problems of communications are simplified, and customers can be more properly serviced. The disadvantages include considerable overlapping of territories and duplication of travel. It is conceivable that four product salesmen would call on the same customer, even on the same day. Customers have mixed feelings about this; some like to deal with the most knowledgeable salesman available, while others resent having so much of their time taken up by one company. The company may lose, too, for a buyer might feel that since he had bought all of his requirements for product A from the company, he would be justified in buying products B, C, and D from other companies. The family concept of products is largely dissipated with the product organization.

Specific assignment of major responsibilities is a requirement of product-structured companies. There follows a discussion of how such responsibilities generally are assigned:

1. Product Research: Product research will probably be under jurisdiction of product managers in a geographically-structured company, and under the sales product manager in a product-structured company. Of course, if the company has a central research department, much of the actual research and development work will be done there.

2. Market Research: Market research usually reports directly to the chief marketing executive. Research is his auditor of past performance against planned objectives; it is his eyes into the future, his source of objectivity. In a factory, quality control rarely reports to the factory superintendent, who is directly in charge of manufacturing the product, but to the chief production manager, who is removed from direct contact with the product. In like manner, market research should not report to the field sales manager, who supervises the salesmen, but to the field sales manager's superior.

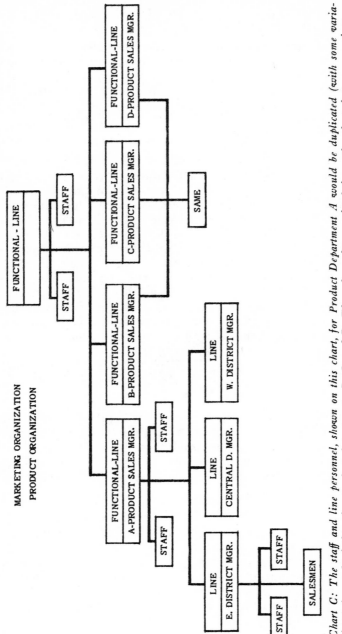

Chart C: The staff and line personnel, shown on this chart, for Product Department A would be duplicated (with some variations) for each of the other product departments, B, C, and D. These have been omitted from the chart for reasons of space limitations. Thus, there would be four product sales managers, each staffed as needed and having separate sales forces. However, two or more product lines might, in some cases, be combined, such as B-C or B-D, under one product sales manager, and sold by one sales force. The blank square at the top represents the position of the marketing chief, who may also be called "vice-president for sales" or "general sales manager."

3. Personnel Administration: Personnel employment and personnel training could report to the field sales manager, who is responsible for the performance of the selling personnel in the field. He should have complete control of who are hired, how they are trained, and what they do.

4. Customer Services: Customer correspondence, sales personnel correspondence, order entry, expediting, and quotations are frequently grouped together under a customer-service manager. This covers all clerical paperwork involved in order soliciting, receiving, checking, pricing, entering and following up on order shipments. The handling of orders remains a part of the sales function until orders are ready in every respect to be turned over to production for manufacture.

Proper service to customers and salesmen is not considered complete until the material reaches the customers and is satisfactorily in use. Some companies requiring two or more correspondents in their customer-service departments divide the work on a geographical basis rather than on a product basis. Thus a customer deals with one salesman and one correspondent; if the work is well done, confidence and enduring relations result.

5. Costing: Estimating is frequently done by the production department, which has the responsibility of making the product. Or it may be done in the customer-service department from cost standards prepared by the production department. Actual quotations are then prepared in the customer-service department with deviations from standards authorized by a high-level marketing man. It is wise for deviations to be made from known standards, rather than to use rough estimates made just to meet a market condition. Losses can thereby be minimized and the full value of special prices capitalized.

6. Sales Services: Sales service and engineering are frequently staff positions under the field sales manager. They are really tools for him to use in maintaining customer satisfaction. The personnel may be drawn from the production department, and the work offers excellent training experience for future salesmen.

7. Advertising: Advertising and sales promotion, in some companies, may be a staff function, but its efficiency, in practice, is determined by how closely it is intertwined with the sales department. In fact, in many organizations, it is an integral part of the sales department, with the advertising manager reporting to the sales manager.

In any event, since the purpose of advertising is to increase sales, the advertising manager must be sales-oriented. He must be sales conscious, rather than simply a channel for producing ads or promotional material. These activities may be left to specialists within the advertising department; the manager, however, should be, first and foremost, a salesman, and all his decisions and efforts must be based on this premise.

In some cases, artists have been appointed advertising managers, and nothing could be wider of the mark. Similarly, copywriters or research men have been elevated to the post of advertising director with the result that the emphasis on sales-producing goals becomes secondary to minor considerations such as four-color brochures, expensive layouts, clever copy themes and odd research projects.

8. Expense Control: Expense checking and recording are frequently done by the accounting department. Forms are prepared by this department along sound accounting lines. Salesmen's expenses are approved by the branch manager, or first principal level of authority over the salesmen (not by gang leaders or sales supervisors, however); the approved expense reports are sent to the accounting department for auditing, recording, and payment. Monthly reports then are sent by this department to the field sales manager, who is responsible for economical field coverage.

Where It All Began

The emphasis on marketing, according to the *Gallagher Report* (volume XV, No. 14), began in package goods, spread to manufacturers of consumer products and finally to industrial and service companies.

The marketing concept received its impetus from advertising directors seeking market services. Out of the struggle for corporate status between the advertising men and sales managers came the creation of the new post of director of marketing. Today, according to Gallagher, more than 50 percent of U.S. advertising managers and 40 percent of the top sales executives report to the marketing director.

Questionnaires mailed to 1,000 leading companies disclosed that corporate presidents rate selling most important, marketing second, and advertising, third. In the next decade, however, the presidents expect marketing to be first, selling second, and advertising third. Three out of every four marketing heads report directly to the president, 87 percent of whom assist in the development of marketing plans. Some 85 percent of the presidents assist in sales planning, while 82 percent confer with the advertising directors. More than half of the presidents make final decisions on test marketing and national distribution of new products.

According to the *Gallagher Report,* companies differ widely on how to organize marketing management. Forty-three place the vice-president, marketing, in charge of sales and advertising. And 31 percent place the marketing, sales, and advertising chiefs on the same level. A growing minority (10.3 percent) place the marketing-and-sales vice-presidents at the same level, with the advertising director reporting to marketing.

The *Gallagher Report* stresses the great need for generalists with a broad knowledge of every phase of marketing: product development, consumer and market research, packaging, pricing, brand management, distribution, advertising, publicity, promotion, merchandising, and sales. Talent must be trained from the ground up and moved from department to department. "Today's marketing departments will provide tomorrow's top corporate executives," said the report. "No single sector of the economy offers a greater or more varied challenge."

PART 2

DEVELOPING
THE
PRODUCT
OR
SERVICE

Chapter 5

DESIGNING TO SELL

THE DESIGN of a product is of primary importance to its success in the market: Improvement of design in an established product is an assured way to increase sales. The strategy is at its best in the packaged-goods field. In the automotive field, new-model designs play an important part in the whole sales strategy. New-car models form the peg on which an intensive and expensive annual advertising and publicity campaign is hung. They create the interest that brings potential customers into the showroom and trade shows. They make people who ordinarily might drive their automobiles several years trade them in for "new models" every two or three years. Were it not for the "annual model" and the frequent change in design of automobiles, it would be impossible for the industry to make and sell millions of cars a year.

A sound business must be built on a sound product or service, one with merits that satisfy user needs. If the product or service is without merit, few people will buy it. If it does not satisfy a need, few people will buy it. This need may be psychological or physical; it may involve a desire for recognition, for security, for pleasure, for alleviation of labor, or any other of the many so-called buying motives. But whatever its character, the product or service must be of a nature to provide satisfaction to the purchaser.

For years it was the tendency of companies to manufacture products which they liked best to manufacture, products which were the easiest, the cheapest, the least complex. Industry is strewn with the corpses of such companies, those that never quite understood that the tastes and needs of the world were changing and passing them by. Others awoke from their dreams, and at great cost and with tremendous effort returned to the practice of serving their customers. Ford with its Model T has long been the classic example of a sleeping giant that awoke; Ford with its Edsel will go down in history as a giant company that for a moment slumbered again; Ford with its Mustang marked the rebirth of a creative and adventure-some spirit within the company.

An Era of Constant Change

Many of the products being marketed today were not available a decade or two ago. In fact, entire new industries have been created since then—the atomic industry, space probes, the application of semiconductors, the utilization of superpressures in the manufacture of diamonds and other perfect crystals, and scores of others, including also such services as computer centers, the credit-card organizations, new forms of investment and insurance, and the car-leasing business.

A recent canvass of a number of leading manufacturers brought an estimate by Bell and Howell that over 80 percent of its current sales were from products that had not existed five years ago—and only 2 percent from products that had been available 10 years ago. A control manufacturer, with approximately three thousand lines, stated that 65 percent of its current products were less than five years old and 99 percent less than 10 years old. General Dynamics, with its two billion dollar production budget, estimated that 95 percent of its sales are of products that did not exist in their present form—or, in many cases, in any form—10 years ago.

By simply changing the design of an oil heater the manufacturer was able to increase sales 400 percent. Streamlining a radio resulted in a 700 percent sales increase. And a well-known vacuum cleaner manufacturer, by changing the design, increased the efficiency of its product 85 percent and sales 150 percent. It is results like these which turn the minds of sales managers toward improving the design of a product, a package, or even a label when selling gets tough and salesmen grow jaded. Very often merely redesigning an old product, or putting it into a new package, will bring profits to a seller far in excess of whatever it costs for designing and production.

Principles of Good Design

Simplicity in design is essential whether it has to do with a train, a building, a display, a product, a store front, or anything else. Industrial design has been defined by Walter Dorwin Teague, one of America's foremost designers, as the external organization of products to reflect their internal efficiency for mass production and mass sales. The two go hand in hand. Good design is aimed at a specific objective, such as to influence acceptance at the point of sale, to stimulate "impulse" buying, to permit the effective use of less costly materials (such as plastics), or to build a desired impression in the public mind. The test of good design is not how "pretty" a product looks, but how effectively it attains its *major* objective. Too many designs miss the mark because they attempt to do too many things.

Function and Design

"Form follows function," a fundamental first voiced by famed architect Louis Sullivan, is a rule of good design which applies to all products, whether objects of impluse buying or studied purchases of lasting value, necessity, or long-felt want. Take the case of a home freezer. Industrial design introduced an economy of production despite the cost of tooling-up for a machine the client did not have. The designer recommended the machine and showed where the cost could be written off in the first year's production. The company needed this machine but, strangely enough, avoided buying because it previously could not justify the investment.

A grinding machine developed into an example of functional excellence because it enabled the operator to man all controls from one station. Originally, controls were on all four sides of the machine. The setup time was reduced, and the new organization of controls provided safety to the operator. Incidentally, the operator was proud of the new machine and its efficiency and his production capacity increased accordingly.

Steps in Designing to Sell

Having selected the designer, the next step is to provide him with the information on the sales objectives sought. Take a hypothetical product—say a fountain pen. How does the designer go about his task? Usually the first thing he will do is to make a survey. He will check with users and those who merchandise the product to determine consumer preferences which should be recognized. Then he searches historical files and patent records to learn what "not to do" and that is important. He will carefully study materials from which the product can be made. Then says Walter Dorwin Teague:

"A look at the production line may lend inspiration. Perhaps time and motion studies alone might cut down production costs. We ask questions, analyze every possibility. A designer must *contribute* something to the product; reduce production steps or cost; and improve the sales appeal.

"Any radical departure in design must have well-founded compensation factors which require studied sales promotion. Progress is spattered with the skeletons of questionable designs. It might be said that design should follow evolution, not revolution.

"A succession of sketches, renderings, conferences, and engineering drawings pass to management. The sales executive who knows the market potential expresses judgment. Visual or working models may be ordered and tested on school children and adults and at stores. Improvements will be incorporated in the designs and production when started.

"Next, the pen must be well-packaged for display. A strong appeal to the eye bolsters sales by giving new breadth to advertising and

A fast and efficient way of getting consumer reactions is through use of the Aptimeter, a machine installed by the A. C. Nielsen Co. in high-volume supermarkets. About the size of a small table-top radio, the machine records consumer preferences on such matters as price, package design, and product characteristics. "Voting" is merely a matter of pressing the buttons adjacent to printed questions, tabulations being easily made from the automatic recordings.

Courtesy, A. C. Nielsen Co.

promotion, Color is very important psychologically. It has attention-dominance, atmosphere, and distinction. Whatever the product, color can be useful as a means of company identification. It can 'trademark' retail chain stores or a company's offices and products. The industrial designer can use color to establish and maintain a consistent theme in product and architectural work. We have all seen examples of design identification in standardized filling stations, reception rooms, trucks, letterheads, employee uniforms, and so on."

Replacement Programming

The development of a new product is a tedious, exacting, long-drawn-out and time-consuming pioneering process. It is surprising that so many manufacturers do not appreciate the length of time involved, and try to enter the market with half-perfected products.

A manufacturer of electrical equipment spent considerable time developing a variable-speed electric drill. The laboratory model had been brought to a point of performance satisfactory to the company's manager of research and development. He had placed about one hundred hand-made samples with potential users to test. No adverse comments had been received, and those comments offered were all favorable. The company was on the verge of placing extensive orders for production equipment when an outside consulting firm was requested to conduct a field investigation for the purpose of confirming the conclusions of the company's engineers.

All the plants which had been supplied with drills for test were visited, only to find that many of the drills had failed early and had been discarded. Since the manufacturer had not followed up on their use, the testing companies had assumed that the manufacturer knew about the inferior condition of the product and so had not notified the manufacturer. Revised samples were prepared and distributed for use under controlled conditions. Most of these eventually failed. The product was never perfected. How tragic it would have been had the manufacturer gone into production as originally intended!

Another company planned to market insulated aluminum wire to be used in the manufacture of motors, transformers, and other electrical apparatus. It had perfected and patented a new process for covering wire; there was a shortage of copper wire; the company's engineers and salesmen had canvassed potential customers and had found the response encouraging; it had approached an investment house which was about ready to make it a sizable loan. At the request of the investment house, a field study was undertaken to verify the company's findings. The same respondents were called on and the same favorable responses received, but with reservations, which had not been pursued by the company. Yes, the manufacturers would use aluminum wire, *provided copper remained in short supply and the price remained high.* In addition, extensive redesign of the motors would be required which would take many months, even years, when proper field testing was included. The project was dropped.

This company had placed too much confidence in the market reports of its own engineers and salesmen; the former had been carried away by the attractiveness of their idea; the latter are inherently optimistic about the salability of anything new.

Under the extreme pressure of competition, many people in a firm get into the mood for taking a chance. Customers push the salesmen; salesmen push the sales manager; the sales manager pushes the director of marketing; the president pushes both the sales department and the research and development manager. The little danger signals that arise are overlooked or ignored, and a new, inadequately designed product hits the market—and money is lost, customers are lost, time is lost.

To safeguard against these dangers, many companies establish strongly organized product-planning departments which are charged with the responsibility of screening all new ideas presented and following them through set steps of product development to completion, including:

Screening and evaluation

Formal approval and assignment of projects for research and development

Laboratory development of the design needed

Field tests of the laboratory model

Refinements resulting from the field tests of the laboratory model

Preparation of production prototypes

Technical and marketing field tests of the production prototypes

Refinements resulting from the field tests of the prototypes

Production of product for distribution

Continued field tests and refinement of the production model

The greatest shakeout of new ideas comes in the screening and evaluation period. Here the mortality rate is amazing. A Bell and Howell executive has estimated that each year his company considers about 200 new product ideas. About one-fourth—or 50—receive research assignment; about half of this group—25—eventually are considered marketable products; but the company, for various reasons, actually markets only 12 of them, 10 of which may prove successful. Thus, out of the original 200 ideas considered, only 10, or 5 percent, are successfully marketed.

Another large company has estimated that out of 100 new product ideas considered, only 1.8 percent emerge as successful new products.

Establishing Pricing Policies

Consideration is given in the design stage to whether pricing policies should be selected for large volume with low margins or for low volume with high margins. In either case, experienced planners set their profit targets higher than normal as a hedge against errors in judgment. Rarely do actual profits exceed targets; usually they are below.

Many firms check anticipated price and profit levels five or six times during the development period. Conditions can change drastically as new data are added. Channels of distribution to be used, programs and manpower for sales solicitation, compensation and incentives, ability to give proper consumer service, general product compatability, availability of adequate and knowledgeable managerial marketing skills, are all given careful consideration.

Screening Procedures Established

Some companies have established screening procedures which include:

Determination and formal application of evaluation criteria

Appraisal, in writing, of all ideas submitted

Preliminary market studies

Advance profit assumption and similar financial safeguards

If an idea for a new product passes these preliminary tests, detailed financial analyses are made which include:

Estimates of possible sales-volume achievement

Probable price levels for various sales-volume attainment

Break-even points in manufacture

Return on capital and marketing investments

Cash flow and financial requirements

In the marketing aspects of these analyses, consideration is given to the company's overall and long-term objectives; to whether the product is being aimed defensively to *maintain* market position or offensively to *broaden* its market position. If the latter, it is kept in mind that all consumer demands in the markets to be invaded are currently being satisfied to a high degree of acceptance; therefore, the problem is to determine what competitive products can be replaced and how to go about doing it.

Time was when a company would have half a dozen package designs made up by an artist, and then call in a few of the girls from the office to decide which one they liked best. Today, scientific equipment is available for measuring the attention-getting values of signs, displays, package designs, and so on. One such type of equipment, designed by Visual Research, Inc., Chicago specialists in visual communication, is described by an executive of that firm:

"The equipment consists of a helmet to which are attached a pair of dark glasses and a small spotlight. The woman doing the appraising sits in a dark room, with the package or display on a slanting shelf in front of her. As she turns her head to examine the item, the photographic light track shows what most attracted the subject's attention, what was skipped, and what was merely glanced at. At the same time, a tape recording is made of the person's comments—giving clues as to whether pauses, for example, are caused by interest or by confusion."

Other types of visual equipment are available for checking consumer reactions to colors, type sizes and type faces, length of line in printed material, and other items of visual communication related to product design and packaging.

Sales managers long have known that redesigning the labels on a product can materially increase its sales. An attractive, well-designed label helps greatly to win attention, which is the first step in making any sale. Labels not only cause the product to stand out on the dealer's shelf, but they add to its advertising possibilities. The more strength a label has the more eye appeal it has. A good label should be simple. It should have the least "copy" consistent with good advertising, a color scheme which can be easily and inexpensively reproduced in advertising literature as well as in outdoor bulletins and magazine ads. It should have bold, easy-to-read lettering. Top-quality art work is required. A few hundred dollars spent in designing a family of labels will work to the advantage of the seller for years to come, and pay dividends out of all proportion to the money invested.

Needless to say, today's label designers must work with one eye on the ever-changing but vitally important U.S. and state government regulations. This is an area in which the sales manager should be an expert. It should not be left to the purchasing agent or advertising manager.

Federal Regulation

A federal packaging law now regulates most product labeling. The principal requirement is that the quantity declaration on packages under 4 pounds or 1 gallon must be stated not only in terms of whole units and fractions, but also in total ounces. Thus, a bottle or can containing 3 pints of liquid must state "1 qt., 16 fl. oz." and also "40 fl. oz." This is a minor label-design problem.

Industry reaction to the law as a whole is summed up by a spokesman for General Foods: "The new federal law seems to us in the food industry to be sound legislation. It preserves for private enterprise the vital right of self-regulation and—what is most important —the essential opportunity to innovate and offer consumers valuable new products and packages."

The main provisions of the federal packaging bill, which went into effect on July 1, 1967, are as follows:

1. The Food and Drug Administration (for food, drugs, and cosmetics) and the Federal Trade Commission (for all other consumer goods) are empowered to issue regulations requiring consumer-goods producers to put on every product package a statement of contents both in ounces and, if applicable, in full pounds, pints, or quarts, plus fractions thereof. This rule would apply only to packages weighing less than four pounds or smaller than one gallon.

2. The FDA and FTC are further empowered to regulate what size packages can be described by such terms as "small," "medium," and "large," and to regulate (but not outlaw) the use of such promotional labels as "cents-off" and "economy size." Food processors who specify the number of servings in the package will be required to state the quantity of these servings. Also, the bill bans slack filling that is "not necessitated by product protection or automatic machine packaging."

3. The Secretary of Commerce is authorized to call on manufacturers and distributors to develop voluntary standards whenever he decides an "undue proliferation [of package sizes]" is making it hard for consumers to make intelligent choices.

Dr. James L. Goddard, FDA commissioner, told Frank Dierson, chairman of the industry committee and general counsel of the Grocery Manufacturers Association, that FDA will not require every package to contain a declaration of "minimum weight," as originally intended.

The concept of minimum weight is something new. It is designed to replace existing practices of labeling the contents of a package in terms of "average weight." Under current practices, some deviation in the weight of the contents of a package is permitted so long as the average weight of all the packages in a lot conforms with the declaration that appears on the label.

Milan Smith, executive vice-president of the National Canners Association, claims that the minimum-weight requirement fails to "give reasonable consideration to utilization of high-speed filling lines, running as many as 1,000 containers per minute." These, he says, have brought economies to consumers.

Harry Schroeter, National Biscuit Company's vice-president for packaging, protested that a minimum-weight proposal would force food companies either to pack more in a box or reduce the stated contents on the label. "Either case increases the cost of doing business," he says, "which, of course, is passed on to the consumer."

Other regulations were forthcoming from FDA dealing with mandatory labeling for drugs and cosmetics under the new law. FTC also is responsible for regulations for other household products such as detergents and paper goods.

But the regulations covering the mandatory sections of the law are only part of the picture. The federal agencies also enforce the second half of the new law—the so-called "optional provisions," designed to cope with such problems as "giant family size," "5 cents off" and the proliferation of package sizes.

As a matter of policy, the new law declares: "Informed consumers are essential to the fair and efficient functioning of a free-market economy. Packages and their labels should enable consumers to obtain accurate information as to the quality of the contents and should facilitate value comparisons."

Part of the problem lies in enforcement of the new law. Authority is split among the Commerce Secretary, the Federal Trade Commission, and the Food and Drug Administration. To compound the confusion, the measure gives the Commerce Department no real power of enforcement.

Through the National Bureau of Standards, the Secretary of Commerce is empowered to determine when, in a specific commodity, there is "undue proliferation" of package sizes or weights that might confuse consumers. If he makes such a finding, he must ask the industry involved to propose a voluntary standard that would remedy the situation.

If, after a year, the Commerce Secretary finds the industry has failed to come up with a viable standard, or if it has developed a standard but fails to conform to it, he then must ask Congress for regulatory authority to deal with the matter.

Under the 1966 measure, FTC is authorized to handle regulations covering packaging and labeling of all consumer goods except foods, drugs, cosmetics, and medical devices—for which FDA is responsible.

Deeper Aspects of Packaging

Designing a package to sell goes deeper than eye appeal. There is, for example, the problem of conserving shelf space if the product is sold through self-service stores. A number of companies found that using a square package rather than the conventional round package helped sales. It reduced the size of shipping cartons, facilitated stacking on the shelf, and brought the full label into view instead of just a part of it. Dairies found square bottles, in place of the conventional round bottles for milk and cream, enabled them to load more bottles into a truck and lengthen routes; and they packed tightly into refrigerators, leaving more room for other things.

Lipsticks sold more readily when designed so that they could be used as a pencil and carried without muss in milady's pocketbook.

Display values naturally play an important part in designing any product to sell. There is a vogue of display cards, for counter or show-window use, which are cut out so that the actual product can be placed in the card, instead of merely illustrating it. This device has great attention value, but the product should be designed for the purpose. By a slight change in design, and the use of this display device, a food product's sales were increased 25 percent.

In the same way sales have been increased by designing a package so that it would have a second use after the product itself was consumed. A manufacturer of food specialties hit the jack pot with a container which would do double duty as an icebox jar. It had a big opening so the housewife could put leftovers in it. Sales of cheese spreads increased when packaged in decorated glass containers which could be used afterwards for serving short drinks. Another popular container can be used, after being emptied, as a flowerpot; still another becomes a kitchen cannister. The typical American housewife is thrifty by instinct. She will switch to a product because of the use she can make of the container, other things being equal.

It was not too long ago that effective packaging was looked upon largely as a means of protecting the product during shipment. But, in the past 10 years significant changes have occurred, resulting from a multiplicity of products on the market and from increased selling and production costs.

Out of these changes has grown a broader and more realistic concept of what effective packaging is—and a new opportunity to reduce the costs of selling and production in addition to adding merchandising impact at point of sale.

Today, effective packaging is generally recognized as a total of six broad areas—consumer use, merchandising, physical distribution, production, product development, and planning.

The "Silent Salesman"

Addressing a meeting of advertising executives, Russell A. Sandgren, of Sandgren & Murtha, Inc., design and marketing consultants, said:

"The package identifies the product—no matter where you see it, under what circumstances you see it, or when you see it. A package is the product's personality, its reality. It has the basic obligation to position the brand in the marketplace, and keep working for that same brand—not just at the supermarket, but in the home.

"In the supermarket, the product is at least 4 feet away—and often it's 12 feet away. Here the consumer hasn't any time to fool around. In fact, she usually has an average of three to four seconds to make up her mind about any one product among the more than 5,000 different items that she is moving past just as fast as she possibly can.

"Packaging also has the further responsibility of providing factual information. Contents. Legal requirements. Ingredients. Recipes. Instructions. Name and address of manufacturer. It occasionally bears news of contests, sweepstakes, prizes, and premiums.

"In some cases, the package inspires the ad. In the current Modess campaign, a design element was transplanted from the original package and incorporated in the advertising—on into the promotion materials, point-of-sale displays, price sheets, and for other collateral materials. It was a perfect example of the synergistic theory behind many brand, marketing, and total communications programs. In this case, it provided a powerful product launching."

Humor is often appropriate in advertising, Mr. Sandgren noted, but most packages have a life expectancy of two to three years, and humor goes stale with prolonged exposure. Warnings were also sounded against the temptation to tamper with a successful, accepted package—simply to be different, or faddish, or to go after a specific market segment.

One company, he noted, changed its packaging to complement a TV commercial series—then canceled the commercials shortly after the new package was introduced. The popularity of aerosol containers led another firm to market an aerosol toothpaste—only to learn that most people prefer squeezing a tube.

Again and again, Mr. Sandgren concluded, it has been found that the package *is* the product.

Packaging redesigns, which are far more numerous than new-product packaging programs, are critical, far more so than the development of packages for new products. A package for a new product can be changed a number of times in test markets before it is finalized.

Joseph M. Murtha, president, Sandgren & Murtha, Inc., New York, writing in *Printers' Ink*, says:

"A redesign can threaten all the equities and investments behind a brand and the disastrous errors, which start with a lack of clearly defined marketing objectives, established criteria, careful analysis, or consideration of possible sensitivity to package change in the product category, come to light only in the test-market situation."

It has been estimated that over 50 percent of all package redesigns never get to market. With shelf environment and competitive packaging constantly undergoing change, the decision to do nothing can result in heavy sales erosion. On the other hand, the decision not to proceed can sometimes save a product from critical losses.

Experience has taught that some products can weather packaging changes better than others. Even slight redesign should be approached very cautiously in circumstances like these:

- If the product category is declining at a steady rate (especially dangerous in a regional market).

- If the product is not capturing new users.

- If the consumer is of low income, education and employment level (brand loyalty is higher in these groups and a package change may weaken loyalty).

- If the product category has not undergone packaging changes for several years.

- If there has not been much new product activity in the category being considered.

- If the product is in a "high anxiety" category. (Hair coloring products and certain drugs, for example, have a higher anxiety level than soap or cereal. In this connection it is, of course, dangerous to generalize since any brand has unique characteristics and the pace of product introduction and supporting communications can serve to alter such "anxiety levels.")

When Not to Change

Sometimes it is better not to make any change in design. Here are some points to be considered:

1. Beware of the new brand manager's desire to innovate.

When a new brand manager appears, the prevailing calm begins to stir with intellectual probes, intoxicating ideas, stimulating thinking—and often, the brand manager's natural desire to innovate and push toward new sales goals. But, in order to reach them, he may feel the need to make a recognizable change in the marketing of the product and finds it easiest to focus on its packaging.

2. Don't change to imitate your competition.

When a direct competitor changes his product, it is always unsettling—especially when the change is as dramatic as packaging changes often are. When your competition makes such a move, you must assume that it's a carefully reasoned one, but it may not be a wise one.

3. Don't change for innovation alone.

New concepts in physical packaging are exciting—sometimes to the point where one can lose sight of the ultimate sales goal and the most direct way of reaching it.

4. Don't change for design values alone.

A poor-looking package might strike the proper note with certain types of audience. Because of its unappealing design, it may clearly say "I'm a bargain" to the price-conscious customer.

5. Don't change when product-package identification is strong.

Some products are so strongly identified in the consumer mind with a specific physical package that change endangers sales.

6. Avoid change which may hurt the branding.

When a product's brand identification is strong, any change must be approached with great care and the brand itself must be treated with something close to reverence. All effort must be directed toward preserving the equities of that brand and its appearance.

William F. May, chairman of the American Can Company, said in a speech before The National Industrial Conference Board:

"In recent years there has been a good deal of talk about how package and product in the end become one. I think some validity has to be given to that point of view, especially now when so often the package won't sell a poor product—certainly not more than once, anyway.

"But from our point of view, the other side of the coin is more important: The man who sells a quality product has a very valuable franchise from the consumer, and that is one thing he cannot jeopardize.

"We've got to make a package that will preserve the integrity and quality of his product; we've got to give him the same degree of protection he has always had, and to make absolutely sure that his product gets to the consumer in the pristine form that he insists on. We can make all kinds of improvements for this customer, but never anything that threatens in any way the quality of what he is selling. We would do everyone—including ourselves—a great disservice if we took that kind of a risk."

Packages and Product Failures

Package designers isolated from the marketplace are partly to blame for the high annual rate of new-product failure, according to Richard C. Christian, president of Marsteller Inc.

"One of your packaging designers comes up with an idea for a new package," he told members of the Packaging Institute. "It is novel. Nobody has ever done anything quite like it. You tend to react to the novelty of the idea, not its real or potential usefulness.

"It is not unusual to carry such an idea all the way to completion, then hand the product to the sales force and tell them to find somebody to sell it to."

The agency executive also said: "Most of your packaging design people are busily engaged in trying to find new and ingenious ways to use up more of the products you produce—paper, aluminum, glass, etc."

He urged that a way be found "to bridge the gap between your customers and your package design people." He added: "There's nothing sacred about an idea; if it has no practical application, there is no reason to preserve it or reward its author.

"When it comes to measuring the success of any idea—evaluating

How consumers rate package characteristics

Which of the following package characteristics seem important to you? Please check (✔) the degree of importance in the corresponding column.

	Very Important	Important	Not Important	No Answer
Keeps contents fresh until they are used up	86	11	1	2
Leakproof	75	22	1	2
Can be tightly re-closed after opening	75	23	1	1
Moistureproof	65	30	3	2
Convenient size & shape for storing	64	32	2	1
Easy to open	62	34	3	2
Fits hand for easy moving about, pouring, etc.	42	48	9	2
Easy to carry	23	49	26	2

This chart and another nearby show the packaging preferences of housewives, based on a survey of consumer opinion on food-store packaging conducted by National Family Opinion, Inc. The survey covered 1,141 homemakers drawn from all age groups, income brackets, and sections of the country. (Reprinted with permission of Sales Management, The Marketing Magazine.)

a package's total contribution to profits, reputation, and growth potential, the customer's success is the only key."

As stated by the chief executive officer of American Can Company: "Home economists look at a package the same way a detective would—analyzing it, trying to find out as much as possible about it. As professionals, it's the only way they can look at it. But the housewife doesn't look at the package that way at all. Her only interest is to get the package home, open it easily, feed its contents to the family and dispose of it quickly.

"Whatever the motives are that lead her to pick up one package instead of another, detective-like analysis isn't one of them. So our

Consumers choose the "best" packages

All things considered, which kind of package or container do you think would be best for each type of food store product listed?

		Plastic	Cardboard	Metal	Glass
Juices	1966	18%	2%	35%	42%
	1960	12	2	42	42
Processed ("canned") fruits and vegetables	1966	4	1	64	28
	1960	3	1	58	35
Frozen fruits	1966	54	32	5	3
	1960	45	35	8	5
Frozen vegetables	1966	46	48	1	1
	1960	38	54	2	2
Dry cereals	1966	16	80	1	1
	1960	12	82	1	2
Dairy products (such as ice cream, cottage cheese, etc.)	1966	61	33	1	2
	1960	49	38	1	8
Pills, capsules, other "dry" medicines	1966	62	2	2	31
Shampoo, hand lotion, other liquid toiletries	1966	85	0	1	12
Cream deodorants, other creamy cosmetics	1966	53	1	2	41
Soft drinks and beer	1966	4	0	35	57

own judgment and our own intuitive sense about what is somehow appealing and right influence us a good deal. Of course we never lose sight of what we have been told by the customer herself.

"When it comes to what the market wants for the future, the job is even harder. It involves determining what the housewife wants but cannot articulate. There is very little point, we have decided, in asking her point-blank what she would really like in a package. She just has never thought about the problem in that way, and she can't express her desires at all clearly. The best way we've been able to find is the strictly pragmatic one of putting the new product before the housewife and saying, 'Here's something we thought you might like better than the one you are now using.' "

Self-Service Store Requirements

The trend toward self-servicing retailing makes the matter of packaging highly important. Since this type of store seldom permits a manufacturer to set up displays in the store, or put up advertising signs, the package and the label must carry the biggest part of the point-of-purchase advertising load. A survey of supermarket and discount-house merchandisers made by the Research Institute of America indicates that the four main factors in designing a package to sell itself on retail counters and display racks are:

1. *Simple design, keyed to the character of the product.* As competition increases, there's a premium on a package that will *stand out* and catch the customer's eye. Obviously, consumer tastes differ, and different products require different package treatment, but as a general guide, note that supermarkets find their best sellers among bright clear reds, yellows, and blues contrasted with black or white. Off-shades, dark colors, and pastels don't usually attract the mass audience. Packages sell better when they build up into an effective mass display. In most cases, retailers prefer clear, large lettering and a striking and uncluttered layout. Colored reproductions of contents and transparent wraps have been particularly successful in food stores. Retailers report that they get attention, put across the idea of quality, and identify the product quickly with the customer.

2. *Strong brand identity is growing in importance.* In case after case, sales have increased when packages were redesigned with an easily recognizable name, distinctive lettering, and an eye-catching trademark or symbol. If a snappy selling message can be incorporated in the package, so much the better.

A distinctive trademark pays extra dividends when a manufacturer adds new lines in new packages. If the company symbol isn't sufficiently distinctive, family identity is lost and with it potential sales. Separate grades and types of products in a given line must, of course, be distinguished; but the identification should be worked out within the framework of the general family design.

Illustration: This is an old principle but its importance has received new proof in recent self-service experience. For instance, when Ralston Purina Co. added a line of farm sanitation products to its cereal and feed business, it created a little outline character called "Sanitation Sam." He's shown on the label doing whatever the contents indicate (scrubbing, spraying, etc.). Another idea that's gaining some acceptance is the use of basic catch phrases from the manufacturer's advertising campaign.

3. *Full, brief information about the product.* What is it? How much does the package hold? How is it used? What does it cost? Retailer surveys show that if the label doesn't answer these questions quickly and completely, the dealer as well as the consumer will turn thumbs down. Informative labeling is increasingly necessary as a sales aid and servicing feature for all types of merchandising today.

Retailers prefer packages which have a "price spot"—a space in which the price can be marked. A recent *Sales Management* survey presents new proof of the influence of price figures. Forty-three percent of the shoppers queried said they were frequently led into unplanned buying when price was shown. Other tests show that sales drop sharply when price is removed.

The importance of pretesting *any* package change *at the point of purchase* is highlighted by the experience of a packer of dried food products. In an attempt to stem a decline in sales, the company decided to change from cellophane bags to a paperboard container. The new design was tested by means of consumer interviews. Eighty percent of the respondents said they preferred the new design, and the company invested $25,000 in new packaging machinery and new cartons. *But* when the paperboard container was put in the stores, it stayed on the shelf while the cellophane bags moved out. Whatever was wrong, the trouble could have been avoided by testing under *actual* selling conditions.

4. *Convenience in handling and use.* The size of your package may or may not be a sales factor, but retailers have voiced complaints which should be noted by manufacturers. Some packages are too large to be handled easily; some are so small that they don't *look* like value. The whole problem of optimum size and weight and number of sizes should be checked at regular intervals, so that changes in retail merchandising and consumer preferences can be reflected.

Using Market Research

Market research is used throughout the product-planning program on a continuous basis. Some companies find it profitable to employ outside management consultants to assist them. Marketing executives who have invested in market research have found benefits as summed up in the following report by the American Management Association:

1. An organization is enabled to build its marketing structure on facts, thus eliminating much of the inefficiency and waste incurred by distributive efforts based wholly on past experience, intuition, and pure chance.

2. Marketing executives and sales personnel, as well as employees generally, are more confident of the soundness of operations and activities which rest on the bedrock of a desirable and acceptable product or service, a favorable competitive position, and tested channels of distribution.

3. Major operating executives in the organization develop an understanding and appreciation of the product or service and of market methods in general, giving them a good reason to become "sales minded."

4. The findings of marketing research indicate the direction which technical research should take by providing concrete data on customer preference relating to composition, design, or other attributes of the product or service.

5. Marketing research fosters goodwill, both in the consumer market and in the industrial market. As the activities become more firmly rooted in scientific methodology and professional viewpoint, a cooperative spirit is introduced—between producer and consumer, between producers of complementary products, between producer and wholesaler, etc.—resulting in improved marketing methods for entire industries.

Modern management must increase the precision of its decisions; it must come to rely more and more on judgments made in the light of adequate facts, or it will find itself outmaneuvered by competition. This process requires a highly objective attitude. We have passed out of the period when vigor and decisiveness alone are enough. They are still vital, of course, but to meet today's conditions, they must be supplemented by an eagerness to get the facts and a willingness to use them objectively. Unless and until that state of mind exists there is little reason for management to spend money on sales research.

An objective attitude may, and in fact should, be a critical and skeptical one. Uncritical acceptance of any set of statistics is not objective. One of the big problems of management is how to distinguish between competent and dependable research and those statistics which "tread a path of mathematical logic between an unwarranted assumption and a preconceived conclusion."

Chapter 6

DIVERSIFICATION AND FLEXIBILITY IN MARKETING

THE MAN who sets out a dish of Alpo dog food for Rover, then pours himself a J&B Scotch highball and lights up a Chesterfield is, in each case, doing business with the Liggett & Myers Tobacco Company.

If he prefers to puff a Camel, sip a glass of Hawaiian Punch and sit down to a plate of Chun King chow mein, he will give a triple boost to the sales of the R. J. Reynolds Tobacco Company, the nation's largest producer of cigarettes.

The acquisition by Reynolds of the Chun King Corporation for $63 million in cash was the latest in a series of diversification moves that have been spreading at an increasing tempo through the tobacco industry in recent years. Although the trend was started almost a decade ago, notably by pioneering Philip Morris, it has picked up most of its momentum since publication of the U.S. Surgeon General's report linking lung cancer to smoking.

Before its purchase of Chun King, which manufactures a variety of 23 canned and frozen Chinese-American foods, Reynolds (Camel, Winston, Salem) was already branching out into the food and beverage line. In 1963, it took over Pacific Hawaiian Products Company, which makes Hawaiian Punch and other fruit-juice products. Later it acquired Penick & Ford, Ltd., which produces Vermont Maid and Brer Rabbit syrups, College Inn tomato cocktail, and My-T-Fine desserts.

Liggett & Myers (Chesterfield, L&M, Lark) went into the liquor business last spring when it moved in on the Paddington Corporation, exclusive U.S. importer of popular J&B Scotch. It bought up Allen Products Company, maker of Alpo, in November 1964.

The American Tobacco Company (Lucky Strike, Pall Mall, Tareyton) announced acquisition of Sunshine Biscuits, Inc.

P. Lorillard Company (Old Gold, Newport, Kent) took over the Golden Nugget Candy Company of San Francisco and a few months earlier bought Usen Products Company, a manufacturer of cat food.

As the granddaddy of tobacco diversifiers, Philip Morris, Inc., started looking around as far back as 1957 when it took over a packaging company, Milprint, Inc. It has since acquired Polymer Industries, Inc., an industrial adhesives maker (1958), American Safety Razor Products Corporation (1960), and the Burma-Vita Co. (Burma Shave) and Clark Gum Company (1963).

The diversifiers insist that they are not trying to hedge their bets on tobacco, and that the Surgeon General's report had nothing to do with their moves. "We just consider diversification a healthy corporate attitude," said Liggett & Myers Tobacco Company president Milton Harrington.

What a "Match Company" Makes

The Universal Match Corporation was engaged in widely diversified activities long before its name was changed to UMC Industries. Here is a *partial* list of the scope of diversification engaged in by UMC:

Match books	Refrigeration equipment for institutions
Special replica packaging	
Vending machines	Metal fabrication and stamping
Refrigerated cabinets	Electronics
Ordnance and defense products	Electromechanical equipment
Uni-pack systems	Magnetic amplifiers
Printing inks	Biochemical research
Ice-making machines	Missile launchers
Metal products for manufacturers	Printing of calendars and labels
Coin-handling devices	Automation machinery
Currency changers	Precision machine tools
Automatic merchandising machines	Roller gear drives

A good example of flexibility and diversification is the Westinghouse Electric Corporation. Drayton Heard, Jr., manager, marketing administration, describes some of the marketing problems involved, as follows:

"As you may have noticed, our middle name is Electric. We make a very wide range of electrical and electronic equipment for homes,

office buildings, manufacturing plants, utilities, and process industries. But we also make exploratory submarines, lasers, varnish,
mass-transportation systems, and kitchen-counter tops. All told,
we have 70 product divisions and about $2½ billion a year in sales.

"Now, how can you impose a rational order on a conglomerate
company like that? We did it by organizing backwards. That is,
instead of starting with the factory we took as our starting point the
markets we serve. We classified our customers into groups according to their wants and needs. As consumers they have one set of
wants. Electric utility people have another set of wants. Manufacturers have still another set. Construction people have another set.
And so on. We wound up with six basic sets of needs. Then we
assigned an appropriate grouping of manufacturing divisions to
the job of satisfying each particular type of customer need. This
gave us, in effect, six companies of manageable size—we call them
groups—each with its own marketing organization and its own
market orientation.

Planning on Two Levels

"So, we're concerned with two levels of planning here: Division
Planning and Group, or Headquarters Planning. Each division
makes and implements its own plans to sell specific products and
goes after specific market opportunities. The division initiates the
plan, communicates it to the salesmen, and they follow through."

Mr. Heard listed the *guiding* rules all divisions are expected to
follow in planning:

1. The plan must be in writing.
2. It must set profitable sales goals.
3. It must be detailed.
4. It must assign responsibilities and include a timetable.
5. The plan must be integrated with field sales.
6. The plan must be communicated to everyone concerned.
7. The plan must have built-in procedures to measure results.
8. And finally, the plan must be consistent with long-range
   strategy.

This is still just a plan on paper until the field sales force learns
about it, Mr. Heard pointed out, so Westinghouse gives the division planning people a set of things to remember when they com-

municate the plan to the field. Again, these are broad enough to apply to most businesses:

1. Give the field measurable short-term volume and profit objectives to shoot at. Not just for the year, but by quarters.

2. Give the salesman a straightforward concept which is easily communicated.

3. Aim at a moving target. Keep the "carrot" moving.

4. Tell the salesmen how this plan takes advantage of current economic conditions and trends.

5. Show the salesmen how this plan plays a part in helping the firm attain its ultimate goal of being "first in performance."

How Sales Executives Lead the Way

The sales executives of corporations which have thus diversified their manufacturing or distribution activities have, more often than not, been in the vanguard of change. When the line on which the company has been concentrating begins to slip, the sales executive is often the first to recognize the situation, and to suggest the possibilities of a merger, purchase, or other method of adding a new string to his company's bow.

It is not only in the area of the multibillion-dollar corporations —General Electric, Westinghouse, Du Pont, Dow Chemical—that diversity is both a challenge and an opportunity for the sales executive; in hundreds of smaller companies, diversification has meant the difference between progress and retrogression, survival or extinction.

Therefore, one inescapable function of sales management is "to keep a weather eye peeled" for opportunities to diversify the line or lines now handled.

Charles A. Cerami, writing in *Nation's Business,* has outlined a number of ways in which diversification may be achieved by adding or dropping product lines. These are:

1. If some of your fringe products are not profitable enough but can't be dropped without weakening your competitive position, you can boost markups on them sharply, or substitute new qualities or models that would yield better margins.

2. If one or a few main products account for most of your sales and profits, and if they are in a growing field, you can consider cutting out all the fringe items and concentrating on the money-makers.

3. If one or a few main products account for most of your sales and profits, but are in a declining or uncertain field, your first job may be to replace them with more dynamic lines.

In some firms any additions to the line have to be worked out in stolen moments by executives busy with other duties. A few fundamentals may be helpful prods to men in this position:

First, use your two "intelligence services"—your sales force and your purchasing men. They are in daily contact with scores of other companies in related lines.

Second, try to make more outside contacts yourself. Just hearing about somebody else's recent experience with a new product may save you expensive mistakes or give you an idea for a variation that will succeed.

Third, explore the possibility of mergers or acquisitions. You're most likely to find these in:

1. Firms that have a good product but an inadequate sales force.

2. Firms with a good idea, but insufficient capital to make it work.

Dangers in Diversification

In an interview with Sylvia Porter, syndicated business and financial newswriter, Wade N. Harris warned that diversification can sometimes be an expensive experiment.

Mr. Harris, president of the Midland-Ross Corporation, a $150,000,000 concern whose products include (literally) everything "from soup"—chemicals for industrial heating—"to nuts"—weld nuts—and from automobile frames to space heaters, warned that diversification for its own sake can be dangerous.

"While it is true that the loss of one big customer or a temporary decline in the market or even a change in production methods or materials sources might put a one-product company on the rocks, the parent company should be sure, before attempting to diversify, that its manufacturing skills and know-how, its sales and distribution setup, and the profit potentials of the new line have a sound relation to the cost of acquisition," Mr. Harris says.

In summary, Mr. Harris warned of several specific dangers, as follows:

1. Diversification merely to get into an industry currently in vogue.

2. Mergers where the parent company must invest heavily to get the acquired company into condition.

3. Taking over a company without reasonable assurance that competent operating management will be willing to come along with it.

4. Falling for the supposed security around the popular word, "diversification," since the move can be disastrous as well as profitable.

J. Paul Austin, president of The Coca-Cola Co., told the American Marketing Association, in Philadelphia, how his company diversified after having concentrated on one product for 69 years.

"We knew the statistics of failure," Austin said. "We heard those who said why tamper with success. We knew that 6,000 new consumer items were introduced each year and only about 500 live beyond their first 12 months. But the world was moving and changing. The world was our customer and we knew we must move with it.

"Testing a new product, even for a full year, is not the result of any arcane lore or secret formula brewed in Atlanta. To put millions of dollars behind a product that does not give reasonable evidence of consumer acceptance would be wasteful. At the same time, to have a product that consumers tell you they like and then not give it everything you've got would be an even greater waste.

"We can share the enthusiasm of 'new product boys' for their latest brainchild. But at the same time, we have to balance carefully the talents of men in research and development and the abilities of the marketing specialists to position the new product with the consumer. And we have to do all this with a profit."

Flexibility in the Banking Field

One of the greatest needs for flexibility has been in the banking field. While dealing every day with business, industry, and consumer, most banks were unaware, to a large extent, of their need for a modern marketing approach.

A. J. Wood, president of A. J. Wood Research Corporation, Philadelphia, told how banks may effectively apply the basic principles of a marketing program to their business. He said:

"Both the term 'marketing concept' and the title 'marketing manager' were a natural development to describe a process that was forced upon industry by the pressures of increasing competition, merchandising complexities, expanding distribution, computer technology and research methodology.

"To cope with these pressures, industry had a variety of skills and disciplines available: sales, production, advertising, public relations, sales promotion, packaging, design, distribution, traffic, research and development, and marketing research—as departments, divisions or executives.

"What business lacked—and what the situation evolved—was a common control entity to coordinate and channel these skills and disciplines into one common and aggressive effort, in a common direction, towards a common goal—for maximum benefit to the company.

"In the early '60's the same necessities began to appear in the banking structure. As banks grew larger and added services to finance their customers and communities better, their problems became more complex, competition grew keener, and business-development problems increased.

"In effect, and almost without realizing it, the banking industry entered the field of mass marketing. Wholesale or strictly commercial banks suddenly found themselves being bypassed or outstripped by their 'retail' competitors. As a result, they wanted to enter the *retail* banking field, and gradually (or quickly by merger) did so.

"Industry had its sales, advertising, packaging, and other departments, divisions, and executives to draw upon in developing a marketing concept and a marketing director—most banks did not.

"One of the reasons for this lag in marketing skill is that few bankers realized that they were handling a 'product.' They did not realize that little difference exists between the retailing of money and that of automobiles, soft drinks, or cigarettes. The distribution techniques may vary but the underlying principles are about the same. Even though their product is money, it must be 'bought' by means of services rendered or interest and dividend payments, and it must be 'sold' at loan and service rates. These transactions are subject to the laws of supply and demand and they are merchandised by means of various instruments created, packaged, and promoted to yield the best return. In short, money as a 'product' is subject to the same marketing needs as are products in industry.

"To meet the challenge of the new marketing concepts, banks had available mainly personal salesmanship at the officer level, and a rather rudimentary marketing function known as new business development. This function typically was headed by a new-business-development director, or a public-relations director.

"But—about the only marketing tools at the disposal of the new-business-development executive were public and community relations activities, descriptive literature, display material and mass-media advertising. Usually, these marketing tools were limited by very modest budget appropriations.

"The alternative is the appointment of a top-level marketing officer who is given the authority to establish and build up a full-fledged marketing department for the permanent growth of the bank's development efforts at the consumer and commercial levels."

Mr. Wood said the marketing officer should have the responsibility of determining just where the bank stands today in relation to:

1. Competition.
2. Its image—to businessmen and the public.
3. Its services.
4. Its people—in relation to their capabilities in advancing the bank's corporate image.
5. Its policies and practices—in all phases of activities that create, change, enhance, or mold public opinion.
6. Its potential—as to the direction and pace of probable growth and achievement in the future.

After a study of these marketing components and their potentials, the marketing officer should then prepare programs of short-range (within a single budgeting year) and long-range objectives (three to five years) on which to concentrate the bank's total marketing resources. This program—which now becomes a marketing concept—should then be approved by the bank's top operating committee as senior management's blueprint for continuing growth or expansion on a planned basis.

Chapter 7

TRADEMARKS AND TRADE NAMES

FOR MANY companies, trademarks are their most important, vital assets. A plant might burn down, or some other catastrophe might occur, but the continuation of their business is assured by virtue of their possession of a well-known established trademark. A forum conducted by the U.S. Trademark Association brought out these points:

A trademark is essentially a symbol of identification. It identifies a product with a given source. That source may not be known as such to the consumer. That is, the consumer may not know the name of the company which makes the item, but the trademark enables the purchaser to recognize a familiar item, either on the basis of a previous satisfactory use of it, or on the basis of a conviction or a persuasion to purchase inspired by advertising and promotion.

A trademark is not a trade name. A trade name identifies a company. A trademark identifies a product.

A trademark is not to be confused with a copyright, nor is it to be confused with a patent. Both of these are, in essence, government monopolies for a limited period of time. The patent pertains to an invention—an invention of a new product or the invention of a new process—and it is granted and extended to you by the government. It does not exist until the government creates it for you, and it exists only for a limited period of time. In the case of a patent, 17 years.

Copyright, on the other hand, pertains to the creation of usually what is termed a work of art. You will recognize it immediately when we speak in terms of a piece of music, literature, or a book of poetry. This is the sort of thing a copyright is designed to protect, and a copyright is also limited in time although for a somewhat longer period.

"Use" Is Key Word for Trademark

It is important to keep in mind that no one gives you a trademark as the government might, for example, with a patent. You create your own rights in a trademark, and a trademark also can be eternal. Those rights will subsist and be protectable so long as you continue to use the mark. That word "use" is the essential word in the field of trademarks.

Your rights in the mark begin automatically with use. You don't need the government to tell you that you have a trademark. It begins from the day you first use the mark. Ultimately you may obtain registration of it, but that simply confers upon you certain procedural advantages. Essentially, the fundamental rights you have are created merely by your use of it, and they will subsist just as long as you continue to use it.

The most important thing about a trademark, whether it be a word, or a symbol or a device or a combination thereof, is that the mark is distinctive enough to be protectable not only on the goods on which the mark is used, but also protectable as to those goods which are related or close to the goods specifically identified by the mark.

If you have a distinctive mark, you are able to effectively enforce your rights in court to prevent infringement. You are able also to obtain a federal registration, if you have use of the mark in interstate commerce, and thereby enjoy the benefits the registration gives you. It is also very important to have a mark which is readily available for expansion of use to other products as you expand your business or come out with new products.

Kinds of Trademarks

There are four categories of trademarks: a coined mark, an arbitrary mark, a descriptive mark, and a suggestive mark.

The *coined mark* constitutes a word which is manufactured and not in the language prior to its adoption.

The classic example of a coined trademark is Kodak.

Other examples of coined words are General Foods' trademark YUBAN for coffee and the trademark SANKA for coffee.

An *arbitrary mark* is a word that is already in the language, but when applied to a certain product does not describe the product in any way.

Examples of this are SHELL petroleum products, LUCKY STRIKE for cigarettes, LILY for paper cups.

The next type of mark is a *suggestive mark*. This suggests to some degree what the product is, or what it does, or what the use of the product is.

There is a fine line between whether a mark is suggestive or descriptive.

An example of a suggestive mark is the COPPERTONE trademark for suntan lotion. Another is KOOL-AID, trademark for a soft-drink mix.

These marks can also be very strong protection, depending upon the notoriety and reputation they have acquired.

Then you get into the area of *descriptive marks*. These are the marks that give company lawyers headaches.

The marketing and advertising people naturally like a mark that describes a product, that tells the consumer what it is. There is nothing wrong with this as long as the owner realizes that there are substantial pitfalls in adopting a mark which describes, because once you use a mark that describes, others can come along and use the same or similar word in its apt descriptive sense.

Examples of descriptive marks include DRY FAST for paint, and DRI-FRI for a vegetable oil.

A descriptive mark is a mark that describes the product, whereas a suggestive mark is a mark that suggests something about the product but does not actually describe it.

The difference between descriptive and suggestive is more a difference in kind than a difference in degree.

A descriptive mark is one that tells you something about the product. It may be geographically descriptive, or descriptive of its qualities.

It is not the generic name of the product—that is something else again.

It describes a quality or something about the origin.

As an example, GRAPHIC was held descriptive for a line of cameras. So was KEEP CLEAN for brushes.

The Trademark as a Monopoly

Fundamentally, the value of the trademark in selling results from the fact that it constitutes a monopoly: A perfectly lawful monopoly which is limited only by the actual use that is made of the mark, and which the courts will protect. There are relatively few products in common use which cannot be imitated successfully, or even duplicated, by the ingenuity of competitors. Any soap manufacturer, for example, can make a white, floating soap; or anyone can buy flour middlings and sell them as farina. There can be, however, only one Ivory Soap and only one Cream of Wheat. The monopoly of those terms for the specific purpose is complete, and includes all the related insignia (package design, wrappers, etc.) which the public associates with them. No competitor may lawfully copy, or even simulate these characteristics, no matter how accurately he may duplicate the products themselves.

The tangible value of such a monopoly depends, of course, upon the reputation for desirability (the goodwill) which the product may acquire. Once such a reputation is established, however, it increases the salability of the product from the standpoint of the trade, and enables the producer to sell on the basis of consumer demand and acceptance, rather than direct comparisons of price or intrinsic quality. It enables the seller, moreover, to stabilize or even standardize the price to the consumer, as well as the margins and terms of sale.

The trademark monopoly also serves as a strong measure of insurance against losses of distribution. A striking instance occurred some years ago, when the Great Atlantic & Pacific Tea Company, following a legal controversy, posted signs in all its stores with the heading: "We do not sell Cream of Wheat." They went on to quote from a Federal Court decision to the effect that the product was merely an advertised brand of farina, and offered the identical product under their own private brands. The effort was a complete failure, and the discarded product went back on the shelves very promptly. Even at a lower price, customers would not readily accept the substitute, and in too many instances were going to other stores where they could buy Cream of Wheat. The impossibility of any confusion between the trademarked product and its competitors was too marked an advantage for even the strongest chain to overcome.

Trademarks and Advertising

It is in the main the trademark which makes it possible to employ national advertising profitably as a selling auxiliary, and trademarks are widely featured in advertising. For this reason it is often assumed that the trademark is an advertising device, intended to recommend the goods or call attention to their quality or utility. Trademarks in this way are sometimes confused with trade characters, slogans, logotypes, etc., and such confusion may result in the selection of a trademark which cannot be protected. It may also result in handling the mark in such a manner as to mislead or confuse the public as to its real significance.

A clear distinction may be made between the function of advertising, which is to describe and recommend the goods, and the function of the trademark, which is to indicate their origin. A trademark may acquire a certain advertising value, but such value is purely incidental and inferential. Unless it does clearly indicate the source or origin, and not the character or quality, of the goods it is not an *exclusive* mark of identification, and the monopoly in its use cannot be protected. This is because any producer or seller of similar goods has an equal right to describe his product and to indicate its quality, utility, features, or general desirability.

It is not essential that you have notices of registration in your advertisements, but if you are in an area where there is a likelihood that the trade press or fashion writers are going to misuse your mark, you probably are taking a step toward preventing that if, when you use your mark, you use it to tell the world, including the editor and the writer, that it is a trademark.

You do not have to use an ® if the mark is registered, but it is advisable because for one thing it means something to the public. The housewife may not have an idea of what the ® means on a grocery product, but she does know it is a badge of ownership.

The Exercise of Diligence

Essentially, it is advertising that creates the meaning for a trademark in the first place, and advertising may change that meaning into a generic term or preserve the validity of the trademark, depending on how it is used. Sydney A. Diamond, member of the New York Bar, stated in *Advertising Age* that sometimes the brand becomes so firmly established by advertising that the public starts to misuse the trademark as if it were a generic term for the product itself. Judge Learned Hand warned of the peril in a famous trademark opinion: "Its very success may prove its failure." If caught in time, this trend can be averted, and even reversed, by advertising directed to the specific objective of education for proper trademark use.

To take a specific example: When American Cyanamid acquired Formica Corp., in 1956, it inherited a problem that tends to affect products in dominant market positions. Formica was so well known that many consumers were unaware of any other name for laminated plastic. This led to substitutions at the retail level and a drop in market share. Cyanamid instituted a corrective program which included a series of educational advertisements designed to strengthen Formica as a trademark.

Another use for the name theme is to explain that a manufacturer's trademark applies to a family of products, not merely one item. An individual product name, therefore, must accompany the trademark for complete identification, and the resulting combination of generic term with trademark is just about the best possible way of preserving the manufacturer's legal rights.

The predecessor company of Chesebrough-Pond's once used a similar approach in an advertisement headed, "What's Their *Whole* Name?" which showed photographs of famous persons with their first names followed by blank spaces for middle and last names. The body copy read:

"Vaseline, the registered trademark owned by the Chesebrough Mfg. Co., is not a complete name for any one product, but the brand word for the whole family of products made by that company.

"It should never be used alone, but always with the name of the product it designates, viz.: 'Vaseline' petroleum jelly, 'Vaseline' hair tonic, 'Vaseline' lip ice pomade, etc. We'd appreciate it if you'd keep this in mind. Many thanks!"

The care a company must take to protect the proper usage of its trademark is indicated by the following letter from Friden, Inc., to a leading business publication:

"We are faced with the continuing problem that incorrect use of a trademark may lead to its loss.

"We would appreciate your assistance in preventing future misuse of our trademark Justowriter automatic composing machine, which appeared in *Sales Management*. In this case it emerged as Adjuster Writer, which is fairly imaginative but incorrect."

Essentials of a Trademark

Trademark rights are acquired only through actual use of the mark as attached to the goods, or in direct association with the goods, in bona fide commercial transactions. No right is created by the mere adoption or invention of a trademark. The right begins when goods bearing the mark are actually placed on the market, and the extent of the rights is proportional to actual use in the market.

A trademark must be distinctive, so far as the kind or class of goods on which it is used is concerned. It must not be identical with or similar to any other trademark used on goods of "the same descriptive properties." Goods are of the same descriptive properties when they are so closely related or generally competitive as to make confusion likely in the public mind. Thus, automobiles are held to be of the same descriptive properties as automobile tires or accessories. Likewise with different articles of furniture, different pharmaceuticals, food products, etc. This, however, does not prevent the use of the same trademark on totally unrelated products, such as automobiles and pianos, for example, or baking powder and plows.

The Selection of a Trademark

Since it is difficult and expensive to make any change in a trademark after it is once adopted and put into use, it is important to give careful attention to the matter of selection. Much expensive litigation may also be avoided, if due care and study are given to this phase of the problem in advance. The courts may be relied upon to protect trademark rights; but they can only protect such rights as actually exist *as a matter of fact* at the time the action is brought. They cannot correct past errors of judgment, and little or no weight can be given to motives and intentions.

First of all, it must be borne clearly in mind that the name or mark selected must be one which the public can use to identify the goods. The public must understand it as meaning goods from a certain source or origin, and it should not be possible for this meaning to be confused. The public bestows its own meanings upon the names it uses in trade, just as it does upon any other words in the language, and the public use of a term cannot be restrained or restricted. Also, the name selected must be one which can be monopolized and used exclusively for the purpose of identification, without interfering with the rights of others.

Thus there are certain groups or classes of words which can be eliminated at the start as not suitable for the purpose. Obviously it is necessary first of all to avoid imitating or duplicating any trademark that is already in use in connection with goods under the same classification. If there is any doubt on this score, an attorney experienced in trademark law should be retained to search the Patent Office records. Other general classes of names it is well to avoid are the following:

1. Descriptive terms, which include all words indicative of the kind or quality or utility of the product, also laudatory adjectives intended to recommend or advertise the quality of the goods (Wonderful Automobile). Such terms are not registrable, and a monopoly in them cannot be sustained since any maker of similar goods may also rightfully use them.

2. Geographical names are equally open to objection as nonregistrable. It is only in exceptional instances, where a "secondary

meaning" can be shown, that a monopoly in a geographical trademark can be sustained.

3. Family names. Though there are a great many well-known family name trademarks (Heinz, Mennen, Smith Brothers, Colgate, etc.) a name of this character is apt to prove troublesome, since others entitled to the same name have the right to use it in connection with their products. The L. E. Waterman Pen Co., for example, was in litigation for many years with a concern making A. A. Waterman pens, carrying the case eventually to the Supreme Court without obtaining adequate relief.

The Trademark Act provides that a mark which is "primarily merely a surname" cannot be registered under normal circumstances. This is based partly on the theory that nobody should be able to take a family name out of circulation by registering it as a trademark, until such time as the purchasing public reacts to it as a trademark rather than just a surname as the result of extensive and exclusive use. Of course, a family name frequently acquires this special kind of status when the product to which it is attached achieves commercial success. Ford, Kellogg, and Wrigley are three well-known examples.

A trademark must be considered in its entirety, not dissected into separate parts. If it is a combination of various elements, it nevertheless makes its impression on the public as a combination, and that is the way in which its registrability should be tested.

Aside from the foregoing, there obviously remains a very wide field from which a choice may be made. A common dictionary word may be chosen which is purely fanciful, as "Ivory" is for soap, "Carnation" for condensed milk, "Cream of Wheat" for farina. Or a purely arbitrary word may be preferred, such as "Star" or "Anchor" or "7-20-4." The main point is to select a name which is easy to recognize, and to pronounce, and which is so obviously fanciful or arbitrary that there is no possible confusion as to its significance as a mark of identification.

Coined Words as Trademarks

Many believe that the best trademark is the coined word: "Kodak," "Vaseline," etc.

Such manufactured words have, as a matter of fact, made up the bulk of the applications for registration in the Patent Office. There is, of course, no technical objection to them, but they have certain disadvantages when used as trademarks, aside from the fact that it is difficult to invent a new word which is entirely distinctive and easy to recognize and pronounce. Radio and television advertising have given added importance to easily remembered names.

For one thing, the adoption of a coined word implies that the public must be taught the meaning of an entirely new term, which in itself is something of a task. For another thing, there is the likelihood that the public will see fit to bestow a meaning of its own upon the mark—to use it in short as a convenient generic term for a certain kind or variety of product. The more widely such marks are advertised, the greater is the possibility of such misconception. Typical instances are "Kodak" which is widely used as synonymous with "camera." "B. V. D." was popularly understood for years as referring merely to a certain athletic style of underwear, making substitution an extremely simple process, and leading to a large crop of vexatious and expensive lawsuits. "Celluloid" is a perfectly valid technical trademark, which only one producer can lawfully use *as a trademark;* that is, as "attached to the goods." But the popular use of the term as referring to a certain substance has been so widespread that any manufacturer of that substance may lawfully sell it as celluloid. Technically, the original proprietor is protected, but practically he is not, since the public use of the term is paramount.

Hence the coined word may quite possibly become a liability, especially where the public does not deal directly with the owner of the trademark, but with irresponsible vendors who may or may not be scrupulous. So far as the right to exclusive use is concerned, the common dictionary word (like "Ivory" or "Carnation," for example) is of equal value, and there is far less likelihood of confusion or misconception as to its significance.

Trademarks on Patented Products

When a product is manufactured under the protection of a patent monopoly, special attention should be given to the trademark problem in order to avoid loss of goodwill when the patent expires. The patent monopoly consists in the right to exclude others from making, using, or selling the product in question for a limited term. At the end of the term, right to make, use, and sell passes to the public, and with it there necessarily passes the right to *describe* the product in terms that ordinarily will be understood. This is inevitable, since the right to make would be of small value without the right to tell what is made. On the other hand, the monopoly of the descriptive phraseology by the original patentee would practically mean indefinite extension of the monopoly.

Hence, if the name that is used as a trademark during the life of the patent is the *only name the public understands* as descriptive of the product, it will pass to the public when the patent expires. A recent specific example is that of "Aspirin," which the courts have decided is the only name the general public understands as referring to a particular chemical compound of acetyl salicylic acid. "Linoleum" is another name originally used as a technical trademark, but now employed generally as an ordinary descriptive term referring to a certain kind of material. The Supreme Court in the famous sewing machine case refused to enjoin a competing manufacturer from using the name "Singer" in connection with machines made under the specifications of Singer patents which had expired.

No general rule of procedure will apply to all cases. The only safe plan is to obtain competent legal advice, as far as possible in advance of the expiration date of the patent. The common error is to delay action until the patent is about to expire, and then adopt some expedient which may actually confuse the situation rather than clarify it. Where patent rights are involved in conjunction with trademarks, competent advice at the start will save many times its cost in ultimate loss of goodwill and unnecessary litigation.

Registration of Trademarks

There was no federal legislation in effect on trademarks until 1870. That year Congress passed an act codifying some of the principles of law which had been applied by common law and in equity courts at that time.

The first federal trademark legislation came under review by the Supreme Court in 1879. The court, while invalidating an enactment because it failed to find constitutional authority to support it, nevertheless recognized and stated the principle that:

"The right to adopt and use a symbol or a device to distinguish the goods or property made or sold by the person whose mark it is, to the exclusion of the use of that symbol by all other persons, has been long recognized by the common law and the chancery courts of England and of this country, and by the statutes of some of the States. It is a property right, for which damages may be recovered in an action at law, and the violation of which will be enjoined by a court of equity, with compensation for past infringement. This property and the exclusive right to its use were not created by the Act of Congress, and do not now depend upon that Act for their enforcement. The whole system of trademark property and the civil remedies for its protection existed long anterior to the Act of Congress, and remain in full force since its passage."

Broadly speaking, therefore, it may be asserted that our law has always recognized the fundamental basis on which trademark protection rests, namely, the principle that business integrity is to be preserved in order that the individual may be protected in his business reputation, and the public may be protected against interlopers who seek to reap where they have not sown. In a word, it has always been the objective of trademark law both on common-law principle and by statute to compel fair play and common honesty in business.

As the Supreme Court said in the case to which reference has been made, this principle exists and is protected quite independently of federal legislation.

The advantage of federal legislation on the subject was recognized by Congress. After the invalidation of the first Trademark Act a new law was enacted in the year 1881.

That act remained without substantial change until 1905, when the whole subject was reviewed and the act of that year, having the objective of extending the scope of protection of trademark owners, became effective.

From time to time the 1905 act was amended, but with the exception of an act passed in 1920, the amendatory acts dealt mainly with procedural matters.

The act of 1920 broadened the scope of subject matter entitled to registration primarily for the purpose of affording protection to American citizens under foreign trademark legislation.

While there was no substantive change in the protection afforded by federal legislation, judicial interpretation developed many uncertainties as to the rights and remedies of trademark owners. A large number of the decisions dealt with principles commonly referred to as unfair competition, and based on encroachments upon business reputation which were independent of technical infringement of registered trademarks. There was a gradual growth of the scope of protection of business outside of the purview of the Trademark Act, and it was recognized by the Supreme Court and other federal tribunals that the essential element in trademark cases was the same as in unfair competition cases unaccompanied by trademark infringement, and that the common law of trademarks was but a part of the broader law of unfair competition. This principle was enunciated by the Supreme Court very clearly in the often-quoted *Hanover Milling Co.* case reported in 240 U.S. 403.

Newer Legislation

Largely because of the uncertainties arising from varying judicial interpretations, and the growth of the law of unfair competition, from time to time agitation for new legislation arose both from within and without Congress. This finally resulted in the enactment of our current law, which was approved July 5, 1946, effective July 5, 1947.

The basic purposes of the 1946 legislation (the Lanham Act) were well stated in a report of the Senate Committee preceding the passage of the act. This report said:

"The purpose underlying any trademark statute is twofold. One is to protect the public so it may be confident that, in purchasing a product bearing a particular trademark which it favorably knows, it will get the product which it asks for and wants to get. Secondly, where the owner of a trademark has spent energy, time, and money in presenting the product to the public, he is protected in his investment from its misappropriation by pirates and cheats. This is a well-established rule of law protecting both the public and the trademark owner."

The 1946 act embraces an extension of the nature of trade indicia, which is subject to federal registration, beyond technical trademarks applied directly to merchandise. This extension of federal recognition of the symbols of goodwill is designed to include prohibition of the use of deceptive and misleading trade indicia which heretofore was cognizable only under the doctrine of unfair competition. The purpose of the new act specifically includes protection against unfair competition and the provisions of the act are designed to prevent fraud and deception by any unfair use of reproductions, copies, counterfeits, or colorable imitations, whereby merchandise or services are distinguished in the course of commerce, whether the indicia be technical trademarks directly applied to the goods, as was the case under prior statutory provision, or whether it is used in other ways in connection with the offer to the public of products or services. The act, therefore, includes not only remedies for technical trademark infringement but also for service marks used in the sale or advertising of services; certification marks, which are marks used in connection with products or services by others than the owner of the mark whereby the origin or certain characteristics of the goods or services are certified; and collective marks, which are marks used by cooperative associations or other groups.

Another important step toward more liberal protection of trademarks may be found in that provision of the Lanham Act which recognizes use of the mark either on the goods themselves or on any displays associated therewith as statutory basis for trademark protection. Under the old act, a trademark was protected by statute only if and when it was actually affixed to the merchandise itself or its container.

No mark can be registered which contains immoral or scandalous matter. It must not include any simulation of the flag or other insignia of the United States, or any state or municipality, or any foreign nation, or any emblem of any philanthropical or fraternal society. Registration is prohibited of any name, emblem, etc., adopted by any institution, organization, club, or society incorporated prior to use by the applicant. Portraits of living individuals are not registrable except upon written consent, and no portrait of a deceased president may be registered during the life of his widow, except by her written consent. No mark which is identical with that used by another on the same class of goods, or which so nearly resembles it as to be likely to cause confusion, can be registered. A mark consisting merely of the name of the applicant can be registered only when it is written distinctively (as a signature, for example) or printed.

The Lanham Act

Under the Lanham Act (1946), which combines and augments the acts of February 20, 1905, and March 19, 1920, the procedures in registering and using trade and service-marks were modernized and liberalized. The new law for example:

1. Gives the owner an "incontestable right" to his trademark if it is consistently used for 5 years after registration under the act—and *provided he is vigilant.*

2. Consolidates all previous trademark legislation and codifies the accumulation of 40 years of legal interpretations and statutes.

3. Protects trademark holders from interference by state legislatures.

4. Assures carrying out U.S. commitments under international trademark agreements.

5. Provides "broader protection" against unfair competition and infringement.

While retaining the old law's prohibition against trademarks which are immoral or scandalous, or those using the seal or insignia of the United States or of any state or municipality, the new legislation adds another forbidden category—marks which "disparage or falsely suggest" a connection with persons living or dead, institutions, beliefs or national symbols, so as to "bring them into contempt or disrepute."

The Lanham Act is more lenient than the old act toward the use of trademarks involving the names of places or persons. Under the old law, the registration of the trademark "Kem" for plastic playing cards was denied because there is a Russian river with this name. The fact that there was a U.S. Senator by the same name, James P. Kem (R., Mo.), would also rule out registration under the old law. But the Lanham Act would permit "Kem" to be registered as a trademark since it is not "primarily" the name of a river or a person, such as "Rhine" or "Smith" would be.

The U.S. Commissioner of Patents termed "extremely fortunate" the Lanham Act's elimination of the "mere existence" of a surname or corporation name as grounds for rejecting a trademark. Take the almost perfect trademark of "Noxon." (It can be spelled forward or backward and read upside down.) Under the old law, it would have been rejected because the Patent Office staff—avid readers of metropolitan telephone directories—would have found a Mrs. Lillian Noxon listed in the Washington directory.

Since the same directory listed a Mrs. Helen Kodak, the office would have had to reject a trademark application for a well-known camera.

The new law also permits the registration of trademarks which have acquired "secondary meanings." For instance, "Philadelphia Cream Cheese" now signifies a certain type of product. Under the old law, this term could not have been registered unless it was exclusively used by the same trader back in 1895—10 years prior to the 1905 Act. The new law rules that "Philadelphia" as it is used here has a "secondary meaning" beyond that of naming a city. Therefore, it may be registered.

Advantages of Registration

Registration does not grant any rights to exclusive use of the trademark that do not actually exist as a matter of fact; such rights are acquired through use, and not through compliance with statutory requirements. The acceptance or rejection of an application by the Patent Office has no effect upon trademark rights *per se,* as the office passes only upon the right to register and not upon the right to exclusive use. Registration is, however, of the highest importance as evidence of the existence of common-law rights, and the owner of a registered mark is in a position of material advantage with respect to the protection of his rights.

Registration is a public record. It also certifies that all prior registrations have been officially examined, and that the registrant is the only known user of the mark in question. Furthermore, it is legal notice of priority, effective with respect to all users of identical or similar marks on the same class of goods.

Federal court jurisdiction is generally advantageous, both with respect to increasing the damages that may be assessed for infringement, and the power of the federal courts to order the seizure and destruction of infringing labels, etc.

Registered trademarks may be filed with the Treasury Department, and the importation of foreign goods bearing infringing marks may be stopped at ports of entry.

Registration in the Patent Office is needed as a prerequisite to registration abroad. Most countries will not register a trademark owned by an alien unless it is registered in the country of origin. Registration abroad is of high importance, since in many instances the *first registrant* is held to be the legal owner of the mark, irrespective of use. This is true in particular of Latin-American countries. Any local resident, a selling agent for example, may register an American-owned trademark in his own name, and place himself in a position to make his own terms with the original user.

Finally, registration is of great value since it is held to be "coterminous with the territory of the United States." The owner of an unregistered mark ordinarily can establish rights only throughout the territory where it is actually used. His rights do not extend beyond the actual market in which he has built up goodwill for the mark. If a competitor later adopts the same mark in other territory, and registers it, he immediately acquires rights throughout the United States *except* the first user's local territory. Thus the first user is practically confined to the local market, and cannot extend the use of his mark into additional territory.

Hence, in general, the advisability of prompt registration of any trademark used in interstate commerce. Neglect of this is far too common, many executives being inclined to regard registration as a formality of slight importance in comparison with more pressing merchandising problems. Even today, there are occasional applications for registration under the "10-year clause," indicating marks in use since 1895 without registration. Registration is so simple and inexpensive that there is no good excuse for neglecting it.

While there are many strong, valid trademarks that are used by major companies that are *not* registered in the Patent Office, yet they can enjoy most of the benefits and protection as if they were registered.

The advantage of having a registration is that it is notice throughout the 50 states that this is your claim of trademark rights. Also, it creates a presumption of exclusive rights to use the mark. It becomes particularly advantageous when you get involved in litigation and you want to establish your priority rights and exclusive rights to the mark.

You can take the certificate of registration and introduce it into evidence without going through the effort of getting sales figures, invoices, and copies of labels.

Valuation and Purchase of Trademarks

A trademark that is widely known is obviously an asset of great value, and sometimes may be the principal asset of a business. Since it represents exclusively the goodwill of the business, however, it is inseparable from all the other assets of the business, and cannot be sold or transferred except in conjunction with them. In any purchase of "trademark rights," it is, therefore, important to make certain that title is also acquired to all the other assets of the business in connection with which the mark has been used. Adequate protection in the courts is difficult, and often impossible to obtain unless the exclusive right to use the trademark includes the exclusive right to manufacture *all of the products* to which the same mark was formerly applied.

When a trademark is acquired through purchase of the assets of a business, it is, however, necessary to appraise its value separately. This value is clearly the value of the goodwill, since possession of the trademark implies possession of the goodwill. The generally recognized formula for an appraisal of goodwill as an asset is in terms of potential earning power, the basis being the average of the annual net profits over a term of years. A trademark in continuous use in connection with a going business may normally be assumed to be worth at least five times the average annual net profits. This is, of course, merely a basis for negotiations, and special circumstances may increase or decrease the figure that is finally agreed upon.

A mark which has been in continuous use in the same business over a long period of years is worth more than a trademark representing the same potential earning more recently established.

A trademark that has been extensively advertised has a greater potential value than a mark advertised less extensively, or only occasionally.

In general, the potential earning power of a trademark increases in proportion to the number of actual customers to whom it is known. On an actuarial basis, goodwill divided among a million customers will die out much more slowly than when there are only a few hundred or a few thousand. Thus trademarks for articles in common daily use among the mass of consumers have a higher potential value proportionately, than those used in connection with products having a more limited sale.

For example, the name "Maxwell House Coffee" was sold at one time for $5 million. The Postum Company paid the Calumet Baking Powder Company $32 million for the Calumet name. The goodwill, and the trademarks of the old *New York World* were sold to Scripps-Howard for $5 million after the paper had been out of publication almost a year! And when Chrysler bought out Dodge in 1926 for $146 million, the purchasers appraised the value of the Dodge name alone as worth $79,341,318.22. Since in nearly every instance names had identifying indicia, the prices paid for them illustrate the balance sheet value of goodwill and the importance of properly protecting it.

Infringement of Trademarks

Trademark infringement in general consists of the copying or simulation of the mark by competitors. The test of infringement is not, however, the degree of similarity between the marks, but the question of fact as to whether customers are misled or deceived. Where the ordinary customer mistakes one mark for another, so that he unintentionally buys one producer's goods while thinking he is buying another's, there is infringement. Where evidence can be brought to show such actual or probable deception of the public, the courts will protect the owner of the original mark by enjoining further use of the offending mark and awarding damages.

When such a situation arises, prompt legal action should be taken, even though the infringer may be operating in limited territory and for the time being doing slight damage. This is important not only because the damage done by an infringer may increase with great rapidity, but also because delay in taking action may reduce or even perhaps destroy the right to protection. Exclusive rights to a trademark cannot be maintained if its use by others is acquiesced in, and to secure relief in the equity courts one must show at least reasonable vigilance in the protection of his rights. Infringement should never be temporized with. The only safe remedy is the legal remedy, and it should be applied as soon as evidence of infringement can be secured.

The first invoice showing a shipment of the goods should be carefully preserved. Not only that, but appropriate copies of the original records, if possible, of the invoices and order to the printer for the first label—any evidence that tends to show when you first went into business on the product—should be kept (and *not* in the regular corporate records which are going to be cleaned out from time to time).

If there is an inside legal department, the records should be kept there, or if the company has outside trademark counsel, it probably should entrust the records to their care.

You may get into litigation 20 or 25 years after the adoption of the mark. If that happens, you may have a great deal of difficulty if you can't find the original records.

International Trademark Problems

The registration of trademarks on a worldwide basis is a serious consideration for companies with international activities on a wide scale. It may be a costly process, but corporations with licensees, subsidiaries, or distributors in foreign markets take every precaution to safeguard their trademarks, at least in principal markets.

In Monaco, an expatriate by the name of Aries had run into the local registrar's office and claimed rights in a series of something like 300 trademarks, most of them owned by United States companies, and a number of them by European companies, and practically all of them extremely valuable and important trademarks, which raises a question of the international considerations in the adoption, use, and protection of a trademark.

In the majority of foreign countries, rights are obtained in a trademark by the mere fact of registration. You do not have to establish that you have used the mark in order to acquire rights in that country, as opposed to the United States where you have to use the mark first and that is when your rights accrue.

When Tidewater Oil started to export to South America, it found it was blocked in practically every country, because somebody had gone around and tied up the Tidewater trademark.

There is quite a problem for a company which intends to use the mark created and initiated domestically, and then uses it internationally.

"Taboo" marks should be considered carefully. For example a company would be certainly rather foolish to attempt to introduce

TRADEMARKS IN CONFLICT

In cases involving registration in the United States Patent Office, a conflict was found between the following marks:

DRAGON (replaceable metal tooth points)	DRAGON (dredges)
BEL-AIR (pneumatic tires and tubes)	BEL-AIR (automotive vehicles and parts)
GLENLOGIE (Scotch whiskey)	GLENUGIE (Scotch whiskey)
JUBILEE FASHION, A (children's wear)	JUBILEE JEANS (denim pants)
PAPER MATE (ballpoint pen inks, etc.)	PEN-MATE (writing paper and envelopes)
SWAGGER (hosiery)	SWAGGER (outer shirts)
PAPER MATE (ball point pens, etc.)	RITE-MATE (fountain pens and pencils)
INTERNATIONAL SET (women's swim suits)	MISS INTERNATIONAL (women's swim suits)
PRINCE IVAN (vodka)	IVAN (vodka)
FANTASY (finger rings)	FANTASY (clocks and watches)
AUTO-MEDIC (lubrication oil)	MOTOR-MEDIC (lubrication oil)
BEAUTY-FOLD (curtain, drapery fixtures)	GLAMOR FOLD (drapery hanging apparatus)
GALEY & LORD (textile fabrics)	GAYLORD (women's skirts, shirts, etc.)
GOOD CUP (ground and instant coffee)	FINE CUP (instant coffee)
RIDE-GUIDE (steering control units for outboard motors)	GUIDE RITE (steering control units for outdoor motors)
ROMA (spaghetti, etc.)	ROMA (vegetable oil)
TOUN HOUSE (mattresses)	TOWN HOUSE (mattresses)
VITA-RICH (milk, cream and cottage cheese)	VITA-N-RICH (eggs)
BAR-RAY (X-ray radiation equipment)	RAY-BAR (X-ray radiation shielding equip.)
BUG (motor driven miniature autos)	ZOOM BUG (motor driven miniature autos)
EVERREADY (electric batteries, etc.)	EVER-READY (hand and power-driven lawn mowers)
E-Z PLANTER (flower seeded mat)	E-Z COME, E-Z GROWN (seeded planters)
GLEN-MORE (suits)	GLENFORD (suits)
MR. BOURBON (bourbon whiskey)	MISS KENTUCKY BOURBON (bourbon whiskey)
NINA RICCI (women's clothing)	RICCI OF HAYMAKER (women's shirts, skirts, dresses)
CHERRY STAR (canned sea foods)	CHERISTAR (dried rice)

Courtesy, The U.S. Trademark Association, New York City, N. Y.

products in South America under the brand-name, *Yankee*. This is a good example, however, of the sort of care that should be given, not only to the literal and formal translation, but also to the vernacular, which may be a quite different thing.

Changing Corporate Names

A final aspect of trademark considerations is that which flows from the changing of a corporate name.

As so well pointed out in *Industrial Marketing*, "the most expensive mania that modern business has fallen victim to is the compulsion to change the company name."

The excuse usually given by companies is that mergers or changes in product lines have made old names irrelevant and misleading. But the fact of the matter is that name-changing became fashionable, with the result that many fine old names—the handles by which markets identified trusted sources of supplies—have given way to some absurd combinations of letters.

American Brake Shoe Company makes many other things besides brake shoes. Changing the name to anything else won't change the opinion the market already has of the company and its products. But changing the name surely will remove from the marketplace an identity which had been built up over the years at substantial cost of promotion and immense investment in good product and good service. And people have to start learning who ABEX is.

If you were naming an American automobile today, you surely wouldn't call it a Chevrolet—a name that's foreign and isn't pronounced the way it is spelled. But those reasons don't compel General Motors to change the name to something modern and American and more easily spelled.

If you made Hotpoint appliances and had built up a reputation for quality in heating appliances, you wouldn't panic and change the name just because a thing that is cold shouldn't have a name that is hot.

Westinghouse is a terrible name if you're going to worry about Western Electric. General Electric is a bad name because so many company names begin with "General." And either Goodrich or Goodyear had better change its name because the names are so close.

Nonsense! The name is just a handle, and there is no reason why International Harvester isn't a good name for trucks, or why U.S. Steel should stay out of the chemicals business, or why Volkswagen should change its spelling because most people spell it wrong.

When Hercules Powder Company changed its name simply by shortening it to Hercules Incorporated, it retained its corporate identity, built up over a period of 53 years. The change was announced in a series of advertisements in the business and technical press.

But the corporate image and industrial design boys have been having a field day doing research and dreaming up new names and designing new logos. With the result that the industrial market is now full of names nobody ever heard of before, and the degree of confusion in the marketplace is only matched by the fees the "imagers" have been dragging out of bug-eyed managements.

Advertising agencies and publications have been benefiting, too, from this craze. Managements which have been withholding funds from legitimate selling promotions eagerly pay for corporate-identification campaigns to tell people that they don't have the same name any more.

On the other hand, there may be valid reasons for changing a corporate name, especially when it is intelligently handled. Because of wide diversification, the severe limitations of the word Powder, and the very important fact that its name could be changed simply by shortening it without losing identity, Hercules Powder Company became Hercules Incorporated.

In announcing the change, the company said:

"For the first six years of existence, commercial explosives . . . were its principal products. Diversification took the company, by 1931, into such new fields of chemistry as derivatives of pine trees and cotton, and materials for the paper and protective-coating industries. Today it is a producer of materials for such widely diversified industries as paper, plastics, coatings, agricultural chemicals, rubber, synthetic fibers, construction, mining, and quarrying.

"These broadening fields of interest in production, sales, and research have resulted in a need for changing its name from one which is descriptive of only a part of its business to one which retains the specific name and 53-year-old reputation and identity of Hercules. Therefore the name of Hercules Powder Company will be replaced by Hercules Incorporated . . . The name Hercules Powder Company will be retained by a subsidiary and will be used and protected in the future."

PART 3

ANALYZING
THE
MARKET

Chapter 8

THE AMERICAN MARKET

THERE is no such thing as *one* American market. This great country, with the greatest purchasing power in the world, is divided into a number of "markets" for individual products and services, each with specific needs and requirements. True, the health of the general economy of the United States will affect these regional "markets," but it may be taken for granted that they underlie all marketing considerations.

Inflation, taxes, the balance of foreign payments, war or peace, all exert tremendous forces affecting the prosperity of industry in general and companies in specific industries. That does not mean to say that the domestic market is not subject to its own fast-changing circumstances and conditions.

Some of these changes, taking place right before our eyes, will determine future marketing success or failure if they are not taken into account by the sales manager.

Kinds of Markets

"What is a market?" asks Jack Sissors in the *Journal of Marketing*. A market usually is identified with a generic class of products. One hears of the beer market, the cake-mix market, or the cigarette market. These are *product markets,* meaning customers who in the past have purchased these products.

For the sake of convenience, these individuals are classified into groups, all of which have similar characteristics. The use of product identification for a market carries with it the assumption that those persons who *will* buy a product in the future will be very much like those who have purchased it in the past. This assumption is usually valid, because purchasers are likely to repurchase the same product in the future if their wants or needs have been satisfied.

Once the market has been identified by *product class, subclass,* or *brand,* purchasers may be described according to: (1) size of the market; (2) geographical locations of purchasers; (3) demographic descriptions of purchasers; (4) social-psychological characteristics; (5) reasons why products are purchased; (6) who makes the actual purchases and who influences the purchaser; (7) when purchases are made, and (8) how purchasing is done. Even more descriptive classifications could be added, such as methods of distribution, effects of pricing changes, or results of sales promotion.

A newer concept is that markets be identified by consumer needs rather than by product classes. Theodore Levitt, writing in the *Harvard Business Review*, argues that a market is composed of persons who have various needs and wants. Ideally, when such needs or wants are recognized by the manufacturer, a special product is made and sold to fulfill them.

Sometimes markets are defined in terms of geographical places. One hears of the Chicago market or the St. Louis market or the suburban market.

But manufacturers may be misled into thinking that their competition consists only of manufacturers of their class of product, when in reality their market is composed of all manufacturers who meet a special consumer need. As an example, the competitors of railroad companies are not just other railway companies, but *all transportation companies*.

Population Changes

According to *Sales Management's* "Survey of Buying Power," while the suburbs are expanding faster than the cities, suburban growth has slowed somewhat in the 1960's while central city growth has quickened slightly. Land annexations by some large cities partly explain this. The population explosion of the 1960's focused on young adult groups, who prefer the apartment life of the big city for income and social reasons. The age groups that first experience the yen for a home in the suburbs, the 30's and early 40's, have either been declining in numbers or just holding their own.

But what concerns city governments everywhere is the trek to the suburbs; the infusion of disadvantaged workers into the core cities. A recent Census Bureau report covering metropolitan changes for the first half of the 1960's notes that the central-city white population declined by 270,000, while city nonwhite population increased by more than two million.

Cities have experienced the influx of disadvantaged people before. But what alarms municipal leaders is that higher-income families are abandoning the city while factory and other laboring jobs that the newcomers rely on are being reduced by modern technology.

The nation's middle-income group now receives more than half of all personal income, according to a study by the National Industrial Conference Board.

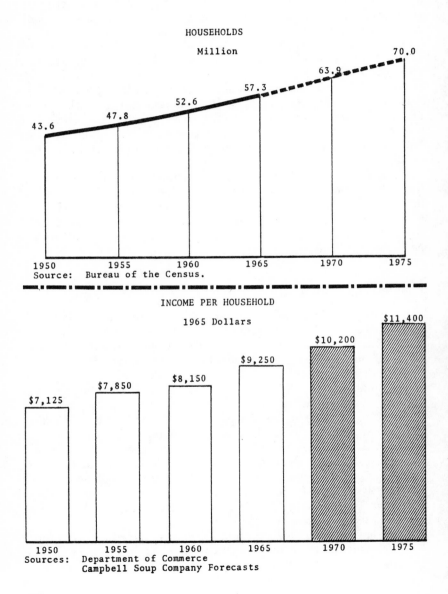

HOUSEHOLDS

Million

70.0

63.9

57.3

52.6

47.8

43.6

1950   1955   1960   1965   1970   1975
Source: Bureau of the Census.

INCOME PER HOUSEHOLD

1965 Dollars

$11,400

$10,200

$9,250

$8,150

$7,850

$7,125

1950   1955   1960   1965   1970   1975
Sources: Department of Commerce
           Campbell Soup Company Forecasts

"The 'bloodless income revolution under contemporary capitalism' is steadily reshaping, almost inverting, the income pyramid," NICB noted.

While two-thirds of the country's households had incomes of less than $5,000 a year in the early 40's (expressed in 1965 dollars), about one-third are now in that bracket. One in four homes currently has an income of $10,000 or more, up from one in 20 some 25 years ago.

THE TRILLION-DOLLAR ECONOMY

Population pressures, rising productivity, the heightened tempo of technology, and the intensification of foreign competition suggest that earlier economic models understated the probable rate of expansion of the American economy. In combination, these forces promise to raise aggregate national output in terms of today's dollar to $1 trillion by 1975 rather than 1980, as earlier projections suggested. Those who are skeptical might well review the record of economic growth thus far in the 1960's. In just six years GNP has already risen from $500 billion to $780 billion. Even after allowance for higher prices, this represents an annual rate of *real* growth of about 5 percent. The rate required to achieve $1 trillion by 1975 is pitched somewhat lower, about 4.25 percent.

MARTIN R. GAINSBRUGH
Senior Vice-President and Chief Economist
National Industrial Conference Board

The Youth Market

The "youth market" has received increased attention in recent years by manufacturers, their advertising agencies, and trade publications, because of the growing percentage of total population represented by consumers under 25 years of age.

In a speech at the annual meeting of the southwest council of the American Association of Advertising Agencies, Robert M. Stelzer maintained that there is no one youth market. "It's four distinctly different markets—children, teens, collegians, and young adults," he said. "Each group must be reached by its own media, influenced by its own motivations, and sold through its own appeals.

"There is one exciting common denominator for young people from 5 to 25. That's their willingness to accept new ideas and try new products. They're eager to spend money, and they have it to spend."

Mr. Stelzer went on to say that the biggest mistake advertisers make "is trying to *talk like teens* to teens. Today, teen-agers are more discriminating in their buying than were their parents, demand better quality and value, and want what's in style for them. What they want most, of course, is to be accepted by their peers."

Ken Hudnall, vice-president and advertising director of Petersen Publishing Co., contended that radio and special-interest magazines are the best ways to reach the youth market.

"The young do not read newspapers to any great degree," he said, and added that the "cost of reaching them through television is high and getting higher." He said general magazines "are costly and inefficient, despite the fact that most of them are now publicizing youth readership."

Ruth Whitney, executive editor of *Seventeen*, advised marketers not to talk down to teens. "They speak English. They really do. Don't patronize them with the 'cool, man, cool' kind of language.

"Simple human dignity and self-respect is what they long for, and their radar, based on years and years of tuning up, can detect a patronizing, palsy-walsy attitude a mile away."

Sampling is more effective than any other audience-measuring surveys for the teen-age market, including Nielsen, ARB, or Hooper, said Gordon McLendon, president of McLendon Corp. "I urge you to sample teen-agers individually and by panel. Even a simple telephone or random sample will be more effective than the above-mentioned surveys can possibly be," he said.

While popular belief has the young-adult group spending as wildly as "the dances it gyrates to," this is a misleading view, argues market researcher Daniel Yankelovich. Addressing the Marketing Science Institute, he said the young-adult market is a trisected one—young married couples, unmarried college students, and unmarried noncollege students. The young marrieds, he holds, find themselves hard-pressed financially, hence tend to be more practical in their shopping than middle-aged adults. "A young woman buying a washing machine will tend to pick the strongest work-horse machine she can find, with great emphasis on trouble-free operation," he says. "The reason: she can't afford service calls." It's also the young marrieds who buy lower-cost nylon carpets, he adds, which leaves, for the people over 35, the wool floor-covering with its thick pile and luxury feel.

CHANGING U.S. AGE PATTERN

Past 24 years 1940-1964

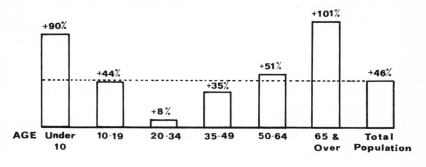

Next 10 years 1964-1974

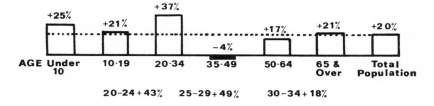

J. Walter Thompson Company.

The college market differs from the other segments, Yankelovich feels, because of its geographical concentration; the separate and distinct campus culture with its own fads, fashions, and values, and the presence of young adults whose values and points of view tend to be at odds with the rest of the young-adult population.

As pointed out in the *Gallagher Report,* campaigns directed at teens reflect differing approaches. Pepsi-Cola added to the vocabulary to launch its chocolate drink, *Devil Shake:* "It's glitzy!" The International Coffee Bureau appealed to youth's intellectual side. Coffee is "the think drink," the thing to imbibe when there's a decision to chew over, the ad copy advised. U.S. Shoe's young men's line emphasized revolt: "Shoes your father would never wear." Arnold Bread invented a dance, "The Giraffe," to sell its new bread of that name to 10-19 year olds. Some advertisers help teens plan ahead. Paillard offered a purse-size career guide with new Hermes typewriters. One advertiser of a medicated skin lotion offered a useful contest prize: a wedding.

According to a *Life* advertisement there are 30,000,000 people in this country aged 10 to 17. They buy two-and-one-half billion gallons of gasoline each year and it is estimated that they buy 20 percent of all cars sold. They account for 44 percent of all camera sales, 55 percent of soft drink sales, and constitute 35 percent of the movie audience.

Of this group, 14 percent own corporate stocks and bonds.

The girls alone buy 20 percent of women's clothes, 33 percent of all hair-dryers, 23 percent of all cosmetics, and spend over 20 million dollars a year on lipstick.

The Women's Market

Today, one out of three married women works as against one of four in 1960. Rising educational levels make women want to do something with what they've learned; in fact, almost half of the nation's women with a college education are working today. Below that the percentage drops off. At the same time, consider the impact of another population trend. The number of men in the 35-44 age group will actually shrink in the next 10 years.

Some ideas that marketing men have about women as consumers are way off base, according to a study by Batten, Barton, Durstine & Osborn, Inc.

The advertising agency claims that marketing experts project their target—the American housewife—in the image of their own wives or as stereotypes from slick magazines. In so doing, they often miss the mark. Instead of being glorified chauffeurs, one-third of all housewives don't even hold driver's licenses. As for women being club joiners, 50 percent don't belong to any kind of group. Liquor also plays a small part in their lives. One-third don't drink at all, and only 5 percent have as much as one drink daily.

More fundamental to the misunderstanding, 93 percent of all U.S. families earn less than $15,000 a year, whereas the income is considerably higher among executives catering to their needs. In addition, the study asserts that after running her household for an average of 22 years, the real Mrs. America is almost impossible to fool about housework.

"Over 60" Market Is Strong

The "elderly" market is nearly 19 million strong and increasing at a rate of more than 800 a day, William D. Bechill, commissioner of the U.S. Administration on Aging, told a government subcommittee. He said the elderly represent 16 percent of today's adult population.

Geneva Mathiasen, executive director of the National Council on the Aging, pointed out that persons over 60 outnumber teen-agers by at least 2,000,000 and that a good percentage of them are well to do.

The Ethnic Groups

The marketing and advertising industries have buried the concept of the "average" consumer and now seek to reach ethnic groups through increasing use of special appeals. Ethnic advertising and marketing are being used to introduce a product of ethnic origin (example: Jewish rye bread) to the general public via general circulation media. They are also being used to promote established national products to ethnic groups.

It is a new field with many unresolved questions yet to be worked out. Meanwhile, advertisers are expanding their appeals to these groups in their own languages. Not only the Negro markets are worth searching out, but also the Italian, German, and so on.

The Negro population in the central cities of the U.S. metropolitan areas increased 24 percent between 1960 and 1966, while the white population in the central cities decreased 2.5 percent. During the same time, white suburban population increased 20 percent while Negro suburban population increased 9 percent.

The Bureau of the Census estimated total Negro population at 12,074,000 in the central cities of the nation's 212 Standard Metropolitan Statistical Areas. This was an increase from 9,705,000 Negroes in the central cities at the time of the 1960 decennial census. During the same six-year period, white population in the central cities dropped from 47,655,000 to 46,444,000.

Citing the ethnic factor as part of the "rhythm of change" that is at work in the U.S., Lippincott & Margulies warns that a marketing man who ignores this factor endangers his product's market share.

"In today's diffuse, competitive market . . . some products benefit significantly by establishing the proper appeals. Because these appeals usually involve limited geographic applications via regional media, we are often unaware of ethnic campaigns—unless they occur inside our immediate marketing areas," says this firm of package researchers and industrial designers.

Food products are especially suited for ethnic appeals because attitudes about them "derive from the deep roots of early upbringing and ancestral habit patterns," say the firm's experts. "For this

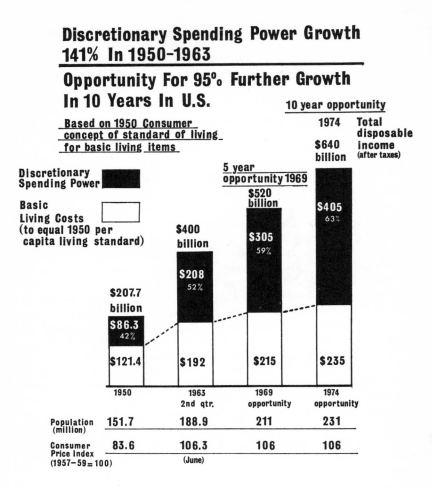

Discretionary Spending Power Growth 141% In 1950-1963

Opportunity For 95% Further Growth In 10 Years In U.S.

10 year opportunity

Based on 1950 Consumer concept of standard of living for basic living items

1974 $640 billion

Total disposable income (after taxes)

Discretionary Spending Power

5 year opportunity 1969 $520 billion

Basic Living Costs (to equal 1950 per capita living standard)

$400 billion

$305 59%

$405 63%

$207.7 billion

$208 52%

$86.3 42%

$121.4

$192

$215

$235

	1950	1963 2nd qtr.	1969 opportunity	1974 opportunity
Population (million)	151.7	188.9	211	231
Consumer Price Index (1957-59=100)	83.6	106.3 (June)	106	106

J. Walter Thompson Company.

reason, the food marketer, in particular, might wisely explore the potential of ethnic factors."

The Service-Oriented Market

Another significant trend for marketers is the increasing portion of the labor force engaged in providing services rather than products. A study by the National Bureau of Economic Research pointed out that the United States is pioneering in a new stage of economic development—one that is a "service economy." The nation is the first in which more than one-half of the employed population is not involved in the production of tangible goods. The shift in employment to services has many implications. Some of these relate to the total economy, the nature of work, the scale of enterprise, unionization, employment stability, and the growing importance of nonprofit organizations.

The Revived Farm Market

Along with the influence of mechanization, good roads, the automobile, and higher prices for farm products and farm lands, improved communications have added to the importance of the farm market. Whereas a generation ago the farmer worked from sunup to sundown, with little or no chance for reading or recreation, the farmer of today has his television set, his radio, a well-edited local newspaper in addition to his sectional farm paper. More important, farm electrification has given him time for reading which he seldom had before. Farming is no longer the drudgery it once was. When the crash of 1930 came, most farms were heavily mortgaged. Today, the heavily mortgaged farm is the exception rather than the rule.

These modern means of communication have given the farmer and his family a desire for the better things in life. He goes places and does things. His wife has an electric kitchen. His children go to the best colleges. When he attends the meeting of his local grange, or the co-op of which he is a member, he goes well-dressed, well-shod, and quite likely in a shiny new automobile. He goes in for blooded livestock. And with a few exceptions, his crops are so planned that a complete crop failure is rare indeed. Market-wise the farmer of today is a very important person, and nobody knows it better than the sales manager.

The Gross National Product

In measuring the well-being of the people of the United States, the figure commonly used is the Gross National Product, sometimes confused with the national income. The estimated total Gross National Product, each year, is reached by multiplying the *amount* of everything we produced by the *price* of everything we produced.

Since an important factor in making marketing plans is the relative size of income groups, the Ready-Reference Section of this handbook should prove useful.

Of late there has been an increasing tendency on the part of marketing men to measure sales potentials in terms of families, rather than on population statistics. Per-capita income might sound nice in a political speech, but in fact it means spreading the national income among all members of the family including the babes in arms, the children in kindergarten, and the old folks who live in the home. In our scheme of living, a family consists of five persons, including children and relatives.

It is not enough that those in sales work properly evaluate the overall purchasing power of the American market. It is equally important to consider the origin of this purchasing power, since marketing, to be most effective, must tap income as its most responsive sources, and those sources which are expanding rather than contracting. In any typical year, the gains in national income have had their roots in the expansion and modernization of our industrial plants.

THE NEGRO MARKET (see discussion on page 131) is worth 30 billion dollars a year in sales. Much of the intelligent development of this special market is being done by black sales and marketing executives like those pictured here.

As vice president of special markets for Greyhound Lines, Joe Black (above), is involved in policies, programs, practices, and procedures in the Negro market. He joined Greyhound in 1962 as a special markets representative.

Radio is a good medium for reaching the Negro market. William A. Manney (left), is general manager of WBEE, in the Chicago area. He was sales manager.

Chicago area sales managers keep an eye on George E. Johnson (right), president of the Johnson Products Co., Inc., a leader in beauty supplies.

Chapter 9

MARKETING AND
DISTRIBUTION TRENDS

A S THE desire for added leisure and comforts grows in our people it is inevitable that the spread between the cost of goods and the cost of distributing them will grow. As we demand more service we must expect to pay for that service. Hence, in approaching the problem of distribution, the sales manager is concerned with methods which will provide as good or better distribution service for a smaller share of the consumer's dollar, rather than cost alone.

It is that objective which underlies the shifts in distribution methods, the many new developments in outlets, and the widespread change in direction. Nearly all of these trends indicate one thing: American consumers are not interested in distribution savings which curtail their comforts, but they are interested in methods which, *while assuring them of greater comfort and convenience, also give them lower prices.*

For example, in many communities cash-and-carry stores have found that in order to compete they *must* render a delivery service as well as extend credit. So they make a small charge for delivery and extend limited credit to homeowners; the point being that in many communities people will not carry out their own groceries and will not pay in cash for what they buy. They *prefer* to pay extra for these conveniences.

Similarly, the cooperative store which places the emphasis on price rather than on service has been an outstanding success in Europe. But only in certain low-income and farm areas has the co-op succeeded in America. American housewives would rather pay a little more and enjoy the satisfaction of "shopping" for what they buy.

In an address to his company's shareholders, Fred Lazarus, Jr., chairman of the board of Federated Department Stores, Inc., noted these trends:

"We are already witnesses to the impact that affluence, youth, and education can have on our affairs. Together they have spawned a revolution in American taste. It is clearly evident in our libraries, museums, and concert halls. As merchants we need go no further than the aisles of our own stores to document the new sense of discrimination that this cultural explosion has brought to the marketplace. The shopworn phrase, 'trading-up,' does not really suggest what has occurred. It seems, rather, that a new generation of customers—younger, wiser, wealthier—is coming to us with new appetites. More and more of them reject the cheap, the gaudy, the ordinary, and the 'pretty good.' They search, instead, for the unique, the tasteful, and the satisfying."

Changes in Distribution

Some of the changes taking place in distribution were outlined by Harry L. Bullock, vice-president, Marketing, Skil Corporation, as follows:

"1. From the manufacturer down, automation being brought on by computerized control of inventories, sales expenses, forecasts, as well as highly sophisticated techniques in physical distribution, are combining to eliminate old-fashioned, cumbersome, and costly steps in distribution.

"2. From the retailer back, the advent of automatic vending and self-service outlets, as well as the application of computers at the retail level is causing changes in distribution. Even the newer forms of credit buying are causing distribution changes.

"More and more manufacturers are performing a time-and-place utility function through strategically located warehouses that supply mass marketers with product at heretofore unheard of speeds. In many cases wholesalers and certain types of distributors are being eliminated or forced into different types of operations than have been in existence since the advent of the industrial revolution.

"As more and more new products are introduced to both the consumer and industrial markets, the complexities of distribution will grow and the dependence upon automated techniques will increase.

"The costs of *physical distribution*, a major factor in food and other packaged goods industries, is forcing streamlining of distribution. As a result of government activity, housewives today are aware of the large share of food dollars going into physical distribution.

"In this one industry, the experts predict that distribution costs can be slashed by more than one billion dollars through the widespread use of such new distribution concepts as the unitized train, palletization, unitization—anything that will reduce the hand or conveyor belt handling of individual pieces. One soft-drink firm found it could save a million dollars a year simply by using computers to plan the delivery route of its truckers.

"The trends in distribution will continue to lead to further streamlining through the elimination of handling steps from the manufacturer to the consumer. More and more consumer durable products will be packaged by the manufacturer in such a manner that they can be displayed as they are received and be delivered to the end user without repackaging.

"During the next decade, distribution costs should drop considerably, the direct result of a new generation of efficiencies in the area of physical distribution."

Avenues of Distribution

There are many ways in which goods and services can be distributed in the American market. Which way is the best way depends upon a variety of factors. The main avenues are as follows:

Selling the Consumer: It is claimed by those who market their products directly to the consumer, as contrasted to those who distribute them through established channels of trade, that it "saves the middleman's profit." It is not unusual for new products to be put on the market which the manufacturer insists can be sold for less than established products because they are "not advertised." Actually, there is little if any difference in the cost of distributing a product through specialty salesmen calling house to house, or by mail, and distributing through established channels of trade. The house-to-house salesman usually gets a commission amounting to as much as, or more than, the dealer's discount. The cost of recruiting, training, and supervising a house-to-house sales organization is considerable. Then there are losses due to overdrafts, misappropriation of funds, theft of samples, etc. The cost of selling direct by mail is likewise more than generally supposed. The percentage of returns from mailings seldom exceeds 2 or 3 percent replies.

Selling for Resale: So-called shopping goods are generally sold through dealers and storekeepers, who retain from 20 to 50 percent of the resale price for performing this service. Merchandise thus distributed falls into two groups: (1) Lower margined staples which require little or no sales effort; and (2) "high ticket" merchandise which calls for specialized selling on the part of the dealer. Outside salesmen are frequently employed by dealers to go out and contact prospects, rather than wait for them to come into the store. This is particularly true of home appliances, automobiles, television sets, and other articles for which a want must be created and competitive values demonstrated. The drawback to this method of distribution is that dealers wait for "consumer demand" to move the goods off their shelves. The average dealer regards himself more as a distributor than a salesman. All too often a manufacturer, having stocked up the trade, feels well satisfied with the sales job he has done. Later he finds his goods are not moving into the hands of consumers.

Because of this, there is a growing tendency among manufacturers to: (1) Stimulate consumer demand by national and point-of-sale advertising, and (2) train and motivate dealers and their salespeople to unload the product after they have stocked it. In fact, some companies go so far as to concentrate their entire sales effort on helping dealers to sell. When you make it possible for a merchant to sell your product quickly he will usually buy more without being asked. The markup on nationally advertised products is slightly less than nonadvertised products, but since the advertised brands usually turn over faster the merchant's real profit is greater.

Selling for Conversion: This means securing economical distribution for products and materials which are built into a machine, or in some other way become a part of another unit—Timken products are a case in point. This type of distribution calls for negotiated selling. Opening up new accounts, as well as expanding the purchases of old accounts, is the main sales objective. Usually manufacturers are hesitant to change a source of supply which has proved satisfactory. The sales strategy therefore is: (1) Demonstrate it as to the converter's advantage to change, and (2) through national advertising or in other ways, to create user acceptance for articles in which your product has been used.

Selling to Institutions: The most commonly used procedure in selling hospitals, schools, homes for the aged, and similar institutions is through supply houses which specialize in serving them. Most wholesalers operate special departments to deal with institutions, but the larger institutions require special discounts, roughly about the same as a manufacturer allows a wholesale distributor. The institutional supply house usually works on a very moderate markup, depending on special "job lot" purchases for his profit.

To introduce products to institutions, and influence this business along desired channels, manufacturers sometimes employ institutional salesmen to concentrate on this type of business. They operate on a regional rather than a territorial basis, and may or may not share credit with the territorial salesmen. As a rule, institutional salesmen are experts in the management of institutions and have a greater technical knowledge of the product. They should be versed in "group selling." It is frequently necessary when dealing with institutions to appear before boards of directors or trustees to get an order. Hence the institutional salesman must be able to talk well on his feet.

The institutional market in the United States is tremendous and steadily growing as new hospitals, schools, orphanages, homes for the aged, convents, etc., are built and equipped.

Selling to Government: The tremendous expansion in government services of all kinds, civilian and military, has given new importance to sales dealings with the various purchasing agencies of federal, state, and local governments. Selling to these varied agencies requires a specialized knowledge of procedures and an acquaintanceship with influential officials. For those reasons most manufacturers interested in government business maintain a special sales staff, usually resident in Washington, to contact federal purchasing agencies. Similar sales units are sometimes maintained at state capitals, when appropriations are large enough to justify the expense. Usually, however, state purchases are handled by the territorial salesman with the help of a home office "pinch hitter" when special situations require it.

Because of the competitive nature of governmental business it is customary to employ representatives for this work on a straight salary, and credit the Washington office with all orders received from any governmental source, regardless of where it originates or where the goods are used. An exception to this practice is equipment which must be serviced by a local office of the manufacturer. In such cases partial credit for governmental sales is usually given to the office or salesman in the territory where the equipment is used.

Smaller manufacturers, not able to afford a Washington office or not especially interested in obtaining this not-too-profitable business, get together with noncompeting manufacturers and maintain joint representation. These joint representatives usually work on a commission basis. Generally speaking this type of representation is unsatisfactory. Even a small commission runs into staggering totals in the event of sudden big-scale purchases, and it is not always feasible to add them to the bid. Some industries depend upon a trade association with Washington headquarters and contacts to keep members informed. The manufacturer or an officer of the company goes to Washington to deal with the proper government agency if and as it may be necessary.

Selling to Railroads: The transportation market includes, in addition to railroads, air lines, trucking companies, bus companies, steamship lines, and interurban railways. It is a big and important market not only for equipment but for almost every conceivable product. While these accounts may be covered by the territorial salesman, the prevailing practice under normal conditions is to employ special salesmen, or sell through railway supply firms and ship chandlers. Selling to transportation companies requires a technical knowledge of the problem involved as well as more than the usual knowledge of the product. This is because railroads and, more especially, steamship companies are ultraconservative and slow to change satisfactory sources of supply.

To get a new product specified, whether it be equipment or supplies, requires patient cultivation of numerous interested persons, beginning with the employee who will use it and following through to the operating official who makes the final decision. While the purchasing agent issues the order, he seldom will take it upon himself to change a source of supply or initiate the purchase of new equipment. This makes the prime users important sales targets.

Most transportation companies operate on a budget, and it frequently happens that toward the end of the budgetary year, certain departments find themselves with "unspent" funds. Rather than have it appear they asked for more funds than they needed, department executives in such a situation are apt to authorize the requisition of equipment and supplies not urgently needed, or to experiment with new equipment. It is important to know when departmental budgets are made up so that the salesman or supply house responsible for an account can redouble his sales effort at the right time.

Selling the Small Towns: One of the most significant merchandising developments is the concentration of the purchases made in smaller cities and county seats in chain and departmental stores. As a result manufacturers underestimate the importance of the small-town market and neglect it for seemingly more attractive sales outlets. Common objections to the small-town market are:

1. Volume is too small to be profitable

2. Small towns buy only low price lines

3. Sales costs are too high

4. Commission salesmen will not work small towns

5. Lines are not suited to small towns.

While there is reason to feel this way about the small-town market, it remains nevertheless a potential outlet for a great volume of goods if a way can be found to reach it *profitably*. Distribution plans can be developed to secure this business without undue sacrifice of profits provided the problem is segregated from the overall distribution policy and the overall pricing policy. An illustration is found in the wearing-apparel field, where manufacturers' salesmen join in putting on traveling "shows." These are held several times a year at key distribution points. The salesmen, using a central promotional organization, invite small-town merchants and buyers to attend these shows, which they are glad to do.

However, the customary method of maintaining distribution in the smaller communities is through alert wholesale houses which understand and service small-town merchants. The average dry-goods wholesaler has about 2,000 customers; but it does not follow that this average wholesaler provides coverage of this group of customers for each line that he sells. He may not sell more than 5 to 10 percent of his lines to any individual merchant. But it is possible he may, through his sales organization, bring a line with attractive resale possibilities to the attention of all his customers. This would mean that 10 "average" dry-goods wholesalers would be in a position, if they elected to do so, to introduce a line to 20,000 stores—more than most manufacturers serve direct.

The small-city and small-town market is not what it used to be, and never again will be as backward as it once was. It will, like the big-city market, have its ups and downs, its good times and its bad times, but it is more stable than the city market, less sensitive to temporary fluctuations.

Whirlpool Looks at Marketing

A perfect summary of the complexities of modern marketing is afforded by Sol Golden, manager, retail marketing, Whirlpool Corporation. His comments are excerpted as follows:

Marketing is a vastly complicated process. The truth is, there are about 40 good ways to take your merchandise to market . . . and there is no one right way for any industry, perhaps not even for any one company.

Let's look at the complexities of Whirlpool distribution. Our business is appliances—but appliances come in assorted shapes, sizes, colors, sometimes with by-products. Appliances are bought by almost every family in the nation and by all sorts of businesses, institutions, and organizations. They're installed in homes, restaurants, hotels, churches, hospitals, and you-name-it. They're sold and serviced by every conceivable type of retailer—including gasoline stations and drug stores.

They're used for everything from cooking food to storing furs. They're powered usually by gas and electricity . . . although some involve power by elbow grease, apron strings, and bobby pins. And some of the newer ones are powered, or about to be powered, by thermo-electricity, solar, sonar, and microwave energy.

For Whirlpool's major business—home appliances—we have a dual-distribution system which involves (1) manufacturing Kenmore and Coldspot lines for Sears; (2) manufacturing and marketing RCA Whirlpool home appliances through independent distributors.

For the RCA Whirlpool line, we must plan and, to a large degree, execute all marketing functions for a vast distributive organization. For this huge hunk of our business, we have 72 customers—who are wholesalers reselling to dealers who resell to ultimate consumers. Fifty-seven of these are independent distributors. Four more are branches of the RCA Victor distributing corporation. These are multiterritory wholesalers who handle all our products plus RCA entertainment appliances.

The others are so-called factory branches—operated by Whirlpool in certain territories where outside distributors are ineffective.

These 72 distributors, in turn, sell to about 15,000 retailers, most of whom carry two or more brands of appliances. These retailers may or may not do their own installation and service work. If they do, fine—life is comparatively simple. If they don't, they may work with our central service associates, the RCA Service Company, or with any of some 35,000 independent service organizations.

Sound complicated? Wait . . . there are also utilities. We make both gas and electric appliances. Because utilities are fiercely competitive, our distributors often must establish separate selling policies. Add to this the fact that some utilities merchandise directly to consumers, while others sell only through dealers.

The next complication is that products don't fit standard distribution patterns. When we merged with Seeger, and acquired our St. Paul plants, we also acquired a healthy business in milk coolers. This called for a different kind of wholesaling system.

Then we came up with a commercial icemaker. The demand for this product is largely from hotels, motels, and the like. For this, we needed still another specialized distribution system—a dual system, one for RCA Whirlpool, another for private labels, including models for one of our biggest competitors, Frigidaire.

Along came coin-operated drycleaning machines—with prices around and above $2,000 each.

Then came residential heating and cooling systems—in electric, gas, and oil.

Consider what we have done in government contracts. We handled the thermoelectric refrigeration system for the nuclear submarine and we helped design the space kitchen for the 14-day orbital flight. For such products, there is only one customer—Uncle Sam.

As if these situations were not complex enough, in the last couple of years Whirlpool has come up with a controlled atmosphere food-processing discovery— TECTROL—which is used by producers, wholesalers, retailers, but not by homemakers. We're still trying to work out logical, profitable distribution systems for this one! From stationary storage in fruit belts, to containers aboard banana boats, to mobile trucks.

All these are the marketing patterns of just one company.

Think of the vast complications in a company like DuPont, which manufactures for dozens of different fields!

The only point of all this is to emphasize that this is a crazy mixed-up distribution world we live in. But mixed-up as it seems, one clear pattern emerges— our big customers are becoming bigger and ever more important; our major accounts are becoming regional and national accounts.

Chapter 10

PRACTICAL SALES RESEARCH

MOST modern sales executives are committed to the need for basing sales plans on facts rather than hunches. Hundreds of companies which once did a superficial sales-planning job have now set up marketing committees and have made a real effort to gather facts which will help them to determine: (a) What to sell; (b) where to sell; and (c) how to sell. Not that these companies had overlooked sales planning before, but they had never gone about it systematically or given it the amount of time and thought it warranted.

Today nearly all progressive companies have research operations under way. These divide themselves into: (a) Product research; (b) market research; (c) methods research; (d) consumer testing; and (e) record analysis. Some of these companies find it profitable to employ outside management-consulting organizations to do this work; others have set up special departments which operate in conjunction with a planning committee. All are finding out a great many things which management might have suspected, but never did very much about.

Major manufacturers have learned that product improvement and development of new products can lead to increased profits. That's why research and development funds constitute the largest appropriation in many corporations' annual budgets. Some companies estimate that 80 percent of their business today comes from products that weren't on the market 10 years ago.

The Benefits of Research

Sales managers who have invested in market research have found the benefits compare favorably with those obtained from laboratory or engineering research activities. A report of their findings to the American Management Association sums up as follows:

1. An organization is enabled to build its marketing structure on facts, thus

eliminating much of the inefficiency and waste incurred by distributive efforts based wholly on past experience, intuition, and pure chance.

2. Marketing executives and sales personnel, as well as employees generally, are more confident of the soundness of operations and activities which rest on the bedrock of a desirable and acceptable product or service, a favorable competitive position, and tested channels of distribution.

3. Major operating executives in the organization develop an understanding and appreciation of the product or service and of market methods in general, giving them a good reason to become "sales minded."

4. The findings of marketing research indicate the direction which technical research should take by providing concrete data on customer preference relating to composition, design, or other attributes of the product or service.

5. Marketing research fosters goodwill, both in the consumer market and in the industrial market. As the activities become more firmly rooted in scientific methodology and professional viewpoint, a cooperative spirit is introduced—between producer and consumer, between producers of complementary products, between producer and wholesaler, etc.—resulting in improved marketing methods for entire industries.

Modern management must increase the precision of its decisions; it must come to rely more and more on judgments made in the light of adequate facts, or it will find itself outmaneuvered by competition. This process requires a highly objective attitude. Vigor and decisiveness alone are not enough. They are still vital, of course, but they must be supplemented by an eagerness to get facts and a willingness to use them objectively. Unless and until that state of mind exists there is little reason for management to spend money on sales research.

An objective attitude may, and in fact should, be a critical and skeptical one. Uncritical acceptance of any set of statistics is not objectivity. One of the big problems of management is how to distinguish between competent and dependable research and those statistics which, as the quip has it, "tread a path of mathematical logic between an unwarranted assumption and a preconceived conclusion."

In the office of one successful marketing expert there appears this bit of business wisdom:

"Find out what people Like and do *more* of it. Find out what people Don't Like and do *less* of it."

Business is keenly aware of this situation, and a number of companies are setting up "proving grounds" for testing customer opinion and customer reactions.

Speaking to a convention of the National Retail Merchants Association, A. W. Zelomek, president of the International Statistical

Bureau, called attention to the fact that American business is involved in a marketing revolution that is in many respects as dramatic as the industrial revolution.

He said in part, "The superstructure of a marketing revolution is now being built more logically and more scientifically on the established foundation of the high-production potential created by the industrial revolution."

The Development of Motivation Research

There are motivational aspects in every purchase—the desire to gain comfort, economy, convenience, savings of effort, prestige, and other benefits. Skillful salesmen have long appealed to these desires, changing their approach and emphasis as conditions demanded. Promotional programs have been attuned to them, trying to match the motives of buyers in the markets at which they were aimed.

As far back as the 1920's, LaSalle Extension University, the Sales Training Institute, and others in sales training were promulgating the idea that certain buying motives are dominant in purchasing, and that the salesman should seek to learn, and to appeal to, these motives. These patterns preceded the work of the psychologists in the management field who, with the help of a few psychiatrists, sociologists, semanticists, and others concerned with the workings of the human mind, formulated Motivation Research. This they described as "the use of social-science techniques to discover and to evaluate the fundamental motivating forces or drives which impel human behavior in the marketplace."

In the late 1940's, some of the large companies, such as those in the automobile industry, adopted this clinical approach to isolate the particular buying motives that applied to their products. Through motivation research these companies determined that certain colors stimulated women in their purchases while others left them unresponsive; that often men who bought sports cars were trying to satisfy an unrecognized desire for raciness; and that those who bought black limousines wished to gain dignified respectability.

While the findings of motivation research in many cases have undoubtedly been entirely sound psychologically, the attempt to project them into every type of sales situation has led to a sort of "complicated oversimplification" which some sales and marketing executives have found difficult to accept.

Furthermore, the cost of nationwide surveys has been beyond the reach of some of the smaller corporations. An executive of a small company, which makes an accessory purchased by fleet owners for the comfort of their truck drivers, believed that his product was purchased as much for prestige as for comfort, and that if he could pinpoint the primary buying motive, he could better promote his product. He considered having a motivation research study made; but after investigation, he decided the cost was beyond his ability to afford. He reported:

"I could use the money more effectively in improving the comfort qualities of my product, and then letting the comfort and economy in use speak for themselves. These are sound buying motives that you can put your teeth in; prestige will take care of itself if the user tells his friends about satisfaction with the product."

To sum up, an understanding of why buyers buy is vital both in selling and in designing to sell; it is only the dangers inherent in the projective techniques of motivation research that have led to the rejection, in some quarters, of this type of market research. Perhaps the answer is in the factor of overconfidence: used as one of many possible tools in market research, motivation studies can be helpful and useful; used as the be-all-and-end-all of market analysis, this tool may lead to multimillion-dollar fiascos.

General Motors' Customer Research Work

General Motors Corporation maintains a highly effective customer-research staff. It is the job of the department to determine what people want in the motor cars of tomorrow. It is set up to get two types of reactions:

1. *Offhand Reactions:* What is the existing state of the public mind as regards a given proposition?

2. *Deliberative Reactions:* What are the reactions to the same proposition after the pros and cons are brought to the customer's attention?

"The former aims to take a cross section of public opinion just as it exists," an executive explained, "without reference to the soundness or the unsoundness of the matter. The latter type concerns itself not with existing attitudes but with what the attitudes will be after the motoring public—through experience or otherwise—has come into possession of the complete facts."

Use of Fact-Finding Questionnaires

The General Motors principal method of testing customer reactions is to use interesting questionnaires, usually prepared in booklet form with plenty of thumbnail illustrations. Recently, however, these general questionnaires have been supplemented with special questionnaires dealing with specific features of product design.

The purpose of customer research by General Motors is to give a true and complete reflection of consumer thinking. Consumer thinking does not follow the pattern of a functional organization chart. The consumer thinks in terms of net results—i.e., how he himself, as an individual, is affected.

Therefore, customer research, if it is to be fully effective, must approach its job from the same viewpoint—namely, a viewpoint from the outside looking in—observing and recording the composite or net effects of all specialized activities on the attitudes and actions of the buyer. Customer research, in its contacts with the consuming public, must lend an attentive ear to any and all kinds of reactions without reference to the more or less arbitrary boundary lines of departmental organization. Then, as a matter of routine procedure and working from effects back to causes, customer research should attempt to segregate and classify the reactions.

Proving the Product Against Competition

In competitive fields greater use is made of experimental testing. In addition to customer questioning, such as General Motors uses, definite comparisons with products now in use should be made to determine consumer preferences. This determines which characteristics are important and should, therefore, be played up, and which are unimportant and should be played down, in sales programs.

In the case of a packing company, tests showed that improvements were necessary in the color, texture, and flavor of the product; these improvements not only reduced its production cost but caused the sales of the improved product to increase rapidly. In another case, tenderness proved to be the dominant consideration while flavor was secondary, although of much importance. However, it seemed practically impossible, at first, to develop a tender product without sacrificing flavor. Later, consumer tests showed that this difficult task had been accomplished to the extent that consumers preferred this company's product on the scores of both tenderness and flavor, and subsequent sales amply justified these measurements.

In a third case, rather ingenious tests were made to learn whether consumers preferred a transparent colorless or a colored wrapper around a product. The colorless wrapper was chosen because the colors distorted the product's natural appearance. On another product, of course, the choice might have been entirely different. Similarly, other products and other product packages have been compared and the information obtained has been most helpful. These studies reveal the gradual changes taking place in consumer tastes and fancies, and enable the company's chemists and production managers to design new products and to modify those already being marketed so as to satisfy consumer demand more completely.

Sometimes this information is obtained by comparison of products at group meetings of consumers, sometimes by family tests, and sometimes by illustrated questionnaires handled by mail. To obtain reliable results from consumer product testing there are a number of technical considerations and safeguards, such as: The selection of testing groups; the avoidance of bias within groups; the comparative advantages of specific and general questions; the proper formulation of inquiries; the proper averaging of people's sense perceptions; control of physical surroundings, including the relationship of light to color; the position of products observed; and many others. All of these should be handled by trained and experienced workers possessing a high degree of imagination.

Suggestions for Surveys

The value of any consumer survey is in proportion to the honesty with which it was made. The bad odor sometimes attached to surveys can be traced to an experience the sales manager had with some survey made to prove a point rather than to chart a condition. The following suggestions may prove helpful in conducting a consumer market study or survey:

1. START OFF WITH A "KNOW-NOTHING" ATTITUDE. This will give you a clear, fresh approach, and such an approach is necessary in order to avoid perverted results.

2. CONDUCT SURVEY TO LEARN—NOT PROVE. If the basic idea behind your survey is to produce sales material, it is best that you forget the whole thing. You will get plenty of good sales material as a by-product of an objective survey.

3. AVOID PRECONCEIVED IDEAS OF RESULTS. If you already know the answers, why make the survey? No honest survey will perfectly follow the pattern you *think* it will take, so don't warp the results by striving to have them parallel your unwarranted conclusions.

4. STRIVE FOR ABSOLUTE ACCURACY. You won't achieve it—no one ever did, but the only way to approach perfection is to make perfection your aim.

5. APPLY STIFF ACCURACY TESTS TO BOTH DESIRABLE AND UNDESIRABLE RESULTS. It is just as easy to go wrong in one direction as another, so either test everything from all angles or let the chips fall where they may.

6. Don't Hide Unpleasant Results—Tell the Whole Truth. It is surprising how much will be added to the believability of your report if you include those few embarrassing results.

7. Use a Scientifically Accurate Sample—There's no Safety in Numbers. Certainly, get an ample number of reports, but most important, the people interviewed must be typically representative of the whole.

8. Include Questions to Check Against Known Facts. This is the best method of testing the accuracy of your sample. When your survey results on these questions parallel recognized statistics such as U.S. Census, you may be sure your sample is both adequate and accurate.

9. Avoid Complicated, Unexplainable Methods. If the basic problem behind your survey is so complex that a complicated method is necessary, call in an outside organization to do the job.

10. Explain Method Fully in All Published Reports. Make certain that you cover the five "W's"—who, what, when, where, and why. Who made the survey, what it's about, when it was made, where it was made, and why it was made. These five things are just as important as your general statements of *how* it was made.

11. Point Out Any Weaknesses or Limitations in Your Method. There is no perfect method, so be sure you enumerate those imperfections. The recipient is just as likely to jump to conclusions as you, so prevent such suicidal leaps by plainly stating all limitations.

12. State Sources Clearly for All Outside Information Used. Some answers can be better qualified if correlated with outside statistical material. Label every item of this type so it won't be confused with survey results.

13. Don't Extend Results to Market Size Unless You Definitely State the Size of Your Sample. Preferably, don't extend results at all, but if you do, make certain that everyone understands how much you have extended them.

14. Don't Try to Learn Too Much from Too Few Reports. Circumstances can affect individual answers, so protect yourself by avoiding conclusions from too few reports. The law of averages cannot function if cramped in space and numbers.

15. Avoid Basing Percentages or Extensions on Small Numbers. An absolute minimum in this respect is 100 reports, because, on anything less, one report will make a difference of more than 1 percent.

16. Keep Your Sales Story Divorced from Your Statistical Report. The recipient is certain to be more interested in your statistics than in your sales story. Cash in on this interest by serving him a pure diet, ungarnished by selling material.

17. Keep Report Brief, with More Details Available on Request. An immense mass of complicated statistics cannot be digested at one sitting, so breeze through it and leave those detailed cross-checks for a future call back. You are most certain to be invited to return.

Research Approach to Selective Selling

Next in importance to knowing what customers want to buy, so that you can more effectively supply their needs, is determining the most profitable selling outlets. Many companies maintain sales-costing systems. In addition to knowing the total cost of sales by products and territories, they know the actual out-of-pocket expense for selling each customer. This provides much factual information of value in establishing discounts, as well as planning future sales activities.

In a study of the operations of a wholesale druggist it was found that 64 percent of his customers (those whose annual purchases were $100 and less) accounted for less than 2 percent of his sales volume. There was an allocated expense of 200 percent of sales in serving those customers whose annual purchases were under $10, and the cost of serving customers whose annual purchases were between $10 and $100 amounted to 59 percent. The average expense for the business as a whole was 16 percent.

A paint distributor analyzed the profitableness of orders by size groups, and found that 75 percent of all his orders were handled at a loss. The remaining 25 percent of his orders, responsible for 78 percent of his sales volume, earned enough profits to offset this loss and to show a profit for the business as a whole.

A meat packer, in studying the business of his wholesale branches,

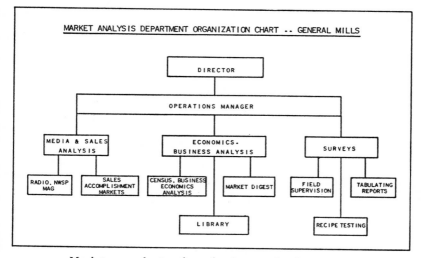

Market research operations of a large national advertiser.

found that 24 percent of his salesmen's personal calls, 26 percent of their telephone calls, and 16 percent of the total number of his deliveries were devoted toward obtaining only 2 percent of the total sales.

Sales managers are scrutinizing each account carefully. They want to know what a customer buys; but more important they want to know what the company has made or lost on that customer in recent months. They want to know the cost of the salesman's time spent on the account, service charges, delivery charges, and other expense ordinarily concealed in lump figures.

Here are some facts brought to light by one company as a result of an account audit. It provided information which the management was able to use effectively in recasting sales territories when salesmen were released from service:

1. Between one-third and one-half of the customers sold in the usual way by competing wholesalers are unprofitable.

2. These unprofitable customers buy only from 5 percent to 15 percent of the individual jobber's volume.

3. The wider margin of gross profit on sales to these customers, arising from higher prices on the small quantities purchased, is not sufficient to cover out-of-pocket expenses.

4. The high rate of expense of serving them is due to the disparity between the volume obtained from large and small buyers and the various kinds of effort expended upon them. Large customers often buy 20 times the volume of small customers, but require only two or three times as many interviews, telephone calls, deliveries, and the like.

5. A shift in effort from unprofitable to profitable types of customers may increase the typical jobber's net profits as much as $10,000 annually if properly carried out.

6. Such a shift in effort must be made according to the needs of each sales territory because unprofitable customers range from 5 percent to 70 percent of the total customers on different routes.

7. By a simple extension of the method, the comparative selling expenses for different products may be obtained, sometimes revealing that certain products cost three times as much to distribute as others in the same line and yield much smaller profits, notwithstanding greater markups.

In food wholesaling, such audits led to the establishment of cash-and-carry depots, where small retailers could share in part of the savings achieved by eliminating deliveries, billing, etc.

Market Research in Small Cities

In a market research program covering small cities the manufacturer should first select the cities, according to studies of buying power, retail outlets available, type of stores, and trading area. This can be done through a study of marketing statistics, available from the U.S. Department of Commerce and business publications.

A number of manufacturers have found it profitable to close many small, weak accounts, where proper merchandising effort is lacking. They have found it far more profitable to select one strong dealer, and help him, than to have three weak dealers none of whom buy enough to make the salesman's visit profitable.

Modern sales management requires top management to make many decisions which were once left to salesmen. Many companies once permitted salesmen to lay out their own routes, and to select the stores to be sold. Today there is less and less of this haphazard selling. Such selling is one of the reasons why so many manufacturers have abandoned the small-city and small-town field.

To profitably sell in small towns, for most manufacturers, means that there must first be a basic list of desirable towns, and then a similarly basic list of desirable dealers.

From this list, distribution is obtained through the dealers who will agree to live up to certain requirements. Each manufacturer must know that it is possible for the dealer to meet the requirements to which he is held. This knowledge usually comes only after careful tests under controlled conditions, or from long experience.

Every town offers special possibilities to certain manufacturers. A school town, with several thousand students, offers a market for special types of merchandise. A railroad-shop town means sales of certain kinds of work clothing. A farm town which has no industry to speak of means sales of certain types of clothing as well as farm implements and supplies.

Similarity in size does not always mean similarity in buying taste and sales possibilities. Schools, industries, mines, railroad activities, tourist trade, farm conditions, proximity to larger cities, weather, and many other factors create many differences in sales possibilities and these factors all need to be known and recorded on sales records of manufacturers who want their product sold in highest possible volume.

Westinghouse Territorial Blueprint

Westinghouse Electric Corporation makes, periodically, a blueprint of each sales territory which it uses advantageously. Westinghouse normally sells the bulk of its products through wholesalers, distributors, or other sales outlets. In order to determine accurately the sales value of these distributors, it is necessary to work through them to obtain the information needed about the customers.

The information is arranged on punched cards which can be run through a tabulating machine. In addition to the customer's name, address, and annual purchases, the card gives his: (a) Industry classification; (b) location of buying control; (c) billings of Westinghouse products through local jobbers and also direct; (d) number of calls scheduled for salesman; (e) number of calls made by salesman.

By analyzing these cards either by territory, by industrial classification, by jobber, or by salesman, information of vital importance may be quickly obtained. Here are a few points upon which light is thrown:

Customer assignment to salesman.

Which salesmen are overloaded or underloaded.

Whether additional or less manpower is needed.

Whether a salesman is located in the right spot.

Whether a salesman is devoting his time to customers from whom sales effort will yield a maximum return.

Sales performance of an individual salesman.

Obviously, a detailed territorial study of this sort requires considerable time. It is also expensive. But it is possible to get the cooperation of distributors, and the study provides data of tremendous value in sales planning.

"Careful selection of customers and proper allocation of marketing effort would reduce delivered costs and enable expanded sales volume to take place through reduced prices," said Donald R. S. Cowan, in an address to the Association of National Advertisers. "The study of the best outlets for particular products would eliminate some costly, haphazard selling. Consideration of whether a product should be marketed by itself or as one of a group is also important in endeavoring to reduce marketing costs. Reduced marketing costs are just as important as reduced factory costs in making possible lower prices and expanded sales volumes.

"It should be borne in mind that the great masses of people are in the low-income brackets, and if the prices of luxury goods now sold mainly to the small high-income market can be reduced, their sales volume to the huge mass market can be multiplied many times. Similarly, the marginal buyers of industrial goods can be induced to buy larger quantities. Analysis of selling and advertising methods may enable the choice of those which will accomplish a given task with least expense." Every progressive company does a certain amount of research work, if only to study the reports of salesmen. But it should be organized.

Attitude Studies and How to Make Them

Another type of research which can profitably be conducted is "opinion checks" to determine negative situations in the current operations of a business. These may have to do with a wide range of activities, any or all of which might have a bearing on the sales operations of the company.

Appraisals of the attitudes of customers, dealers, salesmen, or employees require intelligent interpretation and for that reason the work should be assigned to a man of experience. It cannot be done effectively by the run-of-paper research worker. In the first place he lacks the background for skillful interviewing; in the second place he lacks the judgment necessary to weigh properly information obtained from the persons questioned.

Most companies using attitude studies to help formulate sales policies emphasize the importance of the indirect approach. The most successful method is to employ an executive who has a flair for interviewing.

A skillful interviewer will quickly determine whether a man is sincere or not, and be guided accordingly in making his report. He should also have enough experience in business to recognize men whose opinions and suggestions are valuable and those who are not sound thinkers. Very often the best suggestions and the most important opinions come from relatively young men who have a fresh point of view toward so-called traditional policies.

In a changing world it is essential to get these new viewpoints, as they often provide the peg on which an important shift in policy may be hung.

Testing New Products

In recent years some companies have tested proposed products by trade clinics to determine accurately which qualities the consumer prefers; what price will give the largest sales volume; and what name and package are most likely to "click." This method of pre-determining salability will be even more widely used in the future than in the past. However, to be worthwhile, such tests must be representative of the whole market, and not merely a section or a portion of the market.

Another drawback is that a use test does not tell much about sales possibilities. Many an intrinsically worthy product fails to achieve recognition merely because it is hard to sell, or because it does not have "shelf appeal" or because the price (at least at first) seems high. Use tests do not always reveal these obstacles.

As an alternative, actual sales tests might seem to be the answer. Properly conducted, they can be of great help. This means that they must be carried on under conditions as nearly normal as possible—which rules out tests in stores in the manufacturer's home town, for example.

A New-Product Policy

Experience shows clearly that, to be successful, a new product must fit into the existing company. In developing a sound policy, the human and physical assets and liabilities of the company should be listed and studied.

A partial checklist of important areas is given below. It suggests the kinds of topics which are significant in deciding what kinds of products can be logically considered. Lack of strength in a given area is not necessarily a criticism of current operation. It is rather a reason for avoiding products which depend for success on strength in that particular area.

1. Desires of stockholders and directors.

2. Management abilities, interests, and experience.

3. Technical skills.

4. Types of current production operations.

5. Quality and availability of labor.

6. Sales and distribution arrangements and background.

7. Plant location with respect to markets.

8. Reputation with consumers.

9. Product philosophy (specialty or mass production, high or low price ranges, and so on).

10. Financial condition.

11. Raw materials—availability, cost, location.

12. Transportation.

13. Site utilization.

14. Special competitive factors.

Through a searching, objective study based on this sort of check-list you can uncover a number of limitations on the kinds of new products that you should consider at all. For example, a company with an outstanding reputation for high-quality specialties would be ill-advised to get into the mass production of a cheap item. A well-established and successful sales organization suggests that new products be suited to this strong resource.

Sometimes, a study will suggest that a company should put its present operations in order before considering any new activities at all. Diversification is not a substitute for good day-to-day man-agement of the existing business.

Getting Customer Reactions

There are many ways of submitting samples to consumers for tests. Obviously, the methods used must be adapted to the particular item in question. In any case, it should be remembered:

1. That no one type of test will give all the answers.

2. That it is desirable to test only one variable at a time; hence a series of lesser experiments is preferable to one far-flung effort.

3. That conditions of the test should be as natural as possible, and that respondents should be judged by their acts, rather than by their opinions.

4. That questions having to do with price are likely to elicit un-reliable replies.

5. Provide for a control group. Group A cannot be judged except in comparison with some other group (group B). Moreover, in order to compare group A with group B it may be necessary to compare each of them with a third group (group C).

6. Submit alternative choices rather than a single choice. When asked about a single product, with no alternative choice, reactions all tend to be favorable.

7. In testing a new product, pair it with the nearest comparable, best-known and most successful competitive product.

Preparation of samples for pretests must be done with the ut-most care. It is not enough merely to describe the new product and ask the test consumer whether she would like it. Such hypothetical judgments are unreliable. The product should be actually made up and packaged so that the consumer can see it and try it out under realistic conditions. If the inherent quality of the product is to be tested, the package should be unbranded, carrying merely an identification label and a guaranty of purity, so that questions of brand prestige will be eliminated.

American Can's Strategy

In discussing the development of new products in his company, W. F. May, chairman of the American Can Company, stated:

"The flow of new products is crucial to the future of our company. Only a few new ideas actually develop into large-volume money-makers. That makes it doubly important that we keep the hopper full of new ideas to try out. An obvious source of such ideas is research: Technical information leading to technical breakthroughs that open up for us the prospect of some new opportunity. We are spending more than $20 million annually on research, and that is a big help when it comes to keeping that hopper full.

"But significantly there is another source of these ideas—the marketing organization. Our marketing people must have sandpapered fingertips, and keep them on the pulse of the market— looking for improvements that the customer himself might not have been able to think of, or to put into words. Those perceptions of marketing—and we hope they are keen perceptions—are transmitted to the research organization, so that, in many instances, the market determines the research, instead of the research trying to determine the market."

Campbell Soup Policy

W. B. Murphy, president of Campbell Soup Company, outlines his company's new-product and product-testing policies as follows:

"To illustrate the impact of new products—the average supermarket today carries 6,000 items versus 3,000 10 years ago, and versus 500 for the grocery store of 30 years ago. Today's average supermarket operator is offered each week about 40 items, of which he buys 15 and discontinues about five items previously stocked, for a net addition of 10. You will gather from this that the number of items the store will handle will either continue to increase in the future or there will be a small rate of acceptance or more items dropped. I suspect the last two alternates will take place since the total number cannot go on up, ad infinitum.

"Now as to our procedure. First, we start with an idea. Run-of-the-mill ideas are plentiful, but good ideas are scarce. The ideas may come from almost anywhere. The items may be pure invention

—there have been several in our business—for example, condensed soups, V-8, the TV dinner, several new soups, several new bean products, frozen puff pastry, homemade-quality bread for general use, plus others. The successful blue-chip company generally has a number of these in its history.

"While new ideas may originate almost anywhere, we find mostly they come from within the organization and they come from hard and logical thinking and skillful observation—in other words, from good brains trained to our business.

"A promising product idea must be practical, a sound value, attractive to the buyer, and a source of reasonable profit.

"There are three steps in new-product development once an idea is conceived. These are the laboratory stage, the pilot-plant stage, and the major test.

"The laboratory and pilot-plant experiments are paralleled by a series of investigations of ingredients required—processes and facilities needed—packaging design and experiments—cost calculation—marketing planning. If the pilot-plant work is promising, a major marketing test is begun.

"This careful testing program is needed to avoid costly mistakes. It is important to make one's failures on a small scale for obvious reasons. During the test period so much is learned that sometimes a failure can be converted into a success by product or process revisions. We must watch out for the short, spectacularly successful test. Some products fade rapidly after a wonderful start.

"After all the cautioning about the need for thorough, step-by-step testing, there are times when it is imperative to break the rules and short-cut the ideal testing program. Sometimes new product ideas are judged to be so red-hot that we move to national marketing based on an overwhelmingly favorable consumer-panel test. Our frozen soups, introduced in 1954 and 1955, and barbecue beans, in 1960, are good examples of new ideas that were naturals that developed into successful national businesses almost overnight. The short-cut procedure has the advantage of gaining time over the 'me-too' competitor, but it's risky. Here we need a full measure of experience and cold-blooded objective judgment.

"First—timing is sometimes vitally important. Frozen dinners were test-marketed in 1946 and failed. About nine years later, Swanson introduced TV Brand frozen dinners with almost miraculous success. Apparently the consuming public was not quite ready for this product in the mid-forties. We could detect no other important reason for this contrasting result except timing.

PLAYING TO WIN

The law of the marketplace, like Darwin's theory of evolution, is change or perish. With the persistence of the scientist, we must probe for new concepts, new insights into consumer behavior, new marketing techniques. And with the courage of the explorer, we must be willing to turn from the old that is tarnishing to the new that sparkles with promise—whether it be marketing procedures, new products, or product improvements. There's a great difference between playing not to lose, and playing to win—at American Tobacco we play to win.

Robert B. Walker
President and chairman of the board
The American Tobacco Co.

Printers' Ink

"Second—a product preferred by only a minor proportion of the public can be an outstanding success. In the 1930's a consumer blind-product test showed tomato juice to be overwhelmingly favored over V-8, which is a blend of tomato juice with seven other vegetable juices. Nevertheless, V-8 is now a large volume product, growing each year, winning more and more consumers. Since we make both products, we can watch this performance with dispassion.

"Third—the company executive who looks on a new product idea too fondly, either because he thought it up or because it particularly appeals to him, must be especially careful to be objective. He must learn to laugh at his own ideas for many of them will be flops."

Mr. Murphy said that new products accounted for 57 percent of Campbell's sales increase of $342,000,000 in the last decade.

Speaking before the New York Society of Security Analysts, Mr. Murphy said: "When we acquired Swanson, there were only three TV dinners; now there are 28."

He also noted the success of the new Pepperidge Farm ready-to-serve soups and added that Pepperidge is introducing a new line of layer cakes. "This is a classic product and one which we believe will have a long life."

Quaker Oats Gambles

Before a single package of Life, Quaker Oats Co.'s ready-to-eat cereal, appeared on the shelves, the company had invested $7 million in the product, "the biggest risk in the company's history up to that time."

And before national distribution was achieved, "the gamble" had reached $11,000,000, writes Arthur F. Marquette in *Brands, Trademarks & Good Will*, a history of Quaker Oats Co.

"Management policy required any new product—cereal, cat food, or chemical—to pay its own way, to earn sufficient acceptance, market by market, to warrant further expansion.

"Thus the original budget for the new high-protein cereal was an unheard-of $5 million. When expenses passed $7 million, Quaker's management had begun to experience the facts of life about product introduction. When the total cost had crossed $11 million, even the most optimistic advocates of keeping up with the battle for survival on the supermarket shelf were appalled at the commitment Quaker had undertaken."

Mr. Marquette notes that "fortunately for everyone, the new cereal performed as hoped. It was an instant success. By the end of the first year it had achieved a significant share of the total national market for ready-to-eats and was returning a profit on the promotional investment."

Other Product Histories

Ralph L. Countryman, vice-president, American Bosch Sales Division, American Bosch Arma Corporation, described the 10-point program his company used to gather competitive data when planning to introduce a new product. This included: (1) thorough market investigation, (2) enlisting the sales force to ask customers "what's new in the field," (3) distributor inquiries—"the distributor is usually a forum of what's new in product development," (4) show and convention participation, especially at cocktail parties and in headquarters suites, (5) financial and business publications, (6) clipping bureaus, (7) trade and government publications, (8) competitive catalogs and promotional material, (9) becoming a stockholder in the competitor company and (10) if possible, buying the competitive product.

J. K. Duncan, new-product planning director of S. C. Johnson & Son, recently stated that his company believes that it is the screening of ideas, not the generation of the ideas themselves, that is really the difficult part of new-product planning.

One of the many criteria which determines the feasibility of a new product at S. C. Johnson is whether or not such a product can be easily promoted on TV. As a company executive expressed it:

"We are a heavy buyer of television. We can't afford to buy magazines just for one product, because we don't buy enough magazines to qualify for discounts."

Thus, if a product did not lend itself naturally to TV promotion, this fact alone would weigh heavily against its being considered by the company.

The "Modified" Product

To capture some markets, a new product is often called for. But sometimes, altering an existing product is less risky than developing a totally new item. A modified product can be introduced more quickly and needs little investment, since it may well use the same basic equipment and assembly process as the original.

Sometimes a "new" product may simply be the result of a new process. The newest coffee-processing technique, known as freeze-drying, is the basis of a promotional battle being waged by General Foods Corporation and the Nestle Company, Inc. Both have been competing in test markets with rival brands of freeze-dried instant coffee, which is said to have the aroma and flavor of regularly ground coffee to a degree lacking in most other soluble coffees.

The freeze-drying process, through which water is removed from foods at below-freezing temperatures in a vacuum, has been known in Europe for some time. Its main use there has been for prolonging the freshness, or shelf-life, of dehydrated foods.

It is still too early to tell what effects the freeze-dried coffees will have on coffee-producing countries in the way of price or demands. But it is apparent that the sales stakes are high, since each company is reported to be spending $20 million on test marketing.

Advertising the New Product

No one knows how many thousands of new items and millions of dollars go into test marketing each year, but two things are certain: New-product test marketing is basic to the food business, and no one has come up with the best way of doing it. Manufacturers might spend as much as a quarter-million dollars in testing one item, may saturate a test market with newspaper, regional magazine, radio, and television advertising, flood the mails with samples and coupons, and offer retailers substantial discounts to stock the product and extra allowances for choice display space.

Supermarket executives, well aware that new products often carry a higher price tag than the old (aerosols and frozen foods, for example), grudgingly go along with the manufacturers, hoping to make enough extra profit on the introductory discounts to make up for the extra time and handling. To a chain-store buyer, the most important single factor in a manufacturer's new-product test-marketing program is the advertising campaign.

For new-product introductions, television is usually ranked as the most effective medium, followed by newspaper advertising, with coupons, coupon mailing, sampling, and newspaper advertising without coupons. Regional and local editions of national magazines are relatively new and not yet widely accepted as test-marketing media. But their greater use seems likely, for many test markets extend beyond the coverage of the central city's newspapers and radio and TV stations, and the chains want advertising in all the communities in which they stock the new product.

Heavy advertising is basic to traditional test marketing, in which a new product is introduced on a grand scale with discounts to grocers and consumers and, hopefully, distribution in every store in the test area. But test marketing is also done more quietly and selectively, especially through food brokers. And market research firms now work in conjunction with the manufacturers' salesmen or, in many instances, handle everything—warehousing, distribution, auditing, and cleanup—except the advertising.

Many chains question the value of heavy advertising in test marketing. "Almost any item will move if advertised enough," says Howard Spaulding, chief grocery buyer for the four-store Cooperative Trading group of Waukegan, Illinois. "It is better to use normal advertising and promotion and a market-survey firm." A merchandising vice-president for a nationwide chain of more than 100 stores agrees: "You can get a customer to try anything if you make the offer attractive enough. This is why Kellogg's freeze-dried fruit cereals did so well in test marketing and fell flat afterwards. Advertising should not be so extensive that it distorts the results."

To reduce distortions, manufacturers are turning to market-research firms, of which there are now between 300 and 500. Methods vary among the firms, naturally, and may consist of any combination of consumer diaries, in-store audits, and consumer interviews. For example, Mary O. Young & Associates of Syracuse, one of the largest field-survey firms in the East, first makes a two- or three-month survey of a product category in selected stores to determine shares of market and sales trends. It then introduces the new product on consignment, handling all warehousing, delivery, in-store stocking, displaying, pricing, point-of-purchase promotion, and take-back. Monthly or weekly audits are made during the test period—which may range between six and 24 months—and auditing continues for a time after the product is withdrawn.

The Rainpiper Campaign

Callo and Carroll, Inc., was asked by its client, Aberdeen Manufacturing Co., to test market Aberdeen's Rainpiper, a one-piece umbrella frame molded of polypropylene. There was no question that Aberdeen had come up with a new idea in umbrellas. As described in *Printers' Ink:*

"Two immediate hurdles the company had to face were the traditional place the umbrella occupies as a utilitarian object and the fact that Aberdeen does not make the umbrella, only the frame. The frame, however, would be marketed under a brand name, Rainpiper."

Early discussions turned up the fact that a major characteristic of the umbrella business today is that there is no identity by brand. Another big point was that some buyers look at the umbrella as a bread-and-butter item that sells only because of utility while others see it as an item of fashion.

Goals for the overall marketing approach were set not only to establish a market for a new product but also to increase the total market for women's umbrellas.

Rainpiper created totally new possibilities for umbrella design and promotion. For example, an umbrella could be fashion coordinated for fine stores.

A second objective was to find the most effective, reasonable level of pricing for the item. In the markets used, the umbrella was priced at from $5 to $8.

Third and most important, consumer reaction to the new product, or rather to the new technological contribution, with attendant esthetic change, had to be tested.

Portland, Ore., and Hartford, Conn., were selected as the test areas. Both are fairly urban locations with populations in excess of 250,000. Both have annual rainfalls of 30 to 40 inches.

Results of the test were highly encouraging in both markets. The product was well accepted by women. The primary focus of female reaction was on the fashion and style side.

Nothing definitive was determined about colors. The matching units were as popular as those of contrasting colors.

The most practical price was found to be in the $6 to $7 range. The item sold as effectively with display alone as it did with a live demonstration.

Many Question Test Marketing

But test marketing is not bringing the right products to the right people fast enough. It now takes about two years and at least $500,000 to test a new consumer product to the point where it is ready for national distribution.

The things that can happen in two years are many and forceful. Consumers change their buying habits, competitors introduce similar, or better, products; and packaging advances can affect retailing practices.

Yet the idea persists that test marketing is conducted in a vacuum. There is the erroneous idea that findings gleaned today in one, two, or more test markets are indicative of what will happen to a product in national distribution two years from now. There are just too many variables for that to be true.

In a growing number of companies and agencies, the whole concept of test marketing and new-product introductions is undergoing a shakedown. The reason is that, in some cases, marketing generalists, using experience and intuition, have introduced products cheaply, quickly, and successfully with a minimum of advice from researchers. And there have been too many cases where complex testing procedures have not only slowed down new-product introductions but have also produced inaccurate indications.

"Test marketing historically has not proved to be a dependable ally of the innovator, whether he be an advertiser or an agency. The tests have usually been difficult to arrange, costly to execute, and suffer the added penalty of tipping off competition to the innovator's advance plans. More damaging has been their proclivity to produce equivocal or uncertain results."

That observation comes from Frank Stanton, senior vice-president and director of information management, Benton & Bowles. B&B is among the top three or four agencies in new-product introductions.

In a similar vein, J. K. Duncan, director, new product planning, S. C. Johnson & Son, told an American Marketing Association audience in Chicago that:

"Test marketing these days is passé. It takes too long, costs too much money, and delivers too little in the way of information. More often than not, what is referred to as 'test marketing' today is really the regional rollout of a product that the company is pretty sure will make the grade."

The chief executive of a large container-manufacturing company stated:

"When we put a product into test markets, we are aware that

BORDEN'S TEST MARKETS

The Borden Company has a number of divisions and is constantly test marketing new products from each of them. The following cities are among those used for testing its new food items:

Albany	Harrisburg	Portland, Ore.
Atlanta	Hartford	Providence
Buffalo	Houston	Rochester
Columbus	Knoxville	Sacramento
Dallas	Los Angeles	San Diego
Dayton	Miami	Scranton
Erie	Philadelphia	Syracuse
Fort Wayne	Phoenix	Utica
Grand Rapids		

there can be pitfalls in this approach. Some of the so-called typical markets—South Bend and Indianapolis are among them—have been so overworked as test markets that they are now, in fact, atypical.

"When people become too sophisticated about the test-marketing techniques, they just aren't very reliable indicators any more—they are more like the test marketers themselves. And we take into account, too, the possibility that the competition occasionally might step in and buy up the product just to confuse the results. On the whole, though, we set a good deal of store in test marketing as a helpful indication."

Some Famous Failures

Big companies have their share of failures when it comes to launching new products. Campbell Soup Company discontinued its line of eight Red Kettle dry soup mixes after spending more than $10 million to advertise them, according to *Advertising Age*.

Red Kettle soups were introduced nationally behind a $5-million advertising effort, six months after Corn Products introduced its own dry soup mixes under the Knorr label. Despite lavish expenditures by both companies, neither brand managed to carve out much of a share of the $55- to $65-million dry-soup market, dominated by Thomas J. Lipton Inc., whose share is now approaching 60 percent.

Corn Products' president A. N. McFarlane admitted that the company had "stubbed its toe" on Knorr and that it was no longer producing the soups in the U.S. but was importing them from Europe.

How did Lipton withstand the challenge? "We pushed no panic button," Oscar J. Nickel, director of corporate advertising and public relations, said. "We developed a strategy and we stuck to it. If a company has a good franchise to start with—which we always have had—it's able to withstand the onslaughts of competition."

Edward L. McMenamy, Lipton's vice-president of advertising, observed, "You've got to start with the basic product. A housewife doesn't remember promises about a glorious trip to Moscow or Finland," he said, parodying the Knorr soup ads. "We offered them an excellent value and taste sensations the other products just didn't have."

Lipton drastically increased the number of varieties in its soup line, upped its price from 29 cents to 39 cents, and increased its advertising.

Orienting to the Market

There are many companies in which product planning is not deemed to be solely the province of marketing. It is sometimes done by committees; sometimes the activity is found in research and development; sometimes it is a staff function reporting directly to the president. But in the General Electric Company, reports Dr. Arnold I. Corbin, "product planning is a marketing function because its job is to ferret out, working closely with marketing research, new market opportunities for products and processes, and to provide functional specifications for them to the engineering and research people, who, in turn, produce the design for the factory.

"The marketing manager decides how many will be produced of each of the products in his line. He determines the number needed for a particular period. He schedules production because he is closest to the market and its requirements. Marketing considerations govern. The other executives in this company, whether they be in production, engineering, finance, legal, or anywhere else, are imbued with the same philosophy: the customer is king. This is what is meant by a company that is marketing-minded."

In *Marketing Management in Action*, Victor P. Buell emphasizes the role which is being played by marketing managers in determining the company's product line. This is certainly in keeping with the marketing concept that new products should satisfy customer needs and wants. The marketing manager must establish an effective working relationship with the research director to improve the company's batting average for successful new-product introductions.

Dun & Bradstreet has developed a computer-based Marketing Information System designed to aid in the solution of marketing problems. Its applications include:

Sales performance evaluation, sales quotas, customer profiles, realignment of sales territories, distribution analysis, and plant location. In addition, information is available in magnetic tape form on 40,000 corporations with capital and surplus over a half-million dollars; 35,000 plants employing 20 persons or more; and a census of manufacturing plants, regardless of size, with over 300,000 listings.

Test Territories

Tests are often used to determine the saturation point of a territory, the effect upon dealer sales of inadequate stocks in the hands of distributors, value of advertising in specific types of media, etc. For example, the Silex Company wanted to find out what the probable demand for its products would be if the "pipe lines" of distribution were filled so that anyone wishing to buy a Silex could get it at his dealer's. This was at a time when production was allocated. So Peoria, Illinois, was used for a test. For a given period Peoria distributors were shipped all the coffee brewers they thought they could sell, provided only that they agreed to cooperate in local newspaper advertising. Distributors' salesmen called on all dealers in the Peoria area, got their cooperation, and the Silex market absorption test was under way.

The test proved several things: (1) That the saturation point was nearly 1,760 percent of past sales; (2) that distributors, however good they may be, cannot be depended upon to maintain maximum distribution in a given territory; (3) that the manufacturer through his own trained and controlled salesmen must carry the ball for his distributors. These findings were of great value to the Silex Company (now Proctor-Silex), after the "pent-up" demand for electrical goods had been satisfied by the special promotion.

While "paper" research in connection with evaluating the sales possibilities of a new product is useful, mail questionnaires alone are inadequate; they should be supplemented by retailers in picked locations to help with the testing.

A confectionery company pretests a new product in two different sections of the country; one in New England and one outside New England. In Springfield, Massachusetts, for example, the company has 25 retail outlets in all sections of the city. It goes to them and says: "We have a new item we want to test out. We'll give you this product until you finish the test. We'll give you all you sell of it and you can keep the profit, but in return we want you to keep track of some information. We want to know: The number of initial sales; the number of repeat sales; how soon the repeat sales took place and how many times repeat sales were made during the pretest period." The company then compiles the results, and if it gets a favorable-response majority, it feels fairly safe in launching the product for general sale in all territories.

Tests of this sort yield valuable data for determining marketing policies, and the information resulting can be most effectively used in trade promotional literature and trade-paper advertising as well. Being able to point to specific sales by actual dealers during the test is more convincing than generalities.

Use and Misuse of Questionnaires

It is increasingly difficult to get people to answer questionnaires. Whereas 30 to 40 percent was once considered a good return from questionnaires, the average return has now sunk to 10 percent according to one direct-mail expert.

To get the best returns on questionnaires there should be some definite gain to the person who must fill it out. This should be set forth in the first paragraph of the letter. It may be an offer to send a summary of the returns which would be of value to him; it may be a booklet or a key ring or some other useful personal item. One company reports excellent returns by enclosing a utility booklet and stating in the letter that it was being sent in advance since filling out the blank would take two or three minutes of his time.

Another sales organization, which continuously checks user attitudes, reports exceptionally good returns from questionnaires used to "open up" a new mailing list. In fact, this company has adopted the rule of always conditioning a new mailing list, or a new group of names, with a questionnaire mailing asking questions designed to accomplish a double purpose:

1. Condition the person for the sales effort to follow.

2. Obtain group reactions to the company's present policies, sales methods, and services.

An eastern publishing company which makes an extensive use of questionnaires in its editorial work reports that it never asks a reader to answer more than 10 questions at one time. The editorial director of these papers, who is very close to his readers, contends that detailed and exhaustive questionnaires used by market-research men usually go directly into the wastepaper basket.

It is this editor's experience that, if properly and courteously approached, most men will take a minute or two to jot down answers to a few carefully selected questions; however, he also warns that the questions should be set up so that accurate answers will be obtained and not just "yes" or "no," which do not provide any shade of opinion.

Another market-research man reports good returns when the questions are multilithed on the back of the letter of transmittal, thus saving paper and getting the proposition before the executive in a more concise manner.

A manufacturer of supplies sold to banks uses a questionnaire to determine when the bank will be in the market for certain products. This proved a hard nut to crack. The answer was found by using a letter automatically typed, with appropriate changes in each letter, and making a carbon of each letter. After 10 days, in case the first letter was not answered, the carbon copy was attached to another questionnaire and used as a followup. A very brief note asking for the courtesy of a reply, attached to the carbon copy, did the trick.

A company selling a line of merchandise through dealers had occasion to ask them some questions concerning dealer store layout and the type of sales helps they could use.

The first test of the questionnaire was disappointing. The "sample poll" was inadequate to form accurate conclusions. So another test was made with a partially filled out questionnaire. The dealer's name, his annual purchases for three years back, his credit key, and the name of the salesman who called on him were typed on each questionnaire before it was sent out, instead of after it was received as had been the plan.

A brief letter of transmittal explained that in order to provide the type of sales promotional material dealers could most effectively use, certain information was required by the sales promotion department. Would the dealer please cooperate by completing the enclosed partially filled out questionnaire, after checking it carefully to make sure that the names and addresses were correct?

The average dealer does not have an accurate picture of how much business he gives any particular source of supply over a three-year period, so his interest is aroused. An objection to the plan is that the dealer may think he is giving the company too much business, but this company has not found this to be true. On the contrary, many comments were received from dealers stating they were surprised to see that the orders they had been giving the company showed a falling off, but they would try to increase them next year.

Followup Pays

In his book, *A Procedure for Securing Returns to Mail Questionnaires,* Stanley S. Robin describes a program to secure returns to mail questionnaires which are comparable in quantity to returns obtained by interviews. The steps include:

1. A prequestionnaire letter, intended to pave the way for a sympathetic reception of the questionnaire.

2. The questionnaire itself, a cover letter, and a stamped, self-addressed envelope.

3. First followup letter, reminding the subject of lack of response and mentioning that a stamped envelope was supplied.

4. Second followup letter, along with another copy of the questionnaire and another stamped envelope.

5. Third followup letter, again emphasizing the stamped envelopes sent previously, and inviting the respondent to get in touch with the investigator for another questionnaire if needed.

The results of such a thorough procedure are impressive. Out of nine cases, four had 90 percent or greater response, four more had 80 percent or greater response, and the remaining one had 66 percent response rate.

Practical Uses of Sales Research

In outlining the practical uses of an advanced type of sales research, A. C. Nielsen, a national authority, speaking before the Association of National Advertisers, urged members to be armed with a reliable means of: (1) Detecting each change promptly; (2) determining its importance, its direction, and its rate of change; (3) determining the best means of altering marketing methods, tactics, and policies to meet changed conditions; (4) determining, promptly and accurately, whether each alteration actually does meet the new conditions successfully.

Fourteen practical uses for this type of sales research were outlined, as quoted below. The "index" referred to is the Nielsen Food and Drug Index. These 14 uses, presented in brief from the experiences of nearly a hundred national advertisers offer a guide for many companies in planning to take advantage of changing conditions:

1. Ensuring profitable distribution of advertising and merchandising effort by territories, city-sizes, store-sizes, consumer income levels, etc. This is possible because the *index* reveals the total available market (all brands combined) in each subdivision of the national market, and shows your competitive strength in each subdivision.

2. Ensuring profitable *seasonal* distribution of advertising and merchandising effort. This follows from the fact that the index reveals the true seasonal fluctuations in sales (all brands combined) at the point of consumption. For many products, the *consumer* seasonal curve differs widely from the *factory* seasonal curve.

3. Getting deals properly sized, priced, timed, and distributed. A vast amount of light has been shed on this complex subject, because the index has revealed the *true* effect (i. e., the *consumer* sales increases) resulting from dealer loading operations conducted by hundreds of manufacturers.

4. Detecting profitable or unprofitable advertising appeals, media, or methods. The true effect (on consumers) of every advertising campaign is recorded accurately by the *index*.

5. Detecting profitable or unprofitable merchandising methods, by showing the consumer sales trend following deals, combination offers, premium offers, couponing, sampling, display work, price changes, package changes, etc.

6. Evaluating the effectiveness of the advertising and promotional methods being used either nationally or on a regional basis.

7. Providing *advance* warning of your sales declines or of sales gains by your advertised competitors or by unadvertised brands. Consumer sales usually show a decline or a gain many months before the change is revealed conclusively by *factory* sales records. Time is vital in such cases.

8. Revealing weak spots, either nationally or in any subdivision of the market, e. g., weaknesses in competitive sales position, distribution, inventories, stock-turn, out-of-stock percentages, prices, gross profit, displays, special sales, etc. If, following the detection of any weak spot, an effort is made to improve the situation, the *index* reveals, promptly and accurately, the *result* of the effort.

9. Revealing need for a change in product, for a new product, or for a new size or type of package. Any trend away from your *type* of product is detected instantly. And if you decide to add a new type to your own line, the *index* shows which markets will prove most receptive, what package sizes and types are most popular, how to price the product for maximum profit, etc.

10. Detecting gains or losses in dealer goodwill, by revealing changes in the amount of display and special sales given to your brand.

11. Determining the most profitable consumer price level. This is done by the use of complex cross-analyses revealing the extent to which your competitive sales position in any group of stores is affected by differences in the ratio of your price to competitors' prices.

12. Furnishing a sound basis for setting territorial quotas and measuring quota attainment. The *index* shows how much business is actually being done in each territory (by all brands combined) thus eliminating the use of quotas based on telephones, bank deposits, and other factors whose relationship to the total *consumer* sales of any type of goods cannot be determined by analyzing the *factory* sales of any *single* manufacturer.

13. Predetermining the result of any proposed expenditure. This is done by *testing* the proposed plan in a "laboratory" consisting of 10 cities in one or more specially selected territories.

    While this complex subject cannot be treated in detail here, it should be stated that many common "fetishes" of advertising and merchandising are being exploded by the hundreds of test campaigns being conducted.

    We test not only advertising copy but also advertising quantity, mediums, displays,' deals, sales coverage, detailing, sampling, couponing, price changes, package changes, cooperative advertising, etc.

14. Launching a new product. Certain enterprising manufacturers have used the *index* to decide *whether* to enter a new field and then, after deciding to launch the new product, they have used the *index* as a means of directing their efforts into the most profitable channels.

Making the Research Appropriation Pay

A criticism of sales research as conducted by many companies is that too much data thus obtained gathers dust on some top shelf. Seldom is it put to work making money for the business. Sometimes a research department is set up to meet a specific need, and then after that job has been completed, the research personnel scurries around to find something else to do. Or to go to the other extreme, the department being in operation, every executive in the business becomes suddenly alerted to the need of getting "facts" about this, that, or the other operation to support his own opinions or a position he had previously taken with a superior. On this point an official of Lever Brothers told Dartnell:

"Two things are necessary to prevent misuse of research. The first is to require that a research project either contribute meaningfully to a specific 'action decision' or, at the very least, provide information regarding an area about which little or nothing is known. The second requirement is that all concerned should be committed *in advance of the research* to agreement on exactly what minimum findings will support a proposed decision.

"Actually, certain advances in marketing research in the past several years have tended to make its techniques inherently more actionable, and less prone to misuse. Modern research and information-handling techniques, including computerization, have enabled marketing research to reduce the time it takes to secure and report information, thereby increasing the likelihood that the information will be available in time to be acted on.

"In addition, techniques have been developed to measure the probability of future consumer behavior. This enables marketing research to predict earlier and with greater accuracy what will happen in the marketplace—and why—and will increasingly minimize the necessity of conducting expensive and time-consuming test marketing to evaluate proposed new products, advertising campaigns, and the like."

Analyzing Marketing Costs

Marketing cost analysis is a key to locating unprofitable sales and to determining the losses for which disproportionate spreading of marketing effort is responsible. In a simple form, it can be made from five basic company records: (1) names and locations of customers, (2) types of businesses of customers, (3) number of each customer's orders in a given period, (4) total sales to each customer in the same period, and (5) total sales and gross profits on each product in your line. Most plants will not find it hard to get this information.

A brief description of some of the more advanced marketing cost analysis methods follows. Although a complete, detailed discussion of the procedure involved would be too lengthy and technical here, two basic principles may be readily summarized:

1. *Classifying Costs:* The marketing expenses of a business, which are usually entered in the accounting records on a "natural" expense basis, are reclassified into "functional" cost groups. This brings together all the direct and indirect costs associated with each marketing activity performed by that company. For example, in a natural classification, all expenditures for supplies are grouped together; but with a functional breakdown, the costs of supplies are segregated according to the activity which used them, such as advertising, shipping, and so on.

2. *Allocating Costs:* These functional cost groups are then allocated to territories, to products, to customers, and to any other desired segments of sales. Allocations are based either on known facts or on the product and customer characteristics which control the size of these costs.

Having your records set up to yield a functional classification for your firm's marketing costs is an indispensable step. It has a number of advantages even though you make no further analysis. Remember, of course, that your functional breakdown of marketing costs should parallel the actual organization of your business and the responsibilities for expenditure. Once you get this done, your classification itself will help in controlling marketing expenses just by revealing how money is being spent.

Developing a Classification Basis

The particular functional classification to be used by *your firm* must be developed by a qualified accountant through a detailed study of *your specific marketing activities.* If you make but one product and sell your entire output to a single customer, you can assign every marketing cost you have to that product and customer. In reality, however, things are usually not that simple. Most companies serve diverse markets and produce a number of products. Hence, they have fairly complex marketing organizations and engage

Functional Cost Groups and Bases of Allocation

Functional-cost Groups	To Commodities	To Customers
Investment in finished goods	Average inventory value	(Not allocated)
Storage of finished goods	Floor space occupied	(Not allocated)
Inventory control, finished goods	No. of invoice lines	(Not allocated)
Order assembly (handling)	No. of standard handling units	No. of invoice lines
Packing and shipping	Weight or No. of shipping units	Weight or number of shipping units
Transportation	Weight or No. of shipping units	Weight or number of shipping units
Selling	Time studies	No. of sales calls
Advertising	Cost of space, etc. of specific product advertising	Cost of space, etc. of specific customer advertising
Order entry	No. of invoice lines	No. of orders
Billing	No. of invoice lines	No. of invoice lines
Credit extension	(Not allocated)	Average amount outstanding
Accounts receivable	(Not allocated)	Invoices posted

in a considerable range of marketing activities. For that reason, your company will have to design its own functional classification to reflect local conditions.

It is important that the breakdown you adopt be sufficiently detailed to ensure that all work performed in any one function will be essentially the same. When this is done, you will find it easier to assign an entire functional-cost group to the appropriate segment of sales. However, you will often find it necessary to split up many natural-expense items (as they would appear in the ordinary accounting records) among several functional-cost groups. The reason is that they relate to more than one functional activity. Natural-expense items are distributed to functional-cost groups by means of time study, space measurements, actual counts, managerial estimates, and other methods.

A Dangerous Numbers Game

Any discussion of marketing research must conclude with a word of caution. With so many schools of thought about the methods and techniques employed, questions are bound to arise about their relative merits.

Numbers are important in all marketing research. But without proper evaluation numbers can be dangerous, observed Stephen Dietz, senior vice-president of Kenyon & Eckhardt, New York, in an address before the American Association of Advertising Agencies:

"There are booby traps involved in the numbers game," he said. "Far too many people believe numbers express reality, when in fact, they represent abstractions from reality to a high degree. It's important to remember that they are only shorthand descriptions of pieces of the truth, no more than that."

The booby trap in the numbers game, according to Mr. Dietz is to assume:

That bigger numbers are always better.

That more numbers are always better.

That negative numbers are always bad.

That numerical differences are always meaningful.

That any number is better than no number.

That assigning a number to a guess somehow makes it a reality, not a hypothesis.

That the number descriptions we have today describe the future.

Addressing the American Marketing Association, David C. Wright, director of long-range planning, United States Gypsum Company, said:

"We have made such great strides in developing and refining the techniques of marketing research that many companies today are running the risk of permitting marketing-research methods to become so rarefied that they lose touch with their basic purposes. No matter how sophisticated the techniques and how accomplished the practitioners, marketing research cannot make its full contribution to the success of the company unless it is conducted with a continuing awareness of the principles that make it effective.

"These principles may seem obvious—and, indeed, they should be —but the fact is that a preoccupation with questionnaires, statistical techniques, and other tools of analysis often cause marketing researchers to lose sight of the fundamental purposes of their efforts."

The computer is being used by a number of marketing services and agencies to test the marketing of new products. One of the best known applications thus far is that of Batten, Barton, Durstine & Osborn, Inc., whose executive vice-president, Donald A. Wells, reports as follows:

"Not only is the normal test-market venture an imprecise measure from which to project futures; not only does test marketing require long lead time before going national; but for those companies involved in introducing several new products in the course of a year, test marketing represents a major expense.

"Every test-market failure is a serious setback in the forward movement of the company involved—it's something like tearing a year or two out of the development calendar.

"Now there is a very good possibility of minimizing this wasted money and time.

"For the next few years, most products will continue to be tested along orthodox lines. As time goes on, however, DEMON will assume more and more of the burden during new-product introductions. We believe the test market, as we know it today, will fade in significance."

DEMON is BBDO's total-systems approach in coping with the myriad of variables involved in new-product introduction. It considers all these variables simultaneously against a key objective of management-maximization of profit.

The name DEMON is an acronym for Decision-Mapping Via Optimum Go/No-Go Networks. The system is a little over a year old. It has been put to work on behalf of a half-dozen BBDO clients and several nonclient organizations in the U.S. and abroad.

It is delivering as expected. While it has by no means done away with the test-market phase of the marketing plan, its results clearly forecast the day when test marketing will play a much different role than it does today.

For instance, in one major introduction in which the total-systems approach has been used, a client with a marketing plan that had been previously set elected to run a concurrent test of DEMON-generated plan in one section of his marketing area.

DEMON forecast that the most profitable plan to implement would require advertising and promotion expenditures at one half the level (using standard criteria) that had been recommended for the other area. At the moment, this half-scale plan is producing 73 percent as effectively as the standard plan. The gain in efficiency is 46 percent when measured against the dollar base. This indication of forecasting capacities foreshadows gains in test efficiency.

Checklist for Sales Researchers

Numerous special surveys and similar market investigations have been made by individual publishing organizations and advertising agencies to picture to advertisers a cross section of the market these publishers serve. Some of these are quite valuable in the projecting of a sales program. Others are too limited in their scope to reflect a typical situation, and some are downright deceptive. It is possible to make a survey prove anything. It is just a matter of picking the right people or establishments to survey, and framing the questions so that the desired answers will be obtained. So it is common practice now to double-check information obtained through surveys. The pantry test, where interviewers actually check products in consumers' pantries to determine what products they buy is one example.

To assist sales managers in appraising the true value of sales research and surveys, particularly those made with the idea of selling something, the American Association of Advertising Agencies has prepared and published the following tests:

1. *Who made the survey?*

   Complete information should be given regarding the names of the organizations or individuals who conducted the survey, made the tabulations, and interpreted the results, together with their qualifications and the extent of their interest, if any, in the findings.

2. *Does the title indicate exactly the scope of the survey?*

   No report should bear a title which suggests more than results justify.

THREE MARKETING RULES

The marketing concept in American business has grown increasingly sophisticated and complex. In essence, [its basic principles] are: (1) Find out what the consumer wants and needs; (2) develop or improve products or services that answer those wants and needs better than ever before; (3) find ways to induce the consumer to choose your product and to keep on choosing it.

From an annual report of General Mills

3. *Does the report contain all pertinent data as to how, when, and where the survey was made?*

The following information should be furnished:

1. Reason for making the study.
2. Who financed it?
3. Exact period of time covered in collection of data.
4. Date of issuance or publication.
5. Definition of terms used.
6. Copies of questionnaires and instructions.
7. How field work was conducted and supervised.
8. List of localities where information was gathered, together with number of calls in each locality, and how calls were divided among different sections and different strata of the population.
9. Actual data, as well as percentages and averages.
10. Explanation of bases on which percentages are figured.
11. Sources of collateral data.
12. Description of statistical methods used, together with reasons.

4. *Is the sample ample?*

Lack of adequate sample is one of the commonest weaknesses in market research. There is no rule that can be laid down to cover all cases. In the first place, it must be shown that a true cross section has been selected. Then it must be proved that the size of the sample is adequate—

1. By showing that when results are divided into groups, such as the first 200 or 300, the second 200 or 300, etc., a point has been reached where results are not materially changed by the addition of more instances, or
2. By checks against known facts, or
3. By other acceptable statistical proof.

5. *Have data collected in one city or section been used to draw conclusions for the country as a whole?*

This is a question of the adequacy of the sample. If results obtained in a limited area are projected to cover the entire population, justification for doing so should be established by reasonable evidence.

6. *Are percentages figured for groups or classes that contain too small a number of instances?*

It often happens that although there may be enough data to furnish an adequate total, breakdowns into income groups, or geographical sections, or other forms of groupings, leave too few instances in individual classes to justify figuring of percentages. In other words, the sample becomes too small when broken into parts. When such breakdowns are used, actual figures should be furnished.

7. *Are percentages of increase figured on ample bases?*

Percentages of increase are frequently figured on such small numbers as to be entirely misleading. This is a common error in the case of sales of new products, circulation, and advertising increases, etc. Actual figures should be used in such cases.

8. *Was information obtained by mailed questionnaires?*

Information obtained by mail usually does not represent a true cross section of the market or of the population. When data have been obtained in this way, proof should be furnished that the questions are of such a nature, and that sufficient safeguards have been set up to ensure representative replies.

9. *Is casual relationship attributed to one single factor, when other contributing factors are present?*

It must either be proved that all other factors are held constant, or allowance must be made for the other variable factors.

10. *If questionnaires were used, were questions such as to give fair and adequate answers?*

Care must be taken in interpreting the answers to questions that are too general, that suggest answers, or that are subject to biased replies.

11. *Was information gathered of such a nature that the memories of the people interviewed might have resulted in inaccuracies?*

When any of the so-called "recall" or recognition" methods are used, the results should be looked upon primarily as a measure of the impressions of the people interviewed, rather than as a measure of facts, unless it can be proved that such impressions correspond with such facts.

12. *Can type of information obtained (either by interview or by mail) be relied on as accurate?*

Questions involving income, personal expenditures, personal pride or prejudice, reading habits, education, etc., often do not yield correct answers.

13. *Have any original or unique statistical devices been employed?*

When devices are used, for which there is no well-established, published authority, adequate explanation of the method should be presented, and proof must be furnished that the method is valid.

14. *Are charts misleading?*

In graphic presentations, the titles must be clear, scales must not be exaggerated, the vertical scales should start with zero (except in special cases, as in index numbers that fluctuate over and under 100), curves must be clearly labeled (or easily compared with distinct legends), and simplicity should be the main objective.

Sampling the Market

Researchers have many more classifications of samples than we have room to discuss here, but a few of the most important are worth mentioning. They are described in Dartnell's *The Marketing Campaign*, by Craig S. Rice, as follows:

"The simple, random sample is a little like drawing names from a hat in which every name has been placed. In this method, every member of the universe has an equal opportunity of selection. One way is to select every nth name (such as every 10th) from a list of 'the universe.' This kind of sample has two important advantages; the error is the smallest and can be accurately calculated. The degree of risk taken can be determined. The disadvantage is that the method requires the most time and effort (hence, money) to execute.

"The cluster sample is an economy measure whereby the sample is selected in groups, randomly. For example, if every nth person in a town were to be sampled, the interviewer would have to travel extensively, boosting cost. However, if a number of blocks were selected at random and each resident of each block interviewed, travel time and costs would be reduced. The cluster sample is not as accurate as the random sample, but it is much less expensive.

"The stratified sample is specifically designed to match known facts about the universe. For example, if the universe contains one-third urban families, one-third rural and one-third suburban, the sample would be selected in that way. In this way, some expense is saved. However, each member of the universe does not have an equal chance of selection, unless the selection is random within each stratum. Normally, this is not a random sample and it can have considerable error that cannot be accurately calculated.

"The convenience sample is, basically, just about what it sounds. The sample is selected among those most readily available. They may be all about the same age, location, and income. Consequently, this sample can generate the largest error of all, the error size cannot be calculated, and these errors can lead to serious investment loss.

"From a practical standpoint, the sample should be as random as the budget will permit. In cutting corners, one should recognize that it is almost impossible to find a truly 'typical' person and few researchers know just what such a person would be like. Even successful executives mistakenly believe themselves to be typical of the general population in preferences for product, advertisements, etc.

"True random samples are very rare. Nonrandom samples, if selected with good judgment, are better than swivel-chair guessing. Even fairly crude research can obtain important data. A random sample is not even necessary if the attribute to be measured is randomly distributed.

"The sample size is the second factor affecting sample accuracy. Increasing the size of a random sample will increase the accuracy, but not proportionately. Doubling the sample will not halve the error! We can calculate error for each sample size. However, as the sample increases, it also becomes more expensive, even though it is somewhat more accurate. The key question is, 'How accurate must we be?' or, 'How large an error can we risk?' We must keep in mind the cost of a wrong fact and a campaign failure. On minor decisions, often we can take a chance on data that has a wide range of error.

"A handy little formula has been used to calculate the error for any given sample size. The size of the error is called 'sigma,' or 's.' This error is equal to the square root of an even split in answers obtained from the sample (50 percent in favor, 50 percent against). This calculation is divided by the size of the sample, or as shown in this figure:

$$\text{sigma} = \sqrt{\frac{P\,Q}{n}}$$

"P and Q represent the 50-50 split and 'n' is the sample size. Using this formula, for example, we can see that a random sample of 100 will have an error of 5 percent, which is read plus or minus 5 percent. A sample of 300 has an error of about 2.9 percent (tripling the sample does not quite reduce the error to one half).

"One additional factor tells the degree of confidence that we might place in this estimate. The factor is called 'The Confidence Interval,' or C. I. It is a statement of how many times out of a hundred our estimate is probably correct. For example, if we use just one confidence interval, we are probably right 68 percent of the time. If we use two C. I.'s we are probably right 95 percent of the time.

The C. I. is simply the number of sigmas that we use. If we want to work to one C. I. (and be 68 percent certain), we use one sigma. If we wanted two C. I.'s (or 95 percent certainty) we would use two sigmas."

(Note: This is a highly simplified, rule-of-thumb formula. It will have accuracy only under ideal circumstances, such as a pure random sample, etc. Otherwise, it has definite limitations and good judgment is essential.)

Chapter 11

SOURCES OF MARKETING DATA

IN THE preceding chapter, we discussed market analysis, with consumer research, motivation research, and the determination of consumer preferences, as a means of obtaining quality control in product design. In this chapter, we shall discuss market analysis for quantitative determination. Assuming that the product is in marketable shape, where can it be sold and in what quantities?

This knowledge is necessary on a regional and geographical area basis, as well as on an economic and population-stratification basis. Products that can be sold on the Atlantic coast may have limited demand on the Pacific coast; some may be in demand in the South but not in the North or even in the Midstates. Nationality and racial groups also vary greatly, with Scandinavian families possibly preferring seafood products and families from Latin-American countries leaning toward highly-seasoned dishes; Caucasian ladies wanting lotions to make their hair curly, others seeking hair straighteners.

Not only must the segmented and overall quantities of the product demand be known, but also the growth pattern and probable future trend in demand must be understood. With this knowledge, production requirements can be estimated, cash flow and capital investment demands can be foreseen, sales coverage and personnel requirements can be anticipated, territories and compensation programs can be laid out.

Fortunately, there is a wealth of statistical data available as to past demand and flow of products, and on those economic and geographical factors that contribute to such movements. Some of the important sources for these data are listed in this chapter, together with the major classifications of data included.

Types of Marketing Data

Marketing data fall into two broad classification groups:

1. *Primary,* which originate from company records, the result

of direct interviews with consumers, buyers, dealers and wholesalers.

2. *Secondary,* which, after being collected, are published for use by others. By far the most prolific dispenser of secondary data is the U.S. Government. It collects a wealth of statistics, which, though sometimes late in distribution, is inexpensive, easy to obtain, and often exceedingly useful.

These publications are obtained from the Superintendent of Documents, U.S. Government Printing Office, Washington, D. C., 20025.

Population Statistics: These data are from the Decennial Census of the population of the United States made by the Bureau of the Census. They include statistics on the number of inhabitants for states, counties, other civil divisions (townships, incorporated and unincorporated cities and towns, wards of cities) and for urbanized areas. They also cover such characteristics of the population, by the above geographical and political areas, as race and color, age, nativity, citizenship, country of birth, marital status, household and family units, education, employment status, occupation and industry classification, and income.

These data have been collected, in expanded form, since 1790. Thus they provide valuable information on both current conditions and on trends in population growth and characteristic changes.

A sales executive wishing, for example, to plan ahead for possible sales in a regional market consisting of young-married, native-white, college-educated men in a medium-income bracket could use such data to advantage.

Census of Housing: These data are based upon tabulations from the Decennial Census on Housing. They include such occupancy characteristics for states, standard metropolitan areas, cities, and urbanized areas as: Occupancy and tenure, race and color of occupants, population per occupied dwelling unit, number of persons per room. There are data on such structural characteristics as numbers of rooms per housing unit, type of structure and year built; on such plumbing facilities as water supply, toilets, and baths; on equipment and fuels used, such as electric lighting, radio, television, refrigerators, kitchen sinks, heating and cooking fuels. There are statistics on contract monthly rent, gross monthly rent, value of housing units, and mortgage status.

Thus, a sales executive wishing, for example, to determine the saturation status and the replacement market for refrigerators in a certain area can readily do so with these data.

Census of Manufactures: These data are collected by the Bureau of the Census from manufacturers, trade associations, and government agencies. This census has been made periodically since 1809, and contains a wealth of information on many aspects of our manufacturing economy. Data by geographical area and for many individual industries are available on number of employees, production, related work man-hours, cost and quantity of materials consumed in production, value of shipments made by individual and class of products, value added in manufacture, inventories, expenditures for plant and equipment, fuels consumed, electric energy and water used, horsepower of equipment, selected metalworking operations and equipment employed, distribution of manufacturers' shipments, plant specialization, data on individual groups of companies, and indexes of physical volume of production for many individual and groups of industries.

A sales executive wishing to ascertain the relative importance of two or three markets for his products and in certain industries can do so by comparing such statistics as "value added in manufactures," "capital investment," trends in number of productive workers, "material consumed," or "energy used." Valuable insight into markets can be gained by a company wishing to cater to the employees in the yarn and thread industry in certain states.

Census of Business: The data presented in these reports cover the retail, wholesale, and selected service trades. They are collected by the Bureau of the Census from mail canvasses of business establishments and records of the Internal Revenue Service and the Bureau of Old Age and Survivors' Insurance. There are data on the number of establishments, sales, payrolls, and number of paid employees, for many types of businesses such as food stores, eating and drinking places, general merchandise groups, apparel and accessories stores, furniture and appliance stores, automotive dealers and accessories, lumber and building-material dealers, drugstores, and other retail outlets.

A manufacturer of restaurant china could gain information as to the geographical markets for his products by referring to the statistics on eating places or drinking places. A publisher of books could find equally valuable information on relative sales of bookstores in selected geographical areas.

Data covering the *wholesale trade* include the number of establishments by type of operation and commodity lines, inventories at the year end, operating expenses, payrolls, number of employees, single-unit or multiple-unit operation, credit sales, receivables, bad-debt losses, warehouse space, bulk-storage capacity of petroleum, bulk plants and terminals, sales by merchandise agents and brokers, bin space of grain elevators.

For *selected services,* data covers the number of establishments (by annual receipts groups), receipts, payrolls, number of employees and proprietors. Those selected include (but are not limited to) such personal services as barber and beauty shops, funeral homes, photograph studios, laundries, and Turkish baths. They include such business services as advertising agencies, credit agencies, news syndicates, duplicating services, detective agencies, sign-painting shops, automobile-repair garages, parking lots, watch and clock repair, blacksmiths, and bicycle shops. Many types of amusement services are included, such as motion-picture theaters, poolrooms, bowling alleys, race tracks, baseball fields, golf courses, swimming pools, and dance halls; also hotels (year-round and seasonal), motels, trailer parks, and recreation camps.

Thus, a sales executive could obtain data that would assist him

YEARS WHEN CENSUSES ARE TAKEN

Population and housing censuses. Every 10th year ending in "0"—for example, 1960.

Government census. Every fifth year ending in "2" or "7"—for example, 1957 and 1962.

Business, manufactures, and mineral industries censuses. Every fifth year ending in "3" or "8"—for example, 1958 and 1963.

Agriculture census. Every fifth year ending in "4" or "9"—for example, 1959 and 1964.

in estimating the market for jacks used by service garages, for diving boards used at swimming pools, self-propelled caddy cars used on golf courses, or popcorn sold in motion-picture theaters.

United States Census of Agriculture: This census has been taken periodically since 1840. The current data include information for states and counties as to the number of farms, acreage, value, use, color, and tenure of operator, class of work power and specified equipment, labor force and expenditures, wage rates, livestock and poultry, nursery, greenhouses, forest products, and specified crops harvested.

Should a manufacturer of electric pig-brooders or of garden tractors wish to appraise the potentiality of new markets or their growth trends, he could readily do so by reference to these statistics.

County and City Data Book: Published by the Bureau of the Census, U.S. Department of Commerce.

Mineral Yearbook: Published by the U.S. Bureau of Mines.

Statistical Abstract of the United States: All the above referred data and a great deal more are conveniently summarized in this publication. Convenient as a reference source for these data, and a guide to other statistical publications and sources for more detailed information when needed.

Federal Reserve Bulletin: Current monthly data of significance relating to financial and business developments in the United States are contained in this publication, including department-store sales, consumer-credit estimates, production indexes for an extensive list of industries, construction activities, wholesale and consumer prices for many products, interest rates, security prices, and real-estate credit.

From these data, a sales executive can quickly trace the trends in the production of paper and paper products, in tobacco products, or in construction.

Survey of Current Business: This is a monthly publication issued by the U.S. Department of Commerce. It contains current business statistics of the nature outlined in various census reports and other surveys. Included are many phases of the national income and production, such as personal income, new plant and equipment expenditures, farm income and marketing, industrial production for a broad list of specified industries, wholesale and consumer prices for numerous products, construction expenditures for various classifications of buildings, retail trade, employment and earnings, transportation and equipment, and security prices.

These data are broad in scope, currently maintained, and extend far enough back to provide meaningful trend analyses. This publication is a useful tool for the analytically minded sales executive.

For information on other government publications, reference should be made to the following:

Monthly Catalogue of U.S. Public Documents: A list of current printed material of the federal government, classified by various departments.

Industrial Arts Index: Current technical periodicals on engineering, science, industry, and business subjects are listed and described in detail.

Market Research Sources: A bibliography, revised frequently.

Public Affairs Information Service: A general bibliography of subjects in commerce, business, and economics. It contains the names and addresses of trade associations that collect statistical data.

In preparation for the National Market Conference in Washington, attended by company presidents, marketing executives, and government officials, the Business and Defense Services Administration of the U.S. Department of Commerce prepared a list of publications of interest to the marketing community. It included:

BDSA—How It Works With Business For Business

BDSA Publications List

Bureau of the Census Catalog

Business Cycle Developments

Business Statistics

Businessmen Speak Out For Modernization

Census of Business 1963
  Final Area Reports
  Area Statistics
  Merchandise Line Sales
  Major Retail Centers

Census of Housing 1960 (Final Reports)

Census of Manufactures 1963
  Final Industry Reports
  Final Subject Reports
  Final Area Reports
  Location of Manufacturing Plants

Census of Population 1960
  Characteristics of the Population
  Selected Area Reports
  Subject Reports
  Supplementary Reports
  Census Tracts
  City Blocks

Census of Transportation 1963
  Truck Inventory and Use Survey
  Passenger Transportation Survey (National Travel)
  Commodity Transportation Survey (Production Area Series)
  Commodity Transportation Survey (Shippers Series)

Commerce Business Daily

County Business Patterns

Current Population Reports

Current Retail Trade Reports

Facts for Marketers
  Middle Atlantic
  New England
  East North Central
  East South Central
  Pacific
  West North Central
  West South Central
  South Atlantic
  Mountain

Franchise Company Data For Equal Opportunity in Business

Growth Patterns in Employment by County

Guide to Census Bureau Statistics: Subjects and Areas

Guide to Government Services

Guide to Industrial Statistics

Guide to Negro Marketing Information

How to Succeed by Really Trying

International Commerce

Keeping the American Dollar Strong

Major Programs Providing Federal Funds For Employment and Training

Market Share Reports

Marketing Information Guide

Measuring Markets

Monthly Wholesale Trade Report: Sales and Inventories

Selling Around the World—How Commerce Helps

Semiannual International Business Publications Checklist

Statistical Abstract of the United States

Survey of Current Business

The U.S. Department of Commerce Promotes Economic Growth

What You Should Know About Exporting: A How-to-Get Started Handbook

Other Sources of Statistical Information

Besides the federal government, many states collect information in great detail. They list manufacturers in urban and rural civil areas, showing the types of products manufactured, the number of male and female employees, average yearly sales, and other pertinent data. Chambers of Commerce are also important sources of local information, including local weather conditions, availability of water, taxes, transport, and labor markets.

Many magazines, radio broadcasting and television stations, and newspapers issue periodic reports based on consumer panels and individual surveys. Consumer analyses are published yearly by all major media in principal American cities.

Such data cover the buying habits and the overall use of many types of products in selected markets, as well as the leading brands in consumer preference. Included are items such as baby foods, baking mixes, baked beans, breakfast foods, dog foods, frozen food, juices, pie-crust mix, waxed paper, and many others. There are data on the brand preference of soaps, laundry starch, steel wool, and waxes; on alcoholic beverages, beer, ginger ale, nail polish, electric shavers, toothpaste; on clothes dryers, dishwashers, electric mangles, sewing machines, television receivers; on antifreeze, brassieres, cigars, hosiery, and tires.

From these data, a sales executive can appraise the value of individual markets for instant coffee vs. packaged coffee; for safety razors vs. electric razors; for gas ranges vs. electric ranges; and so on.

Trade associations are prolific collectors and distributors of information concerning the operations of their industries. These data often include operating expenses and salesmen's compensation policies as well as production or sales. Although individual companies contribute to the collection of these data, some of the contributors do not use them to their full advantage.

*The 20 prime markets in the United States, as plotted by the research depart-
ment of The Philadelphia* Inquirer. *The circled areas are in reality highly
irregular trading areas around New York, Los Angeles, Chicago, Philadelphia,
Detroit, San Francisco, Boston, Pittsburgh, Cleveland, St. Louis, Washington,
Milwaukee, Baltimore, Houston, Dallas, New Orleans, Buffalo, Seattle, San
Antonio, and San Diego.*

For example, a manufacturer of work gloves had sent elaborate
sales reports each month for years to his trade association, and had
religiously examined the returned reports received. However, he
had not maintained any continuous time records of his position in
the industry and was amazed to find, when they were presented to
him, that although his sales had grown steadily for the past five
years, he had actually been losing his position in the industry. A
manufacturer of packaged peanut-butter sandwiches was similarly
chagrined when he was presented with time records of his sales
as compared with those of his industry.

Other sources of useful market data include:

Automobile Registrations: Reuben H. Donnelley Corporation, 2000 York, Oak
Brook, Illinois 60521

New Car Registrations: Reuben H. Donnelley Corporation

Construction Contracts Awarded: F. W. Dodge Corporation, 330 W. 42nd
St., New York 10036

Industrial Marketing Annual Market Data and Directory Number: Industrial Marketing, 740 Rush Street, Chicago, Illinois 60611

Survey of Buying Power: Sales Management, Inc., 630 Third Ave., New York 10017

Survey of Industrial Buying Power: Sales Management, Inc.

There are also a number of companies that conduct continuous research programs for their clients, such as the following:

A. C. Nielsen Co., Chicago (sales by retail stores and radio audience)

C. E. Hooper Co., New York (radio audiences)

Daniel Starch and Staff, New York (magazine and newspaper readers)

Although the greatest portion of their findings are private, they also occasionally publish some public information.

Maps also are useful in planning marketing campaigns. Following are some of the sources for map material:

RAND-MCNALLY MARKETING AIDS
Rand-McNally & Co., 124 West Monroe Street, Chicago, Illinois 60603.

Sales Control Map of the United States
Available in two sizes:
4526: 84 inches by 55 inches
4525: 66 inches by 46 inches

Ranally Trading Area Map of United States
4553: 66 inches by 46 inches

City Rating Map
4113: Rolled paper sheet, 52 inches by 41 inches
4114: Cloth mounted, 52 inches by 41 inches

Geographical Handbook
4101: 8½ inches by 11 inches; 160 pages

Commercial Atlas and Marketing Guide
Published annually
15¾ inches by 21 inches; 589 pages

State Pocket Maps
Individual Maps
4049: Complete set of state maps

Standard Highway Mileage Guide
4103: 14⅜ inches by 17½ inches; 338 pages

Railroad Atlas of the United States
4102: 9 inches by 12¼ inches; 64 pages

Trading Area Map of the United States
4549: Two colors; 32 inches by 24 inches

City Rating Map
4836: Two colors; 32 inches by 25 inches

City Rating Guide
4112: 8½ inches by 11 inches; 124 pages

AMERICAN MAP COMPANY, INC.
3 West 61st St., New York 10023.

Cleartype U.S. and Sectional U.S. County-Town Maps.
Ten sizes range from 8½ inches by 6¼ inches at six cents to 75 inches by 50 inches at $10.50. Show only state outline and state names. Available by sections of the U.S.

Cleartype U.S. and Sectional U.S. County-Town Map.
Nine sizes range from 11 inches by 8½ inches at 15 cents to 74 inches by 50 inches at $10.50. Shows state outline, state names, county outlines, and county names. Available by sections of the U.S.

Cleartype U.S. and Sectional U.S. State Outline Maps.
120 inches by 82 inches at $42. Show states and counties, and all towns of 250 population and over; congested metropolitan areas are shown on individual large-scale insets.

Cleartype U.S. and Sectional U.S. County-Town Maps.
82 inches by 56 inches at $21. Show states, counties, and towns of 500 population and over or equivalent in trading value. 34 metropolitan areas shown on large-scale insets.

Cleartype U.S. and Sectional U.S. County-Town Map.
75 inches by 50 inches at $16. Shows states, counties and towns of 1,000 population and over or equivalent in trading value; 25 metropolitan areas shown on large-scale insets. Other sizes range from 11 inches by 8½ inches at 30 cents to 64 inches by 44 inches at $10.00.

Cleartype Master Sales Control Atlas.
Approximately 50 maps, looseleaf. 22 inches by 17 inches. Complete with binder, $175. Individual states with counties, cities and towns of 250 population and over; state capitals, and county seats. Indexed by county, town, and population. Includes a county-town map of the United States.

NEMA STANDARD PATTERNS OF AREA SYSTEMS
The National Electrical Manufacturers Association, 155 East 44th Street, New York 10017, has issued two systems of maps and directories. The first covers 121 industrial trading areas, while the second includes 33 industrial regions.

The maps are wall size (36 inches by 50 inches) and delineate in relief fashion the boundaries of the areas comprising each system. The directories provide for each system a listing of the areas with their specific "county" content, and a listing of the counties with an indication of the areas in which they fall. The directories include a standard coding procedure for automatic business machine treatment.

The maps are also available in 11-inch by 17-inch sizes.

WESTERN UNION

Western Union has gradually expanded its survey services and now plays an important role in marketing research. Through trained interviewers in nearly 1,600 offices throughout the country, covering more than 23,000 communities, Western Union provides the following services:

Check brand preferences

Check buying habits

Check purchases

Provide inventory and inspection service

Check product availability

Make traffic counts

Check retail cooperation

Make TV set counts

Check consumer attitudes

Correct subscription lists

Obtain names and titles of those responsible for purchasing

Determine consumer opinion

MARKETING DEPARTMENT, HEARST MAGAZINES
959 Eighth Avenue, New York 10019

The Consumer Trading Area Map of the United States

County outlines are shown and the trading-area boundaries are indicated with heavier lines. In each case the principal trading center is shown. Size is 30 inches by 50 inches (folds to a convenient 6-inch by 10-inch size). $10 postpaid.

The Marketing Map of the United States

This is a wall map, size 42 inches by 60 inches, printed in five colors on linen-paper stock and mounted top and bottom with metal rods. It shows the 580 principal trading centers of the U.S. and all secondary towns of 2,500 and over population within the respective trading area lines. The 219 SMSA's are shown in outline. $20 postpaid.

Individual State Marketing Maps

Show the 580 principal trading centers and also the secondary towns within the respective trading-area boundary lines. There are 60 maps to a set: one for each of the 50 states and one each for the first 10 standard metropolitan statistical areas. $15 per set. Maps may be purchased separately at 30 cents each. In quantities of 10 or more the charge is 25 cents each.

The General Market Buying-Power Index

An overall index designed especially to help advertisers sell products that have a mass appeal. It is made up of the three basic factors of incomes, population, and retail sales. The index shows the percentage of the national market in each of the 580 principal trading centers as well as their consumer trading areas. $10 postpaid.

Leading Department Stores in Leading Trading Areas

This book contains a great variety of sales information about the top-rated department stores in the United States. Listed are 1,428 stores, their sales volume, resident buying offices and chain-store groups which include many of the important suburban and shopping-center branches. Also shown is each store's handling of some 111 products or items in 32 departments. $5 postpaid.

County Composition of the 580 Consumer Trading Areas

Shows the counties which make up each trading area, as well as an alphabetical listing of every county by state indicating the trading area in which each is located. $2.50 postpaid.

Cosmetics-Toiletries-Drugs Sales Index

Lists the overall U.S. retail sales estimates of cosmetics-toiletries-drugs, broken down by type of outlet. Shows dollar volume in drugstores, food stores, department stores, variety stores and "all others." Then a column showing the total of this group as well as a percentage of the U.S. These are done for all of the 580 consumer trading areas in the United States. $10 postpaid.

Groceries-Other Foods Sales Index

Lists the overall U.S. retail sales estimates of groceries-other foods, broken down by type of outlet. Shows dollar volume in food stores, department stores, general-merchandise stores, variety stores and "all others." Then a column showing the total of this group as well as a percentage of the U.S. These are done for all of the 580 consumer trading areas in the United States. $10 postpaid.

Major Appliance-TV-Radio Sales Index

Lists the overall U.S. retail sales estimates of major appliances-TV-radios broken down by type of outlet. Shows dollar volume in household appliance-radio stores, department stores, furniture-home furnishing stores, general-merchandise stores and "all others." Then a column showing the total of this group as well as a percentage of the U.S. These are done for all of the 580 consumer trading areas in the United States. $10 postpaid.

Women's-Girls' Clothing Sales Index

Lists the overall U.S. retail sales estimates of women's-girls' clothing, broken down by type of outlet. Shows dollar volume in department stores, apparel-accessory stores, variety stores, general-merchandise stores and "all others." Then a column showing the total of this group as well as a percentage of the U.S. These are done for all of the 580 consumer trading areas in the United States. $10 postpaid.

Furniture-Sleep Equipment-Floor Covering Sales Index

Lists the overall U.S. retail sales estimates of furniture-sleep equipment-floor covering, broken down by type of outlet. Shows dollar volume in furniture-home furnishing stores, department stores, general-merchandise stores, household appliance-radio stores and "all others." Then a column showing a total of this group as well as a percentage of the United States. $10 postpaid.

DUN & BRADSTREET MARKETING SERVICES

Dun & Bradstreet provides a wide variety of services for marketing executives. Its *Reference Book* lists alphabetically, within towns and cities, the names of nearly 3,000,000 businesses in the United States and Canada together with information indicating line of business, age, and rating. In addition, the company issues reference books on transportation, manufacturers, and the apparel trades.

The DEB *Reference Book of Transportation* identifies major U.S. truckers. The *Reference Book of Manufacturers* identifies 350,000 U.S. manufacturing establishments in alphabetical order. The apparel-trades book lists over 125,000 retail and wholesale outlets in the apparel industry with lines of merchandise handled and the rating. Other published works include the *Million Dollar Directory,* which lists 31,306 businesses with a net worth of over $1,000,000; the *Middle Market Directory,* which lists 30,000 businesses with net worths between $500,000 and $1,000,000; the *Metalworking Directory,* which lists 45,000 concerns in the metalworking industries with 20 or more employees plus 3,767 metals distributors.

In addition, the Marketing Services Company, a division of Dun & Bradstreet, provides specific marketing services in a variety of formats based upon computerized information taken from its extensive files.

The lists available include 350,000 manufacturing establishments, 20,000 mining establishments, 318,000 contract construction establishments and 100,000 transportation, communications, and public utility establishments.

Practical Use of Marketing Data

Examples of the use of marketing data may suggest possibilities for preliminary research probing by sales executives. More exhaustive and detailed studies should be conducted by trained statisticians and marketing men.

A manufacturer of electric-line power connectors, clamps, fittings, and accessories used in the transmission and distribution of electric energy by utilities, telephone companies, and industrial plants was able to appraise the market potential and his industry position by reference to dollar shipment of pole and transmission hardware (SIC 3611) as reported by the U.S. Department of Commerce, corrected for price inflation by use of price indexes for nonferrous metals and for finished hardware. Although these indexes were not fully applicable, they did represent the cost of nonferrous metals and labor involved in manufacture. By applying them, an indication was obtained of physical volume. From Dun & Bradstreet reports, analysis was also made of competitive sales.

Capital expenditures by the electrical industry in transmission and distribution facilities, for a seven-year period; the number of meters installed each year during that period; a projection of these data by McGraw-Hill's *Electrical Industry Statistics* and the companies' sales for the preceding eight years were studied and compared. This analysis indicated that the connector industry had not grown over the period under study and would probably remain somewhat level in the foreseeable future. On the other hand, the company had enjoyed good growth, considerably better than the industry. With this knowledge, the company was in a position to make sound plans for the future.

Chicago Trade Area

Area 3

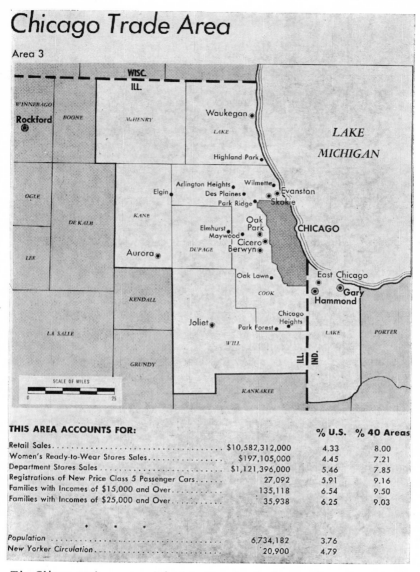

THIS AREA ACCOUNTS FOR:		% U.S.	% 40 Areas
Retail Sales.................................	$10,582,312,000	4.33	8.00
Women's Ready-to-Wear Stores Sales................	$197,105,000	4.45	7.21
Department Stores Sales........................	$1,121,396,000	5.46	7.85
Registrations of New Price Class 5 Passenger Cars......	27,092	5.91	9.16
Families with Incomes of $15,000 and Over..........	135,118	6.54	9.50
Families with Incomes of $25,000 and Over...........	35,938	6.25	9.03
Population	6,734,182	3.76	
New Yorker Circulation........................	20,900	4.79	

The Chicago trade area, as defined by the sales-development department of The New Yorker Magazine. *The magazine identifies 40 major trading areas, many of which overlap state lines.*

Courtesy: *The New Yorker*

A manufacturer of domestic water pumps found by referring to information on water systems (jet, nonjet, and submersible pumps), published by the U.S. Department of Commerce in *Facts for Indus-*

try, that there had been little increase in the number of units sold by the industry during the previous nine years; in fact, there had been a decline for three years. The company, on the other hand, had improved its position slightly each year. This meant that although the number of units it had sold each year had declined in recent years, the trend had been less severe than for the industry as a whole. Future planning for sales was predicated on this knowledge.

A national distributor of residential heating equipment was interested in determining the marketing potentials and trends of air and water heating systems. From the *American Gas Association Directory,* he obtained information as to the number of manufacturers of steam boilers, of central gas furnaces and of unit heaters. From *Facts for Industry,* information was obtained on unit production of boilers and radiation (radiators, convectors and baseboards, both cast iron and nonferrous); from the Department of Commerce and the National Warm Air Heating and Air Conditioning Association, data on unit production of warm air furnaces were obtained. These data permitted the company to compare trends of the two types of systems and of its percentage of the volume sold.

Data on one-family and multifamily, nonframe dwelling units, by geographical areas of the country, were obtained from the U.S. Department of Labor statistics. This permitted the company to measure the relative importance of the different areas and its penetration into those markets. As a result of this study, the company dropped its line of hot-water systems.

A manufacturer interested in the sale of camp trailers wished to appraise the growth possibilities of his market. From reports by the U.S. Department of Agriculture Forestry Service, he obtained information as to the number of people visiting national forests for the primary purpose of camping during each of the previous 10 years. From reports by the U.S. Department of the Interior National Park Service, he obtained similar information as to national and state parks. These data showed a 200 percent increase in visits per year over the period. Camper days at state parks showed the national distribution of interest, California having the highest percentage (23.1 percent of national), Michigan (14.2 percent), and New York (14.1 percent). From these data, he established sales objectives and determined distribution policies.

PART 4

CHANNELS
OF
DISTRIBUTION

Chapter 12

DISTRIBUTING THROUGH WHOLESALERS

HAVING perfected his product and measured markets, a manufacturer must next choose channels of distribution. He may decide to follow the time-honored three-step channel, wholesaler-dealer-consumer; the two-step channel, dealer-consumer; or he may wish to sell directly to the consumer. Each method has its advantages and disadvantages.

Wholesaling as an industry has stood still in the percent of total national sales in the last 30 years. Industrial wholesalers have grown in both volume and wholesaling product groups, while consumer-product wholesalers have had a small decrease in their share of the national total. Consumer-product wholesalers are not as homogenous as the industrials; even the basic classifications of convenience-shopping items and specialty goods are often inadequate because of the difference of products within each category, the variety of outlets, and the overlap of outlets used. At the same time, the three have enough in common to afford some important insights.

The principal headache is the overhead and the slim profit margins, accentuated by price-cutting. Every manufacturer wants special attention given to his product, but the fewer items the distributor carries to make this possible, the better the unit profit has to be to pay the same amount of overhead. This conflict resolves itself to some extent in the degree of exclusiveness of the agency contract made; in fact, a pattern emerges that can be described as follows:

The lower the price and more competitive the product, the more manufacturers lean toward extensive distributions.

The higher the price and the more consumer deliberation in buying, the more is the leaning toward exclusive distribution.

The greater the potential for industrial use, the greater the leaning toward exclusive arrangements.

Over the years many have been meeting the problems of cost by decreasing some services—no credit, no salesmen, sidewalk delivery, cash-and-carry; but at the same time increasing other services to meet the competition from chains, cooperatives, mail-order houses, and department stores. In effect, they have been eliminating those services retailers can do themselves and adding those they cannot.

Distributing Through Wholesalers

In spite of all the talk about "eliminating the jobber," the fact is that selling through the wholesaler remains the most generally used channel. This is because manufacturers discovered that elimination of the wholesaler would not eliminate the cost of the service he performs. Then, too, many jobbers or wholesalers have realized the importance of doing a more thoroughgoing merchandising job, and have not only set their own houses in order, but have also assisted their customers in organizing and modernizing their stores to help them compete with chains and co-ops. That the wholesaler is still the backbone of American distribution is shown in the following tabulation, showing distribution channels for all manufacturing industries, and published by the U.S. Department of Commerce:

Sales to or through own wholesale branches or offices	22.4%
Sales to or through own retail stores	2.1%
Sales to wholesalers and jobbers	25.1%
Sales to export intermediaries	.9%
Sales to retailers for resale	19.6%
Export sales made direct to buyers in other countries	2.3%
Sales to industrial and other large users	26.0%
Sales to consumers at retail	1.6%
	100.0%

Wholesalers render a broad service to the trade. Because of the multiplicity of products and services they distribute, the cost of such service is distributed among more producers with potentialities for lower sales costs to each. This method is most desirable when the product is closely priced, and when sales volume is not a major consideration. The disadvantage of this method of distribution is that sales control, as a rule, rests in the hands of the distributor. When volume is a paramount consideration, it is sometimes difficult to get sufficient creative selling effort behind a product when marketed through this three-step channel.

However, it is noteworthy that companies like Procter & Gamble, which, some years back, elected to eliminate the jobber in order to more evenly spread sales and production, soon found selling costs excessively high in fringe territories. These were territories in which it was too costly to maintain salesmen selling P & G products exclusively. The plan of distribution was therefore changed so that the company now depends upon its own salesmen in large-volume areas, and jobbers' salesmen in fringe areas. However, changing conditions and a trend toward multiple sales organizations in distributing many products make the problems of the wholesaler very acute.

Function of the Wholesaler

Should a wholesaler consider himself primarily responsible to his *customers* or to his *manufacturing sources?*

If the former, he acts as a buying agent and consultant to his customers, stocks those products most suitable for their needs, and may carry only partial lines of a number of manufacturers.

If he is responsible primarily to the manufacturer, he is their representative, their local salesman, promoting the use of their products and carrying their complete lines.

There is, therefore, considerable difference in the philosophy and manner in which a wholesaler conducts his business under these two concepts. Granted the concepts overlap and a wholesaler can straddle them to a great degree, when the chips are down he must follow one philosophy or the other. It is therefore better for him to make the choice in advance as a business principle, then pattern his policies and conduct accordingly.

A distributor can be an active and aggressive part of your field sales organization. Unlike your own salesmen, however, he has a choice. He can sell your product or that of any one of several other companies. When distributors or wholesalers are involved in the marketing of your product, an improvement in their effort can greatly improve the efficiency of your own sales force.

George Needham, Jr., executive vice-president of Biggs Pump and Supply Inc., of Lafayette, Indiana (a plumbing and heating wholesaler) has faced up to this problem and has published to his customers a formal policy of intent, as follows:

GENERAL POLICY OF OPERATIONS

STANDARD PRACTICE INSTRUCTIONS
BIGGS PUMP & SUPPLY, INC.

The basic function of our company is to act as an agent for our customers in the selection of merchandise best suited for their use and in maintaining adequate stocks of such merchandise to supply their needs. We must fulfill this function effectively and efficiently if we are to justify our position in the distribution system and provide real value, in terms of service and savings, to our customers.

With respect to our own internal operations, the application of our general policy may be expressed in terms of product selection, price, service, and personnel.

Product Selection: In order to serve our customers adequately, it is our policy to handle good grades of merchandise. We will carefully screen the manufacturers of the merchandise our customers need in order to provide them with the best combination of quality, price, and service available. We will always keep in mind the integrity of suppliers to insure satisfactory service from their product for years to come.

Our objective is to select suppliers who are the finest in their industry. They must have an equitable sales policy and be morally sound. They must have a superior product at a reasonable price, backed by adequate plant facilities and finances.

Price: We are not in the business of handling low-quality, cut-rate products. Rather, it is our policy to furnish good grades of merchandise at a fair price. We will not always have the lowest price available, but we do intend to be competitive on comparable lines of goods and we will meet competitive situations as we see fit.

Service: As distributors, we can provide a real service to our customers only if we have merchandise available in stock when needed, and if we deliver such merchandise as quickly as possible after it is ordered.

For this purpose, it is our policy to do our utmost to keep adequate merchandise stocks on hand, and thus minimize shortages, and to reduce to a minimum the time required to process an order and make delivery to the customer.

It is also our policy to keep our customers informed of new items and industry trends and to assist them, in every way possible, to do a better job of merchandising or manufacturing.

Personnel: We can do an effective job of serving our customers only through having an effective and competent staff of employees.

For this purpose our basic personnel policy is one of training and promotion from within. We expect to bring our people up through the ranks and train them for the jobs that must be done.

Thus, we use discretion in hiring any person for any job, whether truck drivers, warehouse personnel, or office clerks, since these are the people we expect ultimately to promote to responsible jobs. For this reason, we do our utmost to choose people who have possibilities for advancement.

What Is a Wholesaler?

One question for many years at all trade conventions has been "What is a wholesaler?" The reason for the discussion is because it became the vogue for retailers to claim wholesale status in order to earn jobbing discounts. Sometimes they were entitled to it, sometimes not. Where should the dividing line be in deciding whether a company is a legitimate wholesale house or operates as a retailer with wholesale ambitions?

The National Association of Electrical Distributors recently adopted a "declaration" that applies with comparatively slight modifications to wholesalers in all lines of business. This "declaration" provides that a "legitimate" wholesaler must:

1. Maintain and warehouse an *adequate* stock of standard commodities sufficient to supply the trade.

2. Maintain a showroom to display commodities properly for the benefit of the trade.

3. Maintain delivery service and facilities for pickup service.

4. Maintain a selling organization trained to promote, specify, and quote on electrical commodities, and to handle matters of service or misunderstanding with customers properly.

5. Be prepared to furnish promptly a variety of electrical commodities in one order at a minimum of cost and with greatest convenience to the trade.

6. Advise the trade regarding the most suitable and reliable commodities to purchase and install.

7. Distribute catalogs showing and describing the most essential items in common use in the industry.

8. Extend justified credit to the buyer within his territory upon reasonable terms.

9. Maintain a repair and replacement service to supplement the facilities of the manufacturer and retailer in the handling of defective commodities.

Three Ways of Distribution

There are three ways of distributing through wholesalers:

1. Selling the product without restriction to any wholesaler who will handle it.

2. Selecting the two best wholesalers in a territory and giving them a special arrangement which will permit them to do a good promotional job for the product.

3. The exclusive wholesaler, dividing the country into territories and giving one wholesale distributor in each district the exclusive right to sell your product.

The theory behind the third plan is that the exclusive wholesaler will invest more of his time and money to build up sales volume for you, since he is the certain and sole beneficiary from his effort. This supposition is more imaginary than real. Too often the wholesaler will add a line with the best intentions of energetically pushing it in return for the exclusive sale, but he has so many other lines and products to push that he does much less than he intended doing. For that reason there has been a trend to use the "dual" system of wholesale representation, whereby in some districts two wholesalers, acceptable to each other, are given the line. The principle is that clean competition creates more business, and one will help the other in doing the needed promotional job. As a matter of fact, there are many instances where more than twice as much business has been taken out of a territory under the dual system, and that after the second wholesaler took over the line, the sales of the original distributor usually increased. Great care must be used, however, to make sure both distributors are the sort who will play fair and do a constructive selling job.

A wholesaler can cover his territory economically, because his truck makes many more stops than even a chain-store truck. In a small town, once the wholesaler's salesman is there, he can make several calls at little more cost than if he made a few. In thinly populated country, the wholesaler provides the chief means of supply for essential merchandise. Few retailers could take the time to see salesmen from all the manufacturers whose goods they stock. Distant manufacturers could not give quick delivery. Most businesses need the wholesaler.

Some business is too small to be profitable, but not all small business is unprofitable. The extra volume it provides, beyond the break-even point, may mean the difference between profit and loss. Small customers may be the easiest for wholesalers to keep. Large customers are the easiest to lose to competing wholesalers or to direct-selling manufacturers.

The manufacturer needs wholesalers to obtain complete coverage of his market, and investigation may show that this means using wholesalers to a greater degree than he at first thought necessary.

The Strength of the Wholesaler

The strength of the wholesaler is his service to customers. This is as true of the industrial distributor as of the wholesaler of consumer goods.

The wholesaler, among all those who sell the retailer, is likely to be the one who takes the most interest in the retailer's set of problems, and in keeping him alive—not simply trying to sell him a bill of goods. He is least likely to oversell the retailer—and it must always be remembered that overstocking is a principal cause of retail failures.

The rapid increase in air freight will probably bring new problems and opportunities to wholesalers. Manufacturers of many lines can fly goods to their own warehouses or warehouses of large retailers, if the goods are not too bulky.

Wholesalers themselves have the opportunity of planning to use air freight. New high-speed roads also bring changes. But no transportation development is likely to alter the basic fact that goods flow to the wholesaler from many manufacturers, are broken up into smaller lots, and then are rearranged in different assortments as orders from customers are received.

Wholesalers and retailers do more than "distribute" goods—they *move* them, sell them. They are part of the dynamic mechanism that raises standards of living and creates national wealth. No other nation in the world has developed to such an extent these two tremendous instruments for production of national wealth—the instruments of mass production and organized distribution.

But the special opportunity of the wholesaler is and always has been to build close relations with customers. Over great parts of the nation, and through great parts of its history, the wholesaler has put retailers into business and kept them alive. He has "made merchants out of storekeepers."

Wholesale Distributors

The "wholesale distributor" is a large distributor who sells to smaller wholesalers or jobbers. His operation takes the place of that of manufacturers' sales branches.

In reality, this is a fourth level of distribution, found particularly in the distribution of automotive accessories. Wholesale distributors receive scheduled shipments from their factory sources, carry large inventories, and sell to smaller wholesalers or jobbers, who carry limited stocks, frequently replaced, and who, in their turn, sell to garages, service stations, and similar outlets. These latter sell to the ultimate consumer or car owner, usually on an installed basis.

The function of the wholesale distributor was originally filled by manufacturers' sales-branch warehouses, which sold and delivered to both large and small wholesalers or jobbers. The large wholesalers began to buy in carload lots; then, when they sold to small wholesalers, they received a discount on these reshipments which enlarged their profit on such transactions. Considerable abuse, which arose from the claiming of discounts on shipments not made to small wholesalers, led the manufacturers to seek other means of handling reshipments.

Manufacturers also save in factory handling costs and economical production runs by shipping on predetermined schedules attuned to cyclical and seasonal demand, without being required to maintain factory stocks.

The N.A.P.A. (National Automotive Parts Association) is a nationwide group of wholesale distributors, with 52 independent warehouses serving about 4,000 jobbers. The jobbers order weekly from the wholesale distributors, thus limiting their stocks, maintaining economical turnover and permitting the wholesale distributors to place standing factory orders.

Other Classifications of Wholesalers

In the last Census of Business by the Department of Commerce, there were 47 major groups of products sold through wholesale channels of trade. There were 129 subdivisions of these groups. Not all of these sell consumer goods. Industrial distributors, commonly called mill supply houses, are an important group of wholesalers.

For the purpose of the census, wholesale distributors are divided into six major groups as follows: (1) Merchant wholesalers; (2) manufacturers' sales branches, carrying stocks, and manufacturers' sales offices, which are separate places of business apart from their plants, not carrying stocks; (3) petroleum bulk stations and terminals, and LP gas facilities; (4) merchandise agents and brokers; (5) assemblers of farm products; (6) chain-store warehouses. The first two of these groups involve the following descriptions and subdivisions:

1. *Merchant Wholesalers* are wholesale establishments engaged in the buying and selling of goods on their own account and which are largely independent in ownership: Wholesale Merchants, Voluntary-Group Wholesalers, Converters, Exporters, Importers, Industrial Goods Distributors, Drop Shippers or Desk Jobbers, Cash-and-Carry Wholesalers, Retailer-Cooperative Warehouses, Wagon (Truck) Distributors.

2. *Manufacturers' Sales Branches* are wholesale outlets owned and operated by manufacturers apart from their plants. *Manufacturers' Sales Offices* are establishments maintained by manufacturers apart from their plants for the purpose of selling their products. They are distinguished from sales branches by the fact that the former include facilities for the physical storage, handling, and delivery of merchandise.

Factory Salesrooms

Manufacturers often maintain salesrooms at or near their factories to serve the following purposes:

1. *Display rooms where goods are shown and selections made with delivery and billing of orders by independent dealer outlets.* This type is found in the

building and furniture industries. List prices are frequently, but not always, shown on the goods, to assist the homeowners in making a choice. These display rooms are helpful to the manufacturer because they permit the goods to be displayed under attractive conditions; they are helpful to the dealers in that many cannot afford the cost involved for the volume of business they do. Manufacturers must be careful to show impartiality to their dealer customers, to find out which, if any, dealer sent the homeowner in, and be careful to notify only that dealer of selections made. Wholesalers also install display rooms operating them in the same manner. Manufacturers usually encourage, or help finance, wholesalers to install display rooms using their products; besides assuring good display such investment ties the wholesaler more permanently to the manufacturer.

2. *Display rooms where seconds are sold.* This type is found in the furniture and the textile industries. Usually the goods have small flaws and are rejected by quality control; while they cannot be sold as top-quality goods, their usefulness is not entirely impaired and the goods are sold at a discount. Some bakeries and candy manufacturers sell broken goods which are still edible but are not up to saleable quality.

3. *Display rooms where goods are sold to the consumer.* This type is found especially in the bakery and dairy industries, although any small manufacturer without dealer outlets may use them. Some milk companies that make household deliveries also have dairy and ice-cream bars.

4. *Display rooms where goods are sold only to employees.* This is a type operated by some larger department stores. Also, some manufacturers use them as "company stores." Although desirable as a means of maintaining high employee morale, they sometimes become undesirable through the tendency of relatives of the employees to multiply with unnatural rapidity.

Advantages of Wholesaler Distribution

Some sales managers fail to recognize the overall service that wholesalers render to business and to society. They are so overconcerned with their immediate problem of getting distribution that they don't stop to think what would happen to their retail outlets, and for that matter to the whole scheme of mass distribution as we know it today, if all retailers had to depend upon manufacturers' salesmen for the service they require.

The trend for the past 20 years has been toward branch distribution, but only firms with a full line like General Electric can manage to make them self-supporting over the whole country. Shorter-line companies as large as Philco and Zenith, as well as companies in other industries, have balked at attempting it in more than the major metropolitan areas. They state their preference for independents (because of costs), but cannot afford to settle for what they consider second-rate distributors usually because other brands move better. In such cases, they settle for company-owned branches.

There are a dozen advantages to distribution through wholesalers, when such a procedure is logically within the type of operation and product concerned. These advantages may be listed as follows:

1. Availability of forward stocks.
2. Handling broken stocks, and assembling order requirements.
3. Provision of a ready-made sales force.
4. Frequent customer contact at low cost.
5. Intimate knowledge of local conditions and market demands.
6. Intimate acquaintanceship in the local trade.
7. More knowledgeable granting and handling of credits.
8. Lowered transportation, storage, and delivery costs.
9. Local representation for servicing and handling complaints.
10. Assistance in obtaining local information for product development and market research.
11. Effective means for distribution of product information and promotional literature.
12. Elimination of capital investment in inventory and physical properties.

Wholesaler distribution is particularly advantageous for a manufacturer with a limited line, little concentration of customers, short margin of profit, low demand, or highly seasonal demand.

In the AMA *Marketing for Executives* series, John M. Brion, New York marketing consultant, writes:

A manufacturer's major goal is that his distributors be his inventory and marketing agents in their territories, and he wants them, in this capacity, to:

Carry his full line.

Carry a good stock of each item.

Not carry competing lines.

Not carry too many lines.

Carry sufficient spare parts or components.

Hire salesmen who will make the desired impression.

Train the salesmen on product knowledge and selling.

Develop a network of high-quality retailers.

Cover the product's market intensively and extensively.

Increase the product's share of the market.

Devote the needed time to sell each prospect.

Provide servicing quickly and efficiently.

Cooperate with the manufacturer on planning, sales campaigns, advertising, and promotion.

Provide local advertising and promotion.

Use effectively the advertising, promotion and sales aids provided.

Give the line good window, counter, and floor advertising and display.

Keep facilities and equipment attractive and efficient in operation.

Give prompt delivery service.

Follow the manufacturer's pricing policies.

Provide needed market feedback.

Submit desired sales data on time for analysis.

Cooperate on strategy and tactics.

Make an adequate profit.

This adds up to meeting the demands that one could ordinarily expect only of one's own wholesaling operation; the nearest thing to it with distributors is "keyline status," so such status is frequently a basic goal.

The average distributor actually has only two to eight salesmen, with a volume ranging from $200,000 to about $1.5 million. But his contacts, acceptance and strategic position within his area make a well-planned network of franchised distributors unsurpassable in this respect. A manufacturer obtains maximum coverage, in number of accounts and calls in each geographic area, with resulting greater volume and lower price at a minimum of investment and expense.

Disadvantages of Wholesale Distribution

Disadvantages cited by sales executives generally include one or more of the following:

1. Reluctance by wholesaler to carry adequate stocks.

2. Reduced profit spread to manufacturer.

3. Competitive demand by other manufacturers for salesmen's time and interest.

4. Lack of aggressive sales promotion due to multiple lines carried by the wholesaler.

5. Loss of direct contact with the ultimate customer.

6. Difficulty of providing necessary special and technical services.

Maintenance of contact can be of considerable importance to a manufacturer, particularly should a wholesaler eventually decide to drop its line and replace it with a competitor's product.

Lack of merchandising ability is usually a major objection. Narrow profit margins and stiff competition place constant pressure on distributors to obtain high volume, and the more lines and brands carried, the less attention each gets. Well-advertised major brands as a result often move fairly well, while the products of small manufacturers without comparable ad budgets do not.

Closely related to this is the lack of intensive selling on minor product lines and those that are difficult to sell. Products that *must* be *sold* because of their nature, use, or competition have a rough time starting or growing through most distributors unless a strong incentive is given. This is because the salesmen are admittedly just order-takers for the majority of their products.

The manufacturer's lack of control over the marketing of his product is a third principal disadvantage. Many manufacturers complain that distributors do not always show enough interest in:

Specialized selling

Product success

Ad and promotion care and effort

Missionary work

Service needs

Handling of complaints

Handling of inquiries and followup

Analysis of markets and problems

In addition, manufacturers may also lose control of pricing and control of final condition of product and package. This totals up to inability of the manufacturer to execute marketing strategy because of his remoteness from the actual marketplace, and the conflicting objectives and policies between himself and the market.

Manufacturers are prompted to seek new distributors by:

1. Efforts to gain greater geographic penetration, to sell a new product, or to find new prospects for old products.

2. A need for better coverage in existing territories.

3. Change in the distributive process, such as electing to use distributors instead of selling direct to end-users.

A study conducted by the National Industrial Conference Board revealed that in some industries distributor selection is practically a continuous process, and in these a relatively new executive grade, "manager of distributor sales" (or development), has emerged. Usually, the job responsibility includes all aspects of distributor sales, but sometimes the principal function is to find, develop, and train new distributors or dealers.

Leads to possible new distributors are collected from several sources—trade associations, local civic and business interests, direct-mail solicitation, to name a few—but the brunt of collecting and evaluating information falls on the manufacturer's salesmen.

Sometimes the field sales staff will even make the final decision, but normally corporate headquarters exercises that right after a careful assessment of all relevant information.

What Does a Good Distributor Expect from the Manufacturer?

A study by the National Industrial Conference Board presented some of the things a strong distributor considers before agreeing to take on a new supplier. They are:

The manufacturer's record of financial capacity and stability.

Market potential for the supplier's product in the territory.

Major industries to be served by virtue of carrying the line.

National and local sales position and reputation of the product line.

National and local sales position of the supplier's major competitors.

Information on other distributors and dealers handling the line.

Sales policies of the company (terms, discounts, minimal inventory requirements, and total initial investment required).

Gross margin expectations.

Estimated annual sales volume and profits for the first and succeeding years should the line be added.

Warehousing requirements.

Packaging requirements for the products.

Advertising and sales promotion assistance.

Field sales assistance and training available from the supplier.

In addition, "the principals of almost any well-established, reputable distributor firm will readily admit, or oftentimes complain, that too much of their time is spent seeing representatives of manufacturers who are trying to interest them in selling their product lines," the study discloses.

Distributing Direct to the Dealer

Sometimes there can be no specialized distributive channels that can make the contact between producer and seller. Other manufacturing operations lend themselves to direct dealings with the retailer because of the extent of the market, volume of business, and nature of product.

Among the major advantages of selling direct are: Closer contact with the consumer than under systems which pass through more hands; centralized control over selling to dealers, permitting better promotional cooperation and closer contact with the buying public; and avoidance of the necessity of having to add distributors' margins to the price at which the product is sold to retailers.

From the experience of the Food Machinery and Chemical Corporation, the advantages of direct dealerships are:

1. Closer relations with dealers who actually sell products to the public.

2. Absolute control over distribution of available supply during periods of shortage.

3. Elimination of distributor profit permits pricing of product at a competitive level.

4. Greater profit for manufacturer.

5. Ability to expand dealer organization rapidly by direct efforts rather than on a secondary basis through distributors.

Keeping in close contact with the dealer is one of the headaches in this type of distributive pattern. If the manufacturer is able to get adequate coverage with his organization, the dealers can be one of the most efficient tools at the producer's disposal for measuring consumer acceptance for his product and for gauging market prospects.

This matter was emphasized by Dailey Mills, Inc., producer of poultry and stock feeds:

"Dealers know—or should know—their potential customers, as well as their needs and the feeding problems they must solve, better than anyone farther removed from the consumer. Operation through dealers, we believe, enables the manufacturer to simplify his administrative problems to a minimum, and it eliminates the large staff of field men that any other method would necessitate. We do a minimum of direct selling because of the prohibitive costs of less-than-carload-lot shipments, and because this practice tends to break down the morale of some of the dealers."

What Wholesalers Must Do

To keep abreast of changing conditions, the wholesaler must, if he wants to make a profit, study his relationship to the retailer who, after all, is his main source of income. He should analyze customer accounts, their credit standing, service demands, dealer progressiveness as to location, efficiency of operations, delivery costs, and other factors. Market analysis is also of prime importance. The points to be considered here are:

1. Territorial analysis, such as population pattern, industrial trends, competition, transportation facilities, buying power, etc.

2. Sales quotas to guide executive control and set selling pace for salesmen.

Another important factor in the cost of distributing through wholesalers is the cost of handling orders in some houses. During the last few years various wholesalers have given this obstacle careful consideration, with the result that some of the larger houses have drastically reduced their handling costs, as well as speeded up the shipment of orders, by one-story plant "drag-line" and conveyor systems, short-cutting routines, and the latest mechanical equipment in all departments. Restricting sales to large units is another important development in wholesaling. This is aimed at the small-order headache.

It is the policy of many wholesalers today so to organize their lines and facilities that they will be in a position to supply their customers with merchandise of slightly better quality than the chain stores and mail-order houses offer, at a price which will enable them to compete successfully with these large-scale buying units. By means of special assortments, the excessive cost of handling small orders has been corrected to a large measure.

Dun & Bradstreet, Inc., publishes annually 14 lists of operating ratios in 30 wholesale lines. These reports show that only four of the categories had a median net profit on sales of over 2 percent and 10 had less than 1 percent. Industrial distributors were only slightly better off than consumer-goods distributors.

What are the principal problems distributors face in the conduct of their business?

Profit Margins. Almost all face a continuous problem of survival; few can hope for better than a net profit of 3 to 5 percent of sales and many are consistently around ½ percent to 1½ percent.

Accounts Receivable. A well-run firm may average about a 45-day turnover but still has to pay its sources in 15 days to get the small discount, and within 30 days to retain credit standing. Some manufacturers, in launching a new line, or, in an attempt to "load-up" dealers, sometimes extend much longer terms to both distributors and dealers, but these are special cases.

Credit. Distributors are excellent examples of businessmen who need credit for "accounts receivable" and high inventory costs, yet in periods of tight credit have a difficult time getting it.

Inventories. Even many large distributors do not adequately understand the cost of carrying inventories; sales forecasting; effective methods of analysis and purchasing; and the value of proper product mix and inventory balance.

General Management. Large organizations usually have superior management, even go extensively into automatic data processing, but small and newer firms generally take years to get down to sound management techniques: planning, budgeting, expense control, objectives and policy clarification, market analysis, and training.

Promotion. Distributors cannot always afford to carry out their sources' promotional campaigns. Merchandising displays, in some industries, run as high as $300 in cost; dealers will not pay even a small portion of this. Too, they will not pay for literature, which the distributor must buy from the manufacturer.

Sol Goldin, president of the Institute of Appliance Manufacturers, recently attended a day-long seminar for dealers sponsored by a distributor in Harrisburg, Pa. He was impressed first by the number and caliber of retailers attending this seminar, and by their eagerness to learn the basics of merchandising and management. One dealer said, "Sooner or later we'll have to scratch for sales and then we'll need all the knowledge, skill and help we can get." A major part of this help will be the merchandising experience of local distributors.

"Local" and "independent" were key words, said Mr. Goldin: "In *boom* times, it's all very well to have the factory and factory branches to manage distribution. But in the case of *bum* times, the wholesaler must be far more than an efficient warehouser, shipper, supplier. He also must be a sales manager, a financial adviser, a new-product developer, a headquarters and clearinghouse for *all* services (not just product services), and first lieutenant on the merchandising front line."

The Wholesaler's Sales Organization

Another large area for improving the service which wholesale distributors can render without adding to their cost of operations is to do a more efficient job in selecting, training, and supervising their sales organizations. Relatively few salesmen calling on retailers do any creative selling. Most of them just take orders. The following checklist may be helpful to wholesalers who are not satisfied with the kind of sales job they are doing, or to manufacturers' salesmen who work with distributors in the field:

1. List sales functions and operations now being performed.
2. List other opportunities for promoting sales and expanding customers' sales which might be adopted.

ARE WHOLESALERS RETAILER-ORIENTED?

	Firms Without Salesmen	Firms With Salesmen
Presently offer store-identity or merchandising programs	90%	35%
Of those not already offering, planning to do so	10%	25%
How many stores presently participating	2,097 total	2,822 total
	262 average	99 average
What does your program include for retailers:		
Consumer promotions	100%	97%
Preprinted order forms	75	62
Stock-control plan	55	64
Store identification	100	86
Newspaper advertising	100	71
Preprinted invoices	78	33
Retailer advisory committee	67	61
Modernization assistance	67	71
Accounting advice or service	55	39
Supply catalog service	89%	69%
Supply price-change information	100%	58%
Number of dealers using price service	2,472	8,626
Number of dealers using catalog service	2,472	15,796

Courtesy: Hardware Retailer

3. Where a sales organization is already operating, draw up a chart of organization to make sure all jobs and personnel are covered, and that each has separate consideration.

4. Define the kind of selling job each type of salesman has to perform, starting with a list of the separate operations each salesman goes through. These are the job requirements. Salesmen can help in making this list.

5. Work out a standard operation for each type of salesman. Include the experience of the most successful salesman, and collect information from outside sources.

6. Set up a program for studying each job requirement continuously, having sales supervisors or the sales manager go along with the salesman, so as to work out the best way of doing it.

7. Select for special emphasis the job requirements that prove most profitable.

8. In selecting new salesmen, list the best qualities of the present force and arrange in order of importance.

9. Collect information from outside sources on job analysis, salesmen's selection and training.

10. For new goods requiring specialty selling, consider a plan for sales training by manufacturers' salesmen, sharing the expense with the manufacturer.

11. Standardize the number of calls a salesman should make per day, after analyzing the nature of his route.

12. Review salesmen's routes and territories.

13. Review present methods of compensation to see whether they suit the nature of the business and the job, are understood and accepted by salesmen, and provide incentive rewards for special ability and special sales events. Give special study to results of incentive payment plans that were successfully proved during war production, and consider how these ideas can be applied to salesmen.

14. Analyze sales supervision to see whether it is actively conducted, with the manager regularly in the field with the men.

15. Analyze costs and profitableness of each operation performed in connection with sales, both inside and outside the house.

16. Where salesmen are responsible for collections, analyze methods to make sure they are constructive in building better habits of payment, and also are effective in reducing the average age of accounts and the total amount outstanding.

17. Evaluate the possibility of sales to each customer or potential customer, establish sales objectives, and allocate order solicitation time in accordance with the objectives.

18. Maintain records of sales achievement for review with the salesmen in the preparation and maintenance of sales strategy.

19. Program for the most profitable use of manufacturers' detail men.

20. Examine lost effort and increased costs involved in the distribution of duplicate or competing lines, the carrying of unnecessary slow-moving stock, and poor housekeeping.

Even where the closest relation exists between retailers and a wholesaler, as in the case of voluntary groups in the food field or other instances where salesmen are less needed, the job of promoting sales through customers still remains. In any trade, or with any type of organization, methods of expanding volume of sales need separate consideration.

What Manufacturers Can Do to Help Distributors

A manufacturers-distributors inquiry on the subject of "What are the best distributor sales aids?" produced the following statements:

Hundreds of excellent aids are prepared by manufacturers for the use of distributors and their salesmen. If as much care were taken in distributing these as there was in preparing them, everyone would benefit. The distributor must know what is available to him in order to use it.

> DON PERMODA
> Illinois Tool & Instrument Division
> Illinois Tool Works, Inc.

Although we have the usual assortment of distributors' sales aids . . . there are times when specialized promotions are required to obtain maximum benefits.

> WILLIAM NEEDHAM
> Hewitt-Robins Inc.

The best aids for distributor use are self-contained direct-mail pieces. We favor them because they are relatively inexpensive to produce and more effective than circulars. Some distributors make effective use of these aids, but others do not. It depends on how forceful our distributor sales representative is and on the aggressiveness of the distributor's organization.

> R. F. SCHUSTER
> Owatonna Tool Co.

In my view, the best sales aids are personal calls. Once the user is convinced the product works for him, he wants it delivered and he wants to pay as little as possible. Users are impressed through personal selling and, through their own experience, with consistent service and competitive pricing. It is true that companies that can afford to hit the user wih advertising in every form put their product in a favored position.

> JOHN G. LINCOLN, JR.
> President
> Arizona General Supply Company

What Distributors Say They Need

A questionnaire was sent to all members of the National and Southern Distributors Association to determine distributors' problems with respect to manufacturers' merchandising and promotional programs.

In answer to the question: What does the average customer want to know about the products you handle?, the distributors indicated price, use, and delivery as the most important.

In response to the question: How can distributors be further assisted by manufacturers?, the answers were many and varied. But, in summary, they gave the manufacturers some excellent suggestions for improving their merchandising activities. For instance:

Catalogs and Bulletins
> Contain all the information needed.
> Keep up to date.
> Tell the story simply and show prices.

Display Material
> Limit size.
> New items only.
> Occasional floor or counter units.
> (Some companies thought display was not important.)

Direct Mail
> Very useful.
> Tie-up with distributor.
> Should be colorful.
> Distributors would rather handle.

Advertising
> Very useful.
> Direct to industrial distributors.
> Use appropriate trade publications.

Shipping Practices
> Advise of any delays.
> Use packaging lists.
> Prompt mailing of invoices and documents.
> Not too much weight in one package.

Price Lists
> Keep as simple as possible, but complete.
> Make price lists understandable.
> Standardize.
> Separate from descriptive catalog pages.

In answer to the question, "What are some of the practices you would like to see remedied?" the answers were:
> Acknowledge orders promptly.
> Live up to promises of delivery.
> Have knowledgeable personnel.

How SKF Helped Its Distributors

To help distributors boost their sales, a "Territory Management Plan" was announced by SKF Industries.

The plan was based on the concept that the only way to increase sales volume in a distributor territory is to "prepare and follow a well-defined, comprehensive plan." SKF gave distributors a working outline of the program, which covered creative selling, establishing new accounts, reinstating dormant accounts, followup in-plant seminars, territory sales forecasts by product, and planned expenses.

To assist the distributor, the plan included examples of how to establish sales quotas, increase coverage, and stimulate sales-call activities.

The effective use of maps—so that the individual distributor sales-man or management could see his territory at a glance—was also detailed.

"This plan reflected the best thinking of highly successful men in the industrial sales field," said A. C. Johns, director of distributor program planning. "It grew from requests made by SKF's distributors during seminars held earlier throughout the U.S."

Other Distributor Aids

There are many other examples of how manufacturers aid their distributors and dealers to increase sales:

Westinghouse merely asks its dealers to make the sale. Then Westinghouse takes over; makes the delivery, installs the appliance, and services it. The retailer is relieved of these tasks. Procter & Gamble and General Foods have developed new advanced techniques for improved materials handling and made these available to large food retailers. Campbell Soup Company runs management training seminars for retail food-store personnel. In eight years, over 78,000 attended this manpower development program. Gibson Refrigerator Sales Corporation runs an annual "College of Profit" for retailers and distributors.

E. T. Moe, Di-Acro Division of Houdaille Industries, Inc., describes how his company helps its distributors and their salesmen:

We use a variety of aids to help presell the prospect and also make the salesman's time most productive during his calls. This is done through several methods: Extensive publication advertising, a continuous direct mail program, and displaying our products at most major industrial trade shows. All inquiries generated from these various outlets are turned over to our distributors for followup.

On the distributor level, in addition to personal calls from our district sales managers and factory personnel, we make continuous product mailings throughout the year covering individual models and accessories. This is sent to both inside and outside salesmen. Product mailings include samples or regular backup literature available for handing out. Special literature is also produced to point out and help salesmen better understand specific features.

As an additional sales aid, we try to anticipate many of the questions that prospects will ask and furnish the salesmen with complete series of questions and answers to cover this area. Because we are asking the distributor salesmen to go "a little above and beyond" in becoming as familiar as possible with Di-Acro equipment, we reward him in some way for this extra effort. For instance, we have run a product-knowledge contest that offers merchandise awards during the contest period, plus a choice from a number of world-wide trips as a grand prize.

Our favorite type of distributor aid is direct-mail material. We have found that direct mail is the most effective means of getting past the front office and to the engineering and shop personnel, who specify equipment. You can't force a distributor to use promotional aids, but most of those who have, and who use up-to-date lists and mail with continuity, find that direct mail pays off in increased and traceable sales. Better still, salesmen have found many business opportunities that may not have popped up during their regular sales calls.

The Distributor Salesman

Distributor salesmen have so many different products to sell that they can concentrate their efforts on only a small percentage of them. Second, they often lack complete knowledge of all of the products they handle and the applications of these products. Third, they must produce orders regularly, and hence, can spend very little time on long-range market-development projects.

For the most part, your success with distributors and their salesmen will depend on the quality and frequency of your communications with them. Therefore, part of your advertising program should concern itself with your distributors. It should inform them, motivate them, and help to make it easy for them to sell your product. Distributor salesmen can multiply your efforts in the field substantially, while freeing up your own salesmen to concentrate on the larger, more profitable accounts.

Not all wholesalers are equally dedicated or enlightened about the retailer's changing needs and wants. As described in *Hardware Retailer:*

Many distributors cater to the mediocre retailer's thinking and ignore those aggressive retailers whose needs are different, whose desires are channeled more into merchandising and promotional assistance, not merely in procurement of goods.

It is because this type of retailer had been too much ignored—and still is being ignored in some areas—that types of wholesalers developed who singled these men out to form the nucleus of their own wholesaling organizations which would concentrate efforts only on those services that the retailer felt he needed or wanted.

The idea of dealer-ownership of a wholesale concern is not new. It has boomed during recent years in the food field, where retailers have exhibited even more willingness to subject their individual independence and operational methods to group planning than have hardware retailers.

National Association of Wholesalers

This is a central group of alliance of wholesale associations. Its affiliates (as of the time of publication) include the following:

Air Conditioning and Refrigerating Wholesalers' Association
American Surgical Trade Association

Appliance Parts Jobbers Association

Association of Institutional Distributors

Automotive Service Industrial Association

Farm Equipment Wholesalers Association

Federal Wholesale Druggists Association

Flat Glass Jobbers Association

Hobby Industry Association of America

Independent Shoemen

Laundry and Cleaners Allied Trades Association

National-American Wholesale Lumber Association

National Association of Electrical Distributors

National Association of Musical Merchandise Wholesalers

National Association of Textile and Apparel Wholesalers

National Beer Wholesalers Association

National Building Material Distributors Association

National Candy Wholesalers Association

National Electronic Distributors Association

National Food Distributors Association

National Frozen Food Distributors Association

National Paper Trade Association

National Wheel and Rim Association

National Wholesale Druggists Association

National Wholesale Furniture Association

National Heating and Air Conditioning Wholesalers Association

Optical Wholesalers National Association

Sporting Goods Jobbers Association

Toy Wholesalers Association of America

U.S. Wholesale Grocers Association

Wallcovering Wholesalers Association

Wholesale Stationers Association

Manufacturers seeking ideas for establishing better relations with their wholesalers may receive valuable assistance from any or all of these groups.

There are, of course, many other associations for wholesalers;

most of them make it a point to be helpful to manufacturers. These include:

American Dental Trade Association

American Institutional Wholesale Plumbing and Heating Suppliers Association

American Research Merchandising Institute

American Steel Warehouse Association

Association of Steel Distributors

Central Supply Association

Food Service Equipment Industries

Institutional and Service Distributors Association

National-American Wholesale Grocers Association

National Association of Oil Equipment Jobbers

National Association of Tobacco Distributors

National Coin Machine Distributors Association

National Distributors Council

National Plywood Distributors Association

National Wholesale Hardware Association

Shoe Service Institute of America

Steel Products Warehouse Association

United Fresh Fruit and Vegetable Association

Watch Material Distributors Association of America

Wine and Spirits Wholesalers of America

The National Association of Textile and Apparel Wholesalers is a group of wholesalers of ready-to-wear, piece goods, domestics, floor coverings, notions, underwear, hosiery, furnishings, infants' wear, and other lines. This group has developed timely marketing studies on subjects such as "Salesmen's Compensation" and "Ratio Analysis." It also has developed an excellent advertising program, aimed at retailers expounding the advantages of purchasing from wholesalers. The association sponsors an annual convention, trade show, and educational seminar every January in New York City, open to wholesalers only, which makes it rather unique.

It seems probable that in the future much of the task of building better retailers may be taken over by state associations of whole-salers and retailers, thus freeing the individual wholesaler for the actual work of warehousing and distributing merchandise. For example, a seven-point program of the Wisconsin Pharmaceutical

Association, supported in large measure by the wholesale pharmaceutical houses of that state, was as follows:

1. A pharmacy-school scholarship campaign.
2. A store selling-and-buying service.
3. Aid to pharmacists returning from the armed services.
4. A store-remodeling service.
5. Cooperation with universities.
6. New professional-relations program.
7. New public-relations program.

At the top of the list of things producers can do to help their dealers is to share with them "merchandising know-how" based upon experience with so-called "laboratory stores." This know-how could cover such phases of storekeeping as store arrangement, inventory control, credit policies, advertising and display, personnel problems, customer services. Above all, dealers need help in increasing store traffic.

The Whirlpool Program

In its marketing strategy, Whirlpool Corporation assigned a major role to distributors, particularly with respect to advertising at the local level. The story of this arrangement was told by Joseph A. Schulte, general manager of advertising and promotion for Whirlpool Corporation, at an annual meeting of the Association of National Advertisers.

Detailing the steps that had been taken to create an awareness of the product with the expenditures for advertising out of all proportion to sales, Schulte said that the weaknesses in the marketing effort became apparent at the retail level. The company then set out to line up distributors who would be something more than jobbers "who sent us orders when and if they got orders. This led to the formation of a Distributor Advisory Committee—the 14 best independent thinkers in our distribution system.

"We put in their hands roughly 40 percent of our total selling, advertising, and promotion budget. This money comes to them through co-op funds that are based not only on purchases but have added incentives for increased share of market. As our share of market increases, so do the dollars that it generates. And, their share of our funds has been substantial because our share of market has been steadily rising. Approximately 80 percent of these funds are used in retail advertising, but portions of them are also spent for dealer incentives, including trips."

The Role of the Broker

In reaching his markets, a grocery-product manufacturer or food processor has the choice of maintaining his own sales force or using a food broker. To be successful, brokers must perform certain functions more efficiently than the manufacturers' own sales forces.

Brokers conduct continuing operations in the same area and thus are often able to develop and maintain more effective selling relationships than company sales representatives. They are flexible in their selling efforts, being able to employ extra sales manpower for special promotions or seasonal items. And because they represent several manufacturers, the cost of each sales call is proportionately lower.

How Companies Select a Broker: Before selecting a broker, a manufacturer should analyze his product and his sales need in each market. Questions most frequently asked are:

1. Is the broker willing to represent the company aggressively?

2. Is he oriented toward selling the company's type of product to the buyers the manufacturer wants to reach?

3. Does the broker have contacts in his sales area that will enable him to sell effectively to buyers in that area?

4. Has he a reputation for integrity?

The manufacturer's evaluation of the broker's expressed interest, willingness, and reputation can best be done after personal interviews in the prospective broker's office.

A broker's value to a manufacturer depends on how well he helps the manufacturer achieve sales goals while holding costs at a reasonable level. To reach the target volume, broker and principal must work together to forecast sales accurately and to coordinate the broker's sales and merchandising activities with the manufacturer's promotion and marketing efforts.

Manufacturer Controls Marketing: The broker's primary objective is to maintain good selling relations between his principals and their customers, who are wholesalers, chain-store organizations, industrial users, and other buyers. General marketing management cannot be delegated to brokers. The manufacturer must concern himself with advertising, product development, packaging, research, and pricing policies. The broker frequently assists in physical handling of goods, credit investigation, invoicing, and other nonselling activities.

Food brokers were once free-lance sales representatives lacking any continuing relationship with the companies they represented. Now, they are integrated sales and service organizations operating under contract with the companies. Today's market-oriented brokers must be sufficiently flexible to adjust quickly to the changing requirements of both manufacturers and customers.

Chapter 13

THE INDEPENDENT DEALER

DESPITE the rapid growth of chain stores, discount houses, etc., the independent dealer is still an important factor in our system of mass distribution.

In fact, the independent merchant is today a better merchant, a better salesman, and a more resourceful marketer *because* of the competition of the chains. By adapting new methods of display, self-service, checkout, and the rest, even the small merchant can often survive and make a profit in competition with the mass distributor. Although his prices may be higher, he depends on neighborhood trade and on the millions of consumers who prefer to do business with "the shop around the corner."

While it is customary to think of independents as "small merchants," the classification includes also the large-city specialty stores, department stores, some supermarkets, and exclusive dealers, as well as those tradesmen who operate in the shopping districts of big cities and small cities, suburban shopping centers, county centers, and rural communities, plus the thousands of filling stations and general stores still found at every crossroad.

Small-Town Independents

One of the most intriguing units in the great American market is the small-town and medium-sized city store. Competition for this business is especially keen, with many aggressive and well-managed chains in the field. But there are tremendous sales opportunities for manufacturers whose sales policy pivots around the independent merchant. Actually it is not always necessary to sell through one or the other outlet, for there are many nationally advertised products sold both through independents and through chains.

The key to successful distribution in the small-town market is selecting and selling the stores able and willing to get behind a product and really push it. While some cling to the idea of "100 percent coverage" and seek to sell every store in town able to pay its bills, the more experienced sales executives operate selectively. They find it no longer desirable to leave dealer selection to their salesmen. The salesman as a rule wants an order in a town. If he can't get a profitable order of sufficient size from the best store, he goes to the next best store, and so continues until he gets some kind of an order from any store with any credit rating at all. Such a sales policy may yield volume, but it does not always yield a profit adequate to the effort expended.

Cluett Peabody Methods

The makers of famed Arrow shirts sell to more than 600 key trading centers, including many small towns. This company does not sell to the mail-order chains or mail-order houses, but does sell to department-store chains, to some men's-furnishings chains, and to selected independent retailers. Cluett Peabody makes an intensive study of every community in which it sells, and makes its salesmen approach a dealer at least twice a year (in the big-city stores a Cluett Peabody salesman calls daily), with a detailed plan for selling everything in the Arrow line, including a timetable of all advertising, special events, and promotions.

This organization maintains a continuous market research program, studying consumer preferences and buying habits. It also conducts "in-store" research to help retailers speed turnover and conduct their business on a profitable basis.

Constant checking on styles and consumer wants is maintained, to produce merchandise attractive to consumers. The company, which has grown steadily over a period of 110 years, has been a consistent national advertiser. The image of the company is characterized by style and quality, foregoing entirely low-end merchandising.

Over the years, boys' wear and a Lady Arrow line of shirts and blouses have been added to the regular Arrow men's line of shirts, handkerchiefs, sport knits, jackets, and swim wear.

The manufacturer who is not willing or unable to do a selling job at least partially similar to that of Cluett Peabody in the small cities may become discouraged. For unless the manufacturer's salesman knows how to get his goods properly pushed by the right merchants, and unless that merchandise enjoys consumer demand and is properly advertised, sales volume in the small-city stores may be disappointing.

Two Decisions Necessary

There are two major decisions to be made by the manufacturer who wants business from this small-town sector of the country:

1. To sell to the mass distributors; or

2. To set up selling machinery and methods which will enable independents to sell a fair share of the total, in spite of mass distributor competition.

Now suppose we look at the second alternative, assuming that the manufacturer wants small-town business, but is unwilling or unable to sell to the chains. To hold his own in small towns the manufacturer may have to use one or more of the following methods:

1. To organize and train salesmen to sell smaller merchants direct.

2. To organize and train salesmen to sell independent merchants through wholesalers.

3. To set up his own distributing organization using distributors, branch houses, or warehouses.

4. To organize or promote his own chain of stores.

5. To organize or promote exclusive or "captive" stores to sell his line.

Many of the electrical appliance manufacturers, working through distributors, depend almost wholly on specialty dealers who may handle several lines of appliances. These stores are usually rigidly supervised, and their franchises subject to quick cancellation, if volume fails.

The Scholl Manufacturing Company of Chicago also sets up "captive" dealers to sell its foot appliances and other products exclusively where local dealers produce in sufficient volume. It also has lines for general distribution.

Many other manufacturers have worked out franchise plans which require certain performances from all dealers who sell the lines. This seems to be one of the most successful methods, where the line is big enough to be important to a merchant. All these plans grew out of the fact that, when left to his own devices, the small retailer will seldom produce a profitable volume for any one manufacturer. He is inclined to attempt to sell too many brands, to scatter his efforts, to depend wholly upon voluntary "drop in" business, rather than to develop sales through promotions, program selling, and close cooperation with the manufacturer.

Fairchild Dealer Policies

In a statement to Dartnell, Nat C. Myers, Jr., director, communications products, Fairchild Industrial Products, outlined his company's dealer policy as follows:

As a result of four distinct product lines within a relatively small division of a large company, we developed specific individual patterns of distribution and selling.

There is absolutely no question in our mind with reference to the key factors in our current success. First, foremost, the product has to be well designed, reliable, economically feasible, and capable of performing a valid function. Assuming that that criterion is met, the overriding requirement becomes an effective distribution network with a qualified and "available" service support organization.

With specific reference to our audio-visual and consumer-products lines, we have organized an effective structure. The backbone is a national (and international) network of stocking-service dealers who are, in effect nonexclusive distributors. These dealers work with the franchised dealers within their geographical areas in order to provide sales and service support. We are unusual in this respect. Most audio-visual equipment manufacturers rely upon a one-step sales pattern involving exclusive distributors selling direct to the end user. In those cases support may be provided by manufacturers' representatives or factory-field sales-service liaison personnel. Because we are a meaningful division of a larger corporation we have been able to make cooperative arrangements with sister divisions to function as a support behind the stocking-service dealer structure and the New York, Chicago, and Los Angeles factory-service offices.

As a result, our potential customers, who are dependent upon the equipment once they determine to utilize it, are provided with an effective sales and service support capability. We enjoy sales of about 95 percent of this market despite a number of competitors with somewhat comparable equipment. A good measure of our success is due, I am sure, to the customer confidence engendered by the existence of this network.

In order to establish, maintain, and expand the network we have had to maintain a firm price structure and to avoid accepting "order takers" as dealers. We have, therefore, very few department stores, camera stores, or discount houses as dealers. In some locations organizations of that nature can be counted upon to provide effective selling effort and to maintain the price structure, but, in general, that is not true of large urban areas. Policies of firm price structure and continuous effective dealer support have resulted in a dealer loyalty and a level of dealer selling effort that has proved to be extremely effective in meeting dealer quotas and increasing our overall business.

What the Dealer Wants to Know

Manufacturer-owned retail shops are not a major factor in American retailing. Although a number of firms do own their own stores, the art of retailing is most difficult for manufacturers to understand, let alone master. It is hard for production men to comprehend what goes on in a merchant's mind. This is one of the main criticisms that can be made of manufacturers' salesmen who deal with retailers. Their sales approach is geared primarily to the product and its qualities or characteristics.

The retailer is not as interested in such information as he is in how the product will fit into the rest of his line, its markup and turnover, and *ideas for promoting and merchandising it.* He doesn't concern himself too much with its construction or composition. Unfortunately, too few manufacturers take the time and effort to learn about retailing so that they can sell *from the point of view of their customers,* rather than their products. This represents a tremendous educational opportunity. The more marketing people learn about retail merchandising, the easier it will be for them to win a larger share of the retail market.

An Industry Promotion for Local Dealers

Eleven manufacturers and a trade association banded together to increase summer sales in a classic example of cooperative marketing. The products all had peak sales during the outdoor season, so the group adopted the theme of "Leisure Living."

Styling themselves the Committee for the Great Outdoors were: King-Seeley, Tupperware, American Gas Association, Cessna Aircraft Company, Johnson Motors, Champion Spark Plug Co., International Harvester, Jantzen, Inc., Johnson Reels, Inc., Mobil Oil Corp., Nimrod Division of Ward Manufacturing, Inc., and The Seven-Up Co.

The committee symbol was a stylized logo of a pine tree in a circle.

A Great Outdoors News Service was created, and a 20-page tabloid feature section full of general news stories on subjects ranging from camping in the desert to swimming and cooking in the backyard was made available to newspapers across the country, to be used and edited at will.

King-Seeley received over 800 newspaper requests for product information to include in expanded leisure-living stories.

The committee concentrated its program at the local level. Outdoor special sections were developed by individual newspapers, based on local recreational facilities.

Cooperative Advertising

Since the dealer is right on the firing line when it comes to contact with the customer, most manufacturers go to great lengths to provide advertising and promotional support. This usually takes two forms: The first consists of store merchandisers, window display, and consumer literature; the second assists the dealer to advertise in his local newspapers and over the radio or TV stations in his area. For this purpose many major corporations selling through distributors and dealers have a cooperative advertising policy through which the cost of local advertising is shared among the producer, distributor and dealer.

Basically, a cooperative reserve fund is set up by the manufacturer, based on a certain percentage of the value of each shipment to a distributor. When the local dealer advertises he submits a statement of his expense to the distributor and is credited for 50 percent of the expenditure. The distributor in turn submits the statement to the manufacturer and receives a credit of 50 percent of his own share of the cost. Thus, in theory, at least, the net result is that the dealer pays 50 percent, the distributor 25 percent, and the manufacturer 25 percent but these percentages may vary according to specific industries or companies. The point is that the policy must be uniformly applied to all accounts as required by the Robinson-Patman Act.

That is not to say, however, that in introducing a new line for instance, a manufacturer may not increase his share of the cost. But, if he does, he must do it for *all* his distributors. The advantages or disadvantages of cooperative advertising from the standpoint of the manufacturers' interest are discussed in a later chapter.

Aside from newspaper advertising, the independent dealer does not always take full advantage of the manufacturers' promotional campaigns and advertising material. The reason for this is that he is not too anxious to spend his own money and expects the manufacturer to do it for him. Unlike department stores, many dealers are not aware of the fact that their own store windows are one of their best advertising media. So when a manufacturer launches a very important campaign, in many cases he goes so far as to hire a window-display company to make sure that the dealer properly presents his product to the public.

Some dealers, of course, are very promotion-minded and exploit every promotional opportunity. Mort Farr, well-known appliance dealer in Philadelphia, appears on his own local television programs, advertises extensively, and is active in a variety of community activities.

What of the Future?

In his impressive address, "Is There a Future for the Independent Dealer?" delivered before the NARDA Institute of Management, Sol Goldin, manager, retail marketing, the Whirlpool Corporation, made some challenging points. He said:

As reported by economist Richard Snyder, the U.S. business census shows a drop-off of more than 10,000 appliance-TV dealers in five years—a loss of 25.5 percent.

However, the disappearance of many of these dealers from the list was due to growths, not deaths—some dealers, like Maury Cohen of Lechmere Sales, diversified and were reclassified as department stores rather than appliance dealers. Many more merged, or became parts of other businesses . . . to name a recent example, Kelly & Cohen became a vital part of Shoe Corporation of America.

Let's face the case against us. They tell us we're oversaturated with dealerships.

A second observation is that most dealers carry too many lines of similar products.

A third criticism is that many dealers are undercapitalized.

A fourth area of concern to many analysts is our shortage of information. For instance, we do not understand psychological pricing (as in cosmetics) or floor traffic (as do the food and oil people) and we don't know the values of demonstration (as do automobile dealers).

Some of us seem to believe that merchandising consists solely of offering goods for sale. Others believe that effective merchandising rests solely on buying and pricing. And another school of thought is that merchandising is a matter of wild promotions.

If your primary aim is to buy cheaper, or even to operate cheaper, there is only one route. You must become more efficient. But there is, as you know, a ceiling to efficiency.

But to reach farther for *more markets*—extra sales—there are *no* limits. Not as long as we keep having more kids, more products, more wants, more ambitions. You don't have to be a Sears, a J. C. Penney, or a Gimbel to have chain-type ambitions for broader horizons. But you *do* have to be an independent to be absolutely flexible in your merchandising methods! Isn't this *really* the way to assure your future in appliance retailing? If *saving* money means *making* money, the chains can do it better than you can. But if finding and fitting *new* markets is more profitable then you have a slight advantage in freedom.

If you were to ask 10 independent retailers why chains are becoming chains, I'll bet nine of them would say, "in order to buy cheaper." But if you were to ask 10 *chain* executives why they are expanding, I'll bet all 10 would say, "to reach more markets—to develop more sales."

What a whale of a difference in those two reasons! The first is solely defensive—buying cheaper than what? Cheaper than competition. For what purpose? The answer can only be to get a bigger share of *currently available* business.

The other reason is totally aggressive. When you set out to reach more *markets*—whether by going to another geographic area or by expanding lines to get more *kinds* of business from a present area, or, whether you are going into new price ranges—you are opening up for *extra* business.

I maintain that we are reaching the limits of *buying* as a method of saving and, therefore, of profiting . . . and I submit four reasons: . . .

One . . . the big retailers, your competitors, are approaching peak efficiency in buying.

Two . . . your suppliers are approaching greater efficiency in merchandise handling.

Three . . . government pressures are tending to equalize pricing at all levels.

Four . . . knowledgeability is becoming standardized . . . more college graduates on our staff . . . more books, trade journals . . . consultants, and similar intelligence services.

And that swings the pendulum to merchandising imagination . . . basic merchandising innovation. Not just another contest, another premium plan, or a lower price. There's a lot of innovating to be done.

As far back as 1955, marketing thinkers were saying we may be headed for a rental economy. The lease business did become big business—particularly in the automobile trade. Now in appliances, too, we're following suit. But again, we're doing it *defensively* . . . we're just *going along*.

Aren't there *many* great new merchandising devices yet to be discovered about the leasing of household durables? It doesn't have to stop with a freezer-rental plan any more than it stopped with the borrowing of chairs from funeral parlors.

The overall suggestion here, I'm sure you realize, is diversification. Diversification in your thinking, your planning, your reaching . . . as well as in your markets.

There are, literally, hundreds of markets yet to be explored; hundreds of marketing methods yet to be developed; and hundreds of new-product opportunities coming our way soon. If you were to devote just one or two brainstorming sessions to the many possible directions of diversification, you would spell out great lists of services for the independent appliance store.

Is there a future for the independent dealer? No, only a future for the independent *thinker* . . . only for the *individual* merchandiser. There's no guaranteed, already-thought-out future for anyone.

No matter how big his computer or poolstock warehouse . . . nor how vast the purchasing power of his cooperative . . . nor how skillful his negotiations . . . the future of the independent, just as the future of the chains, must be measured by selling and serving, not by buying and pencil sharpening.

The few strong independent food stores, the thriving drugstores, all the strong independents of every business who are progressing are doing it through innovations. These are the guys who realize we never run out of markets . . . we only run out of sales.

Chapter 14

DEPARTMENT STORES AND DISCOUNT HOUSES

W ITH all its theoretical advantages, such as providing one-stop shopping in a prestige atmosphere with charge accounts and delivery service, the department store is finding it increasingly difficult to compete with independent specialty stores and discount houses.

To meet this competition, many independently owned department stores have pooled their resources and formed cooperative groups. Federated Department Stores is a notable example of such cooperative action. Also, the modern department store avoids a lot of headaches by granting concessions to outsiders to run certain departments which are not greatly profitable or which require technical know-how. Examples of departments which often are run by concessionaires include camera departments, tobacco shops, beauty salons, and millinery departments.

The department-store buyer, however, remains a key man in this industry. The title of "buyer" does not reflect his full importance— he or she makes a lot of advertising, merchandising, and promotion decisions as well as being responsible for buying the stock for his particular department.

The buyer will usually be found in a cubbyhole about the size of a broom closet, when he is not traveling to some large city or even abroad to look at new merchandise. Even when there is centralized purchasing, the buyer has the last word on what will be sold in his department.

Some independent department stores maintain buying offices in cities like New York, Chicago, St. Louis, New Orleans, Dallas, or San Francisco. Frequently a buying office may represent a group of stores.

A few of the largest department stores maintain buying offices in foreign cities; others send their buyers abroad every year to shop the foreign markets, while still others use agents as independent shoppers in the countries in which these agents live. Some of these agents may act as buyers for several U.S. department stores.

It is this wide diversity of practices that makes the problem of selling to department stores a complicated one and that requires marketing executives to study the individual practices of the stores to which they wish to sell.

The Merchandise Manager

The buyer's role is changing dramatically. He is becoming more of a specialist in the distribution of goods as he gives up responsibilities for supervising salespeople and for the collection and tabulation of inventory information.

This change is enhanced by the freedom to concentrate his time and energies on the selection of merchandise, the preparation of assortments, and sales-promotion plans.

The growth of branch operations has wrought the biggest changes in buyer responsibilities. Branch operations have made it necessary in many cases for buyers to relinquish their sales supervisory roles to the branch department manager.

The computer and electronic data processing are rapidly bringing about another change. Electronic data processing is making it possible to relieve the buyer of his responsibilities for inventory and stock-control operations. The buyer, ultimately, will be provided with a stream of fast and accurate information, allowing him to spend less time gathering information and more time interpreting it.

Classification-merchandising techniques will probably bring further changes in the scope and responsibility of the buyer's job. Under the classification-merchandising concepts, departments will gradually give way to classifications, with responsibility assigned by classification rather than by department.

This will give merchandise management more freedom to develop specialized buyers by types of related merchandise, particularly where the added complications of selling responsibilities are removed from the buyer's shoulders.

Divisional merchandise managers, like the buyers, are being relieved of many ancillary responsibilities, including the control of inventories.

The general merchandise manager will continue to be the man directly answerable to top management for merchandise sales and profits. He may have the added responsibility of inventory management by classification thrust upon him.

CHANGES COME FASTER

Change, change, change, continual change. This is the watchword of modern life. We have not only adjusted to it, many of us have begun to revel in it. Conservative scientists have predicted the end of change at various times, but they have always been proved wrong. It seems it must go on forever. In the last two decades, the changes have been coming faster than ever before. Planes have passed the speed of sound, bombs have become incredible and then incredibly squared, men are in orbit; and here below, new countries have proliferated, television has become universal, and every corner of the world is in a state of ferment . . .

John R. Platt, "The Step to Man,"
Science, Vol. 149 (August 6, 1965),
pp. 607-613, at p. 607.

Inventory management is creating a growing corps of new executives to service the merchandise division. The inventory manager (or merchandise controller) relieves the buying department of responsibility for control of merchandise after it is bought and also assumes responsibility for its replenishment.

The new function of inventory manager has been made necessary by the trend to multiunit operations and the advanced development of electronic data processing. His function is to centralize merchandise controls and to present the buying departments with the inventory information necessary to guide them in their buying operations. In some stores the inventory manager will have a rank comparable to that of a divisional merchandise manager; in others he will be attached to the general merchandise manager's office, while some will place him under general management, reflecting the high level of monetary responsibility the inventory manager will have.

Sales-Promotion Responsibility

The function of the sales-promotion manager is also undergoing rapid evolution, particularly in larger stores. The sales-promotion manager's role is no longer merely that of service to the merchandising departments, but is becoming more and more that of participant in every area that affects the store image and the store's relationship with the public.

For example, the rise of storewide events such as import fairs has brought the sales-promotion manager into a closer working relationship with merchandisers, fashion coordinators, salespeople, and sales-supporting personnel. The sales-promotion executive must be concerned with every phase of such a promotion, from initial concept to final sale.

The proliferation of branch stores has presented retailing with a need for better coordination and a closer working relationship between advertising and merchandising. Telephone selling, once only a service or convenience to customers, is emerging as a major promotional tool which the sales-promotion division can help to expand.

The Branch Manager

The branch manager has developed from a hybrid of both line and staff functions. He is expected to be an all-purpose executive, well versed in operations, personnel, merchandising, and sales promotion, as well as in the newer disciplines of data processing and credit management.

The branch manager, however, has a skilled corporate staff at headquarters on which to rely for guidance and assistance.

As branches become less reliant on the main store or corporate headquarters for the day-to-day decisions of store operations and merchandising, the branch manager will become more and more involved with top-management concerns. He will participate in management decisions affecting future plans, rather than simply follow instructions from headquarters.

Eight Problem Areas

In an address before the Institute of Appliance Manufacturers in Washington, D.C., Bernard Zients, executive head of Gimbels, New York department store, cited eight areas in which department stores need help to "increase our effectiveness and cut our costs." The talk strikingly illustrated the relative roles of manufacturer and department store in meeting and satisfying customer needs. The eight points were:

1. Appliances are an expense-creating item to sell. Once the sale is made the store must provide delivery, adjustment, and service facilities. All of these are very expensive and have grown more expensive in recent years . . . while your markup to provide for those services has gone down.

2. You . . . the manufacturers . . . must take on some of the responsibility for the bad service history in the products you make. Customers are not and should not be willing to accept a product that is defective or in need of service the day it arrives in the home.

3. Department stores have a reputation for integrity. This means that the store must exchange the product and help the manufacturer retain his reputation without being compensated for the extra delivery expense, or the markdown . . . if the appliance was used . . . and the expense of the time involved in satisfying the customer.

4. The quality standards set by the manufacturing industry are very weak. Aside from defective operating parts, the packaging leaves a lot to be desired. It might be wise to review what shipping standards are used and what type of inspection procedures are followed. *Very rarely does anyone from a manufacturer solicit the retailer's comments on what his problems are with bad-quality products.*

5. The fair-trade programs sponsored by many manufacturers and administered by their distributors are becoming unrealistic. Someone must take a realistic look into the costs of doing business and heed the retailer's plea for more margin regardless of the unit sale.

6. All of the advances made by your research and development of new products never gave the big retailer anything more to add to his respectability . . . his respectability being his profit.

7. I know that your industry has made studies to prove how much bigger the Sears, Wards, Penneys, Firestones, and Grants are going to become . . . but you don't all sell them . . . some of you are going to have to come back to us.

8. Furthermore, with all of the love-making you have been directing towards the discount stores . . . aren't they now launching a most determined effort to live under the fair-trade banner?

In summary, speaking for major department stores, we are asking for considerable revision of your retailing approaches and policies—not simply to prove we are good purchasing agents, not because we want more and more service for less and less money, not because we're always looking for a better deal.

We ask for reevaluation solely because we know that under the rules, we can deliver more volume than any other class of trade—more profitable volume, too, once you adjust to department-store methods—certainly more stability . . . this I can promise. We marry our suppliers once we find good working partners . . . we stop buying every deal that comes down the street once we establish long-term relationships.

And one more thing I guarantee: If we can work out these basic problems . . . if we can make department stores important to your volume . . . we can deliver a new kind of consumer awareness and confidence, the likes of which your business has not seen for more than 15 years.

Meeting Competition

In discussing the competition of discount stores, Ralph Lazarus, president of Federated Department Stores, Inc., addressing the New York Society of Security Analysts, said in part:

"Our policy is to give each of our stores a character of its own, completely flexible to local customer demands. By adjusting service to the requirements of the market, we can meet—and sometimes better—discount pricing in those departments where price is the shopper's first concern. On top of this we give to our customers the kind of fashion direction that can come only from an organization with resources on a worldwide scale. Fashion is a factor in perhaps 85 percent of the merchandise that crosses our counters.

"There are four principal areas we can look to for growth. First, of course, we know that we have to do a better job with the plant we now occupy. Second, we expect to grow by expanding within trading areas in which we already operate. Third, we can grow by expanding into trading areas where we do not presently operate. Fourth, we expect to be able to do some rather substantial things with the service sales of our business. We want to know what we can do in the restaurant field, in the travel field, in home maintenance, in prepared foods, optometry and repair services."

Markups as a Sales Tool

Not usually considered by suppliers to department stores is the importance of markup as a selling tool. Roger Dickinson, a former buyer for a major department store, now lecturer in marketing at the University of California, writes in the *Journal of Marketing:*

Markup is defined technically as the difference between cost and retail price, an amount usually expressed as a percentage of the retail price.

One notable contribution of markup is as a negotiation tool with actual and potential suppliers. The retailer can gain significant benefits by using markup effectively; and the supplier may benefit by understanding the retailer's use of markup to gain additional advantages.

The success of any commitment depends on the ability of the buyer to communicate it persuasively to the supplier. A buyer for a specific merchandise classification, therefore, might consider only vendor offers with a minimum markup of X percent. This minimum would be set at a realistic level after considering industry practices and those of competitors. If a vendor believes this markup constraint to be a commitment on the part of the retailer, he will meet these requirements if he hopes to sell merchandise to the department.

Any supplier wishing to develop a substantial volume of business through department-store outlets should consider markup requirements when establishing prices through the various channels of distribution. This should result in greater profits accruing to department-store outlets as a group.

Markup is also an effective tool in negotiating with vendors for special merchandise. A buyer may ask a supplier for a mattress with features that, at a markup of 33 percent, will create an exciting value for the consumer. This gives the supplier some latitude, but puts pressure on him for low cost because both buyer and supplier generally know the retail price that a promotional item with specific features must have to excite consumers.

In addition, when the buyer indicates his expected markup, he eliminates some price negotiation because the general range of the alternatives is pre-specified.

Actually, certain markup pressures may induce a buyer to violate the Robinson-Patman Act, by obtaining cost concessions on regular merchandise; but severe markup pressure may induce a buyer to create new products which may be entirely beyond the control of the Robinson-Patman Act.

The Use of Direct Mail

Direct mail is widely used by department stores, as everyone with a charge account knows. In a study published by the National Retail Merchants Association two points were emphasized.

(1) The bigger the store, the more direct mail.

(2) Statement fillers make up 75 percent of direct mail.

However, stores are not happy with statement stuffers, even though they continue to use them. They would like greater discrimination, better selection, and more personalization.

Since nearly all statement enclosures are supplied by vendors, a small drygoods store uses the same glossy mailer as a fashionable department store. So, more stores create their own direct-mail pieces and insist that manufacturers pick up part or all of the cost.

Other facts revealed by the survey are that:

1. Most stores agree on the effectiveness of dated promotions.

2. Cosmetics and hosiery head the list of good direct-mail items, with ready-to-wear at the bottom.

3. Most stores feel that selling the advertised product ranks third in importance. The first two: Bringing customers to the store and increasing the use of charge accounts.

4. A breakdown of the direct-mail dollar cost is:

   43 cents postage

   39 cents production

   18 cents processing

5. The least-used forms of direct mail were postcards, letters, and broadsides.

6. In the stores' opinion, the merchandise itself outweighs the effects of art, copy, and price.

Of the stores surveyed, 95 percent said that direct mail would be increasingly important in the future.

The Credit Manager

The promotional, customer-relations, and financial aspects of credit management in today's department stores are opening opportunities for the development of imaginative, well-rounded, management-oriented executives that are far removed from the usual bookkeeper image of the credit manager.

The credit manager today oversees receivables valued at more than the worth of the store's merchandise inventory. He is concerned with the approximately 60 percent of sales volume which is attributable to credit sales. He is involved with the great majority of the store's best customers, the credit customers. He is, outside of the selling departments, the only store executive continually in direct contact with customers.

Frequently, however, his authority is fragmentized. The sales-promotion department handles credit promotion; the controller's office takes responsibility for the financial and accounting aspects of credit; the personnel department provides training in credit selling. The credit manager is left with only the routine tasks of credit investigation, credit granting, collections, bill adjustments, records maintenance, etc.

But this bookkeeper image of the credit manager is changing. Management in many stores has recognized that a strong credit-management executive can give the overall credit operation more productive direction when he shares responsibility for promotion, selling, and customer relations.

This broadening of the credit-management executive's responsibilities is beginning to extend beyond the immediate store environment, too. He is faced with additional challenges and responsibilities involving trends toward consumer-credit legislation and increasing competition from other forms of consumer credit.

Electronic data processing will eventually relieve the credit-management executive of many of the routine duties that today take so much of his time. At the same time, it will provide him with new information on trends and patterns to use in his promotional and selling efforts.

Effective development of the credit-management executive for tomorrow will depend on how top management views the growing responsibilities of the credit manager. In some stores, there will be credit executives with the ranking of vice-president, participating fully in top-management decisions. In others, the credit department will continue to provide the routine operations, while other departments absorb its more active roles in contributing to store objectives.

Few other areas of executive development, however, offer the potentials that the credit department does for capable persons to create their own opportunities, to demonstrate their value to management, and to climb to greater prominence.

Store Operations

The profit squeeze of recent years has focused greater attention on better utilization of the money spent on store operations.

The challenge of efficient store operations in multiunit organizations has increased greatly, with a corresponding increase in the responsibilities of the operations executive. As this trend continues, the operations manager will have to become a stronger member of the top-management team, being held more and more accountable for profits through more efficient organization and staffing of operating divisions.

It is possible that future department stores will have three pyramids of administration operating out of the central office. One would embrace merchandising and promotion; another would include the physical operations and control of parent and branch units, and the third would deal with coordination and control of all services.

There is a big communications gap from the point at which the manufacturer's salesman meets and sells the department-store buyer and the point where the retail salesperson confronts the customer. The problem lies in the difficulty of transmitting to the selling floor the information which the customer needs as the basis for making a choice or, more importantly, a decision to buy.

Cyrus H. Adams, III, vice-president of Carson Pirie Scott & Co., Chicago, says:

"The real problem is to get this information to the individuals who staff the floors of retail stores, having this communication coincide with the arrival of the merchandise, and giving our salespeople the benefit of all the product selling points as the manufacturer's salesman gave them to the store buyer. The problem is to have the salesperson on the floor able to answer such questions as 'what has this one got that that one hasn't?' or 'what will this do for me?' "

Recruiting Store Personnel

Retail recruiting on the campus will improve when stores cut down the turnover of their two- and three-year employees.

"The bigger retailer needs to pay attention to that second year after a student goes to work for him," said Dr. Paul McWhorter of

North Texas State University, addressing the Retail Personnel Association in Dallas.

"Middle management is probably your biggest problem today. These people have worked two or three years, up through the ranks of the training program, and they're about ready for promotion but they don't know it. They feel as if they don't have a friend in the organization."

Dr. McWhorter believes the turnover rate in retail stores is entirely too high—"and it's highest at the end of two or three years."

"Many students come away from a campus interview with the opinion that the recruiter just wants a clerk or a bookkeeper," said Dr. Paden Neeley at the same meeting. "Challenge marks the major difference in a firm's ability to attract top recruits," he said.

Training Store Personnel

The larger department stores carry on strenuous and continuous attempts to train sales personnel. One of the largest and best known, Marshall Field & Co., of Chicago, produced a film, "By Jupiter," which is shown to all new salespersons; other large stores have film programs, "shopping clinics," and other types of training activities which try to overcome the inertia and disinterest of the average retail clerk.

Merging of stores in the larger cities, self-service, automated selling—all these and other devices have been tried as a partial answer to the difficulty of finding and keeping competent salespeople. Yet despite all efforts, nearly every large city—and many smaller ones—can tell of once-prosperous stores that have fallen by the wayside due to the difficulty of securing adequate sales personnel.

A guide for retailers, published by the Committee for Economic Development, emphasizes that people are more important than a building or merchandise. So a merchant who wants to see his business grow, or a manufacturer who wants to help his dealers to become better dealers, should study its personnel problem especially carefully. The following specific suggestions are offered by CED:

1. With the help of members of the organization, build up a "manual," even if it is only a good-sized notebook, covering the best way to handle each part of the selling job.

2. Make this cover ideas that apply alike to all selling, and also special ideas related to different lines of goods.

3. Collect and file information about the merchandise from wholesalers, manufacturers, and other sources, which salespeople can learn to give them confidence in selling.

4. Train all salespeople carefully to make only true statements about the materials and qualities of goods. This will take on new importance as qualities of goods change for the better, as unfamiliar kinds of goods come into stores, and as prices change.

5. Experiment with methods of training that use "side by side" teaching, and active demonstration by salespeople.

6. Work out methods of incentive compensation for better performance, making them apply to both sales and nonsales personnel.

7. Try to work out a formula for incentive pay that gives better rewards to regular employees of proved ability than to rush-period help, even for equal sales, and that gives recognition to better results obtained in seasons when sales are normally dull.

The Rise of the Discount House

In the 1950's a new kind of retailing establishment—the "discount house"—appeared in America. It was a tentative movement at first. Most of the early discount houses operated on a membership basis, issuing identification cards to government workers, members of labor unions, and similar kindred groups. Gradually, these closed-door discount houses opened to the general public.

The first public discount houses, operating from abandoned warehouses and similar structures, carried little in the way of nationally advertised brands of household goods and appliances. Their development was quite similar to that of the supermarket in food retailing, in that long-established manufacturers were hesitant to sell their merchandise for fear of offending independent retailers.

Like the supermarkets, however, the discount houses prevailed upon brand-name manufacturers to sell them goods. Many discount houses were a double threat to established retailers, in that they carried food as well as soft goods and hardware and appliances.

The early appeal of the discount houses was on price alone—first-quality merchandise was rare, and surroundings were plain and unattractive. Everything was, of course, sold on a self-service basis, and no delivery service was offered.

As discount merchandisers multiplied and competition grew brisk, some upgraded their quality, decorated their stores, and offered some limited but helpful service. In the early 1960's, competition was so brisk that many discount houses failed. But the strongly financed and wisely managed houses survived, and were joined by many old-line retailers. The S. S. Kresge Co. and F. W. Woolworth Co., longtime leaders among chains of low-priced variety stores, came up with their own discount chains—respectively the K-Mart and Woolco stores.

Today many discount houses rival department stores with their fine buildings and interior appointments. Most continue to be largely self-service, and no delivery service is available. But the advent of the bank credit card has made charge-account purchases as easily available in the discount house as in the department store.

The discount house today can justify its claim as a major distribution outlet, according to a study by Perry Meyers, Inc., management consultant firm. Although the survey was restricted to 200 housewives in a New England community, it is of interest in helping to assess the place of the modern discount store in the nation's system of distribution.

Strangely enough, price, the theme of discount-house advertising for years, rated fifth place in the reasons given by the housewives for shopping at these stores. The most common reason given was convenience of location, mentioned by 28 percent of the group. Next most popular reasons were "good parking facilities" and the fact that the women "liked self-service" (each factor rating a 27 percent response). Ten percent of the group interviewed cited evening openings as an advantage.

Voiced as the principal disadvantage by the group, however, was the need to wait in line to check out their purchases, with "too few clerks" given as a second disadvantage. Another peeve (cited by 10 percent) was the "generally poor merchandise" available at discount stores, although only 18 percent thought the wares below average.

The survey further showed that the discount shopper averages 5.2 visits a month, and the lower the income the more frequent the visits. Children's wear, domestic goods, and curtains are the top merchandise "buys" at the discount stores, according to the majority of the group, with furniture and major appliances at the bottom of their list. Biggest losers to the discount stores appear to be the chain department stores and variety stores, particularly in the field of children's wear.

How a Discount Chain Operates

In an interview reported in *The Discount Merchandiser,* Mark Goldman, chairman of the board of Goldmans Bargain Barns, described some of the policies of his chain of discount stores. He noted:

We have upgraded our stores with the newest and most modern fixtures available. We have engaged companies who specialize in store decor. In our new stores, on main traffic aisles, we have changed from tile to terrazzo because the maintenance and housekeeping problem is simpler that way.

We have reappraised our buying staffs and have hired people who are specialists in all areas. We are now buying higher-priced lines than ever before, and are giving our customers more fashion instead of just the lower-end merchandise. In other words, we are taking advantage of the increased gross national product. We know that people want better things.

We used to buy women's blouses that sold for less than $1 each and went to $1.59. Now we buy goods that conventionally sell for $2.98 and $3.98 and discount these lines. A lot of the lower-priced lines we don't even carry any more. We're putting more emphasis on fashion than we ever did, because with TV and magazines, the customer who buys a $10 dress is just as much interested in fine fashion as the one who buys a $100 dress.

We don't buy special promotional merchandise. *We do not want to buy someone else's mistakes.* Of course, if we've been buying an item at $10 and the manufacturer came out with a special on it at $7.50, we'll go out and heavily promote the item. For example, if we had ladies' slips at $1.77 and someone came along with a promotion where we could sell that slip at $1.09 or $1.19 but we couldn't buy the sizes and colors, we would take these $1.77 slips in our regular stock and promote them at $1.19 and fill in our stocks. Our markdowns on that particular sale would be very heavy. However, the total markdown at the end of the season would not be heavy, and it wouldn't affect our gross margin because the thing that kills most stores is the promotional remainders. We eliminate them by promoting from within our stock. After the sale the merchandise goes back to the original price.

We have developed a work schedule whereby we show a breakdown of hours of the day in quarters: 9 to 12, 12 to 2, 2 to 5, and 5 to 9. We know where our peak selling periods are, and therefore, we can schedule our help accordingly.

We give the store managers a budget each quarter, broken down by weeks. Then they have a schedule sheet and break down their schedule by periods during the day. We have a 40-hour week, five days. We'll have part-timers cover the peak periods, and we merchandise our help like we merchandise our merchandise.

In our method of operation we take 95 percent of our promotions out of our everyday merchandise; we don't re-mark items. We count the items and take a markdown on the entire quantity. Then, at the end of the promotion, we recount the items and take a markdown cancellation showing a net markdown on the group.

Trends That Will Improve Retailing

1. Uniform credit reporting centers; regional and, eventually, national.

2. Return to more and better sales assistance on the sales floor. Especially in department stores, self-service is gradually building customer resentment. Shoppers will make fewer shopping trips.

3. Departmental divisions will be reduced and "classification merchandising" will increase. Giant retailers and department store chains will increase their demands for private brand merchandise and perhaps even produce their own.

Chapter 15

SUPERMARKETS AND SHOPPING CENTERS

THE supermarket of today is defined by Super Market Institute as a retail food store with a self-service grocery department, with meat, dairy, and produce departments, and with a combined total sales volume of over $1,000,000 a year. Two factors that favor the growth of the supermarket are the opening up of outlying districts for both low-cost and luxurious housing developments and the constantly increasing number of automobiles on the road. Another factor is the continued popularity of self-service.

The first supermarkets were ramshackle affairs, often housed in deserted garages located in run-down, low-rent neighborhoods on the fringe of a city or community. One reason, of course, for thus locating them was to provide adequate off-the-street parking. Parking has become a major limitation on the business a store located in the heart of a city can hope to do. Because people had their own cars they favored cash-and-carry stores with ample room for parking close to the store.

As the idea of shopping at supermarkets spread there was a tendency to build more suitable homes for them, and some of the supermarkets on the Pacific Coast, such as the Portland Public Market, and the Farmer's Market of Los Angeles, became quite famous. Their success touched off a wave of building and investing. It was not uncommon for as much as $1,500,000 to be invested in a single market. R. H. Macy & Company, Inc., invested $6,000,000 in the Hillside Shopping Center in San Mateo, California.

There are three principal types of supermarkets, as follows:

1. Complete combination food market, highly departmentized, carrying full lines of groceries, meats, delicatessen, dairy products, bakery goods, fruits, and vegetables. Each line is operated as a fully equipped department, generally in charge of a department head who is responsible for a certain percentage of the total profit. These

markets are usually located in the so-called shopping centers, in fine buildings. Some operate in the Main Street areas. They are large advertisers, sell for cash, and frequently offer a delivery service. Their prices usually meet the competition and their net profit, which is small, is based on their huge sales volume. Their sales run from $1,000,000 up to several million annually and because of their large volume they can always obtain their merchandise either direct from the manufacturer at the wholesale price, or they deal with the local wholesaler on a cost-plus basis.

2. A complete food department, but in addition a confectionery, soda and lunch department, gas station, cut-rate drug and toilet-goods department, and a cigar and tobacco department. Occasionally, it features novelties and household articles as special promotions. This type of market also renders limited service, selling mostly on a cash-and-carry basis. Its huge volume is obtained through circus-like promotions and substantial advertising in all types of media.

3. The third type of supermarket features the complete food departments, but, in addition, has added concessions of specialty lines such as hardware, paints, radios, auto accessories, women's apparel, shoes, and shoe repairing, barbershop, beauty parlors, etc. The number of the departments will vary from a dozen to more than 30. The sponsor is usually a wholesale grocer. He uses his grocery department as the leader, counting on his net profits to come from his concessions.

As a rule, the complete food supers are owner-controlled. There are some supers, however, which rent out the meat concession, retaining the rest of the operation for themselves. If the supermarket is opened by a wholesale grocer, as a rule the wholesaler retains only the dry-grocery department and rents out the remaining concessions on a straight rental or a percentage basis. The latter method prevails in the majority of cases. Most of the independent operators follow the procedure of the wholesalers. Worth mentioning is the cooperative supermarket—where the concessionaires pool together, rent a building and each pays its pro-rata share of the operating costs, based on the volume of each department.

Close to the Customer

Supermarkets are in a very unique and sensitive position. In no other retailing activity is there the same degree of daily and consistent contacts with customers.

In inflationary periods food prices are among the first to be affected and consumers become quickly aware of any rise in the cost of living.

As stated by Paul J. Cupp, chairman of Acme Markets, "Most people think food prices are too high. They do not know that the net profit of supermarkets is about 1 cent of each sales dollar. An average $10 food order will net the retailer a profit of 8 to 13 cents. However, interesting and exciting opportunities lie ahead for supermarkets.

"While there has been a leveling of the birth rate recently, the tremendous group of post World War II babies will be forming new households in the next 10 years. There will be 31,000,000 new customers by 1976.

"The application of computers to food retailing has just started and great masses of repetitive details may now be handled at low cost and cost analysis can be produced in minutes, if not seconds.

"The utilization of space will be greatly improved and a new generation of executives will operate in a manner most retailers do not now comprehend.

"The number of women working outside the home grows constantly and so does the popularity of prepared and semiprepared foods. Fully prepared meals also are increasingly being refined."

Supermarkets have for some time emphasized the role of proprietary drugs and some have leased space for prescription services. Recently a number of leading chain-store companies have invaded the business even further; Jewel Tea Company bought a 30-store drug chain which it is operating under the name of Osco Drugs under one roof; Consolidated Foods added drug outlets to some of its food stores; Kroger has made similar moves. A number of large food chains have purchased drug chains that operate near their outlets and thus control their market.

The Shopping Center

The growth of shopping centers in the noncentral communities of the metropolitan cities and larger towns of America and especially in the metropolitan suburbs, has greatly stimulated the increase in the number of supermarkets.

A drawback to the supermarket, at first, was the noncompetitive feature. Inasmuch as they were usually located in areas where there were few other comparable stores, there was little or no opportunity for the shopper to "shop." On the theory that clean competition makes for more business, the current practice is to locate supermarkets close to competitors so that when a woman drives out to the shopping center she will have an opportunity to compare values and prices without having to move her car.

It is not unusual for a modern shopping center to include one or more supermarkets. A typical example is the Colonial Shopping Center in Orlando, Florida. Its key attraction is Belk's, a full-scale department store equal in size and choice of merchandise to any in the downtown area. It makes excellent use of publicity to build "store traffic" for its tenants. A typical promotion was a Mardi Gras Day, when prizes scaling from $2,500 down were awarded by the "landlord" for the most original costumes worn by salespersons working in the center. Full-page newspaper ads invited the public to come and see the fun. And how they came! You could hardly get around the streets.

There are a number of factors which affect the volume of trade which a primary trading center attracts to its stores. The most important of these are: (1) Its relative size as compared with rival trading centers (generally the larger cities have the more attractive stores); and (2) its relative distance from consumers as compared with the rival centers. Obstacles to the movement of traffic, such as mountains, toll bridges, congested roads, etc., could have important effects too. Other factors which may affect the volume of trade drawn to a city are its qualities as a shopping center—the number, size, and character of its stores, parking conditions, variety and types of merchandise carried, prices, and all the other elements which the housewives of the community will consider in determining whether it is a "good place to shop."

The principle that the volume of trade attracted varies with the sizes and distances of rival trading centers has been expressed in a formula known as "the law of retail gravitation." It is that the relative volume of trade which two such centers will draw from an intermediate point is in direct relation to the relative populations of the two centers and in inverse relation to the squares of their distances from the intermediate point.

Annual traffic-building events, such as outdoor art exhibits during fine weather and annual "rummage sales" (perhaps featuring handcarts and street stalls) are conducted, with great success by many shopping centers. Some centers now include "Kiddielands" where shopping mothers may park their children while shopping.

Whether this trend toward community drive-in shopping centers will become increasingly pronounced in the years ahead depends, experts believe, upon how soon the saturation point in automobile operation is reached. The whole problem of traffic and parking is so bad in a great many trading areas, especially suburban areas, that self-protection requires merchants to do something about it. The drive-in store makes it possible for the customer to make many types of purchases without getting out of the car.

While shopping centers are still being developed in the suburbs, retailers are reevaluating the possibilities in downtown areas of large cities, especially those with rebuilding programs.

Encouraged by local banks, a 60,500-square-foot center was built in Lynn, a town 50 miles north of Boston.

In New Haven, Connecticut, a shopping center with enclosed mall and two-level areas providing 160,000 square feet of rentable space, was erected.

Another enclosed mall in an established downtown area is The Mall in New Rochelle, New York. This center will have more than 722,000 square feet, including a three-level R. H. Macy department store.

What Customers Like

A survey reported in *Display World*, sponsored by the Glendale, Calif., Chamber of Commerce was conducted by Latta and Company among local merchants and shoppers to obtain answers to the following question: What do you believe is the most important influence on selling practices and buying habits in the central shopping district? The answers, ranked in order of importance, were:

Fair or competitive prices

Service

Personnel (trained, or courteous)

Ample selection of merchandise

Good or quality merchandise

Attractive stores and displays

Parking

Variety of shops close to each other

Advertising and promotion

Good merchandising

Style (related to fashion goods)

Another phase of the survey showed that 62 percent of the shoppers were influenced by attractive window displays, 58 percent by newspaper advertising, 4 percent by radio and 18 percent by TV.

Chapter 16

CHAIN STORES AND
MASS DISTRIBUTORS

B UYING power is not the only important factor in the amazing
success story of the chain store. Of equal—and sometimes even
greater—importance is the attractiveness of interior display.

Go into any independent store today, and with rarest exception
there is not enough merchandise visible. Stocks may be good, but too
much of the merchandise is high on shelves, in blind packages, under
the counters, and generally out of reach and out of sight of the
customer who has money to spend.

Go into a chain store and the merchandise is piled neatly on open
counters. Oceans of merchandise seem to rise up and tempt the
dollars right out of your pocket. Interior display of the merchandise
itself is all-important, yet the average independent does not seem to
grasp this. In a typical independent drugstore you will see a great
collection of lithographed "cut-outs" advertising cigarettes, cosmetics, laxatives, hair oil, and cigars. In a nearby Walgreen store few if
any of these lithographic nightmares are on display; instead there
are great stacks of merchandise to create "impulse" sales.

Better prices, featuring one low-priced item as bait, but selling
higher-priced lines; better selection; better packages; lighter, bright-
er stores; better advertising, plus a constant succession of "events"
which create customer traffic, are all factors in the success of chains.
But most important is the fact that you can stand at almost any spot
in a chain store and find, within arm's reach, 50 to 100 tempting
items of merchandise. In addition, the chain is more mobile than the
independent. If a store in one community proves unprofitable, it is
promptly closed and the fixtures and merchandise moved to a new
location.

According to *Chain Store Age,* drug chains have been opening
new stores at a rate of 700 to 1,000 new stores a year, most of them
in shopping centers. Remodelings of old stores have numbered 600

to 700 a year, with an increase anticipated in the years ahead due to upcoming renewals of early shopping-center leases.

Today the drug chains are becoming more and more important to all manufacturers in the health and beauty-aids field, as well as in photo, candy, tobacco, stationery, and mass-selling sundries. Pharmaceutical manufacturers are finding that chains, with their professional know-how, the confidence they've earned from both patients and doctors, and their ability to fill the prescription needs of the communities they serve at reasonable prices, account for an increasing share of the nation's prescription business.

In the area of cosmetics, chain volume in the past few years has been phenomenal as chains expand their lines and intensify their training efforts. Toiletry and proprietary-goods manufacturers are returning to their old friends in the chain-drugstore field for promotional exploitation because they know it is the chains that give momentum to new products and promotions.

How Chain Stores Sell

The principal reason, aside from its buying advantages, that the large chain is able to outsell the independent in most communities is better merchandising—particularly in store display. The chain-store theory is that goods well displayed sell themselves if the price is right. Manufacturers interested in chain-store distribution therefore have the problem of adapting their product to display selling, or "concentrated" selling as it is called by merchandising men. Some of the factors which enter into self-service merchandising, as set forth by *Chain Store Age,* are as follows:

1. The package is paramount. Included in the "package" is descriptive, informative labeling or a clear view of its contents, or both. The package must "stack" or be otherwise easy to handle and display. And a recognized brand name helps considerably.

2. The supply lines must be kept open and the merchandise in constant movement. Ordering, warehousing, and transportation systems will undoubtedly receive considerable overhauling as the full weight of concentrated self-service selling makes itself felt.

3. Store layout will be viewed afresh. Customer-traffic patterns will take on new meaning. The entire store will be designed as a selling mechanism—with related selling, trading-up, and all the other sacred cows of service selling taken care of through carefully conceived display, merchandise placement signs, labels.

4. Mass displays will be "punched up" by light coming from fixtures designed for flexibility, as part of the overall scheme to make the display sell.

5. Mechanized handling of merchandise will assume greater importance at the store level.

One trend in chain-store retailing is to group related merchandise into distinctive areas within the store.

Architect Peter Copeland, of Copeland, Novak & Israel, pioneers in the boutique concept and store designers for Grand-Way and other chains, breaks up the "monolithic" look of the bigger stores by creating individual shops for related merchandise. This also creates a more active appearance in contrast to the stiff and formal atmosphere resulting from display techniques of the past.

Merchandise is being presented in casual groupings that serve the interests of the customer, rather than being rigidly grouped to serve the convenience of the merchant.

"Many chains," says Copeland, "are beginning to think in terms of a 'World Concept'—Junior World, Man's World, Leisure World —each composed of at least a half-dozen boutiques."

The Man's World, Copeland explains, includes, in addition to wearing apparel, a smoke shop, greeting-card corner, gift shop (including gifts for women), sporting-goods shop, and camera shop.

The Increase in Self-Service

The phenomenal increase in self-service in grocery and drugstores is rapidly being repeated in hardware, stationery, and discount stores throughout the country. In the grocery field, the increase of self-service has grown from 25 percent to 85 percent in the past decade.

Paralleling the growth of self-service has been the number of items carried in stock. In food distribution, the average supermarket of today carries approximately six times as many items as the food stores of 20 years ago. Statistics on the drug industry indicate a jump from an average of 10,000 items carried 20 years ago to 50,000 items carried today.

What does self-service accomplish? First and foremost, the installation of self-service techniques increases sales volume. Customers tend to buy more on each visit to the store and, in addition, store traffic itself tends to rise. Other benefits which flow logically from increased sales volume are decreased costs of doing business (as a percentage of sales) and the opportunity to show an improved net profit position.

How can increased traffic and sales be handled, assuming no increase in total floor space? One variety-store operator reports that conversion to self-service added 49 percent more effective space. Self-service fixtures (with no "dead" space for clerks), gondola and tiered displays increased the size of selling areas. Step-up selling displayers against a rear wall contributed their share to the total added space.

The principal area of chain-store expansion used to be in the big cities. Then the chain store invaded the small city and town market. Gamble-Skogmo, Inc., for example, started in 1928 in a small Minnesota town, and has since grown into an operation with sales of well over $100 million annually.

But 'it was probably J. C. Penney Co., Inc., that really discovered the possibilities of the smaller-sized city for chain operations. Although Penney is concentrating its efforts more and more on larger-sized markets, 33 percent of its sales still come from towns and cities of less than 100,000 population. With the abandonment of the cash-and-carry policy of the founder and the provision of credit facilities, the company has followed a trend that started long ago in the nation's department stores. The "famous five principles" upon which the Penney stores were originally operated and under which they still function, according to the management, are:

1. *To serve the public, as nearly as we can, to its complete satisfaction.*

2. *To offer the best possible dollar's worth of quality and value.*

3. *To strive constantly for a high level of intelligent and helpful service.*

4. *To charge a fair price for what we offer—and not all the traffic will bear.*

5. *To apply this test to everything we do: "Does it square with what is right and just?"*

Chain-Store Sales Policies

Study of the established principles used so profitably by the chains is useful not only to independent retailers but also to the people who sell to them. You do not find the chain stores going in for any such foolishness as 28 different sizes of shears; nor do you find dead merchandise in their stocks. The reason for this is that the buyers for chains determine accurately what people will buy and stock that and nothing else. In setting up sales policies which will click with the dealers in towns of less than 50,000 population, it is a good idea to study chain buying and selling methods and to develop a sales pattern which is cut after their methods.

The chains have learned to adjust stocks for regional preferences, climatic conditions, and many other factors. The mail-order houses,

LEADING CHAINS OF AMERICA

	Sales for Most Recent Month Available	Number of Stores
VARIETY		
F. W. Woolworth	$ 95,536,000	3,200
S. S. Kresge	64,634,000	916
City Products	33,373,000	677
J. J. Newberry	20,887,000	538
G. C. Murphy	17,717,000	508
GENERAL MERCHANDISE		
Sears, Roebuck	488,756,000	—
J. C. Penney	155,417,000	1,662
Montgomery Ward	106,793,000	—
W. T. Grant	46,097,000	1,106
Gamble-Skogmo	36,539,000	—
Interstate	29,702,000	101
APPAREL		
Lerner Stores	11,921,000	353
Lane Bryant	9,332,000	124
Franklin Stores	4,647,000	169
Mangel Stores	4,417,000	156
GROCERY		
Kroger Co.	227,211,000	1,497
Jewel Tea Co.	102,747,000	—
Grand Union	62,012,000	538
Cook Coffee Co.	30,836,000	—
DRUG		
Walgreen	39,414,000	526
Peoples Drug	12,410,000	241
DISCOUNT		
Zayre	15,006,000	92
Diana Stores	8,238,000	265
Unishops	2,993,000	201
Volume Merchandising	2,284,000	235
Barbara Lynn	1,457,000	—
SHOE		
Melville Shoe	12,244,000	1,305
Edison Bros.	10,405,000	—
AUTO SUPPLY		
Western Auto	29,308,000	—

Courtesy: *Chain Store Age*

at least the larger ones, issue different catalogs for different sections of the country. Yet some manufacturers send out their salesmen armed with facts about some merchandising event which was successful in a great store like Hudson's in Detroit or Gimbel's in New York and wonder why the merchants in Silver City, New Mexico, or Twin Falls, Idaho, show no rising blood pressure or haste to buy when salesmen present the facts.

New Trends in Chain-Store Retailing

High-speed data transmission has shortened the reorder cycle on staple merchandise for more than 200 J. J. Newberry stores. It helps speed warehouse handling of the orders, assures more efficient utilization of trucking capacity, and provides better service to the smaller stores.

The data-transmission network links the stores with their Woodside, N. Y., distribution center through 34 "hub" stores that are equipped with teletypewriters and Data-Phones. Each hub store handles the preparation and transmission of staple orders for itself and several "satellite" stores.

At the hub store, the ordering strips are converted to punched-paper tape on a teletypewriter with an all-numeric keyboard.

The tape is fed into Newberry's computer system, which updates the master inventory record for the Woodside warehouse, charges each store's account for the merchandise ordered, and prints the necessary documents for filling the orders at the warehouse and delivering them to the stores.

In Fort Wayne, Indiana, G. C. Murphy officially unveiled its "A-A store" to downtown shoppers.

The A-A store is designed for high-impact sales, sharply increased customer service and merchandise grouped *the way the shopper expects to find it.*

Murphy president J. S. Mack said:

"Customers today are realizing self-service means no service and they're seeking more guidance as they trade up. Higher prices entitle them to it and their larger expenditures make it desirable. A definite trend toward personal attention is discernible now and this can be given in both quick-service and checkout-type stores.

The A-A store has been tailor-made to answer these pressures. It's broken into nine major shopping units, several of which team up "old-fashioned" departments to create a new kind of department— such as Sweets 'n Eats (a combination of candy, delicatessen, bakery, and specialty-food departments) or Entertainment Center (books, radios, phonographs, sheet music, records, stamps, coins, and cameras all under one umbrella and concentrated in one section of the store). A Sewing Center joins yard goods, sewing notions, and art goods for the first time. And a Fashion Accessories Center sets up shop for jewelry, hosiery, and leather goods for the first time.

Another interesting program is the Compact-Impact plan, originally tested in supermarkets by Philip Morris Incorporated. As a result of the company's testing, audited by Marketing Factors, chains such as the A & P, Safeway, Kroger, Grand Union, Colonial, Shoprite, Stop & Shop, and Jewel Tea Company have adopted it.

Under the plan, all tobacco products and accessories are moved to one department. Brands are then awarded space on an accurately calibrated share-of-sales basis. The more popular the brand, the greater the shelf inventory, and the better the location.

In commenting on the purpose and implementation of the plan, Charles A. Whipple, director of corporate merchandising for Philip Morris, stated: "We realize that every chain and supermarket operator is mainly concerned with profit. Therefore, we developed a program basically designed to improve return on investment and inventory reduction. If a competitive brand outsells our own in a given store, we recommend that it be given its appropriate amount of shelf-space, along with a more favorable position."

The Chain-Store Test Method

For new merchandise, the average chain-store buyer will probably place a small order for tests in typical stores. If the tests prove satisfactory, he may begin negotiations for merchandise to stock the entire chain, or parts of it. Manufacturers who are developing plans to sell merchandise to small-city merchants will be smart to follow this same principle. Tests should be made in typical towns, in several areas, then sales plans built around these tests. In making these tests remember that there are many differences, even in the same states. East Texas and west Texas are very different. There is a considerable range of climate between Florence in northern Alabama and Dothan in southern Alabama. Conditions in the West may depend on which side of a range of mountains a town is situated; in developing any sales plan check every condition which may be a factor in sales: Climate, snowfall, rainfall, crops, industry, temperatures, whether the water is hard or soft.

Affiliated Independents

In order to meet the competition of the large chains, many of the smaller independent retailers in some cities have banded together in buying groups. Their central buying activities led to the organization of central supply houses, the stock of which was owned by the retailers.

In other cities, wholesalers took the initiative themselves. They organized the best retailers in each community, induced them to modernize their stores, and encouraged them to feature private brands.

There are at present the following types of affiliated independents (sometimes referred to as "voluntary chains"):

1. The individual voluntary chain which is operated by a wholesaler on his own plan. This type has no affiliations except local cooperatives.

2. Syndicate voluntary chain. This type is operated by a wholesaler on a franchise plan. National name and trademark used by the wholesaler in an exclusive territory. All buying is done by each wholesaler individually.

3. Retailers' voluntary chains. Primarily operated as a buying pool, but cooperative efforts are extended into advertising, selling, and merchandising channels also. Buys through any source of supply.

4. Retailers' voluntary chains (owning wholesale house). A cooperative buying and advertising group which functions also as a wholesaler. Purpose: To reduce the cost of merchandise to retailer.

5. Retailers' voluntary chains (cooperating with wholesalers). A cooperative buying and advertising group, purchases being made through cooperating wholesalers, with no responsibility for the voluntary chain on the part of the wholesalers.

6. Participating ownership voluntary chains. Under complete control of the wholesaler, with the original owner participating in ownership and profits. Store operating, buying, and management, however, are dominated by headquarters.

7. Syndicate voluntary chain (complete service). This type is operated by the wholesaler on a franchise plan and includes national name, private brands, and trademark. Most of the buying is done by headquarters, all wholesale members pooling their purchases. Includes complete merchandising service.

The chance to buy at a lower price has attracted many retailers to join voluntary groups like the IGA. Some who previously bought from wholesalers with a 15 to 20 percent markup found they could get the same goods through a co-op or voluntary group at a much smaller markup. "Our members save 3 to 4 percent over what it would cost them to buy from a regular wholesaler," says the chairman of one cooperative in the Chicago area, the Certified Grocers of Illinois, Inc.

The IGA Stores

J. Frank Grimes, a Chicago accountant who specialized in auditing the books of wholesale grocery firms, had been watching the new chains gradually putting independent retailers out of business. Why not, he thought, fight the chains with their own weapons—centralized purchasing and hard-hitting merchandising? So in 1926 he organized the Independent Grocers' Alliance, now commonly known as IGA, in Poughkeepsie, N. Y., with five stores as a starter. Today, IGA—the largest of the "voluntary chains"—boasts of more than 5,000 stores whose combined sales total between four and five billion dollars a year.

Approximately 650 of these stores are in Canada, and they have now formed a separate entity. IGA's range all the way from the small country store grossing $50,000 a year to the foodliner equivalent of a supermarket, taking in an average of $2,000,000 a year.

Under the IGA method, the retail outlet purchases merchandise through an IGA supply depot at cost plus a small service charge. The depot acts as a distributor and trucker, rendering retail-store supervision and presenting a retail advertising and merchandising program, all of which are paid for by the retailers. The retailers also receive store-engineering services, insurance, consulting services, the services of a field-operations staff, and a monthly merchandising magazine.

The IGA supply depot receives an order on a preprinted form from each of its retail members once a week on a predetermined schedule. The food retailer receives delivery once a week and pays for the merchandise either at the time of delivery or with the order. Some of the larger stores may receive more than one delivery per week. Liquidity is a prime essential in the extension of credit. Inventory turnover in the supply depot averages from 12 to 15 times a year, sometimes going as high as 18 to 22 times.

Accounts receivable are virtually eliminated from the IGA operations by the retailer through his pledge to observe a cash-and-carry policy in his store, and by the supply depot in requiring retailers to pay cash upon delivery. The only exception is where direct shipments from the manufacturer to the retailer necessarily precede payment by the retailer.

IGA's pricing policy is cited as another reason why its member stores have a competitive advantage. All suggested retail prices on every item are set by the supplier to help the retailer make the strongest price impression on his customers. Individual item-pricing permits a good-sized gross profit on a store's total inventory while making a money-saving impression on shoppers. A complete line of products bearing the IGA name has enabled stores to build the same kind of captive market as that of the company chains.

Mail-Order Houses

Another type of mass distributor, closely allied with the national chain-store group, is the publicly financed company which sells by mail from merchandise catalogs. These distributors serve the rural market principally. In recent years to meet the growing competition from the national chain-store organizations, and because the automobile has made buying from a catalog less necessary to a farmer or small-town resident, these mail-order houses have supplemented their volume by opening up "catalog stores" throughout the country. Since the buying policies and methods of these big mail-order houses follow closely those of the chain store, they require the same sales methods and techniques as prove successful in selling to large chains. The importance of mail-order houses that do not operate chain stores is decreasing.

While some of the larger mail-order houses promote and sell their own brands, others feature national brands. The total volume in the mail-order field is quite impressive, and the companies make their profit on rapid turnover, using highly mechanized order-picking and handling methods.

Consumer Co-Ops

High distribution costs have opened the door for consumer co-operative enterprises in the United States. A group of consumers, usually those living in an agricultural or rural community, pool their resources to obtain greater buying power. They establish a community "store." They pay regular retail prices for what they buy from this warehouse or store, and at the end of the year, after all expenses are met, a dividend is paid to the shareholders. Generally speaking, the importance of these co-ops, both in wholesaling and retailing, has been greatly overemphasized.

Chain Mergers

Mergers of retail chains have come increasingly under the watchful eye of the Federal Trade Commission. The Spartan-Korvette merger, one of the largest in U.S. retailing history, was approved by the FTC only after the agreement by the companies to comply with four provisions. The merged company was required to:

1. Divest itself of the 95 operating and two planned stores in the Spartan's retail division within five years.

2. Divest itself of Korvette's 38 percent stock interest in the Alexander's promotional department-store chain.

3. Not acquire any stores or manufacturing concerns without prior FTC approval for 10 years.

4. Limit purchases by Korvette stores of goods from Spartan's manufacturing facilities to one-third of the stores' requirements for 10 years.

Earlier, National Tea signed a consent order giving up its acquisition rights for 10 years, except with FTC prior approval. More recently, the May Co. signed such an order, and both Allied Department Stores and Federated Department Stores are under similar restrictions.

Thus, it has been evident that the FTC is in no mood to endorse retail chains' acquisition of, or merger with, other retail chains.

The Growth of National Accounts

The term "national accounts" is applied to big-volume companies that buy centrally, or influence buying from a central office, for many geographically dispersed units.

Dr. Arnold Corbin, in a series of lectures in England, later published in the British Institute of Management publication with the title "Implementing the Marketing Concept," states:

With the growth of such large national concerns, the traditional pattern of decentralized selling by product divisions and sales districts is often competitively ineffective. Conversely, in many cases, this is not the way the big customers want to buy. This situation has led to the establishment in more than 300 American companies of a national-accounts manager who represents all or several divisions of the company, and who usually reports to the chief-marketing executive. In several companies he even has a number of national-account salesmen working for him.

Company practice varies with respect to the duties and responsibilities assigned to the national-accounts manager. In some cases, he is primarily a high-level promotional salesman or coordinator. In others, he has line authority to negotiate contracts, set prices, and direct field sales followthrough. In general, he arranges selling procedures and policies with respect to the key accounts assigned to him, distributes information, and develops coordinated sales programs at the headquarters level of the customer. He is a focal contact point for big accounts to whom they can talk, voice their complaints, and get answers with dispatch. Sometimes his authority may extend to working closely with the "trade relations" staff, or even to assuming such responsibility himself. At any rate, it is clear that the new concept of national-account management represents orientation to a large and special market. The national-account management concept is another excellent example of the way alert marketers are adapting to changing market and customer requirements.

The Whirlpool Approach

This fast-growing and significant development in selling to national retail chains was very ably described by Sol Goldin, manager, retail marketing, Whirlpool Corporation, in an address before the American Management Association in New York City. He said:

One result of retail-chain growth is that distributor merchandising territories begin to overlap. Any company's wholesaling geography is bound to be affected because retail chains do not grow in patterns dictated by our wholesale-franchise areas. Today one chain may find it necessary to work through three or five or ten distributors on a given brand . . . this is contrary to his normal central buying policies. Consequently, the manufacturer is pressured to allow central buying. Because this is impracticable for Whirlpool, there is increasing pressure to maintain some sort of national-account control.

All in all, four of the top five retailing groups are turning to low-margin operations—food, department, variety and drugstores. The fifth classification, of course, is the discounters themselves, who already claim $5 billion annual volume. Of the top 50 merchandising firms listed in the latest study by *Fortune,* 29 are now in appliances and 20 of these have announced at least an interest in discount operations.

How will this change the functions of factories and of distributors? Well, no one knows for sure at this date, but several points seem obvious if these new-type retailers meet with any success.

One, the need for a national-accounts manager for every appliance concern and for most other manufacturers will be apparent. It is patently impossible for individual distributors in Florida to decide how to service 300 chain accounts in, say, Minnesota. And these chains may be operating in all distributors' territories along with Minnesota.

Two, there will be increased demands for central buying or its equivalent. For a company like Whirlpool, which is totally dedicated to distribution by independent wholesalers, there may need to be central policy decisions, consolidated product-line offerings, certain standards of supply . . . to prevent central buying. For other companies—perhaps yours—your best interests might be served by a policy of direct selling.

Three, it may change warehousing requirements. Whether the warehouses are owned and operated by the factories or by the distributors or by the chains, they will have to contain vast stocks of varied selections and offer very quick service to many small stores—perhaps even to consumers' homes. Certainly the warehouses will have to be ultramodern and highly automated—which calls for big capital investments by someone.

Fourth, it will require new standards of services to consumers as well as to retailers.

Most of the new chain types of retailers aren't set up for such involved sales. So somehow or other, if the distributor is going to sell to these accounts, he must be able to help in the product-service areas.

In other retailing services, chain-account demands are quite different. For example, they will anticipate help with local advertising money but not with skills—they have vast advertising departments of their own. They'll want sales training, but under their own rules—not those of the distributor or factory. They'll want many aids in market research—because they do not know the appliance business; still the appliance research data will have to be interpreted by someone in authority, because the store manager is a salaried, chain-trained, middle-class manager—not an independent operator. The list of such differences could go on and on and on—for our business has spent many years establishing the right kinds of services for small independent businessmen, virtually no time on the needs of vast professionally managed, salaried-employee chain operations.

A fifth necessity, which encompasses all the other four, is that pricing become more uniform among various geographic areas. Today, one of our distributor's prices may vary 10 to 20 percent on a given model from that of another distributor a few states away. It may vary for good reasons, too—not only because of transportation costs, but also because the number and caliber of services required and supplied may differ greatly.

The point is that the concept of national accounts is going to change the selling policies in my industry, and probably, in all American business.

Chapter 17

HOUSE-TO-HOUSE SELLING

DURING recent years the direct-selling field has expanded tremendously. Today its annual sales volume exceeds $10 billion. Only a small percentage of this volume is accounted for by such outstanding direct-selling firms as Avon Products, which occupies a top position in the nation's cosmetics industry with annual sales of over $170 million.

The main reason for direct-selling's phenomenal growth is that it gives the medium-sized or small company, or the individual free enterpriser, a means for building a nation-spanning sales operation in mere months or even weeks . . . with limited capital and an untried product . . . and without costly national consumer advertising in the initial marketing stages.

Direct-selling sales volume has more than doubled in the last 10 years. In the decade ahead it will double again—or even triple. Two factors alone make this prediction virtually a certainty: First, the constantly accelerating growth of suburbs and, second, the increased leisure which more and more American women are enjoying, making them available in ever-increasing numbers as direct salespeople.

Many of the most famous and successful companies of their kind have been built and have maintained their sales leadership through direct selling: Fuller Brush, Wear-Ever Aluminum, Watkins, Rawleigh, Jewel Tea, National Cash Register, Hoover. Companies like Stanley Home Products, Electrolux, Nutrilite Food Supplements, Real Silk, Studio Girl Cosmetics, to mention only a few, have grown from small local operations to national industrial giants by means of direct selling.

Large corporations, long established in conventional sales channels, now own direct-selling subsidiaries. Such parent corporations include Rexall Drug Company, Ekco Products, Helene Curtis, Alcoa, Vollrath, Presto Industries, and others.

One type of enterprise which direct selling can serve to profitable advantage is the company that has reached a sales "plateau" through conventional channels, a situation that arises with hundreds of concerns of all sizes every year.

A good example is the John D. Brush Company, makers of small safes. Long established, this company sold, and still does, through office-supply outlets. Volume was as good as could be expected when a product is simply placed in the corner of a store, listed in catalogs, and generally expected to sell itself.

Then the company turned to direct selling. Salesmen tested the appeal of a household safe by taking it into homes.

Hundreds of prospects, many of them farmers, instantly responded to the idea of having a safe place to keep their valuables and documents. Most of them had seen small safes in stores but they hadn't bothered to buy one.

By adding the personal presentation and the dramatic demonstration which only direct selling can provide, the independent sales force multiplied the company's sales. Today John D. Brush Company sells the major part of its output through modern direct-selling methods.

Preco, Inc., developed a "Power Brush" attachment for vacuum cleaners and decided to sell them direct to consumers. The immediate response from independent direct salespeople all over the country, according to *Specialty Salesman Magazine,* resulted in sales that exceeded the manufacturer's 1,400-units-per-day production schedule. As a result, Preco began tooling up for a 5,000-daily production as quickly as possible, and a 10,000-units-per-day production within six months.

Witnessing the amazing acceptance of the "Power Brush," major vacuum-cleaner manufacturers contacted Preco, Inc., to arrange to include the "Power Brush" attachment with their standard models. As the manufacturer reported: "Practically every major vacuum-cleaner manufacturer has either ordered substantial quantities, or we are in the process of completing final negotiations toward this end."

Many direct-selling products are not known in the sense that nationally advertised products are known. A clearly stated guarantee of performance or refund *is* important. It's important to successful recruiting of direct-selling men and women, and it's important to the maintenance of a continued demand for the product.

Independent salespeople have many steady customers. Most of them live in the communities in which they sell. They rely upon old customers for referrals to new prospects. They go back to old customers with new products. They always want to be sure they can confidently go back to any customer at any time.

A positive, believable, and lived-up-to guarantee gives this assurance.

A great variety of products is sold through house-to-house methods. One has only to take a look at the products sold by companies with membership in the National Association of Direct Selling Companies to get an idea of their variety.

Included are chemicals, foods, dietary supplements, hygienic products, medicinal articles, toilet articles, cosmetics, children's wear, dresses, foundation garments, hosiery, jackets, knitwear, lingerie, neckties, raincoats, sanitary garments, shirts, shoes, sportswear, men's and women's suits and coats, uniforms, work garments, nursery stock (shrubs, plants, etc.), paints, books, greeting cards, cooking utensils, blankets, brushes, china, fire extinguishers, household furnishings, portraits and frames, roofing and siding, seeds, and vacuum cleaners.

Canvassers and house-to-house salesmen taking orders for future delivery are engaged in interstate commerce, hence are not subject to state license laws. However, most states do have laws which attempt to regulate "peddling." Furthermore, some 800 municipalities have enacted ordinances declaring it a nuisance for salesmen to call at or upon residence premises without having an invitation to call. These ordinances, however, are not state laws. The courts have held (*Robbins* vs. *Taxing District*, 120 U.S. 489) that orders taken by salesmen in the scope of interstate commerce are not subject to local taxation or similar burdens, and it is to avoid that possibility that companies selling house to house are careful to meet both the requirements of the municipal "nuisance" ordinances and federal definitions of interstate commerce.

According to J. M. George, president of the National Association of Direct Selling Companies, about 40 percent of the companies in direct selling sell merchandise outright to house-to-house dealers trading on their own account. These "retailers" often have more than one source of supply.

The independent-contractor type of salesperson can also operate in connection with more than one source of supply. These two categories cover almost the total direct-selling business.

There are very few *employed* salespeople operating in direct selling. They are subject to control as to what they handle. The Treasury Department has ruled that house-to-house canvassers soliciting orders for merchandise of one company under the direction of a crew manager, and working regular hours in assigned territories to which they are provided transportation, are employees for the purpose of withholding income taxes on wages and for federal employment-tax purposes.

Direct selling or house-to-house selling concerns are not price-cutters. Few direct-selling companies claim they can undersell local merchants because of the absence of a middleman in the selling process. Where the direct-selling price of an article is appreciably higher than the over-the-counter price, it is because of the fact that direct-selling merchandise contains, in most cases, special features.

Advantages of Direct Selling

Manufacturers in a number of lines requiring creative salesmanship—especially those making fitted garments, hosiery, special-purpose products such as vacuum cleaners, fire extinguishers, etc.—favor selling direct to the consumer because it gives maximum volume control. It permits the manufacturer to build volume quickly and to increase sales coverage when and where needed. Very often sales volume, as in the case of a company manufacturing vacuum cleaners, depends not so much upon market potential as upon sales manpower. Direct selling provides a way of increasing sales manpower and thus making more sales contacts, and by the ratio of sales to calls, obtaining more orders. Since much direct selling is on a straight commission basis, the plus volume is thus obtained without greatly increasing the cost per unit of sale. Direct selling, quite obviously, depends upon the supply of salesmen available. During a recession, when producers need business, and when there also may be a surplus of salesmen, it has many attractions not present during a boom period.

Other advantages cited by authorities on this type of selling include:

Salesmen carry complete lines of samples (Fuller Brush; Jewel Tea with its wagon stock; etc.).

Salesmen can deliver some products right from the wagon and take orders for the next trip.

Some operations of this nature make use of revolving credit, where customers pay a small amount regularly but keep their balance up to $50 or $100 by regular reorders.

Salesmen can make immediate delivery of perishable goods (bakery and milk products, for example).

Territories can be subdivided and covered by specialized crews.

Specialized markets can be worked. The table-silver companies visit brides-to-be in their homes and set up tables with candles, silverware, and plates, ready for a party. Companies selling pots and pans visit offices and sell to stenographers on a monthly payment plan, at prices often much higher than at retail stores and with margins exceedingly high. Other companies specialize in getting college students to sell clothing or jewelry to other students, and housewives to put on "cosmetic parties" at their homes, to which they invite their neighbors.

Disadvantages of Direct Selling

There may be cases where the larger volume obtained by selling through salesmen direct to the consumer has resulted in production savings. But so far as selling expense goes, it costs the factory approximately as much to sell a single product house to house as it does to utilize an over-the-counter retailer. Commissions to house-to-house salesmen average about 25 percent, and the cost of recruiting, training, and motivating salesmen, the operation of branch and division offices, etc., may amount to as much again, so that the selling expense is usually around 50 percent of the selling price, which is about what it costs to go through the wholesaler and the retailer. Sales administration in the direct-selling field requires great skill, and sales managers must be well compensated to attract men of the needed caliber.

Much of the criticism which has been leveled at some house-to-house selling is created by the door-to-door salesmen who do not worry too much about how they get the order. Manufacturers often take the position that these individuals are in business for themselves, just as a merchant is in business for himself. They require the salesmen to take much of the risk and to make some of the sacrifice which an independent merchant makes in order to succeed.

Direct-Selling Organization

Building a sales organization to do an effective direct-selling job calls for the careful selection of men and women, and for systematic and *continuous* motivation. It is not uncommon, in selling through dealers, for a sales manager to handle 50 to 100 salesmen. In some direct selling there is a sales manager for approximately every 25 men, while others have no manager in the field. Direct-selling managers are of the leader type, able to work with salesmen in the field and to do a certain amount of selling themselves.

In most cases they work on an "overriding" commission, plus any commissions they earn from their own selling effort.

Turnover of salesmen is one of the greatest problems in direct selling. Too many companies overstress the *quantity* of inquiries instead of the *quality* of inquiries, with the result that the men recruited are of a lower type, and turnover, consequently, is high.

Many companies secure the majority of their new salesmen from "salesmen wanted" advertisements in national and specialty salesmen magazines. A booklet is mailed in answer to all inquiries, fully describing the company, its policies, sales plans, terms, and form of payment to salesmen.

Some concerns pay their salesmen a bonus for securing new men. This bonus is usually figured on the cost of recruiting salesmen through advertising.

A nationally known publisher reworks inquiries for sales positions received the preceding year, which were not closed, by sending to each applicant a reproduction of a handwritten letter. The replies to the letter frequently gave reasons why the person did not join the organization the year before and indicate whether his interest is still alive. The company reports that a large number of these prospective salesmen are enlisted the second year.

Some of the problems of the direct-selling field are pointed out by Victor P. Buell, writing in the *Harvard Business Review:*

Manufacturers who use regular distribution methods would be aghast at the turnover rates of door-to-door sales forces. Turnover up to 200 percent a year is not unusual. The reasons for this appear to be nonselective recruiting, straight commission form of compensation, distaste for door-to-door selling, and inadequate training and direction.

Because of the difficulty in obtaining people willing to sell door to door, these companies cannot afford the luxury of careful screening. The recruiting job tends to be one of convincing persons to try door-to-door selling rather than selecting the best applicants from those available. Standards vary widely in this respect, but, generally speaking, screening involves nothing more than weeding out only the more obviously unqualified. Consequently, many persons unsuited to door-to-door selling are persuaded to try it but don't last very long.

In many manufacturing companies sales management has shifted from the inspirational to the factual approach. As more emphasis has been placed on better selection and training of salesmen and concentration of effort on high-potential accounts, the type of sales manager who is strong on inspiration has been gradually disappearing.

This is not so with door-to-door sales management. The door-to-door sales manager, while requiring the same intelligence and business sense as any good sales leader, must also be strong in inspirational techniques and capable of stimulating large groups of people through the spoken and written word.

He must stimulate his field aids to recruit new salespeople constantly and effectively. Also, by his own efforts and through his chain of command, he must inspire his thousands of salespeople to get out and make selling calls. Assuming the product is right and the house-to-house selling approach is right, sales management's job in door-to-door selling boils down to motivating more people to make more calls.

No door-to-door sales organization has ever saturated its market; no company has ever been able to recruit a sales organization large enough to make regular calls on more than a small percentage of potential users. For practical purposes, the market for most companies selling door to door today is "unlimited." That is why sales management's emphasis must be on getting more people to make more sales calls on more prospects.

Training House-to-House Salesmen

More attention is now being given to thorough personal coaching, the elimination of early discouragement and disappointment being recognized as an important aid in reducing turnover. Through personal coaching by the branch manager, the new salesman is taught to feel that the company has a personal interest in him and he is thereby encouraged to do his best and to stick to it. This is one reason why elaborate sales schools and salesmen's conventions at the home office, as well as costly traveling schools where the men are instructed in groups, are being replaced to no little extent by man-to-man contact between the district manager and his salesmen.

One reason for the high rate of turnover in new salesmen is that many become discouraged after failing to earn amounts specified in "help wanted" advertisements. This situation may be avoided by mentioning conservative amounts as possible earnings, coupled with one or two statements of high earnings to show the ultimate possibilities if the salesman will apply himself. This avoids any chance of the salesman expecting large earnings at the start.

Turnover may be further reduced by splitting up the payment of commissions and bonuses to extend over a period of a month, or more, paying an additional bonus for length of service. For instance, one company reports two of the most successful methods it has employed to reduce turnover:

1. To increase the salesman's percentage through constantly increasing bonuses because of length of service.

2. To spread earnings over a period instead of paying in full at any one time. Salesmen receive a daily commission, a monthly bonus, and a quarterly bonus. Each of these tends to hold the salesman to the next period. If he quits, he loses all bonuses on undelivered orders.

Selling Direct Through Agents

With the development of direct-to-consumer selling has come the selling agent, who maintains his own crews of house-to-house salesmen, making his arrangements with the factory for exclusive territory, and paying his men from his gross commissions. The tendency at present is for these men to take on a number of varied lines instead of concentrating on one line exclusively. When this is done, the selling effort is weakened. The agent becomes a jobber and his men become jobbers' salesmen selling door to door. Analysis of direct-to-consumer selling plans indicates, however, that best results are secured when the sales organization is controlled and supervised by the home office through division, district, or branch managers, even though this plan involves the payment of social security taxes by the manufacturer.

Some manufacturers have added materially to their volume of business by organizing subsidiary companies to sell their products under different brand names through an agency plan. In marketing such products as paint specialties, roofing, lubricating oil, etc., it has been found that products can be sold in volume by agents under a plan where the cash-with-order amounts to more than enough to take care of the salesman's commission.

Established Route Selling

Another type of direct selling is through route salesmen who have fixed territories or routes, and who call periodically upon established customers. This method of distribution requires a product, or products, with a high percentage of repeat sales, such as frozen foods, coffee and spices, dairy produce, women's hose, etc. However, an exception is the success of the Fuller Brush Company, which built a large national business using direct door-to-door salesmen.

Since route salesmen call with the consent of the householder, local antipeddler laws do not apply. A commonly used device in this type of distribution is to give the housewife a premium of some sort, to be paid for out of future purchases. Her acceptance of the premium carries with it the request for the salesman to make periodical calls. These routes become quite valuable, and some manufacturers find it profitable to sell the franchise for a profitable route.

Direct-Selling Campaigns

Because the summer season, with school "out" and families away, means a seasonal decline for dairy sales in its area, the Wawa Dairy Company, near Philadelphia, usually schedules incentive campaigns for its driver-salesmen during the period. The programs, based on quotas and a point system for unit sales, affect 150 driver-salesmen, foremen, and division managers.

"We always include executives," states Charles R. Meyers, vice-president. "The incentives are effective all the way to the top. The general manager likes to win a shotgun or hunting rifle just as much as does the driver. So there is more stress on sales all the way up the line."

Incentives for these programs are wide and varied. For one summer program, Meyers recalls, S & H green stamps were the sole incentive for a fruit-drink promotion. With hundreds of items for the home available as prizes, this motivated the driver's wife; and if he wanted to take it easy and coast, she prodded him on to bigger volume and better prizes with green stamps. It was a very successful promotion.

High on Wawa's list of successful personal promotions are the tours of the dairy that attract some 15,000 yearly, including schoolchildren, clubwomen, and teachers. Many proposed premiums are first introduced to the women visitors, who are either given the premiums outright or selected by drawings for "Mother-of-the-Day."

Combining Distribution Channels

The Hoover Company developed one of the most famous trade names in vacuum cleaners via door-to-door methods combined with department-store demonstrations. For a time, Hoover relied principally on the retail store for its distribution, but added door-to-door selling again when it saw some of its competitors, such as Electrolux, shoot ahead through reliance on the direct method.

Wear-Ever Aluminum, which originally sold its products only through door-to-door methods, today also sells through retail stores. This is one of the outstanding examples of a manufacturer who has been able to distribute successfully through both channels while using the same trademark.

But this combination of retail store with door-to-door distribution is not automatically successful. Both Real Silk and Fuller Brush experimented with company-owned retail outlets as supplements to their direct methods, but gave them up after brief and unsuccessful trials.

House-to-house selling will, in all probability, not achieve a major role in the distribution system, or radically increase its present relatively small percentage of retail sales. Along with mail-order selling and vending machines, it will probably continue as an adjunct to the principal method of consumer-goods distribution—the retail store.

However, the system does offer some manufacturers the opportunity of achieving distribution not otherwise readily available. It also offers some competitive advantages, if only on a smaller scale.

Chapter 18

TELEPHONE SELLING

MANY aggressive sales executives use the telephone as an important sales medium. One sales manager who uses phone selling extensively has stated that an experienced solicitor can dial 200 calls in 5 hours, of which she gets 100 answers; 15 of these turn into prospects and five into customers.

The phone is used primarily to open the door for house calls by salesmen, and practically every type of product is promoted in this way. If it is a well-known, inexpensive item, the order may be solicited at the time of the call; otherwise the salesman asks permission to call. In return, a gift may be promised, which is left whether or not a sale results. Maytag, Whirlpool, General Tire and Rubber, and Rexair are among some of the companies that have successfully used this method.

A number of companies which specialize in telephone selling claim that superior selectivity in solicitation is possible. With advertising, inquiries may come from widely scattered locations. A salesman might be able to make only two or three calls a day in followup. But by using directories listing phone subscribers by street address, available in most large cities, solicitations can be localized and face-to-face house calls can be more than doubled.

Some companies employ housewives who can spend an hour or two each day on calls, usually in the evening when people are most likely to be at home. They may be paid by the hour or on a commission basis. Most companies insist that the solicitors adhere to a prepared script to guard against their making unwarranted promises.

Many telephone sales originate with coupons or inquiry cards from direct-mail material and business publications. The business or industrial inquiry has been successfully promoted by trade publications through the use of "bingo cards" on which the inquirer simply circles or checks the number of a company or product in which he is interested and mails in the postage-paid card. The result is usually a letter from the company and a telephone call from its local representative or distributor.

Techniques of Telephone Selling

The American Telephone & Telegraph Company has developed a complete program under the heading of "Phone Power" to aid business organizations in selling by telephone to other companies. As stressed by several AT&T executives, Phone Power is not intended for residential selling.

There are actually six programs which the company uses to train customer salesmen, including such subjects as making appointments, reactivating accounts, inventory cycling, and so forth. Each program is divided into:

1. Precall planning.

2. The call itself.

In addition, a "management resource" unit has been compiled for use by management and this applies to each of the six formal programs.

Samuel McNulty, Phone Power representative of the Bell Telephone Company of Pennsylvania, stresses the importance of adequate preparation in telephoning for appointments. He recommends the following procedure:

Essential Steps of an Appointment Call

I. Preparation.

II. Introduction.

III. "Hinge" for the salesman.

IV. Customer benefit or interest-gaining remark.

V. Close.

Let's look at each step to see what important elements it contains.

I. *Preparation:* Nine out of ten telephone and personal sales calls will fail without it.

    A. Set the goal of your call before you place the call; i.e.,

        1. To sell a policy or product.

        2. To convey information.

        3. To make an appointment.

B. Plan what you are going to say before you place the call. If you improvise your call, you may go right into a sales presentation even though your goal is to make an appointment, thus putting yourself in the precarious position of having the prospect reach a "buy or no-buy" decision on the telephone.

C. Believe in your product or service and your company. Nonbelievers make poor salesmen. How can you hope to convince someone that what you have to sell will benefit him, if you do not believe it yourself?

D. Know the strong points of your product or service, so that you can give your prospects positive benefits.

E. Have a primary and secondary talking point.

F. Beware of a telephone weakness: Loss of "eye contact." We use "eye contact" to judge the impact of our sales presentations on a prospect when we are selling face to face. The loss of this asset on a telephone call is the hidden cause of the uneasy feeling that most salesmen have while making telephone calls. But we still have our sense of hearing and our voice on a telephone call, and we must use these assets to compensate for our loss of eye contact. We can compensate by:

1. Painting word pictures with our voice so that we can use the prospect's imagination to our advantage.

2. Listening intently to what the prospect is saying so that we can judge his reaction to our presentation.

G. Beware of the peculiarities of our speaking and listening capabilities. A person from "our section of the country" speaks at the rate of 125 words per minute as compared to a listening capability of 500 words per minute.

II. *Introduction:* We identify ourselves and our company and confirm that we are talking to the proper person.

III. *"Hinge" for the Salesman:* Something to hang your call on.

A. Leads.

B. Precall mailing. Beware of national direct-mail averages. Less than 5 percent of all mailings are looked at and less than 2 percent of these are returned. Salesmen should hope that these averages are correct because they can then make use of a mailer as a hinge and not be confined by the contents of the mailer. A hinge is not a customer benefit.

SELF-ANALYSIS CHART FOR TELEPHONE SALES APPROACH

	YES	NO

MAYBE I WASN'T PREPARED

Did I have cards, lists, telephone numbers, etc., ready before telephoning? ....
Did I know *exactly* what I was going to say? ....
Did I *anticipate* objections and have answers for these objections? ....
Did I have the attitude that I was going to secure the appointment? ....
Was my *sole* objective to secure an appointment? ....

MAYBE I WASN'T INTERESTED

Did I make the prospect's name an important part of the interview? ....
Did I listen to the prospect's voice, words, vocabulary, and needs? ....
Did I repeat the point in which the prospect expressed an interest? ....
Did I show an interest in *him*? ....
Was I careful not to interrupt, not even *once*? ....

MAYBE HE WASN'T INTERESTED

Did I have a "sizzle" in my approach to gain attention? ....
Did I inspire confidence by being sincere and enthusiastic? ....
Did I project my voice and transmit my personality? ....
Did I use short, vivid, descriptive words? ....
Did I stick to the presentation in a concise, logical order? ....
Was my presentation based on doing something for the *prospect?* ....

MAYBE HE DIDN'T LIKE ME

Did I keep free from arguments and signs of pressure? ....
Did I avoid an apologetic manner or timidity? ....
Did I speak with firmness and authority? ....
Did I smile and hold a level, courteous tone? ....
Did I build prospect's ego rather than talk down to him? ....

MAYBE MY PRESENTATION WAS WEAK

Did I have a "sizzle" to gain prospect's attention? ....
Did I "telegraph" my message? ....
Did I have a "hinge" on which to hang my conversation? ....
Did I give the prospect a "reason" or "benefit" for listening to me? ....
Did I develop and maintain a "customer-you" attitude throughout the call? ....
Did I give the prospect a choice between "something and something"? ....
Did I move smoothly from introduction into presentation into close? ....
Did I answer every objection intelligently? ....
Did I keep the appointment my sole objective? ....
Did I prevent the prospect from giving a definite "no"? ....
Did I ask for the appointment instead of hinting at it? ....

IV. *Customer Benefit or Interest-Gaining Remark:*

    A. Prospect is asking you, *"What is in it for me if I continue listening to you?"* You must answer this question in 15 seconds. If you don't, you will not get an appointment.

    B. Prospect participation. Phrase questions which will make a person say YES, nine out of ten times.

V. *Close:* Use the contained-choice method of closing. Example: "Tonight at 7:10, or would Monday at 8:50 be more convenient for you?"

Questionable Telephone Selling

AT&T draws a sharp line between business selling and "residential selling" by telephone. This is due to the many complaints which are constantly received regarding residential telephone practices indulged in by some companies which reflect on this selling medium.

The Better Business Bureau of Minneapolis, Inc., has issued and distributed a four-page leaflet entitled *What Can I Do About Deceptive or Dishonest Telephone Solicitations?* It reads in part:

Learn to Recognize the Misleading Approach!

For example, when the caller . . .

    Gives no identification;

    Claims to be conducting a survey, then tries to arrange a salesman's interview;

    Says he's not selling anything, but would like to interview you for advertising;

    Reels off prices, costs, offers, and questions so fast that you are confused;

    Describes a "special offer" that sounds too good to be true.

If you consider the call questionable, just interrupt and make some statement such as:

    "Please send me a letter about the matter. I'll consider your offer after I've had a chance to investigate. Thank you for calling. Good-by." (Hang up)

Using this technique you won't cut yourself off from legitimate solicitation, but you will discourage questionable and deceptive uses of the telephone.

Programmed Telephone Selling

Western Utilities Supply programmed long-distance calls to supplement field sales visits. "This helped us keep in closer contact with distant buyers and to time calls to our customers' buying cycles, all at substantial savings," says the president of the company, as reported in *Industrial Distributor News.* "We immediately began profiting by 'plus' sales, business that is handled more economically by phone than face-to-face selling."

Customers are called by long distance on a scheduled basis so that they may place their orders by phone. In a matter of minutes after the conversation, the order is being processed. Confirmation or changes in delivery dates are handled efficiently and economically by phone as well, simply by making a second call to the customer.

"The telephone operation enabled us to place an order in Texas and have the order shipped on a rail car that was going out the next day," said a Western Utilities official. "We recently broke all sales records for the month, and part of it can definitely be attributed to the phone."

SELLING TO INDUSTRY

MANUFACTURERS rely on industrial distributors to move more than $7.5 billion in equipment, tools, materials and supplies to American industry. The distributor fulfills an important role for both buyer and seller.

To the seller, the distributor offers a ready market, physical stocking close to the ultimate users, intimate knowledge of local customers and market requirements, active sales support, and credit.

To the buyer, the distributor often offers immediate delivery from warehouse stocks, a multiplicity of lines from a single source and catalog, product information and technical help, and demonstrable economy in stocking, purchasing, delivery, payment, and credit.

Kinds of Distributors

There are now four types of distributors, when not so long ago there used to be just the mill supply houses. Basically, these are the types of distributors:

The Full-Line Distributor: Despite changing times, the full-line distributor has remained the backbone of industrial marketing, particularly in the smaller markets. Sometimes stocking several hundred product lines, the "industrial department store" renders an invaluable service to both buyers and sellers. However, the very multiplicity and extent of his lines have limited the full-line distributor in his ability to give intensive sales promotion to the products of *all* the manufacturers he represents. It has also limited the degree of technical service he can offer.

Specialized Distributors: Stepping into this "promotional gap" in the services of full-line houses has been a growing group of distributors who specialize in products that may require a high degree of product information, technical service, and application engineering. Common fields for specialization include cutting tools, abrasives, power transmission, materials handling, portable power tools, air and hydraulic equipment, power-plant equipment, welding equipment and supplies, electronics, etc.

Limited-Line Distributors: More recent has been the development of smaller distributors who specialize in a dozen or more profitable lines of unrelated products that require high salesmanship, technical service, rapid delivery, and depth of stock. Relying heavily on merchandising ability and competitive service, this class of distributor keeps an especially close watch on costs, margins, and profits for each line he carries. Sometimes considered to be more a "stocking sales agent," he is constantly seeking new "door openers"— readily salable, high-margin, fast-turnover products providing entrée for his specialty sales team.

Combination Distributors: Aggressive, flexible *full-line* distributors are meeting the challenge of *specialized* and *limited-line* houses by setting up separate departments to sell and service their more profitable "key lines." Thus, in many large distributor organizations there are qualified departmental sales managers and factory-trained salesmen concentrating on power transmission, materials handling, bearings, and other lines that need depth-of-product and application knowledge. This is the modern trend in full-line distribution.

How to Rate a Distributor

In a study by the National Industrial Conference Board entitled "Selecting and Evaluating Distributors," four major points emerged:

1. Elaborate analyses by manufacturers of estimated distributor profit potential from handling a line.

2. The growth of distributor advisory councils, which give the outlets a voice in manufacturer marketing policy by bringing together at regular intervals key manufacturer sales personnel and selected principals from major distributors to consider future plans.

3. Expanded manufacturer sales training for distributor personnel, sometimes on an individual-salesman basis, with the manufacturer often absorbing the whole cost.

4. Advertising and sales-promotion help, business-management counsel and technical sales assistance for distributors by manufacturers.

The Role of Research

Almost all failures in marketing industrial products can be traced to inadequate or faulty market research. The first thing to determine is the potential market. Too often manufacturers undertake an expensive sales and advertising campaign for a product on the assumption that every plant in the country "is a prospect." That is not true. The market for any product, industrial or otherwise, is limited by a number of factors. These include: (1) competition; (2) price; (3) design; (4) freight rates; to say nothing of such intangible factors as a customer's policy in practicing reciprocity in placing orders. It is not unusual for large corporations to go so far as to inquire as to who supplies its suppliers with parts or materials, so that every sales advantage may be considered.

Having determined factually the size of the potential market, the next step is to locate the market. What kind of plants are logical prospects, how many of them are there, and where are they located geographically? It may be more economical, in the beginning at least, to concentrate sales and advertising effort in a few areas rather than to undertake national distribution. It is customary in making such studies to use either a map and tack system or outline maps on which prospects can be "spotted" to visualize the sales management job involved. Colored tacks, or crayons, are used to indicate importance of potential accounts. Thus a blue tack is stuck in the map at a point where a prospect of large buying potential is located; a red tack for a prospect offering a fair potential of business; a yellow tack for a "fringe" prospect whose potential volume is questionable—it might or might not pay to allocate much time to such accounts.

Checking the Price Policy

The pricing of a product is far more important than generally realized. The following questions relating to price policy are listed in the United States Department of Commerce guidebook for manufacturers, *Developing and Selling New Products:*

1. Do you know, in general, what your price policy will be on this product?

2. Have you figured your profit margin as accurately as possible?

3. Have you clearly decided whether you want to follow a big-volume-small-margin price policy or a small-volume-big-margin price policy?

4. If in your price policy you are shooting at a relatively limited group of prospects, should you further reduce the total potential prospects?

5. Are you sure your price schedule on the new product will meet the requirements of all your logical prospects?

6. Have you considered insurance costs as well as manufacturing and selling costs in determining your price?

7. Have you considered all transportation costs, including basic rates, yard and switching charges, if any, and other handling costs?

8. Have you considered packaging and packing costs?

9. How will installation costs, if any, affect the price policies of you and your distributors?

10. Will you service or help service the product? If so, will the user pay you directly for the service?

11. Will you expect your distributor to help service the product?

12. How will performance guarantees, if any, affect your costs and prices and those of your distributors?

13. Will you sell spare parts at cost or at a profit?

14. Have you worked out a complete factory price schedule for spare parts?

15. If your distributors will also handle spare parts for your products, have you worked out spare-parts price schedules for sales to them and suggested prices for resale to users?

16. Have you decided what classes of customers will be entitled to trade discounts?

17. Have you determined the schedule of trade discounts to:
    a. Distributors?
    b. Users (for example, governmental agencies) to whom you may sell direct?

18. Will you offer a cash discount to your customers?

Line of Buying Authority

In industrial selling, it may be necessary for the salesman to "sell" several people before he can walk out with an order. The salesman may first have to "sell" the man who uses the product and get him sufficiently interested to suggest to his immediate supervisor that the salesman's product be specified the next time a requisition is placed. Since few workers are capable of effectively relaying a sales presentation the salesman must also "sell" the supervisor.

After the supervisor requisitions the product, the requisition may go to the works manager or the engineering department for approval. Again the salesman has a selling job to do. He must make sure that these executives understand the engineering advantages of the product. Approved by the engineering or operating department, the requisition next may travel to the controller who approves the budgetary expenditure and passes it along to the purchasing department. The purchasing agent or his assistant may or may not issue a purchase order. But if he runs true to form he will check the price

Wall hanger serves as catalog for maker of industrial markers.

against competition. Some similar product which he thinks is "just as good" may cost less money. So, unless the salesman is on the job, the requisition may travel back to its point of issue to ascertain if the "just as good" product would not be acceptable in view of the "saving."

That is a normal procedure in industrial selling. In the case of equipment which involves a considerable outlay of money, it may be necessary to "sell" several executives *and* the board of directors. There are usually "No men" in every organization who may not have much actual buying authority, but who can, if they are not sold, wreck a sale. A study made some time ago revealed that in less than 1 percent of the companies checked, one person had authority to place orders for industrial equipment. In 9 percent of the transactions two or more people were involved; in 29 percent three persons were involved; in 26 percent four persons were involved; in 13 percent five persons were involved; in 23 percent six or more persons were involved. Even in the purchase of supplies such as oil, less than 16 percent of the purchases studied involved but one person.

Since it is true the line of authority varies with the size and nature of the business, it is important in setting up an industrial sales operation to determine as accurately as possible: (1) Who actually influences the purchase of your products; and (2) how best to reach *all* those in the line of authority with your sales message. Obviously it is impractical and much too costly to depend entirely upon the territorial salesman to penetrate an entire organization.

The Industrial Catalog

The difficulty of maintaining close contact with industrial buyers makes it necessary to develop ways of helping the prospect order between the salesman's calls. This can best be done by: (1) Systematically working a carefully prepared and *well-maintained* list of prospects; (2) establishing your company in the prospective buyer's mind as headquarters for the products you sell; (3) furnishing him with an easily used, well-illustrated catalog describing the products you sell, and issuing *periodical* price lists. In fact, the catalog, next to the salesman, is the most important factor in industrial sales management.

Millions of dollars are wasted on needlessly elaborate catalogs. It is wiser to spend less for producing a catalog, and have more to effectively distribute it. Here are some of the trends observed in recently issued industrial catalogs:

Format: Neatly arranged pages, with inexpensive composition and clean illustrations, produced by the offset process.

Paper: Tough stock, suitable for offset reproduction, in place of highly coated enamel stock which tears easily and is hard to read. Exception is when illustrations show considerable necessary detail which must be faithfully reproduced by fine half-tones or color-process plates.

Size: The size of 8½ by 11 inches fits easily into a catalog file, a letter file, or a desk drawer. It permits issuing supplements which can be mailed in a standard No. 10 envelope. Being the same size as a business letterhead, supplements of that size can be used as enclosures. They can be filed in the customer's correspondence file.

Binding: Most are loose leaf—permitting adding price lists and supplements—or spiral-bound to lay flat when opened on a customer's desk. Since most catalogs are filed on edge, the preference is for post binding which permits stamping the backbone. There is also less danger of contents being taken out and misplaced.

Indexing Supplements: A common weakness of loose-leaf catalogs is that there is no provision for easily inserting supplements in the proper place. It is therefore good practice to use the Dewey decimal system in numbering the sections and pages of industrial catalogs, rather than to number the pages straight through the catalog. This permits giving each supplement a section, page and reference number. It is a simple matter for the clerk to insert each supplement in its proper place in the catalog.

The only sensible procedure to follow in distributing expensive catalogs is to make sure they go only to persons or companies known to have a use for them. If you can get such persons to ask for the catalog, fine, but to refrain from supplying potential customers with a catalog simply because they don't ask for it, seems unwise. It is, however, good practice when sending out catalogs to offer to send return postage if the recipient has no need for it. The same letter can explain how the catalog will be kept up-to-date and ask for the name of the person to whom supplements should be mailed.

"Run On" Cost of Catalogs

It is a common practice in arriving at the cost of a newly issued catalog to add together the editorial, engraving, paper, and printing costs, divide by the number printed and come up with a "cost per copy." From an accounting standpoint that method of arriving at the "cost" is quite all right. But there is a danger that this cost will seem so high that top management will ask for restricted distribution.

For sales promotional purposes the cost of getting the catalog ready for the press should be regarded as a necessary expense which would remain the same regardless of how many copies were printed. In other words, the pro rata cost of the catalog for the first 2,500 copies might be $10 a copy. But the cost of running an additional 2,500 copies to distribute to less important customers might be only $2 a copy. This "run on" figure should be kept in mind when considering a wider distribution for the catalog, rather than the pro rata figure.

In the same way greater value may be obtained from the money invested in preparing copy and engravings for a catalog by "fatting over" some of the pages and binding them as cooperative catalogs, of which there are several published. These cooperative catalogs are one of the most effective ways to secure orders for products which are usually specified by architects, engineers, or others not usually contacted by a salesman.

Other Ways to Reach Buyers

While it may not be considered a catalog from many viewpoints, the telephone directory classified section (yellow pages) is the starting point for any basic classification of a company or its products. No purchasing department is complete without the yellow pages. Although the reference files of a purchasing department may be replete with directories and catalogs of all types, there are many occasions in all corporations when the yellow pages save the day for a harried purchasing agent.

Industrial users often hesitate to adopt a new material or process

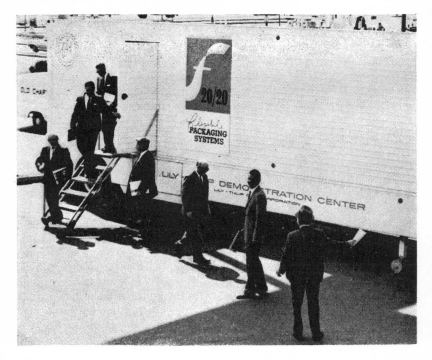

Lily-Tulip Cup. Corporation used this demonstration center on wheels to conduct sales clinics in the field and to show company film on flexible packaging systems to potential buyers.

until consumer acceptance is assured. In such cases, direct advertising is almost essential.

Plenty of case histories prove the point. The garment industry, for instance, would have been much slower in accepting zippers if Talon hadn't done a big job of public education. But remember that building such demand is likely to be very expensive. The consuming public as well as the trade must be educated on a whole new product idea, not merely on a brand name.

Manufacturers selling a wide range of products under a name like General Electric, Goodyear, Du Pont, etc., have a definite advantage when it comes to promoting a material to consumers. Promotion cost per unit is small, and the company can trade on its established reputation. An appliance manufacturer who gets his motor from General Electric is anxious to publicize the fact. The prestige of the branded part is a major selling aid.

More and more industrial companies are moving closer to the ultimate consumers of their materials or products. They are implementing the marketing concept by becoming increasingly ultimate-consumer oriented—that is, concerned with their customers' customers. They are becoming increasingly aware of the truth of the adage: "I'd rather own a market than a mill."

The U. S. Steel Corporation, for instance, is currently running three promotions a year as part of a broad-range campaign to develop the market for its steel products among home-appliance manufacturers.

The company's marketing representatives organize promotions in 30 major markets and work with local members of the industry in 15 secondary markets.

The campaign takes the form of newspaper ads in 15 cities, provides dealers with free display material, sends out editorial material on appliances to 4,000 daily and weekly newspapers, and promotes local-action committees.

The aluminum industry and nickel producers have conducted similar promotions on behalf of their metals.

Don't undertake promotion of a built-in item unless it has definite significance for the ultimate consumer. Failures on this point have been many and costly. A manufacturer of shoe eyelets started a consumer-advertising campaign some years ago; it didn't pan out because eyelets were a negligible selling point with consumers. The same was true of a company that undertook promotion of nuts and bolts; their unit value was too small to justify the expense, and they weren't sufficiently important for people to specify one kind over another.

It is a rough rule of thumb that standard materials or parts shouldn't be promoted directly because the superiority of a single brand is hard to establish. There are exceptions, however, where the item is an important component of a sufficiently important end product. The public can be educated to associate the brand with quality and reliability.

Timken, New Departure, Torrington, and other bearing companies, for example, have done considerable consumer advertising designed to make bearings an important selling point for the product in which they're incorporated.

The key to success in any "hidden" product promotion lies in cooperation between manufacturers and retailers. Unless dealers attach and push your tags and labels, the consumer has no way of recognizing the advertised product at the point of purchase.

Experience of those who have tried shows that you'll have to overcome several obstacles in gaining trade support: Some manufacturers don't want to tie themselves down to one supplier; many retailers as well as manufacturers prefer to build reputation solely on their own name. Where hidden products promotion has been extensive, many retailers regard tags as unnecessary frills and refuse to keep them on; this is particularly true in the soft-goods field. Even physical problems stand in the way. Tags get caught and slow down handling of merchandise in the store. Finally there's apt to be resistance where retailers carry other goods incorporating competitive products; it isn't always feasible to promote all and therefore they prefer not to feature any.

The "Functional Consumer"

The National Automotive Parts Association is an organization of 53 automotive-replacement-parts warehouses that supply the needs of about 4,000 automotive jobbers. The jobbers provide parts for 360,000 automotive service and repair shops.

In discussing how manufacturers try to reach this huge aftermarket, J. R. Degnan, vice-president and general manager of the association, said:

Who are the right people to talk to? Consider the "functional consumer"—the man who does the real consumer's work.

The functional consumer is a person who makes product or brand selections and actually does the buying on behalf of a final user. In markets where they exist, functional consumers are the number one target for sales and communication efforts.

This was amply demonstrated by the "Buying Influences Study" done by Fry Consultants, Inc., a couple of years ago for the Automotive Service Industry

Association and the Automotive Advertisers' Council, which showed that trying to make car owners love your products, or even identify them, let alone insist that they be installed, is a losing battle.

For the past 25 years several manufacturers of replacement parts that lose their identity in an engine overhaul or tune-up, have attempted to establish brand recognition and consumer preference through national advertising.

Of all who have tried the consumer-advertising route, the spark-plug manufacturers, battery makers, and the filter manufacturers have come closest to establishing their brands in the car owner's mind—yet the number of car owners who go into a service station and demand Champion Spark Plugs over AC, or vice versa, is negligible.

The Industrial Distributor

Industrial-product distributors usually have greater stability as a group than those of consumer products because:

1. Their products are sold to buyers who are better capitalized and more durable than the retail buyers of consumer goods.

2. They seldom carry competing lines.

3. The cost of inventories makes new competition more difficult.

4. The demand for technical training and background keeps competition down and the quality of competition up.

5. They are more firmly established in their markets, are not easily substituted by other distributors or company branches.

6. Client relationships are generally stronger and on a higher level.

7. Most products are either on an exclusive or carefully selective contract basis.

8. They have better management know-how.

9. Good distributor associations have fostered high-competitive ethics and mutual respect, and contributed greatly to management education.

This stability has provided a sense of security that permits sound planning and greater effort toward advanced management and marketing. An increasing number of special distribution management courses are being scheduled at universities, consultants are being used more widely, and some of the most modern techniques are being tried and applied.

The industrial distributor's salesmen are the most qualified men a buyer can consult outside his plant for counsel on how to achieve his value-analysis objective, asserted W. H. Lindsey, president of the Pyre-Barker Supply Co., Atlanta, Ga.

As chairman of the modern methods committee of the National & Southern Industrial Distributors' Associations, Mr. Lindsey emphasized that value analysis begins early in a product's planning and continues throughout marketing and servicing.

At every step in this process, there are vast opportunities for the industrial-distributor's salesmen, as well as the buyer, to aid in reducing costs.

A Marketing Plan for Industrial Distributors

Most industrial distributors recognize the need for an effective marketing program in order to compete and survive in today's business world. But many feel they don't have either the money or the manpower to develop such a program. As outlined in *Industrial Distributor News,* there is a simple five-step plan that almost any distributor can follow in developing his own marketing program. It makes use of many sources of information already available to distributors and doesn't require any great expenditure.

In its barest form, it calls for: (1) setting goals, (2) research, (3) planning, (4) action or implementation, and (4) review and evaluation.

Let's examine each phase in detail:

PHASE 1: SETTING GOALS

Distributor management must set realistic goals that are attainable. For example, to increase sales of air hydraulic equipment by 10 percent, or to add 48 new accounts during the coming year, sales to the 21 largest accounts should be increased 14 percent by selling items not now sold to these accounts.

PHASE 2: RESEARCH

The success or failure of a truly effective marketing program hinges on this phase of thorough research concerning market potentials, possibilities, competition, new territories, and methods of qualifying prospects. This means you determine the type of manufacturers that operate in your area; what types of products they make, and whether they are large or small. Knowing the type of products made will give you definite indication about the kind of supplies and tools required in their manufacturing processes.

PHASE 3: PLANNING

Now you are ready to formulate a marketing plan. At the outset, you should analyze the three arms of marketing—advertising, sales promotion, and your sales force. Advertising and sales promotion are the functions necessary to reinforce your sales department. There are two methods of using persuasion. One is printed, the other personal; both have advantages and limitations. Advertising, for instance, can make a thousand calls in a day by direct mail and get the attention of people whose names are not available to the salesman.

PHASE 4: ACTION STAGE

This presumes that the distributor is well organized to handle an order—it is properly selected from stock, packaged, and delivered on time. It also presumes that products will be kept in stock. The best promotion will not produce sales and profits if the distributor has poor inventory control and lacks service.

PHASE 5: REVIEW AND EVALUATION

A good marketing program is self-correcting, thus as certain goals are reached, other goals may then be set by management. As the effectiveness of the advertising and sales campaigns are measured, certain steps are eliminated or stepped up, depending upon their desirability and usefulness.

O.E.M. or P.R.S.?

An electric motor may appear as a part in many kinds of finished products—air conditioners, fans, furnaces, pumping systems, etc. In such cases the motors are called O.E.M. (original equipment manufacturer). The same electric motor may also be used during the manufacturing process or repair of any or all of the products in which it appears as a part. For this kind of use, the motors are called P.R.S. (processing, repair, and service). The only important difference may be the price that is paid and the distributor discounts allowed. Because of the quantities of the motors which may be sold as part of the product, motors qualifying as O.E.M. would be sold (to the same buyer or distributor) at a lower price than the same motors used for P.R.S.

This two-price system for the same or an essentially similar unit has caused a great deal of difficulty among manufacturers, suppliers, and distributors.

The manufacturer of the motors, for instance, may sell direct to pump manufacturers on a lower basis at O.E.M., and allow distributors little discount on the motors when they are ordered for O.E.M. use.

Some difficulty is experienced even in defining the areas. At a recent industry convention, Frank W. Dailey, of A-C Supply Co., Milwaukee, defined an original equipment manufacture (O.E.M.) as follows:

"To qualify for an O.E.M. discount the purchaser must buy a component part of his machine as advertised on the open market. If it is not for sale on the open market, then he is not entitled to an O.E.M. discount."

Robert C. Reese, of T. B. Wood's Sons Co., Chambersburg, Pennsylvania, defined O.E.M. as "pertaining to a company which buys equipment on a repetitive basis for equipment used in the end product it turns out."

John Drollinger, Jr., of Reliance Electric & Engineering Co., Cleveland, defined an O.E.M. customer as "a company that has an engineering department, sales department, and servicing group."

Several of the speakers declared their belief that O.E.M. sales are unprofitable.

"Most O.E.M. sales," said Dailey, "are unprofitable. But by selling related items the overall picture can be made profitable."

Warren M. Pike, of Warren M. Pike Associates, Inc., Boston, stated that "since 75 percent of O.E.M. sales are made at a loss by both manufacturers and distributors," industry should have a standard price system that gives consideration only for quantity. This, he said, would eliminate the O.E.M. discount problem.

Norton's New Plan

The Norton Company, a major manufacturer of abrasive grinding wheels, announced a new marketing plan that bypassed its established distributors on some important accounts. As described in *Industrial Marketing*, the company calculated, on computers, the usage trends and rates of big-volume customers and determined that they could order in large enough lots to provide manufacturing economies. To attract such orders, the company offered to share the savings by supplying customers direct from the factory at reduced prices. The customers had to order a minimum number of certain types and classes of wheels in a 12-month period to get the lower price.

Norton also agreed to set up a minimum inventory for customers who could meet the requirements, at no carrying cost to the customers. Distributors whose annual requirements meet the minimum qualifying quantity can order on the same terms as large customers.

In short order, Carborundum Company and Bay State Abrasives came out with similar plans. They differed to the extent that the qualifying customer could buy through his local distributor or direct from the factory, and distributors could have deferred payments on initial inventory. However, they had to pay the same price on replacement orders as the end users. If they elected not to use the deferred payment option, they could buy the items at a 3 percent discount from the end-user price.

Norton and Carborundum removed restrictions on direct accounts and encouraged distributors to solicit them. This, they said, would increase distributor sales.

The companies have claimed the plan is a success, but at least three large distributors dropped the Norton lines. The National

Industrial Distributors' Association and the Southern Industrial Distributors' Association formally opposed the plan, and a former president of NIDA, Thomas Clynes, said that in several cases it had caused "a serious deterioration in what were formerly splendid distributor-manufacturer relationships."

Supplementary Lines

Frequently, when operating warehouse branches a manufacturer will stock and distribute supplementary lines to improve his service to his dealers. For example, a manufacturer of plumbing fixtures buys heating and electrical appliances, valves, fittings, pipe, kitchen cabinets, and other items for resale to plumbing dealers in order to supply all their needs and to promote the sale of his plumbing fixtures.

This manufacturer faces a policy decision: Shall the warehouse branch be run as a factory outlet for his plumbing fixtures or as a wholesale outlet? If the former, profit margins may be centered in the manufacturing effort and the warehouse merely expected to break even or possibly make a small profit. If the warehouse margin is small, it will be difficult for the warehouse manager to provide services that compete with those of other wholesalers. Furthermore, the factory may be inclined to produce those products most attractive to it, with scant regard to customer preferences.

If the warehouse is run in the manner of an independent wholesaler, then it is more attuned to customers' needs. It can be more demanding on its parent factory for quality products. If, in addition, the warehouse manager is permitted to buy from other than his parent factory and the factory manager is required to meet competitive prices and quality, a strong wholesaling program can be conducted. (General Motors is said to follow this policy; Chevrolet may buy cigarette lighters from any source; G. M. lighter manufacturing plants are expected to compete with outside producers.)

Systems Selling

In discussing the significance of systems selling, the newest concept of marketing, Dr. Arnold Corbin, marketing consultant and instructor, said:

"A systems sale begins when the customer dumps a problem in a vendor's lap and closes when both sign a systems contract. The object is always to solve the problem, not to sell a product, and while the solution—the system—is often complicated, the output is usually extremely simple: power, steam, cement, pellets, thin metal strips, purified water.

"The systems vendor agrees to analyze and define the prospect's problem; to procure additional technology from other divisions within the company or from outside sources; to design, engineer, build, and test the system, and to train customer personnel in its operation and maintenance, agreeing to service the whole system for the length of the contract, which may be years. Every system is a multiproduct, multiservice operation and is wholly self-sustaining."

Why is systems selling a good idea? In the first place, it makes sense from the buyer's point of view, because it simplifies his purchasing and engineering operations; it is much more convenient, and it increases the time and effort he can focus on other aspects of his business. From the seller's point of view, it also offers many advantages. The bigger "packages" (the larger units of sale) make a greater marketing effort worthwhile. Secondly, the seller gets control over all the elements in a sale, not just a specific product at a specific time. Furthermore, when you sell a whole system, in effect, what you are doing is building a continuous "aftermarket." As the customer develops needs for replacements of pieces of the system, he comes back to you again as the source of supply because you sold him the entire system.

Despite some problems, systems selling is here to stay, because it makes sense from the customer's point of view. And if that's the way the buyer wants to buy, then that must be the way the seller must sell, whether it is convenient for him or not. So even though systems selling involves a number of risks and complications, more and more firms are embracing this strategy.

But there's another side to the story. Many companies enamored of the idea of selling a product package rather than separate pieces of hardware, says Rockwell Manufacturing Company sales vice-president Richard E. Love, are bitterly disappointed.

"Producing systems may be something that a company is not equipped to do," says Love, whose company sells both hardware and systems. "If a company produces both systems and hardware, it may need two different people in every job."

The hardware salesman, says Love, must be aggressive, have application and product knowledge, be able to solve problems on the spot, convey his message quickly and concisely, and be a lone wolf.

The systems salesman, on the other hand, should be conservative. "When you think of a system," says Love, "you think of something that is going to entail not only a sale but also a responsibility after the sale. The systems man must be a team player, since the system is a team product."

The Systems Proposal

In selling complicated, expensive systems, marketing executives depend heavily on the engineering department for the development of a basic sales proposal. *Marketing Forum* describes the Westinghouse policy as follows:

From the customer's viewpoint, the sales proposal is the most important medium of communication in the entire process of purchasing.

It is, first and foremost, a *sales* document—designed to persuade the customer. It's also a *technical* document—defining the entire project in sufficient engineering detail so the customer can fully understand what is being proposed. If the sale is made, it becomes also a *legal* document.

The proposal should incorporate the best in professional techniques to exploit the advantages of the system. Drawings, sketches, schematic diagrams, photo drawings, marked photographs, PERT charts, all should be used.

An abbreviated version is prepared for operating management. This tells what the system will do and how it will work, and stresses product quality, production efficiency, flexibility, customer service, and other benefits. For top management and sometimes corporate directors, a short summary is prepared.

Important as the proposal is, it's far from the only communication needed to sell systems. Advancing technology increases the need to simplify the visualization process. Westinghouse often used scale models at the final selling stage. A 3-D model can transmit a concept and the details involved in a matter of minutes, saving hours or even days of poring over drawings. Models can also serve to sell the general concept of systems, and may be used at any stage of selling.

Closely allied to models are exhibits, because they can reach audiences with a predictable interest in what the company offers. Motion pictures are another way to sell the systems concept to an audience which can be tracked down and corralled into one location.

Chapter 20

THE AGRICULTURAL MARKET

THE farm is an industrial market. It will continue to grow as the needs of the United States and the world continue to expand at a great rate.

Many manufacturers of products used primarily in industrial operations have adapted them to the requirements of the agricultural field. In addition, many manufacturers are serving the farm market without knowing too much about it. But a visit to a modern farm reveals the widespread use of mechanical and electrical products.

The well-publicized population growth, the efforts of the United States to alleviate starvation in many countries, and the consequent reduction of surpluses of grains and other price-supported farm products have produced a need for more food. In turn, this has resulted in new and higher-levels of purchasing power in the agricultural field.

Manufacturers who sell to industry should be prepared to take advantage of the growth potential of this market. This may include examining the product line to make sure that products have been adapted where necessary for farm use, and checking distribution to see that products are flowing to this important segment of the industrial market.

The Surpluses Are Gone

The once problem-plagued farm market has experienced a dramatic revival that spells glittering opportunities. As reported in *Sales Management*, "The surpluses that once depressed farm prices and income are now a memory, and powerful forces building up both here and abroad suggest that for the next several years the emphasis will be on boosting rather than curbing output."

Supplier industries sales leaped forward as a result. Farm equipment, for example, scored new sales levels.

Overall prosperity lifted farm buying power to new highs. The average farm in 1964 had a realized new income of $5,024, more than double what it was 10 years before.

One reason that the typical farm shows up so handsomely on the income side is that each year there are fewer of them to split up the total income. The 1964 Census of Agriculture counted 3,157,864 farms, a drop of more than half a million from the 1959 tabulation. Reflecting the mechanical and scientific revolutions that have transformed farming and increased the capital investment needed for survival, the reduction in numbers was confined to smaller units (under 500 acres).

Markets of the Future

Here are some examples of the farm-market opportunities:

Fertilizer potential will be tremendous.

Farm-machinery makers will enjoy rising business from relatively untapped sources.

Food processors, utilizing their nutritional know-how and food technology, will benefit from new products tailored to offset dietary deficiencies.

Research into nontraditional food sources, such as petroleum fermentation, is another promising area.

Until their agricultural economies are more firmly established, the developing nations will continue to rely on the U.S. farmer as a supplier of a large part of their food needs. Shipments under the government's food aid programs currently account for 90 percent of all the aid extended by all countries and international agencies to the diet-short areas.

According to the *Farm Journal*, the next 10 years will see the fastest-growing demands for food in the history of the world. U.S. population will increase by 32 million people—equal to the present population of half our states. World population will add 700 million people—most of them in food-short countries.

Already we supply nearly two-thirds of the grain that hungry nations import—and by 1978 the people in those countries will depend on the U.S. even more to stand between them and starvation. Food aid may be far greater than military aid in the future—and also more effective.

Here at home, markets will soar for meats, fruit, and vegetables—the things affluent people buy. And to supply the baby boom (26 million under five years of age are predicted by 1976; 82 million under 18).

More farm products will be sold on contract—farmers dealing directly with processors with prices set in advance of harvest—and part of the money paid at planting time. Thus (1) a new kind of credit; (2) "guaranteed" market prices negotiated annually; and (3) more certain markets. But this won't be for every farmer—just those who can meet increasing demands for better quality, standard grades, scheduled delivery, and responsive management.

Two kinds of farm programs are ahead: One, mostly a social program for "poverty" farms—those too small to make it full-time in farming. For them, government will buy or retire their land and offer education in new job skills, relocation to where the jobs are, and relocation of industry into "rural" areas. The farm program for "commercial" farms will offer "stop loss" supports and more freedom to plant.

The present nearly 2 million commercial "farm-management units" with sales of more than $2,500 per year will ease off gradually to around 1.5 million in 1976. Other kinds of farms (about 1.5 million now) will fall off more rapidly—and will bring the total to about 2.25 million "farm units" under single management.

Much Higher Income

Family farms will be bigger, more specialized, and more intensified—with much higher incomes. Farm prices may not be much different than now. But gross income for the average farm unit will rise spectacularly—in line with the 7 percent rise in the last 10 years. Average gross income per farm unit will run $25,000 or more.

But the way to make the most profit in farming will be to invest in equipment, fertilizer, irrigation, livestock, feed, and a host of new chemicals. By investing money in these things—instead of in low-return land—tenants also will do well. And good tenants will be able to take their pick of farms.

Farming will remain the nation's biggest business, the country's biggest buyer and supplier; furnishing the most vital products that the nation needs and with more private ownership than in any other place in the economy. Farmers will be the largest group of private-management entrepreneurs in a sea of jobholders.

Within 10 years co-ops will decide their energies are better spent in cooperating rather than fighting, and huge areas will band together to bargain jointly with chain-store buyers and other dealers. Producer co-ops will be reorganized on a regional basis like the Great Lakes Milk Marketing Federation.

Improving the Breeds

A university scientist working with hormones to produce multiple births among cattle stated:

"I think regular twinning is quite possible. I question whether it will be practical under northern range operations, but in farm and pasture setups, where the condition of the cows can be watched more closely, I see no reason why multiple births couldn't be a regular thing. And I think sex determination will be a regular practice within the next generation."

Few lambs will ever see pasture; they'll be weaned early and finished in drylot. With the aid of hormones, many ewes will produce two lamb crops a year. "We'll have three bites of meat in every lamb chop instead of one," predicted one breeder, as a result of selective-breeding programs.

Improvement in pork is expected to come at an even faster clip. There's a big backlog of breeding know-how that hasn't been applied yet.

Carroll Plager, of Geo. A. Hormel & Co., sees a real break-through in processing and merchandising. More and more pork is being sold in completely processed form—defatted and without bone. Busy and diet-conscious homemakers are demanding this, and are getting it by paying higher prices.

New Harvesting Methods

The bulk of fruits and vegetables, whether for processing or the fresh market, will be planted and harvested by "robots"—sophisticated machines requiring skilled operators. A harvester glides along a row of asparagus, selectively cutting by radio impulse only properly matured spears. But machines are only half the answer to the elimination of most hand labors by 1976. Plant varieties need to be and will be developed which are more adaptable to a practical machine.

More truck produce will be sold processed and packaged in convenient-to-use form. "We sold the housewife 35 percent of her potatoes processed in 1964, and that will reach 50 percent to 75 percent in 10 years," predicted J. L. Baxter, Jr., Lamb-Weston Inc., Portland, Ore.

The perfection of methods in food production is just a small part of a larger accomplishment. We have the knowledge and skill to shape nature almost as we please. "That's about the truth," one scientist at Beltsville, Md. said. "The only real problems are time and money. We know what we can do."

Tractors will be larger, faster, more comfortable, and easier to control. Most of them will have air conditioned cabs with two-way radios.

Solid-set and fully automated irrigation systems will turn themselves on and off or move themselves when necessary.

Some hens will lay 300 eggs a year and never see the poultryman.

Recent surveys show that not only are farm wives conversant with plans for making their living in the next few years, but they also have plenty of plans for a good life. Three things loomed large: Education for the children, an attractive, completely up-to-date home and grounds, and recreation!

Water sports, camping, golf, bridge, photography darkrooms, books, flying lessons, riding, hunting, tennis, nature sanctuaries, attending plays and concerts in distant cities—these are the things farm people expect in their futures because of more automated and mechanized farming.

Chapter 21

THE MILITARY MARKET

F IRMS that are interested in entering the military market rapidly find that there is a wealth of information available from both the Department of Defense and private organizations. Many of the suggestions in this chapter for reaching this market come from M. L. Weidenbaum of the Stanford Research Institute, who has prepared similar material for the American Marketing Association.

For the most routine types of equipment, such as standard office supplies, merely getting on the proper bidding lists and submitting responsive bids when requested may be enough. However, in the case of prime or even subcontracts on weapon systems and other military items involving advanced technology, much groundwork generally precedes the submission of a successful proposal.

The Department of Defense and each of the services maintain offices specifically designed to meet with the firm that is new to defense business, and to provide orientation materials and initial introduction to military-procurement personnel.

The Office of the Secretary of Defense maintains a Central Military Information Office in the Pentagon Building in Washington. This agency will supply explanatory brochures on the major procurement programs of the military establishment and make appointments with appropriate personnel in the individual services.

Similarly, the Army maintains an Industrial Assistance and Procurement Information Office in the District of Columbia. This agency is located in the Old Post Office Building in Washington, D.C.

The United States Department of Defense is the largest single customer of American business. It is served by a multitude of large and small manufacturing companies and service organizations which supply the three and one-half million items used.

How the Military Spends

Unlike the private business sector of the economy, the scale and composition of military purchases are determined by the decisions of the federal budget process rather than in response to market trends. The authorization of military-spending programs results from the interaction of many competing demands and requirements —not only of the various military services but of the numerous non-defense programs and of taxpayer groups. Moreover, the federal budget is not determined in isolation but in relation to domestic political and economic conditions, as well as the expected state of international tensions.

In the period since Korea, the Air Force has supplanted the Army as the largest military customer. This shift is evidence of the increased emphasis being placed on strategic-weapon systems, rather than tactical warfare programs involving masses of men and conventional land equipment.

The procurement function may be relatively concentrated in one central agency, as in the Air Force with its Systems Command for major products and the Army with its new Material Development and Logistic Command, or split up among the service's technical bureaus, as in the Navy. Extreme decentralization gives appropriate officials in individual service bases and installations authorization to handle their own procurement of special services and goods.

The various military agencies financing research-and-development activities report that they receive many more proposals than they can accept. For example, virtually all basic proposals submitted to the Office of Naval Research are unsolicited. The three major criteria used by ONR in evaluating research proposals are:

1. *The scientific merit of the proposal.* This evaluation is performed against the background of the importance of the scientific field, the importance of the specific area within the field, and the probable degree to which more knowledge will be accumulated. In essence, is the proposal likely to produce significant new scientific knowledge?

2. *The relevance to the military mission.* The knowledge to be gained from the research is evaluated from the viewpoint of how it will contribute to the long-range technical development and future evolution of the service financing the project. In the case of ONR, that would be the Navy Department.

3. *The competence of the investigator.* The investigator's background, experience, and general knowledge of the field are carefully reviewed.

Typical Government Contracts

A relatively unique aspect of the market for military products is that the price of major weapon systems frequently is set in negotiation with military-procurement officers rather than in response to impersonal market forces. Some explanation of the nature of price formation in the military market may be desirable.

The four major types of contracts which are used for military procurement are (1) cost with no fee, (2) cost with fixed fee, (3) incentive, and (4) firm fixed price. Contrary to some popular misconceptions, contracts for cost plus a percentage of cost do not exist. They are not allowed by the Congressional statute governing military procurement.

Under a cost-with-no-fee contract, the contractor provides supplies or services at actual cost with no fee or profit. Such contractors usually are educational institutions and similar nonprofit organizations performing research.

Cost-plus-fixed-fee contracts have been generally utilized on developmental and initial-production contracts, where experience in the production of the articles contracted for is limited. Cost-plus-fixed-fee contracts (frequently with a ceiling price) are also used for research work by industrial firms.

Under incentive contracts, the producer is given an incentive to cut costs because he shares with the government a portion of the cost reduction. This type of contract operates as follows: Target costs and profits are established early in the program. Upon completion of production, actual costs are compared with target costs. In the case where the actual costs are lower than the target cost, the actual profit is higher than the target profit by a stated percentage of the cost reduction. Conversely, where the actual costs are higher than the target cost, the actual profit is lower than the target profit by a stated percentage of the cost overrun.

Recent statements by government officials indicate that increasing use will be made of incentive-type contracts, even in development and research.

Under the firm-fixed-price contract, supplies are furnished at a specified price with no provision for adjustment.

Cost Not Most Important

Cost is only one of a number of factors considered in awarding contracts for military-weapon systems, and there are many other factors on which rival potential suppliers compete. The previous performance of the company may be an extremely useful indicator of its effectiveness on a future contract.

Following is a list of the factors considered in contracts for a missile program. The relative weight given to each factor is shown. The low importance of cost is clearly shown. It should be borne in mind that previous actual low-cost experience may carry greater weight than optimistic estimates of future low costs on a cost-plus type of contract.

FACTOR	POINTS
Understanding the scope of work	80
Management control in government practices	80
Management availability and capability	100
Management philosophy and organizational experience	100
Resources, skills, and manpower available	100
Weapon-system knowledge and experience	80
Prior experience and performance on like-type projects	80
Labor relations and understanding of human factors	80
Quality-control organization and followup	100
Acceptance of the conditions of contract	70
Acceptance of statement of work	50
Cost and fee	80
Total	1,000

Companies are not automatically placed or kept on bidders lists. The request is initially screened to establish and identify the company's capability as well as the items for which it is qualified. Moreover, a company that has not responded to several consecutive solicitations may be dropped from a bidders list unless it notifies the purchasing office that it desires to remain on the bidders list for future solicitations. Companies not on formal bidders lists may request a copy of the bid invitation or request for proposal.

For the producer of component parts of military-weapon systems, the customer may generally be the industrial company which is the prime contractor (or associate contractor) rather than the military service itself. Each of the major military producers maintains a procurement or material department which is charged to deal with current and potential subcontractors or sub-subcontractors. Again, the prospective seller needs to become aware of the emerging needs of the contractor as they develop.

The announcement of the award of a new major aircraft or missile contract is often interpreted by the uninitiated as a signal for would-be suppliers to contact the winning prime contractor. Generally, this is too late a stage in the procurement process. In the preparation of its proposal, the winning contractor usually has worked with and received assistance from the companies that will become its subcontractors and suppliers.

Chapter 22

THE FRANCHISE INDUSTRY

FOR the businessman with the right talents, a franchise with a successful and reputable firm offers high profits and independence, along with a reassuringly low degree of risk. Many a fortune, in fact, has been built up by men who staked their capital on a franchise, and through flair or good luck, or both, turned it into a gold mine. The sales manager will want to consider the industry as a whole as a potential market.

Some of today's most profitable franchises, for example, are those of Milwaukee-based Manpower, Inc., an organization that provides temporary office help. Two highly successful Manpower franchisees are Toronto's Marvin Goodman and Max Milstone, both in their middle thirties. Although they have only been in business since 1956, they have a "work force" of more than 3,000 girls and probably gross over $1 million a year. Since Manpower estimates that its franchisees often earn (before taxes) about 20 percent of gross, this means that the two men's net income could be in the region of $200,000. And their business is still expanding rapidly. Says Milstone: "I would estimate the full potential of a Manpower franchise in a good location runs to several million dollars gross."

Also much sought after are Howard Johnson Company franchises. Many of Howard Johnson's franchised restaurants and motor lodges, for instance, do an annual business running to half a million dollars or more. One of the most successful of all Howard Johnson licensees is Irving R. Carter, who runs six restaurants and two motels in Connecticut—a chain-within-a-chain built up gradually since the mid-1930's and grossing $2 million a year. Another leading Howard Johnson licensee is William R. Smith of Columbia, Ohio, whose three restaurants and two motor lodges bring in an annual gross of well over $2 million.

Auto-rental franchises can also be built into big business. W. E. Elton of Amarillo, Texas, who with his partner holds the Avis franchises in Amarillo, and Wichita Falls, Texas, and Albuquerque, New

Mexico, started in 1948 "with so little of my own money that I'd be ashamed to tell you." The secret of his success in the rent-a-car business, Elton says, is that he got started early. After working with Avis part-time before he was through college, he was able to get the Avis franchise for a nominal sum, and on the strength of that franchise he was able to borrow $50,000 from a bank to get started. From there, Elton built up his original fleet and also acquired new franchises. Today he is considered one of the most successful operators in the Avis chain.

How Franchises Work

The reasons for the high rewards of franchising are not hard to find. The word *franchise* means many things to many people, but the basic principles of franchising are as follows:

The "parent" company, or franchisor, sets up a chain by licensing independent businessmen to run its establishments, using its trade or brand name and dispensing its services along lines approved by the company. The businessman usually pays a fee for his license and thereafter gives some kind of consideration to the company each year for the privilege of belonging to the chain. He must also have the required sum of capital to put into the business at the outset.

Once he has the franchise, of course, a businessman will have to make additional payments. He will probably have a mortgage to pay off. He may be paying interest on a bank loan. He will have to re-invest part of his earnings in the business as it grows. And most franchising arrangements involve a yearly payment to the franchising company as well as any initial fee. This payment may be in the form of rent for the premises, or it may be a percentage of the gross sales—usually considerably less than 10 percent.

In return for any payments he makes to the parent company, however, the franchisee receives benefits that are worth far more to him. For he has behind him all the leverage offered by the resources of a far larger organization. For one thing, he is selling goods or services that have the incalculable support of a well-known brand name. In addition, whenever the franchising firm conducts a national advertising campaign, he gets a free ride. He will probably be able to buy his supplies at a favorable price through the bulk buying of the "parent" company. And he will share in the benefits from any improvement and upgrading of the product by the parent company.

But perhaps most important of all, the parent company puts management guidance, backed by far larger resources and wider experience than the licensee can hope to demand, constantly at his disposal. As well as providing continuous advice to their franchisees once they are in business, the parent companies usually give them an intensive training course beforehand. "You can hardly go wrong," says Manpower's Milstone, "if you follow the organization's guidance."

Failure Rate Is Low

The rewards of running a franchise business, however, are not measured only in terms of yearly profits. A franchise also offers the businessman a greater degree of security than he could hope for in setting up his own business. The reason is simple: Most companies will go to great lengths to avoid having failed franchisees on their hands. "The franchisor cannot afford failure," says Abraham Tunick, president of the Chicken Delight restaurant chain. "It's not only bad for profits, it's bad for his image."

The "image" of its chain is important to the franchisor because its prosperity depends heavily on the abilities of its franchisees as businessmen and managers. The spectacle of numerous failures would obviously deter the shrewder, more capable, and better-financed prospects from going into it.

Because the franchisor cannot afford to let his franchisee sink, he frequently will go to great lengths to keep him afloat. The result is a phenomenally low failure rate for the industry as a whole. "The experience of the industry," says George M. Otto, executive secretary of the International Franchise Association, "is that much less than 10 percent of all franchisees fail in business." In dramatic contrast with this is the fact that perhaps one out of every two businessmen who start on their own fails within two years.

To qualify for prompt and effective help in business, a franchisee does not even have to be foundering; he merely has to be making less out of his business than the chain thinks he should. Mister Donut of America, for example, claims that the failure rate among its established franchisees is less than 1 percent. "This," says Chairman Harry Winokur, "is because we make it almost impossible for a franchisee to fail."

"If by failure you mean total financial collapse, I don't think we've had any," says Burger Chef Systems' executive vice-president, Robert Wildman. "We have a turnover rate, of course, where franchisees decide to sell out. Every chain does."

It is impossible to generalize about the amount of capital necessary to obtain a franchise. The initial capital needed to secure a Howard Johnson franchise, for example, is around $200,000. Part of this sum can, of course, be raised in the form of a mortgage on the restaurant or motor inn. But the franchisee must still put up a substantial sum in cash and must also pay a flat $10,000 for the license itself. On the other hand, W. E. Elton obtained his Avis franchise with a very low cash payment. And Milstone and Goodman launched their Manpower franchise with only $8,000 in capital.

However, what of the average licensee—the man with the will to work, with a fair share of managerial ability and a few thousand dollars to invest?

John MacDonald is an energetic Mister Donut franchisee. His store at Manchester, a suburb of Hartford, Connecticut, will gross around $140,000 a year. MacDonald had first to prove to Mister Donut that he could find $16,000. Then he had to take an eight-week training course. He was offered a choice of three locations, picked one in Manchester, and opened for business in May, 1961. "I was in the black from the opening day," says MacDonald. "That first year was terrific. I grossed about $145,000." MacDonald estimates that his net runs between 18 percent and 19 percent of gross. He plans to open a satellite store.

Disadvantages of the Franchise System

Operating a franchise has one major drawback: The constant supervision that the parent company maintains over its franchisees is unpalatable to some businessmen of independent temperament. "If the franchisee will just follow our guidance and advice," says President Tunick of the Chicken Delight chain, "his risk of failure is practically nil." Tunick feels that the bigger franchise chains have so carefully researched their operations for all factors that only a local catastrophe could upset their calculations.

Nevertheless, franchisors in general complain that franchisees in general try constantly to change the operations in some way. This is the biggest single cause of conflict. "A franchisee isn't an independent businessman," grumbled one disgruntled operator. "He is as much under the thumb of his supervisor as if he had a boss."

Many prospective franchisees strongly resent being made to undertake a training course. "The first thing we do when we bring a man in for training," says Nick Fiorentino, Mister Donut's director of operations, "is to hand him a mop and tell him to do a little cleaning up. This is a man who has just shown us that he can put up $20,000. Some of them will just throw that mop down and tell us to go jump somewhere."

Mister Donut has its own way of dealing with prospective franchisees who during training display personality traits that seem to cast doubt on their suitability for a franchise. "We give them their money back and let them go," says Fiorentino. "We figure we're doing them a favor as well as ourselves. We don't want to put somebody into a shop who's going to give us problems. We have enough already."

Nevertheless, for hundreds of thousands of businessmen who want a higher income, and can combine a sense of being independent with a willingness and ability to take advice, the advantages of a franchise far outweigh its drawbacks. Not surprisingly, then, the industry is growing very rapidly. This growth cannot be plotted in figures, for it was only in 1963 that the International Franchise Association first published any estimates of the dollar volume of franchising.

Charting the Industry

Franchising has become big business. But just *how* big was anybody's guess until Chicago's newly formed International Franchise Association assembled the figures. The IFA estimated that in the 13 major franchising groups, annual volume totals nearly $60 billion a year.

INDUSTRY	FRANCHISED OUTLETS	ANNUAL VOLUME (MILLIONS)
Automobile and Truck Dealers	33,000	$35,000
Carpet and Upholstery Cleaning Services	4,000	100
Coin-Operated and Regular Laundry and Dry-Cleaning Services	35,700	509
Gasoline and Oil Service Stations	206,302	14,178
Grocery Stores	16,000	4,450
Hearing Aids	3,500	70
Moving Companies	5,000	1,000
Roadside Food, Beverage and Ice-Cream Dispensing Restaurants	24,590	1,410
Soft-Drink Bottlers	4,000	2,001
Swimming Pools	1,000	40
Temporary-Help Services	500	100
Variety Stores	2,400	150
Water-Conditioning Systems and Services	2,300	207
Total	338,292	$59,215

Chapter 23

SELLING OVERSEAS

THE next big challenge to American marketing ingenuity and initiative lies in international trade. There is a world of markets, singly and in groups, private and governmental, industrial and consumer, waiting for U.S. goods and services. That it is a fertile field for sales and profits is evidenced in the annual reports of numerous corporations.

Four Kinds of Markets

International marketing usually falls into four classifications. Most companies sell to independent overseas distributors, who are responsible for "local" (in the foreign country) distribution. As a rule, payment is made through letters of credit and bank drafts. Freight forwarders handle all the details of making shipment abroad. Another channel for international distribution is through export-sales agencies, which usually pay for the merchandise in the U.S., have their own local outlets, and take care of all the shipping details.

Many markets, however, have import restrictions imposed by local governments either to control the flow of their limited supply of United States dollars, to protect local industry, or to encourage the development of new industries.

In this case major American corporations establish manufacturing subsidiaries which import raw materials or the technical components to assemble or manufacture the product locally. These subsidiary companies often enjoy a large measure of autonomy from the parent company since they are in the market and must act quickly to meet changing conditions. In addition, since they must meet local consumer demand by introducing products, models, or parts not made by the parent company, large corporations permit their subsidiaries to buy their requirements from company plants as well as outside plants in any country. This multinational policy is justified on the ground that sales would otherwise be lost. Also, it produces dividends which eventually find their way to the home office.

The fourth international marketing channel is through licensees. Licensing arrangements are justified where imports are restricted or the market is too small to warrant the cost of establishing a subsidiary company plant. Manufacturers license foreign companies to produce their products and to use their trademark, for a contractual fee. Though the fee is usually based on a percentage of sales the parties may agree on a lump sum or annual fee. For this, the American manufacturer provides management, technical, and marketing assistance to the local licensee. The advantages of licensing are that it eliminates the cost and headaches of building a plant and the American manufacturer acquires a ready-built distributing organization. The major disadvantage is reduction of quality control.

For most companies, however, selling to independent distributors is the preferred method. As in the domestic field, the selection of the proper distributor will make or break the position of the manufacturer in any market. Major companies have regional managers or field representatives who will go to a country to investigate the possibilities and to compare the capabilities and resources of local organizations. Other companies depend on information supplied by the U.S. Department of Commerce, banks with international departments, or international transportation firms. The Department of Commerce supplies specific "leads" and will obtain special reports from U.S. consulates and commercial officers abroad at very nominal cost.

Joint Ventures

Joint business ventures in overseas trade are multiplying rapidly and are expected to continue increasing over the next decade, particularly in the developing nations, says a recent study by National Industrial Conference Board.

The vast majority of those surveyed believe that joint ventures (though not the most popular form of investment abroad) can offer widespread advantages. One of the strongest appeals of joint ventures is their reduction of the economic and political risks of foreign investment. The presence of a local partner guards not only against outright expropriation but offers protection against nationalistic sentiment that exists in all nations.

Businessmen cautioned, however, that the benefits of joint ventures can come only from successful, enduring partnerships. The major hazards cited were divergent objectives and management practices, lack of mutual confidence and respect, and failure to anticipate and resolve conflicts of interest before agreements are signed.

Foreign Credit

Until recently, American businessmen were hesitant about offering credit in foreign transactions because of the greater risk. The late President John F. Kennedy realized something had to be done to overcome this uncertainty; the lag in U.S. exports was a factor in our widening balance of payments deficit.

On October 27, 1961, he announced formation of the Foreign Credit Insurance Association (FCIA), an association of domestic insurers, with the full cooperation of the Export-Import Bank. The FCIA, which had an original membership of 14 insurers, now has more than 60 participating insurance companies.

This network of insurers can guarantee the exporter substantial protection in the event a foreign buyer fails to meet his payment obligations due to insolvency, other commercial reasons, or as the result of political risks such as war, expropriation, or currency inconvertibility.

The Multinational Concept

Many leading American corporations have scored outstanding sales results overseas through the application of a broad and forward-looking policy best expressed as "multinational."

Walter P. Margulies, president, Lippincott & Margulies, marketing consultants advises:

"Multinational corporations, drawing on the resources of different national groups, avoiding conflicting interests or domination by any one group, are certain to become dominant factors in the next decade—or less.

"Today there exist relatively few such companies. A majority, especially American firms, are still based in one country and operate in others. But the multinational concept is here and will not be stopped."

Potentials of Overseas Markets

U.S. exports totaled $29.4 billion in 1966, an increase of 10 percent over the previous year. In addition to the usual growth to be expected from any dynamic industry, this increase was, at least in some part, due to the efforts of the government to stimulate export sales through the activities of the National Export Expansion Council, made up of volunteer business executives who are experts in international marketing.

According to some estimates, foreign markets hold a potential 10 times that of the North American markets. In Latin America, for instance, saturation levels for consumer durables are extremely low, while the net population gain from births and immigration is about 14,000 a day.

In some industries, the rate of growth in the European Common Market is up to four times that of the U.S. In 1963, 25 percent of all households in the Netherlands had refrigerators. This is compared with the extremely high saturation of over 95 percent in the U.S. refrigerator market.

The competitiveness of U.S. exports abroad has been underestimated. It is acknowledged that the foreign manufacturer who pays lower wages, makes the same product in equal volume, uses the same process, and employs the same number of workers as the American manufacturer is bound to underprice him. *But the fulfillment of all these conditions by a foreign company is very rare.*

A staff report by the Commerce Committee of the U.S. Senate stated: "With some exceptions, U.S. products generally are not priced out of the markets and that American costs of production are not generally out of line with foreign costs."

According to Senator Charles H. Percy, former president of Bell and Howell, "the true criterion of cost is not dollars per hour of labor, but rather total labor cost per unit produced."

Some Case Histories

According to Lee S. Bickmore, president of the National Biscuit Company, the company's international operations account for about 25 percent of total business, compared with only about 7 percent a few years ago. The company has three plants in Canada, two in England, two in France and one each in Germany, Italy, New Zealand, Australia, Mexico, Venezuela, Spain, Nicaragua and Puerto Rico.

Texas Instruments Supply Company of Dallas, Texas, has been setting up European offices for the distribution of electronic components.

"The overseas market is a fast growing one for electronic products," said a company officer. "In fact, in the next 10 years we expect a 200 percent increase in the distributor market in Europe as opposed to a 50 to 60 percent increase in the U.S. That will be in terms of dollars!"

U.S. DEPARTMENT OF COMMERCE FIELD OFFICES

ALABAMA: 2030 Third Ave., N., Birmingham 35203, (325-3131).

ALASKA: Loussac-Sogn Bldg., Room 306, Anchorage 99501, (272-6331).

ARIZONA: 230 N. First Ave., Phoenix 85025, (261-3285).

CALIFORNIA: 1031 S. Broadway, Los Angeles 90015, (688-2833); Federal Bldg., Box 36013, San Francisco 94102, (566-5864).

COLORADO: 16407 Federal Bldg., Denver 80202, (297-3246).

CONNECTICUT: 18 Asylum St., Hartford 06103, (244-3530).

FLORIDA: 208 Laura St., Jacksonville 32202, (EL 4-7111); 51 S.W. First Ave., Miami 33130, (350-5267).

GEORGIA: 75 Forsyth St., N.W., Atlanta 30303, (526-6000); 125-29 Bull St., Savannah 31402, (232-4321).

HAWAII: 1022 Bethel St., Honolulu 96813, (588977).

ILLINOIS: 219 S. Dearborn St., Chicago 60604, (828-4400).

IOWA: 509 Grand Ave., Des Moines 50309, (284-4222).

LOUISIANA: 610 South St., New Orleans 70130, (527-6546).

MARYLAND: 305 U.S. Customhouse, Baltimore 21202, (PL 2-8460).

MASSACHUSETTS: Room 230, 80 Federal St., Boston 02110, (CA 3-2312).

MICHIGAN: 445 Federal Bldg., Detroit 48226, (226-6088).

MINNESOTA: Room 306, 110 S. Fourth St., Minneapolis 55401, (334-2133).

MISSOURI: Room 2011, 911 Walnut St., Kansas City 64106, (BA 1-7000); 1520 Market St., St. Louis 63103, (MA 2-4243).

NEVADA: Room 2028, Federal Bldg., 300 Booth St., Reno 89502, (784-5203).

NEW MEXICO: U.S. Courthouse, Albuquerque 87101, (247-0311).

NEW YORK: 117 Ellicott St., Buffalo 14203, (842-3208); 350 Fifth Ave., New York 10001, (LO 3-3377).

NORTH CAROLINA: 412 U.S. Post Office Bldg., Greensboro 27402, (275-9111).

OHIO: 550 Main St., Cincinnati 45202, (684-2944); 4th Floor, Federal Reserve Bank Bldg., Cleveland 44101, (241-7900).

OREGON: 520 S.W. Morrison St., Portland 97204, (226-3361).

PENNSYLVANIA: 1015 Chestnut St., Philadelphia 19107, (597-2850); 1000 Liberty Ave., Pittsburgh 15219, (644-2850).

PUERTO RICO: Room 628, 605 Condado Ave., Santurce 00907, (723-4640).

SOUTH CAROLINA: 334 Meeting St., Charleston 29403, (747-4361).

TENNESSEE: 167 N. Main St., Memphis 38103, (534-3214).

TEXAS: Room 1200, 1114 Commerce St., Dallas 75202, (RI 9-3287); 515 Rusk Ave., Houston 77002, (CA 8-0611).

UTAH: 125 S. State St., Salt Lake City 84111, (524-5116).

VIRGINIA: 400 N. 8th St., Richmond 23240, (649-3611).

WASHINGTON: 909 First Ave., Seattle 98104, (583-5615).

WEST VIRGINIA: 500 Quarrier St., Charleston 25301, (343-6196).

WISCONSIN: 238 W. Wisconsin Ave., Milwaukee 53203, (BR 2-8600).

WYOMING: 2120 Capitol Ave., Cheyenne 82001, (634-5920).

Circle Seal Products Co., of Anaheim, California, produces a specialty valve with practically no need of replacement—yet the company increased its foreign industrial export sales 50 percent between 1964 and 1965, double its domestic sales increase, and 133 percent from 1965-66, four times the domestic increase percentage.

The company was honored for this achievement with a Presidential "E" award for export expansion.

Shows, fairs, and expositions are an effective means of selling overseas, Culligan, Inc., a water-softener equipment firm of Northbrook, Illinois, has found. It once picked up $200,000 in business in one home show. In one year Culligan-France participated in 13 different expositions.

Culligan has found foreign business is also good business. Donald L. Porth, a vice-president, told a conference: "In 1957, Culligan had a total sales volume of $7.7 million, with practically no export business. In 10 years, total sales have almost quadrupled to $29 million. At the same time, our overseas companies will do $6.7 million, or almost as much as the parent company did at the time we started exporting."

The *S.S. Mormacwave* sailed from San Francisco with an experimental international room "show." Arranged attractively in two remodeled staterooms on the Moore-McCormack Lines freighter was an array of equipment from Hewlett-Packard Company, manufacturer of electronic, medical, and chemical instrumentation. Over a two-month period, the equipment was displayed and demonstrated to hundreds of customers in seven Latin American countries.

Export Expansion Councils

In order to reduce the balance of payments problem of the United States, the Department of Commerce has organized Regional Export Expansion Councils in all principal cities. These councils, consisting of leading businessmen, bankers, shipping people, and representatives of the Department's field offices, are interested in helping companies enter international markets and their members are available for conferences and discussions.

PART 5

COMPETITIVE
TRADE
PRACTICES

Chapter 24

LEGAL ASPECTS OF COMPETITION

IT IS the will of the American people, as expressed by their voting and by opinion polls, that the public should be protected by government against: (1) The evils of business monopolies on one hand; (2) the evils of unbridled competition on the other. To that end federal laws have been passed and the Federal Trade Commission established. Since it is inevitable that government will exert, through the commission, a wider influence on competitive practices, sales managers should be familiar with these procedures and regulatory agencies.

There are six acts of Congress bearing on the regulation of interstate commerce which must be considered in establishing a sales policy or in making sales decisions. These are as follows:

1. *The Federal Trade Commission Act,* which gave the commission power to act as business police against illegitimate competitive methods.

2. *The Wheeler-Lea Act,* amending the Federal Trade Commission Act, which eliminates the necessity for the Federal Trade Commission to prove injury to competition before a complaint can be made and, for the first time, establishes a fine and imprisonment as possible penalties for violating the prohibitions of the law.

3. *The Robinson-Patman Act,* which prevents unfair price discrimination between competitive purchasers of the same merchandise.

4. *The Sherman Antitrust Act,* the first of the antitrust laws to outlaw contracts, combinations, and conspiracies in restraint of trade.

5. *The Clayton Antitrust Act,* which goes one step further, prohibiting *competitive practices which lead* to monopoly. This law was designed to supplement the Sherman Antitrust Act, which merely forbade *monopoly*— not the *practices* which created that state of restrained competition.

6. *The Fair Labeling and Packaging Act,* which is aimed at correcting abuses tending to mislead or confuse the consumer, such as variations in sizes, quantities, contents.

Trade Practices Considered Unfair

Competition is one of the hallmarks of the U.S. business scene. Any firm must compete successfully if it is to exist and prosper. But competition does not mean "anything goes." There are legal safeguards against unfair competition and discrimination. These safeguards apply to large and small concerns alike.

Valuable protection against unfair competition is provided by the Federal Trade Commission. The FTC administers the Federal Trade Commission Act, the Clayton Act as amended by the Robinson-Patman Act, and six other related statutes. Its main objective is to protect and promote competitive business and to protect the interests of the purchasing public. Among the rights the FTC seeks to preserve are the right to buy as cheaply as competitors, freedom to buy only items and quantities needed, and freedom to sell goods in an open market. In addition, the FTC guards against such unfair competitive methods as rigging prices and markets, illegal price discrimination, granting or receiving discriminatory promotional allowances, false disparagement of competitors, pirating employees, offering fake buying advantages, and using false and misleading advertising.

The commission bases its official legal actions on the facts of each individual case. Its formal procedure involves investigation, complaint, hearings, and if warranted, an order "to cease and desist." Such orders by the commission are subject to review in the courts. In addition, there is a consultation program designed to aid businessmen in understanding the requirements of the law and in complying voluntarily with them. This program involves industrywide trade-practice conferences, and the advisory and assistance work of the Division of Small Business.

FTC field offices are maintained in nine major cities throughout the nation.

Numerous specific practices which tend to injure competition are prohibited by the laws enforced by the Commission. These include (but are not limited to) the following techniques:

Granting Discriminatory Allowances: Granting allowances for advertising, or furnishing services or facilities such as demonstrators, to one or more customers competing in the distribution of similar products, when such allowances or services or facilities are not made available on proportionally equal terms to all competing customers of a supplier.

Manipulating Prices: Agreements or combinations for the purpose and with the effect of raising, depressing, fixing, pegging, or stabilizing the price of a commodity.

Rigging Production and Markets: Agreements or combinations which restrict production, divide territories, establish a so-called "protected market," or divide customers among competitors.

Inducing Discriminatory Allowances: A purchaser's knowingly inducing or receiving payments for advertising allowances from a supplier when such payment is not affirmatively offered or otherwise made available on proportionally equal terms to all other customers competing in the distribution of that supplier's products.

Using Bait Advertising: Engaging in promotional campaigns which offer at an unusually low price certain items in which the public is interested, and which the dealer has no intention of selling but advertises merely to attract potential customers for more expensive merchandise of the same type.

Bribing Patronage: Bribing buyers, purchasing agents, or other employees of customers and prospective customers in order to obtain or hold patronage.

Spying Trade Secrets: Procuring the technical or trade secrets of competitors by espionage, by bribing their employees, or by similar illicit means.

Pirating Employees: Inducing employees of competitors to violate their contracts and enticing them to leave their jobs with the intention and effect of hampering or embarrassing competitors in the operation of their businesses.

Disparaging Competitors: Making false and disparaging statements respecting competitors' products and businesses.

Selling Used Items as New: Selling for new, items that actually are rebuilt, second-hand, renovated or old products, or are made in whole or in part from used or second-hand materials, by representing such articles as new, or by failing to reveal that they are not new, or that they contain second-hand or used materials.

Cornering Competitors' Merchandise: Buying up competitors' merchandise for the purpose of hampering them and stifling or eliminating competition.

Merchandising by Lot or Chance: Selling or distributing punchboards or other lottery devices which are to be or may be used in the sale of merchandise by lot or chance, or using merchandising schemes based on lot or chance.

Offering Fake Buying Advantages: Creating the impression that customers are being offered an opportunity to make purchases under unusually favorable conditions when such is not the case.

Using Misleading Names: Using misleading trade, company, or product names.

Employing Deception: Employing any other false or misleading representation which deceives or has the capacity to deceive or mislead.

The Merger Problem

In a report in *Advertising Age,* Stanley E. Cohen, Washington editor of the publication, stated:

The efforts of the food giants to buy into related product categories have presented antitrusters with sticky problems. In its settlement permitting Procter & Gamble to retain Folger coffee, the Federal Trade Commission tried some remedies which push government deeper into the decision-making functions of the marketing man.

In exchange for letting P&G keep Folger, FTC got what some of its members regard as a good bargain. P&G, which had figured in at least five such product-extension mergers in 10 years, promised not to buy any other domestic grocery products companies in the next seven years without getting FTC consent.

The fact that it was able to pen up P&G was in itself an almost irresistible opportunity for FTC. But it also got other goodies, not the least of them a promise by P&G not to engage in certain kinds of promotional activity which have worried the commission.

P&G, for example, promised not to use any piggyback promotions for coffee which involve tie-ins with other P&G products. Moreover, in computing advertising rates and discounts, the company will not claim rates and discounts for coffee which reflect cumulative purchases by other P&G products.

These concessions presumably were tailored to anticipate FTC concern on issues which were decisive in the Clorox case. Procter & Gamble's promotional power, including its ability to earn discounts of 30 percent or more for network TV, was cited by FTC as a compelling reason why the acquisition of Clorox was likely to bring serious injury to competition in the liquid household bleach industry.

FTC contended that the union between P&G, the sales leader in many grocery items, and Folger, the nation's second largest nonretailer seller of regular coffee and fourth in soluble coffee, upset competitive relationships in the coffee business. FTC stressed P&G's marketing strength, including its "power to create consumer preference for its household consumer products and to obtain valuable grocery store shelf space by mass advertising and consumer sales promotion."

P&G may injure competition, FTC added, because of its ability to "achieve significant cost reductions" in:

The buying of green coffee.

The procuring of financing.

The buying and placement of advertising.

The conducting of consumer and sales promotions.

The buying of containers and packaging materials.

The procuring of warehousing and transportation.

Fair Labeling and Packaging

Congress enacted the Fair Labeling and Packaging Law (public law 89-755) in 1966. This went into effect on July 1, 1967.

The responsibility for administering the law has been divided among the Food and Drug Administration, the Federal Trade Commission, and the Department of Commerce. This has led to some confusion and overlapping of responsibilities which remains to be ironed out.

In essence, the Food and Drug Administration will supervise products and distribution practices in the food, drug, and cosmetics industries. The Federal Trade Commission is responsible for all other household package goods, detergents and paper products, for instance.

323

The FDA and the FTC will issue regulations specifying the typographical arrangements on the basic information panel on all packages.

The Department of Commerce will administer that section of the law which provides for the use of voluntary standards to reduce the proliferation of unnecessary package sizes.

The job of "selling" industry on the use of voluntary standards has been assigned to the Deputy Director of the Institute for Applied Technology in the National Bureau of Standards.

The act makes provision for both mandatory regulation and regulation by administration discretion. As part of the mandatory requirements, packages must bear labels specifying:

1. Identification of the commodity.

2. Name and place of business of the manufacturer or distributor.

3. Net quantity of contents (in terms of weight, measure, or numerical count). The statement of quantity must appear in a uniform location upon the principal display panel of the label.

4. If the package weighs less than four pounds (or one gallon if liquid measure), its weight shall be expressed in both ounces (specified as avoirdupois or fluid ounces) and in pounds, with any remainder in terms of ounces or common or decimal fractions of the pound. Liquid measure shall be shown in the largest whole unit (quarts or pints as appropriate), with any remainder in terms of fluid ounces or common or decimal fractions of the pint or quart. The law also makes specific provision for packages whose contents are commonly specified in length or area, and for random-weight packages.

5. Statements about number of servings must include net weight, measure, or numerical count of each serving.

SUMMARY OF FEDERAL LAWS AFFECTING MARKETING

1. *Interstate Commerce Act* (1887). Controlled rates of interstate freight and passenger carriers and eliminated rebates to large-scale users of their services.

2. *Sherman Antitrust Act* (1890). Prohibited combinations, contracts, or understandings that would stifle, or tend to stifle, competition.

3. *Federal Food and Drug Act* (1906). Made illegal the shipping in interstate commerce of any food or drug that is adulterated or misbranded, or contains decomposed, putrid, or filthy materials.

4. *Clayton Act* (1914). Designed to implement the *Sherman Act*. Prohibited pricing discrimination, and tie-in contracts between purchasers, which leads to monopoly.

5. *Federal Trade Commission Act* (1914). Commonly known as FTC. Designed to check unfair competition, combinations organized for price fixing, price discrimination, false and misleading advertising, and misbranding.

6. *Standard Barrel Act* (1915). Designed to standardize barrel sizes and to eliminate the use of false bottoms, odd sizes, and other questionable practices.

7. *Small Containers Act* (1915). Reduced the number of container sizes for handling produce.

8. *Cotton Futures Act* (1915). Set standards on which price differentials for varying cotton grades could be based.

9. *Grain Standards Act* (1916). Established and administered standards of weights, measures, and commodity grades.

10. *Cotton Standards Act* (1916). Established and administered standards of weights, measures, and commodity grades.

11. *United States Warehouse Act* (1916). Provided for federal licensing of approved commodity warehouses and for the issuance of negotiable warehouse receipts.

12. *Webb-Pomerene Act* (1918). Legalized combinations and monopolies in export trade.

13. *Packers and Stockyards Act* (1921). Gave Secretary of Agriculture the power to prescribe trade practices in the meat-packing industry.

14. *Grain Futures Act* (1922). Promulgated rules to discourage the manipulation of grain prices.

15. *Capper-Volstead Act* (1922). Exempted farmers' cooperatives from provisions of the *Sherman Act*.

16. *Produce Agency Act* (1927) and 17. *Perishable Agricultural Commodities Act* (1930). Controlled unfair trade practices in central markets for fruits and vegetables.

18. *Standard Containers Act* (1928). Attempted to standardize the containers used in the shipment of produce.

19. *Agricultural Marketing Agreement Act* (1929). Created the Federal Farm Board. The first attempt to control minimum farm prices. Also encouraged the formation of farm cooperatives through aid in orderly marketing and offers of loans at low interest rates.

20. *Agricultural Adjustment Acts* (1933, 1938, 1941). Aimed to restrict production and increase farm income. The act of 1933 was declared unconstitutional because of the discriminatory methods used in financing. The two subsequent acts accomplished the same purposes by means of constitutional methods.

21. *National Industrial Recovery Act* (1933). Established the National Recovery Administration (NRA). Shortened work hours, standardized credit terms,

SUMMARY OF FEDERAL LAWS AFFECTING MARKETING

forbade sales below cost, and set up codes of fair competition. Declared unconstitutional in 1935.

22. *Amendment to the Food and Drug Act* (1934). Extended product inspection on a voluntary basis to seafoods.

23. *Robinson-Patman Act* (1936). An amendment to the *Clayton Act*. Prohibited unfair discounts and other forms of price discrimination.

24. *Commodity Exchange Act* (1936). Combined provisions of the *Cotton Futures Act* and the *Grain Futures Act* to correct speculative abuses and prevent market control by large interests. Also encouraged the use of standards in commodity trading.

25. *Miller-Tydings Act* (1937). Permitted resale price maintenance in interstate commerce within limitations set by states, thus safeguarding the manufacturer against antitrust prosecution.

26. *Agricultural Marketing Act* (1937). Allowed the federal government to control marketing agreements of producers to restrict production and fix prices.

27. *Wheeler-Lea Act* (1938). Extended coverage of the *Federal Trade Commission Act* in order to protect consumers from unfair business practices, with special emphasis on the elimination of fraudulent advertising.

28. *Federal Food, Drug, and Cosmetic Act* (1938). Amended *Federal Food and Drug Act* (1906) to include any food, drug, or cosmetic which is adulterated or misbranded. Makes it compulsory to list weight and ingredients on labels.

29. *Wool Products Labeling Act* (1939). Became effective in 1941. Required labels on wool garments indicating percentages of wool, of reprocessed wool, and of reused wool.

30. *Emergency Price Control Act* (1942). Superseded the OPA Act of 1941. Established the Office of Price Administration which endeavored to prevent increases in commodity prices through price regulations. Set up a rationing program for civilian commodities and attempted to protect the consumer from unfair practices arising out of the war emergency.

31. *Lanham Trademark Act* (1946). Stipulated that a properly registered trademark becomes the user's property after five years unless its use is contested within that time.

32. *Office of Price Stabilization* (1950). Reinstated price controls.

33. *Fur Products Labeling Act* (1951). Prohibited false advertising and misleading labeling of fur products.

34. *McGuire Fair Trade Bill* (1952). Reinstated the binding effect of the single-contract agreement whereby one individual agrees to subscribe to a fair trade price. In this way the individual manufacturer or wholesaler compels all other distributors of the product to adhere to the price fixed under the fair trade agreement.

35. *Cigarette Labeling and Advertising Act* (1965; effective 1966). Requires that all cigarette packages carry the following warning: "Caution: Cigarette smoking may be hazardous to your health." Beginning July 1, 1969, this notice was required for all cigarette advertising.

36. *Fair Labeling and Packaging Act* (1966; effective July 1, 1967). This law is aimed at misleading or deceptive labeling or packaging. Responsibility for administering the law is divided among the Food and Drug Administration, the Federal Trade Commission and the Department of Commerce.

HEIDINGSFIELD, MYRON S., AND BLANKENSHIP, ALBERT B.: *Marketing,* Barnes and Noble, New York, 1964.

Chapter 25

BUDGETING FOR SALES

BUDGETING means financial planning. No sales manager with any measurable experience is unaware of the importance of budgeting sales efforts, both on a short- and long-range basis. But budgeting is not an exact science—a foolproof method for forecasting sales results from money expended for sales has not yet been achieved.

Clarence E. Eldridge, former vice-president of marketing for the General Foods Corporation and executive vice-president of the Campbell Soup Company, was commissioned to do a series of essays on budgeting for the Association of National Advertisers. Here is a digest of his main theme:

Management is called upon to make no decisions that are more important, or that can more significantly affect the health, growth, and profitability of the business than those involving the marketing budget. In many companies the cost of marketing is the largest controllable expense; in some companies the cost of marketing the product is even greater than the cost of producing it—including raw materials, labor, and packaging costs.

Of prime importance, of course, is the total amount of the budget. How much money is needed to achieve the agreed-upon marketing objectives? How much is affordable, consistent with the agreed-upon profit objectives? What compromise is permissible between need and affordability—without unduly jeopardizing either the marketing or the profit objectives?

Of almost equal importance are questions such as these:

How should the budget be allocated among the several functions of marketing such as advertising, selling promotion, and marketing research?

How should the money be divided among individual products or groups of products?

How should it be divided among established and new products?

How should it be apportioned geographically?

Finding a foolproof method of determining the marketing budget is not easy, particularly one that gives due consideration to the need for sales volume, the financial and profit needs of the business for the immediate future, and the longer-range health of the business. Perhaps such a method cannot be found, and if so, the more or less fatalistic approach to the subject which is now so typical eventually may be proved to be justified.

At present there are two principal ways—each of which has many variants— by which the amount of the marketing budget is determined. Which of the two ways is used in any given situation depends largely on the relative influence on top management enjoyed by the company controller as compared with the marketing vice-president.

The methods are different, and they both are wrong. The one is wrong because it fails to ascribe to marketing activities (including advertising) any productive role or to recognize any relationship between marketing expenditures and sales results. The other is wrong because it assumes, without adequate proof or evidence, that there is a predictable correlation between expenditures and results and that the correlation can be reduced to a mathematical exactness.

Probably no marketing company, certainly no sophisticated one, uses either of these methods to the exclusion of the other. Most companies try to balance the two—evaluating need against affordability, sales volume against profits ability.

The budget is an indispensable tool of management. It represents, in fact, a profit plan for the period in question, whether it be a year, a quarter, or a month. The estimates of sales volume should be as realistic as possible—if anything underestimating rather than overestimating sales. Product costs can, in most instances, be predicted with almost mathematical accuracy, and marketing expenditures are also subject to absolute and precise determination. Thus, two of the factors that affect profits can be predicted with absolute accuracy. The only unpredictable factor is the sales volume.

Goals of Budgeting

Budgeting or, as its practitioners prefer to call it, financial planning for the future, involves both short-range and long-range goals and methods. Originally they were used mostly as an expenditure-limiting device. But, in recent years they have developed as a basis for planning the business. "To be effective," says Ted J. Olson, assistant to the president of Olin Mathieson Chemical Corporation, "the planning activity must be a continuous process which makes corrections and adjustments in response to changes in the business situation."

Some of the purposes of sales budgets are:

1. They bring into clear focus sales opportunities, sales objectives, and sales quotas for minimum satisfactory performance.

2. They budget reasonable expense investment to attain those objectives.

3. They help stimulate cooperative effort among participants.

4. They encourage broad overall coverage of product lines, balance between sales effort, sales expense, and planned results.

5. They offer a means for evaluating planning and effort.

6. They stimulate maximum attainment through emphasis on profitable lines of products, profitable marketing areas, and profitable present customers and prospective customers.

To attain these objectives and the satisfactory use of budgets, there must be suitable responsibility and authority established. Each department head and manager must be charged with responsibility for the areas which he administers. There must be a suitable accounting system established to identify accurately sales by sales territories, by product lines, and by customer groups, and to properly allocate costs of production, services, and selling and promotional activities to those areas.

No budget can be meaningful unless the source of information used is reliable and accurately maintained. This involves such factors as:

1. Classification of ledger accounts.

2. Perpetual inventory records.

3. Clearly understood and easily used recording and reporting forms.

4. Cooperation and thoroughness on the part of personnel.

Then there must be a well-devised program to distribute reports of results on a regular basis, weekly or monthly.

No sales executive should be asked to participate in budget formation or control in areas beyond his responsibility and authority. To expect a sales executive to meet a profit budget when production costs are rising is foolish. However, given standard production costs, he should be expected to meet a net-profit budget. Budget periods usually extend for a year, but some companies budget for five or ten years or even longer.

Uses of a Break-Even Chart

There are many specific uses to which a break-even chart can be put by management. Some of the more significant ones are the following:

1. *An Aid for Budgetary Control.* It helps to indicate what changes—if any—you need to bring expenses into line with income.

2. *An Aid to Improve and Balance Sales.* It acts as a warning signal to alert you to potential trouble in your sales program. If your sales relative to other things are not as high as you think they should be, this fact will obviously show up on the chart. Then it may be time to reevaluate your sales techniques.

3. *An Aid to Investigate and Credit Control.* It provides answers to specific questions such as the following: (1) How much of the present sales volume can the company lose before profits disappear? (2) How much will profits increase with an increase in volume?

4. *An Aid in Determining Price Policy.* It visualizes the probable effects on profits of price changes in combination with other changes. For example: (1) What changes may be expected in profits with changes in price, assuming all other factors remain constant? (2) If prices are reduced, what is the most practical combination of volume and cost changes to expect and what is the net effect of the combination of changes on profits? (3) Similarly, if prices are increased, what combination of changes and what effect on profits may reasonably be expected?

5. *An Aid in Discussing Wages.* It assists management by: (1) quickly reflecting the probable influence on profits of proposed wage changes (assuming no change in employee efficiency), and (2) providing visual aid in determining possible economies and efficiencies that might protect the profit position of the company.

6. *An Aid in Appraising Merchandising Policies.* It will enable critical examination of the "merchandise mix." A break-even chart for each line is a valuable help in visualizing which products should be pushed and which may be allowed to coast or possibly be eliminated.

7. *An Aid to Assess Further Capitalization and Expansion Decisions.* It provides a visual means of appraising in advance the wisdom of making capital expenditures which may change cost structure of the business.

Defining Expenses

In considering the break-even point, there should be a clear definition and understanding of the difference between variable and fixed expenses. While these differ somewhat in various types of sales work, they can generally be listed somewhat as follows:

Fixed Expenses	*Variable Expenses*
rent	commissions
salaries	postage
insurance	shipping costs
taxes (some)	taxes (some)
essential travel	optional travel
fixed entertainment costs	optional entertainment costs
depreciation	advertising
maintenance	packaging
auto leasing	promotion

In other words, fixed expenses are those which remain constant regardless of the fluctuation of sales volume, while variable expenses can be controlled according to planned determinations after considering sales volume. Rent will be the same, whether sales are good or bad; but the advertising appropriation can be cut or boosted, according to what the figures show on the profit and loss statement.

How to Construct a Break-Even Chart

Break-even charts are useful. A simple one is shown below.

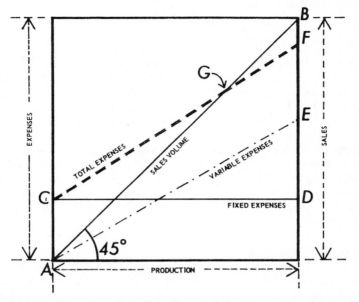

Line A-B indicates the sales-volume line, C-D the fixed-expense line, A-E the variable-expense line, C-F the total-expense line (A-E being moved up to start at Point C) and G, the break-even point.

The two vertical lines represent expenses (left) and sales (right) in dollars, and the horizontal line (bottom) represents production in units or in percentage of capacity. Where the total expense line, C-F, crosses the sales volume line, A-B, is the break-even point. Sales volume less than the amount indicated would generate a loss; volume above this point would generate a profit.

The break-even point can be lowered by lowering either or both fixed and/or variable expenses. If, to obtain added sales volume, the rate of increase in variable expenses rose rapidly, the added volume might generate a loss instead of a profit. The same is true if the fixed expenses were raised. Frequently, profit can be built up faster through the lowering of fixed and variable expenses than by increasing sales volume.

The break-even chart helps to keep management on the alert to find ways and means of improving its margin of safety. If all efforts to reduce the break-even point fail, the chart serves as a constant reminder to management that it is operating on a thin margin of safety. Under such conditions, all decisions must be weighed in the light of their effect upon that margin. As a result, programs may be undertaken to stabilize the margin and to protect it in the event of a business recession.

Fixed expenses increase with increased sales volume but not in direct ratio to it. Examples would include such things as:

opening new territories

adding salesmen to the force

increasing expense allowances

These expenses, once approved, would be fixed for the time being, although sales volume would not increase proportionately. In this respect, sales travel and basic advertising would be fixed, because even if sales dropped drastically the company would still have its salesmen out covering their territories, assisted by advertising and promotional activities.

A marketing executive should take the stepped-up fixed expenses into consideration and reflect them on his break-even chart, probably by adjusting the fixed-expense line at increased volume increments. He should carefully list all of his expenses, indicating those that are fixed, those that are stepped-up-fixed, and those that are variable. This will permit him to create a meaningful budget.

Forecasting the Budget

In most companies the budget for all functions and departments, including sales, is scheduled on a monthly basis. That is no longer enough. Today, with EDP and the increased emphasis on costs and profits, management must have a more immediate picture of the motion and direction of its organization. The fast-changing marketplace no longer allows leisurely budget analysis.

Philco Ford Corporation, for example, has adopted the practice of having its financial analysts interview division heads and department managers about the middle of each month to obtain forecasts of monthly budget performance. This procedure allows managements to maneuver overall company costs and to avoid possible damage caused by the failure of any number of departments to meet their individual budgets. Olin Mathieson also utilizes a monthly system for revising the budget. This is called goal estimating. Through new estimates prepared on the 12th working day of each month, the control-budget figures are updated for the rest of the year.

The Monsanto Company, in forecasting sales for the short range (a year ahead), uses a hybrid approach. According to John L. Gillis, vice-president, this is "partly a gathering of marketers' opinions, partly a jury-of-executive opinion, and partly the computerized treatment of historical data." Monsanto is decentralized and leaves to its operating divisions the choice of a proper approach. As a result, some favor the subjective approach, others the objective, and still others a mixture. The company's library of computer programs for forecasting is fairly extensive and is well used. It covers such techniques as exponential smoothing, adaptive forecasting, trend-curve fitting, regression analysis, and time-series decomposition. Most programs have plotting options.

Cyclical Trends

Like the best-laid plans of mice and men, the best-planned long-range forecasting can be thrown out of kilter by unexpected events —wars, rumors of wars, recessions. What, then, is the best method for establishing cyclical trends?

One method is by plotting unit sales on a time chart, then drawing an "average" line through the dots; this at least gives a rough compensation.

Seasonal trends can be indicated by totaling sales for individual months, over a period of 5 or 10 years; then taking the percentage of distribution for the 12 months.

Cyclical trends can be indicated by fitting curved lines to the dots obtained on the sales-time chart; a refinement can be achieved by using a moving average line developed by statistical methods.

The U.S. Department of Commerce offers a monthly report, prepared primarily for specialists in business-cycle analysis. This report, entitled "Business Cycle Developments," contains basic economic-time series organized in a convenient form for short-term economic analysis and interpretation. It supplements other reports of the Department of Commerce which provide data for analyzing current business conditions.

The presentation and classification of series in this report follow the business-indicator approach. The classification of series is that designated by the National Bureau of Economic Research which, in recent years, has had the leadership in this field of investigation.

Unique features of the report are the arrangement of economic indicators according to their usual timing relations during the course of the business cycle; a cross-classification of these indicators by nine economic processes: employment and unemployment; production, income, consumption, and trade; fixed capital investment; inventories and inventory investment; prices, costs, and profits; money and credit; foreign trade and payments; federal government activities; and the inclusion of special analytical measures and historical cyclical comparisons that help in evaluating the current stage of the business cycle. These measures are made possible by processing on electronic computers.

About 90 principal indicators and over 300 of their components are used for the different measures shown. The movements of the series are shown against the background of the expansions and contractions of the general business cycle, so that "leads" and "lags" can readily be detected and unusual cyclical developments spotted. Almost all the basic data are available in published reports. The chief merits of this report are the speed with which the data for indicators are collected, assembled, and published, and the arrangement of the series for business-cycle studies.

The following principal business indicators are covered in the report: A short list of 25 indicators regarded as especially reliable is distinguished by asterisks (*).

36 LEADING INDICATORS

*Average workweek of production workers, manufacturing.

*Nonagricultural placements.

Accession rate, manufacturing.

Initial claims for unemployment insurance, state programs.

Layoff rate, manufacturing.

*Index of net business formation.

Number of new-business incorporations.

*New orders, durable-goods industries.

Construction contracts, total value.

*Contracts and orders for plant and equipment.

Newly approved capital appropriations, 1,000 manufacturing corporations.

New orders, machinery and equipment industries.

Construction contracts awarded for commercial and industrial buildings, floor space.

New private nonfarm housing units started.

*Index of private housing units authorized by local building permits.

Change in business inventories, all industries.

*Change in book value, manufacturing and trade inventories.

Purchased materials, percent reporting higher inventories.

Change in book value, manufacturers' inventories of materials and supplies.

Buying policy, material, percent reporting commitments 60 days or longer.

Vendor performance, percent reporting slower deliveries.

Change in manufacturers' unfilled orders, durable-goods industries.

*Industrial-materials prices.

*Stock prices, 500 common stocks.

*Corporate profits after taxes.

 Ratio, profits to income originating, all industries.

 Profits per dollar of sales, corporate, manufacturing.

*Ratio, price to unit labor cost, manufacturing.

 Change in money supply and time deposits.

 Change in money supply.

 Total private borrowing.

*Change in consumer installment debt.

 Change in bank loans to businesses.

 Change in mortgage debt.

 Liabilities of business failures.

 Delinquency rate, installment loans.

25 ROUGHLY COINCIDENT INDICATORS

 Nonagricultural job openings, number pending.

 Index of help-wanted advertising in newspapers.

 Man-hours in nonfarm establishments.

*Employees in nonagricultural establishments.

 Total nonagricultural employment.

*Unemployment rate, total.

 Insured unemployment rate.

 Unemployment rate for married males.

 GNP in current dollars.

*GNP in constant dollars.

*Industrial production.

*Personal income.

 Labor income in mining, manufacturing, and construction.

 Final sales.

*Manufacturing and trade sales.

*Sales of retail stores.

 Manufacturers' unfilled orders, durable-goods industries.

 Backlog of capital appropriations, manufacturing.

 Wholesale prices excluding farm products and foods.

 Wholesale price index, manufactured goods.

 Treasury-bill rate.

25 Roughly Coincident Indicators (cont.)

Treasury-bond yields.
Corporate-bond yields.
Municipal-bond yields.
Free reserves.

11 Lagging Indicators

*Unemployment rate, persons unemployed 15 or more weeks.
*Business expenditures, new plant and equipment.
Machinery and equipment sales and business-construction expenditures.
*Book value, manufacturing and trade inventories.
Book value of manufacturers' inventories, finished goods.
Labor cost per dollar of real corporate GNP.
*Labor cost per unit of output, manufacturing.
Consumer installment debt.
*Commercial and industrial loans outstanding.
*Bank rates on short-term business loans.
Mortgage yields, residential.

In addition to these series, classified according to their timing, other U.S. series with business-cycle significance, analytical measures, and international comparisons are included in the report.

The Future Science of Forecasting

The fundamental marketing problem which constantly faces a manufacturer is that of accurately estimating future sales. In all manufacturing and distribution organizations, every effort, every plan, every idea, eventually comes to focus on this all-important problem, beside which all others are secondary!

In production, the path from the drawing board to the finished product is well charted—planned in advance, every stage a definite one, and all based on *precision*. The engineers and production men use every possible device, mechanical or electrical, to measure, test, and control the design, engineering, and manufacture of their product in advance.

With the finished product, however, we move over to the sphere of marketing and here we lose the vital element of precision. The sales department, which originally told the factory the total number of products to manufacture, was guided chiefly by its experience the previous year, plus reports from or conversations with individuals in its distribution channels!

The results are sometimes disastrous. Either the factory makes too many units, or *equally as bad,* not enough. When the distribution men overestimate the market, the result is excessive inventory, price-cutting, additional advertising costs, or outright loss. When the distribution men underestimate the market, potential sales and profits are lost forever.

Obviously, present methods of estimating markets to determine future sales result in high manufacturing costs and lower profits. While industry worries about pricing and packaging, warehousing, and dealer coverage, the main task of developing a practical method of predicting future sales with greater accuracy goes largely unattended.

Regardless of price, package design, number of retailers, efficiency of the sales organization, or anything else, the manufacturer must decide each season how many product units to make. This depends on one thing and one thing only: "How many will we sell?"

The curious thing is that we have had before us, for a long time, two excellent examples pointing to a possible solution of the problem. Magazines and book clubs know *in advance* exactly how many customers they have for their product each and every month. They accomplish this through the simple but all-important expedient of offering buyers a reward for telling them in advance that they intend to buy the product.

The customer who subscribes to a magazine for a year receives a better price than if he buys a newsstand copy each month after publication. The customer who becomes a member of a book club agrees to purchase four books a year and receives a better price plus a premium of two books for merely signing up. In each case, the publisher or the book club knows in advance exactly how many copies are presold!

There is our missing element of precision, so fundamental in production and so sadly lacking in distribution.

Costs of Distribution

Once you get control of distribution costs, you are on your way to higher profits, because there are many ways that you can use cost control in making marketing decisions.

Finding the costs of distributing your products can be almost as complex as running the business itself. Yet unless you bring distribution costs under control, you sacrifice profitability.

"Classic cost analysis," says Albert Bergfeld, president of Case and Company, consultants, "makes the distinction between *fixed* costs—which go on day after day regardless of sales or production volume—and *variable* costs, which vary with activity, whether by volume of production sales or the activity of a particular department."

Modern cost analysis takes the process a step further, by breaking fixed costs into components that Case and Company refers to as "constant costs" and "programmed costs."

"In the distribution function, programmed costs include the cost of new-product development, advertising and promotion, and the amount you must pay salesmen to open new accounts."

Programmed costs are taken on to influence volume, sales revenue, and profits.

Programmed costs can be further separated to show, for example, expenditures made to increase the sale of a particular product. These specific programmed costs should be considered as an offset to revenues from that product.

"Generally speaking, distribution activities are programmed more than are production activities," says Bergfeld. "For example, whether to take on an advertising campaign for one of your products is a management decision that comes up every year. You can raise the advertising appropriation, lower it, or eliminate it entirely."

Distribution-cost analysis can also help you pick the geographical areas where you want to concentrate your marketing effort.

Variable costs include sales commissions, transportation charges, running cost of trucks, order entry, billing, and many credit and collection expenses. These are more easily assigned to product line and product than are specific programmed costs.

Taking a tip from the production side of business, some cost-conscious managers are considering imaginative adaptations of the engineering-developed "value analysis" technique as a means of uncovering some of their true costs of doing business.

The objective is to relate each specific cost to the function, service, or operation purchased by that cost—to make certain that every element of cost (labor, material, supplies, styling, and services) contributes proportionately.

Then imaginative thinking is used to develop a better or less costly means of obtaining the function; and, finally, the most promising alternative is adopted.

Chapter 26

PRICING POLICIES

ONE way to set the price at which a product is to be sold is quite simple. Just add enough to the cost of production to yield the desired profit. This is the "cost plus" method of pricing. But pricing a line of products in a complex and competitive market is not so simple. In fact, it presents one of the most difficult problems in sales management. If the price is set too low the business cannot long remain solvent. If set too high, the product may be priced out of its markets, cutting sales volume below the break-even point. Therefore, setting prices is a compromise between what the producer would like to get and what the buyer is willing to pay. The sound approach is from the viewpoint of the buyer.

Had Henry Ford followed the accounting formula of cost multiplied by x in setting the price on his Model T, it is safe to say there would be no Ford Motor Company today. The cost of manufacturing the first few Ford cars would have been far above what the public was willing to pay. Ford approached the problem by first determining what the public would consider a satisfactory price for a light car. Then he estimated how many people would lay that much on the line for a car at that price within a year after it began to come off the line. Having thus determined how many cars might be sold, he tooled up to produce that many cars and spread his development and overhead charges against them. By that process of pricing Ford found he could not only make a good profit on each car produced, but also could afford to pay his workmen above the "going" rate of wages. This then pioneering approach to price setting was followed by a great many industries where profits depended upon mass production. Many accountants still view this method with much distrust, taking the position that prices should be set more conservatively and with less guessing. They argue, with good logic, that if somebody guesses wrong, the whole year's profits may be lost. But sales managers favor research pricing because it gives them a favorable competitive price. They are usually willing to assume responsibility for getting the required volume if they believe the price is right.

Various Price Techniques

A pricing strategy which works successfully for a producer employing production-line techniques will not work for all. Some products, cement for example, must be priced according to "the market" or the going price in various localities. It is not a question of selling at a price which assures a fair profit; it is a question of producing to a selling price as low or lower than that charged by competitors. The same is true in marketing fresh meat. The large packers are content to show a profit of 2 cents on each dollar of sales. Since they are in competition with local butchers, their competition actually sets the price for them. Because of this problem, the tendency in low-profit industries is for members of an industry to work together as closely as practical in setting prices, without exposing themselves to a charge of illegally fixing prices.

Pricing parts and materials sold to converters affords more leeway, since competition is not so keen and a producer is usually able to get a price above his competitors *if he can prove value.* It is at that point that salesmanship enters the picture. It is the general practice in such cases to add enough to the cost to do a constructive sales job, not only so far as the producer's own salesmen are concerned, but to provide for adequate advertising and sales promotion. In fact, the pricing formula usually allows about as much for marketing the product as the cost of producing it. A commonly used method is to set the price at a figure which will allow one-third for production, one-third for selling, and one-third for administrative expense and profit. The aim is to arrive at a price which will yield 10 percent on sales. In good years the profit may exceed that goal; in poor years it falls below the mark. But over the years it should, if a business is to prosper and grow, average close to 10 percent.

Still different pricing strategy is required when the product is sold for resale. In merchandising practice prices are set backwards —that is to say, a producer starts with the price at which he determines the product can best be sold over the retail counter. This is his catalog or list price. By a system of discounts from that price he arrives at a selling price to his distributors which permits him a fair profit over and above his cost of production, marketing, and administration. It also provides flexibility, since the price can be changed to different classifications of buyers by simply adjusting the discount.

The Pricing Pattern

The sound course to follow in pricing, and this applies especially during a period of changes in the general price index, is to establish a pricing pattern which is flexible enough to meet any condition, and yet which is rigid enough to provide an adequate profit at varying levels of sales production. Dr. Joel Dean, professor of business economics at Columbia University, offers the following suggestions for establishing such a pricing pattern:

1. Alertness and flexibility should be the keynote of your pricing activity. Things are moving fast and prediction of the economic future cannot always pan out. Hence, policies must be continually reviewed and revised. A normal lifetime of price-setting decisions is being concentrated in a few months.

2. A philosophy of pricing is indispensable today. A patchwork of price decisions cannot successfully meet a continuously changing situation. You should formulate a pricing strategy in terms of your long-range objectives and the efficient ways of attaining them. Surprisingly few companies have really done it.

3. Undertake basic research that will lay a sound foundation for more scientific pricing in the future. Price policy is probably the least scientific sector of marketing policy. Though techniques and tools for practical pricing research have definitely proved their usefulness, they are still in an early stage of development. In many instances price rises have not exceeded the increases in unit costs and price changes have lagged behind cost changes.

4. Adjust your costs to current and prospective price levels.

5. Adjust your income statement to fit economic realities. Otherwise the whole set of profit guides becomes distorted.

6. Align your prices with competitive and substitute bench marks to get the kind of buyers' action and market-share results that will attain your company's long-range objectives.

7. Put your price-differential house in order now. In many companies the structure of geographical quantity functional and product-line price differentials have grown haphazardly.

8. Actively recognize the role of public relations in determining your pricing policies. Pricing is a public responsibility, particularly for firms that are pivotal in our economy.

The "Value Added" Pattern

A specific example of pricing policy in a diversified-product company is offered by Metals and Controls, Inc., a corporate division of Texas Instruments, Inc. C. J. Grube, manager, marketing development, reports:

An organization of the size and magnitude of Metals and Controls, Inc., with its great diversification of products, develops a pricing procedure geared to profits. In developing a pricing structure of the various products, factors considered include the amount of the product that will be sold, relationships to material cost, manufacturing expense, overhead, and the cost of all other supporting elements in the manufacturing and marketing phases.

Products that are novel require a different pricing treatment because they are distinctive. The distinctiveness of a proprietary product may maintain its exclusiveness for a time due to patent positions or manufacturing technologies. Products not restricted by these conditions will be readily adopted by competitors who will attempt to take away your market by bringing out substitutes. The speed at which these products lose their uniqueness depends on many factors. Among them are the investment required by competitors to manufacture and market such a product, the strength of patent protection, and the aggressiveness of competitors.

Manufacturing experience and actual cost analysis are acceptable guidelines for pricing of existing products. One could consider pricing policies successful if they achieve the following objectives: Producing profits and maintaining market position in face of strong competition.

The strategy in pricing a product or products relates to a choice between "penetration" and "skimming" pricing. There are many intermediate positions depending upon a broad range of circumstances.

Metals and Controls, with its broad range of product lines, avoids adherence to a specific pattern of pricing and treats each product line individually because of the many variable factors related to the "Create, Make, and Market System." The basis of our computation of pricing for profit is an adaptation of the "value added" formula. "Value added" is the difference between the basic material cost and the selling price.

The Sales Manager's Role

The prime responsibility of the sales executive in pricing is to know, or be able to find out, what the customer will buy, and in what quantities he will buy at varying price ranges. Since the ultimate consumer actually dictates the price of most products, the sales manager should be in a position to advise top management as to the sales and advertising effort required to move a given volume within a certain time onto the market.

At this point, it may be well to differentiate between "markup" and "markon." *Markon* is the amount of profit added to the full cost of an item, while *markup* is the profit expressed in terms of a percentage of the sale price.

Another term of importance in price discussions is "price line." Successful companies are careful to retain their price lines—$2.95, $4.95, $9.95, etc.—for years. While costs may vary, the selling price of a "price-lined" item remains fixed, and profits may shrink or rise in proportion. If the profit grows too small, the seller may jump the price to the next price line, or he may change the specifications of the product to reduce its cost. This practice is found particularly with consumer goods at the retail level but not at the manufacturers' and distributors' level.

No one has yet come up with a convincing explanation of why there is less resistance to buying a product priced at $4.95 than the same item priced at $5.00; it's just one of the facts of life, which, for want of a better term, is called "psychological."

A price may be hopelessly high or low in terms of accounting formulas and still be psychologically correct for maximum sales. The comment which follows is by the vice-president in charge of research of one of the great mail-order chains. Note that three of the six factors in this company's price policy are psychological:

1. *The type of clientele* to which the store caters. X department store regularly gets 45 percent on an article which Y can get only 38 percent for. People who shop at the Y store are very price-conscious and are satisfied with the barren interior, the poor delivery system, and the cheap wrappings.

2. *Price line.* As merchandise increases in price, higher markups are taken. The customers for a pair of $15 shoes are less concerned with price than the customers for a $5 pair.

3. *Tradition.* For several reasons some types of merchandise get a higher markup than others. For example, piece goods and white goods are always sharply marked, while some jewelry gets a high markup.

4. *Cost of selling.* There are two factors involved in this point: Class of salesmanship and hazards of merchandise. When an article requires knowledge of the merchandise and selling ability in the clerk, this higher cost of sales must be recognized and absorbed in the markup. As for hazards, anything with style is vulnerable to quick changes in public taste; a dress, which can become old-fashioned overnight, has to have a higher markup than a keg of nails. Any goods which are fragile, soilable, or perishable must absorb these risks. Mirrors, for instance, get at least a 50 percent markup.

5. *Turnover rate.* Since all merchandise must absorb its share of the overhead, an item with monthly turnover needs less of a markup than one which has an annual rate of turn of 4 or 5 because the unit overhead cost is lower.

6. *Location.* Percentage of markup differs from city to city. For instance, the average markup in Evanston, Illinois, is much higher than in Centralia, Illinois.

The psychological factors are involved in industrial pricing as well as in the pricing of consumer goods. A generator manufacturer said: "Two- and three-kilowatt generators can be manufactured and sold for the same amount, but the profit is better on the three-kilowatt unit because our customers expect the two-kilowatt unit to be cheaper."

Influence of Turnover on Profits

The rate of turnover is the most important factor in business. Offer any merchant two units of merchandise, one of which he can sell at a profit of 10 percent on his investment and the other a profit of 15 percent, and he will invariably take the 15 percent article. He gives but little consideration to the fact that he may be able to sell three of the 10 percent items while he is selling one 15 percent article, and in doing so would make a gross profit on his investment of 30 cents, as against 15 cents on the long profit article.

Computed in terms of annual income a merchant making $30,000 a year with a stock investment of $10,000 would double his income with the same investment if he could turn over his stock twice as often. This principle is clearly explained in the accompanying chart.

Merchants should realize that by handling slow-moving merchandise they have to take losses in the shape of investment, interest, markdowns, salaries and wages which go on just the same, shelf or storage room for which they pay rent, prestige and reputation that are lost through handling unknown brands, and the general inefficiency of a sleepy business.

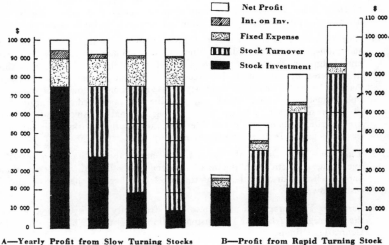

A—Yearly Profit from Slow Turning Stocks on a Given Investment   B—Profit from Rapid Turning Stock on a Given Investment

In the above charts each of the columns in Series A represents sales amounting to $100,000 but the number of turnovers increases from 1 in A-1 to 8 in A-4, and it will be observed that with each increase in turnover the stock investment as well as the interest are cut in two while the amount of profit increases. Series B shows uniform stock investments and costs of interest throughout while the amount of profit increases with the number of turnovers.

LOOK BEFORE YOU CUT PRICES!

You Must Sell More to Break Even

To find the percentage of increase in unit sales which you will need to earn the same gross profits when you cut a price, look in the column headed present gross profit.

If You Cut Your Price	AND YOUR PRESENT GROSS PROFIT IS							
	5%	10%	15%	20%	25%	30%	35%	40%
1%	25.0%	11.1%	7.1%	5.3%	4.2%	3.4%	2.9%	2.6%
2	66.6	25.0	15.4	11.1	8.7	7.1	6.1	5.3
3	150.0	42.8	25.0	17.6	13.6	11.1	9.4	8.1
4	400.0	66.6	36.4	25.0	19.0	15.4	12.9	11.1
5	—	100.0	50.0	33.3	25.0	20.0	16.7	14.3
6	—	150.0	66.7	42.9	31.6	25.0	20.7	17.6
7	—	233.3	87.5	53.8	38.9	30.4	25.0	21.2
8	—	400.0	114.3	66.7	47.1	36.4	29.6	25.0
9	—	1000.0	150.0	81.8	56.3	42.9	34.6	29.0
10	—	—	200.0	100.0	66.7	50.0	40.0	33.3
11	—	—	275.0	122.2	78.6	57.9	45.8	37.9
12	—	—	400.0	150.0	92.3	66.7	52.2	42.9
13	—	—	650.0	185.7	108.3	76.5	59.1	48.1
14	—	—	1400.0	233.3	127.3	87.5	66.7	53.8
15	—	—	—	300.0	150.0	100.0	75.0	60.0
16	—	—	—	400.0	177.8	114.3	84.2	66.7
17	—	—	—	566.7	212.5	130.8	94.4	73.9
18	—	—	—	900.0	257.1	150.0	105.9	81.8
19	—	—	—	1900.0	316.7	172.7	118.8	90.5
20	—	—	—	—	400.0	200.0	133.3	100.0
21	—	—	—	—	525.0	233.3	150.0	110.5
22	—	—	—	—	733.3	275.0	169.2	122.2
23	—	—	—	—	1115.0	328.6	191.7	135.3
24	—	—	—	—	2400.0	400.0	218.2	150.0
25	—	—	—	—	—	500.0	250.0	166.7

Example: Your present gross margin is 25% and you cut your selling price 10%. Locate 10% in the left-hand column. Now follow across to the column headed 25%. You find you will need to sell 66.7% MORE units to earn the same margin dollars as at the previous price. Kinda silly, isn't it?

This "Look Before You Cut Prices!" table has been used by a manufacturer to discourage price-cutters.

Pricing by Customer

The prices and discounts you set should be arranged to make all customers contribute equally to your profits. Since distribution represents the larger part of costs for many products, pricing by customer demands knowledge and control of distribution costs.

The Robinson-Patman Act states that price differences must be specifically traceable to the differing volume or character of your transactions with customers that compete with each other. What it amounts to is marking up the cost of each transaction by the *same percentage* for each customer.

Some customers require costly packaging. Others require special delivery or special facilities for displaying their goods. These can best be handled as extras or rebates, since their specific costs are fairly readily determined and directly assignable to particular customers as they occur.

The Philosophy of Price Cutting

Consideration should be given here to price cutting as a way to increase sales, to move seasonal stock, to reduce inventory, etc. Cuts in price may also take the form of "loss leaders" or "price leaders"; an attractive price which is intended to increase store traffic and to carry over to favorably influence buyers to purchase other products. It has been found that loss leaders attract so much store traffic, which buys other goods at list price, that the loss is more than made up; while to get this same promotional value through advertisements or other promotions is far more costly.

However, when cutting prices, it must be realized that competitors will follow suit immediately with price cuts on the same product or on substitute products. Price wars can become dangerous experiences, and it then may become difficult to raise prices back to normal.

On the other hand, not to meet a cut price is equally dangerous; a competing product may attain recognition or customers may be lost. Price cutting is, therefore, a very serious matter. A company should engage in it with its eyes open and with the pros and cons all carefully considered beforehand.

Chapter 27

TERMS OF SALE AND DISCOUNTS

T HE BUSINESSMAN has a fairly free hand in establishing prices for his products, so long as this is not done in collusion with others for the purpose of restraining competition.

It is in the area of setting terms of sale and establishing discount policies that the sales manager must be alert for an innocently-inspired violation of the provisions of the Robinson-Patman Act and the regulations of the Federal Trade Commission.

The sales manager must remember that whatever terms of sale and discounts his firm offers, these must be available to *all* customers who comply with qualifying requirements for the terms and discounts. Thus, if he allows one wholesaler a large discount for an extremely large order, he must be willing to allow the same discount to any other customer willing to purchase a like quantity of goods. Furthermore, he must offer the same terms of sale. He cannot allow one customer a 2 percent discount if the invoice is paid within 10 days and insist upon the full price from another who pays within 10 days of delivery.

Payment Requirements—Ordinary Terms

Terms establish the conditions under which invoices must be paid. They may be classed as "ordinary," "extra," or "dating ahead" terms.

Net: Terms such as net/30 mean that payment of the face value of the invoice must be made within 30 days or within the number of days stated.

Open Account: Such terms usually imply payment within one week or 10 days or whatever period is agreed upon by the buyer and seller.

F.O.B. (free on board): Normally, this term means that the item sold is placed "free on board" a truck, railway car, or aircraft. Where overseas shipment is involved, the term f.a.s., "free alongside ship," is often used. In both cases, the buyer takes over all transportation costs. In the absence of any contractual terms to indicate a different agreement, the buyer bears the risk of loss when merchandise is shipped F.O.B. Qualifications are often added; for example, "f.o.b. destination," "f.o.b. factory," or "f.a.s. New York."

C.O.D. (cash on delivery): This is used quite frequently, either at the buyer's or seller's request. Under such terms, the seller assumes freight charges both ways if the purchaser refuses to accept shipment unless the merchandise can be sold to another customer in the vicinity.

S.D.B.L. (sight draft—bill of lading): Before shipment will be made, the buyer is required to make immediate payment on a "sight draft" which is attached to an advance bill of lading.

In all the above terms, with the exception of "net," a cash discount may or may not be given. Net terms, as the name implies, carry no cash discount.

Extra or Dating Ahead Terms

E.O.M. or M.O.M. (end of the month or middle of the month): These terms indicate that the credit period starts either on the last day of the month in which the goods are shipped, or on the 15th. For both terms, the purpose is greater convenience for both buyers and sellers. Buyers can make many purchases during a month, pay bills monthly with a single check, and still take advantage of the regular discount. Sellers can cut accounting and billing costs because there are fewer settlements of accounts.

Using E.O.M. terms, for example, you make purchases on August 1, 9, 17, and 25. But all these orders are invoiced to you as of September 1. With terms of 2/10, net 30, you could take your prompt payment discount up to September 10; the full amount would not be due until September 30.

Using M.O.M. terms, you make purchases on September 1, 5, 7, 9, and 12. But all these orders are invoiced to you as of September 15. If you buy on September 16, 20, 22, 26, and 29, those orders are billed as of October 1.

Proximo (specified date in the coming month): Terms 2/10 prox. require payment on the 10th of the month following purchase to secure the 2-percent discount. Actually such terms are the equivalent of 2/10 E.O.M.

R.O.G. or A.O.G. (receipt of goods; arrival of goods): Under these terms, the discount period is based on the date on which the purchaser receives the goods. For example, merchandise with a 2/10, n/30, R.O.G. dating received September 15 must be paid for by September 25 if the discount is to be taken.

R.O.G. terms are employed to meet objections of distant purchasers who would be at a disadvantage if terms were based on "date of invoice." A supplier located in the East with customers throughout the nation must, of necessity, employ R.O.G. terms if he is to meet competition from the customers' local suppliers.

The buyer gets the benefits of R.O.G. terms only when the bill is discounted. If he does not pay the bill in time to take the discount, the net period is measured from the date of the invoice.

"Extra" Terms: Where these terms apply, the discount can be taken until the expiration of the "extra" period. Thus, in the wholesale drygoods trade, you find terms such as 2/10-60 (2 percent 10 days, 60 days extra). These terms allow the buyer a 2-percent discount if he pays his bill within 70 days of the

invoice date. Another term is 3/10, 2/10-60, which allows a 3-percent discount if payment is made within 10 days, but only 2 percent if payment is made after the 10th day.

Close examination of the term 3/10, 2/10-60 reveals that the actual prompt payment discount is only 1 percent, to be taken when the bill is paid within 10 days. The other 2 percent should really be considered a "trade" discount.

Quantity Discounts

The time-honored practice of allowing larger discounts in consideration of larger orders, as has been stated, is sanctioned by the Federal Trade Commission, provided discounts represent actual cost savings, or the buyer renders special service as a consideration. The Robinson-Patman Act also allows different quantity discounts to different customers *if the customers are not in competition with one another*. A sale of merchandise to isolated customers, at larger discounts, for example, is not considered discriminatory, if both customers do an intrastate business and are located in different states. In the same way wholesalers do not compete (in theory) with retailers, so a seller would be in the clear if he gave the wholesaler a larger discount than he gave a retailer in the same territory, even though the retailer claimed to be in competition with the wholesaler on industrial and other accounts. But broadly speaking the test of legality of quantity discounts is the savings which the seller is able to pass on to the buyer by selling in larger quantities.

Functional or Trade Discounts

Whereas quantity discounts are extended to all firms in the same distribution level (horizontally applied), functional or trade discounts are extended to firms in different distribution levels (vertically applied). The accompanying "Discount and Markup Chart—A-From List" illustrates this. Note that the consumer is normally expected to pay the list price of $1. However, at times he may purchase in such quantities as to justify a 10-percent discount. His normal buying quantity is shown on the solid line.

The retailer is expected to buy normally in lots of 1,000 units or more and to receive a 38-percent discount from list, outlined by the solid line. If he sells to the consumer at list price, his markup is 38 percent; if he sells at 10 percent less list, his markup is 31 percent. However, at times he may buy smaller quantities, as for instance 50 units. In this case, his discount is 20 percent; and if he sells to the consumer at list less 10 percent, his markup is only 11 percent.

DISCOUNT AND MARKUP CHART

A—FROM LIST

CONSUMER

Quantity	Discount	Net Price
1-99	—	$1.00 List
100+	10%	.90

RETAILER

Quantity	1-99	100-999	1000+	Extra
Discount	20%	30%	38%	38-5%
Net Price	.80	.70	.62	.589

MARKUP

Quantity	1-99	100-999	1000+	
Retailer	20%	30%	38%	
(Wholesaler)	(12%)	(-)	(Loss)	
Retailer	11%	22%	31%	
(Wholesaler)	(19%)	(7%)	(Loss)	
(Wholesaler)	(31%)	(21%)	(11%)	
(Wholesaler)	(47%)	(28%)	(19%)	(15.1%)

WHOLESALER

Quantity	Discount	Net Price
1-99	30%	.70
100-999	35%	.65
1000-4999	45%	.55
5000+	50%	.50

B—FROM FUNCTIONAL LISTS

Quantity	CONSUMER List $1.00		RETAILER List 80c ($1.00 less 20%)		WHOLESALER List 70c ($1.00 less 30%)	
	Discount	Net Price	Discount	Net Price	Discount	Net Price
1-99	—	$1.00	—	$.80	—	$.70
100-999	10%	.90	12.5%	.70	7.1%	.65
1000-4999			22.5%-	.62	21.4%	.55
5000+			22.5%	.589	28.6%	.50

In the example, the wholesaler normally buys in lots exceeding 5,000 units on which he receives a 50-percent discount. If he sells to the retailer in normal quantities of 1,000 or more units, he receives a markup of 19 percent. If he should extend the retailer an extra 5 percent (list-38 percent-5 percent) the retailer would pay 59 cents and the wholesaler would realize a markup of 15.1 percent.

In lots of 2,000 units, the consumer would receive a discount of 10 percent from list; the retailer 38 percent, and the wholesaler 45 percent.

Functional List Discounts

Another way to handle functional or trade discounts is shown on the same chart under "B-From Functional Lists." Here the consumer quantity discount of 10 percent has been taken from a base of $1. The retailer's quantity discount for normal purchases exceeding 1,000 units has been taken from a base of 80 cents ($1 less 20 percent discount). The base used for the wholesaler is 70 cents ($1 less 30 percent). The resulting markups remain the same as shown in Part "A."

This method of discounting requires the printing of three price lists. These are quite frequently printed in three different identifying colors. When quoting a wholesaler, the manufacturer sends all three lists. The wholesaler sends the retailer the retail and consumer lists, etc.

Some manufacturers issue only one price sheet with quantity discounts shown, and rely upon the quantities purchased to classify the buyers into their respective functional groups.

"Early Order" Discounts

Encouraging buyers to place quantity orders by placing them in a definite yearly purchase classification and giving them a special discount if they order 40 percent in the early portion of the season, has proved successful in many cases where volume is especially important. It can be justified under the Robinson-Patman Act from a cost standpoint. A rubber company used the following plan:

Dealers who buy out of stock and whose annual purchases are over $10,000 receive a discount of 15 percent on their early orders and 10 percent on their fill-in orders. Dealers who buy between $8,000 and $10,000 receive 12½ percent early-order discount and 10 percent on fill-in orders. Dealers who buy from $5,000 to $8,000 receive 10 percent early-order discount and 8 percent on fill-in. Dealers who buy from $2,500 to $5,000 receive 8 percent early-order discount and 5 percent fill-in. Dealers who buy from $1,000 to $2,500 receive a volume rebate at the end of the year of 2½ percent.

Those dealers who receive an early-order discount receive this only when they place a substantial early order of at least 40 percent of the volume classification in which they fall.

Our policy of protecting buyers against price decline applies only to those buyers whose resale price is controlled in any way by our actions. This means that price protection with us is limited only to jobbers who follow our printed prices to retailers.

Our merchandise is very seasonable and therefore we guarantee full price protection on all deliveries of rubber footwear that we make between April 1 and December 1, but in our entire history there has never been a change of price in this period. Therefore, the above statement that our guaranty applies only to jobbers is correct.

In addition to this price guarantee applying to retailers and jobbers, we protect our jobbers against a decline in price after December 1 and up to our initial announcement of prices for the succeeding season, covering all goods that they have on hand that were delivered after December 1, plus all goods they have on hand delivered between April and December 1 up to a total equal to 20 percent of our deliveries to them from April 1 to December 1.

Cash Discounts

Strictly speaking, the cash discount is a financial discount and not sales expense. The Federal Trade Commission recognizes this difference between cash and trade discounts. In actual practice, however, buyers add discounts together and treat them as a trade discount, according to whether or not it is their practice to discount their bills.

Even the most casual inquiry into this matter of cash discount reveals a woeful lack of general understanding among buyers that 2 percent 10 days, net 30 days, is equivalent to 36 percent per annum on their money. There is an equally deplorable lack of understanding on the part of sellers who endeavor to use a slightly increased cash discount as a sales lever, that 3 percent 10 days, net 30 days, is equivalent to 54 percent per annum on the money. In this connection the following table may be useful:

½% 10 days—net 30 days	=	9% per annum
1 % 10 days—net 30 days	=	18% per annum
1½% 10 days—net 30 days	=	27% per annum
2 % 30 days—net 4 mos.	=	8% per annum
2 % 10 days—net 60 days	=	14% per annum
2 % 30 days—net 60 days	=	24% per annum
2 % 10 days—net 30 days	=	36% per annum
3 % 10 days—net 4 mos.	=	10% per annum
3 % 30 days—net 60 days	=	36% per annum
3 % 10 days—net 30 days	=	54% per annum

Unearned Discounts

Some customers deduct the cash discount even though the discount has passed. This amounts to the customer dictating his own terms of payment. If customers are allowed to dictate the terms of sale, it amounts to allowing them to dictate the price at which they will buy. This, of course, is contrary to the Robinson-Patman Act, which requires that no advantages in price or terms be granted one customer that are not allowed all customers under similar conditions.

The usual practice when a customer takes a discount he has not earned is to return the check, thus leaving the account open and the buyer's credit impaired. However, it is not legally necessary that the check be returned. It can be accepted in part payment of the account. If that policy is followed, care must be used to see that endorsement of the check does not constitute receipt in full for the items covered. But no matter how the unearned discount is handled, it invariably leads to unpleasantness, especially with well-rated customers. For that reason some sales managers prefer to accept the loss and allow the discount, rather than make an issue out of the incident. But once the customer finds he can "get away" with taking an unearned discount, he concludes the seller is fearful of losing his business and will soon take other advantages. A courteous, but firm policy is best in the long run, explaining to the customer that it would be unfair to those who pay promptly to get the discount.

Advertising Allowances

The advertising allowance is used mainly by manufacturers of branded products, either as a means of introducing a new product or getting added dealer "push" behind an old product. Properly used, it is an excellent method of stimulating sales.

Many manufacturers have found it profitable to offer an advertising allowance to encourage local retailers to do more advertising, to take advantage of local advertising rates which might not be available to a national manufacturer, and to benefit by the retailer's knowledge of local conditions. When applying this allowance, manufacturers usually insist that a tear sheet of the advertisement accompany the retailer's request for allowance. Otherwise the retailer might take the allowance and add it to his profits, a practice considered unfair under the Robinson-Patman Act.

In some industries advertising allowances are based on a detailed program formally distributed as the company's "cooperative advertising policy." The rules and regulations under which the allowances are made to distributors or dealers are spelled out to avoid possible

Ready Discount Computer

Discount Percent	Equivalent	Net	Discount Percent	Equivalent	Net	Discount Percent	Equivalent	Net
2½	.025	.975	25	.25	.75	30, 7½ & 7½	.4011	.5989
2½ & 2½	.0494	.9506	25 & 2½	.2688	.7312	30, 7½ & 10	.4173	.5827
2½ & 5	.0737	.9263	25, 2½ & 2½	.287	.713	30 & 10	.37	.63
2½, 5 & 2½	.0969	.9031	25, 2½ & 5	.3053	.6947	30, 10 & 2½	.3858	.6142
2½, 5 & 5	.1201	.8799	25, 2½ & 7½	.3236	.6764	30, 10 & 5	.4015	.5985
2½, 5, 5 & 2½	.1421	.8579	25, 2½ & 10	.3419	.6581	30, 10 & 7½	.4173	.5827
2½ & 10	.1225	.8775	25 & 5	.2875	.7125	30, 10 & 10	.433	.567
2½, 10 & 2½	.1444	.8556	25, 5 & 2½	.3053	.6947	32½	.325	.675
2½, 10 & 5	.166	.834	25, 5 & 5	.3231	.6769	32½ & 2½	.3419	.6581
2½, 10, 5 & 2½	.1872	.8128	25, 5 & 7½	.3409	.6591	32½, 2½ & 2½	.3583	.6417
2½, 10 & 10	.2102	.7898	25, 5 & 10	.3588	.6412	32½, 2½ & 5	.3748	.6252
5	.05	.95	25 & 7½	.3063	.6937	32½, 2½ & 7½	.3912	.6088
5 & 2½	.0738	.9262	25, 7½ & 2½	.3236	.6764	32½, 2½ & 10	.4077	.5923
5 & 5	.0975	.9025	25, 7½ & 5	.3409	.6591	32½ & 5	.3588	.6412
5, 5 & 2½	.1201	.8799	25, 7½ & 7½	.3583	.6417	32½, 5 & 2½	.3748	.6252
5, 5 & 5	.1426	.8574	25, 7½ & 10	.3756	.6244	32½, 5 & 5	.3908	.6092
5, 5, 5 & 2½	.164	.836	25 & 10	.325	.675	32½, 5 & 7½	.4068	.5932
5 & 10	.145	.855	25, 10 & 2½	.3419	.6581	32½, 5 & 10	.4229	.5771
5, 10 & 2½	.1664	.8336	25, 10 & 5	.3588	.6412	32½ & 7½	.3756	.6244
5, 10 & 5	.1877	.8123	25, 10 & 7½	.3756	.6244	32½, 7½ & 2½	.3912	.6088
5, 10, 5 & 2½	.2081	.7919	25, 10 & 10	.3925	.6075	32½, 7½ & 5	.4068	.5932
5, 10 & 10	.2305	.7695	27½	.275	.725	32½, 7½ & 7½	.4225	.5775
10	.10	.90	27½ & 2½	.2931	.7069	32½, 7½ & 10	.4381	.5619
10 & 2½	.1225	.8775	27½, 2½ & 2½	.3108	.6892	32½ & 10	.3925	.6075
10 & 5	.145	.855	27½, 2½ & 5	.3285	.6715	32½, 10 & 2½	.4077	.5923
10, 5 & 2½	.1664	.8336	27½, 2½ & 7½	.3461	.6539	32½, 10 & 5	.4229	.5771
10, 5 & 5	.1878	.8122	27½, 2½ & 10	.3638	.6362	32½, 10 & 7½	.4381	.5619
10, 5, 5 & 2½	.2081	.7919	27½ & 5	.3113	.6887	32½, 10 & 10	.4533	.5467
10 & 10	.19	.81	27½, 5 & 2½	.3285	.6715	32½ & 20	.46	.54
10, 10 & 2½	.2103	.7897	27½, 5 & 5	.3457	.6543	32½, 20 & 2½	.4735	.5265
10, 10 & 5	.2305	.7695	27½, 5 & 7½	.3629	.6371	32½, 20 & 5	.487	.513
10, 10, 5 & 2½	.2497	.7503	27½, 5 & 10	.3801	.6199	32½, 20 & 7½	.5005	.4995
10, 10 & 10	.271	.729	27½ & 7½	.3294	.6706	32½, 20 & 10	.514	.486
15	.15	.85	27½, 7½ & 2½	.3461	.6539	32½, 20 & 20	.568	.432
15 & 2½	.1713	.8287	27½, 7½ & 5	.3629	.6371	35	.35	.65
15 & 5	.1925	.8075	27½, 7½ & 7½	.3797	.6203	35 & 2½	.3663	.6337
15, 5 & 2½	.2127	.7873	27½, 7½ & 10	.3964	.6036	35, 2½ & 2½	.3821	.6179
15, 5 & 5	.2329	.7671	27½ & 10	.3475	.6525	35, 2½ & 5	.3979	.6021
15, 5, 5 & 2½	.2521	.7479	27½, 10 & 2½	.3638	.6362	35, 2½ & 7½	.4138	.5862
15 & 10	.235	.765	27½, 10 & 5	.3801	.6199	35, 2½ & 10	.4296	.5704
15, 10 & 2½	.2541	.7459	27½, 10 & 7½	.3964	.6036	35 & 5	.3825	.6175
15, 10 & 5	.2733	.7267	27½, 10 & 10	.4128	.5872	35, 5 & 2½	.3979	.6021
15, 10, 5 & 2½	.2914	.7086	30	.30	.70	35, 5 & 5	.4134	.5866
15, 10 & 10	.3115	.6885	30 & 2½	.3175	.6825	35, 5 & 7½	.4288	.5712
20	.20	.80	30, 2½ & 2½	.3346	.6654	35, 5 & 10	.4443	.5557
20 & 2½	.22	.78	30, 2½ & 5	.3516	.6484	35 & 7½	.3988	.6012
20 & 5	.24	.76	30, 2½ & 7½	.3687	.6313	35, 7½ & 2½	.4138	.5862
20, 5 & 2½	.259	.741	30, 2½ & 10	.3858	.6142	35, 7½ & 5	.4288	.5712
20, 5 & 5	.278	.722	30 & 5	.335	.665	35, 7½ & 7½	.4438	.5562
20, 5, 5 & 2½	.2961	.7039	30, 5 & 2½	.3516	.6484	35, 7½ & 10	.4589	.5411
20 & 10	.28	.72	30, 5 & 5	.3683	.6317	35 & 10	.415	.585
20, 10 & 2½	.298	.702	30, 5 & 7½	.3849	.6151	35, 10 & 2½	.4296	.5704
20, 10 & 5	.316	.684	30, 5 & 10	.4015	.5985	35, 10 & 5	.4443	.5557
20, 10, 5 & 2½	.3331	.6669	30 & 7½	.3525	.6475	35, 10 & 7½	.4589	.5411
20, 10 & 10	.352	.648	30, 7½ & 2½	.3687	.6313	35, 10 & 10	.4735	.5265
			30, 7½ & 5	.3849	.6151	35 & 20	.48	.52

Ready Discount Computer

Discount Percent	Equivalent	Net	Discount Percent	Equivalent	Net	Discount Percent	Equivalent	Net
35, 20 & 2½....	.493	.507	40, 20 & 7½...	.556	.444	45, 20 & 20.....	.648	.352
35, 20 & 5......	.506	.494	40, 20 & 10....	.568	.432	47½..........	.475	.525
35, 20 & 7½....	.519	.481	40, 20 & 20....	.616	.384	47½ & 2½.....	.4881	.5119
35, 20 & 10....	.532	.468	42½..........	.425	.575	47½, 2½ & 2½.	.5009	.4991
35, 20 & 20....	.584	.416	42½ & 2½.....	.4394	.5606	47½, 2½ & 5...	.5137	.4863
37½..........	.375	.625	42½, 2½ & 2½.	.4534	.5466	47½, 2½ & 7½.	.5265	.4735
37½ & 2½....	.3906	.6094	42½, 2½ & 5...	.4674	.5326	47½, 2½ & 10..	.5393	.4607
37½, 2½ & 2½.	.4059	.5941	42½, 2½ & 7½.	.4814	.5186	47½ & 5......	.5013	.4987
37½, 2½ & 5...	.4211	.5789	42½, 2½ & 10.	.4954	.5046	47½, 5 & 2½..	.5137	.4863
37½, 2½ & 7½.	.4363	.5637	42½ & 5.......	.4538	.5462	47½, 5 & 5....	.5262	.4738
37½, 2½ & 10.	.4516	.5484	42½, 5 & 2½...	.4674	.5326	47½, 5 & 7½...	.5386	.4614
37½ & 5......	.4063	.5937	42½, 5 & 5.....	.4811	.5189	47½, 5 & 10...	.5511	.4489
37½, 5 & 2½...	.4211	.5789	42½, 5 & 7½...	.4947	.5053	47½ & 7½.....	.5144	.4856
37½, 5 & 5....	4359	.5641	42½, 5 & 10....	.5084	.4916	47½, 7½ & 2½.	.5265	.4735
37½, 5 & 7½...	.4508	.5492	42½ & 7½.....	.4681	.5319	47½, 7½ & 5...	.5387	.4613
37½, 5 & 10...	.4656	.5344	42½, 7½ & 2½.	.4814	.5186	47½, 7½ & 7½.	.5508	.4492
37½ & 7½.....	.4219	.5781	42½, 7½ & 5...	.4947	.5053	47½, 7½ & 10..	.5629	.4371
37½, 7½ & 2½.	.4363	.5637	42½, 7½ & 7½.	.508	.492	47½ & 10......	.5275	.4725
37½, 7½ & 5...	.4508	.5492	42½, 7½ & 10..	.5213	.4787	47½, 10 & 2½.	.5393	.4607
37½, 7½ & 7½.	.4652	.5348	42½ & 10......	.4825	.5175	47½, 10 & 5...	.5511	.4489
37½, 7½ & 10..	.4797	.5203	42½, 10 & 2½.	.4954	.5046	47½, 10 & 7½.	.5629	.4371
37½ & 10......	.4375	.5625	42½, 10 & 5...	.5084	.4916	47½, 10 & 10..	.5748	.4252
37½, 10 & 2½.	.4516	.5484	42½, 10 & 7½.	.5213	.4787	47½ & 20......	.58	.42
37½, 10 & 5...	.4656	.5344	42½, 10 & 10..	.5343	.4657	47½, 20 & 2½.	.5905	.4095
37½, 10 & 7½..	.4797	.5203	42½ & 20......	.54	.46	47½, 20 & 5...	.601	.399
37½, 10 & 10..	.4938	.5062	42½, 20 & 2½.	.5515	.4485	47½, 20 & 7½..	.6115	.3885
37½ & 20......	.50	.50	42½, 20 & 5...	.563	.437	47½, 20 & 10..	.622	.378
37½, 20 & 2½..	.5125	.4875	42½, 20 & 7½..	.5745	.4255	47½, 20 & 20...	.664	.336
37½, 20 & 5...	.5250	.4750	42½, 20 & 10..	.586	.414	50............	.50	.50
37½, 20 & 7½..	.5375	.4625	42½, 20 & 20...	.632	.368	50 & 2½.......	.5125	.4875
37½, 20 & 10..	.55	.45	45...........	.45	.55	50, 2½ & 2½...	.5247	.4753
37½, 20 & 20...	.60	.40	45 & 2½......	.4638	.5362	50, 2½ & 5....	.5369	.4631
40..........	.40	.60	45, 2½ & 2½...	.4772	.5228	50, 2½ & 7½...	.5491	.4509
40 & 2½......	.415	.585	45, 2½ & 5.....	.4906	.5094	50, 2½ & 10...	.5613	.4387
40, 2½ & 2½...	.4296	.5704	45, 2½ & 7½...	.504	.496	50 & 5.........	.525	.475
40, 2½ & 5....	.4443	.5557	45, 2½ & 10...	.5174	.4826	50, 5 & 2½....	.5369	.4631
40, 2½ & 7½...	.4589	.5411	45 & 5........	.4775	.5225	50, 5 & 5......	.5488	.4512
40, 2½ & 10...	.4735	.5265	45, 5 & 2½....	.4906	.5094	50, 5 & 7½....	.5606	.4394
40 & 5........	.43	.57	45, 5 & 5......	.5036	.4964	50, 5 & 10.....	.5725	.4275
40, 5 & 2½....	.4443	.5557	45, 5 & 7½....	.5167	.4833	50 & 7½.......	.5375	.4625
40, 5 & 5......	.4585	.5415	45, 5 & 10....	.5298	.4702	50, 7½ & 2½...	.5491	.4509
40, 5 & 7½....	.4728	.5272	45 & 7½......	.4913	.5087	50, 7½ & 5....	.5606	.4394
40, 5 & 10....	.487	.513	45, 7½ & 2½...	.504	.496	50, 7½ & 7½...	.5722	.4278
40 & 7½......	.445	.555	45, 7½ & 5....	.5167	.4833	50, 7½ & 10...	.5838	.4162
40, 7½ & 2½...	.4589	.5411	45, 7½ & 7½...	.5294	.4706	50 & 10.......	.55	.45
40, 7½ & 5....	.4728	.5272	45, 7½ & 10....	.5421	.4579	50, 10 & 2½...	.5613	.4387
40, 7½ & 7½...	.4866	.5134	45 & 10.......	.505	.495	50, 10 & 5....	.5725	.4275
40, 7½ & 10...	.5005	.4995	45, 10 & 2½...	.5174	.4826	50, 10 & 7½...	.5838	.4162
40 & 10......	.46	.54	45, 10 & 5....	.5298	.4702	50, 10 & 10...	.595	.405
40, 10 & 2½...	.4735	.5265	45, 10 & 7½...	.5421	.4579	50 & 20........	.60	.40
40, 10 & 5....	.487	.513	45, 10 & 10....	.5545	.4455	50, 20 & 2½...	.61	.39
40, 10 & 7½...	.5005	.4995	45 & 20........	.56	.44	50, 20 & 5.....	.62	.38
40, 10 & 10...	.514	.486	45, 20 & 2½...	.571	.429	50, 20 & 7½...	.63	.37
40 & 20........	.52	.48	45, 20 & 5.....	.582	.418	50, 20 & 10...	.64	.36
40, 20 & 2½...	.532	.468	45, 20 & 7½....	.593	.407	50, 20 & 20....	.68	.32
40, 20 & 5.....	.544	.456	45, 20 & 10....	.604	.396	52½..........	.525	.475

Courtesy MacRae's Blue Book

misunderstandings and to insure compliance with the terms of the policy. Usually the conditions are these:

1. A percentage of the value of each shipment made is reserved in a distributor's individual account. This percentage varies from 1 to 2½ percent depending on the profitability to the company of each model in the line.

2. Advertising claims submitted by distributors, together with evidence of the advertising, are then credited at the rate of 50 percent of the amount actually spent by the distributor.

3. If the advertising originated initially with a dealer, the procedure is for the distributor to credit *him* with 50 percent of the total amount expended. Thus, the division of the total expense becomes dealer 50 percent, distributor 25 percent, manufacturer 25 percent.

4. Credits from the manufacturer must not exceed the amount in each distributor's fund at any given time.

Freight Allowances

The practice of absorbing the freight into prices was held to be discriminatory (except in unusual cases) by the U.S. Supreme Court in the Big Steel basing-point case. This decision empowered the Federal Trade Commission to step in whenever any seller featured "delivered" prices and to determine if his method of selling was not in restraint of trade. Since that decision, many manufacturers have changed over to an f. o. b.-factory basis of pricing.

However, there are ways of granting certain customers an allowance to cover all or part of the freight which are within the law. Pooling shipments to customers in a certain city to get the benefit of the carload rate is one way.

One eastern concern sends a salesman to work the Middle West. In two or three weeks he accumulates about 200 dealers. He then makes the entire shipment in one car, delivering the car to a public warehouse in Chicago. The warehouse notifies the respective purchasers that their shipments are in and they send their trucks to pick them up. By giving the customers the advantage of this freight saving, it is possible for this company to undersell competitors, without in any way cutting profits, and without cutting prices. This same concern has interested several other manufacturers in using the same warehouse, and they pool their Chicago shipments.

Freight is not as inflexible an item of cost as generally supposed. In many cases eastern concerns compete in San Francisco with California manufacturers on a prepaid freight basis. This they are able to do by warehousing their stocks on the coast.

Chapter 28

PREMIUMS AND TRADE DEALS

A LMOST every week the mailman or a special messenger brings to the average home a sample of a new soap, a dentifrice, or other new product. The box of detergent you buy in the super-market may contain a washcloth or a towel or a glass goblet. The top of a cereal box, together with a dollar bill, will obtain by mail a toy airplane that will really fly. New brands of toothpaste come into the market with a "free" toothbrush attached to the package.

The Premium Advertising Association of America has estimated the wholesale value of premiums used as sales aids at more than $2 billion annually, and theorizes that each dollar spent for such premiums helps move $10 worth of goods or services.

The Federal Trade Commission does not prohibit the use of premiums so long as every such deal is available to every customer on the same terms of sale.

Premiums Can Do Many Jobs

A list of sales objectives most frequently achieved by the use of premiums, as compiled from questionnaires received from manufac-turers and wholesalers in a study by Dr. Arnold Corbin of New York University, included:

Introducing a new product.

Getting new customers for existing products.

Achieving regular or more frequent use.

Building goodwill with the trade.

Offsetting competitors' activity.

Beating a slump in sales (seasonal or otherwise).

Increasing the size of orders.

Stimulating the sales force to achieve preset objectives.

Improving shelf position.

Making it easier to get orders, retailer displays, newspaper features, and other promotional support.

Checking on radio and TV results.

Types of Premium Programs

Premium Merchandising Magazine lists 23 types of premiums and some of the ways in which they are used:

Account Opener: Specialized program for banks attracts new depositors or additional deposits by offering free gifts.

Advertising Specialty: Any item that is imprinted with a company's name and given away as an advertising reminder.

Circulation Builders: Premiums in this category are used as incentives by publishers to promote circulation.

Club Plan: "Club secretary" receives a catalog of merchandise ranging from $10 to $100. She collects group's payment, sends in one order per week; gets her reward entirely in form of premiums from general or special catalog.

Container Premiums: Reusable sets of jelly, peanut butter, or cheese packages —salt packed in salt shakers, mustard in squeeze bottles, shortening in canisters.

Contest and Sweepstakes Prizes: Not the big ones—but 500 second prizes make for big premium sales. Profit is usually in the form of heavy national advertising.

Coupon Plan: A variety of merchandise is offered in return for coupons issued with the purchase of sponsoring products. Can run from inexpensive to expensive merchandise.

Dealer Premiums: The battle for shelf and display, or the introduction of new products sometimes necessitates the use of buying incentives for retailers or wholesalers.

Direct Premiums: Simplest and oldest form of premium merchandising. Consumer gets gift at time of purchase.

Door-to-Door Sales: Direct sellers use premiums in variety of ways—from door openers to sales closers. Use modified versions of almost all premium techniques.

Home-Service Routes: Tea and coffee operators offer "advance premium" merchandise given before purchase on condition that consumer continues to buy and "trades out" the premiums.

Package Attachments: Ball-point pen with toothpaste, sponge with soap, pearls with detergent, made part of the package but not in the product.

Package Enclosures: Packed inside the carton with the product—such as china with soap powder, aluminum in oatmeal, kids' items in cereal.

Party Plan: A premium is offered to hostess whose home is used for the party. Sales incentives for demonstrators and managers keep a strong stimulus behind their sales forces.

Sales Incentive: Could be operated by means of an elaborate catalog or consist of individually purchased low- to high-ticket merchandise. This use is booming —prizes can be expensive gifts—almost any category of item.

Self-Liquidator: Normally slanted to women, who send in proof of purchase and cash which completely covers cost of premium, package, mailing, handling— everything but advertising.

Self-Liquidating Dealer Premium: Manufacturer charges full retail price for few extra packages of product. Includes premium. Dealer pays for premium— sells product—makes back payment and gets item free.

Self-Liquidating Traffic Builders: A bargain gift to bring people into a store. Perhaps a $2.50 thermometer for only $1 if a potential customer comes in.

Tape-Redemption Plans: Cash-register tapes saved by consumer and traded, usually with cash, which covers cost of merchandise, for assortment of gifts.

Trading Cards: When the customer has card punched indicating purchases of a certain amount, either a free gift is her reward—or she is entitled to buy an item at about half the retail value.

Trading Stamps: Almost three quarters of a century has seen this plan increase in popularity. Group of retailers combine, buy stamps and merchandise from stamp house. Customers save booksful, redeem either by mail or in centers. Carloads of items promoted in colorful catalogs. One stamp is issued with every 10 cents of purchase, and it takes 1200 to 1500 stamps to fill a book. The retailer spends 2 to 2½ percent of sales for the stamp plan.

Traffic Builders, Free: Items used to get people into a store to look and perhaps to buy. An apron to each woman who looks at a stove, a fistful of marbles to each kid who brings his dad into a service station. Needles at a supermarket opening.

Use the User: Ask a satisfied customer to recommend the names of some friends who might also buy. She gets a premium when the sale is consummated. Cleaners, vacuum sales, refrigerators, diaper service all thrive on this use.

Selecting the Premium

The Whirlpool Corporation has a continuing program of making premium items available to its distributors and dealers for use in supporting their selling efforts. This long-established major-appliance manufacturer generally does not use a single nationally advertised premium, concentrating instead upon local-distributor options in selecting programs.

"Our use of premiums is generally limited to either traffic-builders or sales closers," says Herbert C. Klapp, national sales-promotion manager.

The decision to use a particular item for a particular program is made by the sales promotion executive for the division that will be using it. Working in close liaison with their division colleagues in marketing functions, these men develop a promotional plan to sell their products, then look for the proper items to implement the plan.

There are four criteria for Whirlpool premium acceptability:

1. It must be American-made.

2. It must have adequate intrinsic quality.

3. The price must fall within the budget limitation for the intended program use.

4. It must be an item readily recognizable by the customer, so that no effort is wasted in explaining or promoting the item.

Items suitable for traffic-building by appliance dealers, as opposed to sales closers, constitute a major part of premium activity at Whirlpool. Each plan is carefully worked out and evaluated, and results have been both good and bad—"a couple of bombs and a couple of losers," Klapp recalled.

EXAMPLES OF TIE-IN PREMIUMS

COMPANY	OFFER	REQUIREMENTS
Armstrong	Hildy doll	$1 plus package number of Epic floor wax
Kimberly-Clark Corp.	Pearl pendant	50 cents plus premium seals from Kleenex and Delsey products
Pro-phy-lac-tic Brush Co.	Canister set	$2 plus label from toothbrush
R. J. Reynolds Tobacco Co.	Butane lighter	$1.50 and two empty packs
American Tourister	Da Vinci print	$1.00
Uncle Ben's Inc.	Recipe box with recipes	$1.50 plus boxtop
Musselman's	Lenoxware	$1.25 to $1.75 plus two labels for each set
Kimberly-Clark and Bristol-Myers Co.	Tissue dispenser	$1 plus premium seal from Kleenex and Bufferin packages
American Dairy Assn.	Paper dresses	$1 plus name panel from rolls or butter
Campbell's Soup	Cookbook	50 cents plus three labels

A 10-cent pocket comb and brush set in a polyethylene container was publicized nationally for a two-week period, and given away by dealers at their own option. The promotion lasted 60 days and went over far better than had been anticipated, with about 300,000 sets given out in the period. A Kodak Hawkeye Model R4 camera was recently used as a sales closer for the Whirlpool freezer line.

The Westinghouse Campaign

One very successful premium campaign was employed by the Westinghouse Corporation's appliance and service division in Laurel, Maryland. When sales of black-and-white television sets fell off, the company decided that a strong promotion was needed, based on the use of a good premium. After considering a dozen premium possibilities, an AGFA Isoflash camera kit was selected. The campaign was organized for the months of September through November and the plan was simply that each customer who bought a black-and-white Westinghouse television set would receive the camera outfit as a premium.

The $7 cost of the premium was divided between Westinghouse ($4) and the dealer ($3) provided the dealer bought one television set. "When all the plans were completed," said district sales manager William Lotz, "the campaign was announced through newspaper ads, radio programs, and dealers' show windows." Interest grew and orders poured in for television sets and cameras. A number of dealers who had not been handling Westinghouse products took on the line as a result of the campaign.

"The whole operation," said Mr. Lotz, "was a tremendous success. It brought in new customers and new dealers, and it increased television set sales by more than 10 percent."

Most other concerns which use premiums report that useful articles are the best sales stimulators. It has been found that such articles as razor blades, dishes, silver, and glassware are the most popular. Companies which give salesmen prizes for unusual achievement state that appliances that can be used in the home, gifts that appeal to a woman, smoker's articles, luggage, and similar items are what most appeal to the average man. This is true in the case of dealers also. While articles that will assist him in increasing business appeal to the progressive merchant, he responds most readily when the premium is one that he can use personally.

Many corporations operate their premium programs through one sales manager who reports to the vice-president for sales. Other companies assign these projects to the sales-promotion manager, who works closely with the sales manager or sales vice-president. Still others employ experienced outside premium experts.

Some companies engage manufacturers' agents who specialize in premium sales. Outside consultants are generally paid a fee plus a bonus for sales over a quota, while agents are usually paid standard trade commissions.

Manufacturers of incentive merchandise band together annually in a number of shows and exhibits. These include both general trade shows, such as the National Housewares Manufacturers Exhibit, and special premium shows like the National Premium Buyers Exposition. The interested executive will find up-to-date information in publications like *Premium Practice* and *Sales Management*.

Other Examples of Premium Campaigns

The inner seals from instant-coffee jars played a key role in two promotions conducted by General Foods' Maxwell House division.

In Ohio, where GF wages a battle with heavy advertising support for its Maxim freeze-dried coffee, the company offered a cash refund. Advertised in newspapers by supermarkets such as Big Bear stores in Columbus, the offer involved purchases up to $30, excluding beer, wine, and tobacco.

The refund required mailing a certificate, obtained from a Maxwell House store display, one cash-register tape, and the inner seal from a 6-ounce or larger jar of Maxwell House instant coffee, plus the code number from a can of Maxwell House vacuum-pack coffee.

Another GF coffee promotion offered toys and play equipment in exchange for instant Maxwell House inner seals. For three inner seals each, the customer earned a ball, a magnetic train, and a whale puppet, all for children.

Thirteen larger items, ranging from a wooden wheelbarrow for 260 instant inner seals to a helical slide for 2,825 inner seals, were also offered. Because of the large number of seals required for the large equipment, Maxwell House made direct contact with local dealer organizations to tell them of the promotion. Retail stores were provided with brochures containing order blanks and other point of sale materials.

A promotion in which dealers offered a 10-piece automatic-camera kit along with a rollabout cart as free premiums with the purchase of a portable television set was used by Motorola Consumer Products, Inc. The instant-loading-camera kit had a retail value of $17.95 and included a deluxe case, camera, film cartridge, two batteries, and four flashbulbs. The camera promotion was supported by local newspaper advertising in all parts of the country, and a five-piece banner set for store use was made available through distributors.

The Frigidaire Division of General Motors and Pepsi-Cola Co., combined forces for a wholesale-retail promotional campaign for appliance dealers and bottlers across the nation. Dealers handling Frigidaire appliances were able to offer retail customers seven cases of Pepsi-Cola with each major appliance purchase.

Store Demonstrations

In the marketing of foods and household specialties such as vacuum cleaners and pressure cookers, much importance is attached to store demonstrations.

Manufacturers have broken through entrenched competition by following this practice. In some instances they are willing to pay the dealers, especially department stores, liberally for the use of space. They also stand all expenses of demonstrators, materials, and local advertising. But in most lines the manufacturer makes the dealer share the expense, usually on a fifty-fifty basis, and here again care must be used to see that such store demonstrations are done in a way that no discrimination is shown. The same service must be made available to all customers buying an equal volume of goods.

In a complaint against a group of manufacturers of toilet preparations, the Federal Trade Commission made some significant statements as to the use of factory-paid demonstrators. It alleged that these methods constitute unfair competition—

In that said acts and practices have a tendency to, and do, place a restraint not only upon competition between respondents and other manufacturers, but also upon competition between favored retail customers of respondents and those retail customers of respondents and of other manufacturers who do not receive the benefits of said described unfair methods of competition. The said methods cast upon competitors of the respondents the burden of the loss of business unless they engage in similar acts and practices.

There are among respondents' competitors many manufacturers and distributors of cosmetic products who do not employ demonstrators. As a result of the practices of respondents there has been, and does exist, a tendency to suppress and stifle competition in the sale of cosmetic products in interstate commerce and in the retail sale of said products, and trade has been unfairly diverted to the respondents from their said competitors as well as from those retail customers of respondents and of other manufacturers who do not receive the benefits of such practices to such of respondents' customers who do receive the benefit of said practices, and the ability of said manufacturers to compete successfully with respondents, and of said retail customers to compete with said favored customers, . . . is lessened and injured by the methods of respondents hereinabove set forth.

Use of Premiums to Build Mailing Lists

A concern which used a key container as a premium to a large dealers' list had an interesting experience. First of all the company wrote a letter to half the list advising the dealers that if they would send the names and addresses of 10 jobbers' salesmen they would receive the key case free. Results from this mailing were disappointing, although a number of names were obtained.

The offer was then reversed. Each dealer was sent a key container with a letter from the manufacturers asking the dealer to accept the key case with his compliments. The letter also mentioned that the manufacturer would like to send one of these containers to every jobber's salesman who called on that dealer, if he (the dealer) would send him their names.

The response to this appeal was considerably better. It accomplished the strategic effect of putting the dealer under obligation to reply. The manufacturer then approached the jobbers' salesmen whose names were sent in by the dealers, in the same way. He told them he wanted to send every member of their sales force a key container just like the ones he was sending them, if the salesmen would send him the names of as many of their fellow salesmen as they knew.

In this way, at an amazingly small outlay, the manufacturer built up a most complete list of jobbers' salesmen in a field where it is supposed to be impossible to get such a list.

Classes of Premium Users

Premium users are generally classified into two groups: (1) continual users and (2) special users.

Continual users, as the name implies, purchase standard merchandise of all types for continuing use. Most of these groups publish catalogs and include club plan, coupon plan, home service, route operators, and trading-stamp companies.

In the second group will be found companies which purchase occasional items for special promotion, tie-in sales, and creative sales programs. Since such companies cannot anticipate the exact number of units that will be disposed of, they generally deal with manufacturers who are willing to give them a sliding scale of prices on various quantities.

Popularity of Discount Coupons

Another form of promotion which has become very popular is the use of discount coupons, probably because they are easier to handle and consumers know exactly how much they are worth.

The coupons are used to promote or introduce a vast array of items ranging from soap powder and mouthwash to cereals and salad dressing. Consumers redeem them at grocery stores for credit of perhaps 5, 10 or 15 cents. The store owner relays the coupon to the manufacturer, who then reimburses the retailer for the amount of the coupon plus 2 cents to cover handling costs.

According to Grocery Manufacturers of America, about $100 million a year is redeemed through coupons. Although most of the larger companies in the grocery field issue coupons, there is a difference of opinion among marketing men as to their effectiveness. Coupons do move products, some experts say, but they undermine brand loyalty by appealing solely to the pocketbook. Quite often the coupons are simply turned in for cash and the merchandise is not sold at all.

Supporters of coupons declare that they do more for a good product and do it faster, better, and at less cost than any other medium.

To begin a coupon program, a company decides first on the products to be involved, the size of the discount, and the territory to be covered. Salesmen are then notified of the proposed move. They, in turn, seek cooperation at the retail level. Such cooperation might include large orders during the coupons' effective period and prime display position in stores. Much of this is now arranged by food brokers.

Ten Billion Coupons in Use

"Currently about 800 companies are actively involved in coupon promotions. We estimate that they distribute about 10 billion coupons. Of these, approximately one billion will be redeemed, at a savings of $100,000,000 for U.S. families." These were some of the statistics provided by William R. Bullion, national sales manager, Nielsen Clearing House, A. C. Nielsen Co., in an address to the Merchandising Executives Club of Chicago.

Among the manufacturers who make up the top 10 couponers in the grocery field, eight are also among the top 10 advertisers, according to Mr. Bullion. The 10 top couponers spent $501,400,000 on advertising, combined with 460,800,000 redeemed coupons, to build $11.9 billion in sales in one year.

In regard to the design of coupons, Mr. Bullion suggested using dollar-size or the smaller IBM-punch-card coupons, since many odd sizes and shapes create handling difficulties for retailers. He said the latest technique involves magnetic-encoded coupons which can be read by an electronic reader at the rate of 1,200 per minute.

The Pepsi-Cola Coupon Campaign

Some 30 million magazine coupons, each worth 10 cents off on cartons of Pepsi-Cola or Diet Pepsi supported the Pepsi-Cola Company's "$2,000,000 Worldwide Family Shopping Spree." The coupon appeared as part of a four-color full-page advertisement in leading national magazines.

In addition, free entry blanks in a shopping spree contest were placed in the cartons and reproduced in local newspapers. The national prize winner and his family were given two 30-minute shopping sprees, the first in their home town, the second in any foreign capital served by TWA. The winning family was turned loose in the home town food store of their choice for 30 minutes and given all the groceries they could get into a shopping cart, free of charge. The Pepsi-Cola Company paid the full retail cost of all the food. Later the winners boarded a plane for a two-week stay abroad. Added to all this was $5,000 in expense money.

In addition to the grand prize, there were 520 other national prizes, including ten 1966 Oldsmobile Vista-Cruiser station wagons, each with a supply of equipment and services; ten 15-minute family shopping sprees; and 500 gift certificates ranging in value from $100 to $1,000. About 150,000 additional prizes were awarded by local Pepsi-Cola bottlers.

The Cents-Off Dilemma

In recent years, cents-off promotions were probably more common for coffee than for any other major product. Before they became universal, the cents-off deals undoubtedly built sales of specific brands.

But old-time marketing men had an adage to the effect that you can't increase consumption by giving things away. It proved true in this case. Coffee consumption dropped at the very time cents-off promotions were rampant.

Then the Federal Trade Commission stepped in. It suggested that this is a form of fictitious pricing unless it actually represents a discount from a "regular" price. Paying particular attention to the coffee industry, the Commission asked 22 leading companies to report all forms of "cents off" deals, newspaper coupons, promotional mailings, or any other device affecting regular selling prices.

TYPICAL COUPON AND "CENTS OFF" OFFERS

COMPANY	PRODUCT	INCENTIVE
Johnson and Johnson	Baby powder	Coupon, 6c off
Nestle Company	Nescafe	Coupon, 10c off
Lipton Tea Company	Lipton tea	Coupon, 8c off
Kraft Foods	Sandwich fillings	Coupon, 15c off
W. H. Feronce Co.	Shampoo	Coupon, 10c off
Procter & Gamble	Dash	Coupon, 10c off
Armour & Company	Turkey roast	Coupon, $1 off
Pfeiffer	Salad dressings	Coupon, 25c off
Lever Brothers	Margarine	Coupon, 7c off
Seabrook Farms Co.	Frozen vegetables	Coupon, 7c off
Pillsbury Company	Turnover pastries	Coupon, 5c off
Quaker Oats	Aunt Jemima syrup	Coupon, 7c off
John Morrell & Co.	Wieners	Coupon, 5c off
National Biscuit Co.	Cream of Wheat	Coupon, 7c off
Pacquin	Cold cream	Coupon, 8c off

Coupons and Trading Stamps

Gift-coupon companies have teamed up with trading stamps to broaden the appeal of both merchandising incentives. Rexall's Bonus Gift coupons may be exchanged for any of 60 different trading stamps. Gift Star coupons are exchangeable for the major stamp lines.

The idea obtained most of its support from cigarette companies. American Tobacco offered Bonus Gift coupons with its new Colony brand, and Lorillard announced the availability of Gift Stars with Old Golds, Spring, and York. In one test market, the coupon plan raised sales better than 100 percent, Lorillard said.

Family Fare magazine was market testing in Mercer County, N. J. It contained coupons on 48 products from soap to cigars; was distributed free to housewives who mailed in the coupons with proof of purchase and received a gift certificate negotiable at supermarkets or department stores.

Gift Book Attracts Customers

The largest array of brand-name consumer products and import items were displayed in colorful settings in Gold Bond Stamp Company's gift book. The introduction of the catalog was treated as a major promotional event at many food stores, according to Curtis L. Carlson, Gold Bond president.

"Never before," he said, "has there been such a terrific schedule of full-page introductory newspaper ads, heavy use of radio and television spots, or such widespread and effective utilization of our in-store display materials."

He noted a growing trend among Gold Bond food accounts toward using the gift book introduction as the cornerstone of their efforts to attract and hold customers.

"Once a housewife has selected the gifts she wants for her family from a catalog," he said, "she becomes a regular customer of the food store offering the stamps she needs. Further cementing her loyalty, of course, are coupon specials and other promotions during the year providing bonus stamps and the opportunity to reach her gift goals more rapidly."

How Much Do Trading Stamps Cost?

Although trading stamps were of secondary interest in the report of the National Commission on Food Marketing, it was important to The Sperry and Hutchinson Company (S&H Green Stamps) and the retailing industry.

"In just a few paragraphs of one chapter in that study, the commission staff reached the erroneous conclusion that a food store's volume would have to increase about 40 percent to cover the cost of trading stamps, officials of S&H declared.

Too many variables are involved to put a precise figure on the specific volume needed and it also varies from business to business. In an intensive study of this question, *Effect of Increased Sales on Supermarket Store Operating Profit*, Colorado State University Professor Harvey L. Vredenburg determined a break-even point of about 12 percent in additional sales. In the case of department stores, Professor Vredenburg found that the percentage increase needed could be as low as 6 percent; for drug stores, 8 percent; and hardware stores, 9 percent.

"Trading stamps are not a panacea for poor merchandising practices and a retailer must be prepared to make the most of his increased volume. But history has proven that, everything else being equal, the retailer who is licensed to use the S&H service and who uses it properly is going to enjoy increased volume and—most important—increased profits without increased prices, the Sperry and Hutchinson officials concluded.

PART 6

MODERN
SALES
POLICIES

Chapter 29

SELECTIVE SELLING

THE concept of "selective selling" is one which every sales manager must give attention to at one time or another. What is meant by selective selling? Simply that one customer is *not* just as good as another. Tiffany's, while willing to sell to anyone who can pay the price, creates an affluent clientele by the quality and price level of its luxurious merchandise, by the good taste of the store surroundings and the way in which the goods are displayed, and even the manner of the clerks. On the other hand, because those with affluent tastes are not always affluent with money, Tiffany's has developed good judgment in rating customers on their ability to pay.

The Jupiter discount stores practice selective selling when they attract customers looking for price rather than quality into their stores by giving them a "low price" atmosphere—plain tables piled high with inexpensive wares, sold on a strictly cash and self-service basis. Their goal is high volume on a low profit margin, with quick turnover of cash.

Whether your product is sold to the ultimate consumer, as in house-to-house selling, or to distributors or wholesalers for resale, you will need a policy to guide you in the selection of your customers. This calls for consideration of the following points:

1. *The degree of selectivity in choosing customers.*

2. *The degree of exclusive arrangements with chosen customers.*

3. *The degree to which credit is to be offered.*

4. *The extent of consignment selling, if any.*

5. *The offering of national or private brands, or possibly both.*

6. *Cancellation of orders and acceptance of returned goods.*

7. *The degree to which service and engineering advice should be extended.*

Selective selling can be extremely important in many industries. When any product is sold through distributors and dealers on a nationwide basis, adequate "dealer coverage" determines the degree of success in sales to a large extent. However, it is commonplace in the appliance industry to say that 25 percent of the dealers do 75 percent of the business. In addition to having enough dealers in order to make it convenient for customers to buy, it's equally important to have the right kind of dealers. This is why in the large cities well-known department stores and chain stores are eagerly sought after by manufacturers.

Naturally the choice will be affected by the nature of the industry and the type of product involved. The next step is to determine whether to sell through distributors or directly to dealers. Still, that does not cover the entire situation. Licensing independent organizations (franchising) and selling to national accounts afford additional channels of distribution.

In recent years, many companies have realized the necessity of making the sales force conscious of its role in profit making.

Says Alfred C. Viebranz, senior vice-president, marketing, Sylvania Electric Products Co., "Traditionally, sales managers have been concerned only with sales volume and market share. However, the type of customers sought, the amount of credit extended, and the inventory required to service customers all have a profound effect on return on investment." To make clear the connection between sales decisions and profits, Sylvania developed a three-phase course for all its managers which culminated in a computerized game that compressed a year's business activity into three days. Those participating get the feel of running a complex organization in a realistic setting.

As Viebranz explained at a recent marketing-strategy conference of the Sales Executives Club of New York, the program included a week-long course on management aimed at mastering the principles of hiring, motivating, and appraising personnel.

Factors to Consider

Some of the factors to consider when selecting prospects or customers are:

1. *Credit status.*

2. *Stature in the market.*

3. *Purchase requirements (potentiality).*

4. *Growth possibilities.*

5. *Competitive status in relation to other outlets.*

6. *Location for customer convenience in the shopping area.*

7. *Location for efficient routing of company salesmen.*

8. *Type of goods offered—staple or specialty.*

9. *Relationship with competing manufacturers.*

Obviously, it is of little value to spend time selling a customer who does not pay his bills, or to expect large orders if he is not properly financed. Policies and procedures for extending and handling credit, also the role that salesmen can play in assisting in the proper function of credits in marketing, are discussed elsewhere in this Handbook.

The most respected retail outlet or industrial customer in the market environment should be given first consideration. The prestige of this customer will greatly assist in obtaining other customers. However, sometimes unfavorable considerations may be found in other factors which will mitigate against too close an alliance with the prestige customer.

When going out after orders, it is usually preferable to fish in the larger pools rather than in the smaller ones. A call resulting in a $1,000 order frequently costs no more to make than one producing a $10 order. Furthermore, if a salesman is averaging $10 a call from a customer, and that amount represents the customer's maximum buying power, there is probably little value in the salesman stepping up his sales effort with that customer; whereas, if the customer has a $1,000 potential, the salesman can well invest more selling time with him.

Conversely, even though a customer currently has only $10 per order buying power, he might be young, imaginative, energetic, and on the upgrade. Selling time invested with him should bear attractive returns and he should be selected for the long pull.

Location Important

Sometimes local competitive rivalry makes it almost impossible for a salesman to sell another outlet in the same locality. If a choice has to be made, it is better to select the firm that will give the best representation.

When selling a consumer product, it is well to choose an outlet that is convenient for the ultimate consumers to visit. Frequently you may find it necessary to have many outlets, particularly if your product is an impulse item. If style goods or an appliance, it is preferable to choose outlets that are located near other outlets handling similar items. Better to choose a growing outlet with current low sales in a well-patronized shopping center than a larger one off the beaten path; the latter may often be on the way down. Distributors or industrial goods outlets may not need to be so well located, but even with these, convenient location in a marketing area is preferable.

When routing salesmen, it is important that crisscrossing, backtracking and long dead-end runs be eliminated as much as possible. As is discussed in detail later, the face-to-face sales time of salesmen is absolute and not expandable. Time must be conserved and used judiciously. Customers should be carefully selected, with return per call given careful consideration.

It is possible that in every respect a prospective customer might be attractive, but through the years he has become so closely tied to a competing manufacture that to disrupt the relationship would be too difficult. Or the owner of the store might have a son working for a competitor and nepotism might be too strong to combat.

By-Products of Sales and Cost Analysis

W. G. Archer, owner of the Fulton Supply Company, Atlanta, Georgia, states that local suppliers should have in their records a complete "picture" of each account on their books.

At his own firm, cost analysis of every account has resulted in more effective management control, greater operating efficiency and "a better job done for each customer."

Among the by-products of sales analysis, he said, the distributor would have practical knowledge of what products his customers bought from him, in what quantities, the gross profit realized, and the net profit for each account.

Armed with these figures, Fulton Supply's own salesmen are able to evaluate products by customers and potential by customer, and can plan their time and efforts for the greatest return. They also are able to determine quickly where improvements can be made, and when less time and fewer special services should be given.

How Badger Meter Makes Sales Audits

Badger Meter Manufacturing Company, manufacturer of water meters, conducts customer audits for all its sales territories. The form it uses is shown nearby. Note the instructions at the bottom of the form, whereby the salesman and his district manager are requested to review all municipalities in the territory, both customers and prospects; those of a worthwhile nature are listed on the form. All persons who might be involved in preparing specifications, giving authority to purchase, issuing orders, and even repairing or maintaining meters are shown. It is essential that no important person be overlooked and that the salesman reserve all necessary time for calling on him.

BADGER METER MFG. COMPANY
CUSTOMER-PROSPECT AUDIT

Salesman_____ Territory_____ Date_____ Sheet ___ of __

City	Persons To See	Position	Meters	Yearly Sales		Calls Per Yr.
				Current	Goal	

INSTRUCTIONS: All municipalities, both customers and prospects, of a worthwhile nature are to be listed. All persons with their titles to be seen regular are to be shown; this includes engineers, purchasing agents, elected personnel (mayors, etc.) repair and maintenance people. Insert the estimated number of meters, dollar sales (drop cents) for the current year, the sales goal for the coming year and the expected number of calls to be made on each individual. It is not anticipated that the same number of calls will be made during the year on all persons; the purchasing agent and maintenance department may be seen on each visit, the engineers and elected personnel only once a year. All cities will not be visited on each trip, some may be seen on alternate trips. This form is to be filled in jointly by the salesmen and their district managers.

Then in the fourth column, the estimated number of units that might be purchased from all sources during the ensuing 12 months is inserted. These estimates may not be very accurate the first time they are made, but as time passes they can be revised. In any case, a good, conscientious, objectively considered estimate is much better than no estimate at all. Also, while some will be too low and others too high, they should average out quite accurately. Such estimates of potentiality are exceedingly important in planning sales strategy.

In the next two columns are inserted figures on past sales, which act as bench marks of what might be done against potentials, and what can be reasonably expected as goals for future effort. The goals should not be set so low as to offer no challenge nor so high as not to be attainable. They should be reasonable; the salesman and his district manager should both be satisfied that they are fair.

The last column is for entering the anticipated number of calls that should be made during the year on all individuals listed. It is not expected that the same number of calls will need be made on all individuals listed for a company; the purchasing agent probably should be seen on each call, the maintenance man or engineer might be seen every other call, and the head of the firm only once a year to maintain rapport. Also, all companies need not be seen with the same frequency; a large one demanding a lot of attention may need to be called on once a week, or even daily, while a smaller one may need to be seen only once a month or even only once every three months.

The scheduled number of calls should merely be considered an optimum objective. If conditions change, as may occur when a customer gets ready to place a large order, calls should be stepped up as required; when the period of intense activity ends, the salesman should drop back to his original schedule.

Chapter 30

EXCLUSIVE DISTRIBUTION OUTLETS

WHILE it is undeniably true that many desirable benefits of wide distribution for a "convenience" product are appreciated, it has been found that, in order to get the larger benefits of this method, a product must be nationally advertised.

A dealer won't spend money to promote the sale of a product if he is not sure of getting the reorders. On the other hand, if he can be shown that any money of his own that he spends in building up a demand for a certain product means increased business, and that such business will not go to his competitor, he will get behind the product and push it. The exclusive-agency arrangement is one which protects the dealer and thus encourages him to push your product energetically.

The outstanding advantages of the exclusive, or selected, agency are:

1. Its superiority as a means of increasing the reputation of the goods, and the prestige of the manufacturer. Seldom or never is this system of much value to the manufacturer of goods that are unidentified as to origin by means of trademarks or trade names. To the manufacturer of trademarked goods, however, it is worth the possible sacrifice of a few sales to ensure the standing of his goods in the public mind through adequate presentation of their merits.

2. Dealers who are protected in the enjoyment of exclusive privileges are more apt to make an effort to push a particular line and give it special prominence in display. Special advertising cooperation can be given to exclusive dealers as needed without incurring the ill will of their competitors. It is also much easier to secure advertising cooperation on the part of the dealers. The manufac-

turer can also exercise a direct influence to improve the dealer's selling efforts.

3. Credit risks are obviously reduced when salesmen are calling upon a limited number of dealers who have been selected in advance or already passed upon by the house. Credit is one of the main considerations in appointing a dealer, and closer supervision of his affairs by the company helps to keep his credit good.

4. Salesmen can cover more territory more efficiently when calling on exclusive agencies.

5. When dealers are protected, there is less likelihood of their engaging in unfair price-cutting because they are not subjected to cut-price competition on the same product. Comparatively few dealers are price-cutters from deliberate policy, but are forced to cut to meet competition. It is not difficult to eliminate the deliberate cutters from consideration as agents, which generally takes care of the problem. It goes without saying, of course, that the fear of losing an exclusive agency will often deter a dealer who might otherwise cut prices.

In that connection it will be necessary to determine what your relationship with customers, especially dealers and distributors, will be. Is it best to sell through exclusive agencies, one in each community, or through the dual-agency plan whereby several outlets in each community work together under factory supervision? How should those exclusive dealerships be set up? Should the stock be sold outright or placed with the dealer on a consignment basis? How can resale prices be protected? What provision should there be in the agreement to assure wholehearted sales support for the line? What about advertising and sales-promotion expense? What part, if any, should the dealer assume? These and other questions are vital to the success of any plan for selling to selected accounts.

In this chapter we are concerned only with independents. We are not taking into consideration such elements as company-owned stores (Singer Sewing Machine Company) or chain stores.

The Dual-Agency Plan

A product that is featured by only one or perhaps two stores in a trading center does not assume great importance in the minds of the consumers. But when it is featured on all sides, it assumes a prominence that is difficult to secure otherwise. Advertising alone will accomplish wonders sometimes, but it cannot often give to goods the prestige that is secured by adequate distribution.

This is why most manufacturers of convenience goods who rely upon selected outlets have largely abandoned the exclusive agent for what are generally referred to as dual agencies. Instead of the single agent, who enjoys the complete suppression of local competition, these manufacturers employ two or three or more agencies. These are strategically located to serve the public to the best possible advantage, and at the same time to supplement the efforts of one another in giving the product prominence. This is the policy followed by many of the most successful stores, which will generally all do better than any one of them could do alone. The benefits of such a policy to the manufacturer are fairly obvious. It increases his sales materially as well as the prestige of the goods in the community. It also increases the effectiveness of his advertising, both that which is run over the names of the dealers and that in national mediums.

Sometimes concerns hesitate to employ selected distributors through fear that, in case it is later necessary to make changes, they will offend their most valuable customers and cause them to "throw out the line." Experience seems to show, however, that there is very little substance to that fear. At least there is little danger if the original agreement is drawn properly and the situation handled with tact and restraint. In most cases, the dealer who is large enough to warrant his selection as an exclusive agent is intelligent enough to grasp a sound argument. Very few concerns report any serious difficulty in this connection. In those cases where trouble is experienced it is likely to be due to the fact that rash promises were made in the first place, or the situation was handled in too arbitrary a manner. An occasional dealer may throw out a profitable line in order to spite the manufacturer, or out of belief that the manufacturer cannot get along without it. In the majority of cases, however, they are likely to come back later on when it is clearly demonstrated that they are losing money by the action.

Dangers in Exclusive Agreements

Section 3 of the Clayton Antitrust Act reads in part as follows:

That it shall be unlawful for any person engaged in commerce, in the course of such commerce, to lease or make a sale or contract for sale of goods, wares, merchandise, machinery, supplies, or other commodities, whether patented or unpatented, for use, consumption, or resale within the United States . . . or fix a price charged therefor, or discount from, or rebate upon, such price, on the condition, agreement, or understanding that the lessee or purchaser thereof shall not use or deal in the goods, wares, merchandise, machinery, supplies, or other commodity of a competitor or competitors of the lessor or seller, where the effect of such lease, sale, or contract for sale or such condition, agreement, or understanding may be to substantially lessen competition or tend to create a monopoly in any line of commerce.

It is clear that this covers only those forms of exclusive agency agreements whereby, in return for exclusive territory, the agency or dealer agrees not to handle competing products. It does not apply to the more common practice of leaving the dealer free to handle competing products if he chooses, but making the franchise of sufficient value to induce him to put his main effort into pushing the goods. Furthermore, the addition of the concluding clause makes it unnecessary for the manufacturer of trademarked goods, under ordinary circumstances, to worry about the legality of his exclusive-agency arrangements.

To the great majority of businessmen, the likelihood of any difficulty arising from the above conditions may seem to be very remote. It is only fair to emphasize once more, however, that the enforcement of this section of the Clayton Act is entrusted to the Federal Trade Commission, and a complaint from any individual may inspire an investigation by that body. It is advisable to obtain competent legal counsel before putting into effect specific contracts for exclusive representation.

Formal Contracts Needed

Formal contracts, covering the operation of exclusive agents in detail, are practically necessary under the following conditions:

1. When it is the agent's duty to establish contract relations with his customers by which the company's rights are affected. This applies broadly to such commodities as office and store appliances, machinery, musical instruments, household appliances sold on partial payments, building equipment sold to contractors, heating and lighting equipment, etc. In such cases the agent is acting in part as the direct representative of the company, and his acts must be definitely controlled and his authority definitely limited.

2. When the agent is entrusted with the job of hiring salesmen, who act as representatives of the company, but are not directly under the company's control. The same considerations apply here.

3. When the agent acts as licensee under patents. This does not apply to all commodities that are covered by patent, but only where the patent license is made the basis of representation. In such cases it is necessary to have a definite expression of the company's intention, as well as to control the acts of the agent.

There are also numerous cases where agents render special service in installing equipment, or keep it in working order, either at the company's expense or their own. Under such conditions, when the goodwill of the company largely depends upon the proper installation or operation of the product, many concerns feel that formal contracts are essential. It is necessary, in other words, to specify definitely and in detail, just what the duties of the agent are, and what free service the customer should have.

Aside from the foregoing, however, there seems to be a marked tendency to avoid tying the hands of either party with formal contracts, and to rely upon a general understanding as to terms and conditions. This leaves the company free to make changes promptly when changing local conditions warrant.

Chapter 31

COORDINATING CREDITS AND SALES

SOME executives believe the sales department has no concern with credits or collections. Its job is to get the order. When the order is on the books, it is the job of the credit department to get the money. Back of this thinking is the fear that salesmen, being temperamental, cannot do their best work if they are burdened with credit responsibility in any form. The people who hold this view also feel that the qualities which make a good salesman usually do not make a good credit man.

There may be cases where this is good reasoning. By and large, however, close cooperation between credit and sales pays off. Salesmen waste much time calling on customers who they *think* are good credit risks, only to have the order turned down by the credit department when checked against credit reference books and other data available to the credit manager. When the credit manager works closely with the sales manager, it is possible to rate in advance the prospective customers upon whom the salesman will call. This is known as selective selling. It is widely used today. Before a salesman starts out on a trip the credit department provides him with the credit status of each dealer in his territory. From these data the salesman determines how much time to give different accounts.

Even though salesmen may not be responsible for collections, sales managers know that a salesman can sell more to a customer who is paid up than he can to a customer who is behind in his payments. Thus it is said: "Closed collections make for more sales." So it is the practice to furnish salesmen, calling on established trade, periodical information useful to them in contacting accounts.

Today's marketing manager, with a broad range of responsibility keyed to achieving return on investment, should have greater jurisdiction over credit policies, believes Dr. Michael Schiff, chairman of the accounting and taxation departments of New York University's graduate school of business.

CREDIT LIMIT APPROVAL

LOCATION OF ACTIVITY		ACCOUNT TYPE	

ACCOUNT NAME	ADDRESS	CITY AND STATE

D & B RATING	YEAR STARTED	☐ CORPORATION ☐ PARTNERSHIP ☐ PROPRIETORSHIP	GUARANTEE OR SURETY, IF ANY

SOLD SINCE	PAYMENT RECORD	ESTIMATE OF PURCHASES — IF NEW ACCOUNT OR IF INCREASE IS EXPECTED

CREDIT LIMITS AND TERMS	PRESENT		REQUESTED		APPROVED	
	LINE	TERMS	LINE	TERMS	LINE	TERMS
GENERAL FLOOR PLAN						
EXTRA A/C FLOOR PLAN						
OPEN ACCOUNT						
RADIO PROGRAMS						
OTHER						
TOTAL						

CREDIT EXPERIENCE—OTHER SUPPLIERS

NAME	HOW LONG SOLD	HIGHEST RECENT CREDIT (LAST 6 MONTHS)	TOTAL AMOUNT OWING	TOTAL AMOUNT PAST DUE	TERMS OF SALE	MANNER OF PAYMENTS			
						ANTICI-PATES	DIS-COUNTS	PAYS WHEN DUE	DAYS SLOW

FINANCIAL STATEMENT DATED	TYPE AND SOURCE

FINANCIAL REVIEW

AMOUNT				RATIO			
	19	19	19		19	19	19
NET WORKING CAPITAL				NET WORKING CAPITAL			
TANGIBLE NET WORTH				QUICK ASSET			
TOTAL SALES				T.N.W. TO T.L.			
EARNINGS AFTER TAXES				EARNINGS AS % OF SALES			

CREDIT COMMENTS — SPECIAL CONDITIONS OR CIRCUMSTANCES (USE REVERSE SIDE IF NECESSARY)

ACTIVITY CREDIT MANAGER	DATE	MANAGER OF DISTRIBUTION FINANCING DEPT.	DATE
ASSISTANT TREASURER	DATE	FILE ENCLOSURES ☐ F.S. ☐ D & B REPORT ☐ TRADE CLEARANCE	
CORPORATE CONTROLLER	DATE	☐ BANK REFERENCE ☐ OTHER...............	
REMARKS			

Form used by top corporation as credit record for customers.

Mr. Schiff noted in a talk before a management seminar in Buffalo that the "measure of effectiveness of business management should be return on investment, and not merely sales volume produced, or profit as a percentage of sales." For this reason, he told about 200 Western New York executives, "credit should be a marketing function." Credit policy should not be an all-finance decision handled

SALESMAN'S CREDIT REPORT

Name of Dealer.. Address..

Kind of business...

Please check how long established

Less Than 2 Years ☐
2 to 5 Years ☐
Over 5 Years ☐

Your estimate of the value of stock...

Appearance of store

Good ☐
Fair ☐
Poor ☐

Name of dealer's bank................................... Address..

Please list names of factories or wholesalers from whom dealer principally buys

Name.. Address..

Name.. Address..

Name.. Address..

Name.. Address..

Other Appliances Sold

Article.. Name of manufacturer......................................

Article.. Name of manufacturer......................................

Will our finance plan be used?........................... Did you explain our plan?......................

Name of other finance plans used, or, does dealer carry own paper?...........................

Please give your opinion of financial condition of locality

Good ☐
Fair ☐
Poor ☐

Remarks:..

....

....

....

....

....

....

...................................19   ....
Date   Salesman   Territory

PLEASE ANSWER FULLY

One of several useful forms of salesmen's evaluation of dealer credit rating.

in the treasurer's office, but should be more closely allied to the responsibility of marketing managers.

In order that salesmen may be provided with data they need to concentrate on potentially strong accounts, the credit department should develop background information not only on the desirable accounts, but also on the less desirable accounts. This will permit a salesman in the field to know why the credit department regards the account as "less desirable." He is then in a position to make a field check. If his findings are at variance with the credit department's information he can so report to management. This is important since most credit-reporting services fail to take into consideration important factors affecting the sales value of an account. These factors may include the competitive position of the account in the community, for example, or the certain know-how a dealer may have which would be of considerable importance as far as his ability to succeed is concerned.

It is becoming more and more the practice of companies which practice selective selling to hold meetings at periodical intervals of representatives of both the credit and the sales departments. At these meetings, both sides discuss accounts and compare notes. Whether an account should be placed upon the desirable or the less desirable list is determined by these joint committees rather than by one or the other of the two departments acting alone. By that method of appraisal both points of view are considered and much of the friction which so often develops between the two departments is eliminated. Johns-Manville Corporation, for example, thinks of the credit department as the "business-extension department" and calls credit men "financial consultants."

Keeping Credit Informed

Obtaining the cooperation of the credit department can be facilitated by having a duplicate of the salesman's route sheet sent regularly to the collection department. A well-known paint manufacturer has a duplicate of each route sent to the credit man immediately upon its receipt by the sales department. The credit man then goes over the accounts in various towns on which the salesman is to call and sends to the salesman statements of any accounts which are slow. This gives the salesman all necessary particulars before he sells in the town.

Another point in correlating collection and sales work is to make it a rule not to send dunning letters to any customer without first consulting the sales department. If the man who is responsible for sales has an opportunity to check the collection effort, he will endeavor to secure the money in such a way that the door will be left open for future orders.

The importance of consistent effort in the collection of insurance premiums is evident when it is understood that in the insurance business the company cannot take credit in its annual statement for any outstanding premiums over 90 days old. They have to be carried as a liability, so that insurance sales organizations make every effort to transform outstanding premiums into collected items. In the endeavor to make its salesmen good collectors, one company for many years operated the "Aetna Early Settlers Society." The plan is adaptable to almost any line of business.

For each membership, an annual and sometimes a semiannual reward is offered in the way of a useful diary, a pencil, or some article of value. Early Settlers' pins are also given to those who qualify. A unique diploma is issued by the company to every agent who becomes an Early Settler in the form of a large certificate upon which the agent's name is engraved. The diploma is signed by the president of the company.

Three-quarters of a million dollars were collected from hardware dealers' accounts within two months by a single wholesale house through a special drive taking the form of a contest.

Johns-Manville's Credit Policy

In his book, *Credit as a Sales Tool* (Dartnell), Joseph L. Wood, former credit manager for Johns-Manville, has listed the observations gained in a working lifetime of successful credit management. Here are his conclusions:

Credit is not primarily a financial device—it is a sales technique.

The sole purpose of industrial enterprise is the earning of profit—not merely sales.

The credit department is your full partner. It utilizes the art of credit to increase sales.

Consult your credit manager for help in making important decisions.

Be observant of the progress or lack of progress of your customers and maintain a flow of information to your credit manager.

Make friends with the bankers in each town in your territory and keep regular contact with them for helpful information.

Be familiar with the various types of credit safeguards and understand how, in some cases, they help you make sales which could not otherwise be made.

Requests for financial statements and other credit safeguards help, not hinder, you.

Help your credit manager in collections. You'll be helping yourself. Try to find the reason why the customer has not paid on time and, if possible, offer sound suggestions for correction. If they prove successful, you will have cemented your good relationship with your customer.

Keep the line of communications open both between yourself and the credit manager and between the customer and the credit manager.

Understand cash discount and be adroit in maintaining its principles.

Know the techniques of securing plus sales through secured credit.

Learn the sales channels and approach in selling the manufacturer.

Master the sales and credit aspects in selling the contractor.

Understand why the extension of longer terms would tend to decrease rather than increase sales, and know how to deal with requests for extended terms.

Realize the importance of insurance and, particularly, the *assurance* provided by the intensive training of qualified persons for the eventual assumption of top-management responsibility.

Finally, keep constantly in mind that you, the credit manager, and every member of your company have one responsibility and one aim—the success of the business through the earning of profit.

While the sales manager is not expected to be a credit expert, it is in the best interests of his company that he be at least acquainted with the procedures involved, especially in the granting of credit. There are some indicators, or indexes, with which every sales executive should be familiar.

Credit Control Indexes

Perhaps the best known indexes used in measuring the effectiveness of credit are the rejection percentage and the percentage of change in credit-sales volume. Along with the rejection percentage, you may keep figures on the number of accounts added, the number closed, and the net gain or loss in number of accounts. In addition to the change in credit-sales volume, you can follow such closely related indexes as the ratio of credit sales to total sales volume, the change in the amount of accounts receivable outstanding, the ratio of inactive accounts to total accounts, and the turnover of customers. These ratios have been profiled by the Small Business Administration as follows:

1. *Rejection Percentage:* The rejection percentage is computed by dividing the number of applications for credit declined (for lack of proper requirements or for other reasons) by the total number of applications received. Thus, if 150 applications or first orders are received during a given period and 15 are declined, the rejection percentage would be 0.10 or 10 percent.

If you discover that your rejection percentage is becoming extremely high, you may rightly inquire whether your credit-granting policy is so strict that it is preventing you from enjoying a much greater sales volume. If the percentage seems to be getting excessively low, you should check to see whether this is causing abnormal collection expenses and bad-debt losses.

2. *Trend in Number of Accounts:* You should be interested also in the actual number of applications accepted and the net increase or decrease in the number of accounts on your books. In progressive firms, figures are calculated monthly (and often daily) for the number of new accounts added, the number of accounts closed, and the net gain or loss in number of accounts.

These three figures may be expressed only as percentages of the number of accounts on your books at the beginning of a period. The figures or percentages may be compared with those for the previous period and also with those for the same period in the previous year.

3. *Change in Credit Sales Volume:* Of perhaps even greater interest are measures of increase or decrease in credit-sales volume. To show the percentage of change in credit sales from one period to another, divide the difference between the figures for the two periods by the amount of credit sales for the less recent period.

For example, if your credit sales were $10,000 for last month and $12,500 for the preceding month, divide the difference ($2,500) by the sales for the less recent period ($12,500), giving a percentage of 0.20 or —20 percent.

4. *Ratio of Credit-Sales Volume to Total Sales:* To find this ratio, divide the figure representing the sales made on credit by total sales for the month, or other period. Thus, if your total sales for the past month were $6,200 and $3,410 of this volume was made on credit terms, divide the credit sales of $3,410 by the total sales figure of $6,200, yielding 0.55 or 55 percent.

Your ratio of credit sales to total sales may change with seasonal conditions during the year, or in response to the introduction of new credit plans, different policies, or because of other factors. In short, do not arbitrarily assume that a decline in the ratio is always due to inefficiency in credit granting. By the same token, a rise in the ratio may not always result from credit-sales-promotion efforts alone.

5. *Change in Accounts Receivable Outstanding:* Important, and closely connected with indexes of changes in your firm's credit-sales volume, are measures of your accounts receivable outstanding. In progressive firms, the amount of accounts receivable outstanding (the total amount of money owed to the firm by its customers) is calculated daily. The increase or decrease from the preceding period, or from the same period of the preceding year, is then expressed in percentages.

The dollar figures obtained in these calculations disclose a very important fact; namely, the extent to which your money is tied up in financing customers. Comparative percentage figures reveal the trend.

To find the percentage change in your receivables from one period to another, divide the difference between the amounts outstanding in the two periods by the amount outstanding in the less recent period. For example, if your accounts receivable outstanding amounted to $10,000 at the end of last month and are $12,000 at the end of this month, divide the difference of $2,000 by the outstandings for the less recent period ($10,000), giving a percentage figure of 0.20 or 20 percent.

6. Ratio of Inactive Accounts to Total Accounts: You will find that monthly figures on the number of accounts becoming inactive are important in controlling the correct and full use of accounts. These figures help in maintaining and increasing credit-sales volume.

You find the percentage of inactivity—that is, the proportion of customers not buying on their accounts during the month—by dividing the number of accounts not making any purchases during the month by the total number of accounts on the books at the beginning of the month.

7. Ratio of Turnover of Customers: This ratio expresses the proportion of customers you lost during a given period, usually a year. To obtain this figure, divide the number of accounts removed from your books during the year by the total number of accounts on your books at the beginning of the year.

Changes in this turnover ratio indicate the degree to which you are succeeding or failing in your efforts to keep customers after you have once placed them on your books.

Credit Cards in Modern Sales

The advent of the computer has greatly accelerated the use of credit cards not only as a means of maintaining customer loyalty, but also for such corollary purposes as contests and tie-in sales.

Charge plates, of course, have long been successfully used by department stores and perhaps this was the example which prompted the oil companies and hotel chains to emulate them with tremendous success. In fact some of the oil companies have used credit-card lists to promote the sale of completely unrelated products such as silverware.

Many companies make special arrangements with transportation companies for the use of travel cards by their salesmen. Philco-Ford Corporation, for instance, arranges for international travel cards as well as auto credit cards. Some companies also make arrangements with the telephone company for similar purposes.

There are growing signs that credit cards will assume increasing importance for the sale of all types of goods and services with the utmost ease and convenience for the customer.

Credit Inspires Sales

In the retail field credit is especially important as a sales-producing force. In fact, successful competition often depends in many cases on the nature and extent of the credit offer to consumers.

For instance, in a recent newspaper advertisement, Sears, Roebuck and Co., featured a $52 sewing machine on these terms: No money down, no monthly payments for two months, and up to three years to pay the installments.

Chapter 32

CONSIGNMENT AND
INSTALLMENT SELLING

O NE way to control resale prices as well as merchandising methods is through making the dealer an agent and shipping goods to him on consignment. Under this plan, title to the stock of goods remains in the manufacturer's name until sold, thus giving complete power to dictate how and at what price it will be sold. It also provides the manufacturer with a powerful lever to use in case the dealer does not measure up to a manufacturer's expectations.

It is obvious that such a sales method is costly, and many consider it to be unsound because it makes a banker out of a manufacturer. It takes away the incentive which a dealer needs to push a product in which his own money is invested, and makes it easy for the distributor to carry a larger stock than necessary.

In some fields, consignment selling is on the wane. Manufacturers of pipe, for example, for many years placed pipe on consignment to wholesalers; however, after it was found that millions of dollars of investment were tied up, these manufacturers abandoned the consignment method in favor of selling their products to wholesalers.

Well-financed and well-established dealers usually frown on consignment selling. They feel this practice encourages fly-by-night and underfinanced companies to enter their markets. They prefer to own their stocks and set their own selling policies.

On the other hand, some manufacturers favor consignment selling because it permits placement of adequate stocks in desired locations, particularly with underfinanced distributors or retail outlets; it makes the selling job considerably easier since the buyer is relieved of financing problems; and it permits the manufacturer to have more accurate knowledge of point-of-sale demand, since complete records and reports must be regularly prepared. One substitute for consigned stock is the use of public warehouses. In this way the manufacturer retains control of the stock and maintains complete records.

Legal Pitfalls

Setting aside the uneconomic principles involved in consignment selling, the practice has numerous disadvantages not apparent at first glance. Many of these are legal difficulties which a manufacturer can get into. For this reason, the laws of the individual states should be carefully studied before any concrete steps are taken to enter a new consignment market. The legal technicalities which differentiate conditional sales, absolute sales, bailments, and agency contracts are subtle but important, and should lead the manufacturer to consult his legal counsel before acting.

The Supreme Court at one time ruled that the duty of returning the goods to the manufacturer being established, it matters not that the goods are returned in an altered form. In other words, title to the consigned goods remains in the manufacturer, and when the goods are sold by the dealer at retail, title to the proceeds of the sale is in the manufacturer. The manufacturer, therefore, still retains title to the consigned goods or their proceeds, these being considered as actually the consigned goods in altered form. It follows, of course, that if the manufacturer can compel the return of the consigned goods he can equally compel their return in the altered form.

The altered form may be cash, and if it is, so much the better for the manufacturer. It may also be in notes or other evidences of indebtedness. In either case the contract must be carefully drawn so as to eliminate all doubt of the manufacturer's title to the proceeds.

Installment Selling

It is generally agreed that installment selling is a method which discounts future selling, and in the event of a recession could cause considerable difficulty for both manufacturers and retailers. The argument in its favor is that it stimulates sales and consequently low-cost mass production. It is, however, inflationary. For that reason, and because of the danger of a backing up of merchandise in a period of wide unemployment, many sales managers contend that installment selling should be avoided wherever possible, even though it appears to be an effective way of meeting competition.

CONSIGNMENT AND INSTALLMENT SELLING

The Westinghouse "Equity" Plan

In a buyers' market it is important that a manufacturer help his dealers to finance customer paper without paying the high rates demanded by concerns specializing in that type of financing. Westinghouse recommends to its dealers that they work, when possible, with local banks. To help the dealer make the most advantageous arrangement with his banker, Westinghouse developed what it calls an "equity plan." The dealer agrees to operate on the recommendations of the supplier—namely 10 percent down payment, initial financing period 90 days, and the usual 30-day extension privileges. The operation of the plan is as follows:

1. The dealer signs an "Application for Floor-Plan Accommodations," if such form is required by bank.

2. The dealer submits his financial statement to the bank on whatever form the bank requires. The bank then passes on dealer's credit and usually notifies dealer and distributor of the amount of credit approved.

3. The dealer should sign a "Signature Authorization" form. The use of this form and procedure is optional for both dealer and bank. Many will want to use it, however, because it saves considerable time and effort in the future. The wording of such form is as follows:

"For the convenience of the undersigned in making such arrangements as may be necessary for you to finance undersigned's purchase of merchandise under the terms of the Westinghouse Equity Plan—Wholesale Repurchase Agreement—undersigned hereby requests and authorizes you, through your designated employees, to execute, on behalf of undersigned, such trust receipts or other title retention instruments as you may require in connection with such financing, together with such accompanying notes or drafts as are customary, and including such affidavits or other documents as may be necessary for the filing or recording of such documents. You are to advise undersigned of the execution of any documents pursuant to this authorization. Your authority, hereunder, shall continue until you are notified otherwise in writing."

4. When the dealer places an order for merchandise, either the distributor's representative or bank obtains a down payment of not less than a minimum of 10 percent of the net wholesale invoice, plus transportation or other charges not already included in such invoice. Financing charges should be prepaid by the dealer.

5. The distributor ships the merchandise to his dealer and presents invoice to the bank. Bank should promptly remit the amount due. Country banks may prefer to have their city correspondent bank handle remittances for them when such city correspondent bank is located in the same city as the distributor.

6. The bank executes the Wholesale Repurchase Agreement in duplicate, dating it, in Article 16, the same as the first floor-plan title-retention instrument received from a Westinghouse dealer to whom bank extends floor-plan credit under this agreement. No additional repurchase agree-

ment is required to cover subsequent Westinghouse dealers to whom bank extends floor-plan accommodation. Upon receipt, Westinghouse will sign and return one copy to the bank for its files. Eligible Westinghouse distributors and merchandise are listed and attached to the agreement. Banks having one or more branches need execute only one agreement, following the identical procedure outlined above.

To sum up, therefore, there are certain salient points to consider in consignment selling: The most vital point is, of course, the state in which the dealer does business, since the goods will be in the dealer's possession and the manufacturer's rights will be governed by the laws of the state in which the goods have been attached.

Retail Installment Selling

A number of practical considerations enter into the practice of retail installment selling. Among them are the gross profit (before expenses) that you make on the sale, your ability to get cash from other sources at a cost lower than the discount charged, the extent of your other expenses, and the volume of your installment sales compared to your cash sales.

You will probably sell your installment accounts either to a sales finance company or to a commercial bank. Usually their discount rates are competitive, and both give you and your installment customers similar services.

Installment paper is sold in three different ways—nonrecourse, recourse, and repurchase.

Under the *nonrecourse* plan of purchase, you are not responsible if your customer fails to pay. The financial institution that bought the paper stands the loss. In repossession, the financial institution is fully responsible. It retakes, reconditions, and resells the item and collects any balance the customer owes.

Often whether a retailer can afford to sell an installment credit depends on whether he can find a buyer for his accounts on a nonrecourse basis at an acceptable discount rate.

Under the *recourse* plan of repurchase, you are liable for any balance due in case your customer does not pay. You have to do your own repossessing, reconditioning, and reselling.

Under the *repurchase* plan, you are required to buy back the property for the unpaid balance after the financial institution has retaken it from your customer. Here you share the burden with the institution.

Expenses and Income

What are some of the expenses connected with installment selling? Among them are:

1. Salaries for people to run your credit operations.

2. Expenses of office space, supplies and utilities (you may not have to rent additional space, but you will have to consider the sales you might have made in the space devoted to credit operations).

3. Collection and repossession expenses.

4. Interest on money borrowed to carry on your business.

The longer the contracts, the larger the amount of money you will have to tie up in receivables to do a given amount of installment business. You will also have the advertising bill for announcing and promoting the plan.

If you are selling on cash and on open charge and add installment credit, you will have the problem of separating expenses connected with installment selling from those resulting from open charge accounts. This lets you know whether each credit plan is paying its own way.

You offset such expenses by selling more. Gross income on installment sales should pay for the program.

Customers help cut the expenses by paying a service charge for the privilege of buying on installment. This charge varies with different stores. To find out what is enough for you, you will need an accurate cost study of your expenses in serving installment customers.

How Many Dollars?

Installment payments for any given month are equal to the total of new installment business written in previous months (not including the given month) divided by the contract period.

Installment receivables for a given month are equal to installment receivables of the previous month, plus the new installment business written during the given month, minus installment payments received during the given month. In a table following, the receivables increase by smaller and smaller amounts each month. They reach a peak of $33,390 in the sixth month and remain unchanged thereafter.

With a smaller down payment, your maximum dollars tied up in receivables would increase. However, if you used a contract for three months instead of six months, your number of dollars tied up in receivables would decrease.

Given certain conditions, what would be the maximum number of dollars you could have tied up in installment receivables? Suppose you hope to sell $10,000 of merchandise a month, or $120,000 annually, on installment terms. Suppose also that your contracts call for a 10 percent down payment, 6 months to pay, and a service charge of 1 percent per month. The maximum dollar amount you would have tied up in installment receivables is seen in the table shown here.

MAXIMUM DOLLAR AMOUNT TIED UP IN INSTALLMENT RECEIVABLES

Month	New Business Written	Installment Payments	Month-end Receivables
1	[1] $9,540	....	$ 9,540
2	9,540	$1,590	17,490
3	9,540	3,180	23,850
4	9,540	4,770	28,620
5	9,540	6,360	31,800
6	9,540	7,950	[2] 33,390
7	9,540	9,540	33,390
8	9,540	9,540	33,390
9	9,540	9,540	33,390
10	9,540	9,540	33,390
11	9,540	9,540	33,390
12	9,540	9,540	33,390

[1] Equals installment sales of $10,000 minus down payments of $1,000 plus the service charges of $540 based upon the beginning unpaid balances. [2] Peak.

PROPOSED FEDERAL TRADE COMMISSION GUIDES RELATING TO RETAIL CREDIT TRANSACTIONS

These guides relate to retail credit transactions in the District of Columbia and to transactions in interstate commerce.

GUIDE I—*Disclosure in Advertising and Price Tagging.*

No retailer of any article of merchandise should represent (a) a price in connection with a specified weekly or monthly credit payment or installment, when the aggregate of such credit payments or installments is in excess of the represented price; (b) a specified, weekly, monthly, or other periodic credit payment or installment (e.g., "pay $2.88 weekly," or "payments as low as $12 per month"), unless in immediate conjunction with each such representation there is clear disclosure of either the total number of payments required for payment in full or the total amount of the payments for which the purchaser will be indebted.

GUIDE II—*Disclosure of Costs Prior to Consummation of Credit.*

In a retail credit transaction no seller should fail, before consummation of the credit sale, to furnish the buyer with an itemization in writing separately stating each of the following: (a) the cash price of the article, (b) the amount of any sales, excise or other tax to be paid by the purchaser, (c) the amounts to be credited as downpayment and/or tradein, if any, (d) the unpaid cash balance owed by the buyer to the seller, (e) each finance, credit, service or carrying charge which is to be paid by the purchaser (including any amount covering insurance premiums, service-contract charge and a specification of any other charges, separately stated, which are capable of determination at the point of sale), (f) the amount and the total number of each weekly or monthly installment payment, (g) the total amount for which the purchaser will be indebted, *and* (h) the total credit transaction price (item (g) plus (c) above).

Failure to separately disclose such amounts may have the capacity and tendency to deceive the purchaser as to the nature of his costs in the transaction and may be an unfair method of competition since it does not enable the consumer to make meaningful price and credit comparisons between competitive products.

GUIDE III—*Disclosure of Negotiation to Third Party.*

No seller of any article of merchandise at retail should fail, before consummation of the credit sale, to disclose orally and in writing with such conspicuousness and clarity as likely to be observed and read by the purchaser, that the conditional sale contract and promissory note or other instrument executed by the purchaser may at the option of the seller be negotiated or assigned to a finance company or other third party.

GUIDE IV—*Disclosure of Buyer's Claim to Third Party.*

No seller in a retail credit transaction as defined herein should assist, sell, or otherwise transfer to a finance company or other third person a retail installment contract or other credit instrument after the seller has been notified, either orally or in writing, of any claim or defense respecting the seller's performance, unless the seller makes written disclosure to the transferee of the existence of the buyer's claim or defense.

GUIDE V—*Merchandise as Security for Other Transactions.*

No seller or other party in a retail credit transaction as defined herein should designate merchandise which is the subject of one retail installment contract as security for the buyer's performance under any other retail installment contract.

GUIDE VI—*Passage of Title to Buyer.*

No seller or other party in a retail credit transaction as defined herein should refuse or fail to pass title to the buyer of merchandise purchased under a retail installment contract when the full time price of that merchandise has been paid.

GUIDE VII—*Prorating Payments.*

No seller or other party should prorate a buyer's installment payment among several retail credit installment contracts unless:

1. The buyer is notified in writing that such action is being taken, and

2. The ratio between the amount of the consolidated payment prorated to any one of the contracts and the total amount of the payment is the same as the ratio between the total amount originally due under that contract and the sum of the total amounts originally due on all contracts whose payments have been consolidated.

Chapter 33

NATIONAL VERSUS
PRIVATE BRANDS

A RGUMENTS still wax heavy among sales experts over the
question of whether a manufacturer should produce a national-
brand product, the merchandising and advertising of which he can
fully control, or produce "private label" merchandise for suppliers.

While the argument continues, many manufacturers quietly do
both. The makers of Babbo, a nationally famous cleansing powder,
also produce cleansing powders for chain department, variety, and
food stores under many private labels.

Actually, both kinds of merchandise probably are needed to
provide the merchandise mix demanded by today's large and diversified markets.

Advantages of National Brands

A safe rule in establishing a policy on branding is to use a national
brand if the product lends itself to national distribution and national
advertising. For one thing the manufacturer of a national brand is
in a better trading and operating position. Any goodwill he creates
for his brand, or his company, accrues to him and there are instances where brand names have been sold for millions of dollars.
It is more costly to build national distribution for a product, but
the market thus established cannot easily be taken over by a competitor. Once people accept a national brand and get the habit of asking
for it at their local dealer's store, the dealer will hesitate a long time
before he stops stocking it. So long as the quality of the product is
maintained, and national advertising is adequate, you are assured
of satisfactory sales volume.

Advantages of Private Brands

Producers usually adopt the policy of making goods to be sold
under a distributor's private brand when their competition sells well-

entrenched national brands. Rather than make the investment in national advertising and store-to-store selling required to put another national brand on the market, the manufacturer will go to a sectional distributor and arrange to furnish him with large quantities of the product, bearing his own private brand, at an attractive price. He may or may not allow the distributor an additional sum to be spent for advertising in territories within the distributor's trading zone. He may prefer to take the need of introductory advertising into consideration when setting the price, leaving it to the distributor to decide what to do about advertising. He may wish to put demonstrators in key stores, sample, or do something other than space advertising.

But, as so often happens, these arrangements are only secure so long as a manufacturer can produce the goods for the distributor at a price lower than he can get "just as good" merchandise from a competitor. In fact, it is the history of private brands that in a buyers' market, distributors show no compunction in switching producers if and when they can find somebody to make approximately the same product for a few cents less. The fear that this might happen hangs over all the transactions between the producer and distributor. It places the manufacturer in a tight position, where he must either cut his already small profit or sacrifice volume. There are a few distributors, but not many, smart enough to realize the importance of protecting their sources of supply and who do not constantly try to hammer suppliers down on price. In the long run manufacturers who depend upon making products for large distributors to be sold under brand names owned by the distributors, usually become a department in the distributors' business and find themselves working for the equivalent of a small salary. They end up being the owner of a run-down plant with nothing in the way of goodwill to sell.

The Combination Policy

Sometimes makers of nationally advertised products, in order to spread their overhead over a larger volume, accept large private-brand orders from mail-order houses, co-ops, and other mass producers on what they call a "run-on" basis. While the product supplied on such deals may be equal in most respects to the product carrying the national brand, it is usually slightly different. Such orders, of course, are filled at a price far below what a distributor would pay for the national brand, since no selling expense is involved. Even though much of the manufacturer's overhead expense has been absorbed in the production of the national brands, there is still a chance for his making a fair profit even at a lower price.

While straddling the issue in this way seems attractive, it has its drawbacks. In the first place, it requires a large outlay of capital to create national acceptance for a product under the maker's brand. This must be done before production can reach a point where a manufacturer can shade his price sufficiently to interest the mass distributor, and at the same time make a worthwhile profit himself. In the second place, it soon leaks out—sometimes with the help of the mass distributor who starts a whispering campaign—that the product listed at a greatly reduced price in the catalog is identically the same product as others pay a fancy price for at their local dealer's. The difference, of course, is that the mail-order house doesn't have to pad the price for advertising! All of which doesn't make the independent dealer who handles the nationally advertised product too happy.

Why Some Retailers Favor Advertised Brands

While a few large merchants, like Marshall Field & Company in Chicago, have established sufficient public acceptance for anything they place upon their counters, smaller retailers favor advertised brands even though the profit per sale may be a little less. There are several reasons why this is so. In the first place, well-advertised national brands usually turn over quickly. It takes less time to sell them. Merchants have learned the hard way that profits come from turnovers and not leftovers. In the second place, a store which features well-known advertised products builds a local reputation for handling quality products. That prestige attracts and holds customers.

One of the most important reasons for S. S. Kresge's rapid growth has been its emphasis on national brands, says president Harry B. Cunningham. "They have brand recognition and acceptance. A K Mart isn't always recognized as a Kresge operation when it moves into an area. Manufacturers help by putting up promotional money on their products which K Mart advertises."

Brand lines are now reported to account for more than 50 percent of the total sales of W. T. Grant Company, according to *Home Furnishings Daily*. The chain is described as the second largest network of variety stores and the third largest general merchandise retailer in the country. It has more than 1,100 units in 46 states and owns 34 Diskay Discount Marts. Refrigeration and laundry equipment are made for Grant's under the Bradford label by Franklin

Appliance Division of Studebaker. Gas and electric ranges are manufactured by Hardwick and by Eagle. Other Bradford-brand products sold by Grant's include tape recorders, solid-state stereo combinations and portable phonographs.

Changing Customer Concepts

But there are rumblings of change all over the country among retailers of all types and sizes. They are saying that uniform supermarkets, with standard stock and traditional "catch-all" merchandising, are becoming outdated. Customer loyalty is dwindling. Retailers are becoming increasingly aware that each store unit must tailor its assortment of goods and its merchandising and promotional strategies to appeal to the shopping habits and preferences of the particular families living in the community it serves. Retailers have to know how their customers shop, how they differ from one another—what it takes to please young married couples, or suburban white-collar families, or lower-income working-class households—or whatever other type family lives near their stores. Private brands are one element in this problem, but an important one.

Private brands represent an increasing trend. Dr. Arnold J. Corbin, in *New Trends in American Marketing,* points out that retailers generally find they can promote their own brands within the stores more profitably because they make a wider percentage of profit, even though they sell them at lower prices to their customers. They also have the advantage of being able to display their own brands at eye-level. Although retailer brands are a growing trend, there have been some limitations. There are some chains which have found they are not large enough to do a good job on their own brands. They have found they cannot obtain the rate of turnover fast enough to generate an adequate return on their investment. Even when private-brand percentage margins are greater, if you cannot get as many unit sales within a given period of time as you can with a manufacturer's well-known brand, you are likely then to prefer the manufacturer's brand. However, many retailers believe that by promoting manufacturers' brands they are not building store loyalty; any retailer can carry such brands, but with their own private brands they build loyalty to their own stores.

Chapter 34

CANCELLATIONS AND RETURNED GOODS

IN spite of every effort to eliminate waste, the problem of handling returned goods and permitting cancellation of orders continues to perplex business management. So impregnated has the buyer become with the need of turning his capital quickly that he is growing more and more averse to buying anything beyond his immediate requirements. He is prone to unload back on the manufacturer whatever the manufacturer unloads on him. Competitive conditions make it easy for him to do this and he is utilizing his advantage to the fullest.

A Sales Manager's Responsibility

No business need have a high percentage of cancellations, or more than 2 percent of its total billing returned, if it is willing temporarily to lose some business. The returned-goods problem is nine-tenths a mental condition. It exists for a number of reasons:

1. Management considers it a necessary evil.

2. Salesmen oversell to bolster their orders.

3. Salesmen are permitted to encourage customers to overbuy, with a promise to "fix it up" later.

4. Salesmen are not taught to sell in such a way as to make an order stick.

5. Salesmen are not made to understand that cancellations and returned goods are a reflection on their sales ability.

6. Prices decline, but provisions have not been made to handle the situation.

7. Competitors come in with lower prices and the customer had not been properly sold.

8. Buyers change their minds after the salesman leaves them. This may be due to high-pressure salesmanship without adequate product value.

9. The product might be found to be of low quality or defective.

10. There may have been delays in shipment which caused the buyer to no longer need the goods, or to no longer need them in the quantity ordered.

11. The buyer may have overestimated his requirements, or market needs may have changed after he placed his order.

A check of the work of individual salesmen in a number of different concerns, both manufacturers and jobbers, shows that a liberal returned-goods policy not only does not help sales but, on the contrary, mitigates against a larger volume. Invariably the salesmen who produce the most business have a lower percentage of returned goods and cancellations, whereas the salesmen who produce the smaller volume of business invariably have the highest percentage of returned goods and cancellations. Good salesmen do not need a lax returned-goods policy to lean upon, and the only object such a policy serves is to bolster up the weak sisters, without in any way increasing the productiveness of the stronger men.

A salesman selling oil pumps "slopped over" the sale by attempting to get the contract signed without the buyer reading it, and then "forgetting" to leave a duplicate copy of the order with the customer. Salesmen are prone to do this when the order form is complex, fearing that the various legal clauses in the contract will cause the customer to hesitate and ask questions, thereby getting off the main track. Order forms should be as simple as possible, and free from legal verbiage.

Importance of Clean Orders

One Wisconsin manufacturer with a high percentage of returned goods made a careful analysis of a number of orders. He decided the fault was largely his, because, both directly and indirectly, he had failed to acquaint his customers with his own beliefs and with the basic facts behind his beliefs. As a result of the analysis, he called his 12 salesmen into headquarters. He emphasized the issue by confining the conference to returned goods. As a result, the men thought and talked nothing but returned goods during the two days at headquarters. They sold themselves upon the importance of selling dealers on the exact situation and the remedy. Even though this meant, in some cases, smaller orders, and in all cases a closer supervision of the dealers' stock by the salesmen, there was no hesitancy in accepting both the shrinkage and the responsibility. The salesmen went out with the spirit of crusaders, thoroughly convinced their cause was right, and believing without reservation that they could convince each one of their customers with the fairness of their proposal.

Among the losses that result from canceled orders might be mentioned the following:

1. The cost of making the sale which is wasted.

2. The cost of the office paperwork involved.

3. The cost of handling and shipping the order.

4. The unnecessary capital tied up in expanded inventory.

5. Wear and tear on the goods, which may need to be repaired or refinished, or which possibly may no longer be salable.

6. The possible disappointment of some other customer who has not received his order because the goods were sent elsewhere.

How to Avoid Canceled Orders

Among the practices of companies which have been successful in reducing order cancellations, the following points are considered of importance:

1. Establishing conditions for accepting cancellations, and clearly stating them on the order form.

2. Establishment of procedures to correct any losses due to faulty material, delayed shipments, or other causes under the manufacturer's control.

3. Establishment of procedures for conditions beyond the control of the manufacturer.

4. Establishment of charges to cover costs involved in cancellations.

5. Establishment of routines which give salesmen complete facts on delivery and other details so they will not give incorrect information to their customers.

6. Careful analysis of all cancellations and returned goods, so that identifiable causes can be corrected.

One large wholesale house, which tightened up its returned-goods policy had the following results:

We were very lenient with customers who returned goods at first, cheerfully accepting losses, thinking that gradually the situation would clarify, and that the goodwill of the jobber would reimburse us in future profitable business. Strange as it may seem, the jobbers with whom we were most lenient failed to become good customers, and those with whom we adopted a sterner policy buckled down to learn the "game," instructed their sales forces, and are now doing a very fine business in many cases without any worry to us, the manufacturers.

Our tightening-up policy began with letters of protest to the jobbers, explaining to them why they were failing, and how serious the matter was from the manufacturer's standpoint. This helped with a certain percentage, but others still insisted on sending goods in on slight pretext or no pretext at all, charges collect, and often in damaged condition. Finally we adopted the policy of receiving no merchandise unless permission to return had first been secured from the service department. Goods arriving were refused and a postal notice mailed to the consignor stating the case, informing him that the shipment was being held by the transportation company, and that we would not pick it up unless sent in for repairs, and unless the jobber agreed to stand charges incurred, and agreed to the return of the shipment after inspection or repairs.

This policy brought protests, of course, but after the customer understood our sincerity and earnest desire to be fair, usually he would consent to our terms. Sometimes he would tell us that he was through with us, but fortunately by the time this policy was put into effect the trade had begun to appreciate the profit possibilities of the line and was not anxious to give it up.

The result has been an almost complete stoppage of unjustified losses, a more wholesome relationship between the factory and the jobber, and development of sounder channels of distribution.

Legal Status of Association Agreements

While many returned goods and cancellation problems have been sidetracked through the operation of codes, it should be remembered that the antitrust laws are still in effect and that the courts have held, and will probably hold again, that uniform trade practices constitute restraint of trade if adopted by a group of companies in an industry.

Chapter 35

CUSTOMER-SERVICE POLICIES

CUSTOMER service is the most serious internal problem facing industry today. No matter how big or small the company, how great its reputation or how widely accepted its products, it will, eventually, rise or fall according to the soundness of its customer-service policies.

Arjay Miller, president of Ford Motor Company, addressing the National Automobile Dealers Association, said: "Customer service ranks right beside traffic safety, air pollution, and highway congestion in terms of public interest.

"Nothing will so much affect the future of the franchise system as our ability—and particularly your ability—to meet the car owner's demand for better automotive service. No law, and no change in factory-dealer cost reimbursement, can offer a real solution. The real solution can only be in more effective dealer-factory cooperation in identifying, evaluating, and responding to what the customer expects from us."

While the actual supervision of servicing is not generally a function of the sales manager, yet coordination between the service department, or outside servicing sources, is an important selling responsibility. It goes almost without saying that poor servicing policies or practices can undo all the favorable efforts of salesmen to obtain customer acceptance for their products.

Furthermore, a surprisingly large number of sales executives fail to take full advantage of the profit potentials of servicing. In many lines, service items, parts and supplies may contribute as much as 50 percent or more profit beyond that realized in the original sale.

Variable Factors in Servicing Practices

Analysis of the practices of several hundred companies reveals the following considerations to be of concern to those who determine service policies:

  1. Service is rendered to assist the wholesaler and retailer in the profitable

completion of their functions, and the ultimate consumer in his most satisfactory use of the product.

2. Through service, a manufacturer can gain highly valuable knowledge about his product in use. Careful records should therefore be kept so that product weaknesses can be corrected.

3. To provide service for his product, a manufacturer must either supply it himself or train others to supply it for him.

4. If the manufacturer has others do the servicing of his product, he must educate or train them. This training may be conducted at his factory or by using traveling training schools. Usually the wholesalers or retail outlets pay their own traveling expenses and the manufacturer supplies the trainers, props, and supplies. Some companies give certificates to trainees on completion of the training.

5. For many consumer items, the service is supplied in the form of tags, instruction sheets or labels. Collarbands on shirts may state "Do not starch"; with some synthetic fabrics, tags stating how to wash are attached; a simple appliance may have a user's service manual or instruction sheet included in the package.

6. For industrial goods, more servicing is usually required. This may start with a study of installation problems, to assure proper installation. Also periodical inspection or maintenance after installation may be necessary, to assure proper operations. These services may be charged for as an extra or included in the contract price.

7. Manufacturers may license outside shops to do maintenance and repair work on their products. For example, automobile-jack manufacturers contract with shops which do not sell jacks, merely repair them. The manufacturers protect themselves by selling their parts only to these licensed shops. Or manufacturers may maintain their own local repair shops, as with hearing aids or electric razors.

8. On repairs or replacement of inferior parts, manufacturers may—

   (a) Provide this service for a stated period of time and include labor, material and transportation;

   (b) Limit it to material only.

To control service, many manufacturers provide "Warranty Cards" with their product. This is customary with appliances. The ultimate user is expected to fill in the card, showing the dealer's name, address, date of purchase, and any other pertinent data that the company desires to obtain. From these cards, valuable marketing statistics can be obtained. The trouble is, many people hold the cards for a period of time, thinking they thereby extend the length of warranty. Manufacturers get around this by having the dealer fill out the warranty, giving one copy to the buyer and mailing a copy to the factory or sales office.

Some manufacturers maintain highly trained "preventive maintenance" service departments, and contract for such service. Notable among them are typewriter and other office-equipment manufacturers.

Service—a Tool for Selling

Jim and Tom Anthony have been in the retail appliance-electronics business in Inglewood, California, for 22 years. When asked how their Anthony Bros. store became one of the leading independents in the metropolitan Los Angeles area, they cited service.

"It's not only vital to fulfilling the contract with a customer when he buys from us, it's our bridge to this customer's next purchase," said Jim Anthony, who is in charge of service. "If we do a good job servicing an appliance or electronics product—whether he's bought from us before or not—we're more than halfway toward establishing ourselves as a good place to do business."

The Anthony brothers firmly believe that service is a tool for selling. Salesmen are instructed to refer to the store's complete service facilities during their sales presentations.

"We also try to make certain that everyone who works in this store remembers that service means sales," pointed out Jim Anthony. "Men on house-service calls are in a perfect position to spot a homeowner's need for a new appliance or television set. We pay our men 2 percent of the gross for any business that results from a lead they direct our way."

PART 7

ORGANIZING
FOR
SELLING

Chapter 36

DEPARTMENTAL ORGANIZATION

IN Chapter 4, we briefly examined some of the principal types of modern sales organization, especially with reference to the position of the sales manager in each type of structure.

In this chapter, we shall go into further detail, particularly to examine the relationship of the sales and marketing functions to other functions of a company, and to examine the opportunities for coordination between the departments.

In modern sales organizations, the organization chart is as important a piece of equipment as are the typewriter and adding machine. However, no one organization chart can depict accurately the operation of any considerable number of companies, nor can any two charts be identical, even in similar types of operations.

It is simple enough to develop a sales organization if only one line of products is involved. It becomes a more complex task when a whole series of product lines must be handled, especially if they are diverse or involve several industries. This, too, is where line and staff functions play an important role. An example of this is a market-research department which meets the requirements and needs of the various product managers. Similarly, the advertising department should function for *all* product lines in a company.

Therefore, in preparing an organization chart, such models as are offered in the following pages can be only generally suggestive; they cannot be used as exact patterns to be adopted but rather should be considered as examples to be adapted.

Preparing the Organization Chart

In preparing an organization chart for a specific firm or enterprise of any kind, all functions must be listed. This having been done, the functions are grouped by type and compatibility, and a preliminary charting is sketched along "ideal" lines.

However, the ideal chart is then deviated from, as the skills of present or obtainable personnel require. The final result will be a compromise between the ideal and the practicable. A complete listing of sales management functions will suggest what factors should be included.

The Organization Manual

Once the organization chart has been developed and approved, in many companies it becomes part of the official organization manual. This has many uses of a very practical nature, especially in very large organizations where it is sometimes difficult to keep up with departmental and personnel changes.

The organization manual, however, to serve its purpose fully, must be kept up to date through the issuance of new sections or pages as soon as required.

There is only one way to do this and that is to make it the full responsibility of one officer of the company, preferably the executive responsible for organization planning and development.

Types of Sales Organizations

There are two general types of sales organizations: (1) Those where the direction and administration are strongly centralized in the home office; (2) Those where supervision is decentralized and

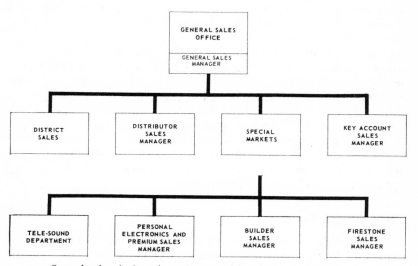

Organizational chart for a large multiproduct sales department.

where the home office functions mainly as a general staff, leaving the actual sales direction to competent divisional managers on the ground. There are advantages and disadvantages to both types of organization. One type may be best for one company, the other best for another. The general trend, however, is toward decentralization under resident vice-presidents or thoroughly capable regional managers.

This trend is in some ways a move back to the earlier method of selling the output of a factory entirely through sales agents, each of whom operated according to his own whims and left the factory with only production to worry about.

Centralized Control

The first company to superimpose central control upon a sales-agency system in the United States was The National Cash Register Company. Soon after John H. Patterson organized that company, he perceived the advantage to the business if methods of the most successful salesmen were taught to *all* salesmen. An administrative sales department was established at Dayton to devise better ways of marketing cash registers and work with the company's agents. He realized how important it was to be sure improved methods were not only devised but also used. The result was that NCR agents began to make more money; turnover of salesmen of the agents fell off; greater sales volume permitted production economies; and, most important of all, many of the successful salesmen in the country were attracted to the NCR waiting list by Mr. Patterson's methods.

Central control of a sales organization affords a greater opportunity to synchronize field selling with sales promotion and advertising. It simplifies administration. It permits manipulating territories more easily. And, to some extent at least, it enables management to quickly put a new sales plan into execution. The need for having to first "sell" the new plan to a group of sales agents, who very often are rugged individualists with a none too high opinion of "swivel chair" plans, is eliminated. Then, too, in the hiring, selection, and supervision of the sales force there is less chance for favoritism and all that goes with it.

Decentralized Control

The objection to centralized sales control is that too many decisions must be made by men thousands of miles away from the scene of action. They have a limited knowledge of territorial conditions,

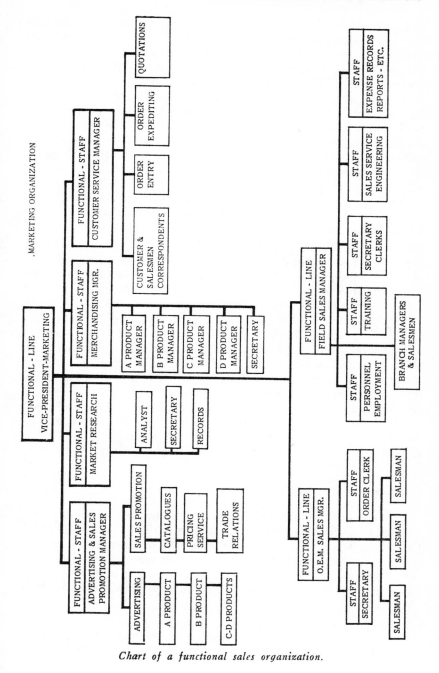

Chart of a functional sales organization.

and may not have the time to work closely with the salesmen. In a survey of salesmen's attitudes made by the Boston Sales Executives Club, the most voiced criticism of sales managers was that they did not spend enough time in the field working with salesmen. Decentralization permits more effective field cooperation with salesmen, because the authority to hire and fire salesmen is vested in the regional manager; he, as far as the salesman is concerned, is really the "big boss." Under centralized control, the division or district manager is too often regarded by salesmen as a sort of "straw boss." As a rule he is a man of limited ability, perhaps an older salesman who was promoted in consideration of long service with the company. In the decentralized type of organization, the regional manager is frequently a "bigger" man than the general sales manager; he invariably makes more money. In fact one Cleveland company makes it a practice to promote its general sales managers to regional sales managers at a higher salary.

Under such a plan a very strong officer personnel is built up, and the sales organization is stimulated by more intelligent and more effective field leadership. Decisions are made on the spot by an executive who is thoroughly conversant with local conditions. There is a concentration of brains upon the problem of selling the company's products. Methods successfully developed by each regional manager become available to all, so that 10 or 12 men with ability as sales executives are giving their entire effort to the sales success of the business. So while the use of high-priced regional managers represents a heavy supervisional expense, the real cost can be measured only in net profits. If through decentralization greater sales volume is obtained for every sales dollar expended, the method is justified regardless of how much the regional executives are paid.

Customer Relations

It is significant that several important companies which have revamped their headquarters organization in order to do a more effective selling job have put additional emphasis on the new importance of public and trade relations. In the case of one well-known manufacturing company the following divisions have been established under a vice-president of distribution, who is responsible for both domestic and foreign sales:

GENERAL SALES ADMINISTRATION: This division in charge of a general sales manager will be responsible for the actual operation of all salesmen and the general execution of all plans adopted by the sales-planning committee.

SALES DEVELOPMENT: This is a new activity with this company and combines the functions of sales research and sales planning. The job of this division is to find and develop new uses for the product, new markets, and new methods of selling and advertising.

SALES PERSONNEL: Formerly this activity was included in the functions of the general sales manager. The management believes that the problem of recruiting and training salesmen will be so important, that it can best be done in the field rather than at the home office. This division will be responsible for the quantity and quality of salesmen.

TRADE RELATIONS: All duties of what is currently called the sales promotion department will be centered in this activity, excepting those which do not bear on trade relations. These will be taken over by the public relations division of the sales department. Trade relations are concerned especially with point-of-sale promotion.

PUBLIC RELATIONS: Consumer advertising, publicity, employee relations, stockholder relations, and similar duties will be handled in this division, and the advertising department, as such, abolished. Many of its functions will be taken over by the advertising agency, including preparation of advertising literature and direct-mail campaigns now handled in the office.

It will be noted that this setup is intended to put more emphasis on what might be termed the "engineering" side of sales management, functioning in the sales organization as a whole somewhat like the general staff functions in a military organization. Its contact with the actual field selling force will be through division managers, of whom there are five in this particular setup. The country is divided between them. They are headquartered at: (1) New York, (2) Chicago, (3) Atlanta, (4) Oklahoma City, and (5) San Francisco. There is also a Canadian sales division with headquarters in Toronto.

Importance of Sales Planning

Advocates of centralized sales control contend that it permits better planning. They contend that a good sales plan is more essential than sales administration and supervision. It is difficult to generalize. In some sales operations, let us say marketing a highly competitive staple through exclusive agents, having the right plan is important. With the right plan almost any salesman who will work can take the "deal" out and sell it. But in marketing an office device where the highest type of creative selling is required, the plan is less essential. In such a case the all-important thing is to find an application for the device in the prospect's business, which is sometimes difficult. That sort of selling takes supervision of the highest order, not at some faraway point, *but* on the job. Even so, sales planning is important, perhaps almost as important as supervision. For these reasons there is a trend toward dividing the sales management job, so that one executive will be in charge of planning, and another, or several, in charge of sales administration.

In many organizations a vice-president in charge of sales is the planning executive. Execution of his plans is in charge of a general sales manager. In the case of small organizations the head of the business usually functions as the sales engineer, and it is significant that at the present time there is a tendency to fill the position of president or general manager with a man who has had sales experience, or at least is salesminded. The actual sales operations, even in the smallest companies, are in charge of a sales manager who heads up the sales department.

Regional Organization

A very successful business, which operated for many years as a highly centralized organization, increased its sales materially when it rearranged its districts into five groups, as follows:

Eastern: Syracuse, Boston, New York, Philadelphia.

Mideastern: Detroit, Pittsburgh, Cincinnati, Richmond.

Southern: Atlanta, Memphis, New Orleans, Dallas, Oklahoma City.

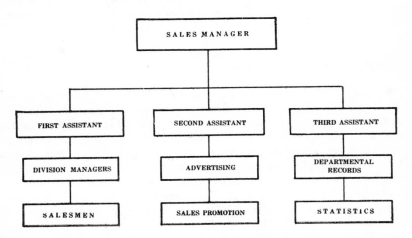

The organization charted here is so planned that the sales manager will have an understudy, the first assistant assuming the title should it become necessary. The sales manager, under this plan, is the central factor of all merchandising activities.

Midwestern: Minneapolis, St. Louis, Chicago, Kansas City, Omaha.

Western: Seattle, Salt Lake City, Denver, San Francisco, Los Angeles.

A regional sales manager responsible for each group of districts is stationed in the New York office. These five division managers and the vice-president in charge of national sales make up the company's sales committee. Thus, this company obtains the advantages of a centralized control while at the same time decentralizing supervision and field administration.

Strengthening the Marketing Department

In reviewing and strengthening the organization of your marketing department, it would be well to keep the following long-recognized and accepted principles in mind:

1. There must be centralized control of all marketing activities within the area of responsibility, and proper authority must be delegated to attain the desired objectives. This means that all responsibility for the marketing of products should be centered in the top sales executive. Responsibility and authority for the various activities or phases of marketing should be delegated to managers, department heads, and successively lower supervisory levels, to assure satisfactory performance in every segment of the marketing organization.

2. Responsibility must be centered in an individual and not in a committee. A committee cannot be held responsible, it is too elusive. It operates too slowly and without sufficient definiteness. The purpose of a committee is that of discussion, whereby objectivity is brought to the fore. A strong executive uses his staff committees to talk out problems as the basis for his decisions; a weak executive hides behind the deliberations of his committees and follows their recommendations. To take a vote of a committee is dangerous; instead, management should give consideration to all pertinent, objective thinking and then make up its own mind for action.

3. Delegated responsibility and authority must be commensurate. Responsibility without adequate authority is meaningless; while authority without responsibility is foolhardy. They must be equal, to obtain satisfactory performance.

4. All activities should be classified and grouped by functions, so that executives and supervisors may become specialists and experts in their fields. This may be accomplished by examining all activities and functions of the organization, then assigning related and homogeneous ones to respective positions. An organization chart, prepared in this theoretical manner without showing names of personnel, can later be adjusted to give recognition to personality traits and skills.

5. The number of subordinates reporting to any position should be limited. Care should be taken that no more responsibilities or subordinates are assigned to an executive than he can properly administer. A rule of thumb is no more than eight or ten subordinates, which, when added to contacts with his executive

superior and contemporaries, keep an executive busy. This rule is flexible; in actual practice a great deal depends on the ability of the executive, the maturity and abilities of his subordinates. Obviously, a district sales manager of an old, well-established district served by knowledgeable and seasoned salesmen, could satisfactorily handle more men than could an equally capable manager in a newly opened district with unseasoned men.

6. Direct responsibility must have full recognition in order that the organization may operate smoothly. There must be widespread understanding of duties, responsibilities, and authority of staff personnel.

7. There must be clear definition of the functions and activities assigned to respective divisions, departments, and sections. All personnel should have complete knowledge as to assignments of associated positions so there will be no conflict or overlapping of effort, and there can be full accountability.

8. All channels of communications must be adequate and open, with complete understanding of them by all personnel. These channels extend from the chief executive officer, functional divisions, staff positions, departments, and section leaders; equally important, they must lead upward from the most minor positions to the highest. It should be recognized and expected that channels of communication crisscross lines of direct authority, and only when it cannot be avoided should they follow formal lines of command.

9. The "Principle of Exception" should be adopted for guidance of all personnel. Under this principle, policies are set forth which cover the usual situations that are encountered at the various levels in the organization. Salesmen are expected to follow those policies that apply to their operations; when an exception is encountered, they refer the problem to their immediate superior. If it falls within his policy coverage, he handles it immediately; otherwise he refers it to the next level above him. The purpose of this principle is to keep decisionmaking at the lowest possible level and close to the events that cause the decision to be made. The further up the ladder a decision is made, the more remote is the arbitrator from actual events; and the more biases may creep in to warp judgment. Personnel in the lower levels tend to shun authority and to look to their superiors for decisions.

COORDINATION WITH PUBLIC RELATIONS

The growing importance which business attaches to building and holding the goodwill of the public, as well as the goodwill of employees, customers, and stockholders, offers the sales department another opportunity to extend its sphere of usefulness to the business. Just as the public relations department helps to make the sales task less difficult, so the sales department can help to make the job of the public relations department lighter.

The Salesman in Community Relations

Another area where the sales department can coordinate its work effectively with public relations is in community relations. The sales executive of one company, for example, was responsible for arranging and staging a successful program to make its city more attractive as a place in which to live and work. Since this sort of project requires skilled salesmanship, it is fitting that sales concern itself with it. The same is true in communities where a company may operate a branch plant or sales office. The managers of such units should be encouraged to become active in civic affairs, to join groups such as Rotary, Kiwanis, local churches, and other organizations interested in community betterment. It is good public relations to have the people in those communities think of the company as a contributor to the community welfare, and not just interested in the money it can take out of the town, as critics charge.

Press Relations

Sales executives, as well as salesmen, travel about the country a good deal and have numerous opportunities, if they seek them, to give interviews to the press. This is an important phase of public relations which too many companies entirely overlook.

It is interesting to note that such an astute corporation as the Standard Oil Company (New Jersey) distributes, to sales executives, salesmen, and certain other employees, a booklet titled "May We Quote You?" This booklet contains suggestions for working with newsmen and commentators.

Sales executives and salesmen, in their travels, often come across human-interest stories reflecting creditably upon the company and its service to society. The public relations department might be able to use these stories to advantage if the material is made known to it. If the public relations department cannot use your story, it is quite probable the advertising department could fit it in somewhere.

Coordination with Advertising

Maynard O. Edwards, advertising manager for the Norfolk & Western Railway, speaking before the Eastern Industrial Advertisers, noted that "In a surprising number of companies there is no common understanding among sales, advertising, and general-management executives of the function of advertising. Advertising is seldom a solo performance; it's the result of a team effort. The lack of informational input from top company management has crippled many well-intended advertising programs."

Clarence E. Eldridge, former vice-president of marketing, General Foods Corporation, and former executive vice-president of marketing, Campbell Soup Company, states: "In many companies the role of the advertising manager has undergone a considerable change in the last 20 to 30 years. Part of this change has come as a result of the widespread adoption of the so-called marketing concept and part for other reasons.

"In earlier years, there were in most companies a sales manager and an advertising manager. Typically, these executives functioned more or less independently of each other, and each reported to the president or general manager. The relative 'status' of the two positions depended largely on the relative importance of the two functions. In fact, it was not unusual to find the two positions combined in a single person with the title of sales and advertising manager, and in such companies the sales managership was usually the more important of the two.

"The 'marketing concept' tended to change all that. Sales and advertising came to be regarded—along with promotion and marketing research—not as separate functions but as parts of a single function which came to be called 'marketing.' "*

In large organizations, the selection and use of an advertising agency is of such prime importance that it involves the most serious consideration of marketing executives and top management. Especially true in the package-goods field, the selection or continued use of a good agency with an appropriate organization to meet a company's marketing requirements can play an important role in the success of its sales efforts. Further, management wishes to be sure that the expenditure of considerable amounts of money in advertising is being channeled efficiently and wisely. Finally, there is the question of establishing the base for agency compensation. In recent years, there has been considerable discussion about the relative merits of several forms of compensating agencies for their services. The traditional practice is the commission paid by the advertising medium. But advertisers have made increasing demands for additional services, such as market research, production of collateral material, package design, etc. Thus, fees, or commission-plus-fees, sometimes with agreed-upon minimum commissions or fees, are coming into more widespread use.

Coordination with Sales Promotion

In some companies, the advertising director is also responsible for sales promotion. In others, the sales-promotion function is important enough to be organized as a separate activity under a sales-promotion manager who reports to the marketing executive.

---

*Clarence E. Eldridge, "The Eldridge Essays"; commissioned by the Association of National Advertisers and republished in *Printers' Ink*, April 1967.

This is especially true when the sales-promotion department's functions, except for media advertising, are all-inclusive; embracing activities such as exhibits, sales meetings, conventions, and field promotions, as well as production of catalogs and house publications.

Relations with advertising agencies are the responsibility of the advertising manager. He is most concerned with guidance and supervision of the agency in producing the themes and content of the advertising in periodicals and through broadcasting media; he is also responsible for involving sales and marketing executives whenever necessary. This is important, because advertising must always be coordinated with product promotion, inventory situations —both at home and in the field—and with corporate policies with which the advertising manager may not always be familiar unless he be a strong, aggressive executive.

Chapter 37

SALES JOB CLASSIFICATIONS

I N the true sense of the word, a salesman is the personal representative of the head of the business and acts for him in customer
relations. In the early days of most business concerns, the president
of the company probably did the selling. The great business of
Swift & Company, for example, had its beginning when Gustavus
Swift bought and butchered calves in Barnstable, Massachusetts,
put them in his "little red wagon" and sold them to the good folks
of Cape Cod. But as the business grew, Swift had to employ others
to help him care for his growing trade. By the time the business
had grown to a point where he moved it to Chicago, Swift had
several men engaged in selling his products. Today there are several
thousand Swift salesmen. To most of the customers these men are
Swift & Company. They are doing, in a more skillful way, what the
founder of the Swift business did in Barnstable those many years
ago—building the Swift business. They represent the Swift management in the company's relations with its customers.

But top Swift people continue to be close to the market. "There
is one development which puts Swift's top management in a selling
role," writes V. G. Lindgren. "Our officers feel the need to keep
in touch with the wants and needs of the trade. Accordingly, they
make personal calls on customers to learn, firsthand, what the company can do to improve its products and services.

"This 'feel of the business pulse' by top management serves to
help the customer and the company. This activity supplements the
efforts of our front-line selling staff in helping build more friends
for Swift."

Kinds of Salesmen

Some sales managers insist that it is not practical to set up job
descriptions or standards because no two sales organizations operate
under the same conditions or have the same objectives.

While it is true salesmen cannot be hedged in with job definitions to the extent production jobs are defined, it is essential to successful sales operations that any program of recruiting, training, and supervising salesmen have its roots in a *clear* understanding between employee and employer as to what the salesman is paid to do. It is not enough that the sales manager should know what he wants his salesmen to do and tell them from time to time. The nature of the job, the knowledge deemed essential, the weight of various duties, etc., should be written out carefully and serve as a basis for the sales personnel program. The program should be, in fact, a blueprint for not only building, but also for activating salesmen and all other personnel in the sales department.

There are at least 15 different kinds of salespeople engaged in distribution in the United States. First in order, beginning at the factory door, are the manufacturer's salesmen who call on the large distributors. There are usually only a few of these salesmen. For example, in marketing automobiles, 10 men representing the home office, stationed in important distributing areas, may be responsible for marketing the entire output of the factory. They contact distributors and arrange for the actual distribution of cars in each district or zone. In smaller organizations this contact work is often done by the head of the business, or by the officers reporting to him. This is especially true when, as in the case of automobiles, the annual output of the factory is contracted for by distributors at the beginning of a "model year." These factory representatives must be capable of negotiating orders involving large amounts of money. They top the list when it comes to compensation; 14 other types of salespeople are as follows:

1. *Brokers' and Distributors' Sales Organizations:* Next in line, when the product is sold through established trade channels for resale to consumers or users, comes the distributor and his selling organization. Not all manufacturers or converters go through distributors. An increasingly large number sell direct to the wholesaler and even to the retailer. A few sell direct to the home. But when a distributor maintains an efficient selling organization it is often advantageous to utilize his services.

In the food field, for example, distributors are called "brokers." They handle exclusive lines in a prescribed territory for a few manufacturers. They call on the wholesalers, institutions, chain stores, and other large-volume buyers and sell at a price which customers in this class would expect to pay the manufacturer if buying direct. Thus the service they render distribution enables a manufacturer to operate without a large sales organization to market his product. The broker or distributor, unlike the wholesaler or jobber who sells thousands of items, many of which are in competition with each other, concentrates on a relatively few *related* lines. Thus his salesmen are in a position to sell several lines with about the same expenditure of time and money as the factory man would have to spend just to sell *one* line. At least that is the theory.

In actual practice, however, depending upon distributors with exclusive franchises to represent the company in a territory leaves much to be desired. The theoretical saving resulting from having one salesman call, where several called before, is offset by the lack of control a manufacturer has over his distribution.

While some manufacturers operating on a mass production basis have found it advantageous to market their products through distributors, there has been a tendency for producers to buy out distributors in order to secure better control of distribution and sales promotional activities. The difficulty of getting independent distributors to train their salesmen properly is another reason why some manufacturers are acquiring financial control of distributing organizations.

2. *Factors and Manufacturers' Agents:* In the early days of the factory system as we know it today, it was customary for producers to give all their attention to manufacturing and procurement, and depend upon others to market their entire output. This procedure still is followed by some manufacturers in Great Britain. In this country there are still textile and paper mills in New England which operate on that basis. It is a hand-me-down from the days of the clipper ships, when great quantities of our manufactures were sold abroad by masters of trading ships, who in turn depended upon factors to finance and furnish them with cargoes. It is an easy way to distribute but seldom the most effective and profitable way. Factors as a rule do little creative selling. A manufacturer depending upon this source of distribution has little or no control over his markets. Should a factor decide to change his source of supply, the manufacturer would be left high and dry without an immediate market.

In an effort to avoid that danger, and at the same time to get some measure of control over sales without diverting working capital to maintaining an expensive sales organization, many companies use manufacturers' agents to market their product at home and abroad. The manufacturers' agent handles the product on an independent contractor basis. The factor, on the other hand, usually operates nationally or even internationally. The contract with the manufacturers' agent may or may not be exclusive. It may or may not restrict his area of operations. Usually it does not. The agent takes on the line, along with other lines and as many as he pleases, employs a sales force, and sells the product wherever he can, but usually to an established clientele which looks to him for certain kinds of merchandise.

Manufacturers' agents are the traditional method of marketing furniture, for example. A manufacturer, let us say, of end tables, would find it costly to sell direct to dealers or even jobbers. But his agent, selling davenports and table lamps as well as tables, is in a position to secure a much larger volume of business for him at a lower selling cost. But again the saving is more theoretical than real, as evidenced by the growing percentage of furniture being sold through "shows" by the manufacturer direct to dealers. The trouble with manufacturers' agents is that they have so many lines to sell, they spread their sales effort too thin. Moreover, a large percentage of their time is spent finding new lines to sell.

Nevertheless, the manufacturers' agent plays an important role in present-day distribution. Some agents operate sizable sales organizations and cover large territories, particularly in sparsely settled areas. But most of them are one-man organizations that confine their sales effort to a circle of customers with whom they enjoy friendly relations. It is most difficult to train and motivate manufacturers' agents and their salesmen. For that reason their function in distribution is to take orders for staple products on a price or friendship basis. They are not very effective when it comes to building volume with modern sales techniques.

3. *Direct-Selling Factory Representatives:* These are salesmen selected, trained, and supervised by a general sales manager at the factory, with or without the help of district and crew supervisors in the field. They may be salaried or commission men, or both. But they are legally employees of the company, subject to company control and discipline, and operating under agreements which require that they devote their entire time to selling the company's products. In this respect they differ from the manufacturers' agent, who is an "independent contractor" *without* company employee status.

These factory representatives may travel out of the home office or out of a branch or they may be resident in their territory. They usually operate on a restricted territory basis. They may sell direct to dealers, to industrial plants and users, to offices and stores in the case of equipment salesmen, or direct to the housewife. They are usually creative salesmen, emphasizing what a product will do for the buyer rather than what it is. For that reason they are highly trained, and as a rule well paid. While salesmen of this type are expensive to employ, and frequently show a selling cost higher than what might otherwise be expected, the large volume of business they produce, as a result of intensive training and supervision, makes using them a most effective way to distribute in a competitive field. It is salesmen of this kind who largely have built our modern mass-production and mass-distribution system.

4. *The Special Representative:* There are situations in sales management which call for the use of a salesman of special experience or ability. It is not always wise nor desirable to have these situations handled by a territorial or general salesman. For example, in selling to the U.S. Government it is common practice to appoint a special representative to handle this business. Selling to the government requires a knowledge of government buying methods not possessed by the average salesman. Moreover the government buys, usually in Washington, for agencies scattered all over the country. To properly follow through on big deals, the special representative may have to go to cities which are within the territorial boundaries of another salesman's area of operations. He therefore requires special status in the organization.

Thus addressing equipment for use by the Weather Bureau Service might be sold in Washington, but the order might depend upon first obtaining requisitions from a number of weather bureaus scattered over the country. It is desirable that one man make these contacts, rather than trusting them to the salesman resident in each territory.

Sometimes company policy considers large buyers, such as Sears, Roebuck & Company, Great Atlantic & Pacific Tea Company, as house accounts. Because of the type of service required they are often handled by a special representative who not only makes a business of knowing their business, but also is free to jump from one company plant to another if the need arises.

5. *The Sales Engineer:* Closely allied with the direct-selling factory representative is the factory representative employed by a manufacturer of a technical product to market it to technical users. These men must not only be good salesmen and capable of negotiating orders running into the thousands of dollars, but they must have a specialized technical or engineering knowledge besides. In the past the tendency was for manufacturers of engineering specialties

and machinery to recruit such salesmen from factory workers or engineering schools. This was on the assumption that to sell the product successfully the man must be an engineer first and a salesman second. Of late there has been a trend toward picking men who were first of all good salesmen, and then giving them a technical training or placing at their disposal the services of a trained engineer to assist them on important deals.

The sales engineer operates largely on his own and does not require, or should not require, the close supervision given general salesmen. He is not as easily controlled through a compensation plan, nor is he easily stimulated by contests and other promotional devices. The typical sales engineer doesn't feel he needs anything more than his technical know-how to make the grade. He is well paid and once established in his job, stays put. The turnover among sales engineers is only a fraction of what it is among other kinds of salesmen.

6. *The Service Salesman:* Like the sales engineer, the service salesman sells a specialty, but instead of selling a product he sells a made-to-order service such as printing, insurance, securities, or even real estate. An understanding of the prospect's needs, plus a considerable amount of technical knowledge, is his distinguishing ability. Unlike the sales engineer he has the problem of making the buyer want something for which no immediate need is felt, as in the case of a salesman selling insurance. Some of the highest paid salesmen in America sell advertising, either for an advertising agency, a publisher or a broadcasting station. This type of selling calls for a high order of intelligence and imagination, plus wide experience and knowledge of the application of the service to the buyer's business.

A different conception of the service salesman is found in the office appliance, household appliance, and related industries. Service men, that is to say, mechanically trained men who are used to service the user's equipment, are often made responsible for the sale of supplies to customers. They receive a small commission on such business. As a rule they are not permitted to sell replacement equipment, which is the job of the regular salesman in the territory, but they work closely with the territorial salesman and are regarded as junior salesmen. Most of them ultimately are promoted to territorial salesmen if they show aptitude for creative selling.

Service salesmen of another kind are found in the shopping lines. They are used to sell "dealer help" advertising and display materials. They carry advertising materials in their cars and help dealers to arrange store and window displays. This is on the theory that dealers value most advertising materials in which they have a cash investment.

7. *The Specialty Salesman:* This term, widely used in sales management, has come to mean any salesman who specializes in selling a product or a service, as contrasted to a salesman who sells a line of products. Thus it is customary to speak of a sales agent for The National Cash Register Company as a specialty salesman, because he devotes his entire thought and effort to creating sales for cash registers. In merchandising, a specialty salesman is considered to be a representative of the factory selling one special line, just as a specialty store has come to mean a store handling a specialty such as women's wear. There was an effort made some years back to call door-to-door canvassers "specialty salesmen"—in fact there is a magazine for such salesmen called *The Specialty Salesman.*

More correctly, however, a specialty salesman is a salesman concentrating on selling a specialty. A good illustration is the packing business where there are car route salesmen who sell practically everything sold through branch houses. Such a salesman will sell meats, soaps, dairy products, lard, and similar products. But, in addition to these car route or general salesmen, Swift & Company, for example, has salesmen attached to each department who sell, exclusively, the products of that department. Thus there are, in addition to general salesmen, specialty salesmen selling soaps, fertilizers, margarine, and many other packing house by-products. These specialty salesmen call on institutions and large buyers of the specialty they sell. For example, soap salesmen get a large volume of business from hotels, which the general salesman would probably never call upon. It is contrary to the policy of large packers to sell meats outside of the established trade.

The specialty salesman, when the term is used in that sense, is important because he is a sort of salesman-at-large for the company, and can develop business outside of the regular channels. By the same token he is usually a better salesman than the general line man. The very fact that he concentrates on selling one product, rather than a hundred or more, in itself assures a greater enthusiasm, a better knowledge of the buyer's problems and a larger measure of promotional salesmanship.

8. *The House-to-House Salesman:* While it is true that every person who sells anything from door to door is broadly classified as a "canvasser," there are a number of hard-hitting sales organizations in this field which have made sales history. Notable among them is

the Fuller Brush Company. It has built up a great national business through controlled door-to-door selling. Such sales operations are closely supervised by district and divisional sales managers. The salesmen are carefully selected, well trained, and work in a restricted sales territory.

9. *The Wholesale Salesman:* These are the traditional American salesmen, once called "drummers." To these men, as much as any other group, must go the credit for the opening up of the West in a distribution sense. They are still one of the most important links in the distribution chain, since they make it possible for the merchant to buy most of his needs in small lots. If, as some persons advocate, the wholesaler were eliminated from the American system of distribution, the only way manufacturers could get the volume of orders needed for mass production would be to employ factory representatives to call on dealers directly. This, of course, would be very costly. A number of manufacturers who experimented with eliminating the wholesaler, learned, to their sorrow, that it did not pay.

10. *The Retail Salesman:* There are two kinds of retail salesmen: the inside or store salesman and the outside salesman. Both are important factors in distribution, since they are the connecting link between the manufacturer and the consumer. Upon their knowledge of the merchandise or product they sell across the counter or in the farmyard depends, more than is generally appreciated, the movement of goods into the hands of the ultimate consumer. If dealers' retail salesmen know how to sell a product, reorders result. If they don't know how to sell it, or are indifferent about selling it, the merchandise will pile up on the top shelves and clog the channels of distribution.

11. *Detail Salesmen or Canvassers:* These salesmen as a rule do not take actual orders but are used to introduce products in a highly competitive territory. They are especially effective in marketing products through professional channels, for example, calling on doctors to bring a product to their attention in the hope the doctor will in turn recommend it to his patients. The patients, in turn, will buy it from their druggist, the druggist will buy it from the wholesaler, and the wholesaler will buy it from the manufacturer who employs the detail man.

Detail salesmen are also used in getting quick distribution for competitive products sold through wholesalers. When a manufacturer introduces such a product the wholesaler will invariably balk at stocking it "until there is a demand." So the manufacturer moves a crew of detail men into the territory. They call on merchants, usually in cooperation with the local newspaper in which advertising for the product is scheduled. The orders thus obtained are cleared through wholesale houses serving the territory, thus inducing them to stock the product. Such a procedure is, of course, costly and for that reason it is usually confined to quick-repeating products, such as coffee, breakfast food, soaps and cleaners, dentifrices, shaving soaps, etc. This type of selling serves as a training operation. Young salesmen who show aptitude are effectively screened out and promoted to better paying sales jobs or brought into the office as administrative assistants. College students frequently take such jobs during their vacations, both as a way of earning tuition money and to gain sales experience.

12. *Store Demonstrators:* These are employed by a manufacturer or a wholesaler to advertise and sell branded products. Orders taken by the demonstrator are filled from the stock of merchandise which the merchant buys in consideration of the manufacturer assigning a demonstrator to the store. It is an effective way to get quick distribution for a new product which sells "on taste."

13. *Route Salesmen:* Some of the great businesses of this country, for example, the Great Atlantic & Pacific Tea Company, have been built by salesmen traveling routes. Basically these salesmen operate stores on wheels. Unlike the door-to-door salesman, who seldom delivers what he sells because of antipeddler ordinances, the route salesman makes his deliveries as he sells. Into this class of salesmen go laundry salesmen, bakery salesmen, towel supply salesmen, milk salesmen, and many others. Lately there has been a trend toward the unionization of such salesmen. There are many thousands of these route salesmen, calling on both homes and stores. As a group they play a very important role in distribution and present a fertile field for sales management. Good route salesmen, who really know their job and work at it, often make two or three times as much money as inside salesmen. A good example of route salesmanship is found in the farm agents used by the Standard Oil Company to market its products in rural territories.

14. *Farmer and Boy Agents:* Last, but by no means least, in distribution come part-time salesmen who sell animal feeds, nursery products, seed, farm machinery, magazine subscriptions and a host of other things to neighbors and town folks. There are many thousands of such salesmen, and their volume of sales would surprise

most people. While they are salesmen by avocation rather than by vocation, nevertheless many of them have built up a considerable following and earn more on their sales work than they do operating a farm. Boy agents are used principally by magazine publishers to obtain subscriptions and distribute their publications as issued. Many a leader of American business today paid his college expenses selling something or other in school. As a result of that experience he found he liked to sell, and later adopted selling as his life career.

On the following pages will be found a detailed job description as might be set forth for a typical salesman in the average sales organization. It may be useful as a guide in preparing job descriptions for your salesmen.

TYPICAL JOB DESCRIPTIONS

TITLE: Salesman

Organizational Relationships

Reports to: Branch Manager

Primary Responsibilities

He is responsible for soliciting orders, selling the company's products assigned to him, and representing the company in accordance with its policies and in the area assigned to him; for maintaining an awareness of local competitive conditions, and for reporting them back promptly to management.

Duties

1. To maintain and increase the sales volume of assigned accounts or territories.

2. To aggressively solicit orders from present and prospective customers for the products assigned to him.

3. To provide useful and practical service to his customers.

4. To aggressively seek new customers, and to formulate and follow plans for such action as directed by the branch manager.

5. To seek new uses and applications for company products with present and prospective customers.

6. To assist present and prospective customers in adopting company products to their own requirements and specifications.

7. To aggressively carry out merchandising programs as directed.

8. To authorize "return" goods in accordance with company policy.

9. To adjust customer complaints in accordance with company policy, and to advise management promptly of any situations beyond his scope of authority.

10. To comply with all company policies, instructions, and directives for the fulfillment of company objectives and for maximum profitable sales.

11. To be alert to competitive products and merchandising practices, and to keep management informed concerning them.

12. To prepare sales audits and analyses of present and prospective customers in accordance with company procedures and instructions.

13. To assist in developing sales forecasts, territory potentials, workload analyses, call programs, and routes.

14. To maintain up-to-date customer record books and other records in accordance with company instructions.

15. To prepare and submit call and expense reports as required.

16. To submit any special reports regarding the operation of the territory, acceptance of products, or competitive conditions as may be requested.

17. To recommend the addition of new products and the modification or deletion of present products to the line as appropriate.

18. To attend and participate in sales meetings, training programs, conventions, and trade shows as directed.

19. To maintain an awareness of likely candidates for the sales force and to call any such to the attention of the branch manager.

20. To assist in the field training of any salesman as requested.

21. To cooperate with all personnel in the branch, department, division and other divisions on the execution of company programs.

22. To assume the obligations of good citizenship and to participate in worthwhile community activities as a public relations asset to the company.

DUTIES OF SALES EXECUTIVES

The duties of a sales manager very naturally depend on the type of organization, the product it sells, the methods of distribution used, and, to a greater extent than may be realized, upon the sales manager's limitations. An analysis of salaries paid sales managers shows the highest compensation is in the specialty field—that is to say, in selling office appliances, insurance, advertising, real estate, automobiles, etc. In those fields sales management has reached the highest state of efficiency, and the duties of the sales executive encompass a wide range of responsibility. In general, he is charged with formulating sales policies, recruiting, training, and supervising the company's entire selling force.

An important responsibility of the general sales manager in some companies is known as "future demands." This has to do not only with the improvement of the products the company makes, but also the development of new ways of selling and using those products. Specifically, these duties, as set forth by one company in its job description, are as follows:

Study new lines of business for the purpose of broadening our field. Devise systems for new or unusual lines of business. Suggest new improvements in present product. Introduce new improvements in present product. Introduce and promote sale of new type of machines. Apply present machines to unusual lines. Suggestion contests for purpose of securing suggestions for improvement of product.

In specialty sales operations, more than in the case of marketing staples through dealers, it is customary for the sales manager to actually devise sales plans and campaigns. Sometimes he has an assistant to do this, but in even the largest organizations that duty is considered so essential to sales production that it is assumed by the sales manager himself, although an assistant may follow through.

Indeed, only the most general sort of job description can hope to cover even a fraction of the duties and responsibilities of the many various types of sales manager. However, the following will serve as a "thought-starter" for drawing up a job specification.

TITLE: Sales Manager

Organizational Relationships

Reports to: Vice-President, Marketing

Supervises: District Sales Manager
Sales Training Manager
Sales Service Manager
Sales Statistics Clerk

Primary Responsibilities

He is responsible for all field sales activities; for the maintenance of an adequate field sales organization; for obtaining maximum sales volume; for hiring of all sales and other personnel in his department, utilizing the facilities of the company's general employment department; for the adequate training and retraining of sales personnel; for sales service and engineering functions; for the flowback of industry and marketing data from customers and on competitive conditions in the field; for maintaining an awareness for and acquaintanceship with those factors that influence sales opportunities and to plan astutely for their realization; for providing adequate forward stocks to assure proper sales and service.

Duties

1. To build, maintain, and direct an efficient, well-trained and effective field sales organization.

2. To develop and recommend to the vice-president, marketing, for his approval, policies and programs relating to:
   a. Size and type of sales organization
   b. Product lines
   c. Distribution channels
   d. Prices
   e. Sales objectives by product and geographical area
   f. Compensation levels
   g. Personnel development and advancements
   h. Sales department budgets
   i. Advertising and sales promotion activities
   j. New product development and improvement of present products
   k. Credit policies
   l. Warehouse and deliveries

3. To establish and execute sales programs in accordance with approved policies.

4. To assign sales objectives to district, branch, and other sales territories; periodically to evaluate performance in their attainment; and to take necessary steps to bring results in line with objectives.

5. To organize, recommend to the proper executives, and administer procedures affecting sales, prices, terms, discounts, allowances on returned goods, sales service and field engineering services.

6. To plan and conduct periodic sales meetings for the purpose of educating, training, and stimulating the sales organization.

7. To supervise the formation and maintenance of an adequate recruitment, hiring, training, and development program for sales personnel.

8. To approve travel and selling expenses of district and other departmental managers, to review related monthly reports, and to institute remedial action when expense policies are violated.

9. To keep management informed of significant sales developments affecting the company.

10. To prepare and recommend selling cost and expense budgets and to strive to operate within approved budgets.

11. To recommend the addition of new products to the line or the modification or elimination of existing items.

12. To achieve adequate profit margins and sales volumes as required to maintain profitable operations.

13. To assist in the preparation of advertising and promotion programs, and to supervise the execution of such programs by sales personnel.

14. To supervise the preparation and interpretation of reports as to sales and markets, and the comparison of sales forecasts with actual sales and sales quotas.

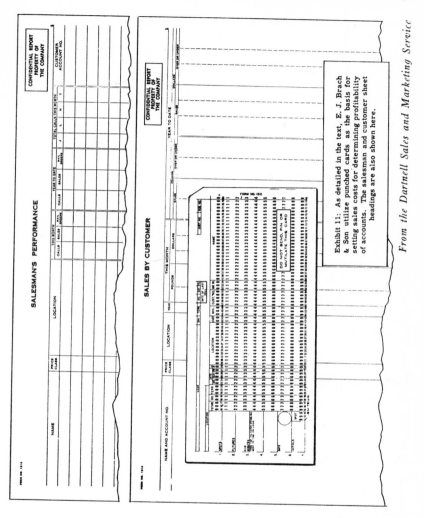

Exhibit 11: As detailed in the text, E. J. Brach & Son utilize punched cards as the basis for setting sales costs for determining profitability of accounts. The salesman and customer sheet headings are also shown here.

From the Dartnell Sales and Marketing Service

15. To correspond with other company personnel and customers as required.

16. To travel in the field, calling on present and prospective customers, consulting and supervising district managers, branch managers, and salesmen as the needs require. Calls on present and prospective customers are to be made in conjunction with the proper field representatives and for the purpose of assisting them by the field sales manager's executive prestige, and in no way should the effectiveness of the company's local representative be impaired.

17. To attend such industry conventions and to participate in industry activities as the vice-president, marketing, may direct.

18. To participate in and contribute to such committee activities as the vice-president, marketing, may direct.

19. To handle all sales distribution problems as assigned by the vice-president, marketing, and to be his assistant and advisor in respect to sales coverage.

20. To interpret company policy in connection with questions arising in the field, and to consult with district managers on matters beyond their authority and experience.

21. To motivate field salesmen through the district managers and branch managers so that they will attain maximum sales volume and product balance.

22. To inspect particularly the operations of district managers, district officers, branch managers, branch offices, and other field facilities to see that policies and instructions are properly executed and customers are properly served, and to take remedial action when required.

23. To cooperate with all executives and other managers in the company, and to require cooperation of all sales, sales training, and sales service personnel with other personnel in the company.

24. To assume the obligations of good citizenship and to participate in worthwhile community and national activities as may be required for sound public relations for the company.

Other jobs closely related to the sales manager's may be outlined as follows:

TITLE: Merchandising Manager

Organizational Relationships

Reports to: Vice-President, Marketing

Supervises: Product Managers

Primary Responsibilities

He is responsible for the development of merchandising programs; for furnishing functional guidance to the field sales organization on all matters pertaining to the merchandising and sale of company products; for maintaining awareness of and for recommendations concerning competitive quality, customer utility, price position, and sales volume of company products; for keeping informed on competitors' products, determining their strong and weak points, and observing customer acceptance of company products relative to competition; for acting as liaison between sales, research, development engineering, and manufacturing departments relative to the design, salability, and utility of company products; for the study of pricing data and pricing policies, price lists, discounts, and gross margins in relation to competition and company needs; and for recommending changes in policy and practice, when required. He has no line authority over the field sales organization or other departments; his is a functional staff department.

Duties

The duties of the merchandising manager may be summarized briefly as follows:

1. To advise and assist the vice-president, marketing, in the development of policies and procedures pertaining to merchandising, pricing, advertising and promotion, packaging, and new product development.

2. To supervise the development of necessary sales tools, including literature or manuals, as may be required by the field force to sell the company's products.

3. To assist the sales training director in the development of training programs for the field sales personnel.

4. To work, and to cause the product managers to work, periodically with the field sales organization and customer personnel, through field calls, correspondence, or telephone, on current trends in industry, styling and customer acceptance. Field work should take at least 20 percent of his time.

5. To recommend, on the advice of the product managers, the addition of new products to the line or the modification or elimination of existing products or lines.

6. To supervise the preparation of and to recommend sales volume budgets for company products.

7. To supervise the product managers in their attention to sales volume, product acceptance, quality and utility of company products, and the competitive situation for these products in the markets.

8. To supervise the accumulation of information concerning competitive products, features, specifications, prices, discounts, terms, merchandising policies and programs, distribution channels and outlets, and customer acceptance; to maintain or direct the maintenance of displays of competitive products for ready comparison and company products.

9. To supervise the review of reports from salesmen regarding product complaints and to take appropriate action.

10. To consult, and to cause the product managers to consult, with factory personnel and engineers on company products.

11. To attend industry conventions and marketing meetings as deemed advisable.

12. To review, and to cause the product managers to review, publications containing industry and trade news.

13. To review pertinent costs of sales and other reports and budgets related to company products.

14. To supervise the preparation of, and give assistance in, the execution of merchandising plans to stimulate sales.

15. To assist in establishing prices for each product line, using price structure forms and percentage "mark-ons" as approved by company policy. Prices and terms are approved by the vice-president, marketing, and the treasurer, and copies are distributed to all principal executives. Once a price structure has been approved by management and the price published, changes may not be made without the formal approval of management.

16. To review sales quotas in cooperation with the vice-president, marketing, field sales managers, and market research managers.

17. To assist in the preparation of bids and proposals.

18. To supervise and direct the activities of all personnel in his department.

19. To supervise the preparation of any regular or special reports that may be requested of his department from the vice-president, marketing.

20. To recommend salary changes, promotions, demotions, or release of personnel under his control.

21. To cooperate with all personnel in the marketing and other divisions, and to cause the personnel of his department to cooperate with all other company personnel.

22. To assume the obligations of good citizenship and to participate in worthwhile community and national activities as may be required for sound public relations for the company.

TITLE: Customer Service Manager

Organizational Relationships

Reports to: Vice-President, Marketing

Supervises: Sales Correspondents
  Order Clerks
  Expediting Clerks
  Quotation Clerks

Primary Responsibilities

He is responsible for handling all correspondence with customers and salesmen dealing with inquiries and quotations, with routing and interpretation of regular and special orders, specifications, prices, shipping dates and other matters of similar nature. He is also responsible for the maintenance of all records, files, preparation of reports that pertain to the department. He has no line authority over the field sales organization or other departments; his is a functional staff department.

Duties

The duties of the customer service manager may be summarized briefly as follows:

1. To supervise the activities of the customer service department.

2. To communicate with company customers and personnel, and others in regard to orders, prices, products, deliveries and other matters of similar nature as required.

3. To supervise and assist in expediting deliveries and in satisfying complaints as required for critical orders or special customer problems.

4. To act as liaison between customers and production on questions concerning orders placed, shipments, production schedules and inventories.

5. To direct the maintaining of records and the preparation of reports as required.

6. To assist in the preparation of production requirements based on sales and other pertinent data.

7. To review reports on shipments, inventories and production and to assist in sales planning in collaboration with the vice-president, marketing, market research manager, merchandising manager, field sales manager, and others designated.

8. To review the methods currently in use in the customer service department, and to make changes, improvements, and revisions as deemed advisable.

9. To delegate duties and work assignments to others in his department, to maintain and train adequate personnel to perform the functions of his department, and to assure good service and dispatch in handling customers' orders.

10. To cooperate with others in preparing the operating budget for his department, and to operate the department within the approved budget program.

11. To cooperate closely with product managers, sales managers, and others, and to handle special assignments as required to assure satisfactory order handling and deliveries.

12. To assume the obligations of good citizenship and to participate in worthwhile community and national activities as may be required for sound public relations for the company.

TITLE: District Manager

Organizational Relationships

Reports to: Field Sales Manager

Supervises: Branch Managers

Primary Responsibilities

He is the direct representative of management in the field sales organization.

Duties

The duties of a district manager may be summarized thus:

1. To direct and supervise the branch managers assigned to his district.

2. To see that all authorized policies, programs, and instructions issued from the general office are put into effect and carried out in all branches.

3. To review branch managers' reports, and to counsel, assist, and direct them as required.

4. To study market analysis figures furnished by the general office, and from them assist the branch managers in preparing sales coverage plans.

5. To review reports on sales activities and compare them with planned activities to assure close adherence to, improvements of, and maximal achievement of results.

6. To aid branch managers in controlling expenses, preparing budgets, call schedules, territory assignments and coverage, and in planning their work.

7. To aid branch managers in the planning of new distributor campaigns, and in the execution of such plans.

8. To make frequent and regular trips to the branches for inspection and counseling.

9. To accompany branch managers and salesmen when necessary in performing any of their duties, such as holding important sales meetings, making important distributor calls, and interpreting major policy decisions within his scope of authority. In all contacts with distributors, it is very important that a district manager build the prestige and recognition of the branch manager and salesmen as the company's sales representatives in their territories.

10. To handle all necessary district sales correspondence.

11. To assist in the hiring of new sales personnel as may be requested by the field sales manager's office.

12. To plan and hold regularly scheduled district and branch conferences within the policy of the company.

13. To attend regularly scheduled district managers' conferences as called by the field sales manager, and to attend industry trade shows and conferences as directed by the field sales manager.

14. To perform required and necessary company entertainment duties with company distributors and prospective distributors.

15. To control expenses and costs within the district, approve expense reports of branch managers, and aid in the building of operating budgets and operating within them.

16. To assist branch managers in determining distributor and sales territory quotas, and in programming related sales effort.

17. To counsel with branch managers and recommend to the field sales manager compensation changes for branch personnel.

18. To fill out and mail promptly and completely all required reports.

19. To maintain awareness for and keep the general office advised of all competitive distribution trends, policies, new products, sales campaigns, prices, discounts, profit structures and "special deals" as these come to his attention.

20. To train and develop branch managers as possible candidates for the position of district manager.

21. To cooperate with all company executives and department heads for the maximum achievement of sales, profits, and satisfied customers.

22. To assume the obligations of good citizenship and to participate in worthwhile community activities as a public relations asset to the company.

TITLE: Branch Manager

Organizational Relationships

Reports to: District Manager

Supervises: Salesmen

Office and Warehouse Personnel

Primary Responsibilities

He is directly responsible for maintenance and development of sales of company products in the areas assigned to him; for the development and maintenance of an effective, well-trained and efficient sales force to aggressively and profitably cover the areas assigned to them; for local interpretation of and compliance with company policy in the operation of the branch and representation of the company to present and prospective customers.

Duties

The duties of a branch manager are summarized as follows:

1. To recruit and select capable branch salesmen. Hiring and severance of salesmen shall be on authority and approval of the district manager and field sales manager.

2. To train branch salesmen in the sale of company products, policies, and procedures of the company, following appropriate sales methods and techniques found to be in good practice; and as developed and outlined by the sales training manager.

3. To maintain an adequate sales force needed to cover the branch areas, to anticipate replacement needs sufficiently in advance so as to have a suitable candidate available for consideration or hire, and to maintain current files of prospective candidates for sales positions. A branch manager may from time to time be requested to suggest the names of possible candidates for hire and assignment to other branches.

4. To assign salesmen to territories, predetermined and balanced for sales opportunities, sales coverage demands within available time, and in line with the salesmen's knowledge and skills.

5. To recommend salary, position, and territory revisions.

6. To see that all company policies, programs, and instructions are put into effect and carried out in the branch assigned to him.

7. To review all salesmen's reports and schedules, and to counsel, advise, assist, and direct the salesmen in their activities.

8. To maintain an awareness of local market and competition conditions, of user preferences and desires, of industry trends, and to transmit such information promptly, with his recommendations, to management.

9. To periodically analyze, jointly with the salesmen, sales objectives for both present and prospective customers, sales and service activity demands, and programs for effective sales coverage.

10. To aid the salesmen in arranging for, planning, and conducting instructive and stimulating meetings, as required, with customer personnel.

11. To make frequent and regular field trips with the salesmen for the purpose of inspecting activities, counseling with them, and generally supervising them.

12. To make field calls with the salesmen when advisable and thus to assist them by his managerial prestige. He is rarely to make calls by himself on customers, as this tends to depreciate the authority and usefulness of the salesmen in the customers' eyes.

13. To review expense reports of the salesman and to take such steps as are advisable for controlling expenses within company policies.

14. To maintain and review records and reports of calls on customers and sales results obtained.

15. To handle correspondence with present and prospective customers, and with company personnel as needful.

16. To supervise the activities of the branch office personnel and the operations of the branch warehouse.

17. To plan and hold regularly scheduled sales meetings.

18. To attend regularly scheduled branch managers' meetings as called by management.

19. To attend such conventions and trade meetings as may be designated by management.

20. To maintain, completely and carefully, all records requested by management, and to fill out and mail promptly all reports requested.

21. To maintain an awareness for promotability of salesmen to more responsible territories or positions in the branch or in the company as a whole, and to assist in the development of those men for such advancement.

22. To cooperate with all company executives, department heads, and other personnel as may be required to assure increased sales volume and satisfied customers.

23. To assume the obligations of good citizenship and to participate in worthwhile community activities as a public relations asset to the company.

TITLE: Market Research Manager

Organizational Relationships

Reports to Vice-President, Marketing

Supervises: Clerical and Statistical Staff

Primary Responsibilities

He is responsible for the execution of economic studies that pertain to company's welfare and growth; for the interpretation of performance data as needed by management in establishing policies, directing marketing operations, and in correlating the planning of company activities; for maintaining data files and records available for company executive and management personnel; for conducting studies in cooperation with the merchandising manager, the product managers, and field sales organization personnel. He has no line authority over the field sales organization or other department; his is strictly a functional staff department.

Duties

His duties may be summarized briefly as follows:

1. To operate the market research department economically and effectively.
2. To consult with other company executives and personnel on performance, marketing, and sales problems.
3. To consult with marketing division personnel on methods best suited for use in dealing with specific statistical and research problems.
4. To study trade and government publications for indication of economic and industry trends and needs.
5. To direct correlation and other studies of company sales and production with available industry and economic data for the purpose of measuring company results, appraising foreseeable probabilities, and determining the company's position and progress.
6. To cooperate with the controller in preparing operating budgets.
7. To participate in industry and trade-association activities and studies on marketing and sales problems.
8. To receive sales, performance, and related reports, and to review and summarize them as required.
9. To prepare reports on sales, performance, products, markets, and economic conditions as requested.
10. To keep up-to-date files for reference as needed.
11. To assist in figuring commissions and bonuses as required.
12. To delegate work to other personnel as required and to supervise and direct their performance.

13. To cooperate with executives and departments as required to assure full use of available data, and to assist them in their problems of supervision, direction, and decision.

14. To assume the obligations of good citizenship and to participate in worthwhile community and national activities as may be required for sound public relations for the company.

TITLE: Vice-President, Marketing

Organizational Relationships

Reports to: President

Supervises: Field Sales Manager
Merchandising Manager
Customer Service Manager
Market Research Manager
Advertising and Sales Promotion Manager

Primary Responsibilities

He is responsible for the general direction of short-range and long-range planning relating to product development and marketing policies; for providing general consultation and advice on all aspects of the company's marketing program; and for the compilation and maintenance of current and complete information on the company's marketing activities and on industry development. He is responsible for the general direction of distribution of the company's products in such a manner as to satisfy customer requirements; for building customer goodwill; for returning the required profit margins, and for providing sufficient volume to permit profitable use of the company's production facilities. His authority extends throughout the entire marketing division in all its varied activities, as required to fulfill the responsibilities assigned to him by the president of the company.

Duties

The duties of the vice-president, marketing, may be summarized briefly as follows:

1. To exercise general supervision over all marketing activities of the company.

2. To supervise the building and maintenance of an aggressive, well-trained, adequately compensated, and well-integrated organization.

3. To maintain equitable compensation and personnel development schedules which will attract and hold competent personnel.

4. To maintain good morale and develop loyalty in the personnel of the marketing organization.

5. To supervise the development of plans for the solicitation of orders and distribution of company products to all worthwhile present and prospective customers.

6. To control selling costs and expenses, approve budgets of sales costs and expenses, and to strive to operate within approved budgets.

7. To approve traveling and selling expenses for all executives and managers in the marketing division, to review related monthly reports, and to institute remedial action when expense policies are violated.

8. To correspond with company personnel, and present and prospective customers, when required.

9. To guide personnel of his division in building goodwill with present and prospective customers.

10. To generally supervise the search for and the analysis of markets for company products.

11. To attain adequate profit margins and sales volumes as required to maintain profitable operations and to enhance the company's position and future growth in the industry.

12. To participate in marketing, distributor, and industry conferences and meetings as necessary to aid in product distribution.

13. To supervise the obtaining of data as to the sales plans, selling effort, markets, products, and prices of competitors to the extent that such data will be beneficial in determining satisfactory marketing policies, developing marketing plans and assisting in programming manufacturing for the company.

14. To give general supervision and approval in the proper development and execution of advertising and sales-promotion plans.

15. To serve on and constructively participate in such committee activities as may be assigned by the president of the company.

16. To supervise the preparation and interpretation of reports as to sales and markets, comparison of sales forecasts with actual sales, and the establishment of sales quotas, as may be needed for the guidance and use of company executives and sales-division personnel.

17. To participate in the review and approval of all requests for research and development projects concerned with new products or new models of old products, as they relate to development in the industry and to customer needs and usage.

18. To anticipate foreseeable marketing conditions and participate in the formation of company plans for future expansion or entrenchment programs.

19. To handle all marketing and distribution problems as assigned by the president and to be the president's advisor with respect to marketing management.

20. To cooperate with all other executives of the company and to require the cooperation of all marketing division personnel with other personnel throughout the company.

21. To assume the obligations of good citizenship and to participate in worthwhile community and national activities as may be required for sound public relations for the company.

Succession

Every sales manager should train a successor. He owes this not alone to his company, but to himself. In an untold number of instances, sales managers who had the qualifications for general executive responsibility have not been advanced to such positions because there was no one available to take over the sales department. The same thing applies, of course, to all sales executive positions. It is the responsibility of the sales head of the business to make sure that his entire second line is secure. There should not only be a good man in each position, but he should have a younger man coming along, qualified and trained to take over his job should the necessity arise. This policy makes for a flexibility of management highly desirable in sales administration. A well-organized sales department, like a well-organized military unit, should be so officered that there is always somebody "coming along" to replace the casualties.

The importance of building a strong second line of officer material has caused larger organizations to institute executive rating systems. These serve to spot men of outstanding leadership ability, and to evaluate them in terms of the proper sales jobs in the organization.

A sales executive who permits his subordinates to flood him with routine decisions is a weak executive; so, too, is one who must approve and sign all reports, letters, and bulletins. A strong executive is one who receives only condensed, summarized, and comparative reports that cover all the elements entering into his management. These summaries should have previously been carefully gone over by an assistant who notes on them all deviations from planned performance, good and bad.

Chapter 38

EQUIPPING THE
SALES DEPARTMENT

THE thoroughness and efficiency with which a sales department discharges its several functions will vary in accordance with its use of modern equipment. Electronic accounting machines, photocopiers, and similar units have greatly speeded up and simplified day-by-day office routines. Electronic data processing is performing miracles of achievement in such marketing areas as warehousing, inventories, and order processing.

In addition, there are many opportunities for saving thousands of dollars through the installation of modern equipment in the sales department for handling names, keeping sales records, and for special operations.

Tabulating and Recording Machines

Many sales executives are not aware of how inexpensively detailed sales statistics may be obtained with the so-called "punched card" system. By simply punching a card for every order received, at the time it is received, these cards may be run through the machine at the close of the day to give the sales manager a detailed report on the day's sales, by salesmen, by products, by territorial divisions, as well as by dollar totals. The same cards tell, at the end of the month, exactly what each salesman has sold. The same record is used by the accounting department to keep the perpetual inventory and to compute the salesmen's commissions. The machines are usually leased by the manufacturer at a surprisingly nominal cost. In some of the larger cities there are establishments which render tabulating service at a fixed fee for the convenience of companies too small to put in their own equipment. Under this system you punch your own cards.

Another type of punched card, widely used in sales analysis, is known as the Keysort system. Pins are used to "take off" desired information from the cards without the need of running them through a sorting machine.

Electronic Machines

Following is a listing by *Business Forms Reporter* of sales-accounting machines in use today in businesses not ready for full-scale computers and print-out equipment. Some of these modern electronic billing and accounting machines produce tapes or cards which may be used as input for computers.

The Friden 5010 Computyper: This electronic billing/accounting machine is a programmed unit that prints dates and invoice numbers; multiplies by fractions, units, hundredths or thousandths; performs horizontal or vertical addition, subtraction or multiplication; prints symbols for operator entry control; computes sales tax or discounts, prints amounts, adjusts extension total; computes and prints subtotals and invoice totals; accumulates fractions and converts to decimals.

Friden Computyper/Model CTP: This machine consists of two basic components, a Flexowriter Programatic writing machine and a console unit containing both automatic programming and computing facilities. The equipment is particularly suited for invoicing and purchase-order operations.

Burroughs E4000: The Burroughs E4000 electronic accounting system has two basic units: an operator's console with alphanumeric keyboard and printer, and an electronic processor with magnetic-core memory.

Burroughs E1400: The Burroughs E1400 electronic computing/accounting machine automatically positions each form for printing and ejects it when posting is completed. The carriage will accommodate two forms side by side plus a continuous journal. Ledgers with one magnetic stripe can be processed by the E1400, permitting the use of two languages, electronic pulses for the machine, and actual visible printing for the operator.

NCR 400: The newest NCR system combines punched-tape programming, magnetic-striped ledger records and a magnetic-disc memory. Various accounting jobs are programmed on loops of punch tape. Programmed instructions may be extensive and unlimited in number.

NRC 395: Cut forms, continuous forms, punched cards, and punched tape are output from this system, depending on the optional devices used. Input may be by keyboard entry or by punched cards. The unit electronically summarizes the data, processes related accounting records, and prints summary information on hard copy.

NCR Compu-tronic 35: This computing/accounting machine processes most data under program control to reduce the need for operator decisions. A visible front-feed carriage accepts several forms simultaneously and permits production of related records at one operation. Optional features include an automatic card reader and a tape punch.

NCR 33: Changeable program bars serve as a mechanical memory for this unit. Bars are set up to meet changing requirements of various accounting operations. They attach to the front of the machine above the keyboard and directly in front of the forms, making them easy to install and providing a constant visual guide to the operator. The carriage accommodates forms up to 26 inches wide.

Litton EBS/1210: Because the printing unit of the EBS/1210 is a standard Model 33 Teletype, remote communications can be realized in conjunction with the regular printing operation. Continuous pin-feed form invoices are used, and seven good copies can be produced.

Olivetti Underwood Mercator 5100: The Mercator 5100 permits automatic posting directly from the invoice or credit memo without reentry of any figures. Balances are electronically verified for accuracy. The machine does not print on the statement and ledger until the balance is correctly entered. Column selection is automatic, with invoices posted as debits and credit memos posted as credits.

Olivetti Underwood Audit Series 1500: The Audit 1500 is advertised as the complete bookkeeping machine that is programmed to think. It verifies the accuracy of balance pickups, computes and prints new balances, selects the debit or credit posting column, dates all posting documents, spaces up after each line, secures forms in place and releases them when completed, senses for typing areas and stores control totals.

IBM 6400: Probably among the best-known machines using magnetic striped ledgers is the IBM 6400. The primary printer has a 22-inch writing line and 220 print positions at 1/10 inch each. Up to 10 legible copies are claimed. Printing can be controlled through the alphanumeric keyboard or through programming. Three different forms may be printed during the same operation. The magnetic ledger processing unit, in a separate cabinet, reads, modifies and re-records up to 252 characters of alphanumeric information stored on the ledger card's magnetic stripe.

Automatic Electric Typewriters

Any company employing salesmen should have at least one electric typewriter and a battery of four of these efficient machines can usually be made to pay handsome dividends. There are now several types of automatic electric typewriters on the market based on the player piano principle, operating through a perforated paper control ribbon. Another type is mechanically operated.

Addressing Equipment

One of the most important factors in business building is an effective mailing list, properly classified and systematically used. Practically all addressing equipment now contemplates maintaining the list with individual plates for each name, these plates or stencils being filed card-index fashion.

There are two general styles of equipment in use: (1) Those which depend upon a paper stencil on which the name is cut with a typewriter, and (2) equipment using embossed metal plates. Both systems have their advantages and disadvantages. The lower first cost of the paper-stencil equipment is usually offset by the greater dependability and durability of the embossed type of metal plate. Where the list is very large, or is of a temporary nature, the paper stencil has decided advantages. Some of the largest mail-order lists are on paper-stencil address cards because of the lower initial cost and the compactness of this system.

For the average-sized mailing list the three-piece card index address plate is recommended. By the use of tabs, lists may be centralized and any desired group of names automatically selected. Machines for printing these name plates are available in a variety of models. The needs of the average-sized department will be well served by one of the hand-fed models with an automatic selecting attachment. When the list is being used continuously it is a good investment to install an automatically fed addressing machine.

The advent of data processing as a means of maintaining mailing lists has greatly increased the potential and use of labeling, addressing, and mailing equipment. To accept the output from high-speed computers, new machines now make it possible for computers to develop, correct, and maintain mailing lists at an incredible fraction of the time formerly required. One example of a computer-fed addressing and labeling machine is the Cheshire Model 514. The Model 10-20 labels or addresses up to 30,000 pieces per hour!

Typical Mail Case Histories

Merrill-Lynch, Pierce, Fenner & Smith Inc., the world's largest brokerage house, mails nine million pieces of proxy material each year. This includes annual reports, notices, and announcements concerning annual meetings of such corporations as U.S. Steel, AT&T, and others. Customer names and addresses at one time were maintained on metal plates. Plate selection for proxy mailings was done by hand, using a computer-printed list as a guide. After each plate was selected, the workers would hand-stencil the envelope and return the plate to the file. Working at top speed, each worker was able to address only 150 envelopes an hour. This was a costly and extremely slow operation.

Customer names and addresses are now stored on magnetic tape and processed by an IBM 7074 computer. Specific mailing lists, as for proxy mailings, are computer-selected, then "printed-out" by an IBM 1403 printer on continuous four-address-wide forms. A Cheshire labeling machine automatically cuts and applies these preaddressed forms as labels to the envelopes at speeds up to 12,000 per hour. Costly hand-stenciling has been completely eliminated.

Sunset House, Los Angeles, California, is one of the largest direct mail users in the country. Each year it mails well over 30 million Sunset House catalogs, distributed in nine different editions, to its mail-order customers and prospects. The entire 3½-million mailing list was converted from metal plates to magnetic tape and is now maintained by a data-processing service bureau. Under the new system, a shipping label is typed at Sunset House on Friden Flexowriters as each customer order is received. This typing operation simultaneously produces a punched paper tape containing the customer name, address, and order data, which is then sent to the service bureau. This paper tape "in-put" is converted to magnetic tape and then match-merged with the Sunset House master customer name file on magnetic tape.

Postage-Metering Machines

Any company handling upward of 50,000 pieces of mail a month should find it profitable to install a stamping and sealing machine—preferably of the metering type. This equipment may be obtained in a variety of low-price models. In addition to the actual saving of time, the use of this equipment guards against the theft of stamps, does away with the 5 o'clock rush in getting the mail out and saves room in the mailing department.

Maps

No well-ordered sales department is complete without up-to-date maps. The most favored are washable maps, mounted on swinging display fixtures. These may be installed in special electrically-lighted cases and arranged so that they may be locked when not in use. While this type of map has become popular, there are many sales managers who prefer the cabinet type of map equipment which provides a separate drawer for every state and is arranged for tacking. Territory lines are indicated on these maps by silk threads strung around tacks. Customers and prospects are indicated by colored tacks, using a different color for each, and various tack signals are used to indicate the volume of business and the degree of sales expectancy in each territory.

Visible Records

It may also be possible to effect a substantial reduction in the cost of record keeping by a greater use of visible index records, in place of the "blind" records generally used in sales departments. Visible systems are especially well suited for customers' control records, a variety of stock forms for this purpose being available. With the visible card record, signal tabs may be used on the lower margin of the card to indicate followup dates, active and passive accounts, and other essential data needed in getting a full quota of business from every account.

Another excellent use for visible indexing is at the order desk, where it permits speedy pricing of orders. The catalog number, the

STOCK RECORD

Model No.

Description

DATE	ORDERED	ALLOC.	ORDER NUMBER	DIST.	SHIPPED			ORDER BAL	COMM. BALANCE	MISC. INV.		REMARKS
					DATE	QTY.	REL. NO.			QTY.	LOC.	

Record card used by one sales department shows the movement and inventory of each product in the company line.

name of the item or product, and the price are carried on the visible section of the card under a transparent protector, different color cards being used to indicate if the item is carried in stock, if it must be ordered from an outside supplier, or if it must be made specially. This information enables the order clerk to route the order to the purchasing department, the production department, or the stock room as the case may be. By using one of the numerous signal devices on the tongue of the card it is possible to "flag" items which must be back-ordered, so that the customer may be so advised in acknowledging the order.

Where prospects are followed up intensively by the home office while the salesman is working on them, sales managers find it profitable to prepare salesmen's reports on new prospects in such a manner that they can be slipped into cellophane carriers in a visible file with the name of the prospect projecting below the card above.

The Microform

The microform, or fiche, is fast becoming a major tool of business in its struggle to cope with the paperwork explosion. Across the country, corporations and other users are compressing scores of cubic feet of conventional documents into microforms that barely fill a shoe box. They are finding it a lot easier to store, update, and retrieve information from microforms than from roll microfilm, states the *Wall Street Journal* in a comprehensive report summarizing the status of the industry and its great potential.

Fiche is the wave of the future in office paperwork simplification, says James Hughes, editor of *Systems,* a magazine dealing with time and space saving in business procedures.

Such a development hinges on the perfection of a low-priced device to "blow up" the microform images so they could be read. Current prices of such "readers" generally range between $100 and $400. "It won't be long, once mass production of microforms takes hold in the popular publishing field, before they could be much less expensive," says Alex Baptie, president of the National Microfilm Association.

At present, the business world is the biggest customer for fiche. Users send their paperwork or roll microfilm to a specialist concern for reduction and get back microforms ready for the reader.

Users of microfiche report big savings in office space and in time taken to retrieve information. National Acme Co., a Cleveland-based machine-tool maker, has spent $35,000 putting 8,000 of its

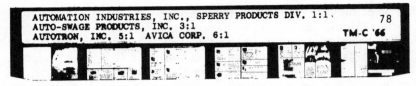

AUTOMATION INDUSTRIES, INC., SPERRY PRODUCTS DIV. 1:1.	78
AUTO-SWAGE PRODUCTS, INC. 3:1	
AUTOTRON, INC. 5:1 AVICA CORP. 6:1	TM-C '66

HERE IS A MICROFICHE — THE "HEART" OF THE THOMAS MICRO-CATALOGS SYSTEM

The 4 x 6" translucent plastic card within this envelope is the key to the Thomas Micro-Catalogs system.

As you can see, each card is able to contain up to six horizontal rows of up to 12 images per row. Each image was originally a full-sized catalog page which has been photographically reduced to what you see here. Thus, up to 72 pages of cataloging can be "stored" on a single card.

An entire file of cards like this are arranged alphabetically by manufacturer's name (see file box at left). All told, the TM-C system has upwards of 30,000 pages of catalogs and is growing rapidly. The Product Index, which cross-references manufacturer to product headings, lists more than 25,000 such headings.

Once the proper catalog microfiche (microfilm card) is located, it is placed in a viewer and blown up for easy reading on a 14" x 14" screen.

11,000 customer files on microfiche. Richard Kozel, National Acme's supervisor of engineering records, says it only takes a clerk 30 seconds to find specifications for replacement parts of retooling on a customer order compared with up to 10 minutes under the conventional file system. Again quoting the *Wall Street Journal:* "It is easier to find a given reference page on fiche than on conventional roll microfilm. Fiche cards can be numbered in columns across the top and rows along the side, and contain an index telling the data seeker where to find the page he wants—say column 40, row 17. The reading machine is capable of moving to the desired reference page quickly.

"The microphoto division of Bell & Howell Co. conducted a study showing that the retrieval of one page of information from 40,000 pages stored on 700 pieces of fiche took an average of 10 seconds.

"There are plenty of other applications for microfiche. The Micro Catalog division of Thomas Publishing Co. has complete descriptions and other information about 21,000 products of 1,350 vendor companies on fiche. Organized into 'microcatalogs,' the information is sold to some 800 subscriber companies who pay $320 for the 'books' and $155 annually for updating.

"The Republic Aviation division of Fairchild Hiller Corp. is now studying better ways to put library material on fiche, under a

$65,000 contract from the Council on Library Resources. Republic has come up with a fiche that will hold 9,801 pages on a 4- by 5-inch piece of film and enable a person to find a given page on it within seconds with the aid of an electronic viewer system."

The Recordak Microfilmer by Kodak records 40 letter-sized documents in about 10 seconds; reduces storage to 2 percent of the space needed for paper originals. According to the company, reference is pushbutton easy, any image out of millions can be retrieved, viewed, and a paper copy made in seconds.

Duplicating Equipment

A study of more than one thousand sales organizations indicates that salesmen's bulletins are most commonly produced on stencil-duplicating (mimeograph) equipment. However, Multilith, Multigraph, and several other processes produce quantities of effective, top-quality copies.

Choosing the most economical method of producing salesmen's bulletins depends largely on the number of salesmen to whom the bulletins are to be sent and on the nature of the copy to be reproduced. The following description of the four principal duplicating processes may be helpful:

Mimeographing: To produce salesmen's bulletins on mimeograph equipment, the operator types or draws directly on the stencil. This operation is the crucial step in obtaining quality copy results. For added effectiveness, however, it is possible to patch preprepared cartoons and illustrations onto the stencil.

The mimeograph process is suited for short, medium, and long runs. It is fast, and it is economical. Stencil duplicator prices cover a wide range. Hand operated models sell for as little as $195; modern, electrically driven models may run up to $850. Speed, versatility, and copy quality results account for the price difference.

The electronic stencil process has been developed recently to help mimeograph attain copy quality results previously reserved for the offset process. These stencils make it possible to reproduce linework, solids, and remarkable halftone facsimiles. From 5,000 to 10,000 copies can be reproduced from one electronic stencil.

Offset Printing: Compared to the cost of other office duplicating equipment, the initial cost of offset equipment is comparatively high. However, only the offset process can produce bulletins with print-like copy quality at a real saving of printing costs—including the reproduction of linework, solid areas, and halftones.

At right, an operator demonstrates the Dennison high-speed copier, which prints 30 copies per minute from one pushbutton control. Above, the Apeco Super-Stat, a desk-top model, makes up to 250 copies, is lightweight, portable, and compact.

Offset equipment can also be used to produce letterheads, office forms, advertising literature, catalog pages, etc.

Any number of bulletins can be economically reproduced with the process at speeds up to 9,000 impressions an hour. Paper masters may economically be used for the production of a few hundred copies, metal plates are more economical when thousands of copies are needed.

A. B. Dick Company, Addressograph-Multigraph Corporation, and Davidson Corporation are among many reliable firms which manufacture office offset equipment.

Photocopy: The photocopy process provides a quick way to obtain from one to several copies of an original document—material temporarily available, reports, letters, invoices, etc. Some photocopiers will even copy pages in bound volumes, photographs and blueprints. Generally, it takes only seconds and costs only a few cents to make a photocopy.

There are many types of copy machines now on the market, ranging from the desk-type unit which produces a few copies for recordkeeping purposes to the elaborate console models which produce 25 copies or more. Copiers also differ according to the technical process used for duplication. Following are just a few examples:

The American Photocopy Equipment Company stresses that its Apeco Super-Stat "is fully automatic, makes up to 250 copies, and is the lowest-cost, electrostatic, three-dimensional copy-maker on the market. It is guaranteed to make a minimum of one million copies without replacement under specified conditions."

The Kodak Readyprint Copier, as advertised by the manufacturer, is neither electrostatic nor 100 percent automatic, but provides one or two clear copies in seconds. It is very simple to use and practically service-free.

The all-electric 3M Model 209 Copier produces copies for as little as 3½ cents each and reproduces fine lines and color pages from bound books.

The 3M Model "107" Copier is a low-cost desk-top unit which the company claims "makes as fine a copy as any copier, at any price."

Another desk-top copying machine is the Electrocopy 400, made by Kee Lox Manufacturing Company, Rochester, N. Y. It copies in sizes up to 11 inches by 17 inches at the rate of six copies a minute. The manufacturer states it will reproduce ink, typing, pencil, crayons, halftones or solids.

The Dennison high-speed copier is a "fast, compact, volume copier featuring one-button control that activates the machine, selects copy size, prints and shuts off the unit. It makes 1,800 copies per hour."

S K & F Uses Television

Smith, Kline & French, a leading marketing innovator, employs television cameras to help train salesmen, speakers-bureau personnel, tour guides, personnel-department executives, public-relations people, and research and development scientists and engineers.

The TV system includes a General Electric monochrome vidicon camera, audio system, and videotape recorder (GE TE-15) and a Sony home videocorder. The initial investment: $18,000.

Heaviest user of the equipment is SK&F's professional sales department.

Chapter 39

THE COMPUTER
AS A SALES TOOL

MANY marketing men are utilizing computers as an aid in sales analysis, sales forecasting, and test marketing, and are enthusiastic about the results obtained. These executives share the opinion that the new "techniques currently being evolved will make it virtually mandatory for any company that wishes to move ahead in the coming decades to use computer techniques." Thus, the sophisticated computer has already proved successful as a marketing tool. There is a clamoring for its extension into other areas of sales and advertising management.

Here is a forecast from the American Federation of Information Processing Societies:

"The full potential of the computer is just now being grasped. The greatest potential payoff in business appears to be in the sophisticated areas which have been out of man's reach so far in his commercial history. These areas include totally integrated management-information systems—i.e., computer-controlled communications from far-flung locations with many pieces of information analyzed and processed to flash instantly to the attention of business executives.

"Now a businessman can take action affecting his business based on information on what is happening *as it is happening.* And the scientist can do the same sort of thing during a rocket launch or a complicated chemical process.

"A recent and significant new development in computer technology will bring many more people into contact with these machines in the next few years. This development is the 'on-line' computer system, in which a large central computer is linked to dozens or even hundreds of telephones or typewriter-sized terminals at different locations—some even thousands of miles away from the computer itself.

"The potential of these new systems is enormous."

Significant future gains in marketing applications of the computer are indicated. Recently, 33 companies surveyed by Booz, Allen & Hamilton, Inc., utilized an average of 12 percent of total computer efforts for such marketing operations as sales forecasting and analysis, market research, and sales order processing. This figure ranged up to 25 percent. Predictable use of computers for marketing purposes in the 1970's raises the average to 16 percent. Gains are also seen for computerization in production and distribution.

Uses for Computers

The uses to which electronic data processing may be applied include: (1) Researching market information and the competitive situation; (2) analyzing sales-territory results; (3) analyzing each product's sales record; (4) sharpening distribution channels; (5) broadening markets; (6) analyzing the structure of the sales force; (7) guiding advertising objectives.

The Research Institute of America predicts that:

"In the immediate future, some computers will not only decide when and how much, but also *who* gets the order. For example, the Large Jet Engine Department of General Electric plans to turn over supplier selection to its GE 225 computer. The machine already determines when to issue requests for quotations. Data on suppliers' performance and other factors are programmed into the computer and when an item is needed the machine supplies the best probable sources. At some future date bids themselves will be fed into the machine for a purchasing *decision*. All the human buyers will have to do is decide which suppliers to ask for bids and which products and services to program *into* the computer."

At a meeting of the American Management Association, in discussing the subject of marketing and the computer, Sidney Schoeffier, General Electric Co. economist, said the computer can enable marketing strategists to learn quickly and thoroughly why the successes of the past were successes and why failures were failures. He said GE is now experimenting with computer analysis that employs a key concept (analyzing past strategies as if they were experiments), the building of a simulation model, and the use of the model to generate "go" decisions.

Kinds of Computers

There are three types of computers. The first is the analogue computer, so-called because it works on analogous relationships.

In the computer-controlled "House of Tomorrow," as envisioned by Philco-Ford Corporation, the lady of the house will shop for food, clothing, and other household requirements projected on a video screen, and make her selections by pushing a button. Above the shopping screen are a household monitor and a video telephone. At a similar console in the den, the man of the house will check his bank balance and conduct other business.

The second is the digital type, which has a prodigious memory, makes rapid calculations, and works in sequences. The third is the hybrid, combining the high-speed processing of the analogue with the storage, decision-making, and control capabilities of the digital. It is expected that the hybrid unit will eventually replace the analogue for most purposes.

What benefits has the computer brought about? By helping business make the most efficient, fullest use of available resources, computers and information processing systems are in effect enabling businessmen to eliminate waste, increase productivity, cut expenses, and thereby offer customers a wider variety of products and services at the lowest possible price.

Outstanding example of the wider services as a result of the computer has been the use of real-time computer systems in air transportation. Computers such as the UNIVAC 490 Real-Time Series have enabled airlines to book and maintain control of millions of reservations and, in addition, even reserve a steak for a passenger's meal aloft. Through computers, airlines reservations clerks in many different cities are able to simultaneously check into seat availability for hundreds of flights and to book them as far as a year in advance. Through data communications, clerks obtain responses to inquiries in seconds. Large-scale systems used by major airlines today are capable of storing complete information on any individual passenger, including his name, address, telephone number, his preference of meals. Computers may also book a rented car or reserve a room at his destination.

These systems are already in operation on several airlines. In the planning stages are still greater management-information systems such as the $56 million system ordered by United Air Lines. Consisting of three giant UNIVAC 1108 computers, the United information system is being designed to handle complete systemwide information on its passenger and fleet operations. In addition to processing some 17 major categories of information for the line, the UNIVAC system will use television-like cathode ray tube sets on a nationwide basis to display data.

A Decision-Making Tool

Drayton Heard, Jr., manager, marketing administration, Westinghouse Electric Corporation, states:

"We have 188 computer programs in the marketing area. They range from sales records to in-warranty reliability studies to negotiation probabilities. Nevertheless, in general, marketing lags behind other company functions in the use of the computer as a decision-making tool. Currently we are exposing marketing staff people to these opportunities through a five-day computer-concepts course. There is also an excellent opportunity to improve the role of the salesman by the use of computerized sales records as a complete program for sales forecasting, order service, engineering modifications, manufacturing information, and purchase requisitions."

Bache & Co., an investment firm, adopted a real-time (practically instantaneous response) computer system which will not only handle much of the firm's vast paperwork but will automatically switch and relay heavy message and business-data traffic throughout its worldwide organization.

The new system, a product of Sperry Rand Corporation, will relay trading instructions directly to Bache members on the floor of the New York Stock Exchange, relay confirmations of sales and purchases to originating offices at electronic speeds, simultaneously and automatically performing all the necessary accounting chores, storing up results in well-ordered fashion in its vast memory. The stored information and accounting data, maintained automatically with up-to-the-second accuracy, can be tapped in almost any form and volume required.

At the heart of Bache & Co.'s new information-accounting-communication system is UNIVAC 494 Real-Time Computer equipment in which the company invested well over $3 million initially.

Small Firms Can Use Computer

A combination of data-processing techniques—including the use of an automatic accounting machine, data-communications equipment, and a service-bureau computer enabled the H. D. Taylor Co., Buffalo, N. Y., to save $600 a month in clerical costs over former manual methods while providing valuable management information which was previously unavailable.

According to Penn Wettlaufer, vice-president of Taylor, this approach to data processing is designed to allow a small industrial supplier to gain benefits usually realized only by much larger firms. "Although we employ only 135 people to handle, control, and sell approximately 57,000 items, we have already automated accounts receivable, payroll, accounts payable, and order-processing applications on our own equipment," he said in an interview with *Industrial Distributor News*.

"Moreover, by making use of the services of a local service bureau, we are obtaining sales and cost-analysis information that would have been impossible to attain by manual or semiautomated methods," Wettlaufer added.

Walgreen Application

A good example of the use of EDP in the field of retail distribution is afforded by the Walgreen chain of drugstores.

Walgreen opened a major distribution center in Houston to serve 130 drugstores and 300 franchised outlets in the Southwest. The fully air-conditioned warehouse covers 275,250 square feet on a 15-acre tract of land.

The new warehouse is tied into the chain's computerized ordering network. Inventory data for it and the Chicago and Jacksonville warehouses is maintained in a central computer in Chicago. All stores produce their orders on optical tape which is airmailed to Chicago for automatic conversion into picking orders at the rate of one per minute. The picking orders are then transmitted over telephone lines to the appropriate warehouses for filling.

Another example is that of the Elm Farm Foods Company computer. Decisions requiring judgment and the consideration of information or conditions not contained in the computer are spotlighted by it in the form of exception reports.

For example, the computerized inventory-control system calculates vendor order quantities on staple items that will maintain the desired level of customer service without creating overstock situations. It employs sophisticated simulation and forecasting techniques and draws upon data from warehouse receivings and store orders plus such stored information as the dimensions and weight of vendor shipping containers and the order-to-delivery lead time.

The Time-Sharing Technique

Historically, the cost of large-scale computers has made them available to only the largest business or organizations. But recent advances in computer technology have extended the benefits of the most powerful data-processing systems to thousands of small users. Through a technique known as computer time-sharing, a number of small users with remote devices in their offices or laboratories can be connected and simultaneously use a large central computer.

In Cambridge, Mass., Keydata Corporation has pioneered a commercial time-sharing service, an information-processing utility that provides data-processing service in much the same way that public utilities provide gas and electricity. Each Keydata subscriber has direct access to the central UNIVAC 491 System and pays only for his shared time on the large-scale computer.

The General Electric Company has introduced time-sharing systems for its 400 series of computers.

The company said the GE 420 would be capable of providing service to 30 users at once. Time-sharing is the simultaneous use of a central computer by a number of persons at various remote locations. The system will be leased for about $17,000 a month and sell for $760,000.

Remote Problem-Solving

IBM's QUIKTRAN is a time-sharing terminal system that enables up to 50 subscribers at the same time to solve problems on a single IBM 7044 computer by using typewriter-like terminals in their own offices—a block or a continent away.

More than 125 subscribers are now using QUIKTRAN in New York and Los Angeles.

Subscribers include large and small organizations from a broad cross-section of business and industrial firms, government agencies, colleges and universities. They use QUIKTRAN for applications

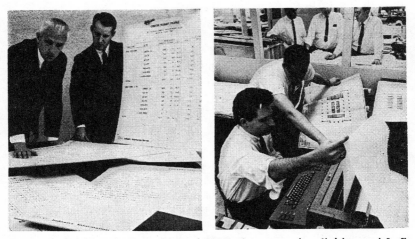

At left, George B. Beitzel, president of IBM's data processing division, and L. E. Donogan, Jr., director of information marketing, check computer-prepared market research reports. The reports are automatically compiled from data banks containing millions of facts and figures on 390,000 businesses. At right, members of the staff at Weiskopf & Pickworth, consulting engineers, use a typewriter-like terminal to "talk over" a problem with a computer located several Manhattan blocks away and time-shared by 49 other users.

ranging from nuclear-research and bridge-design problems to the financial analysis of stock, bond, and other investment opportunities.

The link to the computer for each user is an IBM 1050 tele-processing terminal that communicates with the IBM 7044 over regular voice-grade telephone lines.

In addition to the conversational technique, in which subscribers "talk" to the computer to structure and solve their problems, users can now transmit somewhat larger and previously structured problems to the central computer for overnight processing.

To use the new processing, a subscriber transmits his program, with data and appropriate control instructions. The IBM 7044 will store this information on random-access disk storage files.

During the evening hours, the IBM 7044 will retrieve the program and data from storage, compile and execute the program, and store the results back in the disk storage file. During a subsequent QUIK-TRAN session, the subscriber can instruct the computer to print the results on his terminal.

In standard conversational QUIKTRAN, the subscriber uses his IBM 1050 terminal to converse with the computer in a step-by-step, give-and-take method. He structures his specific mathematical, scientific, or engineering problem, develops a computer program to solve it, enters his data, and quickly receives his answers.

The IBM 7044 at the hub of each QUIKTRAN system can handle processing for a user so fast that there is no appreciable waiting time. The computing technique known as time-sharing which is used in QUIKTRAN gives each person at a terminal the feeling that he alone is controlling the computer.

Two powerful, yet simple, QUIKTRAN languages are available. Both can be mastered within a few hours. The languages—QUIK-TRAN for general scientific and business problems, and QUIK-TRAN/COGO for civil engineering problems—consist of English-like statements and common mathematical symbols.

The IBM Approach

Facts from two electronic "data banks" containing information on some 390,000 businesses and the flow of products and services among industries will be combined in a computer by International Business Machines Corporation. The result will be comprehensive, custom-tailored market research reports for U.S. industries.

The new computerized market research is called Industry Information Service. It is the first product of its kind and represents IBM's entry into the marketing of information services.

Aimed specifically at companies whose products and services are sold to the industrial market, the IBM market research reports will provide detailed analyses of a company's market and of its untapped market potential. The analyses will provide occupancy and share-of-market percentages for each cross-section of the firm's market—by line of business, plant size, sales territory, and combinations of these.

The reports will help businesses determine the size and nature of their markets, how much they can reasonably expect to sell to each market cross-section, and how to direct product development, marketing strategies, and sales tactics to the highest sales potential.

Several large advertising agencies are now using computers. Computerized information services have been designated "the single most pervasive change" that will affect advertising agencies. These systems will provide media data, histories of previous campaigns, records of consumer purchases by brand and price, and field-research statistics and trends. Computerized illustrations will be viewed on cathode ray tubes.

Some Problems Involved

As reported in *Marketing Forum*, conversations with marketing men at a meeting of the American Management Association disclosed frustration with accounting control of EDP. The basic complaint is that marketers were locked into a program format that made it difficult to extract their kind of data.

"My controller isn't interested in a detailed breakdown of the products we sell or the markets we sell to," said one sales manager. He found that to get the information he wants would require considerable specialized programming.

There is a growing feeling that, where it's economically practical, the marketing department should have its own program expert because those setting up accounting formats don't understand marketing problems. It was apparent also that communications between marketing and accounting in general was often poor. Many marketing men said the fundamental problem of financial control could only be solved by ending it and putting EDP either at the top-management level or on neutral ground under management's control.

There were some defenders of accounting people. Their common reaction is that if the marketing man isn't getting what he wants in the way of information, it's because he doesn't know what he wants.

Said one executive: "Most marketing men in the industrial field came up the sales route. And salesmen are not good at the kind of logic required for planning a computer program. Once they decide what they need and why, they'll get it."

SOME COMPUTER ABC's

(Copyright by International Business Machines Corporation)

ALGOL

Algorithmic Oriented Language. An international procedure-oriented language.

ALGORITHM

A prescribed set of well-defined rules for the solution of a problem in a number of finite steps.

ANALOG

Pertaining to data in the form of continuously variable physical quantities, in contrast with *Digital*.

BINARY

A characteristic, property, or condition in which there are but two possible alternatives. The binary code used in computers is expressed in terms of one and zero representing on or off.

BIT

A binary digit.

COBOL

Common Business Oriented Language. A business data processing language.

CODE

A system of symbols for representing data or instructions in a computer.

DEBUG

To detect, locate, and remove mistakes in routines or malfunctions in a computer.

DIGITAL

Pertaining to information in the form of digits, in contrast with *Analog*.

ELECTRONIC

Pertaining to the flow of electrons in vacuum, gas, or semiconductors. Electrons are quantities of electrical energy which course from point to point in a computer, making its high-speed operation possible.

FEEDBACK

Return of part of the output of a system for self-correcting purposes.

FORTRAN

Formula Translating System. Any of several specific procedure-oriented languages.

GAME THEORY

A mathematical process of selecting an optimum strategy in the face of an opponent who has a strategy of his own. The forces of nature might be the "opponent" in a planned space shot. The strategy to overcome these might be "played" on a computer to ascertain an optimum launch date.

HEURISTIC

Pertaining to exploratory methods of problem-solving in which solutions are discovered by evaluation of the progress made toward the final result. Contrast with *Algorithmic*.

INPUT

The data to be processed in a computer.

JUMP

A computer instruction which provides the ability to break the routine program control in order to speed up the processing of specific data items.

KILO

A prefix meaning one thousand. Computer storage capacity can be stated in thousands of addressable locations, i.e. 64K.

LASER

Light amplification by simulated emission of radiation. A beam of light whose waves are coherent, differing from ordinary light as the effect of one pebble tossed into water differs from the effect of a handful.

MEMORY

Storage. Any device into which units of information can be transferred, which will hold information, and from which the information can be obtained at a later time. Memory usually refers to the human function, and storage to the machine function.

NANOSECOND

One billionth of a second. Some computer operations are approaching nanosecond speed.

OUTPUT

Information transferred from the computer to the "outside world." As an adjective—pertaining to the devices which bring information out of the computer.

PROGRAM

The plan for the solution of a problem, including data gathering, processing, and reporting.

QUEUE

The formation of delays or lineups of discrete units of information during processing in a computer.

REAL-TIME

Computation controlling a physical process during the actual moment it transpires, in a sufficiently rapid manner so that the results are available to influence the process being controlled.

SIMULATION

The representation of a physical system by the execution of a computer program.

TRANSDUCER

A device which converts energy from one form to another.

UNKNOWN

Strange, unfamiliar, incalculable, inexpressible. Computers are revolutionizing science as a new research tool of unprecedented power.

VALIDITY

A relative measure of being sound, correct, efficient. A validity check on data ascertains the degree of accuracy of its representation in a computer.

WORD

An ordered set of characters bearing at least one meaning and handled by a computer as a unit.

X-Y PLOTTER

A device used in conjunction with a computer to plot coordinate points in the form of a graph.

ZERO

A numeral normally denoting the lack of magnitude. In a computer there are distinct representations for plus and minus zero.

Chapter 40

RECRUITING SALESMEN

A MERICA'S high schools and colleges are not the only institutions which must cope with "dropout" problems. Each year the approximately 8 percent of all salespersons—recruited and trained at considerable expense—who must be dropped or who leave for reasons of their own, make up a billion-dollar headache for sales managers.

Hank Astwood, director of the Sales Manpower Foundation, a division of the Sales Executives Club of New York, summarizes the problem this way:

"With the average annual turnover of manufacturing salesmen last reported to be 7.7 percent, the 100,055 manufacturing firms in America (that employ 20 or more people) will have approximately 74,898 salesmen drop out or be released during the year. And in addition to replacing these dropouts, these manufacturers will need 42,799 new salesmen to take care of expanding territories, new products, etc., for a total of 117,697 new salesmen."

This turnover rate carries with it an appalling cost, Astwood points out. The 74,898 replacements alone will cost these companies over $664,000,000 in recruitment, selection, and training expenses. Those hired for other reasons will account for the balance of the $1 billion total cost figure.

These manufacturing firms have a total employment of 17,065,000, of which 5.7 percent of personnel (972,705) are salesmen.

"The Foundation's most recent survey indicates that it costs $8,877 to locate, select, train and supervise a manufacturing salesman until productive," Astwood continued. "And this cost—more than $1 billion—is exclusive of the salesman's salary.

"This whopping cost of failure," Astwood stresses, "forcefully drives home to every sales manager that his most important task is to locate and lead top caliber men. And at $8,877 per mistake, he had better pick the right man every time instead of one out of 10!"

The sales manager can improve his score considerably by:

1. Preparing a definite description of the qualifications a salesman needs to sell his company's product or services.

2. Not hiring men under the emergencies created when one of his sales force quits, but instead setting up facilities that will maintain a continuous search for top producers so that he will know where they are when they become available.

3. Hiring every qualified top producer, whether or not there is an opening on the staff—and then using them to replace marginal producers—of which every staff has at least 20 percent.

4. Providing the best initial training program possible and continuing refresher courses at regular intervals.

5. Expecting and demanding top results from every man on the force.

6. Basing salesmen's compensation (salary, commission, bonuses, incentives, etc.) on the results produced.

The Foundation survey revealed that the overall cost of selling $1 of merchandise or service for more than 500 manufacturers averaged 14 percent and rose to as much as 35 percent in some instances! Some comparative averages are: 11.3 percent for the electronics industry, 9.3 percent in the paper industry, 11.1 percent for electrical equipment/appliances, 10 percent for building materials, 7.6 percent for chemicals, 13.3 percent for the consumer advertisers.

The study also shows that the responding firms employ a total of 45,600 persons, 3.2 percent of whom are involved in sales. Another aspect of the survey shows that only 33.2 percent of the companies' salesmen can be placed in the "top producers" category, and that this minority brings in more than 50 percent of the total sales volume. "Average producers" make up 50.9 percent of the sales force and bring in 41.5 percent of the business. "Marginal" salesmen—15.9 percent of the total employed—account for only 8.3 percent of the volume. Of this last group, 22.2 percent are trainees.

What to Look For

Practically all sales managers have differing opinions as to the characteristics of a good salesman. One sales executive listed them as follows: (1) good appearance, (2) a pleasing, well-wearing personality, (3) stability, tenacity, and perseverance; (4) basic character and integrity, and (5) industriousness—willingness to work.

Other sales managers may look for the same qualities in a man but rank them in a different order of importance. It is very interesting to note that many lists place experience at the bottom of the list or omit it entirely.

The productive career salesman is usually a man of only average or slightly below average intelligence, declares Dr. Robert N. Mc-Murry, industrial psychologist who specializes in sales problems. He says:

"One of the most common errors is to seek persons of superior intelligence as sales representatives. Together with poor selection, this is responsible for much of the excessive turnover in sales organizations. Certainly no one who has the other qualifications should be rejected because of mediocre intelligence."

Charles E. Hummel, sales manager for Standard Shannon Supply Company, Philadelphia, drawing on his experience of 28 years and talks with other sales managers, listed the following rules for hiring salesmen for readers of *Industrial Distributor News:*

1. Overcome your prejudices.

2. Don't insist on experience.

3. Advertise your name. Why hide behind a blind box number in your ad? Let the prospect know who you are.

4. Don't hide your story. Has your company experienced terrific growth? Say so in your ad.

5. Keep a reverse file. Even if you don't hire a candidate on the first call, don't throw away all of your applicants' resumes. Keep a file of those candidates who came close.

6. Let someone else interview, too. This is no reflection on your ability to judge applicants. But two heads are better than one in most cases.

7. Check references carefully. Many a poor salesman has listed references that won't check out, figuring you won't check them because you'll assume he wouldn't list a bad reference.

8. Be wary of competitors' men. This is a tough rule and not everyone will agree with it. But the disadvantages may offset any advantages: Their asking price may be high; they may be castoffs who couldn't produce, or prima donnas who won't work your way, or they may simply be job-hoppers who'll leave you the minute a better opportunity shows up.

9. Hire men from related fields. This gives you a man with some experience, yet you avoid the disadvantages of hiring competitors' men.

10. Be flexible. When you hire a man, give him a fair trial. If he's not working out after a reasonable time be prepared to change your own training techniques.

The search for salesmen, as well as for other types of employees, is being simplified through the use of computers. Personnel Information Communication System, a subsidiary of Western Union, has electronically processed the profiles of more than 25,000 individuals, 7,500 of whom are in sales and marketing fields. Skills and abilities are matched with job requirements. To do this PICS classifies job data in the computer in 2,200 different ways. A prospective employer uses the same classifications in detailing his requirements. This employment computer service is available to companies on an annual subscription basis.

Where to Look

Most of the trouble in employing salesmen who will make good can be traced to the method of selection. There are two approaches to this problem: (1) Picking the best men who apply to you for selling positions, and (2) "spotting" likely men and going after them. The trouble with the first method is that, as a rule, the men who will make the best salesmen are usually not out of jobs nor even thinking about changing jobs. They usually have jobs and are making good at them. In the opinion of one sales executive: "There is only one best way of securing salesmen and that is to go right out after them personally by spotting alert, ambitious men who are already employed in chain stores, on farms, as milkmen, in department stores, as preachers, as teachers, as painters, as carpenters, as machinists, etc., and inducing them to take up salesmanship.

"Practically every field of endeavor is a source from which to draw salesmen. Specialty salesmen who are lured from one line to another on the whole are not particularly satisfactory unless you have a proposition of exceptional earning possibilities which tends to advertise itself to other salesmen in other lines."

Some organizations of specialty salesmen are recruited through home-office training schools, and again technically equipped salesmen are hired from retailers or jobbers. As a rule men whose services are sought, rather than the individual who seeks the job, are more desirable from the standpoint of results. It is obvious that such a method of waiting for unsolicited applications would hardly be feasible for companies which employ large staffs of specialty salesmen.

The National Cash Register Co., IBM, and many others in the office-equipment field recruit their best salesmen from the ranks of their servicemen. In fact, it is a rule with many of these companies that in engaging a serviceman, he must have the qualifications which underlie a good salesman. In other industries, the most dependable salesmen are those who come up through the stockroom and know the business thoroughly.

Classified Advertisements

While it is no more possible to indict a *method* than it is a people, for the reason that the conditions under which a method must operate are so very different, the preponderance of experience is decidedly against depending on classified advertisements as the sole means of finding good salesmen. But it is only fair to say that some sales managers still get most of their salesmen that way, and would not think of changing their methods. One sales executive is against classified advertisements on the ground that, "It is a good, reliable, lazy way to get salesmen, but after the prospective salesmen are secured through classified advertising, there is a tremendous amount of work that has to be done in sifting out the applicants and in training the very small percentage that finally stick and develop. Classified advertising attracts a lazy lot of semisalesmen who are looking for a soft job."

Most classified advertisements bring a flood of applications either in person or by mail. The professional ad-answerers are legion. They are the type of men who seem constitutionally unable to hold any position very long. They are the floaters, and advance seekers, the men who want to sell ice cream in the summer and coal in the winter. Weeding out these men requires a lot of interviewing, scanning of many application blanks, and endless investigating of references. Unless an organization is set up to handle applications on a wholesale scale, classified advertising may often prove the most difficult and costly method of recruiting men. This may prove particularly true when only a few men are needed.

While it is true that it requires time and work to weed out the undesirables who answer classified advertisements, many sales executives feel that this work and time are justifiable. In view of the cost of training new salesmen, and in view of the difficulties of finding good men, even one promising letter out of a hundred applications is worth investigating. Many hundreds of letters of application can be scanned in a day, and the good ones can be set aside for further investigation; to find even one good man is worth the effort.

"Situations Wanted"

A salesman is always a salesman, and usually displays his resourcefulness in the manner in which he sells himself. For this reason, a number of concerns make a practice of scanning the "Situations Wanted" columns, claiming that they get a better class of applicants as a rule than through their own advertising. A salesman who takes the trouble to prepare an advertisement and makes the investment in the space is not apt to be a floater. The Equitable Life Assurance Society is a strong believer in this method of securing leads for good life insurance agents.

"KNOCK-OUT" QUESTIONS FOR SALES POSITIONS

Name_____ Address_____ Home telephone_____

Age_____ Marital status_____ No. and ages of children _____ Schooling_____

1. What kind of position are you seeking?_____
   Must be sales

2. What sales experience have you had?_____
   Must have had some experience

3. What are your earnings requirements?_____
   Must be between $_____ and $_____

4. Will you relocate if necessary?_____
   Must be willing to relocate (if job requires)

5. Will you travel if necessary? _____
   Must be willing to travel (if job requires)

6. Will you work nights, Saturdays, and weekends when necessary?_____
   Must be willing (if needed)

7. Do you have a car available for your use?_____
   Must have a car available (if needed)

8. Do you have a valid driver's license?_____
   Must have a license (if needed)

9. Can you be bonded?_____
   Must be bondable (if this applies)

10. Can you pass a physical examination of life insurance standard?._____
    Must be "Yes"

11. Are you presently employed? Yes__No___(If "No")unemployed? How long_____
    Must not exceed eight weeks

12. What is your present or last employment? Company_____

    Dates_____to_____. Job_____ Earnings _____

13. What did you do before this?_____

Disposition: Application sent_____ Appointment made _____

_____
Interviewer

These questions will eliminate unqualified candidates early in an interview or a written application. The form was developed by The McMurry Company and is copyrighted by The Dartnell Corporation.

Using Salesmen to Recruit New Men

Recruiting salesmen through the medium of older salesmen on the force is one of the best methods to build up a sales organization. The only objection is that a salesman is apt to recommend a relative or a friend, being influenced by his personal regard for the candidate rather than by his impartial judgment of him as a possible producer. There is nothing new about this method. For years, a number of companies have delegated this task to their district managers.

A kitchen-furniture company found this practice an effective arrangement for keeping the sales organization adequately staffed. To stimulate interest among salesmen, it operated "The On and Up Club." This organization was established so that proper recognition could be given to those displaying "organizing ability." To be elected to this club, it was necessary for the salesman to recruit one new man for the sales organization.

The sales manager of a plumbing supply house uses only the older and higher type of men for recruiting purposes. These he instructs individually. He does not take the younger men of the force into his confidence. He makes the newer salesmen feel that it is a mark of trust and distinction to be asked to recommend candidates for sales positions—something to strive for.

It has been common practice for insurance companies, bond houses, real-estate concerns, and others to offer salesmen a monetary inducement for securing new men who become good producers. In the past few years, the plan has been adapted to several other related lines of business.

Developing Salesmen Within the Company

There is no question that this method is more effective than any other for the smaller organization, although many large organizations which maintain sales schools also claim that it pays in the long run. Those companies which have been most successful in developing raw material through their factory and office make this distinction, which it is well to bear in mind: Salesmen are not recruited by accident from the shop or the warehouse, but careful attention is given to the employment of these men when they first join the company. Even though a man may be given a job as a delivery man when he is hired, he is sized up at the time as a potential road salesman. In one large tire company, the employment department schedules a certain number of jobs in each department of the factory for future salesmen—these jobs being occupied at all times by men who will later be moved up to positions in the office and then to the sales force. In the automobile-accessory line, it is common practice to promote from stock room to city counter, to city sales, and to the road. The same is true of electrical jobbers. Lumber yards promote from the yards to the mill, to the office, the city counter, and then to road positions.

Recruiting College Graduates

A well-worked source of salesmen is the college campus, not only at those schools which teach salesmanship or marketing but also at liberal-arts and engineering schools.

The very fact that the student has sufficient interest in selling to study it, automatically classifies him as good potential material for a sales organization. This is especially true if, in connection with his studies, the student helped to defray the cost of his education by selling something, either while in school or during his vacations. The larger sales organizations systematically "scout" graduating classes for likely men.

The manager of employment and college relations of Armstrong Cork Company, after checking with divisional general sales managers in early September to determine manpower needs for the next year, schedules visits to selected colleges by the company's recruiting team to meet with members of the administration and faculty, and to interview candidates for Armstrong sales positions.

"In our visits," an Armstrong recruiter explained, "we outline in detail the job opportunities and training offered. We give complete information on our company facilities, products, and scope of activity. When visiting a college, we take a list of its graduates who work for us. This indicates the type of man in whom we are interested and is a good advertisement for the company, since college students look up to graduates and the companies for which they have chosen to work.

"We regularly visit some 100 campuses and interview some 2,500 young men, of whom about 400 are invited to visit our general offices for a day at the expense of the company. Approximately one-half of this number are for the sales divisions. While it is the employee-relations department's responsibility to make the primary selection of candidates, it is the prerogative of the sales divisions to make the final selection. Therefore, at the home office interviews are conducted by as many marketing managers and other executives as possible, as well as by several staff executives who have had long experience in judging and selecting candidates. Unless there is full agreement on an individual by the sales division men, staff executives, and employee relations department personnel, he is not offered a job."

If the employing organization's size does not permit such an extensive canvass, recruiting in local colleges can be used to great advantage. It is imperative that such an organization sell the college on the opportunities offered, for it is only natural that the larger national organizations that have been conducting major recruiting programs hold the appeal for the majority of the students. Local companies will have to draw active attention to their opportunities to be successful in such a program.

What to Look for in College Men

While the qualities which contribute to the success of a college graduate in sales work are the same as those needed to make any salesman successful, there are special considerations to be weighed in recruiting college graduates. These have been summed up by one sales executive as follows:

1. EDUCATION—Except for jobs requiring specific technical training, the course studied is unimportant. We are interested primarily in whether or not the candidate has been taught to think problems through logically and clearly and whether or not he has ability to reach a satisfactory conclusion. We must make certain, nevertheless, that he has a good command of the English language and is able to spell. The breadth of a candidate's vocational interests can be spotted sometimes in educational likes and dislikes.

2. EARNINGS FOR SCHOOL EXPENSES—We are quite interested in men who have worked all or a part of their way through school. We have found that this type of candidate gains valuable practical experience, certainly demonstrates ambition, initiative, self-reliance, and knows the value of a dollar. He usually has confidence, cannot be discouraged easily, and has a more mature attitude toward job procurement and business in general. He views life somewhat more seriously than the student who has been given everything during his college career.

3. LEADERSHIP—Is the candidate a leader? Participation in extracurricular activities is very important to us. Is the candidate sufficiently interested and well-rounded to go beyond the scope of his books in order to obtain a well-rounded education? The ability to get along with fellow men and to gain their respect is essential. Whether a man's interests are in athletics, fraternities, church or welfare work, campus politics, dramatics, or publications is not important to us. Our chief interest is in whether he has the ability to be a leader. Along with this, we are interested in his hobbies, since at times these are indicative of interests, versatility, ambition, and ability to lead.

4. CHARACTER—Good character is naturally a most essential quality. The school record, with faculty impressions and recommendations, should show readiness to accept responsibility and give an indication of the candidate's reputation on the campus. Self-reliance without conceit, and real initiative coupled with tact, are very desirable. Is the man a church member and does he participate with a fair degree of regularity? In many cases, we have found this to be quite indicative of good character.

5. FAMILY AND SCHOOL BACKGROUND—In considering family and social background, our purposes might easily be misconstrued; however, we have obtained some clues from this as to the individual's possibility of success. A young man's

background and family life are very important. Broken homes frequently produce disturbed personalities, while a good pattern of home life generally assures good training. An applicant who has been given good work habits in childhood—a paper route, after-school or Saturday work, etc.—will usually make a better salesman than one who has not had such training.

6. COLLEGE GRADES—Once, concerns tended to emphasize scholastic attainments. But in our case, although there is a general feeling that an outstanding man should be in the first quarter of his class, we are not looking for this type if his scholastic standing has been attained at the expense of a balance between outside work, social life, and leadership and development activities. I might mention here that in the larger group of average or above-average students, some have considerably more to offer than some of those who are in the upper one-tenth or so of the class.

The recruiting officer of a highly successful electronics equipment manufacturing company reports as follows with regard to his experience in college recruiting:

We examine four areas of a candidate's college experience:

1. Grades

2. Extracurricular activities

3. Self-support

4. Personality ratings

For research men, we put top emphasis on grades; for salesmen we do not necessarily want the top-grade man, particularly if he has sacrificed Nos. 2 and 4 to attain those grades. Frankly, we have found a man in the second tenth of his class to be a better salesman than one in the top tenth. The latter are prone to be too reflective and not sufficiently active and aggressive. They think too much before they act; whereas we want salesmen who think a little and act promptly. They spend too much time trying to find the perfect solution, while the somewhat less intellectual man is out getting the order. I have always felt that if you want a good, steady, long-time order producer, he should be just a *little* smarter than his customers, but not *too much* smarter. If he is, you will soon lose him to more challenging work.

To sum up the above, a good sales personality is a must; good grades but not top grades are a must; self-support and extracurricular activities should balance off. By that I mean, a poor boy who had to work his way through college would not be expected to have had much time to engage in extracurricular activities, while a well-financed boy would be expected to go in heavily for such activities.

If the candidate were a fraternity man, we would expect him to have held a high office in the fraternity; so, too, in other social or college organizations. In other words, we want to be sure he has the ability to organize and lead others, that he has demonstrated the ability to sell his ideas.

We want him to demonstrate a willingness to work hard to achieve his aims, an ability to plan his work and to carry out his plan with attention to detail and without too close supervision.

Minority Groups: Minority groups should not be overlooked as a source of sales and marketing manpower. A National Industrial

Conference Board Report states that nearly one thousand college graduates appeared at New York's Summit Hotel for a two-day "Job Opportunity Session" sponsored by Richard Clark Associates, Inc., a large minority-group recruiting firm. IBM screened more than 200 applicants. Other companies which conducted interviews included Air Reduction, Bristol Myers, Celanese, General Electric, Polaroid, Xerox, Westinghouse, and many others. Each applicant had 12 to 15 appointments; some of them paid their own expenses from as far away as Tampa, Florida, and Seattle, Washington.

Other Recruiting Sources

The following additional sources for recruiting salesmen are digested from the plans of more than one thousand concerns which have gone out of the beaten path in their methods. These plans point out fruitful sources for a number of lines of business which have not heretofore taken advantage of them.

Employment Agencies: Comparatively few sales managers use employment agencies as a means of getting applicants for sales positions. As one states, "They are excellent mediums for securing labor, factory help, typists, stenographers, and often executives, but they seem to lack the prerequisites for choosing the type of man that makes a good salesman." However, other executives report good success in recruiting through employment agencies when care is taken to give the selection executive detailed specifications as to exactly the type of man required.

Trade Associations: An activity which has been undertaken by some trade associations on behalf of their members is to plan, either on their own or in cooperation with a university, a practical training course for salesmen. The industry as a whole is in a position to attract young men for sales work, finance the general training required, and then make the salesmen available to members of the association. This idea has been used in recruiting and training printing salesmen, and can be widely applied.

Advantage of this plan is that it would provide the machinery to indoctrinate properly young men and women sincerely interested in selling with a constructive and forward-looking attitude toward their work. If reasonable care in selection is used, the percentage of men who succeed should be relatively high. One good salesman would yield enough profit over a period of time to repay the whole cost.

SELECTION AND EVALUATION SUMMARY

Applicant's Name_____ Date_____ 19____

Position Applied for_____ Job Class_____

CAN-DO FACTORS — Check Each Factor	Above Requirements	Meets Requirements	Marginal	Unacceptable
Appearance, manner			▨	▨
Availability			▨	▨
Education	▨			
Intelligence (as measured by test)	▨			
Experience in this field (if applicable)				▨
Knowledge of the product (if applicable)				
Physical condition, health			▨	▨

WILL-DO FACTORS

CHARACTER TRAITS (Basic Habits)

	A Lot	Some	Not Much	Almost None
STABILITY; maintaining same jobs and interests			▨	
INDUSTRY; willingness to work				
PERSEVERANCE; finishing what he starts				
ABILITY TO GET ALONG WITH OTHERS				▨
LOYALTY; identifying with employer				▨
SELF-RELIANCE; standing on own feet, making own decisions		▨		
LEADERSHIP				

JOB MOTIVATIONS (not already satisfied off the job)

	A Lot	Some	Not Much	Almost None
NEED FOR INCOME or desire for money			▨	▨
NEED FOR SECURITY	▨			
NEED FOR STATUS				
NEED FOR POWER	▨			▨
NEED TO INVESTIGATE	▨			
NEED TO EXCEL (to compete)			▨	
NEED FOR PERFECTION	▨			
NEED TO SERVE				

BASIC ENERGY LEVEL (vigor, initiative, drive, enthusiasm)

	A Lot	Some	Not Much	Almost None
			▨	

DEGREE OF EMOTIONAL MATURITY

	A Lot	Some	Not Much	Almost None
Dependence	▨			
Disregard for consequences			▨	
Incapacity for self-discipline	▨			
Selfishness	▨			
Show-off tendencies				
Pleasure-mindedness				
Destructive tendencies				
Wishful thinking			▨	
Unwillingness to accept responsibility				

Important: Do not add or average these factors in making the Over-all Rating. Match the qualifications of the applicant against the requirements of the *particular position* for which he is being considered, and consider the importance of each mismatch.

Strong Points for This Position_____

Weak Points for This Position_____

Over-all Rating: [1] [2] [3] [4]   Recommendation to Employ: [ ] Yes [ ] No   Rating by_____

Form No. ES-404R-2

This selection and evaluation summary is designed to make it easy for an interviewer to identify strong and weak points of an applicant and record them with pencil shadings.

Competitors' Salesmen: Experience shows it does not pay to hire salesmen from competitors except under unusual circumstances, as when a weak competitor holds a high-class salesman who is bigger than his job. The ethics of modern business demand that the competitor's salesman must make the first advance, and even though he may be hired, there are several reasons why he does not as a rule make as reliable a salesman as a man recruited by another method, or who has been developed within the organization. First, if he is a good man for you, he is worth just as much to his present employer who would not be apt to let him go. Second, he will leave you as quickly as he left the competitor, carrying with him your confidential house policies. Furthermore, he has a lot of "old tricks," learned in another organization, which make it difficult for you to educate him in the policies of your house—so that in the long run the same amount of effort expended on another man will produce equal or better results. Of course, the lure is that he is already trained and has demonstrated what he can do at someone else's expense.

Drawing from Retail Clerks: This is an excellent source for companies selling a seasonal line which may alternate with the busy season in certain retail lines. The salesmen employed can develop their retail connections during one season, and go out on the road for the manufacturer or wholesaler during another season. One company gets most of its applications from men connected with shoe stores—proprietors, buyers, clerks, etc.—who have handled its line at retail. The selling season starts shortly after the first of the year and lasts from three and one-half to five months, and as these months are usually dull ones in the retail shoe store, many of its salesmen are able to handle both jobs satisfactorily. Retailers are also drawn upon by a large number of organizations to recommend salesmen who visit their territory and who they know might be interested in another connection which can be combined with their regular line.

Through Jobbers: Most jobbers' salesmen look upon the position of manufacturer's representative as a step upward and it very often happens that a jobber's salesman will take a particular interest in a certain manufacturer's line, and the jobber is glad to recommend him as it is a certain advantage for him to deal with the manufacturer through a man formerly on his staff.

Recruiting Booklets

The most popular type of literature used to secure applications from desirable salesmen is the brochure which first of all "sells" the reader on the possibilities of selling as a career, and then on the advantages of selling the particular product which that company markets. The Fuller Brush Company used a brochure of this kind called, "Out of the Rut," for many years. Magazine advertising was utilized to get it into the hands of likely applicants. Booklets of this type may also be distributed to bankers, employment agencies, colleges, and others in a position to hear of likely men seeking positions.

One comprehensive and highly effective recruiting booklet is that issued by Goodyear Tire and Rubber Company. It opens with a message from Russell D. Young, chairman of the board, in which he says:

"Choosing a career may be the most important single decision you'll make as you approach graduation. It is a decision that will have a profound effect upon your future. And it is a decision that you alone can make.

"For Goodyear too, your decision is an important one. For we must depend upon the young—upon those who can be counted on to supply the vision and creativity essential to the company's continuing growth and prosperity.

"This booklet is designed to tell you something about Goodyear—about the people, the products and the business. It outlines Goodyear's comprehensive training programs and discusses the career opportunities open to the graduate who is invited to join this organization."

It is divided into four sections starting with "Career Fields," in which the work in a number of divisions in the company is described and the employment opportunities in each is discussed. This is followed by a general information section covering the company plants, corporate history, a product directory and an outline of employee benefits. Next is the section on management training. It ends with a discussion of the work of the aerospace, atomic and international divisions. The final pages cover the subject of "Akron—A Good Place to Live."

Chapter 41

SELECTION PROCEDURES

SUCCESSFUL sales organization requires the selection of men capable of grasping and putting into effect the training they will receive. Loose and haphazard selection of salesmen is not only responsible for the high rate of turnover in salesmen, but is the unsuspected cause of the failure of a great many sales managers. Since a sales manager's success depends so much on his ability to build successful salesmen, it is to his interest to see that his selection methods are up to date. These involve: (1) A sympathetic attitude on the part of top management toward painstaking selection of salesmen and its willingness to appropriate funds for experimental purposes, (2) records which show over a period of years the best sources of salesmen for given sales operations, (3) minimum standards for sales positions based on carefully worked out job definitions, (4) practical tests to assist in determining the qualifications of a man for a certain type of sales work and the proper interpretation of the results of such tests, (5) a standardized procedure of interviewing and grading applicants for sales positions, and (6) dependable checking of references and previous record.

IBM's Procedure

In the course of employing many hundreds of salesmen the International Business Machines Corporation has reached definite conclusions as to what constitutes an effective selection procedure for IBM. This program might not do at all for a business which requires a different type of salesman, for it must be borne in mind that each different sales situation calls for men with special sales qualifications. This is true even in the same sales organization, where there may be salesmen calling on dealers selling for resale, and salesmen selling specialties calling on purchasing agents of industrial plants. But it does suggest factors which one nationally known employer of salesmen uses in establishing his selection pattern.

The procedure for recruiting and selecting marketing representatives for International Business Machines Corporation has two chief objectives:

1. A major portion of the new employees should be recent college graduates.

2. To try, by selecting processes, to balance educational backgrounds to current needs. A certain percentage of new employees should be engineering graduates. Another percentage should come from other technical disciplines, and the remainder should be from a non-technical group; i.e., business and liberal arts.

The selection procedure also consists of two phases. An aptitude examination measures the individual against the work to be performed. No attempt is made to make a definitive judgment from this. It is simply one quantitative measure.

Each individual, however, proceeds through a series of personal interviews. In these interviews his level of interest, desire, communication skills, and other personal characteristics are evaluated by several marketing managers.

"As a result of the aptitude examination, personal interviews, and the individual's interest," states a company official, "those persons whom we feel will be successful in the IBM Corporation are offered employment and entered into the training program."

The Step-by-Step Program*

Because of the large investment which most companies make in each sales representative employed, they can scarcely afford many errors in selection. Yet it is only recently that many sales executives have realized how much a sound personnel selection program can do for them. Two misconceptions were so much a part of their thinking that they could not derive full benefit from their selection efforts.

One misconception was that "selling is selling" and that if a man could sell one company's line, he could handle practically any selling job. This is a completely invalid assumption. Some sales jobs require the ability to entertain customers and to be the center of attention. The major requirement for other sales jobs is the ability to advise customers on highly technical matters, and for others the ability to train retail salesmen.

---

*From *How to Recruit, Select, and Place Salesmen*, by Dr. Robert N. McMurry (Dartnell). The forms referred to are contained in this publication.

As sales jobs differ, so do the kinds of people who can fill them successfully. It is small wonder that sales executives have trouble hiring good men if they keep looking for a universal "sales type" personality. All available evidence indicates that they have done markedly better in predicting job success when they match each applicant's qualifications with the specific requirements of the particular sales job involved.

The Step-by-Step Selection Program calls for as careful and thorough an evaluation of the candidate as possible. Much time is usually required in screening and, particularly, in interviewing. An additional step—the Home Interview—is frequently used before the final hiring decision is made. Because of the difficulty in evaluating all factors essential to success in this field, several executives frequently take part in making the final overall rating of sales applicants. Here, step by step, are stages of the program applied specifically to the selection of salesmen:

Step One: Developing Hiring Specifications. Occasionally, field observers, after detailed analysis in the territory to be covered, supplement the job descriptions given by the sales representatives. Statistical studies frequently yield important specifications.

Step Two: Recruiting. See the previous chapter for specific methods of recruiting sales representatives.

Step Three: Screening. Both rough screening and fine screening are generally used. Sight screening is used occasionally for walk-in applicants, but the more common rough screen is the "Go/No Go" screening based on a brief interview, a letter, a review, or an application. The application is then subjected to very careful diagnostic screening. The Application for Sales Position form is commonly used because of its detail, and some large companies use a specially designed Weighted Application Screening form.

Step Four: Testing. Ordinarily, only mental ability tests are used. Some companies, however, verify interview findings by having an expert administer projective tests.

Step Five: Checking Applicant's History. At least two telephone checks are usually made with previous employers—if necessary, even by long distance. The Telephone Check on Sales Applicant form is usually used. Occasionally, if the man has only a brief work history, the Telephone Check with Schools form is needed. If his present job has been a long one, a personal Credit Report may be useful.

Step Six: The Patterned Interview. The Patterned Interview Form—Sales Position—is generally used because of its completeness and its special coverage of sales activities. Although from 45 minutes to 1½ hours are necessary for each interview, it should be remembered that proper screening and testing will have greatly reduced the number of applicants to whom this step will be applied.

Auxiliary Step: The Home Interview. Many companies have found it profitable when filling sales positions to make a visit to the applicant's home to determine the effect a man's home life might have on his job performance.

Ostensibly, this visit is to acquaint the wife with the job and its opportunities, but actually it is to determine who is dominant in the home—who "wears the pants"—and, if it be the wife, her attitude toward the applicant and the job. This is done primarily by listening and by guiding the conversation—never by a formal interview. The home interview assists materially in evaluating the support which the applicant will receive from home, and the pressures his home life will place upon him.

Step Seven: The Overall Rating. Frequently, several executives will participate in this step. Sometimes they simply make a careful review of all the records concerning the applicant. More often they actually meet and talk with him briefly before they try to evaluate him. This procedure offers two advantages: It provides a check on the field interviewer's judgment. If the major sales executives—both in the home office and in the field—do not approve of the applicant, there is little point in hiring him.

Small companies which cannot provide thorough training for their salesmen usually place considerable stress on the applicant's directly related sales experience. Larger companies are in a better position to hire trainees. In either case, however, "will-do" factors are considered as carefully as "can-do" factors.

All the basic character traits, except leadership, are considered very important for most sales jobs, with special emphasis frequently being given to self-reliance, ability to get along with others, and perseverance. Leadership is important in jobs involving training or supervising others. Emotional maturity and motivation are also given careful scrutiny to be sure that applicant fits the job requirements.

Screening Techniques

It is usually necessary to interview 10 applicants for a salaried sales position to get one likely to "make the grade." Since it costs from $1,000 to $2,000 to get a salesman into profitable production, a selection pattern which eliminates or "screens out" applicants who do not seem to meet a company's minimum standards is essential. This is a matter of observation and the use of a form to spotlight *negative* qualities in the applicant. A sales manager may not be too sure about the qualities required to make a man successful in sales work, but he usually knows pretty well the qualities which make for failure.

One plan is to analyze sales "separations," i.e., salesmen who have been previously employed, but who for one reason or another have been "separated" from the sales payroll, and thus establish a pattern for use by employment managers or branch managers. Since the first task in selection is to weed out the misfits, the use of elimination tests such as the following, prepared by a well-known food manufacturer and based on a careful analysis of the sales records of that company, has considerable practical value.

1. *Former salesmen of leading competitive organizations.*

Experience has taught this company that men from companies in the same line of business have more to unlearn than to learn, and they invariably undermine the work of an instructor putting through a group of salesmen. They know all the answers, or think they do, and the percentage of them who make good is surprisingly small.

2. *Men on whom a doubtful credit report has been received.*

Most of the salesmen collect some money and if they have a bad credit record, too high a percentage of them finally "borrow" a small sum to pay some pressing creditor. Then the trouble begins to pyramid until it must be turned over to the bonding company. Checking with a credit agency has greatly reduced this company's bonding cases.

3. *Men who have had more than five previous jobs.*

Habitual job jumpers are almost always convincing in explaining why they left previous jobs. These reasons often sound so plausible that many a sales manager hires them. Except for vacation jobs, the young man with more than five previous jobs has already established a habit he may never break—quitting when the first cloud rises on his job horizon.

4. *Men who have left previous jobs because of layoff, force reduced, merger, business slump, job discontinued.*

Many applicants think that any of these reasons are excellent ones for being out of work. Actually they may be telltale evidences of weaknesses. Good men do not usually lose jobs because of mergers, slumps, temporary layoffs. At these times the weaker men are eliminated, and to hire such men is merely to pick up the human material which some other company has discarded.

5. *Men whose wives or immediate families are not 100 percent behind them in their desire for the job.*

It is better to find out beforehand than later that a man's wife simply can't bear to have her husband away most of the time. If she does object he finds a thousand excuses to stay home more than is good for his job. Also, you find out in this way whether a man's wife is willing to move to his new headquarters town. Many wives object to leaving their families and established friends.

6. *Men who have domestic difficulties.*

Of course, there are divorced men who are excellent sales material. But when a man is paying alimony or separation allowances, he frequently has too many worries to permit him to think constructively about his job.

7. *Men about whom there is some question as to their physical fitness.*

Just because a man looks healthy and strong to a layman is no sign a doctor's examination may not turn up some condition which will be a severe handicap to success. Get a physical report for every applicant.

8. *Men who have been ill several times for a month or more in recent years.*

Who wants a salesman out of his territory a month or more every year while he stays home or is ill in a hospital? This may sound hard and cruel, but a man who can't keep well is a costly luxury on any sales force.

9. *Men whose salaries, in previous jobs, were more than 50 percent higher than your beginning salary.*

There are men who can accept a big salary reduction, reduce expenses, start over again, live within their means, and make a "go" of a new job which pays much less, particularly if there is a chance to regain their former level within a reasonable period of time, but they are few and far between. Most of them will feel sorry for themselves after they have been on the job awhile.

10. *Men who have heavy financial responsibilities to their families beyond ordinary living expenses, or who are in debt.*

Some sales managers take the attitude that it is none of their business what a man's responsibilities are: Nor do they attempt to pry into a man's personal affairs. But men who have too heavy a drain on their earnings are very doubtful assets in a sales department.

11. *Men who have gone to college more than three years, but did not graduate.*

Here is one which most sales managers could easily overlook on the grounds that any college education is better than none. But the fellow who goes more than three years without graduating often just isn't a "finisher." He starts well but never gets to the finish line. And one thing a salesman must do is "close." Nor can a good salesman ever be made of a quitter.

12. *Men who reformed whether in regard to financial matters or in habits such as drinking.*

The way to judge this question is this: How many men whom you knew in their early twenties ever changed much or reformed? Weren't the habitual drunks, borrowers, cheats, and spendthrifts of your college acquaintances the same fellows who continued these habits through middle age? How many such men have you ever known who really reformed? Of course, you can think of a couple of examples, but they are probably exceptions. Run a sales department, not a reform school.

Application Blanks

It is standard employment practice to first get the applicant's qualifications on paper. Many sales managers devote the first interview to that end. It not only saves a great deal of time, since it enables you to weed out undesirable candidates at the very outset, but having the qualifications of a man in statement form serves as a basis for the second interview. This is the same method that a banker follows in extending credit. The first time you come in for a loan he talks to you briefly, sizes you up as being a man of good character and then gives you a statement to fill out and bring back. There is much to be said in favor of the same plan in hiring salesmen.

Some companies go so far as to give specific weight to the various factors they seek in salesmen, and then arrange their application blanks so that a sales manager can *mathematically* determine how an applicant measures up to the company pattern. But experience with weighted application blanks has not been too good. Many sales managers who tried the plan later discarded it. Prevailing practice is to use the applicant blank as a guide to the interview, and any weighting needed is done in the interview report.

While some qualifications of a salesman cannot be predetermined and must be ascertained by impressions, there are a number which can be reduced to statement form, just as some facts needed in the granting of credit can be reduced to statement form. Five of these are:

Health: No matter how capable a man might be, or how industrious he might seem, he cannot succeed unless he has the physical stamina needed in present-day selling. A sick body cannot nourish a healthy mind. A salesman who tires out cannot do a full day's work. A salesman who is ailing cannot have the fire and fight that count for so much in chalking up a sales victory. So before any man is hired' for a sales position, he should be required to answer in writing such questions as:

Have you had a recent physical examination?

What were the results?

What serious illness have you had within the past 5 years?

What is the present condition of your health?

Are you willing to take a physical examination?

Character: Your applicant might grade perfect on health and be very capable and industrious, but he will fail unless he is honest. He has to be a "square shooter" or he won't wear with his customers and he won't give you a square deal. The best way to judge a man's character is by his past record. So he should be willing to give you in writing:

Five persons whom he knows either personally or in business.

Detailed information about positions previously held.

Names of persons in your employ acquainted with him.

Is he willing to give a surety bond at your expense?

If not—was such a bond ever refused?

What insurance does he carry?

With this information you can send a standard blank to the references given to you which lists various factors that reflect character, as well as capability, and ask each person to mark the applicant "good," "poor," or "indifferent" on each point. You will find this plan more helpful than merely asking for general information, which affords an opportunity for evasion.

Industry: The success which a healthy salesman of good character can attain is directly related to how hard he is willing to work. There is nothing worse than a lazy salesman, because he doesn't produce himself, and he keeps others from working. You can't tell how hard a man will work by how fast he talks. You must find that out by such indirect questions as:

At what age did you commence work?

How many jobs have you held since you left school?

How many accounts did you work in your last position?

How often did you see these accounts?

What were your sales for the past year? Preceding year?

This information should be further supplemented by personally questioning the applicant concerning what he does with his spare time; where he grew up—on a farm, in a small town, or in a big city; possibly he can show you copies of reports for some given period turned in to a previous employer. Still further information will be developed for the reference blanks to be sent to the applicant's references.

Knowledge: This is of growing importance since selling is becoming more and more a matter of knowing your line. Take insurance, investments, or any one of a dozen lines and you find that unless a man knows the business he cannot succeed. But a new man can be taught, *provided he has the capacity to study and learn.* If he is not willing to study, he is a poor risk. How can you find that out on your application blank? Ask indirect questions such as:

What study courses have you completed since leaving school?

To what trade publications do you subscribe?

What books on selling have you read within the past year?

What general business books have you read within the last year?

Also find out details of the man's experience: What territories has he covered? What classes of buyers has he called upon? What products has he sold? What products has he been most successful in selling, etc.? Finally, ask him to write you a letter stating briefly his reasons for wishing to join your organization. This letter will give you an insight into the mental caliber of the man, his ability to organize his thoughts, and his ability to express himself—all indexes of the applicant's receptivity to educational influences.

Previous Sales Record: When an applicant has had previous sales experience, it is useful to ask him to detail that experience. Did he like selling? Why did he change? What problems did he run into?

If a candidate says he increased his sales volume a certain percentage over a certain period of time, he should be asked to outline specifically what he did to achieve this improvement. Perhaps it was a price decrease or changes in the business economy over which he had no control and which merely brought him bigger orders. One long-experienced sales interviewer says:

"I note particularly the attitude of a salesman toward his former sales manager and with regard to the policies of the company for which he worked.

"His attitude and his expression along these lines frequently give a valuable clue as to what we can expect from him."

Dartnell Application Blanks

While there are some companies which have developed an application blank of their own, more than 5,000 sales managers now use the standard application blank developed by Dartnell. They prefer the Dartnell blank because it is in general use, and salesmen are usually familiar with filling it out. It puts the burden of inquisitiveness on the shoulders of a third party, and a sales manager can remove any feeling of resentment by merely explaining that it is a standard blank. The Dartnell standard blank is revised each year to incorporate such changes as users suggest or new legislation requires. It eliminates prying questions which aggravate salesmen and it meets equal opportunity employment requirements.

Another advantage of using Dartnell standard application blanks is their reasonable cost. This is a particular advantage to concerns which use only a few hundred annually. Samples of the blank may be obtained without charge by addressing The Dartnell Corporation, Chicago, Ill. 60640. A standard reference blank, for mailing out to names given by the salesman as references, designed to grade salesmen rather than to generalize about their qualifications, is also available from the same company.

Race, Creed, or Color

Title VII of the Federal Civil Rights Act of 1964 prohibits many hiring practices which might discriminate against applicants because of race, color, sex, religion, or national origin. You or anyone else doing hiring in your organization should become thoroughly familiar with the act in order to avoid incurring penalties. Many questions formerly asked in interviews or on application blanks are now prohibited in all states. You may no longer ask a job applicant to submit a photograph of himself or herself prior to an interview.

Compliance with the provisions of Title VII includes advertising for applicants—you cannot, for instance, specify that you will consider only male applicants if the job opening could conceivably be handled by a woman.

Interviewing the Applicant

The next step in the selection procedure, after applicants have filled out an application for employment, is to determine by personal interview—preferably by more than one executive—those who hold the most promise of succeeding. The interview is by far the most important of the selection procedures.

Successful interviewing is more than a knack. It involves techniques which experience has shown are the best ways to draw from an applicant the information you need to make a decision. That includes information the applicant prefers to withhold. For this reason, large national organizations devote considerable time to coaching those who will interview sales applicants. This training usually is given over a two-day period at the factory under the direction of a consulting psychologist. It is designed to show the interviewer: (1) How to get the facts he needs, (2) how to get them quickly, (3) how to ask questions to prevent calculated answers, (4) how to ask key questions twice in such a way that they appear to be different questions.

Interviewers invite the applicant to talk about himself by saying something like this: "Start with your first job or the job you had 10 years ago (or 3 years or 5 years ago) and tell me as quickly as possible the kind of job it was, why you took it, what you did and how you sold." If applicant has sales ability he should be able to talk intelligently and connectedly.

The Patterned Interview

This technique was developed by Dr. Robert N. McMurry, a Chicago consulting psychologist. It has been successfully employed on a nationwide scale. While the patterned interview is not greatly different from any other method of interviewing, it does require that a written record be made of the interview, and the standard form used for that purpose provides a way for the interviewer to record his judgment. This form has spaces for this purpose and provides a "weighted" average. Dr. McMurry has found, for example, that the ideal employee has the following personality characteristics:

1. He gets along well with people; he has a fair number of friends and makes social contacts easily.

2. He is a stable person; he stays on his jobs an average of two or three years and he also lives in one place a similar length of time.

3. He has a reasonable degree of perseverance; he completes his schooling and gives other evidences of finishing what he starts.

4. He shows traits of leadership; he does things for himself rather than depending on others to do them for him.

5. He is moderately ambitious and shows some initiative; he makes some effort to improve himself and his position.

6. He has matured to the extent that he has become independent of his parents and others and is willing to accept responsibility; he pays his bills and takes into consideration the consequences of what he does.

7. He is capable of loyalty and consideration for other people; he is a good husband and father and is loyal to his employer.

8. He is industrious; his record shows that he works all the time without being pushed.

9. He has motivation to work hard, has dependents to support, a desire to raise his standard of living, and a wish to make money for its own sake or to make a better place for himself with his employer.

It is not essential that the applicant be outstanding in all of the foregoing characteristics in order to be satisfactory as an employee. If these traits are rated on a four-point scale ("1" excellent; "2" good; "3" fair; and "4" unsatisfactory), it is permissible for him to be classed as "3" on one or two traits if there are compensating "1's" on the other traits.

After ratings have been made on these nine characteristics, they are reviewed. *If a man is rated as "4" on any one of them he should be rejected regardless of the number of favorable qualities he may have.* This may seem unnecessarily ruthless. Nevertheless, experience has indicated that this is advisable. For example, a man may have every requisite for success except ambition. Yet that alone will cause him to fail.

Once the ratings on the subtraits have been made, the interviewer should then take the final step—make the overall rating. In making this final judgment, applicants should be classified roughly as follows:

1. Those men who show no evidence of immaturity or disloyalty; indicate they are stable, industrious, persevering, and ambitious; can get along with others; are leaders; are well-motivated; have good

work records; and have proved sales ability in the appliance field should be classified as "1." They constitute the cream of the crop and are the most desirable type of applicant. Not only should the interviewer check them as "1," but he should also indicate in the space allotted for comments, precisely why he feels that they are outstanding.

2. Those who have good work records and are fairly experienced, successful salesmen, but who show some evidences of immaturity or slight instability or tendencies toward lack of perseverance or "lone wolf" characteristics, or a slight lack of industry or ambition, or who may have slight trouble getting along with others, or whose motivation is questionable, or who are not leaders (in other words, those who may have slight deficiencies in one of the nine basic traits) should be regarded as "2." As long as the undesirable traits are not serious, they should not bar the man from consideration. However, in addition to rating the man as "2," the interviewer should also specify exactly wherein the man's major weaknesses lie. This forewarns supervision so that they will know what to expect and how to handle the man should he cause trouble.

3. In the case of men who have little experience and have not demonstrated their ability to sell and at the same time show even moderate evidences of immaturity (even though they are strong otherwise), considerable caution should be exercised. The fact that they have not demonstrated their ability to sell is in itself a sort of danger. It is never possible to know whether or not a man can sell until he has had an opportunity to show what he can do. Therefore, a man who has not demonstrated sales ability may or may not be promising material, depending upon factors of maturity or personality adjustments. Because of this, all applicants who fall into this category should be considered as "3" or marginal men. They should be taken only if the supply of "1's" and "2's" is inadequate.

4. Where the applicant shows serious evidences of immaturity, is not ambitious, industrious, or stable; or where he shows real lack of motivation he should be rejected even though he has demonstrated limited success as a salesman. Even though individuals of this character may have been fair producers, their personality make-up is such that they will almost inevitably be problems, often to such an extent that the supervisor must spend so much time with them that he more than loses any benefits he derives from their sales ability.

The practical worth of applicant ratings depends almost entirely upon the judgment of the executive who does the interviewing. The

McMurry plan does offer a means by which several executives can interview the same applicant, each using the same rating form, and the composite rating thus secured is more dependable than when only one person makes the decision.

Form No. F2507

White

PATTERNED INTERVIEW FORM

Rating: 1 2 3 4   Interviewer _____   Branch (or Distributor) _____   Date _____

Comments: _____
Maturity (as indicated by perseverance; loyalty; industry; stability; self-reliance; _____

ability to get along with people) resourcefulness; motivation

Name _____   Social Security No. _____   Draft status _____

Present address _____   City _____   State _____
Is this a desirable neighborhood? Too high class? Questionable?

Length of time at this address _____   Length of time at previous address _____
Does this indicate stability?

Do you have sole use of your car? _____   What is condition of car? _____

What led you to apply for work here? _____
Get underlying reason. Was it earning possibilities, security, prestige, acquaintance with company employees?

WORK EXPERIENCE. Cover all positions. This information is very important. Interviewer should record last position first. Every month since leaving school should be accounted for. Note military service in work record in continuity with jobs held before and since that time. Experience in Armed Forces should be covered on supplemental form.

Were you in the Service? Yes   No . From _____ to _____ . Why did you fail to return to your pre-service

employer? _____   If 4F or medical discharge—Why? _____

What class of discharge? (honorable, without honor, or dishonorable) If other than honorable—Why? _____
Interviewer must see papers

LAST OR PRESENT POSITION

Company _____   City _____   From _____ 19 to _____ 19
Do these dates check with application?

How was job obtained? _____
Has he shown self-reliance in getting his jobs?

Nature of work at start _____   Starting earnings _____
Get exact description

Nature of work before leaving _____   Final earnings _____
Any supervisory positions? Did he progress?   Any indication of ambition?

What awards, prizes, or sales contests did you win? _____

Supervisor? _____   How did you and your supervisor get along? _____   Any friction?
Name

What did you especially like about the job? _____
Has he been happy and content in his work?

Any special dislikes? _____
Were his dislikes justified?

Reasons for leaving _____
What forced his decision? Why this particular time?

Do you have any part-time jobs? _____
Was this done with employer's knowledge and approval? What kind of work? Will this interfere with his work here?

NEXT TO LAST POSITION

Company _____   City _____   From _____ 19 to _____ 19
Do these dates check with application?

How was job obtained? _____
Has he shown self-reliance in getting his jobs?

Nature of work at start _____   Starting earnings _____
Get exact description

An interview blank designed for The White Motor Company by The McMurry Company. Note suggestions to interviewer (in small print).

The Telephone Check

The third step in the selection procedure for salesmen is to follow through on the interview and check and double check the applicant. Although experience with written references from previous employers has been uniformly bad, it is still common practice. But the principal things you want to know about a prospective salesman, such as whether or not he is overfond of his liquor or is undependable, are seldom brought out except in a man-to-man conversation, either in person or over the telephone. A mail check does not answer the all-important question: "How good is the man, and what has he done to prove he can sell?"

It is to get this type of information, not easily obtained in any other way, that most companies now require a thoroughgoing telephone check (long-distance if necessary) plus a retail credit report. A form is provided: (1) To make sure that the person doing the calling will not overlook any question of importance, and (2) to facilitate preparing a report of the call so that it may be filed with the applicant's other personal history papers. Here, for example, are some of the questions listed on the telephone check blank used by the Pillsbury Company:

PERSONAL OR TELEPHONE CHECKUP

Was Mr. .... employed by your company? Yes........ No........

What were dates of his employment? From ....to..

What was nature of his work? ....

He states he was earning .... at the time he left. Is this true? Yes........No........

If "no" what were his earnings? ....

What were his reasons for leaving? ....

Would you rehire? Yes........ No........ If "no" why not? ....

....

As far as you know, did he have financial trouble? ....

Have his income garnished or assigned? ....

Did he have any domestic trouble which interfered with his work? ....

....

How were his ethics, morals, and habits with respect to drinking and gambling?

....

Photographs of Applicants

These cannot be requested with an application for employment, as explained previously in the discussion of Title VII of the Civil Rights Act. However, once an applicant is hired, there is nothing against requiring a photograph for the company files. It will come in handy later for use in bulletins, company publications, and possibly advertising and publicity. There are other reasons for requiring a photograph after employment: if the employee later proves dishonest or is discovered to have hidden a criminal record, the photograph in the company file will prove valuable to investigating authorities. Photographs are absolutely necessary for some salesmen who are required to wear photographed visitor badges when calling on customers engaged in classified government work.

The Physical Checkup

It is also important that the selection procedure require each applicant, after he has qualified in other ways, to take a physical examination. A regular form is used which the examining medical officer fills out and returns directly to the interested executive. This may seem unimportant, but an applicant who has a foot affliction, or has had a heart condition which might interfere with traveling, or is color blind and cannot see stop lights if he is to drive a company car, can easily let the company in for a lot of expense. Some salesmen refuse point-blank to take a physical examination, and that in itself is a good reason why they should not be employed.

Psychological Testing

During World War I, a professor of psychology from Northwestern University, Evanston, Ill., undertook to screen men in the Armed Services to discover promising officer material. This professor, Dr. Walter Dill Scott, used batteries of so-called "paper-and-pencil" tests to measure aptitudes for leadership, with considerable success. After the war, a number of large sales organizations, including The American Tobacco Company and Remington Rand Inc., used these Scott tests for a time. When Dr. Scott moved up to the presidency of the university, his experiments were carried on by Dr. Samuel Stevens, later president of Grinnell College. Dr. Stevens' contribution to sales-testing procedures was to develop the pattern type of testing.

He first analyzed records of the company so far as present salesmen were concerned, and tested all those who had been successful.

From their profiles he compiled a pattern, and into that pattern he fitted, by using the same battery of tests, applicants for sales positions. It was his theory that if he could give a sales manager more salesmen like his present successful salesmen and eliminate those like his present unsuccessful salesmen, the problem of selection might be solved. When World War II came along, all branches of the service used psychological testing extensively not only for screening recruits, but for promotions and special assignments, too. And in the war plants, workers were upgraded and moved up to supervisory jobs on the strength of these paper-and-pencil tests. When the war ended, and sales organizations had to be rebuilt and expanded, sales managers figured that if testing had worked so well for the Armed Services, it should work for them, too. The number of psychologists employed by industry was more than doubled after the war.

On some subjects, there is considerable unanimity of opinion among experienced sales executives; not so on the subject of psychological testing—or, as it is more commonly called, aptitude testing—for selecting salesmen. There are definitely two schools of thought—those who swear by this process and those who swear at it.

Unfortunately, such testing got off to a bad start in some cities when do-it-yourself aptitude tests were sold to industry and applied by the inexperienced. A specialist in the field of psychological testing, now president of a midwest college, has said, "Do-it-yourself psychological testing has as much validity as do-it-yourself cancer cures." Seeming to substantiate this statement are a number of sales executives who tried this type of testing and were disappointed.

There are, of course, large corporations with psychologists on their staffs or under contract who test all salesmen routinely before employment. Obviously, these companies are convinced of the value of such tests when administered by professionals and—even more importantly—interpreted by the professionals.

Two Types of Tests

The fundamentals of testing salesmen are generally considered in two categories:

1. *Personality*

2. *Sales aptitude*

Tests in the first category are intended to answer the question, *"Does this man have a good sales personality?"* In the second category are tests intended to answer the question, *"Does he have the proper aptitudes for selling?"*

Sometimes these tests are combined, sometimes separate, sometimes administered by the sales executive (who "grades" them with a set of prepared answers and a scoring chart), sometimes by a psychologist on the staff, and sometimes by outside consulting firms, with or without psychologists. Considering the wide variability of practices, it is not surprising that evaluation of such testing is statistically hard to come by.

Personality Tests

Tests for "sales personality" run a gamut of "desirable and undesirable factors" from A to Z. For example, one company specializing in this type of testing lists such factors as:

1. *Aggressiveness*
2. *Business sense*
3. *Confidence*
4. *Dominance*
5. *Enthusiasm*
6. *Foresightedness*
7. *Group sociability*
8. *Happiness*
9. *Incisiveness,* and so on through *Xtra-sensory perceptiveness, Youthful outlook, and Zealousness.*

Those who feel that question-and-answer psychological tests are of limited value list a number of defects. These include:

1. *Oversimplification*
2. *Neglect of potentialities for personality development*
3. *Varying degrees of articulateness of respondent*
4. *Lack of standards for comparison*
5. *Lack of statistical validity*
6. *Lack of self-knowledge*
7. *Tendency to "fake" replies*

Sales Aptitude Testing

Included in, or separate from, the personality tests, a series of "sales aptitudes" is often evaluated.

Practically everything that has been said pro and con with regard to the sales personality tests is repeated with reference to testing for sales aptitudes.

The usual sales aptitude evaluation covers such factors as the following:

1. *Verbal intelligence*
2. *Ability to communicate ideas*
3. *Controlled aggressiveness*
4. *Sales sense*
5. *Insight into higher motivation*
6. *Diplomacy and tact*
7. *Ability to accept criticism*
8. *Resistance to discouragement*
9. *Sales motivation*
10. *Self-discipline*

The overlapping between sales aptitudes and personality qualifications is quite frequent.

Additionally, potential sales executives may be also evaluated for such factors as:

1. *Administrative ability*
2. *Emotional stability*
3. *Ability to inspire others*
4. *Business judgment*
5. *Supervisory capacity*
6. *Initiative*
7. *Resourcefulness*
8. *Maturity*
9. *Organizing ability*
10. *Training skills*

There can be no difference of opinion on the value of determining how a prospective salesman measures up in such factors as those listed above. The difference of opinion arises in the concept of whether valid tests can be made of such factors.

"Home-Made" Tests

Some sales managers and sales recruiters have devised their own informal sales aptitude tests. This process is an adaptation of role playing. They take the applicant into a private office and set up a mock situation, saying, *"I am Mr. Brown, purchasing agent for the XYZ Company. See if you can sell me a carload of nickel-plated widgets."*

They then try to stump the applicant by trotting out questions and objections.

Critics of this type of testing say that, while it does provide the sales executive with some indication of the applicant's ability to think fast and to express himself clearly, it may not measure his actual sales ability. Such critics believe that there is no one correct answer to any given sales situation, and that a tricky question may penalize a prospectively good salesman in a hiring interview; whereas he might, after a few months of experience, handle the same question very successfully. They also point out that such examiners may oversimplify their questions and objections to the point where even potentially poor salesmen can answer them easily, thus leading to an unfortunate amount of turnover.

In commenting on aptitude testing, an officer of a highly successful sales organization in the textiles field reports:

> We use aptitude and psychological tests primarily:
> 1. When hiring a man, to be assured that he will properly fit in with the company and in the job requirements.
> 2. When wishing to upgrade a man, to see if he has the capacity to handle a more complex job.
>
> We never conduct mass testing, believing that:
> 1. The disturbance caused outweighs the added knowledge gained.
> 2. Little will be added to our present knowledge of the individuals. Management already knows if they are doing a good or bad job. If management has been periodically reviewing their work progress and has been counseling with them as it should do, a program for their development is already in progress.

But for even these limited applications there is a considerable difference of opinion among sales managers as to how much dependence can be placed on psychological tests. After four years' experience with a battery of standard self-administered tests, one executive said he thought they were too restricted to count for more than 10 points in a selection procedure. He thought they gave a sales manager a false sense of security. He added:

> "I myself took a sales aptitude test not long ago and was given a very high rating. However, I then took a test with another organization and found that

some of the things in which I had been rated particularly high by the first testing organization were rated low by the second one. Furthermore, some of the qualities in which I know myself actually to be deficient were rated high by both testing organizations. It seems to me, therefore, that there is still a great deal of room for standardization in such testing and that these tests throw more light on the test and the person giving it than on the one who takes it.

"Some sales personnel executives say that aptitude testing for salesmen has prevented a lot of mistakes in hiring. This may be true, particularly in very large sales organizations; but I personally feel that in an organization such as ours where we can sit down and talk with each applicant and become informed of his past successes and failures, we learn more about him than can be divulged by any number of trick questions."

On the other hand, you find considerable enthusiasm for psychological testing in the insurance field. The Life Insurance Sales Research Institute, some years ago, worked out what it calls the "Aptitude Index" for use among member companies, and it proved helpful. Obviously, developing a battery of tests to be applied to applicants selling a special and similar service offers less opportunities for error than when the test is general. It should be noted, however, that these tests are not represented to institute members as being capable of doing the entire selection job, but rather they can be used to check judgments of supervisors after applicants have (1) been screened, (2) been interviewed, and (3) had their references checked.

An executive of one of the major automobile sales organizations had this to say: "We have experimented off and on for about six years with psychological tests and aptitude testing for salesmen. I am personally sold on the value of such tests in general, but I am convinced that there is a lot of testing being done that comes far from hitting the spot, not because the idea is unsound, but because the tests themselves are improperly designed or executed or both. I believe there is a place for scientific testing but there is still a lot of work to be done before a sales manager can feel safe in depending on such tests."

Even though tests are carefully validated—that is to say, tested on the best and worst men in your sales force—they must still be checked for reliability to fully determine their value in the selection procedure. This requires about two years' time.

The Jewel Tea Company of Chicago uses psychological tests for hiring and promoting employees, but only *after* the employee has been hired or promoted by conventional methods. Test results are used to help an employee to cope with his new responsibilities.

Is Psychological Testing Worth It?

As published in the *Home Appliance Builder*, a recent survey among subscribers to the *Harvard Business Review*, conducted by the Research Institute of America, showed that 60 percent of companies with more than 10,000 employees used psychological testing. Another survey of executives under 40 years of age disclosed that 90 percent of these men had taken one or more such tests. Perhaps some extravagant claims have been made for "packaged" test batteries for the selection of salesmen.

Personality tests have been the most vulnerable to attack. According to the report, the greatest success to date in selection techniques has been with what psychologists call the *Biographical Information Blank or Background Survey*. These are based on the premise that the best predictor of the future is the past. In this technique questions are asked about early family background, childhood hobbies and activities, past school performance and extracurricular activities, attitudes toward past experiences, etc. But instead of the applicant answering in his own words (as he would in an interview), he checks one of the several alternative answers that are provided in the questionnaire.

Experience indicates that some types of tests are more likely to predict job success accurately than others, and that is as specific as one can be until the tests have been tried in actual situations.

Efficient Appraisal Procedure

Any appraisal system should include a minimum of four tests and inventories to aid in the appraisal of mental equipment, aptitude for selling, stability, and vocational interest in selling activities. To add more tests frequently measures the same general factor a second time and decreases the emphasis upon and the time for interviews and investigations in the appraisal of personal history.

The appraisal system should include a good personal history blank to aid in the appraisal of physical qualifications; education; occupational experience; financial status and achievement; activities; contacts; marital and family status; financial capacity to survive, and all other factors known to be important. The factors mentioned are best appraised by interviews and investigations, although supplementary steps are recommended to insure sound conclusions.

The system should include a convenient manual of instruction and a good rating form to facilitate appraisal procedure.

Appraising Health and Vitality: The majority of people think of health as the absence of illness. Few understand the substantial differences in the degree of vitality which exist even among persons who appear to be in good health. Far too many salesmen are handicapped by the lack of full vitality, so important to the generation of enthusiasm while engaged in selling activities. This means that the employer and the medical examiner should look for vitality as well as for the negative factors of illness and impairments that will hinder a salesman.

Appraising Mental Equipment: The mental equipment of an individual cannot be appraised as a single unit factor, but must, instead, be appraised in several dimensions. It cannot be appraised by the use of intelligence tests alone, since some highly intelligent people have not yet acquired much knowledge and experience. Neither is mental equipment determined by the number of years of education, nor by the degrees and diplomas received. It has been clearly demonstrated that some high-school graduates are the equal of others who have been graduated from college. It is necessary, therefore, to appraise mental ability, education, and experience.

An accepted method is through the use of a standard mental-ability test with proper adjustments for differences in age. It has been found that as people grow older the speed with which they can complete test items decreases even while their knowledge and experience increase.

The appraiser also must bear in mind that the graduates of each high school and college vary a great deal in the type of courses completed and the quality of work done. Without question, the graduates who earned high grades in recommended courses possess more useful knowledge, on the average, than graduates who earned average or low-average grades, or high grades in courses of doubtful value in business.

The amount and soundness of knowledge possessed by a salesman as related to a given field of work are best determined by a special objective examination developed for the purpose. Such tests are helpful in appraising experienced salesmen or applicants for promotion but much less so in the appraisal of applicants for employment on an apprentice basis. Without such tests, this factor must be appraised in the interview.

Appraising Aggressiveness (Aptitude for Selling): All personality inventories measuring dominance, aggressiveness, and leadership have two important weaknesses which must be corrected in some way. These weaknesses are:

1. Bright persons frequently give the answers which yield high scores and ratings instead of the answers which reflect their true reactions. Such

ABILITY FACTORS (Ability to)

ITEM	Class 1	Class 2	Class 3	Class 4
1. Analyze	Develops essential facts in any situation	Usually gets to bottom of problems	Unable to form conclusions	Often misinterprets facts
2. Create or Invent	Develops and expands his work	Occasionally creates and executes ideas	Fairly aggressive	Waits to be told
3. Visualize or Imagine	Possesses unusual foresight	Quick to grasp possibilities of new plans	Slow to enthuse over changes	Can only comprehend facts proven by experience
4. Make Decisions	Prompt and accurate in his conclusions	Makes few errors in judgment	Usually hesitates between two courses of action	Does many ill-considered things
5. Select and Develop Others	Picks winners and develops them	Chooses good men and trains them well	Occasionally develops a good man	Sometimes spoils potential executives
6. Organize	Creates harmonious efforts among individuals to a constructive end	Secures concrete results by directing efforts of others	Secures loyalty of workers but cannot get results	Cannot secure team work
7. Cooperate	Will help others at personal sacrifice	Good team worker	Strictly an individualist	Selfish and obstructive
8. Be Tactful	Contacts always pleasant	Approach usually good	Occasionally in wrong	Gets in wrong continuously
9. Be Efficient	Puts his effort where it counts the most	Discriminates between important and unimportant matters	Does not always apply himself to best advantage	Takes everything as it comes
10. Express Ideas Clearly and Convincingly	Uses forceful words in effective manner	Logical but not impressive	Cannot put ideas in understandable form	Cannot interest people in his subjects
11. Work Accurately	Others always agree with results	Usually accurate	Makes a few errors	Work always has to be checked
12. Work Rapidly	Exceptionally quick	Can speed up under pressure	Usually behind others	Very slow
13. Remember	Never forgets a thing	Can usually recall salient facts	Has to be occasionally reminded	Cannot retain facts or details

MISCELLANEOUS FACTORS

ITEM	Class 1	Class 2	Class 3	Class 4
1. General Knowledge	Talks intelligently on all subjects	Knows something about most subjects	Well read on a few subjects	Limited to superficial facts
2. Specialized Knowledge	Is an authority on his subject	Thoroughly conversant in his field	Not always certain of his fact	Makes incorrect statements
3. Health Habits	Takes best possible care of self	Follows consistently good habits	Slightly impaired by occasional dissipation	No care of self—habitual dissipation
4. Physical Constitution	Rugged—never sick —stand anything	Occasional sickness	Must take care—cannot overwork	Work impaired by poor health
5. Neatness	Immaculate	Always presentable	Sometimes lax	Careless in appearance of person or work

Executives should be asked to fill out the form to the extent of their personal observation and knowledge of the man in question. During the salesman's employment with a company, such a record, made by a person qualified to do so, is of great value in rating him on his present work or for promotion.

applicants sometimes make good impressions and secure positions for which they are not well qualified.

2. Mere "yes" and "no" answers to questions do not reflect the economic and social level at which personality traits function. The type and quality of aggressiveness must be learned in each case if the ratings for this factor are to mean much.

To overcome the weaknesses mentioned, a set of questions has been developed from the standard inventory measuring aggressiveness. The task of the employer in appraisal procedure is then one of checking or evaluating the responses or examples given for truthfulness, currency, and excellence. The examples given should first be read and then checked by questioning the applicant during a carefully planned interview. The purpose, of course, is to determine whether the individual should be rated as "weak," "marginal," "aggressive," or "very aggressive," and whether the type or quality of aggressiveness will win friends or antagonize prospects in selling interviews. Where examples are not given, or where the examples given are not acceptable, all "yes" responses to the same questions in the standard inventory are changed to "no" and the score lowered accordingly.

These four questions will suggest others:

1. Have you ever argued or talked your way past a guard, doorman, receptionist or secretary? (   ) If so, give circumstances and method used.

   Examples given vary from the crude and offensive to those demonstrating much skill and tact. To be acceptable they should show aptitude for getting by obstacles when seeking interviews.

2. Have you ever asked questions of a public speaker (do not include an instructor or a religious leader) during or after his address? (   ) If so, give speaker's subject, size of audience, nature of questions, and the speaker's responses.

   The examples will vary from clumsy questioning of speakers at inconsequential meetings to poise in questioning distinguished leaders. They should show good poise and intelligent thinking in questioning speakers of consequence.

3. Have you solicited funds for a cause in which you were interested? (   ) If so, give the cause, the circumstances, and amounts raised.

   Funds solicited vary from a few cents for unimportant causes to thousands of dollars for causes of great consequence. The examples should show appreciable achievement in soliciting for causes of importance.

4. Have people ever come to you for advice? (   ) If so, give their ages, educational background, occupation, income level, and the type of advice sought and given.

   Advice given varies from unsound to helpful; from that which deals with trivial matters to that which is very important. The advice given should be sound, deal with important issues, and be likely to influence the recipient.

Chapter 42

COMPENSATION OF
SALES EXECUTIVES

G ENERALLY speaking, there is a pronounced relationship between top executive salary levels and company profitability. Dartnell's survey, *Executive Compensation Practices and Trends*, shows this to be true, and so do others. McKinsey & Company's recent 84-company survey points to this same relationship, as explained by Arch Patton, managing partner:

"In the 84-company survey, we found that the highest paid top-executive group in each industry earned a 50 percent greater return on investment than its average competitor and double the return of the lowest-paid competitor. The survey also showed that a similar pattern existed where top-management pay and profit increases over the past decade were concerned.

"As with the question of which came first, the chicken or the egg, the survey does not *prove* that high compensation means high profits. However, the implication that high pay adds something unusual to the mix of executive motivations is hard to doubt. It seems to me that the consistency with which the top corporate *earners* turn out to be the top *payers* is an eloquent testimonial to the value of high compensation—*if* effectively used.

"The survey findings say to me that if company leadership maintains a demanding, productive environment, it can usually afford to pay its outstanding executives well above going rates in the marketplace, for this premium is returned manifold in the profit column."

Sales Role Enlarges

The ever-increasing importance of the marketing man's role at the top executive level of modern companies was highlighted by two news stories that appeared in *Advertising Age*.

The first reported that Thomas S. Carroll, executive vice-president of marketing of Lever Brothers Company, was elected president and chief executive officer of the firm, one of the nation's top 10 advertisers, with expenditures running close to $100 million per year. Mr. Carroll boasts a broad marketing background, having served as a brand manager at Procter & Gamble and subsequently holding down top marketing posts at both General Foods and Colgate-Palmolive.

The appointment of top marketing men to key corporate executive posts is not new among the "Big Three" in the soaps and detergents field. For many years the top men at the biggest of them all, P&G, have been men who came up through the marketing and advertising ranks.

But it isn't only among the giant advertisers that the marketing man is coming out on top of the executive ladder, and that fact is borne out by another study tracing promotions to three executive positions—president, executive vice-president, and vice-president—in a variety of corporations. The study was conducted by R. M. Schmitz & Co., management consultant, in cooperation with W. A. Owens of Purdue University.

In addition to showing that marketing men are moving up the corporate ladder more quickly than their counterparts in other areas of corporate activity, the Schmitz study also shows that they are getting this executive recognition at an earlier age. The average age of the newly named vice-presidents from marketing was 45; the average age for newly-elected vice-presidents from other areas was 47.

Planning for Results

For the company to gain the greatest return on its compensation investment, it must have its objectives well in mind, and then design its compensation program to give emphasis to the attainment of those objectives, such as the following.

1. Production of maximum sales volume; for, as sales increase beyond the break-even point, profits climb rapidly.

2. Production of maximum profits, which might be gained by selectivity in emphasis on product lines or on customer groups.

3. Expense control, which will contribute to satisfactory profit attainment.

4. Cash retainment for capital expansion, which might be achieved through maximum profits and through investment in facilities.

5. Development and retention of a most efficient managerial group which will assure the continuance of the prosperity of the company.

6. Transition from centralized responsibility to decentralized management.

Sales Management asked six corporate officers to give their views on the subject of compensation for sales and marketing executives. Their comments were:

We offer middle and top executives a base salary realistically competitive with similar responsibility at other firms. This means we must constantly monitor the going salary rate for executives, since the pattern changes constantly. We also offer stock options, group insurance, and recently set up a program that pays up to 60 percent of annual salary if an executive is disabled.

> *John G. Brooks, chairman*
> *Lear Siegler, Inc.*
> *Santa Monica, California*

Salary is and should be a major factor, *if* it is based on performance evaluation. We offer bonuses to all key people who have leverage on results. We use stock options for only the top executive group. Options can be most attractive when stock prices are rising, and the reverse when the situation is otherwise. Options give the recipient incentive to help make the company profitable so the stock will have a higher value when the option is executed. We have lots of fringe benefits, but they are important only defensively.

> *Robert O. Barber, president*
> *Univis, Inc.*
> *Fort Lauderdale, Florida*

The only valid rule I've found is that the real key men are *less* interested in salary and bonus than in an opportunity to grow, financially and in job stature, as the company grows. Job security is also low on the list. The executive worth his pay realizes that his job is only as secure as he makes it.

> *Cass S. Hough, president*
> *Daisy Mfg. Co.*
> *Rogers, Arkansas*

In addition to providing a good environment, we offer a competitive salary range; an incentive plan based on current performance that rewards the outstanding individual but takes full account of basic stockholder interest; a long-term stock option program; and a retirement plan that offers security to the man and his family after retirement age.

> *John W. Field, president*
> *The Warner Bros. Co.*
> *Bridgeport, Connecticut*

For a long time we employed bonuses as a means of motivation and compensation, but we found that cash bonuses involve disadvantages, including the immediate tax burden, the difficulty of relating bonuses to measured performance, and the dangers of inequities which arise from "windfall" situations.

Therefore we have adopted a profit-sharing program that relates directly to the profit performance of the company and which defers income for top executives.

> *W. E. Uzzell, president*
> *Royal Crown Cola Co.*
> *Columbus, Georgia*

We pay unusually high salaries, and high bonuses when results are attained. Stock options are important, and we extend them over as long a period as possible. Pension plan and major medical coverage are reviewed every three years. Our salary-continuation plan covers executives. Should they die before 65, their estate will receive 25 percent of their salary for 10 years.

> *Ralph A. Hart, chairman*
> *Heublein, Inc.*
> *Hartford, Connecticut*

Thus, we find that while there are differences in detail, motivation and performance are the basis for executive compensation plans—as they are for salesmen.

What Management Expects

Perhaps, at a different level of analysis, we may gain an understanding of what management expects by reviewing some recent advertisements for sales executives, chosen at random from the New York *Times:*

NEWSPAPER ADS FOR MARKETING EXECUTIVES

$50,000 TO $100,000 A YEAR OPPORTUNITY
FOR A NATIONAL DIRECT SALES MANAGER

Highly profitable company with a sales volume of over $300 million a year . . .

Wants to employ an outstandingly able sales manager to build and direct a national sales staff.

Our client's products range above $300 in the cultural and educational fields.

Unless you have had a successful record in recruiting and managing salesmen in the direct-to-consumer sales field, don't answer this advertisement.

This is a golden opportunity for the right man.

Replies will be kept in complete confidence.

In answering this advertisement, please give age, education, and complete record of your experience.

Appointments will be made with our client for those who seem to have the desired qualities.

DIRECTOR OF MARKETING
PROFIT BONUS AND STOCK OPTIONS

An outstanding marketing executive with the capacity to move quickly into the position of general manager of a major division of a $100 million company growing at an accelerated rate.

As director of marketing, he will be responsible for development and management of all marketing programs and be expected to make a significant contribution to the overall management of the division.

ASSISTANT BRAND MARKETING MANAGER
CONSUMER PACKAGE GOODS

If you are interested in a challenging position in marketing management, then this immediate opening should be of interest to you. We are one of America's fastest growing consumer-goods manufacturers with plenty of room for future growth. The man we are looking for will not be a "record keeper" but still assume an active role in the marketing of several nationally advertised products. This position is a definite route to a major marketing-management position.

We are seeking an aggressive, professionally competent person with up to three years of experience in brand management or with an advertising agency— preferably some of which is in the package-goods area.

NATIONAL SALES MANAGER

Billion-dollar diversified consumer packaged-goods manufacturer seeking to expand into hardware- and paint-sundries market with established and new-product lines.

We seek a national sales manager who is thoroughly experienced in hardware, sales, and sales administration. The individual will hire and develop a commissioned sales force, be based in our NYC headquarters, and probably will travel up to 50 percent of the time. This should prove to be an unusual opportunity for the qualified applicant seeking a challenge.

SALES MANAGER—UP TO $22,000

Prominent national corporation seeks a professional with top sales-management experience for facility located in a highly industrialized area of southeastern Pennsylvania. Division sales of $50 million to $75 million annually.

Scope of job includes organizing, monitoring, and motivating the sales program, marketing analysis, product orientation, and the coordination of divisional sales office.

Important qualification is demonstrated record of achievement selling to government and private industries.

MARKETING MANAGER—URGENT . . . TO $30,000

Medium-sized company located in the Midwest has an excellent career position available immediately for a marketing manager with solid background in industrial selling, market planning and analysis, and marketing organization. His staff will consist of more than 60 people operating in different states; he will also be responsible for relations with distributors. The man we select will be given unusual freedoms to accomplish the job and will report directly to the president.

FOAM PLASTICS SALES MANAGER

Previous experience necessary, related field considered. Excellent contacts and demonstrated sales record required. Join a growing, exceptionally well-financed corporation. Salary $20,000 to $25,000 plus sales incentives.

MARKETING OPPORTUNITY

Growing national-brand consumer-products company, located in the West, needs an experienced marketing man to administer a multimillion-dollar promotion.

We are not interested in a "hit and run" idea man. The position requires a management approach to sales promotion including responsibility for

... Developing and continuously reviewing plans, policies, and practices for each product and the total company effort.

... Understanding and testing the promotional tools and tactics required to implement promotion strategies and policies.

... Coordinating the implementation of specific promotional programs.

... Evaluating the cost and effectiveness of promotions and promotion programs.

Performance of these responsibilities will require basic insight into the needs of the trade, the consumer, and competitive activity. The sales promotion manager will work closely with product management, the sales department, advertising agencies, and direct the activities of outside promotion consultants.

The man for this responsibility will have had experience in sales promotion and sales management and will possess a fundamental understanding of consumer-goods marketing.

The position will report to the vice-president of marketing services.

MARKETING MANAGER

Our company is seeking an experienced man to head our marketing and sales effort. He must have at least five years' experience in sales, market research, data analysis, product and market expansion. A background in steel distribution or servicing the aircraft industry is preferred.

MARKETING MANAGER—NEW PRODUCTS

Manufacturer of products used industrially and commercially needs experienced product sales manager. Will be responsible for development and introduction of new products as well as for increasing sales of existing products.

Position requires imagination and creativity in preparing marketing plans and involves close liaison with all operating departments. Our candidate must be aggressive and determined to succeed with this outstanding opportunity.

Marketing degree preferred, with MBA in marketing desirable. Must have at least five years' related experience in marketing and/or sales.

SALES MANAGEMENT
ELECTROSTATIC OFFICE COPYING

General Aniline & Film Corporation will soon be entering the electrostatic office copying field, and will have an unusual managerial opportunity available in its systems-products area. We are now looking for an experienced sales-management candidate to share the responsibility for this important area of our marketing activity. Excellent potential for the trained applicant who has proven his supervisory ability in this growing field. Must be flexible as to initial location.

DISTRICT SALES MANAGER
PLASTICS MACHINERY

AAA-1 manufacturer of thermoplastic extruders and post-extrusion systems has outstanding growth opportunity for progressive, forward-looking man to manage N. Y. area sales office. B.S. in M.E., E.E., or Ch.E., plus sales and extrusion experience desired.

Rapidly growing company in fast-moving industry offers attractive salary, incentive, car, expenses, and fringe benefits to right man.

SALES MANAGER

Metropolitan New York company in the public-terminal-warehouse business is seeking to expand present operations in storage of chemical and petroleum products. Individual chosen will head this expansion and should have proven record of sales experience in this or related areas. Selected candidate will be given unusual freedom to accomplish job.

MARKETING PLANNER

Due to the acceptance of our unique products, an immediate opening is now available for a marketing planner to be responsible for our existing-products planning and future-generation expansion.

If you are self-starting E.E., M.E., or I.E. with 2-4 years' experience in market analysis, well-oriented in original equipment and equipment manufacture, with an M.B.A. degree preferred, we would like to speak with you.

Money a Measure of Achievement

Psychologist Marvin Dunnette, of the University of Minnesota, says that money is important to executives as a sign of achievement —points scored in the continual search for recognition. "Beyond a certain amount of buying power," he says, "we cease to strive for extra money for its own sake. But where the additional money ties in directly with a relatively insatiable need such as the need for achievement, then money becomes something more . . . a tangible recognition for achievement."

The Industrial Relations Center at the University of Minnesota conducted a study of executives in three large corporations to find out what the executives themselves really thought about the matter. Were they enchanted with the security their companies provided? Did they look forward with relish to the prospect of assured income at retirement? Or did they want cash *now?*

Responses were highly varied. Nevertheless, certain general conclusions can be drawn from the study. The executives who wanted a larger proportion of their compensation in salary, for instance, were usually those whose present salaries were below average. They tended to be the younger men, with less family income, and with fewer years with their companies.

The executives who were willing to take less salary and more incentive potential instead were those who were already in fairly comfortable circumstances. They were able to take the risk of losing out on a bonus if it should turn out that way. The study showed that age was directly related to desire to postpone receipt of income.

Except for lower-level supervisors, increased compensation in the form of longer vacations was least desired of all.

The study did not include the possibility that stock options might be one form of compensation available to the executives. With that omission, here is how executive preferences were ranked:

1. Salary.

2. Current individual incentives.

3. Current group incentives.

4. Deferred group incentives.

5. Pensions.

6. Deferred individual incentives.

7. Insurance.

8. Vacations.

Natural competitiveness and the need for self-fulfillment are seen by corporate presidents as the motivations driving their executives, says *Dun's Review* as a result of a recent study. Financial motives are generally agreed to be the most straightforward impetus, but a 300-president panel says that other ambitions and desires must be taken into account.

The presidents are almost evenly split between the competitive desire and the desire for self-fulfillment in naming the chief non-financial motive governing an executive's life. Some presidents say they hunt for "fighters," and believe that the competitive instinct is something inborn. Others think it is not only an inborn trait, but present in varying degrees in all men, and certain to "boil to the surface" in those with executive potential.

On the other hand, an equal number of presidents speak of the drive toward self-fulfillment. They seem to feel that "while top management can expect plenty of results from the 'tigers,' it must generally devote more supervision to their work. By the same token, these panelists point out, the manager motivated by a desire to fulfill potential is less self-centered and, therefore, often more valuable to the company."

Compensating Marketing Executives

Executive performance and behavior is, to a large extent, controllable with a compensation plan. Different behavior and different levels of performance will result from different compensation plans. For this reason, if for no other, top-management leaders should keep in mind what it is they wish to do when they develop payment plans for their sales executives. Does the company wish to increase sales, gross margins, reduce inventories, increase its share of the market, improve its public image?

When employees are not properly motivated, their company gets short-changed by not getting the best efforts from its executives. At the same time, the executive gets short-changed because he could and should earn more if he were better measured and motivated.

It's one of the facts of business life that executive base pay usually lags behind company performance. Rewards for good performance in good years must wait until the next fiscal year begins before taking effect. Not so the bonus, however, which can be more closely and immediately related to the earnings statement. A raise in executive base pay means two things: (1) the executive has performed well in the year just ended and is suitably rewarded and (2) the company has hopes, and certainly a reasonable expectation, that he will continue to perform at the same high level, with the same happy effect on the next profit report.

The General Sales Manager

As head of the sales or marketing department, the general manager has overall responsibility for all its activities and all the people in it. The activities vary, however, from company to company, depending on whether or not such functions as advertising, sales promotion, market research, product management, and the rest are under the charge of other executives.

Of the companies taking part in a Dartnell survey, advertising is the direct responsibility of the general sales manager in 34 percent, market research in 33 percent. Pricing of products or services is among his functions in 32 percent of the companies surveyed.

The general sales manager's median salary is $20,400; his total compensation $23,200. He ranks fourth on the compensation chart with 46.4 percent of the chief executive's total pay. His salary has increased over the past five years by 9 percent, his total compensation by 8 percent, both figures well under the all-executives-all-companies average.

Except for a small number of extreme cases, the companies surveyed tend to pay their general sales managers within a fairly narrow range. Even different industry characteristics do not appear to have much to do with variations from the norm. Certainly, there are no such sharp variations as there are in the president's pay.

Base salaries, then, fall within narrow limits. Total compensation (which includes bonuses presumably based on sales performances) relates more closely to company sales and varies more widely. Even so, variations are not as extreme as might be expected.

According to the Sales Manpower Foundation, the compensation rates (salary and commission) for national sales managers as first-level management range from $20,000 to $30,000 with an average of $25,000. This represents a cost factor of .00750.

Vice-President of Sales or Marketing

The top job in sales or marketing very often rates a vice-presidency. As such, the job commands a lot more money than without it. The vice-president in charge of sales or marketing is right up with the leaders in base salary, topped only by the executive vice-president, president, and chairman of the board.

The salary for this position is $28,400, up 9 percent over 1959. Total compensation is $38,400, an increase of 6 percent during the period. The hefty $10,000 bonus which this executive received is 35 percent of his base salary. Large as it is, it is no larger than it was five years ago when the bonus was also measured at $10,000. Because of this, the rate of increase in total pay is low.

Sales Management has culled from public sources the compensation earned by top marketing men in a number of corporations listed on the New York Stock Exchange. Here are a few of them, enough to indicate the general use of the term "marketing" in the man's title and what his position in the company can mean with respect to compensation:

Company	Title	Aggregate Remuneration
The National Cash Register Company	Vice-President and Group Executive— Domestic Marketing	$100,000
Campbell Soup Company	Vice-President— Marketing	88,045
International Minerals and Chemical Corp.	Vice-President—Agricultural Products, Marketing Group	80,250
Pan-American World Airways	Senior Vice-President— Traffic and Sales	73,900
The General Tire and Rubber Company	Vice-President— Marketing	73,318
Eastman Kodak Company	Vice-President— Marketing	70,000
Sunray DX Oil Company	Executive Vice-President—Manufacturing and Marketing	67,900

Selling's Share of the Sales Dollar

As an approach to establishing minimum and maximum salaries for the sales personnel, it is desirable to break down the sales dollar. What part of every sales dollar can a business afford to spend for sales administration, and how should that portion be divided by sales administrative functions? Opinions and practice on this point vary greatly, of course. They vary according to the type of business, the size of the sales operation, and the fairness of the management. They vary, too, according to the capacity of the individual at present holding these positions. But for the purpose of job evaluation, the ability or lack of ability of executives now holding these positions should be disregarded in setting minimum and maximum rates. In other words, there should be an established minimum and maximum for each sales job, and whether an incumbent executive is entitled to the minimum or the maximum or a salary in between should be determined by his ability to get results.

On top of a base salary, provision should be made for some form of *contingent* compensation—compensation which is contingent upon an executive making certain things happen. In no case should the total compensation exceed the maximum which the management has determined the business can afford to pay for that particular sales job. Such determinations should, of course, be dependent upon sales volume reaching the break-even point.

Variations in What Constitutes Sales Expense

It is important to bear in mind that not all companies include the same items or functions as sales expense. This tendency to variation makes difficult a hard-and-fast breakdown of the selling dollar.

For example, one company may consider outgoing freight costs as a cost of distribution (selling expense) while another may classify freight as a production cost. These differences of classification arise because of the divergence of opinions as to where production stops and distribution begins.

Logic suggests that production should be considered finished and sales costs should begin at the moment when the product is ready for shipment to customers or ready for placement in the finished inventory. But this does not completely solve the problem, since the question of warehousing and handling the finished product still may be charged to production by some companies and to sales by others.

One method of fixing the selling price, and working back from that to the compensation of the sales staff, is to call the production cost 33 1/3 percent; the selling cost 33 1/3 percent; leaving 33 1/3 percent for overhead and profit. This method is used in marketing specialties where the selling cost is about equal to the production cost of a product. In breaking down the one-third that is allocated for selling expense, which we will call 100 percent, the salesman gets one-third, another third goes for his supervision (which in this case covers the compensation and operation of branch and division managers, as well as the general sales manager), and the remaining third for administrative expense, taxes, and profits.

Obviously, this method is not universally applicable, since the cost of distribution varies from low, in the distribution of basic materials, to very high, in such specialties as perfumes and cosmetics (where it may reach well above 50 cents of the sales dollar).

Influence of Sales Manager's Duties on Compensation

While the above methods of budgeting selling costs are followed by many concerns which start out from scratch, they are obviously theoretical. In actual practice, such a yardstick is seldom used. Compensation is based as nearly as possible upon a sales manager's contribution to the net earnings of the business, which in turn is determined by the nature of his duties.

There is a growing tendency, however, to consider the sales executive as a part of top management, rather than as a specialist. It is probable that in the future many sales executives now regarded as department managers will be elevated to the board of directors and given official status. As officials of the business they will automatically participate in the top-management bonus. Every activity of the business must be considered a part of the sales program, hence the need for dovetailing the sales executive into the overall management picture.

The highest salaries will be paid to sales executives who are primarily creative sales planners. Men with necessary creative and analytical ability will be scarce. The successful sales director must understand not only the operation of a sales organization, but he must know marketing, sales research, advertising, public relations, and product engineering. Too many sales managers function only as "head salesmen." They concern themselves too much with driving a sales organization to the limit, along with producing a good volume of personal sales, and neglect to analyze the potential opportunity to develop new markets and improve selling techniques.

Incentive Compensation

At a recent convention of the National Retail Merchants Association, James T. Powers, of Peat, Marwick, Mitchell & Co., gave an illuminating address on the subject of sales-executive motivation through incentive-compensation plans. While his comments were directed at the great department store chains, they are applicable to manufacturers and distributors as well:

Executive-compensation methods can be grouped into three general classifications. First, and of prime importance, is money.

The second classification of executive payment involves various deferred-compensation plans. Deferred compensation includes pension plans, profit-sharing plans, group life, accident, and health insurance, stock options, as well as pure deferred dollars.

The third classification of compensating executives might be termed "indirect fringe benefits." Examples of indirect fringe benefits are use of a company car, payment by the company of an employee's country club bills, payment of travel and entertainment expenses at conventions, new carpeting in the office.

The Discretionary Bonus: A recent survey by the Controllers' Congress indicates that bonus plans have not changed substantially in the past decade. One of the most common methods, for example, is still the discretionary bonus which is based upon the judgment of some higher officer or officers in the company.

There are several reservations about the judgment bonus. In the first place, it does not provide a specific method for informing the man receiving the bonus what he did to earn the bonus. Nor does it tell him what he should do better in order to increase his bonus next year.

The discretionary bonus is commonly found in organizations where top management has not prepared a well-defined operating plan. There are exceptions to this, of course, but indirection and discretionary bonuses tend to be found in the same company.

Aside from the judgment bonus, the most common basis of paying cash bonuses among retailers is a percentage of company profits. This method had merit, especially if management believes that a company with no profits should pay no bonuses. We question whether this is either completely rational or completely fair. Certainly, in compensating the chief executive officer, it makes sense. Perhaps it also makes sense in paying the top two or three executives. But what does this method of bonus payment do to motivate a merchandise manager of a women's apparel department who has increased sales and profits 20 percent in his department in a year when two new branches are opened and overall profits decline by 25 percent. Should he receive 25 percent less bonus in that year?

Bonuses based solely on sales can quite often discourage *profitable* performance.

Some companies, however, believe that profits are so elusive a short-term measure of managerial performance that over half their executives' bonuses are based upon nonmonetary factors. Here, for example, is a list of measures which determine the bonus payment of the top executive officers of the various divisions of a large diversified manufacturing and retailing company: Dollar profits, adherence to the budget, return on investment, change in share of market, employee turnover, and percentage of pretax net to gross. It is complicated.

But in some situations, nonfinancial performance measures *should* outweigh the purely profit considerations.

Performance Bonuses: The most direct manner of motivating through compensation is by payment of a performance bonus. In a recent study of bonuses in retailing it was found that about two-thirds of the executives surveyed receive cash bonuses. In the larger stores, they average about 50 percent of base salaries.

However, the sheer size of a bonus has only a limited relationship to its effectiveness as a motivating technique. In order to be an effective incentive device, the bonus must meet certain highly important conditions. *Otherwise, it will not really motivate.* In fact, the wrong kind of bonus plan can quite often have an effect opposite to that desired by the company.

To motivate properly with its bonus program, a company must do several things:

1. The company must identify, or decide upon, a set of specific short- and long-range goals, and these goals must be made explicit.

2. The company must identify the kinds of actions which are required on the part of its executives to assist in achieving these goals.

3. The company must design a bonus plan for a particular executive which will encourage him to take the right kind of actions, and discourage him from taking the wrong kinds of actions.

4. Finally, the company must convince the executive that the kinds of things he is required to do by the terms of his bonus arrangement are the best things for him to do from the standpoint of doing his job most effectively. In short, the plan must be "sold" to the executive.

Formula payments are usually based on the bonus fund being distributed on a set percentage basis among the executives as shown in the following examples:

President	20%
Executive Vice-President	15%
Vice-President, Marketing	12%
Vice-President, Manufacturing	10%
Vice-President, Finance	10%
Managers of the—	
Marketing Division	15%
Manufacturing Division	10%
Finance Division	8%
	100%

Apportionment by salary is another method used for bonus determination. The bonus fund is apportioned according to the relationship of the salary of each individual to the total salaries of the group. This presupposes that the salaries were equitably established in the first place. This system tends to compound any inequities that exist and does not give recognition to current outstanding contributions of individuals to the company's welfare.

A third method is to distribute 70 percent of the fund through one or other of the above formula methods, then to distribute the remaining 30 percent on a discretionary basis, the decisions being made by a finance committee or special bonus committee on advice received from individual executives concerning their subordinates. Usually the bonus committee does not participate in the bonus fund, and the bonus of the president is fixed by the board of directors.

Commission Payments are akin to bonus, as both are usually paid from net profits. But commission payments usually are attuned to the actions of an individual rather than to that of the group as a whole. A marketing executive or sales manager might receive a certain percentage of the profits of his individual division, department, district, or branch, or he may receive a percentage of the total sales volume.

The use of a percentage-of-sales basis is not always looked upon with favor, as it ignores the cost-control element of management and puts the entire emphasis on sales. The executive, if he has any control over prices, could easily sell the company into bankruptcy; or, if he does not apply expense controls, he could readily promote the company into a loss position. Since most executives have some say in pricing and a great deal of say in expense control, net profits are usually used as the base, with or without a minimum net profit earned before commissions are applied.

Frequently companies are combination systems, with half of the extra compensation opportunity represented by results of the executive's operation in his assigned area and the other half through participation in the company's executive bonus plan. In this way the executive receives recognition in proportion to his individual effort, and he is encouraged to cooperate with other executives toward the company's overall benefit.

Profit Sharing frequently takes the form of a certain percentage of profits being paid into a fund which is invested in stock of the company or of other companies, the earnings from which are distributed to the executives in accordance with their bonus or salary payment contributions.

Stock Bonuses are similar to the cash bonus plans, but the earned reward is paid in company stock rather than in cash. The stock payments can be made in a number of ways, depending on the funds of the company and the needs of the executives. The stock can be distributed at once or delayed until retirement. If paid immediately, the value of the stock is subject to normal income tax; if paid on retirement, it is subject to the income tax rate applicable at that time and is not considered capital gain. If current or deferred stock receipts are large, the executive might be short of cash to pay his income tax on their market value. To assist, some companies divide the bonus between stock and cash in order to provide the necessary cash to pay the tax on the stock.

Stock distribution in any form is usually good, but it must be remembered that when given away as treasury stock, it dilutes the stockholders' equities. To overcome this, many companies buy the needed stock on open market and do not use treasury stock.

When payment of stock is deferred, the companies usually pay the dividends currently to the recipients.

Deferred Compensation is becoming increasingly popular, particularly for higher paid and older executives. A man younger than 50 usually prefers immediate payments rather than payments deferred until after retirement. To handle deferred payments, the company enters into a contract with the individual executive whereby, instead of receiving increases in salary or high bonuses, he will receive a sum equal to his present salary, or a percentage of it, for a 5-, 10-, or 15-year period after retirement, in return for which he agrees to act in a consultant capacity for the company and to refrain from going into competition with it.

The company benefits in offering its executives a plan advantageous to them. A hidden danger is that it may be committing itself to higher than desirable fixed expenses, should adversity occur. The executives benefit mainly in reduced income taxes over the remaining period with the company and for the period of the contract.

Stock Options rise and decline in popularity with fluctuations in the economic cycle. When the trend is up, they are highly regarded as the stock grows in value due to improved business conditions and the extra effort of the executives. When the trend is down, the value of the stock may drop, even though the company is doing relatively well.

Stock option plans may be either "restricted" or "unrestricted"; the former is usually used. Under this plan the stockholders vote a certain block of stock which can be used for options.

COMPENSATION OF SALES EXECUTIVES

Stock options were first introduced at top levels of management. They soon filtered down to lower executive ranks, sometimes all the way down. Compensation experts say that this extension of options to larger numbers of company personnel removed the incentive value from them that was originally intended. Reason: The market value of the stock under option is closely related to the efforts and abilities of top management who make the decisions affecting the success of the company. This close relationship between executive ability and company profitability becomes more and more diluted the farther down we go through the executive ranks.

Even with lower tax rates, a man has to earn somewhere around $35,000 before the capital-gains provisions of stock options will do him much good. If an executive earns less than that, he's better off being paid in cash—especially if he can be further rewarded with a bonus. The bonus gives him an immediate reward for his performance, which is a distinct psychological advantage.

On the other hand, once a stock option is exercised, it must be held for at least three years before the capital gains rate takes effect. Theoretically, an executive has to wait three years before he is rewarded for his performance; thus, stock options lose their charm as incentives.

Several of the new rules formulated under the Revenue Act of 1964 have the effect of depressing the value of stock options. One is that the option price must be at least 100 percent of the fair market value of the stock when the option is granted, instead of 85 percent as before.

Before 1964, an unexercised option expired in 10 years; now it's five. It used to be that an option-holder could wait for a long-term market rise to increase the value of his option before exercising it. Now, his chances of benefiting from a sustained rise are less. Short-term ups and downs might even make it unprofitable for him to exercise the option at all.

In order to qualify as a long-term capital gain taxable at no more than 25 percent, it used to be that an executive could hold the stock acquired through his option only six months. The new law changes the holding period to three years. If he sells the stock before the three years are up, he is subject to tax on ordinary income.

Many executives must borrow funds to exercise their options. Under the old six-month holding rule, this was not so bad. The executive could dispose of his stock after six months, pay off his debt and, presumably, still realize a profit on the transaction. It's not so easy now. He must hold onto the stock for at least three years and

523

carry the burden of the interest on his loan for that length of time, at least.

From the company's standpoint, of course, an executive is not expected to unload his stock at the earliest moment the law will allow. The option was given to him so that he might build up a proprietary interest in the company. More often than not, this happens. A Dartmouth College research team sampled 188 executives in 1960 and found that about 40 percent of them still owned all the option stock they had purchased.

But plain facts are plain facts. Under the stress of financial necessity, many executives take their gain when they can get it, and when the cash is needed for other purposes. For these men, the three-year holding requirement represents an inconvenience, if not a hardship.

Retirement Payments: Whereas deferred-compensation contracts can be used for individual executives, retirement programs must include all employees. Although these programs are frequently very generous, expensive to maintain, and highly acceptable to the executives, their motivational value is limited. Lower-paid executives place more value on retirement programs than do higher-paid ones, the former not being in a position to build an estate to the same degree as can the latter group. Because of the uniform company-wide coverage of formal retirement plans, many companies augment them with a form of key-man insurance or other deferred compensation.

Family Benefits: This form of extra compensation may take the form of group insurance, key-man insurance, or a commitment on the part of the company to continue to pay the executive's salary at a reduced rate to his widow or children if he dies. The contingency may be had by stipulating that payment be made, provided the income of the survivors does not exceed a certain amount, or with other qualifications.

Family benefits are sometimes given in the form of educational awards, scholarships, or trips for members of the family.

Contingent Compensation: Profit sharing has been steadily increasing in recent years. The need for all-out effort to get maximum production and employment has forced the wide use of sales incentives. So long as we operate under a profit-and-loss system, the appeal to gain will be required to make it tick. When you eliminate the opportunity a man has to make more money by doing more work, the whole profit system will collapse, and some other incentive will have to be devised.

The most widely used form of contingent compensation for sales executives, both general and division sales managers, is a percentage of sales after an established *break-even* volume has been reached. The complexity of the corporation tax structure has caused many companies which formerly operated profit-sharing plans to discontinue them. The reason is that it is often desirable to make adjustments in the profit-and-loss account which would work a hardship on sales executives compensated on a profit basis. For example, there are times when it is good business for a company to buy a competitor who is operating at a loss. In that case the current profits of the business might be materially reduced through no fault of those sharing in them. While in the long run, they too would gain with the stockholders by the transaction, they would only gain if they continued in the employment of the company. Then, also, under existing tax practice every opportunity is taken to charge off expenses against profits. So everything considered, it is to the advantage of both the sales executive and the company to base the bonus, if it can be fairly done, upon sales volume rather than profits. For obvious reasons it is entirely unsatisfactory to base a bonus on *net* profits in view of fluctuating income tax rates.

How Sears Shares Profits

On July 1, 1916, Julius Rosenwald, then the president of Sears, announced the creation of The Savings and Profit Sharing Pension Fund of Sears, Roebuck and Co. employees as follows:

"To permit eligible employees of the company to share in the profits thereof; to encourage the habit of saving; to provide a plan through which each eligible employee may accumulate his own savings, his portion of the employers' contribution, and the earnings of his accumulations as a means of providing an income for himself at the close of his active business career."

Sales and marketing executives share, as do all other executives and employees, in this fund, which now holds more than $1½ billion in assets, and has an average annual income of over $100 million, in members' deposits, the company's contribution, and income from investments.

Employee members contribute a straight 5 percent of their Sears income, up to a maximum of $500 a year. This ceiling keeps higher-salaried employees from getting a disproportionate share.

Sears' contributions are figured on a sliding scale based on the company's consolidated net income before federal income taxes and dividends. If net income in a year is less than $50 million, the company makes no contribution. But if net income is between $50 million and $100 million, the company contributes 5 percent of its net. The percentage rises to a maximum of 10 percent on net income of $250 million or more.

Because it is primarily a retirement plan, the fund does not benefit all members equally. Those who are approaching retirement and have worked for Sears for many years benefit more than newcomers. Older fund members, in fact, may receive up to four times as much of the company's contribution each year for every dollar they contribute. All regular employees, however, are eligible to join the fund once they have completed one or more years of service.

The following figures (which represent averages) tell the story of what the fund means to participating Sears employees:

Years of Service	Employee's Total Contributions	Retirement Fund
10-15	$2,004	$11,283
15-20	$2,609	$22,950
20-25	$3,939	$51,825
25-30	$4,804	$84,643

Evaluating Executive Compensation Systems

When assaying the worth of any compensation plan, it should be borne in mind that the successful organization is an integration of separate but interrelated parts. For smooth operation, the interrelationship must be recognized. This means that overly-wide separations, dollar-wise or symbol-wise, between groups must be avoided.

The compensation plan must be consistent and must treat all executives with equal consideration and with integrity. It must be *logical,* so that it can be put into practice, administered, understood, and talked about. It should not be a secret in the hands of only one or two people, or of such complexity that calculations are obscure. The executive should clearly understand what it was intended he should do, and what he did for which he received his compensation.

Today, adequate and proper compensation plans for sales executives are a "must" for two vital reasons:

1. A great scarcity of marketing talent makes it imperative that companies do not lose their executives. The high salaries paid competent sales executives proves the need.

2. Companies have large investments of time and money in their sales managers and executives; they cannot afford to jeopardize these investments.

Chapter 43

COMPENSATION OF
MIDDLE MANAGEMENT

WITH competent executives at a premium, many psychologists, personnel experts, compensation planners, and others have tried to measure the pulse of the typical American executive in an attempt to find out what attracts him to a situation, what keeps him there, and what makes him more productive. There is enough consistency in the results of the studies to suggest that executives in particular age groups and business situations react pretty much alike to the same motivating forces.

As a class, junior- and middle-management executives seem to provide the most serious difficulties for their companies. They are too much on the move to suit many employers. They are unwilling to spend a lifetime with the same company. It's not a matter of fickleness, or loyalties that come and go, so much as it is a desire on the part of mobile executives to broaden their base of experience and better themselves financially, while they are doing so.

Companies complain that it costs them upward of $2,500 to recruit and train a promising young executive who, someday, might occupy one of the carpeted offices on the top floor. Long before he gets there, however, he has been lured away to what he considers a better job. Usually it is, too; at least in terms of money and security.

Meeting the Turnover Problem

The waste in executive turnover is unmeasurable but astronomical. Even professional recruiting firms who stand to benefit the most from executive mobility recognize and comment on the waste. Speaking of young executives on the move, one recruiter says: "We now get from 30 to 50 unsolicited queries from these restless young comers each workday, compared to 10 to 15 a decade ago. It's so bad that in order to keep them from pestering me at cocktail parties I always say I'm an insurance man."

Generous and lively profit-sharing also contributes to executive immobility. Companies like General Motors and Eastman Kodak, for example, have attractive profit-sharing arrangements and also low executive turnover.

Some companies report that overlong training programs help make restless young management trainees more restless still. Year-long programs, which are still quite common, are tedious and uninteresting to many young men. Their main interests may already be developed, yet they are exposed to department after department. Anxious to get started, their interest flags and they are sometimes lost to the company before the training program is completed. In these instances, a shortening of the training period has a good effect on turnover.

Apart from the money wasted on recruiting, training, and record-keeping, there is, of course, a loss of efficiency as trained men are lost and replaced by others who must learn their way around. Even more serious, though, according to some personnel people, is the prospect that trained and competent middle-management won't be available to many companies when the time comes to turn over company direction.

One defense against excessive turnover is an active and consistent policy of promoting from within. The companies and industries with the least turnover are almost always the ones which demonstrate by example how their promotion-from-within plan works. They keep their young executives looking to a future with their own companies instead of somewhere else.

Middle management has expense responsibility, so can logically be tied into profit-based plans. It is also closely allied to sales procurement, so can logically be tied into sales-volume attainment plans. Through its close connection with the next higher level of sales management, all of the principles discussed in connection with marketing executives apply just as much to middle management.

The break-even point of the main area of responsibility in middle management can frequently be determined and used as an element in the extra-compensation program. The middle-management sales executive contributes to the general welfare of the company, so he can logically and profitably participate in any bonus fund assigned to the marketing division. He is usually included in retirement plans and can be allotted stock options, though in practice this is rare. Certainly he should receive appropriate status and other so-called intangible compensation.

Frequently, an element of the middle-management sales executive's extra compensation will be based on the results attained by the salesmen who report to him. For example, a manager may have eight salesmen in his branch, each with a quota of $200,000, or a total of $1,600,000. It may be that through no fault of his, there is a high degree of salesman turnover. His salary would then recognize the administration of the eight salesmen, plus the need for locating, hiring, and training one new man each year. Furthermore, rather than setting the quota of his branch at $1,600,000, it would be set at $1,500,000 which would give him a little leeway and not penalize him too heavily when replacements occurred.

Thus his compensation program might include a base salary, an overriding on sales over $1,500,000, a bonus based on profits and expense control, and participation in the executives' bonus fund for his division. However, having more than two elements in the extra compensation plan might make the program too complex, so it might be better if only the ones most directly related to his activities were adopted.

The District Manager

The title given to the first level of sales management above the salesmen varies considerably from company to company. However, 26.2 percent of firms assign their supervision to the district manager, according to a survey conducted by the Sales Manpower Foundation of the Sales Executives Club of New York.

The average total annual earnings of the average first-level district manager for all of the participants on a "salary plus commission" basis is $21,987. This represents a .01379 cost against the average annual sales volume ($2,096,875) from the territory under his supervision. Some 79 percent of the first-level sales executives do personal selling in addition to managing their men. Only 34.7 percent received extra compensation for this personal selling effort.

Regional Sales Manager

Titles, of course, vary from one company to the next. A regional sales manager may be above or below a district manager, depending on the organization chart you happen to be looking at. A Dartnell survey shows general agreement that regional sales managers generally report to division managers, or directly to the top sales executive himself, and that district managers usually report to regional managers.

Whether this terminology is appropriate to any given situation or not, it has been adopted for survey purposes. The regional manager's job is largely supervisory; he hires and fires and administers his area of responsibility either directly or through subordinate managers. He does not usually have direct sales responsibilities, except for tending to a few key or house accounts.

The regional sales manager's median salary is $14,200, at the same level as the assistant general sales manager and almost 70 percent of the general sales manager's salary. His total pay is $15,500—once again, exactly the same as the median for assistant general sales managers and 67 percent of the median for top sales executives.

The five-year gain in the regional sales manager's salary and total compensation has been the same, 9 percent in each case. This is the precise rate of increase for sales management as a whole.

Compensation for Personal Production

A common weakness in compensation plans for field supervisors is that they put the supervisor in competition with the salesman by paying him partly on his own personal production and partly on the production of the men under him. There may be times when this is the only feasible way to operate supervisors. In the long run, however, it undermines the morale of the salesmen, works against the close cooperation which should exist between supervisor and salesman, and usually results in an excessive turnover of salesmen. It is therefore bad practice, however expedient it may seem.

It is a time-tested principle of sales management that every 10 salesmen at work require a field leader, just as a file of soldiers, to be effective, require a corporal to tell them what to do, and show them how to do it, and then see that they do it. It is possible, of course, to get along with fewer supervisors, and under some methods of selective selling one supervisor to 20 men might be adequate. But remember you pay for adequate sales supervision one way or another. You pay for it in a profit on business you should have but are not getting if you have too few supervisors or if you have half-hearted field supervision. So it is good business to provide adequate supervision, and pay the best men you can find what they are worth.

Pitfalls of Branch Compensation Plans

An analysis of several profit-sharing plans which have been tried, and subsequently discontinued, shows that most of them failed because of "loading" by the home-office accounting department. Usually this happened during a year when somebody got the impression the branch manager was making too much money.

One instance of this kind revealed that when the plan was first set up no charge was made against the profits of the branch for the interest on invested capital in the territory. Then a good year came along, and the branches were charged with 6 percent on all consigned stocks in the territory. Since most of the company's business was on a consigned stock basis, this change in accounting practice practically wiped out the profit for the year.

It is, therefore, advisable in setting up a profit-sharing plan for a branch office to include only charges which can be actually controlled by the branch manager. A flat charge to cover home-office overhead, or some other mutually agreeable method, should be used to cover items and charges which the branch manager cannot control.

In the final analysis, whatever plan of compensation may be devised, there will be dissatisfaction and expensive turnover unless those who participate in the plan feel entirely convinced of the fairness and integrity of management.

Qualified-Bonus Compensation Plan

A plan which requires the branch manager to qualify specially over a given period of time before being allowed to participate in the distribution of a bonus that is awarded for the satisfactory operation of his office has proved a valuable aid in encouraging branch managers. One of the large store-equipment companies operates from a unified sales control through district managers who have under them territories which embody several states. In strategic positions throughout the districts, branch offices have been established which are under the immediate supervision of a branch manager. Each branch manager is responsible for both the sales activities and the efficient operation of the office generally. In the conduct of his office the branch manager is given a budgeted expense amount within which he is supposed to confine himself as to the expense of operation.

The compensation of the branch manager is based on a straight salary arrangement, and, in addition, he is given an opportunity to augment his earnings by effecting savings in the operation of his office, also, by qualifying for the bonus which is paid as a reward for keeping his office on a profit basis. Under this arrangement any branch office may operate at a loss for two or three months in succession, or more, and during the time that the office fails to show a profit the branch manager does not share in the bonus that he might have participated in had his office been operated on a profitable basis. If any office has operated at a loss for three months in succession— that is, failed to reach its assigned sales quota or to keep its expenses within the figure established by the home office for that particular branch office—and during the fourth month showed a profit and made its quota, the branch manager has then qualified for the bonus. Then, during the next three months the branch manager receives the bonus to which his office entitles him. If, however, during any month after he has qualified, his office shows a loss, it is necessary for him to qualify again in order to be entitled to his bonus.

Splitting the Credits

To eliminate the haggling over splitting commissions when salesmen sell merchandise to a customer out of their territory, and to develop teamwork for the branch office even though salesmen have exclusive territories, an electrical-mining-machinery manufacturer has worked out a plan to prorate the profits among all of the salesmen.

The plan allows a certain amount of money for each piece of equipment sold. The total amount is divided into three classes: First, the salesman in whose territory the equipment is shipped receives a fixed percentage of the total amount allotted; second, a portion of this allotment is prorated between the salesmen in the district; third, the balance of the allotment is distributed among all of the salesmen. In this way the salesman is interested not only in the equipment which is shipped into his territory, but in the equipment shipped into any other part of the United States.

The compensation plan for regional managers of the Phillips-Van Heusen Corporation, makers of Van Heusen collars and shirts, gives consideration to the opening up of pioneer territories. The plan, with certain modifications, has been in use for a number of years. It is described by an officer of the company as follows:

Our profit-sharing plan for regional managers is a very simple one. After a very close study of our field we know just how much money it should cost us to market our various products. We set up a budget figure for each region to operate on. Out of that budget all expenses for the region must be met: Office rent, salesmen's drawings, traveling expenses, lost samples, etc. The manager's salary is also charged in here. If at the end of the year the manager has been able to save any money on this operation, we go fifty-fifty with him on any surplus he is able to build up, giving him his share in cash as soon as the year's books are closed.

These budget figures, of course, vary according to the cost of doing business in the various territories, but in normal years with normal intelligence and sufficient aggressiveness, a region can operate within our budget figure. It is not a figure that is based on splitting hairs, but it is a perfectly fair, normal operating ratio. So far, this system has worked like a charm. Some of our men have drawn very handsome bonus checks.

If there is a deficit on the region, we take into consideration the cause of the deficit, and if it is some unusual condition over which the manager has absolutely no control, the company meets him halfway and wipes out the deficit. If it is a deficit that has been caused by the manager but we still feel the manager is a good man and worth saving, we charge that deficit against the region and it must be wiped out before any profits can be shown.

On the other hand, if it is a deficit against the region, caused by incompetence on the part of the manager, well the manager gets his. In that way, we're the same as anybody else. In this case, what the manager gets is the "boot."

IBM Rating Plan for Supervisors

The International Business Machines Corporation wanted to lay a foundation for a future sales compensation plan which would provide a reasonable salary to cover a man's living expenses and a commission contingent upon territorial and individual sales production. At one time, IBM operated its sales force on a straight commission basis, but special conditions made it necessary temporarily to revert to a straight salary plan. To provide data necessary for changing over to a salary and commission plan, a system of ratings was established on an experimental basis. Every 90 days, supervisors were required to evaluate the work of each man under their supervision, rating them on these 12 points:

1. Write-ups prepared covering detailed tabulating procedure in specific installations.

2. Time spent out of man's own territory.
   a. Active time.
      In helping to close points not his own, in instructing at Endicott, in performing special assignments, in manning exhibits, etc.
   b. Inactive time—specify cause.
      Illness. Other personal causes.

3. Suggestions made pertaining to sales, sales promotion, engineering, advertising, education, etc.

4. Contributions made to *Business Machines* and *Think* magazines.

5. Speeches, of either business or nonbusiness nature, delivered to outside organizations.

6. Active participation in outside trade, accounting or similar organizations, as member, officer, or director.

7. Trained new salesmen, systems service persons, or other IBM workers.

8. Recommended applicants for IBM employment.

9. Made concessions to customers: Suspended rental—reason. Other concessions—reasons.

10. Customers' attitude toward him.

11. Is this person ready for promotion? Why, or why not?

12. Remarks regarding other significant performances.

Chapter 44

COMPENSATING THE SALESMAN

A SURVEY was conducted by the Sales Manpower Foundation, a division of the Sales Executives Club of New York, to determine compensation methods and rates for sales personnel. In the Foundation's report covering the machinery manufacturers' industry, the study showed that the average overall cost of selling $1 worth of machinery is 11.2 cents. This figure includes salesmen's compensation, their expenses, sales management costs, advertising, merchandising and promotion, cost of servicing, and miscellaneous expenses. The reporting companies indicated that their selling costs ranged from a low of 2 percent to a high of 30 percent of each dollar of sales.

Average Cost of a Sales Call: The survey further revealed that the cost of making a sales call in the machinery industry ranged from $5 to as much as $250 per call. The average was $50.24. Salesmen averaged 14.9 sales calls a week. Salesmen's expenses averaged $132.68.

The average turnover of salesmen averaged 7 percent, but in some cases this rose as high as 35 percent. Of the companies, 85 percent reported that they had difficulty in locating good sales people.

A survey made by the Research Institute of America reveals that compensation plans are in a state of flux. Most companies have made changes in the past five years.

Salesmen are getting more fringe benefits. Even men on "straight commission" are being rapidly embraced in these programs. Less than 10 percent of these now receive no fringe benefits. More than half are now participating in pension and insurance plans. Some, working on "draws," are getting paid vacations.

All in all, companies are basing their compensation plans on "a mixture of security and gamble instead of the old-fashioned and simple straight salary or straight commission."

The most recent report of a nationwide survey conducted by the research editors of the Dartnell Sales and Marketing Service covered more than 17,000 salesmen in 400 statistically selected companies. These represented 29 industries within 18 major industrial classifications. As with every similar survey made by Dartnell over the years, almost half of the respondents (43 percent) have made basic changes in their compensation plans since the last such survey.

Combination plans form an ever-increasing portion of the total number of plans reported. Some 30 percent of the companies reporting changes in their compensation formulas moved into the combination-plan area; 7.5 percent left combination plans to go onto a straight (2.5 percent) or straight commission (5 percent) basis.

The big question about compensating salesmen is, of course, how much they should be paid. In no other occupation do incomes cover so wide a range. From evidence revealed by the most recent survey, it is clear that unlimited opportunities for increasing income await the aggressive, well-motivated man.

It is evident that while the salesman on a combination plan has the widest range of income, it is the salesman on commission who earns the most money. However, an adjustment must be made in comparing net earnings to allow for the expenses paid by the commission man out of his earnings.

New High in Average Earnings

The average salesman has finally reached a five-figure salary—$10,000. Increases, however, have come slower than in previous years. There is developing a leveling trend in the compensation of salesmen. Lowest-paid men have made greater gains in recent years than those in higher income brackets.

There has been a general decline in the compensation of the highest-paid salesmen on salary and commission.

In some companies salesmen are actually overcompensated. The reasons for this are that managers may be uncertain as to the salesman's worth or feel that the men have become indispensable in their territories. Then, too, some sales managers who have come up from the ranks may be biased in favor of high levels of compensation for their sales people.

Despite the increasing gains that have resulted from the use of scientific methods in establishing market potentials, quotas, and supervision of salesmen, there remains a large element of guesswork in determining a salesman's productivity. The combined effects of advertising, product changes, and price shifts frequently cloud the picture of why sales have materialized. Moreover, the impact of personal selling, as is the case with advertising, is often deferred, thereby limiting the opportunity to relate effort and results. And of course there exists the possibility of changing business conditions.

Management may not scrutinize salesmen's costs as closely as other personnel costs. Sales budgets are more flexible and subject to the personal interpretations and evaluations of the sales manager. Although systematic procedures for wage bargaining are the rule in dealing with factory personnel, and to a lesser extent with clerical personnel, they are the exception in dealing with salesmen. For one thing, less than 5 percent of today's outside salesmen are unionized.

Perhaps this tendency to move slowly in adjusting the level of salesmen's earnings reflects the distinctive character of the salesman's job more than management inefficiency. This is no reason, however, for management not to constantly appraise the level of salesmen's earnings in the light of the firm's marketing mix as well as market conditions.

The IBM Compensation Program

The need for *constant* reappraisal of compensation plans was effectively spelled out by C. N. Jones, manager, marketing research and development, International Business Machines Corporation, in a statement to Dartnell. He said:

Marketing chiefs might look carefully at their sales compensation plan if they are not admired, rewarded or appreciated by general management to the degree deemed desirable. Without question, this is one area often taken for granted and overlooked in management's constant search for more profit dollars.

In many companies sales compensation is the largest item in the marketing budget. If marketing expenses are to be materially reduced over a period of time, the sales-compensation expense has to be reduced.

Perhaps the adoption of a viable sales-compensation plan that pays a decreasing *percentage* of sales income to the salesman in succeeding years sounds impractical to many businesses. In fact it may be impossible for a few businesses; but it definitely has not been properly evaluated by all businesses that could benefit by its adoption.

Several conditions have to be present, or planned for, if sales-compensation plans are to produce the optimum number of "extra" dollars of profit that drop into the bottom line without endangering sales morale:

1. Salesmen should receive the major part of their income in the form of commissions or bonuses, as opposed to salary.

2. Salesmen have to be given programs and/or products that will increase the yearly amount of total revenue they can individually generate.

3. Total net income for the average salesman has to increase as revenue generated increases, though not in the same proportion.

   While it is not absolutely mandatory, the sales force should be conditioned to live with change.

4. The sales-compensation plan should be changed every year as a matter of course.

5. New sales territories should be periodically created and it should not be a traumatic experience for a salesman to lose part of his territory.

More than one change will be required and many sacred cows will have to be killed before the above concepts can be imposed on an existing sales force operating under a different philosophy.

The obvious starting point is to make sure that 50 percent to 80 percent of a salesman's total income is dependent on the volume or type of sales generated. There are many pros and cons to a predominantly commission-based sales plan. Some points that are contrary to most ideas on the subject are worthy of comment:

It is often said salaried salesmen's activities can be controlled better than commissioned salesmen's activities. However, there are a number of marketing executives who are convinced: (a) salaried salesmen are more prone to work in "lower gear" than a salesman who participates in every sale, and (b) overall it is easier to direct, motivate, and control commission salesmen.

Most statements on the subject stress that sales-compensation plans should be simple and straightforward. This concept has to be challenged if a marketing organization wants to use its sales compensation to give sales direction and get maximum motivation out of its sales force. There is no argument that each part of the plan has to be easily understood, but if you are to be fair to each salesman regardless of experience, and to each product regardless of its maturity in the marketplace, you need several provisions in your plan which are often interpreted as "complicated."

Many companies pay the same rate of commission or even a decreasing rate of commission as volume increases. Neither of these systems does much to motivate salesmen to bring in a maximum amount of revenue. They might be pleasantly surprised if they adopted a plan that basically *increased* the average commission paid with each new sale made.

In addition to a regular sales plan for the bulk of your sales force, four or five special compensation plans should be adopted if sales management is to have the flexibility needed to maximize sales. This point is not really contrary to popular ideas on the subject, but it is included because many businesses apparently have not adopted a predominantly commission-based compensation plan because it is wrong for a small portion of their sales force.

Once salesmen operate on a plan that has most of the suggested ingredients, management must give careful thought as to what it can do for the salesman that will allow him to increase his productivity in his assigned territory. This can include such items as:

1. Increased education in sales techniques.

2. A broader product line.

3. A new generation of products.

4. Increased financial tools, such as a company-sponsored lease program.

5. Aids to free him for more sales time.

6. More effective sales tools.

After management makes an investment in a product or a program which will increase a salesman's productivity, it has to make a careful evaluation of what this will mean to the average salesman. It is suggested that, for planning purposes, management adopt a philosophy of planning an increase in the average salesman's income of 1 percent for every 3 percent or 4 percent increase in productivity. This approach, in effect, reduces the percentage of total commissions paid. If the saving is greater than the cost of the program (and it should be if the program is properly evaluated), the difference will be available to offset other costs or, more hopefully, become profit. It will also become acceptable to the salesman because he takes home total dollars, not "percents."

Industrial Sales Compensation

In the industrial-distributor field a survey of salesmen's salaries made by an industrial association showed that:

Straight salary is preferred by 12.9 percent of distributors. Salary plus commissions on sales or bonus is used by 24.4 percent. Commission on sales is paid by 13.3 percent. Salary plus commission on gross margin is paid by 20.2 percent, while 25.3 percent pay commissions only on gross margin. The remaining 3.9 percent pay commission based on net profit.

The average annual sales volume for all salesmen is $269,900 per man. Average annual sales by method of compensation were as follows: Straight salary, $275,366; salary plus commission on sales or bonus, $251,750; commission on sales, $285,139; salary plus commission on gross margin, $303,515; commission on gross margin, $240,850; commission on net profit, $262,750.

However, it should be remembered that these are averages. Individual performances ranged from a low of $50,000 a year for a salesman on salary plus commission on gross margin to $1,400,000 a year for salesmen on salary plus commission on sales or a bonus. Two other companies reported salesmen on salary plus commission on gross margin with yearly sales volumes of $1,000,000.

Straight salaried salesmen averaged 6.1 calls per day. Those on salary plus commission on sales and those on salary plus commission on gross margin averaged one more call per day than the straight salaried men—7.1 and 7.2 calls respectively. Those earning commission on net profit averaged 7.5 calls per day while those on commission on gross margin averaged 7.7 calls per day. Those paid commission on sales averaged the most calls per day, 7.9.

Types of Compensation Plans

Straight Commission: The straight commission plans have long been popular because:

1. It is believed they minimized capital investment risks for the company. In a way, this is fallacious, because the expense of selling (living income and travel) is small compared with the business and profits that are lost when a commission salesman fails.

2. They relieve management of the responsibility of management. Frequently top management is too busy to direct its salesmen; in other cases, it does not know how.

3. They encourage salesmen to conduct themselves as though they were in business for themselves, and thus their aggressiveness is increased. At the same time, bad practices may be encouraged which cannot be corrected by management because of the salesman's attitude of independence and his resentment of direction and control. This feeling of independence and sales-territory ownership has frequently reached such heights and intensity that successful well-entrenched commission salesmen have not permitted their sales territories to be reduced in size and have insisted that they be handed down from father to son. The loss in realization of sales opportunities for companies caught in this trap is appalling.

4. They cause selling expenses to vary directly with sales, so that heavy losses do not prevail when sales are off. This permits easy bookkeeping and simplifies budgeting, but in times of high sales volume, companies can have very high sales costs.

5. They attract a type of person who will work hard for high stakes, gambling his time and effort for a big return. But they also attract some men who are less competent than management thinks they are and who overstock their customers, falsely represent the goods, and are inclined to cut corners. The company can do little to correct the situation until after the damage has been done.

Straight commission plans usually pay a commission on shipped orders, with the returns and allowances deducted. The commission varies with different types of products and for different industries. If the product is in great demand and sold in large quantities, the commission rate may be as low as 1 percent or even a fraction of 1 percent of sales. If the product requires intensive selling, or if quantities are small and expenses high, the rate may run as high as 25 percent of sales or higher. Straight commission salesmen usually pay their own expenses.

There is a growing trend for salesmen who work on a commission basis to be given a drawing account which is deducted from their earned commissions. Some sales managers feel that this gives the men the security of a salary, yet is a hedge against company loss, since no further commissions are paid until earned commissions exceed draws; but in reality there is no protection to the company. If the salesman is not able to earn his draw, the company has two alternatives:

1. Fire him and absorb the loss;
2. Keep him and continue his draw.

If the man is fired, there is a break in the company's sales program until a new man can be hired. So when all is said and done, the company would have been just as well off had it paid him a salary, and it would then have had the advantages of control that go with salaries.

Straight Salary: This method of monetary compensation is popular with well-entrenched companies, selling a broad line of products, and requiring a high degree of promotional or engineering work. Those using it claim to have:

1. Better control over their salesmen, particularly for promotional and other activities that do not result in immediate sales.
2. Less turnover, because their men, having a steady income and being well paid (the company assumes), are less inclined to leave.
3. More freedom in changing customers and territories.
4. Realization of greater profits when business is good.

Companies paying straight salaries reason that once a man has become established, increased sales are more often due to improvements in the business economy than in the results of added sales effort. Since the salesman is paid well to do his job, why should he receive an increase for something he did not create?

Of course, things work out differently in a business slump; then the companies are saddled with fixed selling expenses that may cause losses. With the straight salary plan, companies pay all expenses.

Salary Plus Commission: The trend is definitely toward this method. Under this plan, salesmen receive salaries which are expected to take care of their necessities of life and to be in keeping with the market for their characteristics, skills, and knowledge. In return for these salaries, they are expected to do specified jobs and produce satisfactory results. In addition, they have the opportunity to earn extra compensation for accomplishments in excess of the level of satisfactory results for their specified jobs.

Users of this method of compensation feel that they:

1. Obtain good control of their salesmen.
2. Integrate them into the company organization.

3. Cause the salesmen to feel and act as though they were custodians of valuable company property rather than independently in business for themselves.

4. Give the men both the satisfaction of security and incentive motivation.

5. Get flexibility in money income to reflect most truly both tangible and intangible contributions to the company welfare.

6. Have flexibility in changing customers and territories.

7. Control turnover. (However, some degree of turnover is good for a company. While it may become excessive under straight commissions, it may be insufficient under straight salaries.)

8. Achieve maximum cooperation of the salesmen in desirable promotional, engineering, and service activities.

The chart shows how a favorable chain of events can be introduced into a business if productivity per salesman can rise slightly faster than income per salesman, thus bringing down the percentage cost of sales over a period of time. Both the company and the salesmen benefit when such a relationship between constantly rising productivity and salesmen's compensation can be achieved in a sales group.

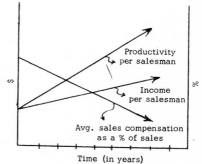

Time (in years)

Setting the base salary is probably the most difficult part of designing a combination plan. If the base is set too high, the salesmen will have too much difficulty in meeting it and the incentive motivation will be lost. If it is set too low, the salesmen will earn more extra compensation than is reasonable.

The term "base" refers to the minimum volume that represents a satisfactory job in relation to the salary paid. "Quota" represents the dollar volume, quantity, or other objective expected that the salesman will sell. It may be the same as the base or it may be higher. Quotas are used in budgetary control. A "goal" is what the salesman and his manager hope to sell if all goes well. It represents their starry-eyed ambitions and is never used for budget controls.

A second difficulty in determining the base arises from cyclical and seasonal variations. In a period of rising economy, it is easy for the salesman to increase his sales. When the economy is declining, he may do a good job but still have his sales drop.

For the foregoing reasons, the base should be adjusted annually, with careful consideration of cyclical trends and seasonal fluctuations. There are a number of ways by which the annual base can be established:

1. *The previous year's sales* may be used as the base. This is not bad when the trend is steadily upward; but as the economy levels off, it becomes more and more difficult for the salesman to reach his base, much less exceed it. The previous year's sales may do for a year or two, or for longer in a newly-opened territory, but usually the program quickly runs out of steam.

2. *A percentage of the previous year's sales,* usually 80 percent, offers the same problems. This plan has the benefit of assuring that the salesman makes some extra monetary compensation if he does a reasonably good job. This money is supposed to whet his appetite and motivate him to greater effort for more of the same.

3. *A three-year moving average,* or 80 percent of such average, is often used. For this, the previous three years are averaged for the following year's base; then, for each subsequent year, the sales figures for the first of the three years are dropped and the immediately previous year's sales are added. This plan smooths out any wide year-to-year fluctuations, yet retains the remaining disadvantages of the two previous methods. An additional disadvantage is that there is a year's lag in giving effect to any change in trend. This works to the salesman's advantage when the trend turns up, but he is fighting quite a battle when the trend turns down.

4. *Expenses including salary* are sometimes capitalized at about 5 percent and the result used as the base.

5. *A percentage of the amount of available business* (potentiality) is sometimes taken. This may not produce any hardship for a well-established territory, but may be exceedingly difficult to attain in a new or underdeveloped territory.

A constructive variation of this is to establish the desirable amount of business based on potentiality, then give the salesman a yearly "grubstake" for five years as he builds the territory to normal realization.

For example, if the base should be $200,000 when the territory has been fully developed, the salesman might be given a grubstake of $150,000 for the first year. Then, if he sold $75,000, that amount added to $150,000 would give him credited sales of $225,000, or $25,000 over the $200,000 base; he would then receive a commission on the $25,000. The second year the grubstake would be reduced to $100,000, the third year to $75,000, the fourth year to $25,000, and after that the full $200,000 base would apply.

The advantage of a grubstake is that the salesman always has the $200,000 full potentiality base before him as a goal. This keeps his eyes on a big figure, whereas if the base were merely raised each year, his eyes would be on lesser figures.

6. *Break-even volumes* are frequently used. Usually it is difficult to determine a break-even point for a sales territory or district which includes all elements of expense. Therefore, the company's break-even volume at anticipated gross margin is determined, plus the volume needed for an adequate minimum return on invested capital. This company volume is then apportioned to the sales territories in accordance with the ratios of their previous three years' sales to total company sales.

This establishes the share of the volume of business that each salesman must attain for the company to reach its break-even point (covering cost of manufacture, overhead expenses, promotional and research expenses, and their own expenses) and to provide a minimum return to the stockholders. The use of the three-year sales figures for the salesmen measures their penetration into their markets. As a salesman's sales increase, he carries a larger share of the break-even volume.

The commission paid may be based on dollar sales over base; or, if salaries are equitable, it may be paid as a percentage of salary.

7. *Arbitrary bases* are sometimes set. Here the manager uses his best judgment on all factors involved—past sales, future possibilities, economic trends, salesman's development—and then arbitrarily picks a base. This is dangerous, as biases are bound to creep in, and some salesmen may not feel that the base chosen is fair to them.

The Problem of Split Credits

The problem of assigning proper sales credit frequently arises when two or more salesmen are involved in a sale. This happens when the buyer of the goods is located in one man's territory, but the shipment is made to the territory of a second man who must service the sale.

Even more complicated is the situation existing when the specifications have been written by an architect or engineer in one man's territory, the goods purchased in a second salesman's and shipment made into the territory of a third salesman. Here three men are involved; if the first man fails to get the material specified, the sale is lost; if the second man fails to get the order, it is lost; if the third man fails to give proper service to the customer, a good customer may be lost.

Some companies handle such situations by giving full credit to the man getting the order, reasoning that although the other two men may lose out at this time, they will receive their full credit on similar orders they get signed.

Other sales managers feel this policy is a shortsighted one, and that the company is taking a risk that the two other men involved will not do their jobs properly and the company will stand a loss.

To guard against such a possibility, to treat all salesmen fairly and to see that due credit is given, many companies split credits. If the situation outlined above is normal, credit is split, with a third to each salesman; if the specifications are written and the order is placed in one territory with shipment to a second one, the first salesman would receive two-thirds credit and the second a third credit.

Mail and Telephone Sales

Most sales organizations give credit to territory salesmen for mail and telephone sales; only a very small minority do not.

The prevailing attitude is that the salesman in the territory has prepared the groundwork for mail orders; he is responsible for the territory as such; hence he should receive credit for the results of his work in that territory.

The counterargument is that mail orders indicate carelessness on the part of the salesman; that the salesman is derelict in his duties; who does not take the order on the occasion of his call, since otherwise he is likely to lose sales to the competitor salesman who is on the spot and aggressively seeking business; that it is the salesman's responsibility to take orders for sufficient quantities so that there will be no need of mail orders to fill in stocks between trips. Certainly this is true in some instances, but it would hardly seem to be realistic generally.

Starting New Territories

When starting a new territory, there is a considerable amount of promotional work to be done, and sales volume may not reach a profitable level for a year or possibly five years. Many companies consider such expenses as a capital investment, even though they might expense the cost currently.

They may pay the salesman assigned to the new territory a larger salary than their other salesmen, knowing that he will be unable to obtain the extra compensation that they do. As the territory becomes better established, the salary would be brought back to normal level with extra compensation being earned.

Some companies have men particularly adept in opening new territories; these men are moved from one new territory to another. Their superior skill justifies their receiving higher salaries than the company's average salesmen.

The "grubstake" plan is a useful method of compensation for new territories. The salesman has a high goal before him at all times. Understanding the program, he feels that the company is assisting him in getting established. Of course the steps in reduction of the grubstake should be explained to him in advance so he will not feel that the company is changing the rules in the middle of the game.

If a company turns a new territory over to a commission salesman, expecting him to carry himself and invest his own time and money in the development of the territory, the salesman has every right to feel that it is his property. The company could hardly take it, or even a portion of it, away from him without reimbursing him in some way.

Transferring Territories

It is relatively easy to transfer men from one territory to another when they are paid straight salaries, but it becomes increasingly difficult as the ratio of variable income (extra compensation) to total anticipated income increases. A popular ratio is for the variable portion (extra compensation) to be 25 percent to 33 percent of total anticipated income, the fixed portion (salary) being 67 percent to 75 percent.

When a salesman who receives a portion of his income as a commission is moved to another territory, his income may be put up considerably due to the purchasing pattern of his new customers, or his income may decline because the territory must be built up. This latter condition prevails when a territory is split; it may take months for the salesman to build up the portion of the territory that he retains to a point where it will be as productive to him as was his old full territory.

Some companies increase a salesman's salary when he loses territory. This may straighten out the situation for the time being, but it may also place the salesman out of step, salarywise, with the other salesmen. Or, if the higher salary is maintained, the income received by the salesman may become too high when the territory becomes fully developed. Some companies guarantee minimum extra compensation to the man for a year, to safeguard him against loss while he is building up his territory.

Other companies follow a split commission program, whereby the salesman losing territory or probable income receives credit for a percentage of sales, from his old territory, such credit being reduced, declining in amount during the year.

House Accounts

One troublesome problem concerns house accounts which are reserved for handling by branch or headquarters management. House accounts should be distinguished from the personal accounts of branch or district managers who receive commissions thereon.

In practice, policies on house accounts are fairly evenly divided. The question of house accounts is more acute in companies where

SALES	COMPANY_____				Form R-366-1
	PERFORMANCE RATING FORM			SCORE_____	
NAME_____	_____JOB TITLE_____			_____DUE BACK_____	
DISCUSSED WITH EMPLOYEE YES[ ] NO[ ] RATED BY____			_____APPROVED BY_____		
DEVELOPMENT OF ACCOUNTS	Cannot hold accounts without assistance	Holds accounts where competition is limited	Can protect vulnerable business against competition	Can open new accounts in established field	Sells new industries and new applications
KNOWLEDGE OF PRODUCT	Inadequate knowledge of product	Requires considerable coaching	Adequate knowledge	Well informed	Excellent technical knowledge
CAPACITY FOR FUTURE GROWTH	Is at the peak	Near his limit	Should advance in normal fashion	Should advance rapidly	Has great possibilities
COOPERATION WITH OTHERS	Uncooperative	Cooperates but unwillingly	Works well with others	Cooperation above average	Exceptionally well-liked and respected
PLANNED USE OF TIME-EFFORT	Work is poorly organized	Needs occasional assistance in planning	Effective under normal circumstances	Effective under difficult circumstances	Efficient, well-organized and planned
VOLUME (except for new territory)	Very poor volume	Approximates three-fourths of previous year's volume	Approximates previous year's volume	Decided improvement over preceding year	Over one-half more volume than preceding year

The modern way of compensating salesmen is on the basis of what they are worth to the company, rather than on sales volume alone. Merit-rating forms like the above used by Reynolds Metals Company are used to measure performance.

salesmen's earnings are directly related to their performance in their territories, but they exist even where salary plans are used because volume of sales is important in the appraisal of performance for promotion or salary increases.

Terminating Salesmen

Companies follow different practices as to termination compensation policies. Some have formal contracts with their salesmen stipulating the program that is to be followed; others have verbal understandings, while many have no stated policy.

With salaried salesmen, many companies expect their salesmen to give from two weeks' to three months' notice before leaving, in order that the company may arrange for replacements. If the men are permitted to leave before that period is up, they receive their full salaries for the period agreed upon. If they leave without notice, many companies merely pay them up to the time of their leaving. Some contracts stipulate that where a man is fired "for cause," he receives his salary up to the time of being fired.

With commission payments, some companies allow commission only on orders that have been shipped prior to the time of the salesman's leaving the company. Other companies pay commissions on all business written by the salesman prior to his leaving and shipped within a specified time after his leaving. The length of time depends on the type of product sold and the amount of work usually required to close an order. It is well to get this down on paper.

Commissions to departing salesmen are sometimes paid on sales entered, but usually on sales shipped less deductions and allowance, the thinking being that a sale is not completely made until it is shipped or even paid for.

Retroactive Sales Base

Companies in industries that have good access to monthly sales data, such as the work-glove industry, for example, frequently adjust their salesmen's base at the end of the year with the trend in the industry's sales.

For example, Salesman A may have a base of $200,000, which is deemed fair in view of the industry's sales trends. But during the year, the economy had a setback and the industry's sales for the year dropped 10 percent below previous year's sales. The salesman's base is also dropped 10 percent, retroactive to the first of the year.

Product Coverage

Salesmen are past masters at spending most of their effort on what they like to sell or on what is the easiest for them to sell. This may or may not be in keeping with the company's desires. In order to overcome this tendency of favoritism or specialization, many companies use the commission portion of their compensation plans to place emphasis on full product coverage or on special products.

To obtain product-coverage emphasis, they may divide the products into groups, with a sales base set for each group. To qualify for commissions, a salesman may have to exceed his sales base in certain important groups, in a certain number of groups, or in all groups. Or the company might pay commissions when the sales base is exceeded for each group, but step up the commission rate as more and more group sales bases are exceeded.

For example, a company has established five product groups; group A, the most profitable, carries a commission of 5 percent when the salary base is exceeded; group B, 4 percent; group C, D, and E, 3 percent. To qualify for any commission, the salesman must exceed the sales base in group A; even though he exceeds his base in groups B, C, D, and E, he receives no commission unless he exceeds his base in group A; if he exceeds his base only in group A, he receives his commission on that group only.

Or the salesman might receive commissions at the rates specified as each sales base is exceeded; but if he qualifies in all three groups, he receives an extra ½ percent on sales above base for the three groups; if he exceeds the base in four groups, he receives an extra ¾ percent for the four groups; if he exceeds the base for all five groups, he receives an override of 1 percent on all sales over the bases.

The Point System

The main object of this method is to develop the salesmen along most profitable lines to themselves and to the company. For those things which the company wants done, a reward is based on points. Annually, the number of points are totaled up and a bonus paid the salesman according to his record. As a matter of fact it is not a bonus, as the money represents what would ordinarily be paid a salesman anyway. The only difference is that what he is paid he earns, and he earns it in such a way that he knows he earns it. Thus, the feeling common among salesmen that they are not being paid all they are entitled to is eliminated.

To determine what number of points to allow on different products, use as a common denominator the work of least resistance. Take the easiest product to sell. A dollar sale of that product is fixed as worth one point, and upon that standard all other values are determined according to the added difficulty in selling. This can be determined easily by consulting the sales records. For example, the sales record might show one product was three times as hard to sell as another, so a salesman would get three points for every dollar sale in the first case; and one in the second.

The following point system was used in a long-term sales contest for distributors by a Canadian electronics manufacturer:

PRODUCT	POINTS
Portable TV—Up to and Including 17 Inch	¼
Portable TV—Over 17 Inch	½
Black and White Console TV—Under $200	½
Black and White Console TV—Over $200	¾
Black and White 3-Way Combinations	1
19 Inch Color TV	1
25 Inch Color TV—Under $700	2
25 Inch Color TV—Over $700	2
25 Inch Color 3-Way Combinations	3

Stereo—Under $300 .... ¾

Stereo—Over $300 1

*6 Portable Phonographs in Package 1

*12 Radios in Package.. 1

White Goods and Air Conditioners .... ½

---

*These products must be purchased as a package. They may not be accumulated to earn points.

Compensation of Sales Trainees

This problem involves two factors: (1) Compensating the trainee who is undergoing training in a company sales school; (2) compensating him after he takes his place in the line as a junior salesman, until such time as he is able to assume responsibility for a territory of his own.

It is customary to pay the trainee a modest weekly salary which will attract him to the job and enable him to care for his obligations. The salary rate varies considerably from line to line; estimates of the going rate for various types of saleswork can best be formed by consulting the sales-trainees-wanted ads in metropolitan newspapers.

Trainees taking a formal training course in a group are generally housed at a company hotel or dormitory. The very large companies sometimes take over an entire hotel, or a whole block of rooms in a hotel, on a permanent basis for this purpose.

Usually the home office carries the expense of training and of paying the trainee until the training period has been completed. In some instances, the home office may carry half the cost of a branch salesman's salary for a period of months, or until the man has become established. By making the branch carry half the expense, the branch manager is encouraged to speed the salesman into production, yet the branch is not required to carry the whole load.

If the salesman is being trained at the request of a distributor or manufacturer's agent, the salary and travel expenses are usually carried by the distributor or agent, while the living expenses and training costs are paid by the company.

When the junior salesman is placed on his "own" in a sales territory, either his "learner's salary" is increased, or he receives supplementary compensation—usually a commission on plus sales or an incentive bonus.

The Challenge of Older Salesmen

All things considered, salesmen retain their usefulness longer than any other group of employees. There are many salesmen working today, and doing their work well, who are far beyond the age at which office and other workers are retired or pensioned. Nevertheless, good management requires that to make room at the top for younger salesmen on the way up, the compensation plan should make it possible for salesmen who have reached age 65 to vacate their territories and retire.

Most companies accomplish this by simply applying their pension plan for office workers and executives (if they have one) to fit members of the sales organization. Some of the larger companies make it mandatory that a salesman or a sales manager must step aside when he reaches retirement age and accept a pension even though he may feel he is still a better salesman than some of the youngsters who are elbowing him out. This policy has been attacked on the grounds that age is not a matter of years but an attitude of mind and physical condition. And that is true. However, as a salesman grows older he also grows set in his ways, is less inclined to cooperate in instituting changes of policy, and is more likely to "crack up" so far as his health is concerned. The kind of competitive selling we have today calls for men with tremendous drive and energy, who can stand up under the hardships of present-day travel.

Consulting Basis for Retirement

Another objection sometimes advanced to retiring salesmen on a pension, especially where the salesman contributes from his earnings to the plan, is that it leaves the salesman free to go to work for a competitor. This is an important consideration since the stock in trade of a salesman is the friends and contacts he has established. So instead of pensioning off a salesman upon reaching retirement age, some firms keep him on the payroll in a consulting capacity and pay him a monthly salary (usually about 40 percent of his average earnings for the last three years) with the understanding that he can be called upon for advice or counsel at any time, or in the event of an emergency he will, if physically able, take over his old territory. Such arrangements usually cover a period of 10 years, beginning at age 65. They expire at age 75. From then on the salesman is on his own, which makes it important that he exert every effort during his high earning period to build up a financial reserve adequate to support his family after he reaches age 75. In accepting such a plan, of course, the salesman remains a full-time employee, which precludes his going to work for a competitor. Some companies require that their salesmen sign an agreement to that effect, in the event the pension plan has any control feature, such as a profit-sharing contribution by the company.

Texas Refinery Pension Plan

Pension plans worked out for commission salesmen are usually a modification of a general plan which takes into account the determination of average earnings of commission salesmen.

One company which has established a retirement fund for salesmen is the Texas Refinery Corporation. Its plan involves a noncontributory fund, based on 10 percent of net profits up to 15 percent of salesmen's total earnings under $5,000, and 7½ percent above $5,000. Salesmen become participants after three years and receive a share in proportion to length of service and income. Men who leave before retirement age receive 15 percent of the amount in their fund after three years' participation, 5 percent more for each additional year, and the full sum after 20 years of participation. There are options as to how these payments are received upon retirement.

Photopress Plan for Dependents

An unusual pension plan is that of Photopress, Incorporated, a Chicago offset printer, whose salesmen themselves worked out the plan. One of the men on the sales force died suddenly, and his accounts were distributed among the other men. The salesmen themselves realized that their incomes were greatly increased by having these accounts dropped in their laps. Since they benefited to such an extent through the business built up by another salesman, they thought his beneficiaries should share in the profits.

After talking the matter over, all concerned agreed upon a legal arrangement by which the beneficiary shares in the income from a salesman's accounts; the plan was also extended to cover a disabled salesman who is compelled to retire.

Benefits are extended over a five-year period. During the first year after the man's retirement, he receives 50 percent of the earnings from his accounts, the second year 40 percent, the third year 30 percent, the fourth year 20 percent, the fifth year 10 percent. If the man dies, his beneficiary receives these benefits.

The plan proved valuable to the company because its accounts were built upon personal contact and friendship, probably to a much greater extent than in the majority of businesses where tangible commodities are offered for sale. The plan helps maintain all the accounts, first, because the customer remembers the former salesman; and second, because the new salesman, if he is smart, establishes a relationship which eventually becomes as cordial as that which previously existed between the consumer and the first salesman.

Chapter 45

SALESMEN'S UNIONS

R ELATIVELY few salesmen carry union cards. Of those who do, the majority are wagon-driver salesmen operating routes in an established territory. However, other fields where salesmen are organizing or are being organized into unions are the liquor trade, electrical appliances, industrial and general-public life insurance, food and drug industries, newspapers and magazines, and automobile agencies. Under federal labor law a salesman is classified as an employee. It has not been too difficult for a union to put pressure on an employer and force him to recognize and bargain with his salesmen. Sales managers who smile at the idea of their salesmen belonging to a union are sometimes shocked to find that the company has had to agree to deal with representatives of salesmen's unions on pay and commission rates, paid vacations, pensions, and other matters which traditionally were settled man-to-man with the salesman. Then the going gets rough for the sales manager who finds himself in such an inflexible position.

Unionization Destroys Sales Control

The experience of those who have contracts with salesmen's unions has seldom been good. For one thing collective bargaining undermines the sales management-salesman relationship which pays salesmen on the basis of what they produce. Union negotiators are not concerned with that angle of sales compensation. They negotiate from the standpoint that the company's salesmen are not getting a fair share of the company's profits, that they are underpaid in relation to other employees; that they are the "forgotten men" of the business. They are deaf to arguments that a company cannot increase selling costs and still meet competition.

No sales manager responsible for producing a needed volume of business at a restricted cost can long operate efficiently under the conditions laid down by most salesmen's unions. Selling usually degenerates into a peddler type of operation, with little or no control over salesmen.

The successful salesman wants no part of a union—not even an independent union such as exists in some business establishments. Salesmen don't want to be restricted as to how much they can earn, or how far they can climb in the ranks of management. Most young salesmen look forward to the day when they will be sales manager of the outfit. It is quite obvious that under a setup such as some unions contemplate, they would remain salesmen, or at best boss salesmen, all their lives. Because of this attitude, efforts to organize salesmen have met with little success. But salesmen would not be human if, looking at what industrial workers have been able to secure through organization, some of them did not wonder if more of the good things in life might not be won through collective bargaining.

Where Organization Begins

The only practical way to maintain a sales organization on an independent basis, free from union control, is to make sure that all "sore points" which can become serious grievances if allowed to fester are recognized and corrected by company policy. This in turn requires that top management formulate a written policy governing the operation and employment of salesmen, and that such a policy be published and lived up to.

Sales and Marketing Executives—International, in an effort to isolate some of the grievances which caused salesmen to organize into unions, prepared a code of recommended employment practices. This code, which represents several years of research work by a special committee under the chairmanship of Paul Heyneman of San Francisco, follows:

1. All salesmen shall receive fair compensation during their initial training period.

2. While recognizing changes in compensation or territory to be functions of sales management, salesmen shall be consulted prior to establishing such changes.

3. Earnings of commission or bonus salesmen shall be unlimited, unless otherwise specified at the time of their employment.

4. When selecting salesmen for promotion, differences in the sales potentials of their territories shall be given full consideration.

5. Salesmen shall receive the same vacation, job or income security, and other employee benefits as are enjoyed by other employees in the same company.

6. The only "house" or "no commission" accounts shall be those clearly defined in advance of solicitation.

7. The paperwork required of any salesman shall be held down to a minimum and its value clearly justified to him.

8. Salesmen's expense reimbursement policies shall be uniform, except when based on clearly justified variations in conditions.

9. A sharp distinction shall be drawn between a salesman's earnings and his expense allowances, and any system which shows a salesman either a profit or a loss on his expense account shall be discouraged.

10. Salesmen shall be given either a contract, agreement, or letter covering such conditions of his employment as might otherwise be the basis for later misunderstandings.

11. If quotas are used—

    (a) Salesmen *may* know how their figures have been determined, and

    (b) The figures shall be based on accurate and adequate criteria or on reliable seasoned personal judgment.

12. A salesman whose health or well-being gives evidence of being prejudiced by the nervous tensions involved in his work shall be given such relief as may be possible.

13. Pressure to achieve results shall be of a constructive nature, avoiding the use of "fear" psychology or threatened loss of employment.

14. No matter where a salesman may be located, he shall be provided with a simple means for stating his grievances, which shall be promptly considered and answered.

Negotiating a Union Contract

Under national labor law, if a majority of the salesmen in "any bargaining unit" of a company doing an interstate business sign cards authorizing a recognized union to represent them in collective bargaining, the National Labor Relations Board will move to certify that union as the official bargaining agent for *all* salesmen in that unit. A bargaining unit might be the salesmen of one sales office, New York City for example. It may include only city salesmen in an office; or it may include all your salesmen. The determination of an "appropriate" unit is made by the National Labor Relations Board usually in open hearing, at which time the employer has the right to protest: (1) The composition of the unit; (2) the validity of the "membership" cards on which the union bases its claim for representation. If a "consent agreement" cannot be reached, then the National Labor Relations Board may call an election to ascertain if a majority of your salesmen in that bargaining unit wish to be represented by the union. If the union wins the election, it is then certified by the board, even though some of your salesmen who signed authorization cards may subsequently refuse to join the union.

Sales managers should carefully note that the law does not require that a majority of your salesmen must be dues-paying members in the union. All the union needs to do is to get more than half the salesmen in what it *thinks* comprises an appropriate bargaining unit to sign cards. Moreover, once a salesman signs such an authorization and turns it over to the union, the union may use it at any future time, *even though the salesman may in the meantime change his mind or job.*

The Abbott Laboratories Case

An important consideration in the determination of representatives under the national labor law is the nature of a salesman's duties. In a close election, as for example in the controversy between the Abbott Laboratories, Inc., of North Chicago and the Drug Trade Salesman's Union, where 28 salesmen were involved, the decision may hinge on whether any of the salesmen are supervisors. In this instance the outcome depended on the status of a challenged vote. The company held one voter was not a salesman but a supervisor. The union lost on appeal. In setting up the bargaining unit, the company contended that all the salesmen working out of the New York branch, and not merely 28 men operating locally, should be included. The board held for the union (Case No. 2-R-6158). The decision was as follows:

IV. The appropriate unit—For the purpose of distributing its products, the company has divided the country into 26 sales districts. Several districts are administered through a branch office. New York has such a branch office consisting of Districts 6, 20, 22, and 24. The union seeks to represent all sales representatives of the company employed in District No. 6. The company, however, contends that the appropriate unit should include the sales representatives of all four districts which make up the New York branch office.

All sales representatives have substantially the same duties, qualifications, and pay range. Their job is to visit physicians, hospitals, retail pharmacies, and wholesale druggists, and sell them the company's products. Nearly all are registered pharmacists.

Each of the four districts maintains its office within the confines of its geographical limits; the sales representatives, however, file daily reports with the New York branch office. The sales representatives of Districts 20, 22, and 24 do considerable traveling, at company expense, and usually by automobile. It is necessary at times for some of these salesmen within the three latter districts to leave their homes for a night or two. The sales representatives of District No. 6, on the other hand, work within the metropolitan area of New York City and with one exception rarely find it necessary to make overnight business trips. Aside from semiannual conventions of two or three days' duration, there is no contact among the sales representatives of the four districts. However, the salesmen within each district meet more often or occasionally to discuss their problems and exchange views. Each district is separately managed by a sales manager who exercises no supervision over sales representatives outside of his own district. District sales managers can hire new salesmen to cover their own districts. If there is a desirable opening available in a certain district, men who have been in that district prior to the opening are given first consideration. For the purpose of sales promotion the company fosters sales competitions wherein prizes for high men are awarded within the district, as well as high men divisionally and nationally. During the last four years there has been but one transfer of a sales representative from one district to another within the New York branch office. The union has confined its organizational efforts to the sales representatives of District No. 6.

In view of the foregoing facts and in the absence of any history of collective bargaining, we believe that a unit consisting exclusively of sales representatives of District No. 6 is appropriate at this time. We therefore find that all sales representatives of the company employed in District No. 6 but excluding the district sales manager and any other supervisory employees with authority to hire, promote, discharge, discipline, or otherwise effect changes in the status of employees or effectively recommend such action, constitute a unit appropriate for the purposes of collective bargaining within the meaning of Section 9 (b) of the Act.

When the union has been certified, either through a consent agreement reached in the NLRB offices or by an election conducted by the NLRB, the union presents its demands, sometimes by letter, sometimes orally. Since the labor law requires that all bargaining be in "good faith," the management is within its rights to ask that the demands be reduced to writing so they may be considered together. Some unions follow the strategy of making one demand at a time, and upping them as they go along. It is desirable, for all concerned, that bargaining should be on the basis of all demands and that they be in writing. Some labor-relations men go further, and ask the union to submit a "tentative" contract rather than a mere statement of demands. Justification for this request lies in the fact that the United States Supreme Court has held that there must be a written agreement between the union and the employer, therefore it is wise to bargain on that basis. Usually the employer prepares the first draft of an initial agreement, which the union can accept or reject.

What the Agreement Should Cover

When the union draft of the proposed contract is presented, and agreement has been reached on each point, it is in order for the company to propose that its attorneys redraft the contract, incorporating the points upon which there has been a meeting of minds, and submit the revised contract at a later meeting for the approval of the bargaining committee of the union.

When, and if, the contract meets the approval of the bargaining committee, it is ready for ratification of the membership of the union. It then becomes binding upon the union. Management, however, should reserve the same right of ratification, and it should be understood that the contract will not be binding upon the company until ratified by the company's board of directors. This protects the company's position while the contract is before the union for ratification.

The simpler a contract is, the better. It should avoid the use of involved legal terms which the average union member cannot understand. It should avoid vague clauses which can be construed in different ways by different parties to the agreement. Wage increases should be expressed in flat amounts rather than percentages. Provision for arbitration of disputed clauses should be made and, if possible, an arbitrator named in the contract. A labor contract, if it is to fulfill its purpose, must be more than an agreement on wages and working conditions; it should lay the foundation for enduring goodwill between management and the union. Too many contracts fail to do that. On the contrary, they become a basis for endless disputes and controversy. The more complicated the wording of the contract, the more danger of stoppages.

The responsibilities of both parties should be clearly set forth, even though this may seem unimportant at the time. For example, we may see a more aggressive effort on the part of labor to place members of the union on the board of directors of the company, or to force management to set up management committees in which labor would have an equal voice with management. It is therefore only common sense that a clause be put into the contract protecting each side from encroachment on the other's rights. Management must be free to manage, or its functions cease.

Union officials and members must likewise have the right to conduct their affairs without interference from the company.

The mutual interest both parties have in maintaining working conditions which provide for the safety and comfort of the worker, and at the same time insure efficient production, should be brought out in the contract. These points are as follows:

1. The right to hire and fire.
2. Protective condition of labor and management in this prerogative, notices, etc.

3. Hours of work:

    a. When overtime starts.

    b. When Sunday starts and ends.

    c. When holidays start and end.

    d. Special periods of work.

    e. Miscellaneous conditions of work.

4. Types of seniority:

    a. Departmental.

    b. Job.

    c. Ability.

    d. Family status.

While it is common practice to include wage schedules, classifications, and differentials in the overall agreement, it is sometimes wiser to have a supplementary agreement covering wages. The overall agreement can then run for a relatively long period with a clause stating that the question of wages can be reopened for discussion under certain specified conditions without affecting the other provisions of the contract. This makes for greater stability of labor relations, and tends to eliminate the need of the union to breach the contract to force a wage increase. Sometimes a clause is inserted to the effect that wage discussions can be started by either side if the cost of living moves up or down a certain number of points, using the U.S. Department of Labor's Cost-of-Living Index for a specified area. In other cases the contract provides for a semiannual or an annual review of wages upon request of either party. In such cases the time is usually stated when one party must notify the other of its desire to review wages, and that date should be carefully considered in relation to the company's sales peaks.

The greatest weakness in labor contracts is when they fail to provide an orderly procedure for handling grievances. The contract should define what is meant by grievances. Does it include wage grievances? The answer to this question is usually no. It should then define carefully the agreed-upon grievance procedure. If possible allow a cooling-off period in the case of disputes between a foreman and a worker by providing for submission of the grievance, in the event it cannot be adjusted by the supervisor, to a grievance committee. Then if that fails to bring about a settlement, the contract should provide for arbitration, either by an arbitrator to be selected by the Federal Conciliation Service, or where there is one, a state board of arbitration, or by some local person in whom both sides have confidence. This last procedure is to be recommended. Sometimes there is a local judge who will act, or the services of the American Arbitration Association may be used.

The contract should not only include an expiration clause, but should preferably state the conditions under which it can be opened up by either party. There is a growing trend to include cost-of-living clauses. The customary arrangement is to make an adjustment whenever there is a five-point fluctuation in living costs, and the adjustment will be on a point-for-point basis.

Agreements on File

The U.S. Bureau of Labor Statistics keeps current a file of approximately 5,000 agreements, all submitted voluntarily. Included in this file are virtually all agreements in the United States covering 1,000 workers or more (about 1,800), but only a small proportion of the smaller agreements. Railroad and airline agreements, which are required to be filed with the National Mediation Board, are not included in the bureau's file.

A few agreements are submitted to the bureau in confidence. With these exceptions, the file is open to public use. The file is located in the offices of the bureau's Division of Industrial and Labor Relations in the General Accounting Office Building, 5th and G Streets, N.W., Washington, D. C. (Room 2336). For information about particular agreements on file, write to the Bureau of Labor Statistics, Washington, D. C. 20212, or call (area code 202) 961-2597.

Chapter 46

MANUFACTURERS' SALES AGENTS

I N some lines of business, manufacturers depend upon independent agents as their main channel of distribution. In other industries small companies have not reached the stage of developing their own sales organizations and they also operate through manufacturers' agents.

Usually a new company just starting in business employs agents as the quickest and most economical way to establish itself on a nationwide basis. Still other companies produce low-cost items, the total volume of which would not support the cost of field representatives. In all these cases manufacturers' sales agents can make definite and valuable contributions to the solution of the sales problems of their principals.

An agent does not take title to the goods, normally sells only a part of a manufacturer's products, and usually does not maintain an inventory. However, the trend over the last few years shows an increasing number of agents warehousing some inventory. In industries where replacement parts or odd sizes are a significant aspect of the customer's operation, agents have found that the added service of carrying emergency stocks enhances their position in the marketplace.

Control over prices, terms, credit, and other conditions of sales generally remains in the hands of the manufacturer. Because of the agent's expertness in a limited line of products, the manufacturers often seek his advice on these matters.

Advantages of the Agent

Although agents come from varied backgrounds, the great majority who are successful are former salesmen. The years of experience acquired as a salesman provide excellent training for the individual whose objective is the establishment of a manufacturers' agency.

The main advantage conceded the representative is low cost of sales coverage. Many newly formed manufacturers, with a minimum of financial resources and little or no market penetration, have relied upon the representative for market coverage.

In the representative, the new manufacturer finds immediate geographical sales coverage. By employing an agent, the manufacturer can concentrate his efforts upon production and product-line expansion, rather than incurring financial risk and expenses associated with establishing company sales offices.

In addition, a new sales force may require many months of nonproductive time for locating potential users and buyers of products. The local representative has established customer contacts and can bring new-product features to the attention of potential buyers without delay.

A manufacturer's agent, by representing a number of manufacturers, usually has many more products to sell than the company salesman. With this wider line, the representative contacts more people per call, spends more time selling and less time traveling between accounts, and consequently becomes more efficient than a company salesman with a limited product line.

The agent who is repeatedly selling a variety of technical products will encounter more customer problems and product applications than will the limited-product-line salesman, and therefore will maintain greater awareness of product uses and customer needs.

Many agent salesmen are graduate engineers who seek the challenge that selling offers, but do not wish to sever their technical and scientific interests. The representative of this caliber is continually associated with stimulating engineering problems whenever confronted with a possible sale.

The income of the agent salesman is dependent entirely upon his sales. His commission is directly related to his performance in the field; the greater his sales, the larger his paycheck. The man who accepts this challenge to significantly better his income level has more confidence in his ability to perform than the man who is satisfied with a steady and more secure income. The agent salesman does take a risk, and his confidence usually is reflected in his sales performance.

Disadvantages of the Agent

Manufacturers' agents usually think in terms of immediate sales. Many have little interest in building for the future, particularly if the company is likely to take its account away from them at some time in the future. They sell hardest those items that are easy for them to sell and on which they will obtain the greatest and quickest return.

A company buying their services may find its products offered as a secondary item or as an afterthought, the agent concentrating on his primary account. The agent is likely to ask himself, *"Why should I cut the selling time on my good accounts to promote a new one, particularly as my net sales commissions would remain exactly the same?"*

For example, suppose the agent spends 75 percent of his time on Company A's product and 25 percent on Company B's, and his income is $7,500 a year. Now Company B urges him to spend half his time on its product. If he does so, and his sales of B products rise while sales of A products fall, and his income still is $7,500, there is no incentive for him to change his work pattern and habits.

Since the main worry of some agents is that a company will take away its account and put in its own salesman, they may try to guard against this by deliberately holding down their sales, so as not to build too attractive a "plum" for the company. Other agents are very secretive about their accounts, and discourage management visits to their areas. They refuse to furnish mailing lists, insist that all customer dealings go through them, and make use of every possible means to protect "their" accounts.

Because agents are independent operators, and therefore individualists in the first place, they are often slow to enter wholeheartedly into company programs. They frequently believe they know a better way, or "the program is a waste of my time." Customer audits, scheduled routes, daily reports, and campaign programs are difficult to install, unless such activities are provided for clearly in the agency agreement.

Manufacturers' agencies, being proprietorships, are subject to all the whims of the agent. He often may have his son, wife, or other relative working for him; they may be competent or they may not be. He may have a partnership or be incorporated, with the surviving partner or owners taking over on his death; and they may be far less capable than he. For these reasons, many companies include termination clauses in case of death or other important change in the operations of the agent.

It is difficult to divide or otherwise geographically change an agent's territory. He believes he has, and actually often does have, a vested interest in all the territory he covers for his combined sources. If one source should decide to transfer a portion of the territory to one of its company offices, the agent would experience a financial setback in trying to operate in that portion with his remaining line.

Commission rates are usually set for purchases in normal quantities. If a large user, such as an O.E.M. (original equipment manufacturer) account becomes interested, the normal commission and even any agent commission might kill the deal. Therefore companies frequently retain the right to sell O.E.M. accounts direct, or use graduated commission rates for increased volume orders.

Finally, an agent may obtain a line with the sole intention of sewing it up so someone else in his area cannot get it, or as a hedge for future promotion, should one of his current lines be lost or go sour. In the meantime the company loses representation and sales.

Territory to Serve

Agents' territories range in size from one city to several states. The sales territory is a geographical expression of a predetermined sales plan. Sales territories of manufacturers' agents are usually custom-made in conformance with the basic requirements of both agent and client. Such territories are almost always handled on an exclusive basis.

When the agent and the manufacturer begin to determine the extent of the area which he can properly cultivate, these fundamental factors should be considered: (1) The nature or type of product will have a substantial influence on the size of the agent's territory; products with a high turnover, many prospects, and repeat sales require a smaller area than products with a slow rate of consumption and few repeat sales; (2) class of customers selected will be a determinant in the size of territory the agent serves; (3) density of the market is an important consideration in setting the boundaries of territory to be covered; (4) frequency of calls is related to buyer density, the class of customer, and type of product. Calls must be made frequently enough to meet competition and to satisfy the needs of the customer without at the same time incurring excessive selling costs. Other fundamentals: The more service and nonselling activities required of the agent the more restricted will be the territory. The stage of market development of the product has considerable influence on the size of territory an agent is able to handle. The degree of competition, if vigorous, will require more frequent calls and restrict the territory an agent can adequately cover. Territories are often established on the basis of political boundaries, which are not necessarily adaptable to efficient marketing; trading areas often form the basis of better territorial boundaries. Other qualitative factors are the strength, size, and location of the agent's organization.

The Sales-Agency Agreement

Some of the provisions that should be included in the sales agreement are:

1. *Territory:* The exact territory to be covered should be delineated. If exclusive representation is to be given, this should be stated.

2. *Products:* The products to be sold by the agent should be designated clearly and it should be stated that the agent will refrain from representing or selling competing lines.

3. *Prices:* The manufacturer will set the prices at which his products are to be sold. The agreement should specify what authority, if any, the agent has to change prices; what discounts are to be allowed, and under what circumstances they may be attained.

4. *Orders:* In some industries the contract provides that all orders are subject to the manufacturer's acceptance. This releases the manufacturer from any liability for errors or other unacceptable factors that may appear in the order as submitted by the agent.

5. *Authority:* The general authority granted the agent by the manufacturer should be precisely described.

6. *Compensation:* The rate of commission and the dates or designation of time where such payments will be made, should be shown.

7. *Expenses:* If there is to be an expense allowance, the type, extent, and liability of the manufacturer should be clearly stated.

8. *Advertising:* Allocation of advertising expense should be designated and a description of the type and extent of such advertising should be given.

9. *House Accounts:* Client manufacturers sometimes retain house accounts. It is essential that the agent and manufacturer have a complete understanding from the outset of the relationship as to house accounts in the agent's given territory.

10. *Termination:* The agreement should stipulate methods for terminating the contract, extent of notice to be given by one party to the other, and the form in which the notice shall be submitted.

Getting Agents to Push a Product

A common complaint of manufacturers' sales agents is that the companies they represent make little or no effort to help them sell a product after they get the line. In most cases about all the sales cooperation the agent receives is a handful of booklets, or perhaps some material for the agent to include in his sales kit. Manufacturers, on the other hand, complain just as loudly that the average sales agent does not try to sell their products, but contents himself with listing them in a price list and waiting for the orders to roll in. Most manufacturers say that in order to give the agent the high discount he demands, there is no margin for sales promotional cooperation. This is especially true of companies which do national advertising.

A Dartnell check of companies selling through manufacturers' agents on an exclusive territory basis indicates that most of them are relatively small concerns with little or no flair for selling. They are primarily producers. They operate on the theory that it costs so much to make a unit, and therefore they must get so much for it, without giving consideration to the effect an increase in sales volume would have on their unit costs. Few of them, it was found, attempted to determine what their break-even point was at varying volumes of sales, or ever stopped to figure how much *more* they could afford to spend to get *added* volume.

Those who have applied the plus-volume reasoning to costs have invariably found they could justify an increase in total selling cost, in order to get a larger sales volume against which fixed expenses could be spread. They have employed contact men to work with their sales agents in the territory and help them to develop a more effective sales presentation. They have induced agents to furnish them with names of their best prospects and customers, which have been consolidated and systematically worked with inexpensive promotional literature. Where the product is well priced, manufacturers have even gone so far as to put on sales contests. Agents who show the largest increase in transactions, open up the most new accounts, or in other ways build new business, win prizes of their own selection.

One of the most effective of all plans, where a company sells a long line of products or a variety of related products, is to select one particular product and build an educational contest around it. The contest lasts one month, and during the month each agent is mailed a weekly bulletin bristling with useful sales suggestions. The next month a different product is pushed. By the end of a year or two, all sales agents get a concentrated education in how to sell from 10 to 20 of a manufacturer's most desirable products. Not only does the knowledge thus acquired help an agent and his salesmen do more profitable business, but the know-how thus developed stands them in good stead for years to come. Most important of all, it puts a manufacturer's products high on the agent's preference list, a matter of no little importance when you consider that most sales agents are trying to sell a hundred different products which, as a rule, they know very little about.

Annual sales conferences at the factory, publishing the standings of agents every month, or requiring them to set up "bogies" to hold their franchise, are other ways to get them to push your products. But a great deal depends upon how much value they attach to their franchise. If they value it lightly, there is not much to be done.

Recognition of the agents' individual salesmen is also very important. Sometimes, manufacturers treat the entire representative organization as if it consisted only of the president. This is often fostered by the organization head, who may resent interference by the factory sales manager. Some companies may hold a two- or three-day meeting for the representatives' managements and then hope that the essential information will be relayed back to the salesmen in a two-hour meeting at the local office. By not holding sales meetings for the individual salesmen, manufacturers lose one of the most direct ways of communicating and motivating these men.

Advertising to Back Up Agents

Failure to get distribution through manufacturers' sales agents can usually be traced to lack of advertising support. It has been proved times without number that salesmen who must sell a product not favorably known to the buyer soon become discouraged and stop trying to sell it. On the other hand, if the buyer has even a slight knowledge of the product from having seen it advertised somewhere, the sales job is simplified and the salesman's task is lightened. Such advertising can be done at a relatively small cost in industrial or business papers slanted directly at specific groups of buyers or markets.

The function of advertising is definitely subordinate to personal selling among manufacturers' agents. Usually, the client assumes the major responsibility for the advertising and promotion. But the agent should be expected to provide close support for his manufacturers' advertising and promotional campaigns. In addition to handling tie-in promotional materials for clients, the agent frequently administers cooperative advertising programs.

In summary, the agent is an educator and problem solver as well as a salesman, and is expected to perform many kinds of presale and postsale activities. These services are necessary and important if the agent expects to compete successfully for the buyer's favor among alternate suppliers.

Chapter 47

CONTRACTS WITH SALESMEN

T HE enactment of federal and state laws affecting the relationship between the company and its salesmen has made it
important that all employment agreements be put in writing. This
not only avoids misunderstandings between employer and employee,
but establishes the salesman's status under the law.

Because of the trend of government to regulate employer-employee
relationships, some employers utilize salesmen as independent contractors rather than as employees of the company. In such cases
both the employment agreement and all correspondence with the
salesman or sales agent must support the independent contractor
status, and neither the basic agreement nor subsequent correspondence should attempt in any way to control the salesman's time. In
fact the agreement should state, "The company does not exercise
any control over the amount of time the agent devotes to the sale
of its products, the number of other lines handled, or the methods
used in canvassing the agent's territory." Such a clause establishes
the agent's independence of action.

Another consideration in determining whether salesmen shall
operate as regular employees or as independent contractors is the
company's liability for acts of the salesman, as, for example, automobile accidents and injuries. Modern courts hold that the term
"independent contractor" signifies one who contracts to do work
according to his own methods, and without being subject to the
broad control of his employer. In other words, an independent contractor is a person who contracts with another to do something but
who is not controlled by the latter as to how or when he does his
work. However, the employer has the legal right to discharge an
independent contractor who does not perform his work satisfactorily,
or in accordance with prior agreements.

Recently a higher court said that the real test of an independent
contractor is whether the employer has any authoritative control

with respect to the manner in which the details of the work are to be performed.

For example, in the recent case of *Peterson* v. *Brinn & Jensen Company*, 277 N. W. 82, it was disclosed that a salesman named Porter used his own automobile and covered his territory about every five weeks. He made sales and collections for his employer. He was paid a commission computed on the gross profit to the company on his orders, and against this he had a drawing account. If at any time the company was dissatisfied with his work he could be discharged.

One day the salesman negligently drove his automobile in collision with another car, seriously injuring the occupants who sued the salesman's employer to recover damages.

When discussing the distinctions between a legal employee and an independent contractor, the court said that under the above arrangement the salesman was an independent contractor. Therefore, in holding the employer not liable, the court said:

"The ultimate test (of whether a salesman is an independent contractor) is determined by the control reserved in the employer. However, in some forms of employment the management (employer) reserves the right to give the most detailed instruction as to the manner and form in which the work is accomplished, even though there is no doubt whatever that the person so directed and instructed is an independent contractor."

Therefore, according to this decision, the fact that an employer instructs a salesman in detail as to how to solicit orders or business does not in the least interfere with their legal relationship of employer and independent contractor.

Notwithstanding the holding of the higher court in this case, there are on record many decisions to the effect that a traveling salesman is a legal employee although he is paid on a commission basis. Among these is *Riggs* v. *Standard*, 130 F. 199. In this case a salesman was paid on a commission basis but the employer treated him as a salaried employee. Therefore, he was held *not* to be an independent contractor.

Nature of Employment

While the contract must specify the kind of employment to be given, it is well not to be too specific. In general contracts the nature of employment is purposely very vague. In sales agreements it is usual to specify the products which the salesman is to sell, thus protecting a territory should a new product be brought out later which the company might wish to sell through a different sales organization. The territory is definitely described, and if there are to be any exceptions or limitations as to the type of trade the salesman is to sell, exceptions should be specifically set forth in the body of the contract.

Many companies have found it good practice to incorporate a clause that the employee agrees to devote his full time to the work. While it is possible that the company will never wish to take advantage of such a clause, nevertheless it has a valuable moral effect and would give the company certain rights in inventions which an employee might develop while in the company's employ. If, however, there is a possibility of that, a separate clause should be used to cover that contingency. A "full time clause" used in employment contracts of The National Cash Register Company, follows:

> Said employee agrees to devote his full time and best endeavor to the business of the company, under the direction of its officers and representatives, and to conform to the rules, regulations, and instructions of the company now in force, or that may hereafter be adopted and mailed to said employee.

Compensation of Employee

It is particularly important that this clause be most specific. There are many opportunities for misunderstandings about compensation. For example, the right of employer to charge commissions on credit losses to salesmen can be challenged, and the courts have held that employers have no right to hold salesmen responsible for credit losses in the absence of a contract covering that point. It should be clearly set forth that the salesman's commissions are not earned until the sale has been completed (i.e., money collected) and that any commission paid prior to the completion of the sale is in the nature of an advance. The most approved method of protecting the company against paying commissions on incompleted orders is to word the clause as follows:

> Said employee, during his continuation in the employment of the company under this contract, shall receive a commission on all monies received from the sales of products sold for the company in the aforementioned territory, as follows:

> (Tabulation of Commission Rates)

> Said employee agrees commission shall not be credited to his account on the company's books until the purchaser has made settlement in full for cash or acceptable notes, in which case the company may withhold payment of the commission, wholly or in part, until the notes are paid.

The above clauses are taken from a contract used by one of the largest corporations in the country.

It is common practice in drawing contracts with salesmen to agree to pay "a commission on sales." Unless the agreement is specific in defining what is meant by sales, the court will construe the agreement in any number of ways. The courts have held a salesman completed his responsibility when he wrote up an order and mailed it to the office. This, of course, is seldom what a sales manager employing a salesman has in mind. He is thinking in terms of "accepted" orders, but the order blank does not specify, as it should, that the order is not an order until accepted by a duly authorized officer of the company at the home office. In one case a salesman's contract provided that he receive commissions on all "sales" within a named territory. He had secured orders under this contract that were not filled until after its termination. The employer maintained that "sales" referred to deliveries; that since deliveries were made after the salesman's employment had ended he did not make the sales and was entitled to no commission.

"We do not agree," said the court. "The word 'sale' or 'sales' does not always include deliveries. As stated by Prof. Williston: These words are constantly used as meaning or including a contract to sell or contract to buy. The salesman's duty was discharged when the contracts or orders were closed and forwarded to his employer. It is simply a question whether he shall be paid for services fully rendered before his discharge and it is not material that the commissions did not become due until after the termination of his contract."

From a lack of understanding between employer and salesman, not only of when the commission is earned but, too, of when it is payable, come the suspicions and distrust that sap the loyalty of any sales organization.

Profit-sharing agreements, both commission agreements with salesmen and agents or profit-sharing agreements with executives and other employees, should carry a clause which requires complaints regarding the commissions or profits shown on the statement be filed within 30 days. Such a clause is helpful in court should an employee sue for an accounting after leaving the company's employ.

Authority of Employee

Under the law an employee's position carries with it certain rights of contract. Frequent decisions have held that when a corporation appoints a sales manager and gives him the authority to use such a title, it then automatically confers upon that individual the right to enter into contracts necessary in the fulfillment of his duties; as, for example, the right to hire salesmen; to enter into advertising contracts; and to do all those things which are essential to managing sales. The same is true in the case of a purchasing agent. The mere granting of the title conveys the authority to enter into purchase agreements, unless a contract limiting the duties of the employee exists.

As a protection to the company against representatives who might be inclined to exceed their authority in such directions it is well to incorporate a clause in all employment contracts specifically stating that the acts of employees are not binding unless ratified by the company. And in the case of salesmen, it should be clearly set forth that no order is binding until it has been accepted by the company. If this is not done, you may find yourself entangled with state laws which hold that you are doing business in their states and that a portion of your business is subject to certain taxes. In a contract of The National Cash Register Company, a clause is included to cover this point, as follows:

When an order is taken, the same shall not be binding until accepted by the company. The company reserves the right to reject an order when in its judgment the register may not be suitable to the business of the customer. The company agrees to fill all orders accepted with practical dispatch according to the instructions endorsed thereon, but failure to do so from any cause shall not make it liable for any commissions thereon.

Drawing Accounts

Where the employment contract calls for the establishment of an account to which profits or commissions will be credited periodically, and against which the employee is permitted to make periodical draws, provision should be made to cover the possibility of overdrafts. There have been a number of different rulings, in different states, as to the ability of an employer to collect monies advanced against such drawing accounts.

Generally speaking, an overdraft cannot be collected unless it has been specifically agreed that it would be repaid, that it is in the nature of a personal loan, or where notes have been given. Without such understanding the court is likely to hold that it was a business partnership, in which the company agreed to finance the employee, and any resulting loss was in the nature of a business loss.

If it is the desire or intention of the employer to treat overdrafts against drawing accounts as a loan, to be set up on the books of the company as an asset, it is imperative that a note should be secured from the salesman for the specific amount of the overdraft, and if possible, it should be endorsed by some responsible person. In that case it is well to cover that point in the contract. The following clause is taken from an agreement used by an oil heating company:

The company will allow a salesman to borrow or draw $............ a week for which he will give the company his personal note to apply against and be deducted from commission credit. This note is payable on demand and may only be satisfied by payment thereof.

Agreements Covering Reports

While it is obviously foolish to expect that getting a salesman to sign an agreement to make periodical reports to the office will entirely solve the report problem, it will help materially. If deemed advisable, a clause covering that point, under the broad title of *Absence from Territory,* should be inserted just ahead of the clause relating to the employee's duties.

Some salesmen's agreements examined are very definite on this point. One reads: "This contract shall be null and void if second party (salesman) does not make complete and full daily reports of all work on company's regular blank for that purpose."

Duties of Employee

The principal advantage of such a clause is to familiarize an employee with the policies of the company and the objective of the business. In the case of general employees the employee merely agrees to adhere to stated policies. It is in the nature of his taking an oath of office. In the case of salesmen and employees engaged to do a specific job, the various phases of that job, in the order of their importance, should be set down, so that there can never be any question as to just what the man is being paid to do.

Points which ought to be covered in defining the duties of a salesman, in addition to living up to the company's standards of practice as well as its rules and regulations are: (1) Maintenance of price, (2) to avoid making any statements which will incriminate the company, (3) giving the company the benefit of any information which will help other salesmen, (4) care of samples, (5) collection and credit cooperation, (6) advertising cooperation, (7) agreement not to handle side lines, (8) agreement to give fidelity bond if required, (9) to cooperate with the home office in every possible way.

Salesmen's Samples

A matter upon which many disagreements have arisen and which should be clearly defined in an agreement with salesmen is the responsibility for samples. The following clauses, taken from the employment contract of Coopers, Inc., of Kenosha, Wisconsin, may be of interest in that connection:

Coopers, Inc., will furnish the salesman, on memorandum charge, as it may deem necessary, trunks, sample cases, sample garments, hosiery, swatches of fabric and swatch book covers, price lists with covers, order books with covers, stationery, business cards, and other supplies, which will aid the salesman in properly exhibiting, soliciting for, and in selling Coopers, Inc., products. All such supplies so furnished by Coopers, Inc., shall at all times remain the property of Coopers, Inc., and shall be returned to it on demand or upon the termination of this agreement. The salesman agrees to conduct all correspondence and dealings with customers, in connection with the sale of goods, on stationery furnished by Coopers, Inc.

The salesman is obligated to return the sample cases, trunks, and other supplies in good condition and to use his best efforts to protect such supplies from waste, damage, and destruction. Upon demand for the return of such supplies or upon the termination of this agreement, the salesman agrees to return such supplies to the office of Coopers, Inc., in Kenosha, Wisconsin, including all old or used order books, files of correspondence, original letters received by him from customers, and copies of letters sent by the salesman relating to the business of Coopers, Inc. For all supplies not returned, the salesman will pay to Coopers, Inc., the invoice price thereof.

Stealing Customers

Is it possible to make an agreement governing an employee's actions after he leaves your employ? Will such contracts hold water? The courts do not like these contracts, but they will enforce them when they are reasonable, because they afford the only way by which the owner of a business can protect his business from appropriation by former employees.

It is important, however, that such a clause be so worded that it will not deprive an employee of his right of livelihood. For example, if the contract prevents a man from following the only trade he knows throughout the entire United States, it could probably not be enforced. But if consideration for the employee's rights were shown by giving him the right to follow his trade in two states, say Arizona and Utah, then it would have a much better chance to be enforced.

The New York State Court of Appeals upheld the case of *Altschuler-Baterson Company* v. *Markowitz* on a contract which had a clause of this kind. The specific wording of the clause was as follows:

That for a period of 12 months after the termination of his employment, for any cause whatsoever, the party of the second part will not, directly or indirectly as employer, employee, or otherwise, engage in the brokerage business of fire insurance, life, marine, accident, fidelity, employers' liability, burglary, plate-glass insurance, and all other kinds of insurance, and in such other business similar thereto, nor act in aid of the business of any rival or competing person, firm or corporation in the same or similar business within the boroughs of Manhattan, Brooklyn, Bronx, Richmond, and Queens in the city of New York.

Businessmen should take care, however, not to make such agreements unreasonably stringent. Anything that goes beyond proper protection is a restriction upon the right of an employee to make a living. It must be limited both as to time and territory and the limitations in both cases must be reasonable.

Should a contract get into court, it will have a much better chance of being enforced if it seems to be an instrument in the employee's interest. The natural sympathy of the court and the jury is with the employee. This point is not generally appreciated, and contracts which are preponderantly in the interests of the house are frequently nullified in court as being "unduly stringent."

In the case of salesmen's contracts the following points should be covered for the protection of the employee: (1) Agreement by company not to put another man in territory, (2) arrangement of split-commission sales, (3) notice from company regarding termination of contract, (4) payment of commissions in event of salesman's death, (5) cooperation and equipment furnished by house, (6) agreement not to cut down territory.

Termination Agreements

An examination of court records discloses that a very large percentage of cases filed against employers by employees who have been dismissed are the result of a misunderstanding as to the termination of employment. Several companies have reported that clauses to cover the matter of a salesman's leaving the employ of the company are the most important of all clauses that go to make up an employment agreement. In fact, some of them consider this matter sufficiently important to make it the basis of their entire agreement with their salesmen. Hotel expenses in the headquarters town and the payment of any balance due in case of the salesman's death may be the only other matters covered by such an agreement.

Common practice in all employment contracts which are in the nature of "a running agreement" is to provide for cancellation by either party giving advance notice in writing. The method of cancellation is important, because it is a point of attack often used by lawyers in breaking down employment contracts. The following points should be incorporated in the termination clause:

1. Thirty days' notice shall begin when the letter or telegram is placed in the hands of the post office or telegraph company.

2. Notice waived if in the sole judgment of the company employee has been guilty of a breach of trust, neglect of the company's interests, or by acts detrimental to the company's interest.

3. Methods of final settlement, in the case of commission salesmen or profit-sharing employees.

In the event the procedure for termination is not specifically covered in the contract, the court will hold, as it has in test cases, that cancellation does not become effective until the *receipt* of the letter of notification. In the famous decision of the Supreme Court of Iowa, *Oldfield* v. *Chevrolet Motor Company of Nebraska,* 199 N. W. 161, the contract did not state the period it would remain in force but contained the wording: "Either party may cancel this contract by five days' written notice to the other."

The company wrote to the salesman stating: "We are canceling your selling agreement with this company. This is in accordance with Clause No. 8 in your contract, and the cancellation becomes effective *within* five days from the date of this letter." The court held that the method used by the company to effect cancellation was not in accordance with the termination clause of the contract and awarded damages to the plaintiff. In this particular case great importance was attached to the use of the word "within," which was held to be contrary to the spirit of the agreement.

Termination of Commission Contracts

There are probably more lawsuits over unpaid commissions after expiration of a contract than any other one thing. Unless this is covered fully, a large area for misunderstanding between the salesman and company is left open. A striking instance of this sort arose in a controversy between the Knox Hat Company of New York City and a sales agent for that company. The commissions were 10 percent on all sales up to $150,000 and 2 percent on sales in excess of that amount. The contract provided a definite date for termination. Some months before that time the contract was ended "by the consent and agreement of both parties." At that time about $6,000 of commissions had been earned but were not payable until later.

These the company refused to pay, insisting that the recision of the contract absolved them from liability since no stipulation for payment of these items had been made when the contract had been terminated. In this they were sustained by the court.

"When the performance of a contract consists in doing on one side and in giving on the other, the doing must take place before the giving. In all contracts for services, therefore, the presumption is that the performance of the service is a condition precedent to the payment for it."

The obligations, both of the salesman and the employer, had ended with the cancellation of the contract. The unpaid commissions, then, became a mere gratuity, for which the salesman was rendering no services to the company and which the former employer was under no obligation to pay.

In every salesman's commission contract these three essentials must be outlined in unmistakable detailed terms and with scrupulous care: The circumstances that determine when the commissions are earned—whether on receipt of the order by the salesman, on its acceptance by the employer, on the shipment of the goods, or on whatever incident that may be agreed upon; the event on which commissions are payable, and a simple, clear setting forth of the disposition of unpaid commissions on the termination of employment.

Providing Against Contradictory State Laws

Many companies using employment contracts in national operations, knowing the conflicting state laws which exist governing many phases of employee relations, insert in their contracts a clause to the effect that in case of dispute the laws of the state in which the company is incorporated apply.

Exclusive Agency Agreements

While the passage of the Clayton Act made illegal many of the agreements that had been used in establishing exclusive agencies, it is still possible to make exclusive contracts with dealers or agents that are not in violation of the provisions of the statute. If your contract does not "substantially lessen competition or tend to create a monopoly" in your line, it violates no provision of the Clayton Act.

It has been held by the Supreme Court (*Standard Fashion Company* v. *Magrane-Houston Company,* 42 Sup. Ct. 360) that any contract which limits the dealer to a single line is illegal, provided the dealer still maintains his status as an independent merchant. In the case cited above the dealer had entered into an agreement whereby he was to become the agent of the Standard Fashion Company for the sale of dress patterns. As a part of the agreement, the dealer was obliged to take and pay for a certain number of patterns and maintain a certain stock on hand at all times. In the event that any of these patterns were not sold, they could be returned to the original seller and an allowance, less than the original price, was to be credited to the dealer. The dealer further agreed that he would not sell or permit to be sold in his store any other patterns of any competitor while this agreement was in force.

The court held that this was not a joint venture, but that when the dealer bought and paid for the patterns they belonged to him. Any agreement that put any limitation on his freedom as an independent merchant was a direct violation of the act and therefore illegal.

For an exclusive agency agreement to be legal, therefore, it must either make the dealer or representative an agent in fact, or it must be binding only on the manufacturer.

It is possible, however, to appoint a dealer an exclusive agent and still be within legal bounds. Where this is done, the contract must be so drawn as to leave the principal the actual owner of the goods and to limit the action of the dealer to that authorized in his agency agreement. It is possible to provide in such a contract that the agent, in return for the agency, may be required to carry a given stock or to meet any other requirement. The point is that the dealer must, under the contract, lose his status as a general dealer, and become, in fact, an agent. In such an agreement it is possible for the principal to decide whether he wants his agent to sell more than one line, just as he could decide in the case of salesmen.

Many firms, however, find that an agency agreement is just as effective when their contracts limit them alone as it was when it used to apply to both parties. Such agreements provide that the manufacturer will grant to a dealer the exclusive right to sell his products in a given area, set up the conditions under which this right is granted, and leave the merchant absolutely free to sell any other or as many other competitive lines as he desires. If the agreement is carefully drawn as to terms, amount of stock to be carried, and rights to be enjoyed, the ultimate effect of such an agreement is about the same as if the dealer had agreed not to offer a competitor's stock. But he is, in fact, not under any obligations to refrain from doing so, and so long as he remains in that status there is no violation of the Clayton Act.

Sales on Contracts

In many lines of business, such as office appliances, machinery, equipment, musical instruments, and so forth, the ultimate sale to the user is based on a contract, partial payment, or otherwise. In such cases the salesman or distributor not only sells the goods, but establishes legal relationships between company and its customers. For the protection of the company's rights it is necessary that the acts of its representatives in this respect be rigidly controlled, and in the case of disputes it must be able to show exactly how far the authority of its representatives extended.

The same considerations apply where valuable patent rights are involved. Patent rights are sometimes adversely affected by acts of salesmen or agents, and it is essential to be able to show exactly what authority is delegated, and what is not.

Following is a sales-representative contract used by American Photocopy Equipment Company. Other sales contracts will be found in the Ready-Reference Section.

APECO SALES-REPRESENTATIVE AGREEMENT

In consideration of my employment or continued employment by American Photocopy Equipment Company (Apeco) and of the salary, commission, and other benefits received or to be received by me in connection with such employment, it is agreed as follows:

1. During my employment I shall devote my best efforts and full time to the performance of such duties as are assigned to me as sales representative and shall comply with all policies and instructions promulgated by Apeco.

2. I agree to such salary, commission, bonus rates, and methods of payment as may be established by Apeco from time to time.

3. Although commissions may be paid to me upon shipment of the merchandise, commissions will not be considered as earned until such time as the merchandise has been shipped, installed and customers' invoices have been paid in full. I shall not be entitled to commissions or bonuses on merchandise returned or refused by a customer and acknowledge that the decision as to accepting any such return or refusal shall be in the sole discretion of Apeco. Further, I shall not hold Apeco liable in any way for failure to meet a delivery date or for defects in merchandise or for any other factor which may create any such return, refusal, or any delinquent account. Any commissions or bonuses which have been paid upon shipment of merchandise shall be charged back against my account in the event of a subsequent return or refusal to accept delivery by the customer or in the event of a customer's delinquency in payment.

4. Upon termination of my employment, I shall immediately return to Apeco all property of Apeco in as good condition as when received by me (normal wear and tear excepted) including records, manuals, promotion materials, equipment, and supplies. For my failure to do so, I shall be liable to Apeco for the following amounts:

Equipment and supplies—Apeco list price

Sales manuals, brochures and promotional materials—$50.00

Customer lists and records pertaining to customer accounts—the monetary value thereof to Apeco.

I authorize Apeco to charge any such amounts of liability against my account.

5. Upon termination of my employment, my final compensation payments shall be made as follows:

a) My final salary payment, prorated to the date of termination, shall be paid on the next regular pay day following receipt of notification of such termination by the Payroll Department.

b) My final commission payment shall not be made to me until a reasonable period of time not in excess of 120 days following termination, to make necessary adjustments for returns, cancellations, allowances, delinquent accounts, and any other similar adjustment item. Any merchandise not fully paid for at the end of said 120-day period shall be considered a delinquent account to the extent of the unpaid amount. In the case of orders obtained by me prior to termination but shipped and fully paid for within said 120 days after termination, I shall receive full commission on any such orders for supplies and one-half ($\frac{1}{2}$) commission on any such order for equipment (the other one-half commission to be payable to my successor who shall have the responsibility for installation, instruction, and servicing).

c) No quarterly bonus payments, Director's Club awards, or payments, or sales-promotion contest awards or payments, shall be made subsequent to the date of termination. I understand and agree that I must be employed by Apeco on the payment date of any quarterly bonuses, special payments and awards in order to be eligible to receive such payments and awards.

6. While employed by Apeco I will acquire a certain amount of confidential information regarding Apeco's business, including but not limited to the following: The names and addresses and purchasing history of Apeco's customers; the name and other pertinent data concerning the persons responsible for purchasing for such customers; the particular needs and applications of such customers for Apeco products and other office copying products and business equipment; information relating to Apeco products, whether presently marketed or in the process of development; research developments, marketing practices, and other business data. This confidential information is a valuable property of Apeco and has been developed over a period of years at great expense to Apeco. Accordingly, I agree that I will not at any time either during or after my employment with Apeco disclose any such confidential information to any third party, or to make any use whatever of such confidential information in any manner detrimental to Apeco, particularly the use of such confidential information in connection with any business activities in competition with Apeco.

7. For a period of one year following the termination of my employment with Apeco, I shall not, directly or indirectly, within any sales territory or within a 25-mile radius of any such territory in which I may have worked for Apeco at any time during the 18-month period prior to termination of my employment with Apeco, accept employment, consult with, or become associated or affiliated with any person, sole proprietorship, partnership or corporation, in any capacity involving activities competitive to Apeco in the photocopy, laminating, or punch-and-bind product industries, or otherwise engage in such competitive activities on my own account.

Without limiting the generality of the foregoing, it is specifically agreed that during such one year period I shall not call on, contact, or communicate with, for any purpose whatsoever, any customers or former customers of Apeco.

8. I agree and acknowledge that the above confidential information non-disclosure and noncompeting covenants are reasonable in that they give Apeco the protection to which it is entitled and yet do not impair my ability to earn a livelihood. Further, since a violation by me of these covenants would result in immediate and irreparable damage to Apeco, I hereby expressly consent to and waive any objections to Apeco's obtaining immediate injunctive relief in a court of law in the event of any such violation, such injunctive relief to be in addition to any rights to damages and any other rights available to Apeco under the law.

9. I understand that I shall have no authority to enter into any contract or agreement on behalf of Apeco or to make collections of accounts for Apeco except where I am given specific written authorization by an officer of Apeco.

10. I agree to abide and be bound by the bylaws and rules and regulations of the Apeco Director's Club as they now exist and as they may be amended from time to time in the future.

11. In the event that any provision of this agreement should be deemed to be unenforceable or void, such invalidity of unenforceability shall not affect the validity or enforceability of any other provision hereof.

12. It is agreed that the provisions of this agreement contain the entire agreement between the parties and cannot be changed, modified, or added to except by a written agreement signed by me and by an officer of Apeco.

Approved and Accepted:

AMERICAN PHOTOCOPY EQUIPMENT COMPANY

By: ....

Dated: ....

....

Sales Representative

Dated: ....

PART 8

OPERATING
THE
SALES
FORCE

TRAINING THE SALESMAN

I N the days made famous by Willie Lohman (central character in
Arthur Miller's play, *The Death of a Salesman*), the training of
a salesman was slow and methodical. Typically, the new man worked
in the plant, then the warehouse, next the office, and finally accompanied an older salesman on his rounds. Perhaps there would
be further orientation while he worked various territories when the
regular men were vacationing. By the time the "new man" was
ready to be assigned his own territory, the sales manager knew
what kind of a man he was and what he could do.

Today's salesmen must be recruited more carefully, trained more
quickly, and sped on their way as salesmen. Whether that training
is better or worse than Willie Lohman and his contemporaries received depends on the company and its sales manager, who must be
responsible for the sales-training program.

The Three Phases of Training

The training of new salesmen, as distinct from "refresher
courses" for experienced men and continuous training activities
such as sales meetings, educational contests, etc., has three phases:
(1) Group-training the new man at the outset of his employment,
similar to the "vestibule" training of production employees (2) field-
coaching new men, and (3) classroom training.

In these three broad divisions of sales training there are four
steps essential to effective training: (1) Tell them; (2) show them;
(3) let them do it; (4) check to be sure they are doing it.

What are the gains to be expected from a sales-training program?
Does formalized sales training really pay off?

We know that the experience of hundreds of successful companies proves that sales-training programs can pay off in many
ways. New business and more sales can be obtained from new customers; larger territories can be covered with less waste of time

and effort; company policies and procedures will be better known and understood; the time and cost of supervisory and administrative efforts can be reduced; costs of turnover can be lowered; goodwill can be increased and returns reduced through reduction, if not total elimination, of ill-advised sales and wrong recommendations.

But these desired accomplishments require careful advance planning and experienced guidance.

The amount of training to be given depends on too many variable factors for generalization: On the product or service to be sold, on its degree of simplicity or complexity, on the market and type of buyers, on the education and previous experience of the salesmen-trainees, and on the extent of information needed to be passed along to salesmen on company policies and procedures. All these factors must be qualified in advance of launching the program.

A Sales-Training Checklist

Sales executives in charge of planning sales training might be guided by considering the following points, in terms of company operations, needs, and special conditions:

1. To what extent do new salesmen need to be indoctrinated and trained before being sent out to sell?

2. How much training is needed and justified for established salesmen whose selling efforts are not up to a reasonable par?

3. How much, and what kind of training, is needed for established men at such times as the following:

   a. When new program or products are being introduced;
   b. When market conditions are changing;
   c. When marketing methods or policies are being changed;
   d. When changes are being made in distribution or pricing policies;
   e. When the status or the organizational position of established men is to be changed.

Whether you are dealing with a single trainee or a group, the sales manager or his delegated substitute must have a planned schedule so that things will start to happen as soon as the trainee walks in—and continue in an orderly fashion. Unfortunately, some managers look upon the indoctrination of a recruit as a necessary but irritating interruption of their usual (and more or less comfortable) routine. They forget that whenever a man reports for duty he already represents a substantial investment by his company in recruiting, screening, investigating—and finally—employment, whether this is done by a central staff office or by the manager himself. An orderly, planned, and organized program to get the new man into

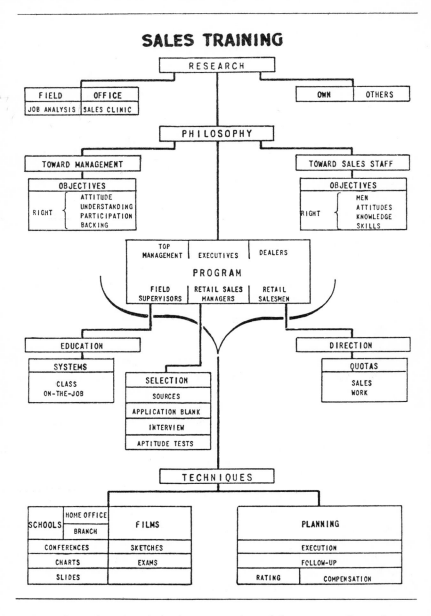

SALES TRAINING

One of the first steps in setting up a sales-training program is to chart the job to be done. The chart shown here is used by one of the large automobile manufacturing companies for this purpose.

productivity with a minimum investment of time and further dollars is one of the job responsibilities of any sales manager.

These same questions should be asked with regard to training order clerks, sales supervisors, and department heads in the sales department, who are too often overlooked in the sales-training program. It is sometimes as important, for example, that the order clerk be aware of sales policies as that the salesman keep abreast of them, since in many cases the men in the home office can contribute to the overall efficiency of the selling operation to a much greater extent than they do when merely blindly following routine.

Why Special Training Is a Necessity

True, a salesman's merely being on the job and going through the process of calling on people, presenting his products or service for purchase and the acceptance of orders, will result in his receiving some training. But how good the training will be, what he learns or does not learn, what work habits and attitudes he does or does not acquire—these are something else. If he is wide awake and above average in observance, he may acquire many favorable fine skills from watching the reactions of his customers. On the other hand, he may learn to be biased in favor of his customers.

Through conversations with other salesmen around motel swimming pools, he may learn what the outstanding salesmen do, or he may learn the wrong things. Such "training" is a gamble with the odds against the company. Special training is the only answer.

To be sure, training costs money. For the company to train its salesmen is expensive; so, too, is it expensive to the company for its salesmen to be *mistrained* by customers or other salesmen. If the company does the training, it can at least appraise and budget all costs. If others do the training, it is anyone's guess how much the cost will be in lost orders, in the poor handling of complaints and requests for undue credits, in the expense of poor routing or indifferent effort, in the headaches of abnormal managerial supervision, in the hiring and eventual rehiring of replacements when the unsuccessful salesmen leave.

If the cost is to be incurred anyway, what will it probably be and how much can a company afford to spend on training? It is difficult to generalize.

For a small company, the training would probably have to be done by the sales manager and the training course would be quite informal.

With a medium-sized company, the sales-training course might be prepared by staff personnel and some class work be given, supplemented by on-the-job direction.

With a large company, there might be a fully staffed training department, well equipped for research and with training tools.

However, the cost per trainee might be about the same in all three types of company, when all expenses, direct and otherwise, are considered.

Who should be trained? Obviously, new salesmen should be trained, and established salesmen should be retrained when the luster goes out of their performance. Sales-office personnel should be trained in *their* work, to assure effective operations and to give them an awareness of how they mesh in with other departments and activities.

Then the trainers themselves should be trained, to be sure they train the way the company wishes them to train.

What Should Training Cover?

The training process is aimed at creating more sales volume through better sales presentations and the better closing of orders. It is also aimed at improving the atmosphere in which the salesman works. It is aimed at improving his knowledge about the history and objectives of the company, its products, its services, its policies, its procedures, and formalities.

It is aimed at contributing to his personal development and advancement in the company, to keeping him interested in staying with the company.

The following suggestions will help you successfully train a new man:

1. *Have a Detailed Plan and Follow It.* Insist that assistants do likewise.

2. *Work at Full Capacity.* Start early and finish late. Remember, nothing that the trainee hears or reads later will affect him as much as what he sees right now. So demonstrate the hard work necessary for success.

3. *Make Company Policies Clear.* No matter what items concerning policy come up, be sure they are fully understood. Explain each one by specific example whenever possible. Where this is not possible, point out how the policy makes sense and assure him that if it were not important to the success of the business it would not exist as a policy.

4. *Put Your Best Foot Forward.* Remember that the trainee is going to want to know what kind of people he is working for. It will not take him long to get to know you. As a new man he is likely to respect your opinions.

5. *Emphasize the Need for Teamwork and Cooperation.* Do this by stressing the importance of each man in your organization. Emphasize the importance of clear, intelligent, factual, and on-time reporting.

6. *Stimulate His Enthusiasm.* Discuss success stories in connection with every phase of the work. Give him some of the romance and history of the organization—its stature in the industry—its growth—and its apparent future.

7. *Earn His Respect.* Conduct yourself at all times as a businessman and a gentleman. Show a good front in all things—your appearance as well as the appearance and condition of your office, warehouse, and equipment. Bear in mind that, even if he does not indicate it, any trainee is studying you very carefully.

8. *Give Him Field Experience* as early as possible, in your presence. Let him carry the ball. Encourage him to think for himself. Correct any errors later, away from the customer.

9. *Make Him Understand That Future Development is Up to Him.* Future training and development cannot be handed to any man on a silver platter. He must do something about them himself.

Selection of Trainers

The success of your orientation program depends on the care used in the selection of the people who will assist you in getting your man off to a sound start. The trainee is quite likely to pattern his own future work habits after those of the people who trained him. If they are prompt in keeping appointments, the trainee will probably be prompt. If they go about their work in a well-planned, organized, and businesslike manner, the trainee will accept these things as standards by which to govern his own future activities. Sound selection of instructors, of course, depends on the objectives desired.

Obviously, in view of the wide diversity of products, company policies, industry conditions, and so forth, it would be folly to try to detail a list of objectives which would apply to all cases. In setting up this program and selecting the people who are to help him implement it, the sales manager will want to keep in mind that the function at this point is threefold:

- To impart knowledge of product, company, methods, procedures, etc.
- To impart and develop skills in performance.
- To inspire enthusiasm for and confidence in the company, product, and industry, as well as self-confidence in the trainee himself.

Before discussing what should go into such a program, however, let's discuss the kind of person who should handle this kind of assignment.

The Trainer's Qualifications

Whether he be a full-time trainer or a man who works with new personnel along with his other duties, there are certain qualifications which must be fully considered if such an appointment is to be successful.

The "natural born" salesman, of whom there are probably a few, rarely makes a good trainer. He intuitively does the right thing at the right time to the right people to get the order, but he seldom knows why he does these things and, since he does not know "why," he is seldom capable of passing on either the "why" or the "how" to someone else. Just as the strong "personal producer" so often fails as a sales manager, he will usually fail to measure up as a successful trainer of new men.

Before a man is appointed to training responsibilities, there are at least three factors which need to be pretty thoroughly investigated. With respect to his experience and background with the company, such questions as these need to be resolved:

Is he loyal to his associates, company, and customers, or is he the type who thinks snide remarks are humorous, and criticizes and ridicules company policy to show his superiority?

Does his experience have breadth and depth in respect to the geography of the territory and acquaintance with all types of customers and industries served, as well as your full line and the application of each line to the customer's needs?

Assuming that he has know-how, to what degree can he pass it along to others so that they, too, can put it to work?

Does he discuss all facets of the work well and effectively, or does he concentrate on those phases which he personally enjoys—like a salesman high-spotting his territory, spending most of his time and effort on the accounts he personally likes, without regard to their buying potential?

The Trainer's Personality

Some feel that all successful salesmen like people and want to be helpful—but experience has proved that too many salesmen are interested only in themselves.

The successful trainer must have a sincere desire to help others and must gain great personal satisfaction from helping others to learn and develop. Many of us can remember certain personalities among the professional teachers under whom we studied who obviously did not possess this attribute. These people, though making their living as teachers, were not truly successful and would not last long as trainers of adults.

Some attributes to be looked for in trainers are:

High Personal Integrity—You are entrusting this man with your trainee's career. You can't afford to settle for less.

Thorough Knowledge of Company Policies and Philosophies—and ability to explain them lucidly and "sell" them loyally.

Good Grooming—never flashy, but dressed to fit the situation, and always in good taste.

Clear and Objective Thinker—who gets to the point and does not allow himself to be lured into meaningless bypaths of time-consuming and unrelated discussions.

Good Vocabulary and Diction—he must do 80 percent of his work through the use of words, so he must have an adequate vocabulary to make his point, and clear diction so the trainee will not have to strain to understand.

Mental and Physical Alertness are Essential. The trainer is always under scrutiny—and always sets the pace—which means he must be the source of both physical and mental energy all the time he is training.

Teaching Ability—A man may have all other attributes, but without teaching ability he is "dead in the water." Unless he has the ability to impart knowledge, develop skills, and inspire enthusiasm for his subject, he is utterly useless as a trainer.

Where do we find such paragons? We don't! Perfect people don't exist. No man possesses all the desirable attributes to the fullest degree, but the real trainer prospect will have most of them in some degree, and be objective enough to try to improve himself in areas where improvement is needed when called to his attention.

A wise procedure for the first-line sales manager who is selecting people to help him break in new men—and is perhaps checking on his own attributes—is to develop a checklist, or set of standards, against which he can score each of his prospective trainers, as shown following:

	Below Average	Average	Above Average
Personal Integrity	....	....	....
Knowledge of Company Policy	....	....	....
Knowledge of Product	....	....	....
Personality	....	....	....
Thinking Ability	....	....	....
Teaching Ability	....	....	....

After applying this "yardstick" to his force, the sales manager at least knows where he stands with respect to trainer talent, how much he can delegate, and how much he must do himself. A side benefit is that the manager will discover weak spots in the regular force which need his action since, ideally, all salesmen should be available to do a good job of breaking in a new man.

Should Old Salesmen Train the New?

The president of one very successful company has this to say on the subject:

As a general rule, I do not believe such men should be assigned to a salesman for training or direction. This, I know, is a long-established practice, but my experience has been that it does not work out satisfactorily.

It is difficult for a person to be an aggressive salesman, thinking and planning his day-to-day actions, and at the same time think in terms of what someone else is to do. Selling requires direct-action thinking for oneself; training requires thinking in terms of action once removed.

If a situation arises where the senior salesman must choose between thinking and acting for himself, or thinking and acting for the junior, he will naturally favor himself. This happens so often that junior salesmen are generally neglected, as I have been repeatedly told by junior salesmen.

Salesmen are notably individualistic, somewhat temperamental, inclined to be critical of management, and have difficulty even managing themselves. Without practice and training, they can only with difficulty successfully manage others.

Unless a salesman is trained in the training he is supposed to give the junior, the company takes considerable risk in requiring him to do so. The branch manager or field sales supervisor should be in the best position to know the needs of the junior man and what he wants him to learn, and to evaluate his training. The trainee should therefore report to this manager.

Trainees and juniors can be used to assist senior salesmen with some of their routine duties at peak times, but *only* at peak times. Senior salesmen gain valuable "sensing" of their territories, customer goodwill, and, if they sell through distributors, the goodwill of the distributor's salesmen, if they handle their own routine work themselves. It is difficult for a salesman to get an intimate, gossipy knowledge of his territory if someone else does this work for him.

It is better to have eight territories, one a training one, than to have seven territories, with one covered by a senior working with a junior salesman.

Field First or Home Office First?

Many sales executives believe men should have their first indoctrination in the field, reading company literature, examining warehouse stocks, handling routine office work, and holding discussions with the local manager, possibly with a few days of observing the work of an established salesman. Then they should be sent to the home office for their training in products and uses, and in company policies and procedures. These executives feel that the men will learn more after their short field experience because they will know what to look for and have some appreciation of how their newly learned information is to be used.

Other executives believe in bringing men to the home office immediately, then sending them to the field for further training. They feel this is the most economical way, and that when the initial training is done in the field, the men just flounder around, not knowing what to do or why they are doing it, and the local manager is too busy to direct them properly.

There is merit to both schools of thought. However, the success of either program depends on how well it has been researched, planned, executed, and followed through.

Evaluation of Training

The results of the training effort should be evaluated in order that mistakes can be corrected in future courses and men who failed to learn can be replaced or properly trained. As distasteful as formal examinations are, it is hard to beat them. There can be a series of informal quizzes; men can be asked to demonstrate sales situations which will show what they have learned, their work can be critically appraised in the field, they can answer "situation" questionnaires.

It is an unescapable responsibility of sales executives to test and find out what their salesmen know and believe, and take remedial action when necessary. To do it subtly is better than to do it crudely; not to do it at all is worse than doing it poorly.

An insight into how one major company evaluates sales training is provided by Drayton Heard, Jr., manager, marketing administration, Westinghouse Electric Corporation. He states:

We feel we must increase the efficiency of the salesman (i.e., his ability to handle more profitable volume) at the same time realizing that his cost to us is going to increase. The demand for our products and services will continue to increase and this will be matched by growth in our physical capacity. However, we do not anticipate that this demand will be matched with a proportionate increase in salesmen. In fact, we anticipate that we would have a great deal of difficulty obtaining and training them if we attempted to do so. Our program to make salesmen more productive consists of these things:

1. "Position" their managers as a manager and not as a super salesman. This we are doing through a continuing series of nine-day courses to increase their understanding of their responsibilities and functions in the areas of planning, pricing, and directing the sales forces as well as inspiring them to improve their own self-development.

2. A six-day marketing course for salesmen who have demonstrated high performance and have exhibited potential for growth.

The two courses focus on sales management as the keystone of our approach to more effective use of salesmen. However, to get at the salesman himself we have two additional steps:

3. Free the salesman from routine paper work, order handling, and followup. Here we are doing such things as "wired order-entry procedures," computer-order followup programs and tape-player communications programs for internal correspondence and product training.

4. Improve the salesman's selling techniques. Much of our business is obtained in large "hunks" or annual commitments. The loss of a single order can be the loss of a single customer's business for the year.

An Industrial View

In an interview with *Industrial Distributor News,* David E. Anderson, general sales manager of the power tool division, Rockwell Manufacturing Company, described his company's training program as follows:

We feel sales training makes distributors' salesmen experts on the products they sell and gives them a distinct edge over competitors.

Rockwell conducts 15 to 18 formal sales-training schools during the year at various points around the country. Several schools are held at our plant locations, which not only give our distributors a chance to learn about our product lines, but to see how we manufacture tools, as well.

Our machine tools and stationary industrial woodworking and metalworking tools are produced at Bellefontaine, Ohio, and Tupelo, Miss. We hold several schools each year at these locations, especially Bellefontaine, where we have a large, well-equipped classroom. School sessions on these products also are conducted at Porterville, Calif.

Sessions at all of these locations are four or five days in length, are attended by 15 to 20 industrial distributor salesmen and managers, and offer complete courses of instruction in Rockwell products.

In my talks with distributors, I believe the greatest good they receive from our sales-training program is sales ideas. To a manufacturer, sales to the ultimate customer is the most important phase in the sales cycle, so we concentrate on presenting ideas which the distributor can use to increase his sales.

Every Man a Beginner

Whatever your final decision as to program, treat every man as a raw, green, inexperienced recruit—no matter how many years he may have worked for competition. The man hired away from competition is a double hazard. Often, you were able to hire him because, for some reason, he just was not "getting along" on the other side of the fence. Then, you'll hear from some such men, "Over at ABC we did it this way." Such people need to be told at the start that they work your way. It is up to you to substitute in their work plan your methods for those of previous employers.

The genuinely new man, perhaps fresh out of school, is an entirely different challenge. How you and your subordinates handle him may well influence the degree of success of his whole career. Someone has said, "Treat 'em all nicely—they may be your boss some day." And it has happened.

The IBM Training Program

The data-processing marketing-training program of International Business Machines Corporation has six key objectives:

Product Proficiency: Sufficient knowledge of the product line to perform the expected job.

Communication Skills: The ability to transmit ideas clearly and persuasively, and development of sales awareness.

Identification with IBM: An understanding and appreciation of IBM's basic beliefs, traditions, and fundamental corporate principles.

Business Concepts: Learning the structure of a business organization, and its need for information processing.

Industry Knowledge: Market orientation and applications peculiar to different industries.

Problem Solving: Enhance capabilities of data-processing problem definition, analysis, and solution.

The training program continues for 15 to 18 months. It is a combination of formal classes and practical application of classroom learning in the marketplace. The emphasis is on the personal growth and development of the individual.

While the emphasis is on development, early productivity is desired. The assistant works with customers in computer application and problem solving. His individual training goals are determined according to the type of territory to which he will be assigned upon qualification as a marketing representative.

The IBM training program requires a new representative to spend a short orientation period in the branch office during his first week with IBM. Here he gains an insight into the typical operations of a branch office, meets the branch personnel, and reviews all functions of the branch office. Following that, he attends class at the local district-education center. These classes are devoted primarily to product instruction. Each of these formal classes is followed by practical experience and application in the field, guided by marketing management and senior marketing representatives.

Upon the successful completion of product schools and field training, the individual goes to one of IBM's divisional education centers at Poughkeepsie, New York, or San Jose, California, to study the techniques used in solving customer problems. He is given an insight into the characteristics, functions, and problems of specific industries. This class is followed by experience in the field under the supervision of senior individuals, including, of course, his manager. During this phase of the field training, he concentrates on gaining experience in customer and prospect calls, presentations, and learning all aspects of the marketing representative's total responsibilities to company and customer.

The final phase of the training program is sales school. Here the objectives are to polish communication and sales skills. The marketing assistant makes practice calls on sales instructors who play the role of the customer. The instructor evaluates the call and counsels the student in areas requiring improvement. Calls are audio- and video-taped for review by the student and instructor.

Sales school also provides training in marketing strategy, practices, and policies. Competitive products and strategies are reviewed as well as business ethics and conduct. Upon graduation from sales school, the now "qualified salesman" returns to his branch office and is assigned to his sales territory.

The training program is broad enough to meet special needs. The man and his manager determine what additional training, or experience is necessary to prepare the individual for his future selling responsibilities.

In IBM, "There is no saturation point in education." Once a man becomes a qualified marketing representative, he continues to receive formal education in products, applications, industry, marketing techniques, and most importantly, personal development.

Armstrong's Merchandising Program

While the need for schooling is greater in the merchandising field than it is in selling specialties, there are relatively few sales organizations that do a thorough sales training job. Many of them tend to treat the training lightly so far as classroom studies are concerned, and are inclined to let the salesmen learn merchandising on the job through observation and personal experience.

Armstrong Cork Company, on the other hand, has found that selling costs can be held down and merchandising made more effective by bringing new salesmen to the general offices for group training. This company, based in Lancaster, Pa., makes resilient flooring and many other products for home and industry. In the case of its flooring products, Armstrong realizes that it cannot appreciably increase sales unless its retailers also increase their sales; so the company carries out an intensive training program to teach its floor-division salesmen how to help flooring retailers and contractors move the goods they buy from Armstrong.

New floor-division salesmen first join other new college-graduate employees for a company-wide orientation program, which lasts about a week. Then the sales trainees begin their specialized four- or five-month training program. They first learn about the flooring products manufactured by Armstrong—how to merchandise them, how to install them, how to sell them. Next they try their hand at practice selling, under the eye of an instructor at Lancaster; videotape "instant replays" help each man evaluate his own skills as they develop. At this stage, the trainees are split up temporarily. Each goes to a major city for about a week, during which he tries his hand at actual selling. The trainees then rejoin in Lancaster for a review of what they have learned during this field experience. This procedure is repeated as the trainee learns about other product categories. And now comes concentrated study of the markets they will be serving—not only retail markets, but also those represented by home builders, architects, interior designers, building managers, and flooring contractors.

One experienced marketing specialist is specifically assigned to coordinate all training activities of the new salesmen. During their program, he makes use of a training library of reference books, technical literature, and visual aids, including some 35 films; visits by guest lecturers who are experts in their fields; conferences with top Armstrong marketing officials, and programmed learning techniques which may be presented.

While at Lancaster, married trainees live with their wives in air-conditioned furnished apartments; single men live in the Armstrong Manor, a stately old homestead recently modernized to accommodate all of Armstrong's unmarried trainees. The company, which provides housing at apartment or manor for a modest rental, feels that the plan helps provide a team spirit among its sales trainees.

Emphasis in the Armstrong program is on merchandising. When the formalized training period is completed, each new salesman is assigned to fill an opening that exists in one of the company's sales districts. He is given immediate responsibility for his own sales territory. In short, he is considered ready to go to work without further on-the-job training. And opportunities for greater responsibility and personal advancement are rapidly provided him as he gains experience and begins making a direct contribution to the company's marketing effort.

Better Hardware Merchandising

Virginia-Carolina Hardware Co., Richmond, Virginia, decided to conduct a program of successive training sessions for its salesmen. Meetings were held every other Saturday over a several-month period. Bob Harrison, vice-president, conducted the meetings, using a series of charts produced by the National Wholesale Hardware Association. Objective was to increase the selling effectiveness of the salesmen so that they could in turn improve the merchandising effectiveness of retailer customers.

As reported in *Hardware Retailer*, nobody preaches at these sales meetings. But everybody participates. Each salesman has to do some homework since the last meeting—perhaps talking to customers about an idea—and then reports on his success.

When one salesman talks, his point is treated to criticism from his fellow salesmen. He can't fake with them; he can't fool them. They don't ignore him either. They listen, evaluate, and learn from his experiences.

Since everyone has multiple opportunities to participate in each of these meetings, one of the techniques is to pose a question, then have everyone write down answers to the problem. Any one of them is liable to be called upon for his thinking on the subject . . . so they all think and write.

Not everybody agrees with everyone else and there is ample opportunity for discussion. In the process, everyone learns. The most striking observation of these men, after putting into practice what they had learned, was that dealers were willing to do more than the salesmen gave them credit for. For instance:

1. Dealers are more interested in inventory control than anything else.

2. NRHA's *Turnover Handbook,* introduced four years ago, is today the dealer's plan for profit.

3. Dealers are so impressed with the enthusiasm and new approach of the men that they want to obtain copies of some of the material so they too can share in this new enthusiasm for the hardware business.

4. Salesmen become conscious of improving their performance. For example, in checking productivity of all salesmen, Virginia-Carolina reports overall sales volume up more than 10 percent over the same period a year ago.

5. Individually, salesmen find new ways to measure their performance.

Sales-Management Training by Goodyear

A major factor in Goodyear's success in the marketplace is the company's emphasis on training. Goodyear salesmen begin with the benefit of an extensive training program. After that, training continues throughout their careers.

There are three separate domestic-sales-management training programs. They are designed to prepare graduates to sell tires and related products, chemicals, or industrial rubber goods. Goodyear International Corporation also offers a comprehensive 60-week-long sales-training program.

Industrial Product Sales: Engineering graduates or men who combined technical courses with business administration majors are eligible for training in industrial-products sales. This work-study program lasts approximately 18 months.

It begins with a three-month factory orientation which is combined with classwork in the training center school. Initial on-the-job training assignments are concentrated in production and development departments of industrial-rubber-goods plants in Akron.

After factory orientation, industrial products sales trainees spend 12 to 15 months on the job, in product-sales departments.

Chemical Products Sales: Men with degrees in chemical engineering or chemistry are eligible for the chemical-products sales-training program. It varies in length from 9 to 12 months and is divided into three sections.

Initially, trainees spend approximately 10 weeks on the job in production departments. They learn Banbury, milling, treadmaking and calendering, curing, and final-inspection operations. They study belt construction and films, flooring, and foam-production techniques.

After production orientation, trainees spend 18 weeks in staff departments.

During production and staff training, candidates attend classes in the training center school. Here they study the corporate structure, rubber manufacturing, personal economics, report writing, speech, finance, cost management, conference leadership, and problems in business organization.

Domestic Tire Sales: The domestic-tire-sales training program prepares college graduates for careers in the renewal tire sales division. Training includes field and Akron plant and staff department assignments, plus related classroom work in the training center school.

Candidates begin their training by spending two months on the job at a company-owned store. Here they are exposed to basic selling practices at the retail level. They return to Akron for six weeks of factory orientation.

Field assignments follow. They include two months' training as a TBA (tires, batteries, accessories) merchandiser and two months as a credit-sales-manager trainee in a company retail store.

Completion of any of the basic sales management training programs prepares the college graduate for his first productive assignment in the Goodyear field-sales organization. From this point on, promotions to positions of increasing responsibilities are based on performance. How fast and how far the career salesman can go with the company are questions that each individual must answer for himself.

Cooperative Schools

In the retail and service field it is not practical for small operators to put on group-training plans of their own. The cost would be prohibitive. However, it is possible for dealers to get together in a city or region and conduct a general training course under the sponsorship of a trade association, a chamber of commerce, or a sales executives' association.

A successful experiment along this line was conducted in Birmingham, Alabama, by the Electrical Appliance Dealers Association. A short training course was prepared by a committee, and 148 salesmen enrolled; 104 passed the grading tests; 72 of these went immediately to jobs with members of the association. The cost of the course was financed by the dealers who contributed $15 each. A one-column advertisement was run for seven consecutive days in each of the three Birmingham papers. The advertisements ran in the want-ad columns of the papers.

An Industry Program

The food industry contributed more than $1 million to establish the Academy of Food Marketing at St. Joseph's College, in Philadelphia, to educate "young men of moral purpose who may be capable of further developing the American food industry." Most of the members of the first graduating class obtained positions with food manufacturers, processors, or distributors at salaries ranging from $6,200 to $7,800. Everyone received two or more offers, reported associate director Samuel Blaskey, and several companies, including General Foods, California Packing Corporation, and Food Fair hired more than one graduate.

The Academy's 165 students make up about 10 percent of the total student body of St. Joseph's. So far, 30 students have been accepted for admission to the academy next fall, but many applicants cannot meet the college's standards. Those who qualify spend their first two years taking a basic liberal-arts course. As upperclassmen and marketing majors, however, they specialize in food-management problems. Courses are taught by a faculty of seven specialists and include physical-distribution management, market research, food science and nutrition, purchasing, processing and packaging, the economics of pricing, world hunger, and world food marketing. During the college year, students tour nearby food industry facilities of Campbell Soup Co., Boscul Coffee and Tea, Inc. and Abbotts Dairies, Inc.

Retraining Salesman

Retraining has been found most valuable to "refresh" salesmen who need to be brought up-to-date on new techniques and also as a device to correct ineffective working habits and improve the selling strategy of older salesmen.

In some cases, the salesmen to be retrained are brought together at some central point for a two-week conference. These are usually men with five or more years of experience. Such a conference is usually presented as a leaders' clinic, executive seminar, or sales management conference rather than as a training program, to get away from the going-to-school idea. One firm, for example, calls the retraining program, a "business management conference." But it is a continuing program, and as fast as one group of dealers is retrained, another group comes in. The company took over a private home which has been especially equipped to house this activity.

Retraining is a continuous process. New demands for volume sales have brought sales managers face to face with the fact that the only way the required business can be produced at a profit, is by more and better training of the salesmen. This is valid for the 30 percent who produce 70 percent of the company's business as well as the newcomers to the organization and the 70 percent who are not doing the business they should. For the topflight men, unless they are exceptions to the rule, run down and get into a groove. They call on many different buyers, most of whom have "gripes" about the company, or the product, or the price. Constant exposure to that sort of thing will wear down any salesman in time.

Then, too, salesmen on their own too long develop "short cuts" which are not always good—such as leaving a sales kit in the back seat of the car instead of using it to get larger orders. It is to guard against salesmen getting off the beam, and to periodically rekindle their enthusiasm by feeding them new ideas, that a number of companies require every salesman who completes his initial training to come back for retraining at least every five years. These companies are too astute, and too experienced in the ways of salesmen, to think the training job is done when the new man graduates from training school. And they have learned the hard way that getting the men together once a year for an annual convention helps, but it still does not do the job of correcting unprofitable work habits.

Refresher training differs from other types of training because it depends upon salesman participation. The men are taught so far as possible by the discussion technique, by far the best way to teach. But it is not always feasible in the case of new salesmen, who might be confused by the arguments. They would lack the field experience necessary to enable them to properly evaluate selling ideas. Then, too, retraining requires, as a first step, ridding the minds of those in the group of any negative ideas which might be impeding their progress. That, of course, is not so important in the case of trainees with little or no sales experience. In fact, it would do more harm than good.

Field Application of Training

To make sure that the utmost return is obtained from the time and effort expended for sales training, Johns-Manville gives particular attention to the use of the training, as well as the training itself. On this particular point, an executive says:

We based the entire Johns-Manville plan of selling on methods developed by successful salesmen in the field. We began surveying and collecting this material six years ago, and we have been at it ever since. Nothing has been passed on to the sales force until it proved itself and until it was proved that average salesmen could use it effectively.

Of course, it costs money, good money, to survey the entire field and find the best selling methods. It's much easier to say, "I guess we ought to know what to tell our salesmen to do." It seems cheaper, too. But it's terrifically expensive to pass on fancy opinions and pet ideas which won't meet the actual needs in the field.

When we provided sound training material we provided also for its use and application in the field. We provided for field supervision and checkups to see that every salesman actually used the recommended methods. We kept checking him until we knew he was using them properly and effectively. We didn't consider that our job was done when we showed films at a sales meeting.

There are sales executives who think they have done their duty when they have passed the information along. The we-did-our-part attitude has cost thousands and thousands of dollars and wrecked many an otherwise worthy training effort. Unless you can follow through to actual, universal use at the point of sale, dissipation of effectiveness is going to increase by the square of the distance from the home office.

The value of refresher training depends upon the use the salesman makes of the information he has been given. Sales executives know this, yet we find many companies do little or nothing to keep the training alive after it has been given to the salesmen. As a result, the men go back to their territories, apply the new methods they have discussed for a while, and soon settle down to using their old methods.

Even the best salesmen forget. To make sure salesmen do not forget, and that the company gets continuing dividends on its investment, it is the growing practice to follow up refresher courses, as well as training courses for new salesmen, with better-methods bulletins.

What are some of the symptoms and signals that suggest it is time for a retraining program?

The following should be considered warning signs that it is time to consider refresher courses of some kind:

1. When the normal keenness of established men appears to dull.
2. When turnover of salesmen increases.
3. When submittal of expense and call reports begins to drag abnormally.
4. When the feed-back about field conditions becomes sluggish or drops off.
5. When sales decline more drastically for the company than for the industry as a whole.
6. When new men outsell established salesmen.

For companies which conduct seasonal programs or campaigns, the occasion of planning and introducing the new program offers an ideal opportunity to retrain the sales force. What baseball or football team would start the new season without an intense rehearsal of the fundamentals and advanced strategy—with no players excused?

When thus closely related to current programming, the cost in time and money of such "refresher" training will not be considered as "extra," but rather as an integral and necessary activity to insure accomplishing the desired selling results.

Besides bringing distributors' salesmen to the home office or other locations for formal training, there can be considerable advantage in holding training meetings at the distributors' places of business. There, meetings are usually handled by manufacturers' salesmen, with various degrees of success. Some companies use specially trained field trainers for such work.

If the company's salesmen do the job, they should be given training in how to conduct these meetings, and they should be supplied with interesting props and other materials. It goes without saying that a manufacturer's salesman who can train his distributor's salesmen to sell the company's products properly will help multiply sales manyfold.

Permacel, manufacturer of pressure-sensitive tapes, uses a railroad car as a traveling classroom for distributor salesmen. In this photo Lawrence A. Gaffney, Permacel's vice-president of marketing, discusses use of the car's audio-visual equipment, including video-tape recorder and closed-circuit TV.

A Training Train

Salesmen with the Arkansas Paper Company (Little Rock) reported on an unusual setting for a series of distributor-dealer training meetings. A three-car private train housed sales meetings conducted by the Permacel Division of Johnson & Johnson, manufacturers of pressure-sensitive tapes.

The train—called The Permacel Express—was taken on a two-year tour of the U.S., with a stop each week or so for training sessions in various cities.

Permacel bought the 45-year-old cars from the Reading Company in Pennsylvania and remodeled and redecorated them in Victorian-age spendor. It was believed the only private train operating on commercial railways in the U.S. The dining-parlor car seats 36; the second car is the classroom car, while the third car contains the equipment needed to make the train self-sufficient.

The train was conceived by Permacel's Lawrence A. Gaffney, vice-president, marketing, as a means of bringing new sales techniques to the distributors in a unique setting.

Training Retail Salesmen

Because of the increasing complexity of merchandise and the growing number of new and different items being added daily to the shelves in the stores, retail training is more important today than ever before. Stores must maximize the efforts of every person regardless of his assignment to do a clean-cut job of public relations and selling.

Large retail stores have training directors and staffs; have their own training manuals, printed materials, and visual aids; and have department heads and buyers to conduct a continuing in-store training program. Others, however, need the help of manufacturers, and sales managers should be alert to the opportunities afforded by their need.

Motivation and morale are the basic purposes of training. Training increases employees' productivity, standardizes store procedure, reduces personnel turnover, and produces a source of trained and experienced personnel to fill supervisory and managerial positions. The employee benefits from greater self-confidence and increased earnings. Training affords the employee additional job security and enhances his opportunity for advancement.

Every store should have a plan for training the new employee and for carrying a continuing training program for all store employees. The plan should include all levels of employees: management, supervisory, sales, and service personnel. New employees should be given information about the operation of the business, store policies, store clientele, employees pay plan and benefits, mechanics of making sales, layaway and credit procedures, stockkeeping procedures, identification of lines of authority, and specific work assignment, stock location, and inventory system.

All employees should be given continuing training in product information and salesmanship techniques.

Supervisory personnel should be given instruction in human relations, psychology, and basic principles of getting work done through other people.

State and local boards of education offer assistance to small stores through distributive education.

Distributive education is a part of the curriculum of many high schools and junior colleges. Students enrolled in distributive education attend school part time and work in local stores part time. Both the student and the store benefit.

Adult classes are also available through distributive education. Classes are conducted for management, supervisory, sales, and service personnel in all types of retail and wholesale establishments.

Numerous colleges and universities now offer noncredit short courses for the retail field. In addition, many undergraduate and graduate courses are available. The student may elect to take the course as a student for degree work or as an auditor for no credit.

Information about instructors and courses may be obtained from the colleges themselves, the state supervisor of distributive education, or the nearest Small Business Administration regional office.

Most trade associations now include educational programs among the services offered to their members. Correspondence courses, films, materials for conducting training programs, management and sales institutes, and traveling instructors are some of the aids provided by trade associations. Many of these services are provided through arrangements with universities and distributive education.

Campbell Retail Training Seminars

Campbell Soup Company conducts management-training seminars aimed at retail personnel. During an eight-year period over 78,000 retail food store owners and supervisory employees attended Campbell's Manpower Development Program (MDP).

In the six workshop sessions that make up the MDP the name "Campbell" is avoided by the instructors and is not mentioned in any of the printed material.

The program is directed to improving the supervisory capabilities of the "students" rather than going into effective use of shelf space, proper produce displaying or other merchandising techniques that could conflict with the existing policies of a store or chain. For example, the first in the series of six workshops is "How to supervise more effectively." Other sessions are devoted to "How to train people for quick effective production," "Managing yourself—developing your leadership ability," "How to insure a favorable store atmosphere by encouraging personal effectiveness," "How to insure a favorable store atmosphere by stimulating personalized customer relations" and "How to insure a favorable store atmosphere by getting things done through communications."

Each of the workshop sessions, normally held from two to four weeks apart, entails enough "enforced participation" on the part of the student to make certain he will come away with something new. There are premeeting assignments. The workshop itself is complete with visual presentations and competitions between groups of students. Postmeeting on-the-job assignments are recorded by the students in specially prepared "activity books."

The MDP evolved from an idea of W. B. Nixon, vice-president, sales. It is his contention that competitive advantages such as size, location, and even merchandising have narrowed over the past few years and will continue to do so in the future. As a result, one of the prime considerations for retail food stores, both chain and private, lies in improving the efficiency and productivity of its employees.

The typical workshop session is held in a hotel, motel or some other location that is not identified with either Campbell or the company giving the course. All material, including films, slidefilms, manuals, and activity booklets, are supplied at no expense to the customer. According to J. M. Vanderford, Campbell's field-force manager, the cost of the material for an average MDP is about $600.

The acceptance of MDP has been well worth the cost of its development, according to Campbell executives. The program is now being given on an international basis as the result of several requests from foreign concerns.

The Whirlpool Program

"Get the story to the man on the floor." That, explained Jim Yund, merchandising manager, air-conditioning department, was the purpose of a Whirlpool Corporation program in taking the story of how to merchandise room air conditioners directly to the retail salesman.

Two teams of Whirlpool executives made a three-week sales-training tour covering about two dozen cities.

With Mr. Yund from the air-conditioning department was Ron Gow, sales promotion manager, while a second team headed by Warren Singer, general manager, included Glen Zerler, sales training manager.

"By meeting directly with the people involved in selling, your message isn't lost," Mr. Yund said. Moreover, he explained, visual aids and displays that a manufacturer can assemble may be beyond the means of many distributors. For maximum effectiveness, he said, "We keep the presentation as documentary as possible."

The Whirlpool merchandising "seminars" are not all unrelieved hard-sell. The presence of retailer wives and an accompanying dinner usually served in conjunction with the presentations are no small factors in the program's success.

THE TOOLS OF SALES TRAINING

Visual Aids in Sales Training

Movies and sound-slidefilms play an important role in modern sales training. Some of the visual aids used by sales managers are amateurish, others highly professional. But regardless of the quality, no better way of reaching a large group of salesmen with a training message has been devised.

A folder issued by the Oravisual Company, Inc., explains why:

"Tests show that we remember only 20 percent of what we hear and only 40 percent of what we see. But when you combine the message orally and visually, we remember 60 percent of what we see and hear."

This means that your meetings using visual aids will be three times more effective than all-talk sessions—your ideas will have that much more impact on the listeners.

The trend is toward short, simple films or sound-slide presentations instead of trying to cover a lot of ground with one long presentation. Each sales problem or objective is given its own frame of reference.

Getting Films Used: One drawback to the use of pictures is the work involved in getting men together for a meeting at which the picture may be shown, and then the effort needed to follow up the showing. The experience of General Motors in this connection is interesting:

"Dealers generally neglect to show the pictures to their staffs unless some factory man comes around and gets it done. Nine salesmen out of 10 won't make the effort they should to show these pictures to prospects. One Chevrolet dealer, for instance, offers his salesmen 50 cents for every time they show the film to a prospect, and it is remarkable how few times he is called upon to pay out this money."

This criticism, however, should not be accepted as an attack on the use of films in selling, because the same objection exists in nearly every type of sales promotion. But in spite of this objection, General Motors has spent up to $1 million a year for sales-promotional and mass selling films.

A large library of promotional films, both moving pictures and sound-slidefilms, is maintained by the Ford Motor Company. Several thousand Ford dealers now own their own projection equipment and, in some cases, pay Ford a monthly service fee for a total of 16 to 20 sound-slidefilm releases during the year. These large users of films divide their functions four ways: (1) Films used for mass advertising; (2) films used to promote dealer and distributor sales efficiency; (3) films used in training the manufacturer's own salesmen; and (4) films used by the salesmen in direct selling as props.

Consumer Educational Films: Commonplace films of this type have been overdone. Such films are by no means as effective in formulating consumer thinking as they used to be and unless backed up with a well-thought-out plan are likely to be expensive advertising. However, there are often delicate situations, peculiar to a business, with which it would be unwise to deal in cold type, but which can be effectively handled with a carefully planned picture.

A common reason for lack of results with this type of promotional activity is that it is dumped into the lap of the dealer and he is expected to look after the details. Those experienced in this selling are careful to work out the whole plan for the dealer, and, if possible, to carry it through for him. The proper coordination of sales promotion and selling is essential to success. To depend too much on the dealer is fatal.

Films for Public Relations: There has been so much agitation about working conditions, customer relations policies, and other matters of broad public interest, that several companies have set up special appropriations for institutional pictures. There are many situations in business which lend themselves to dramatization, and which, if handled in a human-interest way, will insure an extensive, free circulation for the film. Such films can be circulated through distributors for use in meetings of various kinds.

Many outstanding pictures of this type have been produced over the years, some of which have won prizes at international business film festivals. Among these may be mentioned the Dartnell-Borden film, "Overcoming Objections."

Programmed Sales Training

In the sales field as well as in other areas where educational methods are of concern, there is increasing use of the technique called "programmed instruction." One of the best outlines of the origin and development of this method was prepared by Felix F. Kopstein, director, Auto-Instructional Systems Division of the Burroughs Corporation of Detroit:

The subject of "teaching machines," "programmed teaching" or "self-instructional techniques" has attracted considerable public attention. The beginning of this widespread interest is traceable to an article by Professor B. F. Skinner of Harvard University in the AAAS journal, *Science*. Professor Skinner had said much the same thing in an earlier publication in 1954 without attracting much attention, but in 1958 he chose to title his article "Teaching Machines," and this great nation of gadget lovers rose to the bait. Professor Skinner did not invent teaching machines or programmed instruction; neither did Professor Sidney L. Pressey, of Ohio State University, who toyed with these concepts as early as 1925. Indeed, the first teaching machine was patented by one Halcyon Skinner of Bronxville, New York (no relative), in the year 1866. As with most any topic, it is possible to trace the notion back to Socrates, and, if Plato can be believed, Socrates frequently employed a kind of programmed instructional procedure. What Skinner, Pressey, and others did contribute were the scientific underpinnings that make possible progress and improvement in the technique.

Programmed instruction, then, is not new and there is nothing magic about it. Programmed instruction is simply a way of effectively and systematically applying many of the known scientific principles of learning to the instructional process. In programmed instruction, the learner encounters a situation that resembles the relationship between a private tutor and a single student. However, even a private tutor cannot be as sensitive to his student's needs, nor as omniscient about his difficulties.

To understand what programmed teaching is all about, we must first understand what learning is. Scientifically, learning is defined as a change or modification of a person's capability for performing some task as a result of certain experiences. In turn, experiences must be regarded as significant events taking place in the learner's immediate environment. In simpler words, one might say that learning is a change from "can't do" to "can do." Learning is not something about which a learner has a choice. Learning will take place whether the learner wants it to take place or not, given the right kinds of influences in his immediate environment. The best a learner can do is to remove himself from these influences, but, if they are active, learning will inevitably result. Programmed instruction, then, is an optimization of the environment and of the events occurring in it, so as to facilitate the learning process. This optimization relies on the systematic application of known scientific principles that govern learning. It is important to realize that anything which can be taught can be taught in programmed form.

A Powerful Management Control Tool

Programmed instruction is a topic which should be of extreme interest to modern sales and marketing management. Its importance will be appreciated only if it can be viewed as a powerful tool for management control. That it is truly a powerful management control tool will be apparent from the consideration of just some of the advantages that programmed instruction offer:

1. All instruction exists in material form and the effectiveness of the instruction has been objectively established. A human sales-training instructor, no matter how good he may be, is human. That means, among other things, that he is variable and that his effectiveness from day to day and from month to month varies for many reasons. In conventional instruction it is primarily the trainee or student who is evaluated; the quality of the instruction itself is hardly ever measured. When the instruction is evaluated, more often than not it is done on a purely subjective and speculative basis. In programmed instruction the precise characteristics of the instructional material and of its effectiveness are objectively established and can be taken into account during management planning.

2. In programmed teaching the instruction is sent to the trainee instead of his being brought to a central point for the instruction. Since the instruction exists in material form, it can be packaged and mailed to the trainee in the field. That trainee can be active in his territory and need not be removed to journey to a central point where a class might be assembled. Not only does that trainee continue to be active in his terri-

tory, but, also, the cost of his trip and of his sustenance during the instruction can be saved.

3. Programmed instruction exists in material form, therefore it is always ready. Hence, there is never any need to wait in order to form a class. When it is thought that someone needs training, he can be given the training without delay.

4. Obviously, programmed instructional materials can be duplicated into as many sets as necessary or desired. Therefore, it is possible to train as many people at one time as one may wish. If a major sales campaign depends upon training the entire sales force simultaneously, this is potentially possible.

5. With programmed teaching, the instruction can be given and scheduled at the convenience of the trainee rather than the instructor. A salesman-trainee can start the day with an hour of study, then keep a sales appointment or two and return to study when his schedule is free.

6. Most important of all, a graduate of a course of programmed instruction can be relied upon to perform as required. By its very nature, programmed instruction guarantees its own effectiveness. The ability of the overwhelming majority of graduates of programmed instruction to do what is necessary is not hypothetical, but assured. In conventional training, the graduates vary widely in the degree to which they have benefited from the training. In programmed instruction, there is a uniformly high level of attainment and, consequently, management is assured that the trainee is truly able to do what is needed.

The economics of programmed instruction is a complex topic. As a rule of thumb, the development of programmed instructional materials will be warranted only if the total number of people to be trained is relatively large. With a small group with relatively easy subject matter, or where major changes in the subject matter are going to occur frequently, conventional instruction will be the more economic way to proceed. By and large, programmed instruction requires a large initial investment and thereafter very little in incremental costs for the actual implementation of the training program. Conventional instruction, of course, requires relatively little in the way of an initial investment, but thereafter incremental costs, such as instructors' salaries, mount quite rapidly.

To show the potential savings due to programmed instruction, the following example has been selected. This is not a hypothetical example, but represents a fair statement of a real training program in a certain large company. The course to be given normally requires eight weeks. It will be given to approximately 800 people over the period of the next five years. Two instructors will be required to teach this course and their combined salaries total $16,000 per annum. The average travel costs for bringing a trainee to a central point where the course will be given are $150. The costs of lodging and feeding the trainee while away from home amount to $51.50 per week. (Note that this represents a conservative appraisal, since no allowance is made for the trainee's salary during this unproductive period, nor for the loss of his productivity to the company.)

Now let us go through a few fast calculations. Conventional instruction lasts for eight weeks at $51.50 per week, which amounts to $412 per man for the eight-week period. Add to this the $150 of travel expense, and you have a total of $562. Now multiply $562 by the 800 people who will be taking the course.

The total is $449,600. Add to this the costs of the instructors' salaries over the five-year period, and we have an additional increment of $80,000 for a total of $529,600 to administer this hypothetical course in a conventional fashion. A very conservative and extremely liberal estimate for the development of programmed instructional materials to replace the conventional instruction in this course is the sum of $200,000. This amounts to a net savings of $329,600 over the life of this particular training course. Put in a different way, the cost of conventional instruction per man per course will be $662, while the comparable cost for programmed instruction will be $250 per man. Naturally, there will be examples in which the savings that can be effected are even greater, just as there will be instances in which these savings will be far less or even negligible. The decision to resort to programmed instruction first requires a thorough analysis of the specific case.

How to Get Started

Firms interested in applying programmed instruction may want to know how one gets started in this business. The best advice is to find a reputable professional concern and to contract with it for the first trial project. Beware of shady, disreputable, and poorly qualified organizations that have sprung up in profusion. After your first trial project, decide whether you wish to continue on a larger scale while still relying on contractual arrangements, or whether you want to set up your own group. A brief word of advice concerning the setting up of your own programmed-instruction group. To function well, such a group will require certain resources of which some may even seem unreasonable and "plush" to you. The advice is to give them what they need and to remember that you can afford to be generous. If programmed instruction is of value to you at all, it will pay for itself and for its own expenditures many times over. A third possibility that must be mentioned is buying ready-made programs from reputable publishers. In this case, too, beware of a multitude of inferior materials that look like programmed instruction but aren't. A joint committee of the three major professional organizations in the field, the American Psychological Association, the American Educational Research Association, and the Department of Audio-Visual Instruction of the National Educational Association have published criteria by which programmed materials may be assessed. Apply this yardstick before you buy.

A Developing Science

New trends in programmed instruction in the sales field have been traced by Robert C. Jaeger, manager of programmed instruction for the Prudential Insurance Company of America:

We might say that programmed instruction is hardly new, since it has long since proved its value to business. On the other hand, we might argue that it *is* still new, because this training technique is continually changing. Rules which were regarded as inviolable a few years ago are now violated enthusiastically; and techniques which were either unheard of, or were only a gleam in someone's eye previously, are now taken for granted.

Formerly, there was considerable discussion over the relative merits of the linear vs. the branching type of program. In the former, the learner was presented with some information, required to make an immediate response, and was immediately informed of the correct response. This type program was deliberately written so as to minimize practically any likelihood of errors. The matter—the branching type—presented information in larger steps, usually no less than a paragraph, and even as much as a page at a time. The learner responded by making one choice among several. The correct response led him to the next bit of information; an incorrect response was corrected, and he was either told what his response should have been, and he was sent on, or he was referred back to the item where he made his incorrect response. In any case, errors were not only permitted, but in some cases even encouraged.

The dispute has now died down. Instead, at least in our case, linear programming is used to teach basic information—product knowledge for example; branching is used to teach application and use of this basic knowledge.

It wouldn't be accurate to refer to advantages of programmed instruction as being claimed by its proponents. We don't "claim" these advantages: they're very real, and here they are:

1. Learning improves. Our tests have indicated that average test scores improved significantly.

2. Learning becomes uniform over our entire field force. You may not regard this as too important, but it has proved a very real boon to us. We now *know* what our agents are learning much better than we did when they were being taught by conventional class methods, and the individual teachers inevitably brought in their own biases. (At least now the biases are uniform!)

3. The learner takes less time to grasp the same material.

4. Most important, the trainer's time has been reduced astonishingly. Trainers now take less than an hour to introduce programmed material which used to take them more than 13 hours to teach using conventional methods.

One advantage not claimed for programmed instruction is an improvement in retention. Retention does *not* improve, but since the learner knows more to start with, he's still better off a few months later. Moreover, we also know that retention is no problem if the learner continues to use the knowledge he has acquired. And I often wonder why he should teach an agent something he's not going to use?

These are very real advantages of programmed instruction; now what are its disadvantages?

Almost certainly, cost. I hesitate to give any figures because there is such a wide variation in the estimates of what a program will cost. For example, one estimate ranges from $1,700 to $9,000 per average trainee hour of instruction. Perhaps a more realistic range would be from $2,500 to $4,000 per trainee hour of instruction if your programmers are unfamiliar with the material to be written, or $1,500 to $1,600 if they are familiar with the material. These estimates are for writing your own programs, and specifically do *not* include overhead costs. If you were not interested in writing your own material, and could not find any programs commercially available which were suitable for your purposes, you could have a contractor write your programs. But his costs would have to include his overhead and profit margin as well!

Another disadvantage of programmed instruction is the length of time necessary to prepare it. A program which took an average trainee about 12 hours to complete would probably take six months to prepare. Obviously this is a lot longer than would be necessary if you were just to have a training manual written in straight prose. I have known such manuals to be turned out in considerably less than *one* month.

But the very reasons that make programmed instruction so costly and take so long to produce are what assures its success. As I said earlier, the objectives of the program are set out "in performance terms." This means that you must state exactly what your trainees are expected to be able to do upon completion of your course. Are your own *present* training programs that measurable? In order to accomplish these objectives, programmers must write clean, hard prose, with no unnecessary flourishes in it. Furthermore, before the program is published, it is actually tried out on samples of the population, and revised where it failed to do the prescribed job. Obviously this is going to cost money and take time—lots of both.

Obviously, a large part of business and industry in the United States has looked long and hard at these advantages and disadvantages of programmed instruction, and decided in its favor. A list of the companies which are using programming at least to some extent is most impressive.

How about you? Should you use this technique in your training? Consider these points in making your decision:

1. Every salesman is required to have considerable product knowledge. Programmed instruction has proved its ability to impart this knowledge, and almost always in a manner superior to conventional methods.

2. A few years ago there was much doubt as to whether or not programming could be used successfully to teach salesmanship. Now there are programs available commercially. Some are quite inexpensive, others quite costly.

3. Your salesmen all learn the same material uniformly. If this is important to you, programming will do this. You can be assured that they will all learn the same knowledge, without the local interpretation you may not want. This becomes especially important if your salesmen are widely scattered.

4. If they *are* widely scattered, you can send your training material to them at their location, and won't have to bring them in to a central point. Obviously this is going to save a lot of money.

5. If you have a large sales force, and especially if you have a large turnover with the attendant number of new men constantly needing new training, your cost per trainee will be sharply reduced.

6. How important is superior learning to your salesmen? The most knowledgeable salesman isn't always the best, is he?

7. Which automatically brings us to the next point. How good are your best salesmen *as instructors?* Programming will improve the *quality* of your training.

8. How stable is the content of your training courses? If it is volatile and constantly changing, then you would probably be ill advised to go into programmed instruction, in view of what I have already said about costs and time. But if the material *is* stable, and if the other factors above point in that direction, then it would seem like a good idea for you to at least consider programming as a part of your training methods.

If you decide to take this step, how should you start? Probably the best way would be for you to buy an available program which seemed to fit your needs in some areas, and try it out. Send for *Programmed Learning: A Bibliography of Programs and Presentation Devices,* by Carl Hendershot, 4114 Ridgewood Dr., Bay City, Michigan 48707. You'll find listed practically every program on every subject that has been published in the United States and Canada. You're almost certain to find something you can use. If you like the results, then you can go further. (And I'm pretty sure you will like the results.)

Thereafter you can do one of two things: You can contract your material out to be done by one of the many excellent firms now engaged in this effort. This would probably be your best bet if you don't anticipate a continuing need for new programmed material. Or you can decide to prepare your own programs internally. If you do, you will need skilled, trained programmers and at least one editor. They're hard to find and they come high. Incidentally, one of the ways you can get started preparing your own programs is to contract your first program. Many contractors will agree to teach your own people how to write programs as they write yours. If your material has any value elsewhere, and if you let your contractor have the copyright, your costs will go down gratifyingly. Whatever you do though, if you decide to contract out your material, have your lawyer approve the contract first.

The Equitable Life Approach

Ralph A. Drekman, of the manpower development division, of The Equitable Life Assurance Society of the United States, New York City, discusses his company's training philosophy and practice as follows:

Today's training specialist faces a difficult manpower problem: He has to hire the skills he can get and develop them into what his organization needs. To help him bridge that gap, he will rely on training.

One of the most promising training methods is programmed learning. Here is a discussion that may sound familiar to you:

Let's pay more attention to the individual learner and give him a chance to experience achievement.

Okay, but let him learn by doing the thing. He may think he knows it, but we can't be sure until he tries.

Programmers discussing training strategy? No, that's quoting Quintilian and Sophocles in free translation.

Then programmed learning isn't really something new? That's right. You can trace its beginning all the way from Plato's Socratic dialogues to Pavlov's study of conditioned reflexes in dogs, from Thorndike's stimulus-response studies to Pressey's multiple-choice testing machine and Skinner's Ping-Pong playing pigeons.

So why all the excitement about programmed instruction and teaching machines? Because the rediscovery of programmed learning principles may be one of the most significant contributions to human learning in this century. For the first time, behavioral psychologists have taken the results of their scientific experiments out of the laboratory to apply them directly to human learning.

What are some of the psychological principles underlying programmed learning? Most importantly:

Operant conditioning	Discrimination
Reinforcement	Behavior shaping

These principles have to do with habit formation. Here is an oversimplified example: Suppose you want to teach your dog a trick. You want him to retrieve a ball out of the water. By chance you see him run to pick up a stick. He is responding to something, he is showing operant behavior. That is, his behavior operates on the environment.

Right away you give him a piece of Yummy. It's a stimulus. He likes it, feels rewarded, and tries again. You have given him immediate reinforcement. Note that your dog must be active. You cannot reinforce his behavior unless he is busy doing something.

Next you introduce the ball and give him that reinforcing Yummy stimulus *only* when he picks up the ball. Now you are using selective reinforcement to make him react to the difference between ball and stick. You are trying to bring about conditioned discrimination.

By designing a logical, systematic learning sequence, you can eventually train your dog step-by-step to retrieve the ball out of the water. You are shaping his behavior. You are building a new skill. If you help him maintain this behavior, we can observe it and will conclude that he has learned.

You can see that animal trainers have practiced certain principles of programmed learning for centuries. These principles can also be applied to training the human animal. In fact, Brethower and Rummler of the University of Michigan have pointed out that in your daily work with people, you are probably using operant conditioning right now, unwittingly, as a management technique. If you have shaped employees' behavior by deliberately encouraging only desirable practices, you have used operant conditioning.

How do programmers apply these principles to programmed learning? They have designed instructional sequences, called programs, with special characteristics. These training materials are carefully planned to combine typical features:

1. Step-by-Step Build-up
2. Active Response
3. Feedback
4. Self-Pacing

Let's look at each of these features briefly.

1. *Step-by-Step Build-up*

A well-constructed program is organized into clearly defined portions called frames. A frame may range in size from several pages of an overview chapter to the smallest step in a multiplication exercise.

Frames are sequenced in what the programmer perceives to be a logical order. If tryouts of his program show that trainees will learn a process more efficiently in an "illogical" order, he will use that tested order as the most effective training sequence.

Frames are built one upon the other in steps of increasing complexity. An earlier notion that all material to be learned must be broken down into small steps did not prove useful. Instead, the programmer must find the optimum step-size by testing his frames, as they are written, among his intended audience.

2. Active Response

After studying the one specific point presented to him in a frame, the learner must respond. He may have to analyze a diagram, discriminate between typical examples, or form a concept. In this way he is actively engaged in the learning process. He learns by doing.

An earlier "rule" of programming suggested that all active responding should be observable behavior. For example, answering out loud or completing statements in writing. But humans seem to do a great deal of covert responding, hidden but very active. Many learners appear to carry on a silent but incessant dialogue with themselves. They let thoughts race through their minds, manipulate concepts, attempt verbalizations, and keep answering questions to themselves. These too are active responses and must be recognized and acknowledged by the programmer.

3. Feedback

A well-written program will guide the learner through problem-solving exercises which will reveal to him step-by-step that he is answering the questions correctly and finally that he has solved a problem correctly. In addition, the learner will find the correct answer to each frame printed in the program. This will give him a chance to check how he is doing. If he wants to, he can test himself and correct his own work. The printed answer will either confirm that he is right or show that he must correct his response.

At one time programmers thought that such feedback should always follow the frame right away. It would then serve as immediate reinforcement for the learner. But finding out that he made an error was not always a rewarding experience. So, the right answer in the program did not necessarily give reinforcement.

As a result, programmers became preoccupied with the design of programs in which the learner would rarely make a mistake. They wanted programs to be as error-proof as possible. However, many adult learners would only once in a while check for correct answers. They didn't seem to care about immediate confirmation. They became so engrossed in their exercises and action projects that they rejected any interference. All they wanted to do was solve one problem and then still another problem. Never mind some of their errors on the way. After completing the program they too demonstrated that they could perform the task just as well. They had achieved mastery; they had learned.

From these observations programmers concluded that immediate feedback is not always necessary or desirable. They have found out that confirmation is not synonymous with reinforcement. Many adult learners do think: "Let me make my own mistakes. And get off my back, so I can try this by myself."

Training specialists are usually looking for this positive problem-solving behavior in trainees. And they want them to be able to cope with their own mistakes. To be effective, programmed learning materials must therefore modify some of the features developed in the learning laboratory to adapt to practical needs and conditions.

4. Self-Pacing

Since the learner can check his answers without waiting for an instructor, a program can be both self-instructional and self-pacing. Of course, there is nothing new about a self-teaching workbook. It was already popular when Thomas Edison wrote his book, *Telegraphy Self Taught.*

Many learners prefer to work their way through a course at their own speed. The fast learner can go through it in a breeze and the slow learner can take his own good time. Both should be able to perform the training objective after they have completed the program.

Trouble is that some trainees find it difficult to finish a program on their own. Programmed learning may be self-teaching but it is not self-administering. Some time control and selective supervisory monitoring is often helpful. Moreover, if study time varies too much, it may conflict with established training programs. To introduce programmed learning in an organization you must use common sense and suggest reasonable completion schedules.

These four features: Step-by-step build-up, active response, feedback, and self-pacing combine to form a repeating learning cycle. As each segment of knowledge is presented to the learner in frames of increasing complexity, he is required to respond to it in some way, and can then check for feedback to see how he is progressing. On his own, he can speed up this cycle or slow it down, as desired.

How is a program developed? Briefly, here are some of the essential steps used in the process of programming:

1. Examine existing system.
2. Investigate environmental factors.
3. Define trainee's job.
4. Establish need for program.
5. Analyze training task.
6. State training objectives.
7. Write final performance test.
8. Specify course prerequisites.
9. Determine program design.
10. Select suitable media.
11. Write test frames.
12. Write teaching frames.
13. Conduct individual tryouts.
14. Revise program.
15. Validate program through field test by group.
16. Revise, publish, install, and monitor program for next edition.

Let's review some of these steps. The programmer should question:

1. Under what conditions is the program to be used? Is it a hostile environment where line management gives only lip service to training and thinks it's a nuisance? Does top management fully support the training effort?

2. Does the existing system reward the completer or is there a penalty for the trainee who does the job exactly the way it is taught? Does the training program direct trainees one way while their supervisors direct them in another?

3. What is the trainee now doing? What isn't he doing? What is his present repertory? Is it only a minor deficiency that keeps him from doing what you want him to do? Can he, in fact, do it, but doesn't want to? What are his needs?

4. If it is a case of "can do, but won't do," it's not a training problem. Maybe there is a need to improve communications, working conditions, compensation, or leadership. But there is no need for programmed learning materials.

5. Exactly what is the task the learner must accomplish? What are the typical steps in its performance? How does a master performer do it? What experiences do we observe in the field, on the firing line, at the gut level?

6. How do you define in measurable terms the specific behavior you can observe when the trainee demonstrates mastery? Does management accept these terminal behavior specifications as useful performance objectives?

7. Does the final test simulate real-life conditions and the actual job as closely as possible? Is it a valid test? Does it measure what it is supposed to measure?

8. What must the trainee be able to do before he is admitted to the course? What pretest will serve best to screen out those who have not yet met the pre-requisites for taking the program?

9. What teaching strategies will be most effective? Should we use a linear format, a straight-line tell-and-test routine? Do we want to accept the learner's constructed response, such as a written answer, as a receipt that our "goods" have been delivered? Or does this particular training problem call for a fast track in the program? Or for branching into extra drill or refresher loops? Should we use a multiple-choice format and accept selective responses? Can we develop enough plausible choices? Will some combination of these techniques give us a more effective program to let the learner reach his objective as quickly and efficiently as possible?

10. What medium shall we use to communicate? Should the learner look at videotapes, movies, film strips, or slides? Listen to records, audiotapes, or lectures? Read a text? Are teaching machines suitable for this training job? Is computer-assisted instruction practicable for this particular task? Can a multimedia combination perhaps give us an even better simulation of the real-life task? Can we employ other training devices, such as role playing to get the learner into the act of simulating the job for which he trains?

11. How can we create and develop a series of increasingly difficult task-simulation tests to measure the gradual change in behavior, the behavior shaping we want to engineer? How can we make these tests as close to real life as possible so training will transfer to job?

12. Can we develop task-simulators and real-life examples to prepare a sequence of as few learning steps as necessary? Can we develop exercises which will guide the learner quickly to making critical discriminations and solving problems until he can pass each test frame?

13. How can we set up as realistically as possible tryouts with individual members of our intended trainee population to observe how they work their way through the program? Are the instructions in the program clear for proper use? Did we overteach?

14. Do we feel like revising the whole program because we tend to over-listen to the tryout learner? Does a resequencing of materials really improve the program? Did we provide enough practice? Can we trim verbiage to come up with a lean program?

15. Does the program teach what it is supposed to teach under actual field conditions? What are the problems of administering the program to groups in

the field? How does the program fit into the ongoing training effort? Are support equipment and material available when needed? What are the trainer's needs and attitudes?

16. How can we monitor the program's use, after it has been installed, through opinionnaires, routine feedback from reports, or personal observation? What must we do to maintain the skills our trainees have acquired?

This long list of questions is only a sample of the programmer's analytical approach. He is a nosy fellow who wants to find out about things. He is not pleasant to have around, because he can ask a lot of unanswered and uncomfortable questions. Perhaps you would like to ask some of these questions about the task you are now working on.

This review of how a program is developed will now help us in spelling out a definition of programming:

Programming is a systematic process of developing and validating instructional sequences designed to change learner behavior in specific measurable ways.

In programmed learning five key ideas stand out:

1. Systematic analysis.
2. Behavioral objectives.
3. Task simulation.
4. Testing and validation.
5. Focus on the learner.

First, programming means a systematic, organized approach to the analysis and effective coordination of all elements and influencing factors of a training problem.

Second, programmed learning is goal-oriented. A program should separate "nice to know" from "must know." One goes out, perhaps to be recommended as enrichment material; the other goes into the program, because it is necessary for goal achievement.

Third, before we send our astronauts into space, we want them to experience as many contingencies as possible in a task simulator. Before you send your trainee into the cold world to face your precious customers, you want him to handle many real life situations under suitable hothouse conditions.

Fourth, testing and validating will give you vital feedback for accomplishing the programming task. It is at the core of the programming process.

Fifth, programming puts renewed emphasis on the learner. You are selling ideas and he is the consumer. He is the final authority on whether you have communicated. And to serve him is the programmer's ultimate goal.

Are all programs developed in this systematic way? Far from it. We are only looking at guidelines. And they sound much simpler in theory than they are applied in practice. The problem is that humans are so much more than animals. Programming practitioners have convinced themselves that trainees are not learning like dogs or pigeons. For the behavioral psychologist this means going back to the laboratory for reappraisal. That does not mean his approach is not valid. It means that new questions have come up, but no definite answers. As in all science, there may only be an answer and an answer beyond that. Programmed learning has no special claim to solid scientific foundation, as it is practiced now. It is above all an art.

What are the advantages of programmed learning? In hundreds of published studies there is evidence that programs will reduce training time, will reduce training cost, and will help increase the effectiveness of training. Any disadvantages? Yes. You still cannot make a trainee learn, if he does not want to learn. Some learners do not like to be led by the nose—ever. Some like to have a tutor present at all times to lean on when in doubt. Some miss the outside pressure to complete the program. Some training problems do not seem to lend themselves to a programming approach. Other techniques may work better. If so, it does not make sense to program for the sake of programming. Programming is no cure-all.

Who is using programmed learning? Today almost every major organization working with people and concerned about manpower development is making some use of programmed learning. Dr. Ofiesh, an early proponent of the programming method, has published 35 of the many case histories he collected from all branches of the Armed Forces, from a roster of leading industrial companies, banks, insurers, government agencies, giant retailers, and other organizations. Many of these reports tell of remarkable success through judicious application of programmed learning materials.

The important thing to remember is that a program is *not* a product, is *not* a medium! A program is a process. Programming is not the rewriting of training manuals or textbooks to cover prescribed subject matter in a gimmicky way. Programming is a training method, a pedagogic strategy.

Alert training specialists who recognize that all training is basically communication have taken programming concepts and applied them to other communication jobs. For example, management consultants like Dr. Odiorne have used programming principles to propose "management by objectives."

Progressive educators at the Oakland Community College in Michigan have applied the same systematic development and evaluation used in programming to define, design, produce, and implement all elements necessary for an entire institution of higher learning. All performance specifications were identified and defined in behavioral terms. They spell out the knowledge the student should demonstrate at the end of the course. Course content is sequenced meaningfully and based on a flexible time schedule. The student knows what is expected of him and he is kept informed of his progress. Criteria tests serve to evaluate his achievement of interim goals. An array of media is employed to present materials which allow active responding, give feedback, and permit reasonable self-pacing. The entire complex is learner-oriented, from time schedule to physical design of "learning laboratories" which make up the college plant.

Viewed and applied in this way, programmed learning reveals its true scope and great potential. Programmed-learning techniques can be used to develop adjunct training materials to support your present training efforts. Programming can help you develop a year-long training course, redesign your total training program, or even your training center. Properly applied, programmed learning can make a valuable contribution toward more efficient and more effective training for your organization. It will help you solve some of your urgent manpower problems.

CHART OF THE BUYING PROCESS AND THE DOVE-TAILED SELLING PROCESS

PREPARED BY A. D. SELTZ FOR THE CHARLES MORRIS PRICE SCHOOL—FOR USE IN THE CREATIVE SALES CLASS

Step No.	Buymanship	Salesmanship		Salesmanship		
	The Buying Process	Sales Objective	How to Proceed	The Selling Process and Planned Procedure		
				What to Do	S.S.#	Sales Sesames
1.	Mind at ease—state of satisfaction, equilibrium and balance Not interested in any change	To obtain favorable attention from prospect	Sell the "Right to the Interview" by (1) Approaching in a friendly spirit (2) Presenting an arresting, thought-impelling idea (3) Side-stepping the prospect's barriers to an interview	(1) Before you approach obtain all available information about the prospect (2) Feel friendly—Look competent—speak and act courteously (3) Pre-select a forceful, modern, pertinent presentation you will enjoy employing (4) In your approach remember your goal is a friendly response	1. 2. 3. 4. 5. 6. 7. 8.	Mention him and his interests / Show promise of benefits / Use pointed news / Provoke relevant curiosity / Use visual aids / Use current testimonials / Use prophetical case / Ask for opinion
2.	Comparison resulting in a dissatisfaction which shakes complacency and results in mild but growing Interest	To convert attention to interest	Establish the general problem the prospect faces as you discuss and display all buying motives	(1) Build a bridge from your opening to your prospect's interests (2) Know your story—tell it convincingly with enthusiasm (3) Use modern sales aids, verbal proof stories, documentary data	1. 2. 3. 4.	Use product or visual aids / Headline buying motives / Use testimonials and endorsements to show reasons others have bought / Clearly define the general problem that all people face in the same situation
3.	A recognized deficiency established	To intensify interest while displaying and identifying the paramount need	Fix the problem on the prospect by isolating the paramount buying motive or motives using the "fact-finding-listening technique" as you develop the "ideal and perfect" solution	(1) Don't do all the talking (2) Throw him the lead and listen "with enthusiasm" (3) Don't interrupt and don't argue (4) Obtain his aid in setting the pattern of the "ideal solution"	1. 2. 3. 4. 5. 6.	Stop talking and listen / Discover his hopes, desires, ambitions, and inadequacies / If he has a solution, don't attack—congratulate him and aid him in planning the perfect solution / Ask for his aid in solution / Use "if" or "suppose" construction / Inquire—get the facts
4.	State of emotional necessity and drive apparent	To arouse desire by using emotional motivation	Offer the solution by telling and demonstrating how your product or service fills "the ideal" requirements	(1) Use sales visualizers and/or the product as you demonstrate (2) Make him take part in the demonstration as you proceed (3) Be sure he understands each step and what each means in "buying satisfaction" (4) Display all "selling points"	1. 2. 3. 4. 5. 6. 7. 8.	Clearly show how you produce benefits, i.e. how "selling points" deliver "Buying satisfactions" / Show that your product or service is easy, economical, and agreeable to use / Show "only exclusive" features / Show ills avoided by purchase / Show points of contrast or superiority / Show prospect in a favorable light by use of product or service / Appeal to basic emotions / Get agreement and approval on each point as you make it
5.	State of mental turbulence caused by inward struggle to justify emotional urge to buy—and decision reached but undisclosed	To justify desire by using factual motivation (Logical and reasoned proof)	Forestall objections and block-out competition by proving he will gain by buying—and/or answer objections and meet competition	(1) Be sincere and make a background of authority (2) Avoid belligerency (3) Pile buying motive on buying motive (4) Learn the best way to handle objections and competition (5) Use objections as springboards to sales	9. 10. 11. 12. 13.	Dramatize delivery / Demonstrate thoroughly / Guarantee if you can / Use human interest stories / Use testimonials
6.	Procrastination as a defense against spending money—then the climax reached with the "buy" complete and a return to mental equilibrium with inner pleasant feeling of satisfied emotions	To persuade action now and close the sale	Help him to arrive at a mutually favorable action by making it easy for him to buy now	Expect him to buy now and: (1) Use law of assumed consent (2) Use law of contrast (3) Summarize objections (4) Place responsibility on him (5) Ask where you've failed (6) Bring in third person	14. 15. 16. 17. 18. 19.	Give assurances and proofs / Maximize benefits and minimize costs / Give him good reasons for buying / Show benefits by purchase now and ill effects of delay / Show methods of purchase / Hold reserve closing data for refusal to buy now

REMEMBER that good closing begins before the first interview and continues through the entire sales process. Poor closing may be in reality poor prospecting, or poor qualification of the prospect's ability or authority to buy, or it may be the result of the salesman's inferior knowledge of product or service. Certainly everything you do and say in the prospect's presence has a direct bearing on the outcome of the sale. Keep in mind that "closing" is merely the end result of a logical, orderly procedure advancing step by step from start to finish.

The Salesman as a Retail Consultant

It is axiomatic that good salesmanship is based on service to the customer. Salesmen are often called on to make suggestions to the buyer, at his own request, on problems of management, selling, or, in the case of retailers, on advertising, promotion, and on many other subjects, including proposed changes in display, store layout, or even on store modernization. The good sales manager will encourage his men to lend such assistance.

On the subject of store modernization, the Small Business Administration, in its Annual No. 5, offers the following suggestions:

Modernization is not a question solely of painting the walls or acquiring a new neon sign. Its aims are broader, and include:

1. Better physical store appearance (external and internal).

2. Better utilization of space, and better display of merchandise.

3. Up-to-date fixtures and equipment for better display and protection of merchandise and for speeding customer service.

4. Heating, ventilating, and air conditioning, to attract customers and make the store a better place in which to work; and

5. Soundness and safety.

What these five goals add up to is simply this: They convert a store into a "sales builder."

In modernizing a store, keep these points in mind: (1) Before making any changes, look at the overall picture to be sure that whatever changes you do make will blend in with the rest of the physical store makeup, or that future alterations will blend with the ones you are now making; and (2) that changes, particularly exterior changes, harmonize at least in a general way with the physical makeup of other stores.

Changes for changes' sake are not desirable. What you are concerned with are *innovations* that will also be *improvements*. Thus, it may be a good idea to have some assistance in helping to plan a program. There are, of course, specialists whose services are available, and you may wish to turn to them for aid. In addition, you can study trade magazines, and talk to equipment and fixture manufacturers and dealers to get their suggestions and ideas. They provide many services in this field.

The first step is to determine the changes to be made. The following pages of check lists will facilitate analysis and serve as a base from which to make recommendations.

Check (x) condition of item observed	Alter	Install	Paint	Repair	Replace	Refinish	Rearrange	Remove	Conceal	Build	Clean	Other	Enter cost estimate
EXTERIOR — **FACE OF BUILDING**													
Poor appearance..........													
Poor condition............													
Unsuitable color..........													
Unsuitable material.......													
ELECTRIC SIGNS													
Poor appearance..........													
Poor condition............													
Poor color...............													
Illegible.................													
Insecure.................													
Poor position.............													
Improper size.............													
WINDOW LETTERING AND OTHER OUTSIDE SIGNS													
Poor appearance..........													
Poor condition............													
Poor color...............													
Illegible.................													
Poor position............													
Improper size............													
Poor style...............													
Letters missing...........													
Obstructs vision..........													
GLASS IN DISPLAY WINDOWS													
Cracked.................													
Scarred.................													
Frame too heavy.........													
EXTERIOR BASE OF DISPLAY WINDOW													
Poor appearance..........													
Poor condition...........													
Unsuitable color.........													
Unsuitable material.......													
DISPLAY WINDOW PLATFORM (INTERIOR)													
Poor appearance.........													
Poor condition..........													
Improper height.........													
Too shallow.............													

Check (x) condition of item observed	Check (x) treatment needed												Enter cost estimate
	Alter	Install	Paint	Repair	Replace	Refinish	Rearrange	Remove	Conceal	Build	Clean	Other	

EXTERIOR—Con.

DISPLAY WINDOW—SIDE WALLS, CEILING AND REAR PARTITION

Poor appearance.........													
Poor condition..........													
Unsuitable material......													
Unsuitable color.........													

DISPLAY WINDOWS—LIGHTING

Inadequate..............													
Glaring.................													
Unduly noticeable........													
Poor style..............													

VENTILATION

Condensation...........													

AWNINGS

Poor appearance.........													
Poor condition..........													
Poor color..............													
Poor style..............													
Improper height.........													

PLASTIC TRANSPARENT SUN SHADES

Poor appearance.........													
Poor condition..........													
Poor color..............													

ENTRANCE DOORS

Poor appearance.........													
Poor condition..........													
Hard to operate.........													
Wrong location or size....													
Knobs poorly located.....													
Insecure lock............													
Poor lettering...........													
Glass too small..........													
Poor screens (if used).....													

STEPS

Can ramp be built?.......													
Practicable to change floor level?............													

Check (x) condition of item observed	Check (x) treatment needed												Enter cost estimate
	Alter	Install	Paint	Repair	Replace	Refinish	Rearrange	Remove	Conceal	Build	Clean	Other	

EXTERIOR—Con. **CELLAR ENTRANCE**

Insecure door............													
Not flush with sidewalk...													
Unsafe.................													
No elevator.............													
No steps down...........													
Poor interior condition....													
Poor location...........													

OUTSIDE EQUIPMENT—VENDING MACHINES

Poor appearance.........													
Out of order.............													
Obsolete design..........													
Poorly located...........													

CURB OR CAR SERVICE SPACE

Inadequate..............													
Inconvenient............													

PARKING SPACE

Inadequate..............													
Inconvenient............													

INTERIOR **FLOORS**

Poor appearance.........													
Squeaky.................													
Rough..................													
Poorly covered...........													
Unsuitable material......													
Unsuitable color.........													
Hard to clean...........													
Undue moisture..........													

WALLS AND CEILINGS

Poor appearance.........													
Poor condition...........													
Excessive posters, etc.....													
Poor color harmony......													
Partitions needed........													
Unnecessary obstruction..													
Bad skylights............													
Leaks..................													

Check (x) condition of item observed	Check (x) treatment needed												Enter cost estimate
	Alter	Install	Paint	Repair	Replace	Refinish	Rearrange	Remove	Conceal	Build	Clean	Other	

INTERIOR—Con.   OPEN DISPLAY EQUIPMENT

Poor appearance.........													
Poor condition..........													
Excessive..............													
Unsuitable material......													
Unsuitable color........													
Faulty design..........													
Poorly placed..........													

GLASS SHOW CASES

Poor appearance.........													
Poor condition.........													
Excessive..............													
Faulty design..........													
Poorly placed..........													
Glass cracked and scarred.													

HEATING AND HEATING EQUIPMENT

Poor appearance.........													
Poor condition.........													
Inadequate.............													
Poorly placed..........													
Obsolete...............													
Exposed pipes..........													
Inefficient.............													

AIR CONDITIONING

Inefficient.............													
Inadequate.............													

FANS, REGULAR AND DRAUGHT

Poor appearance.........													
Poor conditions.........													
Inadequate.............													
Poorly placed..........													
Noisy.................													
Obsolete...............													

TRANSOMS

Poor appearance.........													
Poor condition.........													
Hard to operate........													
Do not fit.............													

Check (x) condition of item observed	Check (x) treatment needed												Enter cost estimate
	Alter	Install	Paint	Repair	Replace	Refinish	Rearrange	Remove	Conceal	Build	Clean	Other	
INTERIOR—Con. *PIPING, GAS*													
Exposed.................													
Poor condition...........													
Inadequate..............													
TELEPHONE BOOTHS													
Poor appearance..........													
Poor condition...........													
Poor location............													
Improper number........													
LIGHTING FIXTURES AND DEPARTMENTAL SIGNS													
Poor appearance..........													
Poor condition...........													
Insufficient illumination, out of order............													
Obsolete design...........													
Improperly placed........													
Glaring or obscure........													
SHELVES AND WALL CASES													
Poor appearance..........													
Poor condition...........													
Too high................													
Too deep................													
Excessive................													
Insecure.................													
Unsuitable material.......													
Unsuitable color..........													
Drawers stick............													
Doors hide merchandise...													
COUNTERS													
Poor appearance..........													
Poor condition...........													
Improper height..........													
Excessive................													
Unsuitable material.......													
Unsuitable color..........													
Faulty design............													
Long, unbroken lengths...													
Poorly placed............													

Check (x) condition of item observed	Check (x) treatment needed												Enter cost estimate
	Alter	Install	Paint	Repair	Replace	Refinish	Rearrange	Remove	Conceal	Build	Clean	Other	

INTERIOR—Con.   STRUCTURAL OBSTACLES

Columns................													
Projecting columns.......													
Offsets.................													
Partition wall...........													
Bad angles.............													
Low or varying ceilings....													
Varying floor levels.......													
Floor not on street level...													
Elevators...............													
Stairways...............													

PLUMBING

Exposed................													
Poor condition...........													
Inadequate.............													

TOILET ROOMS

Poor appearance..........													
Poor condition...........													
Inadequate number.......													
Poor location............													
Poor ventilation.........													
Poor lighting............													
Unhandy light switch.....													

WASH BASINS, SINKS, AND TOILET BOWLS

Poor appearance..........													
Obsolete design..........													
Out of order.............													
Hard to operate..........													
Unduly noisy............													
Cracks, stains, leaks......													
Unduly exposed..........													

ELECTRIC WIRING

Unpleasantly noticeable...													
Insufficiently protected....													
Inadequate for expansion of lighting equipment...													
Inadequate for present needs................													

Check (x) condition of item observed	Check (x) treatment needed												Enter cost estimate
	Alter	Install	Paint	Repair	Replace	Refinish	Rearrange	Remove	Conceal	Build	Clean	Other	

INTERIOR—Con.   REFRIGERATION, MECHANICAL

Poor appearance													
Out of order													
Poor position													
Poor drainage													
Obsolete													
Inefficient													
Noisy													

WATER COOLERS

Poor appearance													
Out of order													
Obsolete													
Inefficient													
Improper number													

CASH REGISTERS

Poor appearance													
Out of order													
Obsolete													
Inefficient													
Unduly noisy													
Unsuitable type													
Improper number													

BURGLAR ALARM

Poor condition													
Out of order													
Obsolete													
Ineffective													

INCINERATOR, TRASH, AND GARBAGE BOXES

Improper size													
Poor condition													
Improper place													
Insecure													
Fire hazard													

Check (x) condition of item observed	Check (x) treatment needed												Enter cost estimate
	Alter	Install	Paint	Repair	Replace	Refinish	Rearrange	Remove	Conceal	Build	Clean	Other	

INTERIOR—Con. FIRE EXTINGUISHERS

Improper places.........													
Poor condition..........													
Out of order............													
Obsolete................													
Inefficient..............													
Need refilling...........													
Improper number........													

OTHER FIRE EQUIPMENT

Improper places..........													
Poor condition..........													
Out of order............													
Obsolete................													
Inefficient..............													
Need refilling...........													
Improper number........													

OTHER EQUIPMENT (ADD AS REQUIRED)

Poor appearance.........													
Poor condition..........													
Out of order............													
Obsolete................													
Inefficient..............													
Unduly noisy............													
Improper number........													
Improper places..........													

OTHER EQUIPMENT (ADD AS REQUIRED)

Poor appearance.........													
Poor condition..........													
Out of order............													
Obsolete................													
Inefficient..............													
Unduly noisy............													
Improper number........													
Improper places..........													

Chapter 49

SALES MEETINGS
AND CONFERENCES

SALES meetings, conferences, distributors' conventions, dealer meetings, all play a useful and well-justified role in the process of stimulating business. Meetings for distributors especially have widened their functions and intensified their sales objectives. In major companies they have become an indispensable part of the launching of new lines on a national basis.

While sales meetings and conventions are good selling tools, one factor which tends to retard their greater use is that of cost. Some conventions staged by large organizations approach the dimensions of a Broadway production, especially if the meeting be tied in with prize incentive trips for dealers and salesmen. Even here, if total cost is in proper percentage relation to the overall volume of business obtained, the expense is justified.

These major meetings may also have additional sales functions by being made the occasion for interviews with the press and "open house" for local dealers' representatives or salesmen. Too, they afford an excellent opportunity to bring all the elements of a national sales organization together at one place, at one time, with many smaller, private, more intimate contacts between management and the companies comprising its channels of distribution.

In an interview reported in *Advertising Age,* Bert Y. Auger, general manager of the visual products division of 3M Company, and author of *How to Run Better Business Meetings,* said:

"Meetings are vital to 3M. The company holds hundreds annually, and we are deeply concerned with their cost in terms of time and money."

He estimated that about 10,000,000 businessmen participate in all types of business meetings each year, representing an investment of millions of man-hours and dollars. As a rule of thumb to determine the hourly cost of a meeting, double the value of the pay per hour of each person attending, he suggested. To this add the special preparation costs.

Figuring this way, Mr. Auger calculated that at a meeting with 10 participants whose average salary is $10,000 a year, the cost for each hour of the meeting would be $96, plus preparation costs.

What Makes an Effective Sales Meeting?

Ask this of 12 people and you are likely to get a dozen answers.

Walter G. McGuire, director, training and development division, National Biscuit Company, points out that while each of the 12 replies undoubtedly could be correct, a successful sales meeting must contain two basic ingredients—preparation and proper climate. As a matter of fact, the decor of the room alone may have an audience 50 percent sold on a program. McGuire wrote this for *Sales Meetings* magazine:

To aid the discussion leader, we furnish him with a variety of communication tools. One of the most important of these is motion pictures.

A discussion leader, no matter how well prepared, can talk just so much. Therefore, we use films liberally in conjunction with and as a foundation for the overall program. As we use them, films eliminate the lecture as the basis for discussion. They stimulate interpersonal responses that a speaker alone could not generate.

We have built up an extensive library of films that can be used to supplement almost any type of programming assistance requested.

We have a staff group that serves as a consultant for training services to the divisions within the company. The divisions then operate with their own training personnel.

To plan a seminar or workshop, a division merely asks for assistance. Based on its individual goals or objectives, we suggest a program. However, the interested division's training personnel executes and evaluates the particular program.

Most of the sales-management seminars, clinics, workshops, forums, conferences, etc., are held in the New York City headquarters where we have a variety of types and sizes of meeting and presentation rooms. The average room will accommodate 12 to 18 people seated "classroom" style.

Programs for the most part are based on an eight-hour day, with some night assignments, depending on the content activity. While they are carefully planned and prepared, the schedules are distributed to participating speakers but not to the audience. This gives the program an element of surprise and permits last-minute changes without disturbing the audience.

In all, we have nine different films in our library, ranging in subject from dealing with subordinates and their relation to the company to ways of approaching customers.

In the final analysis then, sales meetings, to be effective, should contain these ingredients: Careful planning, proper environment, and a well-prepared discussion leader equipped with the tools to set and maintain the tempo.

Ocean Spray Meeting Plan

Ocean Spray Cranberries' meetings mean business, according to Lester F. Haines, general sales manager.

"Our sales meetings contribute enormously to the success of our $50-million-a-year marketing organization," says Haines. "Normally, we hold three or four such meetings a year. One is always held at the same time as the National Food Brokers' convention. This gives members of our sales and marketing staff an opportunity to review with each broker, the regional sales manager and his assistant, all activities in their area, including our advertising and sales-promotion programs.

"Our organization's own meetings are planned to inform and stimulate the sales organization. We usually have our 12 salesmen, plus myself, my assistant, someone from our advertising department, our director of marketing, our chief executive officer, and a representative of the Nielsen Company. These meetings are normally held in a resort area because it provides a better atmosphere with more opportunity for exchange of ideas without external distractions."

American Oil's Premeeting Guide

The American Oil Company provides those responsible for conducting its sales meetings with a premeeting guide containing the following:

I. PLAN EVERY SALES MEETING AS FAR IN ADVANCE OF MEETING DATE AS POSSIBLE

    a. Anticipate the need for a meeting before it arrives.

    b. Reduce your plan to writing.

    c. Discuss your plan with other members of management.

    d. Check the need for meeting with sales representatives.

    e. Establish time and place when meeting will be most effective.

    f. List the objectives to be accomplished at the meeting.

    g. Eliminate every nonessential from your meeting plan.

II. PREPARE THE MEETING PROGRAM

    a. List the general subjects to be presented at proposed meeting.

    b. Assign subjects to individuals best equipped to present them.

c. Confer with each individual to establish main points that need emphasis in each presentation and to eliminate duplication.

d. Ask for a written, rough draft of each presentation.

e. Arrange the sequence of subjects to be presented so they will fit into an integrated program that will lend emphasis to each item in proportion to its importance.

f. Study all "first rough drafts" in terms of materials available for clues to methods of dramatizing their main points.

   1. Review your inventory of materials and equipment available for making effective presentations.

   2. List materials and equipment available from outside sources that might be helpful in making your proposed meeting more effective.

   3. Study trade journals, house journals and reference materials for showmanship ideas you can adapt to the points needing emphasis.

   4. Suggest to each speaker the methods you recommend for emphasizing with showmanship the points he has indicated and you agree need emphasis.

In addition to their cost—company expense and cost of salesmen's time—meetings can succeed in imparting incorrect information. This

An attractive meeting place adds much to the success-potentials of sales meetings. This Kimberly-Clark Sales Center auditorium seats about 200 persons, and is provided with all facilities for use either as a conference room or a "theater" for skits, playlets, and films, for sales-training and sales-promotion meetings.

was touched upon in the following memo sent by a company's sales manager to his regional and district sales supervisors:

The sales department spends more time in meetings than any other group in our company. These meetings are costly from point of view of actual expense, the time salesmen lose in selling, and the misdirection or misinformation salesmen may carry away because your message was not sharp and clear. Your company can profit from a better organized and more dramatically presented sales message. Some of the areas to be considered are:

I. *Preparation*

  A. Planning (mental activity)

    1. Determining needs

      a. What

      b. How

    2. Establish objective

    3. People to attend

      a. Who should

      b. Why should they

      c. Why do they *think* they should

      d. How much do they already know

      e. What are they to do as a result

      f. Who will object

      g. Who will help

    4. Physical aspects

      a. When

      b. Where

      c. How long

      d. Physical setup

      e. Frequency

    5. Take a second look at objectives

    6. Contact necessary personnel

      a. For information

      b. For assistance

      c. To get them concerned

      d. To delegate responsibility

  B. Organizing

    1. Determine general areas to be covered

    2. Outline

      a. Opening

        (1) Opening remarks

        (2) Introductions

        (3) Purpose of meeting

      b. Select main topics

        (1) Develop

        (2) Arrange

      c. Select methods and techniques

      d. Closing

        (1) Summarize

        (2) Appeal for action

        (3) End on high note

II. *Presentation*

  A. General factors

    1. Methods and techniques

    2. Motivation and climate

    3. Use of props

    4. Change of pace

    5. Pass-out material

    6. Notes

    7. Tempo

    8. Level

  B. Individual factors

    1. Personal appearance

    2. Confidence

    3. Enthusiasm

    4. Sincerity

    5. Knowledge of subject

    6. Vocal habits

    7. Eye contact

    8. Mannerisms

III. *Evaluation*

  A. Methods

MEETING EVALUATION REPORT

Executive's Name
Session
Date

Check Appropriate Box

ITEM	Excellent	Very Good	Good	Fair	Poor	REMARKS:
						REMARKS - PLEASE FILL IN
General Format of Meeting						
Subject Matter: Adequate, Too Much, Too Little						
Organization of Material						
Originality						
Enthusiasm, Sincerity						
Achieve Purpose						

ADDITIONAL REMARKS:

_____

_____

_____

_____

_____

_____

(Use other side if necessary)

As a followup for sales meetings, one company distributes such forms as this to its sales supervisors and other executives who attend the company's periodical sales meetings. The forms are then used as a basis for evaluating each meeting and for planning improvements when needed.

How to Inject Excitement

A national sales meeting that achieved enthusiasm, excitement, interest, and drama was conducted by the Simmons Company. "It was a big, bold, brassy, well-timed sales meeting that left 300 salesmen and guests cheering in the aisles after five solid days," said Richard Jager, director of advertising and merchandising. Here is his account of the affair:

Our selling, advertising, and marketing approaches were packaged with a Western motif with the theme "Sales Stampede '67." We announced the meeting a month in advance with a "wanted" poster shot full of holes. One week before the meeting, we mailed horseshoes with an announcement of an informal get-together on the day of arrival.

Our salesmen were met by costumed cowgirls. A sign hung on the wall read, "Howdy Pardner—Round up Area for Simmons Sales Stampede—Sixty-Seven." They were whisked to the Dorchester Inn in bannered buses.

We made a five-story billboard out of the Dorchester by attaching letters to the exterior to form the message: "Howdy Partners! Welcome to Simmons Sales Stampede Sixty-Seven."

Inside the hotel we set up a message center with three Simmons "cowgirls" and called it the "Hitching Post."

In the lobby, preregistered salesmen picked up room keys and kits, including string ties, sheriff's badges, and meeting instructions, from attractive cowgirls.

First, we made a decision to hold a "big-time" national meeting rather than the regional meetings we used in previous years. We wanted to re-emphasize the leadership of Simmons in the industry. This could not be done in regional meetings. I believe the advantage of a national meeting lies in its opportunity to impress salesmen by assembling top management and key personnel from production, engineering, research, and advertising departments, and overseas personnel.

A second purpose was to permit a thorough presentation of voluminous information to salesmen.

The five-day meeting was divided into two segments. From Monday to Tuesday afternoon, our 16 district managers met for a preview of the program.

On Tuesday, the managers prepared plans and objectives for their teams while rehearsals for the general sales meeting (Wednesday to Friday) were being held. We let the managers spend the rest of the day digesting what they had heard, formulating ideas and questions and relating this information to their districts.

The key elements of the general sales meeting were the presentations in the Ol' Opry House, where every element was carefully chosen to assure variety, and to avoid boredom.

The program required a five-page closely typed outline complete in every respect.

On Wednesday morning, sales vice-president Freir McCollister, garbed in Western attire, opened the meeting with a fusillade of blanks from his six-shooters. From that moment until the climax on Friday, we used every theatrical trick in the book to build interest and suspense, and to prove "The Best Is Even Better."

While the salesmen were at the meeting, their wives received a gift in the mail. Under a special arrangement, *Life* magazine, in which we advertise extensively, mailed a cookbook (retail value $13.95) with a letter to tell wives, "Big things are cooking in Chicago this week . . ."

We taped the songs and will use them at future meetings for our retail salesmen.

When the meeting was over it still had promotional value. We took about 100 of the best photographs and made up a gigantic folder for our salesmen. We mailed extra copies of this folder to salesmen later as a reminder of the excitement of the meeting—with the promise of more and better things to come.

Building Advance Interest

Advance interest is an intangible quality that can assure the success of a meeting before the doors are opened. This is the conviction of specialists who have had an opportunity to watch, analyze, and participate in a large number of sales meetings and conventions conducted by some of America's most sales-conscious companies. Here are some remarks about premeeting promotion by a sales-meeting consultant:

Promotion in relation to sales meetings should not be limited entirely to efforts to lure or increase attendance. Promotional techniques can be very helpful in creating audience interest and receptivity. If, for example, you are assured of maximum attendance because you will have a captive audience of your own sales force, promotion can be used to channel and influence thinking with respect to the meeting. This will give you a valuable head start before your meeting gets underway.

Successful premeeting promotion will also simplify your programing at the meeting: Instead of facing the double task of creating and sustaining interest, you will need only be concerned with the latter problem. And you'll have to admit that it's a big one. What are some ways to promote a sales meeting? A floor-covering company created a corporate character, embodying its trademark, in a meeting it held to introduce its new line, advertising and sales promotion to its distributors. The corporate character had an important role in the meeting itself, appearing throughout the two days. But he also played an equally important role in the preconditioning promotion. Instead of the usual invitation, a special folder was created. This featured a picture of the corporate character that introduced him to the prospective audience and insured his recognition when he appeared early in the meeting. Beyond that, however, it titillated the audience's curiosity and served as a teaser, an attention-getter, and helped to increase reading of the explanatory copy that announced the meeting and explained its aims. The promotion did not just invite. It excited interest, too.

When a bottling company announced a new sales-training program, it used a novel promotion mailing piece. It introduced three films that were to be used. While the films were not in 3D, the promotion piece was.

Other Ways to Get Them to Meetings

Two sunrise seminars conducted at a recent meeting of Sales and Marketing Executives—International in Boston had other benefits besides content of sessions. They relieved the early morning coffee shop rush and helped to start the regular sessions on time. Attendees had continental breakfast at 7:30; went to meetings at 8:00.

To get early registrations, SME ran a contest in which members had to register before December 31. Each member guessed the number of beans in a bean pot; the winner's wife got a free trip to the convention. To get members to pay convention fees early, SME gave the registrant a chance at a five-day, post-convention trip to Bermuda to both the winner and his wife.

To encourage full attendance at business sessions, the American Society of Travel Agents gave points to members. For each session, delegates received a chance on a car that was awarded on the last night of the convention.

Topics for a meeting of the American Society for Association Executives were picked by members. ASAE sent a ballot listing 30 possible subjects. The result was a series of concurrent classroom sessions.

To determine which members will attend the meeting and which ones will stay at home, Direct Mail Advertising Association ran "Conference Sweepstakes." To be eligible, members had to return a card indicating whether or not they were coming. The cards were numbered. Prizes were a round-trip flight to the meeting and 99 other prizes.

Starting Meetings on Time

David F. Schlothauer, of the L. G. Balfour Company, Attleboro, Massachusetts, makes a point of starting sales meetings on time. In a statement to Dartnell, he said:

Our meetings start promptly and finish as scheduled without a lot of "hoopla." Time is valuable, so we insist that even our executives be punctual. We also feel that people who arrive on schedule ought not be penalized for the tardiness of others.

The establishment of a businesslike atmosphere and the fact that our men can count on our following the schedule brings appreciation, respect, and attention.

Since the atmosphere for the meeting must be created by management, we try to add the courteous, thoughtful gestures that make the individual feel we want him at the meeting and appreciate his coming. While there are many ways to do that, one simple gesture helps considerably in this respect. We try always to have at least one member of the management team at the door to greet the attendees or to be at the door during breaks for the purpose of answering questions and helping with problems.

Using Gifts and Gadgets

The Douglas Furniture Corporation also likes to start all its sessions on time. To encourage attendance and punctuality, it gave a handsome cigarette lighter to all salesmen who presented themselves on or before starting time the first session in the morning.

Many executives have found that a gift, whether tied to attendance or punctuality, is a good way to bring a man into a meeting on time and in a pleasant mood. The gift item need not be expensive to work its magic. Those who use them frequently report that the most appreciated gift is one that is unusual and shows evidence of some personal attention.

Douglas Furniture reports that its salesmen are still talking about the pocket handkerchiefs they received several years ago, each one with the man's name embroidered on it so that when correctly folded the name was visible as an identification "badge."

A device that has been rather widely used at big meetings, where attendance is a problem, is the door prize. Many meetings offer cash or merchandise prizes to the holders of lucky ticket stubs. It is generally required that the stub be placed in the ticket box *before the meeting has been started* and that *the winner be present at the end of the meeting* when the drawing takes place.

Here are a few other recommendations for getting the meeting off to a good start:

Have staff members and company executives greet each person as he registers or enters the meeting room.

If the meeting is an early morning one, serve an informal breakfast.

Serve coffee near the registration area or the entrance to the meeting room, but shut off the supply well before the first session starts.

Try to have staff members act as ushers. Don't let hotel employees try to herd your group out of the lobby and into the meeting rooms.

Pay special attention to those who are attending your meeting for the first time. Assign a host or "buddy" to each one. Don't let them get lost, or miss events through lack of knowledge.

In general, try to be the best possible host according to the scale of your operation. Don't overdo things, but consider how you would like to be treated and visualize the guidance needed by a majority of your audience.

Brief your staff on all arrangements. Make sure they know where to turn for help. Try to have a few extra hands available for special assignments. You can be sure that several unexpected things will happen and that you will need help to run messages, move things, and so forth.

Checklist of Physical Facilities

For a meeting to get off to a good start, the physical environment of the room must play its part. To make sure that meeting-room facilities are adequate, The American Oil Company provides this checklist:

1. Are entrance and exit facilities correct for size of audience?

2. Have you provided safety factors—checked fire hazards, floor-load capacity, fire exits, and responsibility of lessor?

3. Have you provided necessary utilities—kinds of electricity, washroom facilities, air conditioning, remote-control switches, adequate fuses, drinking fountains, etc?

4. Have you made certain that meeting room is large enough but not too large for the audience and that it has proper acoustics, light, heat, air, comfortable chairs, window blinds for darkening room if slide or motion-picture projector is to be used, space for room displays, projection facilities, and is away from distracting noises?

5. Does meeting room provide adequate space for setting up and taking down properties planned, and does it have enough height for them? Are backstage entrance and off-stage workroom available, if they will be required?

6. Have you obtained necessary house props, such as blackboards, stage chairs, stage lamps, stage desks, carpets, steps to stage, remote-control switch, P.A. system, and so forth?

7. Have you made arrangements for necessary house services, such as piano, smoking stands, janitor to clean meeting room, electrician with fuses, porter services for house props, and necessary labor for setting up and tearing down?

8. Have you confirmed in writing:

    a. All assignments of speakers to appear on your program?

    b. Date(s) and place(s) of meeting(s) to speakers, audience, and to house management where meeting is to be held?

    c. *To meeting room crew:* To decorate and clean rooms; to arrange seats for correct sight lines; to handle ventilation, heat, etc., during meeting; to distribute materials to audience; to handle guest registrations; to serve as ushers in handling crowd; to post signs that direct audience to meeting room; to provide drinking water for speaker; and to provide drinking fountains and washroom facilities for audience?

    d. *To property men:* To secure and troop props; to crate and uncrate props; to help dress stage; to design, build, and set up room displays, product displays, etc.; to know all prop cues for meeting; to check all fuse boxes, carry extra fuses and stand by during meeting; and to troop working tools and repair materials needed for meeting?

    e. *To projection men,* if projection is being used; to troop projection equipment; to set up projection facilities; to operate projection equipment, signal systems, P.A. system, microphones, remote-control switch on house lights, etc.; to know all projection cues; to correct acoustics, if necessary; and to install window blinds for projection?

f. *To stage manager* (if stage is to be used): To set up stage; to dress stage; to handle traveler during meeting; to handle lights during meeting; to change scenery; to handle sound effects; to strike scenes and sets; and to know all stage cues?

g. *To utility men* (if plans are for a large meeting): To arrange for and handle entertainment, food, refreshments, etc.; to handle emergencies, special props, calls, errands, etc.; to handle special lighting; to serve as prompter on cues; to serve as prompter on stage; to assist in handling crowd; and to assist other departments with special assignments?

Getting Men to Participate

It is generally agreed among sales executives that it is essential for salesmen to take an active part in meetings. A passive audience is likely to be a disinterested, unreceptive one. Here are some hints from "How to Get Group Participation in Sales Training," prepared by the National Society of Sales Training Executives:

1. *Explain Exactly What You Want:* This saves breaking in to correct the man's impression of what he is supposed to do. When you want a salesman to do a task, say, "First I want you to do this; second, this; and third, this. Do I make it clear?" If the man says he understands, ask him to explain what he is going to do and how.

2. *Keep After Them Until They Cooperate:* You can get a group to do anything in a meeting if you keep after it. You asked, "Are there any questions?" The group looks at you as if it hasn't heard. You ask, "Will someone come up and demonstrate this machine for me?" No one moves. If you want questions or participation, keep after the group until it responds. Don't give up.

3. *Illustrate What You Want:* When you ask a salesman to take part, illustrate what you want him to do. Do the demonstration first. Now say, "I'm going to do this again because I am then going to ask one of you to do it." You then ask, "How many think you can do it now?" If you give them enough illustration of what you want, they feel they can't miss.

4. *Start Early in the Session:* If you want the group to take part, start asking for it early in the session. The introductions help to do this. Ask for a show of hands. Have each answer the question: "How long have you been in selling?" Ask the man to stand and give his name and his home town or his company. Get some of this into the first 10 minutes.

5. *Use Numbers:* In describing certain tasks, use numbers to help you explain. Salesmen seem to respond better when the task is broken down into numbered steps.

6. *Let Him Have the Spotlight:* When the salesman starts his performance, step off the stage and take a seat in the audience. Have him do his presentation to the group, not to you. When the leader stands beside the participant, many of the group will be watching the leader to see how he takes the performance.

7. *Use the Compliment:* You can't make a man angry by patting him on the back. Be free with honest praise. Get that word: "honest." But when a man volunteers to try a task for you, he deserves a compliment just for that willingness to try. Usually the man will do some parts of his presentation well. Ask the group if they noticed how well he handled one point.

8. *Be Patient:* A leader needs patience. When you ask a salesman to do a task, let him do it his way. If he is slow, don't break in and take over. Let him finish. Watch what he does with interest. Listen intently. Why should the group listen to him, if you show that you are not listening?

9. *Think of His Self-Esteem:* You will note that many of the suggestions for handling participation help the man keep his self-esteem. The suggestion of courtesy, the compliment, starting with the small bits and going on to the more difficult—all these are designed to give the man recognition, and to help him keep his self-esteem. In a sales meeting, if you hurt the feelings of one participant you draw resentment from the group. Build up always, don't tear down.

10. *Too Much Is Too Much:* While group participation is a big help in meetings, it is possible to use too much. The best meetings are those that have a good balance of all of the methods that help men sell better. Too much audience participation in a session can get tiresome. If the morning is to be given over to practice selling, the wise leader plans so that he can break in at a low point with demonstrations, voice exercises, or other such devices to change the tempo of the session.

The Question-and-Answer Period

Participation can be engendered by a lively question-and-answer period. The most common reasons given by sales managers for using Q&A periods in sales meetings are:

1. To get audience participation in the meeting.

2. To help the audience relate the information to their own situations back home.

3. To rate audience reception and understanding of the information disseminated.

4. To observe which presentations are the most effective.

Variations of the following basic methods may be used to increase the quantity and quality of questions:

Method I—A Guide to Listening: Print or mimeograph a list of categories or areas in which you feel significant questions should be asked. Leave space under each listing of the categories so that each salesman can write any questions that occur to him concerning that category. Call for the questions by category.

Method II—Audience Listening Teams: Divide the audience into teams of approximately equal size, with the number of teams being determined by the specific areas of questions you want "listened for." Assign each team the area in which it will concentrate its questions and instruct each individual to write down questions as they occur to him.

Divide the time allotted for the question period into as many parts as there are listening teams. During this allotted time, team members bring up the questions that concern their particular area.

Another procedure is to ask each member of the audience to write one question in the area of listening to which he has been assigned. These are then picked up, sorted, and answered, section by section.

Method III—Buzz Groups: Ask the salesmen to move their chairs into circles of six or eight. Tell the audience that its task in these buzz groups is to select the one or two most important questions in an assigned area of listening. Each group appoints one of its number as a spokesman to report its findings to the total audience.

Write the questions on a blackboard or project them on a screen. They are then answered from the platform. An interesting variation is to have the buzz-group spokesman join the speakers on the platform to discuss the points developed by the listening teams.

Following are a number of suggestions for making the most of the question-and-answer session:

WHEN THE LEADER ASKS QUESTIONS: The quiz session looks easy—all you need is a list of questions. But don't be fooled. The quiz is a discussion tool. You want it to help your salesmen solve their selling problems. A question such as, "How many benefits does this plan have?" may seem fine when you write it, but how much help will the answer give the group? A question such as, "How would you use this benefit to sell a prospect?" might be better.

The List of Questions: Let's say you come to the session with a list of questions; you can pass out the list and ask one man which question he cannot answer. He says, "Number 5." Ask others the same question and write the numbers mentioned on the blackboard. Then ask, "Who can answer Number 5?" Let the volunteer answer. The numbers on the blackboard might indicate which points have not been clarified.

Start With One Who Can Answer: Some leaders like to start the quiz session by asking the first question of a man the leader feels can come up with a good answer. The quiz might seem unfair if the first few called on fumble in answering. Experience proves that quizzes get off to a better start if the first question is assigned to a man who has a high interest in the subject.

WHEN SALESMEN ASK QUESTIONS: "Are There Any Questions?" This is a weak start for a quiz session. It's weaker when the leader gets no immediate response and then follows the question with, "Well, Mr. Ajax, you must have covered the subject mighty well, for there seems to be no questions." If you want questions, plan to get questions. There are a number of devices you can use to get questions started.

When They Won't Reply: Let's say you ask, "Are there any questions?" The group sits there looking at you as if it hasn't heard. You ask again, and still no response. You can say, "Well, if you know this subject so well, it won't hurt if *I* ask you a few questions about it." You ask the first question, and say, "Joe, you answer that one, please." Usually you will not have to ask more than three questions before the group has thought of a number of questions it wants to ask.

The "Plant" Can Help: To get questions started give out questions to three or four of the group. After a few of these planted questions, the group will start asking.

Have Salesmen Write Out the Questions: Pass out blank cards and have salesmen write out questions that they would like to have answered. Collect these, and sort out the duplicate questions. Have the salesmen sign the cards so that you can give credit to the man who asks it. To make sure you get enough questions from the group, write out some yourself.

GETTING THE QUESTION REPEATED: This is the most difficult problem you have when questions are asked in a meeting. A question is asked by a man in the front row. The leader starts to answer without repeating. The men in the back rows do not hear the question and they wonder what it is all about. Here are some suggestions for getting the question repeated:

The Leader Repeats It: The leader opens the quiz session by asking, "Who has the first question?" When a question is asked, the leader repeats it. This assures that everyone hears, and it gives the leader or speaker a few seconds to think about his answer.

A Sign on the Wall: A sign on the back wall of the meeting room, "Repeat the Question Please," may help. Some companies use a flasher sign. If the speaker starts to answer without repeating, the sign starts to flash. It also helps to have a sign in front of the speaker.

LEADER'S ATTITUDE IN QUIZ SESSION: In a quiz session, the leader is there to help the group. That attitude should show. You are not there to show how much you know, or to get laughs. If, after the session, the salesmen do not know the answers, whose fault is it? Not theirs!

Thus, when a salesman asks a question that shows he did not understand something, say, "Oh, I guess we did not make that point clear." That wording indicates that you are at fault for not making the point clear. In the quiz session, the leader admits that he doesn't know all the answers. It is good to tell the group frankly, "I can answer a lot of them, but not all. I do know where to get the answers, and I'll do my best to get them for you." If you show that you are trying to help, your quiz sessions will go over better.

THE LEADER'S PLAN FOR ANSWERING:

1. *He listens to the question,* all of it. Even though the first words tell him what the question is, he lets the man finish. He doesn't show his impatience in any way.

2. *He repeats the question.* This allows all of the group to hear the question, and gives the man who asked it a chance to agree that the leader has understood.

3. *He answers the question.*

4. *He checks the answer.* He asks the questioner, "Does that answer your question?"

5. *He asks one of the group to repeat the answer.* This is used as a check on whether or not the answer was clear to the group.

Appeal to the Active Senses

The discussion technique offers another way to give salesmen the important sense of being involved in a meeting. It appeals to active senses of seeing, hearing, and feeling. The participant sees the visuals, he hears what others have to say, and he gets into the act himself to ask questions and present his ideas. He writes notes, he reads the visuals and quiz sheets. Salesmen like to talk, to express their ideas, and to listen to other salesmen express theirs.

There are some drawbacks, too. The discussion session takes time, more time than a lecture on the same subject. Further, it takes more planning. While most discussion sessions seem to run without much control, that appearance is a result of planning. Following are some helpful suggestions:

SETTING UP FOR THE DISCUSSION SESSION: To set up for a discussion session you need:

A—An outline of what will be covered.

B—Some notes for opening remarks that sell the group on taking part because of the good each salesman can get out of the discussion.

C—A blackboard or easel pad, with chalk or crayon.

D—Notebooks for the participants. Sell the group on using the notebooks. If you see that they are not making notes, say, "Everybody write this down."

E—Tables or desks on which the participants can write. Arrange these informally. Don't have too much space between the leader and the participants.

The Chairman's Job in the Discussion: The job of the chairman is a lot like that of a committee chairman. He starts the discussion, brings up the points in order, and keeps the discussion on the track.

He makes sure that each point gets the time it should have, he watches to see that one point does not hog all of the time. He sees that the points are summed up, and guides the group in sifting out conclusions.

The Discussion Outline: The leader needs an outline of the subjects to be covered. This can be made up by the chairman or can be made up by the group. If you make it up, list the main points to be covered and the minor points under each main point. Even when the group makes up the outline, it is well for the chairman to have an outline so that he can check the group's suggestions to see if it has forgotten any points that should be covered.

Building-a-Plan Session: This type of session is handled much like the one that builds a sales story. Let's say you want to build a plan for a call on a customer. The leader asks, "What is the first thing you do when you call on a customer?" He asks one participant to describe what he does first, second, third, and so on. Now he asks a second, "Is that the way you do it?" If the man agrees, he asks him to describe his procedure in detail. Then the leader asks, "Who does it differently?" Now he gets more ideas. Each is discussed and in the end the group winds up with a procedure that is approved by the group, and one that the leader will not have much trouble getting the salesmen to try.

The Boasting Session: In this type of session, the salesmen tell how they did a certain job. In organizing such a session, give the men an outline to follow. There never was an unsuccessful boasting session. Salesmen love to tell how they used sales strategy in making a sale. Other salesmen listening to these stories learn from the descriptions of plans that have worked. The leader might ask the salesman to follow the steps of the standard sales procedure. The salesman's story might then be organized to answer the statements below:

My survey showed this........................

Because of this, I used these facts in my approach........................

My presentation covered these points........................

My appeal for action was........................

The objections I got were........................

Here's how I handled each........................

It is not absolutely necessary to have such an outline, but it will help organize the stories and it will not handicap the men.

The Gripe Session: In this type of session the salesman gets his beefs off his chest. This is good for morale, and out of participation in it a man gets ideas that will help him in his job. Salesman A has a complaint. He comes to the session and goes to town on it. Much to his amazement he finds that none of the other salesmen feel that his complaint is important. He learns, too, that other salesmen have found ways of handling this complaint. He goes away resolving to try these ideas and to see if they will work for him.

Perhaps he comes with an idea that one item in the line is a "turkey." He finds that the other fellows are selling it. But he has his say and the attitude of the others convinces him that, perhaps, he is wrong. Maybe he is smarter because he sees the defects in this "turkey." But, if others can sell it, he can too. This kind of session can be called by any name that tells the participant he is going to get his chance to get his gripes off his chest. In this type of session the leader encourages the salesmen to tell all and uses questions to get them started.

Role-Playing in Meetings

The value of role-playing for sales training has been recognized for almost a decade. In the good old standby, one salesman plays the part of a customer, and another plays the salesman. An alternate plan is to have a sales supervisor take the role of the customer while the salesmen try to sell him. Or a top salesman using a toy telephone can show how he secures appointments with hard-to-see prospects.

Several years ago the Brown-Forman Distillers Corporation used a larger cast, including a role-playing "newspaper reporter," to tell the company story at a regional sales meeting. In the hypothetical situation, the reporter was gathering material for a feature story on the history and operations of the company. The scene was a hotel room, and four members of the company's top management in marketing, bottling, financing, and engineering, played themselves.

Keeping closely to an agreed-upon outline, the reporter asked leading questions to which the others could reply from their own broad knowledge and experience. Because the whole setting was informal, the speakers were able to comment upon each other's presentation and reinforce or assist a speaker as he went along.

By eliminating a formal speech, which would probably have had to be either read or memorized, these men, experts in their field and with plenty of product knowledge, were able to relax and to say what they had to say in their own way. This spontaneity made for sincerity and for really effective communication. The audience was "involved" and interested instead of being the object of a lot of speechifying.

This was not a skit with a script, but a spontaneous presentation based on an outline that guided the reporter so that he served as the voice of the audience, with whom the salesmen were able to identify themselves. To reinforce this natural condition, the role of the reporter was played by one of the men in the sales department.

The effectiveness of the presentation was tested by a post-meeting reaction form in which the salesmen were asked to tell how they felt about the meeting and to list the reasons for their likes and dislikes. The most frequent comment from the salesmen related to the number of facts about Brown-Forman products they had gleaned from the presentation. Second most frequent comment dealt with the "sincerity," "informality," and "spontaneity" of the presentation. Another comment was, "The meeting gave me a much better understanding of the company and the men who run it."

Films, visual aids, playlets, all play their parts in sales meetings. But whether a sales manager is designing sessions for new recruits or refresher courses for his salesmen, he cannot do better than to place role-playing of salesmen selling to buyers high on his agenda. That is the way men master lessons, learn from each other, and obtain experience in selling their products which will revitalize them at the course and help them to sell more when they are back on their territories.

Handling "Problem" Personalities

Almost every sales meeting will have at least one "problem" personality—the aggressor who may start out to deflate the status of others, a recognition-seeker who wants to call attention to himself, a playboy who tends to divert the group's activities by offhand (or off-color) remarks, and the like.

An electrical manufacturing company, for example, had one salesman who regularly caused trouble at its sales meetings by his know-it-all attitude. Trouble is, he did know a lot. On one account alone, his commissions amounted to $30,000 a year. Thus, while he was the most troublesome character at the meetings, he was also the most successful. The company soothed, if not solved, the situation by throwing him the load and giving him a dominant role in its meetings so that he was both too busy and too involved himself to snipe and sneer.

Following is a checklist developed by the American Automobile Association to help those who conduct its sales meetings spot potential troublemakers and deal with them.

HOW HE ACTS:	*Professional Heckler*
WHY:	Combative personality or highly argumentative. May be normally good-natured but distracted by personal or job problems.
WHAT TO DO:	Keep your own temper in check . . .
	Don't let other men get excited either.
	Honestly try to find merit in one of his points . . . express your agreement and then move on to something else.
	When he makes an obvious misstatement of facts, toss it to the sales force and let them turn it down.
	As a last resort, talk to this man privately and try to find out what's bothering him . . . see if you can get his cooperation.
HOW HE ACTS:	*Rambler*
WHY:	Can't stay put on subject at hand. One idea leads to another and he gets lost, miles away from original point he was making.
WHAT TO DO:	Watch for the time when he stops for breath, thank him, refocus his attention on pertinent subject, and then move on.
	In a humorous way, tell him point is interesting, but in a friendly manner indicate we are slightly off subject.
	As a last resort, glance at your watch, remarking that time is limited.
HOW HE ACTS:	*Side Conversationalist*
WHY:	Conversation may be related to subject matter, but is usually personal or just plain nonsense.
WHAT TO DO:	Don't embarrass him . . . but call him by name and ask an easy question.
	Also can call him by name, then restate last opinion expressed or last remark, and ask his opinion of it.
	In this case, participating is the best cure for inattention. Get the conversationalist into the act.
HOW HE ACTS:	*Obstinate Guy*

WHY:	This guy won't budge—he's prejudiced in favor of his own viewpoint, regardless of the logic of the other side. He either can't or won't see your point.
WHAT TO DO:	Throw his view out to the sales force, and see if they won't straighten him out. Tell him time is short; you'll be glad to discuss it later. Suggest he accept the group viewpoint for the moment so the subject at hand can be discussed further.
HOW HE ACTS:	*Griper*
WHY:	This salesman either has a pet peeve, gripes for the sake of complaining, or in some cases has a legitimate complaint.
WHAT TO DO:	Point out that policy can't be changed on the spur of the moment at a sales meeting; the problem at hand is to operate as efficiently and cooperatively as possible under the present system. Then indicate you'll discuss the problem with him privately, later.
	In some cases, it works to have a member of the sales force answer instead of you.
HOW HE ACTS:	*Overly Talkative*
WHY:	You'll find this salesman is usually one of four types: (1) an "eager beaver"; (2) a show-off; (3) exceptionally well-informed and anxious to show it; or (4) just plain garrulous.
WHAT TO DO:	Don't be embarrassing or sarcastic . . . you may need his traits at a later time. Instead, slow him down with some difficult questions.
	Or jump in with: "That's an interesting point . . . now let's see what the sales force thinks of it."
	In general, let the group take care of him as much as possible.
HOW HE ACTS:	*Not Understandable*
WHY:	He may be a fair salesman but in front of more than one person he lacks the ability to put his thoughts in proper order. He has an idea but is unable to convey it, and he needs help.
WHAT TO DO:	Don't say, "What you mean is this."
	Say, "Let me repeat that." (Then explain the idea in clear language.)
HOW HE ACTS:	*Definitely Wrong*
WHY:	Salesman who comes up with comment that is obviously incorrect.
WHAT TO DO:	Say, "I can see how you feel," or "That's one way of looking at it," and tactfully correct the comment.

Say, "I see your point, but can we reconcile that with the situation which actually exists?"

Needless to say, this must be handled tactfully, since in effect you are flatly contradicting him.

HOW HE ACTS:	*Won't Talk*
WHY:	This quiet man is either bored, indifferent, superior, timid, or insecure.
WHAT TO DO:	Your action will depend on what you consider the cause for his silence.

If he's bored, arouse interest by asking for his opinion.

If he's indifferent, draw out the fellow next to him, then ask the quiet one to tell the fellow next to him what he thinks of the view expressed.

If he's the superior type, ask for his view after indicating respect for experience. (But don't overdo this, or the other salesmen will resent it.)

If he's timid or insecure, compliment him the first time he does talk. Be sincere!

HOW HE ACTS:	*Quick, Helpful*
WHY:	This salesman is really trying to help. Actually, he makes it difficult, keeps others from participating.
WHAT TO DO:	Cut across him tactfully by questioning others. Thank him, suggest "we put others to work."

Use him for summarizing. This is usually very effective.

HOW HE ACTS:	*Personality Clash*
WHY:	In this situation two or more salesmen clash, and can often divide your sales force into factions, which is dangerous to the success of the meeting.
WHAT TO DO:	Emphasize the points of agreement, minimize the points of disagreement (if possible). Try to draw attention to the objective at hand.

Another method is to cut across with a direct question on the topic, bringing a sound member into the discussion. As a last resort, frankly state that personalities should be omitted in discussing the subject.

How to Tailor a Meeting to Fit Its Objective

Here are the instructions an oil company insists its sales managers follow when planning a sales meeting:

A. Define your objectives clearly and estimate the usefulness of a sales meeting by:

1. Reducing your objectives to writing;

2. Determining whether your objectives are worth the time, energy, and money required for a sales meeting;

3. Satisfying yourself definitely that a sales meeting is necessary to put your objectives across.

B. Don't attempt to cover more than a few objectives at one meeting.

C. Don't hold a meeting unless you can actually accomplish the objectives you set out to accomplish.

D. Here are some typical objectives for sales meetings:

1. To introduce and explain a new product or service, and how to sell it;
2. To review and demonstrate an old product, its quality, and how to sell it;
3. To introduce and explain a new sales campaign;
4. To explain changes in markets for old products;
5. To present best answers to customers' objections;
6. To present and demonstrate the use of new selling tools, advertising, etc., in personal sales contacts;
7. To demonstrate and practice effective sales presentations;
8. To discuss methods of handling competition in sales talks;
9. To discuss ways salesmen can help improve service to customers;
10. To discuss methods of securing new customers and prospects;
11. To assign quotas and discuss use of salesmen's time;
12. To introduce and promote a sales contest;
13. To analyze lost sales and why I lost that sale (clinic);
14. To discuss credits and collections;
15. To explain company sales policies, objectives, etc.;
16. To explain and demonstrate product applications at clinics; e.g., tractor clinics, heating oil clinics, fleet clinics, etc.;
17. To explain and demonstrate use of selling aids and services available to dealers.

Types of Meetings

To help his regional and district sales managers select the type of sales meeting that will provide the best means to their specific objective, the vice-president, marketing, for a large manufacturing company, prepared this comparative analysis:

Objective of Meeting	Type of Meeting Best Suited	Features and Benefits
To disseminate official information; e.g., annual report, etc.	Convention	General session plus committee meetings. Mostly information-giving and voting on official business.
To get facts, plan, solve organization and personal problems.	Work conference	General sessions and face-to-face groups. Usually high participation. Provides more flexible means for doing organization's work.

Objective of Meeting	Type of Meeting Best Suited	Features and Benefits
To train salesmen to gain new knowledge, skills, or insights into problems.	Workshop	General sessions and face-to-face groups. Participants also serve as trainers.
To share experience among experts.	Seminar	Usually a single face-to-face group. Discussion leaders control participants. Provides compact exchange of ideas.
To train in one particular subject.	Clinic	Usually face-to-face grouping but may have general sessions. Staff provides most of training resources and services.
To train in several subjects.	Institute	General sessions and face-to-face groups.
To consider special interests of participants, salesmen, dealers, and others.	Groupings (according to industry, customers, etc.)	Interest generated by discussion of common problems. Usually no action, but findings may be reported.
To apply new skills or information to real-life situations.	Application groups	Mixed composition from total group by interests. Many use trainer to suggest methods. Usually no more than 10. No reporting.
To help salesmen get acquainted.	Orientation groups	A mixed membership from total group. Member of staff at each group to introduce participants and answer questions. Used only for brief period at start of meeting.
To give participants opportunity to react, make suggestions, etc.	Off-the-record sessions	Mixed membership from total group. Officially scheduled "bull session." No reporting but is informal channel to conference staff.
To present information, provide inspiration.	Speech or film	Can convey large quantity of factual information. Residual value must be augmented by takeaway material: lecture outlines, workbooks, booklets, etc.

Objective of Meeting	Type of Meeting Best Suited	Features and Benefits
To present complex information such as new product or service, or details of a new sales and advertising campaign.	Speaker with visuals	More thorough and certain communication with great residual value. Takes more time and money than speaker only.
To present information from diversified points of view.	Symposium	Two or more speakers, each of whom contributes specialized information. Chairman directs and summarizes. Usually a report is published.
To present information from many points of view, sometimes controversial.	Panel	Each member of the panel states his views and discusses with other members. Moderator guides discussion and keeps peace among panelists. Panel members usually hold brief rehearsal. Audience can question and comment.
To develop or ventilate several different sides of an issue.	Forum	Two or more speakers present different aspects of an issue; address salesmen rather than self. Moderator directs and summarizes.
To help salesmen analyze individual or group action in natural setting.	Situation presentation	Salesmen present role-play or case-history example. Commentator may call attention to specific points as "play" progresses.
To dramatize the outer or inner forces that clash in a selling situation.	Conflict presentation	Salesmen present role-play or staged skits. "Ghost" voice talks out loud, revealing inner thoughts of each character. Salesmen gain insight into emotions of prospects.
To demonstrate skills or techniques and show relative effectiveness.	Skill presentation	Salesmen, supervisors, or trainers demonstrate different ways to handle a selling problem. Salesmen in audience observe and then discuss.

Planning Your Meetings

Establishing an orderly and logical planning sequence is vital to achieving a successful sales meeting. Here is a plan used by the 3M Company:

1. The date, place, time, and length of the meeting.
2. The specific objectives you hope to accomplish.
3. Information you plan to give to assist in accomplishing your sales-meeting objectives.
4. The method of presentation you plan to use.
5. The visual and other aids you will need at the meeting.

Many meetings fall apart because the meeting planner failed to be concrete in clearly defining his meeting objectives. What can you do to insure against this? First, write down what you want your meeting to accomplish. Then find out what your salesmen would like your meeting to accomplish.

After you have established your meeting objectives, your next step is to determine what subjects should be included on your meeting agenda to accomplish these objectives. For example:

If one of your meeting objectives is to sell your salesmen on the need for better territory management, you would want to list: "How to profitably manage your time and your customers," as discussion material.

If another of your meeting objectives is to get your salesmen excited about a current promotion, you would want to list: "How this promotion can build sales and profits for us," as a subject for discussion.

If another one of your meeting objectives is to get more effective use of sales tools, advertising, and sales promotional material, you would want to list: "A review of our current selling tools and promotional aids and how their effective use can increase our productivity," as a subject.

If another of your meeting objectives is to get your salesmen to concentrate on selling large-account business, you would want to schedule "How to approach the big business order—whom to see, what to sell, and how to sell."

Adopt a Theme

Your sales meetings will excite more interest if they are built around a theme. A good meeting theme tied in with a popular trend or event—and this can be either past or present—will give your meeting impact. It will cause immediate interest, as well as provide a carryover of enthusiasm for applying the conclusions reached at your meeting.

The one main rule for adopting a theme for your meeting is to make certain that it is tied in with your meeting objectives. Your theme should be immediately identifiable with what you want your salesmen to accomplish.

The Dartnell Sales and Marketing Service, offered monthly by annual subscription, offers a new overall theme for sales departments each year. A typical theme: "Concentrate—Penetrate—Accelerate Sales in '68."

Producing Your Meeting

The first step is to set up a format for the general makeup of your meeting. A typical meeting day for the 3M Company divides into seven major time periods. For example:

1. The meeting opening.
2. Clinic or workshop session.
3. Morning coffee break.
4. Luncheon.
5. Clinic or workshop session continued.
6. Afternoon refreshments.
7. Your meeting close.

Your meeting format represents your meeting skeleton. It is around this skeleton that you build your agenda of subjects to be presented. A practical format assures you that the subjects you wish to present to accomplish your meeting objectives will be presented in the most interesting manner to your salesman audience.

Let us consider a few do's and don'ts to observe in conducting your meeting. These do's and don'ts come out of the experience of literally hundreds of sales managers, like yourself, who have over the years found out what techniques work best in presenting their sales meetings.

1. *Don't create competition for yourself.* You do just that when you pass out material to your salesmen while you are trying to get across a point. It is physically impossible for anyone to concentrate on two things at once. So tell your story, demonstrate, show your chart presentation, or whatever else you might be presenting, and then and only then pass out any material with reference to what you have just covered. However, if you do this, before going on to your next subject, make certain you pick up any of this material so it does not compete for your attention when you take

up your next subject. The same rule applies as far as your use of any of your meeting props. After a prop has served its purpose, get it off-stage or cover it up.

2. *Follow your script!* The meeting control script you have prepared for your meeting will go a long way in preventing interruptions of a non-constructive nature. But, in spite of the best-laid plans of mice and men, you still get the guy who wants to bring up something irrelevant to the subject or particularly personal to his own operation. This requires tactful handling on your part, but your knowledge of these individuals will tell you best how to handle such situations. If, for example, a subject is brought up that your meeting provides for later on in the program, in a nice way inform the individual that you are glad he brought the subject up, but as it will be handled later on in the meeting, you would like to press on. The griper or the guy who brings up the personal problem can be taken care of by saying in a friendly way—"Tom, I'll be very glad to discuss this with you personally after the meeting. I assure you I am interested in your problem and appreciate your concern."

3. Be easy to listen to, and listen yourself.

4. Whenever a controversial discussion takes place, regardless of how you resolve it, be sure to let your salesmen save face.

5. Keep to your time schedule.

6. Keep each subject on a high note.

7. Try to anticipate interruptions and prepare for them accordingly.

8. Don't leave a subject hanging in the air.

And now for a word about the close of your sales meeting. Every good sales meeting, in order to justify the time it took to present it, should ask for action. It should challenge your salesmen to put the ideas and the plans you presented into practice.

Your salesmen should understand that you intend to evaluate their performance following the meeting to determine how successfully they are applying what all of you agreed upon as being necessary to get the results you want.

Develop Good Meeting Leaders

It is an important responsibility of some salesmen to conduct effective meetings in front of groups of customers. The agricultural division of Olin Mathieson Corporation wanted to improve its field representatives' skills in this area. E. Duane Riffel, manager, manpower development and training, offered this report of what was done to accomplish this:

"Some time ago a conference was held on the subject of conducting educational meetings. The panel of specialists at this conference did an outstanding job in presenting visual aids and other material to support their presentations. This material was reproduced as a text and a copy furnished to each of our sales representatives over the nation.

"Since that time, we have evolved a 6- to 8-month orientation program for new sales representatives. This program culminates in a 2½-week training conference. All phases are explored in detail, including organization and preparation of the material to be presented. Finally, the trainees conduct a practice meeting and a critique of their efforts is held including comments by the trainees and their instructors. A second practice meeting is then held to include the recommendations for improvement brought out by the critiques.

"We have found this intensive treatment of a difficult responsibility has resulted in substantial dividends in increased sales effectiveness over the years."

Meetings for Retailers

Sales of appliance manufacturers depend not only on what their salesmen sell but ultimately on *what their dealer salesmen sell*. One company found very little training material directed toward the retail salesmen, particularly the independents, so it developed its own program.

Clyde Dains, director of sales promotion and advertising for Oklahoma Natural Gas Company, of Tulsa, supplemented dealer training through a program which he described as follows:

We assist our dealers with special appliance training meetings conducted by our sales promotion and home service personnel:

Kit Conferences: A 15- to 30-minute meeting is held in the dealer's store. The dealer schedules the date and time. Those participating receive a kit of demonstration aids—a sales-presentation summary, a customer-benefit checklist identifying appliance features, functions, and use. Display material and sample appliance ads are also presented.

Dealer Meal Demo: A one-hour presentation is conducted at an Oklahoma Natural Culino Room—either breakfast, lunch, or dinner. Customer-benefit demonstrations of gas appliance features—how they really work—aid salesmen in "showing and telling" a customer an informed quality-performance story.

Special Training Skits: For a change of pace, we use training skits to launch major sales promotions. Company home economists and sales promotion representatives make up the cast, with one salesman overplaying the "don'ts" of good salesmanship, and another smoothly picking up the pieces with benefit selling. These have been well received by dealer salesmen.

Wholesalers' Meetings

A survey reported by the magazine *Jobber Topics* disclosed that, among its wholesaler readers, Saturday is being less frequently used as a day to hold sales meetings, while Monday is gaining in popularity. Only 41 percent of the participants hold sales meetings on Saturday, in contrast to the 54 percent participating in the survey the magazine conducted 10 years before. Friday also is losing ground; five out of eight favored it previously, but only one of eight do so today.

Sales meetings that last for half a day or a whole day are becoming more popular, *Jobber Topics* reports. They are usually a combination of sales-training and sales-promotion meetings. Until recently, few sales managers tried to make any distinction between the two basic types of meetings. As with members of the Milwaukee Sales Executives Club, meetings that last around two hours are the most common. Some 40 percent of the participants in the *Jobber Topics* survey hold weekly meetings and another 40 percent hold them once a month.

The wholesalers' complaints are instructive. Chief among them is the gripe against the manufacturer's spokesman for being "inexperienced" or "lacking in knowledge of his lines." Sometimes such speakers talk too long or attempt to pass out too much technical and product information instead of sticking to "sales" information. Jobbers think that they can improve the factory representative's talk by finding out in advance the tenor of his "pitch" and suggesting various ways he can make it apply more to the needs and interests of his specific audience.

A Quick Way to Prepare Slides

Slide projections play a helpful role in sales meetings. Some companies would use them more liberally if they were less expensive and could be produced and procured more quickly. A procedure that can produce slides both promptly and cheaply has been developed by the Union Central Life Insurance Company of Cincinnati, as conceived by Robert C. Johnson, the company's comptroller:

We produce transparencies in black and white from prepared charts. The entire process takes only 15 minutes from exposure to slide. We use a standard Polaroid 800 camera using Polaroid No. 46 transparency film. Quickness of the process has proved to be of great value in handling last-minute changes. These slides are inexpensive to produce and compare favorably with professionally produced intensified slides. Projected on a screen, the images have good legibility as far away as 35 to 40 feet.

We have found that sharp contrast is essential to attract attention. Simply presented figures, limited in amount on any one slide, hold interest and get across the point. Involved, complex, or crowded charts are ineffective for our use.

Sound Filmstrips Helpful

The use of sound filmstrips in sales meetings is quite general. Usually they are devoted to specific product information or to the procedure for selling specific products. Other filmstrips, however, feature general selling techniques.

George R. Cheadle, president of Henning and Cheadle Inc., Detroit, states that the "sales film itself can carry the major part of the load in sales meetings, but, of course, its value is increased if the meeting leader is prepared to direct discussion." Accordingly, the company provides meeting leader guides for its sound filmstrips.

The films are also available on a rental basis for home viewing and study. The company sends a projector, the first film, and a study guide to the assigned individual. He is then asked to complete a questionnaire before he may receive the second "session." "One element in the questionnaire," according to Mr. Cheadle, "requires a case history of what happened when the student applied the principles of the film in an actual situation. Needless to say, these case histories are always success stories, and they provide interesting evidence of the effectiveness of this method of training."

Programmer for Exhibits and Displays

Recognizing the need for more interesting, exciting and effective exhibits incorporating complicated lighting sequences, signs, animated devices, audiovisual equipment and other electronic devices, DuKane, among others, has developed an electronic programmer to act as a systems control center.

The programmer provides an organized, dependable, and extremely versatile way of operating complicated sequences—even when live talent is utilized. Now you can easily set up and control special effects that can be operated completely automatically by prerecorded tape and the programmer.

Fully automatic sequences can be set up to run entirely by themselves at the touch of a button. Semiautomatic programs with live speakers or narrators can be run with precision, often by a single operator. The programmer controls spotlights . . . opens curtains . . . turns on room lights . . . lowers screens . . . turns projectors on . . . produces rapid picture advance and shows motion-picture clips.

Show Business in Sales Meetings

Use of music and musicians and other entertainment has long played a role in sales meetings. Many sales executives point out, however, that primarily because of TV, salesmen have become much more sophisticated judges of such presentations and able to react not only to what is being said and shown, but also to *how* it is being said and shown.

A. J. Pocock, account director of the SCI division of Communications Affiliates, Inc., 605 Third Avenue, New York, N. Y. 10017—an organization that plans, creates, and stages sales meetings—had these points to make about the use of professional entertainers:

Professional help in meetings is not a real help if it consists in merely tacking "show biz" or visualization factors onto what is a grueling and disrupting job performed by the executives of the company holding the meeting.

It is undeniable that the "audience" at a sales meeting . . . salesmen; district, branch, and regional managers; brokers; distributors; dealers . . . are all intricately involved with the aims of the host company.

But let's never forget that aside from being a sales or dealer organization, our "audience" are also human beings. And, as such, they are in fact an "audience."

In the physical planning, creation, and staging of the most effective kinds of meetings—both large and small—SCI has developed a full tool kit of methods, approaches, and systems.

A number of these are presented here—some relatively mechanical in nature, but all essential to a smooth-running and effective sales meeting.

1. *USE CAST TO ENFORCE . . . NOT ENTERTAIN.* The use of cast for comedy alone—or "girls" alone—is obviously distracting to the communications job a meeting must do. In a meeting in which a live cast is used, it can be used most effectively to introduce speakers, start and wrap up sessions, dramatize important points, show displays, distribute samples. This requires an integration of all cast material into the meeting subject matter, rather than merely "adding on" a cast number as a meeting brightener. Even a small cast can contribute excitement and an emotional buildup.

2. *SHOW THE REAL THING . . . WHEREVER POSSIBLE.* Of course, slides have an important place in any good meeting.

However, the more of the real thing . . . the real packages, the real point-of-sale material, the real product, the real advertising . . . that can be shown, the better.

In the case of small items, duplicators can be shown by the cast so that all get a closeup look. The aisles, the sides of the room, the coffee-break area—all are also good spots for closeup look. In the case of large items, special meeting-room facilities are desirable.

3. *A TIGHTER, SHORTER PROGRAM.* A mistaken notion of "as long as we've got them here, let's make them work," has often led to sales meetings that last from early morning until well into the evening.

While, in some cases, this kind of a schedule may be necessary, in our experience, a tight, well-planned meeting that ends at 5 p.m. or before is more effective.

Electronic program-control centers aid in the production of smooth-sailing meetings. This DuKane unit controls lights, screens, curtains, projectors; insures appropriate sequences.

Men who are forced to listen to hour after hour of facts, figures, and inspiration tend to become brain-weary. Their attention lags. Their minds wander. They lose more of what they are supposed to be hearing than they retain.

A well-paced meeting—with well-timed coffee breaks and adequate lunch period—can usually do the job right and still release the men at the end of a 7- to 8-hour day.

4. *SCRIPTED SPEECHES AN IMPORTANT CONTROL FACTOR.* If a meeting is to be planned for right timing and smooth running it is of prime importance that speakers use scripts.

In some cases a point outline . . . with specific time limit . . . will be adequate. However, in SCI's experience, scripts for all speakers . . . with the possible exception of a top management speaker or panel . . . provide the best insurance of a good meeting.

5. *ADVANCE REHEARSAL PRODUCES THE BEST RESULTS.* The speakers should be rehearsed by professionals well in advance of the date of the meeting . . . or of travel to the meeting location.

These rehearsals are held in the executives' offices, or in a conference room set aside for that purpose.

6. *A SLIDE-CHECK SAVES CONFUSION, TIME, AND NERVES.* At the scene of the meeting rehearsal, a final check of slides is, of course, necessary. However, the business of having all speakers sit around for hours while speeches are read and slides and slide cues are checked is both wearing to all and actually unnecessary.

By taking only those speakers who will use slides into a separate room—and, there, checking quietly and at close quarters only those portions of their speeches in which slides occur—a more accurate check is provided. And, of course, time and nerves are saved.

7. *A WALK-THROUGH NEED NOT BE A DEATH MARCH.* By carefully segmenting all elements that need checking or rehearsing on the day before the meetings, and then approaching each one on a scheduled basis, the arduous and endless "dress rehearsal" is eliminated.

Such elements include:

The slide-check, previously mentioned.

A test of all speakers' voices for microphone level.

A walk-through with each speaker of where and when he comes up to the lectern or on stage.

A separate, scheduled rehearsal of each speaker who has cast integrated into his session.

8. *THE SKIT vs. DIRECT DRAMATIZATION.* Well known on the sales meeting scene is the so-called skit. One man plays the salesman, another the sales manager . . . or dealer . . . or prospect.

There is a humorous byplay in which the salesman performs his function incorrectly. He is a failure.

Suddenly a third party enters. An angel . . . a devil . . . a sprite . . . another more successful salesman.

He—or it—points out the right way: Our salesman tries it; lo and behold, he becomes a tremendous success.

Variations on this theme have been used—and are being used—in sales meetings of all kinds. Obviously, their intent is to use a lighthearted approach in demonstrating to a salesman the correct way to perform his job.

Unfortunately, however, this approach rarely achieves its objectives; and for very real reasons:

REASON 1: The salesman does not identify with the salesman in the skit. No man thinks of himself as a failure due to his own lack of knowledge.

REASON 2: Contrasted with the highly professional comedy talent to which the salesmen are exposed over and over again on TV, the makeshift "skit" is usually not really as funny as it should be. It sometimes seems corny. It sometimes is embarrassing.

Also, by its very nature, the skit tends to becloud the very points to be communicated.

Much more effective than the skit are any number of other approaches. For example, all of the participation techniques mentioned before, in which the men hear from each other what the real problems, real opportunities, and real selling methods are.

Another effective approach is the use of the cast in a direct manner to get over points via song, giant visuals, or spoken lines.

9. *THE WORKBOOK—EFFECTIVE COMMUNICATION DEVICE.* One problem of the one-, two-, or three-day sales meeting is the mass of material . . . facts, figures, ideas, inspiration . . . to which the men in the audience are exposed.

In direct reverse ratio to the amount of such material is the ability of the men to absorb and retain the information. Yet it is important that much of it be retained in order to be acted upon.

SCI has developed the "workbook" to help accomplish this. The workbook is a simple booklet or looseleaf binder containing pages with headings, some unfinished statements and many blank spaces.

At the close of segments of the sales meeting, "Workbook Summary Sessions" are held. In these, the speaker goes over the highlights of the material just covered and asks the men in the audience to write specific key facts, figures and the like in their workbooks.

In this manner, by getting the audience to participate, several excellent things are accomplished:

The important points are sifted out and spotlighted.

The act of listening is broken by an opportunity to do something—to participate —in this case, by writing in the books.

The men remember the points, because they wrote them down themselves.

Another form of workbook is one that is used concurrently with the meeting talks, themselves. Workbook writing is integrated into the major speeches. This is particularly effective as a training medium.

The workbook, depending on the need, can vary from a simple booklet or looseleaf book to an elaborate book containing pictures, charts, and graphs, as well as write-in sections.

In any case, added to its obvious advantages, it also provides an excellent take-home piece for any meeting—and, of course, can be used for further communication in the field.

10. *FOLLOW-THROUGH—FOR YEAR-ROUND EFFECTIVENESS.* No matter how well planned, created, and staged, a sales meeting is only a one-, two-, or three-day period in a selling year of 365 days. To fully achieve what it can achieve, a sales meeting should, in the last analysis, be the starting point of a six-month or year-long communication effort. Planned with the meeting should be the follow-through activities that will carry the effect of the meeting throughout the year.

Microphone Technique

These excellent suggestions for mastering the microphone were prepared by Shure Brothers, Evanston, Ill., and are excerpts from that company's brochure, "The Microphone in Public Address Systems."

It's amazing how often a speaker, performer, or lecturer "loses" his audience simply because he doesn't take time to master microphone technique. Using one properly is really just a matter of practice and common sense.

One of the most frequent errors occurs when a speaker turns away from the microphone and keeps on talking. His voice is lost—the microphone can't follow him. Face the microphone whenever you're talking . . . if you want to look around at various members of your audience, make the microphone your pivot point.

On the other hand, you should turn away at times. A speaker who clears his throat or coughs directly into the microphone may rock an entire audience.

The sure sign of an amateur speaker is blowing into a microphone to see if it's operating. Yes, it indicates whether sound is coming through or not, but it doesn't give you any idea of the volume at which your voice will be reproduced. Test the sound system by talking . . . "one, two, three, four" is as good as anything else.

All other things being equal, the best sound system is the one that can be operated at minimum volume. Too often, an inexperienced speaker will try to

The LaBelle A. V. Tutor is a dual-track tape player and automatic filmstrip projector combination. A self-contained unit weighing 28 pounds, this machine can be used for closeup showings by utilizing the inside of the cover as a screen, or it may be focused for conventional large-screen showings.

compensate for a bad acoustical condition simply by turning up the volume. This may only result in a disturbing effect for the listeners.

At first, most people in an audience won't complain about sound that is just a little too loud, too soft, or distorted. Unconsciously, perhaps, they will just work harder at listening more carefully, honestly trying to compensate for the inadequacies of the public address system.

But the strain of such careful listening over a period of time takes its toll. Attention wanders and points are missed . . . listeners may become generally irritable, and blame the irritation on the speaker or the people in charge of the arrangements. Quite frequently, a sizable proportion of the audience may just give up and let their minds wander.

In Summary

A Dartnell survey on sales meeting practices covered the policies of 250 companies in the United States and Canada. The results of this survey may be summarized as follows:

Industry seems to be conducting somewhat fewer meetings than in the past. The one-hour weekly get-together is becoming less common and emphasis seems to be shifting to a dozen or fewer "routine" meetings of not more than one day's duration. The annual sales meeting tends to be conducted on a more rigid schedule and the time varies between two and four days. Minor meetings are held in company offices or in nearby motel meeting rooms. Major meetings go outside in increasing numbers—many go to resort areas to create a total company environment away from office distractions. Budgets for meetings range from very small to those practically unlimited.

The overall conclusion is that business meetings have come of age, with positive results expected from every hour and dollar spent.

Chapter 50

EQUIPPING SALESMEN

PROSPECTS want to see what they are being asked to buy. They want to know and understand product features and their importance. They also want printed material that carries the full authority and prestige of the selling company. Purchasing decisions are often made by groups, some members of which cannot be reached or influenced by the salesman and his personal powers of persuasion. With these people, visual aids and literature must perform virtually the total selling task.

To be truly effective, the salesman has to catch and hold the interest of the prospect. It is well established that the average person retains only 25 percent of oral communications. The use in sales presentations of devices such as flip charts, slides, and sales brochures enhances, rather than diminishes, the prestige of the salesman. These visual or audiovisual aids help him to deliver his message in a more complete, more orderly, and more effective manner.

Properly used, they can make the difference between success and failure on many sales calls.

Visual Sales Portfolios

It is a great help to a salesman, in conducting a sales canvass, to have something from which to talk. This serves two purposes: (1) It makes it easier for him to keep on the main track, and to bring out his salient points in proper sequence, and (2) it dramatizes the presentation, thus keeping the prospect's mind on what the salesman is saying. For many years it was the practice to provide salesmen with loose-leaf binders in which they arranged, as best they could, various data useful in building up their canvass. Then there was developed a type of binder, or portfolio, which could be opened up and placed upright on the prospect's desk, instead of lying flat. In using this equipment the salesman turned each page as he shaped his

Sales aids utilizing the slide-rule principle are used by many companies. Both standard and made to order, these are adaptable to almost any line.

Courtesy, Perrygraf Corp.

talk around data on that page, just as was done with the flat binder, but it was not necessary for the prospect to lean over the desk to see it. He could sit back in his chair, and the salesman pointed to the charts or data on the portfolio page with his pencil as he talked. The easel type of portfolio found wide favor with salesmen. Its greatest value is holding attention.

This type of portfolio is recommended for salesmen who sell business executives, dealers, and others working at a desk. It is not so practical for salesmen who are selling door to door, or who must meet and talk to a prospect under unfavorable conditions. It is ideal for building up interest in a specialty which must be sold largely on a basis of what it will do for a buyer, rather than what it is. It is not recommended for selling a line of products, or for selling technical products to engineers who do not take kindly to anything that smacks of high-pressure selling.

The effectiveness of easel portfolios depends, of course, upon the skill with which they are arranged. Too many sales managers make the mistake of turning the preparation of a salesman's presentation kit over to some subordinate in the sales department. It should be realized that upon the proper arrangement and presentation of the sales story, thousands of dollars' worth of business will depend. Not only should the most capable sales executive in the company give personal attention to its development, but expert assistance may be employed profitably. In arranging the sales presentation, as in the case of the sales manual, it should be approached from the standpoint of the buyer. For that reason a person with the buyer's viewpoint can usually do a better job of planning the portfolio, and someone who has a flair for visualization should design the exhibit.

What a Visual Aid Should NOT Do

Visual aids should not undertake to do too much of the salesman's work. A good sales portfolio will high-spot a sales talk so that the salesman's points can be better registered but it never attempts to make the talk for the salesman. That kind of presentation does more harm than good, since it undermines a salesman's individuality

Another consideration in planning sales kits to be used by salesmen is weight. The rapidly growing use of air travel by those in sales work, to say nothing of the aversion of the average salesman to "toting" a heavy sales kit, makes it desirable to keep kits as light as possible. A check of 216 kits provided to salesmen calling on dealers indicated only about half of the data and materials in the kit were used with sufficient regularity to justify their inclusion.

Heavy divider pages, index pages, covers and exhibits also added to both the weight and usefulness. Unless a kit is used it is not worth its cost.

Companies which once required their traveling representatives to carry several sample trunks have been able to condense this sample equipment into one trunk. The growing importance of the merchandising plan, as compared to the actual merchandise, has caused other companies to put more emphasis on the resale plan and their salesmen sell from a "plan" portfolio. Improvements in direct-color photography have further lightened the weight of the salesman's sample kit, and some unusually effective pictorial demonstration portfolios are now being carried by general line salesmen, instead of bulky and costly sample trunks.

Getting Salesmen to Use Portfolios

Various methods are used to convince salesmen of the importance of carrying free equipment in their daily work. Following are a few suggestions which will help the sales executive to solve this problem:

1. Make portfolio convenient to carry. In doing this, great care should be given to size and weight. A design should be selected that will slip easily into the briefcase. It should be quickly displayed and make an attractive exhibit. The weight is important, for the salesman must not consider it a burden.

2. Keep it filled with sales helps—ideas that the salesman can use in his daily work are the things he is looking for, and when these are included in a forceful way, reports show that he is eager to use his portfolio. Some firms furnish strong testimonial letters while others are constantly giving their salesmen facts and statistics that can be used in their sales talk. Information that can be passed along to the customer in the nature of window trims, sales ideas, and direct-mail campaigns has been found to be well received by salesmen.

3. Furnish new material frequently. Giving the salesmen new sales ammunition increases their interest in the sales manual.

The Protection of Papers in Portfolios

This problem can best be solved by the use of cellophane covers as a protective agency. Firms that furnish their salesmen with papers or letters that are repeatedly used by them in their sales work have found that these can be best protected from becoming soiled or damaged by this type of cover. The best arrangement seems to be the placing of such papers or letters in pockets with cellophane windows on each side of the page. The envelopes are punched to file in a standard ring binder. This allows two letters to be placed back to back and easily shown as the page is turned.

Another reason salesmen do not make the best use of photographs in the sales presentation is lack of a way to organize them for instant use. Nothing slows down a sale, or irritates a prospect, more than to have a salesman hunt through a lot of loose photographs or illustrations for documentary evidence to support a sales point he is making. Even mounting the photographs in ring binders, if there are a number of them, is not satisfactory. There has recently been developed a visible index portfolio especially for this purpose. The photographs are mounted in cellophane envelopes, in steps, with an index below each photograph facilitating quick finding.

Easel cards work well. Dean Shaffner, director of sales planning, NBC Television, said that the network prepares its own easel presentations and that one advantage is that they can be turned out fast. "We had a presentation for delivery over a weekend and we keep getting new data in right up until Friday," he said. "We were able to prepare new cards right up until the last minute. And the easel has other advantages. It isn't necessary to darken the room and the speaker is visible."

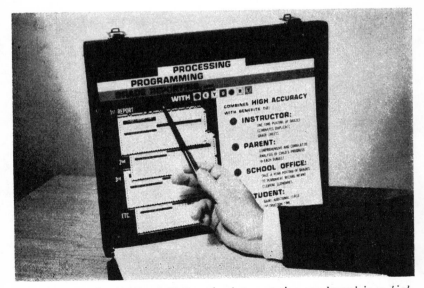

The flip charts in this Royal McBee visual presentation are housed in a high-quality attaché case. They are designed to be used on a "selective" basis, as described in the accompanying text.

The Dangers of Visualizers

No statistics on the subject are available, but if all the prospects and buyers who have been forced to try to listen politely as a salesman turned over page after page of a "visualizer" were laid end to end, they would probably all be sound asleep.

Visualizers were new and clever when first introduced, some years ago; today they are far from novel, and are more likely to bore than to interest the prospect unless they are definitely tailored to his predetermined interests.

It is better not to use a visualizer at all—unless it is (a) very short and snappy and (b) contains something new, novel, or special to attract customer interest.

A businessman was forced to terminate an interview when a young, inexperienced, and thoughtless insurance salesman started to take him—page by page—through a visual. This executive relates:

"I granted the young man an interview as a matter of courtesy, although I am already heavily insured, own my home, and have several grandchildren—matters which it would have been easy for the young man to have ascertained before calling, even if he couldn't guess it by my white hair and my position in the organization. Brightly, the salesman propped up his visualizer and started through it, reading each page—about educating my small children (!), paying off the mortgage on my house, 'What would my widow do for a job? . . .,' etc. Finally, after about 10 pages of this, I had to explain that he was wasting his time and my own. I am sure I hurt his feelings, but I hope he learned something from the experience. Incidentally, I never heard from him—or from his company —again."

How Royal McBee "Tailors" Its Visuals

The other side of the coin is illustrated in a type of visualizer which can be carefully tailored to fit the prospect's needs before the salesman makes his call. This is obviously not possible in rigidly bound visualizers, nor can it be done for every type of selling operation. However, where it is possible to allow for special conditions and situations, this should be done.

In its monthly publication for company personnel, the *Royal McBee Reporter,* that company explains the importance of selecting the pages of the visualizer to fit the needs of the prospect. The visualizer, set up for use, is pictured nearby.

The company instructs its salesmen to carefully study the preapproach information available for each prospect before the call. Then the salesman removes from the visualizer any pages which do not apply, putting the pages in such order of rotation as will most rapidly capture the attention of the individual prospect.

Miniature Models

Another sales tool which is popular among salesmen of engineering specialties is a "pint sized" model of the product, cut away to show the construction. For example, Servel, when introducing a new gas-burning refrigerator, furnished salesmen with a "working" model which the salesman heated by means of a lighted match and the gadget began to refrigerate just as in the actual appliance. The whole device was only about eight inches high. Such working models, in convenient size, help a salesman in demonstrating an engineering principle.

Another device for accomplishing this same purpose is the transparency portfolio. The several working parts of a gas engine, for example, are printed on individual sheets of cellophane fastened at the top. As each leaf or sheet is brought into position, another working part of the engine shows through until finally the engine is completely "built" as the prospect watches and listens.

Portable Projection Equipment

The widespread use of both 8mm. and 16mm. sound film has established it as a potent selling tool and as an effective public relations aid. In some cases, companies are producing their own movies and writing their own scripts. Depending on the scope of the film, it can cost as little as $1,000 or as much as $100,000.

One of the primary reasons why manufacturers use films is their value in demonstrating products to customers in areas where the product is not available or is too large to be carried around.

Vulcan Materials Company, Atlanta, Georgia, faced this problem in its concrete pipe division. Its salesmen reported excellent results in showing the company film, *Precision in Concrete,* to engineers, contractors, and city, county, and state purchasing agents.

There are many kinds and sizes of film projectors to meet a variety of purposes and budgets. Trade magazines and publications such as the *Advertising and Sales Promotion Buyers Guide,* issued annually by Advertising Publications, Inc., Chicago, list or describe the various types of machines on the market. The following units are mentioned merely as examples of the variations in function and design offered by the industry.

La Belle Industries, Inc., offers the Courier, a lightweight (15 pounds) "attaché-case" unit with built-in screen. It is battery-operated.

Technicolor makes a portable model that uses its case top as a projection screen. Fairchild Industrial Products has developed two models, both resembling portable TV sets, one with sound and built-in speaker.

To operate the projector, the salesman inserts the film cartridge and starts the machine. It's fast and simple.

The MPO Videotronic Super 8 is a two-way, cartridge-film repeating unit. It has a built-in screen and projects on wall screens as well.

Filmstrips in Saleswork

Many companies are using custom-made filmstrips either for sales training or as a selling aid. Listed below are 20 reasons why such visual presentations are becoming so popular. This list was drawn up at a visual communications conference of The Kellogg Foundation's National Project in Agricultural Communications. Incidentally, the term "sound-slidefilm" has been replaced by "sound-stripfilm," for greater accuracy.

1. Visual messages illustrate and clarify nonverbal symbols and images, complex relationships, quantitative relationships, abstract concepts, spatial relations, and specific details.
2. They provoke and hold attention.
3. They bring experts (resources) to the platform.
4. They show inaccessible processes, materials, events, things, and changes in time, speed, and space.
5. They promote efficiency in acquisition and retention of learning.
6. They facilitate changes in information, attitudes, behavior, and moods.
7. They permit joint perception and can improve group relations.
8. They increase the prestige of the speaker.
9. They promote a speaker's self-confidence.
10. They facilitate accuracy and standardization of the message intended.
11. They create emotional involvement.
12. They show texture, form, shape, size, and color.
13. They constitute a more universal language than words.
14. They provide objectivity to a delicate or controversial subject.
15. They allow the audience to view an object or process from a variety of reference points.
16. They can economize the effort of understanding.
17. They allow a variety of modes of presentation.
18. They reinforce verbal messages.
19. They promote security—a feeling that the message is true.
20. They are repeatable and durable.

Chapter 51

SALES TASKS AND QUOTAS

I T IS management's responsibility to see that markets are adequately penetrated, sales territories efficiently covered, and that a company's products and prices are fully competitive. It is the sales
manager's duty to see that the salesmen carry out their part of
the job.

This he does not only by supervising the number of calls that
salesmen make in their territories, but also by insuring that they call
on the right kind of prospect. The salesman alone cannot accomplish
this. He must receive the help and guidance of the sales manager
in the home office.

Naturally, the first responsibility of a sales manager is to increase
the sales of his company's products. We have already discussed in
previous chapters the channels of distribution for these products
and we come finally to the efforts of the individual salesman. As the
company's representative in the field, he stands alongside the dealer
on the firing line. Thus we see the significance of the relationship
between the salesman and the prospect and the importance of the
need for adequate supervision to insure its effectiveness.

Forms for Auditing, Evaluating

The best approach calls for an analysis of the sales opportunities
and work demands for each present and prospective account. It also
calls for the establishment of call schedules, and the establishment
of realistic sales goals. Two forms used by the Apex Manufacturing
Company, a Customer-Prospect Audit Form and a Workload Evaluation Form, are shown on following pages.

Customer-Prospect Audit Form: In this form, all customers and
prospective customers are listed in the first column. If there is more
than one important person to be called on regularly, but at different
intervals, their names are included, as shown for the Red Company.

APEX MANUFACTURING COMPANY

SALESMAN _____ Sheet _____ of _____ TERRITORY _____ DATE _____

CUSTOMER-PROSPECT-AUDIT

Names of Companies, Important persons in the companies to be seen individually, and cities to be listed below.		Product Line A	Product Line B	Product Line C	Miscellaneous	Total	Scheduled Calls	Inventories	Dealer Work Men	Dealer Work Days
				SALES OBJECTIVES (Dollars)			WORK SCHEDULE (Per Year)			
First Company 1125 State St.-Chicago	P	5000	2000	-	1000	8000	12	1	-	-
	S	500	100	-	100	700				
	G	1000	500	-	200	1700			-	-
Brown Company 1336 LaSalle St.-Chicago	P	4000	6000	3000	1000	14000	12	-	4	8
	S	1000	-	2000	500	3500				
	G	1500	500	2000	500	4500				
Red Company 142 South St.-Chicago	P	10000	8000	6000	3000	27000		2	6	10
	S	6000	8000	-	1500	15500				
	G	8000	8000	2000	2000	20000				
P. C. Jones, P.A. R. C. Smith, Main	P						24			
	S						24	55		
	G						6			
P. R. Yates, Eng. F. W. Corner, Pres.	P						1			
	S							-	-	-
	G									
White Company Aurora	P	500	300	-	500	1300		-	-	-
	S	100	50	-	100	25				
	G	-	-	-	-	-				
Purple Company Aurora	P	2000	5000	3000	1000	11000	12	-	-	-
	S	-	-	-	-	-				
	G	500	500	300	200	1500				
Last Company St. Charles	P									
	S									
	G									

INSTRUCTIONS: All customers and all worth-while prospective customers are to be listed. "P" refers to potential, the full value of items handled by the Company and purchased from all sources, or the firm's reasonable sales possibilities. "S" refers to the company's sales to the firm during the past 12 months. "G" refers to the sales goal over the coming 12 months. Only dollar sales are to be shown. Individual persons that are to be called on separately are to be listed, and their scheduled calls shown. Prospects are to be scheduled for regular promotional calls. This form is to be filled out jointly by the salesman and his manager. 1 copy for salesman, 1 copy for manager, 1 copy for General Office.

The meaning of the letters "P," "S," and "G" are defined on the form. (It is important that all forms be self-explanatory, so that a salesman required to use them can refresh his memory after their use has been explained to him but forgotten.) "P" stands for potential, the customer's total purchases from all sources in the product area being considered. "S" stands for the company's past year's sales to the customer. "G" stands for the salesman and his manager's planned sales goal for the coming year.

Scheduled calls are then entered, based upon last year's call activity tempered by the coming year's planned activity. For the First Company, 12 calls (once a month) have been planned; for the Red Company, 55 calls have been planned. Note that the salesman would probably visit the Red Company twice a month; he would call on Jones and Smith on each visit, on Yates every fourth visit, and would be sure to see Burton, the president, once during the year.

Inventory checks should be made for the First Company once during the year, and for the Red Company twice a year. Both the Brown Company and the Red Company have salesmen who call on dealers; it is well for salesmen to spend time with these men in the field, calling with them on their customers; time must be reserved for this activity.

The Workload Evaluation: This is merely a summation of the data recorded. Note the full potentiality of the territory is $1,300,000 for the company, its past sales have been $190,000, and it has set its sights for $220,000. There are 150 customers out of the 175 listed who are expected to buy product A.

There have been 1,280 calls scheduled. It takes about a half a day for an inventory, and since the company has set 8 calls per day as an acceptable average, the 25 inventories scheduled are equivalent to 100 calls; the 70 days of dealer work are equivalent to 560 calls. There must always be some time reserved for unscheduled promotional or exploratory work to replace customers lost through normal attrition or if the territory is to grow in volume; 80 calls, or about 5 percent, have been allocated for this work.

A work year has been assumed as 50 weeks (allowing 2 weeks' vacation) with 10 days deducted for holidays, meetings, and sickness. With a five-day week, this equals 240 days a year. With 8 calls a day, the normal workload year would be 1,920 calls. Because of the variation in work habits of salesmen and the need to get a territory started even if it isn't up to full coverage efficiency, the minimum acceptable call load schedule has been shown as 1,760 and the maximum 2,400. If the call load should drop below 1,760, the

APEX MANUFACTURING COMPANY

SALESMAN_ _ _ _ _ _ _   CUSTOMER-PROSPECT AUDIT SUMMARY   _ _ _ _ _ _DATE

SALES GOALS				
PRODUCT LINES	POTENTIAL	CURRENT SALES	SALES GOAL	NUMBER OF CUSTOMERS
A	$ 350,000	$ 65,000	$ 75,000	150
B	250,000	40,000	50,000	175
C	500,000	75,000	85,000	175
Misc.	200,000	10,000	10,000	175
TOTAL	$1,300,000	$190,000	$220,000	175

WORK LOAD			
TYPE OF WORK	AMOUNT SCHEDULED	CALL EQUIVALENT [2]	ADJUSTED CALLS [3]
Calls [1]	1280		1280
Inventories	25	4	100
Days of Dealer Work	70	8	560
Promotional Work Not Scheduled *			80
			2020

[1] Customers, prospects and promotional

[2] It is assumed that the company's call objective
    is 8 per day. To take an average inventory takes
    a half a day, equivalent to 4 calls.

[3] A typical work year is 240 days. This is based
    on 50 five-day work weeks, less 10 days for
    holidays, conventions and sickness. With the company's
    objective of 8 calls per day, a typical work year would
    include 1920 calls.

* Some allowance should be made for promotional and exploratory calls to replace normal
    attrition of established accounts and for growth.

    Territories with Sales Goals less than 150,000 and scheduled adjusted calls less than
    1760 should be increased. Territories with scheduled adjusted calls in excess of 2400
    should be reduced to assure planned coverage and effective sales work.

best part of the territory should be absorbed by an adjoining territory or it should be covered by a manufacturer's agent who has other lines, If the workload exceeds 2,400 calls, the territory should be reduced to assume planned coverage.

A further provision of a minimum sales goal of $150,000 has been shown. Here it is assumed that on sales less than that amount, the company will sustain a loss. However, if management feels that, within a reasonable time, the volume can be brought to well above $150,000, it might open the territory, considering the expense a capital investment.

By this method or similar means, sales opportunities, market coverage, anticipated profit position, workload, and manpower may all be brought into balance.

Some Questions About Quotas

Marketing managers are far from agreed on how to set up and administer a quota system, and a few still hold out against quotas altogether according to Leslie Rich, as quoted in *Dun's Review* and *Modern Industry*. Some of the questions frequently asked are:

- How, in the first place, do you arrive at a fair quota for any individual?
- Should a salesman's quota be higher than you actually expect him to produce? If so, how much higher?
- How can you keep quotas from interfering with the development and service calls so necessary to most companies?
- Should quotas be set in product units or dollars, according to profits?
- Should quotas be the same for everybody, or different according to territory potential, experience, ability?
- What relation should quotas have to salary?
- How can you "sell" salesmen on quotas?
- What do you do when a salesman fails to meet his quota?

Many concerns find that in order to give every man a chance to make a showing it is necessary to take into consideration the salesman operating that territory. A nationally known company gives equal consideration to the salesman's past record, his ability, and conditions and possibilities in his territory. This encourages the salesmen who do not stand at the top of the list in volume and gives each an equal chance to beat his quota. Each man is given a quota of 1,000 points for the year, which represents a certain amount in dollars and cents. While the total number of points is the same for every salesman, the values of the points vary. The value of one point is arrived at by dividing 1,000 into the sales figure set for the year for each salesman.

G. E. Ankeny, sales manager of the Maytag Company, points out that all other reports common in marketing come "after the fact." Only quotas can be used for planning.

In the plumbing and heating division of American-Standard Corp., for example, quotas are tied directly to a budget based on yearly market forecasts. As outlined in *Dun's Review,* the 10-man marketing research department begins to assemble data in October for each of the 13 geographical sales districts. The analysts talk to company people in each district, go over economic bulletins from local banks and building and loan associations, and compare this with national predictions on housing. They try to judge the type of building planned (multiple or single dwelling, for example), the possibility of American-Standard penetration into competitive markets, and the historic comparison of one region's housing with the nation as a whole.

"From all this, we make our considered guess on next year's sales for each of our 20 major products in each district," says Jerome A. Cleveland, division manager of marketing research. "And 'guess' is the correct word."

However, after years of refinement, Cleveland's department now regularly comes within a few percentage points of actual sales each year.

Practical Values of Quotas

In an address entitled "Setting Equitable Quotas for Company Salesmen," delivered at a Midwest Marketing Conference, Edward P. Sheehan, vice-president and general sales manager of the York Corporation, outlined the purposes and practical values of sales quotas. He said:

The quota is the lifeblood of a business and serves both as a goal and as a means of measuring the performance of a company in relation to that goal. It is also a basis for setting sales and operations budgets. For a salesman, it stands as a method of measuring performance and qualifying for advancement. It is a common objective both for the salesman and his company.

In order properly to analyze a salesman's quota, consideration must be given to three other types of quotas upon which the individual salesman's quota is usually based. The first is the long-range quota that sets the stage for projected corporate planning. The second is the national yearly quota, the 12-month objective, which is a steppingstone that leads to ultimate growth potential established by the long-range forecast. The third type is the regional quota which is a breakdown of the national quota.

From all these come the individual salesman's quota, which is generally a breakdown of the regional quota.

There are factors that apply to salesmen's quotas that need not always be considered in setting national or regional quotas which are broader and do not always reflect the market-by-market considerations which must influence salesmen's quotas.

Salesmen's quotas, in general, are more easily determined and controlled in the "institutional" types of business—drugs, opticals, books. These businesses do not suffer from, or profit by, the peaks and valleys that are found in the more volatile types of business, such as clothing, tires, and liquor. Quotas present a greater problem in these volatile businesses where sales often depend upon seasons, weather, fashions, or other hard-to-predict factors.

Regardless of whether yours is a volatile or an institutional type business, there are some fundamentals we should consider when establishing equitable quotas for salesmen:

1. A company should determine what share of the industry it wants, both nationally and in each market area. This, of course, requires a knowledge of what the total industry is doing, along with projections of expected growth. Usually, this data is available from either industry associations or trade magazines. We, at York, use figures supplied by the Air Conditioning and Refrigeration Institute, from the buying-power-index issue of *Sales Management* magazine, and from the National Electrical Manufacturers' Association. We then adjust these data variously, by climatic conditions, so that they will better apply to air conditioning and heating markets, using both industry and buying-power figures.

2. A knowledge of what a company's historical position has been in each market is an important factor, also. We cannot afford not to learn from history— a company must build upon the foundations laid in the past. In other words, consider your heritage, your status, your reputation, and your image in the marketplace.

How well an area has been managed is an important factor to consider when setting an equitable quota for a salesman. Poor management, even in a prime market, may force you to set lower quotas than penetration and industry sales figures might indicate. The comparison of such figures also gives you an insight into whether your present management is strong or weak in any given area.

In short, it is vital that you know what your product's and company's reputation is in each market, and such knowledge should be reflected in each salesman's quota. It is this factor which has the greatest influence on whether the salesman's quota is equitable. A company may nationally enjoy a high percentage of industry volume, but, for any number of reasons, be relatively quite weak in some salesman's territory. We would not be fair to those salesmen to expect them to bring our penetration up to national levels overnight.

3. Consider the national economic outlook—where the experts think the economy is going and how your industry's predictions fit in. For example, a predicted increase in personal income might be offset by industry statistics showing that your product is reaching a saturation point. Of course, new product introductions, a planned product diversification, or other such factors must be considered and should be reflected in the quota.

4. The salesman's quota should be attainable. Setting unrealistic quotas that cannot be met only results in a morale problem and serves no useful purpose.

Too often, management is guilty of fooling itself in putting down figures that are no more than wishful thinking.

The questions now arise as to how do you determine, after having considered these factors, whether or not your quotas were correctly set. As a general rule you have set equitable quotas for salesmen if your weaker salesmen fail to attain them and if your better salesmen either reach them or slightly exceed them.

If a quota is properly and fairly established, it should be the best single measuring stick you can use to evaluate a salesman. Of course, this general rule may not apply in any given case, because of peculiar or extenuating circumstances.

Another rule of thumb is that in the more volatile industries your salesmen's quotas should be at least 10 percent higher than the previous year's performance. The more institutional business may look for more modest increases in the 3 to 5 percent area. This general rule must also be tempered by consideration of local conditions.

It is the responsibility of management or the home-office marketing group to set these quotas and to administer them. It is not usually wise to let field sales representatives have too big a part to play in the establishment of quotas. You need the marketing information from them, as well as records of past performance. However, if given too much authority, you may find that they will endeavor to set higher-than-attainable quotas, particularly if by doing so they can command a higher income. Or, they may desire larger quotas because they will bring with them increased budgets.

Also upon management's shoulders is the responsibility of following up quota performance. It is, I think, apparent that once-a-year checks will not suffice. We, at York, find that monthly checks on performance-to-quota permit us to keep our fingers on the pulse of a salesman's progress. Such checks bring to light any problem areas so that we can give them our immediate attention. Markets making outstanding progress are also checked and the reasons for this success are quickly dispatched to other areas for their consideration.

At first glance, it would seem that money is the primary motive for a salesman to attain quota. Perhaps it is, but this basic motive can be supplemented with sales programs and contests. At York, we have found success with both types. Sales programs and promotions that help salesmen and retailers to sell to the ultimate consumer have proved their worth.

At York we run from two to six contests a year, usually for our salesmen or sales outlets. We've had success when the awards have been exciting and when the contest goals have been within the reach of all. Normally, for contests which constitute an addition to a salesman's income (either with cash or merchandise), special contest quotas are established. Thus, we begin to pay off when more-than-the-normal quota results are attained. Ideally, a contest should motivate salesmen to do more than the yearly quota as prorated over the contest period and, by doing so, give you a sales reserve and frequently bolster sales in product areas which are showing a weakness.

Special quotas should be set for contests, and should be estimated at a higher level of performance. The basic regional quota, as we have said, should be set fairly and realistically. You should expect it to be met in most cases. Therefore, you should not have to reward a man for doing what is basically his job. The contest gives him a reward for above-average performance.

Thus, contests are means of getting extra business. We do not recommend *counting* on contests to help attain the basic yearly quota. This basic quota, as we have said, should be established as an attainable goal without the assistance of contests or special promotions other than the promotional tools or sales programs you may normally provide.

Salaries, commissions, bonuses, and contest prizes may be the keys to quota attainment, but let us not forget one final ingredient—accomplishment.

Salesmen—the hundreds of good ones that we know—are somewhat like professional athletes who, although they perform for financial rewards, play the game to win because they want to win and because they want to better their previous records. This internal feeling of accomplishment is perhaps one of the greatest rewards in life. We are all motivated by our salaries, but we would not have progressed if this were our sole motivation. Just as a batter may try to break 300 for the sake of accomplishment, so, too, will a good salesman work the extra hours to meet or exceed a quota. Although financial gain is a motive, let us not forget man's inborn desire to excel.

A salesman's quota that is equitable for him and for his company provides the best basis for a salesman's earnings as well as the best measuring stick to qualify him for advancement. As such, it provides management with an essential tool for continued growth and sets up for the salesman an attainable goal which he can achieve with justifiable pride.

Extra Discounts as Distributor Incentive

A major corporation in the appliance industry offered its distributors extra discounts as a reward for meeting or exceeding quotas. In a general announcement to all distributors, it outlined the plan as follows:

Starting with this convention, October 1, through September of next year, distributors will be eligible for a special quota fund.

1. If a distributor makes quota in October (four-week month) he will receive 1 percent on all his October sales.
2. If he repeats in November (four-week month) he will receive 1½ percent on all his November sales.
3. If he again repeats in December (five-week month) by doing 100 percent or more of his quota, he will receive 2 percent on all his December sales.
4. The distributor will continue to receive 2 percent for each consecutive month in which he makes quota until October 1 of next year.
5. If a distributor misses quota in any one month, the procedure is repeated beginning with "1."
6. All credits will be issued automatically and in accordance with weekly sales reports.

The Use of Quotas in Incentive Trips

Contests and prize trips as a means of stimulating distributors and dealers to meet their quotas have come into widespread use. Many companies offer their dealers free trips to their annual conventions as a reward for meeting their quotas. Some companies provide incentive trips to such places as Bermuda, Puerto Rico, and Acapulco, Mexico.

Waste King Corporation took 450 distributors and their dealers to Bermuda. This was followed by other trips to Puerto Rico, Holland, and Italy.

Waste King pays for half of the cost of the trip; the distributor pays the other half. When a dealer, plumber, or builder purchases a Waste King product he receives points toward a potential trip. The points were awarded during an 11-month period.

The Primary Purpose of Sales Quotas

Sales quotas provide standards whereby sales volume responsibilities may be distributed, and achievements measured and motivated. Quotas may be based on any of the following factors:

Dollar volume   *New accounts opened*
Unit volume   *Demonstrations made*
Calls made   *Services rendered*

Or they may be based on a combination of these.

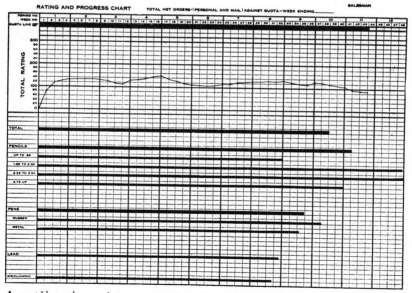

A graphic rating and progress card such as this makes an ideal way of plotting each salesman's work. Every up and down column represents one week. The length of the line shows just what the salesman is, or is not, doing.

Sales quotas also may apply to such concepts as the following:

Geographical areas   *Product lines*

Organizational departments *Market classifications*

When attuned to volume responsibilities distribution, the setting of quotas is:

a. *From top management down*

b. *From the field sales force up*

c. *A combination of both*

Many companies establish quotas by first estimating their total sales for the coming year and then apportioning them to the respective sales divisions, districts, branches, and sales territories. Various means are used in the apportioning process:

Past sales.

Theoretical potentiality.

A combination of past sales and assumed potentiality.

A good guess.

Past sales are certainly an important element, but this basis may compound past inequities. Salesman A might have sales of $150,000, or 1 percent of the firm's total; Salesman B, $300,000, or 2 percent. Should the company anticipate an increase of 10 percent, A's quota would be increased 10 percent to $165,000, while B's quota would go to $330,000. However, A might be having an exceedingly difficult time even in getting his current $150,000 because of limited sales opportunities or severe competition; while B, with his $300,000, may merely be skimming the cream from what could be a very much more lucrative territory. Then too, A may be headed into a bonanza with a surging economy in his territory, whereas B might be headed for trouble through some event such as the death of an important customer.

For these reasons, an increasing number of companies are making valiant efforts to measure the potentiality of their respective sales areas as one basis for distribution of sales responsibility. There are many indices that can be used. One basis is population, wherein the company divides company sales by population figures. This unit is then extended to all the territories, as a measure of past sales opportunities. These estimates are then increased proportionately to reach in total the company's anticipated sales.

(CODE) ITEMS	AMOUNT	% TO U.S.	ESTIMATED SALES				
			Total County Sale % to U.S.	By Salesman % to % to County U.S.	By Mail % to % to County U.S.		
1. Literate Pop over 10 yrs.	81502	0.1045 %					
2. No.of Income Returns	10675	0.1652 %					
3. Net Sales	$ 6141	0.1306 %					
4. Net Sales	$ 6025	0.1843 %					
5.							
6.							
7. S.E.P. (Combined)	7388	0.1372 %					
8.							
9. Eastman							
10. Fuller Brush							
11. Wrigley							
12. Western Co.							
13. Colgate							
14. Quaker Oats							
15.							
16.							
17.							
18.			0.16 %	75% 0.12%	25% 0.04%		

(Table heading: KANE COUNTY STATISTICS STATE ILLINOIS)

Form used by a pencil and pen manufacturer to set territorial quotas by counties. A similar card record is made for each county in the United States. By totaling the estimated sales for all counties included in a territory, a salesman's quota is established. A check of each county quota is obtained by comparing with quotas of other companies.

Another method is to proportion the total sales of the industry by population figures or other indices, then apply the resulting unit to the population indices for the individual areas.

This gives their theoretical full potentiality, which must be reduced by the ratio of the company's anticipated sales to the industry's total sales. The first method is attuned to company average sales; the second method has little reference to company sales.

A third method is to divide the sales of the best territories by population figures or other indices, then apply this unit to the population of the poorer territories as a measure of what they should have done.

Population figures can be very misleading because of inequalities in buying power, tastes, and types of customers in the various geographical, race, nationality, and environmental sections of the nation.

Other indices may be better to use. Among these are data developed by or from—

Sales Management *magazine*	*Automobile Registrations*
The Curtis Publishing Co.	*Manufacturing Statistics*
The Hearst Publications	*Factory Employment Statistics*

Another difficulty arises in using dollar sales rather than physical unit sales. Dollar sales are subject to changes due to price increases or decreases, national economic inflation or deflation. If dollar figures are used, they should be reduced to constant dollars, by dividing sales for each year by cost of living or other indices.

Probably one of the greatest handicaps to basing quotas on management estimates of total sales is the likelihood that salesmen can't or won't perform as management expects them to perform. If management sets its production schedules and operating budgets on such anticipated sales figures and the salesmen fall down, management is in for trouble and the company is in for losses.

Using Salesmen's Estimates

Many companies have their salesmen anticipate their sales for the coming year, adjusting these estimates by branch manager and district manager judgment, totaling the results, and calling the final figure the company's sales goal for the year.

To sharpen the salesmen's estimates, management instructs the men to call on all their customers and discuss with them their anticipated activities and demands.

However, salesmen usually dislike this assignment, as they fear they may antagonize their customers. Customers frequently feel that the salesman is being nosy, and they become cagey and give answers best suited to their own ends. There is a strong possibility that haphazard estimates will be made, hardly reliable enough for company programing.

Then, too, salesmen are, as a class, inclined to be optimistic. If no penalty results from wrong estimates, they will be inclined to place them too high. Or some will place them too low, so that they can make a good showing. In either case, the men are usually not very objective unless held under tight rein.

Defining Quota Terms

Quota, sales goals, and incentive base are three terms frequently used synonymously. However, they have different connotations.

A *quota* is a standard established to measure achievement and used in organizing, programing, budgeting, and controlling company activities. It is carefully, conservatively, and cautiously planned.

A *sales goal* contains more wishful thinking; it is something hoped for and worth striving for, but company budgets (financing, production, and profits) are not geared to it. They are geared to the quota.

An *incentive base* is a measure of minimum satisfactory achievement, often apportioned to the company's quota but more often set

TOWN DEALER		PENCIL	RUBBER PEN	METAL PEN	LEAD	TOTAL
Frank Ward, 145 Main St., Anadarko, Okla	ESTIMATE	100	25	50	50	225
	YOUR PERSONAL SALES					
Weaver-Ellis & Jordon, Formerly Weaver & Jordon, Antlers, Okla.	ESTIMATE	Will	not handle	again		
	YOUR PERSONAL SALES					
Doyle's, 4 Main St., Ardmore, Okla.	ESTIMATE	75	50	75		200
	YOUR PERSONAL SALES					
Gravitt Drug Co., Ardmore, Okla.	ESTIMATE	310		15	5	330
	YOUR PERSONAL SALES					
Rittman Bros., Bartels, Okla.	ESTIMATE		NO	GOOD		
	YOUR PERSONAL SALES					

By listing all accounts in a territory and then having each individual salesman estimate what he feels each account should buy during the year, and averaging these estimates with potential quota, a satisfactory working quota can be established.

a little lower, to provide incentive compensation payments in recognition of achievements above the satisfactory level.

A Combination of Methods

Probably the safest method to follow in setting quotas is to work from both ends, from the top down and from the territories up, and then compromise to reach the final figure.

As management prepares its figures based on economic and market studies, the branch managers conduct customer audits with their individual salesmen. Every attempt is made by the branch managers to obtain realistic sales goals, colored by the characteristics of the salesmen and their individual customers. The sales goals of all the territories are totaled and compared with management's initial quota; if these are reasonably close, management's quota stands.

Working from both ends is a practical method. For unless the branch managers and salesmen can sell the quota on paper, they can hardly be expected to sell it in fact. If top management's initial quota is higher than the field force honestly feels it can produce, management's quota had best be lowered, or new plans projected by the force that will make achievement realistic. Conversely, if the estimate of the field force is high, its program should be searchingly examined; if it still looks reasonable, top management should raise its sights, if practicable.

Scheduling Sales Calls

It is the responsibility of marketing executives to direct the planning of where the company's salesmen go in their sales work, when and with what frequency they make their calls, and what they do when they get there. This may be symbolized by W-W-W: Where, When, and What.

WHERE to Call: Applying the philosophy that markets and sales territories are the property of the company and not of the salesmen, it behooves marketing executives to see that all present and prospective customers are analyzed for sales opportunities and that the salesmen be required to service them well.

In proper sequence, one might say a company should first obtain a suitable product; then a suitable sales force; and last, but far from least, determine where the sales force should go and direct its activities.

Too frequently, salesmen are assigned to territories with no other instructions than to cover them as they deem fit; sometimes prospect cards or customers' names are given to them, but too often they must dig this information out for themselves. Naturally, some salesmen adopt a course best suited to themselves with little regard or thought as to what is best for the company.

Sales calls should be made where the greatest sales opportunities exist; it is wiser to pass by a poor prospect and call on a prospect with greater potentiality, even though more travel time might be consumed, than it is to call on everyone, determinedly and blindly.

An individual salesman, when trained and aggressively working, can make, on an average, only a certain number of calls a day, be that three or five or 15 or more. His time is not elastic; it is fixed in respect to amount. Therefore, it is necessary that policies be adopted that outline how he should expend his time. He is like an army officer with a given number of soldiers to direct; some need to be sent to cover this objective, others sent to cover other objectives. In like manner, the salesman, with a given number of calls available, should be guided and instructed as to how he should deploy them and on whom they should be expended.

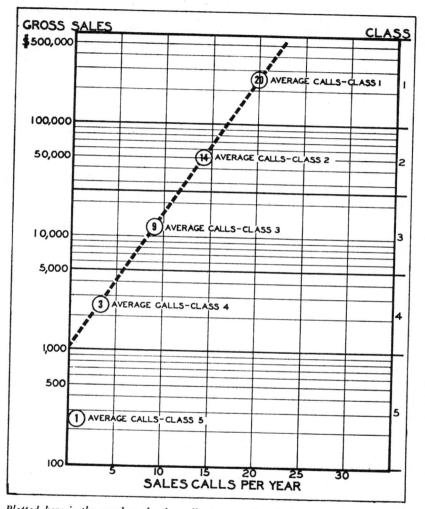

Plotted here is the number of sales calls per year in relation to gross dollar sales for a chemical-products company. To plot the sales cost in relation to customer size (Class), the mean customer size of each class has to be determined. The average call frequency of the class was plotted in relation to the average dollar size of the class. The straight-line relationship on the semilog graph represents an exponential function.

(From *Dartnell Sales and Marketing Service*.)

WHEN to Call: All customers or prospects do not demand the same degree of attention or service. With a prospect, exploratory calls may need to be made only once in six months, while, with a very active and important account, calls may need to be made daily.

Seasonal patterns or buying traditions also enter the picture. Christmas goods are sold early in a year for fall delivery; therefore many calls must be made in the spring during the buying period, but few need be made around Christmas during the retail sales period.

Seasonal patterns also prevail for farm products. In the construction industry, the call activity is increased when contractors are bidding on projects; during the actual building period, calls may become fewer and take on the aspect of service calls.

Besides the different call-demand characteristics of products, industries arid markets, there are differences in the requirements of individual buyers or of personnel in a customer's organization. Some buyers rely heavily on the salesmen with whom they do business; they may open their requisition files to them and expect the salesmen to pick out those which apply to their materials and to enter buying orders for them. Or, as with the retail trade, buyers may expect salesmen to call daily (as with bread) or weekly (canned goods), check inventories, replace stales, and reorder stock. Frequently the buyer merely signs the purchase orders, depending on the salesman not to understock or overstock him.

Customer Audits

It is important that customer audits be conducted regularly at scheduled times, possibly once or twice a year, and jointly by the salesmen and their immediate managers. The sales manager should feel responsible for getting his salesmen to cover their territories wisely; therefore, he must participate in planning the sales strategy. Furthermore, salesmen are inclined to hold their goals low so as to make a good showing. Sales managers need to act as a counterbalance, to keep quotas as high as reasonable in order to provide meaningful challenges.

Whether in a small, moderately sized, or large company, it becomes quite a problem for the chief executive to see that widely separated or even functionally separated executives adhere to company programs simultaneously; and that, where there is repetition of the same operation, each recurrence be similar, no matter how long the time interval between them; or that programed actions take place in proper sequence.

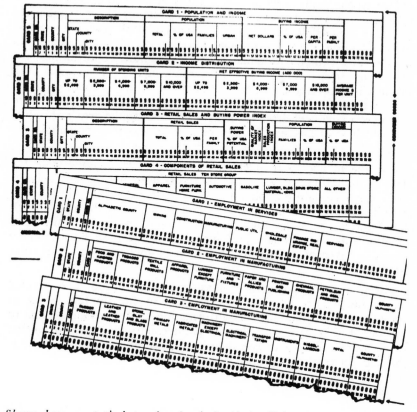

Shown here are typical punchcards of the kind which can be used for fast, automatic territory analysis in conjunction with the Sales Management *"Survey of Buying Power." Companies with their own IBM or Remington Rand equipment can process them automatically, while companies without such equipment can have them analyzed by qualified research consultants. In addition to population, income, employment, and similar factors shown on the cards illustrated above, many other specialized indexes are available on county cards, such as Index of Urban Demand (for styled merchandise), Index of Office Equipment Demand, Index of Resort Activity, Index of Growth Factors (to isolate areas of rapid or slow growth), TV Homes (as of a certain date), age statistics, etc. It is necessary only to determine what factors (or combinations thereof) would reflect demand for your product, then process the cards to determine key marketing factors.*

Courtesy, Market Statistics, Inc., New York City

Using Punch Cards to Evaluate Sales Performance

One of the many uses of punch cards in marketing operations is in connection with the "Annual Survey of Buying Power" published by *Sales Management* magazine. Companies of all sizes are increasingly adapting their accounting procedures and sales records to punch card equipment. This offers many new opportunities for evaluating sales performance. If a sales figure for an area or a product is expressed as a percentage of the company total, comparison with some objective indicator of the potential, also expressed as a percentage, will draw immediate attention to the area or product for which sales are significantly greater or less than potential.

We reproduce on an earlier page actual IBM layout cards, indicating the number and diversity of market factors underlying the data in the "Survey" which can be reproduced for special analyses. IBM cards contain 80 columns which permit including on a single card information on company sales, codes to identify the area (which can refer to states, counties, cities, metropolitan areas, or any combination thereof), alphabetic description of the area, plus as many as six or seven of the market factors most applicable to a particular product.

After a sales manager, or market research head, has decided which factors are of chief concern to him, he can take a set of county cards containing this information and rearrange them to conform to his sales areas, based on the county-by-county definition of each area. The cards can then be run through a listing machine, to yield potentials, subtotaled for each area.

Chapter 52

TERRITORIAL PROFIT CONTROL

S HARE of market is one of the standards by which a company determines the effectiveness of its marketing efforts. A customary practice is for the sales manager to add 10 percent (or any other percentage) to the previous year's share of market. Obviously this is just the beginning, since the increase cannot come from any one sales district or territory.

The next step is to analyze each individual sales territory according to its actual potential.

For example, if electrical power is introduced into a region where none existed before, the potential sales for all kinds of electrically-operated equipment will be greatly improved and the percentage increase in this territory should be much greater in relation to other sales districts. Similarly the addition of new distributers or the assignment of extra salesmen to a territory have a decided influence on the sales to be expected from that particular area.

At one time sales territories followed geographical boundaries or traditional routes. Then sales managers realized that in order to be sure they were getting a full share of the existing business from each territory, more precise information was needed. The question, for example, of which territories should receive intensive sales cultivation and which should be treated as fringe territories can hardly be answered without reliable data on each sales unit. The question of reducing territories, always a headache in sales management, cannot be properly considered unless the sales executive has fairly dependable facts on the territory. Moreover, such information is necessary to "sell" the salesman on taking a smaller territory. Where to direct the advertising and sales promotion effort with the best chances of success can likewise only be properly determined in the light of market data. Today especially, when sales planning is in terms of selective selling rather than seeking all-over coverage, it is most important that each market be carefully studied, appraised, and classified as to its sales potential.

The County as a Unit of Measurement

Marketing men differ in their opinion as to what is the best unit to use in measuring markets. Some favor setting up areas determined by the nature of the business and establishing a sales potential for each area. A notable and widely used plan of this sort was developed by Pacific Mills. The country was broken down into small territorial units; population by income groups was then determined for each unit. The units were gathered into sales territories and the unit potentials added together to get the territory potential. In establishing the potential, known per-capita purchases of the products were used. This per-capita purchase figure was adjusted according to income groups, since it was found there was a definite relationship between a man's income and the number and quality of shirts he was apt to buy. This method, however, can be used only for consumer products on which the government or other agency has made studies to determine per-capita purchases.

Most companies that distribute nationally find the county unit is the most convenient one for measuring sales potentials. This method is not without its drawbacks, not the least of which is the 10-year lapse between taking the U.S. Census. Then, too, it is not always possible to secure the variety of information needed to establish county potentials. But at least when you know the approximate potential in each county, it is a simple matter to combine the counties into sales territories and establish reasonably accurate territorial potentials.

Trading-Area Units

Some marketing organizations, notably publishers selling circulation in concentrated areas, outdoor advertising companies, and TV and radio stations, contend that the county is of questionable value as a sales unit because of the inaccessibility of many counties. They contend, with some logic, that if your salesmen or distributors are unable to maintain sales contact with any given county, that county, however much potential it may have, is of little or no sales worth.

In a talk before a trade association recently, a marketing executive of a highly successful nationally-operating company explained how these trading-area potentials were determined:

For more than 25 years we have been developing the trading-area system of sales control. In brief this is what we have done. We have studied every town in Bradstreet—65,000 of them—and, by a long process of elimination, have reduced the ordinary map of the United States, with all its confusion of political boundaries, its details of mountains, rivers, and deserts, into a simplified "Marketing Map of the United States," which shows the normal flow of trade in this country and the shortest route to the national market.

We have developed and drawn the boundaries for the principal trading areas in the United States. We have been guided by buying habits that pay no attention whatever to political boundary lines. We have used 33 factors to make sure we are right. These 33 factors which determine the principal trading centers and their consumer areas cover such subjects as physical characteristics; people and homes, transportation, communication and distribution machinery; valuation of products and sources of personal income; volume of business, wealth, and standards of living.

In developing the trading-area system of sales potentials, we have broken down the national market as a landscape engineer would break down seven meadows into a fine golf course. We have laid out 613 selling holes, called consumer-trading areas.

The factor of concentration is very important. Selective marketing means concentration. For example, every sales manager should know that most of the business in any town is transacted by a few dealers. He should know that the best 25 percent of his dealers will account for 75 percent of the volume total. So it should not surprise him to learn that of 65,000 towns listed in Bradstreet, the key cities, or principal trading centers of the United States account for more than 70 percent of the total annual retail business in this country.

To search out these important markets, we have analyzed every city. We surveyed the wholesale and retail advantages, the ratings of the stores, and their variety in each community. After this was done, comparative values were made of all places in each section, resulting in the choice of the most dominating commercial center for each area.

Sometimes a city with a smaller population than another has been selected as the key point of a trading area. This is because an impartial examination of all 33 major factors has ultimately resulted in its selection despite its smaller population.

When we have completely analyzed each of the 33 factors, we are ready to determine the extent of the key city influence. We trace the railroad lines, the auto roads, and visualize the flow of trade throughout the section. We trace the buying habits, customs, and trade tendencies in each section. Then we interlock the small pieces of the trade pattern until we have a section which rightly fits against another section—just like a jigsaw puzzle.

The trading-area system offers sales managers the following opportunities for closer sales control:

1. Establishing your sales control by consumer "Trading-Area Units" in contrast to political lines.

2. Revising your sales districts and assigning logical territories of these control units to salesmen.

3. Selecting the principal trading centers in each territory which should receive the greatest amount of sales and advertising energy.

4. Concentrating the time of salesmen in these key cities to obtain greatest results from their time, expense, and selling ability.

5. Checking the sales performance either by months, quarters, or half-year periods against sales potentials.

6. Deciding whether present retail distribution is adequate or justified. This may mean too many or too few retailers in certain markets.

7. Determining the sales potential within each trading-area unit and comparing it with sales performance.

8. Paralleling all your advertising efforts with sales efforts in the most profitable consumer-trading area.

A marketing executive who inherited an old-fashioned marketing setup and turned it into a scientific operation, based on trading areas instead of geographical territories, reported recently as follows:

There can be no question but that trading areas are more meaningful than county lines. Just for one example of many I might mention is St. Louis, Missouri. Much of the marketing area for this city lies across the Mississippi River, in Illinois.

However, this does not mean that county-based geographical territories should be ignored. In many instances, trading areas can be built up, using counties as building units. Of the thousands of counties in the United States, about 75 percent of the national business is concentrated in approximately 25 percent of the counties. It is important, therefore, to study county population and other sales statistics when building trading-area sales territories.

Visualizing Market Potentials

The well-managed business establishment, marketing its products on a national or seminational scale, not only has figures to show where the best sales opportunities lie in every state in which it does business, but it maintains map records on which these data are projected and pictured. Much of the value of sales or marketing facts is lost to a business through the failure of management to utilize them properly after they have been compiled. For the purpose of graphic presentation of market data, it is recommended that outline state maps showing each county in the state, but with no other distracting information, be used. Such maps may be obtained from any sales equipment supplier. Use heavy chart paper, punched so that the maps may be filed in a ring binder. Or wall maps with washable surfaces may be used in special map display fixtures.

A sales manager, to do an effective job, must chart the operations of his salesmen just as a military leader must visualize the movement of troops. To do this requires that sales figures be plotted against sales opportunities in such a way that lost opportunities or neglected markets will be flagged. Here again the outline county map and figures on sales by counties (made easy with punched card accounting machines) are recommended. Territories can be marked

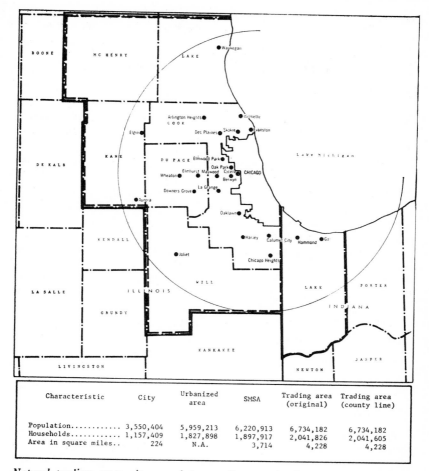

Characteristic	City	Urbanized area	SMSA	Trading area (original)	Trading area (county line)
Population...........	3,550,404	5,959,213	6,220,913	6,734,182	6,734,182
Households...........	1,157,409	1,827,898	1,897,917	2,041,826	2,041,605
Area in square miles..	224	N.A.	3,714	4,228	4,228

Natural trading areas often overlap state lines, as in the case of metropolitan Chicago, which includes the relatively high-ranking consumer communities of Hammond and Gary, Indiana.

Courtesy: The Philadelphia *Inquirer*

out on the map and colored crayons used to indicate the potential sales for each territory, as determined by county quotas, actual sales for the preceding year, the peak sales, and current sales expectancy. This same picture may also be obtained through the use of tacks and similar devices in a map mounted on a soft board.

It is significant that, after experimenting with elaborate market studies, many concerns are coming back to modified population figures as a basis for gauging sales potentials. No matter what line you are in, in the long run you will find it is the number of people in a county, multiplied by their per-capita buying power, that most influences their sales. But, of course, if the product is sold through dealers a great deal depends on the number of stores in the county selling your product. For example, Lake County, Illinois (which lies next to Cook), has a high buying power per capita and a large population. Yet the residents of that county often shop in Chicago, which is in Cook County. Consequently, the number of retail outlets in Lake County is restricted.

By a test of some kind determine just what proportion of the per-capita income is being spent for your product or service. Probably you already have data on this point. But even though you are selling roadgraders or locomotives it is important to have a per-capita basis for working out quota figures. With this information available it is an easy matter to figure the exact business that you should get each year out of a given county. When you have worked out these figures post them with colored crayon on the proper county, leaving room to note beneath them actual yearly sales which show you how far short of the mark you are falling. At the end of a year or two it is possible to combine these figures and thus arrive at what you will find to be a very practical and effective sales potential for each territory. These figures also are available in laying out subterritories, or assigning territories to agents or exclusive dealers, jobbers, and other distributors.

Locating Branch Offices and Sales Agencies

Many companies have not paid any great attention to the efficient location of warehouses, branch offices, or jobber connections. As a result countless orders are being lost through the inability of manufacturers and jobbers to give the prompt service which present merchandising conditions demand.

An outline state map usually is used to decide where to locate jobbers so as to assure the manufacturer of the best distribution facilities in each state. The salesman serving a certain territory is stationed at a point located on the map with a ringed dot. Stocks are carried by local distributors at various cities in each state. These cities are indicated on the map by dots, and territories are assigned on county lines according to accessibility from cities indicated. Territorial boundaries can be outlined by red lines. Either the quota for a particular subterritory or the number of dealers being served by a jobber or whatever information is essential in a particular line of business can be shown by placing the proper figures below the names of the cities. Water colors may be used to distinguish territories.

Trading area maps are usually worth studying with some care. There must be sound reasons for every curve and every indentation. This long arm which projects to the north may indicate a prosperous valley, a good road, or unusually convenient transportation facilities. It may measure also the relative success of your promotional activities.

If you are located in one of the larger cities, it is not safe to assume that you draw trade from the entire city. If you have mapped your local or immediate trading area carefully, you may observe from its outlines that you are getting no business to speak of from certain residential districts to which you have always assumed you made a strong appeal. On the other hand, you may discover that much of your trade comes from districts populated by people whom you had ignored in your merchandising plans or who, for some other reason, have been overlooked. Then, too, the location of paved roads may easily carry your trading territory 50 miles along that highway, whereas it would extend only a few miles if such roads did not exist.

How to Estimate Total Sales in Territory

Having defined your trading area and analyzed it with some care, your next step is to estimate its share of the country's total sales. This can be done in two simple ways; and it is well to use both in order to be able to check one with the other.

The first method is based upon the population of your trading area which usually can be calculated with little difficulty. Divide your estimate of the total population of your trading area by 3.71 (the average number of persons in a family at the present time) in order to get the number of families. Now, estimate the proportions that should be classed, respectively, as rural and as urban (bearing in mind that people living in towns or cities of 2,500 or more are classed as urban, and those living in smaller towns or villages or in the country, as rural) ; figure out the number of families in each of these two groups. If you now multiply the number of rural families by the average for the entire United States, and the number of urban families by the urban average, and add the resulting figures, you will have a rough, yet helpful, estimate.

To check this estimate based upon population alone, consult one of the many excellent national surveys (you probably can secure one from your advertising department), from which you can estimate the approximate percentage of national buying power represented by your trading area. For our purpose it will be safe to assume that sales of your product in your territory should bear about the same ratio to total national sales as the ratio between the buying power credited to your trading area and national buying power.

It may be necessary, however, to make allowances for the effects of current economic forces. If your trading area should be suffering from unusual depression or other conditions unfavorable to retail trade, your estimate should be reduced accordingly. On the other hand, if conditions are unusually good, you should increase your estimate.

Take into account also the habits of the community. If it is largely industrial, families are doubtless moving in and out rapidly; if it is principally farming territory, moves are likely to be relatively infrequent.

The type of population is also a factor to be considered; different races and nationalities not only have different tastes in house furnishings, but also occupy different economic levels.

Metropolitan Market Data

In laying out a sales plan aimed at a group of metropolitan markets rather than a definite marketing area or geographical trading unit, the best source for market information is usually the local newspaper; the next best bet is the Chamber of Commerce.

Other dependable sources of information concerning the relative condition of business in different cities are the United Business Service and Babson's Reports, Inc., both of Boston. Babson publishes, in connection with its service, a map showing which territories are the most active from a sales standpoint each month. Other reliable indexes of this kind are the summary of debits to individual accounts (check transactions) as reported by the Federal Reserve banks, and other government statistics.

Many manufacturers are making wide use of the syndicated services offered by A. C. Nielsen Company of Chicago. Nielsen, in addition to national reports, provides "breakouts" of major markets such as Chicago, New York, Los Angeles, etc. Nielsen has a nationwide staff of field auditors checking grocery, drug, camera, and appliance stores in order to determine the sales of entire market groups (e.g., cake mixes, detergents, cold tablets, etc.) as well as the individual brands within each product group. The raw data,

WISCONSIN

HEARST MAGAZINES
Marketing—Research
57th Street at 8th Ave.
New York 19, N.Y.
WISCONSIN
★ Principal Trading Center
▬▬ Trading Area Boundaries
— County Boundary
SCALE OF MILES
0 10 20 30 40 50

MARKETING MAP OF WISCONSIN
Arranged by the State's Principal Trading Centers and their
Consumer Trading Areas. Boundaries follow county lines since
the county is now generally recognized as the standard marketing unit. The "Principal Trading Centers," designated in red,
are the central marketing points of their areas. These Trading
Areas are economic units and reflect consumer buying habits.

Notice:
This map which is part of the "Trading Area System of
Sales Control" is fully protected by copyright and it may
not be reprinted, either wholly or in part without special
permission.
©1962 by The Hearst Corporation

Base map copyright by C.S. Hammond & Co., N.Y.

*Hearst Magazines Marketing—Research sells state marketing maps, such as the
one for Wisconsin above, which outline the principal trading areas formed by
consumer buying habits. Sales managers may obtain information from Hearst
Magazines Marketing—Research, 57th Street at Eighth Avenue, New York,
N. Y. 10019.*

developed by means of store audits, are projected to regional as well as national totals. In addition to showing sales and sales' share, the report also provides data relative to distribution, inventories, out-of-stock, prices, special factory packs, and so forth. Nielsen service is provided on a continuous basis only so that marketing trends of all types can be evaluated as they occur.

Census of Distribution Data

Among the many useful data available for market analysis purposes is the Census of Distribution made by the Department of Commerce, Bureau of the Census, Washington. The following suggestions for the use of these data in sales planning and market determination are offered:

BASE YOUR DISTRIBUTION ON THE NUMBER OF RETAIL STORES, in any given kind of business, that carry your kind of goods.

LEARN WHAT OTHER STORES MIGHT CARRY YOUR PRODUCTS. By a comparison of the breakdown of sales by commodities in the retail reports, you can learn whether there are other kinds of stores with which your sales department is not familiar, and that might be induced to carry your products.

MAP THE WHOLESALE RESOURCES IN YOUR PROPOSED TERRITORY. By a study of the wholesale census reports, you can discover how many wholesale merchants, brokers, jobbers, and other types of wholesalers there are in any particular section of the country who distribute your kind of goods. To the manufacturer or primary producer, the wholesale statistics enable the producer to follow the principle of selective distribution. By study of the wholesale reports he can determine roughly where his wholesale market lies and the extent of his market. He will find the basic facts to enable him to select brokers or selling agents in territories where they will serve his interests most efficiently. He can select wholesale merchants or jobbers on a scientific basis and he can discover the location and relative strength of chain warehouses. It is possible for him to see how widely other manufacturers have established wholesale branch houses. Information is given for 92 commodities that shows the volume of commodity sales by different trades and by all of the various types of wholesale middlemen operating in those trades. These factors are of inestimable value in formulating an intelligent selective program.

How TO MEASURE YOUR POTENTIAL MARKET. The retail census reports contain schedules showing the commodities sold by each kind of retail store as well as the percentage of sales of each commodity in relation to the total sales of that kind of store. A given commodity is often found in many kinds of stores. To measure your potential market, compile the total sales of all the stores of each kind that sell your products, and apply thereto the percentage that represents the sale of your classification of goods. This can be done for any city, county, state, or combination of states.

ADAPT YOUR SALES POLICIES TO THE REQUIREMENTS OF RETAILERS. Many ambitious sales campaigns are failures because they were not checked in advance by an experienced distribution engineer to insure that they would be acceptable to retailers. Producers should understand the problems that retailers face. In the absence of a retail consultant, manufacturers may, by a careful study of the retail census reports, gain a sympathetic understanding of the many problems faced by retailers. This understanding applies particularly to such factors as operating expenses, customers' returns and allowances, extent and character of competition, credit that must be extended to customers, and the availability of wholesale distributors.

How to Determine Price Policies. You know that the potential market is greater when the price is lower; however, the producer's price cannot disregard the conditions under which the article is finally retailed. Certain retail prices are not popular with the public, and of course increase sales resistance. On account of this the retailer many times finds himself forced to adopt too high or too low retail prices, because the producer did not follow through to the consumer in planning his price policies. A study of the retail and the wholesale census reports will allow the producer to set margins between his price and the planned retail price that make due allowance for distribution costs. If you plan to distribute through any of the several types of wholesale channels, this method is particularly applicable.

The Territory Audit

One of the big problems of the sales manager is keeping on top of what is going on in the individual accounts and prospective accounts in his sales area, says J. V. Fort, marketing training counselor in his Dartnell Executive Report, *Dynamic Sales Leadership*. Here is a digest of his recommendations:

The territory audit correlates the manager's supervision of his men with his job of getting the most business possible from customers, clients, and prospects.

While it is true that most territories are described by geographic lines, many sales organizations are set up by categories of customers and prospects calling for specialized coverage. In these latter industries there may be two or more separate sales "territories" which overlap or are superimposed in the same geographic area.

The territory audit is a useful tool by which the sales manager can do a more effective job of supervising the activities of his men and developing their personal potential.

The procedure also has a training aspect. By going through the territory-audit routine, a great many things can be pointed out to the salesman during the audit which, under ordinary circumstances, might never come to the surface.

PRELIMINARY ARRANGEMENTS

Where is the audit to be conducted? Who is to be involved? This might include someone from the advertising department, accounting department, etc. What will be the timetable?

Where outside departments are involved, a specific timetable and agenda should be set up and appointments made with the other people in advance of the session so that the salesman's time away from his territory can be reduced to a minimum. Of course, a timetable of this sort is not necessary when only manager and man are involved.

Since this "audit" procedure involves more than ordinary digging into the background, information, and progress of each account, some salesmen may feel that this is an invasion of their authority, or shows a lack of confidence of the superior in his subordinates. If there is any suspicion on the part of the sales manager that such a feeling may exist in the mind of the salesman, it would be well to stress that this is not the case.

A good sales manager, once the lines and limitations of authority have been established and mutually understood, will make no decisions which his subordinate should make except as a training procedure. Subsequent decisions on the same matter should be tossed back to the subordinate to make him stand on his own feet. Only thus can he grow and develop.

Prior to the interview or audit with his man, the sales manager must determine what information he needs about each account in order to give the salesman the most effective supervisory guidance.

Here is a list of possible points regarding which the sales manager would like broader information, or which he wishes to discuss with the salesman:

Official business style of the firm.

Names of the heads of the business—and a short estimate of the foibles, capabilities, and the "degree of influence" of each.

Same information about the actual buyer.

Who are "centers of influence" who affect, even remotely, the purchase of our kind of product?

General characteristics of the executives in the account: Are they forward looking and progressive or reactionary? Is their management sound, mediocre, or poor?

Are their business facilities adequate? (Such things as buildings, equipment, machines, trucks.)

How much of our type of product do they use?

What percentage of such material do they buy from us?

Why can we not get a bigger share?

What can we effectively do about it?

Do we have any items to which they have not been introduced? If they have seen and have not bought, why? What can we do about it?

How can or should we improve our service to, and relations with, this account?

How correct is our call frequency? Are we wasting time and money by calling too frequently? Would additional calls generate enough extra volume to justify the expense?

What is the economic climate in this particular market or industry—and what steps should we take to exploit or minimize it?

What are our credit arrangements with this account and would a revision result in more business?

After each individual customer has been covered, each prospect should be investigated in the same manner, with individual plans for action to be taken with each.

SUMMARY FOR TERRITORY

When each customer's status and potential have been explored, and plans for approach to prospects have been developed, it is usually useful to build a summary of general activity for the territory as a whole. This should include such data as the following:

Present gross sales for territory.

Potential of territory (our total sales plus total sales of our kind of product by competition).

Our present penetration (percent of potential we enjoy).

Long-range objectives for territory (possibly three to five years).

Short-range objectives (next few months, but not more than one year).

Matters requiring immediate attention, including opportunities or special events to be exploited, as well as situations to be improved or corrected.

FREQUENCY OF AUDIT

Admittedly, the territory audit is no small task, nor is it easy to do. Obviously it cannot be done so often as to require a burdensome amount of time. In most industries and companies, an annual audit is adequate.

Timing must be determined by each manager to fit his own needs. It is hardly ever practical to take on all men in rotation, day after day. It is more practical to spread these interviews through the year, possibly one man every month or two. The real test is the thoroughness of the job.

Unless yours is an unusual organization, the chances are that even the more experienced men have had very little instruction in planning their time or the sequential order of coverage of their territories. Accordingly, some sales managers feel that the territory audit is not quite complete without constructing, jointly with the salesman, a basic but tentative plan for coverage of the territory —including the geographical progression best suited to cover the territory and the approximate time to be spent in each market.

Such a time-management discussion can be most valuable. Both parties to the "audit" should make notes on the agreed coverage and include the geographical sequence and estimated needed time at each location. After such a plan has been worked out with a salesman a few times, he will become adept at weighing the job to be done in each market and organizing his time accordingly.

The manager can also use the customer and territorial summary as a yardstick in measuring performance as well as in assessing areas where the salesman needs help. Not the least of the benefits to the sales manager is the eventuality that he can use this "audit" information to show his own superiors that he is on top of his job as a planner, coordinator, controller, and man-developer.

Chapter 53

SALES TIME AND
EXPENSE CONTROL

W HILE the salesman is usually out of sight, he is *not* out of mind. Making full use of salesmen's time and capacities has preoccupied management for a long time. New men, especially, unless properly trained and supervised, do not fully appreciate the importance of learning how to make the best use of their time without the guidance and supervision of their managers.

Aside from personal factors, the results achieved by salesmen depend, first, on company policies and, secondly, on the quality of the supervision they receive.

The essence of good supervision can be stated in five lines:

1. Know what you expect a salesman to do.

2. See that he knows what you expect him to do.

3. Know that he does what you expect of him.

4. Let him know you know that he has done it.

5. Let him know you appreciate what he has done.

It is amazing how few sales organizations rate "fair" when measured against these five simple tests. Even supposedly well-managed companies have never set up standards of performance for their salesmen beyond their monthly production. Their salesmen do not know exactly what they are expected to do, nor do their sales superiors.

Importance of Close Supervision

To provide the sales organization with leadership of the type under consideration, as contrasted with the top-sergeant variety, calls for close supervision in the field. Some companies have found that best results are secured when there is one supervisor for approximately every 10 salesmen. Others figure on the basis of one to 20 salesmen. Just as you pay for sales training, either in what you spend for the operation or in the loss of profits on the business you lose as a result of inadequate training, so you pay for sales supervision. Since adequately trained supervisors working closely with salesmen in the field usually produce enough extra business to more than carry their expense, it is foolish indeed for management to attempt to get along with half the supervisors needed, and those only partly trained and qualified for sales leadership.

"We try to avoid making the mistake of training our men and then kidding ourselves that they will stay trained," said the sales manager of The Egry Register Company, Dayton. "We cover all districts with personal visits of the sales staff and executives of the company. We also check very carefully on a list of definite points we have prepared.

"We pay particular attention to how our men use the training we have given them during the year. Thus we not only measure the results of the training we have done, but also uncover information which will assist us to plan the next year's training program."

Supervision is conducted through correspondence, telephone contacts, personal interviews in the home office and in the field, bulletins, manuals, sales meetings, and compensation in its fullest extent. Each medium has its advantages and disadvantages.

Personal contact in the field is probably the most effective; the salesman is more relaxed, the environment that created the supervisory need is around him. However, the supervisor cannot always be on hand when needed, so he must sometimes resort to telephone calls and correspondence. They, too, can be effective.

Telephone calls imply importance, immediate action; while letters provide permanent records for study and restudy. Letters carry authority that may easily become forgotten after mere conversations.

Bulletins and manuals provide ready-reference guidance, while sales meetings provide mass supervision and can be strongly inspirational. While monetary compensation involves the attainment of personal desires, and probably carries the greatest motivational force, the compensation of money alone is not enough for the average salesman, who seeks nonmonetary satisfactions as well.

One element of supervision is the taking of corrective action, when needed. On such occasions, the sales supervisor must hear both sides of the story, the salesman's and the customer's, or whoever else may be involved.

SALES REPRESENTATIVE'S PROGRESS REPORT

REYNOLDS METALS COMPANY
FORM R-366-11

EMPLOYEE'S NAME _____ LOCATION _____

CLASSIFICATION _____ DIVISION _____

EMPLOYMENT DATE _____ BIRTH DATE _____

HOW DO YOU RATE SALES REPRESENTATIVE'S PERFORMANCE ON THE FOLLOWING:	PLANS FOR IMPROVEMENT
1. TOTAL SALES VOLUME	
A. FREQUENCY OF CALLS ON PRESENT AND PROSPECTIVE CUSTOMERS. ☐ ☐ ☐ ☐ ☐ ☐ ☐ ☐ BELOW AVERAGE · · · · ABOVE AVERAGE	
B. PERSONAL ACQUAINTANCE WITH CUSTOMER'S EMPLOYEES WHO ARE INVOLVED IN BUYING DECISIONS. ☐ ☐ ☐ ☐ ☐ ☐ ☐ ☐ BELOW AVERAGE · · · · ABOVE AVERAGE	
C. PLANNING IN ADVANCE TO MAKE SUCCESSFUL SALES PRESENTATION. ☐ ☐ ☐ ☐ ☐ ☐ ☐ ☐ BELOW AVERAGE · · · · ABOVE AVERAGE	
D. PROPER SALES PRESENTATION AND CLOSING ABILITY AT TIME OF SALES INTERVIEW. ☐ ☐ ☐ ☐ ☐ ☐ ☐ ☐ BELOW AVERAGE · · · · ABOVE AVERAGE	
E. USE OF PROPER AVAILABLE REYNOLDS SPECIALISTS IN SERVICING ACCOUNTS. ☐ ☐ ☐ ☐ ☐ ☐ ☐ ☐ BELOW AVERAGE · · · · ABOVE AVERAGE	
2. EFFECTIVE TIME AND ACTIVITY PLANNING	
A. PLANNING TIME FOR PROPER COVERAGE OF TERRITORY. ☐ ☐ ☐ ☐ ☐ ☐ ☐ ☐ BELOW AVERAGE · · · · ABOVE AVERAGE	
C. PUNCTUAL PREPARATION OF REPORTS. ☐ ☐ ☐ ☐ ☐ ☐ ☐ ☐ BELOW AVERAGE · · · · ABOVE AVERAGE	
D. KEEPS SUPERVISOR ADVISED OF SITUATION IN THE TERRITORY. ☐ ☐ ☐ ☐ ☐ ☐ ☐ ☐ BELOW AVERAGE · · · · ABOVE AVERAGE	
E. EFFECTIVE CORRESPONDENCE AND PERSONAL RELATIONS WITH CUSTOMERS AND COMPANY PERSONNEL. ☐ ☐ ☐ ☐ ☐ ☐ ☐ ☐ BELOW AVERAGE · · · · ABOVE AVERAGE	
3. PRODUCT, ORGANIZATION AND POLICY KNOWLEDGE RE:	
A. REYNOLDS. ☐ ☐ ☐ ☐ ☐ ☐ ☐ ☐ BELOW AVERAGE · · · · ABOVE AVERAGE	
B. COMPETITION. ☐ ☐ ☐ ☐ ☐ ☐ ☐ ☐ BELOW AVERAGE · · · · ABOVE AVERAGE	
C. CUSTOMERS. ☐ ☐ ☐ ☐ ☐ ☐ ☐ ☐ BELOW AVERAGE · · · · ABOVE AVERAGE	

SEE INSTRUCTIONS ON BACK OF THIS FORM

Part of a sales representative's progress report used by the Reynolds Metals Company. It is similar to an employee-appraisal form, except that it is tailored to sales work.

Problems of Corrective Action

He should discuss the problem in private and not in open meeting or with other salesmen present. This is vital.

He should maintain an attitude of fairness and display a desire to be fair. There should be no snap judgment; instead, there should be an attempt to reach mutual understanding.

He should speak quietly, at his usual cadence, without anger, and permit the salesman plenty of time to register his comments in a like manner. The salesman should not be made to feel that he is being rushed, and he should also be assured that the conversation will be held confidential.

If the salesman becomes resentful, tries to justify his actions in his own mind and take refuge in emotional intensity, time should be taken to calm him down and if possible to terminate the conference in a friendly but firm manner. Afterward there must be firm and fair followthrough.

To bawl a man out, give directions for future conduct, and then close one's eyes to infractions is bad for morale and future sound supervision.

Qualities Required by the Sales Supervisor

To provide adequate supervisory leadership, the sales supervisor must be familiar with every aspect of each salesman's job; he must have vitality and endurance, and not only he himself, but all his staff and assistants who work with him and represent him. He requires decisiveness, with reasonable promptness in making his decisions.

He requires a keen sense of the responsibility that must always be retained by management, and the degree to which it can be shared with those being supervised.

There must be integrity, emotional stability, and a sincere regard for the private and personal welfare of all those who are being supervised.

There must be a capacity for intellectual growth that will permit the sales supervisor to handle the increasing complexity of marketing problems; the desire and ability to maintain openmindedness with regard to the suggestions of others, including those who are being supervised; and ambition to advance in the company and provide expanded opportunities for those who are striving to come up in the organization.

Good supervision also requires an awareness of needs of other departments in the company and a willingness to assist them by every possible means in satisfying those needs. It should extend

FIELD FACILITIES EXPENSE ANALYSIS

LOCATION _____ MONTH _____

CURRENT MONTH			FACILITIES EXPENSE		YEAR TO DATE	
Actual	Budget	Variance	Acct. No. — Description		Actual	Variance
			101	Office Supervisory Salaries		
			103	Clerical Salaries and Wages		
			134	Overtime Premium		
				TOTAL		
			405	Janitor and Washroom Supplies		
			444	Heat, Light and Janitor Salaries		
			461	Moving, Rearranging and Minor Alter.		
			465	Repairs and Maintenance F & F		
			841	Rent		
			865	Depreciation F & F		
			866	Amortization Leasehold Assets		
				TOTAL		
			414	Postage		
			484	Branch Transportation Expense		
				TOTAL		
			443	Telegraph and Telephone Expense		
			406	Stationery and Office Supplies		
			409	Printing		
			552	Legal Services		
			559	Personal Services—Filing Fee		
			571	Moving Expense—Office Emp. Trans.		
			574	Office Traveling Expense		
			602	Empl.—Doctor's Examinations		
			634	Donations		
			642	Miscellaneous		
				TOTAL		
				TOTAL FACILITIES EXPENSE		
				OPERATOR'S SCHOOL		
			101	School Supervisory Salaries		
			104	Instructor's Salaries		
			134	Overtime Premium		
			406	Departmental Supplies		
			573	Traveling Expense		
			642	Miscellaneous		
				TOTAL SCHOOL EXPENSE		
			901	Less: Revenue—Operator's School		
				NET SCHOOL EXPENSE		

EXHIBIT 6

One of the few breakdowns received in this study showing allowances made for the field facilities provided the sales and service departments. Few companies apparently make this fine a breakdown, generally lumping the figure into the over-all overhead of the branch or the entire company.

A field facilities expense analysis form, from the Dartnell Sales and Marketing Service. The caption is carried in the box on the form.

also to the development of cooperative willingness by the salesmen supervised.

A field sales supervisor is not only the representative of management in the field; he is also the principal contact point between the field salesmen and top management. He interprets the policies and objectives of management to the salesmen; and he reports the salesmen's attitudes, conditions of work, and problems to management.

He relates training objectives and programs to the individual personalities of the salesmen, bringing out the strong points in each and correcting their weaknesses. He does not try to force all the men into one mold, but intermingles character traits and policy objectives astutely to gain the greatest permanent benefit for both the company and the men.

He is the watchdog of local profit attainment, keeping prices in line and expenses under control. Through his ability for leadership, he improves the effectiveness of the salesmen, helping them achieve their results through suggestions and, where needed, through active participation. But he takes no undue credit for himself, letting the results of his men testify as to his leadership.

For the supervisor to discharge his responsibilities, he, too, must have clear-cut objectives established for him; he must have quotas, goals, standards, and the same type of leadership from above as he is expected to give to those under him. His policies, duties and responsibilities must be clearly defined.

The Importance of Field Inspections

It is one of the responsibilities of sales executives to keep informed of field conditions and operations through first-hand knowledge—in other words, through personal inspection. Frequently you hear the fear expressed that the field salesmen may feel that the manager is spying on them or doubts their ability to handle their territories when he visits them for an inspection. In such cases, the misunderstanding is due to failure of the sales manager to let his men know that periodic and thorough inspection is one of his duties.

He should go thoroughly into each man's operations, reviewing all records the salesman is supposed to keep, inspecting samples, stocks of literature, the condition of the salesman's car, and many other pertinent things. If any of these sales tools are sloppily maintained, the manager can blame only himself for permitting the condition to exist.

It is as necessary that well-run territories be inspected as it is to inspect poorly-run ones. There are three reasons for this:

First, because it is a responsibility which the sales manager should not shirk.

Second, because the mere act of inspection places a value and importance to that being inspected which helps contribute to its success.

Third, the sales manager will usually pick up some good ideas which he can pass on to his other salesmen.

Frequently one hears managers say that Salesman A is a good man and does not need to be visited. The truth might well be that Salesman A is a lonely man and yearns for some attention from the home office; or he might be even a better man if management would consult with him about his problems. It is safe to say that erring is more frequent in the direction of too little supervision than too much of it.

Inspection and review of field conditions are needed in sales supervision for four important reasons:

1. To bring management into contact with the realities of performance;

2. To develop morale in the field and respect for authority and for company programs;

3. To assure that proper importance is given to the details of the field work;

4. To determine areas in which corrective action should be taken.

Supervision of men includes consideration in the field, to ascertain the validity of sales objectives. This can be determined only through first-hand knowledge of the territory, its sales opportunities, and the hazards to be encountered in realizing these objectives.

Also included is the element of evaluation, which requires the establishment of standards and the maintenance and study of suitable and meaningful records. Supervisory inspection should culminate in the giving of instructions, encouragement and criticism, in setting examples, in counseling, and, where necessary, in disciplining the salesman.

Methods of Time Control

The wise sales manager teaches his salesmen to learn the buying preferences of their customers and to regulate their calling time accordingly, seeing the "early birds" first.

Two salesmen of the same distributor, on being questioned as to when calls could be made on their customers, gave different replies. One said that since buyers wish to go over their mail the first thing in the morning and to sign their letters late in the afternoon, he made his calls between 9:30 a.m. and 4:00 p.m. The other referred to the same work habit, but said he had a number of customers who would see him at 8:00 a.m. and others who would see him as late as 6:00 p.m. before they closed shop. The first salesman rationalized a short work day, the second one found a way of making the most of his selling time.

In selling, face-to-face selling time is about the only expendable item. A salesman improves his knowledge by sharing it with customers; the same is true of his sales skills and sales personality. Everything used in selling increases by use, except face-to-face selling time; *that* is fully expendable.

An Analysis of Time Distribution: In a recent analysis of the time distribution of a national sales force of about 800 men, it was found:

1. On the average, the men spent ⅓ of their time traveling from customer to customer, ⅓ of their time waiting to see the buyers and ⅓ in face-to-face selling contact. Assuming a nine-hour day, from home or office back to home or office, the salesmen spent three hours in face-to-face selling. If their call contacts averaged 30 minutes a call, the men could make 6 calls a day; if 20 minutes a call, they could make 9 calls. Many salesmen with a well-organized, service type of call schedule can make 10 to 15 calls or more a day. Some cut their travel time by careful routing, or their waiting time by building up receptivity with their customers.

2. Country salesmen made more calls per day than city salesmen. This was due to the ability of the country salesmen to see their customers earlier in the morning and later in the afternoon. Country salesmen took advantage of these opportunities by getting up earlier and being at the place of business of the first customer when he opened up. They did their long-distance traveling between towns in the evening, so as to spend the night in the vicinity of their first call in the morning.

3. Salesmen in the South made as many calls per day as salesmen in the North. Although the southern men seemed to be a little more relaxed and neighborly with their customers than the average northern salesman, they were just as businesslike and maintained just as fast a pace.

It is the sales executive's responsibility to see that the precious, limited, and expendable face-to-face selling time is used to the greatest advantage. Too frequently salesmen are sent out with inadequate preparations as to product knowledge and selling techniques. Knowledge without the ability to convey it to others is useless; selling ability without the strength of product and use knowledge is hollow. Every moment of face-to-face selling time must be put to maximum advantage. Too much time spent in idle chitchat is harmful, as is the monotonous parroting of a "canned" speech. The emphasis here is on "monotonous parroting"; in some lines, prepared sales talks are useful, but they fall flat if they are not given as though they were spontaneous. All sales presentations must be wisely and con-

PRINT NAME		**Cooper TIRES**
		COOPER TIRE AND RUBBER CO.
FOR WEEK ENDING:		**ROUTE LIST -- WORK PLAN**

DATE	SPENDING NIGHT AT —	WORK PLAN FOR DAY
MON.	HOTEL OR MOTEL CITY STATE	NAME OF ACCOUNT ADDRESS-CITY-STATE PHONE NO.
TUES.	HOTEL OR MOTEL CITY STATE	NAME OF ACCOUNT ADDRESS-CITY-STATE PHONE NO.
WED.	HOTEL OR MOTEL CITY STATE	NAME OF ACCOUNT ADDRESS-CITY-STATE PHONE NO.
THURS.	HOTEL OR MOTEL CITY STATE	NAME OF ACCOUNT ADDRESS-CITY-STATE PHONE NO.
FRI.	HOTEL OR MOTEL CITY STATE	NAME OF ACCOUNT ADDRESS-CITY-STATE PHONE NO.
SAT.	HOTEL OR MOTEL CITY STATE	NAME OF ACCOUNT ADDRESS-CITY-STATE PHONE NO.

FORM NO. 04-35

Route list and work plan for Cooper Tire and Rubber Co. salesmen enables home office to get in touch with man if necessary.

structively presented so that every golden moment of customer contact is productive.

Throughout the entire presentation, memorized or "ad libbed," enthusiasm and aggressiveness must be maintained. This management may do by keeping the sales force on its toes. Incentive programs, contests for both monetary gain and honor, change-of-pace tactics, special recognition, and promotions are among the tools that management has at its disposal.

Routing Salesmen Effectively: The problem of routing salesmen most effectively is one of the perpetual problems of sales supervision. There is no one "solution," but only a number of *approaches* to solutions which have a tendency to "come unsolved" after they have been in effect for a time.

The sales executive who expects to set up a routing plan which his salesmen will thenceforward and forever follow implicitly is doomed to a rude awakening.

This does not mean that routing salesmen successfully is an insoluble problem; it merely implies that no system can be depended on to operate automatically in good and bad times and in all sorts of districts. It is an inescapable function of the sales executive to study continually all present and prospective customers and readjust the workload for his salesmen accordingly.

Reduced to its simplest terms, the effective routing of salesmen is merely a matter of arranging calls on the most logical basis. A complex, intricate system is not required; even such a simple plan as that of putting the name of individual companies on colored cards and identifying them by corresponding colored tacks on a large road map works well.

Sales managers feel that if a real job is done in correcting salesmen's attitudes toward time losses, the need for specific help is not great. Several who have attempted ambitious time-control plans, such as hour-by-hour routing of salesmen, have not found results sufficient to justify the expenditure. However, some large employers of salesmen, selling established trade channels, have developed home-office routing to a high degree of efficiency. Two such companies are The American Tobacco Company of New York and Swift & Company of Chicago.

Sales managers also report good results from providing salesmen with route lists prepared by local newspapers for various lines of business. A number of insurance companies have found it effective to furnish salesmen with ruled cards, with space for every hour of the day, on which they can plot their day's work, and keep a record of the result. The backs of these cards may be used for pertinent and timely messages on time economy.

Preparing Routing Sheets: A company selling hospital supplies prepares all routing sheets in its home office. Generally four routes are prepared, each covering a week's time; the salesmen are held responsible for abiding by these routes, and are required to send in daily call reports. The company checks their adherence to the program by phoning them from time to time, to give them price information or other important messages along their routes, management knowing approximately where each man should be at any time each day.

It is better for the home office to prepare these route sheets than the salesmen, as the home office maintains historical records, has seasoned judgment, and is not influenced by the personal desires of the men. Of course, all the salesmen are encouraged to offer constructive criticism and suggestions as to route changes, accounts to be dropped, and new prospects to be added. In fact, if a salesman does not offer such suggestions, management solicits them, calling to the salesman's attention that the making of constructive recommendations is one of his duties and responsibilities.

Another company, in the food field, uses a "manifest" report prepared at headquarters. The names of the customers are typed on Addressograph plates, arranged in the sequence to be called on, then printed on the manifest sheet. If the salesman believes a new name should be added, an old name dropped, or a change made in the sequence, he notifies his manager; and whatever action the manager considers advisable is taken when the next manifest is printed. These manifests are sent to each salesman every Thursday for the following week.

Each man has five routes for covering his territory; thus he sees each customer once a week. However, at times a large customer may appear on two or more routes, depending on how frequently he should be seen. The salesman attaches the forms to a clip-board which he carries in his truck, noting the results of each call; one copy is returned to the company with his cash remittances, one is sent to his branch manager, the third he retains. The figure beside each name (4, 3, 5, etc.) indicates by code his sales goal for each call. Thus the manifest serves as a route sheet to keep him on the track; as an incentive instrument, reminding him of the goals that he and his branch manager have set; as a reporting form as to his sales activity, and as a remittance form for his cash collections.

WEEKLY   ROUTE   AND   PLAN   SHEET

(Airmail Original To Main Office Saturday of Each Week)

Week
Beginning _____

Territory
No. _____   Salesman _____

D A Y	TOWNS TO BE WORKED	PLANNED CALLS CUSTOMERS AND PROSPECTS
MONDAY		
	HOTEL	
TUESDAY		
	HOTEL	
WEDNESDAY		
	HOTEL	
THURSDAY		
	HOTEL	
FRIDAY		
	HOTEL	
SATURDAY		
	HOTEL	

Weekly route and plan sheet of the FWD Corporation.

The salesmen who use the form continuously and thoroughly are the top men; those who use it sloppily are in the lower group—which is probably a reflection of the difference in their general attitude toward their work.

Dramatizing Route Control: A sales manager, in attempting to emphasize the importance of good routing, drew on a large board (about 4 by 5 feet) an outline map of a salesman's territory. He stuck in covered tacks showing location of all the salesman's customers; then with a cord, he traced the salesman's daily travels for a week. The covers on the tacks were then removed showing that some were red, indicating high potentiality; some were blue, indicating fair potentiality; and some were almost colorless, blending with the background, indicating little or no potentiality. The cord was then taken off; it stretched out some 75 feet from the board and indicated dramatically the total amount of time the salesman had available to him for selling during the week. The customers were then analyzed as to past sales and sales opportunities. Goals and call schedules were worked out for each one. Attention to the strong companies was increased as opportunities warranted, the weak and unprofitable customers were dropped. New routes were then designed with the cord placed back on the board to follow the salesman's proposed travel during the week. Final analysis showed the salesman had excellent chances to increase his sales some 20 to 30 percent by calling wisely. He reduced the number of calls and, by routing himself more logically, had about 10 feet of cord left over. This excess cord represented either an expense savings or elbow-room for promotional activities. The demonstration was well accepted by the salesmen, and for years afterwards when a salesman was unable to complete an assigned task, he explained it by saying, "I ran out of string."

Helping Salesmen to Route Themselves: There are conditions which sometimes make it desirable to let the salesmen route themselves as, for example, in cases where salesmen are paid a straight commission. Sales managers very often say: "We hold our salesmen responsible for production only; if they make a mess out of routing themselves that is their hard luck." This is shortsighted, however. After all, it makes no great difference whether a salesman is working on a salary, a commission, or any other kind of compensation plan. The territory assigned to him represents a definite volume of potential business. The more of this business he gets, the more money the company will make. It is, therefore, up to the company to do all it can to help each salesman get the maximum production from his territory. If he is supposed to route himself, at least he should be supervised sufficiently to make sure that he will not waste any more time than necessary in covering his territory.

One thing which costs very little, but which might prove of tremendous value to salesmen, is to prepare a special booklet or brief giving salesmen suggestions for routing themselves to best advantage. A brief used by a display fixture company follows:

In starting out select the towns or cities that you will work within two weeks and carefully prepare in sheet form two lists, each list containing the names and addresses of approximately 75 merchants—all that the average salesman can call on within six working days—mail copy of your list to the Dayton office. Do this again at the end of each week so as always to be ahead of your work two weeks.

Or, if you prefer, plan your trips and mail to the home office a list of the towns and cities that you will work during a week, and a list of merchants will be prepared for circularizing. A copy of those circularized will be mailed to you. Your route list should be mailed a week to two weeks in advance, depending upon how far away you are from the home office.

In the larger cities of from one to several hundred thousand or more population, the leading newspapers usually publish a list of all retail merchants by route. These are usually kept up to date, and are by far the best type of list to use for circularizing, for instead of mailing circulars to merchants located in all sections of the city, the routes only can be circularized as they will be worked.

By working your territory conscientiously and systematically, you will have the advantage of salesmen in other lines who jump from place to place over a large area and whose sales are made at a maximum expense including railroad fare for long rides—valuable time lost in traveling. It must be remembered that train conductors and farmers are not good prospects for Dayton Displays and by devoting to selling the usual time consumed by salesmen making long jumps, your sales will increase. After all, the success of any salesman depends entirely upon how many prospects he interviews each day. By confining your efforts to a smaller area, your selling expense will always be at a minimum, therefore showing a greater profit for you in addition to commission earned on extra sales made possible by devoting more time to actual selling. There are a large number of prospects in your territory and we are entitled to a reasonable volume of business from the same.

* * *

As previously mentioned, you are to work your territory in weekly units consisting of approximately 50 to 75 prospects. It is unprofitable to circularize a large list at one time—experience has proved that it is a disadvantage to the salesmen and a great loss to us.

By mailing out circulars to a list containing several hundred names, you will agree that more than half of the prospects listed will forget having received literature prior to call, which would be several weeks and sometimes an indefinite period after mailing.

As already mentioned, the circulars are mailed to produce inquiries and introduce our method to your prospects. If you are not in a position to call, we most assuredly do not wish to circularize.

An inaccurate list is a great time and money waster, while a good and accurate list is a business producer. A list that is 2 percent inaccurate is so faulty as to be inexcusable. It is therefore to your interest as well as to ours to have the names of the list you wish to have circularized preceding your calls as nearly 100 percent correct as possible.

For the towns and small cities with a population of less than 10,000 we find a Dun & Bradstreet book the best method of compiling names. In the larger cities a telephone book gives a complete list of prospects, usually classified. When making up a list with the aid of Dun & Bradstreet, classify according to type of business; that is, all druggists under heading of druggists and all other prospects under headings such as hardware, jewelry, stationery, grocery, general stores, etc.

Your list should be made on sheets and in duplicate; the towns and cities arranged according to the order in which they will be worked—it will be convenient for you while traveling and enable you to cover the dealers very thoroughly, and this will also help us to determine how to reach you when wishing to advise you of inquiries or take up any other matter.

The circular matter sent out to lists in the above manner is done entirely at our expense, and in order to get the benefit of this circularizing, which will be productive of many sales for you, it will be necessary for you to purchase a late issue of Dun & Bradstreet's pocket reference book. This book is ordered through the home office, and we will gladly do so upon request from you.

The Headquarters "Hounds": In every sales organization there are salesmen who waste a vast amount of time coming back to their homes or headquarters towns far more often than is good for them. Too many of their trips are planned so as to circle out in the morning, then circle back into headquarters in time for the evening meal. It is obvious that such practices use up a lot of gasoline and time which might be better spent face to face with buyers. One company found its men were doing this to such an extent that they were not visiting dealers in the remote sections. The waste of time was terrific. To cut the loss, a plan was devised to send a salesman half his drawing account weekly, then to send the remainder only upon receipt of receipted bills from hotels. In this way the home office could check the salesman's visits, secure the knowledge that the outlying towns were being worked carefully, because the salesmen could obtain only half their expense money if they did not submit hotel bills to show where they had been during the week. This plan was effective in cutting down the time lost rushing back home two or three times a week.

Sales Reports

To provide management and salesmen alike with a results picture, most companies operate some system of sales reports. Some are quite simple; others are quite involved. In all cases, however, they convey information about territorial conditions useful in sales planning. If they do no more than to make it necessary for a salesman to sit down at the close of the day and review his day's work carefully, the effort is worth while. The traditional idea, shared by most salesmen and some sales managers, that daily reports are a kind of portable time clock has largely disappeared. There are still a few sales executives who will tell you they never require salesmen to make out reports, because all they want from salesmen are orders, but there are not many of that school left.

The essentials of good report forms would include the following:

a. Forms should be of convenient size, easy for the men to carry, write on, and mail; easy for the recipient to read, process, act upon, and file.

b. They should provide check spaces for recurring activities that need merely be recorded, not commented upon.

c. They should be so arranged as to discourage any wordy comments about unimportant happenings. It is bad enough for a salesman to spend his time writing verbose reports; it is even worse when they get to the home office and one or more busy executives have to read them. For this reason some sales executives do not approve of equipping salesmen with dictating machines. One sales vice-president comments:

"It seems that when a man gets his hands on one of them, he forgets to stop talking; everything he says must be transcribed by a stenographer and then read by someone else. Better, it seems to me, for the salesman to go through the pangs of penmanship and curtail his wordage. If he can't write, let him print. If the form is well designed so that check marks tell most of the routine story, few words will have to be written."

d. Forms should be instruments of encouragement, motivation, and inspiration. If the salesmen normally average six calls a day, eight or ten spaces can be allowed for recording calls, and the spaces numbered so that the men will automatically see how many calls they have made. As many spaces as possible should appear on the front of the form; if ten spaces are to be provided, at least eight should appear on the front and two on the back of the form. This is better than five on each side, since the salesman may feel his day's work is over when the five on the front have been filled.

e. Carbons should be required only if the salesmen have no other procedure for recording their activities for their own use. Keeping carbon copies just for the sake of maintaining a file is wasteful of time.

f. Summaries should be eliminated if possible. Some managers feel that if the salesmen total their number of calls, sales, demonstrations, etc., it will be instructive and motivating. However, if the form is properly prepared, proper motivation will be provided and the salesmen will be saved the chore of doing unnecessary clerical work, which they greatly dislike. If the statistical work is done in the home office by lower-paid but more efficient clerks, monthly summary data can be sent to the salesmen showing how their activities compare with others or with standards.

g. Reports should not be too inclusive in communication subject areas. If requests for samples or literature go to separate departments, special forms or perforated sections should be provided.

h. Expenses should be recorded on separate reports, as these usually go, after local management approval, to the treasurer's office for reimbursement. If they travel through other departments, they may be delayed or lost. Perforated expense sheets attached to call reports are frequently used; they save time for the sales-

FWD DAILY CALL REPORT							

Day _____ Date _____

Terr. No. _____ Salesman _____

FWD CORPORATION
CLINTONVILLE, WISCONSIN

With Dealer	Alone	Customer - Address and Contact Parties	Cust-omer	Pros-pect	Mar-ket		Remarks or Mailing Instructions

MARKET KEY: H - Highway U - Utility G - Government F - Fire D - Dealer
C - Commercial O - Oil Field P - Pulp Logging T - Transport M - Miscellaneous

Another FWD Corporation form records every customer call.

man, can be approved by local management, detached and sent to the accounting department.

i. Full instructions and a brief description of the use and purpose of the report should be printed on each form to remind and reinstruct the men after the form has been first explained to them.

j. There should be space provided whereby each regular reader or processor of the form initials it and enters the date of completion. This will assure the form receiving proper attention.

k. After a report has served its purpose, it should be destroyed; yesterday's newspaper and last month's reports are equally dead.

What Salesmen Should Report

Aside from the transmission of field activities and market conditions, reports should be used for developing statistics on the number and character of calls, routing, mailing lists, etc. Even when a salesman makes a call and nothing of particular interest transpires, a record of the call should still be made, to assist in the development of work standards based on such data as the following:

- Calls made per day, week or month
- Inventories taken
- Displays set up
- Stocks rearranged
- Literature distributed
- Demonstrations made
- Samples given away
- Sales meetings held
- Call-backs required
- Orders taken

Salesmen should be made to understand that these statistics are not only important for good management but are also important for good salesmanship. Reports should flow back to them as to average and standard activities, so they may have a measure of their own activity. Every man, be he janitor or president, if he has any degree of pride or ambition, wishes to know how he is doing his job in comparison with how others are doing jobs similar to his. Scoreboards are necessary, whether for baseball games or for earning a living.

Reports can be written or verbal. The former are probably needed more by medium-sized and large companies than by small ones. A sales executive with only two or three salesmen whom he sees often can rely on verbal reports. He probably has little need for written reports other than to obtain historical data for the development of standards of activity. A company that sets its salesmen up as independent operators, without direction or assistance, probably needs no written reports. But as the breadth of coverage and complexity of management increase, written reports are more and more needed for good management.

Written reports should be read and acted upon with promptness so that salesmen learn to rely upon them as an important means of communication with the home office. It is incumbent upon top management to report regularly to the board of directors and stockholders. It receives its information from all segments of the company—from the controller as to profit and losses, from the treasurer as to capital investments, from manufacturing as to production, and from sales as to current results and future projections.

The information on sales stems primarily from field activities, sales results, and information as to competitive and market conditions. Unless the channels of communication from the field are adequate and well used, a comprehensive and accurate understanding of field conditions and the company's competitive position will not be obtained. Thus field reports are an important element in corporation knowledge, and the salesmen should be made so to understand.

What Information Should Be Sent Salesmen?

Practice varies among companies as to what information is sent to the salesmen. Some companies send their men copies of all correspondence with present or prospective customers in their territories, copies of all orders as entered, and invoices as issued. Others go farther and send their salesmen summary reports at the end of the month showing dollar value of orders received and shipments made, theoretical profits (if the men are on some profit-sharing plan), expenses incurred by the salesmen, calls made, and other sales data. They may also show a man's standing as compared with a standard or with the average of other men.

What should be sent to the men depends on the nature of the business, the complexity of the selling job, the degree to which the salesmen need to be informed in order to best serve their customers, and to the degree of authority given the salesmen. Certainly a salesman needs to be well informed, and to be in a position to advise his customers about shipments.

If customers send orders direct to the company, the salesman needs to know about it promptly. It is embarrassing for the salesman, and a reflection on the company, for the salesman to ask for an order only to find that the customer has already placed it with his firm. It would be better for the salesman to be able to thank the customer for the order when he first walks into his office.

Salesmen also should have copies of invoices to know when shipments are made and to know about the financial details of the transaction; customers may have questions to ask, or errors may have been made in processing the order. It is better for the salesman to catch these errors than for the customer to find them first.

Some companies rely on copies of invoices to furnish information for their salesmen as to total shipments made during a month to individual customers or for the sales territory as a whole, the salesmen being expected to make their own summations. Some managers, on the contrary, feel that they should not expect their salesmen to do this clerical chore, with all its dangers of error and procrastination, since they may not get around to doing the job.

A Report Form With Inventory Value

GREAT

A hospital supply company has designed a very effective record system for its salesmen. This consists of a standard manila filing folder with a form printed on the inside. The form includes space for the name of the hospital, the address, and the call route number. Vertical lines provide columns; at the top of half of these are printed the names of product groups usually purchased; the remaining columns are left blank for the salesman to fill in. There are horizontal lines about ⅜ inch apart for the salesman to write on. He enters orders as he receives them, and checks them off (dated) when shipped. This gives him a running record of the needs of his customers. As many hospitals do not maintain perpetual inventories, the salesman's records provide this service for them.

When making a call, the salesman opens his folder and notes past order patterns, open orders on hand, and current shipments. If it is time for the hospital to reorder, he can so advise the buyer. Pertinent current mail is kept in the folder for ready reference. Shipping information is obtained from copies of invoices sent to him by the home office.

Some salesmen carry their customer purchase folders with them in a file-box in their cars, bringing them up to date each weekend as to shipments. At that time, they also enter notes to remind themselves of items to cover or purchases to suggest on their next visit. There is usually a direct correlation between the men who use such records and high sales volume, as there is between those who fail to keep up their records and low sales volume.

Salesman's Expense Control

Top management too often regards sales expense as an unavoidable evil, rather than as a profit-returning investment.

The financial executives should never overlook the fact that the purpose of sales expenses is to generate profits.

Of the various practices for handling salesmen's expenses, the most common are the following:

1. *Reimbursement of actual expenses incurred.*

2. *Reimbursement of actual expenses, with top limit.*

3. *Expenses charged to the company.*

4. *Flat expense allowance.*

Reimbursement of Actual Expenses: This is the most commonly followed practice with salaried personnel and is growing in popu-

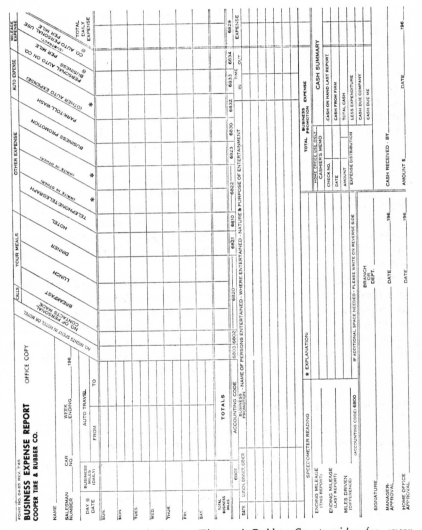

Business expense report of Cooper Tire and Rubber Co. provides for every expense and promotion contingency, and assigns code to each area for the convenience of the accounting department.

larity for commission salesmen. In a study made for the Central Supply Association, plumbing, heating and industrial wholesalers, it was found that of 51 firms in this field which compensated their men through some form of salary plan, 50 reimbursed the men for their actual travel expenses—car, meals, hotels, entertainment, etc. Of 39 firms using some form of commission plan, 14 paid all expenses. Expenses were usually reimbursed on vouchers, expense reports, or expense books. Four firms used flat allowances.

Most marketing executives advance their salesmen a certain amount weekly or monthly as expense money, then reimburse the men as expense reports are submitted. Others require their men to use their own capital for routine selling expenses, reimbursing them weekly or monthly.

However, where salesmen travel from the home office on special trips, it is customary for the company to provide them with air or rail tickets and give them an advance for other expenses, to be accounted for with any balance paid back to the company.

A Company Expense Policy

Properly supervised, the salesmen's expenses are as much an investment as are the expenses incurred in other company operations. It is only by thinking of expenses as *investments for profit attainment* that we bring them into true focus. This is—we repeat—as true of salesmen's expenditures as of any other investment for potential profit.

The company's policy as to paying expenses should be clearly stated to the men and allowable expenses defined. The following example of reimbursement under such an actual expense program is illustrative (from a bulletin from a company to its salesmen):

The company has adopted a policy of paying all allowable expenses incurred by its field organization while on company business. It wants its representatives to look well and to travel in a way that reflects dignity to them as well as to the company. However, unnecessary or excessive expenses will not be approved. The following will explain what expenses are allowable, including automobile, and how they should be reported.

ALLOWABLE EXPENSES:

1. *Public Transportation* (automobile expenses are explained separately). All transportation costs for public carriers, trains, planes, buses, taxicabs, and streetcars shall be approved. Coaches are to be used on short rides; roomettes should be used on overnight rides. Representatives are expected to route themselves in an economical manner, without backtracking, unless this is unavoidable.

2. *Meals.* All meals while away from headquarter cities or while entertaining customers in headquarter cities or elsewhere shall be approved. Ex-

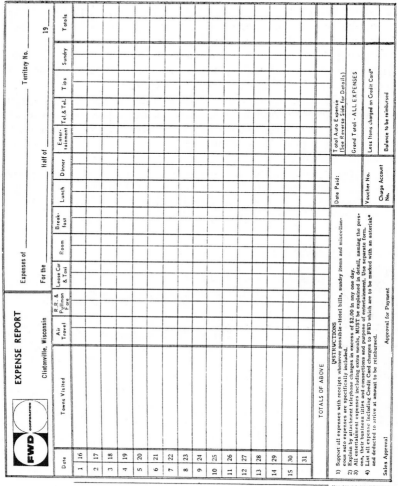

Salesman's expense report used by FWD Corporation, Clintonville, Wisconsin, remains spacious and uncluttered by the use of both sides of the sheet. The reference side (not shown) provides space for listing names of prospects called on and for automobile expense. The weekly route and plan sheet of the FWD Corporation allows the salesman to plan his calls for the week. This report must be airmailed to the home office every Saturday. A companion sheet, the daily call report, provides a record of the results of each call.

ample: a Minneapolis salesman would not be reimbursed for any meals in Minneapolis or St. Paul unless he were entertaining customers, in which case he would be reimbursed for his and their meals. The company expects its men to eat adequately; they are not expected to skimp on meals or to gorge themselves, to eat in inferior restaurants or in the most fashionable and expensive ones.

3. *Lodging.* Rooms in first-class, comfortable hotels or motels are expected and will be approved. The price of rooms should be ascertained before assignment; they should be adequate but not larger or more luxurious than necessary. Necessary telegrams for reservations will be approved. If, when on a regular route, the next stay in the city can be anticipated, a reservation should be made in advance; this will assure accommodations and will save expenses. Checkout times should be observed to forestall unwarranted expenses.

4. *Entertainment.* A reasonable amount of entertainment, preferably limited to meals, will be approved. Tickets to athletic events, fishing trips, presents, and similar expenses will not be approved unless authorized in advance. Customers' wives may be included when advisable, but group entertaining will not be approved. Remember, it takes over $100 of extra sales to make up for $10 of additional expense. The names, positions, and companies of all persons entertained must be shown in the expense report. Coffee expense while doing dealer work will be approved.

5. *Clothing.* Clothes pressing and cleaning, if needed when away from headquarters cities, will be approved. The company wishes its representatives to be neatly dressed at all times. Laundry expenses will be approved only when the representative is required to be away from his headquarters city for 10 days or more.

6. *Tips.* Meal tips should be included with meal expenses, bellboy tips with hotel room expenses, taxicab tips with transportation expenses. Tips to doormen or taxicab starters will not be approved. Other tips should be itemized and shown separately. Overtipping is wasteful and in bad taste and should be carefully avoided.

7. *Miscellaneous.* All postage, telephone, telegraph, road and bridge tolls, and night and day parking charges, when necessary, will be approved. Long-distance calls are to be avoided if airmail will suffice. All miscellaneous charges over $2 are to be itemized.

8. *Personal.* Expenses such as barber shop, personal entertainment without customers, toilet articles, drug products, and similar items will not be approved.

9. *Briefcases.* The company supplies necessary briefcases and display equipment. Purchase costs of personal briefcases, suitcases, portable dictating machines, and similar items will not be approved.

10. *Memberships and Trade Publications.* Membership and trade publication subscriptions will be furnished by the company where advisable. They are to be handled by the district managers and the field sales manager; their costs are not to be shown on the expense accounts.

11. *Automobile Expenses.* The company will reimburse its field representatives for the use of their private automobiles on company business as outlined following:

It is assumed that Fords, Chevrolets, or Plymouths will be used, equipped with radio, heater and turn signals. Station wagons are especially desirable. If a salesman elects to drive a more expensive car, he will be expected to absorb any extra depreciation or operating costs himself (other than the additional costs for station wagons).

EXPENSE CONTROLS:

Suitable records will be maintained by the controller's office to be used in developing allowable expense standards and for controls. The following classifications have been adopted:

1. Automobile.
2. Other transportation.
3. Meals.
4. Lodging.
5. Telephone, telegraph, and postage.
6. Entertainment.
7. Miscellaneous.

The company adopting this program had been using a flat expense allowance for years. The controller was fearful that going to a reimbursable-allowance program would lower the bars and the company's sales expense would soar. Just the opposite happened; expenses dropped and the company was better assured that the expense money was properly used.

Reimbursement of Actual Expenses, With Top Limit

This procedure is similar to the above, but with a ceiling placed on expenses. Such plans are useful when reasonable leeway is allowed; but with plans in which the limit is strictly enforced, the program gets away from the basic concept of selling expenses—that when expenditures are necessary for increased sales, they should be allowed. Curtailment should not be made on the basis of expenses per se, but of unnecessary expenses.

Expenses Charged to the Company: This is similar to the actual reimbursement plan except that all expenses possible are charged to the company through the use of credit cards. There is considerable merit to this plan because it saves the salesman from carrying large amounts of cash and avoids the need of frequently cashing checks when traveling, and it provides the company with reliable vouchers for expense allocation.

Flat Expense Allowance: Few companies today follow this method of expense allotment. It has been generally found undesirable, for the following reasons:

1. It ignores the basic concept of expense investment and treats expenses as a necessary evil.

2. It is difficult to apply fairly. Except in rare cases, a salesman either receives too great an allowance or receives too little and must finance company business from his own pocket. In many instances where men have been on flat expense accounts they have not covered their territories as they should because they were temporarily short of cash or wanted to save the money.

3. A flat expense allowance starts out as being money paid to the salesman for traveling expenses, but quickly it changes its character and becomes part of the salesman's income. He becomes more and more reluctant to spend a part of his "income" on company business.

The IRS on Business Expense

When the Internal Revenue Service launched its much-heralded crackdown on expense accounts in 1963, the main targets of the revised legislation were the categories of expenses lumped under entertainment and expenses for business gifts. The Treasury Department was mainly in pursuit of the big-ticket expense items—personal yachts, country club memberships, private lodges, etc., that were being written off as business entertainment. The regulations were also aimed at the big gift items such as color television, automobiles, and vacation trips. But the new rules had their impact in all areas, as follows:

In general, IRS new regulations call for more detailed recording of expenses. Specifically, the allowable deduction for business gifts was limited to $25 for any one person during a year, and entertainment expenses for any occasion had to be supported by documentation of business purpose of entertainment.

The Internal Revenue Service defines entertainment as any activity generally considered to constitute entertainment, amusement, or recreation. This covers entertaining guests at such places as night clubs, country clubs, theaters, sporting events, and on yachts, or on hunting, fishing, vacation, and similar trips. It may also include satisfying personal living or family needs of any individual, the cost of which represents a business expense to the provider. This would include furnishing food or beverages, a hotel room, or an automobile to a business customer or his family.

The primary criterion for deduction of entertainment expenses is that the expenses must be ordinary and necessary to carrying on your trade or business. The regulations state that lavish or extravagant expenses will not be allowed. Being lavish or extravagant is not necessarily related to a fixed dollar amount or fixed type of entertainment. Judgment will be based on the fact and circumstances of the occasion or purpose of the entertainment. You must be able to show that the entertainment was:

1. Directly related to the active conduct of the trade or business, or

2. Associated with the active conduct of your trade or business, or

3. Other business reason for the expense.

To pass the "directly-related" test for entertainment expenses, you must be able to prove that:

1. There was a specific opportunity to derive income or some other specific benefit *other than goodwill* from the person entertained.

2. The principal purpose was business and not entertainment.

Entertainment expenditures to create goodwill, if they cannot pass the "associated" test, can be deducted as business meals. Business meals, meals furnished to an individual under circumstances which are generally conducive to a business discussion, are not subject to the restrictions on entertainment expenses. In the case of a business meal, it is not essential to show that business was discussed. But you must show that the primary purpose was to further your trade or business.

The regulations on gifts are very clear cut. Deductions in excess of $25 for gifts for any one individual will not be allowed. The definition of an individual includes a family. For example, if you give a customer a gift worth $25 and also give his wife a $25 gift, you can only deduct $25.

The exceptions to the $25 rule on gifts are:

1. An item not costing more than $4 and having your name clearly and permanently imprinted on it which is one of a number of identical items distributed by you.

2. Signs, display racks and other promotional material to be used in the recipient's business.

3. Tickets to a sporting event or the theater given to a customer may be treated as gifts or as entertainment for tax purposes, even if you do not accompany the customer. If you do accompany him, it must be treated as entertainment.

This is only a digest of the basic rules for handling entertainment and gift expenses available in Publication No. 463 (10-65) of the U.S. Treasury Department, Internal Revenue Service.

Expense Account Books and Forms

The practice of furnishing salesmen with expense books is practically universal, whether for Social Security or for income tax purposes. This arrangement for handling expenses is much more convenient than other methods, as it enables salesmen to note such expenses at the time they are made and thus reduces the chances of error where they are recorded later. To meet the requirements of the Social Security Act, salesmen on a straight commission are required to account for their expenses, so proof is available of net income subject to tax; while salesmen on other types of compensation plans are more than ever expected to keep accurate accounts for reimbursable expense outlays.

WEEKLY EXPENSE RECORD

This handy record provides the means for conveniently recording daily expense items as they occur throughout the week. This form can be retained as your permanent expense record.

You can transfer your daily expenses at the end of each day or at the end of the week to the Weekly Expense Report sent to your company.

In accordance with the new IRS rules governing Entertainment Expenses, be sure to be specific and complete when recording entertainment details in the spaces provided under "Details of Entertainment."

FORM SA 8

DATE	19__
BREAKFAST	
LUNCH	
DINNER	
LODGING	
TIPS	
GAS AND OIL	
TELEPHONE - TELEGRAPH	
LAUNDRY	
PARKING	
TOLLS	
PLANE FARE	
RAILROAD FARE	
BUS FARE	
TAXI - LIMOUSINE	
CAR RENTAL	
MILES† @ ¢	
ENTERTAINMENT††	
MISC. (ITEMIZE)	
DAILY TOTAL →	

DETAILS OF TRAVEL
FROM
TO
TO
†DAILY MILEAGE (Enter Above)

WEDNESDAY

DETAILS OF ENTERTAINMENT

COMPANY

INDIVIDUALS

TIME

PLACE

PURPOSE

FOOD	
DRINKS	
TAXI	
TIPS	
TICKETS	
††TOTAL	

In this connection, Dartnell has developed a weekly expense account booklet that is widely used. It is a composite of a large number of forms submitted to The Dartnell Corporation. Its advantages lie in its simplicity and the manner in which it makes possible an analysis of each salesman's expenses.

Traveletter System

A number of companies have found that one way to expedite handling of salesmen's expenses is through a letter-of-credit plan, whereby salesmen are allowed to write their own expense checks up to a limited weekly amount. This plan, sponsored by the Traveletter Corporation, 135 East Putnam Avenue, Greenwich, Conn., and known as the "Traveletter System," has been adopted by several hundred firms.

Not only does this system provide safeguards to prevent the salesman from overdrawing the limits of his expense account, but it avoids confusion as to where each salesman stands each week. Expense reporting is practically automatic, according to companies that use the plan, and salesmen are reported to like the system because it removes all uncertainty about when and where they will receive their expense checks from their company; they no longer have to waste time waiting for reimbursement or filling out expense reports in the headquarters office. The system provides for a continuous record of week-to-week expenses with only a comparatively small amount of paperwork.

Each salesman carries with him a sort of letter of credit, known as a Traveletter Authorization, which includes the name of the man for whose use it is issued, the name and location of the bank at which drafts drawn under it are to be presented, and the weekly limit of the amount that can be drawn. The salesman is also given a book of Travelorder drafts, imprinted with his company's name and that of the bank, and which he can cash wherever he cashes his regular company check or at one of 4,500 hotels and motels that are under agreement to honor these drafts. A list of these places is supplied to the salesman.

Transportation of Salesmen

The first question to be decided in regard to automobile use in sales work is whether the cars should be owned or leased by the company and all expenses paid by the company, or whether the salesman should own the car, and the company allow a certain amount for operating it. Both plans meet with favor; both have advantages and both have disadvantages.

Drawbacks to the company-operated fleet plan are that it requires a larger investment on the company's part; that salesmen take better care of their own cars than they do of cars owned by the company; and that they often use company cars on personal business, which in many cases makes the comparative mileage costs shown by the company's records undependable.

The advantages of the fleet plan are that it gives the company more control over the condition of the cars, and in that way reduces the loss of time due to a salesman's car being out of commission, and permits certain economies in operation. It also enables the company to put its trademark or other advertising on the car, which may, or may not, be of value. With the right kind of automobile allowance plan, the cost of operating salesmen's automobiles in reality is about the same regardless of whether the salesman owns the car or the company owns the car.

Company-owned fleets can be handled more economically and with less trouble if you hire a professional fleet manager. There are also management services which can act for a company in this capacity.

Another trend which has developed in the past few years is renting or leasing automobiles. A survey among members of the National Car Rental System, Inc., revealed that each year sees an increase in the number of companies renting cars for salesmen's use.

Automobile Allowances

For most salesmen, the automobile represents the largest expense item on their job. Some salesmen wear out a car every year, running up 50,000 miles or more. Many salesmen average between 25,000 and 35,000 miles a year. At these rates, salesmen's automobile expenses for companies with large sales forces are a major item, according to the most recent *Dartnell Survey of Business Car Allowances.* Here is a digest:

Basically, the methods used for reimbursing salesmen for use of personal cars on business may be categorized into four plans:

1. Flat mileage allowance.
2. Sliding-scale mileage allowance.
3. Fixed allowance plus mileage.
4. Fixed allowance.

FLAT MILEAGE ALLOWANCE

Consultants on sales policies, auto leasing companies, and others have been preaching for years that the flat mileage allowance method is the most expensive a company can use to reimburse salesmen for automobile expenses. Despite this, it is still a very popular method. Fifty-four percent of the companies in the Dartnell study reported using this method.

The variations in sliding scale plans are so numerous that it is impossible to arrive at averages or medians. Here are some of the reports:

Metal Fabricators

"10 cents first 10,000 miles; 9 cents second 10,000 miles: 8 cents excess of 20,000 miles."

"7 cents per mile—working toward increase to 10 cents per mile (first 15,000 miles) and 7 cents per mile thereafter."

"8 cents first 20,000 miles, 6 cents after that. Salesmen submit mileage or semimonthly expense voucher."

Food Industry

"7 cents per mile first 500 miles, 4 cents per mile over 500 miles each week."

Service Trades

"12 cents per mile first 5,000 miles, 10 cents thereafter. Small car of four cylinders is rated at 10 cents first 5,000 miles, 8 cents thereafter."

Wholesale Trade

"8 cents first 500 miles, 7 cents second 500 miles, 6 cents over 1,000 (per week)."

Canadian Manufacturers

"9 cents first 1,000 per month, 6 cents excess. Mileage allowance is expected to cover all expense except parking and tolls."

"8 cents for first 20,000 per year; 3½ cents thereafter."

FIXED ALLOWANCE PLUS MILEAGE

Another allowance system used frequently to reimburse salesmen for automobile expenses is the fixed allowance with a mileage allowance. Again, the variations in plans made tabulation impossible. Fixed allowance ranged from $45 to $106 a month and mileage rates varied from 3 cents to 7 cents per mile.

FIXED ALLOWANCE

A relatively small proportion of the companies use a fixed allowance for covering salesmen's automobile expenses. The most widely used method is a lump sum paid either weekly, monthly, or annually to cover basic auto expenses. Generally, the fixed allowance is about $1,000 a year, but there were reports of allowances as high as $1,600 and as low as $600. In addition, the company generally pays for all gas and oil, and sometimes insurance, and other expenses.

INCIDENTAL AUTOMOBILE EXPENSES

Parking, tolls, and washing are considered as separate expenses from regular automobile operation by most companies. As a result, these expenses are generally reimbursed separately from other allowances such as mileage or a fixed allowance. Also, companies which furnish a car to their salesmen, either a company-owned or a leased car, generally reimburse salesmen for parking and tolls, and often for washing.

Almost 80 percent of the companies in this study reimburse their salesmen for parking and tolls. Not so many are willing to pay for car washing. Only slightly over 50 percent said they pay for washes.

Relatively few companies operating on a national basis issue oil company credit cards in the company name. The smaller regional companies tend to use credit cards more frequently. These companies have much tighter control over their salesmen and their expenses. Control gets more difficult as the size of the sales force grows. Even fewer companies provide credit cards in the man's name.

Automobile Insurance Practices

The cost of automobile insurance has climbed steadily. Accident costs are higher, repair bills are higher, new car costs are up, and jury awards are more generous than ever.

CAR EXPENSE REPORT SHEET

MONTH OF_____19___

MILEAGE THIS DATE_____

YEAR_____ MAKE_____ FLEET NO_____

MODEL_____ LICENSE NO._____

(State)   (No.)

1. GASOLINE (Misc. Purchases)

Date	Rec. #	No. of Gals.	Amount
TOTALS			

2. OIL

Date	Rec. #	No. of Qts.	Amount
TOTALS			

3. TITLE AND LICENSE EXPENSE

Date	Title State	License No.	Cost

5. AUTO SALES OR USE TAX EXPENSE

Date	Rec. #	%	Taxable Amount	Cost

6. PERSONAL PROPERTY TAX

Date	Rec. #	%	Taxable Amount	Cost

7. TOLL FEES

Tollway	Rec. #	Date	Amount
TOTALS			

4. MAINTENANCE (As listed below — only)

Description	Date	Rec. #	Amount
Filter Cartridges			
Lubrication			
Tire Rotation			
Tire Repairs			
Align Front End			
Adjust Brakes			
Antifreeze			
Wheel Bearing Pack			
U-Joint Pack			
Steering Gear Check			
Differential Grease			
Transmission Fluid			
TOTALS			

8. OTHER REPAIRS

Description	Date	Rec. #	Amount
TOTALS			

9. PARKING FEES

City	Rec. #	Date	Amount
TOTALS			

10. WASH JOBS

Date	Rec. #	Amount
TOTALS		

REIMBURSEMENT CLAIM

	AMOUNT
1. Gasoline	
2. Oil	
3. Title and License Expense	
4. Maintenance	
5. Auto Sales or Use Tax Expense	
6. Personal Property Tax	
7. Toll Fees	
8. Other Repairs	
9. Parking Fees	
10. Wash Jobs	
TOTAL CLAIM	

I CERTIFY THAT THE EXPENSES REPORTED HEREIN ARE MY ACTUAL COSTS OF OPERATING THE ABOVE DESCRIBED AUTOMOBILE DURING THE MONTH REPORTED ABOVE.

SIGNED _____

CHECK TO BE ISSUED TO:

PLEASE PRINT

_____

(Name)

_____

(Street)

LEASE COMPANY USE ONLY

Date Paid_____Check No._____

Amt. Paid_____Initials_____

(City)   (Zone)   (State)

NOTE: Reimbursement will be made according to audit within 5 days after receipt of this report. INSTRUCTIONS ARE PRINTED ON REVERSE HEREOF

Car-expense report sheet for salesman using his own automobile.

What are some of the ways to keep insurance costs controlled? One way, of course, is to self-insure where possible. It is not always easy to tell when this may be the best thing to do, but a common practice is to buy some kinds of insurance from insurance carriers and carry the balance on a self-insured basis.

Another way to keep control of costs is to know how much to buy, when to buy it, and how to buy in combination. This is where many companies say that an insurance manager pays for his keep. He will know, for example, that some insurance companies offer rate discounts to policyholders who enforce fleet speed limitations. He will know that it is possible to get a 15 percent reduction on combined medical payments, death, and disability coverage. He will know, too, that most companies offer lower rates where the drivers are young (but not too young) and are well trained.

Every fleet administrator should provide personal or public liability protection for the cars under his control. And in 99 out of 100 companies using employee-owned cars, salesmen are required to have the same kind of protection before the car leaves the garage on company business.

Most companies insist on property damage coverage, too. Ninety-five percent of those owning or leasing cars carry property damage insurance. In a few instances, coverage is as high as $1 million.

A smaller number of companies, apparently, believe in the necessity for collision coverage. Forty-eight percent of those surveyed require collision insurance for owned or leased cars, while only 26 percent say that salesmen should have this kind of protection for their own automobiles. A number of fleet administrators say that the age of the cars and current values prompt them to leave collision off the insurance list.

Comprehensive coverage, including fire, theft, windstorm, etc., is bought by 40 percent of the companies owning or leasing cars and is required by 21 percent of those whose employees drive their own.

The limits of per-person and per-accident liability have been rising along with all the other aspects of automobile insurance. A few years ago, Dartnell surveys show, it was common for a company to purchase $50,000/$100,000 coverage and regard itself as thoroughly and completely protected. Now, the most popular liability limits are $100,000 per person and $300,000 per accident.

Over two-thirds of all the collision insurance carried by companies surveyed is of the $100-deductible variety. Eighteen percent of it is $250-deductible and higher. These are much larger deductible amounts than were encountered in earlier Dartnell surveys.

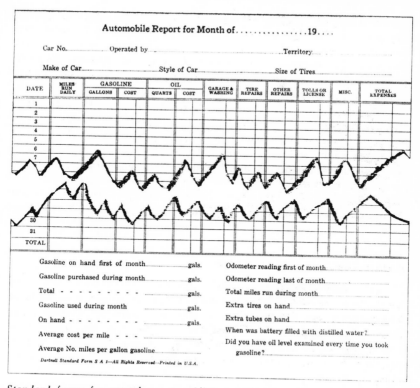

Standard forms for reporting automobilel operating expenses can be utilized in companies where routine car operations are the rule. Here is one example of such a report. (Dartnell Standard Form SA-1)

Who Pays the Premium?

When asked, "Do you pay the insurance premiums for salesmen who drive their own cars on company business?" two-thirds of the replies were in the negative. Many companies make indirect payments, however, in that consideration is given to the high cost of insurance when time-and-mileage allowances are established. The "time" element in the reimbursement plan is intended to help out with the fixed costs the salesman has to cope with, including, of course, his annual insurance bill.

The next most common practice among those companies using employee-owned cars is that of supplementing the employee's privately purchased coverage, whether set at a company-required minimum or not, by some sort of blanket liability coverage. This usually has the effect of stepping up the bodily injury and property damage liability limits bought by the employee. While this is a cooperative insurance purchase plan in a sense, it is considered here in a little different light because it involves no agreement between company and employee on the division of the total premium. Fourteen percent of the companies surveyed fall into this category.

Following close behind, accounting for 13 percent of those reporting, are the companies that pay the entire insurance bill for the employee. This is a practice less popular now than it used to be.

On leased vehicles, the terms of the leasing contract determine how insurance premiums are handled. The tendency is for client companies to pay the insurance bill. Situations where lessor and lessee split the cost (with lessor usually paying for collision, fire and theft, and lessee paying for liability coverage) are also common today.

Automobile Trade-in Practices

The variety of trade-in schedules and plans reported by companies which have contributed to Dartnell surveys are almost without limit. The trade-in age most frequently reported, however, is two years. Among the companies that consider only mileage, the figure mentioned most often is 60,000. The margin between the leaders and the rest is not great, though. There are plenty of companies that say every three years is a good time to trade.

Most of the companies taking part in Dartnell surveys use one of the three basic depreciation methods which have specific Treasury Department approval. Only 8 percent say they have developed their own "homegrown" methods or use combinations of any of the basic plans.

By far the greatest number use the straight-line method of depreciating company cars. Seventy-five percent follow this course. Next most popular are the declining-balance and double-declining-balance methods, which are used by 11 percent.

Whatever the method used to figure depreciation, four-year useful life is still the basis in most companies. Altogether, the three-, four-, and five-year plans account for 91 percent of all companies surveyed. The remaining 9 percent report such depreciation periods as 24 months, 42 months, 50 months, and even 72 months in the case of a very few.

The vast majority of the companies surveyed give the custodian (generally he is a salesman) some authority to have routine repairs made. There is a maximum figure beyond which the user cannot go

AUTOMOBILE EXPENSES

for the Month of

_____

Salesman.................................

Make of Car.............

Type of Car..............

Horsepower..............

ODOMETER RE

First of Month...........

Last of Month...........

Run During Month.......

Average Cost per Mile.....

Form No. SA-20 © Dartnell, U. S

GASOLINE, OIL AND TOLLS

Date	Miles Run Daily	Gasoline	Oil	Tolls	Total
Forward					
18					
19					
20					
21					
22					
23					
24					
25					
26					
27					
28					
29					
30					
31					
Average					

TIRE CHANGE RECORD

Date	Serial Number (OFF)	Serial Number (ON)	Odometer Reading

TIRE PURCHASES AND REP

Date	Make	Serial	Size	
	TOTAL			

SUMMARY FOR MONTH

Gasoline on Hand First of Month...........gals.

Gasoline Purchased During Month...........gals.

Total.....................gals.

Gasoline Used During Month................gals.

Gasoline on Hand..........................gals.

Extra Tires on Hand.......................

Extra Tubes on Hand.......................

EXPENSES FOR MONTH

Gasoline		
Oil and Grease		
Storing and Washing		
Tires and Tubes		
Repairs		
All Other Expenses		
TOTAL		
Average Cost per Mile..........................		

ATTACH RECEIPTS TO THIS REPORT

Another type of standard automobile expense record (Dartnell Standard SA-20), which accordion-folds to pocket size. Spaces for recording storing, washing and other special expenses are provided, in addition to the data shown here, and a page at the end calls for a report on the condition of the car at the end of each month.

without permission from the home office. In the case of emergency repairs, companies generally relax this restriction but require a complete report and explanation afterwards.

The ceiling on the custodian's authority to initiate repairs runs from $15 to $100, with $25 being most frequently cited. One company with 468 cars in a company-owned salesman-operated fleet has three ceilings: The salesman has authority to pay up to $15 for repairs, the district office can authorize repairs costing from $15 to $30; repairs over $30 must be submitted to the automotive department which will issue a purchase order if it approves the project.

The PHH Expense Control Program

A number of management organizations offer special services to sales executives for companies not set up to analyze their own car-expense operations.

As an example of this type of program, Peterson, Howell, & Heater, Baltimore, set up a car-expense-control program planned to give four benefits to the user:

1. *Reimbursement Problem Is Solved*—Salesmen are repaid only for actual car expenses. Inequities to the salesmen are eliminated . . . your men are neither overpaid nor underpaid.

2. *Your Paperwork and Administrative Detail Are Reduced*—in effect, PHH acts as your fleet manager. We analyze basic and overall costs and reports for you . . . reports that let you pinpoint detailed expenses or survey overall costs at a glance.

3. *Effective Control of Car Expenses Is in Your Hands*—You know exactly what your car expenses are each month. There is no guesswork . . . no estimating . . . discrepancies become obvious and can be immediately acted upon.

4. *The Program Is Economical*—Through the use of modern electronic data-processing equipment and specialized techniques, PHH can produce these expense-control reports at far less cost than your company can do on its own.

There are three steps in this particular program as follows:

1. *Salesman submits his expense worksheet for the period along with receipted bills for repairs and other major expenditures.*

2. *Salesman is reimbursed for actual expense as reported.*

3. *Home office accumulates worksheets from all salesmen and sends them once each month to PHH after checking for accuracy and completeness.*

SALES TIME AND EXPENSE CONTROL

CAR EXPENSE REPORT SHEET

MONTH OF_____19____

MILEAGE THIS DATE_____

YEAR_____ MAKE_____ MODEL_____

FLEET NO._____

LICENSE NO._____

(State) (No.)

1. GASOLINE (Misc. Purchases)

Date	Rec. #	No. of Gals.	Amount	
TOTALS				

2. OIL

Date	Rec. #	No. of Qts.	Amount	
TOTALS				

3. TITLE AND LICENSE EXPENSE

Date	Title State	License No.	Cost

4. MAINTENANCE (As listed below — only)

Description	Date	Rec. #	Amount	
Filter Cartridges				
Lubrication				
Tire Rotation				
Tire Repairs				
Align Front End				
Adjust Brakes				
Antifreeze				
Wheel Bearing Pack				
U-Joint Pack				
Steering Gear Check				
Differential Grease				
Transmission Fluid				
TOTALS				

5. AUTO SALES OR USE TAX EXPENSE

Date	Rec. #	%	Taxable Amount	Cost

6. PERSONAL PROPERTY TAX

Date	Rec. #	%	Taxable Amount	Cost

7. TOLL FEES

Tollway	Rec. #	Date	Amount	
TOTALS				

8. OTHER REPAIRS

Description	Date	Rec. #	Amount	
TOTALS				

9. PARKING FEES

City	Rec. #	Date	Amount	
TOTALS				

10. WASH JOBS

	Date	Rec. #	Amount	
TOTALS				

REIMBURSEMENT CLAIM — AMOUNT

	AMOUNT
1. Gasoline	
2. Oil	
3. Title and License Expense	
4. Maintenance	
5. Auto Sales or Use Tax Expense	
6. Personal Property Tax	
7. Toll Fees	
8. Other Repairs	
9. Parking Fees	
10. Wash Jobs	
TOTAL CLAIM	

I CERTIFY THAT THE EXPENSES REPORTED HEREIN ARE MY ACTUAL COSTS OF OPERATING THE ABOVE DESCRIBED AUTOMOBILE DURING THE MONTH REPORTED ABOVE.

SIGNED _____

CHECK TO BE ISSUED TO:

PLEASE PRINT

_____

(Name)

_____

(Street)

_____

(City)   (Zone)   (State)

LEASE COMPANY USE ONLY

Date Paid_____ Check No._____

Amt. Paid_____ Initials._____

NOTE: Reimbursement will be made according to audit within 5 days after receipt of this report. INSTRUCTIONS ARE PRINTED ON REVERSE HEREOF

Lease Company Copy.

This Lease Company Car Expense Report Sheet is prepared for a monthly report by the salesman using the automobile. Full instructions for filling out the form are included on the back of each copy.

Car-Leasing Programs

Typical of the various plans under which cars can be leased are three offered by the Hertz Corporation, one of the largest firms in the car rental or leasing business:

Full Maintenance Leasing: Under this plan Hertz furnishes cars of any make or style desired by a company and assumes responsibility for all repairs, maintenance, and servicing; provides license plates, fire, theft, and collision protection; for all of which there is a flat monthly charge per car. The contract lease usually is for 10 or more cars on a 20- to 24-month replacement basis.

Nonmaintenance Leasing: Essentially the same as the above plan except that all or several of the services are handled by the lessee, at a proportionately lower charge per car.

Finance Leasing: Cars are leased at a monthly charge per car, which includes an amortization reserve based on the original cost of the car. When the car is retired from service and sold, this reserve is used to offset the difference between cost and sales price. All servicing and maintenance costs are paid for by the lessee.

Hertz' finance lease plan is designed for companies operating 25 or more cars. The lease runs for an initial period of one year and may be terminated any time thereafter at the lessee's option. It is renewable on a yearly or monthly basis. The lessee is expected to carry a minimum of $100,000 to $300,000 liability insurance and $25,000 property damage. He must also insure for comprehensive fire, theft, and collision coverage. As an example of how this plan works, Hertz breaks down the average cost for two years' operation of a two-door Chevrolet V8, equipped with fresh air heater and automatic transmission as follows (including freight and federal excise tax costs):

	At 2 Percent Amortization Reserve*		At 2½ Percent Amortization Reserve*	
Original Cost of Car	$2,250.00		$2,250.00	
Dealer's Gross Profit	50.00		50.00	
	$2,300.00		$2,300.00	
	First Year	*Second Year*	*First Year*	*Second Year*
Rental Charge, monthly				
At 0.59%, 1st year	$ 13.57		$ 13.57	
At 0.54%, 2nd year		$ 12.42		$ 12.42
*Amortization Reserve, monthly	46.00	46.00	57.50	57.50
Monthly Charge	$ 59.57	$ 58.42	$ 71.07	$ 69.92
	x 12	x 12	x 12	x 12
	$714.84	$701.04	$852.84	$839.04
Total Cost, 2 Years Operation	$1,415.88		$1,691.88	
Unamortized Cost of Car at Time of Sale (excess of sale price will be returned to lessee)	$1,196.00		$ 920.00	

Chapter 54

MOTIVATING SALESMEN

THERE are many ways to stimulate salesmen to greater effort. As previously pointed out, money is not the sole consideration, although financial reward for self and family is a powerful driving force. However, the desire for promotion, the esteem of associates, the yearning for recognition, and the self-satisfaction derived from excellence in any field are all motivating forces.

How some of these motivating factors were put to work is described by Drayton Heard, Jr., manager, marketing administration, Westinghouse Electric Corporation, as follows:

We adopted a sales plan to put a push behind our entire sales force. The elements were called:

1. Fast Start
2. Half-Time Lead
3. Big Finish

In the fast-start phase, we asked the salesmen—and everybody else concerned—to treat the first part of the year—including the first working day—as if it were the most important selling time of the year. To lend a little urgency to this, the company president telephoned each division manager on January 3rd, and said, "You were asked to get off to a fast start—what did you do yesterday?" He waited for the answer, too. For creating a sense of urgency, a telephone call from the president beats anything else you can do!

Shortly after this, he announced the formation of the *120 Club*. To qualify, a salesman had to be a full 20 percent over his objective at the end of June. The salesman got no cash for making the 120 Club. He did receive a letter from the president; his name went on an honor roll; he got a pin; he was given special recognition at sales meetings. Three-time winners get a silver bowl. Quite a handsome thing, but the real value still is honorary. *We did* some other things to add urgency. We had an unfortunate record in previous years of getting our advertising for the year started in April. I think the idea was to save money by approving the budget late. This year the ads appeared in January.

Twenty percent of the *salesmen* made the 120 Club. And that's not easy, because, like most sales quotas, their loadings were based on the previous year and were higher.

747

Here's how it all came out: For January, February, and March—above average sales—we got the fast start. June was the best month we ever had, and with it we had the orders we needed in the first half to make our profit objective in the second half. Some of that business was borrowed from the following months, but the salesmen did give us a big finish in December. That may not look real big from where you sit, but compared to the previous December, which was below average, it looks pretty fine.

The next year, we followed the same pattern with some evolution. We still had the same problem—we're always going to have it—of getting the bulk of the business in the first half, in order to make the bulk of the profit in the second half. So again we had a fast-start program, an early-lead program, the 120 Club, somewhat expanded, and the big-finish program to top off the year. We added one interesting element last year, though, to help the salesmen plan to meet the objectives we kept putting up before them.

You probably all have observed the human tendency a lot of salesmen have to start off slow and end the year in a blaze of glory. It makes a fascinating pattern when you look at a lot of individual sales records. Not only is the end of the year the time they sell the hardest—if you have a midyear quota, the second quarter is better than the first. It's very clear when you analyze monthly figures and notice *when* the business comes in: The last week is the best week. And that's our problem.

So, as a planning tool for the salesman, we had a program called *Think 7*. The idea was to get our salesmen to plan their months in thirds, rather than a month at a time. We urged them to divide the month up into three periods of seven working days each. We did one thing to encourage them: We put the regular sales records and reports the salesman worked with on a 7-day working basis.

I'm sure it has been obvious what we have really done is just *three things*. We *communicated with* the salesmen, we *motivated* the salesmen, and we *recognized* the salesmen.

It has been our experience that you are never in a position to order a salesman to do anything. Because all too often he's in a position to do other things and to ignore you if the orders don't strike his fancy. In communicating with salesmen, you are pleading your case, just as much as you are in communicating with the customer. So when we communicate with salesmen, we plead, we coax, we reason, we praise, we try to be interesting, and we use liberal amounts of graphic soft-soap.

You know how much time salesmen have to spend in their cars, and you know the amount of reading you would like them to do. Driving's a terrific waste of what could be productive time if we could only figure out a way to use it.

Well, one of our groups is doing this. All of the salesmen have a little black box in their car—a tape recorder. Every Monday morning they get a little cartridge in the mail which snaps into the black box.

And as the salesman drives along, he can simply flip the switch on the black box—and listen.

We ended with a record year in both volume and profits. We got a very fast start, we had a very big lead at midyear, and we had a terrific December—a very strong finish.

The Power of Tangible Rewards

Granting the value of such ego drives as recognition, pride, and appreciation, these psychological stimulants take more time than sales managers have available when a company must increase sales or introduce a new line of products over a limited period. To produce more immediate results, tangible rewards must be offered to stimulate action.

Over the years, sales contests have proved to be the best means of rewarding those who have helped, through outstanding or unusual performance, to attain their company's sales objectives.

Properly used, a sales contest not only pays, but lays the foundation for future selling. It gives salesmen the urge to go out and exert themselves to the limit. In many cases, it involves not only the sales department, but the entire organization. It is the most advanced form of sales promotion; its effectiveness may be measured, its results are definite, and the returns are faster than anything else short of price reduction or doubling the sales force.

According to Henry B. Ostberg, president, Blankenship and Ostberg, Inc., there are two preliminary steps in setting up a contest:

1. *Establishing the Purpose:* Contests can help you accomplish a wide variety of purposes and objectives. An increase in total sales is only one of them. Among some other possible objectives are:

- Selling a particular line or product;

  Picking up new accounts;

  Reactivating lost accounts;

  Overcoming a temporary sales slump;

  Encouraging salesmen to aid dealers in store promotions;

  Getting salesmen to make more calls.

2. *Handicapping:* For one reason or another one salesman sells better than another. This may not be due to differences in sales ability, but to the nature of the territory covered, the length of time in which a salesman has become established, and local economic conditions. Accordingly, it may be desirable to "handicap" the participants. To accomplish this you can:

a. Use a percentage increase in sales over the previous year, rather than total sales, to determine the winner.

b. Set a quota for each salesman, the winner being the one who exceeds his quota the most.

c. Run a contest in which the salesman who brings in the largest number of orders (rather than the highest volume of sales) gets the top prize, or,

d. Declare every salesman a winner who exceeds a minimum standard of performance (say $18,000 worth of sales *during the contest period*).

Popular Uses for Contests

Contests are used in nearly every line of business, but principally in those lines where selling is specialized. They are used less in engineering and related fields where the sale is a matter of negotiation, rather than presentation. The broad uses are as follows:

- 1. To stimulate salesmen to greater effort.
- 2. To educate and interest distributors and their salesmen.
- 3. To win cooperation of jobbers' salesmen.
- 4. To get retail clerks to push your product.
- 5. To arouse consumer interest and get quick demand.
- 6. To cut the time required to put over a new product.
- 7. To open up new accounts and complete distribution.
- 8. To speed up collections.
- 9. To introduce a new sales canvass or program.
- 10. To get added volume on neglected products.
- 11. To get a new name for a product or service.
- 12. To get names of prospects from users.
- 13. To get leads for salesmen.
- 14. To capitalize some special sales situation.
- 15. To secure window and store displays.
- 16. To promote better customer relations.

Types of rewards used include the following:

1. Monetary rewards.
2. Merchandise gifts.
3. Tours and excursions.
4. Pins, badges, emblems, certificates, and similar symbols.
5. Honorary notices in publications.

6. Appointment to honor or advisory committees.

7. Inclusion in honor listings.

8. Letters of congratulation.

9. Election to honor clubs.

10. Various combinations of the above.

The Essentials of a Well-Planned Contest

The first yardstick that must be used in determining whether to have a sales contest is, "What will it do for the salesmen, besides providing an urge for them to strive for 'plus' business?" If the plan is right, a constructive contest should measure up to the following:

1. The contest should be so clearly described that the salesman will have no doubt regarding *what* he should do.

2. Care should be taken to show him *how* he should do it.

3. The anticipated results should be evaluated so that the *cost* of the contest is kept within reasonable bounds.

4. The *objectives* should be well programed. In cases where sales increases are involved, the contest should not be so arranged that the added volume is taken from the sales during previous periods from the following period.

5. The contest period should be *short,* so that payoffs come with reasonable quickness. One month to six weeks is usually considered a good period. It is difficult to keep up interest for longer periods.

6. The wife and entire family should be brought into the act, when possible. Pressure at home is often more effective than that from management.

7. The program should be *planned well in advance,* in order that samples, presentation techniques, product literature, production of material for inventory, promotional bulletins, prize literature, quotas, and goals are ready. If a sales manager is slow in getting a contest underway after it has been announced—if starting dates are made retroactive, or samples are not available, or shipment cannot be made of prize goods—the contest will have two strikes against it at the start.

8. If contests are to be conducted throughout the year, they should be programed for the full year so that the proper sequence of product or activity promotion can be followed.

9. Why should a trip to the home office be a prize or award? If trips to the home office are beneficial to the salesmen, they should be brought in on some predetermined schedule having nothing to do with any contest. An award trip to the home office seems to the salesman to be "two for the company and one for the salesman."

Cash or Merchandise Prizes

An investigation made some time ago showed that only three out of ten companies used cash prizes in sales contests, while seven out of ten preferred merchandise prizes. A smaller group used honor prizes, where some badge of distinction is awarded to those who do a superlative selling job.

In a sales campaign for one of the large eastern insurance companies, the only reward offered was to bind the salesmen's sales reports into a book which was presented to the president of the company. It was a mark of appreciation on the part of the sales force for the effort of the president to help his salesmen build their earning capacity.

Money doesn't mean everything to salesmen. Many of them will work twice as hard to win a TV set which their wives have selected from a prize catalog, as they will for a check for themselves. One salesman has his apartment furnished with prizes which he has earned over a five-year period. That is why the majority of companies reported that merchandise is better than money as a reward for constructive sales achievement. When you set up a prize appropriation, it will go farther in merchandise upon which you get wholesale prices than it will go if paid to the salesmen in money; although, if you ask nine out of ten salesmen which they prefer, they will tell you "money." Usually, they'll use the money to buy the very things that can be found in any good prize book.

Year-Round Contests

There is a current trend toward making competitive activities continuous. Instead of having one or two contests a year, an all-year program of contests is set up and executed, so that there will be a continuing effort behind sales instead of an occasional push. The argument that holding one contest after another dulls interest does not seem to be borne out by experience any more than having a quota for every month of the year. It is, however, important that there be variety to the competition, so that new interest will be added every month.

To illustrate how a program of sales contests may be set up to provide a year-in-and-year-out sales push, without having them become tiresome, the following outline may be of interest. It was followed by a manufacturer of printers' supplies:

JANUARY-MARCH: *Step Ahead Campaign*—During this period, the sales organization was supplied with new tools and new plans to help it to keep out in front during the new year.

APRIL-MAY: *Question Box Contest*—Each week, during the period, salesmen were asked to submit their most effective sales argument for a given product in the line. Those selected as best each week won a $5 bill. The answers, of course, are published and circulated in the company house organ.

JUNE: *Vacation Campaign*—Five products were selected, which the company desired to push, and quotas were given to each salesman. Those making quota received a two weeks' vacation at the company's expense, or a proportion of their expenses if they fell short of quota.

JULY-AUGUST: *Baseball Tournament*—Each branch house constituted a team. Prize points were awarded on prospects reported (hits), sales (runs). Grand prizes to the winning team and to the heavy hitters.

SEPTEMBER: *World's Series Jamboree*—Carrying forward the interest in the baseball tournament, salesmen who qualified in the ball game and who also made quota in September got a free trip to the World's Series.

OCTOBER-NOVEMBER: *Bulls and Bears Stock Market Contest*—A novel campaign in which each salesman is incorporated as a going business, and his stock listed on the "Big Board."

DECEMBER: *President's Month*—Sales this month are a testimonial to the head of the business. A banquet is given during Christmas week to round out the year and make the presentation.

It will be noticed from the foregoing how a variety of interest is maintained. The majority of the contests are educational. Most of them have a definite incentive interest, to permit playing upon salesmen's liking for competitive activities. The schedule is so set up that one contest begins just as soon as the other ends. The successful sales contest—

1. Is built to do a constructive educational job, rather than make a salesman work harder.

2. Is dramatized with a central theme—but showmanship is not permitted to submerge salesmanship.

3. Is planned well ahead of starting time so that it can be effectively "merchandised" to those who must promote it.

4. Makes it possible for every salesman who does a job to win something; it is aimed at the tail-enders rather than the stars.

5. Recognizes all phases of constructive selling as well as the total business obtained by contestants.

6. Is neither too long nor too short—about two months is the best period.

7. Is never allowed to become monotonous. It is a series of surprises which keeps interest alive from beginning to end.

8. Teaches better ways to sell, and rewards those who put those methods into operation.

The time-honored conception of a sales contest was a competition in which the man who got the most business during the period of the contest won a watch. But that practice had one great fault. The same men won most of the watches, and the average salesmen, who comprise about 80 percent of the organization, quickly lost interest.

Since it is more important to stimulate the tail-enders than the few men at the top, sales managers quickly hit upon the idea of handicapping salesmen having above-average territories, to give the less fortunate men a break. The sales task was developed. Each man was given a definite task, and the prizes went to those who succeeded in showing the largest percentage of increase.

The ideal today is to base competition on percentages so calculated that every man will be able to win some prize, and thus be spurred to do his best, rather than discouraged by being an "also-ran."

The Connelly Company, of Ann Arbor, Michigan, for example, takes 80 percent of the previous year's sales as the minimum to qualify, and then pays on a small point unit up to 100 percent, with double the point unit for over 100 percent of that year's sales. The company uses points for merchandise prizes. Thus, everyone gets something, since he is competing merely with himself. Prize catalogs are sent to the salesmen's homes so that the wives and children are also brought into the picture.

Ford Uses Las Vegas

What is probably the largest sales-incentive trip ever conducted up to this year was the "To Vegas on Top Volume" program of the Ford Motor Company.

Day in and day out, for 18 days, commercial flights from all over the United States landed groups of 200-400 Ford dealer-salesmen and their wives, winners in the "To Vegas on Top Volume" incentive program. About 3,000 took the four-day, three-night incentive trip.

In planning the trip, the company's travel agency, E. F. Mac-Donald Co., gave winners in each of Ford's 37 districts a choice of three or four of the 15 contingents. Since the dealers were flown to Las Vegas on commercial flights, the problem of grouping dealer salesmen for charter flights was eliminated.

The incentive program covered a two-month sales period. The plan was introduced at 193 kickoff meetings.

The rules for the incentive trip were:

1. Every salesman could earn prize-point checks based on his sales of new Ford cars and trucks.

2. Bonus prize-point checks were issued to salesmen whose dealership reached a "Fast Start" objective the first month.

3. Trips for two to Las Vegas were awarded to winning dealerships in various competitive groupings. Dealers, in turn, awarded the trips to their top salesmen.

Two months after the contest period, the salesmen and their wives began to fly into Las Vegas.

A CHECKLIST FOR SALES CONTESTS

PLANNING YOUR CONTEST:

Is the contest timed right? You can pay more for extra volume when sales are below the profit break-even point.

Will the contest do a man-building job as well as get extra business? Or do you regard it merely as a "shot in the arm"?

Is your contest designed to bring out the best in the tail-enders, rather than to put a halo on the men at the top of the list?

Will everyone have a chance to win if he makes the special effort required?

Is the contest too short? Will you have ample time to promote it properly?

Is the contest too long? Will the men lose interest so that you can't get up the necessary winning head of steam?

SCORING:

Is your system of credits worked out so that a permanent benefit will result from the contest?

Have you arranged to reward men who come through with a constructive sales suggestion which can be passed along to the others?

Have you provided extra recognition for the salesman who does the best territory development work, such as opening new accounts during the contest?

Have you provided points for those contestants who do a particularly good job in getting point-of-sales advertising?

Have you emphasized the importance of getting window and store displays put in by the customer?

Have you provided extra points for orders which include the neglected items in the line?

Is there a period near the end of the campaign when a man gets double points for double effort? Give the weak sisters a chance to score.

Is your scoring system fair? The most successful contests require men to beat their normal sales expectancy rather than their fellow salesmen.

If you give points on volume alone, is there some equalizing factor so that the weaker salesmen will get a break?

AWARDING PRIZES:

Has each contestant a chance to win a prize of his own selection; or must he take what he gets?

Have you provided prizes of some sort for the wives of the winners, as well as prizes which only men would use?

If prize books are to be used do they feature standard, advertised merchandise or cheap premium-type merchandise which will kill interest in prize contests forever?

Are prizes well displayed in prize book? Remember the success of the contest depends upon the lure of the prize book.

If only a first and second prize are awarded there should be "Honor" prizes for at least the top third of the salesmen. The more winners, the more workers next time.

Will the prize be kept and cherished? Money is seldom as effective as merchandise in the long run.

STAGING THE CONTEST:

Is your contest sufficiently different from your last activity to make it novel and interesting?

Is it dramatic? There should be just enough showmanship and color to awaken interest without detracting from the sales message.

Does it drive home *one* central selling idea which will stick in a salesman's mind long after the contest itself will be forgotten?

Will it click with the men? It should neither be too highbrow nor too clever. One fault is as bad as the other.

Has the office force been put into the picture so that salesmen will feel the eyes of the folks back home are upon them?

Is your starting time far enough ahead so you can do the best possible job of promoting the contest with distributors or dealers?

How about the qualification task? Is it easy to attain so that you will get as many men as possible underway quickly?

Have you provided suitable recognition for those who meet the qualification task—a lapel button, belt buckle, or certificate?

Are your mailings timed so as to reach salesmen on Monday morning? Use airmail or special delivery to far-off points.

Is there a surprise in every mailing? Nothing is more fatal than to let the tempo of a contest drag.

Is the office scoreboard so placed that the entire office organization can see it and comment upon it in letters they may be writing to salesmen?

Is the salesman's family tied in to the contest? Send them duplicate mailings, or provide in some way to get wives and sweethearts into the picture.

PUTTING THE CONTEST OVER:

Is your contest "announcement" sufficiently spectacular? Will it impress your salesmen as it should?

Do you give each salesman an opportunity to go on record as wishing to participate by enclosing a registration card with advance announcement?

Does the advance announcement carry detailed rules, with exact starting and finishing time, what kind of orders count and what kind won't count, etc.?

Have you some simple method by which a salesman can notify the office every time he scores? Such notification cards can be posted on scoreboard.

How frequently do you send progress reports out to the men? Toward the end of the contest they should be mailed daily, using telegrams the last week.

Do you write enough personal letters to contestants suggesting that you are betting on them to beat another salesman of equal ability?

Have you teamed up salesmen by districts and offered a cup or prize on the side for the best team in the league?

Do you write frequent personal letters commenting upon the standings of salesmen to make them keenly aware that you are watching their progress?

What is your plan for awarding the prizes? If possible you should have a president's dinner, with as many men as possible there.

COMMUNICATING WITH SALESMEN

While practically every company operating 10 or more salesmen issues some sort of bulletin, many of these are dull and uninteresting. Although sales managers have abandoned the pep-letter technique which characterized the sales bulletin of 20 years ago, many still make the mistake of using bulletins to preach to their men, clutter them up with instructions and material which should properly be issued as loose-leaf pages for an operating manual, and forget that even a bulletin carrying the sales manager's signature is in competition for the time a busy salesman is able to devote to reading.

An effective sales bulletin should, above all, be newsy. It should be regarded by management as a device for spreading the good news about the business. It should inspire salesmen to renewed effort, strengthen their confidence in the company and its products, bring ideas and suggestions helpful to them in their work, and keep them sold on company policies. It is, in short, the newspaper of the sales organization. And like a good newspaper it should present the news objectively, with a minimum of coloring. It should be well printed and easy to read.

Illustrated Bulletin Stencils

A common criticism of most of the bulletins issued for salesmen, particularly those produced on stencil duplicating machines, is lack of illustrations. In theory the message should be so intensely inter-

Dartnell SALES and MARKETING SERVICE • The Dartnell Corporation • 4660 Ravenswood Ave., Chicago, Ill. 60640

REPRODUCTION PROOF

Note to subscriber: This reproduction proof can be used either to make lithographic plates for offset printing or line engravings for letterpress work.

Sales-oriented cartoons for sales bulletins are supplied monthly to subscribers to the Dartnell Sales and Marketing Service. The reproduction proofs can be used for offset or letterpress printing.

esting that men will read every word without embellishment. Unfortunately practice proves otherwise. Salesmen are not readers. Any sales manager who has had experience in getting salesmen to read even important bulletins on price changes knows that what they should do and what they actually do are entirely different. To get maximum attention and interest, typewritten bulletins should be broken up as much as possible with heads and have at least one pertinent illustration—preferably a cartoon—in each issue.

Arrangements can usually be made with some local cartoonist to prepare a weekly cartoon built up around some subject of timely interest directly on the mimeograph stencil. Another way is to have the cartoons drawn in ink and trace them on to the stencil by means of the mimeoscope and stylus.

There are several bulletin "copy and cut" services which will supply a weekly inset stencil or transferable proof. The cartoons are drawn and then mechanically reproduced in the form of cut stencils, which may be "grafted" or "patched" onto the regular bulletin stencil. Similarly the transfer proof, which is printed in special ink, may be used for illustrating a bulletin to be reproduced by the gelatin copy process.

Cartoons for sales bulletins, ready for reproduction, are included with each month's portfolio of the "Dartnell Sales and Marketing Service."

Preparing Bulletins

The secret of writing successful bulletins or house organs to salesmen is to talk *with* them rather than *at* them. Instead of writing articles telling them to do such and such a thing, use a "let us do it" touch. It is a weakness characteristic of sales managers to make them read like army orders, rather than like intimate, friendly communications designed to help a man do a better selling job.

Another sour touch that spoils many otherwise well-received sales bulletins are signed articles by home-office officials who have nothing particular to write about, so decide to use the space to talk about the value of loyalty, hard work, and care in spending the firm's money. While these are important and worthy of being kept before every salesman, it is better to "say it with news" rather than signed articles. Relating selling experiences and plans of other salesmen and the scoreboard, or comparative standings of salesmen, are generally regarded as the two most important features in sales bulletins. The consensus is that the scoreboard comes first. It is one of the greatest sales stimulators ever invented.

A poll of 3,500 salesmen gives preference to stories of sales, salesmen's experiences and plans, and other material of this nature. They also voted for contests to be operated through the sales bulletin. The demand for more photographs, charts, and cartoons having to do with selling was very great. Some kinds of inspirational articles were strongly commended, but poetry, humor, and general articles received "thumbs down." A majority of the salesmen made clear that their second choice of articles was personal stories about salesmen.

One sales manager makes it a practice to watch sales reports for leads. He selects the most likely looking sales and drops the salesman a line requesting him to write on the opposite side of the sheet just what argument was used in making the sale, what objections had to be overcome, and what point seemed to carry the most weight in clinching the order. The brief replies usually form the basis for building interesting articles.

Motivating Retail Salesmen

Henry Felker of Colder's Furniture Company in Milwaukee, Wisconsin, claims that the main difference between a salesman and a clerk is in the way he is treated by management. He feels his organization has made some outstanding progress in proving this important point.

"First, we believe a prospective salesman must be a cut above the ordinary man," said Felker, president of the three-store furniture and appliance chain. "This means we don't hire just anybody. We tell a new salesman right away that he'll be working for us on a two-week probationary basis. He's paid, of course, which keeps the pressure off while he's learning to sell our way. We also tell him if he can't earn at least $12,000 a year working for us, we had best part company. We pay our men well to do a selling job. We don't want clerks earning clerk's wages—we want professional salesmen . . . who command the salaries of true professional people."

In activating retail salesmen, the experience of Robert Neuman, of L. Fish Furniture Company, headquartered in Chicago, Illinois, will be of interest. As head of its appliance division, he adapted an incentive program for salesmen and store managers.

"This program was originally the idea of one manufacturer," said Neuman. "I found it could be tailored to all our appliance and electronics lines. Sales were so gratifying that we've continued the program ever since!"

L. Fish Furniture Company has 17 branch stores. The incentive program involved approximately 95 salesmen and managers.

"After experimenting with such things as trips, clothing and prizes," said Neuman, "we found cash incentives most effective. Contests are conducted on a point basis—as an example, eight points for a stereo, six for a range, and so forth. These may then be converted to cash awards. In other cases, a straight cash basis is used from the start.

"We establish an overall company goal before starting an incentive drive. Then each store is given a quota based on past performance and overall objectives. If a store meets quota, its manager receives a bonus. Also, we may offer him an extra incentive for going over quota. If he's below quota, he gets nothing. However, the salesmen are paid an incentive on every item sold."

PART 9

READY-
REFERENCE
SECTION

Contents: READY-REFERENCE SECTION

This list of publications, compiled by Juanita Roberts, Dartnell research librarian, offers the reader a choice of reference books most closely related to sales supervision. Because of the fact that prices are subject to change without notice and may include sales taxes or postage, prices are not quoted in this list but can, of course, be ascertained by a phone call to a bookseller.

ALEXANDER, MILTON: *Case Histories in Sales Management*, Pitman Publishing Corporation, New York, 1965.

AMERICAN MANAGEMENT ASSOCIATION: *The Field Sales Manager*, American Management Association, New York, 1960.

AMERICAN MANAGEMENT ASSOCIATION: *Goal Setting and Planning at the District Sales Level*, American Management Association, New York, 1963.

ASPLEY, J. C.: *Aspley on Sales*, The Dartnell Corporation, Chicago, 1966.

ASPLEY, J. C.: *Sales Promotion Handbook*, The Dartnell Corporation, Chicago, 1964.

BAKER, RICHARD: *Salesmanship:* Allyn & Bacon, Inc., Boston, 1966.

BIGELOW, BURTON: *Human Side of Sales Management*, Prentice-Hall, Inc., Englewood Cliffs, N. J., 1961.

CANFIELD, BERTRAND R.: *Sales Administration: Principles and Problems*, Prentice-Hall, Englewood Cliffs, N. J., 1961.

CRISP, RICHARD D.: *Sales Planning and Control*, McGraw-Hill Book Company, New York, 1962.

DAY, RALPH L.: *Salesmen in the Field*, Richard D. Irwin, Inc., Homewood, Illinois, 1963.

FOUNDATION FOR RESEARCH ON HUMAN BEHAVIOR: *Applying Modern Management Principles to Sales Organizations*, Foundation for Research on Human Behavior, Ann Arbor, Mich., 1963.

HAAS, KENNETH BROOKS: *Professional Salesmanship*, Holt, Rinehart & Winston, Inc., New York, 1962.

HODGSON, RICHARD: *Direct Mail and Mail Order Handbook*, The Dartnell Corporation, Chicago, 1964.

HUMMEL, FRANCES: *Market and Sales Potentials*, The Ronald Press Company, New York, 1961.

JOHNSON, H. WEBSTER: *Creative Selling*, South-Western Publishing Company, Cincinnati, 1966.

KUESEL, HARRY N.: *Kuesel on Closing Sales*, Prentice-Hall, Inc., Englewood Cliffs, N. J., 1965.

LAZO, HECTOR: *Management in Marketing: Text and Cases*, McGraw-Hill Book Company, New York, 1961.

LIVINGSTON, J. STERLING: *Cases in Sales Management,* Richard D. Irwin, Inc., Homewood, Ill., 1962.

MATTHEWS, JOHN B.: *Marketing,* McGraw-Hill Book Company, New York, 1964.

MCMURRY, ROBERT N.: *How to Recruit, Select and Place Salesmen,* The Dartnell Corporation, Chicago, 1964.

MELOAN, TAYLOR W.: *Selling: Its Broader Dimensions,* The MacMillan Company, New York, 1960.

PEDERSON, CARLTON A.: *Salesmanship: Principles and Methods,* Richard D. Irwin, Inc., Homewood, Ill., 1966.

PHELPS, DUDLEY M.: *Marketing Management,* Richard D. Irwin, Inc., Homewood, Ill., 1960.

PHILLIPS, CHARLES F.: *Marketing: Principles and Methods,* Richard D. Irwin, Inc., Homewood, Ill., 1964.

RICE, CRAIG: *How to Plan and Execute the Marketing Campaign,* The Dartnell Corporation, Chicago, 1966.

RUSSELL, FREDERICK: *Textbook of Salesmanship,* McGraw-Hill Book Company, New York, 1963.

SHAW, STEVEN: *Salesmanship: Modern Viewpoints on Personal Communications,* Holt, Rinehart & Winston, Inc., New York, 1960.

SMYKAY, EDWARD W.: *Physical Distribution: The New and Profitable Science of Business Logistics,* The Dartnell Corporation, Chicago, 1966.

STANTON, WILLIAM J.: *Management of the Sales Force,* Richard D. Irwin, Inc., Homewood, Ill., 1964.

STEINBRINK, JOHN P.: *Compensation of Salesmen,* The Dartnell Corporation, Chicago, 1965.

STROH, THOMAS F.: *Salesmanship: Personal Communications and Persuasion in Marketing,* Richard D. Irwin, Inc., Homewood, Ill., 1967.

THOMPSON, JOSEPH: *Selling: A Behavioral Approach,* McGraw-Hill Book Company, New York, 1966.

TONNING, WAYLAND: *How to Measure and Evaluate Salesmen's Performance,* Prentice-Hall, Inc., Englewood Cliffs, N. J., 1964.

TRUMP, ROSS: *Essentials of Marketing Management,* Houghton Mifflin Company, Boston, 1966.

WALL STREET JOURNAL: *How They Sell,* by the editors of the *Wall Street Journal,* New York, 1965.

WINGATE, JOHN: *Fundamentals of Selling,* South-Western Publishing Company, Cincinnati, 1964.

ZOBER, MARTIN: *Marketing Management,* John Wiley & Sons, Inc., New York, 1964.

Section B — GLOSSARY OF MARKETING TERMS

The following glossary of sales marketing terms is the result of a report from a joint committee representing principal sales marketing executive groups. All instances where there is a difference of opinion among the groups are acknowledged and identified in the report.

ACCESSORY EQUIPMENT—See Equipment

ADVERTISING—Any paid form of nonpersonal presentation and promotion of ideas, goods, or services by an identified sponsor.

It involves the use of such media as the following:

Magazine and newspaper space
Motion pictures
Outdoor (posters, signs, skywriting, etc.)
Direct mail
Store signs
Novelties (calendars, blotters, etc.)
Radio and television
Cards (car, bus, etc.)
Catalogs
Directories and references
Programs and menus
Circulars

This list is intended to be illustrative, not inclusive.

See "Publicity" for a definition of a kindred activity. It should be noted that retailers often do not regard display as a part of advertising but as a separate activity.

ADVERTISING RESEARCH—See Marketing Research

AGENT MIDDLEMAN—A middleman who negotiates purchases or sales or both but who does not take title to goods.

He usually performs fewer marketing functions than does the merchant middleman. He commonly receives his remuneration in the form of a commission or fee. He commonly does not represent both buyer and seller in the same transaction.

Examples are: Broker, commission merchant, manufacturer's agent, selling agent, and resident buyer.

The Committee recommends that the term Agent rather than Agent Middleman be preferred. The Committee also recommends that the term Functional Middleman no longer be applied to this type of agent. It is hardly logical or consistent in view of the fact that he performs fewer marketing functions than other middlemen.

ASSEMBLING—The marketing function of concentrating goods or their control to facilitate sale or purchase.

The concentration involved here may affect a quantity of like goods or a variety of goods. It includes the assembling of adequate and representative stocks by wholesalers and retailers.

BRANCH HOUSE—An establishment maintained by a manufacturer or a wholesaler, detached from the headquarters establishment and used primarily for the purpose of carrying stocks of, selling, and delivering his product.

BRANCH OFFICE—An establishment maintained by a seller, detached from the headquarters establishment and used for the purpose of selling his product or service.

The characteristic of the branch house that distinguishes it from the branch office is the fact that it is used in the physical storage, handling, and delivery of merchandise. Otherwise the two are identical.

BRANCH STORE—A subsidiary retail business owned and operated by an established store and smaller than, or carrying a much less extensive line of merchandise than, the Parent Store.

See Parent Store for a kindred term.

BRAND—A name, term, symbol, or design, or a combination of them which identifies the goods or services of one seller or group of sellers and distinguishes them from those of competitors.

A brand may include a brand name, a trademark, or both. The term brand is sufficiently comprehensive to include practically all means of identification except perhaps the package and the shape of the product. All brand names and all trademarks are brands or parts of brands but not all brands are either brand names or trademarks. Brand is the inclusive, general term. The others are more particularized.

BRAND NAME—A brand or part of a brand consisting of a word, letter, group of words or letters comprising a name which identifies the goods or services of a seller or group of sellers and distinguishes them from those of competitors.

The brand name is that part of a brand which can be vocalized—the utterable quality resident in it. To illustrate, the brand under which the Buick car is sold is the name "Buick" printed in script and set in the familiar rectangle design which usually appears somewhere on this make of car. This combination also happens to conform to the legal requirements of a trademark. The word "Buick" used orally or set in any kind of type face, whatever its surroundings may be, is the brand name. This is true of the pronounceable part of it regardless of the presence or absence of the usually accompanying designs or symbols.

BROKER—An agent who does not have direct physical control of goods with which he deals but represents either buyer or seller and does business for his principal. His powers as to prices and terms of sale are usually limited by his principal.

BUYING POWER—See Purchasing Power. Purchasing Power is preferred

CANVASSER—See House-to-House Salesman

CASH AND CARRY WHOLESALER—See Wholesaler

CHAIN STORE—A group of retail stores of essentially the same type, centrally owned and with some degree of centralized control of operation.

> *According to the dictionary, two may apparently be construed to constitute a "group." This term may also refer to a single store unit of such a group.*

COLLECTION PERIOD—The number of days that the total of trade accounts and notes receivable (including assigned accounts and discounted notes, if any), less reserves for bad debts, represents when compared with the annual net credit sales. Formula—divide the annual net credit sales by 365 days to obtain the average credit sales per day. Then divide the total of accounts and notes receivable (plus any discounted notes receivable) by the average credit sales per day to obtain the average collection period.

COMMISSARY STORE—A retail store owned and operated by a company or governmental unit to sell primarily to its employees.

Nongovernmental establishments of this type are often referred to as "Company Stores" or "Industrial Stores."

> *Many of these establishments are not operated for profit. The matter of the location of the control over and responsibility for these stores rather than the motive for their operation constitutes their distinguishing characteristic.*

COMMISSION HOUSE—An agent, transacting business in his own name, who usually exercises physical control over the goods consigned to him and negotiates their sale.

The commission merchant usually enjoys broader powers as to prices, methods, and terms of sale than does the broker although he must obey instructions issued by his principal. He generally arranges delivery, extends necessary credit, collects, deducts his fees, and remits the balance to his principal.

> *Most of those who have defined the commission merchant state that he has possession of the goods he handles. In its strict meaning the word "possession" connotes to some extent the idea of ownership; in its legal meaning it involves a degree of control somewhat beyond that usually enjoyed by the commission merchant. Therefore, the phrase, "physical control," was used instead.*
>
> *The fact that many commission merchants are not typical in their operations does not subtract from their status as commission merchants. While the term "merchant" is somewhat of a misnomer when applied to an agent, that fact is disregarded in this definition since this usage is commonly accepted in the trade.*

COMPANY STORE—See Commissary Store

CONSUMER RESEARCH—See Marketing Research

CONSUMER'S COOPERATIVE—An association of ultimate consumers organized to purchase goods and services primarily for use by or resale to the membership.

> *According to this definition the term applies only to the cooperative purchasing activities of ultimate consumers and does not embrace collective buying by business establishments, industrial concerns, and institutions.*

CONSUMERS' GOODS—Goods destined for use by the ultimate household consumer and in such form that they can be used by him without further commercial processing.

Certain articles, for example, typewriters, may be either consumers' goods or industrial goods depending upon whether they are destined for use by the ultimate household consumer or by an industrial, business, or institutional user.

CONVENIENCE GOODS—Those consumers' goods which the customer usually purchases frequently, immediately, and with the minimum of effort.

Examples of merchandise customarily bought as convenience goods are: Tobacco products, soap, most drug products, newspapers, magazines, chewing gum, small packaged confections, and many grocery products.

These articles are usually of small unit value and not bulky. The definition, however, is based on the method of purchase employed by the typical consumer. Its essence lies in consumer attitude and habit. The convenience involved may be in terms of nearness to the buyer's home, easy accessibility to some means of transport, or close proximity to places where people go during the day or evening, for example, downtown to work.

COOPERATIVE MARKETING—The process by which groups composed of producers, middlemen, consumers, or combinations of them act collectively in buying or selling or both.

This term includes only those collective activities that are more or less directly connected with buying and selling.

COST AND FREIGHT: *"C. & F. (named point of destination)"*

NOTE: Seller and buyer should consider not only the definitions but also the "C. & F. Comments" and the "C. & F. and C.I.F. Comments" in order to understand fully their respective responsibilities and rights under "C. & F." terms.

Under this term, the seller quotes a price including the cost of transportation to the named point of destination.

Under this quotation—

Seller must:

1. Provide and pay for transportation to named point of destination;

2. Pay export taxes, or other fees or charges, if any, levied because of exportation;

3. Obtain and dispatch promptly to buyer, or his agent, clean bill of lading to named point of destination;

4. Where received-for-shipment ocean bill of lading may be tendered, be responsible for any loss or damage, or both, until the goods have been delivered into the custody of the ocean carrier;

5. Where on-board ocean bill of lading is required, be responsible for any loss or damage, or both, until the goods have been delivered on board the vessel;

6. Provide, at the buyer's request and expense, certificates of origin, consular invoices, or other documents issued in the country of origin, or of shipment, or of both, which the buyer may require for importation of goods into country of destination and, where necessary, for their passage in transit through another country.

Buyer must:

1. Accept the documents when presented;

2. Receive goods upon arrival, handle and pay for all subsequent movement of the goods, including taking delivery from vessel in accordance with bill of lading clauses and terms; pay all costs of lading, including any duties, taxes, and other expenses at named point of destination;

3. Provide and pay for insurance;

4. Be responsible for loss of or damage to goods, or both, from time and place at which seller's obligations under (4) or (5) above have ceased;

5. Pay the costs of certificates of origin, consular invoices, or any other documents issued in the country of origin, or of shipment, or of both, which may be required for the importation of goods into the country of destination and, where necessary, for their passage in transit through another country.

C. & F. Comments

1. For the seller's protection, he should provide in his contract of sale that marine insurance obtained by the buyer include standard warehouse-to-warehouse coverage.

2. The comments listed under the following C.I.F. terms in many cases apply to C. & F. terms as well, and should be read and understood by the C. & F. seller and buyer.

Cost, Insurance, Freight: *"C.I.F. (named point of destination)"*

Note: Seller and buyer should consider not only the definitions but also the "Comments" at the end of this section, in order to understand fully their respective responsibilities and rights under "C.I.F." terms.

Under this term, the seller quotes a price including the cost of the goods, the marine insurance, and all transportation charges to the named point of destination.

Under this quotation—

Seller must:

1. Provide and pay for transportation to named point of destination;

2. Pay export taxes, or other fees or charges, if any, levied because of exportation;

3. Provide and pay for marine insurance;

4. Provide war risk insurance as obtainable in seller's market at time of shipment at buyer's expense, unless seller has agreed that buyer provide for war risk coverage;

5. Obtain and dispatch promptly to buyer, or his agent, clean bill of lading to named point of destination, and also insurance policy or negotiable insurance certificate;

6. Where received-for-shipment ocean bill of lading may be tendered, be responsible for any loss or damage, or both, until the goods have been delivered into the custody of the ocean carrier;

7. Where on-board ocean bill of lading is required, be responsible for any loss or damage, or both, until the goods have been delivered on board the vessel;

8. Provide, at the buyer's request and expense, certificates of origin, consular invoices, or any other documents issued in the country of origin, or of shipment, or both, which the buyer may require for importation of goods into country or destination and, where necessary, for their passage in transit through another country.

Buyer must:

1. Accept the documents when presented;

2. Receive the goods upon arrival, handle and pay for all subsequent movement of the goods, including taking delivery from vessel in accordance with bill of lading clauses and terms; pay all costs of lading, including any duties, taxes, and other expenses at named point of destination;

3. Pay for war risk insurance provided by seller;

4. Be responsible for loss of or damage to goods, or both, from time and place at which seller's obligation under (6) or (7) above have ceased;

5. Pay the cost of certificates of origin, consular invoices, or any other documents issued in the country of origin, or of shipment, or both, which may be required for importation of the goods into the country of destination and, where necessary, for their passage in transit through another country.

C. &. F. AND C.I.F. COMMENTS

Under C. & F. and C.I.F. contracts there are the following points on which the seller and the buyer should be in complete agreement at the time that the contract is concluded:

1. It should be agreed upon, in advance, who is to pay for miscellaneous expenses, such as weighing or inspection charges.

2. The quantity to be shipped on any one vessel should be agreed upon, in advance, with a view to the buyer's capacity to take delivery upon arrival and discharge of the vessel, within the free time allowed at the port of importation.

3. Although the terms C. & F. and C.I.F. are generally interpreted to provide that charges for consular invoices and certificates of origin are for the account of the buyer, and are charged separately, in many trades these charges are included by the seller in his price. Hence, seller and buyer should agree, in advance, whether these charges are part of the selling price, or will be invoiced separately.

4. The point of final destination should be definitely known in the event the vessel discharges at a port other than the actual destination of the goods.

5. When ocean freight space is difficult to obtain, or forward freight contracts cannot be made at firm rates, it is advisable that sales contracts, as an exception to regular C. & F. or C.I.F. terms, should provide that shipment within the

contract period be subject to ocean freight space being available to the seller, and should also provide that changes in the cost of ocean transportation between the time of sale and the time of shipment be for account of the buyer.

6. Normally, the seller is obligated to prepay the ocean freight. In some instances, shipments are made freight collect and the amount of the freight is deducted from the invoice rendered by the seller. It is necessary to be in agreement on this, in advance, in order to avoid misunderstanding which arises from foreign exchange fluctuations which might affect the actual cost of transportation, and from interest charges which might accrue under letter-of-credit financing. Hence, the seller should always prepay the ocean freight unless he has a specific agreement with the buyer, in advance, that goods can be shipped freight collect.

7. The buyer should recognize that he does not have the right to insist on inspection of goods prior to accepting the documents. The buyer should not refuse to take delivery of goods on account of delay in the receipt of documents, provided the seller has used due diligence in their dispatch through the regular channels.

8. Sellers and buyers are advised against including in a C.I.F. contract any indefinite clause at variance with the obligations of a C.I.F. contract as specified in these Definitions. There have been numerous court decisions in the United States and other countries invalidating C.I.F. contracts because of the inclusion of indefinite clauses.

9. Interest charges should be included in cost computations and should not be charged as a separate item in C.I.F. contracts, unless otherwise agreed upon, in advance, between the seller and buyer; in which case, however, the term C.I.F. & I. (Cost, Insurance, Freight, and Interest) should be used.

10. In connection with insurance under C.I.F. sales, it is necessary that seller and buyer be definitely in accord upon the following points:

(a) The character of the marine insurance should be agreed upon insofar as being W.A. (With Average) or F.P.A. (Free of Particular Average), as well as any other special risks that are covered in specific trades, or against which the buyer may wish individual protection. Among the special risks that should be considered and agreed upon between seller and buyer are theft, pilferage, leakage, breakage, sweat, contact with other cargoes, and others peculiar to any particular trade. It is important that contingent or collect freight and customs duty should be insured to cover Particular Average losses, as well as total loss after arrival and entry but before delivery.

(b) The seller is obligated to exercise ordinary care and diligence in selecting an underwriter that is in good financial standing. However, the risk of obtaining settlement of insurance claims rests with the buyer.

(c) War risk insurance under this term is to be obtained by the seller at the expense and risk of the buyer. It is important that the seller be in definite accord with the buyer on this point, particularly as to the cost. It is desirable that the goods be insured against both marine and war risk with the same underwriter, so that there can be no difficulty arising from the determination of the cause of the loss.

(d) Seller should make certain that in his marine or war risk insurance, there be included the standard protection against strikes, riots, and civil commotions.

(e) Seller and buyer should be in accord as to the insured valuation, bearing in mind that merchandise contributes in General Average on certain bases of valuation which differ in various trades. It is desirable that a competent insurance broker be consulted, in order that full value be covered and trouble avoided.

DEALER'S BRAND—See Private Brands

DEPARTMENT STORE—A retail store which handles a wide variety of lines of goods, such as women's ready-to-wear and accessories, men's and boys' wear, piece goods, small wares and house furnishings, and which is organized into separate departments for purposes of promotion, service, and control.

Examples of department stores are: R. H. Macy and Company in New York; Marshall Field and Company in Chicago; J. L. Hudson Company in Detroit; Jordan Marsh Company in Boston; Rich's, Inc., in Atlanta; The Emporium in San Francisco; Garver Brothers Company in Strasburg, Ohio; and A. B. Wyckoff, Inc., in Stroudsburg, Pennslyvania.

This definition departs from the usual one in that it includes no definite requirement as to classes of goods handled, save only that they shall embrace a wide variety of lines. Most definitions previously suggested for this term set up a list of categories of merchandise which a store must handle before it can be designated as a department store. The emphasis here is placed upon the departmentization feature, provided a wide variety of lines is handled.

This formula probably more nearly conforms to common usage than do those of the more rigid type and at the same time it includes many stores whose problems and characteristics belong to this group but which do not fall within it if a rigid requirement as to classes of goods handled were applied. This is roughly the definition used by the Bureau of the Census.

DEPARTMENTIZED SPECIALTY STORE—See Specialty Store

DIRECT SELLING—The process whereby the producer sells to the user, ultimate consumer, or retailer without intervening middlemen.

The Committee recommends that when this term is used, it be so qualified as to indicate clearly the precise meaning intended (direct to retailer, direct to user, direct to ultimate consumer, etc.).

DISTRIBUTION—The Committee recommends that the term Distribution be regarded and used as synonymous with Marketing.

For a specialized sense in which it is sometimes used in this field see Physical Distribution.

In using this term marketing men should clearly distinguish it from the sense in which it is employed in economic theory, that is, the process of dividing the fund of value produced by industry among the several factors engaged in economic production.

DISTRIBUTION COST ANALYSIS—The study and evaluation of the relative profitability or costs of different marketing operations in terms of customers, marketing units, commodities, territories, warehouses, or services.

DROP SHIPMENT WHOLESALER—See Wholesaler

EQUIPMENT—Those industrial goods that do not become part of the physical product and which are exhausted only after repeated use, such as Major Installations, or Installation Equipment, and Auxiliary Accessories, or Auxiliary Equipment.

Installation Equipment includes such items as boilers, linotype machines, power latches, bank vaults.

Auxiliary Equipment includes such items as trucks, typewriters, filing cases, and most small tools.

Ex—(Point of Origin)

"Ex Factory," "Ex Mill," "Ex Mine," "Ex Plantation," "Ex Warehouse," etc. (named point of origin)

Under this term, the price quoted applies only at the point of origin, and the seller agrees to place the goods at the disposal of the buyer at the agreed place on the date or within the period fixed.

Under this quotation—

Seller must:

1. Bear all costs and risks of the goods until such time as the buyer is obliged to take delivery thereof;
2. Render the buyer, at the buyer's request and expense, assistance in obtaining the documents issued in the country of origin, or of shipment, or both, which the buyer may require either for purposes of exportation, or of importation at destination.

Buyer must:

1. Take delivery of the goods as soon as they have been placed at his disposal at the agreed place on the date or within the period fixed;
2. Pay export taxes, or other fees or charges, if any, levied because of exportation;
3. Bear all costs and risks of the goods from the time when he is obligated to take delivery thereof;
4. Pay all costs and charges incurred in obtaining the documents issued in the country of origin, or of shipment, or of both, which may be required either for purposes of exportation, or of importation at destination.

"Ex DOCK (named port of importation)"

NOTE: Seller and buyer should consider not only the definitions but also the "Ex Dock Comments" at the end of this section, in order to understand fully their respective responsibilities and rights under "Ex Dock" terms.

Under this term, seller quotes a price including the cost of the goods and all additional costs necessary to place the goods on the dock at the named port of importation, duty paid, if any.

Under this quotation—

Seller must:

1. Provide and pay for transportation to named port of importation;
2. Pay export taxes, or other fees or charges, if any, levied because of exportation;

3. Provide and pay for marine insurance;

4. Provide and pay for war risk insurance, unless otherwise agreed upon between the buyer and seller;

5. Be responsible for any loss or damage, or both, until the expiration of the free time allowed on the dock at the named port of importation;

6. Pay the costs of certificates of origin, consular invoices, legalization of bill of lading, or any other documents issued in the country of origin, or of shipment, or of both, which the buyer may require for the importation of goods into the country of destination and, where necessary, for their passage in transit through another country;

7. Pay all costs of landing, including wharfage, landing charges, and taxes, if any;

8. Pay all costs of customs entry in the country of importation;

9. Pay customs duties and all taxes applicable to imports, if any, in the country of importation, unless otherwise agreed upon.

Buyer must:

1. Take delivery of the goods on the dock at the named port of importation within the free time allowed;

2. Bear the cost and risk of the goods if delivery is not taken within the free time allowed.

Ex Dock Comments

This term is used principally in United States import trade. It has various modifications, such as "Ex Quay," "Ex Pier," etc., but it is seldom, if ever, used in American export practice. Its use in quotations for export is not recommended.

General Notes of Caution

1. As foreign trade definitions have been issued by organizations in various parts of the world, and as the courts of countries have interpreted these definitions in different ways, it is important that sellers and buyers agree that their contracts are subject to the latest revised edition of *American Foreign Trade Definitions, Revised,* and that the various points listed are accepted by both parties.

2. In addition to the foreign trade terms listed herein, there are terms that are at times used, such as Free Harbor, C.I.F. & C. (Cost, Insurance, Freight, and Commission), C.I.F.C. & I. (Cost, Insurance, Freight, Commission, and Interest), C.I.F. Landed (Cost, Insurance, Freight, Landed), and others. None of these should be used unless there has first been a definite understanding as to the exact meaning thereof. It is unwise to attempt to interpret other terms in the light of the terms given herein. Hence, whenever possible, one of the terms defined herein should be used.

3. It is unwise to use abbreviations in quotations or in contracts which might be subject to misunderstanding.

4. When making quotations, the familiar terms "hundredweight" or "ton" should be avoided. A hundredweight can be 100 pounds of the short ton, or 112 pounds of the long ton. A ton can be a short ton of 2,000 pounds, or a metric ton of 2,204.6 or a long ton of 2,240 pounds. Hence, the type of hundredweight or

ton should be clearly stated in quotations and in sales confirmations. Also, all terms referring to quantity, weight, volume, length, or surface should be clearly defined and agreed upon.

FACTOR—1. A type of commission merchant who often advances funds to the consignor, identified chiefly with the raw cotton and naval stores trades.

2. A specialized commercial banker, performing the function of financing for producers of and dealers in many varieties of products and occasionally combining this function with that of selling.

The term factor *was formerly synonymous with* commission merchant.

F.A.S. (FREE ALONGSIDE)

"F.A.S. VESSEL (named port of shipment)"

NOTE: Seller and buyer should consider not only the definitions but also the "Comments" given at the end of this section, in order to understand fully their respective responsibilities and rights under "F.A.S." terms.

Under this term, the seller quotes a price including delivery of the goods alongside overseas vessel and within reach of its loading tackle.

Under this quotation—

Seller must:

1. Place goods alongside vessel or on dock designed and provided by, or for, buyer on the date or within the period fixed; pay any heavy lift charges, where necessary, up to this point;

2. Provide clean dock or ship's receipt;

3. Be responsible for any loss or damage, or both, until goods have been delivered alongside the vessel or on the dock;

4. Render the buyer, at the buyer's request and expense, assistance in obtaining the documents issued in the country of origin, or of shipment, or of both, which the buyer may require either for purposes of exportation, or of importation at destination.

Buyer must:

1. Give seller adequate notice of name, sailing date, loading berth of, and delivery time to, the vessel;

2. Handle all subsequent movement of the goods from alongside the vessel:

    (a) Arrange and pay for demurrage or storage charges, or both, in warehouse or on wharf, where necessary;

    (b) Provide and pay for insurance;

    (c) Provide and pay for ocean and other transportation;

3. Pay export taxes, or other fees or charges, if any, levied because of exportation;

4. Be responsible for any loss or damage, or both, while the goods are on a lighter or other conveyance alongside vessel within reach of its loading tackle, or on the dock awaiting loading, or until actually loaded on board the vessel, and subsequent thereto;

5. Pay all costs and charges incurred in obtaining the documents, other than clean dock or ship's receipt, issued in the country of origin, or of shipment, or of both, which may be required either for purposes of exportation or of importation at destination.

F.A.S. Comments

1. Under F.A.S. terms, the obligation to obtain ocean freight space, and marine and war risk insurance, rests with the buyer. Despite this obligation on the part of the buyer, in many trades the seller obtains ocean freight space, and marine and war risk insurance, and provides for shipment on behalf of the buyer. In others, the buyer notifies the seller to make delivery alongside a vessel designated by the buyer and the buyer provides his own marine and war risk insurance. Hence, seller and buyer must have an understanding as to whether the buyer will obtain the ocean freight space, and marine and war risk insurance, as is his obligation, or whether the seller agrees to do this for the buyer.

2. For the seller's protection, he should provide in his contract of sale that marine insurance obtained by the buyer include standard warehouse-to-warehouse coverage.

FIXED ASSETS—The sum of the cost value of land and the depreciated book values of buildings, leasehold improvements, fixtures, furniture, machinery, tools, and equipment—valued at cost or appraised market value.

FUNDED DEBT—Mortgages, bonds, debentures, gold notes, serial notes, or other obligations with maturity of more than one year from statement date.

FREE ON BOARD: *"F.O.B. (named inland carrier at named inland point of departure)"*

NOTE: Seller and buyer should consider not only the definitions but also the "Comments on All F.O.B. Terms" given at end of this section, in order to understand fully their respective responsibilities and rights under the several classes of "F.O.B." terms.

Under this term, the price quoted applies only at inland shipping points, and the seller arranges for loading of the goods on, or in, railway cars, trucks, lighters, barges, aircraft, or other conveyance furnished for transportation.

Under this quotation—

Seller must:

1. Place goods on, or in, conveyance, or deliver to inland carrier for loading;

2. Provide clean bill of lading or other transportation receipt, freight collect;

3. Be responsible for any loss or damage, or both, until goods have been placed in, or on, conveyance at loading point, and clean bill of lading or other transportation receipt has been furnished by the carrier;

4. Render the buyer, at the buyer's request and expense, assistance in obtaining the documents issued in the country of origin, or of shipment, or of both, which the buyer may require either for purposes of exportation, or of importation at destination.

Buyer must:

1. Be responsible for all movement of the goods from inland point of loading, and pay all transportation costs;

2. Pay export taxes, or other fees or charges, if any, levied because of exportation;

3. Be responsible for any loss or damage, or both, incurred after loading at named inland point of departure;

4. Pay all costs and charges incurred in obtaining the documents issued in the country of origin, or of shipment, or of both, which may be required either for purposes of exportation, or of importation at destination.

"F.O.B. (named inland carrier at named inland point of departure) FREIGHT PREPAID TO (named point of exportation)"

Under this term, the seller quotes a price including transportation charges to the named point of exportation and prepays freight to named point of exportation, without assuming responsibility for the goods after obtaining a clean bill of lading or other transportation receipt at named inland point of departure.

Under this quotation—

Seller must:

1. Assume the seller's obligations, as under "Free on Board," except that under (2) he must provide clean bill of lading or other transportation receipt, freight prepaid to named point of exportation.

Buyer must:

1. Assume the same buyer's obligation as under "Free on Board," except that he does not pay freight from loading point to named point of exportation.

"F.O.B. (named inland carrier at named inland point of departure) FREIGHT ALLOWED TO (named point)"

Under this term, the seller quotes a price including the transportation charges to the named point, shipping freight collect and deducting the cost of transportation, without assuming responsibility for the goods after obtaining a clean bill of lading or other transportation receipt at named inland point of departure.

Under this question—

Seller must:

1. Assume the same seller's obligations as under "Free on Board," but deducts from his invoice the transportation cost to named point.

Buyer must:

1. Assume the same buyer's obligations as under "Free on Board," including payment of freight from inland loading point to named point, for which seller has made deduction.

"F.O.B. (named inland carrier at named point of exportation)"

Under this term, the seller quotes a price including the costs of transportation of the goods to named point of exportation, bearing any loss or damage, or both, incurred up to that point.

Under this quotation—

Seller must:

1. Place goods on, or in, conveyance, or deliver to inland carrier for loading;

2. Provide clean bill of lading or other transportation receipt, paying all transportation costs from loading point to named point of exportation;

3. Be responsible for any loss or d•mage, or both, until goods have arrived in, or on, inland conveyance at the named point of exportation;

4. Render the buyer, at the buyer's request and expense, assistance in obtaining the documents issued in the country of origin, or of shipment, or of both, which the buyer may require either for purposes of exportation, or of importation at destination.

Buyer must:

1. Be responsible for all movement of the goods from inland conveyance at named point of exportation;

2. Pay export taxes, or other fees or charges, if any, levied because of exportation;

3. Be responsible for any loss or damage, or both, incurred after goods have arrived in, or on, inland conveyance at the named point of exportation;

4. Pay all costs and charges incurred in obtaining the documents issued in the country of origin, or shipment, or of both, which may be required either for purposes of exportation, or of importation at destination.

"F.O.B. VESSEL (named port of shipment)"

Under this term, the seller quotes a price covering all expenses up to, and including, delivery of the goods upon the overseas vessel provided by, or for, the buyer at the named port of shipment.

Under this quotation—

Seller must:

1. Pay all charges incurred in placing goods actually on board the vessel designated and provided by, or for, the buyer on the date or within the period fixed;

2. Provide clean ship's receipt or on-board bill of lading;

3. Be responsible for any loss or damage, or both, until goods have been placed on board the vessel on the date or within the period fixed;

4. Render the buyer, at the buyer's request and expense, assistance in obtaining the documents issued in the country of origin, or of shipment, or of both, which the buyer may require either for purposes of exportation, or of importation at destination.

Buyer must:

1. Give seller adequate notice of name, sailing date, loading berth of, and delivery time to, the vessel;

2. Bear the additional costs incurred and all risks of the goods from the time when the seller has placed them at his disposal if the vessel named by him fails to arrive or to load within the designated time;

3. Handle all subsequent movement of the goods to destination:
   (a) Provide and pay for insurance;
   (b) Provide and pay for ocean and other transportation;

4. Pay export taxes, or other fees or charges, if any, levied because of exportation;

5. Be responsible for any loss or damage, or both, after goods have been loaded on board the vessel;

6. Pay all costs and charges incurred in obtaining the documents, other than clean ship's receipt or bill of lading, issued in the country of origin, or of shipment, or of both, which may be required either for purposes of exportation, or of importation at destination.

"F.O.B. (named inland point in country of importation)"

Under this term, the seller quotes a price including the cost of the merchandise and all costs of transportation to the named inland point in the country of importation.

Under this question—

Seller must:

1. Provide and pay for all transportation to the named inland point in the country of importation;

2. Pay export taxes, or other fees or charges, if any, levied because of exportation;

3. Provide and pay for marine insurance;

4. Provide and pay for war risk insurance, unless otherwise agreed upon between the seller and buyer;

5. Be responsible for any loss or damage, or both, until arrival of goods on conveyance at the named inland point in the country of importation;

6. Pay the costs of certificates of origin, consular invoices, or any other documents issued in the country of origin, or of shipment, or of both, which the buyer may require for the importation of goods into the country of destination and, where necessary, for their passage in transit through another country;

7. Pay all costs of landing, including wharfage, landing charges, and taxes, if any;

8. Pay all costs of customs entry in the country of importation;

9. Pay customs duties and all taxes applicable to imports, if any, in the country of importation.

NOTE: The seller under this quotation must realize that he is accepting important responsibilities, costs, and risks, and should therefore be certain to obtain adequate insurance. On the other hand, the importer or buyer may desire such quotations to relieve him of the risks of the voyage and to assure him of his landed costs at inland point in country of importation. When competition is keen, or the buyer is accustomed to such quotations from other sellers, seller may quote such terms, being careful to protect himself in an appropriate manner.

Buyer must:

1. Take prompt delivery of goods from conveyance upon arrival at destination;

2. Bear any costs and be responsible for all loss or damage, or both, after arrival at destination.

COMMENTS ON ALL F.O.B. TERMS

In connection with F.O.B. terms, the following points of caution are recommended:

1. The method of inland transportation, such as trucks, railroad cars, lighters, barges, or aircraft should be specified.

2. If any switching charges are involved during the inland transportation, it should be agreed, in advance, whether these charges are for account of the seller or the buyer.

3. The term "F.O.B. (named port)," without designating the exact point at which the liability of the seller terminates and the liability of the buyer begins, should be avoided. The use of this term gives rise to disputes as to the liability of the seller or the buyer in the event of loss or damage arising while the goods are in port, and before delivery to or on board the ocean carrier. Misunderstandings may be avoided by naming the specific point of delivery.

4. If lighterage or trucking is required in the transfer of goods from the inland conveyance to ship's side, and there is a cost therefor, it should be understood, in advance, whether this cost is for account of the seller or the buyer.

5. The seller should be certain to notify the buyer of the minimum quantity required to obtain a carload, a truckload, or a bargeload freight rate.

6. Under F.O.B. terms, excepting "F.O.B. (named inland point in country of importation)," the obligation to obtain ocean freight space, and marine and war risk insurance, rests with the buyer. Despite this obligation on the part of the buyer, in many trades the seller obtains the ocean freight space, and marine and war risk insurance, and provides for shipment on behalf of the buyer. Hence, seller and buyer must have an understanding as to whether the buyer will obtain the ocean freight space, and marine and war risk insurance, as is his obligation, or whether the seller agrees to do this for the buyer.

7. For the seller's protection, he should provide in his contract of sales that marine insurance obtained by the buyer include standard warehouse-to-warehouse coverage.

GENERAL STORE—A retail store which carries a variety of nonrelated items of merchandise, usually including groceries, hard goods, and soft goods, and which is not departmentized.

> *The type is most generally and most typically found in country districts. However, the term is not confined to stores serving the country and village trade but includes retail establishments in cities as well. This conforms roughly to the usage of the Bureau of the Census.*

> *Some country general stores in Western states are departmentized. It is possible that they are departmentized specialty stores instead of general stores, although the term general stores is applied to them as a matter of custom.*

GRADING—Grading is the process of sorting individual units of a product according to predetermined standards or classes.

> *This term is often defined so as to include the work of setting up classes or grades. This work is really a part of the standardization.*

GROSS PROFIT—(for purposes of marketing) Sales less Cost of Goods Sold (adjusted for inventory depreciation and merchandise shortages).

HOUSE-TO-HOUSE SALESMAN—A salesman who is primarily engaged in making sales direct to ultimate consumers in their homes.

> *The term canvasser is often employed as synonymous with house-to-house salesman. Due to its extensive use in fields other than marketing, as for instance in public-opinion polls, this usage is not recommended.*

INDEPENDENT STORE—A retail store which is controlled by its own individual ownership or management rather than from without, except insofar as its management is limited by voluntary group arrangements.

> *This definition includes a member of a voluntary group organization. It is recognized that the voluntary group possesses many of the characteristics of and presents many of the same problems as the chain-store system. In the final analysis, however, the members of the voluntary, groups are independent stores, cooperating, perhaps temporarily, in the accomplishment of certain marketing purposes. Their collective action is entirely voluntary and the retailers engaging in it consider themselves to be independent.*

INDUSTRIAL GOODS—Goods which are destined for use in producing other goods or rendering services as contrasted with goods destined to be sold to the ultimate consumer.

They include land and buildings for business purposes, equipment (installation and accessory), maintenance, repair and operating supplies, raw materials, fabricated materials.

> *The distinguishing characteristics of these goods is the purpose for which they are destined to be used, in carrying on business or industrial activities rather than for consumption by individual ultimate consumers or resale to them. The category also includes merchandise destined for use in carrying on various types of institutional enterprises.*

> *Relatively few goods are exclusively industrial goods. The same article may under one set of circumstances be an industrial goods and under other conditions, a consumers' goods.*

INDUSTRIAL STORE—See Commissary Store

INSTALLATION EQUIPMENT—See Equipment

INVENTORY—The sum of raw material, material in process, and finished merchandise. It does not include supplies.

JOBBER—This term is now widely used as a synonym of *wholesaler.*

> *Formerly the jobber was a dealer in odd lots but this usage has practically disappeared. The term is sometimes used in certain trades and localities to designate special types of wholesalers. This usage is especially common in the distribution of agricultural products. The characteristics of the wholesalers so designated vary from trade to trade and from locality to locality.*

> *Most of the schedules submitted to the Bureau of Census by the members of the wholesale trades show no clear line of demarcation between those who call themselves jobbers and those who prefer to be known as wholesalers. Therefore, it does not seem wise to attempt to set up any general basis of distinction between the terms in those few trades or markets in which one exists. There are scattered examples of special distinctive usage of the term* jobber. *The precise nature of such usage must be sought in each trade or area in which it is employed.*

LIMITED FUNCTION WHOLESALER—See Wholesaler

LIMITED PRICE VARIETY STORE—See Variety Store

MAIL-ORDER HOUSE (retail)—A retail establishment that receives its orders and makes its sales by mail.

> *Other types of retail stores often conduct a mail-order business, usually through departments set up for that purpose, although this fact does not make them mail-order houses. On the other hand, some firms that originally confined themselves to the mail-order business now also operate chain-store systems. For example, Sears, Roebuck and Company and Montgomery Ward and Company are both mail-order houses and chain-store systems.*

MAIL-ORDER WHOLESALER—See Wholesaler

MAJOR INSTALLATIONS—See Equipment

MANUFACTURER'S BRAND—See National Brand

MANUFACTURER'S STORE—A retail store owned and operated by a manufacturer.

Such stores may serve as a channel for the distribution of the manufacturer's products; in other cases they may be used for experimental or publicity purposes.

MANUFACTURERS' AGENTS—An agent who generally operates on an extended contractual basis; sells within an exclusive territory; handles noncompeting but related lines of goods; and possesses limited authority with regard to prices and terms of sale.

He may be authorized to sell a definite portion of his principal's output.

> *The manufacturers' agent has often been defined as a species of broker. In the majority of cases this seems to be substantially accurate. However, in a recent survey, out of 9,048 manufacturers' agents reporting to the Bureau of the Census, 1,423, or about 15.8 percent, carried stocks. It is probably more accurate in seeking to define the entire group, not to classify them as a specialized type of broker but to regard them as a special variety of agent.*

MARKET—1. An aggregate composed of a prospective buyer (or buyers), and a seller (or sellers), that brings to focus the conditions and forces which determine prices.

2. The aggregate demand of the potential buyers of a commodity or service.

3. The place or area in which buyers and sellers function.

4. (As a verb) To perform business activities which direct the flow of goods and services from producer to consumer or user.

In defining this term the Committee sought to include the usages of it commonly found in business, in marketing literature, and in economic theory. It is recommended that when the term is used, the context indicate clearly the sense in which it is employed.

Examples of the usage described in (2) of the definition are the New England Market, the College Market, the Professional Market, the Medical Market, as applied to any product or service.

MARKET ANALYSIS—A subdivision of marketing research which involves the measurement of the extent of a market and the determination of its characteristics.

See also Marketing Research. The activity described above consists essentially of the process of exploring and evaluating the marketing possibilities of the aggregates described in (2) of the definition of Market.

MARKETING FINANCING—That part of the general business function of providing and managing funds and credit which is directly related to the transactions involved in the flow of goods and services from producer to consumer or industrial user.

This definition includes the provision and management of funds needed to finance the carrying of stocks and the granting of mercantile and retail credit, including installment credit. It does not include the provision of funds to purchase a building in which to carry on a marketing enterprise nor does it embrace consumer borrowing on a personal basis. Roughly it embraces financial operations that are undertaken to control or modify the direction of the flow of goods and services in marketing but excludes those which are of a more general nature.

MARKET POTENTIAL—The expected sales of a commodity, a group of commodities, or a service for an entire industry in a market during a stated period.

The use of this concept should be considered in relation to that of Sales Potential.

MARKETING—The performance of business activities that direct the flow of goods and services from producer to consumer or user.

This definition seeks to exclude from marketing those semimanufacturing activities that result in changes in the form of merchandise which represent material modifications in its characteristics or uses. It seeks to include such activities when they result in changes in form primarily designed to make the product more salable and only incidentally to affect its use, such as packaging.

The task of defining Marketing may be approached from at least three points of view.

1. *The "legalistic," of which the following is a good example:*

"Marketing includes all activities having to do with effecting changes in the ownership and possession of goods and services." It seems ob-

viously of doubtful desirability to adopt a definition which throws so much emphasis upon the legal phases of what is essentially a commercial subject.

2. *The "economic," examples of which are:*

   "That part of economics which deals with the creation of time, place, and possession utilities."

   "That phase of business activity through which human wants are satisfied by the exchange of goods and services for some valuable consideration."

Such definitions are apt to assume somewhat more understanding of economic concepts than are ordinarily found in the marketplace.

3. *The "factual or descriptive" of which the definition suggested by the Committee is an example. This type of definition merely seeks to describe its subject in terms likely to be understood by both professional economists and businessmen without reference to legal or economic implications.*

MARKETING FACILITIES AGENCIES—Those agencies which perform or assist in the performance of one or a number of the marketing functions but which neither take title to goods nor negotiate purchases or sales.

Common types are banks, railroads, storage warehouses, commodity exchanges and markets, stockyards, insurance companies, graders and inspectors, advertising agencies, firms engaged in marketing research, cattle loan companies, furniture marts, and packers and shippers.

Writers on Marketing at one time classified these agencies as functional middlemen, including also in that classification all types of nontitle-taking middlemen. This mixture of incongruous elements hardly seems desirable. The groups included in the definition above are not middlemen as that term is defined by the Committee.

MARKETING FUNCTION—A major specialized activity performed in marketing.

There is no generally accepted list of marketing functions. Probably those most generally recognized are Transportation or Traffic Management, Physical Distribution, Storage, Market Financing, Risk Management, Selling, Grading, Assembling, Standardization, and Buying. Merchandising is sometimes included in the list although many students regard it as a broader business function lying between marketing and production.

Some of these activities are broad business functions having special marketing implications. Others are peculiar to the Marketing process. In the first category are Traffic Management, Physical Distribution, Market Financing, and Risk Management. In the second group are Buying, Selling, and Assembling.

Under this term students of marketing have sought to squeeze a heterogeneous and nonconsistent group of activities. For example, the functions of assembling and dividing, if such functions exist, are performed through buying, selling, and transporting. Grading, standardization, and packaging are adjuncts of selling. Such functions as assembling, storage, and transporting are broad general economic functions, while selling and buying are essentially individual in character. All these discrete groups we attempt to crowd into one class and label marketing functions.

MARKETING PLAN—A program covering all methods and procedures for marketing the product or products of a company.

MARKETING POLICY—A course of action established to secure consistency of marketing procedure under recurring and essentially similar circumstances.

MARKETING RESEARCH—The gathering, recording, and analyzing of all facts about problems relating to the transfer and sale of goods and services from producer to consumer.

Among other things it involves the study of the relationships and adjustments between production and consumption, preparation of commodities for sale, their physical distribution, wholesale and retail merchandising, and financial problems concerned. Such research may be undertaken by impartial agencies or by specific concerns or their agents for the solution of their marketing problems.

Marketing Research is the inclusive term which embraces all research activities carried on in connection with the management of marketing work. It includes various subsidiary types of research, such as Market Analysis, Sales Research, *which is largely an analysis of the sales records of a company;* Consumer Research, *which is concerned chiefly with the discovery and analysis of consumer attitudes, reactions, and preferences, and* Advertising Research, *which is carried on chiefly as an aid to the management of advertising work. The term* market research *is often loosely used as synonymous with* marketing research.

MERCHANDISING—The planning involved in marketing the right merchandise or service at the right place, at the right time, in the right quantities, and at the right price.

This term has been used in a great variety of meanings, most of them confusing. The usage recommended by the Committee has the advantage that it adheres closely to the natural and essential meaning of the word. The activity described here might also be called merchandise, or product, planning. Included in the activity are such tasks as selecting the article to be produced or stocked and deciding such details as the size, appearance, form, dressing of the product (packaging, etc.), quantities to be bought or made, time of purchase or production, price lines to be made or carried, etc.

MERCHANDISING CONTROL—The collection and analysis of statistical data of sales, stocks, and pricing practices as a guide to the profitable purchase and sale of merchandise.

MERCHANT MIDDLEMAN—A middleman who takes title to the goods he stocks and sells. Such middlemen usually perform most or all of the distributive functions.

The distinctive feature of this middleman lies in the fact that he takes title to the goods he handles. The extent to which he performs the marketing functions is incidental to the definition. Wholesalers and retailers are the chief types of merchant middlemen.

MERCHANT's BRAND—See Private Brand

MIDDLEMAN—A business concern that specializes in performing functions or rendering services immediately involved in the purchase and/or sale of goods in the process of their flow from producer to consumer.

Middlemen are of two types; Merchants, or Merchant Middlemen, and Agents, or Agent Middlemen.

> *The essence of the middleman's operation is that he plays an active and prominent part in the negotiations leading up to transactions of purchase and sale. This is what distinguishes him from a Marketing Facilitating Agent who, while he performs certain marketing functions, participates only incidentally in negotiations of purchase and sale.*

> *This term is very general in its meaning. The Committee recommends that whenever possible more specific terms be used, such as agent, merchant, retailer, wholesaler.*

MISSIONARY SALESMAN—A salesman employed by a manufacturer to make contact with and work with the customers of his distributors, usually for the purpose of developing goodwill and stimulating demand, helping or inducing them to promote the sale of his employer's goods, helping them train their salesmen to do so, and often taking orders for delivery by such distributors.

> *This term has been used to designate any sort of salesman who is primarily engaged in goodwill work. The definition above gives it a much narrower meaning. The term should not be confused with the so-called "missionary" sales work which usually covers a much more varied type of sales activity than that done by the missionary salesman. Missionary salesmen are sometimes called "detailers." Medical drug salesmen calling on physicians and hospitals are called "detail men."*

NATIONAL BRAND—A manufacturer's or producer's brand, usually enjoying wide territorial distribution.

> *The usage of the terms "National Brand" and "Private Brand" embodied in this report, while generally current and commonly accepted, is highly illogical and nondescriptive. It is recommended that whenever possible more specific and descriptive terms be used, such as Manufacturer's Brand or Producer's Brand.*

NET INCOME—Final income available for proprietary accounts (either before or after deduction of federal and state income taxes as specifically indicated). It includes operating profit together with net other income.

> *Net Profit is recommended as the preferred term among the three.*

NET PROFITS—Profit after full depreciation on buildings, machinery, equipment, furniture, and other assets of a fixed nature; after reserves for federal income and excess profit taxes; after reduction in the value of inventory to cost or market, whichever is lower; after charge-offs for bad debts; after miscellaneous reserves and adjustments; but before dividends or withdrawals.

NET SALES—The dollar volume of business transacted for 365 days net after deductions for returns, allowances, and discounts from gross sales.

Section B — GLOSSARY OF MARKETING TERMS

NET SALES TO INVENTORY—The quotient obtained by dividing the annual net sales by the statement inventory. This quotient does not represent the actual physical turnover, which would be determined by reducing the annual net sales to the cost of goods sold, and then dividing the resulting figure by the statement inventory.

NET WORKING CAPITAL—The excess of the current assets over the current debt.

OPERATING PROFIT—(For purposes of marketing) Gross margin (gross profit), less operating expenses (including salaries of managers, whether proprietors or employees), fixed plant and equipment cost, and sometimes interest on invested capital.

> *Obviously this definition includes only the profit accruing from the trading operations of a mercantile business.*

ORGANIZED MARKET—A group of traders operating under recognized rules for the purpose of buying and selling a single commodity or a small number of related commodities.

> *Examples are the Chicago Board of Trade, the New York Cotton Exchange, and the New York Produce Exchange.*

PARENT STORE—A retail store that owns and operates a *Branch Store* or a group of *Branch Stores*.

PERSONAL SELLING—Oral presentation in a conversation with one or more prospective customers for the purpose of making sales.

> *This definition contemplates that the presentation may be either formal (as a "canned" sales talk), or informal, although it is rather likely to be informal, either in the actual presence of the customer or by telephone although usually the former, either to an individual or to a small group, although usually the former.*

PHYSICAL DISTRIBUTION—The movement and handling of goods from the point of production to the point of consumption or use.

> *The word Distribution is sometimes used to describe this activity. In view of the technical meaning of the word Distribution in economic theory and of the fact that it is used by the Bureau of the Census and increasingly by marketing students and businessmen as synonymous with Marketing, the Committee recommends that its use as a synonym of or substitute for Physical Distribution be discouraged.*

PRICE CUTTING—Offering merchandise or a service for sale at a price below that recognized as usual or standard by the buyers and sellers in a market.

> *One obvious criticism of this definition is that it is indefinite. But that very indefiniteness also causes it to be more accurately descriptive of a concept which is characterized by a high degree of indefiniteness in the mind of the average person affected by price cutting.*
>
> *Traders' ideas of what constitutes price cutting are so vague and indefinite that any precise or highly specific definition of that phenomenon is bound to fail to include all its manifestations. If you ask a group of traders in a specific commodity to define price cutting, you will get as many conflicting formulas as there are traders. But if you ask*

those same traders at any particular time whether selling at a certain price constitutes price cutting, you will probably get a considerable degree of unanimity of opinion. It is precisely this condition which the definition is designed to reflect.

PRIVATE BRANDS—Brands sponsored by merchants or agents as distinguished from those sponsored by manufacturers or producers. In the food industry, sometimes called *"Private Label."*

This usage is thoroughly illogical, since no seller wants his brand to be private in the sense of being secret and all brands are private in the sense that they are special and not common or general in use. But the usage is common in marketing literature and among traders. Therefore the Committee presents it in this report.

It is recommended that, whenever possible, more specific terms, such as Wholesaler's Brand, Retailer's Brand, Dealer's Brand, or Merchant's Brand *be used.*

PRODUCER'S BRAND—See National Brand

PRODUCER'S COOPERATIVE MARKETING—That type of cooperative marketing which primarily involves the sale of goods or services of the associated producing membership.

Many producers' cooperative marketing associations both buy and sell for their members. This fact does not subtract from their status as producers' cooperatives; this is especially true of the farm cooperatives. The term does not include those activities of trade associations that affect only indirectly the sales of the membership. Such activities are the maintenance of credit rating bureaus, design registration bureaus, and brand protection machinery. It does include, however, such things as cooperative advertising.

PUBLICITY—Any form of commercially significant news about a product, an institution, a service, or a person published in space, television or radio time that is not paid for by the sponsor.

In the retail trade this term is often used to include such activities as advertising and display work.

The term Free Publicity is often used as a synonym or substitute for Publicity. The Committee does not recommend this usage because it is a misnomer. It is doubtful if any publicity is ever entirely free.

PURCHASING POWER—The capacity to purchase possessed by an individual buyer, a group of buyers, or the aggregate of the buyers in an area or a market.

RAW MATERIALS—Those industrial goods which in part or in whole become a portion of the physical product but which have undergone no more processing than is required for convenience, protection, or economy in storage, transportation, or handling.

RETAILER—A merchant or business establishment that sells mainly to the ultimate consumer.

The retailer is to be distinguished by the conditions surrounding the sale rather than the procurement of the goods in which he deals. At-

tempts to define the retailer on the basis of the size of the units in which he sells prove indefensible. The size of his sales unit is an incidental rather than a primary element in his character. His essential distinguishing mark is the fact that his typical sale is made to the ultimate consumer.

RETAILER COOPERATIVE—A group of independent retailers organized to buy cooperatively either through a jointly owned warehouse or through a buying club. Their cooperative activities usually include operating under a group name, joint advertising, and cooperative managerial supervision.

RETAILER'S BRAND—See Private Brand

RETAILING—The activities incident to selling to the ultimate consumer. The goods sold may be produced, bought, or carried in stock by the seller.

This definition includes all forms of selling to the ultimate consumer. It embraces the direct-to-consumer sales activities of the producer whether through his own stores, by house-to-house canvass, or by mail order. It does not cover the sale by producers of industrial goods, by industrial supply houses, or by retailers to industrial, commercial, or institutional buyers for use in the conduct of their enterprises.

RISK MANAGEMENT—The function of reducing, spreading, or avoiding the loss of pecuniary value of goods and services during their marketing.

Such losses may occur through physical deterioration, obsolescence, theft, damage, waste, changes in supply or demand, or through changes in the price level.

Some criticism may attach to the designation of this function as Risk Management since it often happens that not much can be done in the way of managing risks. They come as they will regardless of attempts to manage them.

The term has many advantages, however, over risk bearing which is often applied to this type of activity. Not all risks arising in distribution are borne by those engaged in it. Many of them are avoided and many others are changed in character or intensity as a result of good management on the part of marketing concerns. Losses are of two types, those that are insurable, such as fire and accident, and those that are not insurable, such as the losses from changes in price.

SALES BUDGET—An estimate of the probable dollar sales and probable selling costs of a specified period.

The use of this term is sometimes confined to an estimate of future sales. This does not conform to the general use of the term budget, which includes schedules of both receipts and expenditures. If the sales budget is to be used as a device to facilitate sales control and management, it should include the probable cost of getting the estimated volume of sales. The failure to allow proper weight to this item in their calculations is one of the most consistently persistent and fatal mistakes made by American business concerns. It has led to much of the striving after unprofitable volume that has been so costly.

SALES CONTROL—A system of supervision involving the use of such devices as records, statistical analyses, correspondence, and personal contact for the purpose of carrying out or adjusting marketing policies and plans.

The application of this term is often confined to the operation of a system of records and forms from which a picture of sales operations may be obtained. The recommended usage goes much farther and includes the practical use that may be made of such a picture once it is obtained.

SALES FORECAST—An estimate of dollar or unit sales for a specified future period under a proposed marketing plan or program.

The forecast may be for a specified item of merchandise or for an entire line; it may be for a market as a whole or for any portion thereof.

Two sets of factors are involved in making a sales forecast:

1. Those forces outside the control of the firm for which the forecast is made that are likely to influence its sales, and

2. Changes in the marketing methods or practices of the firm that are likely to affect its sales.

In the course of planning future activities the management of a given firm may make several sales forecasts, each consisting of an estimate of probable sales if a given marketing plan is adopted or a given set of outside forces prevails. The estimated effects on sales of a number of marketing plans may be compared in the process of arriving at that marketing program which will, in the opinion of the officials of the company, be best designed to promote its welfare.

SALES MANAGEMENT—The planning, direction, and control of personal selling, including recruiting, selecting, training, equipping, assigning, routing, supervising, paying, and motivating as these tasks apply to the personal sales force.

SALES MANAGER—The executive who plans, directs, and controls the activities of salesmen.

This executive may and often does perform broader functions in the marketing work of his company, but the essential nature of his position lies in his relation to the personal selling work of the firm.

SALES PLANNING—The work of setting up objectives for marketing activity and of determining and scheduling the steps necessary to achieve such objectives.

This term includes not only the work of deciding upon the goals or results to be attained through marketing activity, but also the determination in detail of exactly how they are to be accomplished. The result of this work is a Sales Plan.

SALES POTENTIAL—The share of a market potential which a company expects to achieve.

The portion of the total expected sales of an industry which the managers of a firm expect that firm to get is the Sales Potential for that firm. By means of marketing research a firm may establish a market potential for the industry of which it is a part. Through the use of one or more sales forecasts its managers may determine upon a sales potential for the firm. From this may be derived the sales budget and a sales quota for the entire company or any part of it.

SALES PROMOTION—1. In a specific sense, those sales activities that supplement both personal selling and advertising and coordinate them and help to make them effective, such as displays, shows and expositions, demonstrations, and other nonrecurrent selling efforts not in the ordinary routine.

2. In a general sense, sales promotion includes personal selling, advertising, and supplementary selling activities.

This definition includes the two most logical and commonly accepted among the many confusing and conflicting usages of this term. It is the consensus of the committee that insofar as possible the use of the term should be confined to the first of the two definitions given above.

SALES QUOTA—A sales goal assigned to a marketing unit for use in the management of sales efforts.

It applies to a specified period and may be expressed in dollars or in physical units.

The quota may be used in checking the efficiency, stimulating the efforts, or in fixing the payment of individual salesmen or groups of salesmen or other personnel engaged in sales work.

A quota may be for a salesman, a territory, a branch house, or for the company as a whole. It may be different from the sales figure set up in the sales budget. Since it is a managerial device, it is not an immutable figure inexorably arrived at by the application of absolutely exact statistical formulas but may be set up with an eye to its psychological effects upon the sales personnel or any part of it. Two salesmen, working in territories of identical potentials, may be assigned different quotas in accordance with the anticipated effects of this variation on their sales efforts because of differences in their characters or personalities.

SALES RESEARCH—See Marketing Research

SELECTIVE SELLING—The policy of selling only to dealers and distributors who meet the seller's requirements, such as size of orders, volume of purchases, profitability, or area or type of operations.

While accounts are selected on a variety of bases, probably the most common are size and the kind and amount of reselling service the account is willing and able to give to the goods or services of the seller. Possibly the soundest basis is that of the amount of potential net profit to be derived from the business placed by the account.

SELLING—The personal or impersonal process of assisting and/or persuading a prospective customer to buy a commodity or a service or to act favorably upon an idea that has commercial significance to the seller.

This definition includes advertising and other forms of publicity and sales promotion as well as personal selling.

SELLING AGENT—An agent who operates on an extended contractual basis; sells all of a specified line of merchandise or the entire output of his principal, and usually has full authority with regard to prices, terms, and other conditions of sale. He occasionally renders financial aid to his principal.

SERVICE WHOLESALER—See Wholesaler

SERVICES—Activities or anticipated satisfactions which are offered for sale either as such or in connection with the sale of goods.

Examples are amusements, hotel service, electric service, transportation, the services of barber shops and beauty shops, repair and maintenance service, the work of credit rating bureaus. This list is merely illustrative and no attempt has been made to make it complete. The term also applies to the various activities, such as credit extension, advice and help of salespeople, delivery, by which the seller serves the convenience of his customers.

SHOPPING GOODS—Those consumers' goods which the customer in the process of selection and purchase characteristically compares on such bases as suitability, quality, price, and style.

Examples of goods that most consumers probably buy as *shopping goods* are: Millinery, furniture, dress goods, men's and women's ready-to-wear, shoes, jewelry, and residential real estate (not bought for purposes of speculation).

> *It should be emphasized that the same articles may be bought by one customer as* shopping goods *and by another as* specialty *or* convenience goods. *The general classification depends upon the way in which the average or typical buyer purchases. See Comment under* Specialty Goods.

SIMPLIFICATION—The process of reducing the varieties of goods within a line offered for sale.

> *It involves reducing the number of articles, parts, materials, models, styles, grades, colors, sizes, price lines, brands, designs, etc.*

SPECIALTY GOODS—Those consumers' goods on which a significant group of buyers characteristically insist and for which they are willing to make a special purchasing effort.

Examples of articles that are usually bought as specialty goods are: Specific brands of fancy groceries, watches, men's shoes, and possibly automobiles.

> *There seems to be room for considerable doubt as to whether the distinction between Shopping Goods and Specialty Goods is any longer valid or useful. There is less doubt of the validity of the class Shopping Goods than of Specialty Goods. The term is included here because many students of marketing appear still to find it useful and to desire its retention.*

SPECIALTY SALESMAN—A salesman, other than retail, who specializes in the sale of one product or a few products of a seller's line.

> *A specialty salesman should be contrasted with a General Salesman who handles an entire line. He does not necessarily sell specialty goods.*

SPECIALTY SHOP—See Specialty Store

SPECIALTY STORE—A retail store that makes its appeal on the basis of a restricted class of shopping goods.

Large specialty stores, if organized into departments, are called *Departmentized Specialty Stores*. Small specialty stores in certain trades are sometimes called *Specialty Shops*.

This term should not be used to include stores handling one or a few lines of convenience goods, such as staple groceries, hardware, stationery, or tobacco.

STANDARDIZATION—The determination of basic limits or grades in the form of specifications to which manufactured goods must conform and classes into which the products of agriculture and the extractive industries may be sorted.

This term does not include Grading, *which is the process of sorting units of a product into the grades or classes that have been established through the process of* Standardization.

STORAGE—The marketing function that involves holding goods between the time of their production and their final sale.

Some processing is often done while goods are in storage. It is probable that this should be regarded as a part of production rather than of marketing.

STORE UNIT—A single retail establishment of a chain store system or other group, such as voluntary, cooperative, or ownership group.

SUPPLIES—Those industrial goods which do not become a part of the physical product or which are continually exhausted in facilitating the operation of an enterprise. Examples are fuel, lubricants, stationery, typewriter ribbons, cleaning materials, etc.

TANGIBLE NET WORTH—The sum of all outstanding preferred or preference stocks (if any) and outstanding common stocks, surplus, and undivided profits, less any intangible items in the assets, such as goodwill, trademarks, patents, copyrights, leaseholds, mailing lists, treasury stock, organization expenses, and underwriting discounts and expenses.

TRADEMARK—A brand that is given legal protection because it is capable of exclusive appropriation; because it is used in a manner sufficiently fanciful, distinctive, and arbitrary, because it is affixed to the product when sold, or because it otherwise satisfies the requirements set up by law.

Trademark is essentially a legal term and includes only those brands or parts of brands which the law designates as trademarks. In any specific case a trademark is what the court in that case decides to regard as a trademark.

TRADE NAME—1. The name by which an article or a certain type or grade of an article is known among buyers and sellers.

2. The name under which a business is conducted.

Credit acknowledged to Webster's International.

TRADING AREA—A district whose boundaries are usually determined by the economical buying or selling range for a commodity or group of related commodities from a center of distribution.

Trading areas are not static but are in a constant state of flux. A wholesale trading area may be distinguished chiefly by the economical selling and delivery range of the firms in it; a retail trading area is usually distinguished by the area from which the center draws the buying trade of consumers in significant amounts.

TRAFFIC MANAGEMENT—The planning, selection, and direction of all means of transportation involved in the movement of goods in the marketing process.

This definition is confined to those activities in connection with transportation that have to do particularly with marketing and form an inseparable part of any well-organized system of distribution. It includes the movement of goods in trucks owned by the marketing concern as well as by public carrier. It does not include the movement of goods within the warehouse of a producer or distributor or within the store of a retail concern.

TRUCK WHOLESALER—See Wholesaler

TURNOVER OF TANGIBLE NET WORTH—The quotient obtained by dividing annual net sales by the tangible net worth.

TURNOVER OF NET WORKING CAPITAL—The quotient obtained by dividing annual net sales by the net working capital.

ULTIMATE CONSUMER—One who buys and/or uses goods or services to satisfy personal or household wants rather than for resale or use in business, institutional, or industrial operations.

There seems to be a growing tendency to drop the word "ultimate" from this term. The Committee recommends that this tendency be encouraged.

The definition distinguishes sharply between industrial users and ultimate consumers. A firm buying and using an adding machine, a drum of lubricating oil, or a carload of steel billets is an industrial user of those products, not an Ultimate Consumer of them; under the developing usage it is not even a "consumer" of them. A vital difference exists between the purposes motivating the two types of purchases which in turn results in highly significant differences in buying methods, marketing organization, and selling practices.

VARIETY STORE—A retail store that handles a wide assortment of goods usually of a low or limited price.

Examples are the almost extinct five-and-ten-cent store and the up-to-a-dollar store.

This is often called a "Limited Price Variety Store." The validity of these terms and of the limited price feature of the definition is being dissipated by the tendency of these establishments to handle merchandise within a broader price range.

VOLUNTARY GROUP—A group of retailers each of whom owns and operates his own store and is associated with a wholesaler to carry on joint merchandising activities and who are characterized by some degree of group identity and uniformity of operation. Such joint activities have been largely of two kinds—cooperative advertising and group control of store operation.

WHOLESALER—A merchant middleman who sells to retailers and other merchants and/or to industrial, institutional, and commercial users but who does not sell in significant amounts to ultimate consumers.

In the basic materials, semifinished goods, and tool and machinery trades, merchants of this type are commonly known as "dealers," "distributors," or "supply houses."

Generally these merchants render a wide variety of services to their customers. Those who render all the services normally expected in the wholesale trade are known as "Service Wholesalers"; those who render only a few of the wholesale services are known as "Limited Function Wholesalers." The latter group is composed mainly of "Cash and Carry Wholesalers" who do not render the credit or delivery service, "Drop Shipment Wholesalers" who sell for delivery by the producer direct to the buyer, "Truck Wholesalers" who combine selling, delivery, and collection in one operation, and "Mail-Order Wholesalers" who perform the selling service entirely by mail.

This definition ignores or minimizes two bases upon which the term is often defined; first, the size of the lots in which wholesalers deal, and second, the fact that they habitually sell for resale. The figures show that many wholesalers operate on a very small scale and in small lots. Most of them make a significant portion of their sales to industrial users.

WHOLESALER'S BRAND—See Private Brand

COURT DECISIONS ON DIRECT SELLING

The following* was prepared by legal counsel of the National Association of Direct Selling Companies, Winona, Minn., and includes recent leading cases bearing on the rights and liabilities of companies, their employees and state, county, and town officials:

What Constitutes Interstate Commerce

The taking of orders for the future delivery of merchandise which is at the time located in another state constitutes interstate commerce, and persons so engaged are not subject to the payment of licenses imposed by state law or ordinance. Nippert vs. Richmond, 327 U.S. 416, 66 S. Ct. 586. Real Silk Hosiery Mills vs. Portland, 268 U.S. 325, 45 S. Ct. 525. Best and Co. vs. Maxwell, 311 U.S. 454, 61 S. Ct. 334. Robbins vs. Taxing District, 120 U.S. 489 7 S. Ct. 592. Crenshaw vs. Arkansas, 227 U.S. 389. Rearick vs. Pa., 203 U.S. 507. Best and Co. vs. Omaha, 149 Neb. 868, 33 N. W. (2d) 161, cert. den. 336 U.S. 935. Joseph vs. Carter & Weekes Stevedoring Co., 330 U.S. 422, 67 S. Ct. 815. Railway Express Agency vs. Commonwealth of Virginia, 347 U.S. 359, 74 S. Ct. 558. West Point Wholesale Grocery Co. vs. Opelika, Ala., 354 U.S. 390, 77 S. Ct. 1096. Northwestern States Portland Cement Co. vs. State, 79 S. Ct. 357, 362, 358 U.S. 450. Memphis Steam Laundry Cleaner, Inc. vs. Stone, 342 U.S. 389, 72 S. Ct. 424. Hathaway vs. Texas, 83 S. Ct. 1533.

Taking Deposit Is Proper

The foregoing is true even though the salesperson takes a partial payment in advance of delivery. Nippert vs. Richmond, 327 U.S. 416, 66 S. Ct. 586. Real Silk Hosiery Mills vs. Portland, 268 U.S. 325. Best and Co. vs. Maxwell, 311 U.S. 454, 61 S. Ct. 334. Robbins vs. Taxing District, 120 U.S. 489. West Point Wholesale Grocery Co. vs. Opelika, 354 U.S. 390, 77 S. Ct. 1096. Memphis Steam Laundry Cleaners, Inc. vs. Stone, 342 U.S. 389, 72 S. Ct. 424. Pictorial Review vs. Alexandria, La., 46 Fed. (2d) 337, McCarter vs. Florence, 104 S. 806 (Ala.) In re Dean L. White, No. 8781, Law, U.S. District Ct., District of Utah. Myers vs. Miami, 131 So. 375 (Fla.).

Bond Not Required

Nor may a bond be required in such cases where an advance deposit is taken. Real Silk Hosiery Mills vs. City of Portland, 268 U.S. 325. In re Dean L. White, No. 8781, Law, U.S. Dist. Ct., Dist. of Utah. McCarter vs. City of Florence, 104 So. 806 (Ala.). Myers vs. City of Miami, 131 So. 375 (Fla.). Pictorial Review Co. vs. Alexandria, La., 46 Fed. (2d) 337. Best & Co., Inc. vs. Omaha, 33 N. W. (2d) 161 (Neb.); cert. denied 336 U.S. 935.

---

*While these data are up to date as of the time of going to press, they are offered as information only and not as legal advice.

Section C — LEGAL DATA AND CONTRACT FORMS

Bulk Shipments

Statement contained in first paragraph hereof is also true where the merchandise ordered is sent to the salesperson or to some other representative in bulk, to be broken up and delivered to purchasers according to their individual orders. Caldwell vs. N. C., 187 U.S. 622. Rearick vs. Pa., 203 U.S. 507. Crenshaw vs. Arkansas, 227 U.S. 389. Rogers vs. Arkansas, 227 U.S. 401. Stewart vs. Michigan, 232 U.S. 665. 12 Corpus Juris, Pages 106-107. Jewel Tea Co. vs. Lees Summit, 189 Fed. 280. In re Tyerman, 48 Fed. 167. In re Spain, 47 Fed. 208. In re Nichols, 48 Fed. 164.

A salesperson or dealer may take a number of orders for future delivery, and after such orders are taken may purchase for shipment from another state the exact merchandise ordered, have it shipped to him in bulk, break open the bulk shipment, and fill individual orders, without his being liable for the payment of any local license, fees, or other charges. (Same cases, except the last two.)

Physical Examinations Invalid

State laws or municipal ordinances which seek to interfere, burden, or regulate interstate sales, by requirement of permits, physical examinations, health certificates, elaborate reference and personal information, or other conditions or restrictions, even though a tax or license is not charged, are invalid and unenforceable. Real Silk Hosiery Mills vs. City of Piedmont, 274 U.S. 723. Jewel Tea Co. vs. City of Norman, Equity Case No. 219, U.S. District Ct., Western District, Oklahoma, decided 10-23-17. Jewel Tea Co. vs. Mapleton, Equity Case No. 294, U.S. District Ct., Northern District Iowa Western Division, decided 6-27-31. Shaffer vs. Grain Company, 268 U.S. 189. Buck Stove Company vs. Vicars, 226 U.S. 295. Textbook Company vs. Pigg, 217 U.S. 91. Lemke vs. Grain Company, 258 U.S. 50. Also Ex Parte Edwards, 37 Fed. Supp. 673 (Fla.). Pictorial Review Co. vs. Alexandria, La., 46 Fed. (2d) 337. Nippert vs. Richmond, 327 U.S. 416, 427 66 S. Ct. 586. McCarter vs. Florence, 104 So. 806 (Ala.). Best & Co., Inc., vs. Omaha, 33 N. W. (2d) 161 (Neb.); cert. denied 336 U.S. 935.

Residence of Salesperson Immaterial

The United States Supreme Court has repeatedly held that the taking of orders for the future delivery of merchandise which is at the time located in another state, constitutes interstate commerce. The residence of the salesperson makes no difference whatever, nor does the method of delivery of the merchandise have any bearing on the question. It may be delivered in person by the man who took the order, or by some other representative or person, or by mail, freight, or express. Brennan vs. Titusville, 153 U.S. 289. Caldwell vs. North Carolina, 187 U.S. 622. Stewart vs. Mich., 232 U.S. 655. Crenshaw vs. Ark., 227 U.S. 389.

Police Power Not to Restrict Interstate Commerce

A state or municipality cannot, under the guise of police power, impose licenses, burdens, or other requirements as a condition precedent to engaging in or entering into interstate commerce. See the first paragraph listing court decisions, above. Also: Brennan vs. Titusville, 153 U.S. 289, 300. Shaffer vs. Grain Co., 268 U.S. 189. Lemke vs. Grain Co., 358 U.S. 50. Buck Stove vs. Vicars, 226 U.S. 295. Crutcher vs. Kentucky, 141 U.S. 47. Textbook Co. vs. Pigg, 217 U.S. 91. Real Silk Hosiery Mills vs. Portland, 268 U.S. 325.

When Interstate Commerce Ends

Once the character as interstate commerce attaches to a movement of goods such character continues until the goods reach the point where the parties originally intended that they should arrive. Caldwell vs. N. C., 187 U.S. 622. Illinois Central R. R. Co. vs. Louisiana R. R. Comm., 236 U.S. 157. Western Union Tel. Co. vs. Foster, 247 U.S. 105. Western Oil Refining Co. vs. Lipscomb, 244 U.S. 346. Jewel Tea Co. vs. Camden, 172 S. E. 307 (S. C.).

Additional Interstate Commerce Decisions

Nicholson vs. Forrest City, 228 S. W. (2d) 53 (Ark.). Olan Mills vs. Tallahassee, 43 So. (2d) 521 (Fla.). Wilk vs. Bartow, 86 Fla. 186. Graves vs. Gainesville, 51 S. E. (2d) 58 (Ga.). Winchester vs. Lohrey Pkg. Co., 237 S. W. (2d) 868 (Ky.). Cordell vs. Commonwealth, 254 S. W. (2d) 484 (Ky.). State vs. Best & Co., 195 So. 356 (La.). Waseca vs. Braun, 206 Minn. 154, 288 N. W. 229. Craig vs. Mills, 33 So. (2d) 810 (Miss.). W. K. Vantine Studio vs. Portsmouth, 59 A. (2d) 475 (N. H.). Dimmig vs. Mann, 200 A. 545 (N. J.). Bossert vs. Okmulgee, 260 P. (2d) (Okla.). Leibold vs. Brown, 71 So. (2d) (Ala.). Gadsden vs. Roadway Express, 73 So. (2d) 765 (Ala.). Myers vs. Miami, 131 So. 375 (Fla.). Olan Mills vs. Tallahassee, 43 So. (2d) 521 (Fla.). Olan Mills, Inc. vs. Maysville, 272 S. W. (2d) 460 (Ky.). Olan Mills, Inc., vs. Cape Girardeau, 272 S. W. (2d) (Mo.). Best & Co., Inc., vs. Omaha, 33 N. W. (2d) 161 (Neb.) ; cert. denied 336 U.S. 935. Commonwealth vs. Olan Mills, Inc., 86 S. E. (2d) (Va.).

Customary Method Governs

Salespersons who customarily take orders for the future delivery of merchandise at the time located in another state and who occasionally sell or dispose of a sample or rejected merchandise are still within the scope and protection of interstate commerce and may not be required to take out a license. Commonwealth vs. Farnum, 114 Mass. 267. Kansas vs. Collins, 342 U.S. 344. In re Houston, 47 Fed. 539. Powell vs. Roundtree, 247 S. W. 389 (Ark.). Smith vs. Dickinson, 142 Pac. 1133 (Wash.) Penn. Collier Company vs. McKeever, 87 N. Y. S. 869. Frank vs. State, 42 Tex. Crim. 222, 58 S. W. 1015.

Customer's Refusal of C.O.D.

Where a customer rejects a C.O.D. shipment, his action constitutes a breach of contract, and he is not entitled to recover from the salesman or the company the deposit which he paid. In fact, the company could properly sue him for damages for such breach. Bullard vs. Eames, 106 N. E. 584 (Mass.). Carle vs. Nelson, 130 N. W. 467 (Wis.).

Branch Offices No Bar

A direct selling company or district agent may maintain a branch office in a state other than that where the home office is located, for the purpose of facilitating interstate business, without being compelled to pay a license. Crutcher vs. Ky., 141 U.S. 47. Cheney Bros. vs. Mass., 246 U.S. 146. Railroad Company vs. Pa., 136 U.S. 114. Textbook Company vs Pigg, 217 U.S. 101. Myers vs. City of Miami, 131 So. 375 (Fla.).

Section C — LEGAL DATA AND CONTRACT FORMS

Order Takers Not Peddlers

Even when a person taking orders for the future delivery of merchandise is not engaged in interstate commerce he cannot be required to pay a peddler's license which does not specifically include ordertaking or sales by sample. Crenshaw vs. Arkansas, 227 U.S. 389. State vs. Bristow, 131 Ia. 664. St. Paul vs. Briggs, 85 Minn. 290. DeWitt vs. State, 155 Wis. 249. 40 Am. Jur. p. 916.

Excessive License Fees Invalid

Even when a salesperson is not engaged in interstate commerce he can not be made to pay a license fee which is so excessive as to constitute an indirect prohibition of the business. Such an ordinance is void as being confiscatory, as prohibiting a lawful occupation, and as constituting an illegal discrimination. Real Silk Hosiery Mills vs. Bellingham, 1 Fed. (2d) 934. State vs. Wilson, 249 Ill. 195, 94 N. W. 141. 40 Am. Jur. p. 948.

Peddler Ordinances Do Not Apply

Power granted to a city to license and regulate peddling does not give it power or authority to license or regulate order takers. Village of Cerro Gordo vs. Rawlings, 135 Ill. 36. Ideal Tea Company vs. Salem, 150 Pac. 852 (Ore.). Emmons vs. City of Lewistown, 132 Ill. 380. Village of South Holland vs. Stein, 26 N. E. (2d) 868 (Ill.).

Prohibition of Lawful Business Is Illegal

The power to license or regulate does not carry with it the power to prohibit. A city council cannot, under any powers, pass an ordinance absolutely prohibiting a lawful business. Adams vs. Tanner, 244 U.S. 590. Ralph vs. City of Wenatchee, 209 Pac. (2d) 270 (Wash.).

Green River Ordinance Invalid

The so-called Green River or nuisance type ordinances are invalid in these states: Wilkins vs. City of Harrison, 236 S. W. (2d) 82 (Ark.). Prior vs. White, 180 So. 347 (Fla.), 116 A. L. R. 1176. DeBarry vs. City of LaGrange, 8 S. E. (2d) 146. C. B. Garrison vs. City of Cartersville, 8 S. E. (2d) 154 (Ga.). City of Osceola vs. Blair, 2 N. W. (2d) 83 (Ia.). City of Derby vs. Betty Hiegert, 325 Pac. (2d) 35 (Kans.). City of Mt. Sterling et al. vs. Donaldson Baking Co., 155 S. W. (2d) 237 (Ky.). Jewel Tea Co. vs. Town of Bel Air, 192 A. 417 (Md.). Excelsior Baking Co. vs. City of Northfield, 77 N. W. (2d) 188 (Minn.). Jewel Tea Co. vs. City of Geneva, 291 N. W. 664 (Nebr.). McAlester vs. Grand Union Tea Co., 98 Pac. (2d) 924 (Okla.). Orangeburg vs. O. R. Farmer, 186 S.E. 783 (S. C.). Ex parte Faulkner, 158 S. W. (2d) 525 (Tex.). White vs. Culpeper, 1 S. E. (2d) (Va.).

Officials Liable for Damages

A police official or other person actively participating in causing or making an arrest under a void ordinance can be personally held for general and specific damages. Scott vs. McDonald, 165 U.S. 58 (89). U.S. Code, Title 42, Section 1983.

REGISTRATION OF TRADEMARKS UNDER LANHAM ACT

Service marks may be registered. A service mark is one used in the sale or advertising of services and includes marks, names, symbols, titles, designations, slogans, character names, and distinctive features of television, radio or other advertising used in commerce.

Collective marks may be registered by persons exercising legitimate control over their use. A collective mark is a trademark or service mark used by the members of a cooperative, association, or other collective group or organization.

Certification marks may be registered by persons exercising legitimate control over their use, but who do not themselves engage in the production or marketing of any goods or services to which the mark is applied. A certification mark is one used upon or in connection with the products or services of one or more persons, other than the owner of the mark, to certify regional or other origin, material, mode of manufacture, quality, accuracy or other characteristic of such goods or services, or that the work or labor on the goods or services was performed by members of a union or other organization.

Related companies may use a registered mark, such use inuring to the benefit of the registrant, provided the public is not deceived. A "related company" is one legitimately controlling or controlled by the registrant in respect to the nature or quality of the goods or services in connection with which the mark is used.

Concurrent registration of the same mark to more than one registrant is authorized in cases of concurrent lawful use prior to any filing date; conditions and limitations as to mode, place, or goods are to be prescribed by the Commissioner of Patents.

Registered marks are automatically canceled after six years, unless within the sixth year the registrant files an affidavit showing that the mark is still in use, or excusing nonuse. Abandonment may be presumed after two consecutive years of nonuse.

Assignment of a registered mark, or of a mark for which application to register has been filed, may be made with that part of the goodwill of the business connected with the use of the mark. Assignments should be recorded in the Patent Office.

The requirement for use of the notice "Registered in U.S. Patent Office" or "Reg. U.S. Pat. Off." still stands; but as an alternative it is now optional to display the letter "R" within a circle. No such notice should appear on a mark, however, until it has, in fact, been registered in the Patent Office.

Any mark distinctive of the owner's goods in commerce may be registered, if not immoral, deceptive, scandalous, confusingly similar to a mark in use, etc., and this is true even though the mark is descriptive or geographical or a surname.

Registration is constructive notice of the registrant's claim of ownership of the mark. The purpose of this provision in the law is to make a registrant's rights coterminous with the territory of the United States; thus it becomes impossible for a later comer to acquire, in good faith, adverse rights in a mark in a section of the country (embracing parts of at least two states) where the registrant has not actually used his mark.

Registered marks may become incontestable after any five-year period subsequent to registration on the filing, within the sixth year, of an affidavit setting forth that the mark has been in continuous use for such five years, that there has been no final decision adverse to registrant's claim of ownership, and that no proceeding involving his rights is pending. But "no incontestable right shall be acquired in a mark or trade name which is the common descriptive name of any article or substance, patented or otherwise." An incontestable registration is conclusive evidence of the registrant's exclusive right to use the registered mark. However, incontestability may, paradoxically, be contested on numerous grounds (one being "that the mark has been or is being used to violate the antitrust laws of the United States," and others including fraud and abandonment), and so is limited at best.

To register a trademark, a written, verified application in the form prescribed by the Commissioner of Patents must be filed in the Patent Office. The application must be accompanied by a drawing which complies with the Commissioner's requirements; by five specimens or facsimiles; and by a filing fee of $25.

Certificates of Registration remain in force 20 years (if an affidavit of use is filed during the sixth year). A registration may be renewed for successive 20-year periods. Each renewal fee is $25.

INTRODUCTION TO CONTRACTS AND AGREEMENTS

While the documents reproduced in this book are excellent examples of their kind, they are by no means *representative* examples. The purpose of the collection was not to make a statistically reliable inference of national practices, but to obtain salesmen's agreements that could serve as models for companies seeking to design or redesign employment contracts for their own sales force.

CAVEAT

These forms are not intended to encourage sales executives to practice law. This is a "do-it-yourself" project that holds many dangers. The whole subject of employment contracts is one over which seasoned lawyers differ. Even an expertly drawn agreement with a salesman might prove full of holes when put to a legal test. The forms following are designed only to serve as a source of format and language suggestions useful to an attorney for drafting documents tailored to the specific needs of your company.

CONSIDERATIONS

A good contract can save a lot of time, money, and misunderstanding. Here is a list of factors that especially need to be considered when a contract with a salesman is being drafted:

1. What product(s) and/or service(s) are to be covered by the agreement.

2. Detailed description of the territory or prospect list to be covered by the salesman, including any right the company will retain to split the territory and/or reassign accounts.

3. The established policies and practices to which parties to the contract will agree to adhere at all times.

4. The method of compensation to be used. Where applicable, state policy for handling writeoffs of uncollectible bills; whether commissions are to be paid when order billed, or when bill collected; frequency of payment; and the handling of commission overdrafts. Here are some considerations peculiar to each method of compensation:

   a. *Straight Salary:* Include provision to switch to another method of compensation under certain conditions and after certain period;

   b. *Straight Commission:* State clearly the method of computation that will be the company's normal and accepted accounting method;

   c. *Combinations Involving Draw, Quota:* Include amount of salary or "guaranteed" draw; percent of commission and override; when and how commissions are to be paid; when they are subject to review and revision.

5. Procedure for compensating for orders received from office in salesman's territory but originating from another salesman's territory. Generally these "split accounts" can be handled in one of two ways:

   a. Commission shared by both salesmen at some predetermined rate;

   b. Commission assigned in full to one salesman or the other.

6. Conditions under which contract can be terminated:

   a. Immediately "for cause";

   b. Action of one or the other parties, with advance notice, usually from 30 to 90 days;

   c. Disposition of commissions, if any, earned after termination.

7. The life of the agreement. Standard wording: "The term of this agreement shall be for .... month(s) or year(s), commencing ...., and shall automatically be renewed for similar periods unless written notice of termination be sent by either party to the other not less than .... days prior to the expiration of any such period. Company agrees to accept orders until termination date."

8. Policy regarding expenses, reimbursable and not reimbursable, including clear statement of limitations of authority regarding extraordinary expenses, obligations or liability of any kind in the name of, or for, or on account of the company.

OVERALL COMPANY POLICY

Thomas Truck & Caster Co.
Keokuk, Iowa

The basic marketing program of the Company is designed to provide a thorough sales coverage for all products manufactured, in all areas of each Territory, as well as nationally. The overall growth and strength of the Company, its national competitive position, and the value of Thomas to Representatives, all require adherence to these basic principles.

The basic manufacturing program of the Company, for efficiency of production and all other internal operations, requires an adequate volume of business from every existing and potential surface, ranging from manufacturers who can use Thomas products on the equipment they make, to the homeowner who may only be a one-time, one-item buyer.

The basic problem for the Company resolves itself to the obtaining of an adequate, proportionate, and profitable volume of business for all its products, which requires more than one phase of marketing to produce that result.

The most important and the principal marketing method is by direct sales to the user through commission Representatives, assigned a definite, exclusive territory, and given adequate territory protection and commission compensation in return for their agreement and performance in actively promoting the sale of Company products assigned to them, on that basis.

The other marketing methods used by the Company, in order to obtain an adequate overall volume, are aimed at sources of business which experience has demonstrated requires other methods of selling, except in rare, individual situations. These exceptions to the principal marketing method are specified in the Company Sales Policy and made a part of each Territory Agreement.

Territory

The territory outlined in the Sales Agency Agreement is yours on an exclusive basis for direct sales to users, except as otherwise noted in this Agreement.

The territorial area may be revised by mutual agreement of the Sales Representative and the Company, or by the Company in the event of necessity.

THOMAS TRUCK & CASTER COMPANY
KEOKUK, IOWA

Sales Agency Agreement

DATE_____

This Agreement is between THOMAS TRUCK AND CASTER COMPANY of KEOKUK, IOWA,

hereinafter called the "COMPANY" and_____

of _____, an independent contractor, hereinafter

called the "SALES REPRESENTATIVE".

The COMPANY and the SALES REPRESENTATIVE agree as follows:

A.—The COMPANY hereby appoints_____
its exclusive District Sales Representative in the territory defined in Section B, for the period of
time beginning with the date hereto, until otherwise terminated in accordance with this agreement.

B.—The territory is defined as follows:

C.—It is agreed that the SALES REPRESENTATIVE and the COMPANY will comply with the
rules and regulations as set forth in the "SALES POLICY" of the COMPANY.

D.—This Sales Agency Agreement will be terminated by the COMPANY or the SALES REPRE-
SENTATIVE upon not less than thirty days written notice. This agreement may also be terminated, effective on date written notice is received and without the thirty day notice because of:

> 1. Failure of the SALES REPRESENTATIVE to
> comply with or perform any of the requirements or
> provisions of the SALES POLICY.

> 2. Legislation, court decision or Government rul-
> ing which contravenes any provision of this Agree-
> ment.

After aforesaid written notice terminating this agreement, the COMPANY shall not be liable to
pay commission on any order accepted by the COMPANY, except orders mailed to the COMPANY
by the SALES REPRESENTATIVE, prior to date of termination, and accepted by the COMPANY
and paid for by the customer. Payment of commissions, after notice of termination, will be made
after collection of customer's account by the COMPANY.

E.—This Sales Agency Agreement is approved by the COMPANY at it's home office, KEOKUK,
IOWA and is acceptable to the SALES REPRESENTATIVE.

THOMAS TRUCK AND CASTER COMPANY

-------------------------------------   --
Representatives Signature

-------------------------------------   --
Date

You are not to solicit business, make calls, or in any way attempt to secure
orders for Thomas products in any area outside your exclusive territory, except
with written permission from the Company. Commission credit will not be given
on any order which violates this rule.

Exceptions

Railroad Business

Due to the procedure of selling railroads, the Company has special Railroad Representatives, and other Sales Representatives do not receive commission, except on sales to railroads by resale dealers in their territory.

U.S. Government Business

The Company has a special Government Representative, and other Sales Representatives do not receive commission credit on Government business originating and contracted for at or from Washington, D. C., or the Military General Supply Agency, Richmond, Virginia, except as follows:

U.S. Government and local or area government business, purchased in a Sales Representative's territory, is handled like any other customer. If the purchase on any quotation is transferred to Washington, D. C., the Company is to receive a copy of the quotation and full information without delay, for transmission to the Government Representative. Otherwise, the Sales Representative may not participate in the commission.

Export Business

All inquiries and sales for equipment for export are handled by the Company and our exclusive Export Sales Representatives, except purchases made by a customer in your territory for its own use in a foreign location.

National Accounts

The Company, upon due notification to the Sales Representative, may establish commission rates payable for certain established National Accounts, or may, due to a lack of interest by the Sales Representative in working such accounts, discontinue payment of commission on orders from such accounts.

Other

Any items or products manufactured and sold by the Company which are not cataloged or otherwise offered for sale through the Representative are exempt from commission credit.

Sales Activities

Quotations

Copies of all written quotations on Thomas products are to be sent to the home office for checking of prices and specifications.

Promotion

In return for sales privileges in your territory, we expect you to actively and aggressively promote the sale of Thomas products. We expect you to produce a sales volume satisfactory to the Company, on the entire line and to do this in accordance with the rules of the Sales Policy.

The Sales Representative agrees not to sell items made by another manufacturer that are competitive to items available in the Thomas line of equipment, and will continue to receive exclusive commission protection on those items.

You are an independent contractor and we do not exercise any control over the amount of time you devote to the sale of Thomas products, nor the number of noncompetitive lines you handle, nor in any way intend to regulate you or your activities in such a way as to place you in the category of a direct employee of the Company.

It is agreed that the Sales Representative will make every effort to attend and/or send other personnel when requested or deemed advisable to Product Training Sessions, Sales Meetings, or other legitimate activities at the home office, or at such regional locations as are announced.

TERMS OF SALE

Prices are F.O.B. Keokuk, Iowa. No freight is allowed. Freight charges will not be prepaid, unless the Company agrees in writing to do so, and will be added to the invoice.

Terms for all items are net 30 days from the *date of the invoice*. No deviation is permissible.

PURCHASE. ORDERS

All orders must be signed, and made out to the Company at Keokuk, Iowa, and are subject to approval and acceptance at that point.

Orders should be *complete* and correct as to terms, price, specifications of product, and shipping instructions. Verbal instructions must be confirmed in writing. The Sales Representative will be charged the cost of all errors in an order for which he is responsible, and the Company will stand the cost of any errors for which it is responsible.

An acknowledgment copy of each order, except orders for items to be shipped immediately from stock, will be mailed promptly to both the customer and Representative. The latter should carefully *check* the acknowledgment and immediately notify the Company if not in accord with the sale. In the case of orders for items from stock, your acknowledgment copy is in the form of a commission credit copy, as the item will be shipped promptly.

CREDIT

The Company's Credit Department checks the credit rating of all customers in Dun & Bradstreet. If the customer is not listed or adequately rated, the order is not passed for shipment until the Credit Department is satisfied as to the customer's ability to pay the invoice.

When the Sales Representative has reason to believe the customer is too new in business or otherwise not properly rated, he should send credit references and full information as to the customer's credit standing with the order. Or, attach the customer's check made out to the Company for the full amount of the order. This will avoid delay in entering the order.

The Company reserves the right to debit back all or part of the Sales Representative's commission on an unpaid account. The commission will be reinstated if the customer pays the invoice in full at a later date. If the account has to be given to an attorney for collection, commission will be prorated on the net proceeds.

TRIAL ORDERS

Only certain standard items are available for trial, per specified trial period. A signed purchase order must be obtained from the customer stating: "Subject to return for credit after .... days' trial, f.o.b. Keokuk, Iowa." Consult the Company before offering to submit equipment for trial. Special trucks will not be furnished for *Free* trial.

SPECIAL SAMPLE TRUCKS

On an order for special trucks, the customer may desire to purchase a sample for his approval before we proceed with construction of the entire order. In this case, the sample truck will be shipped and invoiced at the first user discount. Later, when the entire order is shipped, price adjustment will be made to allow the correct quantity discount to apply on the price of the sample. *Sample special trucks cannot be returned for credit,* and this must be agreed to by the purchaser.

SPECIAL FINISH AND MARKING

The Company does not furnish equipment with a special finish or special marking different from its standard finishes and identifying marks, except at an extra charge based upon the extra labor, material, and equipment required.

GUARANTEE

The products of the Company are designed and built for the capacities given in the catalog or quotation, which are based on smooth floors and normal operating conditions. Under such conditions, parts claimed defective within 60 days after shipment and returned prepaid for inspection will be replaced at no charge only if found defective in material or workmanship. All other parts will be sold in the regular way.

Breakage or failure because of defect in our products is rare. It is found that, in most cases, overloading and abuse are common practices, and with uneven elevator entrances, holes in floors or other obstacles which truck wheels or other parts are pushed up against with sharp, heavy impact, breakage may result, which is no fault of the equipment. Sales Representatives should carefully investigate all breakage complaints with these factors in mind, remembering that defects would normally occur within 60 days after shipment.

No payment or credit is allowed for repair work or materials furnished by others, except on *written authority* from the Company, after full investigation.

An order becomes the property of the customer when delivered to the carrier. If breakage or damage occurs in transit, *the customer* should immediately have a damage notation made on the freight bill to support his claim for damage. Parts to repair such damage will be sold in the regular way.

RETURNED GOODS

The Sales Representative is not to authorize a customer to return goods to the factory without first getting authorization and shipping instructions from the home office. In the event such authorization is given and goods are returned to the factory, there will be a refinishing and restocking charge of at least 10 percent to cover actual costs. The Sales Representative will be debited for full commission on any goods returned.

ADVERTISING

Publication

The Company conducts an outstanding national advertising program through its advertising agency at its own expense. This advertising is designed for the benefit of all territories, and inquiries resulting are referred to Sales Representatives for followup.

Direct Mail

From time to time, certain direct mail material is supplied by the Company to any territory at no cost or on a mutual cost basis, as announced at the time of the program.

Local

The Company does not share any part of the expense of local territory advertising of any kind which is not a part of its own advertising program.

Telephone Directory

The Company handles and pays for all Thomas classified telephone-directory advertising through its advertising agency on a *national basis*, using a regular-type, boldface Caster listing, and a trade name listing under "Trucks-Industrial," except in cities where a trademark heading under "Trucks-Industrial" is deemed advisable. In territories where the classified directory has a Material Handling Equipment section, the trade name listing is usually preferred under this section in place of under "Trucks-Industrial."

Cost of the above telephone-directory advertising is divided equally between the Company and the Sales Representative at the time the directory order is placed, and is debited against commission accounts.

Proper notification of a new directory deadline will be sent each territory by the Company in advance, in order that any change necessary can be made.

The Representative is *not to contract locally* for the above telephone-directory advertising.

The *full* name of Thomas Truck & Caster Co. cannot appear in telephone-directory advertising or similar local publications in such a way as to make the Company liable for any local, city, county, state or federal tax.

Use of Company Name

The Sales Representative shall have no right to use the Company name in such way as to make the Company liable for any local, city, county, state or federal tax contribution or expense of any kind.

The full Company name is not to be placed on office doors or building directory. Proper listing is, "Sales Representative for Thomas Trucks, Casters, and Wheels."

The Company must be consulted and its instructions followed in each case where the Sales Representative desires to use the Company name for any publications or listings within his territory.

Operating Expenses

The Company does not pay any part of the Sales Representative's operating expenses.

Types of Accounts—Defined

Regular User Sales

All customers' sales are subject to the *suggested* product quantity discounts of the discount schedule for all items except Skids and Allied Products (see below for skids). Commission rates paid are based on the discount allowed by the Sales Representative.

Sales at discounts other than the user discount specified will carry a commission applying to the next lower user discount.

Orders received by the Company without price will be invoiced at the net figure for the quantity and discount applying, with the appropriate commission rate for that discount.

Skids and Allied Products discounts for users apply only to one item of one size and specification, and not to a miscellaneous assortment. Two or more orders for a single buyer, but for shipment to two or more destinations, may be grouped together to obtain a higher quantity discount, *provided* the orders are for items *of identical specifications* and can be manufactured and shipped on the same date.

Resale Dealers

A person or organization engaged in buying products for sale through them to others, either with shipment direct to the ultimate user, or to the dealer.

Any account in this classification must be approved by the Company, and will be rated as either Class AA, Class A, or Class B, and will have to maintain a satisfactory credit standing.

Class AA: Those dealers who do a substantial volume and who stock or catalog our products, and those that deal in a particular product line on a regional or national basis and who are directly competitive with a Sales Representative.

Class A: Those dealers who regularly buy Thomas products, are generally operating in a normal territorial area, and who work the Thomas line actively.

Class B: All other dealers, not otherwise rated, who occasionally buy Thomas products and who are qualified by the Representative and the Company to receive a dealer discount.

The Representative in whose territory the resale dealer is located will receive the sales commission if qualified, regardless of the destination of the shipment.

Discounts applicable to this classification will be determined by the Company, and will be published discounts.

Sales Representatives' Stock Purchases

Qualified Sales Representatives who purchase Company products for their stock. Prices are f.o.b. Keokuk, Iowa; terms net 30 days.

No special terms, deferred payments, or consignment arrangements are available. The Sales Representative assumes full responsibility for invoicing, collection, and taxes on sales made by him from his stock.

Discounts applicable are as shown, or as otherwise published or established.

Original Equipment Manufacturers (O.E.M.)

Any manufacturer who *regularly* purchases wheels, casters, or other parts for use as an auxiliary or integral part of machinery or products manufactured by such purchaser for sale or lease.

The Company must approve any account in this classification, and will establish discounts and commission rates applicable.

GENERAL

Sales Supplies

The Company furnishes the Sales Representative with an adequate supply of catalogs, bulletins, and sales literature on its products. The Company supplies interoffice letterheads and Company letterheads imprinted with the Sales Representative's name and address at no cost to the Sales Representative.

Telephone and Telegraph

The Sales Representative must pay for all telephone calls and telegrams to the Company. The Company will pay for all telephone calls and telegrams originating from the Company.

When necessary to place collect calls or wires, same will be accepted, but charged back to the Sales Representative as a debit against his commission account.

COMPENSATION

Compensation to the Sales Representative is in the form of commission paid on shipments. Commission is credited at the time the customer is invoiced, and is paid on the 20th of each month on all shipments made during the previous month.

INTERTERRITORY COMMISSIONS

When two or more territories share in a user order, the commission will be divided in proportion to the effort and influence exercised in securing the business.

Commission on jobber or resale dealer sales is paid to the Sales Representative in whose territory such dealer is located, based on billing address and qualification.

The factors that will be used as evidence to substantiate the decision of the Company will be the following:

1. Point at which our equipment is specified.

2. Point at which requisition is issued.

3. Point of issuance of purchase order.

4. Destination of shipment where equipment will be used.

5. Point or points at which specifications are drawn, engineering performed and selling done.

6. Evidence of sales work by territory being considered because of 3 and 4.

In deciding each of the above factors, the Company will be guided entirely by the file of the transaction in our office at the time the order is received. This file will consist of correspondence and quotations, Sales Representative's reports, the formal purchase order, and all other data regarding the sale.

To protect himself, a Sales Representative who has reason to believe that the job he is quoting on may be ordered in another territory, should immediately send full information and the price quoted to the home office. The Sales Representative must not mail a quotation directly to another territory. Interterritory quotations must clear through the home office of the Company.

The commission will be divided as follows:

1. One-third to the territory in which the formal purchase order is issued, except on certain national accounts which merely clear orders of all their plants on an informal basis, and which are not influenced by a Sales Representative at that plant.

2. One-third to the territory in which the equipment is used.

3. One-third to the territory in which the selling and engineering performed causes the Company's product to be purchased.

Exceptions to the above may be made at the discretion of the Company providing the file of the complete transaction clearly proves that two territories equally share part 3, or where buying formalities in certain national firms make part 1 of no consideration.

SALES REPORTS

Monthly reports of sales and the territory position as to sales volume and number of orders will be sent to each territory approximately 15 days after the close of each month. Cumulative reports will be issued in conjunction with the monthly report. Advertising results are also included in this report.

OFFICE BULLETINS

There are three main types of data on general letters sent at various times to each Sales Representative. They are:

1. *"T" Sheet*

   Designed for the man who sells Thomas equipment. A *weekly* news and special feature letter with information of interest including changes in personnel, personal news items, etc., of Sales Representatives.

2. *"G" Letter*

   A "general" letter embodying general material regarding sales, meetings, announcements, etc., issued when required.

3. *"D" Sheet*

   A data sheet embodying technical and price data on the Company's line of equipment, issued when required.

DISTRIBUTOR'S SALES AGREEMENT
WESTINGHOUSE AIR BRAKE CO.
PNEUMATIC EQUIPMENT DIVISION
SIDNEY, OHIO

THIS AGREEMENT, executed as of the................day of........................, 19........., by

WESTINGHOUSE AIR BRAKE COMPANY, Pneumatic Equipment Div.,

hereinafter referred to as the "Manufacturer," and...

....

a .... of

(State whether individual, corporation or co-partnership)

....

(Street address, City and State)

hereinafter referred to as the "Distributor," shall constitute the Agreement governing their business relations.

1. RIGHT TO PURCHASE AND SELL PRODUCTS

A. The Manufacturer grants to the Distributor the right to purchase from the Manufacturer for resale the following described products of the Manufacturer (hereinafter called "Products") :

Class A Products

....

....

Class B Products

....

....

The right to purchase granted herein to Distributor is nonexclusive as to both Class A Products and Class B Products, but it is the Manufacturer's intention that, insofar as is practicable, no corresponding rights to purchase Class A Products for resale to the Industries listed in paragraph 1. C. below will be granted to other distributors within the Territory described in paragraph 1. C.

B. The Manufacturer grants to the Distributor the right to purchase from the Manufacturer for resale, service parts for the aforesaid Products (hereinafter called "Service Parts").

C. It is expected that Distributor will concentrate his efforts in promoting and making sales of Products and Service Parts to customers engaged in the following Industries within the following described territory (hereinafter referred to as "Territory"):

INDUSTRIES:

TERRITORY:

D. The Manufacturer reserves the right to sell any Product or Service Parts to anyone, either within or outside the Territory, without liability to the Distributor, and specifically reserves the right, without in any respect limiting the generality of the foregoing, to sell to the United States or to any State or local government or to any of their agencies or instrumentalities, or to any other vendee for ultimate use by any such governmental authority pursuant to original specifications of that authority, and to sell to purchasers which the Manufacturer classifies as national accounts and which in his opinion can only be served via direct sales.

2. DISCOUNTS, PRICES AND TERMS

Prices to the Distributor shall be the Manufacturer's list price in effect at time of shipment, less the applicable discounts and subject to the Manufacturer's terms. All orders are subject to Credit and Sales Department approval and acceptance by the Manufacturer at Sidney, Ohio and not elsewhere. Unless otherwise stated, prices are f.o.b. plant of manufacturer. Delivery of Product by the Company to a common carrier or to Distributor's own, leased, chartered or authorized conveyance, shall constitute delivery to Distributor. Title and risk of loss shall pass to Distributor upon such delivery, regardless of whether shipments are freight collect, allowed, or prepaid and charged back, except as title may be retained by the Manufacturer as security for payment of the purchase price. The Manufacturer may change list prices, discounts, and terms, in whole or in part, at any time without notice. Any sales, use, excise or other tax applicable to the manufacture, sale, delivery or use of merchandise sold to Distributor shall be added to the price and paid by Distributor. No more than one discount or commission will be allowed on any one sale, and any dispute between the Distributor and other distributors of the Manufacturer, or dealers or supply houses, concerning rights under this or similar agreements relating to the Product shall be determined by the Manufacturer, if he so elects, and any such determination, expressed in writing, shall be final and conclusive.

3. WARRANTY

A. The Manufacturer warrants each new Product sold by the Manufacturer to be free from defects in material and workmanship for six (6) months from date of shipment by Manufacturer but not to exceed ninety (90) days of service, or such other period of time as Manufacturer may agree to in writing. (Except as pertains to unit type air compressors. Warranty on this product covered in attached page.)

B. The obligation under this warranty, statutory or otherwise, is limited to the replacement or repair at the Manufacturer's factory, or at a point designated by the Manufacturer, or such part as shall appear to the Manufacturer, upon inspection at such point, to have been defective in material or workmanship.

C. This warranty does not obligate the Manufacturer to bear the cost of labor or transportation charges in connection with the replacement or repair of defective parts, nor shall it apply to a Product upon which repairs or alterations have been made unless authorized by the Manufacturer.

D. The Manufacturer makes no warranty in respect to accessories, such being subject to the warranties of their respective manufacturers.

E. The Manufacturer shall in no event be liable for consequential damages or contingent liabilities arising out of the failure of any Product or parts to operate properly.

F. No express, implied or statutory warranty other than herein set forth is made by the Manufacturer.

G. The Distributor shall make no warranty or representation on behalf of the Manufacturer with respect to the Product unless authorized in writing by Manufacturer to do so.

4. LISTS AND SALES MANUALS

The Manufacturer issues to the Distributor one or more Sales Manuals, Parts and Price Lists, and/or Schedules setting forth current prices and trade discounts, all of which are subject to change by the Manufacturer at any time. All of this material as revised from time to time is by reference incorporated into and agreed to be made a part of this agreement whether or not attached hereto. Sales Manuals, Parts and Price Lists, unless specifically sold to the Distributor, remain the property of the Manufacturer and shall be returned on termination of this agreement.

5. DELIVERY DELAYS OR SHORTAGES

The Manufacturer shall not be liable to Distributor or any of Distributor's customers for any loss, damage, detention or delay resulting from fires, strikes, lockouts, delays in manufacture, delays in transportation or delivery of materials, embargoes, insurrections or riots, civil or military authority, car shortages, acts of God, acts of the Distributor, or any other cause beyond its reasonable control. Any claims against the Manufacturer for shortages in shipment shall be made in writing within five (5) days after receipt of shipment.

6. TRADEMARKS

The Distributor agrees not to use the Manufacturer's name or registered trademarks or those of Westinghouse Air Brake Company or any marks closely resembling any of them (or the translation of such names or trademarks into any foreign language), as part of the corporation or business name of the Distributorship, or in any manner which the Manufacturer considers misleading, detrimental, or objectionable.

7. RELATIONSHIP OF PARTIES

The relationship contemplated by this agreement is one in which the Manufacturer is vendor and the Distributor is vendee. The Distributor is not an agent, employee, or legal representative of the Manufacturer for any purpose whatever, and shall have no power or authority to incur or create any obligations or liability of any kind for or on behalf of the Manufacturer. The Distributor shall conduct his business as an independent contractor and all persons employed in such business shall be employees of Distributor and all costs and obligations incurred by reason of any such employment shall be for the account and expense of Distributor even though employees of Distributor may be regarded as employees of Manufacturer under a particular law or regulation.

8. FACILITIES AND SALES EFFORTS

A. The Distributor, to the satisfaction of the Manufacturer, will:

1. Make adequate sales and sales promotion efforts;

2. Maintain adequate and suitable sales and display facilities;

3. Maintain at all times adequate service facilities and stocks of genuine Le Roi service parts. The adequacy of the Distributor's stock of genuine Le Roi service parts shall be determined by the Manufacturer upon the basis of the Product populations in the Territory. Obsolete parts in the Distributor's stock shall be purchased, replaced, or allowed as a credit by the Manufacturer to such extent and upon such terms as it may determine;

4. Maintain sufficient qualified sales and service personnel to cover all sources of orders for the Product within the scope of this agreement and to render prompt and adequate service at reasonable prices to all users of the class of Product covered by this agreement within his Territory regardless of when, where, or by whom sold.

5. Avoid in every way such activities or trade practices as may be injurious to the Manufacturer's good name and goodwill, or detrimental to public interest.

B. The Manufacturer will make available to the Distributor such facilities for training of personnel and other assistance as it may deem necessary for adequate distribution and service of the Product.

9. ADVERTISING

A. The Manufacturer shall furnish, without charge to the Distributor, such catalogs, circulars, and other advertising material as are, in the judgment of the Manufacturer, necessary or desirable.

B. The Distributor's advertising shall be at his own expense, and shall include placing an appropriate classified advertisement in his local telephone directory, in the form acceptable to Manufacturer.

10. TERMINATION

A. This agreement shall remain in full force and effect until terminated by either the Manufacturer or the Distributor. Either shall have the right to terminate the agreement at any time upon written notice to the other by registered mail, which termination shall become effective .... days after mailing of such written notice. After termination, the sale or purchase of any Product by the Distributor, or the referring of prospective purchasers by the Manufacturer to the Distributor, shall not be construed as a renewal of this agreement.

B. This agreement shall terminate, at Manufacturer's option and without any notice to Distributor, as of any date on which:

1. Distributor shall become insolvent.

2. Distributor shall become subject to any liquidation, receivership, bankruptcy, reorganization, or creditors' proceedings, either voluntary or involuntary, if such proceeding shall not have been dismissed within thirty (30) days after commencement.

3. Distributor shall attempt to assign this agreement without Manufacturer's written consent.

4. Distributor shall fail to perform any obligation hereunder.

5. Distributor or a partner thereof, if a partnership, shall die or become disabled.

11. EFFECT OF TERMINATION

A. In case the Manufacturer terminates this agreement otherwise than by reason of circumstances stated in paragraph B of paragraph 10, the Manufacturer shall purchase from the Distributor, and the Distributor agrees to sell to the Manufacturer, all new and unsold Products and Service Parts then owned by the Distributor and previously purchased by the Distributor from the Manufacturer, which are, in the opinion of the Manufacturer, unused, undamaged and not obsolete, at 85 percent of the net prices originally charged the Distributor.

B. The Product and Service Parts shall be considered not obsolete for the purpose of this paragraph 11 if it has been produced or sold in like type and size by the Manufacturer within the 12-month period immediately preceding the effective date of termination of this agreement. All Products and/or Service Parts so purchased by the Manufacturer shall be immediately shipped by the Distributor, freight collect, to the destination designated by the Manufacturer.

C. In case the Distributor terminates this agreement, or the agreement is terminated by Manufacturer by reason of circumstances stated in paragraph B of paragraph 10, this paragraph 11 shall apply, at the option of the Manufacturer, to all Products and Service Parts then owned by the Distributor previously purchased by the Distributor from the Manufacturer.

D. Distributor shall be entitled to receive a discount or commission only on orders received and accepted by Manufacturer prior to the date of termination or on orders resulting from outstanding quotations by Distributor which orders are received and accepted by Manufacturer within thirty (30) days following the date of termination, provided, that the Distributor shall have filed written notice with Manufacturer within five (5) days of the date of termination specifying the quotations or orders on which a discount or commission is or will be claimed.

12. ASSIGNMENT

Neither this agreement nor any interest therein is assignable by the Distributor. The benefit of this agreement shall enure to and be binding upon the successors and assigns of the Manufacturer.

13. No Other Agreement—Acceptance By Manufacturer—Law of Performance

This agreement contains the full and entire agreement between the parties hereto, and replaces all previous agreements between Manufacturer and Distributor or Distributor's predecessor in interest or assignor. No agent or representative of the Manufacturer has any authority to make any representations, statements, warranties, or agreements not herein expressed. This agreement shall become valid and binding when signed by a duly authorized representative of Manufacturer at its office at Sidney, Ohio, and when so accepted, this agreement shall be an Ohio contract and shall be construed, enforced, and performed in accordance with the laws of the State of Ohio. If it shall be found that any provision hereof violates the law of any government or governmental division having jurisdiction in the premises, such provision shall be of no force and effect and this agreement shall be treated as if such provision had not been inserted herein.

(Name of Distributor)

By ....

Title ....

Originated by ....

Recommended by ....

Accepted and executed at Sidney, Ohio

WESTINGHOUSE AIR BRAKE COMPANY, Pneumatic Equipment Division

By ....

Title ....

APPLICATION FOR DISPLAY BOOTH AT FAIR OR HOME SHOW

AMWAY CORPORATION

(To be submitted in three copies 90 days *prior* to the event)

To: Distributor Services Department
    Amway Corporation
    7575 East Fulton Road
    Ada, Michigan 49301

In Canada, send to:
    Amway of Canada, Ltd.
    Highway 135, Route 4
    London, Ontario

I (We), the undersigned distributors of Amway products, hereby apply for permission to set up and maintain a booth of a temporary nature at which Amway products will be displayed at the following event:

1. Official name of event:..

....

2. Address of place where event is to be held (include street address and

    name of city and state):...

....

3. Dates on which event is to be held: From..., 19 ....

    to ...., 19 ....

4. Describe exact location of booth:..

....

5. Brief description of booth:...

....

....

I (We) attached hereto proof of reservation or commitment for the space at said event. (Should show *receipt of deposit*)

I (We) understand that approval of our application by Amway is subject to the following conditions:

    1. That we must at all times comply with the rules and regulations relating to the operation of a fair booth as set forth in the Amway Distributors Code of Ethics and Rules of Conduct (SA-323) and in Amway Career Manual (SA-18-108).

    2. That the Amway Fair Booth Kit (AD-60) must be used as the basic decorating material. Any additional signs used must be of a professional

quality. If the Amway trade name is used on such signs, it must be in the proper type style and must be followed by the trademark registration symbol ®. If the Amway red-white-blue logo is used, it must be exactly the same design as the distributor decal (SA-264) and must show the word "distributor" directly under the name "Amway" and must contain the trademark registration symbol ® as in the decal.

3. That any Amway products sold from said display booth shall be sold in conformance with the customer protection rules of The Amway Distributors Association.

4. That at the conclusion of said event, I (we) will promptly remove all displays, signs and products and leave the premises in a neat and presentable condition.

5. That said display booth shall at all times be under the supervision of an Amway Direct Distributor who will assume full responsibility for proper conduct of the booth.

I (We) further understand that, by approving this application, Amway has in no way granted or transferred to me (us) any vested or proprietary interest in the name "Amway" but has instead granted me (us) a limited license for the duration of the above event only.

Dated this .... day of ...., 196..........

....
(signature of distributor)

....
(address of distributor)

SALES AGREEMENT, SALARY PLUS COMMISSION

It is our policy to outline in detail our compensation plan each year. This is an employment contract—the agreement between you and the company which specifies how you will be paid for services you render.

Compensation is divided into "direct" and "supplementary." Our direct compensation plan includes a good base salary, a reasonable expense account, a company leased automobile, and an attractive bonus opportunity.

In addition we provide you with a supplementary compensation plan which includes hospitalization insurance, health and accident policies, major medical, surgical, accidental death, and life insurance. When you have been with the company for five years and have reached the age of 30, you are also eligible for the Blackhawk Retirement Plan.

In order to familiarize yourself again with this insurance, we are enclosing the booklets describing it in detail. We have also spelled out your actual coverage on page nine. Be sure to read this over carefully and then determine how much it would cost to provide this same protection for you and your family.

Often we have a tendency to overlook the importance of supplementary compensation. We may look upon it as "fringe benefits" or believe it is standard procedure with all companies. This is not true in either case. Supplementary compensation is intended to take care of those emergencies which most of us could not otherwise afford and also to build that all-important security for our later years.

Many companies have some form of supplementary compensation but few even approach our plan—our insurance programs are the most complete available.

From time to time we also offer an opportunity to earn important additional money in the form of special contests which help to provide those "extras" which make life more enjoyable.

It is our desire to provide an overall program which will allow you to live comfortably now, provide for the future and, most important, give you the opportunity to grow in proportion to your capabilities.

This covers our agreement with you for the period beginning January 1, 19........, and ending December 31, 19........

1. *Employment.* You are employed by the Blackhawk Mfg. Company, A Division of Applied Power Industries, Inc., hereinafter referred to as "Blackhawk Mfg. Company," as its salesman to sell to the jobbing trade our products exclusively in accordance with prices, terms, conditions, policies and regulations as specified and directed by us from time to time. You are to devote your entire time during business hours to this work, and to use your best efforts and energies to promote the sale of our products in your territory.

2. *Definitions.* The term "our products" wherever used in this agreement shall cover only those standard terms of manufacture regularly offered for sale through jobbers and for which distributor price lists are issued.

The term "specials" wherever used in the agreement shall cover (1) items of manufacture made according to customers' specifications, (2) items embodying changes in our standard items, and (3) products of Dynex, Incorporated (Hydraulic Control products), (4) specific items of Blackhawk Industrial Products Company.

The term "shipments" as used in this agreement shall mean gross shipments of our products to jobbers only, less deductions for returns, allowances, credits, including redistribution credits, less freight if paid by us. The term "shipments" shall not include shipments to anyone of repair parts or repair tools and equipment, specials, or shipments to the United States Government or any of its departments or divisions.

3. *Territory:* Under this agreement you will cover the following territory for the sale of Blackhawk Products as indicated:

4. *Compensation.* Your compensation for your services under this agreement will be calculated and paid on the following basis:

(a) For each month of the contract term you will be paid a salary of $............................ .

(b) In addition, in the event shipments of Lifting Equipment into your territory for the period from January 1, 19........, to December 31, 19........, exceed $............................ ; and the shipments of Porto-Power Equipment into your territory for the period from January 1, 19........, to December 31, 19........, exceed $............................, which amounts are hereinafter referred to as "base shipments," you will be paid a bonus of 4 percent of such excess shipments. This means you must exceed the bases on both Lifting Equipment and Porto-Power Equipment before you are eligible to receive any bonus. This bonus will be paid as follows:

At the end of the contract term the bonus to which you are entitled shall be determined, and shall be paid to you on or before February 15, 19........,

(c) To carry this out properly, we expect you to spend 10 percent of your time on Lifting Equipment and 90 percent of your time on Porto-Power Equipment. We expect you to work out your schedule in accordance with this.

5. *Compensation on Sales of Specials.* On any government business or any business involving specials we reserve the right (1) to deal directly with the government or customer concerned regardless of how or where the business originated, (2) to determine in our discretion what, if any, discount shall be allowed to the jobber; what, if any, special commission shall be allowed to you as a salesman; and what, if any, shipments on such business shall be included in the calculations referred to in paragraph 4 (b) above. If any shipments on such business are not included in the calculations referred to in paragraph 4 (b), and if any special commissions be allowed on such shipments under the provisions of this paragraph 5, said special commission shall be considered earned and payable when the customer's payment has been received in full by us.

6. *Expenses.* It is agreed that the Company will pay the normal expenses you incur in covering your territory away from home. To assist you in determining what should be covered by this expense program, the following information is provided.

(a) Personal Expenses. We will pay for meals and lodging away from home. Hotel receipts must be included with your expense report. If you use transportation other than the car we furnish you, prior permission must be received from your Regional Manager.

(b) Car Expense. We will provide you with a car, as outlined on pages 10 through 15. We will pay for all gas and oil to operate this car for business purposes. This is the only car expense for which the Company is responsible, and receipts must be included with your weekly expense report.

All other service and repairs for these cars are the responsibility of the leasing company, and should be handled directly by you with them.

Your car must be kept clean, and it is your responsibility to see that it is.

(c) Miscellaneous Expenses. Any expenses in addition to those listed above must be described and receipts provided where possible. This can include such items as: telephone expense, customer entertainment, tolls, parking, cab fares, and postage.

(d) Submitting Expenses. It is necessary to submit expense reports only when expenses have been incurred. They must be sent to the Sales Manager for approval, with a copy to your Regional Manager.

(e) Expense Allowance. We think your expenses should average $.............................. per month.

(f) Expenses for Which You Are Responsible. In managing your territory, you will find that there are some expenses which are not covered by our expense allowance. These normal operating expenses are your responsibility and include such items as routine stationery, office supplies, Christmas greeting cards, luggage, brief cases, etc. There may be other expenses which you incur in managing your territory in addition to those itemized above.

7. *Acceptance of Orders.* All orders solicited in your territory are subject to acceptance by an executive of the Company at the home office, and we reserve the right to reject, for any reason whatsoever, any or all orders solicited by you or by any Company salesman in your territory, or any or all orders received at the home office from any jobber located in your territory. Failure of the Company to make shipments on any order or orders whether for causes within or without its control shall not entitle you to compensation with respect to the amount of such order or orders.

8. *Sales Literature and Samples.* The Company will furnish you from time to time such sales literature, samples and data as the company shall deem sufficient to exploit the sale of its products properly. Samples will be charged to your account at our standard jobbing price. All samples furnished to you shall be returned to the Company by you when requested by the Company, and you will be given full credit for all samples returned. In no case shall any samples be sold to anyone.

9. *Termination.* This agreement, unless sooner terminated as hereinafter provided, shall terminate at the close of business on December 31, 19..........

(a) Either of us shall have the right to terminate this agreement at any time, by giving 30 days' prior written notice of intention to terminate.

(b) In the event that the total shipments into your territory as of March 31, 19.........., are 10 percent or more under 25 percent of the "base shipments" or in the event that your total shipments as of June 30, 19.........., are 10 percent or more under 50 percent of the "base shipments" or in the event that your total shipments as of September 30, 19.........., are 10 percent or more under 75 percent of the "base shipments" then we reserve the right to terminate this agreement forthwith.

(c) We reserve the right to terminate this agreement at any time for cause. Cause shall include, but shall not be limited to, your failure or inability for any reason to furnish regular full time services to the Company.

(d) Upon the termination of this contract for any reason, you are to account for all samples furnished to you and all samples you cannot account for shall be paid for by you at the price charged on your account by deducting said amount from any amounts due you by the Company. In the event the amount you owe for samples exceeds the amount which the Company owes you, you shall pay for the balance in cash. In addition, you agree to immediately return to the Company all sales literature and other data in your possession.

(e) Upon termination of this contract for any reason, you shall receive your salary for the full calendar months which have transpired since the beginning of the contract term, plus the proportion of the salary for the month in which the termination occurs which the part of the month worked bears to the full month, less any amounts previously paid to you. In the event you have received on account your salary in an amount in excess of that which you are entitled to under this sub-paragraph, you shall promptly remit the difference to the Company. Payment of any balance of the drawing account due you, which the Company is required to make by the terms of this sub-paragraph shall be made as soon as you have returned or accounted for all of the property of the Company previously delivered to you.

(f) In case of the termination of this agreement by either party prior to December 31, 19........., you shall not be entitled to receive and the Company shall not be liable to pay to you the bonus provided for in paragraph 4.

10. *Construction.* This agreement is executed at West Allis, Wisconsin, and shall be construed and interpreted under the laws of the State of Wisconsin.

11. *Effective Date.* This agreement shall not be binding on either party until accepted by you in writing as provided in the form of acceptance endorsed at the end of this agreement, and returned to the Company's office at 5325 West Rogers Street, West Allis, Wisconsin, within 45 days of the date hereof. When so accepted and returned this agreement shall be effective as of January 1, 19........., and shall supersede and annul all former agreements between the Company and yourself.

> BLACKHAWK MFG. COMPANY
> A Division of
> APPLIED POWER INDUSTRIES, INC.
>
> By...

I hereby acknowledge receipt of the above agreement, and the same is approved and accepted by me.

Date .... (Signed) .... (Seal)

AUTHORITY TO ACKNOWLEDGE ORDERS

A traveling salesman, in the absence of special circumstances, has no authority to bind his house by the acceptance of an order for its product. His function is to solicit orders and forward them to the office of the concern where they are subject to acceptance or rejection. The courts have consistently recognized the limit of the salesman's authority, and have explained closely the acts of the selling house.

An order until accepted in writing, or by the shipment of the goods, or otherwise, is subject to cancellation or rejection. It is customary with many houses to acknowledge the receipt of orders prior to passing upon the customer's credit by dispatching a post card or letter stating that the order has been received and will be given attention. It is not intended, hereby, to *accept* the order.

In Courtney Shoe Co. vs. E. W. Curd & Son, 134 S. W. (Ky.), 146, the acknowledgment read as follows:

"Your order of 8-21-09 to our Mr. Yates is at hand and will receive our prompt and careful attention. Thanking you for same and hoping to merit your future favors, we are, yours truly, The Courtney Shoe Company."

Subsequently the order was rejected. The Kentucky court held that there was no contract. The card was not an acceptance of the order, but a mere acknowledgment of its receipt and a promise that it would receive attention saying:

"In determining what is an acceptance where there is nothing in the conduct of the parties to show an acceptance in fact of the order, we think it a safe and sound rule that the words of the writing should be taken in their ordinary and popular sense, and that they should not be considered to express a meaning they do not naturally convey."

In Stausebach vs. Audubon Paper Stock Company (108 N. Y. Misc. 548) decided by the Appellate Term of the New York Supreme Court, First Department, the order was held accepted because of the conduct of the parties. The facts as stated in the opinion were as follows:

One hundred tons of paper were ordered orally by the plaintiff at defendant's office, and the defendant then stated that it would confirm the order in writing the next day. On the same day defendant wrote to plaintiff the following letter:

"We acknowledge your valued order given us today for 100 No. 2 Overissues in Bundles at 65 cents per cwt., to be shipped to the Thames River Specialties Co., Montville, Conn., via N. Y., N. H. & H. R. R., f.o.b. cars N. Y."

After waiting some time for the goods plaintiff called upon the defendant, who then stated that he would deliver them the following week, and in a final conversation refused to deliver them.

It was stated by Bijur, J.:

"We are not called upon to determine what our view of this interpretation of the language used by commercial men in the ordinary course of business might be were it presented as an original proposition, because there are features in the communication of defendant in the instant case which distinguish it in an important particular. It did not stop with a mere acknowledgment of an order for 'one hundred tons of No. 2 Overissues in Bundles at 65 cts. per cwt.' It might be argued with considerable force that the repetition of the words 'to be shipped to the Thames River Specialties Co. . . . via N. Y., N. H. & H. R. R. Co.' not only indicate a promissory intent upon the part of the writer, but confirm that inference by a reference to detail which would be quite unnecessary to, in fact, contradictory of, the mere purpose to inform the plaintiff that his order has been received.

"But there is an additional element in this case, which, to my mind, is conclusive in plaintiff's favor. At best, as I view it, respondent can claim only that the defendant's communication is ambiguous as to the intent with which it was written, and the subsequent conduct of the parties gives unmistakable evidence that the intent of the defendant had been to accept the order and undertake an obligation to deliver."

Where a buyer, using his own order blank, orders goods and stipulates in the order the terms and conditions thereof, and the order is acknowledged by the seller on a form which sets forth the seller's terms and conditions differing from those proposed by the buyer, the buyer has two courses open to him:

1. He may notify the seller that he will not accept the counter proposals (in which event there is no contract) ; or

2. He may refuse to accept delivery of the merchandise when tendered, pursuant to the terms of the counter offer. If he says nothing, but accepts delivery of the merchandise and treats it as his own, he will be bound by the seller's terms.

BRANCH MANAGER CONTRACT

MEMORANDUM of Agreement by and between .... COMPANY, and .... corporation, duly licensed to do business in ...., and with an office at ...., ..., party of the first part, and ...., party of the second part, made and entered into this .... day of ...., A. D. 19............

WITNESSETH:

.... COMPANY employs the second party as Branch Manager of the .... territory at a salary of .... dollars per month, and his legitimate traveling expenses when absent from his home and engaged upon the business of .... COMPANY, and second party accepts such employment and agrees to give his entire time and undivided attention to the interest of .... COMPANY, and to be governed by and to carry out the instructions of the company, whether embodied in standing rules or special instructions that may be issued from time to time.

As a special incentive to increase activity and watchfulness on the part of the second party, the .... COMPANY agrees to pay the second party a special bonus of .... percent on the net profit of above-mentioned territory, if earned, under and in accordance with the following conditions:

1. The net profit of business obtained from the .... territory shall be ascertained by deducting from orders obtained, which orders have been accepted and filled and for which payment has been received by the company, the total of the following items:

(a) Marginal cost

(b) Commissions

(c) Policy allowances

(d) Interest of one-half of one percent per month on the total inventory of goods on hand and in the hands of the agents in said territory on the first of each month, based upon the marginal cost price established for such goods.

(e) All expenses incurred upon the authority and for the benefit of the .... Branch as recorded on the books of the company in accordance with their regular accounting practice.

2. The marginal costs shall be determined by extending all shipments, upon which credit may be due to second party under paragraph one hereof, at the standard list price, less the discount shown on separate sheet hereto attached, marked "Marginal Cost Discounts."

3. The bonus, if earned, to be calculated monthly and to be accumulated for the six months' period ending .... and .... of each year, and shall be payable semiannually on .... and .... of each year.

4. It is understood and agreed by the parties hereto that this contract, so far as it pertains to the payment of a special bonus, shall be retroactive to ...., 19...........

5. This contract may be terminated by either party hereto giving to the other two weeks' notice in writing, and in case of termination, any amounts earned as bonus shall be calculated as of the date of termination of this contract.

By...

Accepted..   ....

Section C — LEGAL DATA AND CONTRACT FORMS

INFORMAL LETTER OF INTENT

Dear Mr. .... :

This letter constitutes your agreement of employment and itemizes all major details of duties, responsibilities, and compensation.

Effective ...., you will be employed as sales representative for .... in that territory described as the Chicago area. This area is defined as that portion of the State of Illinois north of and including the counties of Vermillion, Champaign, Platt, De Witt, Logan, Menard, Mason, Schuyler and Hancock; that portion of the State of Wisconsin south of and including the counties of Door, Brown, Kewaunee, Outagamie, Winnebago, Waushara, Adams, Juneau, Monroe, and Vernon; the counties of Dubuque, Jackson, Clinton and Scott in the State of Iowa; plus Lake County in the State of Indiana.

Your initial training period of .... through .... will be divided into two periods: the first at .... main office and factory in .... ; the second in the Chicago area. During this preliminary training period your compensation will be based on a $600.00 per month salary prorated over the training period.

Effective ...., you will assume all normal activities as our sales representative in the Chicago area and your compensation will be based on the following:

$325.00 per month salary plus:

Commissions on all orders dated on or after February 1 (which are shipped to some point within the Chicago area) as follows:

0 —$100,000.00	Annual Sales at 3	percent
$100,000.00—$200,000.00	Annual Sales at $3\frac{1}{2}$	percent
$200,000.00—$300,000.00	Annual Sales at $2\frac{1}{2}$	percent
Over $300,000.00	Annual Sales at 2	percent

You will be compensated for expenses incurred in the interests of .... on the basis of actual detailed expenses during the period of .... through .... Effective ...., you will receive an expense allowance of $260.00 per month.

It is definitely understood that your services will be devoted exclusively to the promotion and sale of .... products and that you will assist in any special activity in the company's interest when required.

This Agreement may be terminated by either party, only upon receipt of 30 days' advance notice in writing.

....

Sales Manager

....

Executive Vice-President

....

Sales Representative

FAMOUS FOR QUALITY THE WORLD OVER

PHILCO®

A SUBSIDIARY OF *Ford Motor Company*

APPLICATION FOR LISTING
AS QUALIFIED AUTO RADIO STATION

The undersigned hereby applies for approval for listing as a Qualified Auto Radio Station for Auto Radios manufactured by Philco Corporation.

If approved, I/we agree to:

  a. Maintain an adequate shop facility for the repair of auto radios.
  b. Provide qualified radio repair technicians to perform competent service operations.
  c. Maintain a sufficient supply of Philco or other suitable replacement parts.

Please complete the following in full:

I/we are presently authorized service facilities for:

_____

_____

At the present time, I/we are performing warranty auto radio service for the following automobile dealers:

_____

_____

I/we employ_____full time service technicians.

I/we do, do not have "drive-in" repair facilities.

Application submitted by:

Firm Name:_____

Address:_____
                          Street
           _____
                          City
           _____
                          State

By: _____

Date: _____

PHILCO ® *Famous for Quality the World Over*

A SUBSIDIARY OF *Ford Motor Company,*

SERVICE FACILITY AGREEMENT

FOR PHILCO TELEVISION WARRANTY SERVICE

NOTE: Agreement must be prepared in triplicate. DATE:_____

Agreement between Philco Corporation of Delaware, a subsidiary of Ford Motor Company, with address at Tioga and "C" Streets, Philadelphia 34, Pennsylvania, hereafter called Philco and

_____, hereafter called "Service Facility," located at

_____, _____, telephone number _____

STREET ADDRESS   CITY   STATE

This Agreement defines the participation of SERVICE FACILITY to service PHILCO TELEVISION SETS for customers during "SERVICE OBLIGATION" period; i.e., Ninety (90) days from date of original ownership. The conditions and obligations of SERVICE FACILITY under this Agreement are:

1. To maintain adequate facilities and provide qualified servicemen for the repair of PHILCO TELEVISION.

2. To maintain at least one employee on duty at the address given above during normal working hours.

3. To comply with PHILCO'S Standard Warranty, replacing defective PHILCO parts with genuine PHILCO parts, at no cost to the customer; to exchange defective parts under the terms of the said warranty at the PHILCO Distributor's Parts and Warranty Department; keeping on hand an adequate stock of PHILCO parts so that prompt repairs may be effected for the customer.

4. SERVICE FACILITY and its servicemen will be qualified members of PHILCO FACTORY-SUPERVISED SERVICE ASSOCIATION, and will keep abreast of PHILCO PRODUCT DEVELOPMENT and SERVICE TECHNIQUES as published by PHILCO.

5. SERVICE FACILITY will make its servicemen available when PHILCO training meetings are scheduled in their general area.

6. SERVICE FACILITY and its servicemen agree to identify themselves as PHILCO SERVICE by the use of signs, advertising, and promotional material furnished and/or made available from time to time by the PHILCO Distributor, or PHILCO.

7. SERVICE FACILITY will repair PHILCO TELEVISION and make no charge to the PHILCO customer for parts or labor during the 90-day period of warranty from date or original purchase when such products are serviced by the SERVICE FACILITY. It is understood that defective parts will be exchanged in accordance with the terms of the standard PHILCO Warranty by the PHILCO Distributor; and that the SERVICE FACILITY will receive from PHILCO, an allowance for Labor at the rates printed on schedule (CPD 311) attached to this Agreement.

8. SERVICE FACILITY will conform to all procedures necessary to the efficient operation of PHILCO TELEVISION SERVICE PLAN as outlined in procedure manual attached to the Agreement.

9. Certificate of Adequate Liability Insurance coverage shall be furnished to PHILCO as per "PHILCO Service Facility Insurance Requirements" (CPD 312) attached to this agreement.

10. SERVICE FACILITY understands that PHILCO is under no obligation to solicit or collect any fees for service performed by the SERVICE FACILITY.

11. The SERVICE FACILITY agrees to guarantee, for a period of 30 days, all service workmanship performed on PHILCO TELEVISION by the SERVICE FACILITY or its servicemen.

ORIGINAL — MAIL TO PHILCO SERVICE HEADQUARTERS

DUPLICATE — DISTRIBUTOR'S COPY   TRIPLICATE — SERVICE FACILITY'S COPY

CPD 310
2-63

The parties executing this document agree that, upon acceptance by PHILCO (1) the Agreement may not be transferred or assigned by the SERVICE FACILITY; (2) the Agreement may be cancelled by either party at any time by written notice to the other party, and also if any other contract existing between the SERVICE FACILITY and PHILCO shall, during the term hereof, be terminated other than by expiration, of its stated term, this Agreement shall also then forthwith terminate, anything herein contained to the contrary notwithstanding; (3) upon the cancellation or termination of this Agreement, the SERVICE FACILITY will remove, and not thereafter use, all signs containing the word "PHILCO" and will immediately destroy all stationery, advertising matter, and other printed matter in his possession or under his control containing the word "PHILCO" and the SERVICE FACILITY further convenants and agrees that he will not at any time thereafter use nor permit the use of the word "PHILCO" in any manner in connection with any business by him conducted or in which he may be interested, or otherwise whatsoever, as descriptive of or referring to anything other than PHILCO products; (4) this Agreement contains the full understanding between the parties and there are no other terms or representation except as set forth herein; (5) this Agreement shall not be modified hereafter by any understanding, promise, or representation unless in writing and signed by an officer of the PHILCO Distributor and a duly authorized representative of PHILCO CORPORATION; (6) the SERVICE FACILITY agrees to protect PHILCO CORPORATION and its subsidiaries, and hold them harmless from any loss or damage claim or demand for bodily injury or damage to property, including the loss of use thereof arising out of the installation, service, replacement or repair of products covered by this Agreement, but this indemnification shall apply only to acts or omissions of, or defective workmanship by the Service Facility, his employees, representatives or agents.

Upon the approval and forwarding of this form by the PHILCO Distributor and the acceptance of this Agreement by PHILCO the above terms and the conditions contained therein, shall constitute an Agreement between the SERVICE FACILITY and PHILCO.

PFSS Membership Number_____

Approved and
Forwarded By _____
(PHILCO DISTRIBUTOR)

Authorized SERVICE
FACILITY Signature _____

_____
(ADDRESS)

Title_____

_____
(DISTRIBUTOR SERVICE MANAGER)

Accepted for PHILCO CORPORATION

By_____
PHILCO SERVICE DISTRICT REPRESENTATIVE

Distributor please enter check (X) that the above
Service Facility is a:

Acceptance Date_____

☐ Retail Dealer doing his own service

☐ Non-Retail Service Firm

The Service Facility will fill out this form in triplicate and return all copies to the Distributor for his approval. The Distributor will hold all copies of the Agreement, if approved, for Philco Service District Representative for acceptance. Philco SDR, will forward original copy to Philco Corporation, return duplicate and triplicate for Distributor and Service Facility file.

If the Service Facility is now a PFSS Member, the Membership number must be shown in the space provided.

THE GREATEST BUSINESS BUILDING SERVICE PROGRAM IN THE INDUSTRY
FOR THE INDEPENDENT SERVICE AGENCY

Section D — DIRECTORY OF SALES-TRAINING AIDS

DARTNELL SALES-TRAINING FILMS

For a free copy of the *Dartnell Directory of Sales-Training Films* write:

Ray Linzer, Manager, Film Sales
The Dartnell Corporation
4660 Ravenswood Avenue
Chicago, Illinois 60640

30-MINUTE, 16mm MOTION PICTURES

"What It Takes to Be a Real Salesman" (With Dr. Norman Vincent Peale)

"The Selling Secrets of Ben Franklin"

"How to Take the Butt Out of a Sales Rebuttal" (Featuring Borden and Busse)

"How to Make an Effective Sales Presentation" (Featuring Borden and Busse)

"Opening the Sale" (Featuring Borden and Busse)

"Presenting Your Sales Case—Convincingly" (Featuring Borden and Busse)

"The Power of Enthusiasm" (Starring Hugh Beaumont)

"How to Sell Quality" (Starring Hugh Beaumont)

"Overcoming Objections" (Featuring Borden and Busse)

"Closing the Sale" (Featuring Borden and Busse)

"Solid Gold Hours" (Starring Monty Woolley and Geraldine Brooks)

"The Bettger Story" (Starring Salesman Frank Bettger)

"How to Up Sales by Better Sales Supervision" (Featuring Borden and Busse)

"How to Sell Creatively" (Presenting four of America's top creative salesmen)

"Developing Your Sales Personality" (Featuring Borden and Busse)

"How to Prevent Objections in Selling" (Featuring Borden and Busse)

"The Autopsy of a Lost Sale" (Featuring Borden and Busse)

"How to Succeed in the People Business" (Featuring Dr. Joyce Brothers)

"Second Effort" (Featuring Vince Lombardi)

"The Professional (Starring Van Johnson and Forrest Tucker)

"Make It Happen" (Featuring Julius Boros)

"Take Command" (Featuring Walter M. Schirra)

(Sound tracks are available for some of these films in Danish, Dutch, Finnish, Flemish, French, German, Italian, Japanese, Norwegian, Spanish, and Swedish.)

10-MINUTE, 16mm MOTION PICTURES

"Herman Holds a Sales Meeting"

"Herman's Secrets of Sales Success"

"Why Sales Managers Go Nuts"

SOUND-STRIPFILM KITS

"Keys to Human Relations in Selling" (A kit of five full-color sound stripfilms)

"Selling Against Resistance" (A kit of six black-and-white sound stripfilms)

"Customer Contacts" (A kit of five full-color sound stripfilms)

"Selling . . . The Great Career" (A kit of six full-color sound filmstrips)

30-MINUTE, 16mm EXECUTIVE DEVELOPMENT FILMS

"How to Lead an Effective Sales Conference" (Featuring Porter Henry)

"How to Select Salesmen Who Can and *Will* Sell" (Featuring Dr. Robert N. McMurry)

SOUND-SLIDE TRAINING FILMS

"Keys to Human Relations in Selling"

"How to Write Clear, Concise, Effective Business Letters" (Featuring Robert Gunning)

OTHER SALES-TRAINING FILMS

For an indexed listing of titles, basic data, and descriptions of motion pictures and sound-stripfilms for sales training, together with a directory of sources, write for the *Sales Manager's Film Guide.* Copies can be obtained for 50 cents from:

> Film Guide Library
> BUSINESS SCREEN MAGAZINE
> 7064 North Sheridan Road
> Chicago, Illinois 60626

EQUIPMENT DIRECTORY

The equipment section of this directory lists manufacturers, not distributors. By writing directly to a number of manufacturers for literature, prices, and distributors' names, the sales executive can "shop" for the equipment best suited to his specific needs.

The same "shopping" process can be employed when choosing the services of a sales-training consultant or a film producer.

This directory was designed to be a starting point from which wise buying decisions can be made.

Although the editors have attempted to make this directory as complete as feasible, it is always possible that some firms and individuals will have been missed. Such omission is, of course, no reflection on the firm, nor does inclusion necessarily imply an endorsement by Dartnell.

We invite your comments on the usefulness of this directory, as well as suggestions for its improvement in future editions.

FOR ADDITIONAL HELP

A guide to local distributors of audio-visual equipment is available from the National Audio-Visual Association, Inc., 3150 Spring Street, Fairfax, Virginia 22030. Write directly to the association. The Yellow Pages of your phone book are also an excellent source of information regarding audio-visual equipment retailers.

PROJECTION EQUIPMENT

AUTOMATIC CONTINUOUS
STILL PROJECTORS

ACTION MOTION PICTURE SERVICE
358 West 44th Street
New York, New York 10036

BAUSCH & LOMB OPTICAL CO.
635 St. Paul Street
Rochester, New York 14625

CHARLES BESELER CO.
219 South 18th Street
East Orange, New Jersey 07018

COUSINO PRODUCTS
1941 Franklin Avenue
Toledo, Ohio 43624

DISPLAY-O-VUE CORPORATION OF
AMERICA
25 West 45th Street
New York, New York 10036

EASTMAN KODAK CO.
343 State Street
Rochester, New York 14750

GENARCO, INC.
97-04 Sutphin Boulevard
Jamaica, New York 11435

THE HARWALD CO.
1245 Chicago Avenue
Evanston, Illinois 60202

PICTURE RECORDING CO.
321 Concord Road
Oconomowoc, Wisconsin 53066

HONEYWELL PHOTOGRAPHIC
4800 East Dry Creek Road
Denver, Colorado 80217

REALIST, INC.
N. 93 W 16288 Megal Drive
Menomonee Falls, Wisconsin 53051

AUTOMATIC CONTINUOUS STILL PROJECTORS—CONT.

SPINDLER & SAUPPE, INC.
1239 Grand Central Avenue
Glendale, California 91201

TEL-A-STORY, INC.
517 Main Street
Davenport, Iowa 52805

VIDEOSONICS SYSTEMS
P.O. Box 3310
Fullerton, California 92634

ZEISS IKON VOIGTLANDER
444 Fifth Avenue
New York, New York 10018

FILMSTRIP PROJECTORS

AUDIO-MASTER CORP.
17 East 45th Street
New York, New York 10017

BELL AND HOWELL CO.
7100 McCormick Road
Chicago, Illinois 60645

CHARLES BESELER CO.
219 South 18th Street
East Orange, New Jersey 07018

CAMERA OPTICS MANUFACTURING CORP.
23 Steinway Street
Long Island City, New York 11105

DUKANE CORP.
103 North 11th Avenue
St. Charles, Illinois 60174

EASTMAN KODAK CO.
343 State Street
Rochester, New York 14750

GRAFLEX, INC.
3750 Monroe Avenue
Rochester, New York 14603

HOFFMAN INFORMATION SYSTEMS
2626 South Peck Road
Monrovia, California 91016

HOOVER BROTHERS
1305 North 14th Street
Temple, Texas 76502

MCCLURE PROJECTORS INC.
1215 Washington Street
Wilmette, Illinois 60091

MITCHELL ART PRODUCTIONS
P. O. Box 43173
Los Angeles, California 90043

MUNDUS COMPANY
P. O. Box 356
Riverdale, Maryland 20840

STANDARD PROJECTOR & EQUIPMENT CO.
733 North Harlem Avenue
Chicago, Illinois 60648

TEL-A-STORY, INC.
517 Main Street
Davenport, Iowa 52805

VICTOR ANIMATOGRAPH CORP.
Hultenius Street
Plainville, Connecticut 06062

VIEWLEX, INC.
Veterans Memorial Highway
Holbrook, L. I., New York 11741

OPAQUE PROJECTORS

AMERICAN OPTICAL CO.
Eggert and Sugar Roads
Buffalo, New York 14215

BAUSCH & LOMB OPTICAL CO.
635 St. Paul Street
Rochester, New York 14625

CHARLES BESELER CO.
219 South 18th Street
East Orange, New Jersey 07018

PROJECTION OPTICS CO., INC.
271 11th Avenue
East Orange, New Jersey 07018

SQUIBB-TAYLOR, INC.
P. O. Box 20158
Dallas, Texas 75229

OVERHEAD TRANSPARENCY PROJECTORS

AMERICAN OPTICAL CO.
Eggert and Sugar Roads
Buffalo, New York 14215

APPLIED SERVICES, INC.
12435 Euclid Avenue
Cleveland, Ohio 44106

BAUSCH & LOMB OPTICAL CO.
635 St. Paul Street
Rochester, New York 14625

OVERHEAD TRANSPARENCY PROJECTORS—CONT.

CHARLES BESELER CO.
219 South 18th Street
East Orange, New Jersey 07018

BUHL OPTICAL CO.
1009 Beech Avenue
Pittsburgh, Pennsylvania 15233

GRAFLEX, INC.
3750 Monroe Avenue
Rochester, New York 14603

GREGORY MAGNETIC INDUSTRIES
P. O. Box 10196
Fort Lauderdale, Florida 33305

KEYSTONE VIEW COMPANY
865 Market Street
Meadville, Pennsylvania 16335

E. LEITZ, INC.
468 Park Avenue, S.
New York, New York 10016

PROJECTION OPTICS CO., INC.
271 11th Avenue
East Orange, New Jersey 07018

TECNIFAX CORP.
195 Appleton Street
Holyoke, Massachusetts 01040

H. WILSON CORPORATION
546 West 119th Street
Chicago, Illinois 60628

16mm MOTION PICTURE PROJECTORS

BELL AND HOWELL CO.
7100 McCormick Road
Chicago, Illinois 60645

CARBONS, INC.
10 Saddle Road
Cedar Knolls, New Jersey 07027

BUSCH FILM & EQUIPMENT CO.
214 South Hamilton
Saginaw, Michigan 48602

EASTMAN KODAK COMPANY
343 State Street
Rochester, New York 14750

GRAFLEX, INC.
3750 Monroe Avenue
Rochester, New York 14603

THE HARWALD CO.
1245 Chicago Avenue
Evanston, Illinois 60202

NORTH AMERICAN PHILLIPS, INC.
100 East 42nd Street
New York, New York 10017

RADIO CORPORATION OF AMERICA
Front and Cooper Streets
Camden, New Jersey 08102

MOVIE-MITE CORPORATION
8811 Puritan Street
Detroit, Michigan 48238

TELEPRO INDUSTRIES, INC.
67 West 44th Street
New York, New York 10036

VICTOR ANIMATOGRAPH CORP.
Hultenius Street
Plainville, Connecticut 06062

16mm MOTION PICTURE PROJECTORS/BUILT-IN SCREENS

BUSCH FILM & EQUIPMENT CO.
214 South Hamilton
Saginaw, Michigan 48602

SLIDE PROJECTORS

AIREQUIPT MFG. CO., INC.
20 Jones Street
New Rochelle, New York 10802

ALLIED IMPEX CORP.
300 Park Avenue South
New York, New York 10010

AMERICAN OPTICAL CO.
Eggert and Sugar Roads
Buffalo, New York 10015

BAUSCH & LOMB OPTICAL CO.
635 St. Paul Street
Rochester, New York 14625

BELL AND HOWELL CO.
7100 McCormick Road
Chicago, Illinois 60645

CHARLES BESELER CO.
219 South 18th Street
East Orange, New Jersey 07018

BRUMBERGER CO., INC.
68 34th Street
Brooklyn, New York 11232

SLIDE PROJECTORS—CONT.

CAMERA OPTICS MANUFACTURING CORP.
23 Steinway Street
Long Island City, New York 11105

EASTMAN KODAK CO.
343 State Street
Rochester, New York 14750

THE FR CORP.
951 Brook Avenue
Bronx, New York 10451

GENARCO, INC.
97 Sutphin Boulevard
Jamaica, New York 11435

GRAFLEX, INC.
3750 Monroe Avenue
Rochester, New York 14603

HONEYWELL, INC.
4800 East Dry Creek Road
Denver, Colorado 80217

HOPPMAN CORPORATION
5410 Port Royal Road
Springfield, Virginia 22151

LA BELLE INDUSTRIES, INC.
510 South Worthington Street
Oconomowoc, Wisconsin 53066

E. LEITZ, INC.
468 Park Avenue South
New York, New York 10016

McCLURE PROJECTORS, INC.
1215 Washington Street
Wilmette, Illinois 60091

MITCHELL ART PRODUCTIONS
P. O. Box 43173
Los Angeles, California 90043

NAREN INDUSTRIES, INC.
2104 North Orchard Street
Chicago, Illinois 60614

REALIST, INC.
N. 93 W. 16288 Megal Drive
Menomonee Falls, Wisconsin 53051

VIEWLEX, INC.
Veterans Memorial Highway
Holbrook, L. I., New York 11741

WOLLENSAK/3-M CO.
2501 Hudson Road
St. Paul, Minnesota 55119

SOUND-SLIDE AND FILMSTRIP PROJECTORS

ARGUS, INC.
5950 West Touhy Avenue
Chicago, Illinois 60648

AUDIO-MASTER CORP.
17 East 45th Street
New York, New York 10017

CHARLES BESELER CO.
219 South 18th Street
East Orange, New Jersey 07018

CAMERA OPTICS MANUFACTURING CORP.
23 Steinway Street
Long Island City, New York 11105

DUKANE CORP.
103 North 11th Avenue
St. Charles, Illinois 60174

GRAFLEX, INC.
3750 Monroe Avenue
Rochester, New York 14603

LA BELLE INDUSTRIES, INC.
510 South Worthington Street
Oconomowoc, Wisconsin 53066

McCLURE PROJECTORS, INC.
1215 Washington Street
Wilmette, Illinois 60091

CHARLES MAYER STUDIOS, INC.
776 Commins Street
Akron, Ohio 44307

VICTOR ANIMATOGRAPH CORP.
Hultenius Street
Plainville, Connecticut 06062

VIEWLEX, INC.
Veterans Memorial Highway
Holbrook, L. I., New York 11741

ADAPTER FOR CONVERTING 16mm PROJECTORS INTO BUILT-IN SCREEN UNITS

H. WILSON CORP.
546 West 119th Street
Chicago, Illinois 60628

LIGHTPROOF SHADES, DRAPES, AND BLINDS

AEROSHADE CO.
433 Oakland Avenue
Waukesha, Wisconsin 53186

LIGHTPROOF SHADES, DRAPES, AND BLINDS—CONT.

E. I. Du Pont de Nemours & Co., Inc.
902 Wilmington Trust Building
Wilmington, Delaware 19898

Forse Manufacturing Co.
2347 Sullivan Avenue
St. Louis, Missouri 63107

Plastic Products Inc.
1822 East Franklin Street
Richmond, Virginia 23223

Oliver C. Steele Manufacturing Co.
Spiceland, Indiana 47385

PROJECTION POINTERS

Burke & James, Inc.
333 West Lake Street
Chicago, Illinois 60606

Ednalite Research Corp.
200 North Water Street
Peekskill, New York 10566

E. Leitz, Inc.
468 Park Avenue South
New York, New York 10016

F. Reiter Co.
3340 Bonnie Hill Drive
Hollywood, California 90028

Squibb-Taylor, Inc.
P.O. Box 20158
Dallas, Texas 75229

Williams, Brown & Earle, Inc.
904-906 Chestnut Street
Philadelphia, Pennsylvania 19107

PROJECTION SCREENS

Burleigh-Cashman Company
South Main Street
Franklin, New Hampshire 03235

Commercial Picture Equipment, Inc.
5719 Broadway
Chicago, Illinois 60626

Da-Lite Screen Co., Inc.
Road 15 North
Warsaw, Indiana 46580

Knox Manufacturing Co.
9715 Soreng Avenue
Schiller Park, Illinois 60176

A. J. Nystrom & Co.
3333 Elston Avenue
Chicago, Illinois 60618

Picture Recording Company
321 Concord Road
Oconomowoc, Wisconsin 53066

Polacoat, Inc.
9750 Conklin Road
Blue Ash, Ohio 45242

Radiant Manufacturing Corp.
8220 North Austin Avenue
Morton Grove, Illinois 60053

Frank K. Reid Co.
1210 Westway Boulevard
McAllen, Texas 78501

Standard Projector & Equipment Co., Inc.
733 North Harlem Avenue
Chicago, Illinois 60648

Strobel Vision
917 East Meadow Place
Milwaukee, Wisconsin 53217

PROJECTION TABLES AND STANDS

Advance Products Co.
2300 East Douglas Avenue
Wichita, Kansas 67214

Bausch & Lomb Optical Co.
635 St. Paul Street
Rochester, New York 14625

Jack C. Coffey Co., Inc.
710 Seventeenth Street
North Chicago, Illinois 60064

Colrod Manufacturing Co.
615 Marlboro Avenue
Chattanooga, Tennessee 37411

Commercial Picture Equipment, Inc.
5719 North Broadway
Chicago, Illinois 60626

Cousino Products
1941 Franklin Avenue
Toledo, Ohio 43624

PROJECTION TABLES AND STANDS—CONT.

GRUBER PRODUCTS CO.
5254 Jackman Road
Toledo, Ohio 43613

THE HARWALD CO.
1245 Chicago Avenue
Evanston, Illinois 60202

E. LEITZ, INC.
468 Park Avenue South
New York, New York 10016

HOWARD B. MARKS CO.
2614 Nicollet Avenue
Minneapolis, Minnesota 55408

MILLER MANUFACTURING CO.
P.O. Box 29456
Atlanta, Georgia 30329

NEUMADE PRODUCTS CORP.
250 West 57th Street
New York, New York 10019

SAFE-LOCK, INC.
870 West 25th Street
Hialeah, Florida 33010

SMITH SYSTEM MANUFACTURING CO
56 Emerald Street, S.E.
Minneapolis, Minnesota 55414

SPINDLER & SAUPPE, INC.
1239 Grand Central Avenue
Glendale, California 91201

SQUIBB-TAYLOR, INC.
P. O. Box 20158
Dallas, Texas 75229

VICTOR ANIMATOGRAPH CORP.
Hultenius Street
Plainville, Connecticut 06062

WALLACH AND ASSOCIATES, INC
570 Euclid Avenue
Cleveland, Ohio 44103

H. WILSON CORP.
546 West 119th Street
Chicago, Illinois 60628

REAR PROJECTION SCREENS

PICTURE RECORDING COMPANY
321 Concord Road
Oconomowoc, Wisconsin 53066

VISUAL EQUIPMENT

BACKGROUND PANELS

VISUAL MERCHANDISING
P. O. Box 1408
Beverly Hills, California

EASELS (AND EASEL-MOUNTED BLACKBOARDS, FLIP CHARTS, AND MAGNET BOARDS)

ADVANCE PRODUCTS CO.
2300 East Douglas Avenue
Wichita, Kansas 67214

ARLINGTON ALUMINUM CO.
19303 West Davison Avenue
Detroit, Michigan 48223

CHART-PAK, INC.
1 River Road
Leeds, Massachusetts 01053

CHARLES MAYER STUDIOS, INC.
776 Commins Street
Akron, Ohio 44307

ORAVISUAL CO., INC.
P. O. Box 11150
St. Petersburg, Florida 33733

FLANNEL BOARDS

FLOREZ, INC.
815 Bates Street
Detroit, Michigan 48226

CHARLES MAYER STUDIOS, INC.
776 Commins Street
Akron, Ohio 44307

ORAVISUAL CO., INC.
P. O. Box 11150
St. Petersburg, Florida 33733

PRESENTATION BINDERS (NOTEBOOKS, PORTABLE DISPLAYS)

BELFORD CO.
149 West 24th Street
New York, New York 10011

PRESENTATION BINDERS (NOTEBOOKS, PORTABLE DISPLAYS)—CONT.

CLARENCE H. COMPTON CO.
6210 North Milwaukee Avenue
Chicago, Illinois 60646

GENERAL BINDING CORP.
1101 Skokie Highway
Northbrook, Illinois 60062

JOSHUA MEIER COMPANY, INC.
610 West 26th Street
New York, New York 10011

SALES TOOLS, INC.
1700 West Washington Boulevard
Chicago, Illinois 60612

PRESENTATION PANELS, BULLETIN BOARDS, BLACKBOARDS (UPRIGHT)

SALES TOOLS, INC.
1700 West Washington Boulevard
Chicago, Illinois 60612

LECTERNS

CHARLES MAYER STUDIOS, INC.
776 Commins Street
Akron, Ohio 44307

NEWCOMB AUDIO PRODUCTS CO.
12881 Bradley Avenue
Sylmar, California 91342

ORAVISUAL CO., INC.
P. O. Box 11150
St. Petersburg, Florida 33733

SOUND-CRAFT SYSTEMS
Petit Jean Mountain
Morrilton, Arkansas 72110

POWER MEGAPHONES

ANTREX CORP.
3825 West Montrose
Chicago, Illinois 60647

AUDIO EQUIPMENT CO., INC.
77 Harbor Road
Port Washington, New York 11050

SOUND-CRAFT SYSTEMS
Petit Jean Mountain
Morrilton, Arkansas 72110

PORTABLE TAPE RECORDERS (UNDER 10 POUNDS)

AMERICAN GELOSO ELECTRONICS, INC.
251 Park Avenue South
New York, New York 10010

GEISS-AMERICA
6901 Hamlin Street
Lincolnwood, Illinois 60645

AUDIO EQUIPMENT

RECORD PLAYERS

A/V EQUIPMENT & SUPPLIES
9628 Garden Grove Boulevard
Garden Grove, California 92640

AUDIO-MASTER CORPORATION
17 East 45th Street
New York, New York 10017

AUDIOTRONICS CORPORATION
P. O. Box 151
North Hollywood, California 91605

BOGEN COMMUNICATIONS
P. O. Box 500
Paramus, New Jersey 07652

L. CHARLTON GREENE CO.
The Millstream
Chelmsford, Massachusetts 01824

HAMILTON ELECTRONICS CORP.
2726 Pratt Avenue
Chicago, Illinois 60645

NEWCOMB AUDIO PRODUCTS CO.
12881 Bradley Avenue
Sylmar, California 91342

RHEEM CALIFONE CORP.
5922 Bowcroft Street
Los Angeles, California 90016

RADIO CORPORATION OF AMERICA
Front and Cooper Streets
Camden, New Jersey 08102

VIEWLEX, INC.
Veterans Memorial Highway
Holbrook, Long Island, N. Y. 11741

TAPE RECORDING AND PLAY-BACK EQUIPMENT

AUDIO-MASTER CORP.
17 East 45th Street
New York, New York 10017

BELL AND HOWELL CO.
7100 McCormick Road
Chicago, Illinois 60645

CONCORD ELECTRONICS CORP.
1935 Armacost Avenue
Los Angeles, California 90025

GRAFLEX, INC.
3750 Monroe Avenue
Rochester, New York 14603

LA BELLE INDUSTRIES, INC.
510 South Worthington Street
Oconomowoc, Wisconsin 53066

MAGNECORD
P. O. Box 1526
Tulsa, Oklahoma 74101

NORTH AMERICAN PHILIPS CO.
100 East 42nd Street
New York, New York 10017

PREMIER ELECTRONIC LABORATORIES
382 Lafayette Street
New York, New York 10003

RADIO CORPORATION OF AMERICA
Front and Cooper Streets
Camden, New Jersey 08102

RHEEM CALIFONE CORP.
5922 Bowcroft Street
Los Angeles, California 90016

TANDBERG OF AMERICA, INC.
11 Sintsink Drive, East
Port Washington, New York 11050

FILM PRODUCERS

(Motion Pictures, Slidefilms, and Slides)

METROPOLITAN NEW YORK:

ANIMATIC PRODUCTS, LTD.
15 West 46th Street
New York, New York 10036

CAMPUS FILM PRODUCTIONS, INC.
20 East 46th Street
New York, New York 10017

COLEMAN PRODUCTIONS, INC.
75 West 45th Street
New York, New York 10036

COLOR ILLUSTRATIONS, INC.
4 East 48th Street
New York, New York 10017

DYNAMIC FILMS, INC.
405 Park Avenue
New York, New York 10022

CHARLES ELMS PRODUCTIONS, INC.
163 Highland Avenue
North Tarrytown, New York 10593

WALTER ENGEL PRODUCTIONS, INC.
20 West 47th Street
New York, New York 10036

MATT FARRELL PRODUCTIONS, INC.
213 East 38th Street
New York, New York 10016

STURGIS-GRANT PRODUCTIONS, INC.
328 East 44th Street
New York, New York 10017

UNITED STATES PRODUCTIONS, INC.
5 East 57th Street
New York, New York 10022

VISUALSCOPE, INCORPORATED
103 Park Avenue
New York, New York 10017

ROGER WADE PRODUCTIONS, INC.
16 West 46th Street
New York, New York 10036

WILLARD PICTURES, INC.
45 West 45th Street
New York, New York 10036

NEW YORK STATE:

HOLLAND-WEGMAN PRODUCTIONS
207 Delaware Avenue
Buffalo, New York 14202

NEW YORK STATE—CONT.

INSTITUTE OF VISUAL COMMUNICATIONS, INC.
P. O. Box 268
Scarsdale, New York 10583

MIDDLE ATLANTIC:

CREATIVE ARTS STUDIO, INC.
814 H Street, N. W.
Washington, D. C. 20001

CALVIN-DE FRENES CORPORATION
1909-19 Buttonwood Street
Philadelphia, Pennsylvania 19130

SOUTHEAST:

FOTOVOX, INC.
752 South Somerville
Memphis, Tennessee

EAST CENTRAL:

FLOREZ INCORPORATED
815 Bates Street
Detroit, Michigan 48226

THE JAM HANDY ORGANIZATION, INC.
2821 East Grand Boulevard
Detroit, Michigan 48211

REGAN PRODUCTIONS, INC.
19730 Ralston
Detroit, Michigan 48203

VIDEO FILMS, INCORPORATED
1004 East Jefferson Avenue
Detroit, Michigan 48207

CINECRAFT, INCORPORATED
2515 Franklin Boulevard
Cleveland, Ohio 44113

INDUSTRIAL MOTION PICTURES, INCORPORATED
3211 Payne Avenue
Cleveland, Ohio 44114

METROPOLITAN CHICAGO AREA:

GILBERT ALTSCHUL PRODUCTIONS, INC.
909 W. Diversey Parkway
Chicago, Illinois 60614

ATLAS FILM CORPORATION
1111 South Boulevard
Oak Park, Illinois 60302

CHICAGO FILM LABORATORY, INC.
1322 West Belmont Avenue
Chicago, Illinois 60657

JOHN COLBURN ASSOCIATES, INC.
1215 Washington Avenue
Wilmette, Illinois 60091

DOUGLAS PRODUCTIONS
10 West Kinzie Street
Chicago, Illinois 60610

CAL DUNN STUDIOS, INC.
141 West Ohio Street
Chicago, Illinois 60610

INTERLOCK PRODUCTIONS, INC.
127 South Wacker Drive
Chicago, Illinois 60606

JACK LIEB PRODUCTIONS
1230 W. Washington Boulevard
Chicago, Illinois 60607

FRED A. NILES PRODUCTIONS, INC.
1058 West Washington Boulevard
Chicago, Illinois 60607

PILOT PRODUCTIONS, INCORPORATED
1819 Ridge Avenue
Evanston, Illinois 60201

SARRA-CHICAGO, INC.
16 East Ontario Street
Chicago, Illinois 60611

WILDING, INC.
1345 Argyle Street
Chicago, Illinois 60640

WEST CENTRAL STATES REGION:

CENTRON CORPORATION, INC.
West Ninth Street at Avalon Road
Lawrence, Kansas 66044

EMPIRE PHOTOSOUND INCORPORATED
4444 W. 76th Street
Minneapolis, Minnesota 55435

REID H. RAY FILM INDUSTRIES, INC.
2269 Ford Parkway
St. Paul, Minnesota 55116

WEST CENTRAL STATES REGION—CONT.

CONDOR PRODUCTIONS, INC.
3024 North Lindbergh Blvd.
St. Louis, Missouri 63074

WALTER S. CRAIG FILM PRODUCTIONS
4315 Burt Street
Omaha, Nebraska 68131

SOUTHWEST:

JAMIESON FILM COMPANY
3825 Bryan Street
Dallas, Texas 75204

MOUNTAIN STATES:

SONOCHROME PICTURES, INC.
995 South Clermont Street
Denver, Colorado 80222

WEST COAST—

METROPOLITAN LOS ANGELES:

HARRIS-TUCHMAN PRODUCTIONS, INC.
715 North Highland
Hollywood, California 90038

PARTHENON PICTURES—HOLLYWOOD
2625 Temple Street
Hollywood, California 90026

PICTURES FOR BUSINESS
1260 North Wilcox Avenue
Hollywood, California 90028

QUARTET FILMS, INC.
5631 Hollywood Blvd.
Hollywood, California 90028

ROCKET PICTURES, INC.
1150 W. Olive Avenue
Burbank, California 91506

F. K. ROCKETT PRODUCTIONS, INC.
5451 Laurel Canyon Blvd.
North Hollywood, California 91607

TECHNICAL COMMUNICATIONS, INC.
10340 Santa Monica Blvd.
Los Angeles, California 90025

WEST COAST—SAN FRANCISCO:

MARVIN BECKER FILMS
915 Howard Street
San Francisco, California 94103

ROY NOLAN PRODUCTIONS
181 Second Street
San Francisco, California 94105

PRINCIPAL BUSINESS DIRECTORIES

(Prices subject to change at time of printing)

ACCESSORIES BUYING GUIDE ISSUE OF MOBIL HOME JOURNAL, DAVIS PUBLICATIONS, INC., 505 Park Ave., New York, N. Y. 10022. Published in June. Yearly subscription, $5.

ACCESSORIES DIRECTORY, WOMEN'S WEAR DAILY, FAIRCHILD PUBLICATIONS, INC., 7 E. 12th St., New York, N. Y. 10003. Published in April and October. Price, 50 cents. Lists New York City manufacturers of women's accessories.

ADVERTISING, MARKETING, PUBLIC RELATIONS EDUCATION IN U.S., AMERICAN ADVERTISING FEDERATION, 655 Madison Ave., New York, N. Y. 10021. Price, $3. Includes 1,000 degree-granting U.S. colleges; advertising, marketing.

AEROSPACE YEARBOOK, SPARTAN BOOKS, A DIVISION OF BOOKS, INC., 1250 Connecticut Ave., N.W., Washington, D.C. 20036. Published annually. Price, 1967 edition, $11. Official publication of The Aerospace Industries Association. Pictorial review of aerospace events. A standard reference of U.S. aircraft, missiles, spacecraft, launch vehicles, drones, systems, engines, and sounding rockets. Vital data on leading aerospace manufacturers, government research and development, and civil aviation.

AGRI-BUSINESS BUYERS' REFERENCE, GRAIN TRADE BUYERS' GUIDE Co., 141 W. Jackson Blvd., Chicago, Ill. 60604. Published annually in March. Price, $6. Contains several hundred classified lists of manufacturers and suppliers of equipment for grain, feed, fertilizer, field seed, and farm supply handlers and processors, and of those servicing such equipment.

AGRICULTURAL ENGINEERS YEARBOOK, AMERICAN SOCIETY OF AGRICULTURAL ENGINEERS, 420 Main St., St. Joseph, Mich. 49085. Published annually. Price, $7.50. Includes ASAE standards, recommendations, data; roster of ASAE members; product directory; list of consultants and trade associations.

AIR CONDITIONING, HEATING & REFRIGERATION NEWS DIRECTORY ISSUE, BUSINESS NEWS PUBLISHING Co., 450 W. Fort St., Detroit, Mich. 48226. Issued in December. Included in yearly subscription price of $6. Lists manufacturers and distributors of air conditioning, heating, and refrigerating equipment.

AIR FORCE ALMANAC, AIR FORCE ASSN., 1750 Pennsylvania Ave., N.W., Washington, D.C. 20006. Published in September. Included in yearly subscription price of *Air Force & Space Digest*—$7.

AIR FORWARDER, BUDD PUBLICATIONS, INC., 26 Beaver St., New York, N. Y. 10004. Published annually in July.

AIRLINE GUIDE, OFFICIAL, THE REUBEN H. DONNELLEY CORP., 209 Jackson Blvd., Chicago, Ill. 60606. Published monthly. North American Edition, $2.25 per copy, $18 per year; World-Wide Edition, $2.50 per copy, $24 per year. Also an international Quick Reference Edition at $5 per copy or $48 per year, or North America Quick Reference (twice monthly) at $2.50 per copy or $25 or $40 per year. Contains airline lists, schedules, and fares; alphabetical lists of cities served by air, with the airlines serving them. Quick Reference Edition shows lines and schedules for alphabetical list of cities.

AIRPORT AND BUSINESS FLYING DIRECTORY, AVIATION WEEK MAGAZINE, McGRAW-HILL, INC., 330 W. 42nd St., New York, N. Y. 10036. Published annually. Price, $5. Includes information on 4,500 airports in U.S.

ALCOHOLIC BEVERAGE INDUSTRY, RED BOOK ENCYCLOPEDIA OF, SCHWARTZ PUBLICATIONS, INC., 6 W. 57th St., New York, N. Y. 10019. Issued yearly. Price, $19.50.

AMERICAN ECONOMIC ASSOCIATION DIRECTORY OR HANDBOOK, AMERICAN ECONOMIC ASSOCIATION, 629 Noyes St., Evanston, Ill. 60201. Published irregularly; 1964 edition is available. Single copy, $8. Lists the 11,300 members of the association, including many teachers, with brief biographies of most of them.

AMERICAN FIRMS, SOURCES OF INFORMATION ON, FOR INTERNATIONAL BUYERS, U.S. GOVERNMENT PRINTING OFFICE, Washington, D.C. 20402. Catalog No. C 42.2:Am3/965. Price, 15 cents.

AMERICAN JEWISH ORGANIZATIONS DIRECTORY, FRENKEL MAILING SERVICE, 24 Rutgers St., New York, N. Y., 10002. Price, $10. Includes 4,700 synagogues, Jewish social service organizations, hotels, restaurants, Jewish community leaders.

AMERICA'S EDUCATION PRESS, EDUCATIONAL PRESS ASSOCIATION OF AMERICA, SCHOOL OF JOURNALISM, NEWHOUSE COMMUNICATIONS CENTER, Syracuse University, Syracuse, N. Y. 13210. Educational periodicals. Free to members; $15 to others.

ANALYTICAL CHEMISTRY LABORATORY GUIDE, AMERICAN CHEMICAL SOCIETY, 1155 16th St., N.W., Washington, D.C. 20036. Issued in July. Yearly subscription, $5; to members, $4.

ANNUAL DIRECTORY OF ENGINEERING COLLEGE RESEARCH AND GRADUATE STUDY (1966); AMERICAN SOCIETY FOR ENGINEERING EDUCATION, 1345 Connecticut Ave., N.W., Washington, D.C. 20036. Includes 11,000 research projects in 121 American colleges and universities, administrative officers, personnel engaged in research, etc. Price, $7.

APOTHECARY, APOTHECARY PUBLISHING CO., 375 Broadway, Boston, Mass. 02111. Subscription price, $3.

APPAREL MANUFACTURER DIRECTORY, HAIRE PUBLISHING CO., 111 Fourth Ave., New York, N. Y. 10003. Issued in July. Single copy, $3. Lists suppliers of machinery, equipment, fabrics, trimmings, and services for the apparel industry.

APPAREL TRADES BOOK, CREDIT CLEARING HOUSE DIVISION OF DUN & BRADSTREET, INC., 99 Church St., New York, N. Y. 10008. Includes 120,000 wholesalers and retailers in apparel and accessory lines.

APPLE ASSOCIATION REFERENCE BOOK, INTERNATIONAL, APPLE ASSOCIATION REFERENCE BOOK, 1302 18th St., N.W., Washington, D.C. 20036. Published annually. Includes members of the association in U.S., Canada, and around the world.

ARCHITECTS, AMERICAN DIRECTORY, R. R. BOWKER CO., 1180 Avenue of the Americas, New York, N. Y. 10036. Price, $25. Includes 14,600 architects in U.S., and geographical listing of architectural firms.

ARENA, AUDITORIUM & STADIUM GUIDE, BILLBOARD PUBLISHING CO., 188 W. Randolph St., Chicago, Ill. 60601. Published annually, in October. Single copy, $5. Contains two geographical lists (indoor and outdoor) of U.S. arenas, auditoriums, grandstands, stadiums, and theaters.

ART, AMERICAN, WHO'S WHO IN, R. R. BOWKER CO., 1180 Avenue of the Americas, New York, N. Y. 10036. Published at three-year intervals. Price, $22.50 net prepaid. Contains short biographies of artists, art executives, illustrators, and sculptors, as well as lists of exhibitions, and an index based on geography. In addition, the 1966 edition includes collectors, patrons of art, art critics and editors, plus other leaders in the art field.

ART, COMMERCIAL, & PHOTOGRAPHY, WHO'S WHO IN, DIRECTOR'S ART INSTITUTE, INC., 176 E. 75th St., New York, N. Y. 10021. Published every other year (even years). Price, $20. Lists artists, art directors, photographers, and agents.

ART DIRECTORY, AMERICAN, R. R. BOWKER CO., 1180 Avenue of the Americas, New York, N. Y. 10036. Published every three years. Price, $22.50. Includes art museums, schools and associations in the U.S. and Canada; art magazines, fellowships and scholarships; major museums and art schools abroad; traveling exhibitions.

ARTISTS' GUIDE, published annually by AMERICAN ARTIST, 165 W. 46th St., New York, N. Y. 10036, as an independent publication. Published August 25. Includes product classifications, brand names, manufacturers' index, art books by name of book, author, type and price, also major articles on media and technique. Cost, $1.25 per copy. Sold in art stores and on newsstands.

ATOMIC ENERGY COMMISSION, SELLING TO, PROCUREMENT PROGRAM & ORGANIZATION, PURCHASING OFFICES, ETC., U.S. GOVERNMENT PRINTING OFFICE, Washington, D.C. 20402. Catalog No. Y 3. At 7:2 Se 4/2/966. Price, 20 cents.

AUDIO-VISUAL COMMUNICATIONS, UNITED BUSINESS PUBLICATIONS, INC., 200 Madison Ave., New York, N. Y. 10016. Issued quarterly in 1967, bimonthly in 1968. Single copy, $1.50.

AUDIO-VISUAL EQUIPMENT DIRECTORY, NATIONAL AUDIO-VISUAL ASSN., INC., 3150 Spring St., Fairfax, Va. 22030. Published annually. Price, $6 if invoiced; $5.50 if check accompanies order.

AUDIO-VISUAL MATERIALS, BLUE BOOK OF, EDUCATIONAL SCREEN & AUDIO-VISUAL GUIDE, 434 S. Wabash Ave., Chicago, Ill. 60605. Published annually in August. Price, $1 alone, or $4 as part of an annual subscription to *Educational Screen & Audio-Visual Guide.* Contains classified lists of manufacturers and distributors of audio-visual equipment and materials.

(Automatic Merchandising) DIRECTORY OF MEMBERS, NATIONAL AUTOMATIC MERCHANDISING ASSOCIATION, 7 S. Dearborn St., Chicago, Ill. 60603. Published in June. Single copy, $25. Contains alphabetical listings of vending service companies, machine manufacturers and supplier members of NAMA. Information about the types of products supplied or manufactured is given for each company.

AUTOMOTIVE BUYERS GUIDE, INTERNATIONAL, the November issue of the foreign-circulated monthly publication *Automobile International,* McGRAW-HILL, INC., 330 W. 42nd St., New York, N. Y. 10036. Available to nonsubscribers at $2. Offers highly detailed classified directory of automotive products manufacturers in U.S. and abroad.

(Automotive Cooling Journal) NATIONAL AUTOMOTIVE RADIATOR SERVICE ASSOCIATION, NARSA, INC., 7600 Macomb Rd., Grosse Ile, Mich. 48138. Published bimonthly.

AUTOMOTIVE DIRECTORY, NATIONAL, OF MANUFACTURERS AND THEIR SALES REPRESENTATIVES, W. R. C. SMITH PUBLISHING Co., 1760 Peachtree Rd. N.W., Atlanta, Ga. 30309. Issued in November. Single copy, $5.

(Automotive Engineers) SAE HANDBOOK, SOCIETY OF AUTOMOTIVE ENGINEERS, INC., 485 Lexington Ave., New York, N. Y. 10017. Published annually in December. Price, $25.

AUTOMOTIVE NEWS ALMANAC, SLOCUM PUBLISHING Co., 965 E. Jefferson Ave., Detroit, Mich. 48207. Issued annually in April. Lists automotive companies, along with their executives, branches, and advertising agencies.

AUTOMOTIVE SAFETY PRODUCTS DIRECTORY, BABCOX BUSINESS PUBLICATIONS, INC., 11 S. Forge St., Akron, Ohio 44304. Issued in June.

AVIATION DIRECTORY, WORLD, AMERICAN AVIATION PUBLICATIONS, INC., 1001 Vermont Ave., N.W., Washington, D.C. 20005. Published in June and December. Price, one to nine copies, $18 each; 10 or more, $16 each in U.S. and Canada. Foreign—one to nine copies, $20 each; 10 or more, $18 each.

AVIATION NEWS, GENERAL, BENDER PUBLICATIONS, INC., 4077 W. Pico, Los Angeles, Calif. 90019. Price, $2.50.

AVIATION WEEK & SPACE TECHNOLOGY, BUYERS' GUIDE, McGRAW-HILL, INC., 330 W. 42nd St., New York, N. Y. 10036. Published annually. Price, 75 cents. Information on 1,800 aerospace products for over 4,000 companies.

BAKING INDUSTRY BUYING DIRECTORY, CLISSOLD PUBLISHING Co., 105 W. Adams St., Chicago, Ill. 60603. Published each February. Price, $2 or $5 subscription price including directory issue. Includes classified list of manufacturers of equipment and supplies, index to trade names. 1967 issue now unavailable.

(Baking) PANADERO, LATINOAMERICANO (LATIN AMERICAN BAKERY)— monthly; **BUYERS' GUIDE ISSUE**—special issue. CLISSOLD INTERNATIONAL, INC., 105 W. Adams St., Chicago, Ill. 60603. (Editorial offices: 1602 Harold St., Houston, Tex. 77006.) Published in July, in Spanish. Controlled circulation.

BANK DIRECTORY, AMERICAN, 777 W. Peachtree St., N.E., Atlanta, Ga. 30308. Published semiannually. Price, $25. Includes 14,000 banks in U.S., with names of officers and directors, principal correspondents, condensed statement figures, telephone number, transit number, and mailing address.

BANKER, AMERICAN (a daily), DIRECTORY ISSUES, AMERICAN BANKER, 67 Pearl St., New York, N. Y. 10004. 130 published annually. Daily subscription price, including directory issue(s), $65. Includes "Who's Who" issue, lists banks with $10,000,000 or more deposits; another shows the 300 largest.

BANKER, INDUSTRIAL, AMERICAN INDUSTRIAL BANKERS ASSOCIATION, 1629 K St., N.W., Washington, D.C. 20006. Issued monthly; subscription price, $6 per year. Circulation, 9,500.

BANKERS ALMANAC AND YEAR BOOK, ILIFFE NTP, INC., 300 E. 42nd St., New York, N.Y. 10017. Published annually. Price, $40. Includes an international guide to the principal banks and insurance offices of the world.

BANKERS DIRECTORY, INTERNATIONAL, RAND MCNALLY & Co., Box 7600, Chicago, Ill. 60680. Published twice a year, in April and September. Price, $40. Includes banks around the world, directors, examiners, bankers' associations, clearinghouses, government financial agencies, etc.

BANKERS DIRECTORY, SOUTHERN, MCFADDEN BUSINESS PUBLICATIONS, INC., 777 West Peachtree St., N.E., Atlanta, Ga. 30308. Issued in April. Price, $10.

BANKS' FINANCE MANUAL, MOODY'S, MOODY'S INVESTORS SERVICE, INC., 99 Church St., New York, N. Y. 10007. Published annually with twice weekly News Reports. Price, $115. Contains lists of banks, insurance companies, investment companies in U.S. and Canada.

BEAUTY AND BARBER SUPPLY DEALERS, DIRECTORY OF. NATIONAL BEAUTY AND BARBER MANUFACTURERS ASSOCIATION, National Press Bldg., Washington, D.C. 20004. Includes all suppliers to beauty salons and barbershops.

BEDDING BUYERS' GUIDE & COMPOSITE CATALOG, BEDDING MAGAZINE, Merchandise Mart Plaza, Chicago, Ill. 60654. Published annually. Price, $3. Includes all known supply sources for bedding manufacturers.

BEET SUGAR COMPANIES, AMERICAN, U.S. BEET SUGAR ASSOCIATION, 920 Tower Bldg., Washington, D.C. 20005. Free.

BEVERAGE INDUSTRY NEWS' CALIFORNIA YEARBOOK, INDUSTRY PUBLICATIONS, INC., 703 Market St., San Francisco, Calif. 94103. Published annually in April. Sold for $1.50 in connection with yearly subscription price of $7.50.

BEVERAGE MEDIA BLUE BOOK NUMBER, BEVERAGE MEDIA, LTD., 251 Park Ave., South, New York, N. Y. 10010. Published annually as a second section of the April issue of *Beverage Media*. Included in yearly subscription rate of $5. Lists brewers, distillers, liquor importers and wholesalers, etc., in New York City and upstate.

(Beverages) EL EMBOTELLADOR'S PLANT OPERATING MANUAL & BUYERS DIRECTORY, KELLER PUBLISHING CORP., 9 E. 35th St., New York, N. Y. 10016. Issued in April, in Spanish. Yearly subscription, $4.

BIOGRAPHIC REGISTER, THE DEPARTMENT OF STATE, U.S. GOVERNMENT PRINTING OFFICE, DIVISION OF PUBLIC DOCUMENTS, Washington, D.C. 20402. Price, $3.50. Includes principal officers of U.S. Department of State; U.S. Information Agency; Foreign Operations Administration, with biographies. Catalog No. S1.69:126—1967 ed.

BOARD MILL DIRECTORY, OFFICIAL, BETTENDORF PUBLICATIONS, INC., 228 N. LaSalle St., Chicago, Ill. 60601. Published each December. Price, $2 or $7 subscription in U.S.A. and Canada ($9 elsewhere), including directory. Includes regular and specialty mills, U.S.A. and Canada.

BOAT OWNERS BUYERS GUIDE, YACHTING PUBLISHING CORP., 50 W. 44th St., New York, N. Y. 10036. Issued in March. Price, $1.50.

BOND DEALERS, MUNICIPAL, U.S. DIRECTORY, THE BOND BUYER, 67 Pearl St., New York, N. Y. 10004. Published semiannually. Price, $10. Includes 1,700 municipal bond dealers and their personnel.

BOOK BUYER'S GUIDE, THE BOOK BUYER'S GUIDE, INC., 1405 N. Broad St., Hillside, N. J. 07205. Published every month. Price, $6.

BOOK INDUSTRY TELEPHONE DIRECTORY, THE: NAMES & NUMBERS, R. R. BOWKER CO., 1180 Avenue of the Americas, New York, N. Y. 10036. Published annually as a supplement to the *Literary Market Place*. Price, $10. Alphabetical listing of companies and people in the book publishing industry, with their addresses and telephone numbers.

BOOK OF THE STATES, THE, THE COUNCIL OF STATE GOVERNMENTS, 1313 E. 60th St., Chicago, Ill. 60637. Published in even years, with two supplements in odd years. Price, $11.50 (with supplements, $15). These prices effective with the 1968-69 edition to be published in 1968, scheduled for spring. 1966-67 edition is sold out. Presents authoritative information, including many state-by-state tables, on the structures, administration, finances, and services of all the state governments. Lists selected officers of each state. The supplements contain, respectively, names of newly elected officials and legislators, and classified lists of administrative officials.

BOOK TRADE DIRECTORY, AMERICAN, R. R. BOWKER CO., 1180 Avenue of the Americas, New York, N. Y. 10036. Revised biennially. Price, $35 prepaid. Lists over 9,000 book outlets in U.S. and Canada, with names of key personnel, specialties, sidelines, etc. Includes publishers, U.S. and foreign; wholesalers, book-trade periodicals, etc.

BOWLING AND BILLIARD BUYERS GUIDE, THE NATIONAL BOWLERS JOURNAL, INC., 506 S. Wabash Ave., Chicago, Ill. 60605. Published annually in January. Controlled circulation. Single copy, $4. Lists about 1,500 manufacturers and suppliers.

BOWLING MAGAZINE'S YEARBOOK ISSUE. AMERICAN BOWLING CONGRESS, 1572 E. Capitol Dr., Milwaukee, Wis. 53211. Published in September. Single copy, $1.

BOXBOARD CONTAINERS' SUPPLIER DIRECTORY, MACLEAN-HUNTER PUBLISHING CORP., 300 W. Adams St., Chicago, Ill. 60606. Issued in January. Yearly subscription, $7. This is a classified directory of 1,500 suppliers to the corrugated, folding carton, rigid box and fiber-tube plants, and paperboard mills.

BOYS' WEAR DIRECTORY, FAIRCHILD PUBLICATIONS, INC., 7 E. 12th St., New York, N. Y. 10003. Published in April and October. Price, 50 cents. Includes New York City manufacturers of boys' wear.

BREWER, AMERICAN, BUYERS' GUIDE, AMERICAN BREWER PUBLISHING CORP., 33 Lyons Pl., Mt. Vernon, N. Y., 10553. Published annually; controlled distribution. Includes manufacturers and suppliers to the brewery industry. Single copy, $5 (plus postage).

BREWERIES, WORLD DIRECTORY OF, AMERICAN BREWER PUBLISHING CORP., 33 Lyons Pl., Mt. Vernon, N. Y. 10553. Published each October. Price, $12 (plus postage). Includes breweries around the world.

(Brick & Clay) AUTOCLAYMATION EQUIPMENT & MATERIALS REVIEW OF BRICK & CLAY RECORD, CAHNERS PUBLISHING CO., 5 S. Wabash Ave., Chicago, Ill. 60603. Issued annually in September. Price, $1 alone or $5 as part of yearly subscription. Lists new products in the brick and clay industry, and their manufacturers and distributors.

BROADCASTING YEARBOOK, BROADCASTING PUBLICATIONS, INC., 1735 DeSales St., N.W., Washington, D.C. 20036. Published each January. Price, $10, effective with January 1968 edition. One-book library of television and radio information. Fifty-one directories, 600 pages, fully indexed.

BROOM MANUFACTURERS BUYING GUIDE, BRUSHWARE PUBLICATIONS, INC., 44 N. Dean St., Englewood, N. J. 07631. Issued in June. Included in yearly subscription price of $4.

BRUSH MANUFACTURERS BUYING GUIDE, BRUSHWARE PUBLICATIONS, INC., 44 N. Dean St., Englewood, N. J. 07631. Issued in June. Included in yearly subscription price of $4.

BRUSHWARE BUYERS' GUIDE, BRUSHWARE PUBLICATIONS, INC., 44 N. Dean St., Englewood, N. J. 07631. Published annually as part of subscription to *Brushware Magazine*. Single copies, $1.50.

BUILDING CONSTRUCTION'S DIRECTORY ISSUE, CAHNERS PUBLISHING CO., INC., 5 S. Wabash Ave., Chicago, Ill. 60603. Published annually in May. Price, $3. Contains classified lists of manufacturers of building materials and equipment, and construction equipment.

BUILDING MATERIAL INDUSTRY REVIEW ISSUE, ANNUAL, OF BUILDING NEWS, BUILDING NEWS, 3055 Overland Ave., Los Angeles, Calif. 90034. Published in October. Included in yearly subscription price of $6.

BUILDING PRODUCTS GUIDE, HUDSON PUBLISHING CO., 175 S. San Antonio St., Los Altos, Calif. 94022. Published quarterly in January, April, July, and October.

BUILDING SUPPLY NEWS, CAHNERS PUBLISHING CO., INC., 5 S. Wabash Ave., Chicago, Ill. 60603. Purchasing and Selling File issue, with Specification Tables. Published annually in February. Price of February issue alone is $2.50; annual subscription, $5. Manufacturers of products sold through lumber and building material dealers; jobbers, wholesalers, distributors.

BUSINESS ABROAD, THE INTERNATIONAL TRADE REVIEW, 466 Lexington Ave., New York, N. Y. 10017. Includes annual directory of foreign and international publications and their U.S. representatives.

BUSINESS DIRECTORIES, AMERICAN, GUIDE TO, PUBLIC AFFAIRS PRESS, 419 New Jersey Ave., S.E., Washington, D.C. 20003. Price, $3.75. Includes 1,800 lists of firms, grouped by industries cited and discussed.

BUSINESS PUBLICATION RATES AND DATA, STANDARD RATE & DATA SERVICE, 5201 Old Orchard Rd., Skokie, Ill. 60076. Published monthly with updating bulletins. Price, $44 a year. Includes U.S. trade and other business publications, officers of magazine publishing companies.

BUTANE-PROPANE NEWS, DIRECTORY AND MARKET DATA ISSUE, BUTANE-PROPANE NEWS, 1543 W. Olympic Blvd., Los Angeles, Calif. 90015. Included with July issue of *News*. Includes manufacturers and suppliers to the liquified petroleum gas industry in U.S.

BUYERS BOOK, PHELON'S RESIDENT, PHELON-SHELDON PUBLICATIONS, INC., 32 Union Sq., New York, N. Y. 10003. Published in February. Price, $15. Includes ready-to-wear and dry goods buyers, 700 resident buyers, merchandisers, chain headquarters.

BUYERS PURCHASING DIGEST, BUYERS PURCHASING DIGEST CO., 918 N.E. 20th Ave., Ft. Lauderdale, Fla. 33304. Published monthly.

BUYING GUIDE MAGAZINE, DSC FOUNDATION, INC., 1290 Avenue of the Americas, New York, N. Y. 10019. Published each month except December. Price, 16 cents.

(Cable addresses) MARCONI'S INTERNATIONAL REGISTER, TELEGRAPHIC CABLE & RADIO REGISTRATIONS, INC., 2 Broadway, New York, N. Y. 10004. Price, $20. Lists 50,000 internationally prominent companies with their street addresses, telephone and telex numbers, nature of business, and cable address. Also, alphabetical cable address index. Published annually since 1898.

CALIFORNIA EMPLOYMENT DIRECTORY, CALIFORNIA EMPLOYMENT DIRECTORY, INC., 580 Market St., San Francisco, Calif. 94104. Published in January. Price, $10. Also available in sections, with cover, at $2 each. (Services; electronics; manufacturing, general; retailing/construction; Civil Service.)

(California) ENGINEERING & GRADING CONTRACTORS DIRECTORY, ENGINEERING & GRADING CONTRACTORS ASSOCIATION, 8402 Allport Ave., Santa Fe Springs, Calif. 90670. Published in March.

CALIFORNIA MANUFACTURERS REGISTER, TIMES-MIRROR PRESS, 1115 S. Boyle Ave., Los Angeles, Calif. 90023. Published in January. Price, $35.

CAMPING MAGAZINE, ANNUAL BUYING GUIDE, GALLOWAY CORPORATION, 5 Mountain Ave., North Plainfield, N. J. 07060. Published each March. Price, $6. Subscription price includes *Buying Guide.*

(Canada) DIRECTORY OF DIRECTORIES, THE FINANCIAL POST, 481 University Ave., Toronto 2, Ontario. Published annually in the spring. Price, $17 (Canadian dollars). Contains two alphabetical lists: one of Canadian executives and directors of Canadian companies; and one of Canadian companies, including executives and directors regardless of their place of residence.

CANADA YEAR BOOK, DOMINION BUREAU OF STATISTICS, Ottawa, Ontario. Published annually. Cloth bound, $5; paper bound, $3. Contains textual and statistical material dealing with the physical features of the country; machinery of government; vital statistics; public health and welfare; education; atomic, space, and industrial research; agriculture; transportation; communications; domestic and foreign trade; finance; national income and expenditure; information sources.

CANADIAN ALMANAC & DIRECTORY, THE COPP CLARK PUBLISHING CO., 517 Wellington St., W., Toronto 2B, Ontario. Published annually. Price, $13.75. Contains full astronomical tables, climate, population, etc. Lists Canadian and British government officials, diplomatic personnel in Canada and abroad. Has a complete legal directory, a post office and shipping guide, customs regulations and chambers of commerce, banks, insurance companies, stock exchanges, school boards, colleges, associations and vital statistics. Over 800 pages. Comprehensive index.

CANADIAN ADVERTISING RATES AND DATA, STANDARD RATE & DATA SERVICE, 5201 Old Orchard Rd., Skokie, Ill. 60076, in collaboration with Maclean-Hunter, Toronto, Canada. Published monthly with updating bulletins. Price, $20. Outlines data for Canadian media including business papers, consumer magazines, farm publications, newspapers, radio and television stations, networks, and transit advertising.

CANADIAN TRADE DIRECTORY, FRASER'S, THE MACLEAN-HUNTER PUBLISHING CO., LTD., 481 University Ave., Toronto 2, Canada. Annual. Price, $25. Listing over 30,000 Canadian manufacturers, wholesalers, distributors and agents alphabetically by product. 2,000 pages.

CANDY BUYERS' DIRECTORY, MANUFACTURING CONFECTIONER PUBLISHING CO., 1031 South Blvd., Oak Park, Ill. 60302. Published annually. Price, $5. Includes commercial candy manufacturers and brokers.

CANDY, INDUSTRY CATALOG & FORMULA BOOK, MAGAZINES FOR INDUSTRY, INC., 777 Third Ave., New York, N. Y. 10017. Published annually in April. Price, $5. Lists the industry's sources of equipment, materials, supplies, and services.

CANDY WHOLESALER, NATIONAL, ANNUAL CONVENTION ISSUE, NATIONAL CANDY WHOLESALERS ASSOCIATION, 1343 L St., N.W., Washington, D.C. 20005. Published each August. Price, $5, including the following directories: January—Bulk Confectionery and Packaging Supplies; February—Vending Goods; March—Fountain Supplies; April—Penny Candy; May—5 cent & 10 cent Bars; June—Fund Raising Goods; July—Halloween Candy; September—Christmas Candy; October—Sundries, Toys and Novelties; November—Valentine and Easter Candy; December—Annual Membership Directory.

CANNER/PACKER YEARBOOK, VANCE PUBLISHING CORP., 300 W. Adams St., Chicago, Ill. 60606. Annual. Includes manufacturers and suppliers to food packing industry.

CANNERS DIRECTORY, NATIONAL CANNERS ASSN., 1133 20th St., N.W., Washington, D.C. 20036. Published biennially. Price, $5. Includes geographical list of canners and members of NCA; also members of National Food Brokers Assn., and Canning Machinery & Supplies Assn.

CAR AND LOCOMOTIVE CYCLOPEDIA, SIMMONS-BOARDMAN PUBLISHING CORP., 30 Church St., New York, N. Y. 10007. Price, $20.

CASUAL LIVING DIRECTORY, WILSIR PUBLICATIONS, 301 Sylvan Ave., Englewood Cliffs, N. J. 07632.

CATHOLIC DIRECTORY—THE OFFICIAL, P. J. KENEDY & SONS, 12 Barclay St., New York, N. Y. 10007. Issued annually in May. Hardbound, deluxe edition, $15 (1968 issue will be $17.50); paperbound edition, $13 (1968 edition will be $15).

CATHOLIC EDUCATION, SUMMARY OF, UNITED STATES CATHOLIC CONFERENCE, 1312 Massachusetts Ave., N.W., Washington, D.C. 20005. Gives statistical data on each level of education for two years. Published biennially. Price, $2 prepaid.

CATHOLIC PRESS DIRECTORY, CATHOLIC PRESS ASSOCIATION OF U.S., 432 Park Avenue, S., New York, N. Y. 10016. Price, $5. Includes Catholic publications in U.S. and Canada.

CATHOLIC SCHOOL GUIDE, THE CATHOLIC NEWS PUBLISHING CO., INC., 251 Park Ave. S., New York, N. Y. 10010. Published in four regional editions: Metropolitan New York; New England; Upper New York State; Pennsylvania. Includes all Catholic colleges in U.S.A., Catholic boarding schools in the East, Catholic high schools and grammar schools in the Northeast. Information includes: name, address, phone number, officials, rates, number of students.

CATHOLIC SECONDARY SCHOOLS IN THE U.S.A., A LISTING OF, UNITED STATES CATHOLIC CONFERENCE, Department of Education, 1312 Massachusetts Ave., N.W., Washington, D.C. 20005. Published biennially. Price, $2 per copy prepaid. Complete list of Catholic secondary schools with name and address. Current edition published in July 1967.

CEMETERY DIRECTORY, INTERNATIONAL, AMERICAN CEMETERY ASSOCIATION, 329 E. Broad St., Columbus, Ohio 43215. Price, $40. Lists 10,000 cemeteries, U.S. and Canada.

CERAMIC COMPANIES, ANNUAL DIRECTORY OF, AMERICAN CERAMIC SOCIETY, 4055 N. High St., Columbus, Ohio 43214. Published annually in January. Price, $2.50. Lists ceramic companies.

CERAMIC DATA BOOK, CAHNERS PUBLISHING Co., 5 S. Wabash Ave., Chicago, Ill. 60603. Single copy, $3.50. Includes classified and alphabetical lists of the manufacturers and suppliers to the ceramic industry.

CERAMIC SOCIETY BULLETIN, AMERICAN, ROSTER ISSUE, AMERICAN CERAMIC SOCIETY, INC., 4055 N. High St., Columbus, Ohio 43214. Published annually. Subscription price, including directory issue, $6. Foreign postage, $2. Single copies, $2 (plus postage). Includes members of the society.

(Ceramics) AUTORAMICS ISSUE OF CERAMIC INDUSTRY, CAHNERS PUBLISHING Co., 5 S. Wabash Ave., Chicago, Ill. 60603. Published annually in September. Price, $1, if purchased separately. No charge if part of annual subscription. Describes the year's new automatic machinery and equipment in the ceramics field, with a listing of manufacturers and distributors.

CHAIN STORE AGE BUYERS' REFERENCE ISSUE & DIRECTORY OF MANUFACTURERS, CHAIN STORE AGE, 2 Park Ave., New York, N. Y. 10016, as part of Variety-General Merchandise Editions. Includes listing of manufacturers of resale merchandise sold in variety-general merchandise chains. Also includes merchandising trends and operations figures for major chains. Single copy, $2.

CHEMICAL IMPORTERS AND DEALERS, TRADE LISTS, BUREAU OF INTERNATIONAL COMMERCE, Washington, D.C. 20230. Price, $1. Separate trade lists of foreign business firms available for 55 countries.

CHEMICALS & GASES, SELECTED INORGANIC, DIRECTORY OF MANUFACTURERS OF, 1960, U.S. GOVERNMENT PRINTING OFFICE, Washington, D.C. 20402. Catalog No. C 3.158: M28A (60)-13/supp. 3. Price, 25 cents.

(Chicago) BUILDING CONSTRUCTION EMPLOYERS' DIRECTORY, BUILDING CONSTRUCTION EMPLOYERS' ASSOCIATION, INC., 228 N. LaSalle St., Chicago, Ill. 60601. Published each February. Includes contractors and subcontractors in the Chicago building trades, building trade unions.

CHICAGO BUYERS' GUIDE, CHICAGO ASSOCIATION OF COMMERCE & INDUSTRY, 30 W. Monroe St., Chicago, Ill. 60603. Published annually. Free. This is a list of suppliers in the Chicago metropolitan area.

CHICAGO, FOREIGN CONSULATES IN, CHICAGO ASSOCIATION OF COMMERCE & INDUSTRY, 30 W. Monroe St., Chicago, Ill. 60603. Free to CACI members; 50 cents to others. Contains a list of consulates and their personnel.

CHICAGO, METROPOLITAN, MAJOR EMPLOYERS, CHICAGO ASSOCIATION OF COMMERCE & INDUSTRY, 30 W. Monroe St., Chicago, Ill. 60603. Published periodically. Price, $7. This is a list of Chicago firms employing over 250 people.

CHICAGO TRANSPORTATION FACTS, CHICAGO ASSOCIATION OF COMMERCE & INDUSTRY, 30 W. Monroe St., Chicago, Ill. 60603. Price, $2. A 68-page publication listing Chicago transportation media, maps, and other material of interest to shippers, receivers, and carriers of all types. Includes railroads, motor carriers, airlines, freight forwarders, express companies, steamship lines, conferences and representatives, barge lines, bus lines, warehouses, movers, and commercial piers, wharves, and docks.

CHICAGO AND VICINITY BUILDING TRADES REFERENCE BOOK, BUILDERS' COMMERCIAL AGENCY, INC., 105 N. Oak Park Ave., Oak Park Ill. Published each January. Includes contractors, building material dealers and buyers, banks, mortgage makers. Price, $97.50.

CHILDREN, DIRECTORY FOR EXCEPTIONAL, PORTER SARGENT, 11 Beacon St., Boston, Mass. 02108. Complete listing of all facilities available for the instruction, care, development and encouragement of the exceptional child. Contains descriptions of schools, homes, hospitals, clinics and services for the retarded, disturbed, maladjusted and physically handicapped. Price, $7.

(Children's wear) EARNSHAW'S INFANTS' & CHILDREN'S REVIEW, EARNSHAW PUBLICATIONS, INC., 101 W. 31st St., New York, N. Y. 10001. Published monthly for retailers and manufacturers of clothing for infants and children.

CHINA, GLASS AND TABLEWARE RED BOOK, Ebel-Doctorow Publications, Inc., 23 E. 26th St., New York, N. Y. 10010. Published annually in May. Price, $5. Includes importers, manufacturers, and representatives of chinaware, glassware, and tableware products.

CHURCHES, AMERICAN, YEARBOOK, National Council of Churches, 475 Riverside Dr., New York, N. Y. 10027. Published annually. Price, $7.50. Includes executive officials of national cooperative organizations, religious bodies in U.S. and Canada, general state and local councils, seminaries, colleges, and religious periodicals.

CHURCH MANAGEMENT'S ANNUAL DIRECTORY NUMBER, Church Management, Inc., 13308 Euclid Ave., Cleveland, Ohio 44112. Issued in July. Single copy, $1; per year, $5.

CLUB EXECUTIVE MAGAZINE, THE ANNUAL AUGUST DIRECTORY ISSUE, Army Times Publishing Co., 2201 M St., N.W., Washington, D.C. 20037.

CLUB MANAGEMENT'S EQUIPMENT & HOTEL EXPOSITION ISSUE, Commerce Publishing Co., 408 Olive St., St. Louis, Mo. 63102. Published in October. Included in annual subscription price of $3.

COAL BUYERS MANUAL, KEYSTONE, McGraw-Hill, Inc., 330 W. 42nd St., New York, N. Y. 10036. Published annually in May. Price, $45. Contains directories of coal mines, distributors, exporters, carriers, related associations, and consumer directories for electric utilities, coke and cement plants.

COAT, SUIT & DRESS DIRECTORY, WOMEN'S WEAR DAILY'S, Fairchild Publications, Inc., 7 E. 12th St., New York, N. Y. 10003. Issued June and December. Price, 50 cents.

COKE PLANTS IN THE UNITED STATES AS OF DECEMBER 31, 1960, U. S. Government Printing Office, Washington, D.C. 20402. Catalog No. 1 28:27:8061. Price, 20 cents.

COLLECTION AGENCIES, AMERICAN DIRECTORY, Service Publishing Co., Washington Bldg., 15th and New York Ave., N.W., Washington 20005. Published winter and summer. Price, $7.50 per year. Includes collection agencies and collection attorneys throughout U.S.

COLLEGE BLUE BOOK, Christian Burckel, 1709 W. 8th St., Los Angeles, Calif. 90017. Price, $75. Nine books bound in three volumes. 3,000 pages. Professional reference work of American higher and secondary education.

COLLEGE MEDIA, DIRECTORY OF, B. Klein & Company, 104 Fifth Ave., New York, N. Y. 10011. Price, $15. Geographical register of college newspapers, magazines, etc. Last edition, 1958.

COLLEGE PLACEMENT ANNUAL, College Placement Council, Inc., 35 E. Elizabeth Ave., Bethlehem, Pa. 18018. Released every fall. Material due in spring.

COLLEGE STORES, DIRECTORY OF, B. Klein & Co., 104 Fifth Ave., New York, N. Y. 10036. Published annually in May. Price, $17.50. Contains list of college stores, type of merchandise sold, college name, number of students, and other vital selling information.

(Colleges) ACCREDITED HIGHER INSTITUTIONS, 1960, U.S. Government Printing Office, Washington, D.C. 20402. Catalog No. FS 5.250:50012-64. Price, 70 cents.

COLLEGES AND SPECIALIZED SCHOOLS, Porter Sargeant, 11 Beacon St., Boston, Mass. 02108. Designed for maximum adaptability and unique usefulness to help in matching school programs to individual needs. More than 1,800 institutions are classified under academic, business, technical and creative categories for concise, authoritative reference with admissions' criteria, names of school officers, programs and events, unusual features, special facilities, sports and activities, rules and regulations. Price, $6.

COMMERCE AND INDUSTRY, WORLD WHO'S WHO IN, Marquis—Who's Who, Inc., 210 E. Ohio St., Chicago, Ill. 60611. Price, $27.50. Vol. 14: 30,000 business executives the world over, biographically sketched and key-indexed to over 9,000 leading businesses. Prepublication list price, $30, after-publication list price, $40.

COMMERCIAL CAR JOURNAL FLEET BUYERS DIRECTORY, CHILTON Co., 56th and Chestnut Sts., Philadelphia, Pa. 19139. Published annually in November. Single copy, $2; yearly subscription, $20 in U.S. and Canada.

COMPANIES FILING ANNUAL REPORTS WITH THE SECURITIES & EXCHANGE COMMISSION, ETC., U.S. GOVERNMENT PRINTING OFFICE, Washington, D.C. 20402. Catalog No. SE 1.27:965. Price, $1.50. Companies are listed by industry groups and also alphabetically.

COMPUTER YEARBOOK AND DIRECTORY, AMERICAN DATA PROCESSING, INC., Book Bldg., Detroit, Mich. 48226. Published annually. 1966 edition now available. Not published in 1967. 1968 edition available spring 1968. Price, $25 (plus $1 postage and handling).

(Confectionery Industry) PURCHASING EXECUTIVES BLUE BOOK, MANUFACTURING CONFECTIONER PUBLISHING Co., 1031 South Blvd., Oak Park, Ill. 60302. Published annually in July. Price, $1 (or included in $3 annual subscription). Includes classified lists of manufacturers of equipment and materials.

CONGRESSIONAL DIRECTORY, OFFICIAL, SUPERINTENDENT OF DOCUMENTS, GOVERNMENT PRINTING OFFICE, Washington, D.C. 20402. Price, $3 regular edition or $4.75 thumb-indexed edition. Contains lists and brief biographies of Members of Congress; shows the membership of Congressional committees and the committee assignments of each member, and names of their secretaries; lists the bureaus and other agencies surrounding each cabinet officer and names the principal officials of each, as well as of the White House and of independent agencies; includes sketches of present and retired members of the Supreme Court and present members of various other Federal courts; and lists the personnel of the 10 U.S. Courts of Appeals, and of several other courts; lists our diplomatic and consular offices and many of their officers; names the accredited members of the various press galleries, and their press or other affiliations; and shows the membership of the United Nations and the principal personnel of other important international organizations. Catalog No. Y4.P93/1:1/89-2.

CONSTRUCTION DESIGN CHARTS (revised edition), WESTERN CONSTRUCTION, 609 Mission St., San Francisco, Calif. 94105. 220-page book. Price, $10.

CONSTRUCTION-EQUIPMENT GUIDE FOR CHAIN STORES & SHOPPING CENTERS, CHAIN STORE AGE, LEBHAR-FRIEDMAN PUBLICATIONS, INC., 2 Park Ave., New York, N. Y. 10016. Issued in May. Included in yearly subscription price of $3. Single copies, when available, 50 cents.

CONSUMER FINANCE ROSTER, NATIONAL CONSUMER FINANCE ASSOCIATION, 1000 16th St., N.W., Washington, D.C. 20006. Price, $30. Includes listings of about 22,365 consumer finance offices in the U.S., Guam and Puerto Rico.

CONSUMER MAGAZINE AND FARM PUBLICATION RATES AND DATA, STANDARD RATE & DATA SERVICE, 5201 Old Orchard Rd., Skokie, Ill. 60076. Published monthly with updating bulletins. Reports rates for pertinent data on U.S. and international consumer magazines and farm publications.

CONTACT LENS TRADE DIRECTORY AND BUYERS' GUIDE ISSUE, OCCIDENTAL PUBLISHING Co., 3924 Sunset Blvd., Los Angeles, Calif. 90029. Published in October. Also features WHO'S WHO OF WESTERN OPTOMETRY—a list of names and addresses of every important office holder in the West.

CONTAINER DIRECTORY, OFFICIAL, BETTENDORF PUBLICATIONS, INC., 228 N. LaSalle St., Chicago, Ill. 60601. Published semiannually in May and November. Single copy, $10; per year, $15; three copies to same buyer, $8 each, or $12 per year. Includes box, carton, packaging machinery, and fiber can and drum plants.

CONTRACTORS, ASSOCIATED GENERAL, DIRECTORY ISSUE, AGC INFORMATION, INC., 1957 E St., N.W., Washington, D.C. 20006. Published in July. Price, $25. Lists general contractors in U.S.

CONTRACTORS' ELECTRICAL EQUIPMENT'S GUIDE BOOK ISSUES, SUTTON PUBLISHING Co., INC., 172 S. Broadway, White Plains, N.Y. 10605. The Tool Issue & Guide Book is issued in June; the Electric Heating Issue & Guide Book in August.

(Contractors, Engineers, etc.) ABC DIRECTORY, ABC PUBLISHING Co., 2501 Raymond Dr., Des Moines, Iowa 50310. Issued in March. Price, $25.

CONVENTION DATES MAGAZINE, WORLD, World Convention Dates, 91 N. Franklin St., Hempstead, N. Y. 11550. Published monthly; cumulative semiannually. Price, $20. Includes over 25,000 conventions.

CONVENTION FACILITIES ISSUE, Sales Meetings, 1212 Chestnut St., Philadelphia. Pa. 19107. Published annually in April. Price, $1.50. Lists convention facilities of hotels, etc., around the world; exhibit builders and show suppliers; convention services and products.

(Convention) FAIRS AND EXPOSITIONS, INTERNATIONAL ASSOCIATION OF, Frank H. Kingman, secretary, International Association of Fairs and Expositions, 777 Arbor Rd., Winston-Salem, N. C. Published annually, includes 2,000 county, state, and regional fairs each year.

CONVENTIONS, DIRECTORY OF, Directory of Conventions, Inc., 1212 Chestnut St., Philadelphia, Pa. 19107. Published annually with supplement in July. Price, $15. Includes 18,000 conventions annually in U.S. and Canada; names and titles of executives in charge of event.

CORPORATION DESCRIPTIONS, STANDARD, Standard & Poor's Corp., 345 Hudson St., New York, N. Y. 10014. Published in six alphabetical volumes, each containing seven replaceable sections a year, plus an index of the companies (including cross references in case of merger, name change, etc.). Subscription rate, $236 a year.

CORPORATIONS, DIRECTORS AND EXECUTIVES, POOR'S REGISTER OF, Standard & Poor's Corp., 345 Hudson St., New York, N. Y. 10014. Published each January, plus supplements. Lists 31,000 U.S. and Canadian firms with their officers and directors, 75,000 such executives in an alphabetical list, with home addresses; products in a classified list.

CORRECTIONAL INSTITUTIONS, American Correctional Association, 1000 Shoreham Bldg., Washington, D.C. 20005. Published annually. Price, $2.50. Includes prisons, etc., in U.S. and Canada.

CORSET & BRASSIERE MAGAZINE ANNUAL DIRECTORY, Mackay Publishing Corp., 95 Madison Ave., New York, N.Y. 10016. Issued annually in April. Single copy, $1.50; yearly subscription to magazine, $3.

CORSET & UNDERWEAR REVIEW DIRECTORY, Haire Publishing Co., 111 Fourth Ave., New York, N. Y. 10003. Published annually in April. Price, $1. Lists U.S. corset, girdle, and brassiere manufacturers, supply houses, and trade names for both.

COUNTY AGENTS DIRECTORY, County Agents Directory, 221 N. LaSalle St., Chicago, Ill. 60601. Annual. Price, $5. Geographical arrangement of agricultural extension workers.

CRAFT, MODEL & HOBBY INDUSTRY'S DIRECTORY ISSUE, Hobby Publications, Inc., 229 W. 28th St., New York, N. Y. 10001. Published in April. Yearly subscription, $5.

CURTAIN & DRAPERY DEPARTMENT MAGAZINE'S BUYERS GUIDE, Hall Publishing Co., 230 Fifth Ave., New York, N. Y. 10001. Published annually in April. Single copies, $1. Lists manufacturers and converters of curtain and drapery fabrics and other allied lines, buying offices, and all other sources of supply.

CUSTOM HOUSE GUIDE, Budd Publications, Inc., Box 7, Bowling Green Station, New York, N. Y. 10004. Published each spring. Price, $35. Lists steamship lines, banks, brokers, forwarders, warehouses, etc., at U.S. and territory ports, 26,000 commodities and their U.S. rates of duty.

DAIRY CREDIT BOOK, Dairy Credit Bureau, 1740 Greenleaf Ave., Chicago, Ill. 60626. Published annually. Price, $250. Includes 25,000 plants processing milk and ice cream; mix manufacturers; cheese factories, etc. Executives and financial ratings of each company.

DAIRY INDUSTRIES CATALOG, The Miller Publishing Co., P.O. Box 67, Minneapolis, Minn. 55440. Published annually. Free to qualified dairy processors and dairy equipment suppliers. Directory of equipment, supplies and services available to the dairy industry. List of jobbers, brokers, dairy schools, dairy associations, government agencies and personnel, trade names.

DAIRY INDUSTRY HANDBOOK OF PROCESSES AND SUPPLIES, ICE CREAM
WORLD, 145 Sixth Ave., New York, N. Y. 10013. Issued annually in January.
Price, $5.

(Data Processing) COMPUTER YEARBOOK AND DIRECTORY, AMERICAN DATA
PROCESSING, INC., Book Bldg., Detroit, Mich. 48226. Published annually. Price, $25
(plus $1 postage and handling).

DENTAL DIRECTORY, AMERICAN, AMERICAN DENTAL ASSOCIATION, 211 E. Chicago
Avenue., Chicago, Ill. 60611. Published annually. Price, $25. Includes name, address,
year of birth, dental school, year of graduation, character of practice, and membership status of every dentist in the U.S. whose name and address can be verified.

(Dental Supplies) DENTAL SUPPLY HOUSES, HAYES DIRECTORY OF, EDWARD N.
HAYES, 4229 Birch St., Newport Beach, Calif. 92660. Lists 700 U.S. suppliers and
wholesalers, including financial rating. Issued annually in July. Price, $12.50.

DEPARTMENT STORE DIRECTORIES: SHELDON'S RETAIL TRADE, PHELON-
SHELDON PUBLICATIONS, INC., 32 Union Sq., New York, N. Y. 10003. Published in
February. Price, $25. Includes presidents, advertising, publicity, sales managers, dis-
play managers, divisional merchandisers; all buyers and products bought.

DIESEL AND GAS TURBINE CATALOG, DIESEL ENGINES, INC., P.O. Box 7406,
Milwaukee, Wis. 53213. Published annually. Price, $20. This 1,100-page catalog is a
complete reference information source for diesel, natural gas engines, and industrial
gas turbines, as well as all accessories used in connection with these engines.

DIRECTORS DIRECTORY OF GREAT BRITAIN, THOMAS SKINNER & Co., LTD., 111
Broadway, New York, N. Y. 10006. Published in the summer. Price, $14. Alphabeti-
cal list of 35,000 directors of British companies.

DIRECT MAIL CATALOG OF MAILING AND PROSPECT LISTS, R. L. POLK & Co.,
431 Howard St., Detroit, Mich. 48231. Published annually in January. Free.

DIRECT MAIL LIST RATES AND DATA, STANDARD RATE & DATA SERVICE, 5201 Old
Orchard Rd., Skokie, Ill. 60076. Published semiannually with updating bulletins.
Price, $50 a year. Reports buying data on mailing lists for direct mail advertising.

DIRECT SELLING, NATIONAL ASSOCIATION OF DIRECT SELLING COMPANIES, 165 Center
St., Winona, Minn. 55987. Basic and miscellaneous material on direct selling.

DISCOUNT DEPARTMENT STORES, PHELON-SHELDON PUBLICATIONS, INC., 32 Union
Sq., New York, N. Y. 10003. Lists buying headquarters for 1,200 discount stores and
discount chains. Gives the executives, buyers and lessees of most of the discount
stores and discount chains throughout the U.S. Section of leased department operators
—lines and buyers. Price, $20.

DOMESTICS, LINENS. RUGS & SHOWER CURTAINS DIRECTORY FAIRCHILD'S,
FAIRCHILD PUBLICATIONS, INC., 7 E. 12th St., New York, N. Y. 10003. Issued in
January and June. Price, 50 cents. Includes New York City manufacturers, im-
porters, wholesalers, etc., of the items named.

DRIVE-IN MANAGEMENT GUIDEBOOK, OJIBWAY PRESS, INC., Ojibway Bldg., Duluth,
Minn. 55802. Issued annually. Single copy, $8.50.

DRUG TOPICS RED BOOK, TOPICS PUBLISHING CO., INC., 330 W. 34th St., New York,
N. Y. 10001. Issued annually in September, with two Cumulative Supplements, one in
January and the other in May. Lists drug brand names and their manufacturers.

DRUGGIST DIRECTORY, HAYES, EDWARD N. HAYES, 206 W. 4th, Santa Ana, Calif.
92701. Published annually. Price, $30.

DRUGGIST, AMERICAN, MARKET DIRECTORY: BLUE BOOK, AMERICAN DRUGGIST,
1790 Broadway, New York, N. Y. 10019. Published annually in March. Price, $9.
Includes chains' buying headquarters, department store Rx departments, hospitals.

(Druggists) THE HAYES DRUGGIST DIRECTORY, EDWARD N. HAYES, 4229 Birch
St., Newport Beach, Calif. 92660. Lists 49,000 U.S. retail druggists including credit
rating. Separate list of wholesalers. Published annually in March. Price, $25.

EDIBLE OIL INDUSTRY IN THE U.S., DIRECTORY OF, INSTITUTE OF SHORTENING AND EDIBLE OILS, INC., 815 Connecticut Ave., N.W., Suite 416, Washington, D.C. 20006. Includes companies, brand names.

EDITOR & PUBLISHER INTERNATIONAL YEARBOOK, THE, EDITOR & PUBLISHER Co., 850 Third Ave., New York, N. Y. 10022. Published annually. Price, $10. Lists include U.S. and Canadian daily newspapers and their various officers and editors; news, feature, and picture syndicates; U.S. magazine sections and weekly and foreign language papers; U.S. and Canadian press galleries; American Newspaper Publishers Association members; manufacturers, suppliers, etc., for the newspaper industry; advertising agencies and clubs; journalism schools; Better Business Bureaus; United Nations and London correspondents; European dailies and newspaper groups, and newspapers around the world.

EDUCATION, AMERICAN PATTERSON'S, EDUCATIONAL DIRECTORIES, INC., Box 199, Mt. Prospect, Ill. 60056. Issued annually. Per copy, $25; 3 years, $55.50 (postage extra). Includes as a supplement, Patterson's Source Guide for Educational Materials & Equipment.

EDUCATION, AMERICAN, WHO'S WHO IN, WHO'S WHO IN AMERICAN EDUCATION, 701 Main St., P.O. Box 1898, Hattiesburg, Miss. 39401. Published every other year, in even years. Price, $20. Includes sketches of leaders in various fields of education, including executives.

EDUCATION DIRECTORY, U.S. GOVERNMENT PRINTING OFFICE, Washington, D.C. 20402. Part I—State Governments: not available. Part II—Public School Systems, price, $1.50. Part III—Higher Education: not available. Part IV—Education Associations, price, 55 cents a copy. Part V—Federal Government, out of print. See *Government Organization Manual.*

EDUCATIONAL MATERIAL & EQUIPMENT, PATTERSON'S SOURCE GUIDE FOR, EDUCATIONAL DIRECTORIES, INC., Box 199, Mt. Prospect, Ill. 60056. Issued semiannually in March and October. Price, $1.

EDUCATORS GUIDE TO FREE FILMS, EDUCATORS PROGRESS SERVICE, P.O. Drawer E, Randolph, Wis. 53956. Covers free films for both elementary and secondary schools. Revised annually. Price, $9.50.

EDUCATORS GUIDE TO FREE FILMSTRIPS, EDUCATORS PROGRESS SERVICE, P.O. Drawer E, Randolph, Wis. 53956. Comprehensive listing of free filmstrips and slides with descriptions of 544 titles (42 of which may be retained permanently). 98 sets of free slides included. Price, $7.

EDUCATORS GUIDE TO FREE GUIDANCE MATERIALS, EDUCATORS PROGRESS SERVICE, P.O. Drawer E, Randolph, Wis. 53956. Covers free films, filmstrips, pamphlets, and other materials on guidance for both elementary and secondary schools. Revised annually. Price, $7.50.

EDUCATORS GUIDE TO FREE SCIENCE MATERIALS, EDUCATORS PROGRESS SERVICE, P.O. Drawer E, Randolph, Wis. 53956. Covers free films, filmstrips, pamphlets, and other materials on science for both elementary and secondary schools. Revised annually. Price, $8.25.

EDUCATORS GUIDE TO FREE SOCIAL STUDIES MATERIALS, EDUCATORS PROGRESS SERVICE, P.O. Drawer E, Randolph, Wis. 53956. Covers free films, filmstrips, pamphlets, and other materials on social studies for both elementary and secondary schools. Revised annually. Price, $8.50.

EDUCATORS GUIDE TO FREE TAPES, SCRIPTS, AND TRANSCRIPTIONS, EDUCATORS PROGRESS SERVICE, P.O. Drawer E, Randolph, Wis. 53956. Covers these free aids for both elementary and secondary schools. Revised annually. Price, $6.75.

EDUCATORS INDEX OF FREE MATERIALS, EDUCATORS PROGRESS SERVICE, P.O. Drawer E, Randolph, Wis. 53956. A card index file in a steel container of convenient size. Covers the entire curriculum at both elementary and secondary levels. Revised annually.

EGG AND POULTRY INDUSTRIES, WHO'S WHO, WATT PUBLISHING CO., Sandstone Bldg., Morris, Ill. 61054. Published annually in June. Price, $15. Includes firms, manufacturing poultry equipment and supplies, leading egg and poultry processing plants, wholesalers, jobbers or brokers in marketing services, exporters and export agencies for poultry, processors of liquid and frozen eggs, egg solids, and further processed items, cold-storage warehouses, Federal agencies, national and sectional associations.

ELECTRIC INSTITUTE RATE BOOK, EDISON, EDISON ELECTRIC INSTITUTE, 750 Third Ave., New York, N. Y. 10017. Published periodically; 1967 latest edition. Price, $30. Includes about 200 electric companies and the more than 8,000 companies they serve.

ELECTRICAL BUYERS' GUIDE, MIDWEST, RICKARD PUBLISHING CO., 20 N. Wacker Dr., Chicago, Ill. 60606. Published annually in October. Single copy, $5. Contains an alphabetical list of electrical manufacturers in 12 midwestern states, a geographical list of firms serving as manufacturers' representatives for more than one company, and a directory of 1,000 electrical products and their manufacturers.

ELECTRICAL CONTRACTORS' ASSOCIATION MEMBERSHIP, DIRECTORY OF NATIONAL, NATIONAL ELECTRICAL CONTRACTORS' ASSOCIATION, 610 Ring Bldg., 1200 18th St., N.W., Washington, D.C. 20036. Published annually as part of the March issue, *Qualified Contractor*. Price, $5.

ELECTRICAL SOUTH'S NEW ELECTRICAL PRODUCT & EQUIPMENT & DIREC-TORY ISSUES, W. R. C. SMITH PUBLISHING CO., 1760 Peachtree Rd., N.W., Atlanta, Ga. 30309. The new equipment issue is published in January, and the *Buyer's Guide* issue in October. Yearly subscription rate is $1.50. Lists include manufacturers, manufacturers' agents, and distributors.

ELECTRICAL WEST, BUYERS' GUIDE, MILLER FREEMAN PUBLICATIONS, 500 Howard St., San Francisco, Calif. 94105. Published in December. Price, $1.

ELECTRICAL UTILITIES, DIRECTORY OF, McGRAW-HILL, INC., 330 W. 42nd St., New York, N. Y. 10036. Published annually in July. Price, $60. Listed are light and power companies in the U.S. and Canada, with their executive and operating personnel, in places with over 500 population. Cooperatives and municipal plants are included. There is also an alphabetical list of companies.

ELECTRONIC ENGINEERS MASTER (EEM), UNITED TECHNICAL PUBLICATIONS, INC., Div. Cox Broadcasting Corp., 645 Stewart Ave., Garden City, N. Y. 11530. A 2,133-page catalog section. Directories of manufacturers/sales offices, products, trade names, sales representatives. Distributed to 71,000 engineers and purchasing agents. Published annually.

ELECTRONIC INDUSTRIES ASSOCIATION MEMBERSHIP LIST AND TRADE DIRECTORY, ELECTRONIC INDUSTRIES ASSOCIATION, 2001 Eye St., N.W., Washington, D.C. 20006. Published annually. Contains roster of company members, chief officials, and trade names.

ELECTRONIC SOURCE & PROCUREMENT, including WHO'S WHO IN ELECTRON-ICS, ELECTRONIC PERIODICALS, INC., 33140 Aurora Rd., Cleveland, Ohio 44139. Pub-lished annually in May. Price, $20. Lists include executives, purchasing agents, sales offices, industrial distributors. Special sections detail local sources of products marketed through distribution channels.

ELECTRONICS BUYERS' GUIDE, McGRAW-HILL, INC., 330 W. 42nd St., New York, N. Y. 10036. Published annually in October. Included in $8 yearly subscription to *Electronics*. Lists manufacturers of equipment and materials, and their sales representatives, and suppliers of services.

ELECTRONICS, INTERNATIONAL, ANNUAL BUYERS GUIDE ISSUE, JOHNSTON INTERNATIONAL PUBLISHING CORP., 386 Park Ave., S., New York, N. Y. 10016. Pub-lished in October, in English, Spanish, French, and German.

ELEMENTARY TEACHERS GUIDE TO FREE CURRICULUM MATERIALS, EDU-CATORS PROGRESS SERVICE, P.O. Drawer E, Randolph, Wis. 53956. Lists 1,324 items (628 of which are new) of teacher reference and professional growth materials and 7 teaching units. Price, $8.75.

ENGINEERING, FIRE, DIRECTORY ISSUE, REUBEN H. DONNELLEY CORP., 466 Lexington Ave., New York, N. Y. 10017. Includes manufacturers and suppliers of machinery, equipment, and supplies serving U.S. fire departments. Revised annually. Price, $2.

ENGINEERING & MINING JOURNALS BUYERS' GUIDE, McGRAW-HILL, INC., 330 W. 42nd St., New York, N. Y. 10036. Published annually. Price, $1; also included in $4 yearly subscription rate. Includes classified and alphabetical lists of manufacturers.

ENGINEERS' CAREER DIRECTORY, SPACE AGE PUBLICATIONS, INC., 647 N. Sepulveda Blvd., Bel Air, Calif. 90049. Published annually in December. Price, $2.

ENGINEERS' POWER PLANT DIRECTORY, ROCKWELL F. CLANCY CO., 75 E. Wacker Dr., Chicago, Ill. 60601. Published annually. Price, $25. Includes 6,000 manufacturing and power plants in Illinois, Indiana and Wisconsin.

(Entertainment) CONTACT BOOK, CELEBRITY SERVICE, INC., 171 W. 57th St., New York, N. Y. 10019. Annual. Price, $3.50. Includes producers, directors, etc.; everyone connected with stage, screen, radio, and television in New York, Hollywood, London, Paris, and Rome.

(Entertainment) STUDIO BLU-BOOK, 6605 Hollywood Blvd., Hollywood, Calif. 90028. Published semiannually. Price, $10.66 (prepaid). Includes 2,000 stars, executives, producers, directors, future players, plus other important personnel of the combined motion picture and TV industries.

EXPORT MANAGERS, COMBINATION, DIRECTORY OF, U.S. GOVERNMENT PRINTING OFFICE, Washington, D.C. 20401. Catalog No. S 18.2; Ex 7/(sec.). In three parts: food, feed, and fertilizer: price, 40 cents; fuel: 25 cents; miscellaneous and unclassified: $1.

EXPORT PRODUCTS (INTERNATIONAL) BUYERS GUIDE ISSUE, JOHNSTON INTERNATIONAL PUBLISHING CORP., 386 Park Ave., S., New York, N. Y. 10016. Annual. Published in January in English, Spanish, French, and German.

EXPORTERS AND IMPORTERS, AMERICAN REGISTER OF, AMERICAN REGISTER OF EXPORTERS CORP., 90 W. Broadway, New York, N. Y. 10007. Published annually. Price, $15. Directory of over 30,000 firms.

EXPORTERS' ENCYCLOPEDIA, DUN & BRADSTREET PUBLICATIONS CORP., P.O. Box 3088, Grand Central Station, New York, N. Y. 10017. Published in January. Price, $60.

EYE, EAR, NOSE AND THROAT SPECIALISTS, RED BOOK, THE PROFESSIONAL PRESS, INC., 5 N. Wabash Ave., Chicago, Ill. 60602. Price $5. Published every two years. Includes specialists in U.S. and Canada.

FABRIC, TRIMMINGS AND SUPPLIES DIRECTORY, FAIRCHILD PUBLICATIONS, INC., 7 E. 12th St., New York, N. Y. 10003. Includes New York City manufacturers of fabrics, trimmings, and other clothing supplies. Issued May and November. Single copy, 50 cents.

FAIRS, CAVALCADE AND DIRECTORY OF, BILLBOARD PUBLISHING CO., 188 W. Randolph St., Chicago, Ill. 60601. Published annually in November. Single copy, $5. Contains a geographical list of fairs and exhibitions.

FARM CHEMICALS HANDBOOK, MEISTER PUBLISHING CO., 37841 Euclid Ave., Willoughby, Ohio 44094. Issued annually in November. Single copy, $16. Lists makers of fertilizers and pesticides in U.S., Puerto Rico, and Canada.

FARM STORE BUYER'S GUIDE OF FARM STORE MERCHANDISING, THE MILLER PUBLISHING CO., Box 67, Minneapolis, Minn. 55440. Published in December. Directory issue listing some 1,600 manufacturers of farm supplies by company name, product categories and brand names. Pictorial Products Section describes and illustrates products. Price, $3.

FARM EQUIPMENT RED BOOK OF IMPLEMENT & TRACTOR, IMPLEMENT & TRACTOR PUBLICATIONS, INC., 1014 Wyandotte St., Kansas City, Mo. 64105. Issued in January. Included in annual subscription price of $3.

(Farming) LA HACIENDA'S DIRECTORY ISSUES, CORY PUBLICATIONS, INC., Drawer 891, Kissimmee, Fla. 32741. Directory issues (in Spanish) include Poultry, in January; Mechanized Agriculture, in March; Pesticides, in June; Fertilizers, in July; Transportation and Agriculture, in September; Livestock, in December. Yearly subscription, $4.

FEDERAL STATISTICAL DIRECTORY, U.S. GOVERNMENT PRINTING OFFICE, Div. of Public Documents, Washington, D.C. 20402. Includes professional and technical personnel of federal agencies engaged in statistical activities. Prex. 2.10:965. Price, 70 cents.

FEED BAG RED BOOK, EDITORIAL SERVICE CO., INC., 152 W. Wisconsin Ave., Milwaukee, Wis. 53203. Published annually in March. Single copy, $2. Includes a buyers' guide section listing manufacturers and suppliers to the feed industry.

FENCE MATERIALS, INTERNATIONAL DIRECTORY OF ALL, ELLISON PUBLICATIONS, INC., 127 N. Dearborn St., Chicago, Ill. 60602. Published annually in December. Included in $6 annual subscription rate, or $5 alone. Contains classified and alphabetical lists of fence materials and allied products, and a list of highway engineering officials of all states.

FERTILIZER YEAR BOOK, COMMERCIAL, WALTER W. BROWN PUBLISHING CO., 75 Third St., N.W., Atlanta, Ga. 30308. Annually in December. Price, $12 (U.S.), $20 (foreign). Directory listings include: fertilizer manufacturers, mixers, blenders, formulators (geographical and alphabetical) with their executives in U.S., Canada and Puerto Rico; industry associations; fertilizer control officials; classified supply list. Other data: fertilizer consumption laws and regulations; state grade regulations and materials requirements; fertilizer production aids.

FILM & AUDIO-VISUAL ANNUAL, UNITED BUSINESS PUBLICATIONS, INC., 200 Madison Ave., New York, N. Y. 10016.

(Films) AUDIO-VISUAL COMMUNICATIONS, UNITED BUSINESS PUBLICATIONS, INC., 200 Madison Ave., New York, N. Y. 10016. Issued quarterly in 1967, bimonthly in 1968. Single copy, $1.50.

(Filmstrips) EDUCATORS GUIDE TO FREE FILMSTRIPS, EDUCATORS PROGRESS SERVICE, P.O. Drawer E, Randolph, Wis. 53956. Covers free filmstrips for both elementary and secondary schools. Revised annually. Price, $7.

FINANCE COMPANIES, NATIONAL DIRECTORY, INTER-STATE SERVICE CO., P.O. Box 1, Neosho, Mo. Published every two years. Price, $12. Includes finance and small loan companies.

FIRE ENGINEERING'S BUYER'S GUIDE ISSUE, REUBEN H. DONNELLEY CORP., 466 Lexington Ave., New York, N. Y. 10017. Issued September 1967. Includes manufacturers and suppliers of machinery, equipment, and supplies for fire departments.

FIREARMS ENCYCLOPEDIA, THE, SHELLEY BRAVERMAN, Four Mile Point Rd., Athens, N. Y. 12015. Published annually. Price, $27.50.

FISH AND WILD LIFE SERVICE, U.S. DEPARTMENT OF THE INTERIOR, Bureau of Commercial Fisheries, Washington, D.C. 20240. Includes individual lists on fisheries, fishing gear and equipment.

FISH BOAT'S PRODUCT FILE ISSUE, H. L. PEACE PUBLICATIONS, 624 Gravier St., New Orleans, La. 70130. Published annually in October. Complete marine products buyers' guide.

FISHING GAZETTE'S ANNUAL REVIEW NUMBER AND CLASSIFIED DIRECTORY, FISHING GAZETTE PUBLISHING CORP., 461 Eighth Ave., New York, N. Y. 10001. Published annually in October. Included in yearly subscription price of $3.

FLOOR COVERINGS, MODERN, ANNUAL DIRECTORY, BILL PUBLICATIONS, 630 Third Ave., New York, N. Y. 10017. Published annually in April.

FLOORING'S TRADE DIRECTORY & BUYING GUIDE ISSUE, CANTER PUBLICATIONS, INC., Ojibway Bldg., Duluth, Minn. 55802. Published as December issue. Annual subscription, $4.

FLUID POWER HANDBOOK & DIRECTORY, HYDRAULIC & PNEUMATICS MAGAZINE, 812 Huron Rd., Cleveland, Ohio 44115. Published in November of odd years. Controlled circulation.

(Food Brokers' Association) DIRECTORY OF MEMBERS, NATIONAL FOOD BROKERS ASSOCIATION, 1916 M St., N.W. Washington, D.C. 20036. Published annually in July. Free to firms in the grocery field writing on their letterhead. Contains a geographical list of association members, with the types of products each one handles.

FOOD PROCESSING CATALOG, PUTNAM PUBLISHING CO., 111 E. Delaware Pl., Chicago, Ill. 60611. Published biennially in September of even years. Copies distributed free of charge to selected individuals in the food processing industries. Others, $5 per year. Contains listings of sources and products used by food processors.

Section E — PRINCIPAL BUSINESS DIRECTORIES

FOREIGN CONSULAR OFFICES IN THE UNITED STATES, 1965, U.S. GOVERNMENT PRINTING OFFICE, Washington, D.C. 20402. Catalog No. S 1.69:128. Price, 35 cents.

(Foreign) DIPLOMATIC LIST, U.S. GOVERNMENT PRINTING OFFICE, Washington, D.C. 20402. Catalog No. S 1.8. Published quarterly. Single copy, 35 cents; yearly subscription price, $1.25 (foreign, $2.50). Lists foreign diplomats in and around Washington, D.C.

FOREIGN SERVICE LIST, ETC., U.S. GOVERNMENT PRINTING OFFICE, Washington, D.C. 20402. Published quarterly. Catalog No. S 1.7. Single copy, 65 cents. Yearly subscription, $1.75 (plus 50 cents for foreign mailing). Lists U.S. embassies, legations, consulates, missions, and their personnel, plus field staffs of U.S. Foreign Service, USDA, USIA, and AID.

(Forest Products Industries) CROW'S BUYER'S AND SELLER'S GUIDE OF THE WESTERN FOREST PRODUCTS INDUSTRIES, C. C. CROW PUBLICATIONS, INC., Terminal Sales Bldg., Portland, Ore. 97205. Published biennially. Price, $52.50. Includes names of several thousand manufacturers, jobbers, wholesalers and dealers in lumber, plywood, etc.

FOREST PRODUCTS INDUSTRY, DIRECTORY OF THE, MILLER FREEMAN PUBLICATIONS, 731 S.W. Oak St., Portland, Ore. 97205. Published annually in January. Price, $25.

FOREST PRODUCTS JOURNAL YEARBOOK, FOREST PRODUCTS RESEARCH SOCIETY, 1201 Marshall Ct., Madison, Wis. 53705. Issued in September. Single copy, $5.

FORGING, STAMPING AND HEAT TREATING PLANTS, DIRECTORY OF, STEEL PUBLICATIONS, INC., 624 Grant Bldg., Pittsburgh, Pa. 15230. Published periodically. Price, $17, and tax in certain states. Contains names of approximately 1,900 companies and 17,500 key personnel, such as executives, general and department superintendents, engineers, chemists, metallurgists, foremen, etc.

FORTUNE DIRECTORY, THE, TIME INC., 540 N. Michigan Ave., Chicago, Ill. 60611. Published in two parts: June 15 and September 15. Part I includes lists of the 500 largest U.S. industrials and the 50 largest banks, merchandising, transportation, life insurance and utility companies. Price, 75 cents. Part II lists the 200 largest industrial corporations outside the U.S. Price, 50 cents.

FOUNDATION DIRECTORY, EDITION 3, THE, RUSSELL SAGE FOUNDATION, 230 Park Ave., New York, N. Y. 10017. Price, $12. Includes 6,803 nonprofit U.S. foundations with assets of approximately $100,000 or more, grouped by states. Also alphabetical lists of the foundations themselves, their personnel, and their fields of interest.

FRASER'S CANADIAN TRADE DIRECTORY, THE MACLEAN-HUNTER PUBLISHING Co., LTD., 481 University Ave., Toronto 2, Canada. Annually. Price, $25. Lists over 30,000 Canadian manufacturers, wholesalers, distributors and agents alphabetically by product. 2,000 pages.

FROZEN FOOD FACT BOOK & DIRECTORY, NATIONAL FROZEN FOOD ASSOCIATION, 55 E. 43rd St., New York, N. Y. 10017. Published annually in November. Price, $2.50. This is a current and historical compendium of the statistics of the industry; also a directory of over 1,300 member companies, including distributor, packer, broker, warehouse, and supplier members; also allied associations.

FROZEN FOOD PROCESSORS, QUICK FROZEN FOODS' ANNUAL DIRECTORY OF, E. W. WILLIAMS PUBLICATIONS, 1776 Broadway, New York, N. Y. 10019. Issued annually in June. Price, $10. Contains lists of processors, plants, associations, carriers, warehouses, suppliers, and brand names.

FUEL-BRIQUETTING & PACKAGED-FUEL PLANTS IN UNITED STATES, ETC., 1959, U.S. GOVERNMENT PRINTING OFFICE, Washington, D.C. 20402. Catalog No. 1 28:27:7992. Price, 15 cents.

FUR DIRECTORY, WOMEN'S WEAR DAILY'S, FAIRCHILD PUBLICATIONS, INC., 7 E. 12th St., New York, N. Y. 10003. Published annually in June. Price, 50 cents.

FUR FARMING, BLUE BOOK OF, EDITORIAL SERVICE CO., INC., 152 W. Wisconsin Ave., Milwaukee, Wis. 53203. Published annually in October. Price, $1. Lists distributors of materials and suppliers for the fur farming industry.

FURNITURE PRODUCTION'S BLUE BOOK DIRECTORY OF SUPPLIES, PRODUCTION PUBLISHING CO., 804 Church St., Nashville, Tenn. 37203. Published annually as the December issue of the magazine; included in the yearly subscription rate of $3.

(Garden Supplies) GREEN BOOK BUYERS' GUIDE, HOME & GARDEN SUPPLY MERCHANDISER, 2501 Wayzata Blvd., Minneapolis, Minn. 55405. Annual directory issue lists some 2,000 manufacturers of garden and lawn products by company, product and brand name. Also includes a list of garden associations, manufacturers' representatives and central parts distributors by regions. Pictorial Products Section describes and illustrates products. Price, $3.

(Gas Appliances) DIRECTORY-CERTIFIED APPLIANCES AND ACCESSORIES, AMERICAN GAS ASSOCIATION, INC., Laboratories, 1032 East 62nd St., Cleveland, Ohio 44103. Annual subscription, $5; includes two semiannual issues (January and July), and one supplement for each remaining month. Separate copies of the semiannual issues are $3 each; separate copies of monthly supplements are $1 each. Includes manufacturers of gas equipment and appliances.

GAS COMPANIES, AMERICAN, BROWN'S DIRECTORY, MOORE PUBLISHING CO., Ojibway Bldg., Duluth, Minn. 55802. Price, $60. Includes companies in U.S. and Canada.

GAS HANDBOOK ISSUE OF AMERICAN GAS JOURNAL, PETROLEUM ENGINEER PUBLISHING CO., Box 1589, Dallas, Texas 75221. Issued annually, March 15. Included in yearly subscription. Price, $5. Materials, equipment, engineer-operating reference data.

GAS JOURNAL, AMERICAN, SERVICE GUIDE ISSUE (NEW EQUIPMENT), PETROLEUM ENGINEER PUBLISHING CO., Box 1589, Dallas, Texas 75221. Published annually, July 15. Included in yearly subscription price of $5. Lists new and significant equipment and services available from manufacturers and suppliers to the gas distribution market.

(Gasoline) NATIONAL-GASOLINE & CYCLING PLANTS IN THE UNITED STATES, U.S. GOVERNMENT PRINTING OFFICE, Washington, D.C. 20402. Catalog No. I 28:27:- 8006. Price, 20 cents.

GIFT AND DECORATIVE ACCESSORY BUYERS DIRECTORY, THE, GEYER-MC-ALLISTER PUBLICATIONS, INC., 51 Madison Ave., New York, N. Y. 10010. Published annually in August.

GLASS FACTORY DIRECTORY, NATIONAL GLASS BUDGET, 912-913 Empire Bldg., Pittsburgh, Pa. 15222. Published annually. Price, $3. Includes companies and executives for U.S. and Canada.

GLASS/METAL DIRECTORY, ARTLEE CATALOG, INC., 15 E. 40th St., New York, N. Y. 10016. Published in November. Price, $5.

GLOVES DIRECTORY, HAIRE PUBLISHING CO., 111 Fourth Ave., New York, N. Y. 10003. Published in January. Price, $1.

GOVERNMENT ORGANIZATION MANUAL, U.S., U.S. GOVERNMENT PRINTING OFFICE, Washington, D.C. 20402. Catalog No. GS 4.109:965. Published annually. Price, $2.

GRAIN TRADE BUYERS' GUIDE & MANAGEMENT REFERENCE, GRAIN TRADE BUYERS' GUIDE CO., 141 W. Jackson Blvd., Chicago, Ill. 60604. Published annually in May. Price, $2.50. Contains several hundred classified lists of manufacturers and suppliers of equipment for grain handlers and processors, and of those servicing such equipment.

GRAPHIC SCIENCE'S PURCHASING DIRECTORY, KINELOW PUBLISHING CO., INC., 9 Maiden Lane, New York, N. Y. 10038. Issued in September. Yearly subscription: domestic, $16; Canada, $18; other, $20.

GREAT LAKES RED BOOK, THE PENTON PUBLISHING CO., 1213 W. Third St., Cleveland, Ohio 44113. Issued annually in May. Price, $2. Lists shipping companies operating on the Great Lakes; their vessels, with the masters and engineers; ship builders and repairers, with their executives; sources of equipment or supplies.

GROCER'S BUYING GUIDE & HANDBOOK, GROCERY BULLETIN, 192 S. Alvarado St., Los Angeles, Calif. 90057. Published in December.

GROCERY REGISTER, THOMAS, THOMAS PUBLISHING CO., 461 Eighth Ave., New York, N. Y. 10001. Annually. Price, $15. Includes wholesalers, supermarkets, manufacturers, processors, and brokers in U.S. and Canada.

HANDBAGS & ACCESSORIES DIRECTORY, HAIRE PUBLISHING CO., 111 Fourth Ave., New York, N. Y. 10003. Published in December. Price, $1.

HARDWARE AGE ANNUAL DIRECTORY ISSUE, CHILTON CO., 56th and Chestnut Sts., Philadelphia, Pa. 19139. Published annually in July. Included in yearly subscription price of $2.

HAT LIFE YEARBOOK, HAT LIFE YEAR BOOK, INC., 551 Summit Ave., Jersey City, N. J. 07306. Published annually. Price, $2. Includes manufacturers; wholesalers of men's hats, caps, and straw goods.

HEALTH DIRECTORY, AMERICAN, PUBLIC AFFAIRS PRESS, 419 New Jersey Ave. S.W., Washington, D.C. 20003. Price, $2. Includes official or professional health agencies, lay groups, and research laboratories.

HEALTH ORGANIZATIONS OF THE U.S., CANADA, AND INTERNATIONALLY. Second edition. CLARA SEDACCA WASSERMAN WITH PAUL WASSERMAN. Graduate School of Business and Public Administration, Cornell University, Ithaca, N. Y. 14851. Published 1965. Price, $13.50. A directory of voluntary associations, professional societies, and other groups concerned with health and related fields.

HEARING DEALER, ANNUAL DIRECTORY ISSUE OF, OJIBWAY PRESS, INC., Ojibway Bldg., Duluth, Minn. 55802. Issued in April. Yearly subscription, $5.

(Heating, Air Conditioning, etc.) ASHRAE GUIDE AND DATA BOOK, AMERICAN SOCIETY OF HEATING, REFRIGERATING AND AIR-CONDITIONING ENGINEERS, INC., 345 E. 47th St., New York, N. Y. 10017. *Applications Volume*, issued in May; price, $20. *Systems and Equipment Volume*, issued in May; price, $20.

HEATING, PIPING & AIR CONDITIONING DIRECTORY SECTION, REINHOLD PUBLISHING CORP., Keeney Div., 10 S. LaSalle St., Chicago, Ill. 60603. Published annually in January. Included in annual subscription price of $5.

HIGHER INSTITUTIONS, ACCREDITED, U.S. GOVERNMENT PRINTING OFFICE, DIVISION OF PUBLIC DOCUMENTS, Washington, D.C. 20402. Includes accredited higher institutions in U.S. OE 50012-64. Price, 70 cents.

HIGHWAY & AIRWAY CARRIERS & ROUTES, NATIONAL, NATIONAL HIGHWAY CARRIERS DIRECTORY, 925 W. Jackson Blvd., Chicago, Ill. 60607. Published twice yearly, in spring and fall. Price, $20. Both issues, $30. Lists air and motor freight lines, associations, terminals, etc. Also Interstate Commerce Commission offices.

(Highways) CONSTRUCTIONEER DIRECTORY, CONSTRUCTIONEER, 1 Bond St., Chatham, N. J. 07040. Published annually. Price, $5. Lists about 3,000 manufacturers, distributors of construction equipment, and public officials.

HOBBY INDUSTRY, CRAFT, MODEL, HOBBY PUBLICATIONS, INC., 229 W. 28th St., New York, N. Y. 10001. Price, $5. Includes over 1,000 manufacturers, jobbers of hobby merchandise.

HOME & AUTO RETAILER'S BUYER'S GUIDE, AUTOMOTIVE RETAILER, INC., 75 Station St., Southport, Conn. 06490. Published annually in August. Included in yearly subscription price of $5; $3 each, separately.

HOME & GARDEN SUPPLY MERCHANDISER GREEN BOOK, MILLER PUBLISHING Co., 2501 Wayzata Blvd., Minneapolis, Minn. 55440. Issued annually in October. Single copy, $3; or $10 as part of a year's subscription. Includes classified lists of manufacturers and distributors of lawn and garden supplies and equipment; also brand names.

(Hospital) THE MODERN HOSPITAL DIRECTORY OF HOSPITALS, MCGRAW-HILL PUBLICATIONS, A Division of McGraw-Hill, Inc., 1050 Merchandise Mart, Chicago, Ill. 60654. Lists over 8,500 hospitals, state and federal hospital purchasing agencies in U.S.

HOSPITALS, J.A.H.A., GUIDE ISSUE, Part 2, AMERICAN HOSPITAL ASSOCIATION, 840 N. Lake Shore Dr., Chicago, Ill. 60611. Published annually in August. Price, $12.50 (case-bound edition). Lists include U.S. hospitals; Canadian hospitals; accredited extended care facilities; association institutional, associate, and personal members; health organizations and agencies; schools of pharmacy, nursing, etc.; and vendors of hospital equipment, supplies, and services.

HOTEL-MOTEL GUIDE & TRAVEL ATLAS, LEAHY'S, AMERICAN HOTEL REGISTER Co., 226 W. Ontario St., Chicago, Ill. 60610. Published annually. Price, $7. Includes 40,000 hotels and motels in U.S., Canada, and Mexico.

HOTEL & MOTEL RED BOOK, AMERICAN HOTEL ASSOCIATION DIRECTORY CORP., 221 E. 57th St., New York, N. Y. 10019. Published annually in May. Price, $7.50. Includes hotels and motels in U.S., Canada, and elsewhere.

HOTEL & MOTEL SYSTEMS, DIRECTORY OF, AMERICAN DIRECTORY CORP., 221 W. 57th St., New York, N. Y. 10019. Price, $2. Includes hotel systems with names and locations of affiliated hotels, system officials, referral groups.

HOTEL & TRAVEL INDEX, ELWOOD M. INGLEDUE, 5850 Hollywood Blvd., Los Angeles, Calif. 90028. Published quarterly. Single issue, $7.50; annually, $25. Includes over 11,000 leading hotels, motels—over 3,500 with complete details regarding location.

(House organs) GEBBIE HOUSE MAGAZINE DIRECTORY, GEBBIE DIRECTORY, P.O. Box 1111, Sioux City, Iowa 51102. Price, $24.95. Lists 4,000 house organs with sponsoring company or organization, address, product or service, editors' names and addresses, circulation, printing process, page size, interests (editorial), use of pictures, buys or does not buy free-lance material, printer's name and address.

HYDROCARBON PROCESSING CATALOG, GULF PUBLISHING Co., Box 2608, Houston, Texas 77001. Issued annually in June. Single copy, $18.

(Illinois) BUSINESS, DOING, IN ILLINOIS, CHICAGO ASSOCIATION OF COMMERCE & INDUSTRY, 30 W. Monroe St., Chicago, Ill. 60603. Price, $1.50.

ILLINOIS DENTAL JOURNAL'S DIRECTORY ISSUE, ILLINOIS STATE DENTAL SOCIETY, 1757 W. Harrison St., Chicago, Ill. 60612. Issued annually in August. Included in yearly subscription price of $3. Includes a roster of the society.

(Illinois) LEGISLATIVE DIRECTORY, CHICAGO ASSOCIATION OF COMMERCE & INDUSTRY, 30 W. Monroe St., Chicago, Ill. 60603. Published periodically. Price, $2. Contains lists of Chicago, Cook County, and Illinois State officials.

ILLINOIS MANUFACTURERS DIRECTORY, MANUFACTURERS' NEWS, INC., 3 E. Huron St., Chicago, Ill. 60611. Published annually in February. Price, $50 (or $34.95 if borrowed on a rental-subscription basis). Contains geographic lists covering 754 manufacturing cities and towns, and includes 23,000 companies with a total of 90,000 executives; also an alphabetical list of companies, and 1,500 classified (product) lists.

(Illinois) SULLIVAN'S LAW DIRECTORY FOR THE STATE OF ILLINOIS, SULLI-VAN'S LAW DIRECTORY, 5875 N. Lincoln Ave., Room 224, Chicago, Ill. 60645. Published annually. Price, $9.50 (plus R.O. tax, handling and postage). Lists Illinois lawyers, judges, state, county, and city officials. Also federal officials, and the personnel of federal and local courts, with Illinois jurisdiction; officers of national and local bar associations; banks, title, and abstract companies throughout Illinois.

(Illinois) TAX CALENDAR, 1967, CHICAGO ASSOCIATION OF COMMERCE & INDUSTRY, 30 W. Monroe St., Chicago, Ill. 60603. Published annually. Price, 50 cents.

(Illinois) UNEMPLOYMENT, INSURANCE COSTS, HOW TO CUT, CHICAGO ASSOCIA-TION OF COMMERCE & INDUSTRY, 30 W. Monroe St., Chicago, Ill. 60603. Price, $2.

(Illinois) UNION, CALLS, WHAT TO DO WHEN, CHICAGO ASSOCIATION OF COMMERCE & INDUSTRY, 30 W. Monroe St., Chicago, Ill. 60603. Price, $1.50.

(Illinois) WAGE ASSIGNMENT & WAGE DEDUCTION PROCESS IN ILLINOIS, CHICAGO ASSOCIATION OF COMMERCE & INDUSTRY, 30 W. Monroe St., Chicago, Ill. 60603. Price, $1.

IMPLEMENT & TRACTOR PRODUCT FILE (& BUYER'S GUIDE), IMPLEMENT & TRACTOR PUBLICATIONS, INC., 1014 Wyandotte St., Kansas City, Mo. 64105. Issued annually in March. Included in yearly subscription price of $3.

IMPORTERS, UNITED STATES DIRECTORY OF, JOURNAL OF COMMERCE, 99 Wall St., New York, N. Y. 10005. Includes all import firms in U.S. Price, $50.

INDUSTRIAL, INDIANA DIRECTORY, INDIANA STATE CHAMBER OF COMMERCE, Board of Trade Bldg., Indianapolis, Ind. 46204. Published biennially. Price, $12. Includes summary of state's resources, 12,000 manufacturers, wholesalers, and officials.

INDUSTRIAL MANUAL, MOODY'S, MOODY'S INVESTORS SERVICE, INC., 99 Church St., New York, N. Y. 10007. Published annually with twice weekly News Reports. Price, $150 per year. Contains an alphabetical index of industrial companies in U.S. and Canada, plus a list of companies no longer indexed, because of mergers, name changes, etc.; and individual company summaries which include officers, directors, plants, and subsidiaries, with dates of acquisition, etc., of the latter.

INDUSTRIAL RESEARCH LABORATORIES, IN NEW YORK STATE, DIRECTORY OF, NEW YORK STATE DEPARTMENT OF COMMERCE, 112 State St., Albany, N. Y. 12207. Published periodically. Free. Includes 1,300 laboratories, and names and addresses of executives.

INDUSTRIAL RESEARCH MAGAZINE, INDUSTRIAL RESEARCH, INC., Beverly Shores, Ind. 46301. Thirteen issues: Published monthly, with a *Buyers' Guide* published in the spring. Yearly subscription, $14. *Buyers' Guide*, $5; single issues, $2.

INFANTS', BOYS' & GIRLS' WEAR, EARNSHAW'S GUIDE FOR BUYERS OF, EARNSHAW PUBLICATIONS, INC., 101 W. 31st St., New York, N. Y. 10001. Published in May and December. Price per copy, $1.

INFANTS', CHILDREN'S, GIRLS', SUB-TEENS', TEENS', & YOUNG JUNIORS' WEAR DIRECTORY, WOMEN'S WEAR DAILY, FAIRCHILD PUBLICATIONS, INC., 7 E. 12th St., New York, N. Y. 10003. Issued March and September. Price, 50 cents.

INFORMATION PLEASE ALMANAC, ATLAS & YEARBOOK, INFORMATION PLEASE ALMANAC, ATLAS & YEARBOOK, 160 Central Park, S., New York, N. Y. 10019. Published at year-end. Price, $1.65. Includes world history, sports records, science, income tax, Social Security, crossword puzzle guide, space age chronology, parliamentary procedure, American history, maps.

INSTRUMENTS & CONTROL SYSTEMS' BUYERS' GUIDE, RIMBACH PUBLICATIONS, DIV. OF CHILTON Co., 845 Ridge Ave., Pittsburgh, Pa. 15212. Issued in October. Included in yearly subscription rate of $4 in U.S. and Canada.

INSULATION DIRECTORY/ENCYCLOPEDIA, LAKE PUBLISHING CORP., Box 270, Libertyville, Ill. 60048. Issued in May.

(Insurance) AGENT'S & BUYER'S GUIDE, THE NATIONAL UNDERWRITER Co., 420 E. Fourth St., Cincinnati, Ohio 45202. Contains complete, timesaving "who writes what" market sections for surplus or hard-to-place coverages; provides complete up-to-date information needed for thorough sales-producing surveys, and offers comprehensive treatment of both life and health insurance in language of the general lines man. Published annually in March. Price, $5. (Quantity prices available.)

(Insurance) ARGUS CHART OF HEALTH INSURANCE, THE NATIONAL UNDERWRITER Co., 420 E. Fourth St., Cincinnati, Ohio 45202. Gives all the significant statement items; underwriting results; analyses of group, individual and total health business; non-can.; hospital; and medical. Published annually in June. Price, $3. (Quantity prices available.)

(Insurance) ARGUS FIRE, CASUALTY, AND SURETY CHART, THE NATIONAL UNDERWRITER Co., 420 E. Fourth St., Cincinnati, Ohio 45202. Covers comprehensive financial statements, operating reports, plus underwriting and investment results of some 1,400 property and liability insurers. Price, $4. (Quantity prices available.) Published annually in May.

INSURANCE BAR, THE, THE BAR LIST PUBLISHING Co., State Bank Bldg., Evanston, Ill. 60201. Published annually. Price, $10. Includes 3,000 selected insurance defense lawyers in U.S. and Canada.

INSURANCE IN THE UNITED STATES, CYCLOPEDIA OF, THE INDEX PUBLISHING Co., 327 Totowa Ave., Paterson, N. J. 07502. Price, $8.75. Includes all insurance companies in U.S.

(Insurance) LITTLE GEM LIFE CHART, THE NATIONAL UNDERWRITER Co., 420 E. Fourth St., Cincinnati, Ohio 45202. Full exhibits on 250 companies. Provides policy points of these companies; rates at some 40 "buying" ages—12 or more policies for each company; graded premiums, shown in a simple, easy-to-figure manner. Published annually in April. Price, $6. (Quantity prices available.)

INSURANCE REPORTS, BEST'S, ALFRED M. BEST Co., Park Ave., Morristown, N. J. 07960. Published annually. Includes fire and casualty, $95; life, $40.

(Insurance) TIME SAVER FOR HEALTH INSURANCE, THE NATIONAL UNDERWRITER Co., 420 E. Fourth St., Cincinnati, Ohio 45202. Pocket-size annual reference that analyzes and describes individual policies of 90 leading health insurers with premiums for all ages. Published annually in June. Price, $7. (Quantity prices available.)

(Insurance) UNDERWRITERS' HANDBOOKS, THE NATIONAL UNDERWRITER Co., 420 E. Fourth St., Cincinnati, Ohio 45202. Gives the complete local insurance picture for every community in 36 states, plus Chicago, Washington, D.C., and the U.S., Caribbean. Price, $14 each—except the two California volumes (north and south), which because of their large size are $15 each.

(Insurance) UNIQUE MANUAL & LIFE REPORTS, THE NATIONAL UNDERWRITER Co., 420 E. Fourth St., Cincinnati, Ohio 45202. One volume provides both factual reports on all (some 1,300) companies, and complete data on policies, rates, values, costs, options, etc. Published annually in June. Price, $18. (Quantity prices available.)

(Insurance) WHO WRITES WHAT? THE NATIONAL UNDERWRITER Co., 420 E. Fourth St., Cincinnati, Ohio 45202. Lists what companies will write the unusual in both life and health. Published annually in April. Price, $4.50. (Quantity prices available.)

INTERIOR DESIGNERS, AMERICAN INSTITUTE OF, MEMBERSHIP DIRECTORY, AMERICAN INSTITUTE OF INTERIOR DESIGNERS, 730 Fifth Ave., New York, N. Y. 10019. Price, $25. Includes 4,500 members of the institute with addresses.

INTERIORS' PURCHASING DIRECTORY OF AMERICA'S GREAT SOURCES, WHITNEY PUBLICATIONS, INC., 18 E. 50th St., New York, N. Y. 10022. Issued annually.

INTERNATIONAL YELLOW PAGES (WORLD-WIDE DIRECTORY OF INTERNATIONAL BUSINESS), published by THE REUBEN H. DONNELLEY TELEPHONE DIRECTORY Co., 235 East 45th St., New York, N. Y. 10017. Issued annually in January. Lists addresses and telephone numbers of business firms engaged in international trade under 3,000 classifications in 150 countries. Circulation audited by BPA. Distributed in over 150 countries.

INTERSTATE PORT HANDBOOK, ROCKWELL F. CLANCY Co., 75 E. Wacker Dr., Chicago, Ill. 60601. Published annually in May. Price, $6. Lists harbors and docks of the inland waterways of the United States, and harbors and ports on the Great Lakes of the U.S., and suppliers of marine equipment and services.

INVESTORS REVIEW, VICKERS, VICKERS ASSOCIATES, INC., 48 Elm St., Huntington, N. Y. Published continuously. Price, $50. Reports on the buying and selling of securities by investment companies.

IOWA, ENGINEERING SOCIETY DIRECTORY, IOWA ENGINEERING SOCIETY, 506 Shops Bldg., Des Moines, Iowa 50309. Published annually in September. Included in yearly subscription price of $4 for monthly magazine, *The Exponent*. Contains the society roster.

(Iowa General Contractors) DIRECTORY ISSUE, THE CENTRAL CONTRACTOR, 300 Hubbell Bldg., Des Moines, Iowa 50309. Published annually in April. Included in yearly subscription price of $6. Includes a roster of Associated General Contractors of Iowa; Iowa Limestone Producers Association; Master Builders of Iowa; Iowa Asphalt Paving Association; Iowa Concrete Paving Association; Iowa Ready Mix Producers Association; city, county, and state construction officials. This is a monthly publication with a directory published each April.

IRON AND STEEL PLANTS, DIRECTORY OF, STEEL PUBLICATIONS, INC., 624 Grant Bldg., Pittsburgh, Pa. 15230. Published annually. Price, $17, and tax in certain states. Contains the names of approximately 2,500 companies and 22,000 key personnel, such as executives, general and department superintendents, engineers, chemists, metallurgists, foremen, etc.

IRON AND STEEL WORKS DIRECTORY OF THE U.S. AND CANADA, AMERICAN IRON AND STEEL INSTITUTE, 150 E. 42nd St., New York, N. Y. 10017. Price, $10. Includes iron and steel works in U.S. and Canada; rolling mill descriptions, types of products, etc. 1967 Directory now available.

IRRIGATION ENGINEERING & MAINTENANCE'S ANNUAL, H. L. PEACE PUBLICATIONS, 624 Gravier St., New Orleans, La. 70130. Issued in August. Included in yearly subscription price of $5.

JEWELERS' CIRCULAR-KEYSTONE'S JEWELERS' DIRECTORY ISSUE, CHILTON Co., INC., 56th and Chestnut Sts., Philadelphia, Pa. 19139. Published in midyear. Single copy, $3 in U.S. and its possessions; all other countries, $10.

JEWELERS, MANUFACTURING, BUYERS' GUIDE, MANUFACTURING JEWELERS AND SILVERSMITHS OF AMERICA, S-75 Sheraton-Biltmore Hotel, Providence, R. I. 02902. Published every two years. Free. Includes 500 manufacturers.

JEWELRY TRADE DIRECTORY, AMERICAN DIAMOND AND, MESQUITA AND SILVER, INC., 1200 Avenue of the Americas, New York, N. Y. 10036. Published annually. Includes 10,000 diamond dealers, cutters, setters, and manufacturing jewelers as well as pearl, semi- and precious-stone dealers and importers in U.S. and Canada.

JOBBING TRADE, PHELON-SHELDON PUBLICATIONS, INC., 32 Union Sq., New York, N. Y. 10003. Lists about 6,000-8,000 firms, including over 600 rack jobbers. Gives class of goods each firm buys, buyers' names, and location of New York office. Published biannually. Price, $25.

JUNIOR COLLEGE DIRECTORY, AMERICAN ASSOCIATION OF JUNIOR COLLEGES, 1315 Sixteenth St., N.W., Washington, D.C. 20036. Published annually. Price, $1.50. Includes all junior colleges in the country, with names of directors.

JUVENILE MERCHANDISING'S DIRECTORY ISSUE, WILSIR PUBLICATIONS, 301 Sylvan Ave., Englewood Cliffs, N. J. 07632. Issued in October. Included in yearly subscription price of $4. Contains lists of manufacturers of baby carriages and other juvenile merchandise.

KANSAS MANUFACTURERS AND PRODUCTS, DIRECTORY OF, KANSAS DEPARTMENT OF ECONOMIC DEVELOPMENT, State Office Bldg., Topeka, Kans. 66612. Published biennially in even-numbered years. Price, $5. Register of goods made in Kansas by approximately 4,000 manufacturers and processors, etc.

KITCHEN BUSINESS' DIRECTORY & PRODUCTS ISSUE, GRALLA PUBLISHING CO., 7 E. 43rd St., New York, N. Y. 10017. Issued in February. Included in yearly subscription price of $2 to qualified trade only.

KNIT GOODS TRADE, DAVISON'S, DAVISON PUBLISHING Co., Ridgewood, N. J. 07450. Published annually in the fall. Single copy, $11.

LABOR PRESS DIRECTORY, INTERNATIONAL LABOR PRESS ASSOCIATION, 815 16th St., N.W., Washington, D.C. 20006. Published every two years. Includes 300 labor publications.

LABORATORIES DIRECTORY, AMERICAN COUNCIL OF INDEPENDENT, Douglas Dies, 1026 17th St., N.W., Washington, D.C. 20036. Includes 100 members, index of services, geographic distribution of headquarters.

LANDSCAPE DESIGN & CONSTRUCTION'S PRODUCT DIRECTORY, Miramar Publishing Co., 2048 Cotner Ave., Los Angeles, Calif. 90025. Issued in February. Included in yearly subscription price of $5.

LATHING AND PLASTERING INDUSTRY, WHO'S WHO IN THE, Contracting Plasterers' and Lathers' International Association, 1343 H St., N.W., Washington, D.C. 20005. Published yearly in June. Price, $25. Contains the association membership list; also gives its affiliates, contractors' associations, unions, and manufacturers and suppliers of building industry materials.

LAUNDRY, HOME DIRECTORY, American Home Laundry Manufacturers Association, 20 N. Wacker Dr., Chicago, Ill. 60606. Free. Published annually. Lists association members.

LAW DIRECTORY, Martindale-Hubbell, Inc., Summit, N. J. 07901. Published annually. Price of four volumes, $70. First three volumes contain geographical bar roster of U.S. and Canada, by states and cities, and a roster of patent lawyers. Also, advertising cards of selected title companies, shorthand reporters, examiners of questioned documents; and professional cards of lawyers and law firms. Vol. I includes states, alphabetically, from Alabama through Iowa, a roster of U.S. government lawyers, and a list of colleges and law schools to permit keying each attorney's name to the schools he attended. Vol. II includes Kansas through North Carolina; Vol. III includes North Dakota and balance of states, as well as Canadian and foreign lists. Also, with each named is a well-established bank. Vol. IV contains digests of the laws of each state of the U.S., its possessions, Canada, its 10 provinces, and foreign countries; digests of U.S. patent, copyright, and trademark laws; court calendars, and certain uniform and model acts.

LAW LIBRARIES, DIRECTORY OF, American Association of Law Libraries, 53 W. Jackson Blvd., Chicago, Ill. 60604. Price, $4.

(Law) SULLIVAN'S LAW DIRECTORY FOR THE STATE OF ILLINOIS, Sullivan's Law Directory, 5875 N. Lincoln Ave., Room 224, Chicago, Ill. 60645. Published annually. Price, $9.50, plus R.O. tax, handling and postage. Lists Illinois lawyers, judges, state, county, and city officials. Also federal officials, and the personnel of federal and local courts, with Illinois jurisdiction; officers of national and local bar associations; banks, title, and abstract companies throughout Illinois.

LAWYERS DIRECTORY, The Lawyers Directory, Inc., P.O. Box 768. Charlottesville, Va. 22902. Published annually. Price, $25. Includes lawyers and law firms in U.S. and foreign countries and corporate counsel of more than 1,600 major U.S. corporations.

LEATHER BUYERS GUIDE, Rumpf Publishing Co., 300 W. Adams St., Chicago, Ill. 60606. Published annually in August. Price, $1. Includes lists of U.S. and Canadian leather manufacturers.

LIBRARIES, SPECIAL, DIRECTORY OF, Special Libraries Association, 31 E. 10th St., New York, N. Y. 10003. Published in 1953 and still in print. No plans for a new edition. Price, $5. Includes member libraries, their facilities, and services.

LIBRARY, AMERICAN SCHOOL, DIRECTORY, R. R. Bowker Co., 1180 Avenue of the Americas, New York, N. Y. 10036. Price, $25 per volume. Elementary and secondary school libraries, public and private, in 4 parts: South, West and Southwest, The Midwest and The Northwest. (Each part sold separately.)

LIBRARY ASSOCIATION, AMERICAN, MEMBERSHIP DIRECTORY, American Library Association, 50 E. Huron St., Chicago, Ill. 60611. Published annually. Price, $10. Includes 35,000 members of the association.

LIBRARY DIRECTORY, AMERICAN, R. R. Bowker Co., 1180 Avenue of the Americas, New York, N. Y. 10036. Published biennially in even-numbered years. Price, $25. Includes public, state, club, university, business, and association libraries. In all, it lists 23,000 libraries in U.S., its territories, and Canada, as well as a select list of 4,200 overseas libraries.

LIGHTING BUYERS' GUIDE ISSUE, W. R. C. Smith Publishing Co., 1760 Peachtree Rd., N.W., Atlanta, Ga. 30309. Published in November. Included in yearly subscription price of $4. Lists manufacturers of lighting fixtures classified by type of product; trade names.

LINENS & DOMESTICS DIRECTORY, Select Publications, Inc., 900 Northstar Ctr., Minneapolis, Minn. 55402. Issued annually in December. Included in yearly subscription price of $5. Single copies available at $10 each.

LINGERIE, LOUNGEWEAR, CORSET & BRASSIERE DIRECTORY, WOMEN'S WEAR DAILY, FAIRCHILD PUBLICATIONS, INC., 7 E. 12th St., New York, N. Y. 10003. Issued in May and November. Single copy, 50 cents.

LIQUOR HANDBOOK, THE, GAVIN-JOBSON, INC., 820 Second Ave., New York, N. Y. 10017. Issued annually in May. Price, $7.50.

LITERARY MARKET PLACE, R. R. BOWKER Co., 1180 Avenue of the Americas, New York, N. Y. 10036. Price, $7.45. Business directory to 18,000 book publishers, reviewers, agents, wholesalers, and magazines.

LIVESTOCK REGULATORY ESTABLISHMENTS, STATIONS & OFFICIALS, WORKING REFERENCE OF, U.S. GOVERNMENT PRINTING OFFICE, Washington, D.C. 20402. Catalog No. A 77,221/2:965/11. Published monthly. Single copy, 70 cents; yearly subscription, $6.50 (foreign, $8). Lists include federally inspected meat-packing plants, public stockyards, laboratories, diagnosticians, licensed biological product manufacturers, and state animal disease control officials.

LP-GAS BUYERS' GUIDE ISSUE, MOORE PUBLISHING Co., INC., Ojibway Bldg., Duluth, Minn. 55802. Issued annually in February. Included in yearly subscription price of $3. Lists manufacturers and servicing agencies in the liquefied petroleum gas field.

LUGGAGE & LEATHER GOODS DIRECTORY, HAIRE PUBLISHING Co., 111 Fourth Ave., New York, N. Y. 10003. Issued in July. Price, $1.

LUMBERMEN'S NATIONAL REFERENCE BOOK, LUMBERMEN'S CREDIT ASSOCIATION INC., 608 S. Dearborn St., Chicago, Ill. 60605. Published semiannually. Includes over 45,000 companies and officials in the lumber industry.

LUTHERAN CHURCH, AMERICAN, YEARBOOK OF THE, AUGSBURG PUBLISHING HOUSE, 426 S. Fifth St., Minneapolis, Minn. 55415. Published annually in December. Single copy, $1.25.

MacRAE'S BLUE BOOK, MacRAE'S BLUE BOOK Co., 903 Burlington Ave., Western Springs, Ill. 60658. Published annually in February. Price, $25. Four volumes make a complete industrial reference with more than 50,000 leading U.S. manufacturers, listed alphabetically; over 55,000 product headings, and thousands of additional pages of cataloging and in-depth product information; 60,000 current trade names, and over 300,000 basic listing changes since the 1965 edition.

MAGAZINE DIRECTORY, Vol. II, "THE WORKING PRESS OF THE NATION," THE NATIONAL RESEARCH BUREAU, INC., 221 N. LaSalle St., Chicago, Ill. 60601. Published annually. Price, $30. Contains an alphabetical index of over 3,000 magazines with complete zip-coded addresses and editors' names, according to specialized fields. Information on deadlines, description of editorial interests, readership analysis, charges for publicity copy and cuts.

MAIL ORDER BUSINESS DIRECTORY, B. KLEIN & COMPANY, 104 Fifth Ave., New York, N. Y. 10011. Contains names of more than 3,000 mail order firms whose annual gross business runs into the billions. Each company listed geographically, showing buyers' names, and lines of merchandise carried. Asterisk after a listing denotes a firm whose volume of business ranks it as one of the 500 largest in the country. 1966 edition, $17.50.

MAILING LIST HOUSES, DIRECTORY OF, B. KLEIN & COMPANY, 104 Fifth Ave., New York, N. Y. 10011. Tells at a glance which mailing list houses specialize in the items you need. Saves many hours of research, permitting a quick and easy selection of the exact lists needed. Complete information about each house is provided. 1966 edition, $17.50.

MAINTENANCE SUPPLIERS' BUYERS' GUIDE ISSUE, MacNAIR-DORLAND Co., INC., 254 W. 31st St., New York, N. Y. 10001. Published in November.

MANUFACTURERS' AGENTS NATIONAL ASSOCIATION, DIRECTORY OF MEMBERS, AGENT AND REPRESENTATIVE Co., 626 N. Garfield Ave., Alhambra, Calif. 91802. Contained in the July issue of Agent and Representative Magazine. Price, $5 annually.

MANUFACTURERS' DIRECTORY, CENTRAL ATLANTIC STATES, T. K. SANDERSON ORGANIZATION, 200 E. 25th St., Baltimore, Md. 21218. Price, $40. Geographical arrangement of 20,000 manufacturers, products, and executives in Maryland, Virginia, West Virginia, Delaware, District of Columbia, North Carolina, and South Carolina.

MANUFACTURERS & INDUSTRIAL CLASSIFIED DIRECTORY & BUYERS GUIDE, EASTERN, BELL DIRECTORY PUBLISHERS, INC., 2112 Broadway, New York, N. Y. 10023. Published in January.

MANUFACTURERS, ILLINOIS, DIRECTORY, MANUFACTURERS' NEWS, INC., 3 E. Huron St., Chicago, Ill. 60611. Published annually. Price, $34.95 annual rental; $50, if purchased outright. Includes over 23,000 manufacturers and executives.

MARINE CATALOG, SIMMONS-BOARDMAN PUBLISHING CORP., 30 Church St., New York, N. Y. 10007. Published annually early in the year. Contains alphabetical and classified lists of suppliers of products used in marine industries; also a trade-name index, and names of architects and consultants.

MARKET GUIDE, EDITOR & PUBLISHER, EDITOR & PUBLISHER Co., 850 Third Ave., New York, N. Y. 10022. Issued annually in October. Price, $10. Shows shopping centers, supermarkets, department and variety stores, etc.; and air, rail, bus, and barge lines serving large and small cities in the U.S. and Canada—arranged alphabetically by state or province. Exclusive data on daily newspaper markets. Next issue will have 1968 estimates of population, retail sales, and income; extensive detailed individual market surveys for over 1,500 U.S. and Canadian newspaper markets. Data on retailing and other factors.

MARKETS OF AMERICA, ADVERTISER PUBLISHING Co., 1056 Fifth Ave., New York, N. Y. 10028. Issued annually in March. Price, $5.

MARKING PRODUCTS AND EQUIPMENT, MARKING DEVICES PUBLISHING Co., 18 E. Huron St., Chicago, Ill. 60611. Published annually. Price, $1. Includes classified list of supply sources, trade names.

MATERIAL HANDLING ENGINEERING DIRECTORY & HANDBOOK, THE INDUSTRIAL PUBLISHING Co., DIVISION OF PITTSBURGH RAILROAD Co., 812 Huron Rd., Cleveland, Ohio 44115. Issued in the fall of odd years. Price, $12. Contains classified and alphabetical lists of equipment manufacturers; also lists of sales agents and branches, and of rental sources. Price, $15.

MATERIAL HANDLING/PACKAGING/SHIPPING, WESTERN, BUYERS' GUIDE, BAYMER PUBLICATIONS, INC., 440 N. La Brea Ave., Los Angeles, Calif. 90036. Issued in June. Included in yearly subscription price of $4.

MATERIALS ENGINEERING'S MATERIALS SELECTOR ISSUE, REINHOLD PUBLISHING CORP., 430 Park Ave., New York, N. Y. 10022. Published annually in October.

MECHANICAL ENGINEERS' CATALOG AND PRODUCT DIRECTORY, AMERICAN SOCIETY OF MECHANICAL ENGINEERS, 345 E. 47th St., New York, N. Y. 10017. Issued annually in September. Lists equipment and supply manufacturers in this field.

MEDICAL DIRECTORY OF NEW YORK STATE, MEDICAL SOCIETY OF THE STATE OF NEW YORK, 750 Third Ave., New York, N. Y. 10017. Published every two years. Price, $25 (plus New York State sales tax).

MEDICAL SPECIALISTS, A. N. MARQUIS Co., 200 E. Ohio St., Chicago, Ill. 60611. Vol. 12, out of print. Vol. 13, ready spring, 1968. Price, $27.50. Published every two years. Includes over 90,000 listings of specialists in 19 fields of medicine.

MENNONITE YEARBOOK, MENNONITE PUBLISHING Co., 610-614 Walnut Ave., Scottdale, Pa. 15683. Price, $1.50. Includes 6,000 Mennonite ministers in U.S. and foreign countries.

MEN'S AND BOYS' WEAR DIRECTORY, FAIRCHILD'S, FAIRCHILD PUBLICATIONS, INC., 7 E. 12th St., New York, N. Y. 10003. Issued in March and September. Lists New York manufacturers only. Price, 50 cents.

MEN'S CLOTHING & SPORTSWEAR DIRECTORY, FAIRCHILD'S, FAIRCHILD PUBLICATIONS, INC., 7 E. 12th St., New York, N. Y. 10003. Issued in May and November. Lists New York manufacturers only. Price, 50 cents.

MERCHANDISE MART DIRECTORY, THE MERCHANDISE MART, Chicago, Ill., 60654. Published in January and June. Free. Lists all tenants and exhibitors in the Merchandise Mart, world's largest commercial building.

METAL DIRECTORY, STANDARD, AMERICAN METAL MARKET Co., 525 W. 42nd St., New York, N. Y. 10036. Published every two years. Price, $24. Includes 20,000 foundries, die-casting plants, stamping works, galvanizers, rolling mills and distributors of ores.

METAL FINISHING GUIDEBOOK DIRECTORY, METALS & PLASTICS PUBLICATIONS, INC., 99 Kinderkamack Rd., Westwood, N. J. 07675. Issued annually in summer. Yearly subscription, $5.

METAL STATISTICS, AMERICAN METAL MARKET Co., Metal Statistics, 525 W. 42nd St., New York, N. Y. 10036. Published annually. Price, $5. Includes classified list of supply sources.

METALWORKING DIRECTORY, Dun & Bradstreet, Inc., 99 Church St., New York, N. Y. 10008. Published yearly. National edition, $380. Lists geographically, by product classification, and alphabetically, over 36,000 metalworking plants with 20 or more employees, plus over 2,000 metals distributors. Regional editions sell for $165 or $190.

METALWORKING MACHINERY, 1960, REVISION, U.S. Government Printing Office, Washington, D.C. 20402. Catalog No. D 7.13/3:1 v. 1.2. A complete two-volume revision of the 1956 Directory of Metalworking Machinery. Price per set, $7.50.

METROPOLITAN TRANSPORTATION & PLANNING DIRECTORY, Bobit Publishing Co., 1155 Waukegan Rd., Glenview, Ill. 60025. Published biennially. Next issue, February 1969.

(Michigan) MANUFACTURERS, MICHIGAN, DIRECTORY OF, Manufacturing Publishing Co., 8543 Puritan Ave., Detroit, Mich. 48238. Published biennially. Price, $40. Includes 16,000 manufacturers. Each manufacturer listed three ways: alphabetically, geographically, and by products classified. All Michigan manufacturers listed free of charge. Names and titles of executives; date established; number of employees (male and female); cable code, and export information.

MICRO-CATALOGS: Thomas Micro-Catalogs, Division of Thomas Publishing Co., 461 Eighth Ave., New York, N. Y. 10001. Issued in May, with a supplement in November. Advertising rates: $120 base charge, plus $10 for each additional page up to 50 pages.

MICROWAVE ENGINEERS' HANDBOOK & BUYERS' GUIDE, The Horizon House-Microwave, Inc., 610 Washington St., Dedham, Mass. 02026. Published in December. Price, $8 (including foreign orders).

MIDDLE MARKET DIRECTORY, Dun & Bradstreet, Inc., 99 Church St., New York, N. Y. 10008. Published annually. Price, $108.50. Lists alphabetically, geographically, and by line of business 24,500 business organizations with a net worth between $500,000 and $1,000,000, together with their owners, officers, and directors.

MILITARY MARKET MAGAZINE, THE ANNUAL JULY DIRECTORY ISSUE, Army Times Publishing Co., 2201 M St., N.W., Washington, D. C. 20037. Price, $2.50.

MILITARY, SELLING TO THE, U.S. Government Printing Office, Washington, D.C. 20402. Catalog No. D 1.2: Se 4/966. Price, 30 cents.

MILLINERY, WIGS, HAIR PIECES AND WIG ACCESSORIES DIRECTORY, WOMEN'S WEAR DAILY'S, Fairchild Publications, Inc., 7 E 12th St., New York, N. Y. 10003. Published in June and January. Price. 50 cents. Lists New York City manufacturers of millinery and millinery supplies.

MILLION DOLLAR DIRECTORY, Dun & Bradstreet, Inc., 99 Church St., New York, N. Y. 10008. Published yearly. Price, $108.50, with renewal for $89.50. Lists alphabetically, geographically, and by line of business 28,500 business organizations with a net worth of $1,000,000 or more, together with their owners, officers, and directors.

MINERALS YEARBOOK, Supt. of Documents, Washington, D.C. 20402. Includes iron-ore mines, ferro-alloy producers, etc. 1965 volumes being printed. Vol. I—Metals and Minerals (except fuels): $4.25; Vol. II—Fuels: $2.50; Vol. III—Area Reports, Domestic: $3.75; Vol. IV—Area Reports, International (in preparation—price or date of availability not known).

MINES MEN DIRECTORY, Colorado School of Mines Alumni Association, Golden, Colo. Published in June. Price, $3.50 when included with annual (domestic) subscription to *Mines Magazine.*

MINES REGISTER, American Metal Market Co., 525 W. 42nd St., New York, N. Y. 10036. Price, $36. Includes 7,500 nonferrous metal mining companies throughout the world.

MINNESOTA MEDICINE'S ROSTER ISSUE, Minnesota State Medical Association, 496 Lowery Medical Bldg., St. Paul, Minn. 55102. Issued in June. Yearly subscription, $6.50.

MISSILE & SPACE ALMANAC, Air Force Association, 1750 Pennsylvania Ave., N.W., Washington, D.C. 20006. Published in April. Included in yearly subscription price of *Air Force & Space Digest,* $7.

MOBILE LIFE, Davis Publications, Inc., 505 Park Ave., New York, N. Y. 10022. Published in May. Yearly subscription, $5.

MOP MANUFACTURERS BUYING GUIDE, BRUSHWARE PUBLICATIONS, INC., 44 N. Dean St., Englewood, N. J. 07631. Issued in June. Included in yearly subscription price of $4.

MOTION PICTURE ALMANAC, INTERNATIONAL, QUIGLEY PUBLISHING CO., INC., 1270 Sixth Ave., New York, N. Y. 10020. Issued annually in December. Single copy, $9. Lists photoplay companies, executives, producers, directors, and performers.

MOTION PICTURE HERALD'S MARKET & OPERATING GUIDE EDITION, QUIGLEY PUBLISHING CO., INC., 1270 Sixth Ave., New York, N. Y. 10020. Published annually in March. Yearly subscription, $5.

MOTOR CARRIER DIRECTORY, OFFICIAL, OFFICIAL MOTOR CARRIER DIRECTORY, INC., 1130 S. Canal St., Chicago, Ill. 60607. Issued in March and September. Single copy, $7.50; two-issue subscription, $11.

MOTOR FREIGHT GUIDE, OFFICIAL, OFFICIAL MOTOR FREIGHT GUIDE, INC., 1130 S. Canal St., Chicago, Ill. 60607. Published semiannually as 35 individual city guides, and three for more than one city, including one for four Texas cities. Three guides are issued in January and July, four in February and August, etc. Yearly subscription ranges from $2.50 to $6, depending upon guide ordered. Quantity discounts allowed. Each guide contains a list of carriers in that area.

MUNICIPAL & GOVERNMENT MANUAL, MOODY'S, MOODY'S INVESTORS SERVICE, 99 Church St., New York, N. Y. 10007. Published annually with twice weekly News Reports. Price, $165 a year. Contains an alphabetical list, by states, of municipalities, counties, school districts, irrigation districts, and other public bodies with bonded indebtedness; similar lists for the British Commonwealth, and for various countries in Europe, Latin America, and elsewhere; a utility directory of U.S. and Canadian cities showing their suppliers of electricity, gas, water and transit service; lists of public borrowers, by states, which have issued bonds secured only by the earnings of gas, electric or water utilities, airports, toll roads and bridges, etc., or by tuition payments, dormitory rentals, etc., or by the income from recreational facilities, leased industrial plants, and miscellaneous sources; and lists of officials of the Inter-American Development Bank, and of officials and agents of the European Coal and Steel Community.

MUNICIPAL YEAR BOOK, THE, INTERNATIONAL CITY MANAGER'S ASSOCIATION, 1313 E. 60th St., Chicago, Ill. 60637. Published annually. Price, $12. Lists 2,090 council-manager cities with their city managers. Other cities with a population over 5,000 are divided into two groups, with only mayor and city clerk shown for those under 10,000, but with the chief finance officer, the director of public works, and the police and fire chief also being included for those over 10,000. The book also lists professional organizations of municipal officials, state municipal leagues, and state associations of county officials.

MUTUAL FUND DIRECTORY, IDD, INC., 150 Broadway, New York, N. Y. 10038. Published twice a year in February and August. Price, $6. Includes mutual funds in the U.S. and Canada; contractual plans; tax-exempt bond funds, and exchange funds.

NATION'S RESTAURANT NEWS, LEBHAR-FRIEDMAN PUBLICATIONS, INC., 2 Park Ave., New York, N. Y. 10016. Published biweekly. Price, $2 a year. Includes fortnightly commodity outlook, labor outlook, Washington legislative outlook, plus new technological developments in food service equipment and food products.

NATURALISTS' DIRECTORY (INTERNATIONAL), THE, THE NATURALIST'S DIRECTORY, 376 Turrell Ave., South Orange, N. J. Published biannually. Price, $15. Includes 3,000 naturalists, subjects of interest, natural history museums, and scientific periodicals.

(Naval Academy) ALUMNI, REGISTER OF, ALUMNI ASSOCIATION OF THE UNITED STATES NAVAL ACADEMY, Annapolis, Md. Issued in February. Price, $8 (postpaid)

NAVAL RESERVE REGISTER OF COMMISSIONED & WARRANT OFFICERS OF JULY 1, 1961, U.S. GOVERNMENT PRINTING OFFICE, Washington, D.C. 20402. Catalog No. D 208.12/2/965. Price, $3.

NAVY, U.S., REGISTER OF RETIRED COMMISSIONED & WARRANT OFFICERS, REGULAR & RESERVE, OF THE, U.S. GOVERNMENT PRINTING OFFICE, Washington, D.C. 20402. Catalog No. D 208.12/3:966. Price, $3.

NEBRASKA MANUFACTURERS DIRECTORY, DEPARTMENT OF ECONOMIC DEVELOPMENT, P.O. Box 4666, State Capitol, Lincoln, Neb. 68509. Price, $5.

NETWORK RATES & DATA, SRDS, STANDARD RATE & DATA SERVICE, INC., 5201 Old Orchard Rd., Skokie, Ill. 60076. Published monthly. Yearly subscription, $5. Lists U.S. radio and television networks and affiliated stations for each.

NEW ENGLAND CONSTRUCTION'S DIRECTORY ISSUE, NEW ENGLAND CONSTRUCTION, 27 Muzzey St., Lexington, Mass. 02173. Published in March.

NEW ENGLAND ELECTRICAL BLUE BOOK, NEW ENGLAND ELECTRICAL NEWS, INC., 45 Morrissey Blvd., Boston, Mass. 02125. Published in November. Price, $15.

NEW ENGLAND MANUFACTURERS, GEORGE D. HALL CO., 20 Kilby St., Boston, Mass. 02109. Published annually. Price, $55. Includes 14,000 New England manufacturers listed alphabetically, geographically (by state, then by city or town), by products made, and by brand names.

(New England Road Builders) NERBA ANNUAL DIRECTORY, NEW ENGLAND ROAD BUILDERS ASSOCIATION, 20 Kilby St., Boston, Mass. 02109. Issued annually in October.

NEW JERSEY STATE INDUSTRIAL DIRECTORY, NEW JERSEY STATE INDUSTRIAL DIRECTORY, INC., 111 Eighth Ave., New York, N. Y. 10011. Published in June. Price, $50.

NEWSLETTERS AND REPORTING SERVICES, NATIONAL DIRECTORY OF, GALE RESEARCH CO., The Book Tower, Detroit, Mich. 48226. Price, $20.

NEWSPAPER CIRCULATION ANALYSIS, SRDS, STANDARD RATE & DATA SERVICE, INC., 5201 Old Orchard Rd., Skokie, Ill. 60076. Published annually. Individual newspaper circulations analyzed by state, county, metro area, and city. Relevant consumer market data included. Single copy, $10.

NEWSPAPER DIRECTORY, Vol. I, "THE WORKING PRESS OF THE NATION," THE NATIONAL RESEARCH BUREAU, INC., 221 N. LaSalle St., Chicago, Ill. 60601. Published annually. Price, $30. Leading daily and weekly newspapers are listed geographically and alphabetically. Editorial departments of newspapers are classified by fields of interest. Includes names of editor, managing editor and city editor, etc.; also supplemental information on news services, newsreels, photo services, special interest newspapers, principal foreign-language newspapers in the U.S., and daily newspapers of principal foreign countries printed in England.

(Newspaper) INTERNATIONAL YEARBOOK, EDITOR AND PUBLISHER CO., 850 Third Ave., New York, N. Y. 10022. Published annually in March. Price, $10. Includes daily newspapers, advertising agencies, publishers, editors, etc., in newspaper field in U.S.

NEWSPAPER RATES & DATA, SRDS, STANDARD RATE & DATA SERVICE, INC., 5201 Old Orchard Rd., Skokie, Ill. 60076. Published monthly, with updating bulletins. Yearly subscription rate, $38.50, with Newspaper Circulation Analysis.

NEWSPAPERS AND PERIODICALS, AYER'S DIRECTORY, N. W. AYER & SONS, INC., West Washington Sq., Philadelphia, Pa. 19106. Published annually. Price, $30. Includes newspapers and periodicals in U.S., its territories, Canada, Philippine Islands, Bermuda, and Panama; also alphabetical and classified lists.

NEW YORK IMPORTERS, DIRECTORY OF, COMMERCE & INDUSTRY ASSOCIATION OF NEW YORK, INC., 99 Church St., New York, N. Y. Published periodically. Price, $7 (plus applicable sales tax). Alphabetical and classified lists of 1,700 firms, with date of establishment, bank reference, products imported, countries, brand-names index.

NEW YORK PORT HANDBOOK, PORT RESOURCES INFORMATION COMMITTEE, 1 Broadway, New York, N. Y. 10004. Published in March. Price, $2.50.

NEW YORK STATE INDUSTRIAL DIRECTORY, NEW YORK STATE INDUSTRIAL DIRECTORY, 111 Eighth Ave., New York, N. Y. 10011. Over 800 pages. Lists more than 23,000 firms; 200,000 executives; classified headings of all industry of all 62 counties. Published in January. Price, $75.

NEW YORK STOCK EXCHANGE DIRECTORY, COMMERCE CLEARING HOUSE, 4025 W. Peterson Ave., Chicago, Ill. 60646. Published semiannually, January and June. Price, $3. Includes 2,000 members of the New York Stock Exchange, executives, securities.

NON-FOODS BUYERS, NATIONAL DIRECTORY OF, UNITED PUBLISHING CO., 32 12th St., N.E., Atlanta, Ga. 30309. Price, $25. Geographical listing of over 3,000 firms and 6,000 buyer names in 400 pages. Includes rack jobbers plus non-foods buyers for supermarket chains and voluntary and co-ops.

NORTHWEST FARM EQUIPMENT JOURNAL'S BUYER'S MANUAL, LUMBERMAN PUBLISHING CO., INC., 1011 Upper Midwest Bldg., Minneapolis, Minn. 55401. Published annually in March. Included in yearly subscription price of $2.

NOTION AND NOVELTY REVIEW'S DIRECTORY ISSUE, HAIRE PUBLISHING CO., 111 Fourth Ave., New York, N. Y. 10003. Published annually in May. Price, $1. ($1.50 in Canada and Latin America; $3 outside the Americas.) Contains alphabetical and classified lists of suppliers of notions, novelties, art needlework, etc.

(Nursery furniture) SMALL WORLD, EARNSHAW PUBLICATIONS, INC., 101 W. 31st St., New York, N. Y. 10001. Published monthly for retailers and manufacturers of nursery furniture and wheel goods.

OCCUPATIONAL THERAPY, AMERICAN JOURNAL OF, BUYERS' GUIDE, AMERICAN OCCUPATIONAL THERAPY ASSOCIATION, 251 Park Ave. S., New York, N. Y. 10010. Published annually in March. Included in yearly subscription price of $7.50. Single copies, $1.35.

OFFICE MACHINE INDUSTRY, WHO'S WHO IN, NATIONAL OFFICE DEALERS ASSOCIATION, 1411 Peterson Ave., Park Ridge, Ill. 60068. Published every other year. Price, $50. Contains list of office machine makers and dealers and their executives.

OIL/CHEMICAL BUYERS GUIDE, WORCO INDUSTRIES, INC., Western Saving Fund Bldg., Broad and Chestnut Sts., Philadelphia, Pa. 19107. Published semiannually for the oil, chemical (organic and inorganic), petroleum and petrochemical, machinery and equipment, raw materials, scientific instruments, materials handling, packaging and related industries. Distributed in the U.S. and foreign countries. In addition to product source listings, editorial includes: trade names, new product reviews, engineering and statistical data.

OIL FIELD EQUIPMENT & SERVICES, COMPLETE CATALOG OF, GULF PUBLISHING CO., Box 2608, Houston, Texas 77001. Issued in January of even years. Price, $72.

OIL PRODUCERS MAILING LIST DIRECTORY, PETROLEUM SERVICE BUREAU, P.O. Box 1826, Tulsa, Okla. 74101. Price per single copy, $35. Includes 8,500 operating personnel. Yearly continuous service, with monthly supplement revisions, $75.

OMC, OFFICE MASTER CATALOG, UNITED TECHNICAL PUBLICATIONS, DIV. COX BROADCASTING CORP., 645 Stewart Ave., Garden City, N. Y. 11530. Catalog section, plus directories of products; manufacturers/sales offices; trade names; office supply dealers. Distributed to 83,000 office executives and buyers. Published annually. Price, $15.

OPTICAL INDUSTRY AND SYSTEMS DIRECTORY, OPTICAL PUBLISHING CO., INC., 7 North St., Pittsfield, Mass. 01201. Published annually. Price, $16.50 in U.S. and Canada (postage additional overseas). Includes 2,500 firms supplying the optical industry and its related fields, both in the U.S. and abroad, with product listings, names of executives and officials, alphabetical and geographical breakdowns.

OPTOMETRIC WORLD'S ANNUAL TRADE DIRECTORY & BUYERS GUIDE, OCCIDENTAL PUBLISHING CO., 3924 Sunset Blvd., Los Angeles, Calif. 90029. Special issues: January—Optical Industry Trade Directory and Buyers' Guide; February—California Optometric Association Annual Congress Issue; March—Annual Sunwear Issue; April—Optical Equipment Issue; June—American Optometric Association Annual Congress Issue; October—Contact Lens Trade Directory and Buyers' Guide Issue.

OPTOMETRISTS, BLUE BOOK, THE PROFESSIONAL PRESS, INC., 5 N. Wabash Ave., Chicago, Ill. 60602. Price, $8. Published every two years. Includes specialists in U.S. and Canada.

OREGON MANUFACTURER'S DIRECTORY AND BUYER'S GUIDE, ECONOMIC DEVELOPMENT DIVISION, STATE OF OREGON, 560 State Office Bldg., Portland, Ore. 97201. Price, $5. Lists Oregon manufacturing establishments alphabetically, geographically (by city within county), and by product, using Standard Industrial Classification codes.

OSTEOPATHIC PHYSICIANS, DIRECTORY OF, AMERICAN OSTEOPATHIC ASSOCIATION, 212 E. Ohio St., Chicago, Ill. 60611. Published annually in January. Single copy, $25; extra copies, $12.50 each.

PACIFIC COAST AVIATION DIRECTORY, PACIFIC COAST AND WESTERN STATES AVIATION DIRECTORY, P.O. Box 3001, Stanford, Calif. 94305. Published in June. Lists airports, manufacturers, distributors, and servicing companies, and many of their executives.

PACIFIC HOTEL DIRECTORY & TRAVEL GUIDE, PACIFIC TRAVEL NEWS, 274 Brannan St., San Francisco, Calif. 94107. Published annually in October. Price, $5.

PACIFIC NORTHWEST MARITIME DIRECTORY, MARINE DIGEST PUBLISHING CO., 79 Columbia St., Seattle, Wash. 98104. Published annually. Price, $2. Includes 7,000 companies in commercial shipping.

PACIFIC SOUTHWEST DIRECTORY, FEED, SEED, GRAIN & MILLING (Arizona, California, Hawaii, Nevada, and Utah), CALIFORNIA GRAIN & FEED ASSOCIATION, 3333 Watt Ave., Sacramento, Calif. 95821. Issued each June 30. Price, $5.

PACKAGING DIRECTORY, GOOD PACKAGING'S WESTERN, PACIFIC TRADE JOURNALS, INC., 151 Mission St., San Francisco, Calif. 94105. Issued annually in February. Yearly subscription, $10.

PACKAGING MACHINERY CATALOG, ANGUS J. RAY PUBLISHING CO., 2 N. Riverside Plaza, Chicago, Ill. 60606. Issued in September. Price, $5. Contains classified and alphabetical lists of manufacturers of packaging machinery.

PACKAGING MACHINERY, OFFICIAL DIRECTORY, THE PACKAGING MACHINERY MANUFACTURERS INSTITUTE, INC., 2000 K St., N.W., Washington, D.C. 20006. Contains index of packaging machinery and manufacturers, machinery data, key executives; story of PMMI; 256 pages.

PACKING AND SHIPPING, BONNELL'S DIRECTORY, BONNELL'S PUBLICATIONS, INC., 437 E. Fifth St., Plainfield, N.J. 07060. Published semiannually. Price, $2. Includes 5,000 manufacturers of packing and shipping supplies in U.S.

PAPER & ALLIED TRADES, LOCKWOOD'S DIRECTORY OF THE, LOCKWOOD TRADE JOURNAL CO., INC., 551 Fifth Ave., New York, N. Y. 10017. Published annually in November. Price, $25.

PAPER, FILM & FOIL CONVERTER'S ANNUAL DIRECTORY OF MATERIALS, MACHINERY, EQUIPMENT & SUPPLIES FOR CONVERTERS, PEACOCK BUSINESS PRESS, INC., 200 S. Prospect Ave., Park Ridge, Ill. Issued annually in June. Price, $1.50; yearly subscription, $6. Manufacturers' listings are classified according to product.

(Paper) WALDEN'S ABC GUIDE & PAPER PRODUCTION YEARBOOK, WALDEN SONS & MOTT, INC., 486 Kinderkamack Rd., Oradell, N. J. 07649. Issued annually in February. Price, $15. Contains alphabetical and classified lists of paper manufacturers and converters.

(Paper Wholesalers) SOURCE OF SUPPLY DIRECTORY, PEACOCK BUSINESS PRESS, INC., 200 S. Prospect Ave., Park Ridge, Ill. Issued annually in January. Price, $10. Includes both alphabetical and geographical lists of paper wholesalers and of manufacturers who sell through paper wholesalers.

PAPER YEAR BOOK, THE, OJIBWAY PRESS, Ojibway Bldg., Duluth, Minn. 55802. Available in March. Revised annually. Price, $10.

PARK MAINTENANCE'S ANNUAL BUYER'S GUIDE ISSUE—published in October; ANNUAL SWIMMING POOL ISSUE—March; TURF RESEARCH AND IRRIGATION ANNUAL—July. MADISON PUBLISHING CO., Box 409, Appleton, Wis. 54911. Yearly subscriptions, $4.

PARKS & RECREATION, NATIONAL RECREATION AND PARK ASSOCIATION, 1700 Pennsylvania Ave., N.W., Washington, D.C. 20006. Price, $5.

(Patent Attorneys) ROSTER OF ATTORNEYS & AGENTS REGISTERED TO PRACTICE BEFORE THE U.S. PATENT OFFICE, U.S. GOVERNMENT PRINTING OFFICE, Washington, D.C. 20402. $1 each.

PATTERSON'S SOURCE GUIDE FOR EDUCATIONAL MATERIALS AND EQUIPMENT, EDUCATIONAL DIRECTORIES, INC., Box 199, Mt. Prospect, Ill. 60056. Issued semiannually in March and October. Price, $1 (plus postage).

PERIODICALS DIRECTORY, ULRICH'S, R. R. BOWKER CO., 1180 Avenue of the Americas, New York, N. Y. 10036. Two volumes, published in alternate years, each with annual supplements. Price, $15 per volume. Lists some 27,000 periodicals, foreign and U.S. Vol. I: Scientific Technical and Medical Periodicals; Vol. II: The Arts, Humanities, Social Sciences and Business.

PEST CONTROL'S CHEMICAL DIRECTORY ISSUE, TRADE MAGAZINES, INC., 1900 Euclid Ave., Cleveland, Ohio 44115. Published in March. Included in yearly subscription price of $5.

PEST CONTROL'S EQUIPMENT DIRECTORY ISSUE, TRADE MAGAZINES DIV. HARVEST PUBLISHING CO., 1900 Euclid Ave., Cleveland, Ohio 44115. Published in May. Included in yearly subscription price of $5.

PETROCHEMICAL PLANTS, WORLDWIDE PERSONNEL DIRECTORY OF, THE OIL AND GAS JOURNAL, Directory Dept., Box 1260, Tulsa, Okla. 74101. Published annually October 1. Contains personnel listings as well as statistical surveys on feedstocks, processes, and end products for petrochemical plants throughout the world. More than 7,000 names of key men with titles, addresses and phone numbers in home offices and plants. Information concerning plants that process crude oil, refinery products, natural gas and/or natural-gas liquids to manufacture petrochemicals. Price, $20.

PETROLEUM ENGINEER'S WORLD-WIDE NEW EQUIPMENT GUIDE, PETROLEUM ENGINEER PUBLISHING Co., Box 1589, Dallas, Texas 75202. Published annually in July. Lists manufacturers and suppliers to the oil and gas industry.

PETROLEUM NEWS MID-WAY "FACTBOOK" ISSUE, NATIONAL, McGRAW-HILL, INC., 330 W. 42nd St., New York, N. Y. 10036. Published annually. Yearly subscription, $6. Contains statistics on all facets of oil marketing, including distribution, products, markets, etc.

PETROLEUM REGISTER, INTERNATIONAL, PALMER PUBLICATIONS, 25 W. 45th St., New York, N. Y. 10036. Issued biennially in February; latest issue, 1967. Price, $35. Includes Petroleum Equipment and Service Directory (buyers' guide section).

PETROLEUM REPORT, WORLD, MONA PALMER PUBLISHING Co., 25 W. 45th St., New York, N. Y. 10036. Issued annually in February. Single copy, $12.

PET SHOP MANAGEMENT DIRECTORY, PET SHOP MANAGEMENT, INC., 91 S. Main St., Fond du Lac, Wis. 54935. Published monthly. Single copies, $1.25 when available. Subscription in U.S. and possessions, one year, $9; two years, $14.50; three years, $18. Canada, yearly, $20; foreign, $24. Manufacturers, $15 one year.

(Pharmacy) EL FARMACEUTICO'S BUYERS GUIDE & REFERENCE ISSUE, EL FARMACEUTICO PUBLISHING Co., INC., 50 Main St., Flemington, N. J. 08822. Published in June in Spanish. Circulation 25,000.

PHOTO DEALER DIRECTORY OF THE PHOTOGRAPHIC INDUSTRY, GELLERT PUBLISHING CORP., 33 W. 60th St., New York, N. Y. 10023. Published annually in March. Yearly subscription, $5.

PHOTOGRAPHER'S HANDBOOK, FREE-LANCE, NEW YORK INSTITUTE OF PHOTOGRAPHY, 10 W. 33rd St., New York, N. Y. 10001. Issued annually in June. Single copy, $5.

PHOTOGRAPHIC INDUSTRY, DIRECTORY OF THE, PHOTO DEALER MAGAZINE, 33 W. 60th St., New York, N. Y. 10023. Published annually. Subscription price, $5. Includes manufacturers, distributors, products.

PHOTOGRAPHY, PROFESSIONAL, DIRECTORY OF, PROFESSIONAL PHOTOGRAPHERS OF AMERICA, INC., 1090 Executive Way, Oak Leaf Commons, Des Plaines, Ill. 60018. Published annually in August. Price, $5.

PHYSICIAN AND HOSPITAL SUPPLY HOUSES, HAYES DIRECTORY OF. EDWARD N. HAYES, 4229 Birch St., Newport Beach, Calif. 92660. Lists 1,200 U.S. hospital and physician supply houses, including financial ratings. Issued annually in July. Price, $15.

PIPELINE CATALOG, GULF PUBLISHING Co., Box 2608, Houston, Texas 77001. Published annually in fall. Single copy, $14.

PLANT & PRODUCT DIRECTORY, THE (1966), FORTUNE, FORTUNE PLANT & PRODUCT DIRECTORY, Time & Life Bldg., Rockefeller Center, New York, N. Y. 10020. An offshoot of *Fortune's* annual directory of the 500 largest U.S. corporations. Price, $95 ($80 in lots of five or more). Lists, in two volumes totaling about 1,700 pages, all plants of the 1,000 largest U.S. manufacturing companies.

PLANT ENGINEER & SUPERINTENDENT DIRECTORY & EQUIPMENT GUIDE, ROCKWELL F. CLANCY Co., 75 E Wacker Dr., Chicago, Ill. 60601. Published annually in July. Price, $25. Lists chief engineers, purchasing agents, and plant and building maintenance superintendents and engineers in Illinois, Indiana, and Wisconsin.

PLASTIC DIRECTORY, WESTERN, WESTERN PLASTIC, 274 Brannan St., San Francisco, Calif. 94107. Published annually in January. Price, $4 to qualified subscribers not in 13 western states; free to qualified in western states. Single copy directory, $5.

(Plastic Engineers) SPE JOURNAL'S ROSTER ISSUE, SOCIETY OF PLASTICS ENGINEERS, INC., 65 Prospect St., Stamford, Conn. 06902. Published in August. Annual subscription, $8.

PLASTICS ENCYCLOPEDIA, MODERN, McGRAW-HILL, INC., 1301 Avenue of the Americas, New York, N. Y. 10019. Published as second issue in September. Price, $10. Subscription price includes directory issue. Lists manufacturers, processors, distributors, and supply sources.

PLASTICS, REINFORCED, ANNUAL DIRECTORY ISSUE, CAHNERS PUBLISHING Co., INC., 221 Columbus Ave., Boston, Mass. 02116. Published in November and December. Per issue, $1. Yearly subscription, $4.

PLASTICS WORLD, CAHNERS PUBLISHING CO., INC., 221 Columbus Ave., Boston, Mass. 02116. A directory of the plastics industry. Published in October. Per issue, $2. Yearly subscription, $8.

PLAYTHINGS DIRECTORY ISSUE, GEYER-MCALLISTER PUBLICATIONS, INC., 51 Madison Ave., New York, N. Y. 10010. Includes 1,800 manufacturers of toys and playthings in the U.S.

PODIATRY ASSOCIATION, AMERICAN, DESK REFERENCE OF THE, AMERICAN PODIATRY ASSOCIATION, 3301 16th St., N.W., Washington, D.C. 20010. Issued annually in October.

POISON CONTROL CENTERS, DIRECTORY OF, U.S. GOVERNMENT PRINTING OFFICE, Washington, D.C. 20402. Catalog No. FS 2.2:P75/2/965. Price, 20 cents a copy.

POST EXCHANGE & COMMISSARY DIRECTORY & BUYERS' GUIDE, GLENWOOD PUBLISHING CO., 799 Roosevelt Rd., Bldg. 3, Glen Ellyn, Ill. 60137. Subscription, $10 per year, includes this directory issued in February. Contains product index, product listings, manufacturers' addresses, military representatives, brand names.

POST OFFICES, DIRECTORY OF, SUPT. OF DOCUMENTS, U.S. GOVERNMENT PRINTING OFFICE, Washington, D.C. 20402. Published annually. A list of all post offices, branch post offices, and stations arranged by states, counties within states, Army posts, camps, etc. Catalog No. Pl. 10/4:965. Price, $2.75.

POSTAL AND SHIPPERS GUIDE, BULLINGER'S GUIDES, INC., 60 Woodland Ave., Westwood, N. J. 07675. Published annually. Price, $27. Lists railroad freight stations, post offices with zip codes or nearest post office to any given place in the U.S. and Canada.

(Poultry) WHO'S WHO IN THE EGG & POULTRY INDUSTRIES, WATT PUBLISHING CO., Mt. Morris, Ill. 61054. Published annually in June. Single copy, $15. Lists manufacturers, egg and poultry buyers and processors, further processors, exporters, wholesalers, warehouses, brokers, etc., as well as associations and government agencies in related fields.

POWER TRANSMISSION & BEARING HANDBOOK, THE INDUSTRIAL PUBLISHING CORP., 812 Huron Rd., Cleveland, Ohio 44115. Issued in November of even years. Price, $15.

PREMIUM MERCHANDISING'S DIRECTORY ISSUE, MERCHANDISING PUBLICATIONS, INC., 41 E. 42nd St., New York, N. Y. 10017. Issued in January. Price, $1. Lists premium manufacturers.

PREMIUM PRACTICE DIRECTORY OF SUPPLY SOURCES, BILL BROTHERS PUBLICATIONS, 630 Third Ave., New York, N. Y. 10017. Published in January. Price, $1. Lists suppliers of premium merchandise.

(Premiums) DIRECTORY ISSUES OF INCENTIVES, MAGAZINE OF THE PREMIUM INDUSTRY, HAIRE PUBLISHING CO., 111 Fourth Ave., New York, N. Y., 10003. Published annually in January. Included in yearly subscription price of $4. Contains classified and alphabetical lists of suppliers of products.

(Press) THE WORKING PRESS OF THE NATION, THE NATIONAL RESEARCH BUREAU, INC., 221 N. LaSalle St., Chicago, Ill. 60601. Published annually in four volumes; Vol. 1—The Newspaper Directory; Vol. 2—The Magazine Directory; Vol. 3—The Radio and Television Directory; Vol. 4—The Feature Writer and Syndicate Directory. May be purchased individually at $30 per volume, or as a complete four-volume set for $79.50.

(Printing) EL ARTE TIPOGRAFICO'S BUYERS' GUIDE ISSUE, GRAPHIC MAGAZINES, INC., 61 Hilton Ave., Garden City, N. Y. Published in September in Spanish. Controlled circulation throughout Latin America.

(Printing) INLAND PRINTER/AMERICAN LITHOGRAPHER'S ANNUAL BUYER'S REFERENCE GUIDE FOR EQUIPMENT, SUPPLIES & SERVICES, MAC-LEAN-HUNTER PUBLISHING CORP., 300 W. Adams St., Chicago, Ill. 60606. Issued in December. Part of yearly subscription, $5, or 50 cents alone.

PRINTING PRODUCTION'S "WHERE TO BUY" GUIDE, PENTON PUBLISHING CO., 1213 W. Third St., Cleveland, Ohio 44113. Issued in December. Yearly subscription, $5; 2 years, $8.

PRINTING PURCHASING MANUAL, WALDEN SONS & MOTT, INC., 466 Kinderkamack Rd., Oradell, N. J. 07649. Published annually in August. Single copy, $2.50. Contains classified and alphabetical lists of suppliers of products used in the printing industry; also a list of related associations.

PRINTING TRADES BLUE BOOK, A. F. LEWIS & CO. OF NEW YORK, INC., 853 Broadway, New York, N. Y. 10003. Published in three editions: New York edition annually in February; Northeastern edition in August of even years; Southeastern edition in August of odd years. Price, $25.

PRODUCT ENCYCLOPEDIA, PD&D (PRODUCT DESIGN & DEVELOPMENT) CHILTON Co., 56th and Chestnut Sts., Philadelphia, Pa. 19139. Published annually. Price, $5. Includes a master index of all product classifications (hardware, materials, laboratory equipment, etc.), and a master index of all manufacturers mentioned anywhere in the book.

PUBLIC RELATIONS REGISTER, PUBLIC RELATIONS SOCIETY OF AMERICA, INC., 845 Third Ave., New York, N. Y. 10022. Issued annually in July. Price, $35. Society members are listed by name, area, and affiliated firm.

PUBLIC RELATIONS, WHO'S WHO IN, PR PUBLISHING CO., INC., Meriden, N. H. 03770. Third (1967) edition in preparation. Price, $40. Public relations leaders around the world are listed, both geographically and alphabetically, with brief sketches of each.

PUBLIC UTILITIES FINANCIAL STATISTICS, C. A. TURNER, 327 S. LaSalle St., Chicago, Ill. 60604. Published annually. Price, $27.50. Public utility companies in U.S., 4,000 officials and executives.

PUBLIC UTILITY MANUAL, MOODY'S, MOODY'S INVESTORS SERVICE, INC., 99 Church St., New York, N. Y. 10007. Published annually with twice-weekly news reports. Price, $115 a year. Contains an alphabetical index of utilities in U.S. and Canada, etc.; a table of U.S. and Canadian cities showing suppliers of electricity, gas, water, and transit service for each; and individual company summaries which include officers, directors, plants, service areas, and subsidiaries, with dates of acquisition, etc., of the latter.

PUBLIC WELFARE DIRECTORY, AMERICAN PUBLIC WELFARE ASSOCIATION, 1313 E. 60th St., Chicago, Ill. 60637. Published annually. Price, $15. Includes administrative staffs of federal, state, and local welfare agencies in U.S. and Canada.

PULP & PAPER DIRECTORY, POST'S, MILLER FREEMAN PUBLICATIONS, INC., 370 Lexington Ave., New York, N. Y. 10017. Issued annually in January. Paid circulation.

PULP & PAPER MANUFACTURER'S MILL & PERSONNEL DIRECTORY, SOUTHERN, ERNEST H. ABERNETHY PUBLISHING CO., INC., 75 Third St., N.W., Atlanta, Ga. 30308. Published annually on October 1. Price, $5.

PURCHASING AGENT, SOUTHWESTERN, BUYER'S GUIDE ISSUE, PURCHASING AGENTS ASSOCIATION OF LOS ANGELES, 412 W. 6th St., Los Angeles, Calif. 90014. Issued in November. Included in $6 yearly subscription.

PURCHASING DIRECTORY, CONOVER-MAST, INDUSTRIAL DIRECTORIES, INC., 95 East Putnam Ave., Greenwich, Conn. 06830. Issued in April and October.

RADIO AMATEUR CALLBOOK, RADIO AMATEUR CALLBOOK, INC., 4844 W. Fullerton Ave., Chicago, Ill. 60639. Two sections, U.S. and foreign; both issued quarterly. Single copy of U.S. section, $6.95; yearly subscription, $24. Single copy of foreign section, $4.95; yearly subscription, $16. U.S. section lists approximately 283,000 licensed radio amateurs; the foreign section about 135,000.

RADIO AMATEUR'S HANDBOOK, AMERICAN RADIO RELAY LEAGUE, INC., 225 Main St., Newington, Conn. 06111. Issued in January. Price of yearly subscription to magazine QST, $7.50.

RADIO AND TV DIRECTORY, WORKING PRESS OF THE NATION, NATIONAL RESEARCH BUREAU, INC., 221 N. LaSalle St., Chicago, Ill. 60601. Published annually. Price, $30. Includes stations, executives, public relations contacts, etc.

RADIO-ELECTRONIC MASTER, UNITED TECHNICAL PUBLICATIONS, DIV. COX BROADCASTING CORP., 645 Stewart Ave., Garden City, N. Y. 1,800-page catalog of standard electronic products divided into 32 product categories. Published annually. Single copy, $10.

RADIO AND TELEVISION DIRECTORY, Vol. III, "Working Press of the Nation," NATIONAL RESEARCH BUREAU, INC., 221 N. LaSalle St., Chicago, Ill. 60601. Published annually. Price, $30. Lists all major radio and TV stations in the U.S. geographically, including addresses and personnel. Also included are power and networks. Programing sections by categories contain name and description of program, the master of ceremonies, broadcast days and times, whether guests are used.

RADIO RATES & DATA, SRDS, STANDARD RATE & DATA SERVICE, INC., 5201 Old Orchard Rd., Skokie, Ill. 60076. Published monthly with updating bulletins. Price, $44. Lists U.S. radio stations, grouped by state and city, with rates and other details.

RAILROAD OFFICIALS, POCKET LIST OF, THE RAILWAY EQUIPMENT & PUBLICATION Co., 424 W. 33rd St., New York, N. Y. 10001. Published quarterly in January, April, etc. Single copy, $4; per year, $10.

RAILROADING, WHO'S WHO IN NORTH AMERICA, SIMMONS-BOARDMAN PUBLISHING CORP., 30 Church St., New York, N. Y. 10007. Includes railway supply manufacturers, leaders of railroad labor organizations, members of regulatory bodies, transportation economists, specialists in railway finance, educators concerned with railroad problems, ICC practitioners, and selected group of consultants, authors, and editors.

RAILWAYS, ETC., THE OFFICIAL GUIDE OF THE, NATIONAL RAILWAY PUBLICATION Co., 424 W. 33rd St., New York, N. Y. 10001. Published monthly. Price, $39 per year; single copy, $5. Carries passenger schedules and freight information on U.S., Canadian, and Mexican railways; lists their offices and principal officials; railway associations and their officials; the membership of government commissions, committees, and boards handling railway matters. Also shows steamship lines and their officials, airlines and their principal offices, as well as military posts and hospitals, national parks, and alphabetical lists of points served by rail, air, or water routes.

READY-TO-WEAR DIRECTORY, WOMEN'S WEAR DAILY'S, FAIRCHILD PUBLICATIONS, INC., 7 E. 12th St., New York, N. Y. 10003. Issued in April and October. Price, 50 cents. Lists New York City manufacturers of dresses and women's coats, suits, etc.

(Real Estate) CALIFORNIA REAL ESTATE ROSTER, CALIFORNIA REAL ESTATE ASSOCIATION, 520 South Grand Ave., Los Angeles, Calif. 90017. Published annually in June. Price, $10.

REAL ESTATE HANDBOOK & DIRECTORY, NATIONAL (annual) REAL ESTATE INVESTOR, NATIONAL (monthly), DORNOST PUBLISHING CO., INC., 132 W. 31st St., New York, N. Y. 10001.

REALTORS, NATIONAL ROSTER OF, DIRECTORY, STAMATS PUBLISHING CO., 427 Sixth Ave., S.E., Cedar Rapids, Iowa 52406. Published in the spring.

REFINING AND GAS PROCESSING, WORLD-WIDE PERSONNEL DIRECTORY OF, THE OIL AND GAS JOURNAL, P.O. Box 1260, Tulsa, Okla. 74101. Published annually, May 1. Price, $30. Lists 1,700 refineries, gas processing; compounding and rerefining plants; names of 13,000 key personnel with titles, addresses and phone numbers; statistical surveys showing total plant throughput and downstream processes and capacities; and projects newly completed, under construction or planned. An additional section shows engineering and/or construction firms with services for petroleum processing plants.

(Refrigerated) DIRECTORY OF, REFRIGERATED PUBLIC WAREHOUSES, NATIONAL ASSOCIATION OF REFRIGERATED WAREHOUSES, 1210 Tower Bldg., Washington, D.C. 20005. Published annually. Price, $10. Free to users of public refrigerated warehouses. Includes 500 refrigerated warehouses, executives, services.

RENTAL PRODUCTS, DIRECTORY ISSUE OF RENTAL EQUIPMENT REGISTER, MIRAMAR PUBLISHING CO., 2048 Cotner Ave., Los Angeles, Calif. 90025. Published in June. Yearly subscription, $5.

REPRODUCTIONS ENCYCLOPEDIA, GEYER-McALLISTER PUBLICATIONS, INC., 51 Madison Ave., New York, N. Y. 10010. Incorporated in the July issue of *Reproductions Review*. Issued annually. Price, $2.50. Includes classified lists of the makers of materials and supplies for the duplicating industry.

RESEARCH SOCIETY OF AMERICA, OPERATIONS, DIRECTORY, OPERATIONS RESEARCH SOCIETY OF AMERICA, 428 E. Preston St., Baltimore, Md. 21202. Published annually. Price, $2.50. Includes 5,500 members of the society and their addresses.

RICE ANNUAL, FORT PIPES, 823 Perdido St., New Orleans, La. 70112. Published annually in June, as a 13th issue of *The Rice Journal*. Yearly subscription price, $5. Lists U.S. rice mills and their personnel, and drying and storage plants.

ROOFER, AMERICAN, & BUILDING IMPROVEMENT CONTRACTOR'S MANUAL & DIRECTORY EDITION, SHELTER PUBLICATIONS, 205 W. Monroe St., Chicago, Ill. 60606. Issued annually in March. Subscription, $5; directory issue alone, 75 cents. Contains classified lists of manufacturers, distributors, etc., supplying materials and services for the building and roofing industries.

(Rubber) MATERIALS AND COMPOUNDING INGREDIENTS FOR RUBBER, RUBBER WORLD MAGAZINE, BILL PUBLICATIONS, 630 Third Ave., New York, N. Y. 10017. Profiles every rubber ingredient on the market.

RUBBER RED BOOK, PALMERTON PUBLISHING CO., 101 W. 31st St., New York, N. Y. 10001. Published annually. Price, $20. Includes Section I: rubber manufacturers; Section II: suppliers; Section III: leading people in the industry.

SAFETY-MAINTENANCE DIRECTORY, BEST'S, ALFRED M. BEST CO., INC., Park Ave., Morristown, N. J. 07960. Published in the even years. Price, $10.

(Safety) OCCUPATIONAL HAZARDS' PRODUCT DATA GUIDE ISSUE, THE INDUSTRIAL PUBLISHING CO., 812 Huron Road, Cleveland, Ohio 44115. Published in January. Yearly subscription, $12 in U.S.; single copies, $1.25.

SALESMEN'S DIRECTORY, NATIONAL, H. H. FORD CO., 219 Westfield Blvd., Indianapolis, Ind. 46208. Published annually. Price, $10. Includes 2,500 specialty salesmen, house-to-house wagon jobbers.

SALES PROMOTION ALMANAC, ADVERTISING AND SALES PROMOTION, 740 N. Rush St., Chicago, Ill. 60611. Published annually. Price, $1. Includes 400 special days, weeks and months; conventions, awards.

SANITARY MAINTENANCE'S BUYER'S GUIDE DIRECTORY, TRADE PRESS PUBLISHING CO., 407 E. Michigan St., Milwaukee, Wis. 53201. Issued in January. Included in yearly subscription price of $4.

SANITATION INDUSTRY YEARBOOK, RRJ PUBLISHING CORP., 210 E. 53rd St., New York, N. Y. 10022. Issued in June. Price, $15. Sent free to all subscribers to *Refuse Removal Journal—Solid Wastes Management.* Subscription, $5 annually.

SAVINGS AND LOAN ASSOCIATIONS, AMERICAN DIRECTORY OF, T. K. SANDERSON, 200 E. 25th St., Baltimore, Md. 21218. Published annually. Price, $30. Includes over 6,000 savings, building, loan and cooperative banks in U.S., with names of executives, zip codes, area codes, telephone numbers, branches.

SCHOLARS, AMERICAN, DIRECTORY OF, R. R. BOWKER CO., 1180 Avenue of the Americas, New York, N. Y. 10036. Includes leading American scholars; title, subject, college attended, addresses. Fourth edition in four volumes: Vol. I—History (1963); Vol. II—English, Speech, and Drama (1964); Vol. III—Foreign Languages, Linguistics and Philology (1964); Vol. IV—Philosophy, Religion and Law (1964). Price, $15 net prepaid each volume.

SCHOOL & UNIVERSITY MAGAZINE, AMERICAN, Plant Planning & Purchasing Guide, BUTTENHEIM PUBLISHING CORP., 757 Third Ave., New York, N. Y. 10017. Published in May. Yearly subscription, $8.

SCHOOL ARTS MAGAZINE'S BUYERS GUIDE ISSUE, DAVIS PUBLICATIONS, INC., Printers Bldg., Worcester, Mass. 01608. Issued in February. Included in yearly subscription price of $7.

SCHOOL LIBRARY SUPERVISORS DIRECTORY, R. R. BOWKER CO., 1180 Avenue of the Americas, New York, N. Y. 10036. Published annually. Price, $12.85. Lists school library supervisors by state, county and city; includes statistics on each state's educational and school library systems.

SCHOOLS, PRIVATE INDEPENDENT, BUNTING & LYON, INC., 238 N. Main St., Wallingford, Conn. 06492. Published annually. Price, $15. Includes 960 schools in the U.S. and American schools in territories and foreign countries.

SCHOOL SHOP'S DIRECTORY ISSUE, PRAKKEN PUBLICATIONS, 416 Longshore Dr., Ann Arbor, Mich. 48107. Issued in April. Included in yearly subscription price of $4, or available at single copy price of $1.

SCHOOLS, PUBLIC SECONDARY DAY, DIRECTORY OF, 1958-59, U.S. GOVERNMENT PRINTING OFFICE, Washington, D.C. 20402. Catalog No. FS 5.220:20031. Price, $1.25.

SCHOOLS, SUMMER STUDIES IN PRIVATE INDEPENDENT, BUNTING & LYON, INC., 238 N. Main St., Wallingford, Conn. 06492. Published annually. Price, $6. Includes 153 schools in the U.S. and American schools in foreign countries.

SCIENCE, AMERICAN MEN OF, R. R. BOWKER CO., 1180 Avenue of the Americas, New York, N. Y. 10036. Price, $25 per volume. (Physical and Biological Sciences Section in six volumes.) Includes 135,000 biographies of American and Canadian scientists.

SCIENTIFIC DIRECTORY, NATIONAL INSTITUTES OF HEALTH, U.S. GOVERNMENT PRINTING OFFICE, Washington, D.C. 20402. Catalog No. FS 2.21:41. Price, 55 cents.

(Security Trades) NSTA YEAR BOOK, IDD, INC., 150 Broadway, New York, N. Y. 10038. Issued yearly in the fall. Price, $5. Includes an alphabetical list of the membership of the National Security Traders Association.

SEED TRADE BUYERS' GUIDE, SEED WORLD PUBLICATIONS, P.O. Box 568, LaGrange, Ill. 60525. Issued annually in January. Price, $5. Contains classified lists of suppliers by states.

SELLING TO THE MILITARY, U. S. GOVERNMENT PRINTING OFFICE, Washington, D.C. 20402. Catalog No. D 1.2: Se 4/966. Price, 30 cents.

(Service Distributors) RACK JOBBERS, NATIONAL DIRECTORY OF, UNITED PUBLISHING CO., 32 12th St., N.E., Atlanta, Ga. 30309. Price, $15. Geographical listing of over 3,000 firms and 6,000 buyer names in 400 pages. Includes rack jobbers plus non-foods buyers for supermarket chains and voluntary and co-ops.

SEWERAGE MANUAL & CATALOG FILE, THE, PUBLIC WORKS JOURNAL CORP., 200 S. Broad St., Ridgewood, N. J. 07451. Issued annually in September.

(Shipping) INTERNATIONAL SHIPPING AND SHIPBUILDING DIRECTORY, EDWARD W. SWEETMAN CO., 1 Broadway, New York, N. Y. 10004. Published annually in May. Price, $20. Contains lists of the shipowners, builders and repairers of the world, and of marine engine builders.

(Shipping) LEONARD'S GUIDE, G. R. LEONARD & CO., 123 N. Wacker Dr., Chicago, Ill. 60606. Issued in eight separate editions: New York, January and July; Philadelphia, February and August; Chicago, May and November; St. Louis, June and December; California, January; New England, March; Boston, April; Ohio, May. Each edition is $6 per year (except Philadelphia and California, which are $10 per year). Each lists all motor carriers in its area, and shows which motor carriers serve specific cities throughout the country.

SHIPS, REGISTER OF, LLOYDS REGISTER OF SHIPPING, 17 Battery Pl., New York, N. Y. 10004. Price, $135. Lists owners of more than 100 tons gross, with the builder of each ship, date, length, machinery, etc.

SHOE BUYERS GUIDE, RUMPF PUBLISHING CO., 300 W. Adams St., Chicago, Ill. 60606. Published annually in March. Price, $2. Lists U.S. shoe manufacturers.

SHOPPING CENTERS IN THE U.S. & CANADA DIRECTORY, NATIONAL RESEARCH BUREAU, INC., 221 N. LaSalle St., Chicago, Ill. 60610. Price, $50. Geographical arrangement gives name of center, location, mailing address, owner/developer, manager, size and cost of plant. Comprehensive register covering over 11,000 shopping centers.

(Shows) EXHIBITS SCHEDULE, 1212 Chestnut St., Philadelphia, Pa. 19107. Published annually in September (supplement in April). Price, $25. Includes 5,000 fairs, trade shows, geographical and by date. Gives name and address of executive in charge and sponsoring organization.

SOAP BLUE BOOK, MACNAIR-DORLAND CO., INC., 254 W. 31st St., New York, N. Y. 10001. Published in March. Included in yearly subscription price of $4.

(Social Welfare) SERVICE DIRECTORY, NATIONAL SOCIAL WELFARE ASSEMBLY, 345 E. 46th St., New York, N. Y. 10017. Published every two years. Price, $2.25. Includes national organizations affiliated and associated with the assembly.

SOCIAL WORK, ENCYCLOPEDIA OF, NATIONAL ASSOCIATION OF SOCIAL WORKERS, 2 Park Ave., New York, N. Y. 10016. Price, $13 (includes postage and handling).

SOFT DRINK REVIEW'S TRADE DIRECTORY, OCCIDENTAL PUBLISHING CO., 3924 Sunset Blvd., Los Angeles, Calif. 90029. Published annually in June; combined with an exclusive *Directory of Franchise Company Personnel*. Included in yearly subscription price of $3, or $5 for two years.

SOUND INDUSTRY DIRECTORY, ST. REGIS PUBLICATIONS, INC., 25 W. 45th St., New York, N. Y. 10036. Published annually.

SOYBEAN, THE DIGEST (BLUE BOOK ISSUE), AMERICAN SOYBEAN ASSOCIATION, Hudson, Iowa 50643. Issued annually in March. Price, $10.

SPACE DIRECTORY, WORLD, INCLUDING OCEANOLOGY, AMERICAN AVIATION PUBLICATIONS, INC., 1001 Vermont Ave., N.W., Washington, D.C. 20005. Published in March and September. Price, one to nine copies, $15 each; 10 or more, $13 each.

SPORTING GOODS DIRECTORY, THE, SPORTING GOODS PUBLISHING CO., 2018 Washington Ave., St. Louis, Mo. 63166. Published annually in the spring. $1.50 a copy.

SPORTING GOODS JOBBERS AND MANUFACTURERS REPRESENTATIVES, DIRECTORY OF, SPORTING GOODS PUBLISHING CO., 2018 Washington Ave., St. Louis, Mo. 63166. Published annually. Price, $15. Includes 2,800 jobbers and manufacturers' representatives in the sporting goods field in the U.S.; ratings and executives.

SPORTSWEAR, BLOUSE & SKIRT DIRECTORY, WOMEN'S WEAR DAILY'S, FAIRCHILD PUBLICATIONS, INC., 7 E. 12th St., New York, N. Y. 10003. Issued June and December. Price, 50 cents.

STATESMAN'S YEARBOOK, THE, ST. MARTIN'S PRESS, INC., 175 Fifth Ave., New York, N. Y. 10010. Published annually in September. Price, $12.50. Lists the membership of the U. N.; related organizations, other international organizations (often with bibliographies); governmental units, and usually a few officials, in most of the nations of the world, and in the states or provinces of U.S., Canada, Australia, and U.S.S.R.

STEEL FOUNDRIES, DIRECTORY OF, STEEL FOUNDERS' SOCIETY OF AMERICA, 21010 Center Ridge Rd., Westview Towers, Rocky River, Ohio 44116. Price, $15. Includes over 400 steel foundries and officers in U.S. and Canada.

STEEL SERVICE CENTER INSTITUTE ISSUE OF METAL/CENTER NEWS, AMERICAN METAL MARKET CO., 525 W. 42nd St., New York, N. Y. 10036. Published annually in May. This issue includes the *Directory of Handling and Metal Processing Equipment Manufacturers.*

STEEL SHIPPING CONTAINERS MANUFACTURERS, DIRECTORY, STEEL SHIPPING CONTAINER INSTITUTE, 600 Fifth Ave., New York, N. Y. 10020. Free. Information on addresses of manufacturers' plants and offices.

STOCK EXCHANGE DIRECTORY, NEW YORK, COMMERCE CLEARING HOUSE, 4025 W. Peterson Ave., Chicago, Ill. 60646. Published semiannually. Price, $3. Includes roster of members, officers, member firms.

STOCK EXCHANGE MEMBERSHIP DIRECTORY, AMERICAN, COMMERCE CLEARING HOUSE, INC., 4025 W. Peterson Ave., Chicago, Ill. 60646. Published semiannually. Price, $3. Includes roster of regular and associate members, officers.

STREET & HIGHWAY MANUAL & CATALOG FILE, PUBLIC WORKS JOURNAL CORP., 200 S. Broad St., Ridgewood, N. J. 07451. Issued annually in February.

SUGAR Y AZUCAR YEARBOOK, MONA PALMER, 25 W. 45th St., New York, N. Y. 10036. Issued annually in November. Price, $10.

SWIMMING POOL DATA & REFERENCE ANNUAL, HOFFMAN PUBLICATIONS, Professional Bldg., Sunrise Center, Ft. Lauderdale, Fla. 33304. Published annually for pool builders, service companies, equipment dealers and manufacturers, architects, engineers, public health and recreation officials, colleges, schools, public pool owners and operators, and individuals and groups planning new pools. Price, $5.

SYNTHETIC ORGANIC CHEMICALS, Superintendent of Documents, Washington, D.C. 20402. Includes technical societies, trade association officers. Catalog No. TC 1.33:963. Price, $1.50.

TEA & COFFEE BUYERS GUIDE, TEA & COFFEE TRADE JOURNAL CO., 79 Wall St., New York, N. Y. 10005. Published every 2 years. Price, $5. Includes tea and coffee exporters, etc., wholesale coffee roasters and tea packers, soluble coffee and tea mfrs. in U.S. and abroad.

TEACHERS, ELEMENTARY, GUIDE TO FREE CURRICULUM MATERIALS, EDUCATORS PROGRESS SERVICE, Box 497, Randolph, Wis. 53956. Covers free curriculum materials for the elementary level only. Includes a section on "Teacher Reference and Professional Growth Materials." Revised annually. Price, $8.75.

TEENS' & BOYS' OUTFITTER DIRECTORY, BOYS' OUTFITTER CO., INC., 71 W. 35th St., New York, N. Y. 10001. Published semiannually—April and October. Price, $1. Lists manufacturers of boys' and teenage students' apparel throughout America.

TELEPHONE ENGINEER & MANAGEMENT'S DIRECTORY, BROOKHILL PUBLISHING CO., 402 W. Liberty Dr., Wheaton, Ill. 60187. Issued annually in July. Price, $20 per copy. Contains geographic lists of telephone companies and their personnel around the world; classified lists of makers of telephone equipment and supplies; a telephone department list of the Rural Electrification Administration, and holding companies in the telephone industry.

TELEPHONE DIRECTORY OF THE TELEPHONE INDUSTRY, TELEPHONY PUBLISHING CORP., 53 W. Jackson Blvd., Chicago, Ill. 60604. Issued annually in June. Price, $30 per copy. Lists telephone companies and their principal officials throughout U.S. and Canada, associations of the industry, and public utility commissions. Equipment and supply list is classified. List of manufacturers, suppliers, and service organizations (alphabetical). Comprehensive industry statistics.

TELEVISION ALMANAC, QUIGLEY PUBLISHING CO., INC., 1270 Sixth Ave., New York, N. Y. 10020. Issued annually in January. Single copy, $9.

(Television) RADIO AND TELEVISION DIRECTORY, "THE WORKING PRESS OF THE NATION," THE NATIONAL RESEARCH BUREAU, INC., 221 N. LaSalle St., Chicago, Ill. 60601. Published annually. Price, $30. Lists all major radio and TV stations in the U.S., according to power, news services, name and description of program, the master of ceremonies, broadcast days and times, whether guests are used.

TELEVISION RATES & DATA, SRDS SPOT, STANDARD RATE & DATA SERVICE, INC., 5201 Old Orchard Rd., Skokie, Ill. 60076. Published monthly with updating bulletins. Yearly subscription price, $38.50. Lists U.S. television stations grouped by state and city.

TENNESSEE MUNICIPAL OFFICIALS, MUNICIPAL TECHNICAL ADVISORY SERVICE, The University of Tennessee, Knoxville, Tenn. 37916. Published annually in September. Price, $3.

TEXAS, ALMANAC, DALLAS MORNING NEWS, Young at Houston St., Dallas, Texas 75222. Published every 2 years. Includes state officials, boards, mayors, city managers, county officials.

TEXAS PROFESSIONAL ENGINEER DIRECTORY, TEXAS SOCIETY OF PROFESSIONAL ENGINEERS, Box 2145, Austin, Texas 78767. Published in March. Price, $5.

TEXTBOOKS IN PRINT, R. R. BOWKER Co., 1180 Avenue of the Americas, New York, N. Y. 10036. Published annually. Price, $4 net prepaid. Indexes 14,000 elementary and secondary textbooks, supplementary readers and pedagogical books of 207 U.S. publishers.

TEXTILE BLUE BOOK, DAVISON'S, DAVISON PUBLISHING Co., Ridgewood, N. J. 07450. Issued annually in January. Single deluxe office edition, $20; executives' and salesmen's directories, $8.50 each. Contains state-by-state lists of cotton, knit goods, jute, wool and worsted; synthetic and silk manufacturers; dyers and finishers, "Sanforized" licensees, factors, commission merchants, wool dealers, dry goods dealers and converters, waste and linter dealers. Also textile schools, textile associations, and U.S. and foreign raw cotton firms. And alphabetical U.S. and Canadian indexes of all textile firms mentioned in any of the above classifications.

TEXTILE CATALOGUES & BUYERS GUIDE, DAVISON'S, DAVISON PUBLISHING Co., Ridgewood, N. J. 07450. Issued annually in late spring.

TEXTILE REPORTER, AMERICAN, TEXTILE STATISTICS SECTION, AMERICA'S TEXTILE REPORTER, 286 Congress St., Boston, Mass. 02210. Directory included in price of subscription, $5. Includes 30,000 top executives of all textile firms and mills in geographical order.

THOMAS GROCERY REGISTER, THOMAS PUBLISHING Co., 461 Eighth Ave., New York, N. Y. 10001. Issued in July. Single copy, $15. Lists wholesalers, chains, supermarkets, brokers, manufacturers and processors in U.S., Canada and Puerto Rico; also warehouses, banks, and importers.

TOBACCO BUYERS' GUIDE SUPPLEMENT (annual), LOCKWOOD TRADE JOURNAL Co., 49 W. 45th St., New York, N. Y. 10036. Published last week in October. Subscription, $3.

TOBACCO DIRECTORY, WORLD, TRADE PUBLICATIONS LIMITED, 210 Fifth Ave., New York, N. Y. 10010. Published every two years. Price, $15. Covers the tobacco industry and leaf tobacco trade for each country of the world, including suppliers of machinery, equipment, etc., to the tobacco industry.

TOBACCO JOURNAL SUPPLIER DIRECTORY, UNITED STATES, UNITED STATES TOBACCO JOURNAL, 145 Avenue of the Americas, New York, N. Y. 10013. Published annually in December.

TOMATO YEARBOOK, AMERICAN, BRANDEN PRESS, 36 Melrose St., Boston, Mass. 02116. Published annually. Price, $2. State agricultural colleges, experiment stations and associations, names and addresses of leading men and women engaged in tomato research in U.S.

(Tool & die makers) NTDPMA JOURNAL, NATIONAL TOOL, DIE & PRECISION MACHINERY ASSOCIATION, 1411 K St., N.W., Washington, D.C. 20005. Published annually in October.

TOYS & NOVELTIES DIRECTORY, HAIRE PUBLISHING Co., 111 Fourth Ave., New York, N. Y. 10003. Issued annually in June. Single copy, 50 cents.

TRADE NAMES, MATERIAL, HANDBOOK OF, AND SUPPLEMENTS I, II, III, AND IV, INDUSTRIAL RESEARCH SERVICE, INC., Masonic Bldg., Dover, N. H. 03820. Prices: Handbook, $25; Supplement I, $16; Supplement II, $17; Supplement III, $18; Supplement IV, $25. Include over 50,000 trade-name products manufactured by over 3,000 manufacturers in U.S.

TRAFFIC EXECUTIVES, COMMERCIAL, OFFICIAL DIRECTORY OF, Traffic Publishing Co., Inc., 100 Sixth Ave., New York, N. Y. 10013. Published annually. Price, $8. Includes executives of 7,100 industrial firms, traffic boards, leagues, bureaus, utility commissions.

TRANSIT ADVERTISING RATES & DATA, SR&D, Standard Rate & Data Service, Inc., 5201 Old Orchard Rd., Skokie, Ill. 60076. Published quarterly. Yearly subscription, $10.

TRANSPORTATION MANUAL, MOODY'S, Moody's Investors Service, Inc., 99 Church St., New York, N. Y. 10007. Published annually, with twice weekly News Reports. Price, $120 a year. Contains an alphabetical list of transportation companies in general, and separate sections on U.S. railroad companies, Canadian and other foreign railroad companies, air transport companies, steamship lines, trucking companies, bus and electric railway companies, oil pipeline companies, and miscellaneous (bridge, renting, leasing, etc.) companies.

TRAVEL AGENTS, INTERNATIONAL DIRECTORY, Ronald E. Ingledue, 5850 Hollywood Blvd., Hollywood, Calif. 90028. Price, $15. Includes over 16,000 agents listed geographically throughout the world. Lists detailed information such as addresses, telephone numbers, conference appointments, date established, number of employees, etc.

TRAVEL BLUE BOOK, The American Traveler, Inc., 2 W. 46th St., New York, N. Y. 10036. Issued annually. Lists travel films covering all countries; also yearly report on travel agency business.

TRAVEL INDUSTRY PERSONNEL DIRECTORY, The American Traveler, Inc., 2 W. 46th St., New York, N. Y. 10036. Issued annually. Single copy, $4.

TRAVEL TRAILER & TENT TRAILER BUYING GUIDE ISSUE OF MOBILE HOME JOURNAL, Davis Publications, Inc., 505 Park Ave., New York, N. Y. 10022. Published in April. Yearly subscription, $5.

UNDERWRITERS HANDBOOKS, National Underwriter Co., 420 E. Fourth St., Cincinnati, Ohio 45202. Price, $14 each. Includes insurance agents, adjusters, attorneys, brokers; books cover 36 states.

UNITARIAN UNIVERSALIST ASSOCIATION DIRECTORY, Beacon Press, 25 Beacon St., Boston, Mass. 02108. Published annually. Price, $4. Includes 1,100 churches and fellowships, ministers, statistics, etc.

UNIVERSITIES AND COLLEGES, AMERICAN, American Council on Education, 1785 Massachusetts Ave., N. W., Washington, D.C. 20036. Ninth edition, 1964. Price, $15. Includes geographic list of 1,000 colleges and administrative officers, membership of education associations.

UPHOLSTERING INDUSTRY'S DIRECTORY OF SUPPLY SOURCES, Hall Publishing Co., 230 Fifth Ave., New York, N. Y. 10001. Published annually in August. Single copies, $1.

U.S.A. OIL INDUSTRY, PERSONNEL DIRECTORY OF, The Oil and Gas Journal, Directory Dept., Box 1260, Tulsa, Okla. 74101. Published annually December 15. Contains a complete picture of the hard core of companies in the oil and gas industry, listing key personnel. Grouped in sections indicating fully integrated companies; oil and gas producing; crude oil, products, and natural gas pipeline firms. More than 17,000 names, 290 pages. Price, $35.

USED EQUIPMENT DIRECTORY, 70 Sip Ave., Jersey City, N. J. 07306. Issued monthly. Single copy, $1; yearly subscription, $10. Lists names of dealers in used equipment and tools.

UTAH MANUFACTURERS DIRECTORY, Utah Committee on Industrial and Employment Planning, 174 Social Hall Ave., P.O. Box 11249, Salt Lake City, Utah 84111. Includes over 1,000 manufacturing companies and addresses.

VARIETY DEPARTMENT STORE MERCHANDISER BUYER LISTS OF THE VARIETY-GENERAL MERCHANDISE CHAIN MARKET INCLUDING DISCOUNT CHAINS, Merchandiser Publishing Co., Inc., 419 Park Avenue S., New York, N. Y. 10016. Issued in June. Price, $35. Lists stores, executives, buying offices, manufacturers' representatives, jobbers and wholesalers.

VARIETY-GENERAL MERCHANDISE STORE MARKET DIRECTORY OF VARIETY DEPARTMENT STORE MERCHANDISER, Merchandiser Publishing Co., Inc., 419 Park Ave. S., New York, N. Y. 10016. Issued in June. Price, $45. Lists stores, executives, buying offices, manufacturers (by product and also alphabetically), brand names, manufacturers' representatives, jobbers, and wholesalers.

VEND MARKET DATA AND DIRECTORY EDITION, Billboard Publishing Co., 188 W. Randolph St., Chicago, Ill. 60601. Includes guide to suppliers indexed by type of goods sold.

(Vending Machines) DIRECTORY ISSUE OF VEND, The Billboard Publishing Co., 188 W. Randolph St., Chicago, Ill. 60601. Issued annually in March. Included in yearly subscription price of $7. Includes list of machine manufacturers, technical descriptions of machines, brand name index, classified lists of manufacturers and of product suppliers.

VERMONT YEAR BOOK, National Survey, Chester, Vt. 05143. Published in the spring. Price, $7.50. Includes state and local officials; also schools, clubs, newspapers, business enterprises, etc., by cities.

VETERINARIANS' BLUE BOOK, The Reuben H. Donnelley Corp., 466 Lexington Ave., New York, N. Y. 10017. Issued annually in May. Single copy, $7.50. Lists professional drug products, feed additives, equipment, books.

VOLUNTARY & COOPERATIVE GROUPS MAGAZINE, Mulville-Barks Publications, Inc., 360 N. Michigan Ave., Chicago, Ill. 60601.

(Warehousemen) ROSTER OF MEMBERS, American Warehousemen's Association, 222 W. Adams St., Chicago, Ill. 60606. Includes members of American Warehousemen's Associations in U.S., Canada, Mexico and South America. Published annually. Free.

WASHINGTON LEGISLATIVE MANUAL, State of Washington Legislature, Legislative Bldg., Olympia, Wash. 98501. Free. Includes state and county officials.

WATER POLLUTION CONTROL FEDERATION, JOURNAL OF, DIRECTORY-YEAR-BOOK ISSUE, Water Pollution Control Federation, 3900 Wisconsin Ave., N.W., Washington, D.C. 20016. Published in March. Yearly subscription, $18.50 ($10 to members).

WATER WELL JOURNAL'S BUYERS GUIDE, The Water Well Journal Publishing Co., Box 222, Urbana, Ill. Published in three parts: January (rigs, tools and completion equipment); April (pumps and related equipment); July (water conditioning equipment). Yearly subscription, $6 (domestic); $12 (foreign).

WATER WORKS ASSOCIATION, AMERICAN, JOURNAL'S AWWA DIRECTORY, American Water Works Assn., 2 Park Ave., New York, N. Y. 10016. Issued usually in October. Included in yearly membership fee of $15. Lists AWWA constitution, bylaws, policy statements, manufacturer members, manufacturers agent members, plus water utility bibliography.

WATER WORKS MANUAL & CATALOG FILE, THE, Public Works Journal Corp., 200 S. Broad St., Ridgewood, N. J. 07451. Issued annually in May.

WATERWAYS JOURNAL'S ANNUAL REVIEW & DIRECTORY ISSUE, Waterways Journal, 701 Chemical Bldg., St. Louis, Mo. 63101. Published in December. Included in yearly subscription price of $5.

WEEKLY NEWSPAPER RATES & DATA, SRDS, Standard Rate & Data Service, Inc., 5201 Old Orchard Rd., Skokie, Ill. 60076. Published twice yearly with updating bulletins. Annual subscription, $3. Lists U.S. weekly newspapers.

WELDING DATA BOOK, The Industrial Publishing Co., 812 Huron Rd., Cleveland, Ohio 44115. Contains engineering and application data relating to all areas of metal fabricating and joining, as well as lists of products and trade names used in the welding/fabricating industry. Includes manufacturers' catalogs, local distribution index, and a geographical index of metal fabricating sources. Issued biennially. Price, $15.

WELDING ENCYCLOPEDIA, THE, 16th edition, Monticello Books, Inc., Box 128, Morton Grove, Ill. 60053. Issued in December of odd years. Single copy, $10. Lists manufacturers and associations in the metalworking field, and about 2,000 trade names.

WELDING, HEAT CUTTING & METALLIZING EQUIPMENT, U.S. Government Printing Office, Superintendent of Documents, Washington, D.C. 20402. Catalog No. D 7.13/3:2. Price, $3.25.

WESTERN MATERIAL HANDLING/PACKAGING/SHIPPING, BUYERS' GUIDE, Baymer Publications, Inc., 400 N. La Brea Ave., Los Angeles, Calif. 90036. Issued in September. Included in yearly subscription price of $5.

WHO MAKES IT DIRECTORY, GEYER'S, Geyer-McAllister Publications, Inc., 51 Madison Ave., New York, N. Y. 10010. Issued annually in spring. Lists manufacturers directly and also through a product list.

Section E — PRINCIPAL BUSINESS DIRECTORIES

WHO'S WHO IN AMERICA, MARQUIS, WHO'S WHO, INC., 200 E. Ohio St., Chicago, Ill. 60611. Vol. 35 published spring of '68. Contains sketches of leaders and leading personalities in various fields of achievement and interest. 62,000 listings, 2,492 pages. Price, $32.50.

(Wholesale) THOMAS GROCERY REGISTER, THOMAS PUBLISHING Co., 461 Eighth Ave., New York, N. Y. 10001. Issued in July. Single copy, $15. Lists wholesalers, chains, supermarkets, brokers, manufacturers and processors in U.S., Canada and Puerto Rico; also warehouses, banks and importers.

WHOLESALERS' GUIDE, SOUTHERN, W. R. C. SMITH PUBLISHING Co., 1760 Peach-tree Rd., N.W., Atlanta, Ga. 30309. Published yearly in December.

WINES & VINES ANNUAL DIRECTORY OF THE WINE INDUSTRY, IRVING H. MARCUS, 16 Beale St., San Francisco, Calif. 94105. Published annually in September. Available at $2 to subscribers to monthly *Wines & Vines;* non-subscribers, $5. Lists U.S. wineries and their bottlers, executives, and brand names.

WIRE & WIRE PRODUCTS BUYERS' GUIDE & YEARBOOK OF THE WIRE ASSO-CIATION, HAIRE PUBLISHING Co., INC., 299 Main St., Stamford, Conn. 06901. Issued annually in May. Price, $5 a copy. Lists manufacturers of rod, bar, wire, wire products, and electric wire and cable; machinery, equipment and supplies used by the industry; and officers, directors, and members of the association.

WOMEN, AMERICAN, WHO'S WHO OF, MARQUIS, WHO'S WHO, INC., 200 E. Ohio St., Chicago, Ill. 60611. Issued in odd years. Vol. 5 published September, 1967. Con-tains biographical sketches of several thousand American women, and a table of abbreviations. Price, $27.50.

WOMEN'S SPECIALTY STORES, PHELON-SHELDON PUBLICATIONS, INC., 32 Union Sq., New York, N. Y. 10003. Lists over 15,000 women's wear shops throughout the U.S. (approx. 7,000 better shops) not listed in Sheldon's *Retail Trade.* Each store listing includes store headquarters' name and address; number of stores operated; New York buying office; lines of merchandise bought and sold; name of principal and buyers; store size and price range of merchandise (better, medium, popular). Price, $30.

WOOD & WOOD PRODUCTS REFERENCE DATA/BUYING GUIDE, VANCE PUBLISH-ING CORP., 300 W. Adams St., Chicago, Ill. 60606. Issued annually in October. Single copy, $2; also included in subscription price of from $5 to $10 for from one to three years. Contains list of manufacturers of lumber products for industry, by type of lumber; woodworking machinery manufacturers and dealers; plywood and board products makers; veneer producers; and manufacturers and suppliers to the industry.

WOODWORKING, INDUSTRIAL, ANNUAL DIRECTORY ISSUE, CLEWORTH PUBLISH-ING Co., 1 River Rd., Cos Cob, Conn. Published in May. Single copy, $1, or included in yearly subscription price of $8. Lists suppliers of equipment, materials, and services to the woodworking industry.

WORLD ALMANAC AND BOOK OF FACTS, NEWSPAPER ENTERPRISE ASSOCIATION, 230 Park Ave., New York, N. Y. 10017. Published annually. Price, $1.65 (paper cover), $2.75 (cloth cover).

WORLD MINING'S ANNUAL CATALOG SURVEY & DIRECTORY NUMBER, MILLER FREEMAN PUBLICATIONS, 500 Howard St., San Francisco, Calif. 94105. Published in June.

WORLD SPACE DIRECTORY including OCEANOLOGY, AMERICAN AVIATION PUBLICA-TIONS, INC., 1001 Vermont Ave., N.W., Washington, D.C. 20005. Published in March and September. Price, one to nine copies, $15 each; 10 or more, $13 each.

WYOMING MANUFACTURING & MINING, DIRECTORY OF, WYOMING NATURAL RESOURCE BOARD, 210 W. 23rd St., Cheyenne, Wyo. 82001. Free. Roster of firms engaged in manufacturing; gives company name, address, principal products, number of employees, officials.

(Yachts) LLOYD'S REGISTER OF AMERICAN YACHTS, LLOYD'S REGISTER OF SHIP-PING, 17 Battery Pl., New York, N. Y. 10004. Published annually. Price, $25. Includes yachts, yacht owners, and yacht clubs in U.S. and Canada.

(Zip Code) NATIONAL ZIP CODE DIRECTORY, SUPERINTENDENT OF DOCUMENTS, U.S. POST OFFICE DEPARTMENT, Washington, D.C. 20260. Contains ZIP Code National Area Map, Army posts, camps and stations and Air Force bases, fields and installa-tions, two-letter state abbreviations, alphabetical list of states and cities, numerical list of post offices by ZIP Codes, mandatory pre-sorting list (second- and third-class mail). Price, $7.

BUSINESS AND PROFESSIONAL PUBLICATIONS

Publication	Address
Administrative Management	212 Fifth Ave., New York, N.Y. 10010
Advertising Age*	740 Rush St., Chicago, Ill. 60611
Advertising & Sales Promotion	740 Rush St., Chicago, Ill. 60611
American Banker	67 Pearl St., New York, N. Y. 10036
American Bar Association Journal	1155 E. 60th St., Chicago, Ill. 60637
American Builder*	30 Church St., New York, N. Y. 10007
American City	757 Third Ave., New York, N. Y. 10017
American Druggist*	1790 Broadway, New York, N. Y. 10019
American Engineer (NSPE)	2029 K St., N.W., Washington, D. C. 20006
American Journal of Nursing (ANA)	10 Columbus Circle, New York, N. Y. 10019
Architectural Forum	Rockefeller Center, New York, N. Y. 10020
Army Times	2201 M St., N.W., Washington, D. C. 20037
Automotive News	965 E. Jefferson Ave., Detroit, Mich. 48207
Aviation Week & Space Technology	330 W. 42nd St., New York, N. Y. 10036
Banking (ABA)	90 Park Ave., New York, N. Y. 10016
Billboard*	165 S.W. 46th St., New York, N. Y. 10036
Bowling Magazine (ABC)	1572 E. Capitol Dr., Milwaukee, Wis. 53211
Building Maintenance & Modernization	407 E. Michigan Ave., Milwaukee, Wis. 53201
Building Materials Merchandiser	59 E. Monroe St., Chicago, Ill. 60603
Burroughs Clearing House	P.O. Box 299, Detroit, Mich. 48232
Business Management	22 W. Putnam Ave., Greenwich, Conn. 06830
Business Publication Rates & Data*	5201 Old Orchard Road, Skokie, Ill. 60078
Business Week	330 W. 42nd St., New York, N. Y. 10036
Buyers' Purchasing Digest	918 N.E. 20th Ave., Fort Lauderdale, Fla. 33304
The Carpenter (UBCJA)	101 Constitution, N.W., Washington, D. C. 20001
Case and Comment	Aqueduct Bldg., Rochester, N. Y. 14604
Catholic Building & Maintenance	53 Park Place, New York, N. Y. 10007
Chain Store Age (5 editions)	2 Park Ave., New York, N. Y. 10016
Chemical & Engineering News	430 Park Ave., New York, N. Y. 10022
Chemical Week; Chemical Engineering	330 W. 42nd St., New York, N. Y. 10036
Civil Engineering (ASCE)	345 E. 47th St., New York, N. Y. 10017
Cleaning & Laundry Age	370 Lexington Ave., New York, N. Y. 10017
Commercial Car Journal*	Chestnut & 56th Sts., Philadelphia, Pa. 19139
Commercial & Financial Chronicle	Box 958, Church St. Annex, New York, N. Y. 10007
Construction Equipment	430 Park Ave., New York, N. Y. 10022
Construction Methods & Equipment*	330 W. 42nd St., New York, N. Y. 10036
Contractors & Engineers	757 Third Ave., New York, N. Y. 10017
Cooking for Profit	1202 S. Park St., Madison, Wis. 53715
Credit World (ICCA)	375 Jackson Ave., St. Louis, Mo. 63130
Current Medical Digest	428 E. Preston St., Baltimore, Md. 21202
Daily News Record; Women's Wear*	7 E. 12th St., New York, N. Y. 10003
Dental Survey* (PFA)	4015 W. 65th St., Minneapolis, Minn. 55424
Department Store Economist*	Chestnut & 56th Sts., Philadelphia, Pa. 19139
Dun's Review & Modern Industry	99 Church St., New York, N. Y. 10008
Editor & Publisher, The 4th Estate	850 Third Ave., New York, N. Y. 10022
Electrical Engineering* (IEEE)	72 W. 45th St., New York, N. Y. 10036
Electrical World; Electrical Mdsg. Wk.	330 W. 42nd St., New York, N. Y. 10036
Electrified Industry	20 N. Wacker Dr., Chicago, Ill. 60606
Electronic Industries	Chestnut & 56th Sts., Philadelphia, Pa. 19139
Electronics*	330 W. 42nd St., New York, N. Y. 10036
Electronics World	1 Park Ave., New York, N. Y. 10016
Electronics World*	330 W. 42nd St., New York, N. Y. 10036
Engineering News-Record*	330 W. 42nd St., New York, N. Y. 10036
Factory; Fleet Owner	330 W. 42nd St., New York, N. Y. 10036
Financial World	17 Battery Place, New York, N. Y. 10004
Firemen (NFPA)	60 Batterymarch St., Boston, Mass. 02110
Fleet Management News*	431 S. Dearborn St., Chicago, Ill. 60605
Flying	1 Park Ave., New York, N. Y. 10016
Food Processing	111 E. Delaware Place, Chicago, Ill. 60611
Food Service Magazine	2132 Fordem Ave., Madison, Wis. 53701
Food Topics	205 E. 42nd St., New York, N. Y. 10017
Forbes	70 Fifth Ave., New York, N. Y. 10011
Fortune	1271 Avenue of the Americas, New York, N. Y. 10020
Gasoline Retailer	17 Union Square West, New York, N. Y. 10003
Grade Teacher	420 Lexington Ave., New York, N. Y. 10017
Harvard Business Review	Soldiers Field Station, Boston, Mass. 02163
Heating & Plumbing Merchandiser	1170 Broadway, New York, N. Y. 10001
Home Furnishings Daily	7 E. 12th St., New York, N. Y. 10003
Hospitality Restaurant Combination	5 S. Wabash Ave., Chicago, Ill. 60603
Hospitals (AHA)	840 N. Lake Shore Dr., Chicago, Ill. 60611
Hotel Bulletin	543 Madison Ave., New York, N. Y. 10022
House and Home	330 W. 42nd St., New York, N. Y. 10036
Industrial Bulletin	450 E. Ohio St., Chicago, Ill. 60611
Industrial Equipment News*	461 Eighth Ave., New York, N. Y. 10001
Industrial Machinery News	16171 Meyers Rd., Detroit, Mich. 48235
Industrial Maintenance & Plant Operation	1 West Olney Ave., Philadelphia, Pa. 19120
Industrial Marketing*	740 Rush St., Chicago, Ill. 60611

Courtesy Standard Rate & Data Service, Inc.

BUSINESS AND PROFESSIONAL PUBLICATIONS

Publication	Address
Institutions Magazine*	1801 Prairie Ave., Chicago, Ill. 60616
The Instructor	Dansville, N. Y. 14437
Instrument & Apparatus News*	845 Ridge St., Pittsburgh, Pa. 15212
Insurance Salesman* (life insurance)	1142 N. Meridian St., Indianapolis, Ind. 46204
International Musician (AFM)	39 Division St., Newark, N. J. 07102
Investment Dealers' Digest	150 Broadway, New York, N. Y. 10038
Iron Age; Hardware Age	Chestnut & 56th Sts., Philadelphia, Pa. 19139
Journal of Accountancy (AICPA)	666 Fifth Ave., New York, N. Y. 10019
Journal of American Dental Association*	222 E. Superior St., Chicago, Ill. 60611
Journal of American Medical Association*	535 N. Dearborn St., Chicago, Ill. 60610
Law and Order	72 W. 45th St., New York, N. Y. 10036
Leatherneck	Box 1918, Washington, D. C. 20013
Life Association News (insurance) (NALU)	1922 F St., N.W., Washington, D. C. 20006
Machine and Tool Blue Book*	Hitchcock Bldg., Wheaton, Ill. 60188
Magazine of Wall Street & Business Analyst	120 Wall St., New York, N. Y. 10005
Maintenance	1 River Road, Cos Cob, Conn. 06807
M D Medical Newsmagazine	30 E. 60th St., New York, N. Y. 10022
Mechanical Engineering* (ASME)	345 E. 45th St., New York, N. Y. 10017
Medical Economics	550 Kinderkamack Rd., Oradell, N. J. 07649
Metlfax Magazine	Box 2454, Cleveland, Ohio 44112
Mill and Factory	205 E. 42nd St., New York, N. Y. 10017
Modern Beauty Shop	59 E. Monroe St., Chicago, Ill. 60603
Modern Drugs*	466 Lexington Ave., New York, N. Y. 10017
Modern Medicine*	Southdale Park, Minneapolis, Minn. 55424
Modern Office Procedures	812 Huron Road, Cleveland, Ohio 44115
Modern Photography	165 W. 46th St., New York, N. Y. 10036
Modern Plastics	1301 Avenue of the Americas, New York, N. Y. 10019
Modern Sanitation & Building Maintenance	855 Avenue of the Americas, New York, N. Y. 10001
Motor	250 W. 55th St., New York, N. Y. 10019
Motor Service	549 W. Washington Blvd., Chicago, Ill. 60606
NAHB Journal of Homebuilding	1625 L St., N.W., Washington, D. C. 20006
NARD Journal	1 E. Wacker Dr., Chicago, Ill. 60601
NARGUS Bulletin (retail grocers)	360 N. Michigan Ave., Chicago, Ill. 60601
National Business and Financial Weekly	30 Broad St., New York, N. Y. 10004
National Business Woman (NFBPWC)	2012 Massachusetts Ave., N.W., Wash., D. C. 20006
National Provisioner (meat packing)	15 W. Huron St., Chicago, Ill. 60610
National Safety News* (NSC)	425 N. Michigan Ave., Chicago, Ill. 60611
National Underwriter (insurance; 2 editions)	175 W. Jackson Blvd., Chicago, Ill. 60604
Nation's Business (CCUS)	1615 H St., N.W., Washington, D. C. 20006
New Equipment Digest	726 Penton Bldg., Cleveland, Ohio 44113
Occupational Hazards	812 Huron Road, Cleveland, Ohio 44115
Official Airline Guide	209 W. Jackson Blvd., Chicago, Ill. 60606
Official Guide of the Railways, etc.	424 W. 33rd St., New York, N. Y. 10001
Oil and Gas Journal*	211 S. Cheyenne Ave., Tulsa, Okla. 74101
Oral Hygiene	708 Church St., Evanston, Ill. 60201
Ordnance	P.O. Box 275, Ridgefield, Conn. 06877
Plant Engineering*	308 E. James St., Barrington, Ill. 60010
Power; National Petroleum News; Coal Age	330 W. 42nd St., New York, N. Y. 10036
Practical Builder	5 S. Wabash Ave., Chicago, Ill. 60603
Printers' Ink	501 Madison Ave., New York, N. Y. 10022
Proceedings of the IEEE (radio engineers)	72 W. 45th St., New York, N. Y. 10001
Product Engineering*	330 W. 42nd St., New York, N. Y. 10036
Progressive Grocer	420 Lexington Ave., New York, N. Y. 10017
Protestant Church Buildings & Equipment	27 E. 39th St., New York, N. Y. 10016
Public Works Magazine	200 S. Broad St., Ridgewood, N. J. 07451
QST (American Radio Relay League)	225 Main St., Newington, Conn. 06111
Radio Electronics	154 W. 14th St., New York, N. Y. 10011
Railway Age	30 Church St., New York, N. Y. 10007
Refrigeration & Airconditioning Business	812 Huron Road, Cleveland, Ohio 44115
The Ring	Madison Square Garden, New York, N. Y. 10019
Roads and Streets	209 W. Jackson Blvd., Chicago, Ill. 60606
Sales Management*	630 Third Ave., New York, N. Y. 10017
Salesman's Opportunity	850 N. Dearborn St., Chicago, Ill. 60610
Scholastic Teacher*	50 W. 44th St., New York, N. Y. 10036
School Management	22 W. Putnam Ave., Greenwich, Conn. 06830
Steel; Foundry	Penton Bldg., Cleveland, Ohio 44113
Super Service Station	7300 N. Cicero Ave., Chicago, Ill. 60646
Supermarket News	7 E. 12th St., New York, N. Y. 10003
Textile World	330 W. 42nd St., New York, N. Y. 10036
Today's Business (retailing and electrical)	20 N. Wacker Dr., Chicago, Ill. 60606
Today's Secretary (Gregg shorthand)	330 W. 42nd St., New York, N. Y. 10036
Traffic World	815 Washington Bldg., Washington, D. C. 20005
Transport Topics (ATA)	1616 P St., N.W., Washington, D. C. 20006
TV Guide	Radnor, Pa. 19088
Wall Street Journal	New York; Chicago; Dallas; San Francisco
What's New in Home Economics	466 Lexington Ave., New York, N. Y. 10017
Your Church (Protestant pastors)	122 Old York Rd., Jenkintown, Pa. 19046

*Also one or more related publications

MEDIA FOR ADVERTISING AND PUBLICITY

A selected list of newspapers and radio and television stations for advertising, publicity, and public relations purposes.

State and City	Newspapers	Radio	TV
ALABAMA Birmingham	News (e) Post-Herald (m)	WAPI (NBC) WBRC (MBS) WCRT (ABC)	WAPI-TV (NBC) WBRC-TV (ABC)
Mobile	Press (e) Register (m)	WABB (ABC) WUNI (NBC) WKRG (CBS)	WALA-TV (NBC) WEIQ-TV WKRG-TV (BCS)
Montgomery	Advertiser (m) Journal (e)	WAPX (ABC) WCOV (CBS) WHHY (NBC, KBS)	WCOV-TV (CBS) WSFA-TV (NBC) WSLA-TV (Selma) (ABC)
ALASKA Anchorage	News (e) Times (m)	KENI (ABC) KFQD (CBS)	KENI-TV (ABC, NBC) KTVA (CBS)
Fairbanks	News-Minor (e)	KFRB	KFAR-TV KTVF-TV
Juneau	Empire (e)	KINY	KINY-TV (CBS,ABC,NBC)
ARIZONA Phoenix	Gazette (e) Republic (m)	KOOL (CBS) KOY (ABC) KTAR (NBC)	KOOL-TV (CBS) KTAR-TV (NBC) KTVK (ABC)
Tucson	Citizen (e) Star (m)	KCUB (MBS) KOLD (CBS) KTAN (NBC) KTUC (ABC)	KGUN-TV (ABC) KOLD-TV (CBS) KVOA-TV (NBC)
ARKANSAS Little Rock	Arkansas Democrat (e) Arkansas Gazette (m)	KAAY KARK (NBC) KLRA	KARK-TV (NBC) KATV (ABC) KTVH-TV (CBS)
CALIFORNIA Bakersfield	Californian (e)	KBIS (MBS) KERN (CBS) KGEE (NBC)	KBAK-TV (CBS) KERO-TV (NBC) KLYD-TV (ABC)
Fresno	Bee (e)	KARM (ABC) KFRE (CBS) KMJ (NBC) KYNO (MBS)	KAIL-TV KFRE-TV (CBS) KICU-TV (Visalia) KJEO-TV (ABC)
Long Beach	Independent (m) Press-Telegram (e)	KGER KFOX	
Los Angeles	Citizen-News (Hollywood) (e) Herald Examiner (e) Times (m)	KABC (ABC) KFI (NBC) KGFJ KGBS (MBS) KPOL KMPC KNX (CBS)	KABC-TV (ABC) KCET-TV KMEX-TV KNXT (CBS) KTLA KTTV
Oakland	Tribune (e)	KDIA	KTVU-TV
Sacramento	Bee (e) Union (m)	KCRA (NBC) KFBK (CBS)	KCRA-TV (NBC) KXTV (CBS)
San Diego	Tribune (e) Union (m)	KFMB (CBS) KGB (ABC) KOGO (NBC) KSON	KFMB-TV (CBS) KOGO-TV (NBC) XETV (Tijuana) (ABC)
San Francisco	Chronicle (m) Examiner (m) Wall St. J'l (Pcfc. Ed.)	KCBS (CBS) KFAX KGO (ABC) KNBR (NBC)	KGO-TV (ABC) KPIX (CBS) KRON-TV (NBC) WQED-TV

Courtesy Standard Rate & Data Service, Inc.

MEDIA FOR ADVERTISING AND PUBLICITY

State and City	Newspapers	Radio	TV
CALIFORNIA—*Cont.* Santa Barbara	News-Press (e)	KTMS (NBC, ABC)	KEYT (ABC, NBC)
COLORADO Denver	Post (e) Rocky Mt. News (m)	KBTR (ABC) KHOW KLZ (CBS) KOA (NBC)	KBTV (ABC) KLZ-TV (CBS) KOA-TV (NBC) KRMA-TV
CONNECTICUT Bridgeport	Post (e) Telegram (m)	WICC WNAB (MBS)	
Hartford	Courant (m) Times (e)	WDRC WHCT WTIC (NBC)	WHNB-TV (New Brtn.) (NBC) WNHC-TV (New Hvn.) (ABC) WTIC-TV (CBS)
New Haven	Journal-Courier (m) Register (e)	WAVZ WNHC (ABC)	WNHC-TV (ABC)
DELAWARE Wilmington	News (m) Journal (e)	WDEL (NBC)	
DISTRICT OF COLUMBIA	News (e) Post (m) Star (e)	WMAL (ABC) WRC (NBC) WTOP (CBS)	WMAL-TV (ABC) WRC-TV (NBC) WTOP-TV (CBS)
FLORIDA Jacksonville	Fla. Times-Union (m) Journal (e)	WJAX (NBC) WMBR	WFGA-TV (ABC, NBC) WJCT-TV WJXT (CBS, ABC)
Miami	Herald (m) News (e) Sun (Miami Beach) (e)	WAME (ABC) WIOD (NBC) WKAT (CBS)	WCKT (NBC) WLBW-TV (ABC) WTHS-TV WTVJ (CBS)
Orlando	Sentinel (m) Star (e)	WABR (MBS, ABC) WDBO (CBS) WKIS (NBC)	WDBO-TV (CBS) WMFE-TV WFTV (ABC)
Tampa	Times (e) Tribune (m)	WINQ (CBS) WFLA (NBC)	WEDU-TV WFLA-TV (NBC) WTVT (CBS)
GEORGIA Atlanta	Constitution (m) Journal (e) World (m)	WGST (ABC) WSB (NBC) WYZE	WAGA-TV (CBS) WAII-TV WSB-TV (NBC)
HAWAII Honolulu	Advertiser (m) Star-Bulletin (e) Times (e)	KGMB (CBS) KGU (NBC)	KGMB-TV (CBS) KHVH-TV (ABC)
IDAHO Boise	Statesman (m)	KBOI (CBS) KGEM (ABC)	KBOI-TV (CBS) KTVB (ABC, NBC)
ILLINOIS Chicago	Chicago Today (e) Daily News (e) Sun-Times (m) Tribune (m) Wall Street Journal (Midwest Ed.) (m)	WBBM (CBS) WCFL WGN WIND WJJD WLS (ABC) WMAQ (NBC)	WBBM-TV (CBS) WBKB (ABC) WGN-TV (WPIX) WMAQ-TV WTTW-TV
Peoria	Journal Star (m & e)	WMBD (CBS)	WMBD-TV
Rock Island	Argus (e)	WHBF (CBS)	WHBF-TV (ABC, CBS)
Rockford	Star (m)	WROK (ABC)	WREX-TV (ABC, CBS)

MEDIA FOR ADVERTISING AND PUBLICITY

State and City	Newspapers	Radio	TV
ILLINOIS—*Cont.* Springfield	Ill. State Journal (m) Ill. State Register (e)	WCVS (ABC) WMAY (NBC) WTAX (CBS)	WCIA (Champaign) (CBS) WICS (NBC) WAND-TV (Decatur) (ABC)
INDIANA Bloomington	Herald-Telephone (e)	WTTS (ABC)	WTTV (Indianapolis)
Evansville	Courier (m) Press (e)	WGBF (NBC) WJPS (MBS) WROZ	WEHT-TV (CBS) WFIE-TV (NBC) WTVW (ABC)
Fort Wayne	Journal-Gazette (m) News-Sentinel (e)	WGL (ABC) WKJG (NBC)	WANE-TV (CBS) WKJG-TV (NBC) WPTA (ABC)
Indianapolis	News (e) Star (m)	WFBM WIRE (NBC) WIFE (CBS)	WFBM-TV (NBC) WISH-TV (CBS) WLW-I (ABC) WTTV-TV
South Bend	Tribune (e)	WJVA (MBS) WNDU (ABC) WSBT (CBS)	WNDU-TV (NBC) WSBT-TV (CBS)
IOWA Ames	Tribune (e)	KASI	WOI-TV (ABC)
Des Moines	Register (m) Tribune (e)	KCBC (ABC) KRNT (CBS) WHO (NBC)	KRNT-TV (CBS) WHO-TV (NBC) WOI-TV (Ames) (ABC)
Sioux City	Journal (m & e)	KSCJ (ABC)	KVTV (ABC, CBS)
Waterloo	Courier (e)	KXEL (ABC)	KWWL-TV (NBC)
KANSAS Topeka	Capital (m) State Journal (e)	WIBW (CBS) WREN (ABC)	KTWU-TV WIBW-TV (CBS, ABC, NBC)
Wichita	Eagle (m) Eagle & Beacon (e)	KAKE (ABC) KFH (CBS)	KAKE-TV (ABC) KARD-TV (NBC) KTVH-TV
KENTUCKY Louisville	Courier-Journal (m) Times (e)	WAVE (NBC) WKYW WHAS (ABC)	WHAS-TV (CBS) WFPK-TV WAVE-TV (NBC)
LOUISIANA New Orleans	States-Item (e) Times-Picayune (m)	WDSU (NBC) WSMB (ABC) WWL (CBS)	WDSU-TV (NBC) WVUE (ABC) WWL-TV (CBS)
Shreveport	Journal (e) Times (m)	KRMD (NBC) KWKH	KSLA-TV (CBS) KTBS-TV (ABC)
MAINE Portland	Express (e) Press Herald (m)	WCSH (NBC) WGAN WLOB (CBS)	WCSH-TV (NBC) WGAN-TV (CBS) WMTW-TV (ABC)
MARYLAND Baltimore	News-American (e) Sun (m) Sunday American	WBAL (NBC) WCBM (CBS) WWIN (ABC)	WBAL-TV (NBC) WJZ-TV (ABC) WMAR-TV (CBS)
MASSACHUSETTS Boston	Chr. Sci. Monitor (e) Globe (m & e) Herald (m) Record American (m) Traveler (e)	WBOS (MBS) WBZ WEEI (CBS) WEZE (NBC) WORL (ABC)	WBZ-TV (NBC) WHDH-TV (CBS) WNAC-TV (ABC)
Springfield	News (e) Sunday Republican Union (m)	WHYN WMAS (CBS)	WHYN-TV (ABC) WRLP-TV WWLP (NBC)

MEDIA FOR ADVERTISING AND PUBLICITY

State and City	Newspapers	Radio	TV
MASS.—*Cont.*			
Worcester	Gazette (e) Telegram (m)	WAAB (ABC) WNEB (CBS)	WJZB-TV
MICHIGAN			
Adrian	Telegram (e)	WABJ (CBS)	
Battle Creek	Enquirer & News (e)	WBCK (NBC)	WILX-TV (Lansing) (NBC)
Detroit	Free Press (m) News (e)	WJR (CBS) WKNR WWJ (NBC) WXYZ (ABC)	CKLW-TV (Windsor) WJBK-TV (CBS) WWJ-TV (NBC) WXYZ-TV (ABC)
Flint	Journal (e)	WFDF (NBC) WKMF (ABC) WTRX	WJRT (ABC) WKNX-TV (Saginaw) (CBS)
Grand Rapids	Press (e)	WJEF (CBS) WLAV (ABC) WOOD (NBC)	WOOD-TV (NBC) WZZM-TV (ABC)
Kalamazoo	Gazette (e)	WKZO (CBS)	WKZO-TV (CBS)
Lansing	State Journal (e)	WJIM (CBS)	WJIM-TV (CBS)
Saginaw	News (e)	WSGW (CBS)	WKNX-TV WNEM-TV (NBC)
MINNESOTA			
Duluth	Herald (e) News Tribune (m)	KDAL (CBS) WDSM* (NBC, ABC) WEBC	KDAL-TV (ABC, CBS) WDSE-TV WDSM-TV
Minneapolis	Star (e) Tribune (m)	KRSI (ABC) WCCO (CBS)	KMSP-TV KSTP-TV KTCA-TV WCCO-TV WTCN-TV
St. Paul	Dispatch (e) Pioneer Press (m)	KSTP (NBC)	KSTP-TV (NBC) KTCA-TV KTCI-TV
MISSISSIPPI			
Jackson	Clarion-Ledger (m) News (e)	WSLI (ABC) WJDX (NBC)	WJTV (CBS) WLBT (ABC, NBC)
MISSOURI			
Kansas City	Star (e) Times (m)	KUDL (ABC) KCMO (CBS) WHB	KCMO-TV (CBS) KMBC-TV (ABC) WDAF-TV (NBC)
St. Joseph	Gazette (m) News-Press (e)	KFEQ KKJO (MBS)	KFEQ-TV (CBS)
St. Louis	Globe-Democrat (m) Post-Dispatch (e)	KMOX (CBS) KSD (NBC) KXOK	KETC-TV KMOX-TV (CBS) KSD-TV (NBC) KTVI (ABC)
MONTANA			
Great Falls	Leader (e) Tribune (m)	KARR KMON (ABC)	KFBB-TV (ABC, CBS) KRTV (NBC)
Helena	Independent-Record (e)	KBLL (NBC) KCAP	KBLL-TV (CBS)
NEBRASKA			
Omaha	World-Herald (m & e)	KBON KFAB (NBC) WOW (CBS)	KETV (ABC) KMTV (NBC) WOW-TV (CBS)
NEVADA			
Carson City	Nevada Appeal (e)	KPTL	

*Superior, Wisconsin

MEDIA FOR ADVERTISING AND PUBLICITY

State and City	Newspapers	Radio	TV
NEVADA—*Cont.* Las Vegas	Review-Journal (e) Sun	KLUC (CBS) KORK (MBS)	KLAS-TV (CBS) KORK-TV (NBC) KSHO-TV (ABC)
Reno	Gazette (e) Nev. State Journal (m)	KBET (ABC) KOH (NBC) KOLO (MBS)	KCRL (NBC) KOLO-TV (ABC, CBS)
NEW HAMPSHIRE Concord	Monitor(e)	WKXL (CBS, KBS)	
Manchester	Union Leader (m)	WGIR (NBC)	WMUR-TV (ABC)
NEW JERSEY Jersey City	Jersey Journal (e)		
Newark	News (e) Star-Ledger (m)	WJRZ WNJR	WATV-TV
Trenton	Times (e)	WAAT	
NEW MEXICO Albuquerque	Journal (m) Tribune (e)	KGGM (CBS) KOB (NBC)	KGGM-TV (CBS) KOAT-TV KOB-TV (NBC)
Santa Fe	New Mexican (e)	KTRC (ABC) KVSF (CBS)	
NEW YORK Albany	Knickerb'ker News (e) Times-Union (m)	WOKO (ABC, MBS) WROW (CBS)	WAST (ABC) WTEN-TV
Binghamton	Press (e) Sun-Bulletin (m)	WINR (NBC) WNBF (CBS)	WINR-TV (NBC) WNBF-TV (CBS)
Buffalo	Courier-Express (m) News (e)	WBEN (CBS) WGR (NBC) WKBW KYSL (ABC)	WBEN-TV (CBS) WGR-TV (NBC) KKBW-TV (ABC) WNED-TV
New York City	Journal of Commerce and Commercial (m) Long Island Press (e) Long Isl. Star-J'l (e) Morning Telegraph (m) News (m) Post (e) Times (m) Wall Street Journal (m)	WABC (ABC) WADO WBNX WCBS (CBS) WEVD WHN (MBS) WHOM WINS WLIB WMCA WNBC (NBC) WOR WQXR	WABC-TV (ABC) WATC-TV WCBS-TV (CBS) WNBC-TV (NBC) WNDT-TV WNEW-TV WNYC-TV WOR-TV WPIX-TV
Rochester	Democrat & Chr'cle (m) Times-Union (e)	WHEC (CBS) WROC (NBC)	WHEC-TV (CBS) WOKR-TV WROC-TV (NBC)
Schenectady	Gazette (m)	WGY (NBC)	WGRB-TV
Syracuse	Herald-Journal (e) Post-Standard (m)	WHEN (CBS) WSYR (NBC)	WHEN-TV (CBS) WSYR-TV (NBC)
Utica	Observer-Dispatch (e)	WIBX (CBS)	WKTV (NBC, ABC)
NORTH CAROLINA Charlotte	News (e) Observer (m)	WBT (CBS) WSOC (NBC)	WBTV (CBS, ABC) WSOC-TV (NBC, ABC)
Durham	Herald (m) Sun (e)	WNDC (CBS) WTIK (ABC)	WTVD (CBS)

MEDIA FOR ADVERTISING AND PUBLICITY

State and City	Newspapers	Radio	TV
N. Carolina—*Cont.* Greensboro	News (m) Record (e)	WBIG (CBS) WGBG (ABC)	WFMY-TV (CBS, ABC)
Raleigh	News & Observer (m) Times (e)	WPTF (NBC)	WRAL-TV (ABC, NBC, CBS
Winston-Salem	Journal (m) Twin City Sentinel (e)	WAIR (ABC) WSJS (NBC)	WITN-TV
North Dakota Bismarck	Tribune (e)	KFYR (NBC)	KFYR-TV (NBC)
Fargo	Forum-News (m & e)	WDAY (NBC)	KXJB-TV WDAY-TV (NBC)
Ohio Akron	Beacon Journal (e)	WSLR (CBS)	WAKR-TV (ABC)
Cincinnati	Enquirer (m) Post & Times-Star (e)	WCKY WLW (NBC)	WCET-TV WCPO-TV (CBS) WKRC-TV (ABC) WLWT-TV
Cleveland	Plain Dealer (m) Press & News (e)	WKW WGAR (NBC) WJMO WJW	WKYC-TV (NBC) WEWS (ABC) WJW-TV (CBS)
Columbus	Citizen-Journal (m) Dispatch (e)	WBNS (CBS) WMNI (MBS) WTVN (ABC)	WBNS-TV (CBS) WLWC-TV (NBC) WTVN-TV (ABC)
Dayton	Journal Herald (m) News (e)	WHIO WING	WHIO-TV (CBS) WLWD (ABC, NBC)
Toledo	Blade (e, & Sat. m) Times (m, Mon.-Fri.)	WOHO WSPD (NBC) WTOD	WGTE-TV WSPD-TV (ABC, NBC) WTOL-TV (CBS)
Youngstown	Vindicator (e)	WBBW (MBS) WFMJ (NBC) WKBN (CBS)	WFMJ-TV (NBC) WKBN-TV (CBS) WYTV-TV (ABC)
Oklahoma Oklahoma City	Oklahoman (m) Times (e)	KOCY (NBC) KOMA KTOK (ABC) WKY	KETA-TV KOCO-TV (Enid) (ABC) KWTV (CBS) WKY-TV (NBC)
Tulsa	Tribune (e) World (m)	KOME (ABC) KRMG KVOO (NBC)	KOED KOTV (CBS) KTUL-TV (ABC) KVOO-TV (NBC)
Oregon Portland	Journal (m) Oregon Journal (e) Oregonian (m)	KEX KGW (NBC) KOIN (CBS) KWJJ (ABC)	KOAP-TV KGW-TV (NBC) KOIN-TV (CBS) KPTV (ABC)
Pennsylvania Altoona	Mirror (e)	WFBG WRTA (ABC) WVAM (CBS)	WFBG-TV (CBS, ABC)
Erie	News (m) Times (e)	WICU (ABC) WWGO	WICU-TV (ABC, NBC) WSEE-TV (CBS)
Harrisburg	News (e) Patriot (m)	WHGB (ABC) WHP (CBS) WKBO (NBC)	WHP-TV (CBS) WSBA-TV (York) (CBS) WTPA-TV (ABC)
Johnstown	Tribune-Democrat	WARD (CBS) WCRO (MBS) WJAC (NBC)	WARD-TV (VBS) WFBG-TV (Altoona) WJAC-TV (NBC, ABC)

MEDIA FOR ADVERTISING AND PUBLICITY

State and City	Newspapers	Radio	TV
PENNA.—*Cont.* Lancaster	New Era (e) Intelligencer J'l (m)	WGAL (NBC) WLAN (ABC)	WGAL-TV (NBC)
Lebanon	News (e)	WLBR	WLYH-TV
Philadelphia	Bulletin (e) Inquirer (m) News (e)	WCAU (CBS) WFIL WPEN (NBC) KYW	WCAU-TV (CBS) WFIL-TV (ABC) KYW-TV
Pittsburgh	Post-Gazette (m) Press (e)	KDKA KQV (ABC) WJAS (NBC)	KDKA-TV WIIC (NBC) WTAE (ABC)
Reading	Eagle (e) Times (m)	WEEU (ABC) WHUM (CBS)	
Scranton	Times (e) Tribune (m)	WGBI (CBS) WSCR (NBC)	WDAU-TV (CBS)
Wilkes-Barre	Record (m) Times Lead'r, News (e)	WBRE WILK (ABC)	WBRE-TV WDAU-TV (Scranton) (CBS)
RHODE ISLAND Providence	Bulletin (e) Journal (m)	WEAN (CBS) WJAR (NBC)	WJAR-TV (NBC) WPRI (CBS) WTEV (New Bedfd.) (ABC)
SOUTH CAROLINA Columbia	Record (e) State (m)	WOIC WCOS WIS (NBC)	WIS-TV WNOK-TV
SOUTH DAKOTA Aberdeen	News (e)	KABR KSDN	KXAB-TV
Rapid City	Journal (e)	KOTA (CBS) KRSD	KOTA-TV (CBS, ABC) KRSD-TV
Sioux Falls	Argus Leader (e)	KELO (NBC) KSOO	KELO-TV (CBS)
TENNESSEE Chattanooga	News-Free Press (e) Times (m)	WAPO WDEF WDOD	WDEF-TV (CBS) WRCB-TV WTVC
Knoxville	Journal (m) News-Sentinel (e)	WATE WNOX	WATE-TV WBIR-TV
Memphis	Commercial Appeal (m) Press-Scimitar (e)	WHBQ WMC (NBC) WREC (CBS)	WHBQ-TV (ABC) WMCT (NBC) WREC-TV (CBS)
Nashville	Banner (e) Tennessean (m)	WLAC (CBS) WSIX WSM	WLAC-TV (CBS) WSIX-TV WSM-TV (NBC)
TEXAS Abilene	Reporter-News (m & e)	KRBC (ABC)	KRBC-TV (NBC)
Amarillo	Globe-Times (e) News (m)	KVII (ABC) KGNC (NBC)	KFDA-TV (CBS) KGNC-TV (NBC)
Austin	American (m) Statesman (e)	KNOW KTBC (CBS)	KTBC-TV (ABC, CBS, NBC) KHFI-TV (NBC, ABC, CBS)
Beaumont	Enterprise (m) Journal (e)	KAYC KJET	KFDM-TV (CBS) KBMT-TV (ABC)
Corpus Christi	Caller (m) Times (e)	KCCT KEYS KSIX	KRIS-TV (NBC) KZTV KII (ABC)

MEDIA FOR ADVERTISING AND PUBLICITY

State and City	Newspapers	Radio	TV
TEXAS—*Cont.*			
Dallas	News (m) Times-Herald (e) Wall St. J'l (SW Ed.)	KRLD (CBS) WFAA (ABC, NBC) WRR (MBS)	KRLD-TV (CBS) WFAA-TV (ABC)
El Paso	Herald-Post (e) Times (m)	KHEY KTSM (NBC)	KELP-TV (ABC) KROD-TV (CBS) KTSM-TV (NBC)
Fort Worth	Press (e) Star-Telegram (m & e)	KCUL (MBS) WBAP (ABC, NBC)	KTVT WBAP-TV (NBC)
Galveston	News (m)	KILE KGVC	KGUL-TV
Houston	Chronicle (e) Post (m)	KODA (ABC) KPRC (NBC) KTRH (CBS)	KHOU-TV (CBS) KPRC-TV (NBC) KTRK-TV (ABC) KUHT-TV
Lubbock	Avalanche-J'l (m & e)	KCBD (NBC) KFYO (CBS)	KCBD-TV (NBC) KLBK-TV (CBS, ABC) KTXT-TV
San Antonio	Express (m) Light (e) News (m)	KAPE (ABC) KMAC (CBS) WOAI (NBC)	KENS-TV (CBS) KONO-TV (ABC) WOAI-TV (NBC)
Waco	News-Tribune (m) Times-Herald (e)	KWTX (MBS) WACO (ABC)	KWTX-TV (CBS, ABC)
Wichita Falls	Record-News (m) Times (e)	KNIN (ABC) KWFT (CBS)	KFDX-TV (NBC) KAUZ-TV
UTAH			
Ogden	Standard-Examin'r (e)	KLO (ABC)	KOET-TV KWCS-TV
Salt Lake City	Deseret News-Tlgm. (e) Tribune (m)	KALL (ABC) KCPX (NBC) KSL (CBS)	KCPX-TV (ABC) KSL-TV (CBS) KUTV (NBC)
VERMONT			
Burlington	Free Press (m)	WJOY (ABC) WVMT	WCAX-TV (CBS)
VIRGINIA			
Norfolk	Ledger-Star (e) Virginian-Pilot (m)	WTAR (CBS) WAVY (NBC)	WHRO-TV WAVY-TV (NBC) WTAR-TV (CBS)
Richmond	News-Leader (e) Times-Dispatch (m)	WMBG (ABC) WRNL (CBS) WRVA (NBC)	WRVA-TV (ABC) WTVR (CBS) WXEX-TV (Petrsbg.) (NBC)
Roanoke	Times (m) World-News (e)	WDBJ (CBS) WRIS (MBS) WROV WSLS (NBC)	WDBJ-TV (NBC) WLVA-TV (Lynchbg.) (ABC) WSLS-TV (NBC)
WASHINGTON			
Seattle	J'l of Commerce (m) Post-Intelligencer (m) Times (e)	KING (NBC) KIRO (CBS) KOMO (ABC)	KCTS-TV KING-TV (NBC) KIRO-TV (CBS) KOMO-TV (ABC)
Spokane	Chronicle (e) Spokesman-Review (m)	KGA (CBS) KHQ (NBC) KXLY	KHQ-TV (NBC) KREM-TV (ABC) KXLY-TV (CBS)
Tacoma	News Tribune (e)	KMO	KTNT-TV KPEC-TV KTVW-TV
WEST VIRGINIA			
Charleston	Daily Mail (e) Gazette (m)	WCHS (CBS) WKAZ (NBC)	WCHS-TV (CBS)

MEDIA FOR ADVERTISING AND PUBLICITY

State and City	Newspapers	Radio	TV
W. VIRGINIA—Cont. Huntington	Advertiser (e) Herald-Dispatch (m)	WSAZ (NBC) WWHY (MBS)	WHTN-TV (ABC) WSAZ-TV (NBC)
Wheeling	Intelligencer (m) News-Register (e)	WKWK (MBS) WWVA (ABC)	WSTV-TV (Steubenville) WTRF-TV (NBC, ABC)
WISCONSIN Green Bay	Press-Gazette (e)	WBAY (CBS) WDUZ (ABC)	WBAY-TV (CBS) WLUK-TV (ABC)
La Crosse	Tribune (e)	WKTY (ABC)	WKBT (CBS, ABC, NBC)
Madison	Capital Times (e) State Journal (m)	WIBA (NBC) WISM WKOW (CBS)	WHA-TV WISC-TV (CBS) WKOW-TV (ABC) WMTV (NBC)
Milwaukee	Journal (e) Sentinel (m)	WISN (ABC) WMIL (CBS) WTMJ (NBC)	WISN-TV (CBS) WITI-TV (ABC) WTMJ-TV (NBC)
WYOMING Casper	Star (m) Tribune (e)	KTWO (NBC) KVOC (ABC)	KTWO-TV (ABC, CBS, NBC)
Cheyenne	Wyoming Eagle (m) Wyo. State Tribune (e)	KFBC (ABC) KVWO (MBS)	KFBC-TV (Scottsbluff)

ADVERTISING EXPENDITURES
(A partial list)

Medium	1960		1965 (prelim.)	
	Expenditures*	Percent of Total	Expenditures*	Percent of Total
Total	11,932	100.0	15,120	100.0
National	7,296	61.1	9,269	61.3
Local	4,636	38.9	5,851	38.7
Newspapers	3,703	31.0	4,435	29.4
National	836	7.0	870	5.8
Local	2,867	24.0	3,565	23.6
Radio	692	5.8	889	5.9
Network	43	0.4	60	0.4
Spot	222	1.8	260	1.7
Local	428	3.6	569	3.8
Television	1,590	13.3	2,497	16.5
Network	783	6.6	1,240	8.2
Spot	527	4.4	850	5.6
Local	281	2.3	407	2.7
Magazines	941	7.9	1,198	7.9
Weeklies	525	4.4	610	4.1
Women's	184	1.5	258	1.7
Monthlies	200	1.7	293	1.9
Farm, national	32	0.3	37	0.2
Farm papers	35	0.3	34	0.2
Direct mail	1,830	15.3	2,271	15.0
Business papers	609	5.1	679	4.5

*In millions of dollars

Source: McCann-Erickson, Inc.

RAIL AND PULLMAN FARES BETWEEN CITIES

TO \ FROM	Atlanta	Baltimore	Boston	Buffalo	Chicago	Cincinnati	Cleveland	Dallas	Denver	Detroit	Kansas City	Los Angeles
Albany, N.Y.	SO, SA	PA	NY	NY	NY	NY	NY	TP, MK	UP	NY	WB, MP	SF, UP
Rail fare...	54.82	24.77	15.20	22.15	61.15	54.81	36.16	83.36	101.10	40.71	73.31	146.71
Lower berth	14.45	8.75	6.71	6.71	11.00	10.07	6.71	22.50	23.25	7.76	17.30	35.20
Albuquerque..	SO, WA	PA	NY, NH	NY	SF	BO	NY	FW, SF	SF	NY	SF	SF
Rail fare...	60.95	90.55	128.37	91.70	52.02	69.94	77.76	29.15	18.46	73.51	34.30	34.26
Lower berth	17.00	26.47	29.90	24.46	16.70	21.41	22.46	9.50	......	22.55	12.25	12.25
Amarillo, Tex.	SO, LN	PA	NY, NH	NY	SF	LN	NY	FW, RI	SF	NY	SF, RI	SF
Rail fare...	46.53	77.38	105.07	78.83	39.15	50.93	94.88	14.28	17.96	60.64	21.43	46.84
Lower berth	17.00	21.97	25.49	24.46	13.25	21.41	22.46	5.80	6.70	22.55	8.70	15.50
Atlanta, Ga...		SO	SR	PA	SO	SO, LN	SO	WA	UP	SO	SL	WA
Rail fare...		30.27	60.30	53.45	32.76	23.61	39.52	40.68	62.84	38.37	35.74	91.90
Lower berth		11.25	14.45	11.25	10.00	10.00	10.00	10.20	16.70	10.00	10.00	25.65
Baltimore, Md.	SO, SR	......	NH	PA	CO-BO	CO-BO	PA	TP, MK	UP	CO-BO	SF, RI	SP, SF
Rail fare...	30.27	......	30.25	29.85	55.03	39.21	32.29	66.15	94.98	42.63	57.33	121.61
Lower berth	11.25	......	7.26	6.71	11.00	10.84	6.71	19.75	23.22	12.21	17.30	34.92
Birm'h'm, Ala.	SO, SA	SO	SR	PA	IC	SO	SO	TP, MK	UP	SO	SL, MP	SF, SP
Rail fare...	7.07	37.34	67.37	53.81	27.34	20.77	39.88	29.12	55.77	38.73	31.12	85.25
Lower berth	6.10	12.80	15.45	11.55	9.15	.....	10.70	9.50	14.70	10.70	8.70	25.30
Boston, Mass..	SR	PA	......	NY	NY	NY, PA	NY	TP, MK	UP	NY	SF, RI	UP
Rail fare...	60.30	30.25	......	37.43	76.35	70.02	51.36	91.22	116.30	55.91	94.07	161.91
Lower berth	14.45	7.26	......	6.71	13.20	11.77	8.75	24.95	25.45	10.07	19.50	37.40
Buffalo, N. Y..	SO, LN	PA	NY	......	NY	NY	NY	TP, MK	UP	NY	SF, RI	UP
Rail fare...	49.02	29.85	37.43	......	39.68	33.04	13.96	68.10	79.63	18.48	57.40	125.24
Lower berth	11.25	6.71	6.71	......	7.76	6.71	6.71	19.51	20.01	6.71	14.06	31.96
Calgary, Alta..	SO, LN	BO	BM	NY	CB, CM	NY, PA	NY	FW, SF	CB, CS	NY	RI	SF, SP
Rail fare...	96.88	124.17	120.03	108.82	69.14	91.35	61.65	85.63	48.43	90.63	67.35	89.54
Lower berth	27.70	28.70	30.90	25.46	17.70	24.41	24.41	29.45	25.50	24.41	20.75	......
Charlotte, N.C.	SO	PA	NH	NY, PA	SO	NY		SF, CS	BO	SL, MP	SF, UP	
Rail fare...	11.11	19.23	39.62	48.93	43.66	24.45	41.82	45.68	71.43	39.55	46.78	102.38
Lower berth	6.10	8.20	12.35	12.81	13.90	12.70	12.81	18.20	22.80	12.85	16.30	33.60
Chicago, Ill...	SO, LN	CO-BO	NY	NY	......	NY, PA	NY	SF	SF	NY	SF	SF
Rail fare...	32.76	55.03	76.35	39.68	......	22.23	25.74	37.66	39.95	21.49	17.72	85.56
Lower berth	10.00	11.00	13.20	7.76	......	6.71	6.71	11.75	12.25	6.71	6.30	24.20
Cincinnati, O..	SO, LN	CO-BO	NY	NY	NY	......	NY	TP, MK	UP	CO-BO	NW	UP
Rail fare...	23.61	39.21	70.02	33.04	22.23	......	19.11	61.94	62.18	17.96	37.86	104.64
Lower berth	10.00	7.76	11.77	6.71	6.71	......	6.71	14.80	18.16	6.71	......	29.55
Cleveland, O..	SO, LN	PA	NY	NY	NY	NY	......	SF, TP	UP	CO	SF, RI	UP
Rail fare...	39.52	32.29	51.36	13.96	25.74	19.11	......	58.48	62.19	11.83	43.46	111.30
Lower berth	10.00	6.71	8.75	6.71	6.71	6.71	......	18.16	18.96	6.71	13.01	30.91
Columbus, O..	SO, LN	PA	NY	NY	NY	NY	NY	TP, MK	UP	CO	SF, RI	UP
Rail fare...	27.93	36.81	61.78	24.38	23.75	8.69	10.43	49.46	63.70	11.79	39.31	109.31
Lower berth	*	7.76	11.00	6.71	7.55	6.71	6.71	15.70	18.16	6.71	13.56	29.86
Dallas, Tex...	WA	PA	NY, NH	NY	SF	LN	NY	......	CS, SF	NW	SF	SF
Rail fare...	40.68	67.14	96.03	76.69	37.66	41.94	61.65	......	32.25	54.82	19.94	56.50
Lower berth	10.20	19.75	24.95	19.51	11.75	17.11	18.16	......	16.80	16.80	7.55	17.70
Dayton, Ohio.	SO, LN	PA	NY	NY	PA	CO-BO	NY	TP, MK	SF, RI	BO	SF, RI	UP, SP
Rail fare...	23.15	42.08	66.80	29.65	20.08	3.98	15.70	45.23	53.97	14.41	33.33	99.72
Lower berth	*	7.76	11.00	6.71	6.71	6.71	6.71	15.70	18.16	6.71	13.11	29.86
Denver, Colo..	UP	UP	UP	UP	SF	UP	UP	FW, SF	......	NW	UP	UP
Rail fare...	62.84	94.98	116.30	79.63	39.95	62.18	62.19	32.21	......	57.11	24.65	52.15
Lower berth	16.70	23.22	25.45	20.01	12.25	18.16	18.96	10.20	......	17.85	7.55	17.70
DesMoines, Ia.	LN, SO	BO	NY, NH	NY	RI	NY, PA	NY	SF, MK	UP	NY	RI	SP, UP
Rail fare...	42.62	68.85	90.17	53.50	13.82	36.05	39.56	28.40	26.11	35.31	8.46	72.92
Lower berth	11.75	16.80	19.00	13.56	5.80	12.51	12.51	11.45	9.50	12.80	5.80	22.20
Detroit, Mich..	SO, LN	CO-BO	NY	NY	NY	CO-BO	NY	NW	NW	......	NW	UP
Rail fare...	38.37	42.63	55.91	18.48	21.49	17.96	11.83	54.82	57.11	......	39.21	102.72
Lower berth	10.00	......	10.07	6.71	6.71	6.71	6.71	16.80	17.85	......	13.01	29.55
Duluth, Minn..	SO, LN	BO	NY, NH	NY	CM	NY, PA	NY	RI, MK	RI, CB	NY	RI	UP
Rail fare...	50.45	72.72	94.04	57.37	21.08	39.92	43.43	43.42	40.12	39.18	24.31	122.80
Lower berth	16.40	17.40	19.60	14.16	......	13.11	13.11	17.05	17.05	13.11	12.50	31.85

r abbreviations see page 903.

RAIL AND PULLMAN FARES BETWEEN CITIES

FROM / TO	Atlanta	Baltimore	Boston	Buffalo	Chicago	Cincinnati	Cleveland	Dallas	Denver	Detroit	Kansas City	Los Angeles
El Paso, Tex..	WA	PA	NY, NH	NY	SF	SO, LN	NY	TP	SF, CS	NY	SF, RI	SP
Rail fare...	68.04	94.35	123.29	94.81	56.29	69.15	80.87	30.21	28.18	76.62	37.41	38.15
Lower berth	17.00	27.45	29.90	24.46	16.70	22.50	23.41	9.55	11.45	22.55	12.25	11.75
Gr't Falls, Mt.	SO, LN	BO	NY, NH	NY	GN	NY, PA	NY	FW, RI	CS, CB	NY	CB, MP	SP, UP
Rail fare...	85.29	110.05	131.37	94.70	55.02	77.25	80.76	66.68	34.46	76.51	50.07	54.01
Lower berth	25.00	27.70	29.80	24.46	16.70	23.41	23.41	22.75	12.55	23.41	16.20	21.50
Hartford, Ct.	SO, SA	NH	NY	NY	NY	NY, PA	NY	MK, TP	UP	NY	SF, RI	UP
Rail fare...	43.78	22.26	9.48	32.10	71.02	62.61	46.03	84.77	108.90	50.58	82.28	154.51
Lower berth	14.45	6.71	......	10.07	11.77	11.00	10.07	24.95	25.45	11.77	18.07	35.97
Houston, Tex..	WA	PA	NY	SF	SO, LN	NY	SF		CS, DR	NW		SF
Rail fare...	38.52	67.20	96.14	79.48	47.29	46.44	66.15	10.93	41.84	64.45	29.57	63.43
Lower berth	10.20	20.30	26.20	21.51	13.75	16.60	19.81	5.80	13.25	18.45	10.20	19.10
Indianapolis..	SO, LN	PA	NY, PA	NY	NY	NY	NY	MK, TP	SF, RI		NY	UP
Rail fare...	27.59	49.79	72.29	35.40	13.96	8.29	21.49	42.76	53.91	22.44	29.04	97.33
Lower berth	7.40	10.07	13.20	7.76	6.71	6.71	6.71	14.80	18.16	......	13.01	29.86
Jacksonvl., Fla.	SO	AC	NH	NY	SO	SO	NY	MK, TP	UP	BO	SL	UP
Rail fare...	14.93	36.76	66.79	66.46	46.01	35.34	54.45	47.80	73.58	53.30	47.34	100.41
Lower berth	6.10	12.80	15.45	15.45	13.90	10.70	13.90	14.05	20.15	13.90	14.05	27.50
Kan. City, Mo.	SL	BO	NY, NH	NY	SF	NW	NW	SF	DR	NW		UP
Rail fare...	35.74	72.75	94.07	57.40	17.72	37.86	43.46	19.94	24.65	39.21	......	67.86
Lower berth	10.20	17.30	19.50	14.06	6.30	......	13.01	7.55	7.55	13.01	......	20.80
Little R'k, Ark.	SO, LN	PA	NY, NH	NY	NW	LN, SO	NY	TP	SF, CS	NY	KC, MK	SF, SP
Rail fare...	22.17	51.77	80.71	60.22	26.35	26.07	45.68	15.42	40.35	47.59	19.12	69.16
Lower berth	7.05	18.17	21.50	18.37	8.25	13.11	14.16	6.40	12.25	12.80	6.40	22.90
Los Angeles...	WA	PA	UP	UP	SF	UP	UP	SF	UP	UP	SF	
Rail fare...	91.90	120.94	161.91	125.24	85.56	104.64	111.30	56.50	52.15	102.72	67.86	......
Lower berth	25.65	34.92	37.40	31.96	24.20	29.55	30.91	17.70	17.70	29.55	20.80	......
Louisville, Ky.	LN	CO-BO	PA	NY	PA	LN	NC	MK, TP	UP	BO	RI, SF	UP
Rail fare...	20.24	44.33	73.59	38.16	22.86	5.12	24.23	36.88	55.96	23.08	25.62	90.68
Lower berth	6.10	......	13.20	7.76	6.71	......	6.71	13.85	18.16	6.71	13.11	29.25
Memphis, Tn..	SO, LN	SO	NH	NY	IC, WB	LN	NC	TP, MK	UP	BO	SL	UP
Rail fare...	17.41	47.42	75.58	51.29	21.03	21.25	40.36	19.34	45.43	36.35	20.78	74.49
Lower berth	......	14.10	17.55	12.00	7.05	......	10.70	7.75	12.25	10.00	5.80	23.15
Mexico City..	WA	PA	NY, NH	NY	IC, GM	LN, SO	NY	MK	CS, SF	NY	MK, KC	SP
Rail fare...	65.62	92.68	121.62	100.52	64.91	67.48	84.85	29.26	58.38	86.40	47.84	51.16
Lower berth	......	30.26	36.06	30.51	24.26	25.56	29.12	12.61	21.81	27.76	18.16	*
Miami, Fla....	SO	AC	NH	PA	IC	LN	NY	TP, MK	UP	BO	SL	UP
Rail fare...	30.49	52.32	82.35	82.02	61.57	50.90	68.27	62.85	89.14	66.00	62.90	115.97
Lower berth	10.00	17.35	19.80	19.00	17.55	14.75	18.20	18.10	22.85	18.20	17.70	32.15
Milwaukee...	SO, LN	BO	NY, NH	NY	CM	NY, PA	NC	SF, MK	CM	NY	SF, RI	CM
Rail fare...	36.05	58.32	79.64	42.97	3.29	25.52	29.03	39.11	43.24	24.78	21.01	88.85
Lower berth	12.25	16.80	19.00	13.56	......	12.51	12.51	16.20	......	7.55		
Minneapolis..	SO, LN	BO	NY, NH	NY	CM	NY, PA	NY	RI, SF	CM	NY	RI	NP
Rail fare...	48.46	77.68	92.05	55.38	15.70	37.93	41.44	38.87	50.19	37.19	18.93	122.00
Lower berth	12.25	16.80	19.00	13.56	5.80	12.51	12.51	13.25	......	12.51	6.70	30.90
Montreal, Que.	SO, LN	PA	BM	NY	GT	BO	NY	TP, MK	CB, UP	HT, NY	SF, CB	SP, UP
Rail fare...	57.94	38.66	19.67	21.15	43.21	44.01	35.11	77.35	81.00	26.05	58.77	128.77
Lower berth	15.25	8.75	*	6.71	11.77	11.77	8.75	22.40	23.45	9.13	18.07	35.15
New Orleans..	SO, WA	SO	NH	NY	IC	SO	NY	TP, SP	UP	SO	KC, MP	SF
Rail fare...	21.15	51.42	77.62	65.96	36.29	35.92	55.03	24.30	54.14	53.88	34.14	76.58
Lower berth	7.05	16.00	19.80	15.45	12.00	10.70	13.90	8.30	15.90	13.90	10.20	25.30
N. Y. City....	SO	PA	NH	NY	PA, NY	NY, PA	NY	TP, MK	UP	NY	NW	UP
Rail fare...	44.01	13.96	15.39	32.93	67.38	55.66	42.93	78.04	107.33	51.11	85.10	150.61
Lower berth	13.65	6.71	5.39	6.71	11.77	10.07	7.76	23.52	24.02	8.75	18.07	35.07
Norfolk, Va...	SO, SA	NW	NH	PA	CO-BO	CO-BO	PA	TP, MK	UP	BO	NW	UP
Rail fare...	25.42	13.55	43.58	43.25	58.23	41.70	39.31	62.96	94.07	42.63	72.51	117.31
Lower berth	9.15	8.20	13.59	12.81	13.20	8.75	10.07	23.60	24.65	11.77	......	36.35
Oklahoma City	SO, LN	PA	NY, NH	NY	SF	LN	NY	SF	SF, CS	NW	SF	SF
Rail fare...	35.83	65.43	94.37	71.84	32.56	40.24	57.90	8.69	27.57	49.72	14.84	60.75
Lower berth	12.80	18.70	24.95	19.51	9.50	13.76	14.70	5.80	9.50	......	5.80	19.10

First-class, one-way.

RAIL AND PULLMAN FARES BETWEEN CITIES

FROM / TO	Atlanta	Baltimore	Boston	Buffalo	Chicago	Cincinnati	Cleveland	Dallas	Denver	Detroit	Kansas City	Los Angeles
Omaha, Neb.												
Rail fare	SO, LN 42.62	BO 74.25	NY, NH 95.57	NY 58.90	CM 19.22	BO 41.06	NY 44.96	SF, MK 27.63	20.73	NY 40.71	CB, MP 7.69	UP 67.86
Lower berth	12.55	17.70	19.90	14.46	6.70	13.11	13.41	9.50	7.55	13.41	1.85	20.80
Philadelphia												
Rail fare	SO 37.26	PA 7.17	NH 23.03	PA 31.37	CO-BO 60.92	PA 46.33	PA 36.16	MK, TP 72.19	UP 100.87	BO 47.95	NW 78.64	UP 146.48
Lower berth	12.55	6.71	6.71	6.71	11.00	10.07	6.71	22.75	23.25	8.75	......	35.20
Phoenix, Ariz.												
Rail fare	WA 82.75	PA 111.81	NY, NH 140.75	NY 113.28	SF 73.99	LN, SO 86.61	NY 99.34	TP 50.52	SF 41.06	NY 95.09	SF 56.27	SF 22.35
Lower berth	21.90	32.90	35.10	29.66	21.90	27.80	28.61	14.60	......	27.80	17.70	7.55
Pittsburgh, Pa.												
Rail fare	SO, LN 40.40	PA 22.33	NH 48.43	NY 23.89	CO-BO 33.86	PA 23.09	PA 9.93	MK, TP 61.93	UP 73.81	CO-BO 21.27	NW 51.58	UP 119.42
Lower berth	10.00	6.71	......	6.71	6.71	6.71	6.71	18.45	18.96	6.71	13.01	30.91
Portland, Ore.												
Rail fare	UP 111.64	UP 137.78	SS 158.10	UP 122.45	GN 82.75	UP 104.98	UP 105.00	FW, TP 80.68	UP 53.44	SS	SS 76.29	GN 52.70
Lower berth	29.50	34.92	37.40	31.96	24.20	29.86	30.91	24.50	17.00	......	22.20	15.90
Roch'st'r, N.Y.												
Rail fare	SO, LN 54.10	PA 41.96	NY 32.40	NY 5.08	NY 44.72	NY 38.07	NY 18.96	TP 72.72	UP 80.60	CB, NY 23.49	SF, RI 58.37	UP 130.32
Lower berth	14.45	......	......	*1.43	7.76	7.76	6.71	19.51	20.01	6.71	14.06	31.96
St. Louis, Mo.												
Rail fare	LN 26.44	CO-BO 64.05	NY 87.61	NY 50.94	NY 11.26	NY 26.02	NY 37.00	TP 28.33	DR 36.49	NW 28.11	NW 11.84	SF 78.62
Lower berth	8.30	11.77	15.29	10.07	......	6.71	7.76	10.40	11.45	......	......	23.15
Salt Lake City												
Rail fare	UP 81.04	UP 112.67	UP 133.99	UP 97.32	CM 57.64	UP 79.87	UP 79.85	FW, TP 50.43	DR 22.76	UP 74.80	DR 45.67	UP 30.06
Lower berth	22.50	27.70	29.90	24.46	16.70	23.41	23.41	16.70	8.70	23.10	14.05	10.20
San Antonio												
Rail fare	WA 48.35	PA 76.06	NY, NH 105.00	NY 83.90	NW 53.24	LN, SO 50.86	NY 70.25	PA 11.29	CS, DR 41.76	NY 70.40	MK, SF 31.22	SF 59.01
Lower berth	13.25	22.45	28.00	22.45	16.15	17.50	21.15	5.80	14.05	19.90	10.20	19.30
San Diego												
Rail fare	WA 91.90	UP 138.14	UP 161.91	UP 125.24	SF 85.56	UP 104.64	UP 111.30	TP, SF 56.50	SF 52.68	UP 102.72	SF, RI 67.86	4.87
San Francisco												
Rail fare	WA 99.43	UP 140.59	UP 161.91	UP 125.24	SF, CB 85.56	UP 104.64	UP 111.30	SF 70.91	UP 52.68	UP 102.72	SF 67.86	SP 22.11
Lower berth	26.80	34.92	37.40	31.96	24.20	29.55	30.91	20.15	17.70	29.55	20.80	6.70
Seattle, Wash.												
Rail fare	UP 112.27	UP 137.78	UP 159.10	UP 122.43	GN 82.75	UP 104.98	UP 105.00	FW, TP 85.74	UP 60.50	UP 99.91	UP 75.62	SP 59.76
Lower berth	29.50	34.92	37.40	31.96	24.20	29.55	30.91	24.50	17.00	29.55	20.80	15.90
Shreveport, La.												
Rail fare	SO, LN 31.13	PA 59.37	NY, NH 88.31	NY 68.57	IC, GM 35.05	LN, SO 35.53	NY, NC 54.64	TP 9.01	UP, CS 39.54	NY 56.54	KC 21.67	SP, SF 63.93
Lower berth	7.55	18.40	23.59	18.37	12.00	13.45	16.06	6.40	12.55	14.70	7.55	21.85
Spok'ne, Wash.												
Rail fare	LN, SO 99.70	NP 125.59	NP 146.91	NP 110.24	NP 70.56	NP 92.79	NP 96.30	FW, TP 76.02	UP 53.44	NP 92.05	NP 63.44	SS 67.16
Lower berth	26.50	31.80	34.00	28.56	20.80	26.86	27.51	24.50	15.90	27.51	19.10	18.10
Tampa, Fla.												
Rail fare	SO, AC 23.92	AC 45.75	AC 75.78	PA 75.45	IC 55.00	SO, LN 44.33	NY 61.70	TP, MK 53.66	UP 82.57	BO 59.43	SL 56.33	UP 109.40
Lower berth	7.95	16.00	18.60	17.85	16.30	13.20	17.00	19.00	21.90	17.00	16.20	30.55
Toledo, Ohio												
Rail fare	SO, LN 30.15	CO-BO 39.88	NY 59.38	NY 21.98	NY 17.72	CO-BO 14.16	NY 8.03	SF, TP 51.68	CB, UP 56.06	CO 3.80	SF, RI 33.83	SF, UP 102.51
Lower berth	9.65	8.75	11.00	6.71	6.71	6.71	6.71	16.80	18.16	6.71	13.11	29.55
Toronto, Ont.												
Rail fare	SO, LN 43.14	PA 35.55	NY 43.13	NY 5.70	NY 27.76	NY 28.56	NY 19.66	TP 61.90	UP 66.15	NY, GT 10.60	SF, RI 43.92	SF, UP 113.32
Lower berth	13.60	*	*	......	7.76	7.76	6.71	19.10	20.01	6.38	14.06	31.85
Wash't'n, D.C.												
Rail fare	SO, WA 27.19	CO-BO 2.95	NH 33.11	PA 32.78	PA 57.20	CO-BO 36.26	PA 32.29	MK, TP 63.48	UP 94.98	CO-BO 42.63	NW 72.75	UP 138.14
Lower berth	9.15	*1.40	7.76	6.71	11.00	7.76	6.71	19.75	23.22	8.75	......	34.92
Wichita, Kans.												
Rail fare	SO, LN 42.46	PA 83.13	NY, NH 102.28	NY 65.61	SF 25.93	BO 43.85	NY 51.67	SF 15.33	SF, DR 20.96	NY 47.42	SF 8.21	SF 60.26
Lower berth	15.00	15.90	24.95	19.51	9.50	13.41	14.46	5.80	6.70	13.10	5.80	19.10

*For abbreviations see page 903.

RAIL AND PULLMAN FARES BETWEEN CITIES

FROM / TO	Miami	Milwaukee	Minneapolis	Montreal	New Orleans	New York	Philadelphia	Pittsburgh	St. Louis	San Francisco	Seattle	Washington, D.C.
Albany, N.Y..	SA, FE	CM, CW	CB, CM	DH	LN, SO	NY	PA	PA	NY	UP	UP	PA
Rail fare...	76.87	64.44	71.29	12.99	68.96	10.78	17.55	43.85	72.41	146.71	143.90	27.63
Lower berth	20.40	......	16.80	6.71	16.70	6.71	6.71	7.76	13.20	35.20	35.20	8.75
Albuquerque..	SA, FE	CM, CW	RI	CN	TP	NY, PA	PA	PA	WB, MP	SF	GN, UP	RF, SO
Rail fare...	85.02	55.31	52.94	95.23	50.94	119.40	88.86	75.75	45.06	45.98	73.04	87.47
Lower berth	27.55	......	17.70	28.15	14.70	28.47	27.70	23.41	14.70	13.25	20.80	26.47
Amarillo, Tex.	SA, FE	CM, CW	RI	CN	SP, TP	NY, PA	PA	PA	WB, MP	SF	GN, UP	SO, BO
Rail fare...	70.60	42.44	40.36	80.80	36.41	89.87	83.12	74.55	31.62	58.59	71.48	73.05
Lower berth	22.85	......	15.40	25.02	11.45	24.34	23.40	18.95	10.20	17.00	24.50	21.97
Atlanta, Ga...	SA, FE	CM, CW	CB, CM	CN	SO	SO	PA	PA	LN	WA	UP	PA
Rail fare...	30.49	30.63	48.46	61.56	21.15	44.01	37.26	49.52	26.44	99.43	112.27	27.19
Lower berth	10.00	......	12.51	15.25	7.05	13.65	12.55	10.00	8.30	26.80	29.50	9.15
Baltimore, Md.	AC	CM, CW	CB, BO	DH	SO	PA	PA	PA	CO-BO	UP	UP	CO-BO
Rail fare...	52.32	55.03	77.68	37.76	51.42	13.96	7.17	22.33	64.05	140.59	137.78	2.95
Lower berth	17.35	......	16.80	8.75	16.00	6.71	6.71	6.71	11.77	37.40	34.92	*1.40
Birm'h'm.,Ala.	SO	CM, CW	CB, CM	CN	SO	SO	SO	PA	LN	SF, SP	UP	SO
Rail fare...	34.23	30.63	42.01	61.92	15.21	51.08	44.33	43.86	19.37	85.25	105.20	34.19
Lower berth	10.70	......	12.25	18.37	6.10	14.95	14.10	10.45	7.05	25.30	27.50	10.45
Boston, Mass..	NH	CM, CW	CB, CM	DH	LN, SO	NH	NH	NH	NY	UP	UP	NH
Rail fare...	82.35	79.64	92.05	28.19	80.55	15.39	23.03	48.43	87.61	161.91	159.10	33.11
Lower berth	19.80	......	19.00	6.71	19.80	5.39	6.71	......	15.29	37.40	37.40	7.76
Buffalo, N. Y..	SA, FE	CM, CW	CB, CM	DH	LN, IC	NY	PA	PL	NY	UP	UP	PA
Rail fare...	77.62	42.97	55.38	35.22	68.96	32.93	31.37	23.84	50.94	125.24	122.43	32.78
Lower berth	19.00	......	13.56	6.71	15.45	6.71	6.71	6.71	10.07	31.96	31.96	6.71
Calgary, Alta..	SA, FE	CM, CW	CM	CM	IC	NY, PA	PA	PA	CB, WB	SP	GN	
Rail fare...	124.66	66.36	53.44	98.80	97.44	136.52	130.06	104.54	76.08	73.13	35.79	126.34
Lower berth	35.25	......	14.05	29.47	29.70	29.47	28.70	24.41	23.50	......	......	28.70
Charlotte, N.C.	SA, FE	CM, CW	CB, CM	CN	SO	PA	PA	BO	LN, IC	SF, SP	GN, NP	SO, RF
Rail fare...	33.48	46.75	59.16	65.60	32.19	32.97	26.22	33.80	37.48	102.38	122.40	16.15
Lower berth	13.90	......	18.35	14.85	10.45	10.40	9.50	12.81	14.40	33.60	35.60	6.10
Chicago, Ill...	IC	CM	CM	CN	LN	NY	PA	PA	CO-BO	NW	UP	PA
Rail fare...	61.57	3.29	15.70	43.21	36.29	67.38	60.92	33.86	11.26	85.56	82.75	57.20
Lower berth	17.55	......	5.80	11.77	12.00	11.77	11.00	6.71	......	24.20	24.20	11.00
Cincinnati, O..	SO	CM, CW	CM	CN	SO	NY, PA	CO-BO	PA	NY	PA	NY	PA
Rail fare...	50.90	25.52	37.93	42.66	35.92	53.08	46.33	23.09	26.02	104.64	104.98	36.26
Lower berth	14.75	......	7.55	11.77	10.70	10.07	10.07	6.71	6.71	29.55	29.86	7.76
Cleveland, O..	SA, FE	CM, CW	CB, CM	CN	SO	NY	PA	PA	NY	PA	NY	UP
Rail fare...	67.59	29.03	41.44	38.37	55.03	42.93	36.16	9.93	37.00	111.30	105.00	32.29
Lower berth	18.20	......	8.70	8.75	13.90	7.76	6.71	6.71	7.76	30.91	30.91	6.71
Columbus, O..	SA, FE	CM, CW	CM	CN	LN, SO	NY	PA	PA	PA	UP	PA	PA
Rail fare...	58.42	27.04	37.29	37.84	44.61	47.39	40.67	.14.44	32.29	109.31	106.50	36.81
Lower berth	18.20	......	12.51	11.00	12.00	8.75	8.14	6.71	6.71	29.86	29.86	7.76
Dallas, Tex...	SA, FE	CM, CW	RI	CN	TP	PA	PA	PA	BO	MP, SL	SF	NP, UP	SO, BO
Rail fare...	63.16	40.30	38.87	75.10	24.30	80.88	74.13	70.87	28.33	70.91	85.74	64.06
Lower berth	18.10	......	13.25	22.40	8.30	23.52	22.75	18.45	10.40	20.15	24.50	19.75
Dayton, Ohio.	SA, FE	CM, CW	CB, CM	CN	SO	LN, SO	PA	PA	NY	SF, SP	GN, NP	PA
Rail fare...	53.64	23.37	33.95	39.14	39.61	52.43	45.94	19.71	26.84	99.72	101.00	42.08
Lower berth	15.45	......	12.51	11.25	11.55	10.07	9.13	6.71	6.71	29.86	29.86	7.76
Denver, Colo..	UP	CM	CM	CM	UP	UP	DR	UP	UP	UP	UP	UP
Rail fare...	89.14	43.24	50.19	83.16	54.14	107.33	100.87	73.81	36.49	67.86	60.50	94.98
Lower berth	22.85	......	......	23.45	15.90	24.02	23.25	18.96	11.45	17.70	17.00	23.22
DesMoines, Ia.	SA, FE	CM, CW	RI	CN	KC	NY, PA	PA	PA	CB	UP	UP	PA
Rail fare...	69.78	17.11	10.47	57.03	40.30	81.20	74.74	49.22	14.95	72.92	74.53	71.02
Lower berth	19.10	......	5.80	17.57	12.55	17.57	16.80	12.51	......	22.20	22.20	16.80
Detroit, Mich.	SA, FE	CM, CW	CB, CM	CN	SO	NY	PA	PA	CO-BO	NW	UP	PA
Rail fare...	63.48	24.78	37.19	26.05	53.88	51.11	47.95	21.27	28.11	102.72	99.91	42.63
Lower berth	18.20	......	7.55	9.13	13.90	8.75	8.75	6.71	......	29.55	29.55	8.75
Duluth, Minn.	SA, FE	CM	NP	CN	IC, KC	NY, PA	PA	PA	CB	GM, CB	GN	PA
Rail fare...	79.26	18.30	5.79	59.34	53.87	85.07	78.61	53.09	28.02	104.75	67.87	74.89
Lower berth	23.95	......	5.80	17.57	18.40	18.47	17.40	13.11	12.20	26.80	20.80	17.40

First-class, one-way.

RAIL AND PULLMAN FARES BETWEEN CITIES

FROM / TO	Miami	Milwaukee	Minneapolis	Montreal	New Orleans	New York	Philadelphia	Pittsburgh	St. Louis	San Francisco	Seattle	Washington, D.C.
El Paso, Tex.	SA, FE	CM, CW	RI	CN	SP, TP	NY, PA	PA	PA	MP, WB	SP	NP, UP	SO, BO
Rail fare	88.82	58.42	56.34	96.78	54.52	108.09	101.34	90.53	48.17	60.26	74.10	91.27
Lower berth	28.30	.....	17.70	28.15	16.25	28.47	27.70	23.41	16.15	16.25	21.50	27.45
Gr't Falls, Mt.	SA, FE	CM, CW	GN	CN	IC	GN	PA	PA	CB, MP	SP, WP	GN	PA
Rail fare	115.55	52.21	.....	98.23	82.78	122.40	115.94	90.42	59.50	55.61	29.79	112.22
Lower berth	33.00	.....	13.25	28.47	26.35	28.47	27.70	23.41	16.70	18.45	11.00	27.70
Hartford, Ct.	NH	CM, CW	CB, CM	NH	LN, SO	NH	NH	NH	NY, PA	UP	UP	NH
Rail fare	74.36	74.31	80.26	20.38	72.56	5.59	15.04	41.34	83.03	154.51	151.70	25.12
Lower berth	19.80	.....	17.57	6.71	19.80	.....	6.71	...:..	14.14	35.97	35.97	7.26
Houston, Tex.	SA, FE	CM, CW	RI	CN	SP, MP	PA, NY	PA	PA	MP, IC	SF	NP, UP	SO, RF
Rail fare	56.85	49.21	48.50	84.01	17.37	80.94	73.27	67.43	34.66	79.28	95.37	64.12
Lower berth	18.10	.....	15.90	24.05	6.70	25.20	23.95	20.25	12.05	20.15	26.80	20.30
Indianapolis	SA, FE	CM, CW	CB, CM	CN	SO, LN	NY	PA	PA	NY	UP	UP	PA
Rail fare	59.19	17.25	29.66	45.81	36.29	60.29	53.83	28.00	18.71	97.33	96.71	49.79
Lower berth	15.45	.....	7.55	12.00	10.70	11.77	11.00	6.71	6.71	29.86	29.86	10.07
Jacks'v'le, Fla.	SA, FE	CM, CW	CB, CM	CN	SR	AC	AC	BO	AC	UP	UP	AC
Rail fare	15.56	49.30	60.68	71.68	26.29	50.50	43.75	51.33	38.04	107.94	123.87	33.68
Lower berth	6.10	.....	16.70	16.70	7.95	14.95	14.45	13.90	12.35	27.50	33.20	10.45
Kan. City, Mo.	SL	CM, CW	RI	CN	KC	NW	NW	NW	NW	SF	UP	NW
Rail fare	62.90	21.01	18.93	60.93	38.10	85.10	78.64	51.58	11.84	67.86	75.62	72.75
Lower berth	17.70	.....	6.70	18.07	10.20	18.07	17.30	13.01	.....	20.80	20.80	.....
Little R'k, Ark.	FE, SA	CM, CW	RI	CN	IC, MP	NY, PA	PA	BO	MP, IC	SF, SP	NP, UP	BO
Rail fare	49.33	29.39	37.48	64.19	20.65	65.51	58.76	59.96	14.84	78.62	94.30	48.69
Lower berth	18.10	.....	11.00	18.40	6.40	20.07	19.30	12.55	6.40	23.15	25.00	18.17
Los Angeles	FE, SA	CM	NP	CN	SF	UP	UP	UP	SF	SP	UP	UP
Rail fare	115.41	88.85	122.00	127.21	76.58	150.61	146.48	119.42	78.62	22.11	54.97	138.14
Lower berth	32.15	.....	30.90	35.15	25.30	35.97	35.20	30.91	23.15	6.70	15.90	34.92
Louisville, Ky.	LN	CM, CW	RI	CN	LN	CO-BO	CO-BO	PA	PA	UP	UP	CO-BO
Rail fare	50.73	26.15	31.51	46.27	32.59	58.20	51.45	28.21	21.75	98.09	105.30	41.38
Lower berth	14.75	.....	12.51	13.20	10.00	11.77	11.00	6.71	6.71	29.25	29.86	10.07
Memphis, T'n.	SO	CM, CW	CB, RI	CN	IC	SO	SO	PA	IC	UP	UP	SO
Rail fare	44.57	24.32	34.63	62.40	15.25	61.46	54.41	44.34	21.03	82.02	96.94	44.11
Lower berth	14.75	.....	10.20	18.10	6.10	16.85	16.00	10.70	6.10	23.15	25.00	12.00
Mexico City	SA, FE	CM, CW	RI	CN	SP, MP	PA, NY	PA	BO	MP, IC	SP	NP, UP	SO, BO
Rail fare	82.41	68.20	66.77	103.00	37.29	106.42	99.76	98.77	53.65	73.27	111.91	89.60
Lower berth	27.91	.....	23.61	33.36	16.36	35.16	33.91	29.21	21.36	24.27	29.52	30.26
Miami, Fla.		CM, CW	CB, RI	CN	LN	AC	AC	BO	LN	SF	UP	AC
Rail fare	.....	64.86	76.24	87.24	41.07	66.06	59.31	66.89	53.60	123.50	139.43	49.24
Lower berth	.....	.....	23.35	20.40	12.85	18.80	18.10	18.20	16.30	32.15	39.45	14.45
Milwaukee	SA, FE		CM	CN	IC	NY, PA	PA	BO	WB, GM	CM	CM	PA
Rail fare	64.86	.....	12.90	46.50	39.56	70.67	64.21	37.15	14.55	88.85	79.98	60.49
Lower berth	‡	.....	5.80	‡	‡	‡	‡	‡	‡	‡	‡	‡
Minneapolis	SA, FE	CM		CN	KC, IC	NY, PA	PA	PA	CB, WB	GN	GN	PA
Rail fare	76.24	12.90	.....	57.35	49.76	83.08	76.62	49.56	22.64	103.95	67.04	72.90
Lower berth	23.35	5.80	.....	17.57	14.50	17.57	16.80	12.51	6.70	24.20	20.80	16.80
Montreal, Que.	SA, FE	CM, CW	CM		SO, LN	NY	PA	PA	WB, GM	SF, WP	GN	PA
Rail fare	89.86	46.50	58.91	.....	79.50	23.80	31.44	56.84	54.16	128.77	118.95	40.62
Lower berth	20.40	.....	17.57	.....	20.80	6.71	6.71	13.42	12.00	35.15	35.15	8.75
New Orleans	LN	CM, CW	RI, CB	CN		SO	SO	LN	LN	SF	UP	SO
Rail fare	41.07	39.58	49.85	77.07	.....	65.16	58.41	59.01	27.21	85.56	109.40	48.34
Lower berth	12.85	.....	14.50	20.80	.....	18.80	17.55	13.90	9.65	25.30	30.95	13.90
N. Y. City	AC	CM, CW	RI	CN	LN		PA	PA	NY	UP	UP	PA
Rail fare	66.06	70.67	83.08	23.80	65.16	.....	6.74	33.04	78.00	150.61	147.80	16.82
Lower berth	18.80	.....	17.57	6.71	18.80	.....	6.71	6.71	14.14	35.97	35.97	6.71
Norfolk, Va.	SA, FE	CM, CW	CB, CM	CN	NW	NW	NW	BO	PA, LN	UP	UP	NW
Rail fare	44.29	59.40	68.64	47.72	46.56	27.29	20.54	27.61	51.71	124.85	140.98	10.47
Lower berth	13.90	.....	19.00	14.85	.....	8.20	8.20	12.81	13.20	36.35	36.35	6.10
Oklahoma City	SL	CM, CW	RI	CN	PA, NY	PA	PA	BO	SL	SF	NP, UP	SL
Rail fare	62.99	35.45	33.77	70.28	28.83	79.17	72.42	66.02	23.02	67.86	81.54	81.14
Lower berth	.....	.....	11.00	19.05	9.95	21.19	20.25	15.80	.....	20.15	24.50	.....

‡To Chicago only. *For abbreviations see page 903.

RAIL AND PULLMAN FARES BETWEEN CITIES

FROM / TO	Miami	Milwaukee	Minneapolis	Montreal	New Orleans	New York	Philadelphia	Pittsburgh	St. Louis	San Francisco	Seattle	Washington, D.C.
Omaha. Neb..	SA, FE	CM	CM	CN	LN, SO	NY, PA	PA	PA	WB, MP	UP	UP	PA
Rail fare...	69.78	22.51	29.46	62.43	41.81	86.80	80.14	54.62	16.18	67.86	67.86	76.42
Lower berth	19.85	.....	.....	18.47	13.75	18.47	17.70	13.41	6.40	20.80	20.80	17.70
Philadelphia..	AC	CM, CW	CB, CM	DH	SO	PA	.....	PA	PA	UP	UP	PA
Rail fare...	59.31	64.21	76.62	30.55	58.41	6.74	.....	26.24	71.54	146.48	143.67	10.07
Lower berth	18.10	.....	16.80	6.71	17.55	6.71	.....	6.71	13.20	35.20	35.20	6.71
Phoenix, Ariz..	SA, FE	CM, CW	RI	CN	SP	PA, NY	PA	PA	SF	SF	UP, NP	SO, BO
Rail fare...	82.57	76.89	74.81	116.81	74.34	130.15	118.80	109.00	67.72	34.59	65.69	108.73
Lower berth	32.15	.....	22.50	33.40	21.30	33.67	32.90	28.61	19.85	11.75	20.90	32.90
Pittsburgh, Pa.	SA, FE	CM, CW	CB, CM	DH	LN	PA	PA	.-...	PA	UP	UP	CO-BO
Rail fare...	63.95	38.69	40.19	56.85	59.01	33.04	26.24	.....	46.57	119.42	116.61	21.36
Lower berth	18.20	.....	12.51	13.42	13.90	6.71	6.71	.....	8.75	30.91	30.91	6.71
Portland, Ore..	UP	CM	GN	CN	SS	GN	UP	UP	NW	GN	GN	GN
Rail fare...	138.80	86.04	69.30	119.10	101.52	150.13	143.67	116.61	85.20	34.65	7.06	139.95
Lower berth	39.45	.....	20.80	35.15	30.95	35.97	35.20	30.91	23.15	11.00	5.80	34.92
Roch'st'r, N.Y.	SA, FE	CM, CW	CB, CM	DH	LN, SO	NY	PA	PL	NY	SF, WP	GN, NP	PA
Rail fare...	94.06	48.01	56.55	30.18	71.60	27.97	36.45	28.84	55.98	130.32	123.40	37.86
Lower berth	22.51	.....	13.56	13.42	16.70	6.71	.....	6.71	10.07	31.96	31.96	.....
St. Louis, Mo.	LN	CM, CW	RI, CB	CN	LN	NY	PA	PA		SF	NW	CO-BO
Rail fare...	53.60	14.55	22.64	54.16	27.21	78.00	71.54	46.57	.....	78.62	85.83	61.14
Lower berth	16.30	.....	6.70	12.00	9.65	14.14	13.20	8.75	.....	23.15	23.15	11.77
Salt Lake City	UP	CM	CM	CN	UP	DR	UP	UP	DR	UP	UP	UP
Rail fare...	108.20	60.93	69.29	100.82	72.30	125.02	118.65	91.50	54.60	36.39	41.64	112.67
Lower berth	33.00	.....	.....	28.47	22.50	28.47	27.70	23.41	.....	10.20	13.25	27.70
San Antonio..	SA, FE	CM, CW	RI	CN	SP	PA, NY	PA	PA	MP	SP, SF	NP, UP	SO, BO
Rail fare...	65.79	51.58	50.15	86.38	27.19	89.80	83.05	54.62	40.73	74.99	95.29	72.98
Lower berth	20.15	.....	15.90	25.50	8.75	27.30	26.30	21.15	13.50	22.05	26.50	22.45
San Diego....	UP	CM	CM	CN	UP	UP	UP	UP	SF	SP	UP, GN	UP
Rail fare...	115.97	88.85	95.86	127.21	78.62	150.61	146.48	119.42	78.62	24.97	59.83	138.14
Lower berth									23.15			
San Francisco.	SA, FE	CM	GN	CN	SF	UP	UP	UP	SF		UP	UP
Rail fare...	122.94	88.85	103.95	127.21	85.56	150.61	146.48	119.42	78.62	.....	38.56	140.59
Lower berth	32.15	.....	24.20	35.15	25.30	35.97	35.20	30.91	23.15	.....	11.45	34.92
Seattle, Wash.	UP	CM	GN	CN	UP	UP	UP	UP	NW	UP		PA
Rail fare...	139.43	79.98	67.04	119.10	109.40	147.80	143.67	116.61	85.83	41.71	.....	139.95
Lower berth	39.45	.....	20.80	35.15	30.95	35.97	35.20	30.91	23.15	11.45	.....	34.92
Shreveport, La.	SA, FE	CM, CW	RI	CN	KC	PA, NY	PA	BO	IC	SP, SF	NP, UP	SO, RF
Rail fare...	53.72	38.34	40.55	73.14	14.20	73.11	66.36	68.91	23.79	78.35	93.93	59.09
Lower berth	15.90	.....	14.25	20.30	5.80	22.44	21.50	17.05	8.30	23.15	26.80	18.40
Spok'ne, Wash.	UP	CM	GN	CN	UP	GN	NP	NP	NP	SS	GN	GN
Rail fare...	127.23	67.77	54.84	112.21	97.10	137.94	131.48	104.42	73.38	49.11	12.20	127.76
Lower berth	36.45	.....	17.70	32.15	26.80	32.57	31.80	27.51	20.15	14.05	5.80	31.80
Tampa, Fla...	SA	CM, CW	CM	CN	LN	AC	AC	PA	IC	UP	UP	PA
Rail fare...	11.03	58.29	69.67	80.67	33.72	59.49	52.74	60.32	47.03	116.93	132.88	42.67
Lower berth	.....	.....	20.20	19.35	10.70	17.55	16.85	17.00	14.75	30.55	37.35	13.20
Toledo, Ohio..	SA, FE	CM, CW	CB, CM	CN	LN, SO	NY	PA	BO	NY, PA	SF, WP	GN	CO-BO
Rail fare...	60.64	21.01	31.81	31.03	49.96	50.72	44.76	17.18	28.98	103.28	98.86	39.88
Lower berth	18.20	.....	12.51	9.13	13.20	8.75	8.75	6.71	6.71	29.55	29.55	8.75
Toronto, Ont..	SA, FE	CM, CW	CB, CM	CN, CP	LN, SO	NY	PA	BO	WB, GM	SF, WP	GN	PA
Rail fare...	73.63	31.05	47.79	15.45	58.65	35.09	37.07	40.37	38.71	113.32	103.65	38.48
Lower berth	22.21	.....	13.56	4.50	18.46	6.71	6.71	6.71	8.70	31.85	31.85	7.76
Wash't'n, D.C.	AC	CM, CW	CB, CM	DH	SO	PA	PA	CO-BO	CO-BO	UP	UP	.....
Rail fare...	49.24	57.20	55.64	40.62	48.34	16.82	10.07	21.36	61.14	140.59	137.78	.....
Lower berth	14.45	.....	16.80	8.75	13.90	6.71	6.71	6.71	11.77	34.92	34.92	.....
Wichita, Kans.	SA, FE	CM, CW	RI	CN	MP, SP	PA, NY	PA	PA	WB, MP	UP	SF	NP, UP
Rail fare...	69.62	29.22	27.14	67.58	34.56	93.31	86.85	61.33	18.97	66.94	74.92	83.13
Lower berth	23.00	.....	9.50	18.70	11.45	21.19	20.25	51.80	6.70	19.10	21.50	18.47

First-class, one-way.

RAILROAD ABBREVIATIONS (for use with preceding tables)

AC	Atlantic Coast Line		MN	Monon
BM	Boston & Maine		MP	Missouri Pacific
BO	Baltimore & Ohio		NC	New York, Chicago & St. Louis
CB	Chicago, Burlington & Quincy			(Nickel Plate)
CE	Chicago & Eastern Illinois		NH	New York, New Haven & Hartford
CG	Central of Georgia		NP	Northern Pacific
CM	Chicago, Milwaukee, St. Paul & Pacific		NW	Norfolk & Western
CN	Canadian National		NY	New York Central
CO	Chesapeake & Ohio		PA	Pennsylvania
CP	Canadian Pacific		PL	Pittsburgh & Lake Erie
CS	Colorado & Southern		PS	Pennsylvania-Reading Seashore Lines
CV	Central Vermont		RF	Richmond, Fredericksburg & Potomac
CW	Chicago & North Western		RI	Chicago, Rock Island & Pacific
DH	Delaware & Hudson		SF	Atchison, Topeka & Santa Fe
DR	Denver & Rio Grande Western		SL	St. Louis-San Francisco (Frisco)
E	Erie-Lackawanna		SO	Southern Railway
FE	Florida East Coast		SP	Southern Pacific
FW	Fort Worth & Denver		SR	Seaboard
GM	Gulf, Mobile & Ohio		SS	Spokane, Portland & Seattle
GN	Great Northern		TP	Texas & Pacific
GT	Grand Trunk		UP	Union Pacific
IC	Illinois Central		WA	Western Railway of Alabama
KC	Kansas City Southern		WB	Wabash
LN	Louisville & Nashville		WP	Western Pacific

Some of these railroads are included in current mergers or merger proposals.

AIRLINE ABBREVIATIONS (for tables starting on page 904)

AA	American Airlines	EA	Eastern Air Lines	OZ	Ozark Air Lines
AC	Air-Canada Lines	FL	Frontier Air Lines	PA	Pan American World
AL	Allegheny Airlines	GU	Aviateca (Guatemala)		Airlines
AM	Aeronaves de Mexico	KL	Royal Dutch Airlines	PC	Pacific Air Lines
AS	Alaska Airlines	LC	Lake Central Airlines	PI	Piedmont Airlines
BA	British West Indian	LR	LACSA (Costa Rica)	PN	Pacific Northern Airlines
	Airways	LX	Los Angeles Airways	QF	Qantas Airways
BH	Bahamas Airways	MO	Mohawk Airlines	SO	Southern Airways
BL	Bonanza Air Lines	NA	National Airlines	TA	TACA International
BN	Braniff International	NE	Northeast Airlines	TT	Trans-Texas Airways
	Airways	NI	Lanica Airlines	TW	Trans World Airlines
CN	Central Airlines		(Nicaragua)	UA	United Air Lines
CO	Continental Air Lines	NO	North Central Airlines	VA	VIASA (Venezuela)
CP	Canadian Pacific	NW	Northwest Orient	WA	Western Air Lines
DL	Delta Air Lines		Airlines	WC	West Coast Airlines
DO	Dominican Airlines				

SELECTED NORTH AMERICAN AIR PASSENGER FARES

TO	Atlanta	Baltimore	Buffalo	Chicago	Cincinnati	Cleveland	Dallas	Detroit	Houston	Indianapolis	Jacksonville	Kansas City
Akron, Ohio..	UA	UA	LC	UA	LC	EA, UA	......	EA, UA	......	LC	......	......
Prop. 1st cl..	43.65	24.55	16.35	24.10	18.60	6.00		12.60		21.00		
Pr. economy.	35.20			19.90		6.00		11.25				
Alb.,Troy,Sch.	UA, EA	AA, TW	AA, MO	AA, UA	AA	MO, AA	AA, DL	AA	AA	TW, LC		
Prop. 1st cl...	69.60	24.50	20.75	51.70	43.15	30.80	96.20	35.75	104.10	48.55		
Pr. economy.	56.50		17.40	39.45			72.40	28.65				
Albuquerque..	EA	TW	......	TW	TW, AA	TW, UA	CO	TW, UA	CO	TW, DL		TW
Jet 1st cl.....		127.95		88.05	98.85	111.05	49.30	105.90	65.50	92.60		59.45
Jet economy.		99.85		69.40	77.75	86.90	40.15	83.05	59.45	73.05		47.45
Prop. 1st cl..	97.00						46.20		59.45			55.30
Pr. economy.	74.65						37.15		55.30			41.65
Amarillo, Tex.	......	TW	......	TW			BN, CO		BN, CO	TW		CN, TW
Jet 1st cl...:		103.55		68.00			41.70		46.70	72.35		38.30
Anchorage, Al.	NW, DL			NW		NW, UA		NW, UA				
Jet 1st cl.....	290.90			240.55		260.60		257.70				
Jet economy.	220.80			180.45		202.45		199.35				
Prop. 1st cl...												
Pr. economy.												
Asheville,N.C.	PI, UA			DL	DL, PI					DL	DL	
Prop. 1st cl..	15.05			43.25	25.25					32.40	29.25	
Pr. economy.				34.20	20.70					26.05	23.75	
Atlanta, Ga...		DL, PI	UA	DL, EA	DL	UA, EA	DL	DL, UA	EA, DL	EA, DL	DL	BN, TW
Jet 1st cl.....		49.40		50.40	32.15	47.60	61.60	48.65	60.80	40.00	24.20	58.20
Jet economy.		39.70		40.90	26.55	39.70	49.15	39.10	49.00	33.10	20.55	46.55
Prop. 1st cl..		46.30	60.15	47.40	30.05	44.70	57.50	45.55	56.90	37.00	22.10	54.20
Pr. economy.		33.40	44.70	34.50	24.45	36.50	45.05	36.00	43.60	30.20	18.50	42.55
Austin, Tex...				BN, AA			BN, TT		CO			BN
Prop. 1st cl...				77.50			15.65		15.30			53.00
Pr. economy.				56.50			13.60		12.55			41.05
Baltimore,Md.	DL		AA, UA	UA, TW	LC	UA	AA, DI	UA	BN, DL	TW	EA	TW, UA
Jet 1st cl.....	49.40		38.55	46.80	37.00	27.10	86.25	34.20	93.20		54.55	69.35
Jet economy.	39.70		31.50	37.70	30.30		74.25	28.50	79.60	34.65		57.85
Prop. 1st cl..	46.30			43.70	34.00	25.00	86.25	32.10		39.75	50.40	68.60
Pr. economy.	33.40					19.60	62.55	24.85	71.10		32.70	
Billings, Mont.	NW, EA	UA		NW		NW, UA		NW				FL
Prop. 1st cl..	126.70	120.55		81.40		99.95		94.80				76.00
Pr. economy.	99.60	92.70		63.30		77.25		72.10				
Binghamton..	EA, UA	EA, NA	MO, UA	AA, UA	TW, AA	MO		MO	EA, DL	TW, LC	EA, NA	TW, CO
Prop. 1st cl...	60.30	21.60	16.30	46.75	44.80	28.00		30.00	107.75	44.95	67.30	74.35
Birmingham..	EA	UA	UA	EA, DL		EA, UA	DL	DL, UA	EA	DL	DL, EA	DL
Jet 1st cl.....	15.30			51.30			50.80	52.05	51.90	51.15		33.40	
Jet economy.	14.20			41.90				41.65		41.00		27.45	46.20
Prop. 1st cl...	14.30	52.20	60.75	47.40			47.70	48.95	48.80	48.05	36.30	31.30	
Pr. economy.	13.20	35.00	41.90	38.00			36.55	38.55	39.15	36.50		25.35	36.40
Bismarck,N.D.	NW, EA	NW, UA		UA, NW		NW, UA		NW				FL
Prop. 1st cl...	99.95	93.75		53.60		73.15		66.95				71.60
Pr. economy.	75.90	72.10		42.25		56.65		52.55				
Boston, Mass..	EA	EA, AL	MO, AA	AA, UA	AA	AA, UA	AA, BN	AA, UA	EA, DI	TW, DL	EA, NA	TW, BN
Jet 1st cl...:.	74.40	30.60	32.80	60.85	53.80	43.45	104.70	48.85	115.50	62.20	79.30	93.35
Jet economy.	59.40	26.00	26.90	50.85	44.80	35.30	90.70	39.40	98.30	48.50	62.30	73.90
Prop. 1st cl..	69.50	28.60	30.70	60.85	53.15	40.35	104.70	45.75	115.50	58.05	73.40	88.85
Pr. economy.	51.60	24.00	24.95	47.10	41.70	32.20	81.45	36.30	88.40	44.30	55.50	

For airline abbreviations see page 903.

SELECTED NORTH AMERICAN AIR PASSENGER FARES

FROM / TO	Atlanta	Baltimore	Buffalo	Chicago	Cincinnati	Cleveland	Dallas	Detroit	Houston	Indianapolis	Jacksonville	Kansas City
Buffalo, N. Y..	UA	UA	......	AA, UA	AA	AA	AA	AA, MO	DL, AA	......	......	......
Jet 1st cl....	56.90	38.55		37.10	33.75	17.40	87.80	20.35	94.30			
Jet economy.	47.80	31.50		30.15	27.50	15.10	76.75	17.65	82.65			
Calgary, Alta..	NW			NW		NW		NW, UA				
Prop. 1st cl...	168.25			117.90		122.50		121.70				
Pr. economy.	130.15			89.80		91.20		89.80				
Char'st'n, S. C.	DL, SO	NA, PI		EA, LC	DL	EA	DL	DL	EA, DL	DL	NA, EA	
Prop. 1st cl...	23.45	36.70		59.50	41.90		77.75	56.05	75.25	48.95	16.90	
Pr. economy.	19.35	29.50		46.90	33.20	39.00	60.35		58.45	38.50	14.65	
Char'st'n,W.V.	UA, EA	LC, EA	UA	AA, EA	PI, AA	UA, EA	AA, TW	EA	AA	DL		
Prop. 1st cl...	29.60	23.50		31.95	13.70	19.45	73.10	25.95	79.10	21.00	44.25	
Pr. economy.						16.95		21.75	61.90		35.55	
Charlotte,N.C.	EA	EA		EA	PI	EA	DL	EA	EA	EA	EA	DL
Jet 1st cl....	25.55	33.60		54.30		41.60		47.70	75.20		29.20	
Jet economy.	21.45	28.10		44.30		34.40		38.90	60.00		24.90	
Prop. 1st cl...	23.45	31.60		49.40	32.40	38.70	69.20	44.80	70.30	38.35	27.20	62.45
Pr. economy.	18.40	26.20		39.50		31.40	53.80	33.90	55.10		22.90	48.60
Chattanooga..	DL, EA	DL, PI	UA	DL, EA	DL			DL	EA, DL	DL, EA	DL, EA	
Prop. 1st cl...	12.90	42.30	50.75	40.30	23.05			38.80	58.00	28.75	29.75	
Pr. economy.	11.90	31.65		32.60	19.05				45.30			
Chicago, Ill...	DL, EA	UA, TW	AA, UA		AA	UA	BN, AA	UA, AA	AM	AM	DL, EA	TW, BN
Jet 1st cl....	50.40	46.80	37.10		23.55	26.20	62.95	22.05	75.60	15.30	70.30	32.95
Jet economy.	40.90	37.70	30.15		20.10	22.00	52.95	18.90	63.90	13.60	56.30	27.10
Prop. 1st cl...	47.40	43.70	35.05		21.50	24.10	62.95	19.95	75.60	14.25	65.40	30.85
Pr. economy.	34.50		27.35		18.05	19.65	46.05	15.25		12.55	47.35	24.10
Cincinnati, O..	DL	AA	AA	EA, DL		AA, LC	AA	DL, LC	AA	AA, TW	DL	TW
Jet 1st cl....	32.15	37.00	33.75	24.90		20.70	62.95	21.85	70.00	11.55	53.00	43.75
Jet economy.	26.55	34.00	27.70	21.60		17.85	52.95	18.80	58.95	10.30	42.70	35.50
Prop. 1st cl...	30.05		31.70	23.00		18.60		19.75		10.55	48.95	40.65
Pr. economy.	24.45		25.60	19.70		15.80	49.55	16.70		9.25	38.55	32.40
Cleveland, O..	EA	UA	AA	UA, NO	AA, LC		AA, BN	UA, EA	AA	TW, LC	EA, UA	TW, BN
Jet 1st cl....	47.60	27.10	17.40	26.20	20.70		77.20	11.45	86.10	23.10	64.65	54.85
Jet economy.	39.70		15.10	22.00	17.85		66.20	10.65		19.70	49.40	43.75
Prop. 1st cl...	44.70	25.00	16.35	24.10	18.60		77.20	10.40	86.10	21.00	60.50	51.75
Pr. economy.	36.50	19.60		19.65	15.80			9.50		17.60	44.25	40.55
Columbia,S.C.	EA, PI	EA		EA	DL, EA	EA	DL	EA		EA	EA	
Prop. 1st cl...	21.05	36.40		53.60	35.75	44.05	71.55	50.84		42.75	19.90	
Pr. economy.	17.35	27.35		42.60	28.65		55.55					
Columbus, O..	DL	LC, TW	LC, AA	TW, UA	AA, LC	AA	AA, TW	LC, EA	AA	LC, TW	DL	TW
Jet 1st cl....				26.70	12.90	12.00	72.40		78.50			50.85
Jet economy.				22.35	11.45	11.10	61.40					41.00
Prop. 1st cl...	39.80	27.35	24.00	24.60	11.90	11.00	72.25	17.10	78.50	15.60	56.65	46.70
Pr. economy.	31.00			20.25	10.40	10.05	56.05	15.30	61.40	13.60	43.00	36.85
Dallas, Ft. W.	DL	AA, UA	AA, UA	BN, AA	AA	AA, UA		AA, UA	BN, TT	TW, AA	DL	BN, CN
Jet 1st cl....	61.60	86.25	87.80	62.95	63.70	77.20		75.50	21.70	64.10	77.90	41.65
Jet economy.	49.15	74.25	76.75	52.95	53.70	66.20		64.50	18.85	57.25	62.30	33.85
Prop. 1st cl...	57.50	86.25	87.80	62.95	63.60	77.20		75.50	19.60	64.10	72.00	39.55
Pr. economy.	45.05	62.55	70.45	46.05	49.55			57.30	16.40	53.10	56.40	30.60
Dayton, Ohio.	DL	TW	LC, AA	TW, UA	LC, AA	AA	AA	LC	AA	TW	DL	TW
Jet 1st cl....	37.05		29.90	21.85		15.80	67.40		74.40			46.05
Jet economy.	30.45	27.95	24.75	18.80		13.95	56.75		62.90	10.85		37.40
Prop. 1st cl...	33.95	32.10		19.75	7.10		67.40	16.05		10.85	52.85	41.90
Pr. economy.	27.35			16.70	6.45			14.00		9.75	41.55	32.90

Approximate fares. Taxes not included. *Courtesy Official Airline Guide*

SELECTED NORTH AMERICAN AIR PASSENGER FARES

FROM / TO	Atlanta	Baltimore	Buffalo	Chicago	Cincinnati	Cleveland	Dallas	Detroit	Houston	Indianapolis	Jacksonville	Kansas City
Denver, Colo..	EA	TW, UA		UA, TW	TW, AA	TW	BN	TW	BN, CO			CN, CO
Jet 1st cl....		103.55		66.90		84.85	56.95	81.75	76.50			48.50
Jet economy.		89.05		55.40		72.35	45.55	69.25	60.75			39.00
Prop. 1st cl...	95.05				82.50		52.40		71.35			45.40
Pr. economy.							41.15		55.35			34.50
DesMoines, Ia.				UA, OZ			BN	UA	BN	EA, LC		BN
Prop. 1st cl...				24.55			52.40	41.30	63.40	33.85		15.60
Detroit, Mich.	DL, EU	UA, TW	MO, AA	UA, AA	LC, DL	EA	AA, BN		DL, BN	DL, LC	EA, DL	TW, CO
Jet 1st cl....	48.65	34.20		22.05	21.85	13.40	75.50		87.70	23.05	67.70	50.75
Jet economy.	39.10	28.50		18.90	18.80	12.70	64.50		72.90	19.70	55.00	40.65
Prop. 1st cl...	45.55	32.10	18.30	19.95	19.75	12.40	75.50		84.50	20.95	63.70	47.65
Pr. economy.	36.00	24.85	15.60	15.25	16.70	11.60	57.30		65.80	17.60	49.50	36.15
El Paso, Tex..		AA, UA	AA, UA	AA	AA	AA, UA	AA	AA, UA	CO, AA			CO
Jet 1st cl....		115.65	111.50	87.35	92.40	103.00	43.85	98.05	55.80			70.20
Jet economy.		101.65	97.35	75.85	79.40	89.00	35.60	85.05	44.50			
Prop. 1st cl...			111.50									66.05
Pr. economy.												51.30
Ft. Lauderdale	EA, NW	EA		NW, EA	EA	EA, UA	EA	DL, EA	NA	EA	EA, DL	
Jet 1st cl....	49.30	79.55		94.20	78.15							
Prop. 1st cl...	46.40	74.40		90.25	73.00	84.50	86.20	88.45	74.60	79.30	27.30	
Pr. economy.	35.20	53.70		62.95	55.60	60.65	60.65	65.80	57.85	55.70	22.45	
Grand Rapids.	UA	UA, TW	MO, AA	UA, NO	LC	UA, NO		UA, NO		LC		
Prop. 1st cl...	56.65	43.25	30.50	12.25	27.00	21.55		14.40		22.50		
Grboro., Hi. Pt.	EA, UA	PI		UA, EA	PI	EA	EA	EA		EA	EA	
Prop. 1st cl...	25.90	25.05		45.60	28.45	32.45	74.80	39.60		34.60	31.55	
Gr'nville, S. C.	EA, SO	PI		DL		EA	EA	EA	EA, DL	DL	DL	
Prop. 1st cl...	14.00	36.40		47.05		38.30	67.55	44.80	67.20	36.05	25.40	
Htfd. Hyk., Sp.	EA	AL, EA	MO	UA, TW	TW	UA, AA	AA, BN	MO	EA	TW, DL		TW
Jet 1st cl....	69.70			59.00	51.00	37.35	100.00		43.55	54.00		88.85
Jet economy.	52.40			47.00	40.85	30.35	87.00	90.45	91.30			70.00
Prop. 1st cl...	64.55	21.50	25.40	56.10	47.90	35.25	100.00	35.75	115.35	52.90	68.55	83.70
Pr. economy.	47.25	18.05		42.70	37.75	28.25	79.75	32.15	86.15			63.85
Honolulu.....	NW	UA, TW	UA	UA, NW		NW, AA		UA, NW		TW		TW
Jet 1st cl....	291.10	302.75	297.80	266.55		286.60		283.70		273.20		249.50
Jet economy.	227.60	247.25		215.45		222.00		230.30		219.20		196.00
Prop. 1st cl...	317.05					314.60						
Pr. economy.	241.35					235.55						
H'tSprgs., Ark.				DL			TT, CN		TT, DL	DL		CN
Prop. 1st cl...				51.30			23.00		33.00	43.45		26.40
Houston, Tex..	EA, DL	AA	AA, UA	AA	AA	AA, UA	BN, TT	DL, UA		DL	NA	BN
Jet 1st cl....	60.80	93.20	94.30	75.60	70.00	86.10	21.70	87.70			65.90	54.70
Jet economy.	49.00	79.60	82.65	63.90	58.95	71.80	18.85	72.90		76.00	53.00	44.15
Prop. 1st cl...	56.90	93.20					19.60	84.50		67.60	61.55	50.55
Pr. economy.	43.60	72.20					16.40	65.80		53.20	48.00	39.85
Huntsv'le, Ala.	SO	DL, PI		EA, NW		UA		UA	EA, NA	EA, DL	DL, EA	
Prop. 1st cl...	16.50	47.95		40.55		43.30		44.45	53.95	29.60	35.40	
Indianapolis..	EA, DL	TW, LC	LC	EA, AA	AA, LC	TW	AA, BN	DL, LC	DL	20.95	EA	TW, CO
Jet 1st cl...	40.00			17.10		23.10	64.10			76.00	58.90	36.40
Prop. 1st cl...	37.00	39.75	34.05	16.10	10.55	21.00		20.95	67.60		55.20	34.30
Pr. economy.	30.20			14.50	9.25	17.60		17.60	53.20		40.00	27.35
Jackson, Miss.	DL			DL			DL	DL	TT	DL	DL	
Prop. 1st cl...	29.05			52.00			32.20	61.65	29.25	44.00	46.15	
Pr. economy.	23.70			40.85			26.05	48.15	23.80	35.00	36.50	

For airline abbreviations see page 903.

SELECTED NORTH AMERICAN AIR PASSENGER FARES

FROM / TO	Atlanta	Baltimore	Buffalo	Chicago	Cincinnati	Cleveland	Dallas	Detroit	Houston	Indianapolis	Jacksonville	Kansas City
Jacksonville...	EA	EA	UA	DL, EA	DL	EA, UA	DL	DL	NA	EA	......	DL
Jet 1st cl....	25.50	54.55	......	70.30	53.00	62.80	77.90	67.70	65.90	58.90		86.85
Jet economy.	22.10	......	......	56.30	42.70	52.30	62.30	55.00	53.00	47.60		......
Prop. 1st cl...	23.50	50.40	67.30	65.40	48.95	60.00	72.00	63.70	61.55	55.00		79.60
Pr. economy.	......	37.45		47.50	38.55	44.60	56.40	49.50	48.00	40.00		65.30
Kansas City..	DL, EA	UA, TW	UA	TW, BN	TW, AA	TW, UA	BN, CN	TW, UA	BN	TW	EA	......
Jet 1st cl....	58.20	69.35	......	32.95	43.75	54.85	41.65	50.75	54.70	36.40	86.85	
Jet economy.	46.55	57.85	......	27.10	35.50	43.75	33.85	40.65	44.15	29.70		
Prop. 1st cl...	54.20	68.60	65.90	30.85	40.65	51.75	39.55	47.65	50.55	34.30	79.60	
Pr. economy.	42.55	......	51.45	24.10	32.40	40.55	30.60	36.15	39.85	27.35	65.30	
Knoxville, Tn.	DL	AA, PI	UA	DL, EA	DL	UA	AA	UA	EA, DL	DL		
Prop. 1st cl...	14.05	36.40	46.65	37.30	19.30	34.15	57.50	35.35	63.90	26.35		
Pr. economy.	12.40			29.90	16.40		45.05			21.25		
Las Vegas, Nev.	DL '	UA, TW		TW, UA	TW	UA, TW	DL, AA	UA	NA	TW, DL	NA, DL	TW
Jet 1st cl....	141.10	143.25	......	108.55	128.20	126.25	85.30	122.10	101.15	123.20	161.55	94.90
Jet economy.	111.40	127.75	......	94.05	114.20	111.75	67.40		79.45	99.25	129.75	74.80
Prop. 1st cl...									94.95			
Little Rock...	DL, EA	EA, LC	UA, AA	DL	AA	AA	AA, TT		TT, DL	DL		CN
Prop. 1st cl...	37.55	68.80	70.50	47.85	42.10	57.45	24.80		31.90	39.90		26.40
Los Angeles...	DL	UA, TW	AA, UA	UA, TW	AA, TW	UA, TW	AA, DL	TW, AA	AA	TW, DL	NA, DL	TW, CO
Jet 1st cl....	141.10	152.75	147.80	116.55	128.20	136.60	84.50	133.70	98.30	123.20	161.70	99.50
Jet economy.	117.60	137.25	132.60	105.45	114.20	123.40	72.50	120.30	85.30	109.20	129.75	86.00
Prop. 1st cl...				116.55	128.20	136.60				123.20		
Pr. economy.			108.00	86.90								
Louisville, Ky.	DL, EA	AA, LC	AA	DL	AA, TW	AA, TW	AA, TW	DL	BN	EA	DL, EA	TW
Jet 1st cl....	30.80			23.90				58.10	28.00	83.35	50.80	39.80
Prop. 1st cl...	28.75	39.05	37.75	21.80	9.35	24.75	57.50	25.90	64.65	10.85	47.80	36.80
Pr. economy.	23.40			18.25	8.95		49.10	21.35	50.40	9.80	34.80	
Madison, Wis.	NW	NW		NO		UA, NW		NW				TW, OZ
Prop. 1st cl...	57.65	51.20		11.45		30.60		24.85				35.80
Pr. economy.	43.90	41.75		10.25		25.35		19.25				35.80
Melbourne, Fl.	EA	EA		DL, EA		EA, UA	DL, EA	EA	NA	EA	EA	......
Prop. 1st cl...	35.25	63.40		77.90		73.50	78.90	77.50	68.15	68.25	16.35	......
Memphis, Ten.	SO, DL	AA	UA, AA	DL	AA	AA	AA, TT	DL, UA	TT, DL	DL	DL, EA	DL
Jet 1st cl....	29.70	59.70	62.50	42.05	35.30	51.70	35.70	52.85	44.90	34.20	16.25	29.85
Jet economy.	24.65	51.20	52.20	34.30	28.80	41.40	29.25	42.60	36.65	28.25	14.10	24.20
Prop. 1st cl...	27.65	59.70		38.95			33.60	48.70	40.75	31.10	16.25	29.85
Pr. economy.	22.60			31.25			27.15	38.45	32.50	25.15	14.10	24.20
Mexico City..	EA	AA, UA	AA, UA	AA, MX	AA	AA, UA	BN, AA	AA, UA	PA, AA	AA		BN
Jet 1st cl....	115.40	157.30	157.70	136.40	135.10	146.60	78.50	146.60	61.00	134.70		114.00
Jet economy.	93.50	124.00	127.00	107.00	106.00	118.00	60.00	118.00	46.00	104.40		87.90
Prop. 1st cl...	107.30	147.20							57.00			
Pr. economy.	85.20	114.00							42.00			
Miami, Fla...	EA	NA, EA	UA, MO	DL, EA	DL, EA	EA, UA	EA, DL	DL, EA	NA	EA	DL, EA	TW, DL
Jet 1st cl....	49.40	78.10	......	94.20	76.80	82.10	91.30	92.50	79.30	83.80	29.40	98.25
Jet economy.	40.20	61.20	......	74.70	61.20	70.60	72.80	73.40	63.40	67.00	22.45	77.45
Prop. 1st cl...	46.40	73.20	91.30	88.30	71.90	82.10	84.40	86.60		77.90	27.30	
Pr. economy.	35.20	53.60	60.55	62.40	55.40	60.20	65.80	65.10		55.50	22.45	
Milwaukee....	DL, NW	UA, TW	UA	NW, NO	EA	NW	BN, DL	NW, UA	BN, DL	EA, AA		OZ, TW
Jet 1st cl....	59.90	49.55	......	10.65	......	27.95	......	22.05	92.20			
Jet economy.	50.20			8.85		23.30		18.90	73.40			
Prop. 1st cl...	55.50	46.45	35.05	9.60	30.00	25.85	69.40	19.95	86.00	19.65		37.00
Pr. economy.	42.50	35.90	......	8.85	26.90	20.60		15.65	68.05			

Approximate fares. Taxes not included. *Courtesy Official Airline Guide*

SELECTED NORTH AMERICAN AIR PASSENGER FARES

FROM / TO	Atlanta	Baltimore	Buffalo	Chicago	Cincinnati	Cleveland	Dallas	Detroit	Houston	Indianapolis	Jacksonville	Kansas City
Minapls., St. P.	NW	UA, NW	MO, AA	NW, UA	EA	UA, NW	BN	NW, UA	BN	EA, LC	.....	BN
Jet 1st cl....	75.60	69.70	.....	29.80	.....	47.05	75.45	41.25	88.50	.....	.....	36.60
Jet economy.	65.95	55.80	.....	23.50	.....	38.45	59.70	33.50	70.05	.....	.....	30.05
Prop. 1st cl...	70.70	64.55	56.45	27.70	48.15	43.95	71.30	38.15	82.30	44.25	.....	34.50
Pr. economy.	57.15	50.65	45.90	.....	41.45	35.35	55.25	30.30	63.60	.....	.....	27.85
Mobile, Ala...	EA, UA	EA	UA	EA	.....	UA	.....	UA	EA	EA	NA	.....
Prop. 1st cl..	28.30	67.10	75.50	61.50	.....	62.45	.....	63.60	34.05	51.05	30.75	.....
Montreal.....	EA, UA	EA	.....	AC	.....	AC	BN, AA	AC	BN, DL	EA, LC	EA	TW, BN
Jet 1st cl....	88.35	46.50	.....	71.00	.....	57.00	.....	54.00	.....	.....	.....	.....
Jet economy.	.....	43.60	.....	52.00	.....	42.00	.....	40.00	.....	.....	.....	.....
Pr. economy.	61.50	32.25	.....	48.00	.....	39.00	74.05	40.00	95.60	60.55	63.30	72.10
Nashville, Tn..	EA, TW	EA, LC	AA	EA	AA	AA	AA, BN	UA, AA	AA	EA	.....	TW
Jet 1st cl....	22.00	49.85	.....	35.00	34.15	37.10	50.25	.....	57.40	23.20	.....	.....
Prop. 1st cl..	20.00	46.75	48.15	33.00	.....	.....	47.15	52.05	.....	.....	.....	40.10
New Orleans..	EA, UA	DL, EA	AA	DL	AA	UA, EA	DL, TT	UA, DL	EA, DL	DL	NA	BN, DL
Jet 1st cl....	38.35	74.50	.....	67.60	60.00	85.80	39.85	72.00	27.25	59.10	43.80	57.20
Jet economy.	31.45	63.00	.....	54.40	47.85	.....	32.55	60.50	22.85	47.85	.....	45.75
Prop. 1st cl..	35.25	73.90	83.60	62.70	55.85	70.50	36.75	70.60	25.20	55.20	39.65	54.10
Pr. economy.	28.35	56.90	.....	49.50	43.70	54.70	29.50	55.70	20.80	43.55	31.55	42.45
N. Y., Nwrk..	EA, UA	AA, EA	AA, MO	UA, TW	AA, TW	UA, AL	AA, EA	NW, AL	EA, DL	TW, DL	EA, NA	TW, BN
Jet 1st cl....	59.15	17.30	25.50	52.30	46.25	32.90	96.20	38.35	104.10	51.65	66.60	79.20
Jet economy.	49.65	15.40	21.50	43.70	37.35	27.25	83.20	31.65	89.10	41.45	52.60	66.70
Prop. 1st cl..	57.90	17.00	23.45	51.70	43.15	30.80	96.20	36.30	.....	48.55	61.70	79.20
Pr. economy.	42.90	15.20	19.95	39.45	34.25	25.15	72.40	29.60	79.90	38.35	46.80	60.60
N. N's, Wmsbg..	PI, UA	PI	.....	UA	PI	UA	.....	UA	.....	.....	.....	.....
Prop. 1st cl..	40.95	15.45	.....	53.15	36.95	34.50	.....	41.65	.....	.....	.....	.....
Norfolk, Pmth.	UA, PI	UA, NA	UA	UA, AA	PI	UA	.....	UA	AA	.....	NA	.....
Prop. 1st cl..	40.95	15.45	36.70	53.15	36.95	34.50	.....	41.65	89.50	.....	41.15	.....
Pr. economy.	.....	13.50	30.00	41.70	.....	27.70	.....	33.60	.....	.....	32.85	.....
Oklahoma C..	EA	TW, UA	AA	BN, AA	AA, TW	AA, UA	BN, CN	AA, TW	BN, AA	TW	.....	BN, CN
Jet 1st cl....	.....	82.70	79.40	54.95	57.50	67.95	17.50	65.10	35.00	54.40	.....	28.80
Jet economy.	.....	70.70	66.60	43.80	48.50	56.95	15.50	54.10	28.85	43.55	.....	24.25
Prop. 1st cl..	.....	.....	79.20	51.85	56.55	67.95	15.40	.....	32.95	.....	.....	26.75
Pr. economy.	.....	.....	61.45	39.55	44.35	52.80	13.10	.....	26.30	.....	.....	20.85
Omaha, Neb..	SO	UA, TW	UA	UA, OZ	TW, AA	UA	BN, CN	UA, NW	BN	TW	DL, EA	BN, FL
Jet 1st cl....	.....	73.45	.....	34.60	.....	54.45	54.90	52.35	66.95	.....	.....	16.50
Prop. 1st cl..	.....	.....	67.55	.....	55.50	.....	51.85	49.25	62.85	.....	92.25	15.45
Pr. economy.	.....	.....	.....	.....	.....	.....	40.65	.....	49.00	.....	.....	13.20
Orlando, Fla.	DL, EA	EA, NA	EA	EA	DL	EA	DL, EA	DL	NA, EA	EA	EA, NA	.....
Jet 1st cl....	33.65	64.20	.....	79.30	62.10	73.80	77.90	77.60	65.90	68.90	13.70	.....
Jet economy.	27.70	50.80	.....	63.10	49.90	59.00	62.30	61.90	53.00	55.30	12.45	.....
Prop. 1st cl..	31.60	59.30	76.85	.....	58.10	69.00	72.00	72.80	61.55	64.00	12.70	.....
Pr. economy.	25.60	44.30	.....	.....	45.75	50.80	56.40	55.70	48.00	47.90	11.40	.....
Ottawa, Ont.	.....	EA	.....	AC	.....	AC	.....	.....	.....	.....	EA	.....
Prop. 1st cl..	.....	40.45	.....	69.00	.....	52.00	.....	.....	.....	.....	81.90	.....
Pensacola, Fla.	EA	DL, PI	.....	DL, EA	.....	EA	.....	.....	EA	.....	NA	.....
Prop. 1st cl..	24.70	64.10	.....	61.50	.....	62.45	.....	.....	38.35	.....	26.50	.....
Pr. economy.	21.00	60.70	.....	48.50	.....	48.70	.....	.....	21.70	.....	.....	.....
Philadelphia..	UA	AL, DL	UA	UA, TW	TW, AA	UA, AL	DL, BN	UA, AL	DL, EA	TW, AA	EA, NA	TW, CN
Jet 1st cl....	55.70	9.80	50.90	50.90	42.70	29.05	99.65	34.85	102.80	46.85	60.50	79.35
Jet economy.	44.90	9.20	40.75	40.75	34.60	24.15	78.35	29.45	84.50	37.80	48.00	62.85
Prop. 1st cl..	51.90	8.80	.....	47.80	39.60	26.95	90.35	26.95	100.10	43.75	55.70	74.20
Pr. economy.	37.95	8.15	.....	37.25	31.50	22.05	69.85	22.05	75.40	.....	.....	57.30

For airline abbreviations see page 903.

Section F — COMMUNICATION, TRAVEL, AND TRANSPORT

SELECTED NORTH AMERICAN AIR PASSENGER FARES

FROM / TO	Atlanta	Baltimore	Buffalo	Chicago	Cincinnati	Cleveland	Dallas	Detroit	Houston	Indianapolis	Jacksonville	Kansas City
Phoenix, Ariz..	DL	AA	AA, UA	AA, TW	TW, AA	AA	AA	AA, UA	CO, AA	TW, DL		TW, FL
Jet 1st cl....		135.40	130.50	101.80	111.35	120.75	64.25	117.40	76.20	105.60		85.30
Jet economy..		120.40	114.90	88.80	97.35	106.75	54.25	103.40	65.20	92.60		67.35
Prop. 1st cl..	119.95		130.50		111.35	120.75	63.50	117.40		105.60		80.15
Pr. economy.	92.10		99.00	79.30	90.10		50.10	91.30		83.35		59.45
Pittsburgh, Pa.	UA	UA, AL	UA, AL	TW, UA	TW, AA	UA, NW	AA	NW, UA	AA	TW, LC	EA, UA	TW, CO
Jet 1st cl....	44.45			34.15	24.75	12.75		20.95		19.85	56.00	61.65
Jet economy.	36.60			28.00	20.90	11.70		18.05		17.15	45.50	49.10
Prop. 1st cl..	41.40	16.55	18.25	32.05	22.70	11.70	81.60	18.85	86.10	18.80	52.20	57.50
Pr. economy.	33.50	13.50	16.10	24.75	18.85	10.45		15.70		16.10	39.50	44.95
Portland, Ore.	NW	UA		UA, NW		NW	BN	NW	BN			UA
Jet 1st cl....	166.90	152.75		116.55		136.60		133.70				111.45
Prop. 1st cl..	166.40			116.55		136.60	125.20	133.70	142.75			
Providence...	EA	AL		AA, UA	AA, TW	UA	AA, BN	AA, NW	AA, EA	TW	EA, NA	
Prop. 1st cl..	68.00	25.00	29.75	60.40	52.20	39.55	104.40	44.80	112.70	57.25	71.00	
Pr. economy.	51.00	20.60	24.15	47.10	40.95	31.50	81.45	35.40	90.40		53.50	
Raleigh, N. C.	EA, UA	PI		UA, EA	PI	UA	EA	UA	EA, DL	DL	EA	
Prop. 1st cl..	28.90	21.85		49.40	35.10	38.05	78.00	44.45	78.60	43.95	31.75	
Richmond, Va.	EA	NA, UA		UA, EA	PI	UA, NW		NW, UA	EA, DL		NA	
Prop. 1st cl..	37.80	12.45		50.10	32.55	34.70		41.80	89.60		41.15	
Rochtr., Minn.	NW			NW		NW	BN, CN	NW	BN	EA, LC		BN
Prop. 1st cl..	69.25			23.05		40.65	66.85	34.80	77.75	38.50		29.90
Rochtr., N. Y.	UA	AA	UA, MO	UA, AA	AA	AA	AA	AA, MO	AA			
Prop. 1st cl..	60.15	33.65	7.05	38.80	35.50	20.15	91.00	22.05	99.40			
St. Louis, Mo.	TW	EA, TW	AA	OZ, DL	TW, AA	TW, UA	AA, CN	TW, AA	DL, BN	TW	DL, EA	TW, BN
Jet 1st cl....	42.75	56.20	50.85	22.45	27.20	38.65	50.00	34.80	63.40	19.85	63.20	19.85
Jet economy.	34.70	44.90	40.75	19.25	22.90	31.50	40.10	28.45	50.50	17.15	51.00	17.45
Prop. 1st cl..	39.75	53.10	47.75	20.35	25.10	36.55	46.90	32.70	59.30	18.80	58.30	18.80
Pr. economy.	31.70	41.80	37.65	17.15	20.80	29.40	37.00	26.35	46.35	16.10	46.10	16.40
Salt Lake City		UA		UA, NW		UA, AA	BN	UA, AA	BN			UA, TW
Jet 1st cl....		127.90		92.50		111.25		107.15				81.35
Prop. 1st cl..							83.70		101.50			76.20
San Antonio..	EA, DL	EA, AA	AA	BN, AA	AA, DL	AA, UA	BN, TT	AA, UA	CO, EA		NA	BN
Jet 1st cl....	74.10	96.90	100.70	78.35	78.05	87.70	21.50	87.70	16.75			59.75
Jet economy.	59.20	84.50	87.40	67.35	67.05	76.30	18.70	76.30	16.15			47.95
Prop. 1st cl..	69.20	96.90		78.35	78.05	89.65	19.40	89.60			76.20	55.60
Pr. economy.	52.50	76.60		59.20	61.90	71.45	16.40	70.45			61.05	43.20
San Diego, Cal.	DL	UA, AA	AA, UA	TW, AA	AA, TW	AA, TW	AA, DL	AA	AA, CO	AA, TW	NA, DL	TW
Jet 1st cl....	141.10	152.75	147.80	116.55	128.20	136.60	84.50	133.70	95.15	123.20	161.70	110.85
Jet economy.	117.80	137.25	132.60	105.45	114.20	123.40	72.50	120.30	82.15	109.20	129.75	89.45
Prop. 1st cl..								133.70	95.15	123.20	156.10	
Pr. economy.									97.85	74.45		119.25
San Fr., Oakl.	TW, EA	AA, TW	AA, UA	UA, TW	AA, DL	UA, AA	AA, TW	UA, AA	AA, BN	AA, EA	NA, DL	TW, CN
Jet 1st cl....	152.75	152.75	147.80	116.55	133.75	136.60	103.50	133.70	117.00	128.05	179.15	109.25
Jet economy.	137.25	137.25	132.60	105.45	118.75	123.40	90.50	120.30	102.95	113.05	145.05	94.75
Prop. 1st cl..		152.75				136.60	103.50	133.70		128.05		
Pr. economy.		111.35					77.00	97.85	97.85			
San Juan, P. R.	EA	PA		EA		PA	DL	EA	PA			
Jet 1st cl....	116.65	116.65		154.25		143.75	166.60	150.85	156.10			
Sarasota, Fla..	EA, DL	NA		EA		EA	EA	EA	NA, EA	EA	NA	
Prop. 1st cl..	37.05	66.70		81.10		77.75	75.10	62.50	63.50	70.10	20.45	
Savannah, Ga.	DL	EA		DL, EA	DL		DL		EA, DL		DL, NA	
Prop. 1st cl..	19.40	42.65		66.65	42.45		73.10		69.25		10.95	

Approximate fares. Taxes not included. *Courtesy Official Airline Guide*

SELECTED NORTH AMERICAN AIR PASSENGER FARES

FROM / TO	Atlanta	Baltimore	Buffalo	Chicago	Cincinnati	Cleveland	Dallas	Detroit	Houston	Indianapolis	Jacksonville	Kansas City
Scrant'n, W-B.	......	TW, DL	AA	AA, UA	AA, UA	AL	AA, BN	AL	AA, DL	TW, LC	EA	TW, CO
Prop. 1st cl...	......	22.55	16.20	46.75	38.45	28.60	98.80	31.00	107.05	42.20	64.75	73.25
Seattle, Taco'a	NW	UA, TW	AA, UA	NW, UA	DL, LC	UA, NW	BN	NW, AA	BN	EA, LC	DL, EA	UA, TW
Jet 1st cl.....	166.90	176.45	......	116.55	158.95	136.60	......	133.70	......	......	220.10	133.25
Jet economy.	145.80	137.25	......	105.45	125.50	123.40	......	120.30	......	......	......	103.85
Prop. 1st cl..	166.40	166.15	163.20	116.55	149.65	136.60	134.45	133.70	151.90	142.40	205.60	126.00
Pr. economy.	120.55	111.35	114.25	86.90	104.95	102.55	......	97.85	......	99.45	......	......
Shreveport,La.	DL	DL		DL			DL, TT	DL	DL	DL		BN
Prop. 1st cl...	43.50	34.75	......	60.40	......	......	17.45	70.05	19.40	52.40	......	38.80
Pr. economy.	34.50	28.05	......	47.10	......	......	14.95	54.40	16.40	41.10	......	29.40
Spartanburg..	EA, SO	PI		DL		EA		EA	EA, DL	DL	DL	
Prop. 1st cl...	13.25	36.40	......	47.05	......	38.30	......	44.80	67.20	36.05	25.40	......
Spokane, Wsh.	NW	......		NW		NW, UA		NW, UA				
Jet 1st cl.....	166.90			116.55		136.60		133.70				
Prop. 1st cl...	159.15			108.80		126.35		122.25				
Springf'ld, Mo.	DL	EA, TW	AA	OZ, AA	AA, TW	AA, UA	AA, CN	AA, TW				OZ
Prop. 1st cl...	45.30	66.30	60.95	34.00	39.45	49.75	34.00	45.90				13.25
Syracuse, N.Y.	EA	EA	AA, MO	AA, UA	AA	AA, MO	AA	AA, MO	AA		EA	
Prop. 1st cl...	64.95	28.85	11.90	43.70	40.30	24.95	96.20	26.95	103.40		67.30	
Tampa,St.Pet.	DL	EA, DL	UA	NW, EA	DL, EA	UA, EA	EA	DL, EA	NA, EA	EA	EA	
Jet 1st cl.....	36.25	69.00	......	81.70	64.50	74.00	77.20	80.10	65.20	71.30	20.30	
Jet economy.	30.05	54.40	......	65.20	51.80	62.50	62.30	63.60	52.50	57.10	17.90	
Prop. 1st cl..	34.15	64.10	81.70	76.80	60.50	73.70	71.30	75.20	60.80	66.40	19.40	
Pr. economy.	27.60	46.50	61.70	53.70	47.65	52.90	56.40	57.90	47.45	46.20	16.90	
Toledo, Ohio..	DL	UA	AA	UA	LC, DL	UA, LC	......	LC, DL	EA	DL, LC	EA	TW, BN
Prop. 1st cl...	42.25	29.70	23.65	18.30	15.40	9.50	......	7.65	82.90	17.75	61.10	49.15
Toronto, Ont..	......	AA	EA	AA	......	AC	AA, BN	AC	BN, DL	EA, LC		TW, BN
Prop. 1st cl...	......	44.00	10.00	44.00	......	52.00	102.90	23.00	116.40	55.25		71.85
Tucson, Ariz..	......	TW, AA	AA, UA	AA, TW	AA, TW	AA, UA	AA	AA, UA	CO, AA	TW, DL		TW
Jet 1st cl.....	......	132.05	126.50	101.80	108.00	117.80	60.15	114.70	70.70	102.80	......	85.30
Jet economy.	......	117.05	112.25	88.80	94.00	103.80	50.15	100.70	58.90	89.80	......	67.35
Prop. 1st cl...	......	132.05	126.50	101.80	......	......	......	114.70	......	......	......	80.15
Pr. economy.	......	104.80	93.50	75.95	......	......	......	86.90	......	......	......	59.45
Tulsa, Okla...	EA	TW, EA	AA	AA, BN	AA, TW	AA, UA	BN, CN	AA, TW	BN	......		BN, CN
Jet 1st cl.....	......	76.05	72.00	47.35	52.15	61.35	25.10	58.45	......	......		21.50
Prop. 1st cl...	53.35	76.05	71.65	44.25	49.05	60.50	23.00	56.60	35.40	......		19.45
Pr. economy.	......	......	55.85	35.15	38.65	47.20	19.15	44.30	28.40	......		16.50
Wash't'n,D.C.	UA	TW	UA	UA, AA	AA, LC	NW	AA	NW, UA	EA, BN	TW, AA	EA, NA	TW, BN
Jet 1st cl.....	49.40	......	......	46.80	......	25.00	86.25	34.20	96.90	......	54.40	69.25
Jet economy.	39.70	6.00	......	37.70	......	19.60	74.25	28.50	79.60	33.75	44.10	57.85
Prop. 1st cl...	46.30	6.00	27.20	43.70	31.30	25.00	86.25	32.10	94.80	38.50	50.40	68.60
Pr. economy.	33.40	......	22.85	33.95	......	19.60	62.55	24.85	71.10	30.75	37.45	53.70
W. Palm Beach	EA, UA	NA	UA	DL, EA	DL	EA, UA	EA	DL	NA, EA	EA	EA, DL	......
Prop. 1st cl...	42.40	69.20	89.20	84.30	69.30	80.25	85.60	84.25	74.10	75.05	23.10	......
Pr. economy.	34.20	51.70	66.50	62.40	53.85	......	66.05	63.05	......	......	19.25	......
Wichita, Kans.	......	TW	......	BN, TW	......	......	TW, UA	BN, CN	TW, AA	BN	TW	BN, CN
Jet 1st cl.....		86.65	......	46.85	......		12.30	64.65		50.25		
Prop. 1st cl...		81.50	......	43.75	......		67.90	11.25	60.50	43.60	47.15	16.15
Win'peg, Man.	NW	NW	......	NW		NW, UA		NW, UA				
Jet 1st cl.....	114.55	100.15	......	64.20		70.00		68.00				
Prop. 1st cl...	108.45	95.00	......	62.10		70.00		68.00				
Ygtn.,Wrn.,Sh.	......	LC	LC	LC	LC	UA. LC	......	UA		LC		
Jet 1st cl.....	......	27.00	16.50	31.50	22.70	7.50	......	14.65		23.90		

For airline abbreviations see page 903.

SELECTED NORTH AMERICAN AIR PASSENGER FARES

FROM / TO	Los Angeles	Memphis	Miami	New Orleans	New York	Omaha	Philadelphia	Pittsburgh	St. Louis	San Francisco	Seattle	Washington
Akron, Canton		UA, SO	UA, EA	EA	UA, LC		UA	UA, LC	EA			UA
Prop. 1st cl.		59.70	80.10	70.50	30.80		26.95	11.20	36.55			24.55
Alb.,Troy,Sch.	AA, TW	AA, UA	EA, NA		MO, AA		AA, UA	MO, TW	AA, TW	AA, UA		AA, UA
Prop. 1st cl.	160.90	72.60	98.90		12.50		18.95	28.20	64.00	160.90		27.20
Albuquerque	TW, BL		NA, EA		TW, UA	BN, FL	TW, UA	TW, UA		TW		TW, AA
Jet 1st cl.	56.20		137.35		139.60		134.50	116.80	76.05	80.45		127.95
Jet economy	44.80		107.50		108.85		105.05	91.55	60.15	63.45		99.85
Prop. 1st cl.			129.10		131.35	67.60	125.55			75.30		
Amarillo, Tex.	TW	BN	EA	DL, TT	AA, TW	BN	TW		TW	WA, UA		TW
Jet 1st cl.	76.25	53.85	117.00		115.20		110.10		54.15	100.55		103.55
Anchorage, Al.	NW		NW, EA		NW		NW	NW, UA		NW	PN, NW	NW, UA
Jet 1st cl.	197.25		334.75		284.90		280.60	266.10		177.05	124.00	276.75
Jet economy	160.55		255.15		224.15		221.20	208.45		141.35	89.40	236.25
Prop. 1st cl.											99.00	
Pr. economy											89.40	
Atlanta, Ga.	TW	SO, DL	EA, DL	DL, EA	EA, UA	BN, UA	EA, UA	UA, EA	EA, TW	TW	UA	PI, EA
Jet 1st cl.	141.10	29.70	49.40	38.35	59.15		55.70	44.45	42.80	154.95	176.75	49.50
Jet economy	117.60	24.65	40.20	32.40	49.70		45.20	36.60	34.80	128.50	145.75	40.30
Prop. 1st cl.		27.65	46.20	36.00	57.90	70.15	51.90	41.40	39.75		166.40	46.50
Pr. economy		22.60	35.20	29.50	42.90	50.00	38.60	33.50	31.70		120.55	34.30
Atlantic City	AA, UA	EA			AL, AA		AL	AL				AL
Prop. 1st cl.	179.35	28.80			12.75		7.00	25.00				13.20
Baltimore,Md.	AA, TW	EA	EA, NA	DL, UA	EA	UA, FL	UA, DL	UA	TW, EA	UA, TW	UA	EA, TW
Jet 1st cl.	152.75	64.45	78.10	78.80	19.00	73.45	9.80		56.20	152.75	152.75	
Jet economy	137.25	51.20	61.20	63.00	17.10	66.00	9.20		44.90	137.25	142.45	6.00
Prop. 1st cl.		60.20	73.20	73.90	17.00		8.80	16.55	53.10	166.15		6.00
Pr. economy		45.05	53.60	56.90	15.20		8.15	13.50				
Baton Rouge		SO	NA, EA	EA	EA, DL		DL, EA	UA				UA, EA
Prop. 1st cl.		27.00	57.05	9.80	91.50		85.05	74.70				79.55
Bermuda	PA		PA	PA	PA, EA		PA			PA	PA	EA, PA
Jet 1st cl.	243.80		89.00	165.50	85.00		91.00			243.80	243.80	91.00
Jet economy	204.30		71.00	130.70	63.00		67.00			204.30	204.30	67.00
Billings, Mont.			NW, EA		NW, UA	FL		NW, UA			NW	NW, UA
Prop. 1st cl.			169.95		125.70	63.75		108.15			55.65	120.55
Pr. economy			128.90		97.85			83.45			42.25	92.70
Binghamton	TW, UA	AA, UA	EA, NA		MO		UA, EA	TW, MO	TW, AA	TW, UA		EA
Prop. 1st cl.	160.90	70.25	91.30		15.30		16.75	22.10	59.40	160.90		23.85
Birmingham	DL, NA	EA	DL, EA	EA, SO	EA, UA		UA	UA, EA		DL		UA, DL
Jet 1st cl.	133.10	23.20	53.10	29.30	68.50		62.95			146.95		56.10
Jet economy	109.85	20.20	42.75	24.90	55.00					124.55		45.25
Prop. 1st cl.		21.20	49.10	27.30	63.60		57.50	47.50				52.20
Pr. economy		18.20	35.85	22.90	42.65		38.90	29.95				40.00
Bismarck,N.D.	UA		NW, EA		NW	NO		NW, UA		UA	NW	NW, UA
Prop. 1st cl.	119.15		143.20		98.90	41.00		81.40		123.95	83.45	93.75
Pr. economy			105.20		76.25			62.85			63.90	72.10
Boston, Mass.	TW, AA	AA, NA	AA, NA	EA, DL	EA, NE	UA	EA, NE	TW, AL	AA, TW	AA, TW	UA	AA, NA
Jet 1st cl.	167.25	81.55	106.10	102.80	18.20	95.65	24.00	41.25	72.40	167.25	135.40	32.30
Jet economy	152.25	69.55	81.70	81.20	15.24	75.10	20.50	33.60	61.90	152.25	152.25	26.60
Prop. 1st cl.		81.55	96.30	96.90	17.20		23.40	38.15	72.40	167.25		30.20
Pr. economy		64.40	67.00	74.20	15.20		20.00					24.60
Buffalo, N. Y.	AA, UA	AA	UA, EA	UA	MO, AA	UA, OZ	UA, AL	UA, AL	AA, TW	AA, UA	NW, UA	UA
Jet 1st cl.	147.80	62.50	88.30		25.50	67.50	31.95	20.35	50.85	147.80	147.80	41.30
Jet economy	132.60	52.20	73.00		21.50			26.30	40.75	132.60	132.60	33.55

Approximate fares. Taxes not included. *Courtesy Official Airline Guide*

SELECTED NORTH AMERICAN AIR PASSENGER FARES

FROM / TO	Los Angeles	Memphis	Miami	New Orleans	New York	Omaha	Philadelphia	Pittsburgh	St. Louis	San Francisco	Seattle	Washington
Calgary, Alb.	WA	.....	TC	.....	UA	.....	UA, EA	.....	.....	UA, WC	TC	EA
Prop. 1st cl.	.....	.....	208.90	.....	152.00	.....	161.70	.....	.....	109.95	59.00	169.95
Pr. economy	86.40	.....	157.70	.....	112.00	.....	120.65	.....	.....	.....	44.00	127.35
Caracas, Vzla.	PA	DL	PA, VA	DL, VA	PA, VA	.....	PA	.....	DL	DL	PA	PA
Jet 1st cl.	332.00	238.70	189.00	209.00	228.00	.....	228.00	.....	255.30	332.00	332.00	**228.00**
Jet economy	266.00	190.80	143.00	189.00	175.00	.....	175.00	.....	205.00	266.00	266.00	175.00
Char'st'n, S.C.	DL, CO	.....	NA	DL, EA	NA, EA	.....	EA, NA	.....	.....	DL, UA	.....	EA, NA
Prop. 1st cl.	160.10	.....	40.95	53.30	48.65	.....	42.25	.....	.....	176.55	.....	36.70
Pr. economy	133.90	.....	30.30	41.75	37.05	.....	32.30	.....	.....	144.90	.....	29.50
Char'st'n, W.V.	.....	AA	UA	UA	UA, NA	.....	EA, AL	LC, UA	EA, OZ	TW, AA	.....	EA, AA
Prop. 1st cl.	.....	42.70	68.30	58.05	35.50	.....	29.05	15.45	35.60	142.60	.....	20.80
Charlotte, N.C.	DL	DL, UA	EA	EA, DL	EA, DL	.....	EA	EA, UA	EA	DL, UA	.....	UA, EA
Jet 1st cl.	149.70	.....	54.00	53.40	45.90	.....	39.80	32.60	.....	159.20	.....	33.60
Jet economy	125.55	.....	43.90	43.40	37.70	.....	33.00	27.40	.....	137.40	.....	28.10
Prop. 1st cl.	.....	38.80	50.10	49.40	43.00	.....	36.90	30.60	46.90	.....	.....	31.60
Pr. economy	.....	30.90	.....	39.50	34.70	.....	30.10	25.40	.....	.....	.....	26.20
Chattanooga	.....	SO, UA	EA	UA	EA, UA	.....	EA	UA, EA	EA	.....	.....	EA, AA
Prop. 1st cl.	.....	22.05	53.75	36.05	54.25	.....	47.85	37.50	32.10	.....	.....	42.30
Chicago, Ill.	TW, UA	DL	EA, DL	DL, EA	UA, TW	UA, OZ	UA, TW	UA, TW	DL, OZ	UA, TW	NW, UA	UA, AA
Jet 1st cl.	116.55	42.05	94.20	67.60	52.30	34.60	50.90	34.15	22.45	116.55	116.55	46.80
Jet economy	105.45	34.30	74.70	54.40	43.70	28.60	40.75	28.00	19.25	105.45	105.45	37.70
Prop. 1st cl.	116.55	38.95	88.30	62.70	51.70	32.50	47.80	32.05	20.35	116.55	116.55	43.70
Pr. economy	86.90	31.25	62.40	49.40	39.45	25.10	37.25	25.15	17.15	86.90	86.90	33.95
Cincinnati, O.	AA, TW	AA	DL, EA	DL, SO	AA, TW	BN, UA	TW, AL	TW, LC	TW, AA	UA, AA	.....	AA, LC
Jet 1st cl.	128.20	.....	76.80	60.00	46.25	.....	42.70	24.75	27.20	133.75	158.95	.....
Jet economy	114.20	.....	61.20	47.85	37.35	.....	34.60	20.90	22.90	118.75	125.50	.....
Prop. 1st cl.	.....	33.25	71.90	55.85	43.15	55.50	39.60	22.70	25.10	133.75	149.65	31.30
Pr. economy	.....	26.75	55.40	43.70	34.25	.....	31.50	18.85	20.80	99.00	104.95	.....
Cleveland, O.	AA, UA	AA	UA, EA	DL, EA	UA	UA	UA, AL	UA, NW	AA, TW	UA, TW	NW, UA	UA, NW
Jet 1st cl.	136.60	.....	82.10	85.80	32.90	56.50	29.05	12.75	38.65	136.60	136.60	.....
Jet economy	123.40	.....	70.60	.....	27.25	44.95	24.15	12.00	31.50	122.60	123.40	.....
Prop. 1st cl.	136.60	48.60	82.10	70.50	30.80	.....	26.95	11.70	36.55	130.00	.....	25.00
Pr. economy	102.55	.....	60.65	54.70	25.15	.....	22.05	10.45	29.40	102.55	.....	19.60
Colorado Spgs.	UA, CO	BN	EA	.....	.....	FL, UA	.....	.....	.....	UA, WA	.....	TW, UA
Prop. 1st cl.	79.80	67.35	129.50	.....	.....	43.00	.....	.....	.....	81.60	.....	114.00
Columbia, S.C.	.....	SO, DL	EA	DL, EA	EA, DL	.....	EA	.....	EA	.....	.....	PI, EA
Prop. 1st cl.	.....	46.10	40.95	.....	48.65	.....	42.25	41.05	56.10	.....	.....	34.60
Columbus, O.	AA, TW	AA	EA, DL	.....	TW, UA	.....	TW, LA	TW, LC	TW, AA	TW, UA	.....	UA, LC
Jet 1st cl.	134.75	44.95	.....	.....	39.80	.....	.....	.....	.....	136.60	.....	.....
Jet economy	119.75	36.30	.....	.....	32.55	.....	.....	.....	.....	122.60	.....	.....
Prop. 1st cl.	134.75	41.85	77.40	.....	36.70	.....	31.40	14.10	31.20	136.60	.....	26.15
Pr. economy	105.10	33.20	60.50	.....	29.45	.....	25.40	12.45	25.15	105.30	.....	21.50
Corpus Christi	.....	TT	.....	EA	.....	BN	.....	.....	AA, DL	.....	.....	BN, EA
Prop. 1st cl.	.....	54.40	87.10	37.70	121.55	76.45	115.20	102.70	72.95	.....	.....	109.60
Dallas, Ft. W.	DL, BN	AA, TT	EA, DL	EA, TT	DL, BN	BN	AA, UA	AA, TW	AA, CN	AA, DL	UA	AA, BN
Jet 1st cl.	84.50	35.70	91.30	40.40	96.20	54.90	90.35	81.60	50.00	103.50	.....	86.25
Jet economy	72.50	29.25	72.80	33.50	83.20	44.05	78.35	.....	40.10	90.50	.....	74.25
Prop. 1st cl.	84.50	33.60	84.40	37.50	96.20	51.85	90.35	81.60	46.90	103.50	134.45	86.25
Pr. economy	66.05	27.15	65.80	30.60	72.40	40.65	69.85	.....	37.00	77.00	.....	62.55
Dayton, Ohio	TW, UA	AA	DL, UA	.....	TW, UA	.....	TW, AL	TW	TW, AA	TW, UA	.....	TW
Jet 1st cl.	129.90	.....	.....	.....	44.60	.....	39.25	20.95	.....	134.00	.....	.....
Jet economy	114.90	.....	.....	.....	36.00	.....	32.05	18.20	26.35	119.00	.....	27.05
Prop. 1st cl.	129.90	37.10	78.80	.....	41.50	.....	36.15	18.85	21.65	.....	.....	30.90

Section F — COMMUNICATION, TRAVEL, AND TRANSPORT

SELECTED NORTH AMERICAN AIR PASSENGER FARES

TO \ FROM	Los Angeles	Memphis	Miami	New Orleans	New York	Omaha	Philadelphia	Pittsburgh	St. Louis	San Francisco	Seattle	Washington
Denver, Colo..	UA, CO	BN	EA	TT	UA, TW	UA, FL	UA, TW	UA, TW	BN, TW		TW	UA, AA
Jet 1st cl....	68.10	74.75	.....	96.80	109.60	38.80	106.65	92.85	.....	73.75	81.60	103.55
Jet economy.	61.00	59.20	.....	78.10	95.10	31.45	92.15	79.35	.....	62.25	70.10	89.05
Prop. 1st cl..		70.65		86.05		36.70			60.95			106.30
Pr. economy.		54.80		71.85		28.45			50.85			80.30
Des Moines, Ia.	UA, CO	DL	.....	BN, FL	UA, TW	UA	UA	UA	UA	BN		UA
Jet 1st cl....	120.70	.....	.....	70.10	.....	12.30	74.20	.....	24.50	.....	.....	
Prop. 1st cl..	113.45	41.65	.....	66.00	72.95	11.25	69.05	53.35	22.45	.....	.....	64.90
Detroit, Mich.	AA, UA	DL	EA, DL	DL, UA	AA, NW	UA, BN	UA, AL	NW, UA	AA, TW	AA, UA	NW, UA	UA, NW
Jet 1st cl....	133.70	52.85	92.50	72.00	38.35	52.35	34.85	20.45	34.80	133.70	133.70	34.20
Jet economy.	120.30	42.60	73.40	60.50	31.65	41.85	29.45	18.05	28.45	120.30	120.30	28.50
Prop. 1st cl..	133.70	48.70	86.60	70.60	36.30	49.25	32.75	18.85	32.70	133.70		32.10
Pr. economy.	97.85	38.45	65.10	55.50	29.60		27.35	15.70	26.35	97.85	97.85	24.85
Edmont'n,Alb.			AC		AC		UA, EA			UA, WC	UA, AC	EA, NA
Prop. 1st cl..			208.90		152.00		150.70			106.95	62.00	168.95
Pr. economy.			112.00		112.00		112.65				46.00	119.35
El Paso, Tex..	CO, AA	AA, TT	AA, CO	EA	AA, EA	FL, BN	AA, UA	TW, UA	AA, CN	AA, WA	UA	AA, BN
Jet 1st cl....	54.30	71.85	137.25	83.05	125.90		120.85	123.20	73.00	75.60	135.20	115.65
Jet economy.	45.30	60.85	109.55	67.35	110.90		106.85	98.40	62.00	64.15	107.10	101.65
Prop. 1st cl..	53.70	71.15	126.95	77.90	125.90	88.25	120.85	106.80	73.00	75.60	126.90	115.65
Pr. economy.	42.20	55.75	99.10	62.20	101.95		98.50			59.00	95.35	92.10
Evansv'le,Ind.		DL	EA	EA	EA, UA		EA	TW, AA	EA			EA
Prop. 1st cl..		20.60	71.65	45.00	56.50		52.10	33.05	16.10			44.20
Fargo, N. D..			NW		NW	NO		NW, UA			NW	NW, UA
Prop. 1st cl..			132.90		85.50	33.00		68.00			96.85	80.35
Pr. economy.			97.20		65.95			52.80			72.00	61.80
Ft. Lauderdale		DL, EA	MK	NA, EA	EA		EA	UA, EA	EA		UA	EA
Jet 1st cl....				57.50	94.40		86.15		87.80		210.75	79.55
Jet economy.				46.60	71.90						181.40	61.70
Prop. 1st cl..		64.80		52.60	84.60		78.50	76.35	82.65		204.25	73.20
Pr. economy.			2.50	41.45	58.30		57.90	48.60	51.30		149.85	53 60
Ft. Smith, Ark.		BN	EA	BN	TW, EA	BN, FL			CN			AA
Prop. 1st cl..		21.30	83.55	37.60	93.95	35.55			28.85			75.65
Ft.Wayne,Ind.	UA, TW				UA, TW	UA	AL, TW	UA				UA
Prop. 1st cl..	141.60				43.60	42.80	43.35	22.85				36.05
Grand Rapids.				UA, EA	UA		UA	UA, AL				UA
Prop. 1st cl..				99.75	47.40		45.00	30.00				43.25
Great Falls...	WA			NW, EA	NW		NW	NW, UA		UA, WA	NW	NW, UA
Prop. 1st cl..				187.95	138.05		137.45	121.55		79.40	45.50	132.90
Pr. economy.	66.65			140.55	106.10		106.10	91.70			34.00	102.00
Grboro.,Hi.Pt.			UA	EA		EA, UA		EA	EA			UA, EA
Prop. 1st cl..			43.60	55.30		37.05		30.55	23.95	46.90		22.30
Gr'nville, S. C.			EA	DL	EA	EA, UA		EA		EA		EA
Prop. 1st cl..			33.20	49.45	45.20	48.50		42.40		33.35		37.10
Guatemala....	GU		PA, GU	TA, PA	PA		PA			PA	PA	PA
Jet 1st cl....	189.00		122.00	120.00	213.00		206.90			189.00	189.00	200.00
Jet economy.	137.00		92.00	86.00	159.60		154.80			137.00	137.00	149.70
Prop. 1st cl..			71.15	110.00								
Halifax, N. S..			AC		AC		UA, EA				UA, AC	EA
Prop. 1st cl..			160.70		63.00		67.70				219.40	75.95
Pr. economy.			116.40		46.00		51.65				163.90	58.35
Harrisburg.Pa.					AL, TW		AL	AL, TW	TW	TW		AL, UA
Prop. 1st cl..	156.60				14.75		9.00	14.40	53.10	156.50		11.25

SELECTED NORTH AMERICAN AIR PASSENGER FARES

FROM TO	Los Angeles	Memphis	Miami	New Orleans	New York	Omaha	Philadelphia	Pittsburgh	St. Louis	San Francisco	Seattle	Washington
Htfd.,H'k.,Sp.	AA, TW	AA, UA	EA	......	EA, AA	UA	AA	AL, UA	TW	UA, TW	UA	AL, EA
Jet 1st cl....	163.60	78.80	102.90		10.55	90.45	18.10	35.20	74.65	163.60	191.30	26.35
Jet economy.	148.40	67.80	77.75		9.95	71.20		29.05	68.45	148.40	148.40	22.25
Prop. 1st cl...	181.00	77.90	92.60		9.50			32.10	68.45	181.00		24.25
Honolulu.....	PA, UA		PA	PA	NW,TW	UA, BN	PA, TW	NW,TW	TW	UA, PA	NW, PA	NW,TW
Jet 1st cl....	150.00		327.90	274.35	310.90	248.40	306.60	292.10	260.60	150.00	180.75	302.75
Jet economy.	110.00		250.10	211.60	255.10	194.90	251.40	237.90	206.60	100.00	110.00	247.25
Prop. 1st cl...										178.00	178.00	338.90
Pr. economy.											133.00	245.45
Houston, Tex.	CO, NA	DL, TT	NA, EA	EA, NA	DL, EA	BN	EA, DL	AA, UA	DL, AA	NA, AA	UA	DL
Jet 1st cl....	98.30	44.90	79.30	27.25	108.30		104.00	86.10	63.40	117.00		96.90
Jet economy.	85.30	36.65	63.40	22.85	89.10		84.50		50.50	102.95		79.60
Prop. 1st cl..	102.65	40.75	74.60	25.20	106.10	62.85	100.10	86.10	59.30	117.00	151.90	94.80
Pr. economy.	77.70	32.50	53.75	20.80	79.90	49.00	75.40		46.35	102.95		71.10
Huntsv'le, Ala.	AA	SO, UA	EA	EA, SO	UA, EA		EA, UA	UA				UA
Prop. 1st cl...	133.85	16.45	55.80	32.85	59.90		53.50	43.15	33.05			45.20
Indianapolis.	TW, AA	DL	EA, DL	DL	TW, AA	BN	TW, AL	TW	TW, OZ	TW, AA	NW, UA	AA, TW
Jet 1st cl....	123.20			60.00	51.65		46.85	19.85	19.85	128.05		
Prop. 1st cl...	109.20	31.10	79.30	55.20	48.55	49.75	43.75	18.80	18.80	113.05	142.40	38.50
Pr. economy.		25.15	55.70	43.55	38.35		34.70	16.10	16.10		99.45	30.75
Jackson, Miss.	......	DL, SO	EA, DL	DL, SO	DL, EA							
Prop. 1st cl...		16.25	59.05	14.70	80.95				34.85			69.00
Jacksonville...	DL, SO	SO, DL	EA, NA	NA	EA, NA	BN, UA	EA, NA	UA, EA	EA, TW	DL, UA	UA	EA, NA
Jet 1st cl....	161.70	53.90	29.40	43.80	66.60		60.50	56.10	63.20	179.15	220.10	54.40
Jet economy.	129.75	45.20	24.50	35.70	52.60		48.00	45.50	51.00	145.05		44.10
Prop. 1st cl..		49.75	27.30	39.65	61.70	92.15	55.70	52.20	58.30		205.60	50.40
Pr. economy.		41.10	22.45	31.55	46.60		41.90	39.60	46.10			37.45
Kansas City..	CO, TW	DL	TW, EA	BN, DL	TW, AA	BN, FL	TW, UA	TW, UA	TW, BN	UA, TW	UA	TW, UA
Jet 1st cl....	99.50	29.85	98.25		79.20		79.35	61.65	19.85	109.25	133.25	69.25
Jet economy.	86.00	20.50	77.45		66.70		62.85	49.10	17.45	94.75	61.75	57.85
Prop. 1st cl.		29.85		54.10	79.20	15.45	74.20	57.50	18.80			68.60
Pr. economy.		24.20		42.45	60.60	13.20	57.30	44.95	16.40			53.70
Kingston, J'ca	PA	DL	BA, KL	DL	TW, BA		PA	......	DL	DL		PA
Jet 1st cl....	247.00	151.70	81.00	125.00	171.00		165.00		168.80	268.40		159.10
Knoxville, Tn.	AA, DL	SO, UA	EA, DL	UA	UA, AA		AA, UA	UA	......	AA, TW		UA, PI
Prop. 1st cl...	131.00	27.15	60.25	41.95	48.40		41.95	31.65		149.70		33.65
LasVegas,Nev.	WA, BL		NA	NA, DL	UA, TW	UA	UA, TW	UA, TW	TW	UA	WA	UA, TW
Jet 1st cl....	23.85		175.25	124.70	149.20	88.90	146.35	133.25	110.60	42.30	95.35	143.25
Jet economy.	20.35		136.40	97.60	133.70	70.05	130.85	117.75	87.55	32.55	74.90	127.75
Prop. 1st cl..	17.15			115.80	....	83.75			25.70			
Little Rock..	AA, TW	AA	EA	TT, DL	SO		BN	AA	TW, UA	CN, DL	AA, UA	AA
Jet 1st cl....	103.10	13.15	75.40	35.10	80.00	40.35	74.50	62.30	30.75	118.00		68.80
Jet economy.	90.70	12.15		28.15	68.05		63.20		24.95	104.55		55.95
Los Angeles...	......	AA	TW, DL	NA, DL	AA, TW	UA, BN	UA, TW	UA, TW	TW, AA	WA, UA	UA, WA	AA, TW
Jet 1st cl....		111.40	175.80	124.35	160.90	98.40	156.60	142.10	110.60	28.45	73.25	152.75
Jet economy.		97.40	140.10	101.60	145.10	84.90	141.40	127.90	96.60	23.70	61.75	137.25
Prop. 1st cl..		111.40		120.55	160.90		156.60		110.60	26.00	73.05	145.00
Pr. economy.		90.05	129.65	93.35	112.45	90.00	111.35		83.65	16.95	53.15	
Louisville, Ky.	AA	AA	EA, DL	SO	AA		TW, EA	TW, AA	EA, OZ	TW, AA	NW, UA	EA, PI
Jet 1st cl....	125.35	29.25	75.50	59.15	53.40		47.90	30.80	24.70	130.10	159.30	42.60
Jet economy.	111.35	24.30	60.30	49.05	42.85		39.00	25.50	21.40	115.10	125.70	35.00
Prop. 1st cl..	125.35	27.15	70.60	54.80	49.25		44.60	28.80	21.25		149.95	37.10
Pr. economy.	98.30	22.20	50.30		38.35		33.65	23.50	17.80		105.15	30.30

For airline abbreviations see page 903.

SELECTED NORTH AMERICAN AIR PASSENGER FARES

FROM / TO	Los Angeles	Memphis	Miami	New Orleans	New York	Omaha	Philadelphia	Pittsburgh	St. Louis	San Francisco	Seattle	Washington
Madison, Wis.	UA, TW	.....	EA, NW	.....	NW, UA	OZ, UA	.....	.....	OZ	.....	NW	NW
Prop. 1st cl..	139.60	.....	100.65	.....	56.50	32.50	.....	.....	31.80	.....	126.70	51.20
M'caibo, Vzla.	PA	.....	VA	VA	PA	.....	PA	.....	.....	.....	.....	PA
Jet 1st cl....	317.00	.....	169.00	209.00	228.00	.....	228.00	.....	.....	.....	.....	228.00
Melbourne, Fl.	NA	EA	NA, EA	NA	EA, NA	.....	EA	UA, EA	EA, TW	NA	.....	EA
Jet 1st cl....	.....	.....	16.60	49.30	81.40	.....	.....	.....	.....	179.15	.....	.....
Prop. 1st cl..	.....	57.80	14.50	46.20	75.40	.....	69.30	65.40	71.65	.....	.....	64.10
Memphis, Ten.	ᴀA, DL	.....	EA, DL	DL, SO	UA, AA	BN, FL	AA, AL	UA	DL	AA, UA	UA	AA, UA
Jet 1st cl....	111.40	.....	69.70	29.70	71.50	.....	66.35	55.75	24.00	125.25	.....	59.70
Jet economy.	97.40	.....	55.90	24.75	61.10	.....	56.35	44.40	20.50	111.40	.....	51.20
Prop. 1st cl..	111.40	52.65	64.80	27.65	71.20	45.30	65.85	.....	21.90	125.25	154.45	59.70
Pr. economy.	90.05	.....	50.95	22.70	56.15	27.40	51.20	.....	18.40	98.50	.....	45.05
Mexico City ..	WA, MX	.....	PA, AG	EA	PA, AM	.....	PA	EA, TW	EA, CN	WA	WA	EA
Jet 1st cl....	117.00	.....	102.00	77.80	168.00	.....	163.90	.....	.....	145.50	195.20	157.30
Jet economy.	93.00	.....	86.00	62.70	127.00	.....	124.00	.....	.....	116.70	154.80	121.00
Prop. 1st cl..	109.00	.....	.....	72.80	.....	.....	.....	142.00	118.30	102.00	.....	147.20
Miami, Fla....	TW, UA	DL, EA	.....	NA, EA	EA, NA	BN	EA, NA	UA, EA	EA, TW	NA, TW	NW	EA, NA
Jet 1st cl....	175.80	69.70	.....	57.50	94.40	.....	84.40	76.30	86.00	194.80	217.70	78.10
Jet economy.	140.10	55.90	.....	46.80	71.90	.....	66.40	64.80	68.30	157.05	181.40	61.20
Prop. 1st cl..	.....	64.80	.....	52.60	84.60	107.80	78.50	75.10	81.10	.....	204.25	73.20
Pr. economy.	129.65	50.95	.....	41.90	58.30	.....	57.90	55.00	58.10	.....	149.85	53.60
Milwaukee, W.	UA, CO	.....	EA, NW	.....	NW	UA	UA, TW	NW, UA	AA	AA, UA	NW	NW, UA
Jet 1st cl....	135.40	.....	94.20	.....	52.30	.....	50.90	36.35	.....	.....	135.40	46.80
Prop. 1st cl..	128.15	.....	114.60	.....	51.70	37.40	47.80	32.05	25.75	116.55	128.15	43.70
Pr. economy.	.....	.....	86.45	.....	39.45	.....	.....	25.15	.....	.....	86.90	33.95
Minapls., St.P.	WA, TW	.....	NW, EA	BN	NW, UA	BN, OZ	UA	NW, UA	BN, OZ	WA, UA	NW	NW, UA
Jet 1st cl....	130.65	.....	122.90	89.10	72.25	27.65	68.55	54.10	52.25	130.65	116.55	67.30
Jet economy.	101.60	.....	100.30	70.95	60.75	23.30	57.05	44.60	36.25	101.60	91.95	55.80
Prop. 1st cl..	.....	.....	117.30	83.30	69.80	25.55	65.90	52.40	41.40	.....	111.25	64.55
Pr. economy.	94.35	.....	98.20	65.60	55.60	21.15	.....	41.50	32.90	92.80	83.45	50.65
Mobile, Ala...	DL, NA	SO	EA, NA	NA	EA, UA	.....	NA	UA	.....	NA, DL	.....	UA, NA
Prop. 1st cl..	130.20	27.65	43.85	14.10	77.60	.....	72.60	62.25	.....	149.20	.....	66.30
Pr. economy.	101.60	.....	34.75	13.00	60.70	.....	56.20	.....	.....	115.25	.....	52.00
M'line,Rl.,Dv.	.....	.....	.....	.....	UA	UA	.....	UA, TW	OZ	.....	.....	UA
Prop. 1st cl..	.....	.....	.....	.....	61.55	22.65	.....	45.15	18.15	.....	.....	53.55
M't'goB'y,J'ca	DL	DL	BA, PA	DL	PA, BA	.....	PA	.....	DL	DL	.....	PA
Jet 1st cl....	247.00	151.70	81.00	125.00	171.00	.....	167.20	.....	168.80	268.40	.....	160.60
Jet economy.	182.00	113.80	61.00	90.00	116.00	.....	116.00	.....	128.70	201.00	.....	116.00
Montreal.....	UA, TW	.....	EA	DL, EA	EA	UA, OZ	NE, EA	.....	EA, OZ	UA, TW	UA, AC	EA
Jet 1st cl....	.....	.....	109.00	.....	32.00	.....	38.90	.....	.....	.....	177.00	46.50
Jet economy.	.....	.....	.....	.....	24.00	.....	33.00	.....	.....	.....	131.00	38.00
Prop. 1st cl..	194.15	.....	81.00	109.40	.....	98.50	38.00	.....	74.55	194.15	.....	43.60
Nashville,Ten.	AA	AA, SO	EA	SO	AA, BN	.....	AA, AL	AA	EA, TW	NW, AA	.....	AA, BN
Jet 1st cl....	122.05	18.90	65.80	.....	59.00	.....	55.40	42.15	.....	130.10	.....	49.85
Prop. 1st cl..	130.25	16.80	60.80	41.15	58.75	.....	52.30	39.05	24.60	105.35	.....	44.00
Pr. economy	.....	14.55	45.20	.....	45.85	.....	41.05	.....	20.30	.....	.....	35.00
Nassau, B'mas	PA	.....	BH, PA	PA	PA	.....	PA	.....	.....	PA	PA	PA
Jet 1st cl....	202.10	.....	25.00	80.90	119.00	.....	111.20	.....	.....	202.10	202.10	104.60
New Orleans..	DL, NA	DL, SO	EA	.....	EA, DL	BN	DL, EA	UA	DL	NA, DL	UA	UA, EA
Jet 1st cl....	124.35	29.70	57.50	.....	84.90	.....	79.40	75.45	50.45	143.35	185.75	74.50
Jet economy.	101.60	24.75	46.80	.....	72.40	.....	67.90	.....	40.75	118.75	148.20	63.00
Prop. 1st cl..	.....	27.65	52.60	.....	84.90	66.35	79.20	70.30	46.30	.....	174.40	73.90
Pr. economy..	.....	22.70	41.90	.....	65.50	51.70	61.10	.....	.....	.....	.....	56.90

Approximate fares. Taxes not included. *Courtesy Official Airline Guide*

SELECTED NORTH AMERICAN AIR PASSENGER FARES

FROM / TO	Los Angeles	Memphis	Miami	New Orleans	New York	Omaha	Philadelphia	Pittsburgh	St. Louis	San Francisco	Seattle	Washington
N. Y., Newark	TW, AA	AA, UA	EA, NA	EA, DL	......	UA	UA, EA	UA, AL	TW, AA	UA, TW	NW, UA	EA, NA
Jet 1st cl.	160.90	71.50	94.40	84.90	......	86.10	10.75	28.00	63.30	160.90	160.90	21.60
Jet economy	145.10	61.10	71.90	72.40	......	67.95	9.70	23.35	53.80	145.10	145.10	18.10
Prop. 1st cl.	160.90	71.20	84.60	84.90	......	80.95	9.70	25.90	63.30	160.90	......	19.60
Pr. economy	111.35	56.15	58.30	65.50	......	......	8.65	20.80	48.25	112.45	......	17.10
Norfolk, Pmth.	AA, TW	......	NA	NA	NA, UA	......	NA, UA	UA	EA, OZ	......	......	UA, NA
Prop. 1st cl.	175.35	......	65.20	67.55	25.20	......	21.05	26.05	64.35	......	......	12.75
Pr. economy	152.10	......	50.85	52.50	21.35	......	17.65	21.35	......	......	......	11.15
Oklahoma City	AA, TW	BN	EA	TT	AA, TW	BN	TW, EA	AA	AA, TW	AA, UA	......	AA, BN
Jet 1st cl.	85.10	39.60	104.60	......	92.95	41.70	86.90	78.55	37.80	104.65	......	82.70
Jet economy	73.10	32.25	......	......	79.95	33.85	76.00	62.50	31.00	91.65	......	70.70
Prop. 1st cl.	......	37.50	98.40	50.05	......	39.65	......	......	......	......	......	82.70
Omaha, Neb.	UA, CO	DL	DL	BN	UA, NW	......	BN, TW	UA	BN, TW	UA, TW	UA	UA, AA
Jet 1st cl.	108.40	......	......	70.50	86.10	......	......	65.50	......	113.30	124.45	82.70
Prop. 1st cl.	102.20	45.30	110.80	66.35	......	......	83.25	52.00	30.40	......	97.25	......
Orlando, Fla.	DL, NA	DL	EA	NA, EA	EA, NA	......	EA	EA	......	DL, UA	......	EA
Jet 1st cl.	161.70	59.60	20.70	42.70	76.60	......	69.60	66.10	......	179.15	......	64.20
Jet economy	129.75	47.90	18.50	34.65	60.30	......	55.80	53.20	......	145.05	......	50.80
Prop. 1st cl.	......	55.70	18.70	39.65	70.70	......	64.70	61.20	......	......	......	59.30
Pr. economy	......	40.60	16.60	31.55	52.90	......	48.50	45.80	......	......	......	44.30
Ottawa, Ont.	......	EA	EA	EA	TC, EA	......	EA	......	EA	......	UA, TC	EA
Prop. 1st cl.	......	87.40	105.25	109.40	40.00	......	37.10	......	74.55	......	169.40	43.60
Pan. City, Fl	DL	......	NA	NA, SO	NA, EA	......	NA	......	......	NA, DL	......	NA, EA
Prop. 1st cl.	143.80	......	38.75	23.25	76.50	......	70.05	......	......	163.50	......	64.55
Pr. economy	109.95	......	30.85	19.30	58.80	......	54.30	......	......	123.55	......	50.20
Pan. City, Pan.	PA	......	BN, PA	PA	PA	......	PA	......	......	PA	......	EA, PA
Jet 1st cl.	285.00	......	130.00	188.00	218.00	......	216.00	......	......	285.00	......	203.60
Jet economy	204.00	......	95.00	142.00	167.00	......	162.20	......	......	204.00	......	156.70
Prop. 1st cl.	......	......	120.00	......	206.00	......	......	......	......	......	......	194.40
Pensacola, Fla.	DL, NA	......	NA, EA	EA, NA	EA	......	EA	EA	......	DL	......	NA
Prop. 1st cl.	133.00	......	39.60	16.40	77.00	......	71.90	61.45	......	152.00	......	65.60
Pr. economy	104.80	......	31.50	14.15	60.30	......	55.70	......	......	118.40	......	51.50
Philadelphia	UA, AA	UA, AA	EA, NA	DL, EA	EA	UA	......	AL, TW	AA	UA, TW	UA, NW	UA, TW
Jet 1st cl.	156.60	66.35	84.40	85.10	10.75	76.50	......	22.65	63.85	156.60	156.60	12.55
Jet economy	141.40	56.35	66.40	67.90	9.70	65.00	......	19.50	51.00	141.40	141.40	11.50
Prop. 1st cl.	156.60	65.85	78.50	79.20	9.70	77.00	......	20.55	58.70	156.60	......	11.50
Pr. economy	111.35	51.20	57.90	61.10	8.65	......	......	17.40	45.95	111.35	111.35	10.05
Phoenix, Ariz.	AA, CO	AA, DL	NA, EA	......	AA, TW	FL, UA	......	TW, UA	AA, TW	WA, AA	WA	AA, TW
Jet 1st cl.	30.30	91.85	......	......	143.45	......	139.80	125.10	91.85	53.55	104.35	135.40
Jet economy	25.10	79.85	......	......	128.45	......	124.80	111.10	79.85	42.80	81.60	120.40
Prop. 1st cl.	28.20	91.85	147.50	......	143.45	84.00	139.80	......	91.85	50.45	......	135.40
Pr. economy	23.00	......	113.10	......	107.00	......	105.85	......	72.65	37.85	......	105.85
Pittsburgh, Pa.	TW	AA	AA	UA	UA, AL	AL, TW	......		TW	TW, UA	UA	NW, UA
Jet 1st cl.	142.10	......	76.10	75.45	28.00	65.50	22.65	......	45.05	142.10	166.25	......
Jet economy	127.90	......	64.80	......	23.35	52.00	19.50	......	36.40	127.90	129.35	......
Prop. 1st cl.	142.10	52.65	75.10	70.30	25.90	61.35	20.55	......	41.95	142.10	156.95	16.55
Pr. economy	109.15	......	55.00	......	20.80	......	17.40	......	......	109.15	109.10	13.50
Portland, Ore.	UA, WA	......	NW	......	NW, UA	UA	UA	UA, TW	......	UA, WA	UA, NW	NW, UA
Jet 1st cl.	68.00	......	217.70	......	186.90	115.30	181.95	166.25	......	43.85	13.50	176.45
Jet economy	53.85	......	180.15	......	145.10	90.40	141.40	129.35	......	35.50	12.20	137.25
Prop. 1st cl.	......	......	210.15	......	176.60	108.05	171.65	156.95	......	40.75	12.45	166.15
Providence	AA, TW	AA, UA	EA, NA	EA, DL	AA	......	AL, EA	AL, MO	AA, TW	AA, UA	......	AL, EA
Prop. 1st cl.	167.25	81.55	93.90	96.85	13.00	......	19.45	35.65	72.90	167.25	......	28.90

For airline abbreviations see page 903.

SELECTED NORTH AMERICAN AIR PASSENGER FARES

FROM / TO	Los Angeles	Memphis	Miami	New Orleans	New York	Omaha	Philadelphia	Pittsburgh	St. Louis	San Francisco	Seattle	Washington
Raleigh, N. C.	......	UA	EA	EA, DL	EA, UA	......	EA	EA, UA	EA	......	......	UA, EA
Prop. 1st cl..	......	47.60	55.60	58.05	34.70	......	28.60	29.55	52.50	......	......	20.70
Richmond, Va.	UA	......	EA, NA	NA	EA	......	EA, AL	UA	......	......	......	UA, EA
Prop. 1st cl...	175.85	......	64.50	67.55	25.80	......	19.60	23.00	......	......	......	11.80
Rochtr., Minn.	NW	DL	......	DL	NW	OZ	......	NW	OZ	......	NW	NW
Prop. 1st cl...	69.25	55.90	......	80.25	66.45	22.15	......	49.10	36.70	......	115.40	61.25
Rochtr., N. Y.	AA, UA	AA	UA, EA	......	MO, AA	......	UA, NA	UA	AA	AA, UA	......	UA, AA
Prop. 1st cl...	151.00	65.50	91.30	......	21.70	......	28.10	22.00	51.45	151.00	......	36.40
Pr. economy.	112.45	......	67.00	......	18.70	......	......	18.95	40.45	112.45	......	......
Sacramento...	UA, WA	......	......	......	UA, AA	......	UA, TW	UA, TW	......	UA, PC	WC, UA	UA, TW
Pr. economy.	20.85	......	......	......	112.45	......	111.35	109.15	......	7.30	42.15	118.65
St. Louis, Mo.	TW, AA	DL	EA, TW	DL	TW	BN, UA	TW	TW, UA	......	TW, AA	UA	AA, TW
Jet 1st cl....	110.60	24.00	86.00	50.45	63.30	......	37.80	45.05	......	114.75	......	56.20
Jet economy..	96.60	20.50	68.30	40.75	53.80	......	31.00	36.40	......	100.75	......	44.90
Prop. 1st cl..	110.60	21.90	81.10	46.30	63.30	30.40	......	41.95	......	......	......	53.10
Salt Lake City	WA, UA	......	58.10	......	UA	UA	UA	UA, TW	......	UA, WA	UA, WC	UA
Jet 1st cl....	68.90	......	......	......	134.95	66.25	132.00	119.00	......	51.00	61.10	127.90
Jet economy..	42.15	......	......	......	119.45	55.75	116.50	104.50	......	40.85	48.40	113.40
Prop. 1st cl..	49.60	......	......	......	......	......	......	......	......	33.95	......	......
San Antonio..	CO, AA	TT	NA, EA	EA, DL	AA, EA	BN	AA, AL	AA, TW	AA, DL	AA, UA	WA	BN, EA
Jet 1st cl....	90.45	52.85	......	41.35	108.30	......	102.80	94.30	62.40	109.35	177.00	96.90
Jet economy..	78.45	42.50	......	33.60	95.00	......	89.50	82.65	53.40	96.35	138.95	84.50
Prop. 1st cl..	......	......	87.65	38.25	......	67.90	......	......	62.40	......	166.65	96.90
Pr. economy.	......	......	67.80	30.50	......	52.90	......	......	49.10	......	......	75.60
San Diego, Cal.	UA	AA, DL	NA, TW	NA, DL	UA, AA	UA	UA, TW	UA, TW	TW, AA	TW, PC	WA, UA	AA, TW
Jet 1st cl....	11.75	111.40	177.90	124.35	160.90	99.30	156.60	142.10	110.60	35.90	79.10	152.75
Jet economy..	10.90	97.40	140.10	101.60	145.10	85.80	141.40	127.90	96.60	29.25	67.60	137.25
Prop. 1st cl..	10.70	......	169.90	120.55	160.90	......	......	142.10	110.60	33.80	......	......
Pr. economy.	8.25	......	129.65	93.35	112.45	......	......	109.15	86.65	23.10	......	......
San Fr., Oakl.	WA, UA	AA, BN	NA, EA	NA, DL	AA, UA	UA, BN	AA, TW	UA, TW	AA	......	UA, WA	UA, TW
Jet 1st cl....	28.45	125.25	194.80	143.35	160.90	113.30	156.60	142.10	114.75	......	53.05	152.75
Jet economy..	13.50	111.25	157.05	118.75	145.10	88.60	141.40	127.90	100.75	......	42.35	137.25
Prop. 1st cl..	......	125.25	......	143.15	160.90	107.10	156.60	142.10	114.75	......	49.95	152.75
Pr. economy.	......	98.50	......	104.30	112.45	......	111.35	109.15	......	......	......	111.35
San Juan, P. R.	PA, DL	DL	PA, EA	DL	PA, EA	......	PA, EA	EA	DL	DL	......	PA
Jet 1st cl....	251.10	145.00	75.30	132.80	116.65	......	116.65	135.30	159.45	269.40	......	116.65
Jet economy..	184.05	100.10	52.85	90.55	78.30	......	78.30	93.90	122.05	201.00	......	78.30
Sarasota, Fla.	NA	SO, DL	NA, EA	NA, EA	NA	......	NA	UA, EA	EA, TW	......	......	NA
Prop. 1st cl..	159.60	54.59	15.65	41.60	79.55	......	73.10	69.65	73.15	......	......	67.55
Savannah, Ga.	CO	......	NA	EA, DL	EA, NA	......	NA	......	......	DL, UA	......	EA, NA
Prop. 1st cl..	156.10	......	35.00	47.25	54.65	......	48.25	......	......	176.55	......	42.65
Pr. economy.	129.30	......	28.10	37.25	42.80	......	38.10	......	......	140.30	......	33.80
Scrant'n,W.-B..	TW, UA	......	EA, NA	......	AL	......	EA	AL, TW	TW, DL	TW, UA	......	EA, AL
Prop. 1st cl..	156.80	......	92.05	......	10.60	......	12.10	19.05	57.70	156.80	......	19.05
Seattle,Tac'ma	UA, WA	BN	NW	DL, TT	NW, UA	UA	UA, TW	UA, TW	BN, TW	UA, WC	......	NW, UA
Jet 1st cl....	73.25	......	217.70	185.75	160.90	111.75	156.60	142.10	......	53.05	......	176.45
Jet economy..	61.75	......	181.35	148.20	145.10	97.25	141.40	129.35	......	42.35	......	137.25
Prop. 1st cl..	73.05	154.45	210.15	174.40	......	......	......	......	144.85	49.95	......	166.15
Shreveport,La.	DL, AA	DL, TT	......	DL, TT	UA, AA	BN, FL	......	......	DL	......	......	AA, UA
Prop. 1st cl..	104.45	24.65	......	22.60	96.95	51.10	......	......	43.25	......	......	85.00
Pr. economy.	81.00	20.30	......	18.80	77.75	......	......	......	34.30	......	......	66.65
So. Bend, Ind.	UA. TW	......	......	......	UA	UA	......	UA	DL, OZ	......	......	NW, UA
Prop. 1st cl..	136.45	......	......	......	47.05	37.55	......	27.45	28.65	......	......	44.00

Approximate fares. Taxes not included. *Courtesy Official Airline Guide*

SELECTED NORTH AMERICAN AIR PASSENGER FARES

TO \ FROM	Los Angeles	Memphis	Miami	New Orleans	New York	Omaha	Philadelphia	Pittsburgh	St. Louis	San Francisco	Seattle	Washington
Spartanburg..		EA	DL	DL, EA	EA, UA		EA		EA			EA
Prop. 1st cl...		33.20	49.45	45.20	48.00		41.95		43.20			36.40
Spokane, W'sh.	NA, WA		NW		NW, UA		NW	NW, UA		UA, WC	NW, WC	NW
Jet 1st cl....	101.30		210.75		160.90		156.63	142.10			23.10	152.75
Prop. 1st cl...	94.05		206.60		146.85		154.85	132.55		61.90	21.00	138.60
Springf'ld, Mo.	AA, TW	DL			AA, TW		TW, EA	TW, UA	OZ, AA	UA, TW		AA, EA
Prop. 1st cl...	106.30	19.80			77.35		71.85	56.30	16.50	120.70		66.30
Syracuse, N.Y.	AA, UA	AA	EA, UA	EA	MO, AA		AA	MO	AA	AA, UA		AA
Jet 1st cl....	155.00	70.80	89.30	92.20	17.90		25.35	23.95	56.90	155.00		33.65
Prop. 1st cl...	139.05		68.60		16.35		23.30		56.35			31.30
Tallahassee...	DL, NA		EA	NA	NA		EA, UA		EA	DL, UA		NA
Prop. 1st cl...	146.05		30.85	28.80	72.10		66.85		56.50	167.75		60.80
Pr. economy.	111.80		25.05	23.35	56.40		51.90		43.90	127.65		47.75
Tampa, St. Pet.	NA, DL	DL	NA, EA	NA, EA	NA, EA		NA, EA	UA, NW	EA, TW	NA, TW	UA	EA, NA
Jet 1st cl....	161.70	55.80	19.15	41.90	81.40		74.20	70.90	74.20	179.50	202.80	64.10
Jet economy.	129.75	44.75	16.80	34.00	64.10		59.20	56.05	59.30	145.05	171.35	46.25
Prop. 1st cl...		51.65	17.05	38.80	75.50		69.30	66.75	69.30	156.80	109.40	64.10
Pr. economy.		40.60	14.75	31.05	55.10		50.75	47.80	47.80	130.25	140.70	46.50
Toledo, Ohio..	UA, TW		EA		UA, AA	UA	UA, TW	UA	TW, OZ	UA, TW		UA, NW
Prop. 1st cl...	146.45		85.15		36.30	47.60	32.75	17.95	36.55	146.45		29.70
Toronto, Ont..	UA, CO		EA, NA	DL, EA	AC, AA	UA, OZ	AA, EA			UA, TW	UA, AC	EA
Jet 1st cl....			99.00		34.00		40.45					
Prop. 1st cl...	169.15			104.35	32.00	73.50	34.50			169.15	160.40	36.20
Pr. economy.	116.90			79.40	26.00	55.10	29.85			116.90	119.90	31.85
Tucson, Ariz..	AA, CO	AA, DL	TW, EA		AA	FL, UA	AA, TW	UA, TW	AA	AA, WA		TW
Jet 1st cl....	37.75	87.25	150.50		140.55		136.50	135.95	88.75	58.35		132.05
Prop. 1st cl...	35.65	87.25			140.55	89.50	136.50	122.50	88.75	57.80		132.05
Pr. economy.	28.70	69.05			105.85		104.80	97.85	70.45	43.55		104.80
Tulsa, Okla...	AA, TW	BN	EA	BN	AA, TW	BN	TW, EA	TW, AA	AA, TW	AA	UA	AA, UA
Jet 1st cl....	91.75		97.65		86.30		82.30	70.05	29.30	104.65		76.05
Jet economy.	79.75		76.90		74.30		69.25	55.45	24.40	91.65		65.05
Prop. 1st cl...	91.75	29.25	91.45	45.55	86.30	31.00	82.30		27.20	104.65	126.05	76.05
V'couver, B.C.	UA		AC		AC, AA		UA, EA	65.90		UA	UA, AC	EA, NA
Jet 1st cl....	86.90		232.60							62.85	17.00	
Prop. 1st cl...	81.75				174.00		189.70			58.70	13.00	197.95
Waco, Tex....	DL, AA	AA, TT			AA, BN	BN			AA, CN			AA, BN
Prop. 1st cl...	91.10	40.20			106.40	58.35			53.50			94.35
Wash't'n, D.C.	AA, TW	UA, AA	EA, NA	EA, UA	EA	UA, OZ	EA, TW	UA, NW	AA	UA, TW	NW, UA	
Jet 1st cl....	152.75	59.70	78.10	78.80	20.05		12.55		56.20	152.75	152.75	
Jet economy.	137.25	51.20	61.20	63.00	16.40		11.50		44.90	137.25		
Prop. 1st cl...	152.75	59.70	73.20	73.90	17.95	72.95	11.50	16.55	53.00	152.75	152.75	
Pr. economy.	111.35	45.05	53.60	56.90	15.35	56.15	10.05	13.50		111.35		
W. Palm Beach	NA, DL	DL, EA	EA, NA	NA, NA	EA		EA		EA, TW	NA, TW		EA, NA
Jet 1st cl....	174.30		8.50	56.00	86.50		80.40			193.30		74.10
Prop. 1st cl...	173.40	64.60	7.50	52.10	80.60		74.50	72.05	78.40	193.10		69.20
Pr. economy.	133.55		6.80	40.90	57.70		57.70	52.60		144.55		51.70
Wichita, Kans.	TW, DL			TW, UA	BN, DL	TW, UA	TW, UA	TW, UA	TW, UA	TW, UA	UA	TW
Jet 1st cl....	91.75		109.45	55.15	97.75	28.95	93.20	75.45	33.75	132.75	121.55	86.65
Win'peg, Man.			NW		NW, AC		UA	NW		UA, WC	NW	NW
Jet 1st cl....			148.15		92.00		95.00	82.75			117.45	100.15
Prop. 1st cl...			148.15		92.00		95.00	81.70		161.20	111.25	95.00
Ygtn., Wrn., Sh.	UA, TW				UA, TW		UA	UA				UA
Prop. 1st cl...	155.25				28.45		25.55	8.25				21.55

For airline abbreviations see page 903.

AUTOMOBILE MILEAGE—PRINCIPAL CANADIAN CITIES

FROM / TO	Calgary	Edmonton	Halifax	Hamilton	London	Montreal	Ottawa	Quebec	Regina	St. John, N.B.	Toronto	Vancouver	Windsor	Winnipeg
Calgary	.....	189	3149	*2175	*2099	2325	2199	2492	473	2918	2130	652	*1981	830
Edmonton	189	.....	3173	*2199	*2123	2349	2223	2516	497	2942	2154	841	*2005	854
Halifax	3149	3173	.....	1206	1286	824	950	657	2676	276	1164	3801	1398	2319
Hamilton	*2175	*2199	1206	.....	78	382	290	549	*1702	975	42	*2827	194	*1345
London	*2099	*2123	1286	78	.....	454	362	621	*1626	1055	122	*2751	118	*1269
Montreal	2325	2349	824	382	454	.....	126	167	1852	593	340	2977	574	1495
Ottawa	2199	2223	950	290	362	126	.....	293	1726	719	248	2851	474	1369
Quebec	2492	2516	657	549	621	167	293	.....	2019	426	507	3144	741	1662
Regina	473	497	2676	*1702	*1626	1852	1726	2019	.....	2445	1657	1125	*1508	357
Saint John, N.B.	2918	2942	276	975	1055	593	719	426	2445	.....	933	3570	1167	2088
Toronto	2130	2154	1164	42	122	340	248	507	1657	933	.....	2782	234	1300
Vancouver	652	841	3801	*2827	*2751	2977	2851	3144	1125	3570	2782	.....	*2633	1482
Windsor	*1981	*2005	1398	194	118	574	474	741	*1508	1167	234	*2633	.....	*1151
Winnipeg	830	854	2319	*1345	*1269	1495	1369	1662	357	2088	1300	1482	*1151	.....

*Via Detroit, Chicago, Madison, Minneapolis, Fargo, and Emerson to Winnipeg, from which the distances are computed via the shortest route.
Courtesy Canadian Travel Bureau

FIRST-CLASS RAILWAY FARES—CANADIAN CITIES

FROM / TO	Calgary	Halifax	London, Ont.	Montreal	Ottawa	Quebec	Regina	St. John, N.B.	Toronto	Vancouver	Windsor	Winnipeg
Calgary	.....	61.00	48.00	48.00	47.00	51.00	19.00	59.00	47.00	24.00	49.00	24.00
Edmonton	6.80	61.00	45.00	45.00	44.00	48.00	14.20	56.00	44.00	21.00	46.00	21.00
Halifax	61.00	.....	29.00	21.00	24.00	19.00	52.00	9.20	28.00	72.00	33.00	45.00
Hamilton	47.00	30.00	3.15	12.30	9.90	15.00	38.00	28.00	1.95	52.00	6.70	29.00
London	48.00	28.00	.....	13.30	12.30	17.00	38.00	28.00	4.00	54.00	4.00	31.00
Montreal	48.00	21.00	13.30	.....	4.00	6.10	39.00	20.00	11.40	54.00	15.50	31.00
Ottawa	47.00	24.00	12.30	4.00	.....	9.50	38.00	22.00	8.40	52.00	14.20	29.00
Quebec	51.00	19.00	17.00	6.10	9.50	.....	42.00	16.50	14.70	58.00	20.00	34.00
Regina	19.00	52.00	38.00	39.00	38.00	42.00	.....	51.00	36.00	28.00	39.00	13.70
Saint John, N. B.	59.00	9.20	28.00	20.00	22.00	16.50	51.00	.....	26.00	71.00	31.00	44.00
St. John's Nfld.	80.00	26.00	47.00	39.00	41.00	36.00	72.00	30.00	44.00	87.00	49.00	61.00
Toronto	47.00	28.00	4.00	11.40	8.40	14.70	36.00	26.00	.....	52.00	7.50	29.00
Vancouver	24.00	72.00	54.00	54.00	52.00	58.00	28.00	71.00	52.00	.....	56.00	33.00
Victoria	29.52	77.52	59.52	59.52	57.52	63.52	33.52	76.52	57 52	5.52	61.52	38.52
Windsor	49.00	33.00	4.00	15.50	14.20	20.00	39.00	31.00	7.50	56.00	.....	33.00
Winnipeg	24.00	45.00	31.00	31.00	29.00	34.00	13.70	44.00	29.00	33.00	33.00	.....

Courtesy Canadian National Railways   Fares subject to change.

MARKET DATA—PRINCIPAL CANADIAN CITIES

Province and Urban Centres	Population 1961	Establishments 1962*	Selling Value of Factory Shipments 1962*	Province and Urban Centres	Population 1961	Establishments 1962*	Selling Value of Factory Shipments 1962*
Newfoundland....	457,853	331	$ 143,925,293	Ontario—Cont.			
St. John's......	63,633	72	28,862,895	Cornwall........	43,639	53	$ 94,801,188
				Fort William....	45,214	57	74,316,333
Prince Edw. Island	104,629	157	35,129,798	Galt...........	27,830	96	108,945,018
Charlottetown...	18,318	31	17,268,789	Guelph..........	39,838	117	122,061,065
				Hamilton........	273,991	526	1,182,093,371
Nova Scotia......	737,007	1,030	426,676,746	Kingston........	53,526	66	73,410,593
Amherst........	10,788	25	11,225,672	Kitchener.......	74,485	203	266,838,653
Halifax.........	92,511	98	70,464,922	Leaside.........	18,579	49	113,558,934
Lunenburg......	3,056	14	8,848,730	London.........	169,569	292	334,535,694
New Glasgow....	9,782	26	6,946,019	New Toronto....	13,384	32	166,471,712
Truro...........	12,421	30	13,027,383	Niagara Falls....	22,351	95	144,763,846
Yarmouth.......	8,636	25	11,315,513	Orillia..........	15,345	55	28,166,321
				Ottawa.........	268,206	226	152,059,399
New Brunswick...	597,936	722	401,142,111	Owen Sound.....	17,421	40	28,284,842
Fredericton......	19,683	36	11,298,188	Peterborough....	47,185	79	130,183,193
Moncton........	43,840	63	34,303,618	Port Arthur.....	45,276	55	51,049,453
Saint John......	55,153	88	136,121,112	St. Catharines...	84,472	152	221,242,272
				St. Thomas......	22,469	59	39,476,390
Quebec..........	5,259,211	11,104	7,936,346,113	Sarnia..........	50,976	49	368,798,177
Beauharnois.....	8,704	14	37,138,770	Sault Ste. Marie..	43,088	39	†
Cap-de-la-Madelei ne	26,925	40	55,634,588	Stratford........	20,467	67	58,987,856
Drummondville..	27,909	72	96,109,362	Toronto.........	672,407	2,722	1,938,150,380
Granby.........	31,463	82	107,209,428	Trenton.........	13,183	31	30,957,405
Grand'Mere.....	15,806	33	32,331,421	Waterloo........	21,366	68	70,493,809
Hull............	56,929	50	58,628,460	Welland.........	36,079	59	149,964,503
Joliette.........	18,088	55	36,289,749	Weston.........	9,175	60	39,420,933
Lachine.........	38,630	81	215,107,412	Windsor.........	114,367	289	463,772,748
LaSalle.........	30,904	58	186,078,880	Woodstock......	20,486	59	81,688,094
Longueuil.......	24,131	33	12,817,592				
Montreal........	1,191,062	3,782	2,414,286,285	Manitoba........	921,686	1,461	836,573,390
Montreal East...	5,884	39	654,058,789	Brandon........	28,166	38	13,360,888
Outremont......	30,753	77	38,957,358	St. Boniface.....	37,600	84	177,133,262
Quebec..........	171,979	361	230,681,830	Winnipeg........	265,429	748	337,894,845
St. Hyacinthe....	22,354	91	57,838,857				
St. Jean........	26,988	81	78,862,446	Saskatchewan.....	925,181	720	375,222,535
St. Jerome......	24,546	69	47,592,190	Moose Jaw......	33,206	47	50,201,703
St. Laurent......	49,805	134	329,297,492	Prince Albert....	24,168	27	23,642,655
Shawinigan......	32,169	45	122,529,334	Regina..........	112,141	122	105,133,146
Sherbrooke......	66,554	116	124,859,068	Saskatoon.......	95,526	138	101,533,480
Three Rivers....	53,477	83	147,108,367				
Valleyfield......	27,297	50	57,441,166	Alberta..........	1,331,944	1,681	1,017,236,000
Verdun.........	78,317	68	18,790,293	Calgary.........	294,641	394	280,131,709
Victoriaville.....	18,720	59	33,947,141	Edmonton.......	281,027	453	292,653,996
Westmount......	25,012	36	25,299,158	Lethbridge......	35,454	70	42,461,091
				Medicine Hat....	24,484	40	39,653,540
Ontario..........	6,236,092	12,586	13,342,556,967				
Barrie..........	21,169	45	49,652,482	British Columbia..	1,629,082	3,622	2,194,598,563
Belleville.......	30,655	64	51,654,757	New Westminster	33,654	104	111,398,029
Brantford.......	55,201	160	151,005,397	North Vancouver.	23,656	71	44,862,594
Brockville.......	17,744	42	64,311,857	Vancouver.......	384,522	1,158	543,775,371
Chatham........	29,826	80	108,012,045	Victoria.........	54,941	174	67,872,595

*Latest available statistics †Confidential *Courtesy Dominion Bureau of Statistics*

Telephones	1-1-58	1-1-59	1-1-60	1-1-61	1-1-62	1-1-63	1-1-64
Newfoundland.....	41,434	46,994	51,882	58,006	61,969	69,777	74,099
Prince Edw. Island.	15,333	16,244	17,321	18,573	20,362	22,251	23,550
Nova Scotia.......	151,413	158,219	166,629	173,971	183,848	194,605	202,874
New Brunswick....	112,687	116,886	122,205	128,557	136,809	144,994	152,922
Quebec............	1,277,627	1,363,627	1,448,795	1,520,622	1,611,294	1,709,943	1,815,331
Ontario...........	1,990,158	2,088,922	2,204,922	2,324,875	2,421,915	2,529,095	2,644,045
Manitoba.........	237,677	250,630	269,515	282,800	298,838	311,331	324,904
Saskatchewan......	206,010	217,979	230,975	241,435	251,130	260,668	272,449
Alberta.....:.....	299,417	326,213	362,661	392,844	422,164	452,990	477,337
British Columbia...	495,167	532,756	563,686	585,038	604,102	632,305*	666,190*
Yukon............	212	224	231	230	223	†	†
N.W. Territories...	....	....	201	1,216	1,361	1,489	2,912
Totals........	4,827,135	5,118,293	5,439,023	5,728,167	6,014,015	6,329,448	6,656,613

*Includes Yukon. †Included with British Columbia

AUTOMOBILE MILEAGE BETWEEN CITIES

FROM / TO	Albany, N.Y.	Atlanta, Ga.	Baltimore, Md.	Boston, Mass.	Buffalo, N.Y.	Chicago, Ill.	Cincinnati, Ohio	Cleveland, Ohio	Columbus, Ohio	Dallas, Tex.	Denver, Colo.	Detroit, Mich.	Houston, Tex.	Indianapolis, Ind.	Kansas City, Mo.	Little Rock, Ark.
Albany, N. Y.	....	988	*333*	*170*	*286*	*810*	*728*	*476*	*620*	1713	1848	*534*	1835	*774*	1268	1393
Amarillo, Tex.	1807	1152	1714	2110	1521	1092	1136	1333	1207	362	438	1305	654	1033	622	611
Asheville, N. C.	831	212	508	*904*	745	671	359	557	439	1007	1593	627	1132	485	872	667
Atlanta, Ga.	988	....	669	1068	877	695	461	686	549	805	1401	726	814	508	810	505
Baltimore, Md.	333	669	....	399	345	687	494	351	408	1458	1701	*511*	1449	580	1099	1086
Birmingham, Ala.	996	152	787	1185	902	656	476	716	579	653	1282	741	662	480	706	386
Bismarck, N. D.	*1681*	1543	1535	1823	1377	850	1143	1191	1207	1175	685	1123	1417	1035	783	1188
Boise, Idaho	2553	2218	2418	2705	2258	1731	1944	2072	2001	1607	842	1999	1797	1836	1410	1798
Boston, Mass.	*170*	1068	399	....	*449*	975	*876*	*632*	769	1819	1989	*735*	1916	*941*	1456	1494
Buffalo, N. Y.	*286*	877	*345*	*449*	....	529	*430*	*186*	*323*	1373	1543	247	1470	*495*	1010	1048
Calgary, Alta. (Can.)	2565	2511	2496	2678	2279	1802	1906	2151	2115	1929	1129	2062	2172	1988	1662	2121
Charleston, W. Va.	*729*	497	391	*803*	444	468	197	267	169	1075	1366	359	1172	305	785	750
Chattanooga, Tenn.	952	120	660	1056	887	589	349	603	457	703	1422	611	890	445	731	464
Cheyenne, Wyo.	1790	1456	1656	1943	1496	969	1182	1310	1239	875	102	1238	1117	1074	648	1040
Chicago, Ill.	*810*	695	*687*	975	529	....	295	343	359	936	1016	*275*	1085	187	499	644
Cincinnati, Ohio	*728*	461	494	*876*	*430*	295	....	244	107	943	1169	265	1040	108	590	618
Cleveland, Ohio	*476*	686	*351*	*632*	*186*	343	244	....	137	1187	1357	*167*	1284	309	824	862
Colorado Spgs., Colo.	1880	1493	1672	2057	1594	1195	1216	1406	1280	760	67	1378	1027	1106	612	951
Columbia, S. C.	852	215	508	906	770	785	517	655	557	1020	1605	746	1029	601	1001	720
Columbus, Ohio	*620*	549	*408*	*769*	*323*	359	107	137	....	1050	1233	189	1147	172	656	725
Dallas, Tex.	1713	805	1458	1819	1373	936	943	1187	1050	....	784	1188	242	882	499	325
Denver, Colo.	1848	1401	1701	1989	1543	1016	1169	1357	1233	784	....	1284	1026	1061	604	957
Des Moines, Ia.	1151	894	1025	1311	865	338	571	*679*	695	736	679	606	946	483	213	573
Detroit, Mich.	*534*	726	*511*	*735*	247	275	265	*167*	189	1188	1284	....	1337	277	751	896
Duluth, Minn.	1203	1183	1177	1465	1022	492	785	833	849	1109	1002	765	1351	677	610	978
El Paso, Tex.	2175	1427	2034	2391	1945	1434	1524	1759	1595	*622*	654	1686	755	1423	935	947
Evansville, Ind.	964	415	*718*	*1100*	654	296	224	468	331	734	1027	444	834	167	423	409
Fargo, N. D.	1498	1390	1367	1677	1207	670	957	1019	975	1136	955	957	1379	846	669	1077
Ft. Smith, Ark.	1422	696	1272	1602	1126	710	741	938	849	295	815	910	497	638	309	154
Ft. Wayne, Ind.	674	*610*	*556*	*844*	398	176	154	212	152	999	1156	160	1114	117	585	697
Galveston, Tex.	1877	896	1550	1957	1592	1160	1150	1404	1258	293	1093	1355	*50*	1007	814	500
Great Falls, Mont.	2366	2174	2235	2525	1981	1538	1809	1867	1837	1556	756	1805	1799	1699	1323	1791
Greensboro, N. C.	675	352	320	716	688	786	*479*	536	*442*	1166	1686	630	1254	*589*	1042	852
Harrisburg, Pa.	285	719	80	398	279	657	472	321	*368*	1418	1666	*481*	1474	*540*	1132	1094
Hartford, Conn.	*103*	972	303	*102*	380	903	752	562	*650*	1690	1883	*731*	1752	*822*	1306	1365
Helena, Mont.	2309	2053	2163	2451	2005	1478	1770	1819	1835	1571	792	1751	1813	1663	1261	1666
Houston, Tex.	1835	814	1449	1916	1470	1085	1040	1284	1147	242	1026	1337	....	997	741	441
Indianapolis, Ind.	774	508	580	*941*	495	187	108	309	172	882	1061	277	997	....	484	562
Jacksonville, Fla.	978	314	793	1191	1067	1009	775	952	854	994	1708	996	911	822	1123	812
Kansas City, Mo.	1268	810	1099	1456	1010	499	590	824	656	499	604	751	741	484	....	405
Knoxville, Tenn.	840	195	548	948	775	559	280	534	388	890	1481	582	1002	373	783	555
Las Vegas, Nev.	2696	2026	2563	2873	2410	1886	2010	2235	2081	1236	841	2158	1501	1907	1496	1485
Lexington, Ky.	*813*	384	579	*948*	511	367	85	339	177	962	1242	347	1036	181	598	627
Lincoln, Neb.	1369	1076	1197	1535	1058	548	741	882	805	640	493	809	883	631	225	633
Little Rock, Ark.	1393	505	1086	1494	1048	644	618	862	725	325	957	896	441	562	405	....
Los Angeles, Cal.	2931	2197	2695	3052	2606	2095	2186	2420	2245	1403	1134	2347	1553	2080	1596	1701
Louisville, Ky.	*836*	394	604	*986*	540	301	110	354	217	833	1120	375	930	114	516	508
Memphis, Tenn.	1239	366	947	1355	909	544	479	723	586	464	1035	713	561	436	459	139

Italics denote shortest routes using one or more turnpikes.

AUTOMOBILE MILEAGE BETWEEN CITIES

TO \ FROM	Albany, N.Y.	Atlanta, Ga.	Baltimore, Md.	Boston, Mass.	Buffalo, N.Y.	Chicago, Ill.	Cincinnati, Ohio	Cleveland, Ohio	Columbus, Ohio	Dallas, Tex.	Denver, Colo.	Detroit, Mich.	Houston, Tex.	Indianapolis, Ind.	Kansas City, Mo.	Little Rock, Ark.
Miami, Fla.........	1461	665	1144	1542	1418	1360	1126	1303	1205	1309	2046	1347	1216	1173	1470	1144
Milwaukee, Wis.....	898	784	776	1064	618	91	384	432	448	1015	1040	364	1174	276	580	723
Minneapolis-St. Paul	1235	1105	1097	1385	939	412	705	753	769	956	841	685	1198	597	457	825
Mobile, Ala........	1433	365	1052	1448	1218	870	742	1030	850	599	1389	1038	537	748	853	445
Montgomery, Ala...	1245	169	838	1236	979	748	568	793	656	650	1374	833	659	572	798	478
Montreal, Que......	228	1230	562	324	393	848	820	576	713	1763	1862	573	1860	885	1324	1438
Nashville, Tenn....	1036	256	725	1165	719	451	290	533	396	686	1158	555	783	294	554	361
New Orleans, La....	1383	493	1138	1536	1253	925	820	1063	926	498	1282	1085	359	805	821	416
New York, N. Y....	167	855	187	216	445	843	659	507	557	1607	1851	667	1636	729	1319	1282
Oklahoma City, Okla.	1545	845	1321	1684	1308	797	844	1052	915	215	615	1049	457	743	347	349
Omaha, Neb.....	1296	1012	1163	1449	1003	476	691	817	748	656	540	744	898	583	205	610
Philadelphia, Pa....	237	766	97	304	365	762	578	426	476	1526	1770	586	1546	648	1238	1201
Phoenix, Ariz.......	2531	1810	2325	2682	2236	1722	1816	2050	1882	1005	818	1977	1155	1710	1226	1330
Pittsburgh, Pa......	465	697	230	598	217	461	284	125	182	1232	1482	285	1319	354	937	897
Portland, Me.......	241	1173	501	109	524	1048	968	712	858	1833	2086	796	1976	1088	1506	1605
Portland, Ore.......	3002	2654	2816	3085	2639	2112	2405	2453	2469	2043	1278	2385	2233	2297	1846	2234
Providence, R. I....	172	1033	364	45	444	982	848	626	711	1751	1944	795	1813	883	1367	1426
Quebec, Que.......	401	1462	734	399	582	1038	1024	760	916	2045	2089	766	2073	1038	1532	1631
Raleigh, N. C.......	636	402	353	699	671	838	559	616	522	1216	1720	710	1331	645	1127	919
Rapid City, S. D....	1817	1599	1624	1994	1531	909	1247	1271	1235	1235	406	1279	1405	1137	761	1325
Richmond, Va......	477	533	148	546	468	796	508	460	453	1310	1805	620	1347	609	1109	985
Sacramento, Cal....	2919	2614	2792	3096	2626	2109	2336	2438	2403	1815	1181	2376	1961	2226	1810	2038
St. Joseph, Mo.....	1274	905	1056	1440	978	500	600	790	664	581	561	767	818	490	54	462
St. Louis, Mo......	1015	558	817	1178	802	291	338	546	409	654	856	543	794	237	252	353
Salt Lake City, Utah	2250	1900	2118	2405	1958	1431	1644	1772	1701	1241	512	1700	1431	1536	1116	1456
San Antonio, Tex.†..	1978	1016	1703	2099	1697	1271	1282	1536	1390	274	965	1552	169	1183	801	600
San Diego, Cal.....	2836	2125	2803	3199	2610	2181	2225	2416	2296	1176	1191	2394	1994	2122	1711	1700
San Francisco, Cal...	3007	2523	2876	3163	2716	2189	2402	2530	2459	1806	1270	2458	1955	2294	1874	2027
Santa Fe, N. M.....	2110	1387	1817	2219	1773	1262	1353	1587	1410	630	360	1514	820	1247	763	891
Sault Ste. Marie....	967	1083	921	951	553	444	604	509	530	1429	1389	366	1555	520	907	1113
Scranton, Pa.......	175	884	219	310	248	747	564	369	462	1570	1761	500	1712	635	1166	1232
Seattle, Wash......	2921	2756	2748	3036	2590	2063	2356	2404	2420	2112	1347	2336	2302	2248	1872	2277
Shreveport, La......	1589	627	1314	1710	1308	882	893	1147	1001	187	977	1066	241	794	565	200
Sioux City, Ia......	1318	1149	1207	1497	1027	510	782	839	819	785	613	777	1028	672	318	726
Sioux Falls, S. D....	1396	1237	1265	1555	1085	568	870	897	867	873	695	835	1116	760	406	814
Spokane, Wash.....	2626	2467	2459	2747	2301	1774	2067	2115	2131	1891	1112	2047	2138	1959	1583	1988
Springfield, Ill......	962	611	754	1147	701	191	300	515	364	746	869	442	895	192	309	454
Springfield, Mo.....	1245	649	1037	1468	1022	511	558	766	629	425	752	763	640	457	176	229
Syracuse, N. Y.....	134	1083	327	311	156	680	598	344	490	1583	1718	408	1616	644	1138	1234
Tampa, Fla........	1298	467	981	1379	1248	1162	928	1122	985	1077	1814	1193	984	975	1238	912
Toledo, Ohio.......	585	668	454	742	296	241	207	110	132	1154	1250	58	1247	221	717	783
Toronto, Ont.......	386	969	468	563	106	510	542	288	429	1497	1561	241	1545	510	1004	1103
Tulsa, Okla........	1431	783	1219	1650	1204	693	740	948	811	271	693	945	513	641	258	287
Vancouver, B. C....	3038	3002	2887	3139	2717	2193	2589	2542	2506	2296	1412	2465	2642	2379	2155	2538
Washington, D. C...	372	630	39	437	437	687	492	351	392	1372	1696	511	1410	564	1048	1047
Wichita, Kans......	1486	895	1297	1654	1208	697	697	1022	852	384	507	949	612	682	198	473
Wilmington, N. C...	731	423	398	794	766	1008	696	697	634	1246	1930	822	1308	791	1209	965
Winnipeg, Man.....	1650	1631	1615	1805	1382	921	1217	1270	1234	1344	1194	1203	1587	1107	908	1316

†To Mexico City, 920 miles

Section F — COMMUNICATION, TRAVEL, AND TRANSPORT

AUTOMOBILE MILEAGE BETWEEN CITIES

TO \ FROM	Los Angeles, Cal.	Louisville, Ky.	Memphis, Tenn.	Miami, Fla.	Minneapolis-St. Paul	New Orleans, La.	New York, N.Y.	Omaha, Neb.	Philadelphia, Pa.	Richmond, Va.	St. Louis, Mo.	Salt Lake City, Utah	San Francisco, Cal.	Seattle, Wash.	Spokane, Wash.	Washington, D.C.
Albany, N. Y.	2931	836	1239	1461	1235	1383	167	1296	237	477	1015	2250	3007	2921	2626	372
Amarillo, Tex.	1124	1059	750	1708	1042	852	1902	628	1785	1599	792	899	1445	1791	1671	1567
Asheville, N. C.	2399	371	578	789	1096	747	696	1087	604	367	645	1956	2720	2915	2552	479
Atlanta, Ga.	2197	394	366	665	1105	493	855	1012	766	533	558	1900	2523	2576	2467	630
Baltimore, Md.	2695	604	947	1144	1097	1138	187	1163	97	148	817	2118	2876	2748	2459	39
Birmingham, Ala.	2056	366	247	803	1066	351	974	911	884	716	476	1781	2393	2575	2286	748
Bismarck, N. D.	1649	1146	1266	2184	428	1604	1691	581	1610	1689	980	960	1633	1213	924	1531
Boise, Idaho	962	1929	1869	3066	1422	2105	2566	1255	2485	2482	1660	366	658	505	391	2411
Boston, Mass.	3052	986	1355	1542	1385	1536	216	1449	304	546	1178	2405	3163	3036	2747	437
Buffalo, N. Y.	2606	540	909	1418	939	1253	445	1003	365	468	802	1958	2716	2590	2301	437
Calgary, Alta. (Can.)	1609	2102	1989	3064	1262	2409	2446	1271	2563	2806	1728	993	1514	760	465	2257
Charleston, W. Va.	2381	269	611	1043	875	925	591	885	510	311	533	1838	2596	2529	2240	352
Chattanooga, Tenn.	2199	316	330	795	1014	505	848	943	756	614	474	1933	2520	2744	2470	599
Cheyenne, Wyo.	1169	1162	1107	2255	794	1373	1806	493	1725	1719	898	462	1220	1267	1022	1650
Chicago, Ill.	2095	301	544	1360	412	925	843	476	762	796	291	1431	2189	2063	1774	687
Cincinnati, Ohio	2186	110	479	1126	705	820	659	691	578	508	338	1644	2402	2356	2067	492
Cleveland, Ohio	2420	354	723	1303	753	1063	507	817	426	460	546	1772	2530	2404	2115	351
Colorado Spgs., Colo.	1128	1136	1090	2141	985	1239	1813	621	1768	1738	819	586	1345	1478	1177	1747
Columbia, S. C.	2417	499	581	656	1190	697	694	1184	605	368	749	2109	2738	2846	2557	469
Columbus, Ohio	2245	217	586	1205	769	926	557	748	476	453	409	1701	2459	2420	2131	392
Dallas, Tex.	1403	833	464	1309	956	498	1607	656	1526	1310	654	1241	1806	2112	1891	1372
Denver, Colo.	1134	1120	1035	2046	841	1282	1851	540	1770	1805	856	512	1270	1347	1122	1696
Des Moines, Ia.	1801	569	608	1627	252	989	1173	139	1092	1122	336	1094	1852	1773	1484	1018
Detroit, Mich.	2347	375	713	1347	685	1085	667	744	586	620	543	1700	2458	2336	2047	511
Duluth, Minn.	2059	791	958	1880	153	1359	1333	514	1252	1238	665	1352	2064	1652	1363	1177
El Paso, Tex.	798	1450	1086	1998	1339	1114	2254	1040	2173	1950	1180	869	1200	1740	1601	1983
Evansville, Ind.	2029	125	273	1088	706	642	888	622	807	705	172	1539	2297	2357	2068	716
Fargo, N. D.	1925	960	1103	2058	241	1504	1516	457	1427	1458	803	1190	1949	1459	1164	1363
Ft. Smith, Ark.	1581	664	290	1330	773	576	1394	521	1304	1159	397	1326	1914	2140	1845	1233
Ft. Wayne, Ind.	2181	216	553	1340	586	926	712	616	631	665	354	1571	2329	2237	1948	556
Galveston, Tex.	1616	1042	639	1316	1278	372	1749	972	1646	1435	861	1554	2041	2395	2090	1468
Great Falls, Mont.	1323	1873	1811	2835	1007	2053	2384	1171	2275	2316	1567	588	1292	706	411	2231
Greensboro, N. C.	2584	518	713	837	1201	876	508	1179	416	230	785	2230	2947	2964	2669	281
Harrisburg, Pa.	2729	582	953	1225	1067	1163	186	1127	105	219	777	2081	2839	2718	2429	119
Hartford, Conn.	2895	862	1226	1439	1317	1445	121	1371	207	503	1059	2326	3076	2955	2666	342
Helena, Mont.	1234	1777	1720	2896	1056	2070	2319	1056	2238	2391	1498	500	1134	611	322	2163
Houston, Tex.	1553	930	561	1216	1198	359	1636	898	1546	1347	794	1431	1955	2302	2138	1410
Indianapolis, Ind.	2080	114	436	1173	597	805	729	583	648	609	237	1536	2294	2248	1959	564
Jacksonville, Fla.	2397	708	603	359	1419	570	980	1326	890	655	872	2207	2799	3070	2718	754
Kansas City, Mo.	1596	516	459	1470	457	821	1319	205	1238	1109	252	1116	1874	1872	1583	1048
Knoxville, Tenn.	2290	259	416	867	984	617	736	995	644	433	533	1969	2611	2742	2447	509
Las Vegas, Nev.	292	1933	1624	2674	1729	1726	2736	1400	2684	2473	1686	441	595	1208	1088	2425
Lexington, Ky.	2319	74	445	1063	792	769	705	771	670	503	341	1753	2512	2443	2148	616
Lincoln, Neb.	1663	749	715	1757	423	1093	1359	59	1265	1263	482	928	1687	1697	1402	1194
Little Rock, Ark.	1701	508	139	1144	825	416	1282	610	1201	985	353	1456	2027	2277	1988	1047
Los Angeles, Cal.	....	2017	1831	2712	1940	1901	2915	1662	2721	2682	1848	734	403	1145	1227	2644
Louisville, Ky.	2017	....	369	1059	711	710	769	689	688	580	264	1632	2390	2362	2073	596
Memphis, Tenn.	1831	369	....	1011	840	401	1138	664	1057	846	294	1534	2157	2331	2042	908

AUTOMOBILE MILEAGE BETWEEN CITIES

TO \ FROM	Los Angeles, Cal.	Louisville, Ky.	Memphis, Tenn.	Miami, Fla.	Minneapolis-St. Paul	New Orleans, La.	New York, N.Y.	Omaha, Neb.	Philadelphia, Pa.	Richmond, Va.	St. Louis, Mo.	Salt Lake City, Utah	San Francisco, Cal.	Seattle, Wash.	Spokane, Wash.	Washington, D.C.
Miami, Fla.	2712	1059	1011	....	1770	875	1330	1738	1224	1006	1269	2607	3270	3582	3265	1075
Milwaukee, Wis.	2176	390	624	1472	326	1013	932	500	851	886	370	1455	2213	1977	1688	776
Minneapolis-St. Paul	1940	711	840	1770	....	1241	1253	358	1172	1206	546	1239	1997	1641	1352	1097
Mobile, Ala.	2042	634	373	775	1304	152	1240	1062	1148	926	642	1877	2444	2701	2406	1013
Montgomery, Ala.	2056	458	339	730	1158	324	1024	1003	935	738	572	1873	2456	2667	2378	799
Montreal, Que.	2920	930	1299	1689	1258	1640	388	1317	467	705	1116	2273	3031	2697	2408	600
Nashville, Tenn.	2058	180	222	932	861	530	949	756	868	629	302	1670	2410	2512	2223	685
New Orleans, La.	1901	710	401	875	1241	....	1325	1026	1235	1026	695	1739	2303	2610	2392	1099
New York, N. Y.	2915	769	1138	1330	1253	1325	....	1312	92	334	966	2267	3025	2904	2615	225
Oklahoma City, Okla.	1357	770	479	1518	813	678	1472	454	1391	1337	506	1108	1678	1962	1714	1307
Omaha, Neb.	1662	689	664	1738	358	1026	1312	....	1230	1256	454	955	1713	1667	1378	1156
Philadelphia, Pa.	2721	688	1057	1224	1172	1235	92	1230	....	245	885	2186	2944	2823	2324	136
Phoenix, Ariz.	398	1757	1466	2411	1630	1503	2459	1335	2464	2323	1478	653	800	1541	1369	2274
Pittsburgh, Pa.	2533	394	758	1276	871	1093	386	942	305	311	591	1890	2648	2522	2233	230
Portland, Me.	3223	1076	1465	1645	1430	1591	313	1534	409	645	1253	2488	3241	3004	2709	567
Portland, Ore.	970	2412	2305	3519	1690	2541	2953	1691	2872	2935	2096	802	652	175	360	2797
Providence, R. I.	2956	923	1287	1558	1381	1506	182	1435	268	511	1120	2390	3140	3019	2730	403
Quebec, Que.	3213	1122	1482	1862	1334	1754	547	1524	638	878	1338	2478	3272	2908	2613	773
Raleigh, N. C.	2654	598	780	847	1204	914	491	1259	399	159	865	2231	2619	3031	2736	264
Rapid City, S. D.	1421	1251	1267	2274	563	1613	1790	549	1696	1769	1005	686	1444	1254	959	1638
Richmond, Va.	2682	580	846	1006	1206	1026	334	1256	245	....	844	2225	2983	2857	2568	109
Sacramento, Cal.	386	2334	2174	3189	1953	2322	2976	1636	2882	2868	2067	670	89	794	785	2789
St. Joseph, Mo.	1772	578	544	1586	436	922	1246	158	1156	1122	311	1072	1831	1866	1571	1053
St. Louis, Mo.	1848	264	294	1269	546	695	966	454	885	844	....	1368	2126	2109	1820	801
Salt Lake City, Utah	734	1632	1534	2607	1239	1739	2267	955	2186	2225	1368	....	759	871	732	2111
San Antonio, Tex.	1379	1120	739	1484	1265	581	1898	994	1799	1577	971	1426	1803	2315	2109	1630
San Diego, Cal.	135	2148	1839	2742	2241	1879	2849	1743	2899	2688	1881	784	528	1302	1344	2764
San Francisco, Cal.	403	2390	2157	3270	1997	2303	3025	1713	2944	2983	2126	759	....	827	915	2869
Santa Fe, N. M.	868	1285	1021	2016	1136	1128	2014	817	2001	1896	1015	611	1189	1482	1343	1811
Sault Ste. Marie	2526	634	964	1756	537	1385	937	837	946	1065	749	1820	2578	2111	1816	960
Scranton, Pa.	2860	718	1112	1366	1162	1415	125	1229	122	341	873	2163	2922	2919	2629	257
Seattle, Wash.	1145	2362	2331	3582	1641	2610	2904	1667	2823	2857	2109	871	827	....	289	2748
Shreveport, La.	1673	731	352	1159	935	315	1509	777	1410	1188	582	1465	1994	2330	2121	1241
Sioux City, Ia.	1714	829	808	1830	336	1186	1336	106	1247	1326	562	996	1755	1640	1345	1203
Sioux Falls, S. D.	1752	917	896	1918	248	1274	1414	194	1325	1414	650	1053	1812	1555	1260	1261
Spokane, Wash.	1227	2073	2042	3265	1352	2392	2615	1378	2534	2568	1820	732	915	289	....	2459
Springfield, Ill.	1905	279	378	1310	478	779	1010	410	929	820	101	1357	2115	2063	1774	854
Springfield, Mo.	1637	484	283	1391	596	645	1186	381	1105	1132	220	1251	1958	2048	1759	1021
Syracuse, N. Y.	2855	706	1114	1477	1114	1548	262	1166	262	471	885	2120	2879	2840	2444	366
Tampa, Fla.	2480	861	779	259	1547	643	1167	1443	1078	853	1016	2313	2882	3110	2821	942
Toledo, Ohio.	2313	317	686	1358	651	1027	610	710	529	542	509	1670	2428	2302	2013	454
Toronto, Ont.	2685	608	954	1594	990	1354	484	996	493	612	751	1950	2707	2504	2269	507
Tulsa, Okla.	1461	668	417	1481	715	689	1370	385	1289	1166	404	1191	1776	2038	1749	1205
Vancouver, B. C.	1320	2593	2638	3677	1759	2704	3043	1916	2975	3111	2376	1032	1011	143	412	2790
Washington, D. C.	2644	596	908	1075	1097	1099	225	1156	136	109	801	2111	2869	2748	2459	....
Wichita, Kans.	1402	714	529	1603	655	833	1517	303	1369	1266	450	1005	1721	1852	1563	1246
Wilmington, N. C.	2700	685	826	777	1442	923	586	1371	494	251	982	2441	3117	3252	2889	359
Winnipeg, Man.	2209	1221	1355	2305	480	1755	1771	696	1753	1719	1042	1474	2232	1473	1178	1619

Source: American Automobile Association

SIMPLE INTEREST TABLE (Interest on $100—360-Day Basis)

Days	3%	4%	5%	6%	7%	Days	3%	4%	5%	6%	7%
1	$0.0083	$0.0111	$0.0139	$0.0167	$0.0194	16	$0.1333	$0.1778	$0.2222	$0.2667	$0.3111
2	.0167	.0222	.0278	.0333	.0389	17	.1417	.1889	.2361	.2833	.3306
3	.0250	.0333	.0417	.0500	.0583	18	.1500	.2000	.2500	.3000	.3500
4	.0333	.0444	.0556	.0667	.0778	19	.1583	.2111	.2639	.3167	.3694
5	.0417	.0556	.0694	.0833	.0972	20	1667	.2222	.2778	.3333	.3889
6	.0500	.0667	.0833	.1000	.1167	21	.1750	.2333	.2917	.3500	.4083
7	.0583	.0778	.0972	.1167	.1361	22	1833	.2444	.3056	.3667	.4278
8	.0667	.0889	.1111	.1333	.1556	23	.1917	.2556	.3194	.3833	.4472
9	.0750	.1000	.1250	.1500	.1750	24	.2000	.2667	.3333	.4000	4667
10	.0833	.1111	.1389	1667	.1944	25	.2083	.2778	.3472	.4167	.4861
11	.0917	.1222	.1528	.1833	.2139	26	.2167	.2889	.3611	.4333	.5056
12	.1000	.1333	.1667	.2000	.2333	27	.2250	.3000	.3750	.4500	.5250
13	.1083	.1444	.1806	.2167	.2528	28	.2333	.3111	.3889	.4667	.5444
14	.1167	.1556	.1944	.2333	.2722	29	.2417	.3222	.4028	.4833	5639
15	.1250	.1667	.2083	.2500	.2917	30	.2500	.3333	.4167	.5000	.5833

Months	1%	1½%	2%	2¼%	3%	3½%	4%	5%	6%	7%
2	$0.1667	$0.2500	$0.3333	$0.3750	$0.5000	$0.5833	$0.6667	$0.8333	$1.0000	$1.1667
3	.2500	.3750	.5000	.5625	.7500	.8750	1.0000	1.2500	1.5000	1.7500
4	.3333	.5000	.6667	.7500	1.0000	1.1667	1.3333	1.6667	2.0000	2.3333
5	.4167	.6250	.8333	.9375	1.2500	1.4583	1.6667	2.0833	2.5000	2.9167
6	.5000	.7500	1.0000	1.1250	1.5000	1.7500	2.0000	2.5000	3.0000	3.5000
7	.5833	.8750	1.1667	1.3125	1.7500	2.0417	2.3333	2.9167	3.5000	4.0833
8	.6667	1.0000	1.3333	1.5000	2.0000	2.3333	2.6667	3.3333	4.0000	4.6667
9	.7500	1.1250	1.5000	1.6875	2.2500	2.6250	3.0000	3.7500	4.5000	5.2500
10	.8333	1.2500	1.6667	1.8750	2.5000	2.9167	3.3333	4.1667	5.0000	5.8333
11	.9167	1.3750	1.8333	2.0625	2.7500	3.2083	3.6667	4.5833	5.5000	6.4167
12	1.0000	1.5000	2.0000	2.2500	3.0000	3.5000	4.0000	5.0000	6.0000	7.0000

$1.00 AT COMPOUND INTEREST

Years	1%	2%	2½%	3%	4%	5%	6%	7%
1	$1.0100	$1.0200	$1.0250	$1.0300	$1.0400	$1.0500	$1.0600	$1.0700
2	1.0201	1.0404	1.0506	1.0609	1.0816	1.1025	1.1236	1.1449
3	1.0303	1.0612	1.0769	1.0927	1.1249	1.1576	1.1910	1.2250
4	1.0406	1.0824	1.1038	1.1255	1.1699	1.2155	1.2625	1.3108
5	1.0510	1.1041	1.1314	1.1593	1.2167	1.2763	1.3382	1.4026
6	1.0615	1.1262	1.1597	1.1941	1.2653	1.3401	1.4185	1.5007
7	1.0721	1.1487	1.1887	1.2299	1.3159	1.4071	1.5036	1.6058
8	1.0829	1.1717	1.2184	1.2668	1.3686	1.4775	1.5938	1.7182
9	1.0937	1.1951	1.2489	1.3048	1.4233	1.5513	1.6895	1.8385
10	1.1046	1.2190	1.2801	1.3439	1.4802	1.6289	1.7908	1.9672
12	1.1268	1.2682	1.3449	1.4258	1.6010	1.7959	2.0122	2.2522
15	1.1610	1.3459	1.4483	1.5580	1.8009	2.0789	2.3966	2.7590
20	1.2202	1.4859	1.6386	1.8061	2.1911	2.6533	3.2071	3.8697
25	1.2824	1.6406	1.8539	2.0938	2.6658	3.3864	4.2919	5.4274
30	1.3478	1.8114	2.0976	2.4273	3.2434	4.3219	5.7435	7.6123

STANDARD ANNUAL SALARY TABLE
40 Hours a Week—5 Days of 8 Hours

Annual Rate	Quarterly	Monthly	Weekly	Daily	Hourly	¼ Hour
$ 2,400	$ 600.00	$ 200.00	$ 46.15	$ 9.23	$1.15	$0.29
2,500	625.00	208.33	48.08	9.62	1.20	.30
3,000	750.00	250.00	57.69	11.54	1.44	.36
3,500	875.00	291.67	67.31	13.46	1.68	.42
4,000	1,000.00	333.33	76.92	15.38	1.92	.48
4,500	1,125.00	375.00	86.54	17.30	2.16	.54
5,000	1,250.00	416.67	96.15	19.23	2.40	.60
5,500	1,375.00	458.33	105.77	21.15	2.64	.66
6,000	1,500.00	500.00	115.38	23.08	2.88	.72
6,500	1,625.00	541.67	125.00	25.00	3.13	.78
7,000	1,750.00	583.33	134.62	26.92	3.37	.84
7,500	1,875.00	625.00	144.23	28.85	3.60	.90
8,000	2,000.00	666.67	153.85	30.76	3.84	.96
8,500	2,125.00	708.33	163.59	32.72	4.09	1.02
9,000	2,250.00	750.00	173.08	34.62	4.33	1.08
9,500	2,375.00	791.67	182.70	36.54	4.57	1.14
10,000	2,500.00	833.33	192.31	38.46	4.81	1.20
11,000	2,750.00	916.67	211.54	42.31	5.29	1.32
12,000	3,000.00	1,000.00	230.77	46.15	5.77	1.44

STANDARD MONTHLY SALARY TABLE

Monthly Rate	Annual	Quarterly	Weekly	Daily	Hourly	¼ Hour
$ 150	$ 1,800	$ 450	$ 34.62	$ 6.92	$0.87	$0.22
175	2,100	525	40.38	8.08	1.01	.25
185	2,200	555	42.69	8.54	1.07	.27
200	2,400	600	46.15	9.23	1.15	.29
210	2,520	630	48.46	9.69	1.21	.30
225	2,700	675	51.92	10.38	1.30	.32
235	2,820	705	54.23	10.85	1.36	.34
240	2,880	720	55.38	11.07	1.38	.35
250	3,000	750	57.69	11.54	1.44	.36
260	3,120	780	60.00	12.00	1.50	.37
265	3,180	795	61.15	12.23	1.53	.38
275	3,300	825	63.46	12.69	1.59	.40
285	3,420	855	65.77	13.15	1.64	.41
300	3,600	900	69.23	13.85	1.73	.43
325	3,900	975	75.00	15.00	1.87	.47
350	4,200	1,050	80.77	16.15	2.02	.51
375	4,500	1,125	86.54	17.31	2.16	.54
400	4,800	1,200	92.31	18.46	2.31	.58
425	5,100	1,275	98.08	19.62	2.45	.61
450	5,400	1,350	103.84	20.77	2.60	.65
475	5,700	1,425	109.61	21.92	2.74	.69
500	6,000	1,500	115.38	23.08	2.88	.72
550	6,600	1,650	126.92	25.38	3.17	.79
600	7,200	1,800	138.46	27.69	3.46	.87
800	9,600	2,400	184.61	36.92	4.62	1.16
900	10,800	2,700	207.69	41.54	5.19	1.30
950	11,400	2,850	219.23	43.85	5.48	1.37
1,000	12,000	3,000	230.77	46.15	5.77	1.44

TABLE OF PROFITS AND MARKUPS

Cost per Dozen	Each	Profit Percentage on Selling Price							
		20%	23.10%	25%	28.57%	33⅓%	37½%	42.86%	50%
$0.12	.01	.013	.013	.013	.014	.015	.016	.018	.02
.15	.013	.016	.016	.017	.014	.019	.02	.022	.025
.20	.017	.021	.022	.022	.023	.025	.027	.029	.033
.24	.02	.025	.026	.027	.028	.03	.032	.035	.04
.25	.021	.026	.027	.028	.029	.031	.033	.037	.042
.30	.025	.031	.033	.033	.035	.038	.04	.044	.05
.35	.030	.037	.038	.039	.041	.044	.047	.051	.058
.36	.03	.038	.039	.04	.042	.045	.048	.053	.06
.40	.033	.042	.043	.044	.047	.05	.053	.058	.067
.45	.038	.047	.049	.05	.053	.056	.06	.066	.075
.48	.04	.05	.052	.053	.056	.06	.064	.07	.08
.50	.042	.053	.055	.056	.059	.063	.067	.074	.084
.60	.05	.063	.065	.067	.07	.075	.08	.088	.10
.72	.06	.075	.078	.08	.084	.09	.096	.105	.12
.75	.063	.078	.081	.083	.088	.094	.10	.11	.125
.84	.07	.088	.091	.093	.098	.105	.112	.123	.14
.96	.08	.10	.101	.107	.112	.12	.128	.148	.16
1.00	.083	.104	.108	.111	.116	.125	.133	.145	.166
1.20	.10	.125	.13	.133	.14	.15	.16	.175	.20
1.25	.104	.13	.135	.139	.146	.156	.166	.182	.208
1.50	.125	.156	.163	.167	.175	.188	.20	.219	.25
1.75	.146	.183	.19	.195	.204	.219	.234	.256	.292
2.00	.167	.209	.217	.223	.234	.251	.267	.292	.334
2.25	.188	.235	.244	.251	.263	.282	.30	.329	.376
2.50	.208	.26	.27	.277	.291	.312	.333	.364	.416
2.75	.229	.286	.298	.305	.321	.344	.366	.40	.458
3.00	.25	.312	.325	.333	.35	.375	.40	.437	.50
3.25	.27	.337	.351	.36	.378	.405	.432	.473	.54
3.75	.312	.39	.406	.416	.437	.468	.499	.546	.624
4.00	.333	.416	.433	.444	.466	.50	.533	.583	.666
4.25	.354	.443	.460	.472	.496	.531	.566	.62	.708
4.50	.375	.469	.488	.50	.525	.563	.60	.656	.75
5.00	.417	.524	.542	.556	.584	.626	.667	.73	.834
6.00	.50	.625	.65	.667	.70	.75	.80	.875	1.00
6.50	.541	.676	.703	.721	.757	.812	.866	.947	1.08
6.75	.562	.703	.731	.749	.787	.843	.899	.984	1.12
7.00	.583	.729	.758	.777	.816	.875	.933	1.02	1.17
7.25	.604	.755	.785	.805	.846	.906	.956	1.06	1.21
7.50	.625	.781	.813	.833	.875	.938	1.00	1.09	1.25
8.00	.666	.833	.866	.888	.932	.999	1.07	1.17	1.33
8.50	.708	.885	.92	.944	.991	1.06	1.13	1.24	1.41
9.00	.75	.938	.975	1.00	1.05	1.13	1.20	1.31	1.50
10.50	.88	1.09	1.14	1.17	1.23	1.31	1.40	1.53	1.75
12.00	1.00	1.25	1.30	1.33	1.40	1.50	1.60	1.75	2.00
13.50	1.13	1.41	1.46	1.50	1.58	1.69	1.80	1.97	2.25
15.00	1.25	1.56	1.63	1.66	1.75	1.88	2.00	2.19	2.50
16.50	1.38	1.72	1.79	1.83	1.93	2.06	2.20	2.41	2.75
18.00	1.50	1.87	1.95	2.00	2.00	2.25	2.40	2.63	3.00
19.50	1.63	2.04	2.12	2.17	2.28	2.45	2.61	2.85	3.26
21.00	1.75	2.19	2.28	2.33	2.45	2.63	2.80	3.06	3.50
22.50	1.88	2.34	2.44	2.50	2.63	2.81	3.00	3.28	3.75
24.00	2.00	2.50	2.60	2.67	2.80	3.00	3.20	3.50	4.00
27.00	2.25	2.81	2.93	3.00	3.15	3.38	3.60	3.96	4.50
30.00	2.50	3.12	3.25	3.33	3.50	3.75	4.00	4.38	5.00
33.00	2.75	3.44	3.58	3.67	3.85	4.13	4.40	4.81	5.50
36.00	3.00	3.75	3.90	4.00	4.20	4.50	4.80	5.25	6.00
39.00	3.25	4.06	4.23	4.33	4.55	4.88	5.20	5.69	6.50
42.00	3.50	4.37	4.55	4.67	4.90	5.25	5.60	6.12	7.00
45.00	3.75	4.69	4.88	5.00	5.25	5.63	6.00	6.56	7.50
48.00	4.00	5.00	5.20	5.33	5.60	6.00	6.40	7.00	8.00
54.00	4.50	5.62	5.85	6.00	6.30	6.75	7.20	7.87	9.00
60.00	5.00	6.25	6.50	6.67	7.00	7.50	8.00	8.75	10.00
72.00	6.00	7.50	7.80	8.00	8.40	9.00	9.60	10.50	12.00
Per Doz.	Each	25%	30%	33⅓%	40%	50%	60%	75%	100%
		Profit Percentage on Cost							

DEPRECIATION AND COST TABLE

Original Cost	Value in 10 Years	Yearly Depreciation*	Annual Interest	Yearly Cost	Monthly Cost	Daily Cost
$ 10.00	$ 2.50	$ .75	$ .60	$ 1.35	$ .11	$ .0037
30.00	7.50	2.25	1.80	4.05	.34	.01
50.00	12.50	3.75	3.00	6.75	.56	.02
75.00	18.75	5.63	4.50	10.13	.84	.03
100.00	25.00	7.50	6.00	13.50	1.13	.04
125.00	31.25	9.38	7.50	16.88	1.41	.05
150.00	37.50	11.25	9.00	20.25	1.69	.06
175.00	43.75	13.13	10.50	23.63	1.97	.07
200.00	50.00	15.00	12.00	27.00	2.25	.08
225.00	56.25	16.88	13.50	30.38	2.53	.08
250.00	62.50	18.75	15.00	33.75	2.81	.09
275.00	68.75	20.63	16.50	37.13	3.09	.10
300.00	75.00	22.50	18.00	40.50	3.38	.11
325.00	81.25	24.38	19.50	43.88	3.66	.12
350.00	87.50	26.25	21.00	47.25	3.94	.13
375.00	93.75	28.13	22.50	50.63	4.22	.14
400.00	100.00	30.00	24.00	54.00	4.50	.15
425.00	106.25	31.88	25.50	57.38	4.78	.16
450.00	112.50	33.75	27.00	60.75	5.06	.17
475.00	118.75	35.63	28.50	64.13	5.35	.18
500.00	125.00	37.50	30.00	67.50	5.63	.19
525.00	131.25	39.38	31.50	70.88	5.91	.20
550.00	137.50	41.25	33.00	74.25	6.19	.21
575.00	143.75	43.13	34.50	77.63	6.47	.22
600.00	150.00	45.00	36.00	81.00	6.75	.22
625.00	156.25	46.88	37.50	84.38	7.03	.23
650.00	162.50	48.75	39.00	87.75	7.31	.24
675.00	168.75	50.63	40.50	91.13	7.59	.25
700.00	175.00	52.50	42.00	94.50	7.87	.26
725.00	181.25	54.38	43.50	97.88	8.16	.27
750.00	187.50	56.25	45.00	101.25	8.44	.28
775.00	193.75	58.13	46.50	104.63	8.72	.29
800.00	200.00	60.00	48.00	108.00	9.00	.30
825.00	206.25	61.88	49.50	111.38	9.28	.31
850.00	212.50	63.75	51.00	114.75	9.56	.32
875.00	218.75	65.63	52.50	118.13	9.84	.33
900.00	225.00	67.50	54.00	121.50	10.12	.34
925.00	231.25	69.38	55.50	124.88	10.41	.35
950.00	237.50	71.25	57.00	128.25	10.69	.36
975.00	243.75	73.13	58.50	131.63	10.97	.37
1,000.00	250.00	75.00	60.00	135.00	11.25	.38
2,000.00	500.00	150.00	120.00	270.00	22.50	.75
3,000.00	750.00	225.00	180.00	405.00	33.75	1.13
4,000.00	1,000.00	300.00	240.00	540.00	45.00	1.50
5,000.00	1,250.00	375.00	300.00	675.00	56.25	1.88
10,000.00	2,500.00	750.00	600.00	1,350.00	112.50	3.75
25,000.00	6,250.00	1,875.00	1,500.00	3,375.00	281.25	9.38
50,000.00	12,500.00	3,750.00	3,000.00	6,750.00	562.50	18.75
100,000.00	25,000.00	7,500.00	6,000.00	13,500.00	1,125.00	37.50
500,000.00	125,000.00	37,500.00	30,000.00	67,500.00	5,625.00	187.50

*Based on 7½% of full cost

PRORATING TABLE FOR RENTS, TAXES, AND INSURANCE

Number of Years Months or Days	Rents One Month — Days to Month		Taxes and Insurance One Year		Insurance — Three Years			Insurance — Five Years			Number of Years Months or Days
	30	31	Months	Days	Years	Months	Days	Years	Months	Days	
1	.0333	.0323	.0833	.0028	.3333	.0278	.0009	.2000	.0167	.0006	1
2	.0667	.0645	.1667	.0056	.6667	.0556	.0019	.4000	.0333	.0011	2
3	.1000	.0968	.2500	.0083	1.0000	.0833	.0028	.6000	.0500	.0017	3
4	.1333	.1290	.3333	.0111		.1111	.0037	.8000	.0667	.0022	4
5	.1667	.1613	.4167	.0139		.1389	.0046	1.0000	.0833	.0028	5
6	.2000	.1935	.5000	.0167		.1667	.0056		.1000	.0033	6
7	.2333	.2258	.5833	.0194		.1944	.0065		.1167	.0039	7
8	.2667	.2581	.6667	.0222		.2222	.0074		.1333	.0044	8
9	.3000	.2903	.7500	.0250		.2500	.0083		.1500	.0050	9
10	.3333	.3226	.8333	.0278		.2778	.0093		.1667	.0056	10
11	.3667	.3548	.9167	.0306		.3056	.0102		.1833	.0061	11
12	.4000	.3871	1.0000	.0333		.3333	.0111		.2000	.0067	12
13	.4333	.4194		.0361			.0120			.0072	13
14	.4667	.4516		.0389			.0130			.0078	14
15	.5000	.4839		.0417			.0139			.0083	15
16	.5333	.5161		.0444			.0148			.0089	16
17	.5667	.5484		.0472			.0157			.0094	17
18	.6000	.5806		.0500			.0167			.0100	18
19	.6333	.6129		.0528			.0176			.0106	19
20	.6667	.6452		.0556			.0185			.0111	20
21	.7000	.6774		.0583			.0194			.0117	21
22	.7333	.7097		.0611			.0204			.0122	22
23	.7667	.7419		.0639			.0213			0128	23
24	.8000	.7742		.0667			.0222			.0133	24
25	.8333	8065		.0694			.0231			.0139	25
26	.8667	.8387		.0722			.0241			.0144	26
27	.9000	.8710		.0750			.0250			.0150	27
28	.9333	.9032		.0778			.0259			.0156	28
29	.9667	.9355		.0806			.0269			.0161	29
30	1.0000	.9677		.0833			.0278			.0167	30
31		1.0000									31

EXAMPLE
Rent $135.00 a month.

To find value of 23 days of a 31-day month.

From Table:
23 days = .7419

.7419 × $135 = $100.16

EXAMPLE
Taxes = $1,215.12.

To find value of 7 months and 19 days.

From Table:
7 mos. = .5833
19 days = .0528

7 mos. 19 days = .6361

6361 × $1,215.12
= $772.94

EXAMPLE
3-Year Policy Premium is $58.75.

To find the value of 1 yr. 3 mos. 11 days.

From Table:
1 year = .3333
3 mos. = .0833
11 days = .0102

1 yr. 3 mos. 11 days = .4268

.4268 × $58.75
= $25.07

EXAMPLE
5-Year Policy Premium is $312.82.

To find value of 3 yrs. 4 mos. 13 days.

From Table:
3 yrs. = .6000
4 mos. = .0667
13 days = .0072

3 yrs. 4 mos. 13 days = .6739

.6739 × $312.82
= $210.81

Courtesy Chicago Title and Trust Co.

HIGH COST OF WASTE

Showing Sales Required to Equalize Wasted Dollars at a Given Percent of Net Profit to Sales

Percent of Profit	WASTE—(Time lost, breakage, lost shipments, bad credits, etc.)								
	$1.00	$2.00	$3.00	$4.00	$5.00	$6.00	$7.00	$8.00	$9.00
1	$100.00	$200.00	$300.00	$400.00	$500.00	$600.00	$700.00	$800.00	$900.00
1½	66.67	133.33	200.00	266.67	333.33	400.00	466.67	533.33	600.00
2	50.00	100.00	150.00	200.00	250.00	300.00	350.00	400.00	450.00
2½	40.00	80.00	120.00	160.00	200.00	240.00	280.00	320.00	360.00
3	33.33	66.67	100.00	133.33	166.67	200.00	233.33	266.67	300.00
3½	28.57	57.14	85.71	114.29	142.86	171.43	200.00	228.57	257.14
4	25.00	50.00	75.00	100.00	125.00	150.00	175.00	200.00	225.00
4½	22.22	44.44	66.67	88.89	111.11	133.33	155.56	177.78	200.00
5	20.00	40.00	60.00	80.00	100.00	120.00	140.00	160.00	180.00
5½	18.18	36.36	54.55	72.73	90.91	109.09	127.27	145.45	163.64
6	16.67	33.33	50.00	66.67	83.33	100.00	116.67	133.33	150.00
6½	15.38	30.77	46.15	61.54	76.92	92.31	107.69	123.08	138.46
7	14.29	28.57	42.86	57.14	71.43	85.71	100.00	114.29	128.57
7½	13.33	26.67	40.00	53.33	66.67	80.00	93.33	106.67	120.00
8	12.50	25.00	37.50	50.00	62.50	75.00	87.50	100.00	112.50
8½	11.76	23.53	35.29	47.06	58.82	70.59	82.35	94.12	105.88
9	11.11	22.22	33.33	44.44	55.56	66.67	77.78	88.89	100.00
9½	10.53	21.05	31.58	42.11	52.63	63.16	73.68	84.21	94.74
10	10.00	20.00	30.00	40.00	50.00	60.00	70.00	80.00	90.00
12½	8.00	16.00	24.00	32.00	40.00	48.00	56.00	64.00	72.00

Percent of Profit	WASTE—(Time lost, breakage, lost shipments, bad credits, etc.)						
	$10.00	$20.00	$25.00	$30.00	$40.00	$50.00	$60.00
1	$1,000.00	$2,000.00	$2,500.00	$3,000.00	$4,000.00	$5,000.00	$6,000.00
1½	666.67	1,333.33	1,666.67	2,000.00	2,666.67	3,333.33	4,000.00
2	500.00	1,000.00	1,250.00	1,500.00	2,000.00	2,500.00	3,000.00
2½	400.00	800.00	1,000.00	1,200.00	1,600.00	2,000.00	2,400.00
3	333.33	666.67	833.33	1,000.00	1,333.33	1,666.67	2,000.00
3½	285.71	571.43	714.29	857.14	1,142.86	1,428.57	1,714.29
4	250.00	500.00	625.00	750.00	1,000.00	1,250.00	1,500.00
4½	222.22	444.44	555.56	666.67	888.89	1,111.11	1,333.33
5	200.00	400.00	500.00	600.00	800.00	1,000.00	1,200.00
5½	181.82	363.64	454.55	545.45	727.27	909.09	1,090.91
6	166.67	333.33	416.67	500.00	666.67	833.33	1,000.00
6½	153.85	307.69	384.62	461.54	615.38	769.23	923.08
7	142.86	285.71	357.14	428.57	571.43	714.29	857.14
7½	133.33	266.67	333.33	400.00	533.33	666.67	800.00
8	125.00	250.00	312.50	375.00	500.00	625.00	750.00
8½	117.65	235.29	294.12	352.94	470.59	588.24	705.88
9	111.11	222.22	277.78	333.33	444.44	555.56	666.67
9½	105.26	210.53	263.16	315.79	421.05	526.32	631.58
10	100.00	200.00	250.00	300.00	400.00	500.00	600.00
12½	80.00	160.00	200.00	240.00	320.00	400.00	480.00

POPULATION OF THE UNITED STATES

Region, division and state	April 1, 1960 census	April 1, 1950 census	Pct. + or −	1960 Census			Rank	
				Urban	Rural	Percent urban	1960	1950
UNITED STATES	179,323,175	151,325,798	18.5	125,268,750	54,054,425	69.9		
DIVISIONS								
New England.......	10,509,367	9,314,453	12.8	8,031,795	2,477,572	76.4		
Middle Atlantic.....	34,168,452	30,163,533	13.3	27,808,345	6,360,107	81.4		
E. No. Central......	36,225,024	30,399,368	19.2	26,434,937	9,790,087	73.0		
W. No. Central.....	15,394,115	14,061,394	9.5	9,046,317	6,347,798	58.8		
So. Atlantic........	25,971,732	21,182,335	22.6	14,851,516	11,120,216	57.2		
E. So. Central.....	12,050,126	11,477,181	5.0	5,830,569	6,219,557	48.4		
W. So. Central.....	16,951,255	14,537,572	16.6	11,478,165	5,473,090	67.7		
Mountain..........	6,855,060	5,074,998	35.1	4,600,852	2,254,208	67.1		
Pacific............	21,198,044	15,114,964	40.2	17,186,254	4,011,790	81.1		
NEW ENGLAND								
Maine.............	969,265	913,774	6.1	497,114	472,151	51.3	36	35
New Hampshire.....	606,921	533,242	13.8	353,766	253,155	58.3	45	44
Vermont...........	389,881	377,747	3.2	149,921	239,960	38.5	47	46
Massachusetts......	5,148,578	4,690,514	9.8	4,302,530	846,048	83.6	9	9
Rhode Island.......	859,488	791,896	8.5	742,897	116,591	86.4	39	36
Connecticut........	2,535,234	2,007,280	26.3	1,985,567	549,667	78.3	25	28
MID. ATLANTIC								
New York..........	16,782,304	14,830,192	13.2	14,331,925	2,450,379	85.4	1	1
New Jersey.........	6,066,782	4,835,329	25.5	5,374,369	692,413	88.6	8	8
Pennsylvania.......	11,319,366	10,498,012	7.8	8,102,051	3,217,315	71.6	3	3
E. No. CENTRAL								
Ohio..............	9,706,397	7,946,627	22.1	7,123,162	2,583,235	73.4	5	5
Indiana...........	4,662,498	3,934,224	18.5	2,910,149	1,752,349	62.4	11	12
Illinois............	10,081,158	8,712,176	15.7	8,140,315	1,940,843	80.7	4	4
Michigan..........	7,823,194	6,371,766	22.8	5,739,132	2,084,062	73.4	7	7
Wisconsin..........	3,951,777	3,434,575	15.1	2,522,179	1,429,598	63.8	15	14
W. No. CENTRAL								
Minnesota.........	3,413,864	2,928,483	14.5	2,122,566	1,291,298	62.2	18	18
Iowa..............	2,757,537	2,621,073	5.2	1,462,512	1,295,025	53.0	24	22
Missouri..........	4,319,813	3,954,653	9.2	2,876,557	1,443,256	66.6	13	11
North Dakota.....	632,446	619,636	2.1	222,708	409,738	35.2	44	41
South Dakota......	680,514	652,740	4.3	267,180	413,334	39.3	40	40
Nebraska..........	1,411,330	1,325,510	6.5	766,053	645,277	54.3	34	33
Kansas............	2,178,611	1,905,299	14.3	1,328,741	849,870	61.0	28	31
SO. ATLANTIC								
Delaware..........	446,292	318,085	40.3	292,788	153,504	65.6	46	47
Maryland..........	3,100,689	2,343,001	32.3	2,253,832	846,857	72.7	21	24
Dist. of Col........	763,956	802,178	−4.8	763,956		100.0		
Virginia...........	3,966,949	3,318,680	19.5	2,204,913	1,762,036	55.6	14	15
West Virginia.......	1,860,421	2,005,552	−7.2	711,101	1,149,320	38.2	30	29
North Carolina.....	4,556,155	4,061,929	12.2	1,801,921	2,754,234	39.5	12	10
South Carolina.....	2,382,594	2,117,027	12.5	981,386	1,401,208	41.2	26	27
Georgia...........	3,943,116	3,444,578	14.5	2,180,236	1,762,880	55.3	16	13
Florida............	4,951,560	2,771,305	78.7	3,661,383	1,290,177	73.9	10	20
E. SO. CENTRAL								
Kentucky..........	3,038,156	2,944,806	3.2	1,353,215	1,684,941	44.5	22	19
Tennessee.........	3,567,089	3,291,718	8.4	1,864,828	1,702,261	52.3	17	16
Alabama..........	3,266,740	3,061,743	6.7	1,791,721	1,475,019	54.8	19	17
Mississippi........	2,178,141	2,178,914		820,805	1,357,336	37.7	29	26
W. SO. CENTRAL								
Arkansas..........	1,786,272	1,909,511	−6.5	765,303	1,020,969	42.8	31	30
Louisiana..........	3,257,022	2,683,516	21.4	2,060,606	1,196,416	63.3	20	21
Oklahoma.........	2,328,284	2,233,351	4.3	1,464,786	863,498	62.9	27	25
Texas.............	9,579,677	7,711,194	24.2	7,187,470	2,392,207	75.0	6	6
MOUNTAIN								
Montana..........	674,767	591,024	14.2	338,457	336,310	50.2	41	42
Idaho.............	667,191	588,637	13.3	317,097	350,094	47.5	42	43
Wyoming..........	330,066	290,529	13.6	187,551	142,515	56.8	48	48
Colorado..........	1,753,947	1,325,089	32.4	1,292,790	461,157	73.7	33	34
New Mexico........	951,023	681,187	39.6	626,479	324,544	65.9	37	39
Arizona...........	1,302,161	749,587	73.7	970,616	331,545	74.5	35	37
Utah..............	890,627	688,862	29.3	667,158	223,469	74.9	38	38
Nevada............	285,278	160,083	78.2	200,704	84,574	70.4	49	49
PACIFIC								
Washington........	2,853,214	2,378,963	19.9	1,943,249	909,965	68.1	23	23
Oregon............	1,768,687	1,521,341	16.3	1,100,122	668,565	62.2	32	32
California.........	15,717,204	10,586,223	48.5	13,573,155	2,144,049	86.4	2	2
Alaska............	226,167	128,643	75.8	85,767	140,400	37.9	50	50
Hawaii............	632,772	499,794	26.6	483,961	148,811	76.5	43	45

Source: *Bureau of the Census and The World Almanac*

BUYING POWER BY STATES AND SECTIONS

Sections and States	Population Estimate December 31, 1964			Effective Buying Income 1964 Estimate			Retail Sales 1964 Estimate	
	Total (in thousands)	% of U.S.A.	Households*	Net Dollars (in thousands)	% of U.S.A.	Per Capita	Dollars (in thousands)	% of U.S.A.
NEW ENGLAND								
Connecticut.....	2,785.7	1.4451	821.4	$7,775,987	1.8128	$2,791	$4,156,495	1.6014
Maine.........	993.2	.5153	287.2	1,856,161	.4327	1,869	1,250,134	.4817
Massachusetts...	5,380.6	2.7912	1,596.6	13,641,445	3.1801	2,535	7,792,310	3.0020
New Hampshire..	636.6	.3303	188.8	1,360,510	.3171	2,137	934,236	.3599
Rhode Island....	905.2	.4696	269.4	1,988,469	.4636	2,197	1,180,971	.4550
Vermont........	396.2	.2055	112.7	769,259	.1794	1,942	558,486	.2151
MIDDLE ATLANTIC								
New Jersey......	6,648.1	3.4487	1,968.8	17,320,237	4.0379	2,605	9,889,374	3.8099
New York.......	17,696.5	9.1801	5,486.2	47,924,170	11.1724	2,708	25,310,292	9.7510
Pennsylvania....	11,676.8	6.0574	3,448.5	25,877,835	6.0328	2,216	14,441,648	5.5637
EAST N. CENTRAL								
Illinois.........	10,649.4	5.5244	3,239.9	27,789,676	6.4786	2,610	16,266,936	6.2670
Indiana.........	4,929.7	2.5573	1,466.4	10,952,787	2.5534	2,222	6,844,616	2.6369
Michigan........	8,259.7	4.2847	2,356.0	19,486,956	4.5430	2,359	11,658,100	4.4913
Ohio............	10,471.2	5.4320	3,068.1	23,403,356	5.4559	2,235	13,522,523	5.2096
Wisconsin.......	4,215.3	2.1867	1,221.8	8,845,618	2.0621	2,098	5,490,506	2.1153
WEST N. CENTRAL								
Iowa...........	2,818.3	1.4620	859.8	5,980,114	1.3941	2,122	3,965,891	1.5279
Kansas.........	2,268.7	1.1769	701.1	4,630,603	1.0795	2,041	2,987,522	1.1509
Minnesota.......	3,600.5	1.8678	1,039.5	7,515,460	1.7520	2,087	4,772,656	1.8387
Missouri........	4,484.8	2.3265	1,404.8	10,161,427	2.3689	2,266	6,289,209	2.4230
Nebraska.......	1,464.0	.7595	450.4	3,138,606	.7317	2,144	2,155,371	.8304
North Dakota...	640.4	.3322	175.6	1,213,219	.2828	1,894	874,065	.3368
South Dakota....	706.8	.3666	202.9	1,311,032	.3056	1,855	891,287	.3433
SOUTH ATLANTIC								
Delaware........	501.3	.2601	143.5	1,395,326	.3252	2,783	762,362	.2937
Dist. of Columbia	800.2	.4151	264.1	2,403,226	.5603	3,003	1,515,010	.5836
Florida.........	5,871.6	3.0459	1,840.5	11,492,146	2.6791	1,957	8,493,866	3.2723
Georgia.........	4,203.9	2.1808	1,144.2	7,379,146	1.7203	1,755	4,926,392	1.8980
Maryland.......	3,444.3	1.7867	953.7	8,542,056	1.9914	2,480	4,646,528	1.7901
North Carolina..	4,805.2	2.4927	1,270.8	8,188,632	1.9090	1,704	5,308,302	2.0450
South Carolina...	2,549.8	1.3227	645.3	3,790,805	.8837	1,487	2,425,151	.9343
Virginia........	4,341.6	2.2522	1,174.5	8,382,750	1.9542	1,931	5,137,396	1.9793
West Virginia....	1,780.8	.9238	500.0	3,171,549	.7394	1,781	1,845,601	.7110
EAST S. CENTRAL								
Alabama........	3,415.9	1.7720	925.6	5,252,920	1.2246	1,538	3,524,397	1.3577
Kentucky.......	3,109.8	1.6132	871.9	5,245,879	1.2230	1,687	3,367,466	1.2973
Mississippi......	2,216.1	1.1496	579.0	3,076,643	.7173	1,388	2,016,895	.7770
Tennessee.......	3,738.8	1.9396	1,055.7	6,274,293	1.4627	1,678	4,322,303	1.6652
WEST S. CENTRAL								
Arkansas........	1,833.9	.9514	539.2	2,857,669	.6662	1,558	2,067,374	.7965
Louisiana.......	3,515.8	1.8238	962.5	5,800,705	1.3523	1,650	3,659,364	1.4098
Oklahoma.......	2,411.2	1.2508	759.5	4,562,432	1.0637	1,892	3,052,569	1.1760
Texas..........	10,480.9	5.4370	3,038.0	19,952,520	4.6515	1,904	13,303,043	5.1251
MOUNTAIN								
Arizona.........	1,611.0	.8357	453.0	3,156,815	.7359	1,960	2,131,939	.8214
Colorado........	1,985.4	1.0299	604.0	4,471,512	1.0425	2,252	2,844,202	1.1111
Idaho..........	697.5	.3618	204.3	1,268,910	.2958	1,819	976,686	.3762
Montana........	718.1	.3725	215.5	1,439,401	.3355	2,004	981,267	.3780
Nevada........	400.3	.2076	127.7	1,199,960	.2798	2,998	732,701	.2823
New Mexico.....	1,037.3	.5381	275.1	1,845,852	.4303	1,779	1,218,710	.4695
Utah..........	998.0	.5177	268.7	1,931,202	.4502	1,935	1,318,029	.5078
Wyoming.......	350.8	.1819	105.3	776,537	.1810	2,214	510,122	.1965
PACIFIC								
Alaska..........	273.6	.1420	69.2	660,299	.1540	2,413	291,964	.1125
California.......	18,355.0	9.5221	5,783.5	48,751,396	11.3653	2,656	29,059,792	11.1954
Hawaii..........	730.7	.3790	175.3	1,539,144	.3588	2,106	797,829	.3074
Oregon..........	1,907.0	.9892	606.1	4,253,187	.9915	2,230	2,869,463	1.1055
Washington.....	3,055.9	1.5853	953.9	6,945,136	1.6191	2,273	4,188,811	1.6137
U. S. TOTALS......	192,770.2	100.0000	56,876.2	428,951,435	100.0000	2,225	259,568,162	100.0000

*In thousands. *Source: Sales Management Survey of Buying Power*

THE 100 LARGEST U.S. CITIES

Rank	City	Population 1960	Population 1950	Rank	City	Population 1960	Population 1950
1	New York, N.Y.	7,781,984	7,891,957	51	Wichita, Kans.	254,698	168,279
2	Chicago, Ill.	3,550,404	3,620,962	52	Richmond, Va.	219,958	230,310
3	Los Angeles, Calif.	2,479,015	1,970,358	53	Syracuse, N. Y.	216,038	220,583
4	Philadelphia, Pa.	2,002,512	2,071,605	54	Tucson, Ariz.	212,892	45,454
5	Detroit, Mich.	1,670,144	1,849,568	55	Des Moines, Iowa	208,982	177,965
6	Baltimore, Md.	939,024	949,708	56	Providence, R. I.	207,498	248,674
7	Houston, Texas	938,219	596,163	57	San Jose, Calif.	204,196	95,280
8	Cleveland, Ohio	876,050	914,808	58	Mobile, Ala.	202,779	129,009
9	Washington, D. C.	763,956	802,178	59	Charlotte, N. C.	201,564	134,042
10	St. Louis, Mo.	750,026	856,796	60	Albuquerque, N. M.	201,189	96,815
11	Milwaukee, Wisc.	741,324	637,392	61	Jacksonville, Fla.	201,030	204,517
12	San Francisco, Calif.	740,316	775,357	62	Flint, Mich.	196,940	163,143
13	Boston, Mass.	697,197	801,444	63	Sacramento, Calif.	191,667	137,572
14	Dallas, Texas	679,684	434,462	64	Yonkers, N. Y.	190,634	152,798
15	New Orleans, La.	627,525	570,445	65	Salt Lake City, Utah	189,454	182,121
16	Pittsburgh, Pa.	604,332	676,806	66	Worcester, Mass.	186,587	203,486
17	San Antonio, Texas	587,718	408,442	67	Austin, Texas	186,545	132,459
18	San Diego, Calif.	573,224	334,387	68	Spokane, Wash.	181,608	161,721
19	Seattle, Wash.	557,087	467,591	69	St. Petersburg, Fla.	181,298	96,738
20	Buffalo, N. Y.	532,759	580,132	70	Gary, Ind.	178,320	133,911
21	Cincinnati, Ohio	502,550	503,998	71	Grand Rapids, Mich.	177,313	176,515
22	Memphis, Tenn.	497,524	396,000	72	Springfield, Mass.	174,463	162,399
23	Denver, Colo.	493,887	415,786	73	Nashville, Tenn.	170,874	174,307
24	Atlanta, Ga.	487,455	331,314	74	Corpus Christi, Texas	167,670	108,287
25	Minneapolis, Minn.	482,872	521,718	75	Youngstown, Ohio	166,689	168,330
26	Indianapolis, Ind.	476,258	427,173	76	Shreveport, La.	164,372	127,206
27	Kansas City, Mo.	475,539	456,622	77	Hartford, Conn.	162,178	177,397
28	Columbus, Ohio	471,316	375,901	78	Fort Wayne, Ind.	161,776	133,607
29	Phoenix, Ariz.	439,170	106,818	79	Bridgeport, Conn.	156,748	158,709
30	Newark, N. J.	405,220	438,776	80	Baton Rouge, La.	152,419	125,629
31	Louisville, Ky.	390,639	369,129	81	New Haven, Conn.	152,048	164,443
32	Portland, Ore.	372,676	373,628	82	Savannah, Ga.	149,245	119,638
33	Oakland, Calif.	367,548	384,575	83	Tacoma, Wash.	147,979	143,673
34	Fort Worth, Texas	356,268	278,778	84	Jackson, Miss.	144,422	98,271
35	Long Beach, Calif.	344,168	250,767	85	Paterson, N. J.	143,663	139,336
36	Birmingham, Ala.	340,887	326,037	86	Evansville, Ind.	141,543	128,636
37	Oklahoma City, Okla.	324,253	243,504	87	Erie, Pa.	138,440	130,803
38	Rochester, N. Y.	318,611	332,488	88	Amarillo, Texas	137,969	74,246
39	Toledo, Ohio	318,003	303,616	89	Montgomery, Ala.	134,393	106,525
40	St. Paul, Minn.	313,411	311,349	90	Fresno, Calif.	133,929	91,669
41	Norfolk, Va.	304,869	213,513	91	South Bend, Ind.	132,445	115,911
42	Omaha, Nebr.	301,598	251,117	92	Chattanooga, Tenn.	130,009	131,041
43	Honolulu, Hawaii	294,194	248,034	93	Albany, N. Y.	129,726	134,995
44	Miami, Fla.	291,688	249,276	94	Lubbock, Texas	128,691	71,747
45	Akron, Ohio	290,351	274,605	95	Lincoln, Nebr.	128,521	98,884
46	El Paso, Texas	276,687	130,485	96	Madison, Wisc.	126,706	96,056
47	Jersey City, N. J.	276,101	299,017	97	Rockford, Ill.	126,706	92,927
48	Tampa, Fla.	274,970	124,681	98	Kansas City, Kans.	121,901	129,553
49	Dayton, Ohio	262,332	243,872	99	Greensboro, N. C.	119,574	74,389
50	Tulsa, Okla.	261,685	182,740	100	Topeka, Kans.	119,484	78,791

Source: Bureau of the Census and The World Almanac

LEGAL HOLIDAYS IN THE 50 STATES, D.C., AND PUERTO RICO

HOLIDAYS WIDELY OBSERVED

January 1, New Year's Day: All states, D. C., Puerto Rico.

February 12, Lincoln's Birthday: Alaska, Arizona, California, Colorado, Connecticut, Delaware, Illinois, Indiana, Iowa, Kansas, Kentucky, Maryland, Michigan, Minnesota, Missouri, Montana, Nebraska, New Jersey, New Mexico, New York, North Dakota, Ohio, Oregon, Pennsylvania, South Dakota, Tennessee, Utah, Vermont, Washington, West Virginia, Wisconsin, Wyoming.

February 22, Washington's Birthday: All states[1] (except Louisiana, Nevada); D. C., Puerto Rico.

May 30, Memorial (or Decoration) Day: All states (except Alabama, Georgia, Louisiana, Mississippi, South Carolina, Texas); D. C., Puerto Rico.

July 4, Independence Day: All states, D. C., Puerto Rico.

September (1st Monday), Labor Day: All states, D. C., Puerto Rico.

October 12, Columbus Day: All states (except Alaska, Arkansas, D. C., Hawaii, Idaho, Iowa, Kansas, Louisiana, Maine, Mississippi, Nevada, North Carolina, Oregon, South Carolina, South Dakota, Tennessee, Virginia, Wyoming), Puerto Rico.

November (1st Tuesday after 1st Monday), Election Day: Arizona, Arkansas, California, Colorado, Delaware, Florida, Hawaii, Illinois, Indiana, Iowa, Louisiana, Maryland, Michigan, Missouri, Montana, New Hampshire, New Jersey, New York, North Carolina, North Dakota, Ohio, Oregon, Pennsylvania, Rhode Island, South Carolina, South Dakota, Tennessee, Texas, Vermont, Virginia, Washington, West Virginia, Wisconsin, Wyoming, Puerto Rico.

November 11, Veterans Day (formerly Armistice Day): All states (except Louisiana); D. C., Puerto Rico.

November (4th Thursday) Thanksgiving Day: All states, D. C., Puerto Rico.

December 25, Christmas: All states,[2] D. C., Puerto Rico.

OTHER HOLIDAYS

January 6, Three Kings' Day: Puerto Rico.

January 11, De Hostos' Birthday Puerto Rico.

January 19, Robert E. Lee's Birthday: Alabama, Arkansas, Florida, Georgia, Kentucky, Mississippi, North Carolina, South Carolina, Tennessee, Texas, Virginia.[3]

January 20, Inauguration Day (every 4 yrs.): D. C.

January 30, F. D. Roosevelt's Birthday: Ky.

February 14, Admission Day: Arizona.

March (first Tuesday), Town Meeting Day: Vt.

March 2, Texas Independence Day.

March (second Friday), Arbor Day: New Mexico.

March 15, Andrew Jackson's Birthday: Tennessee.

March or April (2 days before Easter), Good Friday: California (noon–3 P.M.), Connecticut, Delaware, Florida, Hawaii, Illinois, Indiana, Louisiana, Maryland, Minnesota, New Jersey, North Dakota, Pennsylvania, Tennessee, Wisconsin (11 A.M.–3 P.M.), Puerto Rico.

March or April (1 day after Easter), Easter Monday: North Carolina.

March 22, Emancipation Day: Puerto Rico.

March 25, Maryland Day.

March 26, Kuhio Day: Hawaii.

March 30, Seward's Day: Alaska.

April (date set by governor), Arbor Day: Wyo.

April 12, Halifax Resolutions Anniversary: N. C.

April 13, Thomas Jefferson's Birthday: Alabama, Missouri, Oklahoma, Virginia.

April 16, De Diego's Birthday: Puerto Rico.

April 19, Patriots' Day: Maine, Massachusetts.

April 21, San Jacinto Day: Texas.

April 22, Oklahoma Day.

April 22, Arbor Day: Nebraska.

April 26, Confederate Memorial Day: Alabama, Florida, Georgia, Mississippi.

April (4th Monday), Fast Day: New Hampshire.

April (last Friday), Arbor Day: Utah.

May 4, Rhode Island Independence Day.

May (2nd Sunday), Mother's Day: Oklahoma.

May 10, Confederate Memorial Day: North Carolina, South Carolina.

May 20, Mecklenburg Independence Day: N. C.

June 3, Jefferson Davis' Birthday: Alabama, Florida, Georgia, Kentucky, Mississippi, South Carolina, Tennessee, Texas.

June 9, Senior Citizens' Day: Oklahoma.

June 11, Kamehameha Day: Hawaii.

June 14, Flag Day: Pennsylvania.

June 17, Bunker Hill Day: Massachusetts (in Suffolk Co. only).

June 20, West Virginia Day.

July (on day designated by governor), Onate Day: New Mexico.

July 13, Nathan Bedford Forrest's Birthday: Tenn.

July 17, Munoz Rivera's Birthday: Puerto Rico.

July 24, Pioneer Day: Utah.

July 25, Constitution Day: Puerto Rico.

July 27, Barbosa's Birthday: Puerto Rico.

August 1, Colorada Day.

August 3, Ernie Pyle Day: New Mexico.

August 14, Victory Day: Rhode Island.

August 14, V-J Day: Arkansas.

August 16, Bennington Battle Day: Vermont.

August 30, Huey P. Long Day: Louisiana.

September 9, Admission Day: California.

September 12, Defenders' Day: Maryland.

September 16, Cherokee Strip Day: Oklahoma.

October 10, Oklahoma Historical Day.

October 18, Alaska Day.

October 31, Nevada Day.

November 1, All Saints' Day: Louisiana.

November 4, Will Rogers Day: Oklahoma.

November 19, Discovery Day: Puerto Rico.

---

[1]Designated *President's Day* in Hawaii.   [2]Two days in South Carolina (Dec. 25-26).
[3]Called *Lee-Jackson Day*.   *Source: Information Please Almanac*

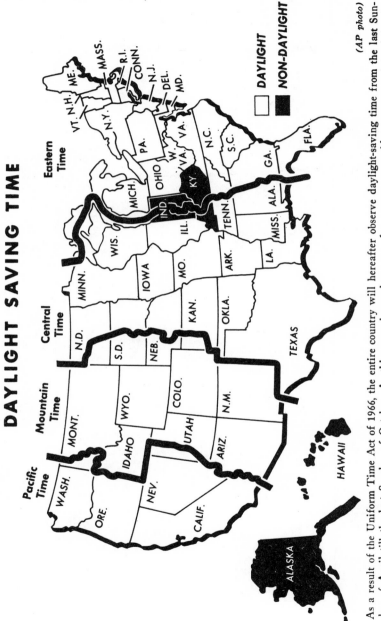

DAYLIGHT SAVING TIME

□ DAYLIGHT
■ NON-DAYLIGHT

(AP photo)

As a result of the Uniform Time Act of 1966, the entire country will hereafter observe daylight-saving time from the last Sunday of April till the last Sunday of October. As this map shows, however, four states were able to exempt themselves, for various reasons, in 1967.

INDEX

INDEX

A-A Store, 258
A-C Supply Co., 293
Abbott Laboratories, Inc., 556-557
Abbotts Dairies, Inc., 601
Abbreviations in contracts, 776
Aberdeen Manufacturing Co., 164
Ability factors, 504-505
Academy of Food Marketing, St. Joseph's College, 600
Accessory equipment, 767
Account opener, 358
Acknowledgment of orders, 826-827
Acme Markets, Inc., 250
Adams, Cyrus H., III, 243
Adapter for converting 16mm. projectors into built-in screen units, 838
Addressing equipment, 447-448
Administrative Behavior, 57
Advertisers, Association of National, 30, 154

ADVERTISING
advantage to independent dealer, 232
allowances, 353
assistance to distributors, 219
attempts to reduce cost of distribution, 26
campaign, importance of, 163-164
consumer, 289
cooperative, 232
distributors, 817
equipment, 767, 835
expenditures, 896
intertwining with sales department, 67
manufacturer, 817
media, 767, 886-896
profitable distribution of, 172-173
research, 767, 787
role of distributors, 224
slanted at specific markets, 567
specialty, 358
strategy, 27
trademarks, 103
Advertising Age, 104, 166, 322-323, 506, 632
Advertising manager, 419
Advertising and Sales Promotion Buyers Guide, 674
Aetna Early Settlers Society, 385
Agent, 767
Agent middleman, 767
Aggressiveness, 503-505
National Council on, 131

AGING
U. S. Administration on, 130-131
Agricultural Adjustment Acts, 325-326
Agricultural market, 298-302
Air Conditioning and Refrigeration Institute, 682
Air Conditioning and Refrigeration Wholesalers Association, 221
Air Conditioning Wholesalers Association, National Heating and, 222
Air freight, 206
Airline abbreviations, 903
Air passenger fares, 904-918
Alcoa, 266
Alexander, Milton, 765
Altschuler-Baterson Co. v. Markowitz, 575-576
Amendment to the Food and Drug Act, 326
American Association of Advertising Agencies, 127, 178-181
American Bosch Arma Corporation, 161
American Brake Shoe Co., 119
American Can Company, 19, 87, 158
American Cyanamid Co., 104
American Dental Trade Association, 223
American Educational Research Association, 612
American Foreign Trade Definitions, Revised, 776
American Gas Association Directory, 198
American Institutional Wholesale Plumbing and Heating Suppliers Association, 223
American Management Association, 90, 264, 457, 464, 765
American Map Co., Inc., 193
American market, 124-128
American Marketing Association, 18, 20, 165, 177, 303
American Oil Co., 634-637, 642
American Photocopy Equipment Co., 580-582
American Psychological Association, 612
American Research Merchandising Institute, 223
American Safety Razor Products Corp., 93
American Society for Association Executives, 640
American Society of Travel Agents, 640
American-Standard Corp., 681
American Steel Warehouse Association, 223
American Surgical Trade Association, 222
American Telephone & Telegraph Co., 276

IMPORTANT REFERENCE DATA

The *Dartnell Sales Manager's Handbook* contains much valuable reference material in the form of charts, maps, tables, checklists and other summary forms of information needed by the sales executive. Because this source material may be overlooked in the index, the reader is urged to familiarize himself with the following list of the most important reference data contained in this handbook: